THE MODERN LIBRARY

of the World's Best Books

THE SHOCK

OF

RECOGNITION

The publishers will be pleased to send, upon request, an illustrated folder setting forth the purpose and scope of THE MODERN LIBRARY, and listing each volume in the series. Every reader of books will find titles he has been looking for, handsomely printed, in definitive editions, and at an unusually low price.

THE SHOCK
OF
RECOGNITION

THE DEVELOPMENT OF LITERATURE
IN THE UNITED STATES
RECORDED BY THE MEN
WHO MADE IT

EDITED BY
EDMUND WILSON

THE MODERN LIBRARY
NEW YORK

WITH ILLUSTRATIONS BY
ROBERT F. HALLOCK

Random House IS THE PUBLISHER OF *The Modern Library*
BENNETT CERF • DONALD S. KLOPFER
Manufactured in the United States of America

For genius, all over the world, stands hand in hand, and one shock of recognition runs the whole circle round.

HERMAN MELVILLE

FOREWORD

THIS BOOK is not a critical anthology, but a collection of
literary documents. It is an attempt to present a chronicle
of the progress of literature in the United States as one finds
it recorded by those who had some part in creating that
literature.

But this statement requires qualification. I have had to
exclude general discussions, even where these were interesting, of literary principles and tendencies, and to confine
myself to pieces which deal with particular writers, because
I should not have had space to cover both kinds of criticism
in a manageable volume. The best way to understand the
general is, in any case, to study the concrete; and in the
course of these examinations of individual writers, one gets,
though by glimpses, a fairly complete view of the larger
backgrounds and movements. But even within these limitations I have restricted the scope further by excluding essays
and reviews by professional literary critics. There would, of
course, be a large field to choose from in this department,
but a collection of critical essays would be quite another
kind of anthology. I was aiming to show the effect on one
another of the first-rate American figures; and these writers,

FOREWORD

though, like Poe or Howells, they have sometimes practiced criticism, have never simply been scholars or reviewers, but have always expressed themselves in literature in some more direct way. What I am trying to present, in fact, is the developing self-consciousness of the American genius from the moment in the middle of the last century when we first really had a literature worth talking about to the moment toward the end of the second decade of ours when it was plain that, following the cultural slump of the period after the Civil War, a new movement had got under way.

For this purpose I have brought together materials of the most varied shapes and styles: essays, monographs, memoirs, journals, letters, satires, dialogues, poems. And I have violated my American canon by admitting a few pieces by foreigners that show the repercussions of American books thrown back to us from abroad and the consciousness of Europe of *us*. I have also departed from the program suggested by my title of showing only the moments when genius becomes aware of its kin by including a few examples of the shock of recognition which occurs when the very good writer is confronted by the very bad. It requires gifts just as rare—since they are just the same gifts—to be fully aware of the bad as to be fully aware of the good.

As a hater of extracts and omissions, I have printed the whole of everything.

The following acknowledgments are due for permission to use copyrighted material: to Houghton Mifflin Company for letters from *The Life of James Russell Lowell* by Horace E. Scudder, letter and quotations from *Walt Whitman* by Bliss Perry, quotations from *My Own Story* by John Taylor Trowbridge, Emerson's *Journals* and *Whitman and Burroughs, Comrades* by Clara Barrus, and *A Critical Fable* by Amy Lowell; the Columbia University Press for Emerson letters and quotation from Mr. Rusk in *Letters of Ralph Waldo Emerson* edited by Ralph L. Rusk; Doubleday, Doran and Company, Inc., for quotations from *Walt Whitman in Camden* by Horace Traubel and selections from *Collected Prose Works* of Walt Whitman; The Macmillan Company for

FOREWORD

quotations from *Days with Walt Whitman* by Edward Carpenter; the Harvard University Press for a quotation from *Whitman's Workshop* by Clifton Joseph Furness and Mrs. Frank J. Sprague, who owns the original manuscript of this dialogue; for quotations from *Reminiscences of Walt Whitman* by W. S. Kennedy; Harper and Brothers for *The Literary Offenses of James Fenimore Cooper* by Mark Twain and a selection from *My Mark Twain* by William Dean Howells; Charles Scribner's Sons for *Emerson* by J. J. Chapman and essays on *William James* and *Josiah Royce* from *Character and Opinion in the United States* by George Santayana; Mr. H. G. Wells for *Stephen Crane from an English Standpoint;* Miss Mildred Howells for selections from *My Mark Twain* by William Dean Howells; Miss Elizabeth Lodge for *The Life of George Cabot Lodge* by Henry Adams; Mr. T. S. Eliot for his essays on Henry James; Viking Press, Inc., for *Studies in Classic American Literature* by D. H. Lawrence, copyright 1923 by Thomas Seltzer, Inc., 1951 by Frieda Lawrence; Alfred A. Knopf, Inc., for essays from *A Book of Prefaces and Prejudices, First* and *Fifth Series* by H. L. Mencken, copyright 1917, 1926, 1945 by Alfred A. Knopf, Inc.; Mr. Mencken and *The Nation* for *A Short View of Gamalielese;* Mr. John Dos Passos for his review of E. E. Cummings' *The Enormous Room;* and Mrs. Sherwood Anderson, Mr. Van Wyck Brooks and Little, Brown & Co. for *Letters of Sherwood Anderson* from the book of the same title, edited by Howard Mumford Jones and Walter B. Rideout, copyright 1953 by Eleanor Anderson.

I have especially to thank the authorities of the Harvard University Library, who have greatly facilitated my researches; Mr. Clifton Joseph Furness of Cambridge, who has generously advised me out of his immense knowledge of Walt Whitman, and who has loaned me materials and allowed me to quote from his own unpublished manuscripts; Mr. Ferris Greenslet and Mr. R. N. Linscott of Houghton Mifflin, to whom I am indebted for loan of materials and help of other kinds; and Miss Helen Gould, who has worked with me with expert skill on the mechanical side of the book.

FOREWORD TO THE SECOND EDITION

I HAVE ADDED, in this new edition, with the permission of Harper and Brothers, a second section of Mark Twain's essay, *Fenimore Cooper's Literary Offenses,* discovered recently among the Mark Twain papers by Mr. Bernard De Voto and published in the *New England Quarterly.* I may also take this opportunity to mention another piece which I should have liked to include in *The Shock of Recognition* but for which I was unable to get permission: the essay called *Mark Twain: An Inquiry,* which stands as the last chapter of Howells' book *My Mark Twain* and which should stand here beside the personal memoir. This essay, which first appeared in the *North American Review* of February, 1901, was written to celebrate the occasion of Mark Twain's return to the United States, after his five years spent abroad, and of the first publication of his collected works. Mark Twain had left the States a popular humorist and had come back a great public figure, who had been praised and made much of in Europe, and who was now taken seriously at home by the younger generation as he had hardly ever been by his contemporaries. This essay is the most extensive critical study that Howells devoted to the work of his friend, and it has a unique interest in attempting to explain this work in terms of Mark Twain's Western origins, which Howells was in a position to understand so much better than the Eastern critics.

FOREWORD TO SECOND EDITION

I should like to recommend, also, as supplementary reading, Thomas Beer's little book on Stephen Crane: *Stephen Crane: A Study in American Letters*—to which, on rereading it since *The Shock* was compiled, I have felt that I have done something less than justice in my introduction to the section on Crane. The more recent and scholarly writers on Crane complain that Beer is most unreliable, that his book is full of errors of fact; but it will serve to fill in, by its picture of Crane's period, a chapter of our literary history which I have otherwise rather slighted: the Bohemian "end of the century," when people like Stephen Crane and Harold Frederic and Henry Harland would begin as American realists, champions of Art and Truth, fighting the genteel tradition, and end up in Paris or London as journalists or fashionable novelists. Thomas Beer—not himself a writer on a level with the figures in this book—had a special relish for the nineties and the early nineteen hundreds and has given the sense of this moment of Mouquin's and *M'lle New York,* of Hearst papers and President McKinley, of *Yellow Book* writers and of young correspondents conducting themselves gallantly in minor wars, of efforts to grow in American soil the windblown seeds from Europe of Aestheticism and Naturalism, as no other non-contemporary has been able to give it.

I have taken the occasion, also, to correct a number of errors of the kind that can be easily corrected; but I shall have to explain here—to avoid more extensive changes in the plates—that Mr. Ferris Greenslet of Houghton, Mifflin has been able to set me right in my account, in the last paragraph of page 743, of the biography of John Hay that Herbert Croly was discouraged from wr'ting by an interview with Henry Adams. It was the publishers, it seems, not the Hay family, who had selected Herbert Croly to do the biography of Hay, and he had actually signed a contract and been at work for some time on Hay's papers when his desolating meeting with Adams had the effect of making him throw up the job.

CONTENTS

CONTENTS

CONTENTS

THE SHOCK OF RECOGNITION

THE SHOCK OF RECOGNITION

THIS ESSAY BY LOWELL on Poe was written at Poe's request
for a series called *Our Contributors* in *Graham's Magazine*.
It appeared in the issue of February 1845. Poe at that time
was thirty-six and Lowell was twenty-six. They had both
briefly in the early eighteen forties been editors of magazines
and had published one another's writings; and their letters
to one another had been cordial and full of appreciation.
This essay is characteristic of the generous early Lowell. But
when Poe died in 1849 and Rufus Griswold, his literary ex-
ecutor, was getting out his edition of Poe's work, this article
of Lowell's appeared in it in a curiously different form. The
praise of Poe as a critic in the early part of the essay had completely disappeared, and the original ending had been
clipped, and a new and rather disparaging one substituted.

It is true that Poe had in the meantime persistently attacked Longfellow for plagiarism, that he had sneered at the
Abolitionists, with whose cause the young Lowell had allied
himself, and that he had finally published a review of
Lowell's *Fable for Critics* in which he had characterized it
as "an irrevocable *faux pas*" and said that it had "lowered"
Lowell "at least 50 per cent in the literary public opinion."

On the other hand, it is possible, as Mr. A. H. Quinn, the biographer of Poe, suggests, that Griswold may have forged these alterations. Griswold detested Poe: he lied about him in his memoir, he circulated false scandals about him, and he completely rewrote those letters of Poe's which he quoted in this edition, in such a way as to put himself in a favorable light and Poe in an unfavorable one. One of Griswold's chief sources of income was the editing of anthologies of American writing, and Lowell's sarcastic description of the "babble" that "is kept up about a national literature" and the feebleness of American criticism would have been contrary to Griswold's interests.

Lowell did not repudiate this version of his essay, but on the other hand he never reprinted it. Touchy though he sometimes was, he seems, on the basis of his letters, to have preserved in relation to Poe a certain equanimity. He wrote to his friend Charles F. Briggs in January 1845, just before his notice had come out: "From a paragraph I saw yesterday in the *Tribune* I find that Poe has been at me in the *Mirror*. He has at least that chief element of a critic—a disregard of persons. He will be a very valuable coadjutor to you." (Poe and Briggs were both on the staff of the *Broadway Journal*.) His opinion of Griswold appears in a later letter to Briggs, who had written him that Griswold had been circulating "some abominable lies" about Poe: "The Rev. Mr. Griswold is an ass, and, what's more, a knave, and even if he had said anything against Poe, I should not have believed it. But neither he nor anyone else ever did. I remain of my old opinion about the allusion to Mrs. Longfellow.[1] I remain of my old opinion about Poe, and I have no doubt that Poe

---

[1] Poe had been attacking Longfellow and another poet named James Aldrich; and an anonymous writer who called himself "Outis" had made an attempt to defend them. In his *Reply to "Outis,"* Poe had just written: "There can be no doubt in the world . . . that 'Outis' considers me a fool: the thing is sufficiently plain; and this opinion on the part of 'Outis' is what mankind have agreed to denominate an idea; and this idea is also entertained by Mr. Aldrich, and by Mr. Longfellow—and by Mrs. 'Outis' and her seven children —and by Mrs. Aldrich and hers—and by Mrs. Longfellow and hers —including the grandchildren and great grandchildren, if any, who

estimates Longfellow's poetical abilities more highly than I do perhaps, but I nevertheless do not like his two last articles. I still think Poe an invaluable contributor, but I like such articles as his review of Miss Barrett better than these last." Later, Lowell called on Poe in New York. Poe had been drinking, says Briggs, and Lowell seems to have got rather a bad impression of him: "Poe, I am afraid," he wrote Briggs on August 21, 1845, "is wholly lacking in that element of manhood which, for want of a better name, we call character. It is something quite distinct from genius—though all great geniuses are endowed with it. Hence we always think of Dante Alighieri, of Michelangelo, of Will Shakespeare, of John Milton—while of such men as Gibbon and Hume we merely recall the works, and think of them as the author of this and that. As I prognosticated, I have made Poe my enemy by doing him a service.

"In the last *Broadway Journal* he has accused me of plagiarism, and misquoted Wordsworth to sustain his charge.

> Armor rustling on the walls,
> On the blood of Clifford calls,

he quotes, italicizing *rustling* as the point of resemblance. The word is really *rusting*—you will find the passage in Wordsworth's *Song Sung at Brougham Castle,* etc. My metaphor was drawn from some old Greek or Roman story which was in my mind, and which Poe, who makes such a scholar of himself, ought to have known. There is a similar incident in Chaucer's *Knight's Tale,* probably from the same source. Anyone who had ever read the whole of Wordsworth's poem would see that there was no resemblance between the two passages. Poe wishes to kick down the ladder by which he rose. He is welcome. But he does not attack me at a weak point. He probably cannot conceive of anybody's writing for anything but a newspaper reputation or for posthumous fame, which is much the same thing magnified by

will be instructed to transmit the idea in unadulterated purity down an infinite vista of generations yet to come."

Lowell had complained to Briggs of what he called "the grossness and vulgarity" of this.

distance. I have quite other aims." In the *Fable for Critics,* though he still speaks of Poe's "genius," he deals with him perfunctorily and briefly, and he makes the same kind of criticism—"the heart somehow seems all squeezed out by the mind"—as in the new ending to the *Graham's* article. Since, however, the *Fable for Critics* had come out in 1848, Griswold might have been echoing this.

The version of Lowell's article published in the Griswold edition of Poe has been reprinted in the Woodberry and the Stoddard editions; but the original, as far as I know, though it is quoted by Mr. Quinn in his biography, is here reprinted for the first time in full. I have indicated the later changes and made only a few corrections of what are obviously typographical errors. Poe had substituted *Lenore* for another poem quoted by Lowell. He wrote Lowell that he was making this change: one wonders whether it was Poe himself who added: "How exquisite, too, is the rhythm!"

The essay, though it did not appear till February 1845, had been written in 1844, so that Lowell does not mention *The Raven,* which had come out the month before and created a considerable sensation.

JAMES RUSSELL LOWELL

EDGAR ALLAN POE

THE SITUATION of American literature is anomalous. It has no center, or, if it have, it is like that of the sphere of Hermes. It is divided into many systems, each revolving round its several sun, and often presenting to the rest only the faint glimmer of a milk-and-watery way. Our capital city, unlike London or Paris, is not a great central heart, from which life and vigor radiate to the extremities, but resembles more an isolated umbilicus, stuck down as near as may be to the center of the land, and seeming rather to tell a legend of former usefulness than to serve any present need. Boston, New York, Philadelphia, each has its literature almost more distinct than those of the different dialects of Germany; and the Young Queen of the West has also one of her own, of which some articulate rumor barely has reached us dwellers by the Atlantic. Meanwhile, a great babble is kept up concerning a national literature, and the country, having delivered itself of the ugly likeness of a paint-bedaubed, filthy savage, smilingly dandles the rag baby upon her maternal knee, as if it were veritable flesh and blood, and would grow timely to bone and sinew.

But, before we have an American literature, we must have

an American criticism. We have, it is true, some scores of
"American Macaulays," the faint echoes of defunct originalities, who will discourse learnedly at an hour's notice upon
matters, to be even a sciolist in which would ask the patient
study and self-denial of years—but, with a few rare exceptions, America is still to seek a profound, original, and
aesthetic criticism. Our criticism, which from its nature
might be expected to pass most erudite judgment upon the
merit of thistles, undertakes to decide upon

The plant and flower of light.

There is little life in it, little conscientiousness, little reverence; nay, it has seldom the mere physical merit of fearless-
ness. It may be best likened to an intellectual gathering of
chips to keep the critical pot of potatoes or reputation
a-boiling. Too often, indeed, with the cast garments of some
pigmy Gifford, or other foreign notoriety, which he has
picked up at the ragfair of literature, our critic sallies forth,
a self-dubbed Amadis, armed with a pen, which, more wonderful even than the fairy-gifts in an old ballad, becomes at
will either the lance couched terribly at defiant windmills,
or the trumpet for a halfpenny pæan.[1]
  Perhaps there is no task more difficult than the just criticism of contemporary literature. It is even more grateful to
give praise where it is needed than where it is deserved, and
friendship so often seduces the iron stylus of justice into a
vague flourish, that she writes what seems rather like an
epitaph than a criticism. Yet if praise be given as an alms,
we could not drop so poisonous a one into any man's hat.
The critic's ink may suffer equally from too large an infusion
of nutgalls or of sugar. But it is easier to be generous than
to be just, though there are some who find it equally hard to
be either,[2] and we might readily put faith in that fabulous
direction to the hiding-place of truth, did we judge from the
amount of water which we usually find mixed with it.

[1]This paragraph and the last sentence of the paragraph before are
omitted in the text of 1850. E. W.

[2]*Though there are some who find it equally hard to be either* is
omitted in the text of 1850. E. W.

We were very naturally led into some remarks on American criticism by the subject of the present sketch. Mr. Poe is at once the most discriminating, philosophical, and fearless critic upon imaginative works who has written in America. It may be that we should qualify our remark a little, and say that he *might be,* rather than that he always *is,* for he seems sometimes to mistake his phial of prussic-acid for his inkstand. If we do not always agree with him in his premises, we are, at least, satisfied that his deductions are logical, and that we are reading the thoughts of a man who thinks for himself, and says what he thinks, and knows well what he is talking about. His analytic power would furnish forth bravely some score of ordinary critics. We do not know him personally, but we suspect him for a man who has one or two pet prejudices on which he prides himself. These sometimes allure him out of the strict path of criticism,[1] but, where they do not interfere, we would put almost entire confidence in his judgments. Had Mr. Poe had the control of a magazine of his own, in which to display his critical abilities, he would have been as autocratic, ere this, in America, as Professor Wilson has been in England; and his criticisms, we are sure, would have been far more profound and philosophical than those of the Scotsman. As it is, he has squared out blocks enough to build an enduring pyramid, but has left them lying carelessly and unclaimed in many different quarries.[2]

Remarkable experiences are usually confined to the inner life of imaginative men, but Mr. Poe's biography displays a vicissitude and peculiarity of interest such as is rarely met with. The offspring of a romantic marriage, and left an orphan at an early age, he was adopted by Mr. Allan, a wealthy Virginian, whose barren marriage bed seemed the warranty of a large estate to the young poet. Having received a classical education in England, he returned home and entered the University of Virginia, where, after an

[1]We cannot but think that this was the case in his review of W. E. Channing's poems, in which we are sure that there is much which must otherwise have challenged Mr. Poe's hearty liking. J. R. L.

[2]This paragraph is omitted in the text of 1850. E. W.

extravagant course, followed by reformation at the last extremity, he was graduated with the highest honors of his class. Then came a boyish attempt to join the fortunes of the insurgent Greeks, which ended at St. Petersburg, where he got into difficulties through want of a passport, from which he was rescued by the American consul and sent home.[1] He now entered the military academy at West Point, from which he obtained a dismissal on hearing of the birth of a son to his adopted father, by a second marriage, an event which cut off his expectations as an heir.[2] The death of Mr. Allan, in whose will his name was not mentioned, soon after relieved him of all doubt in this regard, and he committed himself at once to authorship for a support. Previously to this, however, he had published (in 1827) a small volume of poems, which soon ran through three editions, and excited high expectations of its author's future distinction in the minds of many competent judges.

That no certain augury can be drawn from a poet's earliest lispings there are instances enough to prove. Shakespeare's first poems, though brimful of vigor and youth and picturesqueness, give but a very faint promise of the directness, condensation, and overflowing moral of his maturer works. Perhaps, however, Shakespeare is hardly a case in point, his *Venus and Adonis* having been published, we believe, in his twenty-sixth year. Milton's Latin verses show tenderness, a fine eye for nature, and a delicate appreciation of classic models, but give no hint of the author of a new style in poetry. Pope's youthful pieces have all the sing-song, wholly

---

[1]This trip to Europe was a myth, invented by Poe to cover up the fact that, after quarreling with Allan, his foster father, in 1827, he had enlisted in the United States Army as "Edgar A. Perry" and had, first as private, then as sergeant major, served from May 26, 1827, to April 15, 1829, in Boston Harbor and Charleston Harbor. E. W.

[2]Poe announced his intention of getting himself dismissed from West Point in a letter of January 3, 1831; John Allan's first child by his second wife was not born till August 23. Mr. A. H. Quinn says that it is nevertheless true that Allan's second marriage had something to do with Poe's decision to give up his military career. E. W.

unrelieved by the glittering malignity and eloquent irreligion
of his later productions. Collins' callow namby-pamby died
and gave no sign of the vigorous and original genius which
he afterward displayed. We have never thought that the
world lost more in the "marvelous boy," Chatterton, than a
very ingenious imitator of obscure and antiquated dullness.
Where he becomes original (as it is called) the interest of
ingenuity ceases and he becomes stupid. Kirke White's
promises were endorsed by the respectable name of Mr.
Southey, but surely with no authority from Apollo. They
have the merit of a traditional piety, which, to our mind,
if uttered at all, had been less objectionable in the retired
closet of a diary, and in the sober raiment of prose. They do
not clutch hold of the memory with the drowning pertinacity
of Watts'; neither have they the interest of his occasional
simple, lucky beauty. Burns, having fortunately been rescued
by his humble station from the contaminating society of the
"best models," wrote well and naturally from the first. Had
he been unfortunate enough to have had an educated taste,
we should have had a series of poems from which, as from
his letters, we could sift here and there a kernel from the
mass of chaff. Coleridge's youthful efforts give no promise
whatever of that poetical genius which produced at once the
wildest, tenderest, most original and most purely imaginative
poems of modern times. Byron's *Hours of Idleness* would
never find a reader except from an intrepid and indefatigable
curiosity. In Wordsworth's first preludings there is but a dim
foreboding of the creator of an era. From Southey's early
poems, a safer augury might have been drawn. They show
the patient investigator, the close student of history, and the
unwearied explorer of the beauties of predecessors, but they
give no assurances of a man who should add aught to [the]
stock of household words, or to the rarer and more sacred
delights of the fireside or the arbor. The earliest specimens
of Shelley's poetic mind already, also, give tokens of that
ethereal sublimation in which the spirit seems to soar above
the region of words, but leaves its body, the verse, to be entombed, without hope of resurrection, in a mass of them.
Cowley is generally instanced as a wonder of precocity. But

his early insipidities show only a capacity for rhyming and for the metrical arrangement of certain conventional combinations of words, a capacity wholly dependent on a delicate physical organization, and an unhappy memory. An early poem is only remarkable when it displays an effort of *reason,* and the rudest verses in which we can trace some conception of the ends of poetry are worth all the miracles of smooth juvenile versification. A schoolboy, one would say, might acquire the regular seesaw of Pope merely by an association with the motion of the playground tilt.

Mr. Poe's early productions show that he could see through the verse to the spirit beneath, and that he already had a feeling that all the life and grace of the one must depend on and be modulated by the will of the other. We call them the most remarkable boyish poems that we have ever read. We know of none that can compare with them for maturity of purpose, and a nice understanding of the effects of language and meter. Such pieces are only valuable when they display what we can only express by the contradictory phrase of *innate experience.* We copy one of the shorter poems written when the author was only *fourteen!*[1] There is a little dimness in the filling up, but the grace and symmetry of the outline are such as few poets ever attain. There is a smack of ambrosia about it.

To Helen

Helen, thy beauty is to me
　　Like those Nicéan barks of yore,
That gently, o'er a perfumed sea,
　　The weary, way-worn wanderer bore
　　To his own native shore.

On desperate seas long wont to roam,
　　Thy hyacinth hair, thy classic face,
Thy Naiad airs have brought me home
　　To the glory that was Greece
　　And the grandeur that was Rome.

[1]The first version of *To Helen* may have been written when Poe was a boy, but it was included only in his third book of poems, published in 1831, and then in a form much inferior to the final version

> Lo! in yon brilliant window-niche
> How statue-like I see thee stand!
> The agate lamp within thy hand,
> Ah! Psyche, from the regions which
> Are Holy Land!

It is the *tendency* of the young poet that impresses us. Here is no "withering scorn," no heart "blighted" ere it has safely got into its teens, none of the drawing-room sansculottism which Byron had brought into vogue. All is limpid and serene, with a pleasant dash of the Greek Helicon in it. The melody of the whole, too, is remarkable. It is not of that kind which can be demonstrated arithmetically upon the tips of the fingers. It is of that finer sort which the inner ear alone can estimate. It seems simple, like a Greek column, because of its perfection. In a poem named *Ligeia,* under which title he intended to personify the music of nature, our boy-poet gives us the following exquisite picture:

> Ligeia! Ligeia!
>   My beautiful one,
> Whose harshest idea
>   Will to melody run,
> *Say, is it thy will*
>   *On the breezes to toss,*
> *Or, capriciously still,*
>   *Like the lone albatross,*
> *Incumbent on night,*
>   *As she on the air,*
> *To keep watch with delight*
>   *On the harmony there?*

John Neal, himself a man of genius, and whose lyre has been too long capriciously silent, appreciated the high merit of these and similar passages, and drew a proud horoscope for their author. The extracts which we shall presently make from Mr. Poe's later poems fully justify his predictions.[1]

Mr. Poe has that indescribable something which men

given by Lowell. This version was not published till 1843, when Poe was thirty-four. E. W.

[1] This sentence is omitted in the text of 1850. E. W.

have agreed to call *genius*. No man could ever tell us precisely what it is, and yet there is none who is not inevitably aware of its presence and its power. Let talent writhe and contort itself as it may, it has no such magnetism. Larger of bone and sinew it may be, but the wings are wanting. Talent sticks fast to earth, and its most perfect works have still one foot of clay. Genius claims kindred with the very workings of Nature herself, so that a sunset shall seem like a quotation from Dante or Milton, and if Shakespeare be read in the very presence of the sea itself, his verses shall but seem nobler for the sublime criticism of ocean. Talent may make friends for itself, but only genius can give to its creations the divine power of winning love and veneration. Enthusiasm cannot cling to what itself is unenthusiastic, nor will he ever have disciples who has not himself impulsive zeal enough to be a disciple. Great wits are allied to madness only inasmuch as they are possessed and carried away by their demon, while talent keeps him, as Paracelsus did, securely prisoned in the pommel of its sword. To the eye of genius, the veil of the spiritual world is ever rent asunder, that it may perceive the ministers of good and evil who throng continually around it. No man of mere talent ever flung his inkstand at the devil.

When we say that Mr. Poe has genius, we do not mean to say that he has produced evidence of the highest. But to say that he possesses it at all is to say that he needs only zeal, industry, and a reverence for the trust reposed in him, to achieve the proudest triumphs and the greenest laurels. If we may believe the Longinuses and Aristotles of our newspapers, we have quite too many geniuses of the loftiest order to render a place among them at all desirable, whether for its hardness of attainment or its seclusion. The highest peak of our Parnassus is, according to these gentlemen, by far the most thickly settled portion of the country, a circumstance which must make it an uncomfortable residence for individuals of a poetical temperament, if love of solitude be, as immemorial tradition asserts, a necessary part of their idiosyncrasy. There is scarce a gentleman or lady of respectable moral character to whom these liberal dispensers of the laurel creation of Beauty,[1] and perhaps it is only in the definition of that word that we disagree with him. But in what we shall say of his writings we shall take his own standard as our guide. The temple of the god of song is equally accessible from every side, and there is room enough in it for all who bring offerings, or seek an oracle.

In his tales, Mr. Poe has chosen to exhibit his power chiefly in that dim region which stretches from the very utmost limits of the probable into the weird confines of superstition and unreality. He combines in a very remarkable manner two faculties which are seldom found united: a power of influencing the mind of the reader by the impalpable shadows of mystery, and a minuteness of detail which does not leave a pin or a button unnoticed. Both are, in truth, the natural results of the predominating quality of his mind, to which we have before alluded, analysis. It is this which distinguishes the artist. His mind at once reaches forward to the effect to be produced. Having resolved to bring about certain emotions in the reader, he makes all subordinate parts tend strictly to the common center. Even his mystery is mathematical to his own mind. To him x is a known quantity all along. In any picture that he paints, he understands the chemical properties of all his colors. However vague some of his figures may seem, however formless the shadows, to him the outline is as clear and distinct as that of a geometrical diagram. For this reason Mr. Poe has no sympathy with *Mysticism*. The Mystic dwells *in* the mystery, is enveloped with it; it colors all his thoughts; it affects his optic nerve especially, and the commonest things get a rainbow edging from it. Mr. Poe, on the other hand, is a spectator *ab extra*. He analyzes, he dissects, he watches.

> ——with an eye serene,
> The very pulse of the machine,

for such it practically is to him, with wheels and cogs and piston rods all working to produce a certain end. It is this that makes him so good a critic. Nothing balks him, or

[1] Mr. P.'s proposition is here perhaps somewhat too *generally* stated. Editor of *Graham's Magazine*.

have not given a ticket to that once sacred pr.
may elbow Shakespeare and Milton at leisur.
visitor, such as a critic must necessarily be, sees
mate proprietors in common, parading their sacrec
as thick and buzzing as flies, each with "Entered a
to act of Congress" labeled securely to his back. Forme.
Phœbus, a foreigner, we believe, had the monopoly of \
porting all passengers thither, a service for which he provi
no other conveyance than a vicious horse, named Pegasu
who could, of course, carry but one at a time, and even that
but seldom, his back being a ticklish seat, and one fall proving generally enough to damp the ardor of the most zealous
aspirant. The charges, however, were moderate, as the poet's
pocket formerly occupied that position in regard to the rest
of his outfit which is now more usually conceded to his head.
But we must return from our little historical digression.[1]

Mr. Poe has two of the prime qualities of genius, a faculty
of vigorous yet minute analysis, and a wonderful fecundity
of imagination. The first of these faculties is as needful to
the artist in words, as a knowledge of anatomy is to the artist
in colors or in stone. This enables him to conceive truly, to
maintain a proper relation of parts, and to draw a correct
outline, while the second groups, fills up, and colors. Both
of these Mr. Poe has displayed with singular distinctness in
his prose works, the last predominating in his earlier tales,
and the first in his later ones. In judging of the merit of an
author, and assigning him his niche among our household
gods, we have a right to regard him from our own point of
view, and to measure him by our own standard. But, in
estimating[2] his works, we must be governed by his own
design, and, placing them by the side of his own ideal, find
how much is wanting. We differ with[3] Mr. Poe in his opinions of the objects of art. He esteems that object to be the

[1]The latter part of this paragraph, from the sentence that begins,
There is scarce a gentleman or lady . . ., is omitted in the text of
1850. E. W.

[2]In the text of 1850 this phrase reads, *in estimating the amount
of power displayed in his works.* E. W.

[3]*With* has been changed to *from* in the edition of 1850. E. W.

throws him off the scent, *except now and then a prejudice.*[1]

This analyzing tendency of his mind balances the poetical, and, by giving him the patience to be minute, enables him to throw a wonderful reality into his most unreal fancies. A monomania he paints with great power. He loves to dissect one of these cancers of the mind, and to trace all the subtle ramifications of its roots. In raising images of horror, also, he has a strange success; conveying to us sometimes by a dusky hint some terrible *doubt* which is the secret of all horror. He leaves to imagination the task of finishing the picture, a task to which only she is competent.

> For much imaginary work was there;
> Conceit deceitful, so compact, so kind,
> That for Achilles' image stood his spear
> Grasped in an armed hand; himself behind
> Was left unseen, save to the eye of mind.

We have hitherto spoken chiefly of Mr. Poe's *collected* tales, as by them he is more widely known than by those published since in various magazines, and which we hope soon to see collected. In these he has more strikingly displayed his analytic propensity.[2]

[1] The last two sentences of this paragraph are omitted in the text of 1850. Lowell was evidently referring to Poe's prejudice against New England. E. W.

[2] Since the publication of the *Tales of the Grotesque and Arabesque*, Mr. P. has written, for this and other journals, the following tales, independently of essays, criticisms, etc.: *The Mystery of Marie Rogêt, Never Bet Your Head, A Tale of the Ragged Mountains, The Masque of the Red Death, The Colloquy of Monos and Una, The Landscape Garden, The Pit and the Pendulum, The Tell-Tale Heart, The Black Cat, The Man of the Crowd, The System of Doctors Tarr and Fether, The Spectacles, The Elk, The Business Man, The Premature Burial, The Oblong-Box, Thou Art the Man, Eleonora, Three Sundays in a Week, The Island of the Fay, Life in Death, The Angel of the Odd, The Literary Life of Thingum-Bob, The Descent into the Maelstrom, The 1002d Tale of Scheherazade, Mesmeric Revelation, The Murders in the Rue Morgue, The Purloined Letter,* and *The Gold-Bug.* He is also the author of the late *Balloon-Hoax.* The *Grotesque and Arabesque* included twenty-five tales.

This paragraph with its note is omitted in the text of 1850. E. W.

Beside the merit of conception, Mr. Poe's writings have also that of form. His style is highly finished, graceful, and truly classical. It would be hard to find a living author who had displayed such varied powers. As an example of his style we would refer to one of his tales, *The House of Usher,* in the first volume of his *Tales of the Grotesque and Arabesque.* It has a singular charm for us, and we think that no one could read it without being strongly moved by its serene and somber beauty. Had its author written nothing else it would alone have been enough to stamp him as a man of genius, and the master of a classic style. In this tale occurs one of the most beautiful of his poems. It loses greatly by being taken out of its rich and appropriate setting, but we cannot deny ourselves the pleasure of copying it here. We know no modern poet who might not have been justly proud of it.

THE HAUNTED PALACE

In the greenest of our valleys,
By good angels tenanted,
Once a fair and stately palace—
Radiant palace—rear'd its head.
In the monarch Thought's dominion—
It stood there!
Never seraph spread a pinion
Over fabric half so fair!

Banners yellow, glorious, golden,
On its roof did float and flow,
(This—all this—was in the olden
Time, long ago,)
And every gentle air that dallied,
In that sweet day,
Along the ramparts plumed and pallid,
A winged odor went away.

Wanderers in that happy valley,
Through two luminous windows, saw
Spirits moving musically,
To a lute's well-tuned law,

Round about a throne where, sitting
  (Porphyrogene!)
In state his glory well befitting,
  The ruler of the realm was seen.

And all with pearl and ruby glowing
  Was the fair palace door,
Through which came flowing, flowing, flowing,
  And sparkling evermore,
A troop of Echoes, whose sweet duty
  Was but to sing,
In voices of surpassing beauty,
  The wit and wisdom of their king.

But evil things, in robes of sorrow,
  Assail'd the monarch's high estate.
(Ah, let us mourn!—for never morrow
  Shall dawn upon him desolate!)
And round about his home the glory
  That blush'd and bloom'd,
Is but a dim remember'd story
  Of the old time entomb'd.

And travelers, now, within that valley,
  Through the red-litten windows see
Vast forms, that move fantastically
  To a discordant melody,
While, like a ghastly rapid river,
  Through the pale door,
A hideous throng rush out forever,
  And laugh—but smile no more.

Was ever the wreck and desolation of a noble mind so musically sung?

A writer in the *London Foreign Quarterly Review*, who did some faint justice to Mr. Poe's poetical abilities, speaks of his resemblance to Tennyson. The resemblance, if there be any, is only in so sensitive an ear to melody as leads him sometimes into quaintness, and the germ of which may be traced in his earliest poems, published several years before the first of Tennyson's appeared.

We copy one more of Mr. Poe's poems, whose effect cannot fail of being universally appreciated.

LENORE

Ah, broken is the golden bowl!—the spirit flown forever!
Let the bell toll!—a saintly soul floats on the Stygian river.
And, Guy De Vere, hast *thou* no tear?—weep now or never
    more!
See, on yon drear and rigid bier, low lies thy love, Lenore!
Ah, let the burial rite be read—the funeral song be sung—
An anthem for the queenliest dead that ever died so young—
A dirge for her the doubly dead in that she died so young!

Wretches! ye loved her for her wealth and hated her for her
    pride,
And, when she fell in feeble health, ye blessed her—that she
    died.
How shall the ritual then be read?—the requiem how be sung
By you—by yours the evil eye—by yours the slanderous tongue,
That did to death the innocence that died and died so young?

Peccavimus; but rave not thus! and let a Sabbath song
Go up to God so solemnly the dead may feel no wrong.
The sweet Lenore hath "gone before," with Hope that flew be-
    side,
Leaving thee wild for the dear child that should have been thy
    bride—
For her the fair and *debonair* that now so lowly lies,
The life upon her yellow hair but not within her eyes—
The life still there, upon her hair—the death upon her eyes.

Avaunt!—tonight my heart is light; no dirge will I upraise,
But wait the angel on her flight with a pæan of old days!
Let *no* bell toll!—lest her sweet soul, amid its hallowed mirth,
Should catch the note as it doth float up from the damnéd earth.
To friends above, from fiends below, the indignant ghost is
    riven—
From Hell unto a high estate far up within the Heaven—
From moan and groan to a golden throne beside the King of
    Heaven.

How exquisite, too, is the rhythm!

    Beside his *Tales of the Grotesque and Arabesque,* and
some works unacknowledged, Mr. Poe is the author of
Arthur Gordon Pym, a romance, in two volumes, which has

run through many editions in London; of a system of
Conchology, of a digest and translation of Lemmonnier's
Natural History, and has contributed to several reviews in
France, in England, and in this country. He edited the
Southern Literary Messenger during its novitiate, and by his
own contributions gained it most of its success and reputation. He was also, for some time, the editor of this magazine,
and our readers will bear testimony to his ability in that
capacity.

Mr. Poe is still in the prime of life, being about thirty-two
years of age, and has probably as yet given but an earnest of
his powers. As a critic, he has shown so superior an ability
that we cannot but hope that he will collect his essays of this
kind and give them a more durable form. They would be a
very valuable contribution to our literature, and would fully
justify all we have said in his praise. We could refer to many
others of his poems than those we have quoted, to prove that
he is the possessor of a pure and original vein. His tales and
essays have equally shown him a master in prose. It is not for
us to assign him his definite rank among contemporary
authors, but we may be allowed to say that we know of
none who has displayed more varied and striking abilities.

In the text of 1850 the sentence which here introduces The
Haunted Palace *is changed to read as follows:* In this tale
occurs, perhaps, one of the most beautiful of his poems; *and
it is made to end the paragraph. The following new ending
has been substituted:*

The great masters of imagination have seldom resorted to
the vague and the unreal as sources of effect. They have not
used dread and horror alone, but only in combination with
other qualities, as means of subjugating the fancies of their
readers. The loftiest muse has ever a household and fireside
charm about her. Mr. Poe's secret lies mainly in the skill
with which he has employed the strange fascination of
mystery and terror. In this his success is so great and striking
as to deserve the name of art, not artifice. We cannot call
his materials the noblest or purest, but we must concede to
him the highest merit of construction.

As a critic, Mr. Poe was aesthetically deficient. Unerring in his analysis of dictions, meters, and plots, he seemed wanting in the faculty of perceiving the profounder ethics of art. His criticisms are, however, distinguished for scientific precision and coherence of logic. They have the exactness, and, at the same time, the coldness of mathematical demonstrations. Yet they stand in strikingly refreshing contrast with the vague generalisms and sharp personalities of the day. If deficient in warmth, they are also without the heat of partisanship. They are especially valuable as illustrating the great truth, too generally overlooked, that analytic power is a subordinate quality of the critic.

On the whole, it may be considered certain that Mr. Poe has attained an individual eminence in our literature, which he will keep. He has given proof of power and originality. He has done that which could only be done once with success or safety, and the imitation or repetition of which would produce weariness.

LOWELL's *A Fable for Critics* was published anonymously in 1848. It presents a panorama of the American writers as they appeared by the middle of the century to an alert and well-read man of letters. We had by this time been a nation long enough and had produced enough respectable writing so that a taking of stock was in order. The time for mere boosting was past, and the moment had come to discriminate. Lowell's *Fable* appears logically and naturally at a time when Edgar Allan Poe was near the end of his career as a critic, his effort month by month in his reviews to establish comparative values, and it does its best to supply the summary which Poe never lived to make.

In the *Fable,* as in all Lowell's writing, the wit is some-times clumsy or silly, and the learned illusions a bore. It is true, also, as Poe was to complain, that Lowell's ear was rather defective, so that some of the versification is rocky. Yet the *Fable* was of the best of the early Lowell, and the early Lowell was the best. He is capable of straight thought, of bold utterance, and of intellectual exhilaration. He wants a native American literature just as he wants the slaves to be freed, and in the *Fable* the first of these causes calls forth his full shrewdness and enthusiasm and humor, as the second was to do in the *Biglow Papers*. Poe is probably right, however, in insisting that political and regional prejudice made Lowell unfair to the writers of the South.

The following prefatory note appeared with the second edition:

This *jeu d'esprit* was extemporized, I may fairly say, so rapidly was it written, purely for my own amusement and with no thought of publication. I sent daily instalments of it to a friend in New York, the late Charles F. Briggs. He urged me to let it be printed, and I at last consented to its anonymous publication. The secret was kept till after several persons had laid claim to its authorship.

JAMES RUSSELL LOWELL

*Reader! walk up at once (it will soon be too late),
and buy at a perfectly ruinous rate*

A FABLE FOR CRITICS:

OR, BETTER,

(I LIKE, AS A THING THAT THE READER'S FIRST FANCY MAY STRIKE,
AN OLD-FASHIONED TITLE-PAGE,
SUCH AS PRESENTS A TABULAR VIEW OF THE VOLUME'S CONTENTS),

A GLANCE AT A FEW OF OUR LITERARY PROGENIES

(MRS. MALAPROP'S WORD)

FROM THE TUB OF DIOGENES;

A VOCAL AND MUSICAL MEDLEY,

THAT IS,

A SERIES OF JOKES

By A Wonderful Quiz,

WHO ACCOMPANIES HIMSELF WITH A RUB-A-DUB-DUB, FULL OF
SPIRIT AND GRACE, ON THE TOP OF THE TUB.

*Set forth in October, the 31st day,
In the year '48, G. P. Putnam, Broadway.*

It being the commonest mode of procedure, I premise a
few candid remarks

To the Reader:

This trifle, begun to please only myself and my own private
fancy, was laid on the shelf. But some friends, who had seen it,
induced me, by dint of saying they liked it, to put it in print.
That is, having come to that very conclusion, I asked their
advice when 'twould make no confusion. For though (in the
gentlest of ways) they had hinted it was scarce worth the while,
I should doubtless have printed it.

I began it, intending a Fable, a frail, slender thing, rhyme-
ywinged, with a sting in its tail. But, by addings and alterings
not previously planned, digressions chance-hatched, like birds'
eggs in the sand, and dawdlings to suit every whimsey's demand
(always freeing the bird which I held in my hand, for the
two perched, perhaps out of reach, in the tree),—it grew by
degrees to the size which you see. I was like the old woman
that carried the calf, and my neighbors, like hers, no doubt,
wonder and laugh; and when, my strained arms with their
grown burthen full, I call it my Fable, they call it a bull.

Having scrawled at full gallop (as far as that goes) in a
style that is neither good verse nor bad prose, and being a

person whom nobody knows, some people will say I am rather
more free with my readers than it is becoming to be, that I
seem to expect them to wait on my leisure in following wherever I wander at pleasure, that, in short, I take more than a
young author's lawful ease, and laugh in a queer way so like
Mephistopheles that the Public will doubt, as they grope
through my rhythm, if in truth I am making fun *of* them or
with them.

So the excellent Public is hereby assured that the sale of my
book is already secured. For there is not a poet throughout the
whole land but will purchase a copy or two out of hand, in the
fond expectation of being amused in it, by seeing his betters
cut up and abused in it. Now, I find, by a pretty exact calculation, there are something like ten thousand bards in the nation,
of that special variety whom the Review and Magazine critics
call *lofty* and *true,* and about thirty thousand (*this* tribe is increasing) of the kinds who are termed *full of promise* and
pleasing. The Public will see by a glance at this schedule, that
they cannot expect me to be over-sedulous about courting *them,*
since it seems I have got enough fuel made sure of for boiling
my pot.

As for such of our poets as find not their names mentioned
once in my pages, with praises or blames, let them SEND IN
THEIR CARDS, without further DELAY, to my friend G. P.
PUTNAM, Esquire, in Broadway, where a LIST will be kept with
the strictest regard to the day and the hour of receiving the
card. Then, taking them up as I chance to have time (that is,
if their names can be twisted in rhyme), I will honestly give
each his PROPER POSITION, at the rate of ONE AUTHOR to each
NEW EDITION. Thus a PREMIUM is offered sufficiently HIGH
(as the magazines say when they tell their best lie) to induce
bards to CLUB their resources and buy the balance of every
edition, until they have all of them fairly been run through the
mill.

One word to such readers (judicious and wise) as read books
with something behind the mere eyes, of whom in the country,
perhaps, there are two, including myself, gentle reader, and you.
All the characters sketched in this slight *jeu d'esprit,* though, it
may be, they seem, here and there, rather free, and drawn
from a somewhat too cynical standpoint, are *meant* to be faithful, for that is the grand point, and none but an owl would
feel sore at a rub from a jester who tells you, without any
subterfuge, that he sits in Diogenes' tub.

A Preliminary Note to the Second Edition,

though it well may be reckoned, of all composition, the species at once most delightful and healthy, is a thing which an author, unless he be wealthy and willing to pay for that kind of delight, is not, in all instances, called on to write, though there are, it is said, who, their spirits to cheer, slip in a new title-page three times a year, and in this way snuff up an imaginary savor of that sweetest of dishes, the popular favor,—much as if a starved painter should fall to and treat the Ugolino inside to a picture of meat.

You remember (if not, pray turn backward and look) that, in writing the preface which ushered my book, I treated you, excellent Public, not merely with a cool disregard, but downright cavalierly. Now I would not take back the least thing I then said, though I thereby could butter both sides of my bread, for I never could see that an author owed aught to the people he solaced, diverted, or taught; and, as for mere fame, I have long ago learned that the persons by whom it is finally earned are those with whom *your* verdict weighed not a pin, unsustained by the higher court sitting within.

But I wander from what I intended to say,—that you have, namely, shown such a liberal way of thinking, and so much aesthetic perception of anonymous worth in the handsome reception you gave to my book, spite of some private piques (having bought the first thousand in barely two weeks), that I think, past a doubt, if you measured the phiz of yours most devotedly, Wonderful Quiz, you would find that its vertical section was shorter, by an inch and two tenths, or 'twixt that and a quarter.

You have watched a child playing—in those wondrous years when belief is not bound to the eyes and the ears, and the vision divine is so clear and unmarred, that each baker of pies in the dirt is a bard? Give a knife and a shingle, he fits out a fleet, and, on that little mud-puddle over the street, his fancy, in purest good faith, will make sail round the globe with a puff of his breath for a gale, will visit, in barely ten minutes, all climes, and do the Columbus-feat hundreds of times. Or, suppose the young poet fresh stored with delights from that Bible of childhood, the *Arabian Nights,* he will turn to a crony and cry, "Jack, let's play that I am a Genius!" Jacky straightway makes Aladdin's lamp out of a stone, and, for hours, they enjoy each his own supernatural powers. This is all very pretty and pleasant, but then suppose our two urchins have grown into men, and both have turned authors,—one says to his brother, "Let's play we're the American somethings or other—say Homer or Sophocles, Goethe or Scott (only let them be big enough, no matter what). Come, you shall be Byron or Pope, which you choose: I'll be Coleridge, and both shall write mutual reviews." So they both (as mere strangers) before many days send each other a cord of anonymous bays. Each, piling his epithets, smiles in his sleeve to see what his friend can be made to believe; each, reading the other's unbiased review, thinks—Here's pretty high praise, but no more than my due. Well, we laugh at them both, and yet make no great fuss when the same farce is acted to benefit us. Even I, who, if asked, scarce a month since, what Fudge meant, should have answered, the dear Public's critical judgment, begin to think sharp-witted Horace spoke sooth when he said that the Public *sometimes* hit the truth.

In reading these lines, you perhaps have a vision of a person in pretty good health and condition; and yet, since I put forth my primary edition, I have been crushed, scorched, withered, used up and put down (by Smith with the cordial assistance of Brown), in all, if you put any faith in my rhymes, to the number of ninety-five several times, and, while I am writing,— I tremble to think of it, for I may at this moment be just on the brink of it,—Molybdostom, angry at being omitted, has begun a critique,—am I not to be pitied?[1]

Now I shall not crush *them* since, indeed, for that matter, no pressure I know of could render them flatter; nor wither, nor scorch them,—no action of fire could make either them or their articles drier; nor waste time in putting them down—I am thinking not their own self-inflation will keep them from sinking; for there's this contradiction about the whole bevy: though without the least weight, they are awfully heavy. No, my dear honest bore, *surdo fabulam narras,* they are no more to me than a rat in the arras. I can walk with the Doctor, get facts from the Don, or draw out the Lambish quintessence of John, and feel nothing more than a half-comic sorrow, to think that they all will be lying tomorrow tossed carelessly up on the waste-paper shelves, and forgotten by all but their half-dozen

---

[1]The wise Scandinavians probably called their bards by the queer-looking title of Scald, in a delicate way, as it were, just to hint to the world the hot water they always get into.

selves. Once snug in my attic, my fire in a roar, I leave the
whole pack of them outside the door. With Hakluyt or Purchas
I wander away to the black northern seas or barbaric Cathay;
get *fou* with O'Shanter, and sober me then with that builder
of brick-kilnish dramas, rare Ben; snuff Herbert, as holy as a
flower on a grave; with Fletcher wax tender, o'er Chapman grow
brave; with Marlowe or Kyd take a fine poet-rave; in Very, most
Hebrew of Saxons, find peace; with Lycidas welter on vext Irish
seas; with Webster grow wild, and climb earthward again,
down by mystical Browne's Jacob's-ladder-like brain, to that
spiritual Pepys (Cotton's version) Montaigne; find a new
depth in Wordsworth, undreamed of before, that marvel, a poet
divine who can bore. Or, out of my study, the scholar thrown
off, Nature holds up her shield 'gainst the sneer and the scoff;
the landscape, forever consoling and kind, pours her wine and
her oil on the smarts of the mind. The waterfall, scattering its
vanishing gems; the tall grove of hemlocks, with moss on their
stems, like plashes of sunlight; the pond in the woods, where
no foot but mine and the bittern's intrudes, where pitcher-
plants purple and gentians hard by recall to September the blue
of June's sky; these are all my kind neighbors, and leave me no
wish to say aught to you all, my poor critics, but—pish! I've
buried the hatchet: I'm twisting an allumette out of one of you
now, and relighting my calumet. In your private capacities,
come when you please, I will give you my hand and a fresh
pipe apiece.

As I ran through the leaves of my poor little book, to take
a fond author's first tremulous look, it was quite an excitement
to hunt the *errata,* sprawled in as birds' tracks are in some kinds
of strata (only these made things crookeder). Fancy an heir
that a father had seen born well-featured and fair, turning
suddenly wry-nosed, club-footed, squint-eyed, hair-lipped,
wapper-jawed, carrot-haired, from a pride become an aversion,—
my case was yet worse. A club-foot (by way of a change) in a
verse, I might have forgiven, an *o*'s being wry, a limp in an *e*,
or a cock in an *i*,—but to have the sweet babe of my brain served
in *pil* I am not queasy-stomached, but such a Thyestean banquet as that was quite out of the question.

In the edition now issued no pains are neglected, and my
verses, as orators say, stand corrected. Yet some blunders remain
of the Public's own make, which I wish to correct for my personal sake. For instance, a character drawn in pure fun and
condensing the traits of a dozen in one, has been, as I hear,

by some persons applied to a good friend of mine, whom to stab in the side, as we walked along chatting and joking together, would not be *my* way. I can hardly tell whether a question will ever arise in which he and I should by any strange fortune agree, but meanwhile my esteem for him grows as I know him, and, though not the best judge on earth of a poem, he knows what it is he is saying and why, and is honest and fearless, two good points which I have not found so rife I can easily smother my love for them, whether on my side or t'other.

For my other *anonymi*, you may be sure that I know what is meant by a caricature, and what by a portrait. There *are* those who think it is capital fun to be spattering their ink on quiet, unquarrelsome folk, but the minute the game changes sides and the others begin it, they see something savage and horrible in it. As for me I respect neither women nor men for their gender, nor own any sex in a pen. I choose just to hint to some causeless unfriends that, as far as I know, there are always two ends (and one of them heaviest, too) to a staff, and two parties also to every good laugh.

A FABLE FOR CRITICS

PHŒBUS, sitting one day in a laurel-tree's shade,
Was reminded of Daphne, of whom it was made,
For the god being one day too warm in his wooing,
She took to the tree to escape his pursuing;
Be the cause what it might, from his offers she shrunk,
And, Ginevra-like, shut herself up in a trunk;
And, though 'twas a step into which he had driven her,
He somehow or other had never forgiven her;
Her memory he nursed as a kind of a tonic,
Something bitter to chew when he'd play the Byronic,
And I can't count the obstinate nymphs that he brought over
By a strange kind of smile he put on when he thought of
    her.
"My case is like Dido's," he sometimes remarked;
"When I last saw my love, she was fairly embarked
In a laurel, as *she* thought—but (ah, how Fate mocks!)
She has found it by this time a very bad box;
Let hunters from me take this saw when they need it:

You're not always sure of your game when you've treed it.
Just conceive such a change taking place in one's mistress!
What romance would be left?—who can flatter or kiss trees?
And, for mercy's sake, how could one keep up a dialogue
With a dull wooden thing that will live and will die a log,—
Not to say that the thought would forever intrude
That you've less chance to win her the more she is wood?
Ah! it went to my heart, and the memory still grieves,
To see those loved graces all taking their leaves;
Those charms beyond speech, so enchanting but now,
As they left me forever, each making its bough!
If her tongue *had* a tang sometimes more than was right,
Her new bark is worse than ten times her old bite."

Now, Daphne—before she was happily treeified—
Over all other blossoms the lily had deified,
And when she expected the god on a visit
('Twas before he had made his intentions explicit),
Some buds she arranged with a vast deal of care,
To look as if artlessly twined in her hair,
Where they seemed, as he said, when he paid his addresses,
Like the day breaking through the long night of her tresses;
So whenever he wished to be quite irresistible,
Like a man with eight trumps in his hand at a whist-table
(I feared me at first that the rhyme was untwistable,
Though I might have lugged in an allusion to *Cristabel*),—
He would take up a lily, and gloomily look in it,
As I shall at the ——, when they cut up my book in it.

Well, here, after all the bad rhyme I've been spinning,
I've got back at last to my story's beginning:
Sitting there, as I say, in the shade of his mistress,
As dull as a volume of old Chester mysteries,
Or as those puzzling specimens which, in old histories,
We read of his verses—the Oracles, namely,—
(I wonder the Greeks should have swallowed them tamely,
For one might bet safely whatever he has to risk,
They were laid at his door by some ancient Miss Asterisk,
And so dull that the men who retailed them outdoors

Got the ill name of augurs, because they were bores,)
First, he mused what the animal substance or herb is
Would induce a mustache, for you know he's *imberbis;*
Then he shuddered to think how his youthful position
Was assailed by the age of his son the physician;
At some poems he glanced, had been sent to him lately,
And the meter and sentiment puzzled him greatly;
"Mehercle! I'd make such proceeding felonious,—
Have they all of them slept in the cave of Trophonius?
Look well to your seat, 'tis like taking an airing
On a corduroy road, and that out of repairing;
It leads one, 'tis true, through the primitive forest,
Grand natural features, but then one has no rest;
You just catch a glimpse of some ravishing distance,
When a jolt puts the whole of it out of existence,—
Why not use their ears, if they happen to have any?"
—Here the laurel-leaves murmured the name of poor
    Daphne.

"Oh, weep with me, Daphne," he sighed, "for you know
    it's
A terrible thing to be pestered with poets!
But, alas, she is dumb, and the proverb holds good,
She never will cry till she's out of the wood!
What wouldn't I give if I never had known of her?
'Twere a kind of relief had I something to groan over:
If I had but some letters of hers, now, to toss over,
I might turn for the nonce a Byronic philosopher,
And bewitch all the flats by bemoaning the loss of her.
One needs something tangible, though, to begin on,—
A loom, as it were, for the fancy to spin on;
What boots all your grist? it can never be ground
Till a breeze makes the arms of the windmill go round;
(Or, if 'tis a water mill, alter the metaphor,
And say it won't stir, save the wheel be well wet afore,
Or lug in some stuff about water 'so dreamily'—
It is not a metaphor, though, 'tis a simile);
A lily, perhaps, would set *my* mill a-going,
For just at this season, I think, they are blowing.

Here, somebody, fetch one; not very far hence
They're in bloom by the score, 'tis but climbing a fence;
There's a poet hard by, who does nothing but fill his
Whole garden, from one end to t'other, with lilies;
A very good plan, were it not for satiety,
One longs for a weed here and there, for variety;
Though a weed is no more than a flower in disguise,
Which is seen through at once, if love give a man eyes."

Now there happened to be among Phœbus's followers,
A gentleman, one of the omnivorous swallowers,
Who bolt every book that comes out of the press,
Without the least question of larger or less,
Whose stomachs are strong at the expense of their head,—
For reading new books is like eating new bread,
One can bear it at first, but by gradual steps he
Is brought to death's door of a mental dyspepsy.
On a previous stage of existence, our Hero
Had ridden outside, with the glass below zero;
He had been, 'tis a fact you may safely rely on,
Of a very old stock a most eminent scion,—
A stock all fresh quacks their fierce boluses ply on,
Who stretch the new boots Earth's unwilling to try on,
Whom humbugs of all shapes and sorts keep their eye on,
Whose hair's in the mortar of every new Zion,
Who, when whistles are dear, go directly and buy one,
Who think slavery a crime that we must not say fie on,
Who hunt, if they e'er hunt at all, with the lion
(Though they hunt lions also, whenever they spy one),
Who contrive to make every good fortune a wry one,
And at last choose the hard bed of honor to die on,
Whose pedigree, traced to earth's earliest years,
Is longer than anything else but their ears;—
In short, he was sent into life with the wrong key,
He unlocked the door, and stept forth a poor donkey.
Though kicked and abused by his bipedal betters
Yet he filled no mean place in the kingdom of letters;
Far happier than many a literary hack,
He bore only paper-mill rags on his back

(For it makes a vast difference which side the mill
One expends on the paper his labor and skill);
So, when his soul waited a new transmigration,
And Destiny balanced 'twixt this and that station,
Not having much time to expend upon bothers,
Remembering he'd had some connection with authors,
And considering his four legs had grown paralytic,—
She set him on two, and he came forth a critic.

Through his babyhood no kind of pleasure he took
In any amusement but tearing a book;
For him there was no intermediate stage
From babyhood up to strait-laced middle age;
There were years when he didn't wear coattails behind,
But a boy he could never be rightly defined;
Like the Irish Good Folk, though in length scarce a span,
From the womb he came gravely, a little old man;
While other boys' trousers demanded the toil
Of the motherly fingers on all kinds of soil,
Red, yellow, brown, black, clayey, gravelly, loamy,
He sat in the corner and read *Viri Romæ*.
He never was known to unbend or to revel once
In base, marbles, hockey, or kick up the devil once;
He was just one of those who excite the benevolence
Of your old prigs who sound the soul's depths with a ledger,
And are on the lookout for some young men to "edger-
cate," as they call it, who won't be too costly,
And who'll afterward take to the ministry mostly;
Who always wear spectacles, always look bilious,
Always keep on good terms with each *mater-familias*
Throughout the whole parish, and manage to rear
Ten boys like themselves, on four hundred a year:
Who, fulfilling in turn the same fearful conditions,
Either preach through their noses, or go upon missions.

In this way our Hero got safely to college,
Where he bolted alike both his commons and knowledge;
A reading machine, always wound up and going,
He mastered whatever was not worth the knowing,

Appeared in a gown, with black waistcoat of satin,
To spout such a Gothic oration in Latin
That Tully could never have made out a word in it
(Though himself was the model the author preferred in it),
And grasping the parchment which gave him in fee
All the mystic and-so-forths contained in A. B.,
He was launched (life is always compared to a sea)
With just enough learning, and skill for the using it,
To prove he'd a brain, by forever confusing it.
So worthy St. Benedict, piously burning
With the holiest zeal against secular learning,
Nesciensque scienter, as writers express it,
Indoctusque sapienter a Roma recessit.

'Twould be endless to tell you the things that he knew,
Each a separate fact, undeniably true,
But with him or each other they'd nothing to do;
No power of combining, arranging, discerning,
Digested the masses he learned into learning;
There was one thing in life he had practical knowledge for
(And this, you will think, he need scarce go to college for),—
Not a deed would he do, nor a word would he utter,
Till he'd weighed its relations to plain bread and butter.
When he left Alma Mater, he practiced his wits
In compiling the journals' historical bits,—
Of shops broken open, men falling in fits,
Great fortunes in England bequeathed to poor printers,
And cold spells, the coldest for many past winters,—
Then, rising by industry, knack, and address,
Got notices up for an unbiased press,
With a mind so well poised, it seemed equally made for
Applause or abuse, just which chanced to be paid for:
From this point his progress was rapid and sure,
To the post of a regular heavy reviewer.

And here I must say he wrote excellent articles
On Hebraical points, or the force of Greek particles;
They filled up the space nothing else was prepared for,
And nobody read that which nobody cared for;

If any old book reached a fiftieth edition,
He could fill forty pages with safe erudition:
He could gauge the old books by the old set of rules,
And his very old nothings pleased very old fools;
But give him a new book, fresh out of the heart,
And you put him at sea without compass or chart,—
His blunders aspired to the rank of an art;
For his lore was engraft, something foreign that grew in him,
Exhausting the sap of the native and true in him,
So that when a man came with a soul that was new in him,
Carving new forms of truth out of Nature's old granite,
New and old at their birth, like Le Verrier's planet,
Which, to get a true judgment, themselves must create
In the soul of their critic the measure and weight,
Being rather themselves a fresh standard of grace,
To compute their own judge, and assign him his place,
Our reviewer would crawl all about it and round it,
And, reporting each circumstance just as he found it,
Without the least malice,—his record would be
Profoundly aesthetic as that of a flea,
Which, supping on Wordsworth, should print, for our sakes,
Recollections of nights with the Bard of the Lakes,
Or, lodged by an Arab guide, ventured to render a
Comprehensive account of the ruins at Denderah.

　　As I said, he was never precisely unkind,
The defect in his brain was just absence of mind;
If he boasted, 'twas simply that he was self-made,
A position which I, for one, never gainsaid,
My respect for my Maker supposing a skill
In His works which our Hero would answer but ill;
And I trust that the mold which he used may be cracked,
　　or he,
Made bold by success, may enlarge his phylactery,
And set up a kind of a man-manufactory,—
An event which I shudder to think about, seeing
That Man is a moral, accountable being.

　　He meant well enough, but was still in the way,
As dunces still are, let them be where they may;

Indeed, they appear to come into existence
To impede other folks with their awkward assistance;
If you set up a dunce on the very North Pole
All alone with himself, I believe, on my soul,
He'd manage to get betwixt somebody's shins,
And pitch him down bodily, all in his sins,
To the grave polar bears sitting round on the ice,
All shortening their grace, to be in for a slice;
Or, if he found nobody else there to pother,
Why, one of his legs would just trip up the other,
For there's nothing we read of in torture's inventions,
Like a well-meaning dunce, with the best of intentions.

A terrible fellow to meet in society,
Not the toast that he buttered was ever so dry at tea;
There he'd sit at the table and stir in his sugar,
Crouching close for a spring, all the while, like a cougar;
Be sure of your facts, of your measures and weights,
Of your time,—he's as fond as an Arab of dates;
You'll be telling, perhaps, in your comical way,
Of something you've seen in the course of the day;
And, just as you're tapering out the conclusion,
You venture an ill-fated classic allusion,—
The girls have all got their laughs ready, when, whack!
The cougar comes down on your thunderstruck back!
You had left out a comma,—your Greek's put in joint,
And pointed at cost of your story's whole point.
In the course of the evening, you find chance for certain
Soft speeches to Anne, in the shade of the curtain:
You tell her your heart can be likened to *one* flower,
"And that, O most charming of women's the sunflower,
Which turns"—here a clear nasal voice, to your terror,
From outside the curtain, says, "That's all an error."
As for him, he's—no matter, he never grew tender,
Sitting after a ball, with his feet on the fender,
Shaping somebody's sweet features out of cigar smoke
(Though he'd willingly grant you that such doings are
    smoke);
All women he damns with *mutabile semper,*

And if ever he felt something like love's distemper,
'Twas tow'rd a young lady who spoke ancient Mexican,
And assisted her father in making a lexicon;
Though I recollect hearing him get quite ferocious
About Mary Clausum, the mistress of Grotius,
Or something of that sort,—but, no more to bore ye
With character-painting, I'll turn to my story.

   Now, Apollo, who finds it convenient sometimes
To get his court clear of the makers of rhymes,
The *genus*, I think it is called, *irritabile*,
Every one of whom thinks himself treated most shabbily,
And nurses a—what is it?—*immedicabile*,
Which keeps him at boiling point, hot for a quarrel,
As bitter as wormwood, and sourer than sorrel,
If any poor devil but look at a laurel—
Apollo, I say, being sick of their rioting
(Though he sometimes acknowledged their verse had a
    quieting
Effect after dinner, and seemed to suggest a
Retreat to the shrine of a tranquil siesta),
Kept our Hero at hand, who, by means of a bray,
Which he gave to the life, drove the rabble away;
And if that wouldn't do, he was sure to succeed,
If he took his review out and offered to read;
Or, failing in plans of this milder description,
He would ask for their aid to get up a subscription,
Considering that authorship wasn't a rich craft,
To print the "American drama of Witchcraft."
"Stay, I'll read you a scene,"—but he hardly began,
Ere Apollo shrieked "Help!" and the authors all ran:
And once, when these purgatives acted with less spirit,
And the desperate case asked a remedy desperate,
He drew from his pocket a foolscap epistle
As calmly as if 'twere a nine-barreled pistol,
And threatened them all with the judgment to come,
Of "A wandering Star's first impressions of Rome."
"Stop! stop!" with their hands o'er their ears, screamed the
    Muses,

"He may go off and murder himself, if he chooses,
'Twas a means self-defense only sanctioned his trying,
'Tis mere massacre now that the enemy's flying;
If he's forced to 't again, and we happen to be there,
Give us each a large handkerchief soaked in strong ether."

I called this a *Fable for Critics;* you think it's
More like a display of my rhythmical trinkets;
My plot, like an icicle, 's slender and slippery,
Every moment more slender, and likely to slip awry,
And the reader unwilling *in loco desipere,*
Is free to jump over as much of my frippery
As he fancies, and, if he's a provident skipper, he
May have like Odysseus control of the gales,
And get safe to port, ere his patience quite fails;
Moreover, although 'tis a slender return
For your toil and expense, yet my paper will burn,
And, if you have manfully struggled thus far with me,
You may e'en twist me up, and just light your cigar with
    me:
If too angry for that, you can tear me in pieces,
And my *membra disjecta* consign to the breezes,
A fate like great Ratzau's, whom one of those bores,
Who beflead with bad verses poor Louis Quatorze,
Describes (the first verse somehow ends with *victoire*),
As *dispersant partout et ses membres et sa gloire;*
Or, if I were over desirous of earning
A repute among noodles for classical learning,
I could pick you a score of allusions, i-wis,
As new as the jests of *Didaskalos tis;*
Better still, I could make out a good solid list
From authors recondite who do not exist,—
But that would be naughty: at least, I could twist
Something out of Absyrtus, or turn your inquiries
After Milton's prose metaphor, drawn from Osiris;
But, as Cicero says he won't say this or that
(A fetch, I must say, most transparent and flat),
After saying whate'er he could possibly think of,—
I simply will state that I pause on the brink of

A mire, ankle-deep, of deliberate confusion,
Made up of old jumbles of classic allusion:
So, when you were thinking yourselves to be pitied,
Just conceive how much harder your teeth you'd have
    gritted,
An 'twere not for the dullness I've kindly omitted.

I'd apologize here for my many digressions,
Were it not that I'm certain to trip into fresh ones
('Tis so hard to escape if you get in their mesh once);
Just reflect, if you please, how 'tis said by Horatius,
That Mæonides nods now and then, and, my gracious!
It certainly does look a little bit ominous
When he gets under way with *ton d' apameibomenos.*
(Here a something occurs which I'll just clap a rhyme to,
And say it myself, ere a Zoïlus have time to,—
Any author a nap like Van Winkle's may take,
If he only contrive to keep readers awake,
But he'll very soon find himself laid on the shelf,
If *they* fall a-nodding when he nods himself.)

Once for all, to return, and to stay, will I, nill I—
When Phœbus expressed his desire for a lily,
Our Hero, whose homœopathic sagacity
With an ocean of zeal mixed his drop of capacity,
Set off for the garden as fast as the wind
(Or, to take a comparison more to my mind,
As a sound politician leaves conscience behind),
And leaped the low fence, as a party hack jumps
O'er his principles, when something else turns up trumps.

He was gone a long time, and Apollo, meanwhile,
Went over some sonnets of his with a file,
For, of all compositions, he thought that the sonnet
Best repaid all the toil you expended upon it;
It should reach with one impulse the end of its course,
And for one final blow collect all of its force;
Not a verse should be salient, but each one should tend
With a wavelike upgathering to break at the end;

So, condensing the strength here, there smoothing a wry
    kink,
He was killing the time, when up walked Mr. D——;[1]
At a few steps behind him, a small man in glasses
Went dodging about, muttering, "Murderers! asses!"
From out of his pocket a paper he'd take,
With a proud look of martyrdom tied to its stake,
And, reading a squib at himself, he'd say, "Here I see
'Gainst American letters a bloody conspiracy,
They are all by my personal enemies written;
I must post an anonymous letter to Britain,
And show that this gall is the merest suggestion
Of spite at my zeal on the Copyright question,
For, on this side the water, 'tis prudent to pull
O'er the eyes of the public their national wool,
By accusing of slavish respect to John Bull
All American authors who have more or less
Of that anti-American humbug—success,
While in private we're always embracing the knees
Of some twopenny editor over the seas,
And licking his critical shoes, for you know 'tis
The whole aim of our lives to get one English notice;
My American puffs I would willingly burn all
(They're all from one source, monthly, weekly, diurnal)
To get but a kick from a transmarine journal!"

So, culling the gibes of each critical scorner
As if they were plums, and himself were Jack Horner,
He came cautiously on, peeping round every corner,
And into each hole where a weasel might pass in,
Expecting the knife of some critic assassin,
Who stabs to the heart with a caricature,
Not so bad as those daubs of the *Sun*, to be sure,
Yet done with a dagger-o'-type, whose vile portraits
Disperse all one's good and condense all one's poor traits.

Apollo looked up, hearing footsteps approaching,
And slipped out of sight the new rhymes he was broaching,—

[1]Evert Augustus Duyckink. E. W.

"Good day, Mr. D——, I'm happy to meet,
With a scholar so ripe, and a critic so neat,
Who through Grub Street the soul of a gentleman carries;
What news from that suburb of London and Paris
Which latterly makes such shrill claims to monopolize
The credit of being the New World's metropolis?"

      "Why, nothing of consequence, save this attack
On my friend there, behind, by some pitiful hack,
Who thinks every national author a poor one,
That isn't a copy of something that's foreign,
And assaults the American Dick—"

                                        "Nay, 'tis clear
That your Damon there's fond of a flea in his ear,
And, if no one else furnished them gratis, on tick
He would buy some himself, just to hear the old click;
Why, I honestly think, if some fool in Japan
Should turn up his nose at the *Poems on Man*,
(Which contain many verses as fine, by the bye,
As any that lately came under my eye,)
Your friend there by some inward instinct would know it,
Would get it translated, reprinted, and show it;
As a man might take off a high stock to exhibit
The autograph round his own neck of the gibbet;
Nor would let it rest so, but fire column after column,
Signed Cato, or Brutus, or something as solemn,
By way of displaying his critical crosses,
And tweaking that poor transatlantic proboscis,
His broadsides resulting (this last there's no doubt of)
In successively sinking the craft they're fired out of.
Now nobody knows when an author is hit,
If he have not a public hysterical fit;
Let him only keep close in his snug garret's dim ether,
And nobody'd think of his foes—or of him either;
If an author have any least fiber of worth in him,
Abuse would but tickle the organ of mirth in him;
All the critics on earth cannot crush with their ban
One word that's in tune with the nature of man."

"Well, perhaps so; meanwhile I have brought you a book,
Into which if you'll just have the goodness to look,
You may feel so delighted (when once you are through it)
As to deem it not unworth your while to review it,
And I think I can promise your thoughts, if you do,
A place in the next *Democratic Review.*"

"The most thankless of gods you must surely have thought
      me,
For this is the forty-fourth copy you've brought me,
I have given them away, or at least I have tried,
But I've forty-two left, standing all side by side
(The man who accepted that one copy died),—
From one end of a shelf to the other they reach,
'With the author's respects' neatly written in each.
The publisher, sure, will proclaim a Te Deum,
When he hears of that order the British Museum
Has sent for one set of what books were first printed
In America, little or big,—for 'tis hinted
That this is the first truly tangible hope he
Has ever had raised for the sale of a copy.
I've thought very often 'twould be a good thing
In all public collections of books, if a wing
Were set off by itself, like the seas from the dry lands,
Marked *Literature suited to desolate islands,*
And filled with such books as could never be read
Save by readers of proofs, forced to do it for bread,
Such books as one's wrecked on in small country taverns,
Such as hermits might mortify over in caverns,
Such as Satan, if printing had then been invented,
As the climax of woe, would to Job have presented,
Such as Crusoe might dip in, although there are few so
Outrageously cornered by fate as poor Crusoe;
And since the philanthropists just now are banging
And gibbeting all who're in favor of hanging
(Though Cheever has proved that the Bible and Altar
Were let down from Heaven at the end of a halter,
And that vital religion would dull and grow callous,
Unrefreshed, now and then, with a sniff of the gallows),—

And folks are beginning to think it looks odd,
To choke a poor scamp for the glory of God;
And that He who esteems the Virginia reel
A bait to draw saints from their spiritual weal,
And regards the quadrille as a far greater knavery
Than crushing His African children with slavery,—
Since all who take part in a waltz or cotillon
Are mounted for hell on the Devil's own pillion,
Who, as every true orthodox Christian well knows,
Approaches the heart through the door of the toes,—
That He, I was saying, whose judgments are stored
For such as take steps in despite of His word,
Should look with delight on the agonized prancing
Of a wretch who has not the least ground for his dancing,
While the State, standing by, sings a verse from the Psalter
About offering to God on His favorite halter,
And, when the legs droop from their twitching divergence,
Sells the clothes to a Jew, and the corpse to the surgeons;—
Now, instead of all this, I think I can direct you all
To a criminal code both humane and effectual;
I propose to shut up every doer of wrong
With these desperate books, for such term, short or long,
As by statute in such cases made and provided,
Shall be by your wise legislators decided:
Thus: Let murderers be shut, to grow wiser and cooler,
At hard labor for life on the works of Miss ——;[1]
Petty thieves, kept from flagranter crimes by their fears,
Shall peruse *Yankee Doodle* a blank term of years,—
That American Punch, like the English, no doubt,—
Just the sugar and lemons and spirit left out.

"But stay, here comes Tityrus Griswold, and leads on
The flocks whom he first plucks alive, and then feeds on,—
A loud-cackling swarm, in whose feathers warmdrest,
He goes for as perfect a—swan as the rest.

"There comes Emerson first, whose rich words, every one,
Are like gold nails in temples to hang trophies on,

[1] Margaret Fuller. E. W.

Whose prose is grand verse, while his verse, the Lord knows,
Is some of it pr— No, 'tis not even prose;
I'm speaking of meters; some poems have welled
From those rare depths of soul that have ne'er been excelled;
They're not epics, but that doesn't matter a pin,
In creating, the only hard thing's to begin;
A grass-blade's no easier to make than an oak;
If you've once found the way, you've achieved the grand
    stroke;
In the worst of his poems are mines of rich matter,
But thrown in a heap with a crash and a clatter;
Now it is not one thing nor another alone
Makes a poem, but rather the general tone,
The something pervading, uniting the whole,
The before unconceived, unconceivable soul,
So that just in removing this trifle or that, you
Take away, as it were, a chief limb of the statue;
Roots, wood, bark, and leaves singly perfect may be,
But, clapt hodge-podge together, they don't make a tree.

"But, to come back to Emerson (whom, by the way,
I believe we left waiting),—his is, we may say,
A Greek head on right Yankee shoulders, whose range
Has Olympus for one pole, for t'other the Exchange;
He seems, to my thinking (although I'm afraid
The comparison must, long ere this, have been made),
A Plotinus-Montaigne, where the Egyptian's gold mist
And the Gascon's shrewd wit cheek-by-jowl coexist;
All admire, and yet scarcely six converts he's got
To I don't (nor they either) exactly know what;
For though he builds glorious temples, 'tis odd
He leaves never a doorway to get in a god.
'Tis refreshing to old-fashioned people like me
To meet such a primitive Pagan as he,
In whose mind all creation is duly respected
As parts of himself—just a little projected;
And who's willing to worship the stars and the sun,
A convert to—nothing but Emerson.
So perfect a balance there is in his head,

That he talks of things sometimes as if they were dead;
Life, nature, love, God, and affairs of that sort,
He looks at as merely ideas; in short,
As if they were fossils stuck round in a cabinet,
Of such vast extent that our earth's a mere dab in it;
Composed just as he is inclined to conjecture her,
Namely, one part pure earth, ninety-nine parts pure lecturer;
You are filled with delight at his clear demonstration,
Each figure, word, gesture, just fits the occasion,
With the quiet precision of science he'll sort 'em,
But you can't help suspecting the whole a *post mortem.*

"There are persons, mole-blind to the soul's make and
    style,
Who insist on a likeness 'twixt him and Carlyle;
To compare him with Plato would be vastly fairer,
Carlyle's the more burly, but E. is the rarer;
He sees fewer objects, but clearlier, truelier,
If C.'s as original, E.'s more peculiar;
That he's more of a man you might say of the one,
Of the other he's more of an Emerson;
C.'s the Titan, as shaggy of mind as of limb,—
E. the clear-eyed Olympian, rapid and slim;
The one's two thirds Norseman, the other half Greek,
Where the one's most abounding, the other's to seek;
C.'s generals require to be seen in the mass,—
E.'s specialties gain if enlarged by the glass;
C. gives nature and God his own fits of the blues,
And rims common-sense things with mystical hues,—
E. sits in a mystery calm and intense,
And looks coolly around him with sharp common sense;
C. shows you how every-day matters unite
With the dim transdiurnal recesses of night,—
While E., in a plain, preternatural way,
Makes mysteries matters of mere every day;
C. draws all his characters quite *à la* Fuseli,—
Not sketching their bundles of muscles and thews illy,
He paints with a brush so untamed and profuse,
They seem nothing but bundles of muscles and thews;

E. is rather like Flaxman, lines strait and severe,
And a colorless outline, but full, round, and clear;—
To the men he thinks worthy he frankly accords
The design of a white marble statue in words.
C. labors to get at the center, and then
Take a reckoning from there of his actions and men;
E. calmly assumes the said center as granted,
And, given himself, has whatever is wanted.

"He has imitators in scores, who omit
No part of the man but his wisdom and wit,—
Who go carefully o'er the sky-blue of his brain,
And when he has skimmed it once, skim it again;
If at all they resemble him, you may be sure it is
Because their shoals mirror his mists and obscurities,
As a mud-puddle seems deep as heaven for a minute,
While a cloud that floats o'er is reflected within it.

"There comes ——,[1] for instance; to see him's rare sport,
Tread in Emerson's tracks with legs painfully short;
How he jumps, how he strains, and gets red in the face,
To keep step with the mystagogue's natural pace!
He follows as close as a stick to a rocket,
His fingers exploring the prophet's each pocket.
Fie, for shame, brother bard; with good fruit of your own,
Can't you let Neighbor Emerson's orchards alone?
Besides, 'tis no use, you'll not find e'en a core,—
——[2] has picked up all the windfalls before.
They might strip every tree, and E. never would catch 'em,
His Hesperides have no rude dragon to watch 'em;
When they send him a dishful, and ask him to try 'em,
He never suspects how the sly rogues came by 'em;
He wonders why 'tis there are none such his trees on,
And thinks 'em the best he has tasted this season.

"Yonder, calm as a cloud, Alcott stalks in a dream,
And fancies himself in thy groves, Academe,

[1] This is supposed to refer to William Ellery Channing, the poet. E. W.

[2] This is supposed to refer to Henry David Thoreau. E. W.

With the Parthenon nigh, and the olive-trees o'er him,
And never a fact to perplex him or bore him,
With a snug room at Plato's when night comes, to walk to,
And people from morning till midnight to talk to,
And from midnight till morning, nor snore in their listen-
    ing;—
So he muses, his face with the joy of it glistening,
For his highest conceit of a happiest state is
Where they'd live upon acorns, and hear him talk gratis;
And indeed, I believe, no man ever talked better,—
Each sentence hangs perfectly poised to a letter;
He seems piling words, but there's royal dust hid
In the heart of each sky-piercing pyramid.
While he talks he is great, but goes out like a taper,
If you shut him up closely with pen, ink, and paper;
Yet his fingers itch for 'em from morning till night,
And he thinks he does wrong if he don't always write;
In this, as in all things, a lamb among men,
He goes to sure death when he goes to his pen.

"Close behind him is Brownson, his mouth very full
With attempting to gulp a Gregorian bull;
Who contrives, spite of that, to pour out as he goes
A stream of transparent and forcible prose;
He shifts quite about, then proceeds to expound
That 'tis merely the earth, not himself, that turns round,
And wishes it clearly impressed on your mind
That the weathercock rules and not follows the wind;
Proving first, then as deftly confuting each side,
With no doctrine pleased that's not somewhere denied,
He lays the denier away on the shelf,
And then—down beside him lies gravely himself.
He's the Salt River boatman, who always stands willing
To convey friend or foe without charging a shilling,
And so fond of the trip that, when leisure's to spare,
He'll row himself up, if he can't get a fare.
The worst of it is, that his logic's so strong,
That of two sides he commonly chooses the wrong;
If there *is* only one, why, he'll split it in two,

And first pummel this half, then that, black and blue.
That white's white needs no proof, but it takes a deep fellow
To prove it jet-black, and that jet-black is yellow.
He offers the true faith to drink in a sieve,—
When it reaches your lips there's naught left to believe
But a few silly- (syllo-, I mean,) -gisms that squat 'em
Like tadpoles, o'erjoyed with the mud at the bottom.

"There is Willis, all *natty* and jaunty and gay,
Who says his best things in so foppish a way,
With conceits and pet phrases so thickly o'erlaying 'em,
That one hardly knows whether to thank him for saying
    'em;
Overornament ruins both poem and prose,
Just conceive of a Muse with a ring in her nose!
His prose had a natural grace of its own,
And enough of it, too, if he'd let it alone;
But he twitches and jerks so, one fairly gets tired,
And is forced to forgive where one might have admired;
Yet whenever it slips away free and unlaced,
It runs like a stream with a musical waste,
And gurgles along with the liquidest sweep;
'Tis not deep as a river, but who'd have it deep?
In a country where scarcely a village is found
That has not its author sublime and profound,
For someone to be slightly shallow's a duty,
And Willis's shallowness makes half his beauty.
His prose winds along with a blithe, gurgling error,
And reflects all of Heaven it can see in its mirror:
'Tis a narrowish strip, but it is not an artifice;
'Tis the true out-of-doors with its genuine hearty phiz;
It is Nature herself, and there's something in that,
Since most brains reflect but the crown of a hat.
Few volumes I know to read under a tree,
More truly delightful than his *A l'Abri*,
With the shadows of leaves flowing over your book,
Like ripple-shades netting the bed of a brook;
With June coming softly your shoulder to look over,
Breezes waiting to turn every leaf of your book over,

And Nature to criticise still as you read,—
The page that bears that is a rare one indeed.

"He's so innate a cockney, that had he been born
Where plain bare-skin's the only full-dress that is worn,
He'd have given his own such an air that you'd say
'T had been made by a tailor to lounge in Broadway.
His nature's a glass of champagne with the foam on 't,
As tender as Fletcher, as witty as Beaumont;
So his best things are done in the flush of the moment;
If he wait, all is spoiled; he may stir it and shake it,
But, the fixed air once gone, he can never remake it.
He might be a marvel of easy delightfulness,
If he would not sometimes leave the r out of sprightfulness;
And he ought to let Scripture alone—'tis self-slaughter,
For nobody likes inspiration-and-water.
He'd have been just the fellow to sup at the Mermaid,
Cracking jokes at rare Ben, with an eye to the barmaid,
His wit running up as Canary ran down,—
The topmost bright bubble on the wave of The Town.

"Here comes Parker, the Orson of parsons, a man
Whom the Church undertook to put under her ban
(The Church of Socinus, I mean),—his opinions
Being So- (ultra) -cinian, they shocked the Socinians;
They believed—faith, I'm puzzled—I think I may call
Their belief a believing in nothing at all,
Or something of that sort; I know they all went
For a general union of total dissent:
He went a step farther; without cough or hem,
He frankly avowed he believed not in them;
And, before he could be jumbled up or prevented,
From their orthodox kind of dissent he dissented.
There was heresy here, you perceive, for the right
Of privately judging means simply that light
Has been granted to *me,* for deciding on *you;*
And in happier times, before Atheism grew,
The deed contained clauses for cooking you too:
Now at Xerxes and Knut we all laugh, yet our foot

With the same wave is wet that mocked Xerxes and Knut,
And we all entertain a secure private notion,
That our *Thus far!* will have a great weight with the ocean.
'Twas so with our liberal Christians: they bore
With sincerest conviction their chairs to the shore;
They brandished their worn theological birches,
Bade natural progress keep out of the Churches,
And expected the lines they had drawn to prevail
With the fast-rising tide to keep out of their pale;
They had formerly dammed the Pontifical See,
And the same thing, they thought, would do nicely for P.,
But he turned up his nose at their mumming and shamming,
And cared (shall I say?) not a d—— for their damming;
So they first read him out of their church, and next minute
Turned round and declared he had never been in it.
But the ban was too small or the man was too big,
For he recks not their bells, books, and candles a fig
(He scarce looks like a man who would *stay* treated shabbily,
Sophroniscus' son's head o'er the features of Rabelais);—
He bangs and bethwacks them,—their backs he salutes
With the whole tree of knowledge torn up by the roots;
His sermons with satire are plenteously verjuiced,
And he talks in one breath of Confutzee, Cass, Zerduscht,
Jack Robinson, Peter the Hermit, Strap, Dathan,
Cush, Pitt (not the bottomless, *that* he's no faith in),
Pan, Pillicock, Shakespeare, Paul, Toots, Monsieur Tonson,
Aldebaran, Alcander, Ben Khorat, Ben Jonson,
Thoth, Richter, Joe Smith, Father Paul, Judah Monis,
Musæus, Muretus, hem,— μ Scorpionis,
Maccabee, Maccaboy, Mac—Mac—ah! Machiavelli,
Condorcet, Count d'Orsay, Conder, Say, Ganganelli,
Orion, O'Connell, the Chevalier D'O,
(See the Memoirs of Sully,) $\tau\grave{o}$ $\pi\tilde{\alpha}\nu$, the great toe
Of the statue of Jupiter, now made to pass
For that of Jew Peter by good Romish brass,
(You may add for yourselves, for I find it a bore,
All the names you have ever, or not, heard before,
And when you've done that—why, invent a few more.)
His hearers can't tell you on Sunday beforehand,

If in that day's discourse they'll be Bibled or Koraned,
For he's seized the idea (by his martyrdom fired)
That all men (not orthodox) *may be* inspired;
Yet though wisdom profane with his creed he may weave in,
He makes it quite clear what he *doesn't* believe in,
While some, who decry him, think all Kingdom Come
Is a sort of a, kind of a, species of Hum,
Of which, as it were, so to speak, not a crumb
Would be left, if we didn't keep carefully mum,
And, to make a clean breast, that 'tis perfectly plain
That *all* kinds of wisdom are somewhat profane;
Now P.'s creed than this may be lighter or darker,
But in one thing, 'tis clear, he has faith, namely—Parker;
And this is what makes him the crowd-drawing preacher,
There's a background of god to each hard-working feature,
Every word that he speaks has been fierily furnaced
In the blast of a life that has struggled in earnest:
There he stands, looking more like a plowman than priest,
If not dreadfully awkward, not graceful at least,
His gestures all downright and same, if you will,
As of brown-fisted Hobnail in hoeing a drill;
But his periods fall on you, stroke after stroke,
Like the blows of a lumberer felling an oak,
You forget the man wholly, you're thankful to meet
With a preacher who smacks of the field and the street,
And to hear, you're not overparticular whence,
Almost Taylor's profusion, quite Latimer's sense.

"There is Bryant, as quiet, as cool, and as dignified,
As a smooth, silent iceberg, that never is ignified,
Save when by reflection 'tis kindled o' nights
With a semblance of flame by the chill Northern Lights.
He may rank (Griswold says so) first bard of your nation
(There's no doubt that he stands in supreme ice-olation),
Your topmost Parnassus he may set his heel on,—
But no warm applauses come, peal following peal on,
He's too smooth and too polished to hang any zeal on:
Unqualified merits, I'll grant, if you choose, he has 'em,
But he lacks the one merit of kindling enthusiasm;

If he stir you at all, it is just, on my soul,
Like being stirred up with the very North Pole.

"He is very nice reading in summer, but *inter*
Nos, we don't want *extra* freezing in winter;
Take him up in the depth of July, my advice is,
When you feel an Egyptian devotion to ices.
But, deduct all you can, there's enough that's right good in
    him,
He has a true soul for field, river, and wood in him;
And his heart, in the midst of brick walls, or where'er it is,
Glows, softens, and thrills with the tenderest charities—
To you mortals that delve in this trade-ridden planet?
No, to old Berkshire's hills, with their limestone and granite.
If you're one who *in loco* (add *foco* here) *desipis,*
You will get of his outermost heart (as I guess) a piece;
But you'd get deeper down if you came as a precipice,
And would break the last seal of its inwardest fountain,
If you only could palm yourself off for a mountain.
Mr. Quivis, or somebody quite as discerning,
Some scholar who's hourly expecting his learning,
Calls B. the American Wordsworth; but Wordsworth
May be rated at more than your whole tuneful herd's worth.
No, don't be absurd, he's an excellent Bryant;
But, my friends, you'll endanger the life of your client,
By attempting to stretch him up into a giant:
If you choose to compare him, I think there are two per-
-sons fit for a parallel—Thompson and Cowper;[1]
I don't mean exactly,—there's something of each,
There's T.'s love of nature, C.'s penchant to preach;
Just mix up their minds so that C.'s spice of craziness
Shall balance and neutralize T.'s turn for laziness,
And it gives you a brain cool, quite frictionless, quiet,
Whose internal police nips the buds of all riot,—
A brain like a permanent strait jacket put on

[1]To demonstrate quickly and easily how per-
-versely absurd 'tis to sound this name *Cowper,*
As people in general call him named *super,*
I remark that he rhymes it himself with horse-trooper.

The heart that strives vainly to burst off a button,—
A brain which, without being slow or mechanic,
Does more than a larger less drilled, more volcanic;
He's a Cowper condensed, with no craziness bitten,
And the advantage that Wordsworth before him had written.

"But, my dear little bardlings, don't prick up your ears
Nor suppose I would rank you and Bryant as peers;
If I call him an iceberg, I don't mean to say
There is nothing in that which is grand in its way;
He is almost the one of your poets that knows
How much grace, strength, and dignity lie in Repose;
If he sometimes fall short, he is too wise to mar
His thought's modest fullness by going too far;
'Twould be well if your authors should all make a trial
Of what virtue there is in severe self-denial,
And measure their writings by Hesiod's staff,
Which teaches that all has less value than half.

"There is Whittier, whose swelling and vehement heart
Strains the strait-breasted drab of the Quaker apart,
And reveals the live Man, still supreme and erect,
Underneath the bemummying wrappers of sect;
There was ne'er a man born who had more of the swing
Of the true lyric bard and all that kind of thing;
And his failures arise (though he seem not to know it)
From the very same cause that has made him a poet,—
A fervor of mind which knows no separation
'Twixt simple excitement and pure inspiration,
As my Pythoness erst sometimes erred from not knowing
If 'twere I or mere wind through her tripod was blowing;
Let his mind once get head in its favorite direction
And the torrent of verse bursts the dams of reflection,
While, borne with the rush of the meter along,
The poet may chance to go right or go wrong,
Content with the whirl and delirium of song;
Then his grammar's not always correct, nor his rhymes,
And he's prone to repeat his own lyrics sometimes,
Not his best, though, for those are struck off at white heats

When the heart in his breast like a triphammer beats,
And can ne'er be repeated again any more
Than they could have been carefully plotted before:
Like old what's-his-name there at the battle of Hastings
(Who, however, gave more than mere rhythmical bastings).
Our Quaker leads off metaphorical fights
For reform and whatever they call human rights,
Both singing and striking in front of the war,
And hitting his foes with the mallet of Thor;
Anne haec, one exclaims, on beholding his knocks,
Vestis filii tui, O leather-clad Fox?
Can that be thy son, in the battle's mid din,
Preaching brotherly love and then driving it in
To the brain of the tough old Goliath of sin,
With the smoothest of pebbles from Castaly's spring
Impressed on his hard moral sense with a sling?

"All honor and praise to the right-hearted bard
Who was true to The Voice when such service was hard,
Who himself was so free he dared sing for the slave
When to look but a protest in silence was brave;
All honor and praise to the women and men
Who spoke out for the dumb and the downtrodden then!
It needs not to name them, already for each
I see History preparing the statue and niche;
They were harsh, but shall *you* be so shocked at hard words
Who have beaten your pruning hooks up into swords,
Whose rewards and hurrahs men are surer to gain
By the reaping of men and of women than grain?
Why should *you* stand aghast at their fierce wordy war, if
You scalp one another for Bank or for Tariff?
Your calling them cutthroats and knaves all day long
Doesn't prove that the use of hard language is wrong;
While the World's heart beats quicker to think of such men
As signed Tyranny's doom with a bloody steel pen,
While on Fourth of Julys beardless orators fright one
With hints at Harmodius and Aristogeiton,
You need not look shy at your sisters and brothers
Who stab with sharp words for the freedom of others;—

No, a wreath, twine a wreath for the loyal and true
Who, for sake of the many, dared stand with the few,
Not of blood-spattered laurel for enemies braved,
But of broad, peaceful oak leaves for citizens saved!

"Here comes Dana, abstractedly loitering along,
Involved in a paulo-post-future of song,
Who'll be going to write what'll never be written
Till the Muse, ere he think of it, gives him the mitten,—
Who is so well aware of how things should be done,
That his own works displease him before they're begun,—
Who so well all that makes up good poetry knows,
That the best of his poems is written in prose;
All saddled and bridled stood Pegasus waiting,
He was booted and spurred, but he loitered debating;
In a very grave question his soul was immersed,—
Which foot in the stirrup he ought to put first;
And, while this point and that he judicially dwelt on,
He, somehow or other, had written *Paul Felton*,
Whose beauties or faults, whichsoever you see there,
You'll allow only genius could hit upon either.
That he once was the Idle Man none will deplore,
But I fear he will never be anything more;
The ocean of song heaves and glitters before him,
The depth and the vastness and longing sweep o'er him,
He knows every breaker and shoal on the chart,
He has the Coast Pilot and so on by heart,
Yet he spends his whole life, like the man in the fable,
In learning to swim on his library table.

"There swaggers John Neal, who has wasted in Maine
The sinews and cords of his pugilist brain,
Who might have been poet, but that, in its stead, he
Preferred to believe that he was so already;
Too hasty to wait till Art's ripe fruit should drop,
He must pelt down an unripe and colicky crop;
Who took to the law, and had this sterling plea for it,
It required him to quarrel, and paid him a fee for it;
A man who's made less than he might have, because

He always has thought himself more than he was,—
Who, with very good natural gifts as a bard,
Broke the strings of his lyre out by striking too hard,
And cracked half the notes of a truly fine voice,
Because song drew less instant attention than noise.
Ah, men do not know how much strength is in poise,
That he goes the farthest who goes far enough,
And that all beyond that is just bother and stuff.
No vain man matures, he makes too much new wood;
His blooms are too thick for the fruit to be good;
'Tis the modest man ripens, 'tis he that achieves,
Just what's needed of sunshine and shade he receives;
Grapes, to mellow, require the cool dark of their leaves;
Neal wants balance; he throws his mind always too far,
Whisking out flocks of comets, but never a star;
He has so much muscle, and loves so to show it,
That he strips himself naked to prove he's a poet,
And, to show he could leap Art's wide ditch, if he tried,
Jumps clean o'er it, and into the hedge t' other side.
He has strength, but there's nothing about him in keeping;
One gets surelier onward by walking than leaping;
He has used his own sinews himself to distress,
And had done vastly more had he done vastly less;
In letters, too soon is as bad as too late;
Could he only have waited he might have been great;
But he plumped into Helicon up to the waist,
And muddied the stream ere he took his first taste.

"There is Hawthorne, with genius so shrinking and rare
That you hardly at first see the strength that is there;
A frame so robust, with a nature so sweet,
So earnest, so graceful, so lithe and so fleet,
Is worth a descent from Olympus to meet;
'Tis as if a rough oak that for ages had stood,
With his gnarled bony branches like ribs of the wood,
Should bloom, after cycles of struggle and scathe,
With a single anemone trembly and rathe;
His strength is so tender, his wildness so meek,
That a suitable parallel sets one to seek,—

He's a John Bunyan Fouqué, a Puritan Tieck;
When Nature was shaping him, clay was not granted
For making so full-sized a man as she wanted,
So, to fill out her model, a little she spared
From some finer-grained stuff for a woman prepared,
And she could not have hit a more excellent plan
For making him fully and perfectly man.
The success of her scheme gave her so much delight,
That she tried it again, shortly after, in Dwight;
Only, while she was kneading and shaping the clay,
She sang to her work in her sweet childish way,
And found, when she'd put the last touch to his soul,
That the music had somehow got mixed with the whole.

"Here's Cooper, who's written six volumes to show
He's as good as a lord: well, let's grant that he's so;
If a person prefer that description of praise,
Why, a coronet's certainly cheaper than bays;
But he need take no pains to convince us he's not
(As his enemies say) the American Scott.
Choose any twelve men, and let C. read aloud
That one of his novels of which he's most proud,
And I'd lay any bet that, without ever quitting
Their box, they'd be all, to a man, for acquitting.
He has drawn you one character, though, that is new,
One wildflower he's plucked that is wet with the dew
Of this fresh Western world, and, the thing not to mince,
He has done naught but copy it ill ever since;
His Indians, with proper respect be it said,
Are just Natty Bumppo, daubed over with red,
And his very Long Toms are the same useful Nat,
Rigged up in duck pants and a sou'wester hat
(Though once in a Coffin, a good chance was found
To have slipped the old fellow away underground).
All his other men figures are clothes upon sticks,
The *dernière chemise* of a man in a fix
(As a captain besieged, when his garrison's small,
Sets up caps upon poles to be seen o'er the wall);
And the women he draws from one model don't vary,

All sappy as maples and flat as a prairie.
When a character's wanted, he goes to the task
As a cooper would do in composing a cask;
He picks out the staves, of their qualities heedful,
Just hoops them together as tight as is needful,
And, if the best fortune should crown the attempt, he
Has made at the most something wooden and empty.

"Don't suppose I would underrate Cooper's abilities;
If I thought you'd do that, I should feel very ill at ease;
The men who have given to *one* character life
And objective existence are not very rife;
You may number them all, both prose writers and singers,
Without overrunning the bounds of your fingers,
And Natty won't go to oblivion quicker
Than Adams the parson or Primrose the vicar.

"There is one thing in Cooper I like, too, and that is
That on manners he lectures his countrymen gratis;
Not precisely so either, because, for a rarity,
He is paid for his tickets in unpopularity.
Now he may overcharge his American pictures,
But you'll grant there's a good deal of truth in his strictures;
And I honor the man who is willing to sink
Half his present repute for the freedom to think,
And, when he has thought, be his cause strong or weak,
Will risk t'other half for the freedom to speak,
Caring naught for what vengeance the mob has in store,
Let that mob be the upper ten thousand or lower.

"There are truths you Americans need to be told,
And it never'll refute them to swagger and scold;
John Bull, looking o'er the Atlantic, in choler
At your aptness for trade, says you worship the dollar;
But to scorn such eye-dollar-try's what very few do,
And John goes to that church as often as you do.
No matter what John says, don't try to outcrow him,
'Tis enough to go quietly on and outgrow him;
Like most fathers, Bull hates to see Number One
Displacing himself in the mind of his son,

And detests the same faults in himself he'd neglected
When he sees them again in his child's glass reflected;
To love one another you're too like by half;
If he is a bull, you're a pretty stout calf,
And tear your own pasture for naught but to show
What a nice pair of horns you're beginning to grow.

"There are one or two things I should just like to hint,
For you don't often get the truth told you in print;
The most of you (this is what strikes all beholders)
Have a mental and physical stoop in the shoulders;
Though you ought to be free as the winds and the waves,
You've the gait and the manners of runaway slaves;
Though you brag of your New World, you don't half believe
    in it;
And as much of the Old as is possible weave in it;
Your goddess of freedom, a tight, buxom girl,
With lips like a cherry and teeth like a pearl,
With eyes bold as Herë's, and hair floating free,
And full of the sun as the spray of the sea,
Who can sing at a husking or romp at a shearing,
Who can trip through the forests alone without fearing,
Who can drive home the cows with a song through the grass,
Keeps glancing aside into Europe's cracked glass,
Hides her red hands in gloves, pinches up her lithe waist,
And makes herself wretched with transmarine taste;
She loses her fresh country charm when she takes
Any mirror except her own rivers and lakes.

"You steal Englishmen's books and think Englishmen's
    thought,
With their salt on her tail your wild eagle is caught;
Your literature suits its each whisper and motion
To what will be thought of it over the ocean;
The cast clothes of Europe your statesmanship tries
And mumbles again the old blarneys and lies;—
Forget Europe wholly, your veins throb with blood,
To which the dull current in hers is but mud;
Let her sneer, let her say your experiment fails,

In her voice there's a tremble e'en now while she rails,
And your shore will soon be in the nature of things
Covered thick with gilt driftwood of castaway kings,
Where alone, as it were in a Longfellow's *Waif*,
Her fugitive pieces will find themselves safe.
O my friends, thank your god, if you have one, that he
'Twixt the Old World and you set the gulf of a sea;
Be strong-backed, brown-handed, upright as your pines,
By the scale of a hemisphere shape your designs,
Be true to yourselves and this new nineteenth age,
As a statue by Powers, or a picture by Page,
Plow, sail, forge, build, carve, paint, make all over new,
To your own New-World instincts contrive to be true,
Keep your ears open wide to the Future's first call,
Be whatever you will, but yourselves first of all,
Stand fronting the dawn on Toil's heaven-scaling peaks,
And become my new race of more practical Greeks.—
Hem! your likeness at present, I shudder to tell o't,
Is that you have your slaves, and the Greek had his helot."

Here a gentleman present, who had in his attic
More pepper than brains, shrieked, "The man's a fanatic,
I'm a capital tailor with warm tar and feathers,
And will make him a suit that'll serve in all weathers;
But we'll argue the point first, I'm willing to reason 't,
Palaver before condemnation's but decent;
So, through my humble person, Humanity begs
Of the friends of true freedom a loan of bad eggs."
But Apollo let one such a look of his show forth
As when ἤιε νύκτι ἐοικώς, and so forth,
And the gentleman somehow slunk out of the way,
But, as he was going, gained courage to say,—
"At slavery in the abstract my whole soul rebels,
I am as strongly opposed to 't as anyone else."
"Ay, no doubt, but whenever I've happened to meet
With a wrong or a crime, it is always concrete,"
Answered Phœbus severely; then turning to us,
"The mistake of such fellows as just made the fuss
Is only in taking a great busy nation

For a part of their pitiful cotton plantation.—
But there comes Miranda,[1] Zeus! where shall I flee to?
She has such a penchant for bothering me too!
She always keeps asking if I don't observe a
Particular likeness 'twixt her and Minerva;
She tells me my efforts in verse are quite clever;—
She's been traveling now, and will be worse than ever;
One would think, though, a sharp-sighted noter she'd be
Of all that's worth mentioning over the sea,
For a woman must surely see well, if she try,
The whole of whose being's a capital I:
She will take an old notion, and make it her own,
By saying it o'er in her Sibylline tone,
Or persuade you 'tis something tremendously deep,
By repeating it so as to put you to sleep;
And she well may defy any mortal to see through it,
When once she has mixed up her infinite *me* through it.
There is one thing she owns in her own single right,
It is native and genuine—namely, her spite;
Though, when acting as censor, she privately blows
A censer of vanity 'neath her own nose."[2]

Here Miranda came up, and said, "Phœbus! you know
That the Infinite Soul has its infinite woe,
As I ought to know, having lived cheek by jowl,
Since the day I was born, with the Infinite Soul;
I myself introduced, I myself, I alone,
To my Land's better life authors solely my own,
Who the sad heart of earth on their shoulders have taken,
Whose works sound a depth by Life's quiet unshaken,
Such as Shakespeare, for instance, the Bible, and Bacon,
Not to mention my own works; Time's nadir is fleet,
And, as for myself, I'm quite out of conceit——"

"Quite out of conceit! I'm enchanted to hear it,"
Cried Apollo aside. "Who'd have thought she was near it?

[1] Margaret Fuller, E. W.
[2] Lowell made an attempt at the last moment to suppress the last four lines of this passage. E. W.

To be sure, one is apt to exhaust those commodities
One uses too fast, yet in this case as odd it is
As if Neptune should say to his turbots and whitings,
'I'm as much out of salt as Miranda's own writings'
(Which, as she in her own happy manner has said,
Sound a depth, for 'tis one of the functions of lead).
She often has asked me if I could not find
A place somewhere near me that suited her mind;
I know but a single one vacant, which she,
With her rare talent that way, would fit to a T.
And it would not imply any pause or cessation
In the work she esteems her peculiar vocation,—
She may enter on duty today, if she chooses,
And remain Tiring-woman for life to the Muses."

Miranda meanwhile has succeeded in driving
Up into a corner, in spite of their striving,
A small flock of terrified victims, and there,
With an I-turn-the-crank-of-the-Universe air
And a tone which, at least to *my* fancy, appears
Not so much to be entering as boxing your ears,
Is unfolding a tale (of herself, I surmise,
For 'tis dotted as thick as a peacock's with I's).
Apropos of Miranda, I'll rest on my oars
And drift through a trifling digression on bores,
For, though not wearing earrings *in more majorum,*
Our ears are kept bored just as if we still wore 'em.
There was one feudal custom worth keeping, at least,
Roasted bores made a part of each well-ordered feast,
And of all quiet pleasures the very *ne plus*
Was in hunting wild bores as the tame ones hunt us.
Archæologians, I know, who have personal fears
Of this wise application of hounds and of spears,
Have tried to make out, with a zeal more than wonted,
'Twas a kind of wild swine that our ancestors hunted;
But I'll never believe that the age which has strewn
Europe o'er with cathedrals, and otherwise shown
That it knew what was what, could by chance not have
        known

(Spending, too, its chief time with its buff on, no doubt)
Which beast 'twould improve the world most to thin out.
I divide bores myself, in the manner of rifles,
Into two great divisions, regardless of trifles;—
There's your smoothbore and screw-bore, who do not much
    vary
In the weight of cold lead they respectively carry.
The smoothbore is one in whose essence the mind
Not a corner nor cranny to cling by can find;
You feel as in nightmares sometimes, when you slip
Down a steep slated roof, where there's nothing to grip;
You slide and you slide, the blank horror increases,—
You had rather by far be at once smashed to pieces;
You fancy a whirlpool below white and frothing,
And finally drop off and light upon—nothing.
The screw-bore has twists in him, faint predilections
For going just wrong in the tritest directions;
When he's wrong he is flat, when he's right he can't show it,
He'll tell you what Snooks said about the new poet,[1]
Or how Fogrum was outraged by Tennyson's *Princess;*
He has spent all his spare time and intellect since his
Birth in perusing, on each art and science,
Just the books in which no one puts any reliance,
And though *nemo,* we're told, *horis omnibus sapit,*
The rule will not fit him, however you shape it,
For he has a perennial foison of sappiness;
He has just enough force to spoil half your day's happiness,
And to make him a sort of mosquito to be with,
But just not enough to dispute or agree with.

    These sketches I made (not to be too explicit)
From two honest fellows who made me a visit,
And broke, like the tale of the Bear and the Fiddle,
My reflections on Halleck short off by the middle;
I sha'n't now go into the subject more deeply,
For I notice that some of my readers look sleep'ly;
I will barely remark that, 'mongst civilized nations,

[1](If you call Snooks an owl, he will show by his looks
That he's morally certain you're jealous of Snooks.)

There's none that displays more exemplary patience
Under all sorts of boring, at all sorts of hours,
From all sorts of desperate persons, than ours.
Not to speak of our papers, our State legislatures,
And other such trials for sensitive natures,
Just look for a moment at Congress,—appalled,
My fancy shrinks back from the phantom it called;
Why, there's scarcely a member unworthy to frown
'Neath what Fourier nicknames the Boreal crown;
Only think what that infinite bore-pow'r could do
If applied with a utilitarian view;
Suppose, for example, we shipped it with care
To Sahara's great desert and let it bore there;
If they held one short session and did nothing else,
They'd fill the whole waste with Artesian wells.
But 'tis time now with pen phonographic to follow
Through some more of his sketches our laughing Apollo:—

"There comes Harry Franco,[1] and, as he draws near,
You find that's a smile which you took for a sneer;
One half of him contradicts t' other; his wont
Is to say very sharp things and do very blunt;
His manner's as hard as his feelings are tender,
And a *sortie* he'll make when he means to surrender;
He's in joke half the time when he seems to be sternest,
When he seems to be joking, be sure he's in earnest;
He has common sense in a way that's uncommon,
Hates humbug and cant, loves his friends like a woman,
Builds his dislikes of cards and his friendships of oak,
Loves a prejudice better than aught but a joke,
Is half upright Quaker, half downright Come-outer,
Loves Freedom too well to go stark mad about her,
Quite artless himself, is a lover of Art,
Shuts you out of his secrets and into his heart,
And though not a poet, yet all must admire
In his letters of Pinto his skill on the liar.

[1]Charles Frederick Briggs, who wrote a novel called *The Adventures of Harry Franco*. E. W.

"There comes Poe, with his raven, like Barnaby Rudge,
Three-fifths of him genius and two-fifths sheer fudge,
Who talks like a book of iambs and pentameters,
In a way to make people of common sense damn meters,
Who has written some things quite the best of their kind,
But the heart somehow seems all squeezed out by the mind,
Who—— But hey-day! What's this? Messieurs Mathews and
    Poe,
You mustn't fling mud balls at Longfellow so,
Does it make a man worse that his character's such
As to make his friends love him (as you think) too much?
Why, there is not a bard at this moment alive
More willing than he that his fellows should thrive;
While you are abusing him thus, even now
He would help either one of you out of a slough;
You may say that he's smooth and all that till you're hoarse,
But remember that elegance also is force;
After polishing granite as much as you will,
The heart keeps its tough old persistency still;
Deduct all you can, *that* still keeps you at bay;
Why, he'll live till men weary of Collins and Gray.
I'm not overfond of Greek meters in English,
To me rhyme's a gain, so it be not too jinglish,
And your modern hexameter verses are no more
Like Greek ones than sleek Mr. Pope is like Homer;
As the roar of the sea to the coo of a pigeon is,
So, compared to your moderns, sounds old Melesigenes;
I may be too partial, the reason, perhaps, o't is
That I've heard the old blind man recite his own rhapsodies,
And my ear with that music impregnate may be,
Like the poor exiled shell with the soul of the sea,
Or as one can't bear Strauss when his nature is cloven
To its deeps within deeps by the stroke of Beethoven;
But, set that aside, and 'tis truth that I speak,
Had Theocritus written in English, not Greek,
I believe that his exquisite sense would scarce change a line
In that rare, tender, virginlike pastoral *Evangeline*.
That's not ancient nor modern, its place is apart

Where time has no sway, in the realm of pure Art,
'Tis a shrine of retreat from Earth's hubbub and strife
As quiet and chaste as the author's own life.

"There comes Philothea,[1] her face all aglow,
She has just been dividing some poor creature's woe,
And can't tell which pleases her most, to relieve
His want, or his story to hear and believe;
No doubt against many deep griefs she prevails,
For her ear is the refuge of destitute tales;
She knows well that silence is sorrow's best food,
And that talking draws off from the heart its black blood,
So she'll listen with patience and let you unfold
Your bundle of rags as 'twere pure cloth of gold,
Which, indeed, it all turns to as soon as she's touched it,
And (to borrow a phrase from the nursery) *muched* it;
She has such a musical taste, she will go
Any distance to hear one who draws a long bow; ,
She will swallow a wonder by mere might and main,
And thinks it Geometry's fault if she's fain
To consider things flat, inasmuch as they're plain;
Facts with her are accomplished, as Frenchmen would say—
They will prove all she wishes them to either way,—
And, as fact lies on this side or that, we must try,
If we're seeking the truth, to find where it don't lie;
I was telling her once of a marvelous aloe
That for thousands of years had looked spindling and sallow,
And, though nursed by the fruitfullest powers of mud,
Had never vouchsafed e'en so much as a bud,
Till its owner remarked (as a sailor, you know,
Often will in a calm) that it never would blow,
For he wished to exhibit the plant, and designed
That its blowing should help him in raising the wind;
At last it was told him that if he should water
Its roots with the blood of his unmarried daughter
(Who was born, as her mother, a Calvinist, said,
With William Law's serious caul on her head),
It would blow as the obstinate breeze did when by a

'Lydia Maria Child, who wrote a novel called *Philothea*. E. W.

Like decree of her father died Iphigenia;
At first he declared he himself would be blowed
Ere his conscience with such a foul crime he would load,
But the thought, coming oft, grew less dark than before,
And he mused, as each creditor knocked at his door,
If *this* were but done they would dun me no more;
I told Philothea his struggles and doubts,
And how he considered the ins and the outs
Of the visions he had, and the dreadful dyspepsy,
How he went to the seer that lives at Po'keepsie,
How the seer advised him to sleep on it first,
And to read his big volume in case of the worst,
And further advised he should pay him five dollars
For writing **Hum, Hum,** on his wristbands and collars;
Three years and ten days these dark words he had studied
When the daughter was missed, and the aloe had budded;
I told how he watched it grow large and more large,
And wondered how much for the show he should charge,—
She had listened with utter indifference to this, till
I told how it bloomed, and, discharging its pistil
With an aim the Eumenides dictated, shot
The botanical filicide dead on the spot;
It had blown, but he reaped not his horrible gains,
For it blew with such force as to blow out his brains,
And the crime was blown also, because on the wad,
Which was paper, was writ 'Visitation of God,'
As well as a thrilling account of the deed
Which the coroner kindly allowed me to read.

"Well, my friend took this story up just, to be sure,
As one might a poor foundling that's laid at one's door;
She combed it and washed it and clothed it and fed it,
And as if 'twere her own child most tenderly bred it,
Laid the scene (of the legend, I mean) far away a-
-mong the green vales underneath Himalaya,
And by artistlike touches, laid on here and there,
Made the whole thing so touching, I frankly declare
I have read it all thrice, and, perhaps I am weak,
But I found every time there were tears on my cheek.

"The pole, science tells us, the magnet controls,
But she is a magnet to emigrant Poles,
And folks with a mission that nobody knows,
Throng thickly about her as bees round a rose;
She can fill up the *carets* in such, make their scope
Converge to some focus of rational hope,
And, with sympathies fresh as the morning, their gall
Can transmute into honey,—but this is not all;
Not only for those she has solace, oh say,
Vice's desperate nursling adrift in Broadway,
Who clingest, with all that is left of thee human,
To the last slender spar from the wreck of the woman,
Hast thou not found one shore where those tired drooping
    feet
Could reach firm mother earth, one full heart on whose beat
The soothed head in silence reposing could hear
The chimes of far childhood .throb back on the ear?
Ah, there's many a beam from the fountain of day
That, to reach us unclouded, must pass, on its way,
Through the soul of a woman, and hers is wide ope
To the influence of Heaven as the blue eyes of Hope;
Yes, a great heart is hers, one that dares to go in
To the prison, the slave hut, the alleys of sin,
And to bring into each, or to find there, some line
Of the never completely outtrampled divine;
If her heart at high floods swamps her brain now and then,
'Tis but richer for that when the tide ebbs agen,
As, after old Nile has subsided, his plain
Overflows with a second broad deluge of grain;
What a wealth would it bring to the narrow and sour
Could they be as a Child but for one little hour!

"What! Irving? thrice welcome, warm heart and fine
    brain,
You bring back the happiest spirit from Spain,
And the gravest sweet humor, that ever were there
Since Cervantes met death in his gentle despair;
Nay, don't be embarrassed, nor look so beseeching,
I shan't run directly against my own preaching,

And, having just laughed at their Raphaels and Dantes,
Go to setting you up beside matchless Cervantes;
But allow me to speak what I honestly feel,—
To a true poet heart add the fun of Dick Steele,
Throw in all of Addison, *minus* the chill,
With the whole of that partnership's stock and good will,
Mix well, and while stirring, hum o'er, as a spell,
The fine *old* English Gentleman, simmer it well,
Sweeten just to your own private liking, then strain,
That only the finest and clearest remain,
Let it stand out-of-doors till a soul it receives
From the warm lazy sun loitering down through green
   leaves,
And you'll find a choice nature, not wholly deserving
A name either English or Yankee,—just Irving.

   "There goes,—but *stet nominis umbra,*—his name
You'll be glad enough, some day or other, to claim,
And will all crowd about him and swear that you knew him
If some English critic should chance to review him.[1]
The old *porcos ante ne projiciatis*
Margaritas, for him you have verified gratis;
What matters his name? Why, it may be Sylvester,
Judd, Junior, or Junius, Ulysses, or Nestor,
For aught *I* know or care; 'tis enough that I look
On the author of *Margaret,* the first Yankee book
With the *soul* of Down East in 't, and things farther East,
As far as the threshold of morning, at least,
Where awaits the fair dawn of the simple and true,
Of the day that comes slowly to make all things new.
'T has a smack of pine woods, of bare field and bleak hill,
Such as only the breed of the *Mayflower* could till;
The Puritan's shown in it, tough to the core,
Such as prayed, smiting Agag on red Marston Moor:
With an unwilling humor, half choked by the drouth
In brown hollows about the inhospitable mouth;
With a soul full of poetry, though it has qualms

[1]Sylvester Judd, whose novel *Margaret* was published anonymously.
E. W.

About finding a happiness out of the Psalms;
Full of tenderness, too, though it shrinks in the dark,
Hamadryad-like, under the coarse, shaggy bark;
That sees visions, knows wrestlings of God with the Will,
And has its own Sinais and thunderings still."

  Here, "Forgive me, Apollo," I cried, "while I pour
My heart out to my birthplace: O loved more and more
Dear Baystate, from whose rocky bosom thy sons
Should suck milk, strong-will-giving, brave, such as runs
In the veins of old Graylock—who is it that dares
Call thee peddler, a soul wrapped in bank books and shares?
It is false! She's a Poet! I see, as I write,
Along the far railroad the steam snake glide white,
The cataract throb of her mill hearts I hear,
The swift strokes of trip hammers weary my ear,
Sledges ring upon anvils, through logs the saw screams,
Blocks swing to their place, beetles drive home the beams:—
It is songs such as these that she croons to the din
Of her fast-flying shuttles, year out and year in,
While from earth's farthest corner there comes not a breeze
But wafts her the buzz of her gold-gleaning bees:
What though those horn hands have as yet found small time
For painting and sculpture and music and rhyme?
These will come in due order; the need that pressed sorest
Was to vanquish the seasons, the ocean, the forest,
To bridle and harness the rivers, the steam,
Making those whirl her mill wheels, this tug in her team,
To vassalize old tyrant Winter, and make
Him delve surlily for her on river and lake;—
When this New World was parted, she strove not to shirk
Her lot in the heirdom, the tough, silent Work,
The hero share ever, from Herakles down
To Odin, the Earth's iron scepter and crown:
Yes, thou dear, noble Mother! If ever men's praise
Could be claimed for creating heroical lays,
Thou hast won it; if ever the laurel divine
Crowned the Maker and Builder, that glory is thine!
Thy songs are right epic, they tell how this rude

Rock rib of our earth here was tamed and subdued;
Thou hast written them plain on the face of the planet
In brave, deathless letters of iron and granite;
Thou hast printed them deep for all time; they are set
From the same runic type fount and alphabet
With thy stout Berkshire hills and the arms of thy Bay,—
They are staves from the burly old *Mayflower* lay.
If the drones of the Old World, in querulous ease,
Ask thy Art and thy Letters, point proudly to these,
Or, if they deny these are Letters and Art,
Toil on with the same old invincible heart;
Thou art rearing the pedestal broad-based and grand
Whereon the fair shapes of the Artist shall stand,
And creating, through labors undaunted and long,
The theme for all Sculpture and Painting and Song!

"But my good mother Baystate wants no praise of mine,
She learned from *her* mother a precept divine
About something that butters no parsnips, her *forte*
In another direction lies, work is her sport
(Though she'll curtsy and set her cap straight, that she will,
If you talk about Plymouth and red Bunker's hill).
Dear, notable goodwife! by this time of night,
Her hearth is swept neatly, her fire burning bright,
And she sits in a chair (of home plan and make) rocking,
Musing much, all the while, as she darns on a stocking,
Whether turkeys will come pretty high next Thanksgiving,
Whether flour'll be so dear, for, as sure as she's living,
She will use rye-and-injun then, whether the pig
By this time ain't got pretty tolerable big,
And whether to sell it outright will be best,
Or to smoke hams and shoulders and salt down the rest,—
At this minute, she'd swop all my verses, ah, cruel!
For the last patent stove that is saving of fuel;
So I'll just let Apollo go on, for his phiz
Shows I've kept him awaiting too long as it is."

"If our friend, there, who seems a reporter, is done
With his burst of emotion, why, *I* will go on,"

Said Apollo; some smiled, and, indeed, I must own
There was something sarcastic, perhaps, in his tone;—

"There's Holmes, who is matchless among you for wit;
A Leyden jar always full-charged, from which flit
The electrical tingles of hit after hit;
In long poems 'tis painful sometimes, and invites
A thought of the way the new Telegraph writes,
Which pricks down its little sharp sentences spitefully
As if you got more than you'd title to rightfully,
And you find yourself hoping its wild father Lightning
Would flame in for a second and give you a fright'ning.
He has perfect sway of what I call a sham meter,
But many admire it, the English pentameter,
And Campbell, I think, wrote most commonly worse,
With less nerve, swing, and fire in the same kind of verse,
Nor e'er achieved aught in 't so worthy of praise
As the tribute of Holmes to the grand *Marseillaise*.
You went crazy last year over Bulwer's *New Timon*;
Why, if B., to the day of his dying, should rhyme on
Heaping verses on verses and tomes upon tomes,
He could ne'er reach the best point and vigor of Holmes.
His are just the fine hands, too, to weave you a lyric
Full of fancy, fun, feeling, or spiced with satiric
In a measure so kindly, you doubt if the toes
That are trodden upon are your own or your foes'.

"There is Lowell, who's striving Parnassus to climb
With a whole bale of *isms* tied together with rhyme,
He might get on alone, spite of brambles and boulders,
But he can't with that bundle he has on his shoulders,
The top of the hill he will ne'er come nigh reaching
Till he learns the distinction 'twixt singing and preaching;
His lyre has some chords that would ring pretty well,
But he'd rather by half make a drum of the shell,
And rattle away till he's old as Methusalem,
At the head of a march to the last new Jerusalem.

"There goes Halleck, whose *Fanny*'s a pseudo *Don Juan*,
With the wickedness out that gave salt to the true one,

He's a wit, though, I hear, of the very first order,
And once made a pun on the words soft Recorder;
More than this, he's a very great poet, I'm told,
And has had his works published in crimson and gold,
With something they call 'Illustrations,' to wit,
Like those with which Chapman obscured Holy Writ,[1]
Which are said to illustrate, because, as I view it,
Like *lucus a non*, they precisely don't do it;
Let a man who can write what himself understands
Keep clear, if he can, of designing men's hands,
Who bury the sense, if there's any worth having,
And then very honestly call it engraving.
But, to quit *badinage*, which there isn't much wit in,
Halleck's better, I doubt not, than all he has written;
In his verse a clear glimpse you will frequently find,
If not of a great, of a fortunate mind,
Which contrives to be true to its natural loves
In a world of back offices, ledgers, and stoves.
When his heart breaks away from the brokers and banks,
And kneels in his own private shrine to give thanks,
There's a genial manliness in him that earns
Our sincerest respect (read, for instance, his *Burns*),
And we can't but regret (seek excuse where we may)
That so much of a man has been peddled away.

"But what's that? a mass meeting? No, there come in lots,
The American Bulwers, Disraelis, and Scotts,
And in short the American everything elses,
Each charging the others with envies and jealousies;—
By the way, 'tis a fact that displays what profusions
Of all kinds of greatness bless free institutions,
That while the Old World has produced barely eight
Of such poets as all men agree to call great,
And of other great characters hardly a score
(One might safely say less than that rather than more),
With you every year a whole crop is begotten,
They're as much of a staple as corn is, or cotton;
Why, there's scarcely a huddle of log huts and shanties

[1](Cuts rightly called wooden, as all must admit.)

That has not brought forth its own Miltons and Dantes;
I myself know ten Byrons, one Coleridge, three Shelleys,
Two Raphaels, six Titians, (I think) one Apelles,
Leonardos and Rubenses plenty as lichens,
One (but that one is plenty) American Dickens,
A whole flock of Lambs, any number of Tennysons,—
In short, if a man has the luck to have any sons,
He may feel pretty certain that one out of twain
Will be some very great person over again.
There is one inconvenience in all this, which lies
In the fact that by contrast we estimate size,[1]
And, where there are none except Titans, great stature
Is only the normal proceeding of nature.
What puff the strained sails of your praise will you furl at, if
The calmest degree that you know is superlative?
At Rome, all whom Charon took into his wherry must,
As a matter of course, be well *issimust* and *errimust*,
A Greek, too, could feel, while in that famous boat he tost,
That his friends would take care he was ιστοst and ωτατοst,
And formerly we, as through graveyards we past,
Thought the world went from bad to worst fearfully fast;
Let us glance for a moment, 'tis well worth the pains,
And note what an average graveyard contains;
There lie levelers leveled, duns done up themselves,
There are booksellers finally laid on their shelves,
Horizontally there lie upright politicians,
Dose-a-dose with their patients sleep faultless physicians,
There are slave drivers quietly whipped underground,
There bookbinders, done up in boards, are fast bound,
There card players wait till the last trump be played,
There all the choice spirits get finally laid,
There the babe that's unborn is supplied with a berth,
There men without legs get their six feet of earth,
There lawyers repose, each wrapped up in his case,
There seekers of office are sure of a place,

[1]That is in most cases we do, but not all,
Past a doubt, there are men who are innately small,
Such as Blank, who, without being 'minished a tittle,
Might stand for a type of the Absolute Little.

There defendant and plaintiff get equally cast,
There shoemakers quietly stick to the last,
There brokers at length become silent as stocks,
There stage drivers sleep without quitting their box,
And so forth and so forth and so forth and so on,
With this kind of stuff one might endlessly go on;
To come to the point, I may safely assert you
Will find in each yard every cardinal virtue;[1]
Each has six truest patriots: four discoverers of ether,
Who never had thought on 't nor mentioned it either;
Ten poets, the greatest who ever wrote rhyme:
Two hundred and forty first men of their time:
One person whose portrait just gave the least hint
Its original had a most horrible squint:
One critic, most (what do they call it?) reflective,
Who never had used the phrase ob- or subjective:
Forty fathers of Freedom, of whom twenty bred
Their sons for the rice swamps, at so much a head,
And their daughters for—faugh! thirty mothers of Gracchi:
Non-resistants who gave many a spiritual black eye:
Eight true friends of their kind, one of whom was a jailer:
Four captains almost as astounding as Taylor:
Two dozen of Italy's exiles who shoot us his
Kaiership daily, stern pen-and-ink Brutuses,
Who, in Yankee back parlors, with crucified smile,[2]
Mount serenely their country's funereal pile:
Ninety-nine Irish heroes, ferocious rebellers
'Gainst the Saxon in cis-marine garrets and cellars,
Who shake their dread fists o'er the sea and all that,—
As long as a copper drops into the hat:
Nine hundred Teutonic republicans stark
From Vaterland's battles just won—in the Park,
Who the happy profession of martyrdom take
Whenever it gives them a chance at a steak:
Sixty-two second Washingtons: two or three Jacksons:
And so many everythings else that it racks one's

[1](And at this just conclusion will surely arrive,
That the goodness of earth is more dead than alive.)
[2]Not forgetting their tea and their toast, though, the while.

Poor memory too much to continue the list,
Especially now they no longer exist;
I would merely observe that you've taken to giving
The puffs that belong to the dead to the living,
And that somehow your trump-of-contemporary-doom's tones
Is tuned after old dedications and tombstones."

    Here the critic came in and a thistle presented—[1]
From a frown to a smile the god's features relented,
As he stared at his envoy, who, swelling with pride,
To the god's asking look, nothing daunted, replied,—
"You're surprised, I suppose, I was absent so long,
But your godship respecting the lilies was wrong;
I hunted the garden from one end to t'other,
And got no reward but vexation and bother,
Till, tossed out with weeds in a corner to wither,
This one lily I found and made haste to bring hither."

    "Did he think I had given him a book to review?
I ought to have known what the fellow would do,"
Muttered Phœbus aside, "for a thistle will pass
Beyond doubt for the queen of all flowers with an ass;
He has chosen in just the same way as he'd choose
His specimens out of the books he reviews;
And now, as this offers an excellent text,
I'll give 'em some brief hints on criticism next."
So, musing a moment, he turned to the crowd,
And, clearing his voice, spoke as follows aloud:

    "My friends, in the happier days of the muse,
We were luckily free from such things as reviews;
Then naught came between with its fog to make clearer
The heart of the poet to that of his hearer;
Then the poet brought heaven to the people, and they
Felt that they, too, were poets in hearing his lay;
Then the poet was prophet, the past in his soul
Precreated the future, both parts of one whole;
Then for him there was nothing too great or too small,

[1]Turn back now to page — goodness only knows what,
And take a fresh hold on the thread of my plot.

For one natural deity sanctified all;
Then the bard owned no clipper and meter of moods
Save the spirit of silence that hovers and broods
O'er the seas and the mountains, the rivers and woods;
He asked not earth's verdict, forgetting the clods,
His soul soared and sang to an audience of gods;
'Twas for them that he measured the thought and the line,
And shaped for their vision the perfect design,
With as glorious a foresight, a balance as true,
As swung out the worlds in the infinite blue;
Then a glory and greatness invested man's heart,
The universal, which now stands estranged and apart,
In the free individual molded, was Art;
Then the forms of the Artist seemed thrilled with desire
For something as yet unattained, fuller, higher,
As once with her lips, lifted hands, and eyes listening,
And her whole upward soul in her countenance glistening,
Eurydice stood—like a beacon unfired,
Which, once touched with flame, will leap heav'nward
    inspired—
And waited with answering kindle to mark
The first gleam of Orpheus that pained the red Dark.
Then painting, song, sculpture did more than relieve
The need that men feel to create and believe,
And as, in all beauty, who listens with love
Hears these words oft repeated—'beyond and above,'
So these seemed to be but the visible sign
Of the grasp of the soul after things more divine;
They were ladders the Artist erected to climb
O'er the narrow horizon of space and of time,
And we see there the footsteps by which men had gained
To the one rapturous glimpse of the never-attained,
As shepherds could erst sometimes trace in the sod
The last spurning print of a sky-cleaving god.

"But now, on the poet's dis-privacied moods
With *do this* and *do that* the pert critic intrudes;
While he thinks he's been barely fulfilling his duty
To interpret 'twixt men and their own sense of beauty,

And has striven, while others sought honor or pelf,
To make his kind happy as he was himself,
He finds he's been guilty of horrid offenses
In all kinds of moods, numbers, genders, and tenses;
He's been *ob* and *sub*jective, what Kettle calls Pot,
Precisely, at all events, what he ought not,
You have done this, says one judge; *done that,* says another;
You should have done this, grumbles one; *that,* says t'other;
Never mind what he touches, one shrieks out *Taboo!*
And while he is wondering what he shall do,
Since each suggests opposite topics for song,
They all shout together *you're right!* and *you're wrong!*

"Nature fits all her children with something to do,
He who would write and can't write can surely review,
Can set up a small booth as critic and sell us his
Petty conceit and his pettier jealousies;
Thus a lawyer's apprentice, just out of his teens,
Will do for the Jeffrey of six magazines;
Having read Johnson's lives of the poets half through,
There's nothing on earth he's not competent to;
He reviews with as much nonchalance as he whistles,—
He goes through a book and just picks out the thistles;
It matters not whether he blame or commend,
If he's bad as a foe, he's far worse as a friend:
Let an author but write what's above his poor scope,
He goes to work gravely and twists up a rope,
And, inviting the world to see punishment done,
Hangs himself up to bleach in the wind and the sun;
'Tis delightful to see, when a man comes along
Who has anything in him peculiar and strong,
Every cockboat that swims clear its fierce (pop) gun deck at
     him,
And make as he passes its ludicrous Peck at him—"

Here Miranda came up and began, "As to that——"
Apollo at once seized his gloves, cane, and hat,
And, seeing the place getting rapidly cleared,
I too snatched my notes and forthwith disappeared.

Poe, at the time of his death in 1849, had had the intention of publishing a book on *The Authors of America in Prose and Verse*. He had already worked over to a considerable extent the material of his articles and reviews; and the collection of critical writing printed by Griswold after his death is something between a journalistic chronicle like Bernard Shaw's dramatic notices and a selected and concentrated volume like Eliot's *The Sacred Wood*.

Poe as a critic has points of resemblance both to Eliot and to Shaw. He deals vigorously and boldly with books as they come into his hands day by day, as Shaw did with the plays of the season, and manages to be brilliant and arresting even about works of no interest; and he constantly insists, as Eliot does, on attempting, in the practice of this journalism, to formulate general principles. His literary articles and lectures, in fact, surely constitute the most remarkable body of criticism ever produced in the United States. Henry James, as will be seen in his study of Hawthorne, called it "probably the most complete and exquisite specimen of *provincialism* ever prepared for the edification of men." But, though Poe had his share of provincialism as all American writers did in that period, the thing that most strikes us today is his success in keeping himself above it. Intellectually he stands on higher ground than any other American writer of his time. He is trying to curb the tendency of the Americans to overrate or overpraise their own books, and at the same time he is fighting a rearguard action against the overinflation of British reputations and the British injustice to American writers; and he has also a third battle: to break down the monopolistic instincts of the New Englanders, who tended to act as a clique and to keep out New Yorkers and Southerners.

On one plane, Poe grapples realistically with the practical problems of writers in the United States of that time: the copyright situation and the growth of the American magazine, with its influence on literary technique; and on another plane, he is able to take in the large developments of Western literature. With his general interest in method, he has definite ideas about the procedures in a variety of departments of literature: fiction, poetry, satire, travel, criticism. And he can be elevated, ironic, analytical, as the subject in hand requires. His prose is as taut as in his stories, but it has cast off the imagery of his fiction to become simply sharp and precise: our only first-rate classical prose of this period. His mind is like a bright vivid shaft that picks out the successive objects in the American literary landscape just as the searchlight on the Albany night-boat picks out houses along the Hudson; so that, just as we are drawn to gaze at even undistinguished mansions in their new relief of spectral intensity, so with Poe we read even the articles on insignificant figures whose dead faces the critic irradiates in the process of speeding them to oblivion. When we have put the whole picture together, we seem to behold it as clearly as the geography of the surface of the moon under an unattainably powerful telescope. There is no other such critical survey in our literature.

But Poe had tweaked the beard of Longfellow, and he had made people laugh at a Channing, and the lurking rancor of New England seems to have worked against the acceptance of his criticism. There is an anecdote in W. D.

Howells' book, *Literary Friends and Acquaintance,* which
shows both the attitude of New England and the influence
of this attitude on others. Howells had visited Boston for
the first time when he was twenty-three, and he had gone to
see Emerson in Concord. Poe had been dead ten years.
"After dinner," says Howells, "we walked about in [Emer-
son's] 'pleached garden' a little, and then we came again
into his library, where I meant to linger only till I could
fitly get away. He questioned me about what I had seen of
Concord, and whom besides Hawthorne I had met, and
when I told him only Thoreau, he asked me if I knew the
poems of Mr. William Ellery Channing. I have known
them since, and felt their quality, which I have gladly
owned a genuine and original poetry; but I answered then
truly that I knew them only from Poe's criticisms: cruel
and spiteful things which I should be ashamed of enjoying
as I once did. 'Whose criticisms?' asked Emerson. 'Poe's,' I
said again. 'Oh,' he cried out, after a moment, as if he had
returned from a far search for my meaning, *'you mean the
jingle-man.'*
"I do not know why this should have put me to such confusion, but if I had written the criticisms myself I do not
think I could have been more abashed. Perhaps I felt an
edge of reproof, of admonition, in a characterization of Poe
which the world will hardly agree with; though I do not
agree with the world about him, myself, in its admiration.
At any rate, it made an end of me for the time, and I remained as if already absent, while Emerson questioned me
as to what I had written in the *Atlantic Monthly.*"
It is true that Poe had not much admired Emerson and had
written rather insultingly about him in *A Chapter of Autog-
raphy;* and that Channing had been a sort of disciple
and protégé of Emerson's. But an entry in Emerson's journal for 1855 shows that his private opinion of Channing was
not so very different from Poe's: "Ellery Channing's poetry
has the merit of being genuine, and not the metrical commonplaces of the magazines, but it is painfully incomplete.
He has not kept faith with the reader; 'tis shamefully insolent
and slovenly. He should have lain awake all night to find the

true rhyme for a verse, and he has availed himself of the first one that came; so that it is all a babyish incompleteness."

The prejudice of New England against Poe was supported by the bad reputation that had been given him by Griswold's mendacious memoirs. It is not so long ago that it was possible for President Hadley of Yale to explain the refusal of the Hall of Fame to admit Poe among its immortals on the ground that he "wrote like a drunkard and a man who is not accustomed to pay his debts"; and it was only in 1941 that Professor A. H. Quinn showed the lengths to which Griswold had gone, by producing the originals of Poe's letters and printing them side by side with Griswold's falsifications.

We have often been told of Poe's criticism that it is spiteful; that it is pretentious; that it is vitiated by Poe's acceptance of the sentimental bad taste of his time. In regard to the first two of these charges, it must be admitted that the essays do give us unpleasant moments: they do have their queer knots and wrinkles; they are neurotic as all Poe's work is neurotic, and the distortions do here sometimes throw us off as they do not do in the stories, because it is here a question of judgment, whereas in his fiction the distortion itself is the subject of the story. It is true, as Mr. Joseph Wood Krutch has said, that there is constantly felt in Poe's criticism the same element of obsessive cruelty that inspires his tales of horror. Yet certainly Poe in his criticism makes an effort to hold this tendency in check—with an occasional effect of inconsistency, of opinion as well as of tone, as when he will begin by telling us that certain passages in some book he is reviewing are among the best things of their kind to be found in contemporary poetry, and then go on to pick the poet to pieces slowly, coldly, and at a length of many pages. It is also true that Poe pretends sometimes, or at least sometimes lets us infer, that he has read things he has not read. The psychology of the pretender is always a factor to be reckoned with in Poe.

The child of a fascinating actress, who died when he was two years old, he had been adopted by a Scotch merchant in Richmond, brought up as a Southern gentleman, and then cast off with no job and no income at the end of his first year of college. His foster father had even failed to provide money for his necessary expenses, so that Poe, as he said, had been unable to associate with any students "except those who were in a similar situation with myself." He had always been in the false situation of not being Allan's son and of knowing that in the society he was bred to his parents had been *déclassés;* and now he was suddenly deprived of his role of a well-heeled young Southern gentleman with prospects of inheriting a fortune, and found himself a poor man with no backing who had to survive in the American Grub Street. He had the confidence of faith in superior abilities, and the reports of his work at his English school and at the University of Virginia show that he excelled as a student. But his studies had been aborted at the same time as his social career, and a shade of the uncertainty of the "gentleman" was communicated also to the "scholar." Perhaps, also, though Poe's mind was a first-rate one, there was in him a dash of the actor who delights in elaborating a part. Out of this consciousness of being a pretender, at any rate, with its infliction of an habitual secretiveness, came certainly Poe's love of cryptograms, his interest in inventing and solving crimes, and his indulgence in concocting and exposing hoaxes. If Poe sometimes plays unavowed tricks by cheating the reader a little as to what he has written or read, the imposture is still almost as gratuitous, as innocent, and as unimportant as Stendhal's disguises and aliases and his weakness for taking ladies from the provinces through Paris and misinforming them about the public monuments. And with this we must also write off Poe's rather annoying mania of accusing his contemporaries of plagiarism—a harsh name he is in the habit of brandishing to indicate borrowings and echoes of a kind which, whether more or less abject, are usually perfectly harmless. Poe himself was certainly guilty —in his imitations of Chivers, for example—of borrowings of precisely the same kind. But the consciousness of borrowing at all was enough to touch off the pretender.

As for the charge of Poe's acquiescence in the mawkish bad taste of his period, it is deserved to only a slight degree. He more often ran counter to this taste, as when he came

down on Fitz-Greene Halleck; and, for the rest, his excessive
enthusiasm for poets like Mrs. Osgood is attributable to
the same sort of causes as, say, the praises of Bernard Shaw
for the plays of Henry Arthur Jones: the writer who is
potentially a master sees in the inferior writer a suggestion of
the kind of thing that he wants to do himself—a kind of
thing of which the possibility will hardly be plain to anyone else till the master himself has made it actual.

We must recognize these warpings of Poe's line; but we
must not allow them as serious impugnments of the validity
of his critical work. His reading *was* wide and great; and
his culture was derived from a plane of the world of thought
and art which had hardly been visited by Longfellow, with
his patient, persistent transposition of the poetry of many
lands and ages into terms of his own insipidity or by Lowell
with his awful cozy titles for the collections of his literary
essays: *My Study Windows* and *Among My Books*. The
truth was that literary America has always resented in Poe
the very superiority which made him so quickly an international figure. He must have been a difficult person, with
his accesses of hatefulness and depression, though certain
people seem to have got on very well with him; but it
seems hard to explain the virulence with which Griswold
pursued him after his death and the general hostility toward
him which has haunted us ever since, except on the ground
that he puts us out by making so much of our culture seem
second-rate. In our childhood we read *The Gold Bug* and
The Murders in the Rue Morgue, and everybody knows
Annabel Lee and *Ulalume* and *The Raven* and *The Bells;*
but Poe is not, as he is with the French and as he ought to
be with us, a vital part of our intellectual equipment. It is
rare that an American writer points out, as Waldo Frank
once did, that Poe does not belong at all with the clever con-
trivers of fiction like O. Henry and S. S. Van Dine, but, in
terms of his more constricted personality, with the great inquiring and versatile minds like Goethe. So that in any presentation of American writing it is still necessary to insist on
his value. In the darkness of his solitary confinement, Poe is
still a prince.

EDGAR ALLAN POE

J. G. C. BRAINARD

February 1842[1]

AMONG all the *pioneers* of American literature, whether prose or poetical, there is *not one* whose productions have not been much overrated by his countrymen. But this fact is more especially obvious in respect to such of these pioneers as are no longer living; nor is it a fact of so deeply transcendental a nature as only to be accounted for by the Emersons and Alcotts. In the first place, we have but to consider that gratitude, surprise, and a species of hyper-patriotic triumph have been blended, and finally confounded with mere admiration, or appreciation, in respect to the labors of our earlier writers; and, in the second place, that Death has thrown his customary veil of the sacred over these commingled feelings, forbidding them, in a measure, to be *now* separated or subjected to analysis. "In speaking of the deceased," says that excellent old English Moralist, James Puckle, in his *Gray Cap for a Green Head*, "so fold up your discourse that their virtues may be outwardly shown, while their vices are wrapped up in silence." And with somewhat too inconsiderate a promptitude have we followed the spirit of this quaint advice. The mass of American readers have been, hitherto, in no frame of mind to view with calmness,

[1] The dates given here are the dates of the first publication of Poe's essays in contemporary periodicals. E. W.

and to discuss with discrimination, the true claims of the few who were *first* in convincing the mother country that her sons were not all brainless, as, in the plenitude of her arrogance, she, at one period, half affected and half wished to believe; and where any of these few have departed from among us, the difficulty of bringing their pretensions to the test of a proper criticism has been enhanced in a very remarkable degree. But even as concerns the living: is there anyone so blind as not to see that Mr. Cooper, for example, owes much, and that Mr. Paulding owes *all* of his reputation as a novelist to his early occupation of the field? Is there anyone so dull as not to know that fictions which neither Mr. Paulding nor Mr. Cooper *could* have written are daily published by native authors without attracting more of commendation than can be crammed into a hack newspaper paragraph? And, again, is there anyone so prejudiced as not to acknowledge that all this is because there is no longer either reason or wit in the query,—"Who reads an American book?" It is not because we lack the talent in which the days of Mr. Paulding exulted, but because such talent has shown itself to be common. It is not because we have *no* Mr. Coopers; but because it has been demonstrated that we might, at any moment, have as many Mr. Coopers as we please. In fact, we are now strong in our own resources. We have, at length, arrived at that epoch when our literature may and must stand on its own merits, or fall through its own defects. We have snapped asunder the leading-strings of our British grandmamma, and, better still, we have survived the first hours of our novel freedom,—the first licentious hours of a hobbledehoy braggadocio and swagger. At last, then, we are in a condition to be criticized —even more, to be neglected; and the journalist is no longer in danger of being impeached for *lèse majesté* of the Democratic Spirit, who shall assert, with sufficient humility, that we have committed an error in mistaking Kettell's *Specimens* for the Pentateuch, or Joseph Rodman Drake for Apollo.

The case of this latter gentleman is one which well illustrates what we have been saying. We believe it was about 1835 that Mr. Dearborn republished *The Culprit Fay,* which

then, as at the period of its original issue, was belauded by
the universal American press, in a manner which must have
appeared ludicrous—not to speak *very* plainly—in the eyes of
all unprejudiced observers. With a curiosity much excited
by comments at once so grandiloquent and so general, we
procured and read the poem. What we found it we ventured to express distinctly, and at some length, in the pages
of the *Southern Messenger*. It is a well-versified and sufficiently fluent composition, without high merit of any kind.
Its defects are gross and superabundant. Its plot and conduct, considered in reference to its scene, are absurd. Its
originality is none at all. Its imagination (and this was
the great feature insisted upon by its admirers) is but a
"counterfeit presentment,"—but the shadow of the shade of
that lofty quality which is, in fact, the soul of the Poetic
Sentiment, but a drivelling *effort to be fanciful,* an effort
resulting in a species of hop-skip-and-go-merry rodomontade,
which the uninitiated feel it a duty to call ideality, and to
admire as such, while lost in surprise at the impossibility of
performing at least the latter half of the duty with anything
like satisfaction to themselves. And all this we not only
asserted, but without difficulty *proved*. Dr. Drake has written
some beautiful poems, but *The Culprit Fay* is not of them.
We neither expected to hear any dissent from our opinions,
nor did we hear any. On the contrary, the approving voice
of every critic in the country whose *dictum* we had been
accustomed to respect was to us a sufficient assurance that
we had not been very grossly in the wrong. In fact, the public taste was then approaching the right. The truth indeed
had not, as yet, made itself heard; but we had reached a
point at which it had but to be plainly and boldly put, to be
at least tacitly admitted.

This habit of apotheosizing our literary pioneers was a
most indiscriminating one. Upon all who wrote, the applause
was plastered with an impartiality really refreshing. Of
course, the system favored the dunces at the expense of true
merit; and, since there existed a certain fixed standard of
exaggerated commendation to which all were adapted after
the fashion of Procrustes, it is clear that the most meritorious

required *the least stretching*,—in other words, that although all were much overrated, the deserving were overrated in a less degree than the unworthy. Thus with Brainard: a man of indisputable genius, who, in any more discriminate system of panegyric, would have been long ago bepuffed into Demi-Deism; for if *M'Fingal*, for example, is in reality what we have been told, the commentators upon Trumbull, as a matter of the simplest consistency, should have exalted into the seventh heaven of poetical dominion the author of the many graceful and vigorous effusions which are now lying, in a very neat little volume, before us.

Yet we maintain that even these effusions have been overpraised, and materially so. It is not that Brainard has not written poems which may rank with those of any American, with the single exception of Longfellow; but that the general merit of our whole national Muse has been estimated too highly, and that the author of *The Connecticut River* has, individually, shared in the exaggeration. No poet among us has composed what would deserve the tithe of that amount of approbation so innocently lavished upon Brainard. But it would not suit our purpose just now to enter into any elaborate analysis of his productions. It so happens, however, that we open the book at a brief poem, an examination of which will stand us in good stead of this general analysis, since it is by this very poem that the admirers of its author are content to swear, since it is the fashion to cite it as his best, since thus, in short, it is the chief basis of his notoriety, if not the surest triumph of his fame.

We allude to *The Fall of Niagara,* and shall be pardoned for quoting it in full:

> The thoughts are strange that crowd into my brain
> While I look upward to thee. It would seem
> As if God poured thee from His hollow hand,
> And hung His bow upon thy awful front;
> And spoke in that loud voice which seemed to him
> Who dwelt in Patmos for his Savior's sake
> The "sound of many waters;" and had bade
> Thy flood to chronicle the ages back,
> And notch his centuries in the eternal rocks.

Deep calleth unto deep. And what are we
That hear the question of that voice sublime?
Oh, what are all the notes that ever rung
From war's vain trumpet, by thy thundering side?
Yea, what is all the riot man can make
In his short life to thy unceasing roar?
And yet, bold babbler, what art thou to HIM
Who drowned a world and heaped the waters far
Above its loftiest mountains?—a light wave
That breaks and whispers of its Maker's might.

It is a very usual thing to hear these verses called not merely the best of their author, but the best which have been written on the subject of Niagara. Their positive merit appears to us only partial. We have been informed that the poet had seen the great cataract before writing the lines; but the Memoir prefixed to the present edition denies what, for our own part, we never believed, for Brainard was truly a poet, and no poet could have looked upon Niagara, in the substance, and written thus about it. If he saw it at all, it must have been in fancy—"at a distance"—ἑκάς—as the lying Pindar says he saw Archilochus, who died ages before the villain was born.

To the two opening verses we have no objection; but it may be well observed, in passing, that had the mind of the poet been really "crowded with strange thoughts," and not merely *engaged in an endeavor to think,* he would have entered at once upon the thoughts themselves, without allusion to the state of his brain. His subject would have left him no room for self.

The third line embodies an absurd and impossible, not to say a contemptible image. We are called upon to conceive a similarity between the *continuous* downward sweep of Niagara and the momentary splashing of some definite and of course trifling quantity of water *from a hand;* for, although it is the hand of the Deity Himself which is referred to, the mind is irresistibly led, by the words "poured from His hollow hand," to that idea which has been *customarily* attached to such a phrase. It is needless to say, moreover, that the bestowing upon Deity a human form is at best a low and most unideal conception. In fact, the poet has committed the grossest of errors in likening the fall to any material object; for the human fancy can fashion nothing which shall not be inferior in majesty to the cataract itself. Thus bathos is inevitable; and there is no better exemplification of bathos than Mr. Brainard has here given.[1]

The fourth line but renders the matter worse, for here the figure is most inartistically shifted. The handful of water becomes animate; for it has a front—that is, a forehead, and upon this forehead the Deity proceeds to hang a bow, that is, a rainbow. At the same time He "speaks in that loud voice," etc.; and here it is obvious that the ideas of the writer are in a sad state of fluctuation; for he transfers the idiosyncrasy of the fall itself (that is to say, its sound) to the One who pours it from His hand. But not content with all this, Mr. Brainard commands the flood to *keep a kind of tally*; for this is the low thought which the expression about "notching in the rocks" immediately and inevitably induces. The whole of this first division of the poem embraces, we hesitate not to say, one of the most jarring, inappropriate, mean, and in every way monstrous assemblages of false imagery which can be found out of the tragedies of Nat Lee or the farces of Thomas Carlyle.

In the latter division, the poet recovers himself, as if ashamed of his previous bombast. His natural instinct (for

[1] It is remarkable that Drake is, perhaps, the sole poet who has employed, in the description of Niagara, imagery which does not produce a bathetic impression. In one of his minor poems he has these magnificent lines:

How sweet 'twould be, *when all the air
In moonlight swims,* along thy river
    To couch upon the grass, and hear
Niagara's everlasting voice
    Far in the deep blue West away—
That dreaming and poetic noise
    We mark not in the glare of day;
Oh, how unlike its torrent-cry
    When o'er the brink the tide is driven,
*As if the vast and sheeted sky
    In thunder fell from Heaven!*

E. A. P.

Brainard was no artist) has enabled him to feel that *subjects which surpass in grandeur all efforts of the human imagination are well depicted only in the simplest and least metaphorical language*—a proposition as susceptible of demonstration as any in Euclid. Accordingly, we find a material sinking in tone, although he does not at once discard all imagery. The "Deep calleth unto deep" is nevertheless a great improvement upon his previous rhetoricianism. The personification of the waters above and below would be good in reference to any subject less august. The moral reflections which immediately follow have at least the merit of simplicity; but the poet exhibits no very lofty imagination when he bases these reflections only upon the cataract's superiority to man *in the noise it can create;* nor is the concluding idea more spirited, where the mere difference between the quantity of water which occasioned the flood and the quantity which Niagara precipitates is made the measure of the Almighty Mind's superiority to that cataract which it called by a thought into existence.

But although *The Fall of Niagara* does not deserve all the unmeaning commendation it has received, there are, nevertheless, many truly beautiful poems in this collection, and even more certain evidences of poetic power. *To a Child, the Daughter of a Friend,* is exceedingly graceful and terse. *To the Dead* has equal grace, with more vigor, and, moreover, a touching air of melancholy. Its melody is very rich, and in the monotonous repetition, at each stanza, of a certain rhyme, we recognize a fantastic yet true imagination. *Mr. Merry's Lament for Long Tom* would be worthy of all praise were not its unusually beautiful rhythm an imitation from Campbell, who would deserve his high poetical rank, if only for its construction. Of the merely humorous pieces we have little to say. Such things are not *poetry.* Mr. Brainard excelled in them, and they are very good in their place; but that place is not in a collection of poems. The prevalent notions upon this head are extremely vague; yet we see no reason why any ambiguity should exist. Humor, with an exception to be made hereafter, is directly antagonistical to that which is the soul of the Muse proper; and the omni-prevalent belief, that melancholy is inseparable from the higher manifestations of the beautiful, is not without a firm basis in nature and in reason. But it so happens that humor and that quality which we have termed the soul of the Muse (imagination) are both essentially aided in their development by the same adventitious assistance—that of rhythm and of rhyme. Thus the only bond between humorous verse and poetry, properly so called, is that they employ in common a certain tool. But this single circumstance has been sufficient to occasion, and to maintain through long ages, a confusion of two very distinct ideas in the brain of the unthinking critic. There is, nevertheless, an individual branch of humor which blends so happily with the ideal that from the union result some of the finest effects of legitimate poesy. We allude to what is termed *"archness"*—a trait with which popular feeling, which is unfailingly poetic, has invested, for example, the whole character of the fairy. In the volume before us there is a brief composition entitled *The Tree Toad* which will afford a fine exemplification of our idea. It seems to have been hurriedly constructed, as if its author had felt ashamed of his light labor. But that in his heart there was a secret exultation over these verses for which his reason found it difficult to account, *we know;* and there is not a really imaginative man within sound of our voice today, who, upon perusal of this little *Tree Toad*, will not admit it to be one of the truest poems ever written by Brainard.

LONGFELLOW'S BALLADS

April 1842

"Il y a à parier," says Chamfort, *"que toute idée publique, toute convention reçue, est une sottise, car elle a convenu au plus grand nombre,"*—"One would be safe in wagering that any given public idea is erroneous, for it has

been yielded to the clamor of the majority"; and this strictly philosophical, although somewhat French, assertion has especial bearing upon the whole race of what are termed maxims and popular proverbs, nine-tenths of which are the quintessence of folly. One of the most deplorably false of them is the antique adage, "*De gustibus non est disputandum*"— "There should be no disputing about taste." Here the idea designed to be conveyed is that any one person has as just right to consider his own taste *the true*, as has any one other —that taste itself, in short, is an arbitrary something, amenable to no law, and measurable by no definite rules. It must be confessed, however, that the exceedingly vague and impotent treatises which are alone extant have much to answer for as regards confirming the general error. Not the least important service which, hereafter, mankind will owe to *Phrenology*, may, perhaps, be recognized in an analysis of the real principles and a digest of the resulting laws of taste. These principles, in fact, are as clearly traceable, and these laws as readily susceptible of system, as are any whatever.

In the meantime, the insane adage above mentioned is in no respect more generally, more stupidly, and more pertinaciously quoted than by the admirers of what is termed the "good old Pope" or the "good old Goldsmith school" of poetry, in reference to the bolder, more natural, and more ideal compositions of such authors as Coëtlogon and Lamartine[1] in France; Herder, Körner, and Uhland in Germany; Brun and Baggesen in Denmark; Bellman, Tegner, and Nyberg[2] in Sweden; Keats, Shelley, Coleridge, and Tennyson in England; Lowell and Longfellow in America. "*De gustibus non*," say these "good-old-school" fellows; and we have no doubt that their mental translation of the phrase is —"We pity your taste—we pity everybody's taste but our own."

It is our purpose to controvert the popular idea that the poets just mentioned owe to novelty, to trickeries of expression, and to other meretricious effects, their appreciation by

[1]We allude here chiefly to the *David* of Coëtlogon, and *only* to the *Chute d'un Ange* of Lamartine. E. A. P.

[2]Julia C. Nyberg, author of the *Dikter von Euphrosyne*. E. A. P.

certain readers; to demonstrate (for the matter is susceptible of demonstration) that such poetry, and *such alone,* has fulfilled the legitimate office of the Muse; has thoroughly satisfied an earnest and unquenchable desire existing in the heart of man.

This volume of *Ballads and Tales* includes, with several brief original pieces, a translation from the Swedish of Tegner. In attempting (what never should be attempted) a literal version of both the words and the meter of this poem, Professor Longfellow has failed to do justice either to his author or himself. He has striven to do what no man ever did well, and what, from the nature of language itself, never can be well done. Unless, for example, we shall come to have an influx of spondees in our English tongue, it will always be impossible to construct an English hexameter. Our spondees, or, we should say, our spondaic words, are rare. In the Swedish they are nearly as abundant as in the Latin and Greek. We have only "compound," "context," "footfall," and a few other similar ones. This is the difficulty; and that it is so will become evident upon reading *The Children of the Lord's Supper,* where the sole readable verses are those in which we meet with the rare spondaic dissyllables. We mean to say readable as hexameters; for many of them will read very well as mere English dactylics with certain irregularities.

Much as we admire the genius of Mr. Longfellow, we are fully sensible of his many errors of affectation and imitation. His artistical skill is great, and his ideality high. But his conception of the aims of poesy is all wrong; and this we shall prove at some future day, to our own satisfaction, at least. His didactics are all out of place. He has written brilliant poems, by accident; that is to say, when permitting his genius to get the better of his conventional habit of thinking, a habit deduced from German study. We do not mean to say that a didactic moral may not be well made the undercurrent of a poetical thesis; but that it can never be well put so obtrusively forth, as in the majority of his compositions.

We have said that Mr. Longfellow's conception of the aims of poesy is erroneous; and that thus, laboring at a disadvantage, he does violent wrong to his own high powers;

and now the question is, what are his ideas of the aims of the Muse, as we gather these ideas from the general tendency of his poems? It will be at once evident that, imbued with the peculiar spirit of German song (in pure conventionality), he regards the inculcation of a moral as essential. Here we find it necessary to repeat that we have reference only to the general tendency of his compositions; for there are some magnificent exceptions, where, as if by accident, he has permitted his genius to get the better of his conventional prejudice. But didacticism is the prevalent tone of his song. His invention, his imagery, his all, is made subservient to the elucidation of some one or more points (but rarely of more than one) which he looks upon as truth. And that this mode of procedure will find stern defenders should never excite surprise, so long as the world is full to overflowing with cant and conventicles. There are men who will scramble on all fours through the muddiest sloughs of vice to pick up a single apple of virtue. There are things called men who, so long as the sun rolls, will greet with snuffling huzzas every figure that takes upon itself the semblance of truth, even although the figure, in itself only a "stuffed Paddy," be as much out of place as a toga on the statue of Washington, or out of season as rabbits in the days of the dog star.

We say this with little fear of contradiction. Yet the spirit of our assertion must be more heeded than the letter. Mankind have seemed to define Poesy in a thousand, and in a thousand conflicting, definitions. But the war is one only of words. Induction is as well applicable to this subject as to the most palpable and utilitarian; and by its sober processes we find that, in respect to compositions which have been really received as poems, the imaginative, or, more popularly, the creative portions alone have insured them to be so received. Yet these works, on account of these portions, having once been so received and so named, it has happened, naturally and inevitably, that other portions totally unpoetic have not only come to be regarded by the popular voice as poetic, but have been made to serve as false standards of perfection, in the adjustment of other poetical claims. Whatever has been found in whatever has been received as a poem

has been blindly regarded as *ex statu* poetic. And this is a
species of gross error which scarcely could have made its
way into any less intangible topic. In fact, that license, which
appertains to the Muse herself, it has been thought decorous,
if not sagacious, to indulge, in all examination of her character.

Poesy is a response—unsatisfactory, it is true—but still in
some measure a response, to a natural and irrepressible demand. Man being what he is, the time could never have
been in which Poesy was not. Its first element is the thirst
for supernal BEAUTY—a beauty which is not afforded the
soul by any existing collocation of earth's forms—a beauty
which, perhaps, no possible combination of these forms
would fully produce. Its second element is the attempt to
satisfy this thirst by novel combinations among those forms
of beauty which already exist—or by novel combinations *of
those combinations which our predecessors, toiling in chase
of the same phantom, have already set in order.* We thus
clearly deduce the *novelty,* the *originality,* the *invention,* the
imagination, or lastly the *creation* of BEAUTY (for the terms
as here employed are synonymous), as the essence of all
Poesy. Nor is this idea so much at variance with ordinary
opinion as, at first sight, it may appear. A multitude of antique dogmas on this topic will be found, when divested of
extrinsic speculation, to be easily resoluble into the definition
now proposed. We do nothing more than present tangibly
the vague clouds of the world's idea. We recognize the idea
itself floating, unsettled, indefinite, in every attempt which
has yet been made to circumscribe the conception of "Poesy"
in words. A striking instance of this is observable in the fact
that no definition exists in which either "the beautiful," or
some one of those qualities which we have above designated
synonymously with "creation," has not been pointed out as
the chief attribute of the Muse. "Invention," however, or
"imagination," is by far more commonly insisted upon. The
word ποιῆσις itself (creation) speaks volumes upon this
point. Neither will it be amiss here to mention Count Biel-
feld's definition of poetry as *"L'art d'exprimer les pensées par
la fiction."* With this definition (of which the philosophy

is profound to a certain extent) the German terms *Dicht-kunst,* the art of fiction, and *dichten,* to feign, which are used for "poetry" and "to make verses," are in full and re-markable accordance. It is, nevertheless, in the combination of the two omni-prevalent ideas that the novelty, and, we believe, the force of our own proposition is to be found.

The elements of that beauty which is felt in sound may be the mutual or common heritage of Earth and Heaven. Con-tenting ourselves with the firm conviction that music (in its modifications of rhythm and rhyme) is of so vast a moment to Poesy as never to be neglected by him who is truly poetical —is of so mighty a force in furthering the great aim intended that he is mad who rejects its assistance—content with this idea, we shall not pause to maintain its absolute essentiality for the mere sake of rounding a definition. That our defini-tion of poetry will necessarily exclude much of what, through a supine toleration, has been hitherto ranked as poetical, is a matter which affords us not even momentary concern. We address but the thoughtful, and heed only their approval— with our own. If our suggestions are truthful, then "after many days" shall they be understood as truth, even though found in contradiction of all that has been hitherto so under-stood. If false, shall we not be the first to bid them die?

We would reject, of course, all such matters as Armstrong on *Health,* a revolting production; Pope's *Essay on Man,* which may well be content with the title of an *Essay in Rhyme; Hudibras,* and other merely humorous pieces. We do not gainsay the peculiar merits of either of these latter compositions, but deny them the position held. In a notice of Brainard's poems, we took occasion to show that the common use of a certain instrument (rhythm) had tended, more than aught else, to confound humorous verse with poetry. The observation is now recalled to corroborate what we have just said in respect to the vast effect or force of melody in itself —an effect which could elevate into even momentary confu-sion with the highest efforts of mind compositions such as are the greater number of satires or burlesques.

We have shown our ground of objection to the general themes of Professor Longfellow. In common with all who claim the sacred title of poet, he should limit his endeavors to the creation of novel moods of beauty, in form, in color, in sound, in sentiment; for over all this wide range has the poetry of words dominion. To what the world terms "prose" may be safely and properly left all else. The artist who doubts of his thesis may always resolve his doubt by the single question—"might not this matter be as well or better handled in prose?" If it may, then is it no subject for the Muse. In the general acceptation of the term "Beauty" we are content to rest; being careful only to suggest that, in our peculiar views, it must be understood as inclusive of the sublime.

Of the pieces which constitute the present volume, there are not more than one or two thoroughly fulfilling the ideas we have proposed; although the volume, as a whole, is by no means so chargeable with didacticism as Mr. Longfellow's previous book. We would mention as poems nearly true, *The Village Blacksmith, The Wreck of the* Hesperus, and especially *The Skeleton in Armor.* In the first-mentioned we have the beauty of simple-mindedness as a genuine thesis; and this thesis is inimitably handled until the concluding stanza, where the spirit of legitimate poesy is aggrieved in the pointed antithetical deduction of a moral from what has gone before. In *The Wreck of the* Hesperus we have the beauty of childlike confidence and innocence, with that of the father's stern courage and affection. But, with slight exception, those particulars of the storm here detailed are not poetic subjects. Their thrilling horror belongs to prose, in which it could be far more effectively discussed, as Professor Longfellow may assure himself at any moment by experiment. There are points of a tempest which afford the loftiest and truest poetical themes—points in which pure beauty is found, or, better still, beauty heightened into the sublime by terror. But when we read, among other similar things, that

> The salt sea was frozen on her breast,
> The salt tears in her eyes,

we feel, if not positive disgust, at least a chilling sense of the inappropriate. In *The Skeleton in Armor* we find a pure and perfect thesis artistically treated. We find the beauty of bold courage and self-confidence, of love and maiden devotion, of reckless adventure, and finally of life-contemning grief. Combined with all this, we have numerous points of beauty apparently insulated, but all aiding the main effect or impression. The heart is stirred, and the mind does not lament its mal-instruction. The meter is simple, sonorous, well-balanced, and fully adapted to the subject. Upon the whole, there are fewer truer poems than this. It has but one defect—an important one. The prose remarks prefacing the narrative are really necessary. But every work of art should contain within itself all that is requisite for its own comprehension. And this remark is especially true of the ballad. In poems of magnitude the mind of the reader is not, at all times, enabled to include, in one comprehensive survey, the proportions and proper adjustment of the whole. He is pleased, if at all, with particular passages; and the sum of his pleasure is compounded of the sums of the pleasurable sentiments inspired by these individual passages in the progress of perusal. But, in pieces of less extent, the pleasure is unique, in the proper acceptation of this term—the understanding is employed, without difficulty, in the contemplation of the picture as a whole; and thus its effect will depend, in great measure, upon the perfection of its finish, upon the nice adaptation of its constituent parts, and, especially, upon what is rightly termed by Schlegel *the unity or totality of interest*. But the practice of prefixing explanatory passages is utterly at variance with such unity. By the prefix, we are either put in possession of the subject of the poem, or some hint, historic fact, or suggestion is thereby afforded, not included in the body of the piece, which, without the hint, is incomprehensible. In the latter case, while perusing the poem, the reader must revert, in mind at least, to the prefix, for the necessary explanation. In the former, the poem being a mere paraphrase of the prefix, the interest is divided between the prefix and the paraphrase. In either instance the totality of effect is destroyed.

Of the other original poems in the volume before us there is none in which the aim of instruction, or truth, has not been too obviously substituted for the legitimate aim, beauty. We have heretofore taken occasion to say that a didactic moral might be happily made the undercurrent of a poetical theme, and we have treated this point at length, in a review of Moore's *Alciphron*; but the moral thus conveyed is invariably an ill effect when obtruding beyond the upper current of the thesis itself. Perhaps the worst specimen of this obtrusion is given us by our poet in *Blind Bartimeus* and *The Goblet of Life*, where it will be observed that the sole interest of the upper current of meaning depends upon its relation or reference to the under. What we read upon the surface would be *vox et præterea nihil* in default of the moral beneath. The Greek *finales* of *Blind Bartimeus* are an affectation altogether inexcusable. What the small, second-hand Gibbonish pedantry of Byron introduced is unworthy the imitation of Longfellow.

Of the translations we scarcely think it necessary to speak at all. We regret that our poet will persist in busying himself about such matters. His time might be better employed in original conception. Most of these versions are marked with the error upon which we have commented. This error is, in fact, essentially Germanic. *The Luck of Edenhall*, however, is a truly beautiful poem; and we say this with all that deference which the opinion of the *Democratic Review* demands. This composition appears to us one of the very finest. It has all the free, hearty, obvious movement of the true ballad-legend. The greatest force of language is combined in it with the richest imagination, acting in its most legitimate province. Upon the whole, we prefer it even to the *Sword-Song* of Körner. The pointed moral with which it terminates is so exceedingly natural, so perfectly fluent from the incidents, that we have hardly heart to pronounce it in ill taste. We may observe of this ballad, in conclusion, that its subject is more physical than is usual in Germany. Its images are rich rather in physical than in moral beauty. And this tendency, in Song, is the true one. It is chiefly, if we are not mistaken—it is chiefly amid forms of physical loveliness (we use the word *forms* in its widest sense as embracing modifications of sound and color) that the soul seeks the realization of its dreams of BEAUTY. It is to her demand in this sense especially that the poet, who is wise, will most frequently and most earnestly respond.

The Children of the Lord's Supper is, beyond doubt, a true and most beautiful poem in great part, while, in some particulars, it is too metaphysical to have any pretension to the name. We have already objected, briefly, to its meter—the ordinary Latin or Greek hexameter—dactyls and spondees at random, with a spondee in conclusion. We maintain that the hexameter can never be introduced into our language, from the nature of that language itself. This rhythm demands, *for English ears,* a preponderance of natural spondees. Our tongue has few. Not only does the Latin and Greek, with the Swedish, and some others, abound in them; but the Greek and Roman ear had become reconciled (why or how is unknown) to the reception of artificial spondees—that is to say, spondaic words formed partly of one word and partly of another, or from an excised part of one word. In short, the ancients were content to read *as they scanned,* or nearly so. It may be safely prophesied that we shall never do this; and thus we shall never admit English hexameters. The attempt to introduce them, after the repeated failures of Sir Philip Sidney, and others, is, perhaps, somewhat discreditable to the scholarship of Professor Longfellow. The *Democratic Review,* in saying that he has triumphed over difficulties in this rhythm, has been deceived, it is evident, by the facility with which some of these verses may be read. In glancing over the poem, we do not observe a single verse which can be read, *to English ears, as a Greek hexameter.* There are many, however, which can be well read as mere English dactylic verses; such, for example, as the well-known lines of Byron, commencing

Know ye the | land where the | cypress and | myrtle.

These lines (although full of irregularities) are, in their perfection, formed of three dactyls and a cæsura—just as if we should cut short the initial verse of the *Bucolics* thus:

Tityre | tu patu | læ recu | bans . . .

The "myrtle," at the close of Byron's line, is a double rhyme, and must be understood as one syllable.

Now a great number of Professor Longfellow's hexameters are merely these dactylic lines, *continued for two feet*. For example:

Whispered the | race of the | flowers and | merry on | balancing | branches.

In this example, also, "branches," which is a double ending, must be regarded as the cæsura, or one syllable, of which alone it has the force.

As we have already alluded, in one or two regards, to a notice of these poems which appeared in the *Democratic Review,* we may as well here proceed with some few further comments upon the article in question, with whose general tenor we are happy to agree.

The *Review* speaks of *Maidenhood* as a poem "not to be understood but at the expense of more time and trouble than a song can justly claim." We are scarcely less surprised at this opinion from Mr. Langtree than we were at the condemnation of *The Luck of Edenhall.*

Maidenhood is faulty, it appears to us, only on the score of its theme, which is somewhat didactic. Its meaning seems simplicity itself. A maiden on the verge of womanhood, hesitating to enjoy life (for which she has a strong appetite) through a false idea of duty, is bidden to fear nothing, having purity of heart as her lion of Una.

What Mr. Langtree styles "an unfortunate peculiarity" in Mr. Longfellow, resulting from "adherence to a false system," has really been always regarded by us as one of his idiosyncratic merits. "In each poem," says the critic, "he has but one idea, which, in the progress of his song, is gradually unfolded, and at last reaches its full development in the concluding lines; this singleness of thought might lead a harsh critic to suspect intellectual barrenness." It leads *us,* individually, only to a full sense of the artistical power and knowledge of the poet. We confess that now, for the first time, we hear unity of conception objected to as a defect. But Mr. Langtree seems to have fallen into the singular error of supposing the poet to have absolutely *but one idea* in each of his ballads. Yet how "one idea" can be "gradually unfolded" without other ideas is, to us, a mystery of mysteries. Mr. Longfellow, very properly, has but one leading idea which forms the basis of his poem; but to the aid and development of this one there are innumerable others, of which the rare excellence is that all are in keeping, that none could be well omitted, that each tends to the one general effect. It is unnecessary to say another word upon this topic.

In speaking of *Excelsior,* Mr. Langtree (are we wrong in attributing the notice to his very forcible pen?) seems to labor under some similar misconception. "It carries along with it," says he, "a false moral which greatly diminishes its merit in our eyes. The great merit of a picture, whether made with the pencil or pen, is its truth; and this merit does not belong to Mr. Longfellow's sketch. Men of genius may, and probably do, meet with greater difficulties in their struggles with the world than their fellow men who are less highly gifted; but their power of overcoming obstacles is proportionably greater, and the result of their laborious suffering is not death but immortality."

That the chief merit of a picture is its truth is an assertion deplorably erroneous. Even in Painting, which is, more essentially than Poetry, a mimetic art, the proposition cannot be sustained. Truth is not even the aim. Indeed it is curious to observe how very slight a degree of truth is sufficient to satisfy the mind, which acquiesces in the absence of numerous essentials in the thing depicted. An outline frequently stirs the spirit more pleasantly than the most elaborate picture. We need only refer to the compositions of Flaxman and of Retzch. Here all details are omitted—nothing can be farther from truth. Without even color the most thrilling effects are produced. In statues we are rather pleased than disgusted with *the want of the eyeball.* The hair of the Venus de Medici *was gilded.* Truth indeed! The grapes of Zeuxis as well as the curtain of Parrhasius were received as indisputable evidence of the truthful ability of these artists— but they were not even *classed among their pictures.* If truth

is the highest aim of either Painting or Poesy, then Jan
Steen was a greater artist than Angelo, and Crabbe is a more
noble poet than Milton.

But we have not quoted the observation of Mr. Langtree
to deny its philosophy; our design was simply to show that
he has misunderstood the poet. *Excelsior* has not even a
remote tendency to the interpretation assigned it by the
critic. It depicts the *earnest upward impulse of the soul*—an
impulse not to be subdued even in Death. Despising danger,
resisting pleasure, the youth, bearing the banner inscribed
"Excelsior!" ("higher still!") struggles through all difficulties
to an Alpine summit. Warned to be content with the elevation attained, his cry is still *"Excelsior!"* and, even in falling
dead on the highest pinnacle, his cry is *still "Excelsior!"*
There is yet an immortal height to be surmounted—an ascent
in Eternity. The poet holds in view the idea of never-ending
progress. That he is misunderstood is rather the misfortune
of Mr. Langtree than the fault of Mr. Longfellow. There is
an old adage about the difficulty of one's furnishing an
auditor both with matter to be comprehended and brains for
its comprehension.

FLACCUS—THOMAS WARD

March 1843

THE POET now comprehended in the *cognomen* FLACCUS
is by no means our ancient friend Quintus Horatius, nor
even his ghost, but merely a Mr. —— Ward, of Gotham,
once a contributor to the New York *American* and to the
New York *Knickerbocker Magazine*. He is characterized by
Mr. Griswold, in his *Poets and Poetry of America*, as a
gentleman of elegant leisure.

What there is in "elegant leisure" so much at war with
the divine afflatus it is not very difficult, but quite un-

necessary, to say. The fact has been long apparent. Never sing the Nine so well as when penniless. The *mens divinior* is one thing, and the *otium cum dignitate* quite another.

Of course Mr. Ward is not, as a poet, altogether destitute of merit. If so, the public had been spared these paragraphs. But the sum of his deserts has been footed up by a clique who are in the habit of reckoning units as tens in all cases where champagne and "elegant leisure" are concerned. We do not consider him, at all points, a "Pop Emmons," but, with deference to the more matured opinions of the *Knickerbocker*, we may be permitted to entertain a doubt whether he is either Jupiter Tonans or Phœbus Apollo.

Justice is not, at all times, to all persons, the most desirable thing in the world; but then there is the old adage about the tumbling of the heavens, and simple justice is all that we propose in the case of Mr. Ward. We have no design to be bitter. We notice his book at all, only because it is an unusually large one of its kind, because it is here lying upon our table, and because, whether justly or unjustly, whether for good reason or for none, it has attracted some portion of the attention of the public.

The volume is entitled, somewhat affectedly, *Passaic, a Group of Poems touching that river: with Other Musings, by Flaccus,* and embodies, we believe, all the previously published effusions of its author. It commences with a very pretty *Sonnet to Passaic;* and from the second poem, *Introductory Musings on Rivers,* we are happy in being able to quote an entire page of even remarkable beauty:

> Beautiful Rivers! that adown the vale
> With graceful passage journey to the deep,
> Let me along your grassy marge recline
> At ease, and, musing, meditate the strange
> Bright history of your life: yes, from your birth
> Has beauty's shadow chased your every step;
> The blue sea was your mother, and the sun,
> Your glorious sire, clouds your voluptuous cradle,
> Roofed with o'erarching rainbows; and your fall
> To earth was cheered with shouts of happy birds,
> With brightened faces of reviving flowers,

And meadows, while the sympathizing west
Took holiday, and donned her richest robes.
From deep mysterious wanderings your springs
Break bubbling into beauty; where they lie
In infant helplessness awhile, but soon,
Gathering in tiny brooks, they gambol down
The steep sides of the mountain, laughing, shouting,
Teasing the wild flowers, and at every turn
Meeting new playmates still to swell their ranks;
Which, with the rich increase resistless grown,
Shed foam and thunder, that the echoing wood
Rings with the boisterous glee; while, o'er their heads,
Catching their spirit blithe, young rainbows sport,
The frolic children of the wanton sun.

Nor is your swelling prime, or green old age,
Though calm, unlovely; still, where'er ye move,
Your train is beauty; trees stand grouping by,
To mark your graceful progress; giddy flowers
And vain, as beauties wont, stoop o'er the verge
To greet their faces in your flattering glass;
The thirsty herd are following at your side;
And water-birds in clustering fleets convoy
Your sea-bound tides; and jaded man, released
From worldly thraldom, here his dwelling plants,
Here pauses in your pleasant neighborhood,
Sure of repose along your tranquil shores;
And, when your end approaches and ye blend
With the eternal ocean, ye shall fade
As placidly as when an infant dies,
And the Death-Angel shall your powers withdraw
Gently as twilight takes the parting day,
And, with a soft and gradual decline
That cheats the senses, lets it down to night.

There is nothing very original in all this; the general idea
is, perhaps, the most absolutely trite in poetical literature;
but the theme is not the less just on this account, while we
must confess that it is admirably handled. The picture embodied in the whole of the concluding paragraph is perfect.
The seven final lines convey not only a novel but a highly
appropriate and beautiful image.

What follows, of this poem, however, is by no means worthy so fine a beginning. Instead of confining himself to the true poetical thesis, the beauty or the sublimity of river scenery, he descends into mere meteorology—into the uses and general philosophy of rain, etc., matters which should be left to Mr. Espy, who knows something about them, as we are sorry to say Mr. Flaccus does not.

The second and chief *poem* in the volume is entitled *The Great Descender*. We emphasize the "poem" merely by way of suggesting that *The Great Descender* is anything else. We never could understand what pleasure men of talent can take in concocting elaborate doggerel of this order. Least of all can we comprehend why, having perpetrated the atrocity, they should place it at the door of the Muse. We are at a loss to know by what right, human or divine, twattle of this character is intruded into a collection of what professes to be *poetry*. We put it to Mr. Ward, in all earnestness, if *The Great Descender*, which is a history of Sam Patch, has a single attribute, beyond that of mere versification, in common with what even Sam Patch himself would have had the hardihood to denominate a poem.

Let us call this thing a rhymed *jeu d'esprit*, a burlesque, or what not?—and, even so called and judged by its new name, we must still regard it as a failure. Even in the loosest compositions we demand a certain degree of keeping. But in *The Great Descender* none is apparent. The tone is unsteady, fluctuating between the grave and the gay, and never being precisely either. Thus there is a failure in both. The intention being never rightly taken, we are, of course, never exactly in condition either to weep or to laugh.

We do not pretend to be the Oracle of Dodona, but it does really appear to us that Mr. Flaccus intended the whole matter, in the first instance, as a solemnly serious thing; and that, having composed it in a grave vein, he became apprehensive of its exciting derision, and so interwove sundry touches of the burlesque, behind whose equivocal aspect he might shelter himself at need. In no other supposition can we reconcile the spotty appearance of the whole with a belief in the sanity of the author. It is difficult, also, in any other

view of the case, to appreciate the air of positive gravity
with which he descants upon the advantages to Science
which have accrued from a man's making a frog of himself.
Mr. Ward is frequently pleased to denominate Mr. Patch "a
martyr of science," and appears very doggedly in earnest in
all passages such as the following:

> Through the glad Heavens, which tempests now conceal,
> Deep thunder-guns in quick succession peal,
> As if salutes were firing from the sky,
> To hail the triumph and the victory.
> Shout! trump of Fame, till thy brass lungs burst out!
> Shout! mortal tongues! deep-throated thunders, shout!
> For lo! electric *genius*, downward hurled,
> Has startled *Science*, and illumed the world!

That Mr. Patch was a genius we do not doubt; so is Mr.
Ward; but the science displayed in jumping down the Falls
is a point above us. There might have been some science in
jumping *up*.

The Worth of Beauty; or a Lover's Journal, is the title
of the poem next in place and importance. Of this composition Mr. Ward thus speaks in a Note: "The individual to
whom the present poem relates, and who had suffered
severely all the pains and penalties which arise from the
want of those personal charms so much admired by him in
others, gave the author many years since some fragments of
a journal kept in his early days, in which he had bared his
heart and set down all his thoughts and feelings. This prose
journal has here been transplanted into the richer soil of
verse."

The narrative of the friend of Mr. Flaccus must, originally, have been a very good thing. By "originally," we
mean before it had the misfortune to be "transplanted in the
richer soil of verse"—which has by no means agreed with its
constitution. But, even through the dense fog of our author's
rhythm, we can get an occasional glimpse of its merit. It
must have been the work of a heart on fire with passion, and
the utter abandon of the details reminds us even of Jean-

Jacques. But alas for this "richer soil"! *Can* we venture to present our readers with a specimen?

> Now roses blush, and violets' eyes
> And seas reflect the glance of skies;
> And now *that frolic pencil* streaks
> With quaintest tints the tulips' cheeks;
> Now jewels bloom in secret worth,
> Like blossoms of the inner earth;
> Now painted birds are pouring round
> The beauty and the wealth of sound;
> Now sea-shells glance with quivering ray,
> Too rare to seize, too fleet to stay,
> And hues outdazzling all the rest
> Are dashed profusely on the west,
> While rainbows seem to palettes changed,
> Whereon the motley tints are ranged.
> But soft the moon *that pencil* tipped,
> As though, in liquid radiance dipped,
> A likeness of the sun it drew,
> But flattered him with pearlier hue,
> Which haply spilling runs astray,
> And blots with light the Milky Way;
> While stars besprinkle all the air,
> Like spatterings of *that pencil* there.

All this by way of *exalting* the subject. The moon is made a painter, and the rainbow a palette. And the moon has a pencil (*that* pencil!) which she dips, by way of a brush, in the liquid radiance (the colors on a palette are *not* liquid) and then *draws* (not paints) a likeness of the sun; but, in the attempt, plasters him too "pearly," puts it on too thick; the consequence of which is that some of the paint is spilt, and "runs astray" and besmears the Milky Way, and "spatters" the rest of the sky with stars! We can only say that a very singular picture was spoilt in the making.

The versification of *The Worth of Beauty* proceeds much after this fashion; we select a fair example of the whole from page 43:

> Yes! pangs have cut my soul with grief
> So keen that gashes were relief,

> And racks have wrung my spirit-frame
> To which the strain of joints were tame,
> And battle strife itself were nought
> Beside the inner fight I've fought, etc., etc.

Nor do we regard any portion of it (so far as rhythm is concerned) as at all comparable to some of the better ditties of William Slater. Here, for example, from his Psalms, published in 1642:

> The righteous shall his sorrow scan
> And laugh at him, and say, "Behold!
> What hath become of this here man
> That on his riches was so bold?"

And here, again, are lines from the edition of the same Psalms, by Archbishop Parker, which we most decidedly prefer:

> Who sticketh to God in sable trust,
> As Sion's mount he stands full just,
> Which moveth no whit nor yet can reel,
> But standeth forever as stiff as steel.

The Martyr and *The Retreat of Seventy-six* are merely Revolutionary incidents "done into verse," and spoilt in the doing. *The Retreat* begins with the remarkable line,

> Tramp! tramp! tramp! tramp!

which is elsewhere introduced into the poem. We look in vain here for anything worth even qualified commendation.

The Diary is a record of events occurring to the author during a voyage from New York to Havre. Of these events a fit of seasickness is the chief. Mr. Ward, we believe, is the first of the *genus irritabile* who has ventured to treat so delicate a subject with that grave dignity which is its due:

> Rejoice! rejoice! already on my sight
> Bright shores, gray towers, and coming wonders reel;
> My brain grows giddy—is it with delight?
> A swimming faintness, such as one might feel
> When stabbed and dying, gathers on my sense—
> It weighs me down—and now—help!—horror!—

But the "horror," and indeed all that ensues, we must leave to the fancy of the poetical.

Some pieces entitled *Humorous* next succeed, and one or two of them (for example, *The Graham System* and *The Bachelor's Lament*) are not so *very* contemptible in their way, but the way itself is beneath even contempt.

To an Infant in Heaven embodies some striking thoughts, and, although feeble as a whole, and terminating lamely, may be cited as the best composition in the volume. We quote two or three of the opening stanzas:

> Thou bright and starlike spirit,
>   That in my visions wild
> I see 'mid heaven's seraphic host—
>   Oh! canst thou be my child?
>
> My grief is quenched in wonder,
>   And pride arrests my sighs;
> A branch from this unworthy stock
>   Now blossoms in the skies.
>
> Our hopes of thee were lofty,
>   But have we cause to grieve?
> Oh! could our fondest, proudest wish
>   A nobler fate conceive?
>
> The little weeper tearless!
>   The sinner snatched from sin!
> The babe to more than manhood grown,
>   Ere childhood did begin!
>
> And I, thy earthly teacher,
>   Would blush thy powers to see!
> Thou art to me a parent now,
>   And I a child to thee!

There are several other pieces in the book—but it is needless to speak of them in detail. Among them we note one or two poetical effusions, and one or two which are (satirically?) termed satirical. All are worthless.

Mr. Ward's imagery, at detached points, has occasional vigor and appropriateness; we may go so far as to say that, at times, it is strikingly beautiful—by accident, of course. Let us cite a few instances. At page 53 we read,

> Oh, happy day!—earth, sky is fair,
> And fragrance floats along the air;
> *For all the bloomy orchards glow*
> *As with a fall of rosy snow.*

At page 91,

> How flashed the overloaded flowers
> With gems, a present from the showers!

At page 92,

> No! there is danger; all the night
> I saw her like a starry light
> More lovely in my visions lone
> Than in my day-dreams' truth she shone.
> 'Tis naught when on the sun we gaze,
> If only dazzled by his rays;
> But, when our eyes his form retain,
> Some wound to vision must remain.

And again, at page 234, speaking of a slight shock of an earthquake, the earth is said to tremble

> As if some wing of passing angel, bound
> From sphere to sphere, had brushed the golden chain
> That hangs our planet to the throne of God.

This latter passage, however, is, perhaps, not altogether original with Mr. Ward. In a poem now lying before us, entitled *Al Aaraaf,* the composition of a gentleman of Philadelphia,[1] we find what follows:

> A dome by linkèd light from heaven let down
> Sat gently on these columns as a crown;
> A window of one circular diamond there
> Looked out above into the purple air,
> And rays from God shot down that meteor chain
> And hallowed all the beauty twice again,
> Save when, between the Empyrean and that ring,
> Some eager spirit flapped his dusky wing.

[1]Poe himself. E. W.

But if Mr. Ward's imagery is, indeed, at rare intervals good, it must be granted, on the other hand, that in general it is atrociously inappropriate or low. For example:

> Thou gaping chasm! whose wide devouring throat
> Swallows a river, *while the gulping note*
> *Of monstrous deglutition gurgles loud,* etc.
>
> (*Page 24.*)

> Bright Beauty! child of starry birth,
> The grace, the gem, the flower of earth,
> The *damask livery* of Heaven! (*Page 44.*)

Here the mind wavers between gems, and stars, and taffety—between footmen and flowers. Again, at page 46,

> All thornless flowers of wit, all chaste
> And delicate essays of taste,
> All playful fancies, wingèd wiles,
> That from their pinions scatter smiles,
> All prompt resource in stress or pain,
> *Leap ready-armed* from woman's brain.

The idea of "thornless flowers," etc., leaping "*ready-armed*" could have entered few brains except those of Mr. Ward.

Of the most ineffable *bad taste* we have instances without number. For example, page 183,

> And, straining, fastens on her lips a kiss
> That seemed to *suck the life-blood from her heart!*

And here, very gravely, at page 25,

> Again he's roused, *first cramming in his cheek*
> *The weed, though vile, that props the nerves when weak.*

Here again, at page 33,

> Full well he knew, where food does not refresh,
> The shriveled soul sinks inward with the flesh—
> That he's best armed for danger's rash career,
> *Who's crammed so full there is no room for fear.*

But we doubt if the whole world of literature, poetical or prosaic, can afford a picture more utterly *disgusting* than the following, which we quote from page 177:

> But most of all good eating cheers the brain,
>   Where other joys are rarely met—at sea—
> Unless, indeed, we lose as soon as gain—
>   Ay, there's the rub, so baffling oft to me.
> Boiled, roast, and baked—*what precious choice of dishes*
> *My generous throat has shared among the fishes!*
>
> 'Tis sweet to leave, in each forsaken spot,
>   Our footprints there, if only in the sand;
> 'Tis sweet to feel we are not all forgot,
>   That some will weep our flight from every land;
> And sweet the knowledge, when the seas I cross,
> *My briny messmates! ye will mourn my loss.*

This passage alone should damn the book—ay, damn a dozen such.

Of what may be termed the *niaiseries*—the sillinesses—of the volume, there is no end. Under this head we might quote two thirds of the work. For example:

> Now lightning, with convulsive spasm
> Splits heaven *in many a* fearful chasm.
>
> *It takes the high trees by the hair*
> And, as with *besoms,* sweeps the air.
>
> Now breaks the gloom and through the *chinks*
> The moon, in search of opening, *winks—*

all seriously urged, at different points of page 66. Again, on the very next page,

> Bees buzzed, and wrens that thronged the rushes
> Poured round incessant twittering gushes.

And here, at page 129,

> And now he leads her to the slippery brink
> Where ponderous tides headlong plunge down the horrid *chink.*

And here, page 109,

> And, like a ravenous vulture, *peck*
> The smoothness of that cheek and neck.

And here, page 111,

> While through the skin worms *wriggling* broke.

And here, page 170,

> And ride the *skittish* backs of untamed waves.

And here, page 214,

> Now clasps its mate in holy prayer,
> Or *twangs* a harp of gold.

Mr. Ward, also, is constantly talking about "thunder-guns," "thunder-trumpets," and "thunder-shrieks." He has a bad habit, too, of styling an eye "a weeper," as for example, at page 208,

> Oh, curl in smiles that mouth again
> And wipe that *weeper* dry.

Somewhere else he calls two tears "two sparklers"—very much in the style of Mr. Richard Swiveller, who was fond of denominating Madeira "the rosy." "In the nick," meaning in the height, or fullness, is likewise a pet expression of the author of *The Great Descender*. Speaking of American forests, at page 286, for instance, he says, "let the doubter walk through them in the nick of their glory." A phrase which may be considered as in the very nick of good taste.

We cannot pause to comment upon Mr. Ward's most extraordinary system of versification. *Is* it his own? He has quite an original way of conglomerating consonants, and seems to have been experimenting whether it were not possible to do altogether without vowels. Sometimes he strings together quite a chain of impossibilities. The line, for example, at page 51,

> Or, only such as seashells flash,

puts us much in mind of the schoolboy stumbling-block, beginning, "The cat ran up the ladder with a lump of raw liver in her mouth," and we defy Sam Patch himself to pronounce it twice in succession without tumbling into a blunder.

But we are fairly wearied with this absurd theme. *Who*

calls Mr. Ward a poet? He is a second-rate, or a third-rate, or perhaps a ninety-ninth-rate poetaster. He is a gentleman of "elegant leisure," and gentlemen of elegant leisure are, for the most part, neither men, women, nor Harriet Martineaus. Similar opinions, we believe, were expressed by somebody else—was it Mr. Benjamin?—not very long ago. But neither Mr. Ward nor the *Knickerbocker* would be convinced. The latter, by way of defense, went into a treatise upon Sam Patch, and Mr. Ward, "in the nick of his glory," wrote another poem against criticism in general, in which he called Mr. Benjamin "a wasp" and "an owl," and endeavored to prove him an ass. An owl is a wise bird—especially in spectacles—still, we do not look upon Mr. Benjamin as an owl. If all are owls who disbelieve in this book (which we now throw to the pigs), then the world at large cuts a pretty figure, indeed, and should be burnt up in April, as Mr. Miller desires—for it is only one immense aviary of owls.

WILLIAM ELLERY CHANNING

August 1843

IN SPEAKING of Mr. William Ellery Channing, who has just published a very neat little volume of poems, we feel the necessity of employing the indefinite rather than the definite article. He is *a*, and by no means *the*, William Ellery Channing. He is only *the son* of the great essayist deceased.[1] He is just such a person, in despite of his *clarum et venerabile nomen*, as Pindar would have designated by the significant term τις. It may be said in his favor that nobody ever heard of him. Like an honest woman, he has always succeeded in keeping himself from being made the subject of gossip. His book contains about sixty-three things,

[1] William Ellery Channing was not the son but the nephew of the famous Boston divine of the same name. E. W.

which he calls poems, and which he no doubt seriously supposes so to be. They are full of all kinds of mistakes, of which the most important is that of their having been printed at all. They are not precisely English—nor will we insult a great nation by calling them Kickapoo; perhaps they are Channingese. We may convey some general idea of them by two foreign terms not in common use—the Italian *pavoneggiarsi*, "to strut like a peacock," and the German word for "sky-rocketing," *schwärmerei*. They are more preposterous, in a word, than any poems except those of the author of Sam Patch; for we presume we are right (are we not?) in taking it for granted that the author of Sam Patch is the very worst of all the wretched poets that ever existed upon earth.

In spite, however, of the customary phrase about a man's "making a fool of himself," we doubt if anyone was ever a fool of his own free will and accord. A poet, therefore, should not always be taken too strictly to task. He should be treated with leniency, and, even when damned, should be damned with respect. Nobility of descent, too, should be allowed its privileges not more in social life than in letters. The son of a great author cannot be handled too tenderly by the critical Jack Ketch. Mr. Channing must be hung, that's true. He must be hung *in terrorem*—and for this there is no help under the sun; but then we shall do him all manner of justice, and observe every species of decorum, and be especially careful of his feelings, and hang him gingerly and gracefully, with a silken cord, as the Spaniards hang their grandees of the blue blood, their nobles of the *sangre azul*.

To be serious, then; as we always wish to be if possible. Mr. Channing (whom we suppose to be a *very* young man, since we are precluded from supposing him a *very* old one) appears to have been inoculated, at the same moment, with *virus* from Tennyson and from Carlyle. And here we do not wish to be misunderstood. For Tennyson, as for a man imbued with the richest and rarest poetic impulses, we have an admiration, a reverence unbounded. His *Morte D'Arthur*, his *Locksley Hall*, his *Sleeping Beauty*, his *Lady of Shalott*, his *Lotos Eaters*, his *Œnone*, and many other poems, are not surpassed, in all that gives to poetry its distinctive value, by the compositions of anyone living or dead. And his leading error, that error which renders him unpopular—a point, to be sure, of no particular importance—that very error, we say, is founded in truth, in a keen perception of the elements of poetic beauty. We allude to his quaintness, to what the world chooses to term his affectation. No true poet, no critic whose approbation is worth even a copy of the volume we now hold in our hand, will deny that he feels impressed, sometimes even to tears, by many of those very affectations which he is impelled by the prejudice of his education or by the cant of his reason to condemn. He should thus be led to examine the extent of the one and to be wary of the deductions of the other. In fact, the profound intuition of Lord Bacon has supplied, in one of his immortal apothegms, the whole philosophy of the point at issue. "There is no exquisite beauty," he truly says, "without some *strangeness* in its proportions." We maintain, then, that Tennyson errs, not in his occasional quaintness, but in its continual and obtrusive excess. And, in accusing Mr. Channing of having been inoculated with *virus* from Tennyson, we merely mean to say that he has adopted and exaggerated that noble poet's characteristic defect, having mistaken it for his principal merit.

Mr. Tennyson is quaint only; he is never, as some have supposed him, obscure, except, indeed, to the uneducated, whom he does not address. Mr. Carlyle, on the other hand, is obscure only; he is seldom, as some have imagined him, quaint. So far he is right; for although quaintness, employed by a man of judgment and genius, may be made auxiliary to a poem, whose true thesis is beauty, and beauty alone, it is grossly, and even ridiculously, out of place in a work of prose. But in his obscurity it is scarcely necessary to say that he is wrong. Either a man intends to be understood, or he does not. If he write a book which he intends not to be understood, we shall be very happy indeed not to understand it; but if he write a book which he means to be understood, and, in this book, be at all possible pains to prevent us from understanding it, we can only say that he is an ass—

and this, to be brief, is our private opinion of Mr. Carlyle, which we now take the liberty of making public.

It seems that having deduced, from Tennyson and Carlyle, an opinion of the sublimity of everything odd, and of the profundity of everything meaningless, Mr. Channing has conceived the idea of setting up for himself as a poet of unusual depth and very remarkable powers of mind. His airs and graces, in consequence, have a highly picturesque effect, and the Boston critics, who have a notion that poets are porpoises (for they are always talking about their running in "schools"), cannot make up their minds as to what particular school he must belong. *We* say the Bobby Button school, by all means. He clearly belongs to that. And should nobody ever have heard of the Bobby Button school, that is a point of no material importance. We will answer for it, as it is one of our own. Bobby Button is a gentleman with whom, for a long time, we have had the honor of an intimate acquaintance. His personal appearance is striking. He has quite a big head. His eyes protrude and have all the air of saucers. His chin retreats. His mouth is depressed at the corners. He wears a perpetual frown of contemplation. His words are slow, emphatic, few, and oracular. His "the's," "ands," and "buts" have more meaning than other men's polysyllables. His nods would have put Burleigh's to the blush. His whole aspect, indeed, conveys the idea of a gentleman modest to a fault, and painfully overburdened with intellect. We insist, however, upon calling Mr. Channing's school of poetry the Bobby Button school, rather because Mr. Channing's poetry is strongly suggestive of Bobby Button than because Mr. Button himself ever dallied, to any very great extent, with the Muses. With the exception, indeed, of a *very* fine *Sonnet to a Pig*—or rather the fragment of a sonnet, for he proceeded no farther than the words "*O* piggy wiggy," with the *O* italicized for emphasis —with the exception of this, we say, we are not aware of his having produced anything worthy of that stupendous genius which is certainly *in* him, and only wants, like the starling of Sterne, "to get out."

The best passage in the book before us is to be found at

page 121, and we quote it, as a matter of simple justice, in full:

> Dear friend, in this fair atmosphere again,
> Far from the noisy echoes of the main,
> Amid the world-old mountains, and the hills
> From whose strange grouping a fine power distills
> The soothing and the calm, I seek repose,
> The city's noise forgot and hard stern woes.
> As thou once saidst, the rarest sons of earth
> Have in the dust of cities shown their worth,
> Where long collision with the human curse
> Has of great glory been the frequent nurse,
> *And only those who in sad cities dwell*
> *Are of the green trees fully sensible.*
> *To them the silver bells of tinkling streams*
> *Seem brighter than an angel's laugh in dreams.*

The four lines italicized are highly meritorious, and the whole extract is so far decent and intelligible that we experienced a feeling of surprise upon meeting it amid the doggerel which surrounds it. Not less was our astonishment upon finding, at page 18, a fine thought so well embodied as the following:

> *Or see the early stars, a mild sweet train,*
> *Come out to bury the diurnal sun.*

But, in the way of commendation, we have now done. We have carefully explored the whole volume, in vain, for a single additional line worth even the most qualified applause.

The utter abandon—the charming *négligé*—the perfect looseness (to use a Western phrase) of his rhythm, is one of Mr. Channing's most noticeable, and certainly one of his most refreshing traits. It would be quite a pleasure to hear him read or scan, or to hear anybody else read or scan, such a line as this, at page 3, for example:

> Masculine almost though softly carved in grace,

where "masculine" has to be read as a trochee, and "almost" as an iambus; or this, at page 8:

> That compels me on through wood, and fell, and moor,

where "that compels" has to be pronounced as equivalent to the iambus "me on"; or this, at page 18:

> I leave thee, *the* maid spoke to *the* true youth,

where both the "the's" demand a strong accent to preserve the iambic rhythm; or this, at page 29:

> So in our steps strides truth and honest trust,

where (to say nothing of the grammar, which *may* be Dutch, but is not English) it is quite impossible to get through with the "steps strides truth" without dislocating the under jaw; or this, at page 32:

> The *serene* azure. *The* keen stars are now;

or this, on the same page:

> Some*time* of sorrow. Joy to *thy* Future;

or this, at page 56:

> *Harsh action, even in repose inwardly harsh;*

or this, at page 59:

> Provides am*plest* enjoyment. O my brother;

or this, at page 138:

> *Like the swift petrel, mimicking the wave's measure;*

about all of which the less we say the better.

At page 96 we read thus:

> Where the untrammeled soul on her wind-pinions,
> *Fearlessly sweeping, defies my earthly woes,*
> There, there upon that infinitest sea
> *Lady, thy hope, so fair a hope, summons me.*

At page 51 we have it thus:

> The river calmly flows
> Through shining banks, through lonely glen
> Where the owl shrieks, though ne'er the cheer of men
> Has stirred its mute repose;
> *Still if you should walk there you would go there again.*

At page 136 we read as follows:

> Tune thy clear voice to no funereal song,
> *For O Death stands to welcome thee sure.*

At page 116 he has this:

> These graves, you mean;
> Their histo*ry* who knows bet*ter* than I?
> For in the busy street strikes on my ear
> *Each sound, even inaudible voices*
> Lengthen the long tale my memory tells.

Just below, on the same page, he has,

> I see but little difference tru*ly,*

and at page 76 he fairly puts the climax to metrical absurdity in the lines which follow:

> The spirit builds his house in *the* least flowers—
> A beautiful mansion; how the colors live,
> In*tri*cately de*li*cate!

This is to be read, of course, intrikkittly delikkit, and "intrikkittly delikkit" it is—unless, indeed, we are very especially mistaken.

The affectations—the Tennysonisms of Mr. Channing—pervade his book at all points, and are not easily particu-larized. He employs, for example, the word "delight" for "delighted"; as at page 2:

> Delight to trace the mountain-brook's descent.

He uses, also, all the prepositions in a different sense from the rabble. If, for instance, he was called upon to say "on," he wouldn't say it by any means, but he'd say "off," and endeavor to make it answer the purpose. For "to," in the same manner, he says "from"; for "with," "of," and so on; at page 2, for example:

> Nor less in winter, mid the glittering banks
> Heaped *of* unspotted snow, the maiden roved.

For "serene," he says "*se*rene"; as at page 4:

> The influences of this *se*rene isle.

For "subdued," he says *"sub*dued"; as at page 16:

> So full of thought, so *sub*dued to bright fears.

By the way, what kind of fears *are* bright?
  For "eternal," he says "eterne"; as at page 30:

> Has risen, *and* an eterne sun now paints.

For "friendless," he substitutes "friend*less*"; as at page 31:

> Are drawn in other figures. Not friend*less*.

To "future," he prefers "fu*ture*"; as at page 32:

> Sometime of sorrow. Joy to thy fu*ture*.

To "azure," in the same way, he prefers "a*zure*"; as at page 46:

> Ye stand each separate in the a*zure*.

In place of "unheard," he writes *"un*heard"; as thus, at page 47:

> Or think, though *un*heard, that your sphere is dumb.

In place of "perchance," he writes *"per*chance"; as at page 71:

> When *per*chance sorrow with her icy smile.

Instead of "more infinite," he writes "infi*nit*er," with an accent on the "nit"; as thus, at page 100:

> Hope's child, I summon infi*nit*er powers.

And here we might as well ask Mr. Channing, in passing, what idea he attaches to infinity, and whether he really thinks that he is at liberty to subject the adjective "infinite" to degrees of comparison. Some of these days we shall hear, no doubt, of "eternal," "eternaler," and "eternalest."

Our author is quite enamored of the word "sumptuous," and talks about "sumptuous trees" and "sumptuous girls," with no other object, we think, than to employ the epithet at all hazards and upon all occasions. He seems unconscious that it means nothing more than expensive, or costly; and we are not quite sure that either trees or girls are, in America, either the one or the other.

For "loved" Mr. Channing prefers to say "was loving," and takes great pleasure in the law phrase "the same." Both peculiarities are exemplified at page 20, where he says:

> The maid was loving this enamored same.

He is fond, also, of inversions and contractions, and employs them in a very singular manner. At page 15 he has

> Now may I thee describe a Paradise.

At page 86 he says:

> Thou lazy river, flowing neither way
> Me figurest, and yet thy banks seem gay.

At page 143 he writes:

> Men change that Heaven above not more;

meaning that men change so much that Heaven above does not change more. At page 150 he says:

> But so much soul hast thou within thy form
> Than luscious summer days thou art the more;

by which he would imply that the lady has so much soul within her form that she is more luscious than luscious summer days.

Were we to quote specimens under the general head of "utter and irredeemable nonsense," we should quote nine tenths of the book. Such nonsense, we mean, as the following, from page 11:

> I hear thy solemn anthem fall,
> Of richest song upon my ear,
> That clothes thee in thy golden pall
> As this wide sun flows on the mere.

Now let us translate this: He hears (Mr. Channing) a solemn anthem, of richest song, fall upon his ear, and this anthem clothes the individual who sings it in that individual's golden pall, in the same manner that, or at the time when, the wide sun flows on the mere—which is all very delightful, no doubt.

At page 37 he informs us that,

> It is not living,
> To a soul believing,
> To change each noble joy,
> Which our strength employs,
> For a state half rotten
> And a life of toys,

and that it is

> Better to be forgotten
> Than lose equipoise.

And we dare say it is, if one could only understand what kind of equipoise is intended. It is better to be forgotten, for instance, than to lose one's equipoise on the top of a shot tower.

Occupying the whole of page 88, he has the six lines which follow, and we will present anyone (the author not excepted) with a copy of the volume, if anyone will tell us what they are all about:

> He came and waved a little silver wand,
> He dropped the veil that hid a statue fair,
> He drew a circle with that pearly hand,
> His grace confined that beauty in the air,
> Those limbs so gentle now at rest from flight,
> Those quiet eyes now musing on the night.

At page 102 he has the following:

> Dry leaves with yellow ferns, they are
> Fit wreath of Autumn, while a star
> Still, bright, and pure, our frosty air
> Shivers in twinkling points
> Of thin celestial hair
> And thus one side of Heaven anoints.

This we think we can explain. Let us see. Dry leaves, mixed with yellow ferns, are a wreath fit for autumn at the time when our frosty air shivers a still, bright, and pure star with twinkling points of thin celestial hair, and with this hair, or hair plaster, anoints one side of the sky. Yes—this is it—no doubt.

At page 123 we have these lines:

> My sweet girl is lying still
>   In her lovely atmosphere;
> The gentle hopes her blue veins fill
>   With pure silver warm and clear.
>
> Oh, see her hair, oh, mark her breast!
>   Would it not, oh, comfort thee,
> If thou couldst nightly go to rest
>   By that virgin chastity?

Yes; we think, upon the whole, it would. The eight lines are entitled a *Song*, and we should like very much to hear Mr. Channing sing it.

Pages 36, 37, 38, 39, 40, and 41 are filled with short *Thoughts* in what Mr. Channing supposes to be the manner of Jean Paul. One of them runs thus:

> How shall I live? In earnestness.
> What shall I do? Work earnestly.
> What shall I give? A willingness.
> What shall I gain? Tranquillity.
> But do you mean a quietness
> In which I act and no man bless?
> Flash out in action infinite and free,
> Action conjoined with deep tranquillity,
> Resting upon the soul's true utterance,
> And life shall flow as merry as a dance.

All our readers will be happy to hear, we are sure, that Mr. Channing is going "to flash out." Elsewhere, at page 97, he expresses very similar sentiments:

> My empire is myself and I defy
> The external; yes, I rule the whole or die!

It will be observed here that Mr. Channing's empire is himself (a small kingdom, however), that he intends to defy "the external," whatever that is—perhaps he means the infernal—and that, in short, he is going to rule the whole or die; all which is very proper, indeed, and nothing more than we have to expect from Mr. Channing.

Again, at page 146, he is rather fierce than otherwise. He says:

> We surely were not meant to ride the sea,
>   Skimming the wave in that so prisoned small,
> Reposing our infinite faculties utterly.
>   Boom like a roaring sunlit waterfall,
>   Humming to infinite abysms: speak loud, speak free!

Here Mr. Channing not only intends to "speak loud and free" himself, but advises everybody else to do likewise. For his own part, he says, he is going to *"boom"*—"to hum and to boom"—to "hum like a roaring waterfall" and "boom to an infinite abysm." What, in the name of Beelzebub, *is* to become of us all?

At page 39, while indulging in similar bursts of fervor and of indignation, he says:

> Thou meetest a common man
> With a delusive show of *can,*

and this passage we quote by way of instancing what we consider the only misprint in the book. Mr. Channing could never have meant to say:

> Thou meetest a common man
> With a delusive show of *can;*

for what *is* a delusive show of *can?* No doubt it should have been:

> Thou meetest a little pup
> With a delusive show of tin-cup.

A can, we believe, is a tin cup, and the cup must have been tied to the tail of the pup. Boys *will* do such tricks, and there is no earthly way of preventing them, we believe, short of cutting off their heads—or the tails of the pups.

And this remarkable little volume is, after all, by William Ellery Channing. A great name, it has been said, is, in many cases, a great misfortune. We hear daily complaints from the George Washington Dixons, the Socrates Smiths, and the Napoleon Buonaparte Joneses, about the inconsiderate ambition of their parents and sponsors. By inducing invidious comparison, these *prænomina* get their bearers (so they say) into every variety of scrape. If George Washington Dixon, for example, does not think proper, upon compulsion, to distinguish himself as a patriot, he is considered a very singular man; and Socrates Smith is never brought up before his honor the Mayor without receiving a double allowance of thirty days; while his honor the Mayor can assign no sounder reason for his severity than that better things than getting toddied are to be expected of Socrates. Napoleon Buonaparte Jones, on the other hand, to say nothing of being called Nota Bene Jones by all his acquaintance, is cowskinned, with perfect regularity, five times a month, merely because people *will* feel it a point of honor to cowskin a Napoleon Buonaparte.

And yet these gentlemen—the Smiths and the Joneses— are wrong *in toto,* as the Smiths and the Joneses invariably are. They are wrong, we say, in accusing their parents and sponsors. They err in attributing their misfortunes and persecutions to the *prænomina*—to the names assigned them at the baptismal font. Mr. Socrates Smith does not receive his double quantum of thirty days because he is called Socrates, but because he is called Socrates *Smith.* Mr. Napoleon Buonaparte Jones is not in the weekly receipt of a flogging on account of being Mr. Napoleon Buonaparte, but simply on account of being Mr. Napoleon Buonaparte *Jones.* Here, indeed, is a clear distinction. It is the surname which is to blame, after all. Mr. Smith must drop the Smith. Mr. Jones should discard the Jones. No one would ever think of taking Socrates—Socrates solely—to the watch house; and there is not a bully living who would venture to cowskin Napoleon Buonaparte *per se.* And the reason is plain. With nine individuals out of ten, as the world is at present happily constituted, Mr. Socrates (without the Smith) would be taken for the veritable philosopher of whom we have heard so much, and Mr. Napoleon Buonaparte (without the Jones) would be received implicitly as the hero of Austerlitz. And should Mr. Napoleon Buonaparte (without the Jones) give an opinion upon military strategy, it would be heard with the profoundest respect. And should Mr. Socrates (without the Smith) deliver a lecture or write a book, what critic so bold as not to pronounce it more luminous than the logic of Emerson, and more profound than the Orphicism of Alcott. In fact, both Mr. Smith and Mr. Jones, in the case we have imagined, would derive, through their own ingenuity, a very material advantage. But no such ingenuity has been needed in the case of Mr. William Ellery Channing, who has been befriended by Fate, or the foresight of his sponsors, and who has *no* Jones or Smith at the end of his name.

And here, too, a question occurs. There are many people in the world silly enough to be deceived by appearances. There are individuals so crude in intellect—so *green* (if we may be permitted to employ a word which answers our purpose much better than any other in the language), so green, we say, as to imagine, in the absence of any indication to the contrary, that a volume bearing upon its title page the name of William Ellery Channing must necessarily be the posthumous work of that truly illustrious author, the *sole* William Ellery Channing of whom anybody in the world ever heard. There are a vast number of uninformed young persons prowling about our bookshops, who will be raw enough to buy, and even to read half through this pretty little book (God preserve and forgive them!) mistaking it for the composition of another. But what then? Are not books made, as well as razors, to sell? The poet's name *is* William Ellery Channing—is it *not*? And if a man has not a right to the use of his own name, to the use of what has he a right? And could the poet have reconciled it to his conscience to have injured the sale of his own volume by any uncalled-for announcement upon the title page, or in a preface, to the effect that he is not his father, but only his father's very intelligent son? To put the case more clearly by reference to our old friends, Mr. Smith and Mr. Jones. Is either Mr. Smith, when mistaken for Socrates, or Mr. Jones, when accosted as Napoleon, bound, by any conceivable species of honor, to inform the whole world—

the one, that he is not Socrates, but only Socrates Smith; the other, that he is by no means Napoleon Buonaparte, but only Napoleon Buonaparte Jones?

SIMMS'S *THE WIGWAM AND THE CABIN*

January 1846

MR. SIMMS, we believe, made his first, or nearly his first, appearance before an American audience with a small volume entitled *Martin Faber,* an amplification of a much shorter fiction. He had some difficulty in getting it published, but the Harpers finally undertook it, and it did credit to their judgment. It was well received both by the public and the more discriminative few, although some of the critics objected that the story was an imitation of *Miserrimus,* a very powerful fiction by the author of *Pickwick Abroad.* The original tale, however—the germ of *Martin Faber*—was written long before the publication of *Miserrimus.* But independently of this fact, there is not the slightest ground for the charge of imitation. The thesis and incidents of the two works are totally dissimilar; the idea of resemblance arises only from the absolute identity of *effect* wrought by both.

Martin Faber was succeeded, at short intervals, by a great number and variety of fictions, some brief, but many of the ordinary novel size. Among these we may notice *Guy Rivers, The Partisan, The Yemassee, Mellichampe, Beauchampe,* and *Richard Hurdis.* The last two were issued anonymously, the author wishing to ascertain whether the success of his books (which was great) had anything to do with his mere name as the writer of previous works. The result proved that popularity, in Mr. Simms's case, arose solely from intrinsic merit, for *Beauchampe* and *Richard Hurdis* were the most popular of his fictions, and excited very general attention and curiosity. *Border Beagles* was another of his anonymous novels, published with the same end in view, and, although disfigured by some instances of bad taste, was even more successful than *Richard Hurdis*.

The "bad taste" of the *Border Beagles* was more particularly apparent in *The Partisan*, *The Yemassee*, and one or two other of the author's earlier works, and displayed itself most offensively in a certain fondness for the purely disgusting or repulsive, where the intention was or should have been merely the horrible. The writer evinced a strange propensity for minute details of human and brute suffering, and even indulged at times in more unequivocal obscenities. His English, too, was, in his efforts, exceedingly objectionable—verbose, involute, and not unfrequently ungrammatical. He was especially given to pet words, of which we remember at present only "hug," "coil," and the compound "old-time," and introduced them upon all occasions. Neither was he at this period particularly dexterous in the conduct of his stories. His improvement, however, was rapid at all these points, although, on the two first counts of our indictment, there is still abundant room for improvement. But whatever may have been his early defects, or whatever are his present errors, there can be no doubt that from the very beginning he gave evidence of genius, and that of no common order. His *Martin Faber*, in our opinion, is a more forcible story than its supposed prototype, *Miserrimus*. The difference in the American reception of the two is to be referred to the fact (we blush while recording it) that *Miserrimus* was understood to be the work of an Englishman, and *Martin Faber* was known to be the composition of an American as yet unaccredited in our Republic of Letters. The fiction of Mr. Simms gave indication, we repeat, of genius, and that of no common order. Had he been even a Yankee, this genius would have been rendered immediately manifest to his countrymen, but unhappily (*perhaps*) he was a Southerner, and united the Southern pride, the Southern dislike to the making of bargains, with the Southern supineness and general want of tact in all matters relating to the making of money. His book, therefore, depended entirely upon its own intrinsic value and resources, but with these it made its way in the end. The "intrinsic value" consisted first of a very vigorous imagination in the conception of the story; secondly, in artistic skill manifested in its conduct; thirdly, in general vigor, life, movement—the whole resulting in deep interest on the part of the reader. These high qualities Mr. Simms has carried with him in his subsequent books; and they are qualities which, above all others, the fresh and vigorous intellect of America should and does esteem. It may be said, upon the whole, that while there are several of our native writers who excel the author of *Martin Faber* at particular *points,* there is, nevertheless, not one who surpasses him in the aggregate of the higher excellences of fiction. We confidently expect him to do much for the lighter literature of his country.

The volume now before us has a title which may mislead the reader. *The Wigwam and the Cabin* is merely a generic phrase, intended to designate the subject matter of a series of short tales, most of which have first seen the light in the Annuals. "The material employed," says the author, "will be found to illustrate, in large degree, the border history of the South. I can speak with confidence of the general truthfulness of its treatment. The life of the planter, the squatter, the Indian, the negro, the bold and hardy pioneer, and the vigorous yeoman—these are the subjects. In their delineation I have mostly drawn from living portraits, and, in frequent instances, from actual scenes and circumstances within the memories of men."

All the tales in this collection have merit, and the first has merit of a very peculiar kind. *Grayling, or Murder Will Out,* is the title. The story was well received in England, but on this fact no opinion can be safely based. The *Athenæum,* we believe, or some other of the London weekly critical journals, having its attention called (no doubt through personal influence) to Carey and Hart's beautiful annual *The Gift,* found it convenient, in the course of its notice, to speak at length of some one particular article, and *Murder Will Out* probably arrested the attention of the sub-editor who was employed in so trivial a task as the patting on the head an American book—arrested his attention first from its title (murder being a taking theme with the cockney), and secondly, from its details of Southern forest scenery. Large quotations were made, as a matter of course, and very ample commendation bestowed—the whole criticism proving nothing, in our opinion, but that the critic had not read a single syllable of the story. The *critique*, however, had at least the good effect of calling American attention to the fact that an American might possibly do a decent thing (provided the possibility were first admitted by the British sub-editors), and the result was, first, that many persons read, and secondly, that all persons admired, the "excellent story in *The Gift* that had actually been called 'readable' by one of the English newspapers."

Now had *Murder Will Out* been a much worse story than was ever written by Professor Ingraham, still, under the circumstances, we patriotic and independent Americans would have declared it inimitable; but, by some species of odd accident, it happened to deserve all that the British "sub-sub" had condescended to say of it, on the strength of a guess as to what it was all about. It is really an admirable tale, nobly conceived, and skillfully carried into execution —the best ghost story ever written *by an American*—for we presume that this is the ultimate extent of commendation to which we, as an humble American, dare go.

The other stories of the volume do credit to the author's abilities, and display their peculiarities in a strong light, but there is no one of them so good as *Murder Will Out.*

WILLIAM CULLEN BRYANT

April 1846

MR. BRYANT's position in the poetical world is, perhaps, better settled than that of any American. There is less difference of opinion about his rank; but, as usual, the agreement is more decided in private literary circles than in what appears to be the public expression of sentiment as gleaned from the press. I may as well observe here, too, that this coincidence of opinion in private circles is in all cases very noticeable when compared with the discrepancy of the apparent public opinion. In private it is quite a rare thing to find any strongly marked disagreement—I mean, of course, about mere authorial merit. The author accustomed to seclusion, and mingling for the first time freely with the literary people about him, is invariably startled and delighted to find that the decisions of his own unbiased judgment—decisions to which he has refrained from giving voice on account of their broad contradiction to the decision of the press—are sustained and considered quite as matters of course by almost every person with whom he converses. The fact is, that, when brought face to face with each other, we are constrained to a certain amount of honesty by the sheer trouble it causes us to mold the countenance to a lie. We put on paper with a grave air what we could not for our lives assert personally to a friend without either blushing or laughing outright. That the opinion of the press is not an honest opinion—that necessarily it is impossible that it should be an honest opinion—is never denied by the members of the press themselves. Individual presses, of course, are now and then honest, but I speak of the combined effect. Indeed, it would be difficult for those conversant with the *modus operandi* of public journals to deny the general falsity of impression conveyed. Let, in America, a book be published by an unknown, careless, or uninfluential author; if he publishes it "on his own account," he will be confounded at finding that no notice of it is taken at all. If it has been intrusted to a publisher of caste, there will appear forthwith in each of the leading business papers a variously phrased critique to the extent of three or four lines, and to the effect that "we have received, from the fertile press of So and So, a volume entitled This and That, which appears to be well worthy perusal, and which is 'got up' in the customary neat style of the enterprising firm of So and So." On the other hand, let our author have acquired influence.

experience, or (what will stand him in good stead of either)
effrontery, on the issue of his book he will obtain from
his publisher a hundred copies (or more, as the case may
be) "for distribution among friends connected with the
press." Armed with these, he will call personally either at
the office or (if he understands his game) at the private
residence of every editor within his reach, enter into conversation, compliment the journalist, interest him, as if incidentally, in the subject of the book, and finally, watching
an opportunity, beg leave to hand him "a volume which,
quite opportunely, is on the very matter now under discussion." If the editor seems sufficiently interested, the rest is
left to fate; but if there is any lukewarmness (usually indicated by a polite regret on the editor's part that he really
has "no time to render the work that justice which its importance demands"), then our author is prepared to understand and to sympathize; has, luckily, a friend thoroughly
conversant with the topic, and who (perhaps) could be
persuaded to write some account of the volume, provided
that the editor would be kind enough just to glance over
the critique and amend it in accordance with his own particular views. Glad to fill half a column or so of his editorial
space, and still more glad to get rid of his visitor, the journalist assents. The author retires, consults the friend, in-
structs him touching the strong points of the volume and,
insinuating in some shape a *quid pro quo,* gets an elaborate
critique written (or, what is more usual and far more simple,
writes it himself), and his business in this individual quarter
is accomplished. Nothing more than sheer impudence is
requisite to accomplish it in all.

Now the effect of this system (for it has really grown to
be such) is obvious. In ninety-nine cases out of a hundred,
men of genius, too indolent and careless about worldly
concerns to bestir themselves after this fashion, have also
that pride of intellect which would prevent them, under
any circumstances, from even insinuating, by the presentation of a book to a member of the press, a desire to have
that book reviewed. They, consequently, and their works,
are utterly overwhelmed and extinguished in the flood of

the *apparent* public adulation upon which in gilded barges are borne triumphant the ingenious toady and the diligent quack.

In general, the books of the toadies and quacks, not being read at all, are safe from any contradiction of this self-bestowed praise; but now and then it happens that the excess of the laudation works out in part its own remedy. Men of leisure, hearing one of the toady works commended, look at it, read its preface and a few pages of its body, and throw it aside with disgust, wondering at the ill taste of the *editors* who extol it. But there is an iteration, and then a continuous reiteration of the panegyric, till these men of leisure begin to suspect themselves in the wrong, to fancy that there may really be something good lying *perdu* in the volume. In a fit of desperate curiosity they read it through critically, their indignation growing hotter at each succeeding page till it gets the better even of contempt. The result is, that reviews now appear in various quarters entirely at variance with the opinions so generally expressed, and which, but for these indignation reviews, would have passed universally current as the opinion of the public. It is in this manner that those gross seeming discrepancies arise which so often astonish us, but which vanish instantaneously in private society.

But although it may be said, in general, that Mr. Bryant's position is comparatively well settled, still for some time past there has been a growing tendency to underestimate him. The new licentious "schools" of poetry—I do not now speak of the transcendentalists, who are the merest nobodies, fatiguing even themselves, but the Tennysonian and Barrettian schools—having, in their rashness of spirit, much in accordance with the whole spirit of the age, thrown into the shade necessarily all that seems akin to the conservatism of half a century ago,—the conventionalities, even the most justifiable *decora* of composition, are regarded, *per se*, with a suspicious eye. When I say *per se*, I mean that, from finding them so long in connection with conservatism of thought, we have come at last to dislike them, not merely as the outward visible signs of that conservatism, but as things evil in themselves. It is very clear that those accuracies and elegancies of style, and of general manner, which in the time of Pope were considered as *prima facie* and indispensable indications of genius, are now conversely regarded. How few are willing to admit the possibility of reconciling genius with artistic skill! Yet this reconciliation is not only possible, but an absolute necessity. It is a mere prejudice which has hitherto prevented the union, by studiously insisting upon a natural repulsion which not only does not exist but which is at war with all the analogies of nature. The greatest poems will not be written until this prejudice is annihilated; and I mean to express a very exalted opinion of Mr. Bryant when I say that his works in time to come will do much towards the annihilation.

I have never disbelieved in the perfect consistency, and even congeniality, of the highest genius and the profoundest art; but in the case of the author of *The Ages,* I *have* fallen into the general error of undervaluing his poetic ability on account of the mere "elegancies and accuracies" to which allusion has already been made. I confess that, with an absolute abstraction from all personal feelings, and with the most sincere intention to do justice, I was at one period beguiled into this popular error; there can be no difficulty, therefore, on my part, in excusing the inadvertence in others.

It will never do to claim for Bryant a genius of the loftiest order, but there has been latterly, since the days of Mr. Longfellow and Mr. Lowell, a growing disposition to deny him genius in any respect. He is now commonly spoken of as "a man of high poetical talent, very 'correct,' with a warm appreciation of the beauty of nature and great descriptive powers, but rather too much of the old-school manner of Cowper, Goldsmith, and Young." This is the truth, but not the whole truth. Mr. Bryant has genius, and that of a marked character, but it has been overlooked by modern schools, because deficient in those externals which have become in a measure symbolical of those schools.

Dr. Griswold, in summing up his comments on Bryant, has the following significant objections: "His genius is not versatile; he has related no history; he has not sung of the passion of love; he has not described artificial life. Still the tenderness and feeling in *The Death of the Flowers, Rizpah, The Indian Girl's Lament,* and other pieces, show that he might have excelled in delineations of the gentler passions, had he made them his study."

Now, in describing *no* artificial life, in relating *no* history, in *not* singing the passion of love, the poet has merely shown himself the profound artist, has merely evinced a proper consciousness that such are not the legitimate themes of poetry. That they are not, I have repeatedly shown, or attempted to show; and to go over the demonstration now would be foreign to the gossiping and desultory nature of the present article. What Dr. Griswold means by "the gentler passions" is, I presume, not very clear to himself; but it is possible that he employs the phrase in consequence of the gentle, unpassionate emotion induced by the poems of which he quotes the titles. It is precisely this "unpassionate emotion" which is the limit of the true poetical art. Passion proper and poesy are discordant. Poetry, in elevating, tranquillizes *the soul.* With *the heart* it has nothing to do. For a fuller explanation of these views I refer the reader to an analysis of a poem by Mrs. Welby—an analysis contained in an article called *Marginalia,* and published about a year ago in the *Democratic Review.*

The editor of *The Poets and Poetry of America* thinks the literary precocity of Bryant remarkable. "There are few recorded more remarkable," he says. The first edition of *The Embargo* was in 1808, and the poet was born in 1794; he was more than thirteen, then, when the satire was printed, although it is reported to have been written a year earlier. I quote a few lines:

> Oh, might some patriot rise, the gloom dispel,
> Chase Error's mist and break the magic spell!
> But vain the wish; for, hark! the murmuring meed
> Of hoarse applause from yonder shed proceed.
> Enter and view the thronging concourse there,
> Intent with gaping mouth and stupid stare;
> While in the midst their supple leader stands,
> Harangues aloud. and flourishes his hands,

> To adulation tunes his servile throat,
> And sues successful for each blockhead's vote.

This is a fair specimen of the whole, both as regards its satirical and rhythmical power. A satire is, of course, no *poem*. I have known boys of an earlier age do better things, although the case is rare. All depends upon the course of education. Bryant's father "was familiar with the best English literature, and perceiving in his son indications of superior genius, attended carefully to his instruction, taught him the art of composition, and guided his literary taste." This being understood, the marvel of such verse as I have quoted ceases at once, even admitting it to be thoroughly the boy's own work; but it is difficult to make any such admission. The father *must* have suggested, revised, retouched.

The longest poem of Bryant is *The Ages*—thirty-five Spenserian stanzas. It is the one improper theme of its author. The design is, "from a survey of the past ages of the world, and of the successive advances of mankind in knowledge and virtue, to justify and confirm the hopes of the philanthropist for the future destinies of the human race." All this would have been more rationally, because more effectually, accomplished in prose. Dismissing it as a poem (which in its general tendency it is not), one might commend the force of its argumentation but for the radical error of deducing a hope of progression from the cycles of physical nature. The sixth stanza is a specimen of noble versification (within the narrow limits of the iambic pentameter):

> Look on this beautiful world, and read the truth
> In her fair page; see, every season brings
> New change to her of everlasting youth;
> Still the green soil with joyous living things
> Swarms; the wide air is full of joyous wings;
> And myriads still are happy in the sleep
> Of Ocean's azure gulfs, and where he flings
> The restless surge. Eternal Love doth keep
> In his complacent arms, the earth, the air, the deep.

The cadences here at "page," "swarms," and "surge," cannot be surpassed. There are comparatively few consonants. Liquids and the softer vowels abound, and the partial line after the pause at "surge," with the stately march of the succeeding Alexandrine, is one of the finest conceivable *finales*.

The poem, in general, has unity, completeness. Its tone, of calm, elevated and hopeful contemplation, is well sustained throughout. There is an occasional quaint grace of expression, as in,

> Nurse of full streams, and lifter-up of proud
> Sky-mingling mountains that o'erlook the cloud!

or of antithetical and rhythmical force combined, as in,

> The shock that hurled
> To dust, in many fragments dashed and strown,
> The throne whose roofs were in another world,
> And whose far-stretching shadow awed our own.

But we look in vain for anything more worthy commendation.

Thanatopsis is the poem by which its author is best known, but is by no means his best poem. It owes the extent of its celebrity to its nearly absolute freedom from defect, in the ordinary understanding of the term. I mean to say that its negative merit recommends it to the public attention. It is a thoughtful, well-phrased, well-constructed, well-versified poem. The concluding thought is exceedingly noble, and has done wonders for the success of the whole composition.

The Waterfowl is very beautiful, but like *Thanatopsis* owes a great deal to its completeness and pointed termination.

Oh, Fairest of the Rural Maids! will strike every poet as the truest poem written by Bryant. It is richly ideal.

June is sweet, and perfectly well modulated in its rhythm, and inexpressibly pathetic. It serves well to illustrate my previous remarks about passion in its connection with poetry. In *June* there is, very properly, nothing of the intense *passion* of grief; but the subdued sorrow which comes up, as if perforce, to the surface of the poet's gay sayings about his

grave, we find thrilling us to the soul, while there is yet a
spiritual *elevation* in the thrill:

> And what if cheerful shouts at noon
>   Come, from the village sent,
> Or songs of maids, beneath the moon
>   With fairy laughter blent?
> And what if, in the evening light,
> Betrothed lovers walk in sight
>   Of my low monument?
> I would the lovely scene around
> Might know no sadder sight nor sound.
>
> I know that I no more should see
>   The season's glorious show,
> Nor would its brightness shine for me,
>   Nor its wild music flow;
> But if, around my place of sleep,
> The friends I love should come to weep,
>   They might not haste to go;
> Soft airs, and song, and light, and bloom,
> Should keep them lingering by my tomb.

The thoughts here belong to the highest class of poetry,
the imaginative-natural, and are of themselves sufficient to
stamp their author a man of genius.

I copy at random a few passages of similar cast, inducing
a similar conviction:

> The great heavens
> *Seem to stoop down upon the scene in love,—*
> A nearer vault, and of a tenderer blue,
> Than that which bends above our eastern hills.

> Till twilight blushed, and lovers walked, and wooed
> In a forgotten language, and *old tunes*
> *From instruments of unremembered form*
> *Gave the soft winds a voice.*

> Breezes of the South!
> *Who toss the golden and the flame-like flowers,*
> *And pass the prairie hawk that, poised on high,*
> *Flaps his broad wings, yet moves not.*

On the breast of Earth
I lie, and listen to her mighty voice:
A voice of many tones—sent up from streams
That wander through the gloom, from woods unseen
Swayed by the sweeping of the tides of air;
From rocky chasms where darkness dwells all day,
And hollows of the great invisible hills,
And sands that edge the ocean, stretching far
Into the night—a melancholy sound!

All the green herbs
Are stirring in his breath; *a thousand flowers*
By the roadside and the borders of the brook,
Nod gayly to each other.

There is a fine "echo of sound to sense" in "the borders
of the brook," etc.; and in the same poem from which these
lines are taken, *The Summer Wind*, may be found two
other equally happy examples:

For me, I lie
Languidly in the shade, where the thick turf,
Yet virgin from the kisses of the sun,
Retains some freshness.

And again:

All is silent, save the faint
And interrupted murmur of the bee
Settling on the sick flowers, and then again
Instantly on the wing.

I resume the imaginative extracts:

Paths, homes, graves, ruins from the lowest glen
To where life shrinks from the fierce Alpine air.

And the blue gentian flower that in the breeze
Nods lonely, of her beauteous race the last.

A shoot of that old vine that made
The nations silent in the shade.

But 'neath yon crimson tree,
Lover to listening maid might breathe his flame,
Nor mark, within its roseate canopy,
Her flush of maiden shame.

The mountains that infold,
In their wild sweep, the colored landscape round,
Seem *groups of giant kings in purple and gold*
That guard the enchanted ground.

This latter passage is especially beautiful. Happily to endow inanimate nature with sentience and a capability of action is one of the severest tests of the poet.

There is a Power whose care
Teaches thy way along *that pathless coast—*
The desert and illimitable air—
Lone wandering, but not lost.

Pleasant shall be thy way *where meekly bows*
The shutting flower, and darkling waters pass,
And where the o'ershadowing branches sweep the grass.

Sweet odors in the sea air, sweet and strange,
Shall tell the homesick mariner of the shore,
And, listening to thy murmur, he shall deem
He hears the rustling leaf and running stream.

In a *Sonnet, To* ——, are some richly imaginative lines. I quote the whole:

Ay, thou art for the grave; thy glances shine
Too brightly to shine long; another Spring
Shall deck her for men's eyes, but not for thine,
Sealed in a sleep which knows no wakening.
The fields for thee have no medicinal leaf,
And the vexed ore no mineral of power;
And they who love thee wait in anxious grief
Till the slow plague shall bring the fatal hour.
Glide softly to thy rest, then: death should come
Gently to one of gentle mold like thee,
As light winds wandering through groves of bloom,
Detach the delicate blossom from the tree.
Close thy sweet eyes, calmly, and without pain,
And we will trust in God to see thee yet again.

The happiest *finale* to these brief extracts will be the magnificent conclusion of *Thanatopsis.*

So live, that, when thy summons comes to join
The innumerable caravan, which moves

> *To that mysterious realm where each shall take*
> *His chamber in the silent halls of death,*
> Thou go not, like the quarry slave at night
> Scourged to his dungeon, but, sustained and soothed
> By an unfaltering trust, approach thy grave,
> *Like one who wraps the drapery of his couch*
> *About him and lies down to pleasant dreams.*

In the minor morals of the Muse, Mr. Bryant excels. In versification (as far as he goes) he is unsurpassed in America—unless, indeed, by Mr. Sprague. Mr. Longfellow is not so thorough a versifier, within Mr. Bryant's limits, but a far better one upon the whole, on account of his greater range. Mr. Bryant, however, is by no means always accurate —or defensible, for accurate is not the term. His lines are occasionally unpronounceable through excess of harsh consonants, as in

As if they loved to breast the breeze that sweeps the cool clear sky.

Now and then he gets out of his depth in attempting anapæstic rhythm, of which he makes sad havoc, as in

> And Rizpah, once the loveliest of all
> That bloomed and smiled in the court of Saul.

Not unfrequently, too, even his pentameters are inexcusably rough, as in

> Kind influence. Lo! their orbs burn more bright,

which can only be read metrically by drawing out "influence" into three marked syllables, shortening the long monosyllable "Lo!" and lengthening the short one "their."

Mr. Bryant is not devoid of mannerisms, one of the most noticeable of which is his use of the epithet "old" preceded by some other adjective, *e. g.*:

> In all that proud old world beyond the deep;

> There is a tale about these gray old rocks;

> The wide old woods resounded with her song;

> And from the gray old trunks that high in heaven,

etc., etc., etc. These duplicates occur so frequently as to
excite a smile upon each repetition.

Of merely grammatical errors the poet is rarely guilty.
Faulty constructions are more frequently chargeable to him.
In *The Massacre of Scio* we read:

> Till the last link of slavery's chain
> Is shattered, to be worn no more.

What shall be worn no more? The chain, of course—but
the link is implied. It will be understood that I pick these
flaws only with difficulty from the poems of Bryant. He is,
in the "minor morals," the most generally correct of our
poets.

He is now fifty-two years of age. In height, he is, perhaps,
five feet nine. His frame is rather robust. His features are
large but thin. His countenance is sallow, nearly bloodless.
His eyes are piercing gray, deep set, with large projecting
eyebrows. His mouth is wide and massive, the expression
of the smile hard, cold—even sardonic. The forehead is
broad, with prominent organs of ideality; a good deal bald;
the hair thin and grayish, as are also the whiskers, which
he wears in a simple style. His bearing is quite distinguished,
full of the aristocracy of intellect. In general, he looks in
better health than before his last visit to England. He seems
active—physically and morally energetic. His dress is plain
to the extreme of simplicity, although of late there is a
certain degree of Anglicism about it.

In character no man stands more loftily than Bryant. The
peculiarly melancholy expression of his countenance has
caused him to be accused of harshness, or coldness of heart.
Never was there a greater mistake. His soul is charity itself,
in all respects generous and noble. His manners are undoubtedly reserved.

Of late days he has nearly, if not altogether, abandoned
literary pursuits, although still editing with unabated vigor
the New York *Evening Post*. He is married (Mrs. Bryant
still living), has two daughters (one of them Mrs. Parke
Godwin), and is residing for the present at Vice-Chancellor
McCown's, near the junction of Warren and Church streets.

SARAH MARGARET FULLER

August 1846

MISS FULLER was at one time editor, or one of the editors of the *Dial,* to which she contributed many of the most forcible and certainly some of the most peculiar papers. She is known, too, by *Summer on the Lakes,* a remarkable assemblage of sketches, issued in 1844, by Little and Brown, of Boston. More lately she has published *Woman in the Nineteenth Century,* a work which has occasioned much discussion, having had the good fortune to be warmly abused and chivalrously defended. At present, she is assistant editor of the New York *Tribune,* or rather a salaried contributor to that journal, for which she has furnished a great variety of matter, chiefly notices of new books, etc., etc., her articles being designated by an asterisk. Two of the best of them were a review of Professor Longfellow's late magnificent edition of his own works (with a portrait), and an appeal to the public in behalf of her friend Harro Harring. The review did her infinite credit; it was frank, candid, independent—in even ludicrous contrast to the usual mere glorifications of the day, giving honor only where honor was due, yet evincing the most thorough capacity to appreciate and the most sincere intention to place in the fairest light the real and idiosyncratic merits of the poet.

In my opinion it is one of the very few reviews of Longfellow's poems, ever published in America, of which the critics have not had abundant reason to be ashamed. Mr. Longfellow is entitled to a certain, and very distinguished, rank among the poets of his country; but that country is disgraced by the evident toadyism which would award to his social position and influence, to his fine paper and large type, to his morocco binding and gilt edges, to his flattering portrait of himself, and to the illustrations of his poems by

Huntingdon, that amount of indiscriminate approbation which neither could nor would have been given to the poems themselves.

The defense of Harro Harring, or rather the philippic against those who were doing him wrong, was one of the most eloquent and well-*put* articles I have ever yet seen in a newspaper.

Woman in the Nineteenth Century is a book which few women in the country could have written, and no woman in the country would have published, with the exception of Miss Fuller. In the way of independence, of unmitigated radicalism, it is one of the "Curiosities of American Literature," and Doctor Griswold should include it in his book. I need scarcely say that the essay is nervous, forcible, thoughtful, suggestive, brilliant, and to a certain extent scholarlike—for all that Miss Fuller produces is entitled to these epithets—but I must say that the conclusions reached are only in part my own. Not that they are too bold, by any means—too novel, too startling, or too dangerous in their consequences, but that in their attainment too many premises have been distorted, and too many analogical inferences left altogether out of sight. I mean to say that the intention of the Deity as regards sexual differences—an intention which can be distinctly comprehended only by throwing the exterior (more sensitive) portions of the mental retina *casually* over the wide field of universal analogy—I mean to say that this intention has not been sufficiently considered. Miss Fuller has erred, too, through her own excessive subjectiveness. She judges woman by the heart and intellect of Miss Fuller, but there are not more than one or two dozen Miss Fullers on the whole face of the earth. Holding these opinions in regard to *Woman in the Nineteenth Century,* I still feel myself called upon to disavow the silly, condemnatory criticism of the work which appeared in one of the earlier numbers of the *Broadway Journal.* That article was *not* written by myself, and *was* written by my associate, Mr. Briggs.

The most favorable estimate of Miss Fuller's genius (for high genius she unquestionably possesses) is to be obtained, perhaps, from her contributions to the *Dial*, and from her *Summer on the Lakes*. Many of the descriptions in this volume are unrivaled for graphicality (why is there not such a word?)—for the force with which they convey the true by the novel or unexpected, by the introduction of touches which other artists would be sure to omit as irrelevant to the subject. This faculty, too, springs from her subjectiveness, which leads her to paint a scene less by its features than by its effects.

Here, for example, is a portion of her account of Niagara:

Daily these proportions widened and towered more and more upon my sight, and I got at last a proper foreground for these sublime distances. Before coming away, I think I really saw the full wonder of the scene. After awhile it *so drew me into itself as to inspire an undefined dread, such as I never knew before, such as may be felt when death is about to usher us into a new existence.* The perpetual trampling of the waters seized my senses. *I felt that no other sound, however near, could be heard, and would start and look behind me for a foe.* I realized the identity of that mood of nature in which these waters were poured down with such absorbing force with that in which the Indian was shaped on the same soil. For continually upon my mind came, unsought and unwelcome, *images, such as had never haunted it before, of naked savages stealing behind me with uplifted tomahawks.* Again and again this illusion recurred, and even *after I had thought it over and tried to shake it off, I could not help starting and looking behind me.* What I liked best was to sit on Table Rock close to the great fall; *there all power of observing details, all separate consciousness was quite lost.*

The truthfulness of the passages italicized will be felt by all; the feelings described are, perhaps, experienced by every (imaginative) person who visits the fall; but most persons, through predominant subjectiveness, would scarcely be conscious of the feelings, or, at best, would never think of employing them in an attempt to convey to others an impression of the scene. Hence so many desperate failures to convey it on the part of ordinary tourists. Mr. William W. Lord, to be sure, in his poem *Niagara,* is sufficiently objective; he describes not the fall, but very properly the effect of the fall upon *him*. He says that it made him think of his *own* greatness, of his *own* superiority, and so forth, and so forth; and it is only when we come to think that the thought of Mr. Lord's greatness is quite idiosyncratic, confined exclusively to Mr. Lord, that we are in condition to understand how, in despite of his objectiveness, he has failed to convey an idea of anything beyond one Mr. William W. Lord.

From the essay entitled *Philip Van Artevelde,* I copy a paragraph which will serve at once to exemplify Miss Fuller's more earnest (declamatory) style, and to show the tenor of her prospective speculations:

At Chicago I read again *Philip Van Artevelde,* and certain passages in it will always be in my mind associated with the deep sound of the lake, as heard in the night. I used to read a short time at night, and then open the blind to look out. The moon would be full upon the lake, and the calm breath, pure light, and the deep voice, harmonized well with the thought of the Flemish hero. When will this country have such a man? It is what she needs—no thin Idealist, no coarse Realist, but a man whose eye reads the heavens while his feet step firmly on the ground, and his hands are strong and dexterous in the use of human instruments. A man, religious, virtuous, and— sagacious; a man of universal sympathies, but self-possessed; a man who knows the region of emotion, though he is not its slave; a man to whom this world is no mere spectacle or fleeting shadow, but a great, solemn game, to be played with good heed, for its stakes are of eternal value, yet who, if his own play be true, heeds not what he loses by the falsehood of others. A man who lives from the past, yet knows that its honey can but moderately avail him; whose comprehensive eye scans the present, neither infatuated by its golden lures nor chilled by its many ventures; who possesses prescience, as the wise man must, but not so far as to be driven mad today by the gift which discerns tomorrow. When there is such a man for America, the thought which urges her on will be expressed.

From what I have quoted, a general conception of the prose style of the authoress may be gathered. Her manner, however, is infinitely varied. It is always forcible—but I am not sure that it is always anything else, unless I say picturesque. It rather indicates than evinces scholarship. Perhaps only the scholastic, or, more properly, those accustomed to look narrowly at the structure of phrases, would be willing to acquit her of ignorance of grammar—would be willing to attribute her slovenliness to disregard of the shell in anxiety for the kernel, or to waywardness, or to affectation, or to blind reverence for Carlyle—would be able to detect, in her strange and continual inaccuracies, a capacity for the accurate:

I cannot sympathize with such an apprehension; the spectacle is *capable to* swallow *up* all such objects.

It is fearful, too, to know, as you look, that whatever has been swallowed by the cataract, is *like* to rise suddenly to light.

I took our *mutual* friends to see her.

It was always obvious that they had nothing in common *between them.*

The Indian cannot be looked at truly *except* by a poetic eye.

McKenney's *Tour to the Lakes* gives some facts not to be met *with* elsewhere.

There is that mixture of culture and rudeness in the aspect of things *as* gives a feeling of freedom, etc., etc., etc.

These are merely a few, a very few instances, taken at random from among a multitude of willful murders committed by Miss Fuller on the American of President Polk. She uses, too, the word "ignore," a vulgarity adopted only of late days (and to no good purpose, since there is no necessity for it) from the barbarisms of the law, and makes no scruple of giving the Yankee interpretation to the verbs "witness" and "realize," to say nothing of "use," as in the sentence, "I used to read a short time at night." It will not do to say, in defense of such words, that in such senses they may be found in certain dictionaries—in that of Bolles, for instance;—*some* kind of "authority" may be found for *any* kind of vulgarity under the sun.

In spite of these things, however, and of her frequent unjustifiable Carlyleisms (such as that of writing sentences which are no sentences, since, to be parsed, reference must be had to sentences preceding), the style of Miss Fuller is one of the very best with which I am acquainted. In general effect, I know no style which surpasses it. It is singularly piquant, vivid, terse, bold, luminous; leaving details out of sight, it is everything that a style need be.

I believe that Miss Fuller has written much poetry, although she has published little. That little is tainted with the affectation of the transcendentalists (I use this term, of course, in the sense which the public of late days seem resolved to give it), but is brimful of the poetic sentiment. Here, for example, is something in Coleridge's manner, of which the author of *Genevieve* might have had no reason to be ashamed:

> A maiden sat beneath a tree;
> Tear-bedewed her pale cheeks be,
> And she sighed heavily.
>
> From forth the wood into the *light*
> A hunter strides with carol *light*,
> And a glance so bold and bright.
>
> He careless stopped and eyed the maid:
> "Why weepest thou?" he gently said;
> "I love thee well, be not afraid."
>
> He takes her hand and leads her on—
> She should have waited there alone,
> For he was not her chosen one.
>
> He *leans* her head upon his breast—
> She knew 'twas not her home of rest,
> But, ah, she had been sore distrest.
>
> The sacred stars looked sadly down;
> The parting moon appeared to frown,
> To see thus dimmed the diamond crown.
>
> Then from the thicket starts a deer—
> The huntsman, seizing *on* his spear,
> Cries, "Maiden, wait thou for me here."
>
> She sees him vanish into night—
> She starts from sleep in deep affright,
> For it was not her own true knight.

Though but in dream Gunhilda failed,
Though but a fancied ill assailed,
Though she but fancied fault bewailed,—

Yet thought of day makes dream of night;
She is not worthy of the knight;
The inmost altar burns not bright.

If loneliness thou canst not bear—
Cannot the dragon's venom dare—
Of the pure meed thou shouldst despair.

Now sadder that lone maiden sighs;
Far bitterer tears profane her eyes;
Crushed in the dust her heart's flower lies.

To show the evident carelessness with which this poem was constructed, I have italicized an identical rhyme (of about the same force in versification as an identical proposition in logic) and two grammatical improprieties. *To lean* is a neuter verb, and "seizing *on*" is not properly to be called a pleonasm, merely because it is—nothing at all. The concluding line is difficult of pronunciation through excess of consonants. I should have preferred, indeed, the antipenultimate tristich as the *finale* of the poem.

The supposition that the book of an author is a thing apart from the author's self is, I think, ill-founded. The soul is a cipher, in the sense of a cryptograph; and the shorter a cryptograph is, the more difficulty there is in its comprehension—at a certain point of brevity it would bid defiance to an army of Champollions. And thus he who has written very little, may in that little either conceal his spirit or convey quite an erroneous idea of it—of his acquirements, talents, temper, manner, tenor, and depth (or shallowness) of thought—in a word, of his character, of himself. But this is impossible with him who has written much. Of such a person we get, from his books, not merely a just, but the most just representation. Bulwer, the individual, personal man, in a green velvet waistcoat and amber gloves, is not by any means the veritable Sir Edward Lytton, who is discoverable only in *Ernest Maltravers*, where his soul is de-

liberately and nakedly set forth. And who would ever know
Dickens by looking at him or talking with him, or doing
anything with him except reading his *Old Curiosity Shop?*
What poet, in especial, but must feel at least the better
portion of himself more fairly represented in even his commonest sonnet (earnestly written) than in his most elaborate
or most intimate personalities?

I put all this as a general proposition, to which Miss
Fuller affords a marked exception—to this extent, that her
personal character and her printed book are merely one and
the same thing. We get access to her soul *as* directly from the
one as from the other—no *more* readily from this than from
that—easily from either. Her acts are bookish, and her books
are less thoughts than acts. Her literary and her conversational manner are identical. Here is a passage from her
Summer on the Lakes:

> The rapids enchanted me far beyond what I expected; they
> are so swift that they cease to *seem* so—you can think only of
> their *beauty.* The fountain beyond the Moss islands I discov-
> ered for myself, and thought it for some time an *accidental*
> beauty which it would not do to *leave,* lest I might never see it
> again. After I found it *permanent,* I returned many times to
> watch the play of its crest. In the little waterfall beyond, Nature
> seems, as she often does, to have made a *study* for some larger
> design. She delights in this—a sketch within a sketch—a dream
> within *a dream.* Wherever we see it, the lines of the great but-
> tress in the fragment of stone, the hues of the waterfall, copied
> in the flowers that *star* its bordering mosses, we are *delighted;*
> for all the lineaments become *fluent,* and we mold the scene
> in congenial thought with its *genius.*

Now all this is precisely as Miss Fuller would speak it.
She is perpetually saying just such things in just such
words. To get the conversational woman in the mind's eye,
all that is needed is to imagine her reciting the paragraph
just quoted; but first let us have the personal woman. She
is of the medium height; nothing remarkable about the
figure; a profusion of lustrous light hair; eyes a bluish gray,
full of fire; capacious forehead; the mouth when in repose
indicates profound sensibility, capacity for affection, for

love—when moved by a slight smile, it becomes even beautiful in the intensity of this expression; but the upper lip, as
if impelled by the action of involuntary muscles, habitually
uplifts itself, conveying the impression of a sneer. Imagine,
now, a person of this description looking you at one moment earnestly in the face, at the next seeming to look only
within her own spirit or at the wall; moving nervously every
now and then in her chair; speaking in a high key, but
musically, deliberately (not hurriedly or loudly), with a
delicious distinctness of enunciation—speaking, I say, the
paragraph in question, and emphasizing the words which I
have italicized, not by impulsion of the breath (as is usual)
but by drawing them out as long as possible, nearly closing
her eyes the while—imagine all this, and we have both the
woman and the authoress before us.

HAWTHORNE'S *TALES*

November 1847

THE REPUTATION of the author of *Twice-Told Tales* has
been confined, until very lately, to literary society; and I
have not been wrong, perhaps, in citing him as *the* example,
par excellence, in this country, of the privately-admired and
publicly-unappreciated man of genius. Within the last year
or two, it is true, an occasional critic has been urged, by
honest indignation, into very warm approval. Mr. Webber,
for instance (than whom no one has a keener relish for
that kind of writing which Mr. Hawthorne has best illustrated), gave us, in a late number of the *American Review,* a cordial and certainly a full tribute to his talents;
and since the issue of the *Mosses from an Old Manse* criticisms of similar tone have been by no means infrequent
in our more authoritative journals. I can call to mind few
reviews of Hawthorne published *before* the *Mosses.* One I

remember in *Arcturus* (edited by Mathews and Duyckinck)
for May 1841; another in the *American Monthly* (edited by
Hoffman and Herbert) for March 1838; a third in the
ninety-sixth number of the *North American Review*. These
criticisms, however, seemed to have little effect on the popular taste; at least, if we are to form any idea of the popular
taste by reference to its expression in the newspapers, or by
the sale of the author's book. It was never the fashion (until
lately) to speak of him in any summary of our best authors.

The daily critics would say, on such occasions, "Is there
not Irving, and Cooper, and Bryant, and Paulding, and—
Smith?" or, "Have we not Halleck, and Dana, and Longfellow, and—Thompson?" or, "Can we not point triumphantly to our own Sprague, Willis, Channing, Bancroft,
Prescott, and—Jenkins?" but these unanswerable queries
were never wound up by the name of Hawthorne.

Beyond doubt, this inappreciation of him on the part of
the public arose chiefly from the two causes to which I
have referred—from the facts that he is neither a man of
wealth nor a quack; but these are insufficient to account for
the whole effect. No small portion of it is attributable to
the very marked idiosyncrasy of Mr. Hawthorne himself.
In one sense, and in great measure, to be peculiar is to be
original, and than the true originality there is no higher
literary virtue. This true or commendable originality, however, implies not the uniform, but the continuous peculiarity
—a peculiarity springing from ever-active vigor of fancy—
better still if from ever-present force of imagination, giving
its own hue, its own character, to everything it touches, and,
especially, *self-impelled to touch everything*.

It is often said, inconsiderately, that very original writers
always fail in popularity, that such and such persons are too
original to be comprehended by the mass. "Too peculiar,"
should be the phrase, "too idiosyncratic." It is, in fact, the
excitable, undisciplined, and childlike popular mind which
most keenly feels the original.

The criticism of the conservatives, of the hackneys, of
the cultivated old clergymen of the *North American Review*,
is precisely the criticism which condemns, and alone con-

demns it. "It becometh not a divine," saith Lord Coke, "to
be of a fiery and salamandrine spirit." Their conscience allowing them to move nothing themselves, these dignitaries
have a holy horror of being moved. "Give us *quietude*," they
say. Opening their mouths with proper caution, they sigh
forth the word "*Repose*." And this is, indeed, the one thing
they should be permitted to enjoy, if only upon the Christian principle of give and take.

The fact is, that if Mr. Hawthorne were really original,
he could not fail of making himself felt by the public. But
the fact is, he is not original in any sense. Those who speak
of him as original mean nothing more than that he differs
in his manner or tone, and in his choice of subjects, from
any author of their acquaintance—their acquaintance not
extending to the German Tieck, whose manner, in *some* of
his works, is absolutely identical with that *habitual* to Hawthorne. But it is clear that the element of the literary originality is novelty. The element of its appreciation by the
reader is the reader's sense of the new. Whatever gives him
a new, and, insomuch, a pleasurable emotion, he considers
original; and whoever frequently gives him such emotion,
he considers an original writer. In a word, it is by the sum
total of these emotions that he decides upon the writer's
claim to originality. I may observe here, however, that there
is clearly a point at which even novelty itself would cease
to produce the legitimate originality, if we judge this originality, as we should, by the effect designed; this point
is that at which *novelty becomes nothing novel*, and here
the artist, *to preserve his originality*, will subside into the
commonplace. No one, I think, has noticed that, merely
through inattention to this matter, Moore has comparatively
failed in his *Lalla Rookh*. Few readers, and indeed few
critics, have commended this poem for originality—and, in
fact, the effect, originality, is not produced by it; yet no
work of equal size so abounds in the happiest originalities,
individually considered. They are so excessive as, in the end,
to deaden in the reader all capacity for their appreciation.

These points properly understood, it will be seen that
the critic (unacquainted with Tieck) who reads a single

tale or essay by Hawthorne, may be justified in thinking him original; but the tone, or manner, or choice of subject, which induces in this critic the sense of the new, will—if not in a second tale, at least in a third and all subsequent ones—not only fail of inducing it, but bring about an exactly antagonistic impression. In concluding a volume, and more especially in concluding all the volumes of the author, the critic will abandon his first design of calling him "original," and content himself with styling him "peculiar."

With the vague opinion that to be original is to be unpopular, I could, indeed, agree, were I to adopt an understanding of originality which, to my surprise, I have known adopted by many who have a right to be called critical. They have limited, in a love for mere words, the literary to the metaphysical originality. They regard as original in letters only such combinations of thought, of incident, and so forth, as are, in fact, absolutely novel. It is clear, however, not only that it is the novelty of effect alone which is worth consideration, but that this effect is best wrought, for the end of all fictitious composition, pleasure, by shunning rather than by seeking the absolute novelty of combination. Originality, thus understood, tasks and startles the intellect, and so brings into undue action the faculties to which, in the lighter literature, we least appeal. And thus understood, it cannot fail to prove unpopular with the masses, who, seeking in this literature amusement, are positively offended by instruction. But the true originality—true in respect of its purposes—is that which, in bringing out the half-formed, the reluctant, or the unexpressed fancies of mankind, or in exciting the more delicate pulses of the heart's passion, or in giving birth to some universal sentiment or instinct in embryo, thus combines with the pleasurable effect of *apparent* novelty a real egotistic delight. The reader, in the case first supposed (that of the absolute novelty), is excited, but embarrassed, disturbed, in some degree even pained, at his own want of perception, at his own folly in not having himself hit upon the idea. In the second case, his pleasure is doubled. He is filled with an intrinsic and extrinsic delight. He feels and intensely enjoys the seeming novelty of the thought, enjoys it as really novel, as absolutely original with the writer—*and* himself. They two, he fancies, have, alone of all men, thought thus. They two have, together, created this thing. Henceforward there is a bond of sympathy between them—a sympathy which irradiates every subsequent page of the book.

There is a species of writing which, with some difficulty, may be admitted as a lower degree of what I have called the true original. In its perusal, we say to ourselves, not "how original this is!" nor "here is an idea which I and the author have alone entertained," but "here is a charmingly obvious fancy," or sometimes even, "here is a thought which I am not sure has ever occurred to myself, but which, of course, has occurred to all the rest of the world." This kind of composition (which still appertains to a high order) is usually designated as "the natural." It has little external resemblance, but strong internal affinity to the true original, if, indeed, as I have suggested, it is not of this latter an inferior degree. It is best exemplified, among English writers, in Addison, Irving, and *Hawthorne*. The "ease" which is so often spoken of as its distinguishing feature, it has been the fashion to regard as ease in appearance alone, as a point of really difficult attainment. This idea, however, must be received with some reservation. The natural style is difficult only to those who should never intermeddle with it—to the unnatural. It is but the result of writing with the understanding, or with the instinct, that the *tone,* in composition, should be that which, at any given point or upon any given topic, would be the tone of the great mass of humanity. The author who, after the manner of the "North Americans," is merely at *all* times *quiet,* is, of course, upon *most* occasions, merely silly or stupid, and has no more right to be thought "easy" or "natural" than has a cockney exquisite, or the sleeping beauty in the waxworks.

The "peculiarity," or sameness, or monotone of Hawthorne, would, in its mere character of "peculiarity," and without reference to what *is* the peculiarity, suffice to deprive him of all chance of popular appreciation. But at his failure to be appreciated, we can, of course, no longer wonder, when we find him monotonous at decidedly the worst of all possible points—at that point which, having the least concern with Nature, is the farthest removed from the popular intellect, from the popular sentiment, and from the popular taste. I allude to the strain of allegory which completely overwhelms the greater number of his subjects, and which in some measure interferes with the direct conduct of absolutely all.

In defense of allegory (however or for whatever object employed) there is scarcely one respectable word to be said. Its best appeals are made to the fancy—that is to say, to our sense of adaptation, not of matters proper, but of matters improper for the purpose, of the real with the unreal; having never more of intelligible connection than has something with nothing, never half so much of effective affinity as has the substance for the shadow. The deepest emotion aroused within us by the happiest allegory, *as* allegory, is a very, very imperfectly satisfied sense of the writer's ingenuity in overcoming a difficulty we should have preferred his not having attempted to overcome. The fallacy of the idea that allegory, in any of its moods, can be made to enforce a truth, that metaphor, for example, may illustrate as well as embellish an argument, could be promptly demonstrated; the converse of the supposed fact might be shown, indeed, with very little trouble; but these are topics foreign to my present purpose. One thing is clear, that if allegory ever establishes a fact, it is by dint of overturning a fiction. Where the suggested meaning runs through the obvious one in a *very* profound undercurrent, so as never to interfere with the upper one without our own volition, so as never to show itself unless *called* to the surface, there only, for the proper uses of fictitious narrative, is it available at all. Under the best circumstances, it must always interfere with that unity of effect which, to the artist, is worth all the allegory in the world. Its vital injury, however, is rendered to the most vitally important point in fiction— that of earnestness or verisimilitude. That *The Pilgrim's Progress* is a ludicrously overrated book, owing its seeming popularity to one or two of those accidents in critical literature which by the critical are sufficiently well understood, is a matter upon which no two thinking people disagree; but the pleasure derivable from it, in any sense, will be found in the direct ratio of the reader's capacity to smother its true purpose, in the direct ratio of his ability to keep the allegory out of sight, or of his *in*ability to comprehend it. Of allegory properly handled, judiciously subdued, seen only as a shadow or by suggestive glimpses, and making its nearest approach to truth in a not obtrusive and therefore not unpleasant *appositeness*, the *Undine* of De La Motte Fouqué is the best, and undoubtedly a very remarkable specimen.

The obvious causes, however, which have prevented Mr. Hawthorne's *popularity* do not suffice to condemn him in the eyes of the few who belong properly to books, and to whom books, perhaps, do not quite so properly belong. These few estimate an author, not as do the public, altogether by what he does, but in great measure—indeed, even in the greatest measure—by what he evinces a capability of doing. In this view, Hawthorne stands among literary people in America much in the same light as did Coleridge in England. The few, also, through a certain warping of the taste, which long pondering upon books as books merely never fails to induce, are not in condition to view the errors of a scholar as errors altogether. At any time these gentlemen are prone to think the public not right rather than an educated author wrong. But the simple truth is that the writer who aims at impressing the people is *always* wrong when he fails in forcing that people to receive the impression. How far Mr. Hawthorne has addressed the people at all, is, of course, not a question for me to decide. His books afford strong internal evidence of having been written to himself and his particular friends alone.

There has long existed in literature a fatal and unfounded prejudice, which it will be the office of this age to overthrow, the idea that the mere bulk of a work must enter largely into our estimate of its merit. I do not suppose even the weakest of the *Quarterly* reviewers weak enough to maintain that in a book's size or mass, abstractly considered, there is anything which especially calls for our admiration. A mountain, simply through the sensation of physical magnitude which it conveys, does, indeed, affect us with a sense of the sublime, but we cannot admit any such influence in the contemplation even of *The Columbiad*. The Quarterlies themselves will not admit it. And yet, what else are we to understand by their continual prating about "sustained effort"? Granted that this sustained effort has accomplished an epic—let us then admire the effort (if this be a thing admirable), but certainly not the epic on the effort's account. Common sense, in the time to come, may possibly insist upon measuring a work of art rather by the object it fulfills, by the impression it makes, than by the time it took to fulfill the object, or by the extent of "sustained effort" which became necessary to produce the impression. The fact is, that perseverance is one thing and genius quite another; nor can all the transcendentalists in Heathendom confound them.

II

The pieces in the volumes entitled *Twice-Told Tales* are now in their third republication, and, of course, are thrice-told. Moreover, they are by no means *all* tales, either in the ordinary or in the legitimate understanding of the term. Many of them are pure essays; for example, *Sights from a Steeple, Sunday at Home, Little Annie's Ramble, A Rill from the Town Pump, The Toll-Gatherer's Day, The Haunted Mind, The Sister Years, Snow Flakes, Night Sketches,* and *Footprints on the Sea Shore.* I mention these matters chiefly on account of their discrepancy with that marked precision and finish by which the body of the work is distinguished.

Of the essays just named, I must be content to speak in brief. They are each and all beautiful, without being characterized by the polish and adaptation so visible in the tales proper. A painter would at once note their leading or predominant feature, and style it *repose*. There is no attempt at effect. All is quiet, thoughtful, subdued. Yet this repose may exist simultaneously with high originality of thought; and Mr. Hawthorne has demonstrated the fact. At every turn we meet with novel combinations; yet these combinations never surpass the limits of the quiet. We are soothed as we read; and withal is a calm astonishment that ideas so apparently obvious have never occurred or been presented to us before. Herein our author differs materially from Lamb or Hunt or Hazlitt—who, with vivid originality of manner and expression, have less of the true novelty of thought than is generally supposed, and whose originality, at best, has an uneasy and meretricious quaintness, replete with startling effects unfounded in nature, and inducing trains of reflection which lead to no satisfactory result. The essays of Hawthorne have much of the character of Irving, with more of originality, and less of finish; while, compared with *The Spectator,* they have a vast superiority at all points. *The Spectator,* Mr. Irving, and Hawthorne have in common that tranquil and subdued manner which I have chosen to denominate *repose;* but, in the case of the two former, this repose is attained rather by the absence of novel combination, or of originality, than otherwise, and consists chiefly in the calm, quiet, unostentatious expression of commonplace thoughts, in an unambitious, unadulterated Saxon. In them, by strong effort, we are made to conceive the absence of all. In the essays before me the absence of effort is too obvious to be mistaken, and a strong undercurrent of *suggestion* runs continuously beneath the upper stream of the tranquil thesis. In short, these effusions of Mr. Hawthorne are the product of a truly imaginative intellect, restrained, and in some measure repressed, by fastidiousness of taste, by constitutional melancholy, and by indolence.

But it is of his tales that I desire principally to speak. The tale proper, in my opinion, affords unquestionably the fairest field for the exercise of the loftiest talent, which can be afforded by the wide domains of mere prose. Were I bidden to say how the highest genius could be most advantageously employed for the best display of its own powers, I should answer, without hesitation—in the composition of a rhymed poem, not to exceed in length what might be perused in an hour. Within this limit alone can the highest order of true poetry exist. I need only here say, upon this topic, that, in almost all classes of composition, the unity of effect or impression is a point of the greatest importance. It is clear, moreover, that this unity cannot be thoroughly preserved in productions whose perusal cannot be completed at one sitting. We may continue the reading of a prose composition, from the very nature of prose itself, much longer than we can persevere, to any good purpose, in the perusal of a poem. This latter, if truly fulfilling the demands of the poetic sentiment, induces an exaltation of the soul which cannot be long sustained. All high excitements are necessarily transient. Thus a long poem is a paradox. And, without unity of impression, the deepest effects cannot be brought about. Epics were the offspring of an imperfect sense of Art, and their reign is no more. A poem *too* brief may produce a vivid, but never an intense or enduring impression. Without a certain continuity of effort—without a certain duration or repetition of purpose—the soul is never deeply moved. There must be the dropping of the water upon the rock. De Béranger has wrought brilliant things, pungent and spirit-stirring; but, like all immassive bodies, they lack *momentum,* and thus fail to satisfy the Poetic Sentiment. They sparkle and excite, but, from want of continuity, fail deeply to impress. Extreme brevity will degenerate into epigrammatism; but the sin of extreme length is even more unpardonable. *In medio tutissimus ibis.*

Were I called upon, however, to designate that class of composition which, next to such a poem as I have suggested, should best fulfill the demands of high genius—should offer it the most advantageous field of exertion—I should unhesitatingly speak of the prose tale, as Mr. Hawthorne has here exemplified it. I allude to the short prose narrative, requiring from a half-hour to one or two hours in its perusal. The ordinary novel is objectionable, from its length, for reasons already stated in substance. As it cannot be read at one sitting, it deprives itself, of course, of the immense force derivable from *totality.* Worldly interests intervening during the pauses of perusal, modify, annul, or counteract, in a greater or less degree, the impressions of the book. But simple cessation in reading would, of itself, be sufficient to destroy the true unity. In the brief tale, however, the author is enabled to carry out the fullness of his intention, be it what it may. During the hour of perusal the soul of the reader is at the writer's control. There are no external or extrinsic influences—resulting from weariness or interruption.

A skillful literary artist has constructed a tale. If wise, he has not fashioned his thoughts to accommodate his incidents; but having conceived, with deliberate care, a certain unique or single *effect* to be wrought out, he then invents such incidents—he then combines such events as may best aid him in establishing this preconceived effect. If his very initial sentence tend not to the outbringing of this effect, then he has failed in his first step. In the whole composition there should be no word written, of which the tendency, direct or indirect, is not to the one pre-established design. And by such means, with such care and skill, a picture is at length painted which leaves in the mind of him who contemplates it with a kindred art, a sense of the fullest satisfaction. The idea of the tale has been presented unblemished, because undisturbed; and this is an end unattainable by the novel. Undue brevity is just as exceptionable here as in the poem; but undue length is yet more to be avoided.

We have said that the tale has a point of superiority even over the poem. In fact, while the *rhythm* of this latter is an essential aid in the development of the poem's highest idea —the idea of the Beautiful—the artificialities of this rhythm are an inseparable bar to the development of all points of thought or expression which have their basis in *Truth*. But Truth is often, and in very great degree, the aim of the tale. Some of the finest tales are tales of ratiocination. Thus the field of this species of composition, if not in so elevated a region on the mountain of Mind, is a tableland of far vaster extent than the domain of the mere poem. Its products are never so rich, but infinitely more numerous, and more appreciable by the mass of mankind. The writer of the prose tale, in short, may bring to his theme a vast variety of modes or inflections of thought and expression (the ratiocinative, for example, the sarcastic, or the humorous)— which are not only antagonistical to the nature of the poem, but absolutely forbidden by one of its most peculiar and indispensable adjuncts; we allude, of course, to rhythm. It may be added, here, *par parenthèse,* that the author who aims at the purely beautiful in a prose tale is laboring at a great disadvantage. For Beauty can be better treated in the poem. Not so with terror, or passion, or horror, or a multitude of such other points. And here it will be seen how full of prejudice are the usual animadversions against those *tales of effect,* many fine examples of which were found in the earlier numbers of *Blackwood.* The impressions produced were wrought in a legitimate sphere of action, and constituted a legitimate although sometimes an exaggerated interest. They were relished by every man of genius: although there were found many men of genius who condemned them without just ground. The true critic will but demand that the design intended be accomplished, to the fullest extent, by the means most advantageously applicable.

We have very few American tales of real merit—we may say, indeed, none, with the exception of *The Tales of a Traveller* of Washington Irving, and these *Twice-Told Tales* of Mr. Hawthorne. Some of the pieces of Mr. John Neal abound in vigor and originality; but, in general, his compositions of this class are excessively diffuse, extravagant, and indicative of an imperfect sentiment of Art. Articles at random are, now and then, met with in our periodicals which might be advantageously compared with the best effusions of the British magazines; but, upon the whole, we are far behind our progenitors in this department of literature.

Of Mr. Hawthorne's *Tales* we would say, emphatically, that they belong to the highest region of Art—an Art subservient to genius of a very lofty order. We had supposed, with good reason for so supposing, that he had been thrust into his present position by one of the impudent cliques which beset our literature, and whose pretensions it is our full purpose to expose at the earliest opportunity; but we have been most agreeably mistaken. We know of few compositions which the critic can more honestly commend than these *Twice-Told Tales*. As Americans, we feel proud of the book.

Mr. Hawthorne's distinctive trait is invention, creation, imagination, originality—a trait which, in the literature of fiction, is positively worth all the rest. But the nature of the originality, so far as regards its manifestation in letters, is but imperfectly understood. The inventive or original mind as frequently displays itself in novelty of *tone* as in novelty of matter. Mr. Hawthorne is original in *all* points.

It would be a matter of some difficulty to designate the best of these tales; we repeat that, without exception, they are beautiful. *Wakefield* is remarkable for the skill with which an old idea—a well-known incident—is worked up or discussed. A man of whims conceives the purpose of quitting his wife and residing *incognito,* for twenty years, in her immediate neighborhood. Something of this kind actually happened in London. The force of Mr. Hawthorne's tale lies in the analysis of the motives which must or might have impelled the husband to such folly, in the first instance, with the possible causes of his perseverance. Upon this thesis a sketch of singular power has been constructed. *The Wedding Knell* is full of the boldest imagination—an imagination fully controlled by taste. The most captious critic could find no flaw in this production. *The Minister's Black Veil* is a masterly composition of which the sole defect is that to the rabble its exquisite skill will be *caviare.* The obvious meaning of this article will be found to smother its insinuated one. The moral put into the mouth of the dying minister will be supposed to convey the true import of the narrative; and that a crime of dark dye (having reference to the "young lady") has been committed, is a point which only minds congenial with that of the author will perceive. *Mr. Higginbotham's Catastrophe* is vividly original and managed most dexterously. *Dr. Heidegger's Experiment* is exceedingly well imagined, and executed with surpassing ability. The artist breathes in every line of it. *The White Old Maid* is objectionable, even more than *The Minister's Black Veil*, on the score of its mysticism. Even with the thoughtful and analytic, there will be much trouble in penetrating its entire import.

The Hollow of the Three Hills we would quote in full, had we space; not as evincing higher talent than any of the other pieces, but as affording an excellent example of the author's peculiar ability. The subject is commonplace. A witch subjects the Distant and the Past to the view of a mourner. It has been the fashion to describe, in such cases, a mirror in which the images of the absent appear; or a cloud of smoke is made to arise, and thence the figures are gradually unfolded. Mr. Hawthorne has wonderfully heightened his effect by making the ear, in place of the eye, the medium by which the fantasy is conveyed. The head of the mourner is enveloped in the cloak of the witch, and within its magic folds there arise sounds which have an all-sufficient intelligence. Throughout this article also, the artist is conspicuous—not more in positive than in negative merits. Not only is all done that should be done, but (what perhaps is an end with more difficulty attained) there is nothing done which should not be. Every word *tells,* and there is not a word which does *not* tell.

In *Howe's Masquerade* we observe something which resembles a plagiarism,—but which *may be* a very flattering coincidence of thought. We quote the passage in question.

With a dark flush of wrath upon his brow, they saw the General *draw his sword* and *advance to meet* the figure *in the cloak* before the latter had stepped one pace upon the floor. "*Villain, unmuffle yourself,*" cried he. "You pass no farther!" The figure, without blenching a hair's breadth from the sword which was pointed at his breast, made a solemn pause, and *lowered the cape of the cloak* from about his face, yet not sufficiently for the spectators to catch a glimpse of it. But Sir William Howe had evidently seen enough. The sternness of his countenance gave place to a look of wild amazement, if not horror, while he recoiled several steps from the figure, *and let fall his sword* upon the floor. ii. 21.

The idea here is, that the figure in the cloak is the phantom or reduplication of Sir William Howe; but in an article called *William Wilson*, one of the *Tales of the Grotesque and Arabesque*,[1] we have not only the same idea, but the same idea similarly presented in several respects. We quote two paragraphs, which our readers may compare with what has been already given. We have italicized, above, the immediate particulars of resemblance.

The brief moment in which I averted my eyes had been sufficient to produce, apparently, a material change in the arrangement at the upper or farther end of the room. A large mirror, it appeared to me, now stood where none had been perceptible before: and as I stepped up to it in extremity of terror, mine own image, but with features all pale and dabbled in blood, *advanced* with a feeble and tottering gait to meet me.

Thus it appeared, I say, but was not. It was Wilson, who then stood before me in the agonies of dissolution. Not a line in all the marked and singular lineaments of that face which was not even identically mine own. *His mask and cloak lay where he had thrown them, upon the floor.* ii. 57.

Here, it will be observed that, not only are the two general conceptions identical, but there are various *points* of similarity. In each case the figure seen is the wraith or duplication of the beholder. In each case the scene is a masquerade. In each case the figure is cloaked. In each there is a quarrel,—that is to say, angry words pass between the parties. In each the beholder is enraged. In each the cloak and sword fall upon the floor. The "villain, unmuffle yourself," of Mr. Hawthorne is precisely paralleled by a passage at page 56 of *William Wilson*.

III

I must hasten to conclude this paper with a summary of Mr. Hawthorne's merits and demerits.

He is peculiar and not original—unless in those detailed fancies and detached thoughts which his want of general originality will deprive of the appreciation due to them, in

[1] By Poe himself. E. W.

preventing them from ever reaching the public eye. He is infinitely too fond of allegory, and can never hope for popularity so long as he persists in it. This he will not do, for allegory is at war with the whole tone of his nature, which disports itself never so well as when escaping from the mysticism of his *Goodman Browns* and *White Old Maids* into the hearty, genial, but still Indian-summer sunshine of his *Wakefields* and *Little Annie's Rambles*. Indeed, his spirit of "metaphor run mad" is clearly imbibed from the phalanx and phalanstery atmosphere in which he has been so long struggling for breath. He has not half the material for the exclusiveness of authorship that he possesses for its universality. He has the purest style, the finest taste, the most available scholarship, the most delicate humor, the most touching pathos, the most radiant imagination, the most consummate ingenuity; and with these varied good qualities he has done *well* as a mystic. But is there any one of these qualities which should prevent his doing doubly as well in a career of honest, upright, sensible, prehensible, and comprehensible things? Let him mend his pen, get a bottle of visible ink, come out from the Old Manse, cut Mr. Alcott, hang (if possible) the editor of the *Dial*, and throw out of the window to the pigs all his odd numbers of the *North American Review*.

LOWELL'S *A FABLE FOR CRITICS*

February 1849

WHAT have we Americans accomplished in the way of satire? *The Vision of Rubeta*, by Laughton Osborn, is probably our best composition of the kind: but, in saying this, we intend no excessive commendation. Trumbull's clumsy and imitative work is scarcely worth mention; and then we have Halleck's *Croakers*, local and ephemeral; but what is there besides? Park Benjamin has written a clever address, with the title *Infatuation,* and Holmes has an occasional scrap, piquant enough in its way; but we can think of nothing more that can be fairly called "satire." Some matters we have produced, to be sure, which were excellent in the way of burlesque—the *Poems* of William Ellery Channing, for example—without meaning a syllable that was not utterly solemn and serious. Odes, ballads, songs, sonnets, epics, and epigrams, possessed of this unintentional excellence, we should have no difficulty in designating by the dozen; but in the particular of direct and obvious satire, it cannot be denied that we are unaccountably deficient.

It has been suggested that this deficiency arises from the want of a suitable field for satirical display. In England, it is said, satire abounds, because the people there find a proper target in the aristocracy, whom they (the people) regard as a distinct race with whom they have little in common; relishing even the most virulent abuse of the upper classes with a gusto undiminished by any feeling that they (the people) have any concern in it. In Russia, or Austria, on the other hand, it is urged, satire is unknown; because there is danger in touching the aristocracy, and self-satire would be odious to the mass. In America, also, the people who write are, it is maintained, the people who read; thus in satirizing the people we satirize only ourselves, and are never in condition to sympathize with the satire.

All this is more verisimilar than true. It is forgotten that no individual considers himself as one of the mass. Each person, in his own estimate, is the pivot on which all the rest of the world spins round. We may abuse *the people* by wholesale, and yet with a clear conscience, so far as regards any compunction for offending any one from among the multitude of which that "people" is composed. Everyone of the crowd will cry *"Encore!*—give it to them, the vagabonds! —it serves them right." It seems to us that, in America, we have refused to encourage satire—not because what we have had touches us too nearly—but because it has been too pointless to touch us at all. Its namby-pambyism has arisen, in part, from the general want, among our men of letters, of that minute polish, of that skill in details, which, in combination with natural sarcastic power, satire, more than any other form of literature, so imperatively demands. In part, also, we may attribute our failure to the colonial sin of imitation. We content ourselves, at this point, not less supinely than at all others, with doing what not only has been done before, but what, however well done, has yet been done *ad nauseam*. We should not be able to endure infinite repetitions of even absolute excellence; but what is *McFingal* more than a faint echo from *Hudibras?*—and what is *The Vision of Rubeta* more than a vast gilded swill-trough overflowing with *Dunciad* and water? Although we are not all Archilochuses, however—although we have few pretensions to the ἠχεῆντες ἰάμβοι—although, in short, we are no satirists ourselves, there can be no question that we answer sufficiently well as subjects for satire.

The Vision is bold enough, if we leave out of sight its anonymous issue, and bitter enough, and witty enough, if we forget its pitiable punning on names, and long enough (Heaven knows), and well constructed and decently versified; but it fails in the principal element of all satire—sarcasm —because the intention to be sarcastic (as in the *English Bards and Scotch Reviewers,* and in all the more classical satires) is permitted to render itself manifest. The malevolence appears. The author is never very severe, because he is at no time particularly cool. We laugh not so much at his victims as at himself, for letting them put him in such a passion. And where a deeper sentiment than mirth is excited— where it is pity or contempt that we are made to feel—the feeling is too often reflected, in its object, from the satirized to the satirist, with whom we sympathize in the discomfort of his animosity. Mr. Osborn has not many superiors in downright invective; but this is the awkward left arm of the satiric Muse. That satire alone is worth talking about which at least appears to be the genial, good-humored outpouring of irrepressible merriment.

The *Fable for Critics*, just issued, has not the name of its author on the title page; and but for some slight foreknowledge of the literary opinions, likes, dislikes, whims, prejudices, and crotchets of Mr. James Russell Lowell, we should have had much difficulty in attributing so very loose a brochure to him. The *Fable* is essentially "loose"—ill-conceived and feebly executed, as well in detail as in general. Some good hints and some sparkling witticisms do not serve to compensate us for its rambling plot (if plot it can be called) and for the want of artistic finish so particularly noticeable throughout the work—especially in its versification. In Mr. Lowell's prose efforts we have before observed a certain *disjointedness*, but never, until now, in his verse; and we confess some surprise at his putting forth so unpolished a performance. The author of *The Legend of Brittany* (which is decidedly the noblest poem, of the same length, written by an American) could not do a better thing than to take the advice of those who mean him well, in spite of his fanaticism, and leave prose, with satiric verse, to those who are better able to manage them; while he contents himself with that class of poetry for which, and for which alone, he seems to have an especial vocation—the poetry of *sentiment*. This, to be sure, is not the very loftiest order of verse, for it is far inferior to either that of the imagination or that of the passions; but it is the loftiest region in which Mr. Lowell can get his breath without difficulty.

Our primary objection to this *Fable for Critics* has reference to a point which we have already touched in a general way. "The malevolence appears." We laugh not so much at the author's victims as at himself, for letting them put him in such a passion. The very title of the book shows the want of a due sense in respect to the satirical essence, *sarcasm*. This *Fable*—this severe lesson—is meant *"for Critics."* "Ah!" we say to ourselves at once—"we see how it is. Mr. Lowell is a poor-devil poet, and some critic has been reviewing him, and making him feel very uncomfortable; whereupon, bearing in mind that Lord Byron, when similarly assailed, avenged his wrongs in a satire which he called *English Bards and Scotch Reviewers,* he (Mr. Lowell), imitative as usual, has been endeavoring to get redress in a parallel manner—by a satire with a parallel title—*A Fable for Critics.*"

All this the reader says to himself; and all this tells against

Mr. Lowell in two ways—first, by suggesting unlucky comparisons between Byron and Lowell, and, secondly, by reminding us of the various criticisms in which we have been amused (rather ill-naturedly) at seeing Mr. Lowell "used up."

The title starts us on this train of thought, and the satire sustains us in it. Every reader versed in our literary gossip is at once put *dessous des cartes* as to the particular provocation which engendered the *Fable*. Miss Margaret Fuller, some time ago, in a silly and conceited piece of Transcendentalism, which she called an *Essay on American Literature*, or something of that kind, had the consummate pleasantry, after selecting, from the list of American poets, Cornelius Mathews and William Ellery Channing for especial commendation, to speak of Longfellow as a booby, and of Lowell as so wretched a poetaster "as to be disgusting even to his best friends." All this Miss Fuller said, if not in our precise words, still in words quite as much to the purpose. Why she said it, Heaven only knows—unless it was because she was Margaret Fuller, and wished to be taken for nobody else. Messrs. Longfellow and Lowell, so pointedly picked out for abuse as the worst of our poets, are, upon the whole, perhaps, our best—although Bryant, and one or two others, are scarcely inferior. As for the two favorites, selected just as pointedly for laudation by Miss Fuller—it is really difficult to think of them, in connection with poetry, without laughing. Mr. Mathews once wrote some sonnets *On Man*, and Mr. Channing some lines on *A Tin Can*, or something of that kind; and if the former gentleman be not the very worst poet that ever existed on the face of the earth, it is only because he is not quite so bad as the latter. To speak algebraically: Mr. Mathews is *e*xecrable, but Mr. Channing is $x + 1$-ecrable.

Mr. Lowell has obviously aimed his *Fable* at Miss Fuller's head, in the first instance, with an eye to its ricocheting so as to knock down Mr. Mathews in the second. Miss Fuller is first introduced as "Miss ——," rhyming to "cooler," and afterwards as "Miranda"; while poor Mr. Mathews is brought in upon all occasions, head and shoulders; and now and then a

sharp thing, although never very original, is said of them or
at them; but all the true satiric effect wrought is that produced by the satirist against himself. The reader is all the
time smiling to think that so unsurpassable a—(what shall
we call her?—we wish to be civil)—a transcendentalist as
Miss Fuller should, by such a criticism, have had the power
to put a respectable poet in such a passion.

As for the plot or conduct of this *Fable,* the less we say
of it the better. It is so weak, so flimsy, so ill put together,
as to be not worth the trouble of understanding: something,
as usual, about Apollo and Daphne. Is there no originality
on the face of the earth? Mr. Lowell's total want of it is
shown at all points—very especially in his preface of rhyming
verse written without distinction by lines or initial capitals
(a hackneyed matter, originating, we believe, with *Fraser's
Magazine*), very especially also in his long continuations of
some particular rhyme—a fashion introduced, if we remember aright, by Leigh Hunt, more than twenty-five years ago,
in his *Feast of the Poets,* which, by the way, has been Mr.
Lowell's model in many respects.

Although ill-temper has evidently engendered this *Fable,*
it is by no means a satire throughout. Much of it is devoted
to panegyric; but our readers would be quite puzzled to know
the grounds of the author's laudations, in many cases, unless
made acquainted with a fact which we think it as well they
should be informed of at once. Mr. Lowell is one of the most
rabid of the Abolition fanatics; and no Southerner, who does
not wish to be insulted, and at the same time revolted by a
bigotry the most obstinately blind and deaf, should ever
touch a volume by this author.[1] His fanaticism about slavery
is a mere local outbreak of the same innate wrong-
headedness which, if he owned slaves, would manifest itself
in atrocious ill-treatment of them, with murder of any abolitionist who should endeavor to set them free. A fanatic of

[1] This *Fable* for Critics—this *literary* satire—this benevolent *jeu
d'esprit,* is disgraced by such passages as the following:

> Forty fathers of Freedom, of whom twenty bred
> Their sons for the rice swamps, at so much a head,
> And their daughters for—faugh!   E. A. P.

Mr. Lowell's species is simply a fanatic for the sake of fanaticism, and must be a fanatic in whatever circumstances you place him.

His prejudices on the topic of slavery break out everywhere in his present book. Mr. Lowell has not the common honesty to speak well, even in a literary sense, of any man who is not a ranting abolitionist. With the exception of Mr. Poe (who has written some commendatory criticisms on his poems), no Southerner is mentioned at all in this *Fable*. It is a fashion among Mr. Lowell's set to affect a belief that there is no such thing as Southern literature. Northerners, people who have really nothing to speak of as men of letters, are cited by the dozen, and lauded by this candid critic without stint, while Legaré, Simms, Longstreet, and others of equal note, are passed by in contemptuous silence. Mr. Lowell cannot carry his frail honesty of opinion even so far South as New York. All whom he praises are Bostonians. Other writers are barbarians, and satirized accordingly, if mentioned at all.

To show the general manner of the *Fable,* we quote a portion of what he says about Mr. Poe:

There comes Poe with his Raven, like Barnaby Rudge,
Three-fifths of him genius and two-fifths sheer fudge,
Who talks like a book of iambs and pentameters,
In a way to make all men of common sense damn meters,
Who has written some things quite the best of their kind,
But the heart somehow seems all squeezed out by the mind.

We may observe here that profound ignorance on any particular topic is always sure to manifest itself by some allusion to "common sense" as an all-sufficient instructor. So far from Mr. Poe's talking "like a book" on the topic at issue, his chief purpose has been to demonstrate that there exists no book on the subject worth talking about; and "common sense," after all, has been the basis on which he relied, in contradistinction from the uncommon nonsense of Mr. Lowell and the small pedants.

And now let us see how far the unusual "common sense" of our satirist has availed him in the structure of his verse.

First, by way of showing what his intention was, we quote three accidentally accurate lines:

> But a boy | he could ne | ver be right | ly defined.

> As I said | he was ne | ver precise | ly unkind.

> But as Ci | cero says | he won't say | this or that.

Here it is clearly seen that Mr. Lowell intends a line of four anapæsts. (An anapæst is a foot composed of two short syllables followed by a long.) With this observation, we will now simply copy a few of the lines which constitute the body of the poem; asking any of our readers to *read them if they can;* that is to say, we place the question, without argument, on the broad basis of the very commonest "common sense."

They're all from one source, monthly, weekly, diurnal.

Disperse all one's good and condense all one's poor traits.

The one's two-thirds Norseman, the other half Greek.

He has imitators in scores who omit.

Should suck milk, strong-will-giving brave, such as runs.

Along the far railroad the steam-snake glide white.

From the same runic type-fount and alphabet.

Earth has six truest patriots: four discoverers of ether.

Every cockboat that swims clear its fierce (pop) gun deck at him.

Is some of it pr—— No, 'tis not even prose.

O'er his principles, when something else turns up trumps.

But a few silly-(syllo-I mean) gisms that squat 'em.

Nos, we don't want *extra* freezing in winter.

Plow, sail, forge, build, carve, paint, make all over new.

But enough: we have given a fair specimen of the general versification. It might have been better—but we are quite sure that it *could not have been worse.* So much for "common sense," in Mr. Lowell's understanding of the term. Mr. Lowell should not have meddled with the anapæstic rhythm: it is exceedingly awkward in the hands of one who knows nothing about it and who *will* persist in fancying that he can write it by ear. Very especially, he should have avoided this rhythm in satire, which, more than any other branch of Letters, is dependent upon seeming trifles for its effect. Two thirds of the force of the *Dunciad,* may be referred to its exquisite finish; and had the *Fable for Critics* been (what it is *not*) the quintessence of the satiric spirit itself, it would, nevertheless, in so slovenly a form, have failed. As it is, no failure was ever more complete or more pitiable. By the publication of a book at once so ambitious and so feeble, so malevolent in design and so harmless in execution, a work so roughly and clumsily yet so weakly constructed, so very different in body and spirit from anything that he has written before, Mr. Lowell has committed an irrevocable *faux pas* and lowered himself at least fifty per cent in the literary public opinion.

BAYARD TAYLOR

April 1849

I BLUSH TO SEE, in the *Literary World,* an invidious notice of Bayard Taylor's *Rhymes of Travel.* What makes the matter worse, the critique is from the pen of one who, although undeservedly, holds, himself, some position as a poet; and what makes the matter worst, the attack is anonymous, and (while ostensibly commending) most zealously endeavors to damn the young writer "with faint praise." In his whole life. the author of the criticism never published a poem, long

or short, which could compare, either in the higher merits or
in the minor morals of the Muse, with the worst of Mr.
Taylor's compositions.

Observe the generalizing, disingenuous, patronizing tone:

> It is the empty charlatan, to whom all things are alike im-
> possible, who attempts everything. He can do one thing as well
> as another; for he can really do nothing. . . . Mr. Taylor's
> volume, as we have intimated, is an advance upon his previous
> publication. We could have wished, indeed, something more
> of restraint in the rhetoric, *but,* etc., etc., etc.

The concluding sentence, here, is an excellent example of
one of the most ingeniously malignant of critical ruses—that
of condemning an author, in especial, for what the world,
in general, feel to be his principal merit. In fact, the
"rhetoric" of Mr. Taylor, in the sense intended by the critic,
is Mr. Taylor's distinguishing excellence. He is, unquestionably, the most terse, glowing, and vigorous of all our poets,
young or old,—in point, I mean, of *expression.* His sonorous,
well-balanced rhythm puts me often in mind of Campbell
(in spite of our anonymous friend's implied sneer at "mere
jingling of rhymes, brilliant and successful for the moment"), and his rhetoric in general is of the highest order.
By "rhetoric," I intend the mode generally in which thought
is presented. Where shall we find more magnificent passages
than these?

> First queenly Asia, from the fallen thrones
>   Of twice three thousand years,
> Came *with the woe a grieving goddess owns*
>   *Who longs for mortal tears.*
> The dust of ruin to her mantle clung
>   And dimmed her crown of gold,
> While *the majestic sorrows of her tongue*
>   *From Tyre to Indus rolled:*

> "Mourn with me, sisters, in my realm of woe
>   *Whose only glory streams*
> *From its lost childhood, like the arctic glow*
>   *Which sunless Winter dreams!*
> *In the red desert molders Babylon,*
>   *And the wild serpent's hiss*

Echoes in Petra's palaces of stone
And waste Persepolis."

. . . . . .

Then from her seat, *amid the palms embowered*
That shade the Lion-land,
Swart Africa in dusky aspect towered,
The fetters on her hand.
Backward she saw, from out her drear eclipse,
The mighty Theban years,
And the deep anguish of her mournful lips
Interpreted her tears.

I copy these passages first, because the critic in question
has copied them, without the slightest appreciation of their
grandeur—for they are grand; and secondly, to put the question of "rhetoric" at rest. No artist who reads them will deny
that they are the perfection of skill in their way. But thirdly,
I wish to call attention to the glowing imagination evinced
in the lines italicized. My very soul revolts at such efforts (as
the one I refer to) to depreciate such poems as Mr. Taylor's.
Is there no honor—no chivalry left in the land? Are our most
deserving writers to be forever sneered down, or hooted
down, or damned down with faint praise, by a set of men
who possess little other ability than that which assures temporary success to *them,* in common with Swaim's Panacea or
Morrison's Pills? The fact is, some person should write, at
once, a magazine paper exposing—*ruthlessly* exposing—the
dessous des cartes of our literary affairs. He should show
how and why it is that the ubiquitous quack in letters can
always "succeed," while *genius* (which implies self-respect,
with a scorn of creeping and crawling) must inevitably succumb. He should point out the "easy arts" by which anyone,
base enough to do it, can get himself placed at the very head
of American Letters by an article in that magnanimous journal, the —— *Review.* He should explain, too, how readily
the same work can be induced (as in the case of Simms) to
vilify, and vilify personally, anyone not a Northerner, for a
trifling "consideration." In fact, our criticism needs a thorough regeneration, *and must have it.*

HEADLEY'S *THE SACRED MOUNTAINS*

October 1850[1]

THE *Reverend* Mr. Headley (why *will* he not put his full title in his title pages?) has in his *Sacred Mountains* been reversing the facts of the old fable about the mountains that brought forth the mouse—*parturiunt montes: nascitur ridiculus mus*—for in this instance it appears to be the mouse —the little *ridiculus mus*—that has been bringing forth the *Mountains,* and a great litter of them, too. The epithet, "funny," however, is perhaps the only one which can be considered as thoroughly applicable to the book. We say that a book is a "funny" book, and nothing else, when it spreads over two hundred pages an amount of matter which could be conveniently presented in twenty of a magazine; that a book is a "funny" book—"only this and nothing more" —when it is written in that kind of phraseology in which John Philpot Curran, when drunk, would have made a speech at a public dinner; and, moreover, we do say, emphatically, that a book is a "funny" book, and nothing but a "funny" book, whenever it happens to be penned by Mr. Headley.

We should like to give some account of *The Sacred Mountains,* if the thing were only possible, but we cannot conceive that it is. Mr. Headley belongs to that numerous class of authors who must be read to be understood, and who, for that reason, very seldom are as thoroughly comprehended as they should be. Let us endeavor, however, to give some general idea of the work. "The design," says the author, in his preface, "is to render more familiar and lifelike some of the scenes of the Bible." Here, in the very first sentence of his preface, we suspect the Reverend Mr. Headley of fibbing: for his design, as it appears to ordinary apprehension, is merely that of making a little money by selling a little book.

[1]Poe had died October 7, 1849. E. W.

The mountains described are Ararat, Moriah, Sinai, Hor, Pisgah, Horeb, Carmel, Lebanon, Zion, Tabor, Olivet, and Calvary. Taking up these, one by one, the author proceeds, in his own very peculiar way, to *elocutionize* about them: we really do not know how else to express what it is that Mr. Headley does with these eminences. Perhaps if we were to say that he stood up before the reader and "made a speech" about them, one after the other, we should come still nearer the truth. By way of carrying out his design, as announced in the preface—that of rendering "more familiar and lifelike some of the scenes" and so forth—he tells not only how each mountain is, and was, but how it might have been and ought to be, in his own opinion. To hear him talk, anybody would suppose that he had been at the laying of the corner stone of Solomon's Temple—to say nothing of being born and brought up in the ark with Noah, and hail-fellow-well-met with every one of the beasts that went into it. If any person really desires to know how and why it was that the deluge took place—but especially *how*—if any person wishes to get minute and accurate information on the topic, let him read *The Sacred Mountains,* let him only listen to the Reverend Mr. Headley. He explains to us precisely how it all took place—what Noah said, and thought, while the ark was building, and what the people, who saw him building the ark, said and thought about his undertaking such a work; and how the beasts, birds, and fishes looked, as they came in, arm in arm; and what the dove did, and what the raven did not—in short, all the rest of it: nothing could be more beautifully posted up. What *can* Mr. Headley mean, at page 17, by the remark that "there is no one who does not lament that there is not a fuller antediluvian history"? We are quite sure that nothing that ever happened before the flood has been omitted in the scrupulous researches of the author of *The Sacred Mountains.*

He might, perhaps, wrap up the fruits of these researches in rather better English than that which he employs:

Yet *still* the water rose around them till all through the valleys nothing but little black islands of human beings *were* seen on the surface. . . . The more fixed the irrevocable

decree, *the heavier* he leaned on the Omnipotent arm. . . .
And lo! a solitary cloud comes drifting along the morning sky
and *catches* against the top of the mountain. . . . At length
emboldened by their own numbers they *assembled* tumultu-
ously *together*. . . . Aaron never appears *so perfect* a character as Moses. . . . As he advanced from rock to rock the sob-
bing of the multitude that *followed after* tore his heart-strings.
. . . Friends were *following after* whose sick Christ had
healed. . . . The steady mountain threatened *to lift* from its
base and be carried away. . . . Sometimes God's hatred of
sin, sometimes His care for His children, sometimes the disci-
pline of His church, *were* the motives. . . . Surely it was His
mighty hand that *laid* on that trembling, tottering mountain.

These things are not exactly as we could wish them, perhaps; but that a gentleman should know so much about
Noah's ark and know anything about anything else, is
scarcely to be expected. We have no right to require English
grammar and accurate information about Moses and Aaron
at the hands of one and the same author. For our parts, now
we come to think of it, if we only understood as much about
Mount Sinai and other matters as Mr. Headley does, we
should make a point of always writing bad English upon
principle, whether we knew better or not.

It may well be made a question, moreover, how far a man
of genius is justified in discussing topics so serious as those
handled by Mr. Headley, in any ordinary kind of *style*. One
should not talk about Scriptural subjects as one would talk
about the rise and fall of stocks or the proceedings of Congress. Mr. Headley has seemed to feel this and has therefore
elevated his manner—a little. For example:

The fields were smiling in verdure before his eyes; the perfumed breezes *floated* by. . . . The sun is *sailing* over the
encampment. . . . That cloud was God's pavilion; the thunder
was its sentinels; and the lightning the lances' points as they
moved round the sacred trust. . . . And how could he part
with his children whom he had *borne on his brave heart* for
more than forty years? . . . Thus everything conspired to render Zion the spell-word of the nation and on its summit the
heart of Israel seemed to lie and throb. . . . The sun died in

the heavens; *an earthquake thundered* on to complete the dismay, etc., etc.

Here no one can fail to perceive the beauty (in an antediluvian, or at least in a Pickwickian, sense) of these expressions in general, about the floating of the breeze, the sailing of the sun, the thundering of the earthquake, and the throbbing of the heart as it lay on the top of the mountain.

The true artist, however, always rises as he proceeds, and in his last page or so brings all his elocution to a climax. Only hear Mr. Headley's *finale*. He has been describing the crucifixion, and now soars into the sublime:

How Heaven regarded this disaster, and the Universe felt at the sight, I cannot tell. I know not but tears fell like raindrops from angelic eyes when they saw Christ spit upon and struck. I know not but there was silence on high for *more* than "half an hour" when the scene of the crucifixion was transpiring [a scene, as well as an event, always "transpires" with Mr. Headley], a silence unbroken save by the solitary sound of some harp string on which unconsciously fell the agitated, trembling fingers of a seraph. I know not but all the radiant ranks on high, and even Gabriel himself, turned with the deepest solicitude to the Father's face, to see if He was calm and untroubled amid it all. I know not but His composed brow and serene majesty were all that restrained Heaven from one universal shriek of horror when they heard groans on Calvary—*dying* groans. I know not but they thought God had given His glory to another, but one thing I *do* know [Ah, there *is* really one thing Mr. Headley knows!]—that when they saw through the vast design, comprehended the stupendous scene, the hills of God shook to a shout that never before rung over their bright tops, and the crystal sea trembled to a song that had never before stirred its bright depths, and the "Glory to God in the Highest" was a sevenfold chorus of hallelujahs and harping symphonies.

Here we have direct evidence of Mr. Headley's accuracy not less than of his eloquence. "I know not but that" one is as vast as the other. The one thing that he does know he knows to perfection:—he knows not only what the chorus was (it was one of "hallelujahs and harping symphonies") but also how much of it there was—it was a "sevenfold chorus." **Mr. Headley** is a mathematical man. Moreover, he is a modest man; for he confesses (no doubt with tears in his eyes) that really there is one thing that he does not know. "How Heaven regarded this disaster, and the Universe felt at the sight, I cannot tell." Only think of that! *I* cannot!—*I*, Headley, really cannot tell how the Universe "felt" once upon a time! This is downright bashfulness on the part of Mr. Headley. He *could* tell if he would only try. Why did he not inquire? Had he demanded of the Universe how it felt, can anyone doubt that the answer would have been— "Pretty well, I thank you, my dear Headley; how do you feel yourself?"

"Quack" is a word that sounds well only in the mouth of a duck; and upon our honor we feel a scruple in using it:— nevertheless the truth should be told; and the simple fact is, that the author of *The Sacred Mountains* is the Autocrat of all the Quacks. In saying this, we beg not to be misunderstood. We mean no disparagement to Mr. Headley. We admire that gentleman as much as any individual ever did except that gentleman himself. He looks remarkably well at all points—although perhaps best, ἑκάς—at a distance—as the lying Pindar says he saw Archilochus, who died ages before the vagabond was born:—the reader will excuse the digression; but talking of one great man is very apt to put us in mind of another. We were saying—were we not?—that Mr. Headley is by no means to be sneered at as a quack. This might be justifiable, indeed, were he only a quack in a small way—a quack doing business by retail. But the wholesale dealer is entitled to respect. Besides, the Reverend author of *Napoleon and his Marshals* was a quack to some purpose. He knows what he is about. We like perfection wherever we see it. We readily forgive a man for being a fool if he only be a *perfect* fool—and this is a particular in which we cannot put our hands upon our hearts and say that Mr. Headley is deficient. He acts upon the principle that if a thing is worth doing at all it is worth doing well:—and the thing that he "does" especially well is the public.

THIS ELOQUENT ESSAY by Melville on Hawthorne appeared
in a weekly called *The Literary World* for August 17 and
August 24, 1850.

Melville has of course, for the purposes of his essay, assumed a fictitious character. He was not a Southerner but
a New Yorker. In the autumn of 1850, he bought a house
in the Berkshires near Lenox, where Hawthorne was already
living. Hawthorne was working on *The House of Seven
Gables,* and he had published *The Scarlet Letter* that April
—so that it is perhaps a little strange that Melville should
declare that *Mosses from an Old Manse,* published in 1846,
would be "ultimately accounted his masterpiece." Melville
had started *Moby Dick* in the latter part of the summer of
1850 and, working with terrific intensity, finished it the
following summer. His remarks about Shakespeare, thus
uttered on the brink of his own great moment of creative
energy, must have been inspired by his sense of his own
genius rather than by any clear perception of the quality of
Hawthorne's.

He seems to have laid siege to his neighbor, tried to carry
Hawthorne along with him into his own world of fierce frus-

trations and apocalyptic visions; and Hawthorne, who was fifteen years the older, seems to have let Melville dash past him as he did many other things. The story is that the two men at first were rather shy of one another till they had been driven one day by a thunderstorm to take shelter under the same rocks. They saw thereafter a good deal of one another. Mr. Raymond M. Weaver, the biographer of Melville, regards this relationship as a tragedy for Melville; but, though it is true that Melville hardly found in Hawthorne the ideal companion he desired and seems usually to be in the position of seeking out the more recessive man, they evidently had some good evenings "that lasted pretty deep into the night," during which they drank cider or brandy and talked "about time and eternity," as Hawthorne says of one such occasion, "things of this world and of the next, and books, and publishers, and all possible and impossible matters." Julian Hawthorne tells a story of a visit Melville paid them one evening, in the course of which he entertained them with an account of a fight between some natives that he had seen in the South Seas. The next day Hawthorne inquired of his wife: "Where is that club with which Mr. Melville was laying about him so?" Hawthorne thought that Melville had taken it home; Mrs. Hawthorne thought he had put it in a corner. But there had never been a club.

It will be noted that Melville here, in his enthusiasm for native literature and no doubt in the pride of his own genius, recommends a policy the opposite of Poe's and one which it would always have been dangerous to follow: "Let America first praise mediocrity even, in her children, before she praises . . . the best excellence in the children of other lands."

HERMAN MELVILLE

HAWTHORNE AND HIS *MOSSES*
By a Virginian Spending July in Vermont

A PAPERED CHAMBER in a fine old farmhouse, a mile from any other dwelling, and dipped to the eaves in foliage—surrounded by mountains, old woods, and Indian pools, —this, surely, is the place to write of Hawthorne. Some charm is in this northern air, for love and duty seem both impelling to the task. A man of a deep and noble nature has seized me in this seclusion. His wild witch voice rings through me; or, in softer cadences, I seem to hear it in the songs of the hillside birds that sing in the larch trees at my window.

Would that all excellent books were foundlings, without father or mother, that so it might be we could glorify them, without including their ostensible authors! Nor would any true man take exception to this; least of all, he who writes, "When the artist rises high enough to achieve the beautiful, the symbol by which he makes it perceptible to mortal senses becomes of little value in his eyes, while his spirit possesses itself in the enjoyment of the reality."

But more than this. I know not what would be the right name to put on the title page of an excellent book; but this I feel, that the names of all fine authors are fictitious ones, far more so than that of Junius; simply standing, as they do, for the mystical, ever-eluding spirit of all beauty, which ubiquitously possesses men of genius. Purely imaginative as this fancy may appear, it nevertheless seems to receive some warranty from the fact that on a personal interview no great author has ever come up to the idea of his reader. But that dust of which our bodies are composed, how can it fitly express the nobler intelligences among us? With reverence be it spoken, that not even in the case of one deemed more than man, not even in our Savior, did his visible frame betoken anything of the augustness of the nature within. Else, how could those Jewish eyewitnesses fail to see heaven in his glance!

It is curious how a man may travel along a country road, and yet miss the grandest or sweetest of prospects by reason of an intervening hedge, so like all other hedges, as in no way to hint of the wide landscape beyond. So has it been with me concerning the enchanting landscape in the soul of this Hawthorne, this most excellent Man of Mosses. His *Old Manse* has been written now four years, but I never read it till a day or two since. I had seen it in the bookstores —heard of it often—even had it recommended to me by a tasteful friend, as a rare, quiet book, perhaps too deserving of popularity to be popular. But there are so many books called "excellent," and so much unpopular merit, that amid the thick stir of other things, the hint of my tasteful friend was disregarded, and for four years the *Mosses on the Old Manse* never refreshed me with their perennial green. It may be, however, that all this while the book, likewise, was only improving in flavor and body. At any rate, it so chanced that this long procrastination eventuated in a happy result. At breakfast the other day, a mountain girl, a cousin of mine, who for the last two weeks has every morning helped me to strawberries and raspberries, which, like the roses and pearls in the fairy tale, seemed to fall into the saucer from those strawberry beds, her cheeks—this delightful creature, this charming Cherry says to me—"I see you spend your mornings in the haymow; and yesterday I found there Dwight's *Travels in New England*. Now I have something far better than that, something more congenial to our summer on these hills. Take these raspberries, and then I will give you some moss." "Moss!" said I. "Yes, and you must take it to the barn with you, and good-by to Dwight."

With that she left me, and soon returned with a volume, verdantly bound, and garnished with a curious frontispiece in green; nothing less than a fragment of real moss, cunningly pressed to a fly-leaf. "Why, this," said I, spilling my raspberries, "this is the *Mosses from an Old Manse.*" "Yes," said Cousin Cherry, "Yes, it is that flowery Hawthorne." "Hawthorne and Mosses," said I, "no more it is morning: it is July in the country: and I am off for the barn."

Stretched on that new-mown clover, the hillside breeze blowing over me through the wide barn door, and soothed by the hum of the bees in the meadows around, how magically stole over me this Mossy Man! and how amply, how bountifully, did he redeem that delicious promise to his guests in the Old Manse, of whom it is written: "Others could give them pleasure, or amusement, or instruction— these could be picked up anywhere; but it was for me to give them rest—rest, in a life of trouble! What better could be done for those weary and world-worn spirits? . . . what better could be done for anybody who came within our magic circle than to throw the spell of a tranquil spirit over him?" So all that day, half buried in the new clover, I watched this Hawthorne's "Assyrian dawn, and Paphian sunset and moonrise from the summit of our eastern hill."

The soft ravishments of the man spun me round about in a web of dreams, and when the book was closed, when the spell was over, this wizard "dismissed me with but misty reminiscences, as if I had been dreaming of him."

What a wild moonlight of contemplative humor bathes that Old Manse!—the rich and rare distilment of a spicy and slowly-oozing heart. No rollicking rudeness, no gross fun fed on fat dinners, and bred in the lees of wine,—but a humor so spiritually gentle, so high, so deep, and yet so richly relishable, that it were hardly inappropriate in an angel. It is the very religion of mirth; for nothing so human but it may be advanced to that. The orchard of the Old Manse seems the visible type of the fine mind that has described it—those twisted and contorted old trees, "they stretch out their crooked branches, and take such hold of the imagination that we remember them as humorists and odd-fellows." And then, as surrounded by these grotesque forms, and hushed in the noonday repose of this Hawthorne's spell, how aptly might the still fall of his ruddy thoughts into your soul be symbolized by: "In the stillest afternoon, if I listened, the thump of a great apple was audible, falling without a breath of wind, from the mere necessity of perfect ripeness." For no less ripe than ruddy are the apples of the thoughts and fancies in this sweet Man of Mosses.

Buds and Bird Voices. What a delicious thing is that! "Will the world ever be so decayed, that spring may not renew its greenness?" And the *Fire Worship.* Was ever the hearth so glorified into an altar before? The mere title of that piece is better than any common work in fifty folio volumes. How exquisite is this: "Nor did it lessen the charm of his soft, familiar courtesy and helpfulness that the mighty spirit, were opportunity offered him, would run riot through the peaceful house, wrap its inmates in his terrible embrace, and leave nothing of them save their whitened bones. This possibility of mad destruction only made his domestic kindness the more beautiful and touching. It was so sweet of him, being endowed with such power, to dwell day after day, and one long lonesome night after another, on the dusky hearth, only now and then betraying his wild nature by thrusting his red tongue out of the chimney top! True, he had done much mischief in the world, and was pretty certain to do more; but his warm heart atoned for all. He was kindly to the race of man; and they pardoned his characteristic imperfections."

But he has still other apples, not quite so ruddy, though full as ripe: apples that have been left to wither on the tree, after the pleasant autumn gathering is past. The sketch of *The Old Apple Dealer* is conceived in the subtlest spirit of sadness; he whose "subdued and nerveless boyhood prefigured his abortive prime, which likewise contained within itself the prophecy and image of his lean and torpid age." Such touches as are in this piece cannot proceed from any common heart. They argue such a depth of tenderness, such a boundless sympathy with all forms of being, such an omnipresent love, that we must needs say that this Hawthorne is here almost alone in his generation—at least, in the artistic manifestation of these things. Still more. Such touches as these—and many, very many similar ones, all through his chapters—furnish clues whereby we enter a little way into the intricate, profound heart where they originated. And we see that suffering, sometime or other, and in some shape or other—this only can enable any man to depict it in others. All over him, Hawthorne's melancholy rests like an Indian summer, which, though bathing a whole country in one softness, still reveals the distinctive hue of every towering hill and each far-winding vale.

But it is the least part of genius that attracts admiration. Where Hawthorne is known, he seems to be deemed a pleasant writer, with a pleasant style,—a sequestered, harmless man, from whom any deep and weighty thing would hardly be anticipated—a man who means no meanings. But there is no man in whom humor and love, like mountain peaks, soar to such a rapt height as to receive the irradiations of the upper skies; there is no man in whom humor and love are developed in that high form called genius; no such man can exist without also possessing, as the indispensable complement of these, a great, deep intellect, which drops down into the universe like a plummet. Or, love and humor are only the eyes through which such an intellect views this world. The great beauty in such a mind is but the product of its strength. What, to all readers, can be more charming than the piece entitled *Monsieur du Miroir;* and to a reader at all capable of fully fathoming it, what, at the same time, can possess more mystical depth of meaning?—yes, there he sits and looks at me—this "shape of mystery," this "identical MONSIEUR DU MIROIR!" "Methinks I should tremble now were his wizard power of gliding through all impediments in search of me to place him suddenly before my eyes."

How profound, nay, appalling, is the moral evolved by the *Earth's Holocaust;* where—beginning with the hollow follies and affectations of the world—all vanities and empty theories and forms are, one after another, and by an admirably graduated, growing comprehensiveness, thrown into the allegorical fire, till, at length, nothing is left but the all-engendering heart of man; which remaining still unconsumed, the great conflagration is naught.

Of a piece with this is the *Intelligence Office,* a wondrous symbolizing of the secret workings in men's souls. There are other sketches still more charged with ponderous import.

The Christmas Banquet and *The Bosom Serpent* would be fine subjects for a curious and elaborate analysis, touching the conjectural parts of the mind that produced them. For spite of all the Indian-summer sunlight on the hither side of Hawthorne's soul, the other side—like the dark half of the physical sphere—is shrouded in a blackness, ten times black. But this darkness but gives more effect to the ever-moving dawn, that forever advances through it, and circumnavigates his world. Whether Hawthorne has simply availed himself of this mystical blackness as a means to the wondrous effects he makes it to produce in his lights and shades; or whether there really lurks in him, perhaps unknown to himself, a touch of Puritanic gloom,—this, I cannot altogether tell. Certain it is, however, that this great power of blackness in him derives its force from its appeals to that Calvinistic sense of Innate Depravity and Original Sin, from whose visitations, in some shape or other, no deeply thinking mind is always and wholly free. For, in certain moods, no man can weigh this world without throwing in something, somehow like Original Sin, to strike the uneven balance. At all events, perhaps no writer has ever wielded this terrific thought with greater terror than this same harmless Hawthorne. Still more: this black conceit pervades him through and through. You may be witched by his sunlight—transported by the bright gildings in the skies he builds over you; but there is the blackness of darkness beyond; and even his bright gildings but fringe and play upon the edges of thunder-clouds. In one word, the world is mistaken in this Nathaniel Hawthorne. He himself must often have smiled at its absurd misconception of him. He is immeasurably deeper than the plummet of the mere critic. For it is not

the brain that can test such a man; it is only the heart. You
cannot come to know greatness by inspecting it; there is no
glimpse to be caught of it, except by intuition; you need not
ring it, you but touch it, and you find it is gold.

Now, it is that blackness in Hawthorne, of which I have
spoken, that so fixes and fascinates me. It may be, nevertheless, that it is too largely developed in him. Perhaps he does
not give us a ray of light for every shade of his dark. But
however this may be, this blackness it is that furnishes the
infinite obscure of his background—that background against
which Shakespeare plays his grandest conceits, the things
that have made for Shakespeare his loftiest but most circum-
scribed renown, as the profoundest of thinkers. For by
philosophers Shakespeare is not adored, as the great man of
tragedy and comedy: "Off with his head; so much for Buck-
ingham!" This sort of rant, interlined by another hand,
brings down the house—those mistaken souls, who dream
of Shakespeare as a mere man of Richard the Third humps
and Macbeth daggers. But it is those deep, far-away things
in him; those occasional flashings-forth of the intuitive Truth
in him; those short, quick probings at the very axis of reality,
—these are the things that make Shakespeare, Shakespeare.
Through the mouths of the dark characters of Hamlet,
Timon, Lear, and Iago, he craftily says, or sometimes insin-
uates the things which we feel to be so terrifically true that
it were all but madness for any good man, in his own proper
character, to utter, or even hint of them. Tormented into
desperation, Lear, the frantic king, tears off the mask, and
speaks the same madness of vital truth. But, as I before said,
it is the least part of genius that attracts admiration. And
so, much of the blind, unbridled admiration that has been
heaped upon Shakespeare has been lavished upon the least
part of him. And few of his endless commentators and critics
seem to have remembered, or even perceived, that the immediate products of a great mind are not so great as that undeveloped and sometimes undevelopable yet dimly-
discernible greatness to which those immediate products are
but the infallible indices. In Shakespeare's tomb lies infinitely more than Shakespeare ever wrote. And if I magnify

Shakespeare, it is not so much for what he did do as for what he did not do, or refrained from doing. For in this world of lies, Truth is forced to fly like a sacred white doe in the woodlands; and only by cunning glimpses will she reveal herself, as in Shakespeare and other masters of the great Art of Telling the Truth, even though it be covertly and by snatches.

But if this view of the all-popular Shakespeare be seldom taken by his readers, and if very few who extol him have ever read him deeply, or, perhaps, only have seen him on the tricky stage (which alone made, and is still making him, his mere mob renown)—if few men have time, or patience, or palate, for the spiritual truth as it is in that great genius—it is then no matter of surprise that in a contemporaneous age Nathaniel Hawthorne is a man as yet almost utterly mistaken among men. Here and there, in some quiet armchair in the noisy town, or some deep nook among the noiseless mountains, he may be appreciated for something of what he is. But unlike Shakespeare, who was forced to the contrary course by circumstances, Hawthorne (either from simple disinclination, or else from inaptitude) refrains from all the popularizing noise and show of broad farce and blood-besmeared tragedy; content with the still, rich utterance of a great intellect in repose, and which sends few thoughts into circulation, except they be arterialized at his large warm lungs, and expanded in his honest heart.

Nor need you fix upon that blackness in him, if it suit you not. Nor, indeed, will all readers discern it; for it is, mostly, insinuated to those who may best understand it, and account for it; it is not obtruded upon everyone alike.

Some may start to read of Shakespeare and Hawthorne on the same page. They may say that if an illustration were needed, a lesser light might have sufficed to elucidate this Hawthorne, this small man of yesterday. But I am not willingly one of those who, as touching Shakespeare at least, exemplify the maxim of Rochefoucauld, that "we exalt the reputation of some, in order to depress that of others"—who, to teach all noble-souled aspirants that there is no hope for them, pronounce Shakespeare absolutely unapproachable. But Shakespeare has been approached. There are minds that

have gone as far as Shakespeare into the universe. And
hardly a mortal man, who, at some time or other, has not felt
as great thoughts in him as any you will find in Hamlet. We
must not inferentially malign mankind for the sake of any
one man, whoever he may be. This is too cheap a purchase
of contentment for conscious mediocrity to make. Besides,
this absolute and unconditional adoration of Shakespeare
has grown to be a part of our Anglo-Saxon superstitions. The
Thirty-Nine Articles are now forty. Intolerance has come to
exist in this matter. You must believe in Shakespeare's un-
approachability, or quit the country. But what sort of a
belief is this for an American, a man who is bound to carry
republican progressiveness into Literature as well as into
Life? Believe me, my friends, that men not very much inferior to Shakespeare are this day being born on the banks
of the Ohio. And the day will come when you shall say,
Who reads a book by an Englishman that is a modern? The
great mistake seems to be, that even with those Americans
who look forward to the coming of a great literary genius
among us, they somehow fancy he will come in the costume
of Queen Elizabeth's day; be a writer of dramas founded
upon old English history or the tales of Boccaccio. Whereas,
great geniuses are parts of the times, they themselves are the
times, and possess a corresponding coloring. It is of a piece
with the Jews, who, while their Shiloh was meekly walking
in their streets, were still praying for his magnificent coming; looking for him in a chariot, who was already among
them on an ass. Nor must we forget that, in his own lifetime, Shakepeare was not Shakespeare, but only Master
William Shakespeare of the shrewd, thriving business firm
of Condell, Shakespeare and Co., proprietors of the Globe
Theater in London; and by a courtly author, of the name
of Chettle, was looked at as an "upstart crow," beautified
"with other birds' feathers." For, mark it well, imitation is
often the first charge brought against originality. Why this
is so, there is not space to set forth here. You must have
plenty of sea-room to tell the Truth in; especially when it
seems to have an aspect of newness, as America did in 1492,
though it was then just as old, and perhaps older than Asia,

only those sagacious philosophers, the common sailors, had never seen it before, swearing it was all water and moonshine there.

Now I do not say that Nathaniel of Salem is a greater man than William of Avon, or as great. But the difference between the two men is by no means immeasurable. Not a very great deal more, and Nathaniel were verily William.

This, too, I mean: that if Shakespeare has not been equaled, give the world time, and he is sure to be surpassed in one hemisphere or the other. Nor will it at all do to say that the world is getting gray and grizzled now, and has lost that fresh charm which she wore of old, and by virtue of which the great poets of past times made themselves what we esteem them to be. Not so. The world is as young today as when it was created; and this Vermont morning dew is as wet to my feet as Eden's dew to Adam's. Nor has nature been all over ransacked by our progenitors, so that no new charms and mysteries remain for this latter generation to find. Far from it. The trillionth part has not yet been said; and all that has been said but multiplies the avenues to what remains to be said. It is not so much paucity as superabundance of material that seems to incapacitate modern authors.

Let America, then, prize and cherish her writers; yea, let her glorify them. They are not so many in number as to exhaust her goodwill. And while she has good kith and kin of her own to take to her bosom, let her not lavish her embraces upon the household of an alien. For believe it or not, England, after all, is in many things an alien to us. China has more bonds of real love for us than she. But even were there no strong literary individualities among us, as there are some dozens at least, nevertheless, let America first praise mediocrity even, in her children, before she praises (for everywhere, merit demands acknowledgment from everyone) the best excellence in the children of any other land. Let her own authors, I say, have the priority of appreciation. I was much pleased with a hot-headed Carolina cousin of mine, who once said, "If there were no other American to stand by, in literature, why, then, I would stand by Pop Emmons and his

Fredoniad, and till a better epic came along, swear it was not very far behind the *Iliad.*" Take away the words, and in spirit he was sound.

Not that American genius needs patronage in order to expand. For that explosive sort of stuff will expand though screwed up in a vise, and burst it, though it were triple steel. It is for the nation's sake, and not for her authors' sake, that I would have America be heedful of the increasing greatness among her writers. For how great the shame, if other nations should be before her, in crowning her heroes of the pen! But this is almost the case now. American authors have received more just and discriminating praise (however loftily and ridiculously given, in certain cases) even from some Englishmen, than from their own countrymen. There are hardly five critics in America; and several of them are asleep. As for patronage, it is the American author who now patronizes his country, and not his country him. And if at times some among them appeal to the people for more recognition, it is not always with selfish motives, but patriotic ones.

It is true that but few of them as yet have evinced that decided originality which merits great praise. But that graceful writer who perhaps of all Americans has received the most plaudits from his own country for his productions—that very popular and amiable writer, however good and self-reliant in many things, perhaps owes his chief reputation to the self-acknowledged imitation of a foreign model, and to the studied avoidance of all topics but smooth ones.[1] But it is better to fail in originality than to succeed in imitation. He who has never failed somewhere, that man cannot be great. Failure is the true test of greatness. And if it be said that continual success is a proof that a man wisely knows his powers, it is only to be added that, in that case, he knows them to be small. Let us believe it, then, once for all, that there is no hope for us in these smooth, pleasing writers that know their powers. Without malice, but to speak the plain fact, they but furnish an appendix to Goldsmith and other English authors. And we want no American Goldsmiths,

[1]Washington Irving. E. W.

nay, we want no American Miltons. It were the vilest thing
you could say of a true American author that he were an
American Tompkins. Call him an American and have done,
for you cannot say a nobler thing of him. But it is not meant
that all American writers should studiously cleave to nationality in their writings; only this, no American writer
should write like an Englishman or a Frenchman; let him
write like a man, for then he will be sure to write like an
American. Let us away with this leaven of literary flunkey-
ism toward England. If either must play the flunkey in this
thing, let England do it, not us. While we are rapidly preparing for that political supremacy among the nations which
prophetically awaits us at the close of the present century,
in a literary point of view, we are deplorably unprepared for
it; and we seem studious to remain so. Hitherto, reasons
might have existed why this should be; but no good reason
exists now. And all that is requisite to amendment in this
matter is simply this: that while fully acknowledging all
excellence everywhere, we should refrain from unduly lauding foreign writers, and, at the same time, duly recognize the
meritorious writers that are our own; those writers who
breathe that unshackled, democratic spirit of Christianity in
all things, which now takes the practical lead in this world,
though at the same time led by ourselves—us Americans.
Let us boldly condemn all imitation, though it comes to us
graceful and fragrant as the morning; and foster all originality, though at first it be crabbed and ugly as our own
pine knots. And if any of our authors fail, or seem to fail,
then, in the words of my Carolina cousin, let us clap him on
the shoulder and back him against all Europe for his second
round. The truth is, that in one point of view this matter of
a national literature has come to such a pass with us, that in
some sense we must turn bullies, else the day is lost, or
superiority so far beyond us, that we can hardly say it will
ever be ours.

And now, my countrymen, as an excellent author of your
own flesh and blood—an unimitating, and, perhaps, in his
way, an inimitable man—whom better can I commend to
you, in the first place, than Nathaniel Hawthorne? He is

one of the new, and far better generation of your writers. The smell of young beeches and hemlocks is upon him; your own broad prairies are in his soul; and if you travel away inland into his deep and noble nature, you will hear the far roar of his Niagara. Give not over to future generations the glad duty of acknowledging him for what he is. Take that joy to yourself, in your own generation; and so shall he feel those grateful impulses on him, that may possibly prompt him to the full flower of some still greater achievement in your eyes. And by confessing him you thereby confess others; you brace the whole brotherhood. For genius, all over the world, stands hand in hand, and one shock of recognition runs the whole circle round.

In treating of Hawthorne, or rather of Hawthorne in his writings (for I never saw the man; and in the chances of a quiet plantation life, remote from his haunts, perhaps never shall); in treating of his works, I say, I have thus far omitted all mention of his *Twice-Told Tales* and *Scarlet Letter*. Both are excellent, but full of such manifold, strange, and diffusive beauties, that time would all but fail me to point the half of them out. But there are things in those two books which, had they been written in England a century ago, Nathaniel Hawthorne had utterly displaced many of the bright names we now revere on authority. But I am content to leave Hawthorne to himself, and to the infallible finding of posterity; and however great may be the praise I have bestowed upon him, I feel that in so doing I have served and honored myself, rather than him. For, at bottom, great excellence is praise enough to itself; but the feeling of a sincere and appreciative love and admiration toward it, this is relieved by utterance, and warm, honest praise ever leaves a pleasant flavor in the mouth; and it is an honorable thing to confess to what is honorable in others.

But I cannot leave my subject yet. No man can read a fine author, and relish him to his very bones while he reads, without subsequently fancying to himself some ideal image of the man and his mind. And if you rightly look for it, you will almost always find that the author himself has somewhere furnished you with his own picture. For poets (whether in prose or verse), being painters by nature, are like their brethren of the pencil, the true portrait-painters, who, in the multitude of likenesses to be sketched, do not invariably omit their own; and in all high instances, they paint them without any vanity, though at times with a lurking something that would take several pages to properly define.

I submit it, then, to those best acquainted with the man personally, whether the following is not Nathaniel Hawthorne; and to himself, whether something involved in it does not express the temper of his mind—that lasting temper of all true, candid men—a seeker, not a finder yet:

A man now entered, in neglected attire, with the aspect of a thinker, but somewhat too roughhewn and brawny for a scholar. His face was full of sturdy vigor, with some finer and keener attribute beneath; though harsh at first, it was tempered with the glow of a large, warm heart, which had force enough to heat his powerful intellect through and through. He advanced to the Intelligencer, and looked at him with a glance of such stern sincerity, that perhaps few secrets were beyond its scope.

"I seek for Truth," said he.

Twenty-four hours have elapsed since writing the foregoing. I have just returned from the haymow, charged more and more with love and admiration of Hawthorne. For I have just been gleaning through the *Mosses,* picking up many things here and there that had previously escaped me. And I found that but to glean after this man is better than to be in at the harvest of others. To be frank (though, perhaps, rather foolish), notwithstanding what I wrote yesterday of these *Mosses,* I had not then culled them all; but had, nevertheless, been sufficiently sensible of the subtle essence in them as to write as I did. To what infinite height of loving wonder and admiration I may yet be borne, when by repeatedly banqueting on these *Mosses* I shall have thoroughly incorporated their whole stuff into my being— that, I cannot tell. But already I feel that this Hawthorne has dropped germinous seeds into my soul. He expands and deepens down, the more I contemplate him; and further and

further, shoots his strong New England roots into the hot
soil in my Southern soul.

By careful reference to the table of contents, I now find
that I have gone through all the sketches; but that when I
yesterday wrote, I had not at all read two particular pieces,
to which I now desire to call special attention—*A Select
Party* and *Young Goodman Brown*. Here, be it said to all
those whom this poor fugitive scrawl of mine may tempt to
the perusal of the *Mosses*, that they must on no account
suffer themselves to be trifled with, disappointed, or deceived by the triviality of many of the titles to these sketches.
For in more than one instance the title utterly belies the
piece. It is as if rustic demijohns containing the very best
and costliest of Falernian and Tokay were labeled "Cider,"
"Perry," and "Elderberry wine." The truth seems to be, that
like many other geniuses, this Man of Mosses takes great
delight in hoodwinking the world—at least, with respect to
himself. Personally, I doubt not that he rather prefers to be
generally esteemed but a so-so sort of author; being willing
to reserve the thorough and acute appreciation of what he
is, to that party most qualified to judge—that is, to himself.
Besides, at the bottom of their natures, men like Hawthorne,
in many things, deem the plaudits of the public such strong
presumptive evidence of mediocrity in the object of them,
that it would in some degree render them doubtful of their
own powers did they hear much and vociferous braying concerning them in the public pastures. True, I have been
braying myself (if you please to be witty enough to have
it so), but then I claim to be the first that has so brayed in
this particular matter; and, therefore, while pleading guilty
to the charge, still claim all the merit due to originality.

But with whatever motive, playful or profound, Nathaniel
Hawthorne has chosen to entitle his pieces in the manner
he has, it is certain that some of them are directly calculated
to deceive—egregiously deceive, the superficial skimmer of
pages. To be downright and candid once more, let me cheerfully say that two of these titles did dolefully dupe no less
an eager-eyed reader than myself; and that, too, after I had
been impressed with a sense of the great depth and breadth

of this American man. "Who in the name of thunder" (as the country people say in this neighborhood), "who in the name of thunder would anticipate any marvel in a piece entitled *Young Goodman Brown?*" You would, of course, suppose that it was a simple little tale, intended as a supplement to *Goody Two Shoes*. Whereas, it is deep as Dante; nor can you finish it without addressing the author in his own words—"It shall be yours to penetrate, in every bosom, the deep mystery of sin." . . . And with Young Goodman, too, in allegorical pursuit of his Puritan wife, you cry out in your anguish:

"Faith!" shouted Goodman Brown, in a voice of agony and desperation; and the echoes of the forest mocked him, crying, "Faith! Faith!" as if bewildered wretches were seeking her all through the wilderness.

Now this same piece entitled *Young Goodman Brown* is one of the two that I had not all read yesterday; and I allude to it now, because it is, in itself, such a strong, positive illustration of the blackness in Hawthorne which I had assumed from the mere occasional shadows of it, as revealed in several of the other sketches. But had I previously perused *Young Goodman Brown*, I should have been at no pains to draw the conclusion, which I came to at a time when I was ignorant that the book contained one such direct and un-qualified manifestation of it.

The other piece of the two referred to is entitled *A Select Party*, which, in my first simplicity upon originally taking hold of the book, I fancied must treat of some pumpkin-pie party in old Salem; or some chowder party on Cape Cod. Whereas, by all the gods of Peedee, it is the sweetest and sublimest thing that has been written since Spenser wrote. Nay, there is nothing in Spenser that surpasses it, perhaps nothing that equals it. And the test is this. Read any canto in *The Faerie Queene* and then read *A Select Party*, and decide which pleases you most, that is, if you are qualified to judge. Do not be frightened at this; for when Spenser was alive, he was thought of very much as Hawthorne is now—was generally accounted just such a "gentle," harmless

man. It may be that to common eyes the sublimity of Hawthorne seems lost in his sweetness,—as perhaps in that same
Select Party of his; for whom he has builded so august a
dome of sunset clouds, and served them on richer plate
than Belshazzar when he banqueted his lords in Babylon.

But my chief business now is to point out a particular
page in this piece, having reference to an honored guest,
who under the name of the Master Genius but in the guise
"of a young man of poor attire, with no insignia of rank or
acknowledged eminence," is introduced to the Man of Fancy,
who is the giver of the feast. Now, the page having reference to this Master Genius so happily expresses much of
what I yesterday wrote, touching the coming of the literary
Shiloh of America, that I cannot but be charmed by the
coincidence; especially when it shows such a parity of ideas,
at least in this one point, between a man like Hawthorne
and a man like me.

And here let me throw out another conceit of mine touching this American Shiloh, or Master Genius, as Hawthorne
calls him. May it not be that this commanding mind has
not been, is not, and never will be, individually developed
in any one man? And would it, indeed, appear so unreasonable to suppose that this great fullness and overflowing
may be, or may be destined to be, shared by a plurality of
men of genius? Surely, to take the very greatest example
on record, Shakespeare cannot be regarded as in himself the
concretion of all the genius of his time; nor as so immeasurably beyond Marlowe, Webster, Ford, Beaumont, Jonson,
that these great men can be said to share none of his power?
For one, I conceive that there were dramatists in Elizabeth's
day, between whom and Shakespeare the distance was by
no means great. Let anyone, hitherto little acquainted with
those neglected old authors, for the first time read them
thoroughly, or even read Charles Lamb's *Specimens* of them,
and he will be amazed at the wondrous ability of those
Anaks of men, and shocked at this renewed example of the
fact that Fortune has more to do with fame than merit,—
though without merit, lasting fame there can be none.

Nevertheless, it would argue too ill of my country were

this maxim to hold good concerning Nathaniel Hawthorne, a man who already in some few minds has shed "such a light as never illuminates the earth save when a great heart burns as the household fire of a grand intellect."

The words are his—in the *Select Party;* and they are a magnificent setting to a coincident sentiment of my own, but ramblingly expressed yesterday, in reference to himself. Gainsay it who will, as I now write, I am Posterity speaking by proxy—and after-times will make it more than good, when I declare that the American who up to the present day has evinced, in literature, the largest brain with the largest heart, that man is Nathaniel Hawthorne. Moreover, that whatever Nathaniel Hawthorne may hereafter write, *Mosses from an Old Manse* will be ultimately accounted his masterpiece. For there is a sure, though secret sign in some works which proves the culmination of the powers (only the developable ones, however) that produced them. But I am by no means desirous of the glory of a prophet. I pray Heaven that Hawthorne may yet prove me an impostor in this prediction. Especially, as I somehow cling to the strange fancy that, in all men, hiddenly reside certain wondrous, occult properties—as in some plants and minerals—which by some happy but very rare accident (as bronze was discovered by the melting of the iron and brass at the burning of Corinth) may chance to be called forth here on earth; not entirely waiting for their better discovery in the more congenial, blessed atmosphere of heaven.

Once more—for it is hard to be finite upon an infinite subject, and all subjects are infinite. By some people this entire scrawl of mine may be esteemed altogether unnecessary, inasmuch "as years ago" (they may say) "we found out the rich and rare stuff in this Hawthorne, whom you now parade forth, as if only you *yourself* were the discoverer of this Portuguese diamond in your literature." But even granting all this—and adding to it the assumption that the books of Hawthorne have sold by the five thousand—what does that signify? They should be sold by the hundred thousand; and read by the million; and admired by every one who is capable of admiration.

HENRY DAVID THOREAU died in 1862, and both Emerson and Lowell wrote about him.

Emerson had read an address at Thoreau's funeral, and his essay is based on this. It came out in *The Atlantic Monthly* in the summer of 1863. Thoreau had been born in Concord, and Emerson, whose father's family came from Boston, went to live there when he was thirty-one. The two men were constant companions; and Thoreau, who was fourteen years the younger, became a sort of disciple of Emerson's.

In August 1837, in an oration called *The American Scholar* before the Phi Beta Kappa Society at Cambridge, Emerson had spoken as follows: "The scholar is that man who must take up into himself all the ability of the time, all the contributions of the past, all the hopes of the future. He must be an university of knowledges. If there be one lesson more than another which should pierce his ear, it is, The world is nothing, the man is all; in yourself is the law of all nature, and you know not yet how a globule of sap ascends; in yourself slumbers the whole of Reason; it is for you to know all; it is for you to dare all. Mr. President and Gentlemen, this confidence in the unsearched might of man belongs, by all motives, by all prophecy, by all preparation, to the American Scholar. We have listened too long to the courtly muses of Europe. The spirit of the American freeman is already suspected to be timid, imitative, tame. Public and private avarice make the air we breathe thick and fat. The scholar is decent, indolent, complaisant. See already the tragic consequence. The mind of this country, taught to aim at low objects, eats upon itself. There is no work for any but the decorous and the complaisant. Young men of the fairest promise, who begin life upon our shores, inflated by the mountain winds, shined upon by all the stars of God, find the earth below not in unison with these, but are hindered from action by the disgust which the principles on which business is managed inspire, and turn drudges, or die of disgust, some of them suicides. What is the remedy? They did not yet see, and thousands of young men as hopeful now crowding to the barriers for the career do not yet see, that if the single man plant himself indomitably on his instincts, and there abide, the huge world will come round to him. Patience—patience; with the shades of all the good and great for company; and for solace the perspective of your own infinite life; and for work the study and the communication of principles, the making those instincts prevalent, the conversion of the world. Is it not the chief disgrace in the world, not to be an unit; not to be reckoned one character; not to yield that peculiar fruit which each man was created to bear, but to be reckoned in the gross, in the hundred, or the thousand, of the party, the section, to which we belong; and our opinion predicted geographically, as the north, or the south? Not so, brothers and friends,—please God, ours shall not be so. We will walk on our own feet; we will work with our own hands; we will speak our own minds."

Thoreau's life and work were like an exemplification of this text. Alone at Walden Pond, in his hut, with his ax and his Indian meal, with his head full of Greek poetry and oriental wisdom, and in his heart the contempt of commercial New England, he lived and wrote *Walden*, the masterpiece of prose that Emerson lacked the concentration to make.

Lowell's essay was written in 1865, and it is written by a different Lowell from the author of the paper on Poe and the *Fable for Critics*. The change in Lowell has often been noted, and has been attributed to the death of his first wife in 1853. Maria White Lowell had herself been a poet, and it was she who had enlisted Lowell for the Abolitionist cause. Her death left him suddenly blank, in the discomfiting and dreary situation of living alone in Cambridge with the daughter who had been the only one of their children to survive. He employed as a governess a Boston lady who had some taste for literature but did not enjoy Lowell's humor, and a few years later married her. From being a young and brilliant journalist living in the center of things, he became a Harvard professor and later our minister to Spain and England. He grew more official and snobbish, complained much, after his return from England, about the way things were done in America. He had returned to live at Elmwood, the eighteenth-century house where he had been born; and Cambridge eventually closed over him.

We shall see his growing hostility to Whitman; and the tone of this paper on Thoreau is not merely grudging but surly. It is occupied almost entirely with jeering at the Transcendentalists in general and pointing out the limitations of Thoreau, and it would not be appropriate to include it here if it were not that just before the end the old frank and generous Lowell reasserts himself, rather startlingly after what has gone before, with the declaration that, after all, a master is a master; and goes on in the small margin he has left himself to pay Thoreau one of the aptest of tributes.

RALPH WALDO EMERSON

THOREAU

> A queen rejoices in her peers,
> And wary Nature knows her own,
> By court and city, dale and down,
> And like a lover volunteers,
> And to her son will treasures more,
> And more to purpose, freely pour
> In one wood walk, than learned men
> Will find with glass in ten times ten.
>
> It seemed as if the breezes brought him,
> It seemed as if the sparrows taught him,
> As if by secret sign he knew
> Where in far fields the orchis grew.

HENRY DAVID THOREAU was the last male descendant of a French ancestor who came to this country from the Isle of Guernsey. His character exhibited occasional traits drawn from this blood, in singular combination with a very strong Saxon genius.

He was born in Concord, Massachusetts, on the twelfth of July, 1817. He was graduated at Harvard College in 1837, but without any literary distinction. An iconoclast in literature, he seldom thanked colleges for their services to him, holding them in small esteem, whilst yet his debt to them was important. After leaving the University, he joined his brother in teaching a private school, which he soon renounced. His father was a manufacturer of lead pencils, and Henry applied himself for a time to this craft, believing he could make a better pencil than was then in use. After completing his experiments, he exhibited his work to chemists and artists in Boston, and having obtained their certificates to its excellence and to its equality with the best London manufacture, he returned home contented. His friends congratulated him that he had now opened his way to fortune. But he replied that he should never make another pencil. "Why should I? I would not do again what I have done once." He resumed his endless walks and miscellaneous studies, making every day some new acquaintance with Nature, though as yet never speaking of zoölogy or botany, since, though very studious of natural facts, he was incurious of technical and textual science.

At this time, a strong, healthy youth, fresh from college, whilst all his companions were choosing their profession, or eager to begin some lucrative employment, it was inevitable that his thoughts should be exercised on the same question, and it required rare decision to refuse all the accustomed paths and keep his solitary freedom at the cost of disappointing the natural expectations of his family and friends: all the more difficult that he had a perfect probity, was exact in securing his own independence, and in holding every man to the like duty. But Thoreau never faltered. He was a born protestant. He declined to give up his large ambition of knowledge and action for any narrow craft or profession, aiming at a much more comprehensive calling, the art of living well. If he slighted and defied the opinions of others, it was only that he was more intent to reconcile his practice with his own belief. Never idle or self-indulgent, he preferred, when he wanted money, earning it by some piece of manual labor agreeable to him, as building a boat or a fence, planting, grafting, surveying, or other short work, to any long engagements. With his hardy habits and few wants, his skill in woodcraft, and his powerful arithmetic, he was very competent to live in any part of the world. It would cost him less time to supply his wants than another. He was therefore secure of his leisure.

A natural skill for mensuration, growing out of his mathematical knowledge and his habit of ascertaining the measures and distances of objects which interested him, the size of trees, the depth and extent of ponds and rivers, the height of mountains, and the air-line distance of his favorite summits —this, and his intimate knowledge of the territory about Concord, made him drift into the profession of land surveyor. It had the advantage for him that it led him continually into new and secluded grounds, and helped his studies of Nature. His accuracy and skill in this work were readily appreciated, and he found all the employment he wanted.

He could easily solve the problems of the surveyor, but he was daily beset with graver questions, which he manfully confronted. He interrogated every custom, and wished to settle all his practice on an ideal foundation. He was a protestant *à outrance*, and few lives contain so many renunciations. He was bred to no profession; he never married; he lived alone; he never went to church; he never voted; he refused to pay a tax to the State; he ate no flesh, he drank no wine, he never knew the use of tobacco; and, though a naturalist, he used neither trap nor gun. He chose, wisely no doubt for himself, to be the bachelor of thought and Nature. He had no talent for wealth, and knew how to be poor without the least hint of squalor or inelegance. Perhaps he fell into his way of living without forecasting it much, but approved it with later wisdom. "I am often reminded," he wrote in his journal, "that if I had bestowed on me the wealth of Crœsus, my aims must be still the same, and my means essentially the same." He had no temptations to fight against—no appetites, no passions, no taste for elegant trifles. A fine house, dress, the manners and talk of highly cultivated people were all thrown away on him. He much preferred a good Indian, and considered these refinements as impediments to conversation, wishing to meet his companion on the simplest terms. He declined invitations to dinner parties, because there each was in everyone's way, and he could not meet the individuals to any purpose. "They make their pride," he said, "in making their dinner cost much; I make my pride in making my dinner cost little." When asked at table what dish he preferred, he answered, "The nearest." He did not like the taste of wine, and never had a vice in his life. He said, "I have a faint recollection of pleasure derived from smoking dried lily stems, before I was a man. I had commonly a supply of these. I have never smoked anything more noxious."

He chose to be rich by making his wants few, and supplying them himself. In his travels, he used the railroad only to get over so much country as was unimportant to the present purpose, walking hundreds of miles, avoiding taverns, buying a lodging in farmers' and fishermen's houses, as cheaper, and more agreeable to him, and because there he could better find the men and the information he wanted.

There was somewhat military in his nature, not to be subdued, always manly and able, but rarely tender, as if he did not feel himself except in opposition. He wanted a fallacy to expose, a blunder to pillory, I may say required a little sense of victory, a roll of the drum, to call his powers into full exercise. It cost him nothing to say No; indeed he found it much easier than to say Yes. It seemed as if his first instinct on hearing a proposition was to controvert it, so impatient was he of the limitations of our daily thought. This habit, of course, is a little chilling to the social affections; and though the companion would in the end acquit him of any malice or untruth, yet it mars conversation. Hence, no equal companion stood in affectionate relations with one so pure and guileless. "I love Henry," said one of his friends, "but I cannot like him; and as for taking his arm, I should as soon think of taking the arm of an elm tree."

Yet, hermit and stoic as he was, he was really fond of sympathy, and threw himself heartily and childlike into the company of young people whom he loved, and whom he delighted to entertain, as he only could, with the varied and endless anecdotes of his experiences by field and river; and he was always ready to lead a huckleberry party or a search for chestnuts or grapes. Talking, one day, of a public discourse, Henry remarked that whatever succeeded with the audience was bad. I said, "Who would not like to write something which all can read, like *Robinson Crusoe?* and who does not see with regret that his page is not solid with a right materialistic treatment which delights everybody?" Henry objected, of course, and vaunted the better lectures which reached only a few persons. But, at supper, a young girl, understanding that he was to lecture at the Lyceum, sharply asked him, "Whether his lecture would be a nice, interesting story, such as she wished to hear, or whether it was one of those old philosophical things that she did not care about." Henry turned to her, and bethought himself, and, I saw, was trying to believe that he had matter that might fit her and her brother, who were to sit up and go to the lecture, if it was a good one for them.

He was a speaker and actor of the truth, born such, and was ever running into dramatic situations from this cause. In any circumstance it interested all bystanders to know what part Henry would take, and what he would say; and he did not disappoint expectation, but used an original judgment on each emergency. In 1845 he built himself a small framed house on the shores of Walden Pond, and lived there two years alone, a life of labor and study. This action was quite native and fit for him. No one who knew him would tax him with affectation. He was more unlike his neighbors in his thought than in his action. As soon as he had exhausted the advantages of that solitude, he abandoned it. In 1847, not approving some uses to which the public expenditure was applied, he refused to pay his town tax, and was put in jail. A friend paid the tax for him, and he was released. The like annoyance was threatened the next year. But, as his friends paid the tax, notwithstanding his protest, I believe he ceased to resist. No opposition or ridicule had any weight with him. He coldly and fully stated his opinion without affecting to believe that it was the opinion of the company. It was of no consequence if everyone present held the opposite opinion.

On one occasion he went to the University Library to procure some books. The librarian refused to lend them. Mr.
Thoreau repaired to the President, who stated to him the
rules and usages, which permitted the loan of books to
resident graduates, to clergymen who were alumni, and to
some others resident within a circle of ten miles' radius from
the College. Mr. Thoreau explained to the President that
the railroad had destroyed the old scale of distances,—that the
library was useless, yes, and President and College useless,
on the terms of his rules,—that the one benefit he owed to the
College was its library,—that, at this moment, not only his
want of books was imperative but he wanted a large number
of books, and assured him that he, Thoreau, and not the
librarian, was the proper custodian of these. In short, the
President found the petitioner so formidable, and the rules
getting to look so ridiculous that he ended by giving him a
privilege which in his hands proved unlimited thereafter.

No truer American existed than Thoreau. His preference
of his country and condition was genuine, and his aversation
from English and European manners and tastes almost
reached contempt. He listened impatiently to news or *bon
mots* gleaned from London circles; and though he tried to be
civil, these anecdotes fatigued him. The men were all imitating each other, and on a small mold. Why can they not
live as far apart as possible, and each be a man by himself?
What he sought was the most energetic nature; and he
wished to go to Oregon, not to London. "In every part of
Great Britain," he wrote in his diary, "are discovered traces
of the Romans, their funereal urns, their camps, their roads,
their dwellings. But New England, at least, is not based on
any Roman ruins. We have not to lay the foundations of our
houses on the ashes of a former civilization."

But, idealist as he was, standing for abolition of slavery,
abolition of tariffs, almost for abolition of government, it is
needless to say he found himself not only unrepresented in
actual politics, but almost equally opposed to every class of
reformers. Yet he paid the tribute of his uniform respect to
the Anti-Slavery party. One man, whose personal acquaintance he had formed, he honored with exceptional regard.

Before the first friendly word had been spoken for Captain John Brown, he sent notices to most houses in Concord that he would speak in a public hall on the condition and character of John Brown, on Sunday evening, and invited all people to come. The Republican Committee, the Abolitionist Committee, sent him word that it was premature and not advisable. He replied, "I did not send to you for advice, but to announce that I am to speak." The hall was filled at an early hour by people of all parties, and his earnest eulogy of the hero was heard by all respectfully, by many with a sympathy that surprised themselves.

It was said of Plotinus that he was ashamed of his body, and 'tis very likely he had good reason for it,—that his body was a bad servant, and he had not skill in dealing with the material world, as happens often to men of abstract intellect. But Mr. Thoreau was equipped with a most adapted and serviceable body. He was of short stature, firmly built, of light complexion, with strong, serious blue eyes, and a grave aspect—his face covered in the late years with a becoming beard. His senses were acute, his frame well knit and hardy, his hands strong and skillful in the use of tools. And there was a wonderful fitness of body and mind. He could pace sixteen rods more accurately than another man could measure them with rod and chain. He could find his path in the woods at night, he said, better by his feet than his eyes. He could estimate the measure of a tree very well by his eye; he could estimate the weight of a calf or a pig, like a dealer. From a box containing a bushel or more of loose pencils, he could take up with his hands fast enough just a dozen pencils at every grasp. He was a good swimmer, runner, skater, boatman, and would probably outwalk most countrymen in a day's journey. And the relation of body to mind was still finer than we have indicated. He said he wanted every stride his legs made. The length of his walk uniformly made the length of his writing. If shut up in the house he did not write at all.

He had a strong common sense, like that which Rose Flammock the weaver's daughter in Scott's romance commends in her father, as resembling a yardstick, which, whilst

it measures dowlas and diaper, can equally well measure
tapestry and cloth of gold. He had always a new resource.
When I was planting forest trees, and had procured half a
peck of acorns, he said that only a small portion of them
would be sound, and proceeded to examine them and select
the sound ones. But finding this took time, he said, "I think
if you put them all into water the good ones will sink";
which experiment we tried with success. He could plan a
garden or a house or a barn; would have been competent to
lead a "Pacific Exploring Expedition"; could give judicious
counsel in the gravest private or public affairs.

He lived for the day, not cumbered and mortified by his
memory. If he brought you yesterday a new proposition, he
would bring you today another not less revolutionary. A very
industrious man, and setting, like all highly organized men,
a high value on his time, he seemed the only man of leisure
in town always ready for any excursion that promised well,
or for conversation prolonged into late hours. His trenchant
sense was never stopped by his rules of daily prudence, but
was always up to the new occasion. He liked and used the
simplest food, yet, when someone urged a vegetable diet,
Thoreau thought all diets a very small matter, saying that
"the man who shoots the buffalo lives better than the man
who boards at the Graham House." He said: "You can sleep
near the railroad, and never be disturbed: Nature knows
very well what sounds are worth attending to, and has made
up her mind not to hear the railroad whistle. But things
respect the devout mind, and a mental ecstasy was never
interrupted." He noted what repeatedly befell him, that,
after receiving from a distance a rare plant, he would presently find the same in his own haunts. And those pieces of
luck which happen only to good players happened to him.
One day, walking with a stranger, who inquired where
Indian arrowheads could be found, he replied, "Everywhere," and, stooping forward, picked one on the instant
from the ground. At Mount Washington, in Tuckerman's
Ravine, Thoreau had a bad fall, and sprained his foot. As
he was in the act of getting up from his fall, he saw for the
first time the leaves of the *Arnica mollis*.

His robust common sense, armed with stout hands, keen perceptions, and strong will, cannot yet account for the superiority which shone in his simple and hidden life. I must add the cardinal fact, that there was an excellent wisdom in him, proper to a rare class of men, which showed him the material world as a means and symbol. This discovery, which sometimes yields to poets a certain casual and interrupted light, serving for the ornament of their writing, was in him an unsleeping insight; and whatever faults or obstructions of temperament might cloud it, he was not disobedient to the heavenly vision. In his youth, he said, one day, "The other world is all my art; my pencils will draw no other; my jack-knife will cut nothing else; I do not use it as a means." This was the muse and genius that ruled his opinions, conversation, studies, work, and course of life. This made him a searching judge of men. At first glance he measured his companion, and, though insensible to some fine traits of culture, could very well report his weight and caliber. And this made the impression of genius which his conversation sometimes gave.

He understood the matter in hand at a glance, and saw the limitations and poverty of those he talked with, so that nothing seemed concealed from such terrible eyes. I have repeatedly known young men of sensibility converted in a moment to the belief that this was the man they were in search of, the man of men, who could tell them all they should do. His own dealing with them was never affectionate, but superior, didactic, scorning their petty ways—very slowly conceding, or not conceding at all, the promise of his society at their houses, or even at his own. "Would he not walk with them?" "He did not know. There was nothing so important to him as his walk; he had no walks to throw away on company." Visits were offered him from respectful parties, but he declined them. Admiring friends offered to carry him at their own cost to the Yellowstone River, to the West Indies, to South America. But though nothing could be more grave or considered than his refusals, they remind one, in quite new relations, of that fop Brummel's reply to the gentleman who offered him his carriage in a shower, "But where will *you* ride, then?"—and what accusing silences, and what searching and irresistible speeches, battering down all defenses, his companions can remember!

Mr. Thoreau dedicated his genius with such entire love to the fields, hills, and waters of his native town that he made them known and interesting to all reading Americans, and to people over the sea. The river on whose banks he was born and died he knew from its springs to its confluence with the Merrimack. He had made summer and winter observations on it for many years, and at every hour of the day and night. The result of the recent survey of the Water Commissioners appointed by the State of Massachusetts he had reached by his private experiments several years earlier. Every fact which occurs in the bed, on the banks, or in the air over it; the fishes, and their spawning and nests, their manners, their food; the shad flies which fill the air on a certain evening once a year, and which are snapped at by the fishes so ravenously that many of these die of repletion; the conical heaps of small stones on the river shallows, the huge nests of small fishes, one of which will sometimes overfill a cart; the birds which frequent the stream, heron, duck, sheldrake, loon, osprey; the snake, muskrat, otter, woodchuck, and fox, on the banks; the turtle, frog, hyla, and cricket, which make the banks vocal,—were all known to him, and, as it were, townsmen and fellow creatures; so that he felt an absurdity or violence in any narrative of one of these by itself apart, and still more of its dimensions on an inch rule, or in the exhibition of its skeleton, or the specimen of a squirrel or a bird in brandy. He liked to speak of the manners of the river, as itself a lawful creature, yet with exactness, and always to an observed fact. As he knew the river, so the ponds in this region.

One of the weapons he used, more important to him than microscope or alcohol receiver to other investigators, was a whim which grew on him by indulgence, yet appeared in gravest statement, namely, of extolling his own town and neighborhood as the most favored center for natural observation. He remarked that the flora of Massachusetts embraced almost all the important plants of America—most of the oaks, most of the willows, the best pines, the ash, the maple, the beech, the nuts. He returned Kane's *Arctic Voyage* to a friend of whom he had borrowed it, with the remark that "Most of the phenomena noted might be observed in Concord." He seemed a little envious of the Pole, for the coincident sunrise and sunset, or five minutes' day after six months: a splendid fact, which Annursnuc had never afforded him. He found red snow in one of his walks, and told me that he expected to find yet the *Victoria regia* in Concord. He was the attorney of the indigenous plants, and owned to a preference of the weeds to the imported plants as of the Indian to the civilized man, and noticed, with pleasure, that the willow bean poles of his neighbor had grown more than his beans. "See these weeds," he said, "which have been hoed at by a million farmers all spring and summer, and yet have prevailed, and just now come out triumphant over all lanes, pastures, fields, and gardens, such is their vigor. We have insulted them with low names, too— as Pigweed, Wormwood, Chickweed, Shad-blossom." He says, "They have brave names, too—Ambrosia, Stellaria, Amelanchier, Amaranth, etc."

I think his fancy for referring everything to the meridian of Concord did not grow out of any ignorance or depreciation of other longitudes or latitudes, but was rather a playful expression of his conviction of the indifferency of all places, and that the best place for each is where he stands. He expressed it once in this wise: "I think nothing is to be hoped from you, if this bit of mold under your feet is not sweeter to you to eat than any other in this world, or in any world."

The other weapon with which he conquered all obstacles in science was patience. He knew how to sit immovable, a part of the rock he rested on, until the bird, the reptile, the fish, which had retired from him, should come back and resume its habits, nay, moved by curiosity, should come to him and watch him.

It was a pleasure and a privilege to walk with him. He knew the country like a fox or a bird, and passed through it as freely by paths of his own. He knew every track in the snow or on the ground, and what creature had taken this path before him. One must submit abjectly to such a guide, and the reward was great. Under his arm he carried an old music book to press plants; in his pocket, his diary and pencil, a spyglass for birds, microscope, jackknife, and twine. He wore a straw hat, stout shoes, strong gray trousers, to brave scrub oaks and smilax, and to climb a tree for a hawk's or a squirrel's nest. He waded into the pool for the water plants, and his strong legs were no insignificant part of his armor. On the day I speak of he looked for the Menyanthes, detected it across the wide pool, and, on examination of the florets, decided that it had been in flower five days. He drew out of his breast pocket his diary, and read the names of all the plants that should bloom on this day, whereof he kept account as a banker when his notes fall due. The Cypripedium not due till tomorrow. He thought that, if waked up from a trance, in this swamp, he could tell by the plants what time of the year it was within two days. The redstart was flying about, and presently the fine grosbeaks, whose brilliant scarlet "makes the rash gazer wipe his eye," and whose fine clear note Thoreau compared to that of a tanager which has got rid of its hoarseness. Presently he heard a note which he called that of the night warbler, a bird he had never identified, had been in search of twelve years, which always, when he saw it, was in the act of diving down into a tree or bush, and which it was vain to seek; the only bird which sings indifferently by night and by day. I told him he must beware of finding and booking it, lest life should have nothing more to show him. He said, "What you seek in vain for, half your life, one day you come full upon, all the family at dinner. You seek it like a dream, and as soon as you find it you become its prey."

His interest in the flower or the bird lay very deep in his mind, was connected with Nature,—and the meaning of Nature was never attempted to be defined by him. He would not offer a memoir of his observations to the Natural History Society. "Why should I? To detach the description from its connections in my mind would make it no longer true or valuable to me: and they do not wish what belongs to it." His power of observation seemed to indicate additional senses. He saw as with microscope, heard as with ear trumpet, and his memory was a photographic register of all he saw and heard. And yet none knew better than he that it is not the fact that imports, but the impression or effect of the fact on your mind. Every fact lay in glory in his mind, a type of the order and beauty of the whole.

His determination on Natural History was organic. He confessed that he sometimes felt like a hound or a panther, and, if born among Indians, would have been a fell hunter. But, restrained by his Massachusetts culture, he played out the game in this mild form of botany and ichthyology. His intimacy with animals suggested what Thomas Fuller records of Butler the apiologist, that "either he had told the bees things or the bees had told him." Snakes coiled round his leg; the fishes swam into his hand, and he took them out of the water; he pulled the woodchuck out of its hole by the tail and took the foxes under his protection from the hunters. Our naturalist had perfect magnanimity; he had no secrets: he would carry you to the heron's haunt, or even to his most prized botanical swamp—possibly knowing that you could never find it again, yet willing to take his risks.

No college ever offered him a diploma, or a professor's chair; no academy made him its corresponding secretary, its discoverer, or even its member. Perhaps these learned bodies feared the satire of his presence. Yet so much knowledge of Nature's secret and genius few others possessed; none in a more large and religious synthesis. For not a particle of respect had he to the opinions of any man or body of men, but homage solely to the truth itself; and as he discovered everywhere among doctors some leaning of courtesy, it discredited them. He grew to be revered and admired by his townsmen, who had at first known him only as an oddity. The farmers who employed him as a surveyor soon discovered his rare accuracy and skill, his knowledge of their lands, of trees, of birds, of Indian remains and the like, which enabled him to tell every farmer more than he knew before of his own farm: so that he began to feel a little as if Mr. Thoreau had better

rights in his land than he. They felt, too, the superiority of
character which addressed all men with a native authority.
Indian relics abound in Concord—arrowheads, stone
chisels, pestles, and fragments of pottery; and on the riverbank, large heaps of clam shells and ashes mark spots which
the savages frequented. These, and every circumstance touching the Indian, were important in his eyes. His visits to
Maine were chiefly for love of the Indian. He had the satisfaction of seeing the manufacture of the bark canoe, as well
as of trying his hand in its management on the rapids. He
was inquisitive about the making of the stone arrowhead,
and in his last days charged a youth setting out for the
Rocky Mountains to find an Indian who could tell him that:
"It was well worth a visit to California to learn it." Occa
sionally, a small party of Penobscot Indians would visit Concord, and pitch their tents for a few weeks in summer on
the riverbank. He failed not to make acquaintance with the
best of them; though he well knew that asking questions of
Indians is like catechizing beavers and rabbits. In his last
visit to Maine he had great satisfaction from Joseph Polis,
an intelligent Indian of Oldtown, who was his guide for
some weeks.

He was equally interested in every natural fact. The depth
of his perception found likeness of law throughout Nature,
and I know not any genius who so swiftly inferred universal
law from the single fact. He was no pedant of a department.
His eye was open to beauty, and his ear to music. He found
these, not in rare conditions, but wheresoever he went. He
thought the best of music was in single strains; and he found
poetic suggestion in the humming of the telegraph wire.

His poetry might be bad or good; he no doubt wanted a
lyric facility and technical skill, but he had the source of
poetry in his spiritual perception. He was a good reader and
critic, and his judgment on poetry was to the ground of it.
He could not be deceived as to the presence or absence of the
poetic element in any composition, and his thirst for this
made him negligent and perhaps scornful of superficial
graces. He would pass by many delicate rhythms, but he
would have detected every live stanza or line in a volume,

and knew very well where to find an equal poetic charm in prose. He was so enamored of the spiritual beauty that he held all actual written poems in very light esteem in the comparison. He admired Æschylus and Pindar; but, when someone was commending them, he said that Æschylus and the Greeks, in describing Apollo and Orpheus, had given no song, or no good one. "They ought not to have moved trees, but to have chanted to the gods such a hymn as would have sung all their old ideas out of their heads, and new ones in." His own verses are often rude and defective. The gold does not yet run pure, is drossy and crude. The thyme and marjoram are not yet honey. But if he want lyric fineness and technical merits, if he have not the poetic temperament, he never lacks the casual thought, showing that his genius was better than his talent. He knew the worth of the Imagination for the uplifting and consolation of human life, and liked to throw every thought into a symbol. The fact you tell is of no value, but only the impression. For this reason his presence was poetic, always piqued the curiosity to know more deeply the secrets of his mind. He had many reserves, an unwillingness to exhibit to profane eyes what was still sacred in his own, and knew well how to throw a poetic veil over his experience. All readers of *Walden* will remember his mythical record of his disappointments:

"I long ago lost a hound, a bay horse, and a turtle-dove, and am still on their trail. Many are the travelers I have spoken concerning them, describing their tracks, and what calls they answered to. I have met one or two who have heard the hound, and the tramp of the horse, and even seen the dove disappear behind a cloud; and they seemed as anxious to recover them as if they had lost them themselves."[1]

His riddles were worth the reading, and I confide that if at any time I do not understand the expression, it is yet just. Such was the wealth of his truth that it was not worth his while to use words in vain. His poem entitled *Sympathy* reveals the tenderness under that triple steel of stoicism, and the intellectual subtilty it could animate. His classic poem on *Smoke* suggests Simonides, but is better than any poem

[1] *Walden:* p. 20. R. W. E.

of Simonides. His biography is in his verses. His habitual thought makes all his poetry a hymn to the Cause of causes, the Spirit which vivifies and controls his own:

> I hearing get, who had but ears,
> And sight, who had but eyes before;
> I moments live, who lived but years,
> And truth discern, who knew but learning's lore.

And still more in these religious lines:

> Now chiefly is my natal hour,
> And only now my prime of life;
> I will not doubt the love untold,
> Which not my worth nor want have bought,
> Which wooed me young, and woos me old,
> And to this evening hath me brought.

Whilst he used in his writings a certain petulance of remark in reference to churches or churchmen, he was a person of a rare, tender, and absolute religion, a person incapable of any profanation, by act or by thought. Of course, the same isolation which belonged to his original thinking and living detached him from the social religious forms. This is neither to be censured nor regretted. Aristotle long ago explained it, when he said, "One who surpasses his fellow citizens in virtue is no longer a part of the city. Their law is not for him, since he is a law to himself."

Thoreau was sincerity itself, and might fortify the convictions of prophets in the ethical laws by his holy living. It was an affirmative experience which refused to be set aside. A truth-speaker he, capable of the most deep and strict conversation; a physician to the wounds of any soul; a friend, knowing not only the secret of friendship, but almost worshiped by those few persons who resorted to him as their confessor and prophet, and knew the deep value of his mind and great heart. He thought that without religion or devotion of some kind nothing great was ever accomplished: and he thought that the bigoted sectarian had better bear this in mind.

His virtues, of course, sometimes ran into extremes. It was easy to trace to the inexorable demand on all for exact truth that austerity which made this willing hermit more solitary even than he wished. Himself of a perfect probity, he required not less of others. He had a disgust at crime, and no worldly success would cover it. He detected paltering as readily in dignified and prosperous persons as in beggars, and with equal scorn. Such dangerous frankness was in his dealing that his admirers called him "that terrible Thoreau," as if he spoke when silent, and was still present when he had departed. I think the severity of his ideal interfered to deprive him of a healthy sufficiency of human society.

The habit of a realist to find things the reverse of their appearance inclined him to put every statement in a paradox. A certain habit of antagonism defaced his earlier writings— a trick of rhetoric not quite outgrown in his later, or substituting for the obvious word and thought its diametrical opposite. He praised wild mountains and winter forests for their domestic air, in snow and ice he would find sultriness, and commended the wilderness for resembling Rome and Paris. "It was so dry, that you might call it wet."

The tendency to magnify the moment, to read all the laws of Nature in the one object or one combination under your eye, is of course comic to those who do not share the philosopher's perception of identity. To him there was no such thing as size. The pond was a small ocean; the Atlantic, a large Walden Pond. He referred every minute fact to cosmical laws. Though he meant to be just, he seemed haunted by a certain chronic assumption that the science of the day pretended completeness, and he had just found out that the *savans* had neglected to discriminate a particular botanical variety, had failed to describe the seeds or count the sepals. "That is to say," we replied, "the blockheads were not born in Concord; but who said they were? It was their unspeakable misfortune to be born in London, or Paris, or Rome; but, poor fellows, they did what they could, considering that they never saw Bateman's Pond, or Nine-Acre Corner, or Becky Stow's Swamp; besides, what were you sent into the world for, but to add this observation?"

Had his genius been only contemplative, he had been fitted to his life, but with his energy and practical ability he seemed born for great enterprise and for command; and I so much regret the loss of his rare powers of action that I cannot help counting it a fault in him that he had no ambition. Wanting this, instead of engineering for all America, he was the captain of a huckleberry party. Pounding beans is good to the end of pounding empires one of these days; but if, at the end of years, it is still only beans!

But these foibles, real or apparent, were fast vanishing in the incessant growth of a spirit so robust and wise, and which effaced its defeats with new triumphs. His study of Nature was a perpetual ornament to him, and inspired his friends with curiosity to see the world through his eyes, and to hear his adventures. They possessed every kind of interest.

He had many elegancies of his own, whilst he scoffed at conventional elegance. Thus, he could not bear to hear the sound of his own steps, the grit of gravel; and therefore never willingly walked in the road, but in the grass, on mountains, and in woods. His senses were acute, and he remarked that by night every dwelling house gives out bad air, like a slaughterhouse. He liked the pure fragrance of melilot. He honored certain plants with special regard, and, over all, the pond lily,—then, the gentian, and the *Mikania scandens*, and "life-everlasting," and a bass tree which he visited every year when it bloomed, in the middle of July. He thought the scent a more oracular inquisition than the sight—more oracular and trustworthy. The scent, of course, reveals what is concealed from the other senses. By it he detected earthiness. He delighted in echoes, and said they were almost the only kind of kindred voices that he heard. He loved Nature so well, was so happy in her solitude, that he became very jealous of cities and the sad work which their refinements and artifices made with man and his dwelling. The ax was always destroying his forest. "Thank God," he said, "they cannot cut down the clouds!" "All kinds of figures are drawn on the blue ground with this fibrous white paint."

I subjoin a few sentences taken from his unpublished

manuscripts, not only as records of his thought and feeling, but for their power of description and literary excellence:

Some circumstantial evidence is very strong, as when you find a trout in the milk.

The chub is a soft fish, and tastes like boiled brown paper salted.

The youth gets together his materials to build a bridge to the moon, or, perchance, a palace or temple on the earth, and, at length the middle-aged man concludes to build a woodshed with them.

The locust z-ing.

Devil's-needles zigzagging along the Nut-Meadow brook.

Sugar is not so sweet to the palate as sound to the healthy ear.

I put on some hemlock boughs, and the rich salt crackling of their leaves was like mustard to the ear, the crackling of un-countable regiments. Dead trees love the fire.

The bluebird carries the sky on his back.

The tanager flies through the green foliage as if it would ignite the leaves.

If I wish for a horsehair for my compass sight I must go to the stable; but the hair-bird, with her sharp eyes, goes to the road.

Immortal water, alive even to the superficies.

Fire is the most tolerable third party.

Nature made ferns for pure leaves, to show what she could do in that line.

No tree has so fair a bole and so handsome an instep as the beech.

How did these beautiful rainbow tints get into the shell of the fresh-water clam, buried in the mud at the bottom of our dark river?

Hard are the times when the infant's shoes are second-foot.

We are strictly confined to our men to whom we give liberty.

Nothing is so much to be feared as fear. Atheism may comparatively be popular with God himself.

Of what significance the things you can forget? A little thought is sexton to all the world.

How can we expect a harvest of thought who have not had a seed-time of character?

Only he can be trusted with gifts who can present a face of bronze to expectations.

I ask to be melted. You can only ask of the metals that they be tender to the fire that melts them. To nought else can they be tender.

There is a flower known to botanists, one of the same genus with our summer plant called "Life-Everlasting," a *Gnaphalium* like that, which grows on the most inaccessible cliffs of the Tyrolese mountains, where the chamois dare hardly venture, and which the hunter, tempted by its beauty, and by his love (for it is immensely valued by the Swiss maidens), climbs the cliffs to gather, and is sometimes found dead at the foot, with the flower in his hand. It is called by botanists the *Gnaphalium leontopodium,* but by the Swiss *Edelweiss,* which signifies *Noble Purity.* Thoreau seemed to me living in the hope to gather this plant, which belonged to him of right. The scale on which his studies proceeded was so large as to require longevity, and we were the less prepared for his sudden disappearance. The country knows not yet, or in the least part, how great a son it has lost. It seems an injury that he should leave in the midst his broken task which none else can finish, a kind of indignity to so noble a soul that he should depart out of Nature before yet he has been really shown to his peers for what he is. But he, at least, is content. His soul was made for the noblest society; he had in a short life exhausted the capabilities of this world; wherever there is knowledge, wherever there is virtue, wherever there is beauty, he will find a home.

In Emerson's journal of 1863, the following note is found:

April 28

I have never recorded a fact, which perhaps ought to have gone into my sketch of *Thoreau* that, on the 1st August 1844, when I read my Discourse on Emancipation (in the British West Indies), in the Town Hall, in Concord, and the selectmen would not direct the sexton to ring the meeting-house bell, Henry went himself, and rung the bell at the appointed hour.

THOREAU

WHAT CONTEMPORARY, if he was in the fighting period of
his life (since Nature sets limits about her conscription for
spiritual fields, as the state does in physical warfare), will
ever forget what was somewhat vaguely called the "Transcendental Movement" of thirty years ago? Apparently set
astir by Carlyle's essays on the *Signs of the Times,* and on
History, the final and more immediate impulse seemed to
be given by *Sartor Resartus.* At least the republication in
Boston of that wonderful Abraham à Sancta Clara sermon
on Falstaff's text of the miserable forked radish gave the
signal for a sudden mental and moral mutiny. *Ecce nunc
tempus acceptabile!* was shouted on all hands with every
variety of emphasis, and by voices of every conceivable pitch,
representing the three sexes of men, women, and Lady Mary
Wortley Montagues. The nameless eagle of the tree Ygdrasil
was about to sit at last, and wild-eyed enthusiasts rushed
from all sides, each eager to thrust under the mystic bird
that chalk egg from which the new and fairer Creation was
to be hatched in due time. *Redeunt Saturnia regna*—so far
was certain, though in what shape, or by what methods, was
still a matter of debate. Every possible form of intellectual

and physical dyspepsia brought forth its gospel. Bran had its prophets, and the presartorial simplicity of Adam its martyrs, tailored impromptu from the tar pot by incensed neighbors, and sent forth to illustrate the "feathered Mercury," as defined by Webster and Worcester. Plainness of speech was carried to a pitch that would have taken away the breath of George Fox; and even swearing had its evangelists, who answered a simple inquiry after their health with an elaborate ingenuity of imprecation that might have been honorably mentioned by Marlborough in general orders. Everybody had a mission (with a capital M) to attend to everybody else's business. No brain but had its private maggot, which must have found pitiably short commons sometimes. Not a few impecunious zealots abjured the use of money (unless earned by other people), professing to live on the internal revenues of the spirit. Some had an assurance of instant millennium so soon as hooks and eyes should be substituted for buttons. Communities were established where everything was to be common but common sense. Men renounced their old gods, and hesitated only whether to bestow their furloughed allegiance on Thor or Budh. Conventions were held for every hitherto inconceivable purpose. The belated gift of tongues, as among the Fifth Monarchy men, spread like a contagion, rendering its victims incomprehensible to all Christian men; whether equally so to the most distant possible heathen or not was unexperimented, though many would have subscribed liberally that a fair trial might be made. It was the pentecost of Shinar. The day of utterances reproduced the day of abuses and anagrams, and there was nothing so simple that uncial letters and the style of Diphilus the Labyrinth could not turn it into a riddle. Many foreign revolutionists out of work added to the general misunderstanding their contribution of broken English in every most ingenious form of fracture. All stood ready at a moment's notice to reform everything but themselves. The general motto was:

> And we'll *talk* with them, too,
> And take upon 's the mystery of things
> As if we were God's spies.

Nature is always kind enough to give even her clouds a humorous lining. I have barely hinted at the comic side of the affair, for the material was endless. This was the whistle and trailing fuse of the shell, but there was a very solid and serious kernel, full of the most deadly explosiveness. Thoughtful men divined it, but the generality suspected nothing. The word "transcendental" then was the maid of all work for those who could not think, as "Pre-Raphaelite" has been more recently for people of the same limited housekeeping. The truth is that there was a much nearer metaphysical relation and a much more distant aesthetic and literary relation between Carlyle and the Apostles of the Newness, as they were called in New England, than has commonly been supposed. Both represented the reaction and revolt against *Philisterei*, a renewal of the old battle begun in modern times by Erasmus and Reuchlin, and continued by Lessing, Goethe, and, in a far narrower sense, by Heine in Germany, and of which Fielding, Sterne, and Wordsworth in different ways have been the leaders in England. It was simply a struggle for fresh air, in which, if the windows could not be opened, there was danger that panes would be broken, though painted with images of saints and martyrs. Light, colored by these reverend effigies, was none the more respirable for being picturesque. There is only one thing better than tradition, and that is the original and eternal life out of which all tradition takes its rise. It was this life which the reformers demanded, with more or less clearness of consciousness and expression, life in politics, life in literature, life in religion. Of what use to import a gospel from Judaea, if we leave behind the soul that made it possible, the God who keeps it forever real and present? Surely Abana and Pharpar *are* better than Jordan, if a living faith be mixed with those waters and none with these.

Scotch Presbyterianism as a motive of spiritual progress was dead; New England Puritanism was in like manner dead; in other words, Protestantism had made its fortune and no longer protested; but till Carlyle spoke out in the Old World and Emerson in the New, no one had dared to proclaim, *Le roi est mort: vive le roi!* The meaning of which proclamation was essentially this: the vital spirit has long since departed out of this form once so kingly, and the great seal has been in commission long enough; but meanwhile the soul of man, from which all power emanates and to which it reverts, still survives in undiminished royalty; God still survives, little as you gentlemen of the Commission seem to be aware of it—nay, will possibly outlive the whole of you, incredible as it may appear. The truth is that both Scotch Presbyterianism and New England Puritanism made their new avatar in Carlyle and Emerson, the heralds of their formal decease, and the tendency of the one toward Authority and of the other toward Independency might have been prophesied by whoever had studied history. The necessity was not so much in the men as in the principles they represented and the traditions which overruled them. The Puritanism of the past found its unwilling poet in Hawthorne, the rarest creative imagination of the century, the rarest in some ideal respects since Shakespeare; but the Puritanism that cannot die, the Puritanism that made New England what it is, and is destined to make America what it should be, found its voice in Emerson. Though holding himself aloof from all active partnership in movements of reform, he has been the sleeping partner who has supplied a great part of their capital.

The artistic range of Emerson is narrow, as every well-read critic must feel at once; and so is that of Æschylus, so is that of Dante, so is that of Montaigne, so is that of Schiller, so is that of nearly everyone except Shakespeare; but there is a gauge of height no less than of breadth, of individuality as well as of comprehensiveness, and, above all, there is the standard of genetic power, the test of the masculine as distinguished from the receptive minds. There are staminate plants in literature that make no fine show of fruit, but without whose pollen, quintessence of fructifying gold, the garden had been barren. Emerson's mind is emphatically one of these, and there is no man to whom our aesthetic culture owes so much. The Puritan revolt had made us ecclesiastically and the Revolution politically independent, but we were still socially and intellectually moored to English thought, till Emerson cut the cable and gave us a chance at the dangers and the glories of blue water. No man young enough to have felt it can forget or cease to be grateful for the mental and moral *nudge* which he received from the writings of his high-minded and brave-spirited countryman. That we agree with him, or that he always agrees with himself, is aside from the question; but that he arouses in us something that we are the better for having awakened, whether that something be of opposition or assent, that he speaks always to what is highest and least selfish in us, few Americans of the generation younger than his own would be disposed to deny. His oration before the Phi Beta Kappa Society at Cambridge, some thirty years ago, was an event without any former parallel in our literary annals, a scene to be always treasured in the memory for its picturesqueness and its inspiration. What crowded and breathless aisles, what windows clustering with eager heads, what enthusiasm of approval, what grim silence of foregone dissent! It was our Yankee version of a lecture by Abelard, our Harvard parallel to the last public appearances of Schelling.

I said that the Transcendental Movement was the protestant spirit of Puritanism seeking a new outlet and an escape from forms and creeds which compressed rather than expressed it. In its motives, its preaching, and its results, it differed radically from the doctrine of Carlyle. The Scotchman, with all his genius, and his humor gigantesque as that of Rabelais, has grown shriller and shriller with years, degenerating sometimes into a common scold, and emptying very unsavory vials of wrath on the head of the sturdy British Socrates of worldly common sense. The teaching of Emerson tended much more exclusively to self-culture and the independent development of the individual man. It seemed to many almost Pythagorean in its voluntary seclusion from commonwealth affairs. Both Carlyle and Emerson were disciples of Goethe, but Emerson in a far truer sense; and while the one, from his bias toward the eccentric, has degenerated more and more into mannerism, the other has clarified steadily toward perfection of style—exquisite fineness of material, unobtrusive lowness of tone and simplicity of fashion, the most high-bred garb of expression. Whatever may be said of his thought, nothing can be finer than the delicious limpidness of his phrase. If it was ever questionable whether democracy could develop a gentleman, the problem has been affirmatively solved at last. Carlyle, in his cynicism and his admiration of force in and for itself, has become at last positively inhuman; Emerson, reverencing strength, seeking the highest outcome of the individual, has found that society and politics are also main elements in the attainment of the desired end, and has drawn steadily manward and worldward. The two men represent respectively those grand personifications in the drama of Æschylus, Βία and Κράτος.

Among the pistillate plants kindled to fruitage by the Emersonian pollen, Thoreau is thus far the most remarkable; and it is something eminently fitting that his posthumous works should be offered us by Emerson, for they are strawberries from his own garden. A singular mixture of varieties, indeed, there is—alpine, some of them, with the flavor of rare mountain air; others wood, tasting of sunny roadside banks or shy openings in the forest; and not a few seedlings swollen hugely by culture, but lacking the fine natural aroma of the more modest kinds. Strange books these are of his, and interesting in many ways—instructive chiefly as showing how considerable a crop may be raised on a comparatively narrow close of mind, and how much a man may make of his life if he will assiduously follow it, though perhaps never truly finding it at last.

I have just been renewing my recollection of Mr. Thoreau's writings, and have read through his six volumes in the order of their production. I shall try to give an adequate report of their impression upon me both as critic and as mere reader. He seems to me to have been a man with so high a conceit of himself that he accepted without questioning, and insisted on our accepting, his defects and weaknesses of character as virtues and powers peculiar to himself. Was he indolent, he finds none of the activities which attract or employ the rest of mankind worthy of him. Was he wanting in the qualities that make success, it is success that is contemptible, and not himself that lacks persistency and purpose. Was he poor, money was an unmixed evil. Did his life seem a selfish one, he condemns doing good as one of the weakest of superstitions. To be of use was with him the most killing bait of the wily tempter Uselessness. He had no faculty of generalization from outside of himself, or at least no experience which would supply the material of such, and he makes his own whim the law, his own range the horizon of the universe. He condemns a world, the hollowness of whose satisfactions he had never had the means of testing, and we recognize Apemantus behind the mask of Timon. He had little active imagination; of the receptive he had much. His appreciation is of the highest quality; his critical power, from want of continuity of mind, very limited and inadequate. He somewhere cites a simile from Ossian, as an example of the superiority of the old poetry to the new, though, even were the historic evidence less convincing, the sentimental melancholy of those poems should be conclusive of their modernness. He had none of the artistic mastery which controls a great work to the serene balance of completeness, but exquisite mechanical skill in the shaping of sentences and paragraphs, or (more rarely) short bits of verse for the expression of a detached thought, sentiment, or image. His works give one the feeling of a sky full of stars—something impressive and exhilarating certainly, something high overhead and freckled thickly with spots of isolated brightness; but whether these have any mutual relation with each other, or have any concern with our mundane matters, is for the most part matter of conjecture—astrology as yet, and not astronomy.

It is curious, considering what Thoreau afterwards became, that he was not by nature an observer. He only saw the things he looked for, and was less poet than naturalist. Till he built his Walden shanty, he did not know that the hickory grew in Concord. Till he went to Maine, he had never seen phosphorescent wood, a phenomenon early familiar to most country boys. At forty he speaks of the seeding of the pine as a new discovery, though one should have thought that its gold dust of blowing pollen might have earlier drawn his eye. Neither his attention nor his genius was of the spontaneous kind. He discovered nothing. He thought everything a discovery of his own, from moonlight to the planting of acorns and nuts by squirrels. This is a defect in his character, but one of his chief charms as a writer. Everything grows fresh under his hand. He delved in his mind and nature; he planted them with all manner of native and foreign seeds, and reaped assiduously. He was not merely solitary, he would be isolated, and succeeded at last in almost persuading himself that he was autochthonous. He valued everything in proportion as he fancied it to be exclusively his own. He complains in *Walden* that there is no one in Concord with whom he could talk of Oriental literature, though the man was living within two miles of his hut who had introduced him to it. This intellectual selfishness becomes sometimes almost painful in reading him. He lacked that generosity of "communication" which Johnson admired in Burke. De Quincey tells us that Wordsworth was impatient when anyone else spoke of mountains, as if he had a peculiar property in them. And we can readily understand why it should be so: no one is satisfied with another's appreciation of his mistress. But Thoreau seems to have prized a lofty way of thinking (often we should be inclined to call it a remote one) not so much because it was good in itself as because he wished few to share it with him. It seems now and then as if he did not seek to lure others up "above our lower region of turmoil," but to leave his own name cut on the mountain peak as the first climber. This itch of originality infects his thought and style. To be misty is not to be mystic. He turns commonplaces end for end, and fancies it makes something new of them. As we walk down Park Street, our eye is caught by Dr. Winship's dumbbells, one of which bears an inscription testifying that it is the heaviest ever put up at arm's length by any athlete; and in reading Mr. Thoreau's books we cannot help feeling as if he sometimes invited our attention to a particular sophism or paradox as the biggest yet maintained by any single writer. He seeks, at all risks, for perversity of thought, and revives the age of *concetti* while he fancies himself going back to a preclassical nature. "A day," he says, "passed in the society of those Greek sages, such as described in the Banquet of Xenophon, would not be comparable with the dry wit of decayed cranberry vines and the fresh Attic salt of the moss beds." It is not so much the True that he loves as the Out-of-the-Way. As the Brazen Age shows itself in other men by exaggeration of phrase, so in him by extravagance of statement. He wishes always to trump your suit and to *ruff* when you least expect it. Do you love Nature because she is beautiful? He will find a better argument in her ugliness. Are you tired of the artificial man? He instantly dresses you up an ideal in a Penobscot Indian, and attributes to this creature of his otherwise-mindedness as peculiarities things that are common to all woodsmen, white or red, and this simply because he has not studied the pale-faced variety.

This notion of an absolute originality, as if one could have a patent right in it, is an absurdity. A man cannot escape in thought, any more than he can in language, from the past and the present. As no one ever invents a word, and yet language somehow grows by general contribution and necessity, so it is with thought. Mr. Thoreau seems to me to insist in public on going back to flint and steel when there is a matchbox in his pocket which he knows very well how to use at a pinch. Originality consists in power of digesting and assimilating thought, so that they become part of our life and substance. Montaigne, for example, is one of the most original of authors, though he helped himself to ideas in every direction. But they turn to blood and coloring in his style, and give a freshness of complexion that is forever charming. In Thoreau much seems yet to be foreign and unassimilated, showing itself in symptoms of indigestion. A preacher-up of Nature, we now and then detect under the surly and stoic garb something of the sophist and the sentimentalizer. I am far from implying that this was conscious on his part. But it is much easier for a man to impose on himself when he measures only with himself. A greater familiarity with ordinary men would have done Thoreau good, by showing him how many fine qualities are common to the race. The radical vice of his theory of life was that he confounded physical with spiritual remoteness from men. A man is far enough withdrawn from his fellows if he keep himself clear of their weaknesses. He is not so truly withdrawn as exiled, if he refuse to share in their strength. "Solitude," says Cowley, "can be well fitted and set right but upon a very few persons. They must have enough knowledge of the world to see the vanity of it, and enough virtue to despise all vanity." It is a morbid self-consciousness that pronounces the world of men empty and worthless before trying it, the instinctive evasion of one who is sensible of some innate weakness, and retorts the accusation of it before any has made it but himself. To a healthy mind, the world is a constant challenge of opportunity. Mr. Thoreau had not a healthy mind, or he would not have been so fond of prescribing. His whole life was a search for the doctor. The old mystics had a wiser sense of what the world was worth. They ordained a severe apprenticeship to law, and even ceremonial, in order to the gaining of freedom and mastery over these. Seven years of service for Rachel were to be rewarded at last with Leah. Seven other years of faithfulness with her were to win them at last the true bride of their souls. Active Life was with them the only path to the Contemplative.

Thoreau had no humor, and this implies that he was a sorry logician. Himself an artist in rhetoric, he confounds thought with style when he undertakes to speak of the latter. He was forever talking of getting away from the world, but he must be always near enough to it, nay, to the Concord corner of it, to feel the impression he makes there. He verifies the shrewd remark of Sainte-Beuve, *"On touche encore à son temps et très-fort, même quand on le repousse."* This egotism of his is a Stylites pillar after all, a seclusion which keeps him in the public eye. The dignity of man is an excellent thing, but therefore to hold one's self too sacred and precious is the reverse of excellent. There is something delightfully absurd in six volumes addressed to a world of such "vulgar fellows" as Thoreau affirmed his fellowmen to be. I once had a glimpse of a genuine solitary who spent his winters one hundred and fifty miles beyond all human communication, and there dwelt with his rifle as his only confidant. Compared with this, the shanty on Walden Pond has something the air, it must be confessed, of the Hermitage of La Chevrette. I do not believe that the way to a true cosmopolitanism carries one into the woods or the society of musquashes. Perhaps the narrowest provincialism is that of Self; that of Kleinwinkel is nothing to it. The natural man, like the singing birds, comes out of the forest as inevitably as the natural bear and the wildcat stick there. To seek to be natural implies a consciousness that forbids all naturalness forever. It is as easy—and no easier—to be natural in a *salon* as in a swamp, if one do not aim at it, for what we call unnaturalness always has its spring in a man's thinking too much about himself. "It is impossible," said Turgot, "for a vulgar man to be simple."

I look upon a great deal of the modern sentimentalism about Nature as a mark of disease. It is one more symptom of the general liver complaint. To a man of wholesome constitution the wilderness is well enough for a mood or a vacation, but not for a habit of life. Those who have most loudly advertised their passion for seclusion and their intimacy with nature, from Petrarch down, have been mostly sentimentalists, unreal men, misanthropes on the spindle side, solacing an uneasy suspicion of themselves by professing contempt for their kind. They make demands on the world in advance proportioned to their inward measure of their own merit, and are angry that the world pays only by the visible measure of performance. It is true of Rousseau, the modern founder of the sect, true of Saint Pierre, his intellectual child, and of Châteaubriand, his grandchild, the inventor, we might almost say, of the primitive forest, and who first was touched by the solemn falling of a tree from natural decay in the windless silence of the woods. It is a very shallow view that affirms trees and rocks to be healthy, and cannot see that men in communities are just as true to the laws of their organization and destiny; that can tolerate the puffin and the fox, but not the fool and the knave; that would shun politics because of its demagogues, and snuff up the stench of the obscene fungus. The divine life of Nature is more wonderful, more various, more sublime in man than in any other of her works, and the wisdom that is gained by commerce with men, as Montaigne and Shakespeare gained it, or with one's own soul among men, as Dante, is the most delightful, as it is the most precious, of all. In outward nature it is still man that interests us, and we care far less for the things seen than the way in which they are seen by poetic eyes like Wordsworth's or Thoreau's, and the reflections they cast there. To hear the to-do that is often made over the simple fact that a man sees the image of himself in the outward world, one is reminded of a savage when he for the first time catches a glimpse of himself in a looking glass. "Venerable child of Nature," we are tempted to say, "to whose science in the invention of the tobacco pipe, to whose art in the tattooing of thine undegenerate hide not yet enslaved by tailors, we are slowly striving to climb back, the miracle thou beholdest is sold in my unhappy country for a shilling!" If matters go on as they have done, and everybody must needs blab of all the favors that have been done him by roadside and river brink and woodland walk, as if to kiss and tell were no longer treachery, it will be a positive refreshment to meet a man who is as superbly indifferent to Nature as she is to him. By and by we shall have John Smith, of No. –12–12th Street, advertising that he is not the J. S. who saw a cow lily on Thursday last, as he never saw one in his life, would not see one if he could, and is prepared to prove an alibi on the day in question.

Solitary communion with Nature does not seem to have been sanitary or sweetening in its influence on Thoreau's character. On the contrary, his letters show him more cynical as he grew older. While he studied with respectful attention the minks and woodchucks, his neighbors, he looked with utter contempt on the august drama of destiny of which his country was the scene, and on which the curtain had already risen. He was converting us back to a state of nature "so eloquently," as Voltaire said of Rousseau, "that he almost persuaded us to go on all fours," while the wiser fates were making it possible for us to walk erect for the first time. Had he conversed more with his fellows, his sympathies would have widened with the assurance that his peculiar

genius had more appreciation, and his writings a larger circle
of readers, or at least a warmer one, than he dreamed of. We
have the highest testimony[1] to the natural sweetness, sincerity, and nobleness of his temper, and in his books an equally
irrefragable one to the rare quality of his mind. He was not
a strong thinker, but a sensitive feeler. Yet his mind strikes
us as cold and wintry in its purity. A light snow has fallen
everywhere in which he seems to come on the track of the
shier sensations that would elsewhere leave no trace. We
think greater compression would have done more for his
fame. A feeling of sameness comes over us as we read so
much. Trifles are recorded with an over-minute punctuality
and conscientiousness of detail. He registers the state of his
personal thermometer thirteen times a day. We cannot help
thinking sometimes of the man who

> Watches, starves, freezes, and sweats
> To learn but catechisms and alphabets
> Of unconcerning things, matters of fact,

and sometimes of the saying of the Persian poet, that
"when the owl would boast, he boasts of catching mice
at the edge of a hole." We could readily part with some of
his affectations. It was well enough for Pythagoras to say,
once for all, "When I was Euphorbus at the siege of Troy";
not so well for Thoreau to travesty it into "When I was
a shepherd on the plains of Assyria." A naïve thing said
over again is anything but naïve. But with every exception,
there is no writing comparable with Thoreau's in kind that
is comparable with it in degree where it is best; where it
disengages itself, that is, from the tangled roots and dead
leaves of a second-hand Orientalism, and runs limpid and
smooth and broadening as it runs, a mirror for whatever is
grand and lovely in both worlds.

George Sand says neatly that "Art is not a study of positive
reality" (*actuality* were the fitter word), "but a seeking after
ideal truth." It would be doing very inadequate justice to
Thoreau if we left it to be inferred that this ideal element

[1]Mr. Emerson, in the Biographical Sketch prefixed to the *Excursions.*

did not exist in him, and that, too, in larger proportion, if less obtrusive, than his nature worship. He took nature as the mountain path to an ideal world. If the path wind a good deal, if he record too faithfully every trip over a root, if he botanize somewhat wearisomely, he gives us now and then superb outlooks from some jutting crag, and brings us out at last into an illimitable ether, where the breathing is not difficult for those who have any true touch of the climbing spirit. His shanty life was a mere impossibility, so far as his own conception of it goes, as an entire independency of mankind. The tub of Diogenes had a sounder bottom. Thoreau's experiment actually presupposed all that complicated civilization which it theoretically abjured. He squatted on another man's land; he borrows an ax; his boards, his nails, his bricks, his mortar, his books, his lamp, his fishhooks, his plow, his hoe, all turn state's evidence against him as an accomplice in the sin of that artificial civilization which rendered it possible that such a person as Henry D. Thoreau should exist at all. *Magnis tamen excidit ausis.* His aim was a noble and a useful one, in the direction of "plain living and high thinking." It was a practical sermon on Emerson's text that "things are in the saddle and ride mankind," an attempt to solve Carlyle's problem (condensed from Johnson) of "lessening your denominator." His whole life was a rebuke of the waste and aimlessness of our American luxury, which is an abject enslavement to tawdry upholstery. He had "fine translunary things" in him. His better style as a writer is in keeping with the simplicity and purity of his life. We have said that his range was narrow, but to be a master is to be a master. He had caught his English at its living source, among the poets and prose writers of its best days; his literature was extensive and recondite; his quotations are always nuggets of the purest ore: there are sentences of his as perfect as anything in the language, and thoughts as clearly crystallized; his metaphors and images are always fresh from the soil; he had watched Nature like a detective who is to go upon the stand; as we read him, it seems as if all out-of-doors had kept a diary and become its own Montaigne; we look at the landscape as in a Claude Lorraine glass; compared with his, all other books of similar aim, even White's *Selborne,* seem dry as a country clergyman's meteorological journal in an old almanac. He belongs with Donne and Browne and Novalis; if not with the originally creative men, with the scarcely smaller class who are peculiar, and whose leaves shed their invisible thought-seed like ferns.

Emerson's letter to Whitman on reading the first edition of *Leaves of Grass* is like a spark that sets off a smoldering fire. It has been said by Mr. Ralph L. Rusk, the editor of Emerson's letters, that "the printing of this letter, with its later public use by Whitman, was perhaps an event of greater importance in the history of American literature than the printing of any other letter has ever been."

The relations between Emerson and Whitman that date from this occasion may be clearly traced in their writings and in the memoirs of their friends; and they provide a curious drama, sometimes comic, sometimes moving. Among our serious writers (leaving aside Mrs. Stowe) these two men were certainly the most influential in the United States of their time. They both seemed to give exalted expression to ideas, to ways of feeling, to forces, that had come out of the American situation: both had the Protestant belief in the importance of the individual and his right to speak for himself; and both were trying to help the new country to formulate its new self-consciousness in relation to the rest of the world.

But Emerson and Whitman, who at moments seem to

merge under the pressure of their common purpose, sometimes repel one another. Whitman tends to expand his ego so as to identify himself with and include all the other human beings in the United States; he wants to feel through physical and moral contact that he is of the same stuff as they. Emerson, more bourgeois and cannier, shrinks from promiscuous contacts; and if he fights dead convention on the one hand, he dreads vulgarization on the other.

Whitman (1818–92) was younger than Emerson (1803–82), and outlived him and in a sense superseded him. The commercial-industrial domination that followed the Civil War was a defeat for the idealism of both; but where it crushed the poet-preacher like Emerson, it still left people free to glorify the experience of the common man, though this common man had often been reduced in the progress of our mechanical development to something that seemed even more featureless than the types in the catalogues of Whitman.

RALPH WALDO EMERSON AND
WALT WHITMAN

DOCUMENTS ON THEIR RELATIONS

In 1855, *the first edition of* Leaves of Grass *was printed in Brooklyn. Walt Whitman himself set up the type. Only about a thousand copies were made. Whitman had the greatest difficulty inducing the New York bookstores to put the book on sale. One bookdealer on Nassau Street, after looking into the volume, told Whitman that he could not stock it because he was a religious man; and the poet was obliged to resort to a "phrenological depot" on Broadway. Those shops in Brooklyn, New York, and Boston that consented to stock it did not sell it.*

Even aside from the book's unconventional contents, it presented a queer and unkempt appearance. It was a quarto with enormous pages; and it was bound in dark green, with the title in gilt on both covers. The letters of the words Leaves of Grass *exfoliated irregularly and disturbingly in long gold tendrils of grass blades and grass roots. The author's name was not given on the title page, but there was a large portrait of Whitman opposite—a picture which showed him wearing a slouch hat and an open flannel shirt, one hand resting nonchalantly on his hip and the other in his trousers pocket. The text itself was not the book we know, but a sort of early version of the* Song of Myself, *divided into sections with no subtitles but simply a reiterated* Leaves of Grass.

Whitman sent several copies to the press and to prominent men of letters, and did his best to attract attention to the book by himself writing three reviews and publishing them anonymously in different places. But the press was either silent or hostile. The Boston Intelligencer *declared that* Leaves of Grass *was "a heterogeneous mass of bombast, egotism, vulgarity, and nonsense. . . . The beastliness of the author is set forth in his own description of himself, and we can conceive of no better reward than the lash for such a violation of decency. The author should be kicked from all decent society as below the level of the brute. He must be some escaped lunatic raving in pitiable delirium."*

At this damping and humiliating moment, Whitman received a letter from Emerson, to whom, though he did not know him, he had sent a copy of his book:

CONCORD, MASSACHUSETTS, 21 *July, 1855*

DEAR SIR—I am not blind to the worth of the wonderful gift of *Leaves of Grass.* I find it the most extraordinary piece of wit and wisdom that America has yet contributed. I am very happy in reading it, as great power makes us happy. It meets the demand I am always making of what seemed the sterile and stingy Nature, as if too much handiwork, or too much lymph in the temperament, were making our Western wits fat and mean.

I give you joy of your free and brave thought. I have great joy in it. I find incomparable things said incomparably well, as they must be. I find the courage of treatment which so delights us, and which large perception only can inspire.

I greet you at the beginning of a great career, which yet must have had a long foreground somewhere, for such a start. I rubbed my eyes a little, to see if this sunbeam were no illusion; but the solid sense of the book is a sober certainty. It has the best merits, namely, of fortifying and encouraging.

I did not know until I last night saw the book advertised

in a newspaper that I could trust the name as real and available for a post-office. I wish to see my benefactor, and have felt much like striking my tasks and visiting New York to pay you my respects.

R. W. EMERSON

Two months later Emerson wrote as follows to James Elliot Cabot:

CONCORD, 26 *Sept. 1855*

MY DEAR CABOT,

I fear you will lend me no more books. After straining your good nature as I have done by these, I will not add to my offense by detailing the causes that have hindered their return to your shelves. Meantime, I am heartily thankful for the books. I did not find my way into Hegel as readily as I hoped, nor was I as richly rewarded as probably better scholars have been. The Eastern poetry I looked through, but find the Persian still the best by far, and shall stay by the Van Hammer with all the more content. Have you seen the strange Whitman's poems? Many weeks ago I thought to send them to you, but they seemed presently to become more known & you have probably found them. He seems a Minotaur of a man, with such insight and equal expression, but hurt by hard life & too animal experience. But perhaps you have not read the American poem. . . .

And on October 1, 1855, he asked, in a letter to W. H. Furness:

Have you read that wonderful book—with all its formlessness & faults *Leaves of Grass?*

In the meantime, Charles Eliot Norton had written to Lowell, who was then abroad:

Sept. 23, 1855

A new book called *Leaves of Grass* has just come out which is worth knowing about. It is a quarto volume of unmetrical poetry, and its author, according to his own account, is

"Walt Whitman, one of the roughs, a Kosmos." It is a book which has excited Emerson's enthusiasm. He has written a letter to this "one of the roughs," which I have seen, expressing the warmest admiration and encouragement. It is no wonder that he likes him, for Walt Whitman has read *The Dial, Nature,* and combines the characteristics of a Concord philosopher with those of a New York fireman. There is little original thought but much original expression in it. There are some passages of most vigorous and vivid writing, some superbly graphic description, great stretches of imagination—and then passages of intolerable coarseness—not gross and licentious, but simply disgustingly coarse. The book is such, indeed, that one cannot leave it about for chance readers, and would be sorry to know that any woman had looked into it past the title page. I have got a copy for you, for there are things in it that you will admire, and it is worth having merely as a literary curiosity, for the external appearance of it, the covers, the portrait, the print, are as odd as the inside. . . .

Lowell replied as follows—forgetting his Fable for Critics *of only seven years before, in which he had ridiculed the kind of man who "could gauge the old books by the old set of rules," but who, given "a new book just out of the heart," was at once put "at sea without compass or chart":*

DRESDEN, *Monday, Oct. 12, 1855*

I thank you for having thought of me in the copy of Whitman's book. Whitman—I remember him of old—he used to write for the *Democratic Review* under Sullivan. He used to do stories then à la Hawthorne. No, no, the kind of thing you describe won't do. When a man aims at originality, he acknowledges himself consciously *un*original, a want of self-respect which does not often go along with the capacity for great things. The great fellows have always let the stream of their activity flow quietly—if one splashes in it he may make a sparkle, but he muddies it too, and the good folks down below (I mean posterity) will have none of it. We have a feeling of quick and easygoing power in the really great that makes us willing to commit ourselves with them. Sometimes I have thought that Michel Angelo cocked his hat a little wee bit too much, but after seeing his Prophets and Sybils (i y) you'll say I'm a wretch. It is not the volcanoes, after all, that give a lasting and serene delight, but those quick old giants without a drop of fireblood in their veins that lie there basking their unwarmable old sides in the sun no more everlasting than they—patent unshiftable ballast that keep earth and human thought trimmed and true on an even keel. Ah, the cold-blooded old monsters, how little they care for you and me! Homer, Plato, Dante, Shakespeare, Cervantes, Goethe—are they not everlasting boundary-stones that work the limits of a noble reserve and self-restraint, and seem to say, "Outside of us is Chaos—go there if you like—we know better—it is a dreary realm where moan the ghosts of dead-born children, and where the ghost of mad old Lear is king"?

My dear Norton, upon my word I am not giving you an extract from my next lecture. . . .

On October 10, Charles A. Dana, the editor of the New York Tribune, who was a friend of both Emerson's and Whitman's and who had published a favorable review of Leaves of Grass, printed Emerson's letter to Whitman in the Tribune.

An acquaintance of Emerson's, Frank Bellew, in an article called Emerson and Walt Whitman in the Tribune of June 22, 1884, has left a record of Emerson's reaction to this:

One day, when I was calling upon Emerson, he drew my attention to an unbound volume of poems he had just received from New York, over which he was in raptures. It was called *Leaves of Grass*, by Walt Whitman. "I have just written off post-haste to thank him," he said. "It is really a most wonderful production, and gives promise of the greatest things, and if, as he says, it is his first writing, seems almost incredible. He must have taken a long run to make such a jump as this."

He read me some passages, raising his eyebrows here and there, remarking that it was hardly a book for the seminary or parlor table. Shortly after this I went off to the Wachusett Mountains, where I remained two months. On my return to Concord I again met Emerson, who was still enthusiastic over *Leaves of Grass*. "I wrote at once," he said, "a letter to the author, congratulating him." "Yes," I replied, "I read it." "How? When? Have you been to New York?" "No, I read it in the New York *Tribune*." "In the New York *Tribune?* No, no! Impossible! He cannot have published it!" he exclaimed, with much surprise. I assured him that I had read it a few weeks before in that paper.

"Dear! dear!" he muttered, "that was very wrong, very wrong indeed. That was merely a private letter of congratulation. Had I intended it for publication I should have enlarged the *but* very much—enlarged the *but*," repeating "enlarged the *but*" twice and biting the "but" off with his lips, and for a moment looking thoughtfully out of the window.

And on November 25, 1855, a Mr. J. P. Lesley, a geologist in Philadelphia, whose work Emerson knew, wrote Emerson,[1] "that he had examined the 'profane and obscene' *Leaves of Grass* and thought the author a pretentious ass without decency; then he had been confronted by a newspaper clipping containing what purported to be a letter of respect and gratitude to that same author over the name of one whom, of all American thinkers, he most revered. He asked now for Emerson's confirmation of his own immediate assertion that the quoted letter was not genuine but only a malicious jest."

Emerson to Thomas Carlyle the next spring:

CONCORD, 6 *May, 1856*

DEAR CARLYLE,—There is no escape from the forces of time and life, and we do not write letters to the gods or to

[1]The letter has been paraphrased by Mr. Ralph L. Rusk in his edition of Emerson's correspondence.

our friends, but only to attorneys, landlords, and tenants. But the planes and platforms on which all stand remain the same, and we are ever expecting the descent of the heavens, which is to put us into familiarity with the first named. When I ceased to write to you for a long time, I said to myself,—if anything really good should happen here, —any stroke of good sense or virtue in our politics, or of great sense in a book,—I will send it on the instant to the formidable man; but I will not repeat to him every month, that there are no news. Thank me for my resolution, and for keeping it through the long night. One book, last summer, came out in New York, a nondescript monster which yet had terrible eyes and buffalo strength, and was indisputably American,—which I thought to send you; but the book throve so badly with the few to whom I showed it, and wanted good morals so much, that I never did. Yet I believe now again, I shall. It is called *Leaves of Grass*,—was written and printed by a journeyman printer in Brooklyn, New York, named Walter Whitman; and after you have looked into it, if you think, as you may, that it is only an auctioneer's inventory of a warehouse, you can light your pipe with it. . . .

Ever affectionately yours,
R. W. EMERSON

A few weeks later, in June 1856, Whitman brought out Leaves of Grass in a second edition, also published by himself and also distributed by the phrenological bookstore. On the back of this volume, under a title which was sprouting large plantain and clover of a phalliform appearance, Whitman had had stamped in gold a quotation from Emerson's earlier letter: "I greet you at the beginning of a great career. R. W. Emerson"; and in an appendix, along with selections from the reviews of the first edition, he printed Emerson's letter to him in toto with the following reply:

BROOKLYN, *August 1856*

Here are thirty-two Poems, which I send you, dear Friend and Master, not having found how I could satisfy myself with sending any usual acknowledgment of your letter. The first edition, on which you mailed me that till now un-answered letter, was twelve poems—I printed a thousand copies, and they readily sold; these thirty-two Poems I ster-eotype, to print several thousand copies of. I much enjoy making poems. Other work I have set for myself to do, to meet people and The States face to face, to confront them with an American rude tongue; but the work of my life is making poems. I keep on till I make a hundred, and then several hundred—perhaps a thousand. The way is clear to me. A few years, and the average annual call for my Poems is ten or twenty thousand copies—more, quite likely. Why should I hurry or compromise? In poems or in speeches I say the word or two that has got to be said, adhere to the body, step with the countless common footsteps, and remind every man and woman of something.

Master, I am a man who has perfect faith. Master, we have not come through centuries, caste, heroisms, fables, to halt in this land today. Or I think it is to collect a ten-fold impetus that any halt is made. As nature, inexorable, on-ward, resistless, impassive amid the threats and screams of disputants, so America. Let all defer. Let all attend respect-fully the leisure of These States, their politics, poems, liter-ature, manners, and their free-handed modes of training their own offspring. Their own comes, just matured, certain, numerous and capable enough, with egotistical tongues, with sinewed wrists, seizing openly what belongs to them. They resume Personality, too long left out of mind. Their shadows are projected in employments, in books, in the cities, in trade; their feet are on the flights of the steps of the Capitol; they dilate, a larger, brawnier, more candid, more democratic, lawless, positive native to The States, sweet-bodied, com-pleter, dauntless, flowing, masterful, beard-faced, new race of men.

Swiftly, on limitless foundations, the United States too are founding a literature. It is all as well done, in my opinion, as could be practicable. Each element here is in condition. Every day I go among the people of Manhattan Island, Brooklyn, and other cities, and among the young men, to discover the spirit of them, and to refresh myself. These are to be attended to; I am myself more drawn here than to those authors, publishers, importations, reprints, and so forth. I pass coolly through those, understanding them perfectly well, and that they do the indispensable service, outside of men like me, which nothing else could do. In poems, the young men of The States shall be represented, for they out-rival the best of the rest of the earth.

The lists of ready-made literature which America inherits by the mighty inheritance of the English language—all the rich repertoire of traditions, poems, histories, metaphysics, plays, classics, translations, have made, and still continue, magnificent preparations for that other plainly signified liter-ature, to be our own, to be electric, fresh, lusty, to express the full-sized body, male and female—to give the modern meanings of things, to grow up beautiful, lasting, commen-surate with America, with all the passions of home, with the inimitable sympathies of having been boys and girls together, and of parents who were with our parents.

What else can happen The States, even in their own despite? That huge English flow, so sweet, so undeniable, has done incalculable good here, and is to be spoken of for its own sake with generous praise and with gratitude. Yet the price The States have had to lie under for the same has not been a small price. Payment prevails; a nation can never take the issues of the needs of other nations for noth-ing. America, grandest of lands in the theory of its politics, in popular reading, in hospitality, breadth, animal beauty, cities, ships, machines, money, credit, collapses quick as light-ning at the repeated, admonishing, stern words, Where are any mental expressions from you, beyond what you have copied or stolen? Where the born throngs of poets, literats, orators, you promised? Will you but tag after other nations? They struggled long for their literature, painfully working their way, some with deficient languages, some with priest-craft, some in the endeavor just to live—yet achieved for their times, works, poems, perhaps the only solid consolation left to them through ages afterwards of shame and decay. You are young, have the perfectest of dialects, a free press, a free government, the world forwarding its best to be with you. As justice has been strictly done to you, from this hour do strict justice to yourself. Strangle the singers who will not sing you loud and strong. Open the doors of The West. Call for new great masters to comprehend new arts, new perfections, new wants. Submit to the most robust bard till he remedy your barrenness. Then you will not need to adopt the heirs of others; you will have true heirs, begotten of yourself, blooded with your own blood.

With composure I see such propositions, seeing more and more every day of the answers that serve. Expressions do not yet serve, for sufficient reasons; but that is getting ready, beyond what the earth has hitherto known, to take home the expressions when they come, and to identify them with the populace of The States, which is the schooling cheaply procured by any outlay any number of years. Such schooling The States extract from the swarms of reprints, and from the current authors and editors. Such service and extract are done after enormous, reckless, free modes, characteristic of The States. Here are to be attained results never elsewhere thought possible; the modes are very grand too. The instincts of the American people are all perfect, and tend to make heroes. It is a rare thing in a man here to understand The States.

All current nourishments to literature serve. Of authors and editors I do not know how many there are in The States, but there are thousands, each one building his or her step to the stairs by which giants shall mount. Of the twenty-four modern mammoth two-double, three-double, and four-double cylinder presses now in the world, printing by steam, twenty-one of them are in These States. The twelve thousand large and small shops for dispensing books and newspapers—the same number of public libraries, any one of which has all the reading wanted to equip a man or woman for American reading—the three thousand different newspapers, the nutriment of the imperfect ones coming in just as usefully as any—the story papers, various, full of strong-flavored romances, widely circulated—the one-cent and two-cent journals—the political ones, no matter what side—

the weeklies in the country—the sporting and pictorial papers
—the monthly magazines, with plentiful imported feed—
the sentimental novels, numberless copies of them—the low-
priced flaring tales, adventures, biographies—all are prophetic; all waft rapidly on. I see that they swell wide, for
reasons. I am not troubled at the movement of them, but
greatly pleased. I see plying shuttles, the active ephemeral
myriads of books also, faithfully weaving the garments of a
generation of men, and a generation of women, they do not
perceive or know. What a progress popular reading and
writing has made in fifty years! What a progress fifty years
hence! The time is at hand when inherent literature will
be a main part of These States, as general and real as steam-
power, iron, corn, beef, fish. First-rate American persons are
to be supplied. Our perennial materials for fresh thoughts,
histories, poems, music, orations, religions, recitations, amusements, will then not be disregarded, any more than our
perennial fields, mines, rivers, seas. Certain things are established, and are immovable; in those things millions of years
stand justified. The mothers and fathers of whom modern
centuries have come, have not existed for nothing; they too
had brains and hearts. Of course all literature, in all nations
and years, will share marked attributes in common, as we
all, of all ages, share the common human attributes. America
is to be kept coarse and broad. What is to be done is to withdraw from precedents, and be directed to men and women—
also to The States in their federalness; for the union of the
parts of the body is not more necessary to their life than the
union of These States is to their life.

A profound person can easily know more of the people
than they know of themselves. Always waiting untold in
the souls of the armies of common people, is stuff better
than anything that can possibly appear in the leadership of
the same. That gives final verdicts. In every department of
These States, he who travels with a coterie, or with selected persons, or with imitators, or with infidels, or with
the owners of slaves, or with that which is ashamed of
the body of a man, or with that which is ashamed of the
body of a woman, or with any thing less than the bravest

and the openest, travels straight for the slopes of dissolution. The genius of all foreign literature is clipped and cut small, compared to our genius, and is essentially insulting to our usages, and to the organic compacts of These States. Old forms, old poems, majestic and proper in their own lands here in this land are exiles; the air here is very strong. Much that stands well and has a little enough place provided for it in the small scales of European kingdoms, empires, and the like, here stands haggard, dwarfed, ludicrous, or has no place little enough provided for it. Authorities, poems, models, laws, names, imported into America, are useful to America today to destroy them, and so move disencumbered to great works, great days.

Just so long, in our country or any country, as no revolutionists advance, and are backed by the people, sweeping off the swarms of routine representatives, officers in power, book-makers, teachers, ecclesiastics, politicians, just so long, I perceive, do they who are in power fairly represent that country, and remain of use, probably of very great use. To supersede them, when it is the pleasure of These States, full provision is made; and I say the time has arrived to use it with a strong hand. Here also the souls of the armies have not only overtaken the souls of the officers, but passed on, and left the souls of the officers behind out of sight many weeks' journey; and the souls of the armies now go en-masse without officers. Here also formulas, glosses, blanks, minutiæ, are choking the throats of the spokesmen to death. Those things most listened for, certainly those are the things least said. There is not a single History of the World. There is not one of America, or of the organic compacts of These States, or of Washington, or of Jefferson, nor of Language, nor any Dictionary of the English Language. There is no great author; every one has demeaned himself to some etiquette or some impotence. There is no manhood or life-power in poems; there are shoats and geldings more like. Or literature will be dressed up, a fine gentleman, distasteful to our instinct, foreign to our soil. Its neck bends right and left wherever it goes. Its costumes and jewelry prove how little it knows Nature. Its flesh is soft; it shows less and less of the indefinable hard something that is Nature. Where is any thing but the shaved Nature of synods and schools? Where is a savage and luxuriant man? Where is an overseer? In lives, in poems, in codes of law, in Congress, in tuitions, theaters, conversations, argumentations, not a single head lifts itself clean out, with proof that it is their master, and has subordinated them to itself, and is ready to try their superiors. None believes in These States, boldly illustrating them in himself. Not a man faces round at the rest with terrible negative voice, refusing all terms to be bought off from his own eyesight, or from the soul that he is, or from friendship, or from the body that he is, or from the soil and sea. To creeds, literature, art, the army, the navy, the executive, life is hardly proposed, but the sick and dying are proposed to cure the sick and dying. The churches are one vast lie; the people do not believe them, and they do not believe themselves; the priests are continually telling what they know well enough is not so, and keeping back what they know is so. The spectacle is a pitiful one. I think there can never be again upon the festive earth more bad-disordered persons deliberately taking seats, as of late in These States, at the heads of the public tables—such corpses' eyes for judges—such a rascal and thief in the Presidency.

Up to the present, as helps best, the people, like a lot of large boys, have no determined tastes, are quite unaware of the grandeur of themselves, and of their destiny, and of their immense strides—accept with voracity whatever is presented them in novels, histories, newspapers, poems, schools, lectures, every thing. Pretty soon through these and other means, their development makes the fibre that is capable of itself, and will assume determined tastes. The young men will be clear what they want, and will have it. They will follow none except him whose spirit leads them in the like spirit with themselves. Any such man will be welcome as the flowers of May. Others will be put out without ceremony. How much is there anyhow, to the young men of These States, in a parcel of helpless dandies, who can neither fight, work, shoot, ride, run, command—some of them devout, some quite insane, some castrated—all second-hand, or third, fourth, or fifth hand—waited upon by waiters, putting not this land first, but always other lands first, talking of art, doing the most ridiculous things for fear of being called ridiculous, smirking and skipping along, continually taking off their hats—no one behaving, dressing, writing, talking, loving, out of any natural and manly tastes of his own, but each one looking cautiously to see how the rest behave, dress, write, talk, love—pressing the noses of dead books upon themselves and upon their country—favoring no poets, philosophs, literats here, but dog-like danglers at the heels of the poets, philosophs, literats, of enemies' lands—favoring mental expressions, models of gentlemen and ladies, social habitudes in These States, to grow up in sneaking defiance of the popular substratums of The States? Of course they and the likes of them can never justify the strong poems of America. Of course no feed of theirs is to stop and be made welcome to muscle the bodies, male and female, for Manhattan Island, Brooklyn, Boston, Worcester, Hartford, Portland, Montreal, Detroit, Buffalo, Cleveland, Milwaukee, St. Louis, Indianapolis, Chicago, Cincinnati, Iowa City, Philadelphia, Baltimore, Raleigh, Savannah, Charleston, Mobile, New Orleans, Galveston, Brownsville, San Francisco, Havana, and a thousand equal cities, present and to come. Of course what they and the likes of them have been used for, draws toward its close, after which they will all be discharged, and not one of them will ever be heard of any more.

America, having duly conceived, bears out of herself offspring of her own to do the workmanship wanted. To freedom, to strength, to poems, to personal greatness, it is never permitted to rest, not a generation or part of a generation. To be ripe beyond further increase is to prepare to die. The architects of These States laid their foundations, and passed to further spheres. What they laid is a work done; as much more remains. Now are needed other architects, whose duty is not less difficult, but perhaps more difficult. Each age forever needs architects. America is not finished, perhaps never will be; now America is a divine true sketch. There are Thirty-Two States sketched—the population thirty millions. In a few years there will be Fifty States. Again in a few years there will be A Hundred States, the population hundreds of millions, the freshest and freest of men. Of course such men stand to nothing less than the freshest and freest expression.

Poets here, literats here, are to rest on organic different bases from other countries; not a class set apart, circling only in the circle themselves, modest and pretty, desperately scratching for rhymes, pallid with white paper, shut off, aware of the old pictures and traditions of the race, but unaware of the actual race around them—not breeding in and in among each other till they all have the scrofula. Lands of ensemble, bards of ensemble! Walking freely out from the old traditions, as our politics has walked out, American poets and literats recognize nothing behind them superior to what is present with them—recognize with joy the sturdy living forms of the men and women of These States, the divinity of sex, the perfect eligibility of the female with the male, all The States, liberty and equality, real articles, the different trades, mechanics, the young fellows of Manhattan Island, customs, instincts, slang, Wisconsin, Georgia, the noble Southern heart, the hot blood, the spirit that will be nothing less than master, the filibuster spirit, the Western man, native-born perceptions, the eye for forms, the perfect models of made things, the wild smack of freedom, California, money, electric-telegraphs, free-trade, iron and the iron mines—recognize without demur those splendid resistless black poems, the steam-ships of the seaboard states, and those other resistless splendid poems, the locomotives, followed through the interior states by trains of rail-road cars.

A word remains to be said, as of one ever present, not yet permitted to be acknowledged, discarded or made dumb by literature, and the results apparent. To the lack of an avowed, empowered, unabashed development of sex, (the only salvation for the same,) and to the fact of speakers and writers fraudulently assuming as always dead what every one knows to be always alive, is attributable the remarkable non-personality and indistinctness of modern productions in books, art, talk; also that in the scanned lives of men and women most of them appear to have been for some time past of the neuter gender; and also the stinging fact that in orthodox society today, if the dresses were changed, the men might easily pass for women and the women for men.

Infidelism usurps most with fœtid polite face; among the rest infidelism about sex. By silence or obedience the pens of savans, poets, historians, biographers, and the rest, have long connived at the filthy law, and books enslaved to it, that what makes the manhood of a man, that sex, womanhood, maternity, desires, lusty animations, organs, acts, are unmentionable and to be ashamed of, to be driven to skulk out of literature with whatever belongs to them. This filthy law has to be repealed—it stands in the way of great reforms. Of women just as much as men, it is the interest that there should not be infidelism about sex, but perfect faith. Women in These States approach the day of that organic equality with men, without which, I see, men cannot have organic equality among themselves. This empty dish, gallantry, will then be filled with something. This tepid wash, this diluted deferential love, as in songs, fictions, and so forth, is enough to make a man vomit; as to manly friendship, everywhere observed in The States, there is not the first breath of it to be observed in print. I say that the body of a man or woman, the main matter, is so far quite unexpressed in poems; but that the body is to be expressed, and sex is. Of bards for These States, if it come to a question, it is whether they shall celebrate in poems the eternal decency of the amativeness of Nature, the motherhood of all, or whether they shall be the bards of the fashionable delusion of the inherent nastiness of sex, and of the feeble and querulous modesty of deprivation. This is important in poems, because the whole of the other expressions of a nation are but flanges out of its great poems. To me, henceforth, that theory of any thing, no matter what, stagnates in its vitals, cowardly and rotten, while it cannot publicly accept, and publicly name, with specific words, the things on which all existence, all souls, all realization, all decency, all health, all that is worth being here for, all of woman and of man, all beauty, all purity, all sweetness, all friendship, all strength, all life, all immortality depend. The courageous soul, for a year or two to come, may be proved by faith in sex, and by disdaining concessions.

To poets and literats—to every woman and man, today or any day, the conditions of the present, needs, dangers, prejudices, and the like, are the perfect conditions on which we are here, and the conditions for wording the future with undissuadable words. These States; receivers of the stamina of past ages and lands, initiate the outlines of repayment a thousand fold. They fetch the American great masters, waited for by old worlds and new, who accept evil as well as good, ignorance as well as erudition, black as soon as white, foreign-born materials as well as home-born, reject none, force discrepancies into range, surround the whole, concentrate them on present periods and places, show the application to each and any one's body and soul, and show the true use of precedents. Always America will be agitated and turbulent. This day it is taking shape, not to be less so, but to be more so, stormily, capriciously, on native principles, with such vast proportions of parts! As for me, I love screaming, wrestling, boiling-hot days.

Of course, we shall have a national character, an identity. As it ought to be, and as soon as it ought to be, it will be. That, with much else, takes care of itself, is a result, and the cause of greater results. With Ohio, Illinois, Missouri, Oregon—with the states around the Mexican sea—with cheerfully welcomed immigrants from Europe, Asia, Africa—with Connecticut, Vermont, New Hampshire, Rhode Island—with all varied interests, facts, beliefs, parties, genesis —there is being fused a determined character, fit for the broadest use for the freewomen and freemen of The States, accomplished and to be accomplished, without any exception whatever—each indeed free, each idiomatic, as becomes live states and men, but each adhering to one enclosing general form of politics, manners, talk, personal style, as the plenteous varieties of the race adhere to one physical form. Such character is the brain and spine to all, including literature, including poems. Such character, strong, limber, just, openmouthed, American-blooded, full of pride, full of ease, of passionate friendliness, is to stand compact upon that vast basis of the supremacy of Individuality—that new moral American continent without which, I see, the physical continent remained incomplete, may-be a carcass, a bloat—that newer America, answering face to face with The States, with ever-satisfying and ever-unsurveyable seas and shores.

Those shores you found. I say you have led The States there—have led Me there. I say that none has ever done, or ever can do, a greater deed for The States, than your deed. Others may line out the lines, build cities, work mines, break up farms; it is yours to have been the original true Captain who put to sea, intuitive, positive, rendering the first report, to be told less by any report, and more by the mariners of a thousand bays, in each tack of their arriving and departing, many years after you.

Receive, dear Master, these statements and assurances through me, for all the young men, and for an earnest that we know none before you, but the best following you; and that we demand to take your name into our keeping, and that we understand what you have indicated, and find the same indicated in ourselves, and that we will stick to it and enlarge upon it through These States.

WALT WHITMAN

But the new edition of Leaves of Grass *contained a good deal of new material, including pieces intended to combat that "infidelism about sex" of which Whitman complained in his epistle.*

Of the effect of all this on Emerson the following account has been left by Josiah P. Quincy of Boston[1]:

Mr. Emerson came into his study at Concord where I was sitting, bearing in his hand a book which he had just received. This was the new edition of Whitman's book with the words "I greet you at the beginning of a great career. R. W. Emerson," printed in gold letters upon the cover. Emerson looked troubled, and expressed annoyance that a

[1] Quoted in Bliss Perry's *Walt Whitman.*

sentence from a private letter should be wrenched from its context and so emblazoned. He afterwards gave me the book, saying that the inside was worthy attention even though it came from one capable of so misusing the cover. I noted the incident because at no other time had I seen a cloud of dissatisfaction darken that serene countenance.

Of this second edition Henry Thoreau wrote as follows in a letter to Harrison Blake[1]:

December 7 (1856)

That Walt Whitman, of whom I wrote to you, is the most interesting fact to me at present. I have just read his second edition (which he gave me), and it has done me more good than any reading for a long time. Perhaps I remember best the poem of Walt Whitman, an American, and the Sun-Down Poem. There are two or three pieces in the book which are disagreeable, to say the least; simply sensual. He does not celebrate love at all. It is as if the beasts spoke. I think that men have not been ashamed of themselves without reason. No doubt there have always been dens where such deeds were unblushingly recited, and it is no merit to compete with their inhabitants. But even on this side he has spoken more truth than any American or modern that I know. I have found his poem exhilarating, encouraging. As for its sensuality,—and it may turn out to be less sensual than it appears,—I do not so much wish that those parts were not written, as that men and women were so pure that they could read them without harm, that is, without understanding them. One woman told me that no woman could read it,—as if a man could read what a woman could not. Of course Walt Whitman can communicate to us no experience, and if we are shocked, whose experience is it that we are reminded of?

On the whole, it sounds to me very brave and American, after whatever deductions. I do not believe that all the sermons, so called, that have been preached in this land put together are equal to it for preaching.

[1]Quoted in Bliss Perry's *Walt Whitman.*

We ought to rejoice greatly in him. He occasionally suggests something a little more than human. You can't confound him with the other inhabitants of Brooklyn or New York. How they must shudder when they read him! He is awfully good.

To be sure I sometimes feel a little imposed on. By his heartiness and broad generalities he puts me into a liberal frame of mind prepared to see wonders,—as it were, sets me upon a hill or in the midst of a plain,—stirs me well up, and then—throws in a thousand of brick. Though rude, and sometimes ineffectual, it is a great primitive poem,—an alarum or trumpet-note ringing through the American camp. Wonderfully like the Orientals, too, considering that when I asked him if he had read them, he answered, "No; tell me about them."

I did not get far in conversation with him,—two more being present,—and among the few things which I chanced to say, I remember that one was, in answer to him as representing America, that I did not think much of America or of politics, and so on, which may have been somewhat of a damper to him.

Since I have seen him, I find that I am not disturbed by any brag or egoism in his book. He may turn out the least of a braggart of all, having a better right to be confident. He is a great fellow.

Emerson to Caroline Sturgis Tappan, an American friend then in Europe:

CONCORD *Octr 13, 1857*

DEAR CAROLINE,

You will never write me again, I have been so ungrateful, I who value every line & word from you, or about you. Perhaps 'tis my too much writing in youth that makes it so repulsive now in these old days. What to tell you now that I have begun—you that are in the land of wine & oil, of us in the land of meal? Italy cannot excel the banks of glory wh. sun & mist paint in these very days on the forest by lake & river. But the Muses are as reticent as Nature is flamboyant, & no fireeyed child has yet been born. 'Tis strange that the relations of your old friends here remain unchanged to the world of letters & society, I mean, that those who held of the Imagination & believed that the necessities of the New World would presently evoke the mystic Power, & we should not pass away without hearing the Choral Hymns of a new age & adequate to Nature, still find colleges & books as cramp & sterile as ever, & our discontent keeps us in the selfsame suspicious relation to beauties & elegant society. We are all the worse that you, & those who are like you, if any such there be, as there are not,—but persons of positive quality, & capacious of beauty—desert us, & abdicate their power at home. Why not a mind as wise & deep & subtle as your Browning, with his trained talent? Why can we not breed a lyric man as exquisite as Tennyson; or such a Burke-like *longanimity* as E. Browning (whom you mention in interesting positions, but do not describe to me)? Our wild Whitman, with real inspiration but choked by Titanic abdomen, & Delia Bacon,[1] with genius, but mad, & clinging like a tortoise to English soil, are the sole producers that America has yielded in ten years. Is all the granite & forest & prairie & superfoetation of millions to no richer result? If I were writing to any other than you, I should render my wonted homage to the gods for my two gossips, Alcott & Henry T., whose existence I impute to America for righteousness, though they miss the fame of your praise. Charles Newcomb, too, proves the rich possibilities in the soil, tho' his result is zero. So does Ellery. But who cares? As soon as we walk out of doors Nature transcends all poets so far, that a little more or less skill in whistling is of no account. Out of doors we lose the lust of performance, & are content to pass silent, & see others pass silent, into the depths of a Universe so resonant & beaming. . . .

[1]Delia Bacon, the first exponent of the "Baconian theory," believed that Shakespeare's plays had been written by a group including Bacon, Raleigh, and Spenser, and that they contained a cipher which would reveal an esoteric system of thought. That year she published a book called *Philosophy of the Plays of Shakespeare Unfolded.* E. W.

But the second edition of Leaves of Grass *provoked notices as angry as the first one, and the publishers who had been handling it became frightened and dropped it. Whitman, however, went on working on his book, revising it and adding to it, and in the May of 1860 he brought out a third edition.*

This edition was published in Boston, and Whitman went on to supervise it. Emerson came to see him. The Children of Adam *poems were appearing for the first time as a special section, which Whitman tried to veil a little by making it* Enfans [sic] d'Adam; *and Emerson made an attempt to dissuade him from having them printed. Whitman has left in* Specimen Days *an account of this conversation, written in 1881 on the occasion of a later trip to Boston:*

Up and down this breadth by Beacon street, between these same old elms, I walk'd for two hours, of a bright sharp February[1] mid-day twenty-one years ago, with Emerson, then in his prime, keen, physically and morally magnetic, arm'd at every point, and when he chose, wielding the emotional just as well as the intellectual. During those two hours he was the talker and I the listener. It was an argument-statement, reconnoitring, review, attack, and pressing home, (like an army corps in order, artillery, cavalry, infantry,) of all that could be said against that part (and a main part) in the construction of my poems, *Children of Adam.* More precious than gold to me that dissertion—it afforded me, ever after, this strange and paradoxical lesson; each point of E.'s statement was unanswerable, no judge's charge ever more complete or convincing, I could never hear the points better put—and then I felt down in my soul the clear and unmistakable conviction to disobey all, and pursue my own way. "What have you to say then to such things?" said E., pausing in conclusion. "Only that while I can't answer them at all, I feel more settled than ever to adhere to my own theory, and exemplify it," was my candid response. Whereupon we went and had a good dinner at the American House. And

[1]It appears from a letter from Whitman written to a friend at the time that his walk with Emerson took place, not in February, but just after the middle of March.

thenceforward I never waver'd or was touch'd with qualms, (as I confess I had been two or three times before.)

And Whitman amplified this account in a conversation with Horace Traubel on April 20, 1888:

Emerson's objections to the outcast passages in *Leaves of Grass* were neither moral nor literary, but were given with an eye to my worldly success. He believed the book would sell—said that the American people should know the book: yes, would know it but for its sex handicap: and he thought he saw the way by which to accomplish what he called "the desirable end." He did not say I should drop a single line —he did not put it that way at all: he asked whether I could consent to eliminate certain popularly objectionable poems and passages. Emerson's position has been misunderstood: he offered absolutely no spiritual argument against the book exactly as it stood. Give it a chance to be seen, give the people a chance to want to see it—that was the gist of his contention. If there was any weakness in his position it was in his idea that the particular poems could be dropped and the *Leaves* remain the *Leaves* still: he did not see the significance of the sex element as I had put it into the book and resolutely there stuck to it—he did not see that if I had cut sex out I might just as well have cut everything out— the full scheme would no longer exist—it would have been violated in its most sensitive spot.

Whitman also on the occasion of this visit saw the once famous writer of boys' books, John Taylor Trowbridge, who has left in his autobiography a report of a conversation with Whitman, in which the latter discussed the influence on him of Emerson:

Much of the talk was about himself and his poems, in every particular of which I was profoundly interested. He told me of his boyhood in Brooklyn; going to work in a printing office at the age of fourteen; teaching school at seventeen and eighteen; writing stories and sketches for periodicals under his full name, Walter Whitman (his first

Leaves of Grass was copyrighted by Walter Whitman, after which he discarded "Walter" for "Walt"); editing newspapers and making political speeches, on the Democratic side; leading an impulsive, irregular sort of life, and absorbing, as probably no other man ever did, the common aspects of the cities he was so proud of, Brooklyn and New York. His friendships were mostly with the common people—pilots, drivers, mechanics; and his favorite diversions crossing the ferries, riding on the top of omnibuses, and attending operas. He liked to get off alone by the seashore, read Homer and Ossian with the salt air on his cheeks, and shout their winged words to the winds and waves. The book he knew best was the Bible, the prophetical parts of which stirred in him a vague desire to be the bard or prophet of his own time and country.

Then, at the right moment, he read Emerson.

I was extremely interested to know how far the influence of our greatest writer had been felt in the making of a book which, without being at all imitative, was pitched in the very highest key of self-reliance. In his letter to Emerson, printed in the second edition of *Leaves of Grass,* speaking of "Individuality, that new moral American continent," Whitman had averred: "Those shores you found; I say, you led the States there—have led me there." And it seemed hardly possible that the first determined attempt to cast into literature a complete man, with all his pride and passions, should have been made by one whose feet were not already firmly planted on "those shores." Then there was the significant fact of his having mailed a copy of his first edition to Emerson.

Whitman talked frankly on the subject, that day on Prospect Hill, and told how he became acquainted with Emerson's writings. He was at work as a carpenter (his father's trade before him) in Brooklyn, building with his own hands and on his own account small and very plain houses for laboring men; as soon as one was finished and sold, beginning another—houses of two or three rooms. This was in 1854; he was then thirty-five years old. He lived at home with his mother; going off to his work in the morning and returning at night, carrying his dinner pail like any common laborer. Along with his pail he usually carried a book, between which and his solitary meal he would divide his nooning. Once the book chanced to be a volume of Emerson; and from that time he took with him no other writer. His half-formed purpose, his vague aspirations, all that had lain smoldering so long within him, waiting to be fired, rushed into flame at the touch of those electric words—the words that burn in the prose-poem *Nature,* and in the essays on *Spiritual Laws, The Over-Soul, Self-Reliance.* The sturdy carpenter in his working-day garb, seated on his pile of boards; a poet in that rude disguise, as yet but dimly conscious of his powers; in one hand the sandwich put up for him by his good mother, his other hand holding open the volume that revealed to him his greatness and his destiny,— this is the picture which his simple narrative called up, that Sunday so long ago, and which has never faded from my memory.

He freely admitted that he could never have written his poems if he had not first "come to himself," and that Emerson helped him to "find himself." I asked him if he thought he would have come to himself without that help. He said, "Yes, but it would have taken longer." And he used this characteristic expression: "I was simmering, simmering, simmering; Emerson brought me to a boil."

It was in that summer of 1854, while he was still at work upon his houses, that he began the *Leaves of Grass,* which he wrote, rewrote, and re-rewrote (to quote again his own words), and afterward set in type with his own hand.

I make this statement thus explicit because a question of profound personal and literary interest is involved, and because it is claimed by some of the later friends of Whitman that he wrote his first *Leaves of Grass* before he had read Emerson. When they urge his own authority for their contention, I can only reply that he told me distinctly the contrary, when his memory was fresher.

The Emersonian influence is often clearly traceable in Whitman's early poems; seldom in the later. It is in the first line of the very first poem in which he struck the keynote of his defiant chant: "I celebrate myself." And at times Emerson's identical thought reappears with slight change in the *Leaves*. Two or three instances out of many will suffice. Emerson wrote: "Suppose you should contradict yourself, what then? With consistency a great soul has simply nothing to do." Whitman says:

> Do I contradict myself?
> Very well, then, I contradict myself,
> I am large, I contain multitudes.

Emerson: "Shall I skulk and dodge and duck, with my unreasonable apologies?" Whitman:

> I see that the elementary laws never apologize . . .
> We have had ducking and deprecating about enough.

Emerson: "The unstable estimates of men crowd to him whose mind is filled with a truth as the heaped waves of the Atlantic follow the moon." Whitman:

> Surely whoever speaks to me in the right voice, him or her I
>   shall follow,
> As the waters follow the moon, silently, with fluid steps, any-
>   where around the globe.

Yet the form Whitman chose for his message was as independent of Emerson's as of all other literary forms whatsoever. Outwardly, his unrhymed and unmeasured lines resemble those of Tupper's *Proverbial Philosophy;* but in no other way are they akin to those colorless platitudes. To the music of the opera, for which he had a passion, more than to anything else, was due his emancipation from what he called the "ballad-style" of poetry, by which he meant poetry hampered by rhyme and meter. "But for the opera," he declared, that day on Prospect Hill, "I could never have written *Leaves of Grass.*"

Entry in Emerson's journal of February 1862:

Thoreau. Perhaps his fancy for Walt Whitman grew out of his taste for wild nature, for an otter, a woodchuck, or a loon. He loved sufficiency, hated a sum that would not prove: loved Walt and hated Alcott.

In 1863, Emerson helped Whitman to raise money for the sick and wounded soldiers of the Civil War, whom Whitman was visiting in hospitals; and the following note by Whitman (from a manuscript in the Library of Congress) was found written on the back of a pamphlet which dealt with the activities of an organization called The United States Christian Commission, with which Whitman was associated at the beginning of that year.

His quality, his meaning has the quality of the light of day, which startles nobody. You cannot put your finger upon it yet there is nothing more palpable, nothing more wonderful, nothing more vital and refreshing. There are some things in the expression of this philosoph, this poet, that are full mates of the best, the perennial masters, and will so stand in fame and the centuries. America in the future, in her long train of poets and writers, while knowing more vehement and luxuriant ones, will, I think, acknowledge nothing nearer [than] this man, the actual beginner of the whole procession—and certainly nothing purer, cleaner, sweeter, more canny, none, after all, more thoroughly her own and native. The most exquisite taste and caution are in him, always saving his feet from passing beyond the limits, for he is transcendental of limits, and you see underneath the rest a secret proclivity, American maybe, to dare and violate and make escapades.

That winter James Russell Lowell wrote as follows to the Rev. W. L. Gage:

ELMWOOD, 7ᵗʰ Decʳ 1863

MY DEAR SIR,—When I was editing the *Atlantic Monthly*, I was in the habit of sending all the new books which came to me as editor, to the College Library. I suppose *Leaves of Grass* must have been one of them. It is a book I never looked into farther than to satisfy myself that it was a solemn humbug. Still, I think the business of a library is to have *every* book in it, and I should be sorry to have it supposed that I thought well of every volume I have sent to Gore Hall— nay, that I did not think ill of many of them.

As for the evil influence of this particular book, I doubt if so much harm is done by downright *animality* as by a more refined sensuousness. There is worse in Schleiermacher. Wordsworth would have tabooed *Wilhelm Meister*. Where shall the line be drawn? Would you have a library without Byron? or a Byron with his most characteristic work left out? For my own part I should like to see a bonfire made of a good deal of ancient and modern literature—but 'tis out of the question.

I am obliged to you, however, for calling my attention to a part of this book of which I knew nothing, and I will take care to keep it out of the way of the students.

Very truly yours

J. R. LOWELL

Emerson had also sent Whitman two letters of recommendation to prominent New England political figures, Charles Sumner and Salmon P. Chase.

In December 1863 Trowbridge was in Washington visiting Chase, then Secretary of the Treasury in Lincoln's cabinet. Whitman was also in Washington, and Trowbridge describes what happened as follows:

I thought no man more than Whitman merited recognition and assistance from the government, and I once asked him if he would accept a position in one of the departments. He answered frankly that he would. But he believed it improbable that he could get an appointment, although (as he mentioned casually) he had letters of recommendation from Emerson.

There were two of these, and they were especially interesting to me, as I knew something of the disturbed relations existing between the two men, on account of Whitman's indiscreet use of Emerson's famous letter to him, acknowledging the gift copy of the first *Leaves of Grass*. Whitman not only published that letter without the writer's authority, but printed an extract from it, in conspicuous gold, on the back of his second edition: "I greet you at the beginning of a great career;" thus making Emerson in some sense an indorser not only of the first poems, but of others he had never seen, and which he would have preferred never to see in print. This was an instance of bad taste, but not of intentional bad faith, on the part of Whitman. Talking of it once, he said, in his grand way: "I supposed the letter was meant to be blazoned; I regarded it as the chart of an emperor." But Emerson had no thought of acting the imperial part toward so adventurous a voyager. I remember hearing him allude to the incident shortly after that second edition appeared. Speaking of the attention the new poet was attracting, he mentioned an Englishman who had come to this country bringing a letter to Whitman from Monckton Milnes (afterward Lord Houghton). "But," said Emerson, "hearing that Whitman had not used me well in the matter of letters, he did not deliver it." He had afterwards made a strenuous effort to induce Whitman to omit certain objectionable passages from his edition of 1860, and failed. And I knew that the later writings of Whitman interested him less and less. "No more evidence of getting into form," he once remarked,—a singular comment, it may be thought, from one whose own chief defect as a writer seemed to be an imperfect mastery of form.

With these things in mind, I read eagerly the two letters from Emerson recommending Whitman for a government appointment. One was addressed to Senator Sumner; the other, I was surprised and pleased to find, to Secretary Chase. I had but a slight acquaintance with Sumner, and the letter to him I handed back. The one written to Chase I wished to retain, in order to deliver it to the Secretary with my own hands, and with such furthering words as I could summon in so good a cause. Whitman expressed small hope in the venture, and stipulated that in case of the failure he anticipated, I should bring back the letter.

As we left the breakfast table, the next morning, I followed the Secretary into his private office, where, after some pleasant talk, I remarked that I was about to overstep a rule I had laid down for myself on entering his house. He said, "What rule?" I replied, "Never to repay your hospitality by asking of you any official favor." He said I needn't have thought it necessary to make that rule, for he was always glad to do for his friends such things as he was constantly called upon to do for strangers. Then I laid before him the Whitman business. He was evidently impressed by Emerson's letter, and he listened with interest to what I had to say of the man and his patriotic work. But he was troubled. "I am placed," he said, "in a very embarrassing position. It would give me great pleasure to grant this request, out of my regard for Mr. Emerson"; and he was gracious enough to extend the courtesy of this "regard" to me, also. But then he went on to speak of *Leaves of Grass* as a book that had made the author notorious; and I found that he judged it, as all but a very few persons then did, not independently, on its own merits, but by conventional standards of taste and propriety. He had understood that the writer was a rowdy—"one of the roughs"—according to his descriptions of himself.

I said, "He is as quiet a gentleman in his manners and conversation as any guest who enters your door."

He replied: "I am bound to believe what you say; but his writings have given him a bad repute, and I should not know what sort of a place to give to such a man"—with more to the same purpose.

I respected his decision, much as I regretted it, and, persuaded that nothing I could urge would induce him to change it, I said I would relieve him of all embarrassment in the business by withdrawing the letter. He glanced again at the signature, hesitated, and made this surprising response:

"I have nothing of Emerson's in his handwriting, and I shall be glad to keep this."

I thought it hardly fair, but as the letter was addressed to him, and had passed into his hands, I couldn't well reclaim it against his wishes.

Whitman seemed really to have formed some hopes of the success of my mission, after I had undertaken it, as he showed when I went to give him an account of my interview with the Secretary. He took the disappointment philosophically, but indulged in some sardonic remarks about Chase and his department, regarding which some choice

scandals were then afloat. "He is right," he said, "in preserving his saints from contamination by a man like me!"
But I stood up for the Secretary, as, with the Secretary,
I had stood up for Whitman. Those very scandals had no
doubt rendered him cautious in making appointments. And
could anyone be blamed for taking the writer of *Leaves of
Grass* at his word when, in his defiance of conventionality,
he had described himself as "rowdyish," "disorderly," and
worse? "'I cock my hat as I please, indoors and out,'" I
quoted. Walt laughed, and said, "I don't blame him; it's
about what I expected." He asked for the letter, and showed
his amused disgust when I explained how it had been
pocketed by the Secretary.

I should probably have had no difficulty in securing the
appointment if I had withheld Emerson's letter, and called
my friend simply Mr. Whitman, or Mr. Walter Whitman,
without mentioning *Leaves of Grass*. But I felt that the
Secretary, if he was to appoint him, should know just whom
he was appointing; and Whitman was the last person in
the world to shirk the responsibility of having written an
audacious book.

Whether the same candor was used in procuring for him
a clerkship in the Interior Department, to which he was
appointed later, I do not know. He had been for some time
performing the duties of that position, without exciting any
other comment than that he performed them well, when a
new Secretary (James Harlan), coming in under Johnson,
and discovering that the grave and silent man at a certain
desk was the author of a reprehensible book, dismissed him
unceremoniously.

*John Burroughs in his journal of December 21, 1871,
reports the following conversation with Whitman*[1]:

Walt said a friend of his, Mr. Marvin, met Emerson in
Boston the other day. When Walt was mentioned, "Yes,"
said Mr. Emerson, "Walt sends me all his books. But tell

[1] This quotation and the next are from *Whitman and Burroughs,
Comrades,* by Clara Barrus.

Walt I am not satisfied—not satisfied. I expect—him—to make—the songs of the Nation—but he seems—to be contented to—make the inventories."

Walt laughed and said it tickled him much. It was capital. But it did not disturb him at all. "I know what I am about better than Emerson does. Yet I love to hear what the gods have to say." And continuing, he said, "I see how I might easily have wandered into other and easier paths than I did—paths that would have paid better, and gained me popularity; and I wonder how my feet were guided as they were. Indeed, I am more than satisfied with myself for having the courage to do what I have."

Later in the same year John Burroughs, in a letter to Myron B. Benton, described a conversation with Emerson, whom he had met in the station at Washington:

He was alone and had ten or fifteen minutes to spare, so I got him aboard the train and sat down beside him. He has not changed much since we saw him, except perhaps his nose is a little more hooked, and his hair a little thinner. I drew him out on Walt and found out what was the matter. He thought Walt's friends ought to quarrel a little more with him, and insist on his being a little more tame and orderly—more mindful of the requirements of beauty, of art, of culture, etc.—all of which was very pitiful to me, and I wanted to tell him so. But the train started just then and I got off. However, I wrote him a letter telling what I thought, and sent him my book. I do not expect to hear from it, but I was determined to give him a shot.

In notes on conversations with Whitman in the winter of 1876–77,[1] Herbert Gilchrist reports the following observations:

Talking of the Bostonians, Mr. Whitman said:

W.: "They are supercilious to everybody. Emerson is the only sweet one among them, and he has been spoilt by them. Yes, it is a stifling atmosphere for him. Yes, that is just

[1] Printed in *Walt Whitman's Workshop* by Clifton Joseph Furness.

what I should say. There are certain recognized parlor laws of propriety which are remembered and allowed. But to carry their notions of suitor drawing-room proprieties into poetry . . . it's too absurd! They are a most supercilious set. Look down on everybody. It is bad enough with Vic Hugo and [the] Parisians."

Herbert Gilchrist: "Ah, there is Patriotism!"

Whitman: "Well, yes, and *they* have done something, but Bostonians have not, like Paris, got beautiful works of accomplished art, yet they consider themselves the salt of the earth."

In 1877 Edward Carpenter, an English disciple of Whitman's, visited the United States. He reports, in Days with Walt Whitman, *the following conversation with Emerson:*

On the occasion of my . . . visit to the States in 1877, I stayed a night at Emerson's house at Concord—most pleasantly and hospitably received—and enjoyed greatly his talk as we walked up and down the old-fashioned garden, or sat in his book-lined study. When I spoke of Whitman and asked what he thought of him, he laughed (a little nervously, I thought) and said, "Well, I thought he had some merit at one time: there was a good deal of promise in his first edition—but he is a wayward fanciful man." (He used a third epithet beside *wayward* and *fanciful,* something like *violent,* but I hardly think as strong as that.) "I saw him in New York and asked him to dine at my hotel. He shouted for a 'tin mug' for his beer. Then he had a noisy fire-engine society. And he took me there, and was like a boy over it, as if there had never been such a thing before." He went on, in words which I do not recall, to object to the absence of meter in *Leaves of Grass;* and ended, I remember, by taking down a volume by Tennyson from the shelf—handling it affectionately and showing me the author's autograph on the fly-leaf and dwelling on the beauty of the Tennysonian diction and meter.

Whitman in his later years, October 19, 1888, gave Horace Traubel the following account of what—since Emerson lectured in Newark in December 1855—is perhaps the same occasion:

"Yes—he was very beautiful, very serene: there were always new revelations of it in our intercourse. Did I ever tell you the story of a visit he paid me once on the way to lecture at Newark? Emerson called—I was in Brooklyn at the time: it was early afternoon: he was free from then on to the lecture hour: he said to me at once: 'I have a lecture to deliver at Newark this evening: I therefore have three hours to spend with you.' I invited him to take a bite or two, but he answered: 'No—it is but a little after dinner: I am stopping at the Astor House: you don't want anything now? Nor do I.' I was entirely satisfied. He asked me how we should go: we lived three miles from the ferry: I answered him that I would rather walk. He was agreeable to that: so we went along in that way talking: the long stroll being very happy, memorable. We went to New York—to the Astor House. Emerson left me here: took me into the office: spoke of his engagement in the evening—of his anxiety to be on time: said that he would go out for a few minutes—see about the trains, make sure of everything: meanwhile I should go to his room. He left—I looked up one of the hotel men. I asked him if he knew Mr. Emerson's room. He said, 'Yes.' I then asked: 'Have you the pass-key?' He said again, 'Yes.' I then told him what I wanted. He was reluctant. I asked: 'Will you open the room for me so I can wait there till Mr. Emerson comes?' He still hesitated. I asked: 'You won't do it?' and he answered: 'I'd rather not.'" W. stopped here—laughed heartily—took some liberal gulps of water from the pitcher on the floor. "After about ten minutes Emerson came back—took in the situation at a glance: seemed anxious, annoyed, flustrated—even inclined to be angry. I was not a bit mad myself—I was thoroughly composed, satisfied: on the contrary, I commended the waiter: he had done the one thing the right kind of a man in his position was bound to do. We went up to Emerson's room together—Emerson still seemed exercised—made no attempt to disguise his annoyance. We sat down. Emerson said: 'We have had quite a long walk: you must be thirsty: wouldn't you like to have something to drink?' I answered, 'Yes.' So we had some drink together. I can't now remember what. Emerson still continued in a sort of fretful mood: I saw there was danger he would break loose on, be sharp to, the waiter. I think I said to him—I am sure I said to him—about it: 'Let it pass—don't say anything about it: he did his duty—that was all.'" "Did Emerson see it?" "I should say so—like a flash." Then he added: "Why, Emerson had the cutest, justest, brain of all our world: saw everything, literally everything, in right perspective—things personal, things general. We got into some discussion at dinner: were perfectly free together: sometimes things would get hot, stormy (for us): we differed sharply in some things—never hesitated to express our differences—doing so this day rather loudly—more positively than usual. The question up was of national character: Emerson had just published *English Traits*—naturally was full of the English—English power, characteristics, and so forth. We talked and talked: Emerson inclined to favor the English—to accept them in a more favorable light than the Scotch-Irish. My own choice would have been hard to tell—I embrace, include, all. I am especially fond of the Scotch, though I can never be partial in the last analysis to one nation as above another: fond of the Scotch, who, after we admit their gloomy, despotic, reverse side, are still to be credited with some of the most marvelous qualities of which any race can boast. At one moment, the discussion running along this line, Emerson was saying: 'I like the English—I do not like the Scotch so well: and as for the Irish——': here he suddenly stopped (suddenly, as Hicks used to haul himself to in the moment of his canting spells): I didn't know what had happened. A young waiter who had been standing back of us left the room. Emerson looked at me quietly and said: 'I was going to say more—more about the Irish: but it suddenly struck me that the young man there was himself Irish and might not find what I was going to say pleasant.' It was thoroughly characteristic—just like him: like his consideration, courtesy, unfailing tact. His temperament was almost ideal." Then he said: "Whatever may be the truth of what Clifford says about me, I hope there may never stray out of my work anywhere a note of dissatisfaction, disappointment, despair: indeed, I may say I am sure there does not—sure of it."

In 1881, the firm of James R. Osgood and Company in Boston offered to bring out a definitive edition of Leaves of Grass. *Whitman went on at the end of August to supervise the printing. He had insisted that "the sexuality odes about which the original row was started and kept up so long" must be "retained and go in the same as ever."* Leaves of Grass *was not only to appear for the first time with a regular publisher's imprint, but to be brought out by one of the leading American publishers.*

An account of a visit to Concord appears in his journal for September of that year (Specimen Days):

Concord, Mass. Out here on a visit—elastic, mellow, Indian-summery weather. Came today from Boston (a pleasant ride of 40 minutes by steam, through Somerville, Belmont, Waltham, Stony Brook, and other lively towns), convoy'd by my friend F. B. Sanborn, and to his ample house, and the kindness and hospitality of Mrs. S. and their fine family. Am writing this under the shade of some old hickories and elms, just after 4 P.M., on the porch, within a stone's throw of the Concord river. Off against me, across stream, on a meadow and side-hill, haymakers are gathering and wagoning-in probably their second or third crop. The spread of emerald-green and brown, the knolls, the score or two of little haycocks dotting the meadow, the loaded-up wagons, the patient horses, the slow-strong action of the men and pitchforks—all in the just-waning afternoon, with patches of yellow sunsheen, mottled by long shadows—a cricket shrilly chirping, herald of the dusk—a boat with two figures noiselessly gliding along the little river, passing under the stone bridge-arch—the slight settling haze of aerial moisture, the sky and the peacefulness expanding in all directions and overhead—fill and soothe me.

Same Evening. Never had I a better piece of luck befall me: a long and blessed evening with Emerson, in a way I couldn't have wish'd better or different. For nearly two hours he has been placidly sitting where I could see his face in the best light, near me. Mrs. S.'s back-parlor well fill'd with people, neighbors, many fresh and charming faces, women, mostly young, but some old. My friend A. B. Alcott and his daughter Louisa were there early. A good deal of talk, the subject Henry Thoreau—some new glints of his life and fortunes, with letters to and from him—one of the best by Margaret Fuller, others by Horace Greeley, Channing, *etc.*— one from Thoreau himself, most quaint and interesting. (No doubt I seem'd very stupid to the roomful of company, taking hardly any part in the conversation; but I had "my own pail to milk in," as the Swiss proverb puts it.) My seat and the relative arrangement were such that, without being rude, or anything of the kind, I could just look squarely at E., which I did a good part of the two hours. On entering, he had spoken very briefly and politely to several of the company, then settled himself in his chair, a trifle push'd back, and, though a listener and apparently an alert one, remain'd silent through the whole talk and discussion. A lady friend quietly took a seat next him, to give special attention. A good color in his face, eyes clear, with the well-known expression of sweetness, and the old clear-peering aspect quite the same.

Next Day.—Several hours at E.'s house, and dinner there. An old familiar house (he has been in it thirty-five years), with surroundings, furnishment, roominess, and plain elegance and fullness, signifying democratic ease, sufficient opulence, and an admirable old-fashioned simplicity—modern luxury, with its mere sumptuousness and affectation, either touch'd lightly upon or ignored altogether. Dinner the same. Of course the best of the occasion (Sunday, September 18, '81) was the sight of E. himself. As just said, a healthy color in the cheeks, and good light in the eyes, cheery expression, and just the amount of talking that best suited, namely, a word or short phrase only where needed, and almost always with a smile. Besides Emerson himself, Mrs.

E., with their daughter Ellen, the son Edward and his wife, with my friend F. S. and Mrs. S., and others, relatives and intimates. Mrs. Emerson, resuming the subject of the evening before (I sat next to her), gave me further and fuller information about Thoreau, who, years ago, during Mr. E.'s absence in Europe, had lived for some time in the family, by invitation.

Though the evening at Mr. and Mrs. Sanborn's, and the memorable family dinner at Mr. and Mrs. Emerson's, have most pleasantly and permanently fill'd my memory, I must not slight other notations of Concord. I went to the old Manse, walk'd through the ancient garden, enter'd the rooms, noted the quaintness, the unkempt grass and bushes, the little panes in the windows, the low ceilings, the spicy smell, the creepers embowering the light. Went to the Concord battle ground, which is close by, scann'd French's statue, "the Minute Man," read Emerson's poetic inscription on the base, linger'd a long while on the bridge, and stopp'd by the grave of the unnamed British soldiers buried there the day after the fight on April, '75. Then riding on (thanks to my friend Miss M. and her spirited white ponies, she driving them), a half hour at Hawthorne's and Thoreau's graves. I got out and went up of course on foot, and stood a long while and ponder'd. They lie close together in a pleasant wooded spot well up the cemetery hill, "Sleepy Hollow." The flat surface of the first was densely cover'd by myrtle, with a border of arbor-vitæ, and the other had a brown headstone, moderately elaborate, with inscriptions. By Henry's side lies his brother John, of whom much was expected, but he died young. Then to Walden pond, that beautiful embower'd sheet of water, and spent over an hour there. On the spot in the woods where Thoreau had his solitary house is now quite a cairn of stones, to mark the place; I too carried one and deposited [it] on the heap. As we drove back, saw the "School of Philosophy," but it was shut up, and I would not have it open'd for me. Near by stopp'd at the house of W. T. Harris, the Hegelian, who came out, and we had a pleasant chat while I sat in the wagon. I shall not soon forget those Concord drives, and especially that charming Sunday forenoon one with my friend Miss M., and the white ponies.

Emerson died the following year, April 27, 1882, at the age of seventy-nine. Whitman noted the event in his journal:

May 6, '82.

We stand by Emerson's new-made grave without sadness —indeed a solemn joy and faith, almost hauteur—our soul-benison no mere

Warrior, rest, thy task is done,

for one beyond the warriors of the world lies surely symbol'd here. A just man, poised on himself, all-loving, all-inclosing, and sane and clear as the sun. Nor does it seem so much Emerson himself we are here to honor—it is conscience, simplicity, culture, humanity's attributes at their best, yet applicable if need be to average affairs, and eligible to all. So used are we to suppose a heroic death can only come from out of battle or storm, or mighty personal contest, or amid dramatic incidents or danger (have we not been taught so for ages by all the plays and poems?) that few even of those who most sympathizingly mourn Emerson's late departure will fully appreciate the ripen'd grandeur of that event, with its play of calm and fitness, like evening light on the sea.

How I shall henceforth dwell on the blessed hours when, not long since, I saw that benignant face, the clear eyes, the silently smiling mouth, the form yet upright in its great age—to the very last, with so much spring and cheeriness, and such an absence of decrepitude, that even the term *venerable* hardly seem'd fitting.

Perhaps the life now rounded and completed in its mortal development, and which nothing can change or harm more, has its most illustrious halo, not in its splendid intellectual or esthetic products, but as forming in its entirety one of the few (alas! how few!) perfect and flawless excuses for being of the entire literary class.

We can say, as Abraham Lincoln at Gettysburg: It is not we who come to consecrate the dead—we reverently come to receive, if so it may be, some consecration to ourselves and daily work from him.

On May 28, Whitman sent William O'Connor the following memorandum in a letter[1]:

I doubt whether there is anything more affecting or emphatic in Emerson's whole career—a sort of last corruscation in the evening twilight of it—than his driving over to Frank Sanborn's in Concord Sept. 1881 to deliberately pay those 'respects' for which he had obligated himself twenty-five years before. Nor was the unusual compliment of the hospitable but formal dinner made the next day for Walt Whitman by Mr. and Mrs. Emerson, without a marked significance. It was a beautiful autumn Sunday. And if that afternoon, with its occurrences there in his own mansion, surrounded by all his family, wife, son, daughters, sons-in-law, nearest relatives and two or three very near friends—some fourteen or fifteen in all—if that does not mean how Emerson by this simple, yet almost solemn rite, wished before he departed to reiterate and finally seal his verdict of 1856 [1855], then there is no significance in human life or its emotions or actions.

In the autumn of the same year, Whitman published Specimen Days and Collect, *which included the following essay on Emerson:*

In the regions we call Nature, towering beyond all measurement, with infinite spread, infinite depth and height—in those regions, including Man, socially and historically, with his moral-emotional influences—how small a part (it came in my mind to-day) has literature really depicted—even summing up all of it, all ages. Seems at its best some little fleet of boats, hugging the shores of a boundless sea, and never venturing, exploring the unmapp'd—never, Columbus-like, sailing out for New Worlds, and to complete

[1]Quoted in Bliss Perry's *Walt Whitman.*

the orb's rondure. Emerson writes frequently in the atmosphere of this thought, and his books report one or two things from that very ocean and air, and more legibly address'd to our age and American polity than by any man yet. But I will begin by scarifying him—thus proving that I am not insensible to his deepest lessons. I will consider his books from a democratic and Western point of view. I will specify the shadows on these sunny expanses. Somebody has said of heroic character that "wherever the tallest peaks are present, must inevitably be deep chasms and valleys." Mine be the ungracious task (for reasons) of leaving unmention'd both sunny expanses and sky-reaching heights, to dwell on the bare spots and darkness. I have a theory that no artist or work of the very first class may be or can be without them.

First, then, these pages are perhaps too perfect, too concentrated. (How good, for instance, is good butter, good sugar. But to be eating nothing but sugar and butter all the time! even if ever so good.) And though the author has much to say of freedom and wildness and simplicity and spontaneity, no performance was ever more based on artificial scholarships and decorums at third or fourth removes (he calls it culture), and built up from them. It is always a *make,* never an unconscious *growth.* It is the porcelain figure or statuette of lion, or stag, or Indian hunter—and a very choice statuette, too—appropriate for the rosewood or marble bracket of parlor or library; never the animal itself, or the hunter himself. Indeed, who wants the real animal or hunter? What would that do amid astral and bric-a-brac and tapestry, and ladies and gentlemen talking in subdued tones of Browning and Longfellow and art? The least suspicion of such actual bull, or Indian, or of Nature carrying out itself, would put all those good people to instant terror and flight.

Emerson, in my opinion, is not most eminent as poet or artist or teacher, though valuable in all those. He is best as critic, or diagnoser. Not passion or imagination or warp or weakness, or any pronounced cause or specialty, dominates him. Cold and bloodless intellectuality dominates him. (I

know the fires, emotions, love, egotisms, glow deep, perennial, as in all New Englanders—but the façade, hides them
well—they give no sign.) He does not see or take one side,
one presentation only or mainly (as all the poets, or most
of the fine writers anyhow)—he sees all sides. His final
influence is to make his students cease to worship anything—
almost cease to believe in anything, outside of themselves.
These books will fill, and well fill, certain stretches of life,
certain stages of development—are, (like the tenets or theology the author of them preach'd when a young man,)
unspeakably serviceable and precious as a stage. But in old
or nervous or solemnest or dying hours, when one needs
the impalpably soothing and vitalizing influences of abysmic
Nature, or its affinities in literature or human society, and
the soul resents the keenest mere intellection, they will not
be sought for.

For a philosopher, Emerson possesses a singularly dandi-
fied theory of manners. He seems to have no notion at all
that manners are simply the signs by which the chemist or
metallurgist knows his metals. To the profound scientist,
all metals are profound, as they really are. The little one,
like the conventional world, will make much of gold and
silver only. Then to the real artist in humanity, what are
called bad manners are often the most picturesque and significant of all. Suppose these books becoming absorb'd, the
permanent chyle of American general and particular character—what a well-wash'd and grammatical, but bloodless
and helpless, race we should turn out! No, no, dear friend;
though the States want scholars, undoubtedly, and perhaps
want ladies and gentlemen who use the bath frequently,
and never laugh loud, or talk wrong, they don't want
scholars, or ladies and gentlemen, at the expense of all the
rest. They want good farmers, sailors, mechanics, clerks,
citizens—perfect business and social relations—perfect fathers
and mothers. If we could only have these, or their ap-
proximations, plenty of them, fine and large and sane and
generous and patriotic, they might make their verbs disagree from their nominatives, and laugh like volleys of
musketeers, if they should please. Of course these are not

all America wants, but they are first of all to be provided
on a large scale. And, with tremendous errors and escapades,
this, substantially, is what the States seem to have an intuition of, and to be mainly aiming at. The plan of a select
class, superfined (demarcated from the rest), the plan of
Old World lands and literatures, is not so objectionable in
itself, but because it chokes the true plan for us, and indeed
is death to it. As to such special class, the United States can
never produce any equal to the splendid show (far, far
beyond comparison or competition here) of the principal
European nations, both in the past and at the present day.
But an immense and distinctive commonalty over our vast
and varied area, West and East, South and North—in fact, for
the first time in history, a great, aggregated, real PEOPLE,
worthy the name, and made of develop'd heroic individuals,
both sexes—is America's principal, perhaps only, reason for
being. If ever accomplish'd, it will be at least as much (I
lately think, doubly as much) the result of fitting and
democratic sociologies, literatures and arts—if we ever get
them—as of our democratic politics.

At times it has been doubtful to me if Emerson really
knows or feels what Poetry is at its highest, as in the Bible,
for instance, or Homer or Shakspere. I see he covertly or
plainly likes best superb verbal polish, or something old or
odd—Waller's *Go, Lovely Rose,* or Lovelace's lines *To
Lucusta*—the quaint conceits of the old French bards, and
the like. Of *power* he seems to have a gentleman's admiration—but in his inmost heart the grandest attribute of God
and Poets is always subordinate to the octaves, conceits,
polite kinks, and verbs.

The reminiscence that years ago I began like most
youngsters to have a touch (though it came late, and was
only on the surface) of Emerson-on-the-brain—that I read
his writings reverently, and address'd him in print as "Master," and for a month or so thought of him as such—I retain
not only with composure, but positive satisfaction. I have
noticed that most young people of eager minds pass through
this stage of exercise.

The best part of Emersonianism is, it breeds the giant

that destroys itself. Who wants to be any man's mere follower? lurks behind every page. No teacher ever taught,
that has so provided for his pupil's setting up independently
—no truer evolutionist.

*In 1887 Whitman wrote the following letter to W. S.
Kennedy, who prints it in his* Reminiscences of Walt Whitman. *It will be noted that Whitman here contradicts the
statement he made to Trowbridge: that he had been influenced by Emerson in a decisive way before he wrote*
Leaves of Grass.

CAMDEN, *Feb. 25, '87—Noon*

DEAR W. S. K.—It is of no importance whether I had read
Emerson before starting *L. of G.* or not. The fact happens
to be positively that I had *not.* The basis and body and
genesis of the *L[eaves]* differing I suppose from Em[erson]
and many grandest poets and artists [—] was and is that I
found and find everything in the *common concrete,* the
broadcast materials, the flesh, the common passions, the
tangible and visible, etc., and in *the average,* and that I
radiate, work from, these outward—or rather hardly wish
to leave here but to remain and celebrate it all. Whatever
the amount of this may be or not be, it is certainly *not
Emersonian,* not Shakspeare, not Tennyson—indeed, the
antipodes of E. and the others in essential respects. But I
have not suggested or exprest myself well in my book unless
I have in a sort included them and their sides and expressions too—as this orb the world means and includes all
climes, all sorts, *L. of G.'s* word is *the body, including all,*
including the intellect and soul; E.'s word is mind (or intellect or soul).

If I were to unbosom to you in the matter I should say
that I never cared so very much for E.'s writings, prose or
poems, but from his first personal visit and two hours with
me (in Brooklyn in 1866 or '65?)[1] I had a strange attachment
and love for *him* and his contact, talk, company, magnetism.
I welcomed *him* deepest and always—yet it began and con-

[1] "The query mark his," notes Kennedy. "He means '55 or '56."

tinued *on his part,* quite entirely; HE always sought ME. We probably had a dozen (possibly twenty) of these meetings, talks, walks, etc.—some five or six times (sometimes New York, sometimes Boston) had good long dinners together. I was very happy—I don't think I was at my best with him—he always did most of the talking—I am sure he was happy too. That visit to me at Sanborn's, by E. and family, and the splendid formal-informal family dinner *to me,* next day, Sunday, Sept. 18, '81, by E., Mrs. E. and all, I consider not only a victor-event in my life, but it is an after-explanation of so much and offered as an apology, peace-offering, justification of much that the world knows not of. My dear friend, I think I know R. W. E. better than anybody else knows him—and loved him in proportion, but quietly. Much was revealed to me.

WALT WHITMAN.

Whitman also told John Burroughs that he had never read Emerson at all before he wrote Leaves of Grass. *He gave Burroughs the same account that he had given Trowbridge of reading Emerson on the beach at Coney Island, but he put this in the summer of 1885, just after his book had been published, instead of in the summer before. It is probable that Whitman was telling the truth in his original story to Trowbridge. Mr. Clifton Joseph Furness, who is distinguished both for his exhaustive knowledge of Whitman and for his common sense in dealing with the subject, has shown that Whitman, as he grew older, desired to pass for and to believe himself a completely original poet with no sources and no kin; and he attributes to this desire the tendency to repudiate Emerson which appears in Whitman's later years. He was always, Mr. Furness points out, extremely vague about facts, told quite different stories at different times about important events in his life, and probably did not, especially as he got older, always know the truth himself.*

Yet his respect and affection for Emerson remained, as is touchingly shown in certain passages of Horace Traubel's

With Walt Whitman in Camden. *Whitman was now just turning seventy. He was to die in March 1892.*

April 23, 1888

W. got talking of Emerson again: "The world does not know what our relations really were—they think of our friendship always as a literary friendship: it was a bit that but it was mostly something else—it was certainly more than that—for I loved Emerson for his personality and I always felt that he loved me for something I brought him from the rush of the big cities and the mass of men. We used to walk together, dine together, argue, even, in a sort of a way, though neither one of us was much of an arguer. We were not much for repartee or sallies or what people ordinarily call humor, but we got along together beautifully—the atmosphere was always sweet, I don't mind saying it, both on Emerson's side and mine: we had no friction—there was no kind of fight in us for each other—we were like two Quakers together. Dear Emerson! I doubt if the literary classes which have taken to coddling him have any right to their god. He belonged to us—yes, to us—rather than to them." Then after a pause: "I suppose to all as well as to us—perhaps to no clique whatever."

July 12, 1888

Asked me: "You remember our talk about Lowell yesterday? Yes? Well—I have thought a lot of it since. The New England crowd has always seemed to be divided about me, with Emerson, Alcott, Longfellow on the one side—Lowell, Whittier, and Holmes on the other. Sometimes I seem to be divided about myself—don't quite get myself of one mind about myself. I understand that Lowell is in the habit of saying sore things about me—yes, very severe things—Holmes passes me off in a joke: but Whittier? Well—Whittier took me in dead earnest at the very start—my book was an evil book—he would shake his head—a sort of ah me!" The Whittier picture of horror amused W.

July 14, 1888

"I often say of Emerson that the personality of the man—the wonderful heart and soul of the man, present in all he writes, thinks, does, hopes—goes far towards justifying the whole literary business—the whole raft good and bad, the entire system. You see, I find nothing in literature that is valuable simply for its professional quality: literature is only valuable in the measure of the passion—the blood and muscle —with which it is invested—which lies concealed and active in it."

July 31, 1888

"I seem to have various feelings about Emerson, but I am always loyal at last. Emerson gratified me as a young man by what he did—he sometimes tantalized me as an old man by what he failed to do. You see, I both blaspheme and worship." I reminded him: "You once addressed Emerson as Master." He nodded his assent. "So I did—and master he was, for me, then. But I got my roots stronger in the earth—master would not do any more: no, not then: would no longer do." "And when you say your last word about Emerson—just before you shut up shop for good— what will it be?" He laughed mildly. "It will be loyal," he said "—after all the impatiences, loyal, loyal."

August 12, 1888

W. spoke of Emerson: "I shall never forget the first visit he paid me—the call, the first call: it was in Brooklyn: no, I can never forget it. I can hear his gentle knock still— the soft knock—'so'"—indicating it on the chair-arm—"and the slow sweet voice, as my mother stood there by the door: and the words, 'I came to see Mr. Whitman': and the response, 'He is here'—the simple unaffected greeting on both sides—'How are you, Mr. Whitman,' 'How are you, Waldo' —the hour's talk or so—the taste of lovableness he left behind when he was gone. I can easily see how Carlyle should have likened Emerson's appearance in their household to the apparition of an angel."

W. liked what Burroughs said of Emerson: "To me Emerson filled nearly the whole horizon in that direction." W.
said: "I guess I enjoy that: I guess I do." He had had me
read the line over again. "John was right: Emerson *was*
the whole horizon: Ralph Waldo: Emerson: the gentle,
noble, perfect, radiant, consolatory, Emerson. I think of
something Emerson said in one of our talks: he said: 'I
agree with you, Mr. Whitman, that a man who does not
live according to his lights—who trims his sails to the current breeze—is already dead—is as many times dead as he is
untrue.' Emerson lived according to his lights—not according to libraries, books, literature, the traditions: he was
unostentatiously loyal: no collegian, overdone with culture:
so gifted, so peculiarly tremendous, that, if I may say so,
knowing too much did not as it so often does with the
scholar hurt him." "Didn't you tell me that he expressed
regrets to your face one day—saying some sort of apologetic
thing about his book learning?" W. nodded. "Yes—more
than once: said he felt like athletes—some athletes: overtrained: that a scholar, like an athlete, overtrained, is apt
to go stale. He said he felt that culture had done all it could
do for him - then it had done something for him which had
better been left undone." "Did he seem very serious in that
self-analysis or did he say it all quizzically?" W. answered:
"Oh! he was serious enough in it: he said to me (speaking
of Thoreau) that, 'as strange as it may seem, Henry being
an outdoor man (he called him Henry)—he shrinks from
some formidable things in you—in your book, in your
personality—over which I rejoice!' And he said this too: 'I
don't say it by way of flattery at all—I would as readily say
it to any man like you who had not written a book—but I
say that meeting you is a peculiar refreshment to me—puts
something needed into my tissue which I do not seem to
get in my own established environment.' Yes, Horace: he
was in dead earnest about it all: not plaintive at all: no,
nothing of that sort: but soberly free." I asked: "Did some
of this happen in that Boston Common walk?" "Yes—some

of it: but I recall that some of it occurred that Astor House day in New York."

December 23, 1888

W. gave me one of what he calls his "soger boy letters": his draft of such a letter: he even had me read it to him. I don't like to read these letters aloud. They move me too much. I notice that he too is stirred strangely over them hearing them again. But I read. I could not get out of it. It was spread out over ten different slips of paper which were folded in a Sanitary Commission envelope on which he had written: "to Hugo Aug. 7 '63." He said: "Yes it was from the midst of things—to the midst of things: when I went to New York I would write to the hospitals: when I was in the hospitals I would write to New York: I could not forget the boys—they were too precious." . . .

The text of the letter follows.

I said to W.: "That's not so serious as you led me to believe." He smiled: "The undertone is serious: they were grave times: I was not feeling gay and festive in those years: never could get away from the terrible experiences. Emerson asked me: 'Mr. Whitman, how can you stand it? I do not think I could endure it. It would take too much out of me: too much—too much——.'" I asked W.: "Did Emerson always address you as Mister?" "Generally—I may say always. Once or twice he addressed me as Whitman: but he looked a bit uncertain after he had done so as if possibly he might have taken too much liberty."

W. lay on the bed as I left. The tangerines and a book beside him: he played with them. I was happy. He seemed so well.

December 24, 1888

Harned asked W.: "Do you always feel as if it was quite certain that Emerson will size up in history ultimately bigger than Thoreau?" W. replied: "Tom, you've a hell of a habit of putting the most difficult questions to me when

I'm least prepared for them." T. got back: "But that's not answering the question. Do you?" W. took his glasses off his nose and said: "Tom, I'm not dead sure on that point either way: my prejudices, if I may call them that, are all with Emerson: but Thoreau was a surprising fellow—he is not easily grasped—is elusive: yet he is one of the native forces—stands for a fact, a movement, an upheaval: Thoreau belongs to America, to the transcendental, to the protesters: then he is an outdoor man: all outdoor men, everything else being equal, appeal to me. Thoreau was not so precious, tender, a personality as Emerson: but he was a force—he looms up bigger and bigger: his dying does not seem to have hurt him a bit: every year has added to his fame. One thing about Thoreau keeps him very near to me: I refer to his lawlessness—his dissent—his going down his own absolute road, let hell blaze all it chooses."

December 25, 1888

Traubel had just read Whitman a draft of a letter he had written in 1863 to the soldier mentioned above.

I looked up as I finished reading. Walt's eyes were full of tears. He wiped the tears away with the sleeve of his coat. Put on a make-believe chuckle. "It's very beautiful, Walt: right on the ground: where the people are." "I hope so: that's where I belong: right on the ground." W. added: "Emerson said when we were out together in New York and Boston—said it more than once: 'I envy you your capacity for being at home with anybody in any crowd.' Then he asked me on another occasion: 'Don't you fear now and then that your freedom, your ease, your nonchalance, with men may be misunderstood?' I asked him: 'Do you misunderstand it?' He put his hand on my arm and said: 'No: I see it for what it is: it is beautiful.' Then I said to him: 'Misunderstood? Yes: it will be misunderstood. But what is there I do that is not misunderstood?' He smiled in his sweet gentle way and murmured: 'true! true!'"

BAYARD TAYLOR (1825–78), who had a considerable reputation in his own time, is hardly known to ours save as the author of a translation of *Faust*. He wrote some novels, a great deal of poetry, and many volumes of travels. Part English Quaker and part Pennsylvania Dutch, he passed through a variety of literatures as he visited a variety of countries without adding much that was interesting to the adventures of the human spirit. Yet Taylor was a man of the world in the experience both of books and of men as were few American writers of his time. He read poetry aloud, says R. H. Stoddard, with a "boyish exultation," and his head was always humming with the verse of his extraordinary repertory of tongues. His own poems, though not especially inspired, are literate and competent in a sense that much of our poetry of that period is not. It was as if the sound tradition of English verse were steadily being washed away by the demands of the magazines—as if the poets were getting to feel that it was necessary to put into a poem only enough of art to last a month; and Taylor, under these conditions, maintains what seems by comparison a certain solidity and style. If his verse, as has been said, is all rhetoric, it is at least not a messy rhetoric.

In the latter part of his life, Bayard Taylor wrote a set of imitations of his contemporaries which he embodied in a series of dialogues. These were first published anonymously in the *Atlantic Monthly* in 1872 as *Diversions of the Echo Club,* and afterwards, in 1876, in a volume under the author's name. The book had had its origin in the fifties in the games of parody-writing which Taylor, Stoddard, Fitz-James O'Brien, and Thomas Bailey Aldrich had been in the habit of playing on Saturday nights in New York, when Taylor had lived on Washington Square; and they present an idealized picture of the literary life of Pfaff's Restaurant, the beer-cellar on Broadway above Bleecker Street which the New York writers had frequented in the decade before the Civil War. The *Echo Club* is perhaps the most attractive relic of the Bohemian New York of that period. But it has also a real critical value. Taylor said that he tried "under the guise of fun" to put into it "a good deal of serious matter," and "to give a few earnest hints in regard to certain aspects of our popular literature." The dialogues in their day fell completely flat. It was not, one supposes, a kind of thing particularly well understood in a literary world dominated by Boston. Taylor found when he went to Rome that the American painters there had been much delighted by them, and they won him a compliment from Browning; but at home they remained unread.

We can appreciate them better today. The little book opens an unexpected window—the window of a non-provincial and cultivated mind—on the whole poetic landscape of the middle nineteenth century. Taylor gives us a view from the seventies just as Poe gave us a view from the forties. His parodies, like Poe's derisive extracts, paint in for us the background of inferior verse with which the first-rate figures partly blend and from which they partly emerge; and Taylor in every case provides a very clear little picture of the artistic personality of the poet. When we go among even the pages of selections in Bryant's or Stedman's anthology, we find that it is hard to enjoy or to judge because we breathe again the air of the period, we are back in an old, closed-in atmosphere of half-remembered houses and people. But Taylor has somehow got free of this murkiness of the family poets and the family magazines: he has somehow risen above it into the light, lively New York air, where one can hear the whistles of steamboats departing for all the ports of the world; and one can look at the whole thing with the eyes of a returned traveller, who has just come in through the Narrows and landed at Christopher Street.

It may serve to emphasize the difference between the literary atmospheres of New England and New York to add here Walt Whitman's tribute to Pfaff's in his journal of August 16, 1881:

"Chalk a big mark for today," was one of the sayings of an old sportsman-friend of mine, when he had had unusually good luck—come home thoroughly tired, but with satisfactory results of fish or birds. Well, today might warrant such a mark for me. Everything propitious from the start. An hour's fresh stimulation, coming down ten miles of Manhattan Island by railroad and 8 o'clock stage. Then an excellent breakfast at Pfaff's restaurant, 24th street. Our host himself, an old friend of mine, quickly appear'd on the scene to welcome me and bring up the news, and, first opening a big fat bottle of the best wine in the cellar, talk about ante-bellum times, '59 and '60, and the jovial suppers at his then Broadway place, near Bleecker street. Ah, the friends and names and frequenters, those times, that place. Most are dead—Ada Clare, Wilkins, Daisy Sheppard, O'Brien, Henry Clapp, Stanley, Mullen, Wood, Brougham, Arnold—all gone. And there Pfaff and I, sitting opposite each other at the little table, gave a remembrance to them in a style they would have themselves fully confirm'd, namely, big, brimming, fill'd-up champagne-glasses, drain'd in abstracted silence, very leisurely, to the last drop. (Pfaff is a generous German *restaurateur*, silent, stout, jolly, and I should say the best selecter of champagne in America.)

BAYARD TAYLOR

DIVERSIONS OF THE ECHO CLUB

Introduction

THE PAPERS which make up this volume are sufficiently described by its title. They are literary "Diversions,"—the product of a good many random hours of thoughtless (or, at least, only half-thoughtful) recreation and amusement,—nothing else. More than as many burlesque imitations of authors, living or dead, as are here contained had been written before any thought of publication was suggested. The fact that there was no such original design requires that the form in which the diversions are now presented should be explained to the reader.

The habit originated, very much as it is described in the *First Evening*, at least twenty years ago, in a small private circle. Three or four young authors found not only amusement, but an agreeable relaxation from their graver tasks, in drawing names and also subjects as from a lottery wheel, and improvising imitations of older and more renowned poets. Nothing was further from their minds than ridicule, or even incidental disparagement, of the latter, many of whom were not only recognized, but genuinely revered, by all. One form of intellectual diversion gradually led to another: the parodies alternated with the filling up of end-

rhymes (usually of the most difficult and incongruous character), with the writing of double or concealed acrostics,
spurious quotations from various languages, and whatever
else could be devised by the ingenuity of the company. I
may mention that some years before Mr. Lewis Carroll
delighted all lovers of nonsense with his ballad of *The Jab-
berwock* we tried precisely the same experiment of introducing invented words. The following four lines may serve as
a specimen of one attempt:

> Smitten by harsh, transcetic thuds of shame,
> My squelgence fades: I mogrify my blame:
> The lupkin world, that leaves me yole and blant,
> Denies my affligance with looks askant!

Of course nothing further than amusing nonsense was
ever contemplated. A few of the imitations found their way
into print, but they were comparatively unnoticed in the
flood of burlesque with which the public was then supplied
from many other quarters. As a participant, for several years,
in a variety of fun which was certainly harmless so long as
it remained private, I was of the opinion that very little
could be made public without some accompanying explanation. The idea of setting the imitations in a framework of
dialogue which should represent various forms of literary
taste and opinion seemed, first, to make the publication possible. But when I came to examine the scattered leaves with
a view to this end, I was at once struck with their inadequacy
to the purpose of comical illustration. Removed from the
genial atmosphere in which they had spontaneously grown,
many of them seemed withered and insipid. Many others
were simply parodies of particular poems, instead of being
burlesque reproductions of an author's manner and diction.
The plan demanded that they should be rewritten, in con-
sonance with the governing conception of the work as a
whole. This was accordingly done; and not more than three
or four of the following poems belong to the original private
"diversions."

There is scarcely a more hazardous experiment which an
author can make than to attempt to draw amusement from

the intellectual characteristics of his contemporaries. If I had not been firmly convinced that the absence of any conscious unfriendliness on my part *must* make itself evident to many who were old and honored friends, I never should have dared it. In addition to this, I ventured on a number of private tests, and was further assured by finding that the subject of each travesty accepted his share with the greatest good nature. I have yet to learn that the publication has given other than a very slight momentary annoyance, and that only in one or two cases. It is doubtful whether the same experiment could be made in any of the other arts, with a similar result. I am satisfied that opera singers, actors, composers, sculptors, painters, theologians even, have a better right to be called the *genus irritabile* than the literary guild. The more devotedly an author aspires towards his ideal of achievement, the less he is concerned with all transitory estimates of his work. Looking back now, four years since the papers appeared in the *Atlantic Monthly*, I see more clearly how much was ventured, and I am profoundly grateful to find that no serious wound was given.

Some of my friends have suggested that the characters introduced in the Echo Club, and the course of their dialogues, might have been made more interesting to the reader. This is probably true; but, on the other hand, all work of the kind has but an ephemeral interest, and the leisure of mind which produced it seems now so remote, so beyond recall, that I have not undertaken to make any change. The four principal characters were designed to represent classes, not individuals. In "The Ancient" I endeavored to express something of the calmer judicial temper, in literary matters, which comes from age and liberal study. The name of "Zoïlus" (the *Homeromastix*, or "Scourge of Homer") explains his place: he is the carping, cynical, unconsciously arrogant critic,— though these qualities could not be given with entire dramatic truth. "Galahad" is the young, sensational, impressive element in the reading public; admiration, in him, is almost equivalent to adoration. "The Gannet"—a name suggested by a poem written by a member of the class long ago— represents brilliancy without literary principle, the love of technical effect, regardless of the intellectual conception of a work. This is a class which is always large, and always more or less successful—for a time. It was not necessary that each character should keep rigidly within the limits of his part, and thus each of them may be occasionally inconsistent. I need hardly explain that the author's own views, though scattered here and there through the dialogues, together with their exact opposites, are not specially expressed by any one of the four persons.

The papers were meant to be anonymous, but the secret was soon betrayed—not, however, before some amusing illustrations of the personal character of much so-called criticism were furnished. The comments of certain writers for the press, before and after the authorship was known, formed a curious and instructive contrast. In London, the papers were collected and published as a volume more than two years ago; and there may be possibly enough diversion still lingering about them to satisfy the indolent mood of a summer afternoon. More than this is not intended by their appearance in the present form.

I have added some other specimens of the same kind of fooling, partly in order to put everything of the sort in its place and leave it behind me, and partly because a good many personal friends have been amused, and hence some unknown friends may also be. This prelude is no doubt longer than necessary; but on completing and offering to others a diversion which will never be repeated, one may be pardoned for an overscrupulousness in explaining circumstances and justifying motives.

B. T.

New York, June 1876.

Night The First

If it were not that the public cherishes rather singular and fluctuating notions with regard to the private and familiar intercourse of authors, the reports which follow would need no prologue. But between the two classes of readers, one of which innocently supposes T. Percy Jones to be the strange and terrible being whom they find represented in his *Firmilian,* while the other, having discovered, by a few startling disillusions, that the race of authors is Janus-faced, is sure that T. Percy Jones is the exact opposite of his poetical self, there has arisen a confusion which it may be well to correct.

The authors themselves, I am aware, are chiefly responsible for these opposite impressions. When Joaquin Miller at Niagara, standing on the brink of the American precipice, kisses his hands grandly to Canada, exclaiming, "England, I thank you!" or when Martin Farquhar Tupper, in a speech at New York, cries out with noble magnanimity, "America, be not afraid, *I* will protect you!" the public might reasonably expect to find all poets visibly trailing their mantles in our streets. But when an eager listener, stealing behind Irving and Halleck at an evening party, found them talking of—shoe leather! and a breathless devotee of Thackeray, sitting opposite to him at the dinner table, saw those Delphian lips unclose only to utter the words, "Another potato, if you please!"—they had revelations which might cast a dreadful suspicion over the nature of the whole tribe of authors.

I would not have the reader imagine that the members of the Echo Club are represented by either of these extremes. They are authors, of different ages and very unequal places in public estimation. It would never occur to them to seat themselves on self-constructed pyramids, and speak as if The Ages were listening; yet, like their brethren of all lands and all times, the staple of their talk is literature. What Englishmen call "the shop" is an inevitable feature of their conversation. They can never come together without discussing the literary news of the day, the qualities of prominent authors, living or dead, and sometimes their own. However the enlightened listener might smile at the positiveness of their opinions, and the contradictions into which they are sometimes led in the lawless play and keen clash of the lighter intellect, he could not fail to recognize the sovereign importance they attach to their art. Without lifting from their intercourse that last veil of mystery, behind which only equals are permitted to pass, I may safely try to report the mixture of sport and earnest, of satire and enthusiasm, of irreverent audacity and pure aspiration, which met and mingled at their meetings. If the reader cannot immediately separate these elements, it is no fault of mine. He is most desirous, I know, to be present at the private diversions of a small society of authors, and to hear them talk as they are wont to talk when the wise heads of the world are out of earshot.

The character which the society assumed for a short time was entirely accidental. As one of the Chorus, I was present at the first meeting, and of course I never failed afterwards. The four authors who furnished our entertainment were not aware that I had written down, from memory, the substance of the conversation, until our evenings came to an end; and I have had some difficulty in obtaining their permission to publish my reports. The Ancient and Galahad feared that certain poets whom they delight to honor might be annoyed, not so much at the sportive imitation of their manner, as at the possible misconception of its purpose by the public. But Zoïlus and the Gannet agreed with me that where no harm is meant none can be inflicted, that the literature of our day is in a sad state of bewilderment and confusion, and that a few effervescing powders would perhaps soothe a public stomach which has been overdosed with startling effects.

At last the Ancient said: "So be it, then! Take the poems, but don't bring your manuscript to us for correction! I am quite sure you have often reported us falsely, and if our masks of names are pulled off, we will have that defense."

I have only to add that the three or four gentlemen comprising the Chorus are not authors by profession. The Ancient is in the habit of dividing the race of artists into active and passive—the latter possessing the artistic temperament, the tastes, the delights, the instincts of the race—everything, except that creative gadfly which stings to expression. In every quality except production they are the equals of the producers, he says; and they are quite as necessary to the world as the active artists, since they are the first to recognize the good points of the latter, to strengthen them with warm and intelligent sympathy, and to commend them to the slower perceptions and more uncertain tastes of the mass of readers. I am sure, at least, that our presence and participation in the amusements was a gentle stimulus to the principal actors. We were their enthusiastic audience, and kept them fresh and warm to their work. I do not record our share in the conversation, for there is sufficient diversity of opinion without it; and I made no notes of it at the time. —THE NAMELESS REPORTER.

In the rear of Karl Schäfer's lager-beer cellar and restaurant—which everyone knows is but a block from the central part of Broadway—there is a small room, with a vaulted ceiling, which Karl calls his *Löwengrube*, or Lions' Den. Here, in their Bohemian days, Zoïlus and the Gannet had been accustomed to meet to discuss literary projects and read fragments of manuscript to each other. The Chorus, the Ancient, and young Galahad gradually fell into the same habit, and thus a little circle of six, seven, or eight members came to be formed. The room could comfortably contain no more; it was quiet, with a dim, smoky, confidential atmosphere, and suggested Auerbach's Cellar to the Ancient, who had been in Leipzig.

Here, authors, books, magazines, and newspapers were talked about; sometimes a manuscript poem was read by its writer; while mild potations of beer and the dreamy breath of cigars delayed the nervous, fidgety, clattering-footed American Hours. One night they chanced upon a discussion of Morris' *Earthly Paradise,* which Galahad rapturously admired, while the Ancient continued to draw him out, at first by guarded praise, then by critical objections to the passages which Galahad quoted. The conversation finally took this turn:

GALAHAD. Indeed, you are not just! Tell me, have you read the whole work?

THE ANCIENT. Yes; I had it with me on my last trip to Havana, and read all three volumes under the most favorable auspices,—lying on deck in the shadow of a sail, with the palms and mangroves of the Bahamas floating past in the distance. Just so I floated through the narrative poems, one after the other, admiring the storyteller's art, heartily enjoying many passages, accepting even the unnecessary quaintness of the speech, and at first disposed to say, "Here is a genuine poet!" But I was conscious of a lack of something, which, in my lazy mood, I did not attempt to analyze. When the lines and scenes and characters began to fade in my mind (which they did almost immediately), I found that the final impression which the work left behind was very much like the Hades of the Greeks,—a gray, misty, cheerless land, full of wandering shadows,—a place, where there is no sun, no clear, conscious, joyous life, where even fortunate love is sad, where hope is unknown to the heart, and there is nothing in the distance but death, and nothing after death. There had been a languid and rather agreeable sense of enjoyment; but it was followed by a chill.

GALAHAD. Oh!

THE GANNET. How often have I told you, Galahad, that you're too easily taken off your feet! He's very clever, I admit; but there's a deal of trick in it, for all that. His revival of obsolete words, his imitation of Chaucer——

GALAHAD (*impatiently*). Imitation!

THE GANNET. Well,—only half, and half similarity of talent. But no writer can naturally assume a manner of speech which has long fallen into disuse, even in literature: so far as he does so, he is artificial. And this artifice Morris carries into his pictures of sentiment and passion. You cease to feel with and for his characters long before he has done with them.

GALAHAD. As human beings, perhaps; but as conceptions of beauty, they have another existence.

THE GANNET. When I want a Greek frieze, let me have it in marble! Yes, he's a skillful workman, and a successful one, as his popularity proves. And he's lucky in producing his canned fruit after Swinburne's curry and pepper sauce; but it is *canned*. I don't say I could equal him in his own line, for that requires natural inclination as well as knack, yet I think I could give you something exactly in his style in ten minutes.

THE ANCIENT. Challenge him, Galahad!

THE GANNET. Get me paper and pencil! I will at least try. Now, Galahad, put up your watch; I only stipulate that you don't time me too exactly. Stay!—take another sheet and try the same thing yourself.

(*They write; meanwhile the others talk.*)

THE GANNET (*after twenty minutes*). I have failed in time, because I began wrong. I tried to write a serious passage in Morris' manner, and my own habit of expression immediately came in as a disturbing influence. Then I gave up the plan of producing something really earnest and coherent—that is, I kept in mind the manner, alone, and let the matter come of itself. Very little effort was required, I found: the lines arranged themselves easily enough. Now, lend me your ears: it is a passage from *The Taming of Themistocles*, in the ninth volume of the *Earthly Paradise*. (*Reads.*)

> "He must be holpen; yet how help shall I,
> Steeped to the lips in ancient misery,
> And by the newer grief appareléd?
> If that I throw these ashes on mine head,
> Do this thing for thee,—while about my way
> A shadow gathers, and the piteous day,
> So wan and bleak for very loneliness,
> Turneth from sight of such unruthfulness?"
> Therewith he caught an arrow from the sheaf,
> And brake the shaft in witlessness of grief;
> But Chiton's vest, such dismal fear she had,
> Shook from the heart that sorely was a-drad,
> And she began, withouten any pause,
> To say: "Why break the old Ætolian laws,
> Send this man forth, that never harm hath done
> Between the risen and the setten sun?"
> And next, they wandered to a steepy hill,
> Whence all the land was lying gray and still,
> And not a living creature there might be,
> From the cold mountains to the salt, cold sea;
> Only, within a little cove, one sail
> Shook, as it whimpered at the cruel gale,
> And the mast moaned from chafing of the rope;
> So all was pain: they saw not any hope.

Zoïlus. But that is no imitation! You have copied a passage out of—out of—pshaw! I know the poem, and I remember the lines.

The Gannet (*indignantly*). Out of Milton, why not say? —where you'll be just as likely to find them. Now, let me hear yours, Galahad; you were writing.

Galahad (*crushing the paper in his hand*). Mine is neither one thing nor the other,—not the author's poetic dialect throughout, nor hinting of his choice of subjects. I began something, which was really my own, and then gradually ran into an echo. I think *you* have hit upon the true method; and we must try again, since we know it.

The Gannet. Why not try others—a dozen of them? By Jove, I should like some mere gymnastics, after the heavy prose I've been writing! And you, too, Galahad, and the Ancient (if his ponderous dignity doesn't prevent it); and here's Zoïlus, the very fellow for such a diversion! We can come together, here, and be a private, secret club of Parodists, —of Echoes,—of Iconoclasts, of——

The Ancient. Of irreverent satirists, I fear. That would be a new kind of a *Hainbund*, indeed; but, after all, it need not be ill-natured. At least, to insure yourselves against relapsing into mere burlesque and incidental depreciation—which is a tempting, but nearly always a fatal course for young writers—I must be present. My indifferentism, as you call it, which sometimes provokes you when I cannot share all your raptures, may do good service in keeping you from rushing into the opposite extreme. As for taking part in the work, I won't promise to do much. You know I am a man of uncertain impulses, and can get nothing out of myself by force of resolution.

Omnes. Oh, you must take part! It will be capital sport.

The Ancient (*deliberately, between the whiffs of his cigar*). First of all, let us clearly understand what is to be done. To undertake *parodies,* as the word is generally comprehended—that is, to make a close imitation of some particular poem, though it should be characteristic of the author —would be rather a flat business. Even the Brothers Smith and Bon Gaultier, admirable as they are, stuck too closely to selected models; and Phoebe Cary, who has written the best American parodies, did the same thing. I think the Gannet has discovered something altogether more original and satisfactory—a simple echo of the author's tone and manner. The choice of a subject gives another chance of fun.

(*He takes up* THE GANNET'S *imitation and looks over it.*)

Here the dialect and movement and atmosphere are suggested; the exaggeration is neither coarse nor extreme, and the comical effect seems to lie mainly in the circumstance that it *is* a wilful imitation. If we were to find the passage in one of Morris' poems, we might think it carelessly written, somewhat obscure, but still in the same key with what precedes and follows it. Possibly, nay, almost certainly, it would not amuse us at all; but just now I noticed that even Galahad could not help laughing. A diversion of this sort is less a labor and more a higher and finer recreation of the mind, than the mechanical setting of some given poem, line by line, to a ludicrous subject, like those endless and generally stupid parodies of Longfellow's *Excelsior* and Emerson's *Brahma*. For heaven's—no, Homer's—sake, let us not fall into that vein!

THE GANNET. Thou speakest well.

GALAHAD. But how shall we select the authors? And shall I be required to make my own demigods ridiculous?

ZOÏLUS. Let me prove to you, by one of your own demigods, that nothing can be either sublime or ridiculous. Poetry is the Brahma of literature—above all, pervading all, self-existent, though so few find her (and men of business reckon ill who leave her out), and therefore quite unmoved by anything we may do. Don't you remember the lines?——

> Far or forgot to me is near,
>   Shadow and sunlight are the same;
> The vanished gods to me appear,
>   And one to me are shame and fame.

THE ANCIENT. You are right, Zoïlus, in spite of your sarcasm. Besides, it is an evidence of a poet's distinct individuality, when he can be amusingly imitated. We can only make those the objects of our fun whose manner or dialect stamps itself so deeply into our minds that a new cast can be taken. We are sporting around great, and sometimes little names, like birds or cats or lizards around the feet, and over the shoulders, and on the heads of statues. Now, there's an idea for a poem, Galahad. But, seriously, how would you imitate Pollok's *Course of Time,* or Young's *Night Thoughts,* or Blair's *Grave,* or any other of those masses of words, which are too ponderous for poetry and too respectable for absurdity! Either extreme will do for us, excellence or imbecility; but it must have a distinct, pronounced character.

THE GANNET. Come, now. I'm eager for another trial.

THE ANCIENT. Let us each write the names of three or four poets on separate slips of paper, and throw them into my hat; then let each draw out one slip as his model for tonight. Thus there will be no clashing of tastes or inclinations, and our powers of imitation will be more fairly tested.

(They write three names apiece, THE CHORUS *taking part. Then all are thrown into* THE ANCIENT's *hat and shaken up together.)*

GALAHAD *(drawing).* Robert Browning.

THE GANNET. So is mine.

ZOÏLUS. Edgar A. Poe.

THE ANCIENT. Some of us have written the same names. Well, let it be so tonight. If we find the experiment diverting, we can easily avoid any such repetition next time. Moreover, Browning alone will challenge echoes from all of us; and I am curious to see whether the several imitations will reflect the same characteristics of his style. It will, at least, show whether the stamp upon each mind has any common likeness to the original.

THE GANNET. A good idea! But Zoïlus is already possessed by the spirit of Poe: not, I hope, in the manner of Dr. Garth Wilkinson of London, whose volume of poems dictated by the spirits of the dead authors is the most astonishing collection I ever saw. He makes Poe's "wet locks" rhyme to his "fetlocks"! It is even worse than Harris' *Epic of the Starry Heavens,* dictated to him in forty-eight hours by Dante. By the by, we have a good chance to test this matter of possession; the suggestion nimbly and sweetly recommends itself to my fancy. But since I was your pioneer tonight, I'll even rest until Zoïlus has finished; then, let us all start fairly.

ZoïLUS (*a few minutes later*). If this is at all good, it is not because of labor. I had an easier task than the Gannet. (*Reads.*)

THE PROMISSORY NOTE

In the lonesome latter years,
   (Fatal years!)
To the dropping of my tears
Danced the mad and mystic spheres
In a rounded, reeling rune,
   'Neath the moon,
To the dripping and the dropping of my tears.

Ah, my soul is swathed in gloom,
   (Ulalume!)
In a dim Titanic tomb,
For my gaunt and gloomy soul
Ponders o'er the penal scroll,
O'er the parchment (not a rhyme),
Out of place—out of time—
I am shredded, shorn, unshifty,
   (Oh, the fifty!)
And the days have passed, the three,
   Over me!
And the debit and the credit are as one to him and me!

'Twas the random runes I wrote
At the bottom of the note
   (Wrote and freely
   Gave to Greeley),
In the middle of the night,
In the mellow, moonless night,
When the stars were out of sight,
When my pulses, like a knell,
   (Israfel!)
Danced with dim and dying fays
O'er the ruins of my days,
O'er the dimeless, timeless days,
When the fifty, drawn at thirty,
Seeming thrifty, yet the dirty
Lucre of the market, was the most that I could raise!

Fiends controlled it,
　　(Let him hold it!)
Devils held for me the inkstand and the pen;
　　Now the days of grace are o'er,
　　　　(Ah, Lenore!)
　　I am but as other men:
　　What is time, time, time,
　　To my rare and runic rhyme,
　　To my random, reeling rhyme,
　　By the sands along the shore,
Where the tempest whispers, "Pay him!" and I answer,
　　　　"Nevermore!"

GALAHAD. What do you mean by the reference to Greeley?

ZOÏLUS. I thought everybody had heard that Greeley's only autograph of Poe was a signature to a promissory note for fifty dollars. He offers to sell it for half the money. Now, I don't mean to be wicked, and to do nothing with the dead except bone 'em, but when such a cue pops into one's mind, what is one to do?

THE ANCIENT. Oh, I think you're still within decent limits! There was a congenital twist about poor Poe. We can't entirely condone his faults, yet we stretch our charity so as to cover as much as possible. His poetry has a hectic flush, a strange, fascinating, narcotic quality, which belongs to him alone. Baudelaire and Swinburne after him have been trying to surpass him by increasing the dose; but his Muse is the natural Pythia, inheriting her convulsions, while they eat all sorts of insane roots to produce theirs.

GALAHAD (eagerly). Did you ever know him?

THE ANCIENT. I met him two or three times, heard him lecture once (his enunciation was exquisite), and saw him now and then in Broadway,—enough to satisfy me that there were two men in him: one, a refined gentleman, an aspiring soul, an artist among those who had little sense of literary art; the other——

ZOÏLUS. Go on!

THE ANCIENT. "Built his nest with the birds of Night." No more of that! Now let us all invoke the demigod, Browning.

GALAHAD. It will be a task.

ZOÏLUS. I don't think so; it's even simpler than what we've done. Why, Browning's manner is as distinctly his own as Carlyle's, and sometimes as wilfully artificial. In fact, he is so peculiarly himself that no younger poet has dared to imitate his fashion of speech, although many a one tries to follow him in the choice and treatment of subjects. Browning is the most dramatic of poets since Shakespeare; don't you think so, Ancient?

THE ANCIENT. In manner and language, perhaps. I should prefer to call him a psychologist. His subtile studies of all varieties of character are wonderful, if you look at the substance only; but every one of them, from first to last, speaks with the voice of Browning. Take *The Ring and the Book* for instance,—and I consider it one of the most original and excellent poems in the English language,—and in each of the twelve divisions you will find exactly the same interruptions, parentheses, ellipses, the same coinage of illustration and play of recondite hints under what is expressed. I should guess that he writes very rapidly, and concerns himself little with any objective theories of art. You ought to copy his manner easily enough.

ZOÏLUS. I can. I have caught the idea already.

(He takes a pencil and writes rapidly. GALAHAD *and* THE GANNET *also begin to write, but slowly.)*

THE CHORUS *(to* THE ANCIENT*).* Why don't you begin?

THE ANCIENT. I was deliberating; what a range of forms there is! He is as inexhaustible as Raphael, and he always expresses the same sense of satisfaction in his work. Well, anything will do for a subject. *(Writes.)*

ZOÏLUS *(after a few minutes).* Hearken! I must read at once, or I shall go on writing forever; it bewilders me. *(Reads.)*

> Who *wills,* may hear Sordello's story told
> By Robert Browning: warm? (you ask) or cold?
> But just so much as seemeth to enhance—
> The start being granted, onward goes the dance
> To its own music—the poet's inward sense;
> So, by its verity . . . nay, no pretense

Avails your self-created bards, and thus
By just the chance of half a hair to us,
If understood . . . but what the odds to you,
Who, with no obligations to pursue
Scant tracks of thought, if such, indeed, there be
In this one poem,—stay, my friend, and see
Whether you note that creamy tint of flesh,
Softer than bivalve pink, impearled and fresh,
Just where the small o' the back goes curving down
To orbic muscles . . . ha! that sidelong frown
Pursing the eye, and folded, deeply cleft
I' the nostril's edge, as though contempt were left
Just o'er the line that bounds indifference. . . .
But here's the test of any closer sense
(You follow me?) such as I started with;
And there be minds that seek the very pith,
Crowd close, bore deep, push far, and reach the light
Through league-long tunnels——

GALAHAD (*interrupting*). But that *is* Sordello you're reading!

ZOÏLUS. Yes, mine. I am one of the few who have bored their way through that amazing work. Browning's *Sordello* (if you ever read it, you will remember) begins with something about "Pentapolin o' the Naked Arm." It is not any particular passage, but the manner of the whole poem which I've tried to reproduce; a little exaggerated, to be sure, but not much. Now, I call this perplexity, not profundity. Wasn't it the Swedish poet, Tegner, who said, "The obscurely uttered is the obscurely thought"?

THE ANCIENT. Yes; and it is true in regard to poetry, however the case may be with metaphysics. But we have a right to be vexed with Browning, when, in the dedicatory letter to the new edition of *Sordello,* he says that he had taken pains to make the work something "which the many *might,* instead of what the few *must,* like," but, after all, did not choose to publish the revised copy. There is a touch of arrogance in this expression which I should rather not have encountered. The *"must"* which he flings at the few is far more offensive than utter indifference to all readers would have been; and not even those few can make us accept

Sordello. However, *multum creavit* is as good a plea as *multum dilexit.* Browning has a royal brain, and we owe him too much to bear malice against him. Only we must not encourage our masters in absolute rule, or they will become tyrants.

ZOÏLUS. I don't acknowledge any masters!

THE ANCIENT. We all know that. Now, Galahad, what have you done?

GALAHAD (*reads*):

BY THE SEA

(*Mutatis mutandis*)

I

Is it life or is it death?
  A whiff of the cool salt scum,
As the whole sea puffed its breath
  Against you,—blind and dumb,
This way it answereth.

II

Nearer the sands it shows
  Spotted and leprous tints;
But stay! yon fisher knows
  Rock-tokens, which evince
How high the tide arose.

III

How high? In you and me
  'Twas falling then, I think;
Open your heart's eyes, see
  From just so slight a chink
The chasm that now must be.

IV

You sighed and shivered then,
  Blue ecstasies of June
Around you, shouts of fishermen,
  Sharp wings of sea-gulls, soon
To dip—the clock struck ten!

v

Was it the cup too full
    To carry it you grew
Too faint, the wine's hue dull,
    (Dulness, misjudged untrue!)
Love's flower unfit to cull?

vi

You should have held me fast
    One moment, stopped my pace,
Crushed down the feeble, vast
    Suggestions of embrace,
And so be crowned at last.

vii

But now! . . . Bare-legged and brown
    Bait-diggers delve the sand,
Tramp i' the sunshine down
    Burnt-ochre vestured land,
And yonder stares the town.

viii

A heron screams! I shut
    This book of scurf and scum,
Its final page uncut;
    The sea-beast, blind, and dumb,
Done with his bellowing? All but!

THE GANNET. It seems we have all hit upon the obvious
characteristics, especially those which are most confusing.
There is something very like that in the *Dramatis Personæ*,
or there seems to be. Now, I wonder how my attempt will
strike you? (*Reads.*)

ANGELO ORDERS HIS DINNER

I Angelo, obese, black-garmented,
Respectable, much in demand, well fed
With mine own larder's dainties,—where, indeed,
Such cakes of myrrh or fine alyssum seed,
Thin as a mallow-leaf, embrowned o' the top,
Which, cracking, lets the ropy, trickling drop

Of sweetness touch your tongue, or potted nests
Which my recondite recipe invests
With cold, conglomerate tidbits—ah, the bill!
(You say) but given it were mine to fill
My chests, the case so put were yours, we'll say
(This counter, here, your post, as mine, today),
And you've an eye to luxuries, what harm
In smoothing down your palate with the charm
Yourself concocted? There we issue take;
And see! as thus across the rim I break
This puffy paunch of glazed embroidered cake,
So breaks, through use, the lust of watering chaps
And craveth plainness: do I so? Perhaps;
But that's my secret. Find me such a man
As Lippo yonder, built upon the plan
Of heavy storage, double-naveled, fat
From his own giblets' oils, an Ararat
Uplift o'er water, sucking rosy draughts
From Noah's vineyard . . . crisp, enticing wafts
Yon kitchen now emits, which to your sense
Somewhat abate the fear of old events,
Qualms to the stomach——I, you see, am slow
Unnecessary duties to forego——
You understand? A venison haunch, *haut goût,*
Ducks that in Cimbrian olives mildly stew,
And sprigs of anise, might one's teeth provoke
To taste, and so we wear the complex yoke
Just as it suits——my liking, I confess,
More to receive, and to partake no less,
Still more obese, while through thick adipose
Sensation shoots, from testing tongue to toes
Far-off, dim-conscious, at the body's verge
Where the froth-whispers of its waves emerge
On the untasting sand. Stay, now! a seat
Is bare: I, Angelo, will sit and eat.

THE CHORUS. There's no mistaking any of them!

THE ANCIENT. And yet what a wealth of forms and moods there is left! You have only touched the poet on two or three of his shifting sides. Whoever should hear these imitations first, and then take up the original works, would recognize certain fashions here and there, but he would be wholly unprepared for the special best qualities of Browning.

THE CHORUS. How, then, have *you* fared?

THE ANCIENT. I'm afraid I've violated the very law I laid down at the beginning. But I took the first notion that came into my head, and I could not possibly make it either all imitation or all burlesque. However, hear, and then punish me as you like! (*Reads.*)

ON THE TRACK

Where the crags are close, and the railway-curve
    Begins to swerve
From its straight-shot course i' the level plain
    To the hills again,
At the end of the twilight, when you mark
    The denser dark

Blown by the wind from the heights, that make
    A cold, coiled snake
Round the shuddering world, as a Midgards-orm·
    like, sinuous form,—
With scant-cut hosen, jacket in hands,
    The small boy stands.

Clipt by the iron ways, shiny and straight,
    You see him wait,
'Twixt the coming thunder and the rock,
    To fend the shock,
As a mite should stay, with its wiggling force,
    A planet's course.

Even as he dances, leaps, and stoops,
    The black train swoops
Up from the level: wave jacket, cry!
    Must all then die?
Sweating, the small boy smiles again;
    He has stopped the train!

GALAHAD. Well, that somehow suggests to me two poems: his *Love among the Ruins,* and the *Incident of the French Camp,* yet it is not an imitation of either. I should only apply to it the same criticism as to my own,—that it gives no hint of Browning's subtile and ingenious way of dealing with the simplest subjects. He seems always to seek some other than the ordinary and natural point of view. I believe he could change *Mother Hubbard* and *Kits, Cats, Sacks, and Wives* into profound psychological poems.

THE ANCIENT. Now, why didn't you say that before we began? I might have made, at least, a more grotesque failure. But, O Gambrinus! our glasses have been empty this hour. Ring for the waiter, Galahad; let us refresh our wearied virtue, and depart!

OMNES (*touching glasses*). To be continued!

[*Exeunt.*

Night The Second

THE friends came together again in the Lions' Den a little earlier than their wont; but they did not immediately take up the chief diversion of the evening. In intellectual, as in physical acrobatics, the joints must be gradually made flexible, and the muscles warm and elastic, by lighter feats; so the conversation began as mere skylarking and mutual chaffing, as empty and evanescent, when you attempt to catch it, as the foam-ripples on a swift stream. But Galahad had something on his mind; he had again read portions of the *Earthly Paradise,* and insisted that the atmosphere of the poems was not gray and overcast, but charged with a golden, luminous mist, like that of the Indian summer. Finally, he asked the Ancient:

"Granting the force of your impression, might not much of it come from some want of harmony between your mood or temper of mind and the author's? In that case, it would not be abstractly just."

THE ANCIENT. I don't think that we often can be "abstractly just" towards contemporary poets; we either exalt or abase them too much. For we and they breathe either the same or opposite currents in the intellectual atmosphere of the time, and there can be no impartial estimate until those winds have blown over. This is precisely the reason why you sometimes think me indifferent, when I am only trying to shove myself as far off as the next generation; at least, to get a little outside of the fashions and whims and prejudices of this day. American authors, and also their publishers, are often charged with an overconcern for the opinion of the English literary journals. I think their interest quite natural——

Zoïlus (*with energy*). Now, you surely are not going to justify that sycophantic respect for the judgment of men who know so much less than we do of our own literature?

The Ancient. I condemn *all* sycophancy, even to the great, triumphant, overwhelming American spirit! But, until we have literary criticism of a more purely objective character in this country,—until our critics learn to separate their personal tastes and theories from their estimate of the executive and artistic quality of the author; or, which amounts to the same thing, to set this quality, this creative principle, higher than the range of themes and opinions,—the author will look to the judgment of critics, whose distance and whose very want of acquaintance with our prejudices and passions assure him of a certain amount of impartiality. The feeling is reciprocal; I venture to say that an intelligent American criticism has more weight with an English author than that of one of his own Reviews.

Zoïlus. Do you mean to say that we have *no* genuine criticism?

The Ancient. By no means; we have some that is admirable. But it is only recognized at its true value by a very small class; the great reading public is blissfully ignorant of its existence. It adds to the confusion that many of our writers have no definite ideas of literary excellence apart from the effect which immediately follows their work; and readers are thus actually misled by those who should guide them. Why, a year ago, the most popular book in the whole country was one which does not even belong to literature; and the most popular poem of late years was written, not from a poetic, but from a high moral, inspiration! Somebody must set up a true aesthetic standard; it is high time this were done, and a better criticism must be the first step.

The Gannet. Why don't you undertake it yourself?

The Ancient. I'm too fond of comfort. Think what a hor-

net's nest I should thrust my hand into! Moreover, I doubt
whether one could force such interests beyond their natural
growth; we are still suffering from the intellectual demor-
alization which the war left behind it. But where's the hat?
We are spoiling ourselves by all this serious prose. Let us
throw in a few more names, and try our luck again.

(*They draw the lots as before.*)

THE GANNET. John Keats! How shall I wear his mantle?

ZOÏLUS. I'm crushed, buried under an avalanche of—well,
not much, after all. Don't ask me who it is, until I try my
hand. You would confuse me with your laughter.

THE ANCIENT. I shall keep mine specially for you, Zoïlus.

GALAHAD. I have drawn one of the names I wrote myself;
but you have already so demoralized me, that I will try to
parody him as heartily as if I didn't like his poetry.

THE ANCIENT. You are getting on. But I think the Gannet
ought to draw another name; it is best not to go back of our
own day and generation. I propose that we limit ourselves
to the poets who stand nearer to our own minds, under
whom, or beside whom, or above whom (as each chooses to
estimate himself), we have grown and are now growing.
The farther we withdraw from this atmosphere, the more
artificial must our imitations be.

THE GANNET. Let it pass this once, I pray thee, for I have
caught my idea! But, even taking your limitation, who is
nearer us than Keats? Not alone in his own person, though
there he stands among us; he is in Tennyson, in Morris, in
Swinburne, and, more remotely, in the earlier poems of
Browning and Lowell, besides a host of small rhymers. He
still approaches us, while Shelley and Byron withdraw. I
think it's a fair exception; and if you won't admit it, I'll
take the sense of the company.

OMNES. Go on!

(*All write busily for fifteen minutes, except* THE ANCIENT,
who talks in a lower tone to THE CHORUS.)

THE GANNET (*looking up*). Zoïlus, you were ready first.

ZOÏLUS. Could you guess whom I represent?

THE GANNET. Tupper?

ZOÏLUS. He? He is his own best parody. No; it is a lyrical

inanity, which once was tolerably famous. The Ancient's rule as to what is properly parodiable doesn't apply here; for it is neither excellent nor imbecile. I think I had the right to reject the name, but I have tried to see whether a respectable jingle of words, expressing ordinary and highly proper feelings, can be so imitated as to be recognized. Here it is. (*Reads.*)

Obituary

ON THE DEATH OF THE REV. ELIJAH W. BATEY

Ay, bear him to his sainted rest,
    Ye mourners, but be calm!
Instead of dirge and sable crest,
    Raise ye thanksgiving psalm!
For he was old and full of years,
    The grandsire of your souls;
Then check ye now your heaving tears,
    And quench the sigh that rolls!

Ye heard him from yon pulpit preach,
    For sixty years and more,
Still battering with unwearied speech
    The ceiling, pews, and floor;
As, hour by hour, his periods fell,
    Your pious hopes arose,
And each one murmured, "All is well,"
    Long ere the sermon's close.

Think ye the voice that spake so long
    Can anywhere be dumb?
Before him went a goodly throng,
    And wait for him to come.
He preaches still, in other spheres,
    To saved and patient souls;
Then, mourners, check your heaving tears,
    And quench the sigh that rolls!

Omnes (*shouting*). Mrs. Sigourney!

Zoïlus. I *have* succeeded, then! But, oh! my friends, is the success a thing over which I should rejoice? Do not, I beg of you, do not congratulate me!

GALAHAD. Come, now, don't abuse good old Mother Sigourney! For a long time she was almost our only woman-poet; and I insist that she was not a mere echo of Felicia Hemans.

ZOÏLUS (*ironically*). Of course not! None but herself could ever have written that exquisite original poem, *On Finding a Shred of Linen*. One passage I can never forget:

> Methinks I scan
> Some idiosyncrasy, which marks thee out
> A defunct pillow-case.

GALAHAD. You are incorrigible; but we wait for the Gannet and the idea he has caught.

THE GANNET. It was better in anticipation than it seems after execution. However, Keats is too dainty a spirit to be possessed in a few minutes. (*Reads.*)

ODE ON A JAR OF PICKLES

I

A sweet, acidulous, down-reaching thrill
    Pervades my sense; I seem to see or hear
The lushy garden-grounds of Greenwich Hill
    In autumn, when the crispy leaves are sere;
And odors haunt me of remotest spice
    From the Levant or musky-aired Cathay,
Or from the saffron-fields of Jericho,
        Where everything is nice;
    The more I sniff, the more I swoon away,
And what else mortal palate craves, forego.

II

Odors unsmelled are keen, but those I smell
    Are keener; wherefore let me sniff again!
Enticing walnuts, I have known ye well
    In youth, when pickles were a passing pain;
Unwitting youth, that craves the candy stem,
    And sugar-plums to olives doth prefer,
And even licks the pots of marmalade
        When sweetness clings to them;
    But now I dream of ambergris and myrrh,
Tasting these walnuts in the poplar shade.

III

Lo! hoarded coolness in the heart of noon,
 Plucked with its dew, the cucumber is here,
As to the Dryad's parching lips a boon,
 And crescent bean-pods, unto Bacchus dear;
And, last of all, the pepper's pungent globe,
 The scarlet dwelling of the sylph of fire,
Provoking purple draughts; and, surfeited,
   I cast my trailing robe
O'er my pale feet, touch up my tuneless lyre,
And twist the Delphic wreath to suit my head.

IV

Here shall my tongue in other wise be soured
 Than fretful men's in parched and palsied days;
And, by the mid-May's dusky leaves embowered,
 Forget the fruitful blame, the scanty praise.
No sweets to them who sweet themselves were born,
 Whose natures ooze with lucent saccharine;
Who, with sad repetition soothly cloyed,
   The lemon-tinted morn
Enjoy, and for acetic darkness pine:
Wake I, or sleep? The pickle-jar is void.

Zoïlus. Not to be mistaken; but you have almost stepped over the bounds of our plan. Those two odes of Keats are too immediately suggested, though I find that only two lines are actually parodied. I agree with the Ancient; let us stick to the authors of our own day! Galahad, you look mysterious; are we to guess your singer from the echo?

GALAHAD. Are you all ready to hear me chant, in rare and rhythmic redundancy, the viciousness of virtue?

THE CHORUS. O Swinburne! chant away!

GALAHAD (reads):

THE LAY OF MACARONI

As a wave that steals when the winds are stormy
 From creek to cove of the curving shore,
Buffeted, blown, and broken before me,
 Scattered and spread to its sunlit core;

As a dove that dips in the dark of maples
  To sip the sweetness of shelter and shade,
I kneel in thy nimbus, O noon of Naples,
  I bathe in thine beauty, by thee embayed!

What is it ails me that I should sing of her?
  The queen of the flashes and flames that were!
Yea, I have felt the shuddering sting of her,
  The flower-sweet throat and the hands of her!
I have swayed and sung to the sound of her psalters,
  I have danced her dances of dizzy delight,
I have hallowed mine hair to the horns of her altars,
  Between the nightingale's song and the night!

What is it, Queen, that now I should do for thee?
  What is it now I should ask at thine hands?
Blow of the trumpets thine children once blew for thee?
  Break from thine feet and thine bosom the bands?
Nay, as sweet as the songs of Leone Leoni,
  And gay as her garments of gem-sprinkled gold,
She gives me mellifluous, mild macaroni,
  The choice of her children when cheeses are old!

And over me hover, as if by the wings of it,
  Frayed in the furnace by flame that is fleet,
The curious coils and the strenuous strings of it,
  Dropping, diminishing down, as I eat;
Lo! and the beautiful Queen, as she brings of it,
  Lifts me the links of the limitless chain,
Bidding mine mouth chant the splendidest things of it,
  Out of the wealth of my wonderful brain!

Behold! I have done it: my stomach is smitten
  With sweets of the surfeit her hands have unrolled.
Italia, mine cheeks with thine kisses are bitten:
  I am broken with beauty, stabbed, slaughtered, and sold!
No man of thine millions is more macaronied,
  Save mighty Mazzini, than musical Me:
The souls of the Ages shall stand as astonished,
  And faint in the flame I am fanning for thee!

The Ancient (*laughing*). O Galahad, I can fancy your
later remorse. It is not a year since you were absolutely
Swinburne-mad, and I hardly dared, in your presence, to

object even to *Anactoria* and *Dolores*. I *would not* encourage you, then, for I saw you were carried away by the wild rush of the rhythm, and the sparkle of epithets which were partly new and seemed wholly splendid; but now I will confess to you that as a purely rhythmical genius I look on Swinburne as a phenomenon in literature.

GALAHAD (*eagerly*). Then you admit that he is great?

THE ANCIENT. Not as you mean. I have been waiting for his ferment to settle, as in the case of Keats and Shelley; but there are no signs of it in his last volume. How splendidly the mind of Keats precipitated its crudity and redundancy, and clarified into the pure wine of *Hyperion!* In Shelley's case the process was slower, but it was steadily going on; you will find the same thing in Schiller, in Dryden, and many other poets, therefore I mean to reserve my judgment in Swinburne's case, and wait, at least until his next work is published. Meanwhile, I grant that he has enriched our English lyric poetry with some new and admirable forms.

THE GANNET. He has certainly made a "sensation" in the literary world; does that indicate nothing?

THE ANCIENT. That depends. I declare it seems to me as if the general taste were not quite healthy. To a very large class reading has become a form of lazy luxury, and such readers are not satisfied without a new great poet every four or five years. Then, too, there has been an amazing deal of trash written about the *coming* authors,—what they should be, how they must write, and the like; and so those luxurious readers are all the time believing they have discovered one of the tribe. Why, let a man take a thought as old as Confucius, and put it into some strange, jerky, convulsed form, and you will immediately hear the cry, "How wonderful! how original!" You all remember the case of Alexander Smith; it seems incredible, now, that the simulated passion and forced sentiment of his *Life-Drama* should have been accepted as real, yet, because of this book, he was hailed as a second Shakespeare. This hunger of the luxurious reader for new flavors is a dangerous thing for young poets.

ZOÏLUS. I almost think I hear my own voice. We don't often agree so thoroughly.

THE ANCIENT. So much the better. I wonder if you'll be as well satisfied with the task I have in store for you; here is the name. (*Giving him the slip of paper.*)

ZOÏLUS. Emerson! I think I can guess why.

THE ANCIENT. Yes, I remember what you wrote when *Brahma* was first published, and what you said to Galahad the other evening. I confess I was amazed, at the time, that the newspapers should so innocently betray their ignorance. There was a universal cry of "incomprehensible!" when the meaning of the poem was perfectly plain. In fact, there are few authors so transparently clear, barring a few idiosyncrasies of expression, which one soon learns, as just Emerson.

ZOÏLUS. Then explain to me those lines from *Alphonso of Castile:*

> Hear you then, celestial fellows!
> Fits not to be overzealous;
> Steads not to work on the clean jump,
> And wine and brains perpetual pump!

THE ANCIENT. That is simply baldness of language (which Emerson sometimes mistakes for humor), not obscurity. I will not explain it! Read the whole poem over again, and I'm sure you will not need to ask me. But now, to your work! Who will draw again?

THE GANNET (*drawing*). Ha! A friend, this time; and I wish he were here with us. Nobody would take more kindly to our fun than he.

GALAHAD. I shall try no more tonight. My imitation of Swinburne has exhausted me. I felt, while writing, as Zoïlus did when he was imitating Browning,—as if I could have gone on and on forever! Really there is some sort of possession or demoniac influence in these experiments. They fascinate me, and yet I feel as if a spirit foreign to my own had seized me.

THE ANCIENT. Take another cigar! I wish we had the Meleager, or the Farnese torso, here; five minutes of either would surround you with a different atmosphere. I know precisely how it affects you. Thirty years ago—O Tempus Edax, must I say *thirty?*—when I dreamed hot dreams of fame, and walked the streets in a mild delirium, pondering

over the great and godlike powers pent within me, I had
the same chills and fevers. I'm not laughing at you, my dear
Galahad; God forbid! I only pray that there may be more
vitality in the seeds which your dreams cover than in mine.
Waiter! Our glasses are empty.

(ZOÏLUS *and* THE GANNET *continue to write; meantime,
fresh glasses of beer are brought, and there is a brief silence.*)

ZOÏLUS. I suspect the Ancient will want to knock me on
the head for this. (*Reads.*)

ALL OR NOTHING

Whoso answers my questions
    Knoweth more than me;
Hunger is but knowledge
    In a less degree:
Prophet, priest, and poet
    Oft prevaricate,
And the surest sentence
    Hath the greatest weight.

When upon my gaiters
    Drops the morning dew,
Somewhat of Life's riddle
    Soaks my spirit through.
I am buskined by the goddess
    Of Monadnock's crest,
And my wings extended
    Touch the East and West.

Or ever coal was hardened
    In the cells of earth,
Or flowed the founts of Bourbon,
    Lo! I had my birth.
I am crowned coeval
    With the Saurian eggs,
And my fancy firmly
    Stands on its own legs.

Wouldst thou know the secret
    Of the barberry-bush,
Catch the slippery whistle
    Of the moulting thrush.

> Dance upon the mushrooms,
>   Dive beneath the sea,
> Or anything else remarkable,
>   Thou must follow me!

THE ANCIENT. Well, you have read somewhat more than
I imagined, Zoïlus. This is a fair imitation of the manner
of some of Emerson's earlier poems; but you may take heart,
Galahad, if you fear the power of association, for not one
of the inimitable, imperishable passages has been suggested.

ZOÏLUS. Now, seriously, do you mean to say that there
are such?

THE ANCIENT.

> Still on the seeds of all he made
>   The rose of beauty burns;
> Through times that wear, the forms that fade,
>   Immortal youth returns.

GALAHAD (*drawing a long breath*). How beautiful!

THE ANCIENT.

> Thou canst not wave thy staff in air,
>   Or dip thy paddle in the lake,
> But it carves the bow of Beauty there,
>   And the ripples in rhyme the oar forsake.

ZOÏLUS. *Peccavi!*

THE ANCIENT. Then I will lock up my half-unbolted
thunders. The Master does not need my vindication; and
I should do him a poor service by trying to drive anyone
towards the recognition of his deserts, when all who think
for themselves must come, sooner or later, to know him.

THE GANNET. But I never saw those stanzas!

THE ANCIENT. Yet they are printed for all the world. The
secret is simply this: Emerson cut from his limbs, long ago,
the old theological fetters, as every independent thinker
must. Those who run along in the ruts made by their grand-
fathers, unable to appreciate the exquisite fiber of his intellect, the broad and grand eclecticism of his taste, suspect a
heresy in every sentence which they are too coarsely textured
to understand. No man of our day habitually lives in a purer
region of thought.

ZoïLus (*looking at his watch*). Now, we must know what the Gannet has been doing.

THE GANNET. My name is Edmund Clarence Stedman.

THE ANCIENT. One of the younger tribes, with some of whom I'm not so familiar. I have caught many of his "fugitives" in their flight, finding them of a kind sure to stay where they touch, instead of being blown quietly on until they pass forever out of the world. There's a fine masculine vibration in his lines: he sings in the major key, which young poets generally do not. I'd be willing to bet that your imitation has a sportive, not a solemn, character.

THE GANNET. Why, in spite of your disclaimer, you're not so ignorant. Your guess is right: therefore, listen! (*Reads.*)

THE GOLD-ROOM

AN IDYL

They come from mansions far up-town,
    And from their country villas,
And some Charybdis' gulf whirls down,
    And some fall into Scylla's.
Lo! here young Paris climbs the stairs
    As if their slope were Ida's,
And here his golden touch declares
    The ass's ears of Midas.

It seems a Bacchic, brawling rout
    To every business-scorner,
But such, methinks, must be an "out,"
    Or has not made a "corner."
In me the rhythmic gush revives;
    I feel a classic passion:
We, also, lead Arcadian lives,
    Though in a Broad-Street fashion.

Old Battos, here, 's a leading bull,
    And Diomed a bear is,
And near them, shearing bankers' wool,
    Strides the Tiltonian Charis;
And Atys, there, has gone to smash,
    His every bill protested,
While Cleon's eyes with comfort flash,—
    I have his funds invested!

> Mehercle! 'tis the same thing yet
> As in the days of Pindar:
> The Isthmian race, the dust and sweat,
> The prize—why, what's to hinder?
> And if I twang my lyre at times,
> They did so then, I reckon;
> That man's the best at modern rhymes
> Whom you can draw a check on!

OMNES (*clapping their hands*). Bravo!

THE ANCIENT. To think of Stedman's being the only voice in our literature which comes out of the business crowds of the whole country! The man who can spend his days in a purely material atmosphere, and sing at night, has genuine pluck in him. It's enough to make any green poet, who wails about the cruel world, and the harsh realities of life, and the beautiful realm of the ideal, ashamed of himself!

GALAHAD (*annoyed*). You don't mean as much as you say! Every poet, green or not, must have faith in an ideal.

THE ANCIENT (*gently*). Ay, but if it make him

> Pamper the coward heart
> With feelings all too delicate for use,

as Coleridge translates Schiller, it is a deceit and a snare to him. Your Shakespeare, Dante, Cervantes, Goethe were made of different clay.

ZOÏLUS. Here's to their sublime Shades, wherever they may be wandering! Out, to the last drop! We are in the small hours; the *Donnerwetters!* are all silent in the saloon, and Karl Schäfer is probably snoring over his counter, waiting for us. Come!

[*Exeunt.*

Night The Third

WHEN the sportive tilting with light lances, the reciprocal, good-natured chaffing, in which the members of the Club were wont to indulge on coming together, had subsided, the conversation took the following turn:

ZOÏLUS (*to* THE ANCIENT). I've been considering what you said the last time, about the prevalent literary taste not being entirely healthy. How far would you apply that verdict to the authors? Their relative popularity is your only gauge for the character of the readers.

THE ANCIENT. I don't think I had any individual authors in my mind, at the time. But a great deal of all modern literature is ephemeral, created from day to day, to supply a certain definite demand, and sinking out of sight, sooner or later. Nine readers out of ten make no distinction between this ephemeral material and the few works which really belong to our literary history; that is, they confound the transitory with the permanent authors.

ZOÏLUS. So far, I agree with you. Now the inference would be that those nine readers, who lack the finer judgment, and who, of course, represent the prevalent taste, are responsible for the success of the transitory authors. But they do not make the latter; they do not even dictate the character of their works: hence the school, no matter how temporary it may be, must be founded by the authors,—which obliges us to admit a certain degree of originality and power.

THE ANCIENT. I see where you are going; let us have no reasoning in a ring, I pray you! If you admit the two classes of authors, it is enough. I have already seen one generation forgotten, and I fancy I now see the second slipping the cables of their craft, and making ready to drop downstream with the ebb tide. I remember, for instance, that in 1840 there were many well-known and tolerably popular names, which are never heard now. Byron and Mrs. Hemans then gave the tone to poetry, and Scott, Bulwer, and Cooper to fiction. Willis was, by all odds, the most popular American author; Longfellow was not known by the multitude, Emerson was only "that Transcendentalist," and Whittier "that Abolitionist." We young men used to talk of Rufus Dawes, and Charles Fenno Hoffman, and Grenville Mellen, and Brainard, and Sands. Why, we even had a hope that something wonderful would come out of Chivers!

OMNES. Chivers?

THE ANCIENT. Have you never heard of Chivers? He is a phenomenon!

THE GANNET. Doesn't Poe speak of him somewhere?

THE ANCIENT. To be sure. Poe finished the ruin of him which Shelley began. Dr. Thomas Holley Chivers, of Georgia, author of *Virginalia, The Lost Pleiad, Facets of Diamond,* and *Eonchs of Ruby!*

ZOÏLUS. What! Come, now, this is only a *ben trovato.*

THE ANCIENT. Also of *Nacoochee, the Beautiful Star;* and there was still another volume,—six in all! The British Museum has the only complete set of his works. I speak the sober truth, Zoïlus; a friend of mine has three of the volumes, and I can show them to you. One of the finest things in modern poetry is in his *Apollo:*

> Like cataracts of adamant, uplifted into mountains,
> Making oceans metropolitan, for the splendor of the dawn!

ZOÏLUS. Incredible!

THE ANCIENT. I remember also a stanza of his *Rosalie Lee:*

> Many mellow Cydonian suckets,
>   Sweet apples, anthosmial, divine,
> From the ruby-rimmed beryline buckets,
>   Star-gemmed, lily-shaped, hyaline;
> Like the sweet golden goblet found growing
>   On the wild emerald cucumber-tree,
> Rich, brilliant, like chrysoprase glowing,
>   Was my beautiful Rosalie Lee!

ZOÏLUS. Hold, hold! I can endure no more.

THE ANCIENT. You see what comes of a fashion in literature. There was many a youth in those days who made attempts just as idiotic, in the columns of country papers; and perhaps the most singular circumstance was that very few readers laughed at them. Why, they are expressions, epithets, images, which run all over the land, and sometimes last for a generation. I once discovered that with both the English and German poets of a hundred years ago, evening is always called *brown,* and morning either *rosy* or *purple.* Just now the fashion runs to jewelry; we have ruby lips, and topaz light, and sapphire seas, and diamond air. Mrs. Browning even says:

> Her *cheek's pale opal* burnt with a red and restless spark!

What sort of a cheek must that be? Then we have such a wealth of gorgeous color as never was seen before,—no quiet half-tints, but pure pigments, laid on with a pallet knife. Really, I sometimes feel a distinct sense of fatigue at the base of the optic nerve, after reading a magazine story. The besetting sin of the popular—not the best—authors is the intense.

Zoïlus. Why do you call intensity of expression a sin?

The Ancient. I mean intensity of *epithet*: the strongest expression is generally the briefest and barest. Take the old ballads of any people, and you will find few adjectives. The singer says: "He laughed; she wept." Perhaps the poet of a more civilized age might say: "He laughed in scorn; she turned away and shed tears of disappointment." But nowadays the ambitious young writer must produce something like this: "A hard, fiendish laugh, scornful and pitiless, forced its passage from his throat through the lips that curled in mockery of her appeal; she covered her despairing face, and a gust and whirlwind of sorrowing agony burst forth in her irresistible tears!"

Omnes (*clapping their hands*). Go on! Go on!

The Ancient. It is enough of the Bowery for tonight.

Galahad. Oh, you forget the intenser life of our day! I see the exaggeration of which you speak, but I believe something of it comes from the struggle to express more. All our senses have grown keener, our natures respond more delicately, and to a greater range of influences, than those of the generations before us. There is a finer moral development; our aims in life have become spiritualized; we may have less power, less energy of genius, but we move towards higher and purer goals.

Zoïlus. The writers of Queen Anne's time might have compared themselves in the same way with their predecessors in Charles II's. What if your own poems should be considered coarse and immoral a hundred years hence?

Galahad (*bewildered*). What has that to do with the question?

The Ancient. Only this; that there are eternal laws of

Art, to which the moral and spiritual aspirations of the author, which are generally relative to his own or the preceding age, must conform, if they would also become eternal.

THE GANNET. Very fine, indeed; but you are all forgetting our business.

ZOÏLUS. Let us first add a fresh supply of names.

THE GANNET. Write them yourself; we shall otherwise repeat.

(ZOÏLUS *writes a dozen or more slips, whereupon they draw.*)

GALAHAD. Dante Rossetti!

ZOÏLUS. I have Barry Cornwall.

THE GANNET. And I—Whittier.

OMNES. Whittier must not be parodied.

GALAHAD (*earnestly*). Draw another name!

THE ANCIENT. Why?

GALAHAD. There is at once an evidence of what I said! Where are your jewelry and colors? On the other side, where will you find an intenser faith, a more ardent aspiration for truth and good? The moral and spiritual element is so predominant in him,—so wedded for time and eternity to his genius as a poet,—that you cannot imitate him without seeming to slight, or in some way offend, what should be as holy to us as to him!

THE ANCIENT (*laying his hand on* GALAHAD's *shoulder*). My dear boy, Whittier deserves all the love and reverence you are capable of giving him. He is just as fine an illustration of my side of the question: his poetic art has refined and harmonized that moral quality in his nature, which, many years ago, made his poetry seem partisan, and, therefore, not unmixed poetry. But the alloy (in a poetic sense only) has been melted out in the pure and steady flame of his intellect, and the preacher in him has now his rightful authority because he no longer governs the poet. As for those poems which exhale devotion and aspiration as naturally as a violet exhales odor, there is no danger of the Gannet imitating them; he has not the power even if he had the will. But Whittier has also written——

THE GANNET. Don't you see I'm hard at work? What do you mean by dictating what I may or may not do? I am already launched, and (*declaiming*) "I see no change; and, least of all, such change as you would give me!"

THE ANCIENT. I can't help you, Galahad; go on with your own work now. I have drawn one of the youngsters, this time, and mean to turn him over to you when you have slaughtered Rossetti.

GALAHAD. Who is he?

THE ANCIENT. A brother near your throne.

ZOÏLUS (*to* THE ANCIENT). I have done Barry Cornwall; it's an easy task. He is nearly always very brief. His are not even short swallow flights of song, but little hops from one twig to another. While Galahad and the Gannet are finishing theirs, repeat to me something more of Chivers!

THE ANCIENT. I can only recall fragments here and there. The refrain to a poem called *The Poet's Vocation*, in the *Eonchs of Ruby*, is:

> In the music of the morns,
> Blown through the Conchimarian horns,
> Down the dark vistas of the reboantic Norns,
> To the Genius of Eternity,
> Crying: "Come to me! Come to me!"

ZOÏLUS. Ye gods! It is amazing. Why can't you write a stanza in his manner?

THE ANCIENT (*smiling*). I think I can even equal him.

(*He takes a pencil and writes rapidly. Just as he finishes,* GALAHAD *and* THE GANNET *lay down their pencils and lean back in their seats.*)

THE CHORUS (*eagerly*). We must first hear the Ancient! He is a medium for the great Chivers.

THE ANCIENT. I have been merciful towards you. One stanza will suffice. (*Reads.*)

> Beloved of the wanderer's father
> That walks mid the agates of June,
> The wreaths of remorse that I gather
> Were torn from the turrets of Rune;

When the star-patterns broidered so brilliant
Shone forth from the diapered blue,
And the moon dropped her balsam scintilliant,
Soul-nectar for me and for you!

THE GANNET. Send for a physician; tie a wet towel around his head! A thousand years hence, when the human race comes back to polytheism, Chivers will be the god of all crack-brained authors.

THE ANCIENT. I recognize a fantastic infection. Come, Zoïlus, give me a tonic!

ZOÏLUS. Wine has become a very fashionable tonic, and that is just what I have put into Barry Cornwall's mouth. (Reads.)

SONG

Talk of dew on eglantine,—
Stuff! the poet's drink is wine.
Black as quaffed by old King Death.
That which biteth, maddeneth;
For my readers fain would see
What effect it has on me.

Nose may redden, head may swim,
Joints be loose in every limb,
And the golden rhymes I chant
Sheer away on wings aslant,
Whale may whistle, porpoise roll,
Yet I'll drain the gentle bowl!

Pleasure's dolphin gambols near;
Virtue's mackerel looks austere;
Duty's hippopotamus
Waddles forward, leaving us;
Joy, the sturgeon, leaps and soars,
While we coast the Teian shores!

THE ANCIENT. What a fearful Bacchanalian you have made of good and gentle Barry Cornwall! You must have been possessed by Poe's "Imp of the Perverse," to yoke his manner to such a subject I was expecting to hear some-

thing of spring and clover and cowslips. Faith! I believe
I could improvise an imitation. Wait a second! Now:

> When spring returneth,
>   And cowslips blow,
> The milkmaid churneth
>   Her creamy snow,
> The mill-wheel spurneth
>   The stream below;
> The cherry-tree skippeth in earth and air,
> The small bird calleth: beware, prepare!
> And all is fair!

OMNES. Another stanza!

THE ANCIENT. Oh, you have but to turn things upside
down, and there it is:

> The cold wind bloweth
>   O'er brake and burn,
> The cream o'erfloweth
>   The tilted churn,
> The mill-wheel sloweth,
>   And fails to turn;
> The cherry-tree sheddeth her leaves in the fall,
> The crow and the clamoring raven call,
> And that is all!

But, seriously, Galahad, after what Zoïlus has done, I am
a little afraid of the Gannet's work. Suppose he should make
our beloved Whittier

> Troll a careless tavern catch
> Of Moll and Meg, and strange experiences
> Unmeet for ladies?

GALAHAD (earnestly). Then I should withdraw from the
Club.

THE GANNET. Prythee, peace, young hotspur! I'll agree
to start with you for Massachusetts by tomorrow morning's
express train, and lay before the poet what I've written.
If he doesn't laugh heartily on reading it, I'll engage to
come all the way back afoot.

THE ANCIENT. We can decide for him: read!

THE GANNET. It is a ballad of New England life which you shall hear. (*Reads.*)

THE BALLAD OF HIRAM HOVER

Where the Moosatockmaguntic
Pours its waters in the Skuntic,
    Met, along the forest-side,
    Hiram Hover, Huldah Hyde.

She, a maiden fair and dapper,
He, a red-haired, stalwart trapper,
    Hunting beaver, mink, and skunk,
    In the Woodlands of Squeedunk.

She, Pentucket's pensive daughter,
Walked beside the Skuntic water,
    Gathering, in her apron wet,
    Snakeroot, mint, and bouncing-bet.

"Why," he murmured, loath to leave her,
"Gather yarbs for chills and fever,
    When a lovyer, bold and true,
    Only waits to gather you?"

"Go," she answered, "I'm not hasty;
I prefer a man more tasty:
    Leastways, one to please me well
    Should not have a beasty smell."

"Haughty Huldah!" Hiram answered;
"Mind and heart alike are cancered:
    Jest look here! these peltries give
    Cash, wherefrom a pair may live.

"I, you think, am but a vagrant,
Trapping beasts by no means fragrant,
    Yet—I'm sure it's worth a thank—
    I've a handsome sum in bank."

Turned and vanished Hiram Hover;
And, before the year was over,
    Huldah, with the yarbs she sold,
    Bought a cape, against the cold.

Black and thick the furry cape was;
Of a stylish cut the shape was;
　　And the girls, in all the town,
　　Envied Huldah up and down.

Then at last one winter morning,
Hiram came without a warning:
　　"Either," said he, "you are blind,
　　Huldah, or you've changed your mind.

"Me you snub for trapping varmints,
Yet you take the skins for garments:
　　Since you wear the skunk and mink,
　　There's no harm in me, I think."

"Well," said she, "we will not quarrel,
Hiram: I accept the moral.
　　Now the fashion's so, I guess
　　I can't hardly do no less."

Thus the trouble all was over
Of the love of Hiram Hover;
　　Thus he made sweet Huldah Hyde
　　Huldah Hover, as his bride.

Love employs, with equal favor,
Things of good and evil savor;
　　That, which first appeared to part,
　　Warmed, at last, the maiden's heart.

Under one impartial banner,
Life, the hunter, Love, the tanner,
　　Draw, from every beast they snare,
　　Comfort for a wedded pair!

Zoïlus. The Gannet distances us all tonight. Even Galahad is laughing yet, and I saw, when the reading began,
that he was resolved not to smile, if he could help it. What
does our Ancient think?

The Ancient. It does, certainly, suggest the style of some
of Whittier's delightful ballads, only substituting a comical

for an earnest motive. Change that motive and a few expressions, and it would become a serious poem. The Gannet was lucky in striking the proper key at the start. And here, perhaps, is one result of our diversions, upon which we had not calculated, over and above the fun. I don't see why poets should not drill themselves in all that is technical, as well as painters, sculptors, opera singers, or even orators. All the faculties called into play to produce rhythm, harmony of words, richness of the poetical dialect, choice of keys and cadences, may be made nimbler, more active, and more obedient to command, by even mechanical practice. I never rightly believed in the peculiar solemnity of the poet's gift; every singer should have a gay, sportive side to his nature. I am sure the young Shakespeare would have heartily joined in what we are here doing; the young Goethe, we know, did many a similar thing. He was a capital *improvvisatore;* and who knows how much of his mastery over all forms of poetry may not have come from just such gymnastics?

GALAHAD. Might not an aptness in representing the manner of others—like that of an actor who assumes a different character every night—indicate some lack of original force?

THE ANCIENT. The comparison is deceptive. An actor's sole business is to assume other individualities. What we do is no more than every novelist does, in talking as a young girl, an old man, a saint, or a sinner. If anything of yourself is lost in the process, and you can't get it back again, why—let it go!

ZOÏLUS. You have it now, Galahad!

GALAHAD. Well, I'll cover my confusion by transferring myself into Dante Gabriel Rossetti. (*Reads.*)

CIMABUELLA

I

Fair-tinted cheeks, clear eyelids drawn
    In crescent curves above the light
Of eyes, whose dim, uncertain dawn
    Becomes not day: a forehead white
Beneath long yellow heaps of hair:
She is so strange she must be fair.

II

Had she sharp, slant-wise wings outspread,
　　She were an angel; but she stands
With flat dead gold behind her head,
　　And lilies in her long thin hands:
Her folded mantle, gathered in,
Falls to her feet as it were tin.

III

Her nose is keen as pointed flame;
　　Her crimson lips no thing express;
And never dread of saintly blame
　　Held down her heavy eyelashes:
To guess what she were thinking of
Precluded any meaner love.

IV

An azure carpet, fringed with gold,
　　Sprinkled with scarlet spots, I laid
Before her straight, cool feet unrolled:
　　But she nor sound nor movement made
(Albeit I heard a soft, shy smile,
Printing her neck a moment's while);

V

And I was shamed through all my mind
　　For that she spake not, neither kissed,
But stared right past me. Lo! behind
　　Me stood, in pink and amethyst,
Sword-girt and velvet-doubleted,
A tall, gaunt youth, with frowzy head,

VI

Wide nostrils in the air, dull eyes,
　　Thick lips that simpered, but, ah me!
I saw, with most forlorn surprise,
　　He was the Thirteenth Century,
I but the Nineteenth; then despair
Curdled beneath my curling hair.

VII

O, Love and Fate! How could she choose
　　My rounded outlines, broader brain,

And my resuscitated Muse?
　　Some tears she shed, but whether pain
　　Or joy in him unlocked their source,
　　I could not fathom which, of course.

VIII

But I from missals, quaintly bound,
　　With cither and with clavichord
Will sing her songs of sovran sound:
　　Belike her pity will afford
　　Such faint return as suits a saint
So sweetly done in verse and paint.

THE GANNET. O Galahad! Who could have expected this of you?

GALAHAD. You know I like Rossetti's poems, but, really, I couldn't help it, after I once got under way.

THE GANNET. Rossetti is picturesque, whatever else he may not be. His poetry has a delicate flavor of its own, and that is much to me, in these days, when so many dishes seem to be cooked with the same sauce. A poet is welcome to go back to the thirteenth century, if he only fetches us pictures. Poetry belongs to luxurious living, as much as painting and music; hence we must value color, rhythmical effect, quaint and unexpected play of fancy, and every other quality that makes verse bright and sparkling. The theme is of less importance. Take, for instance, Victor Hugo's *Orientales*.

ZOÏLUS. Pray, let us not open that discussion again! You know, already, how far I go with you, and just where Galahad and the Ancient stand. We should rather confine ourselves directly to the authors we imitate. Now, I think Rossetti's book on the Early Italian Poets better than his own poems. Perhaps it was the attempt to reproduce those poets in English which has given the mediaeval coloring to his verse. We cannot undertake to say how much of the manner is natural, and how much assumed; for a thirteenth or even a second century nature may be born nowadays. But it is none the less out of harmony with our thought and feeling, and the encouragement of such a fashion in literature strikes me as being related to the Pre-Raphaelite hallucination in art. I should like to have the Ancient's opinion on this point.

THE ANCIENT. Here is your other name, Galahad. (*Gives him a slip of paper.*) If there were not so much confusion of taste, Zoïlus,—such an uncertainty in regard to the unchanging standards of excellence, in literature and art,—I could answer you in a few words. We must judge these anachronistic developments (as they seem) by those which provoked them. A movement may be false in itself, yet made necessary by some antecedent illusion or inanity. If you want to leave port, almost any craft will answer. I might carry out the image, and add that we never can foresee what side-winds may come to force the vessel to some other shore than that for which she seems bound. I have carefully read Rossetti's book, as one of the many phenomena of the day. It seems to me that there is a genuine thread of native poetry in him, but so encumbered with the burden of color, sensuous expression, and mediaeval imagery and drapery, that it often is nearly lost. What I have heard of the author explains to me the existence of the volume; but its immediate popularity is something which I should not have anticipated.

GALAHAD. I have written.

THE GANNET. Already? Who was it, then?

GALAHAD. A personal friend, whose poems I know by heart,—Thomas Bailey Aldrich. Therefore, I couldn't well avoid violating our rule, for a special little rhyme popped into my head, and imitated myself. If Aldrich were not living in Boston, we should have him here with us tonight, and he would be quite ready to burlesque himself. (*Reads.*)

PALABRAS GRANDIOSAS

I lay i' the bosom of the sun,
Under the roses dappled and dun.
I thought of the Sultan Gingerbeer,
In his palace beside the Bendemeer,
With his Afghan guards and his eunuchs blind,
And the harem that stretched for a league behind.
The tulips bent i' the summer breeze,

Under the broad chrysanthemum-trees,
And the minstrel, playing his culverin,
Made for mine ears a merry din.
If I were the Sultan, and he were I,
Here i' the grass he should loafing lie,
And I should bestride my zebra steed,
And ride to the hunt of the centipede:
While the pet of the harem, Dandeline,
Should fill me a crystal bucket of wine,
And the kislar aga, Up-to-Snuff,
Should wipe my mouth when I sighed, "Enough!"
And the gay court-poet, Fearfulbore,
Should sit in the hall when the hunt was o'er,
And chant me songs of silvery tone,
Not from Hafiz, but—mine own!

Ah, wee sweet love, beside me here,
I am not the Sultan Gingerbeer,
Nor you the odalisque Dandeline,
Yet I am yourn, and you are mine!

THE ANCIENT. There's a delicate, elusive quality about Aldrich's short lyrics, which I should think very difficult to catch. I have an indistinct recollection of poor George Arnold writing something.

ZOÏLUS. It was all about a mistake Aldrich made, years ago, in the color of a crocus. He called it *red,* and there may be red crocuses for aught I know; but yellow or orange is the conventional color. Of course we didn't let the occasion slip; we were all unmerciful towards each other. I remember I wrote something like this:

I walked into the garden, ruffled with rain,
Through the blossoms of every hue;
And I saw the pink, with its yellow stain,
And the rose with its bud of blue.

George Arnold's lines were:

And all about the porphyry plates were strewn
The blue arbutus of the early June,
The crimson lemon and the purple yam,
And Jainties brought from Seringapatam!

THE GANNET. They are better than yours. Well, I'm glad that Galahad has not confused our color, at least. I especially like Aldrich; for he is faithful to his talent, and gives us nothing that is not daintily polished and rounded. Some of his fragments remind me of Genoese filigree-work—there seems to be so much elaboration in a small compass; yet only sport, not labor, is suggested. He, also, has ceased to sing in the minor key; but I don't think he ever affected it much.

THE ANCIENT (*earnestly*). I'm glad to hear it! O ye cheerful gods of all great poets, shall we never have an end of weeping and wailing and lamentation! Is the world nothing but a cavern of sorrow, and the individual life a couch of thorns? Must we have always bats, and never skylarks, in the air of poetry?

ZOÏLUS. Hear, hear! I have not seen the Ancient so roused this many a day.

THE ANCIENT. The truth always excites.

GALAHAD. Before you put on your hats, let us have one more "lager." (*The glasses are filled.*) Now, to the health of all our young authors!

THE GANNET. Here's to them heartily,—for that includes ourselves.

THE ANCIENT. As the youngest, I return thanks.

[*Exeunt.*

Night The Fourth

ALL the members of the club were assembled, but the Ancient had not yet made his appearance. He was dining that evening, as it happened, with a wealthy banker, and there was no possibility of omitting one of the seventeen courses, or escaping before the coffee and *liqueurs.* As the oldest of the members, the duties of chairman were always conferred on him whenever a decision became necessary, and all assumed, as a matter of course, that the Diversions should be suspended until his arrival. But the conversation, meanwhile, settled upon him as its subject. Zoïlus and one of the Chorus were not as old acquaintances as the Gannet and

Galahad, which circumstance led, after his nature had been genially discussed, to the following digression:

ZOÏLUS (to THE GANNET). I had not often met him familiarly, in this way, before. He is a good, mellow-natured companion, and not at all dogmatic, that is, in a direct way; but I can see the influence of his Boston associations. There is a great deal of external tact and propriety in that city. Now *our* impetuous, keen, incisive atmosphere——

THE GANNET (interrupting). Spare me the "incisive"! It has been overdone, as an effect, and will be the ruin of you yet. If I had as much faith as Galahad there, I should believe as the Ancient does. But, since you will have the "incisive," where can you find sentences more clearly cut—the very intaglio of style—than in Holmes?

ZOÏLUS (angrily). And do you remember what he wrote of our New York authors:

> Whose fame, beyond their own abode,
> Extends—for miles along the Harlem road?

THE GANNET. Yes, and don't you know who they were? Why, their fame doesn't reach up to Twenty-third Street now! It was a deliberate attempt, by a small clique, to manufacture the Great American Literature. The materials were selected in advance, the style and manner settled, and then the great authors went to work. Like the Chinese mechanics who copied a steamboat, the external imitation was perfect; but there were no inside works and it wouldn't move a paddle! When you speak of our legitimate authors, here in New York, what name first comes to your lips? Bryant, of course; and have you forgotten how Holmes celebrated him? and how his was the only garland of verse thrown upon Halleck's grave?

ZOÏLUS. Nevertheless, they systematically depreciate what we do; they are only kind and considerate towards one another. You remember Poe's experience?

THE ANCIENT (entering the room). Which one, pray?

ZOÏLUS. Of Boston. But they did not and have not put *him* down!

THE ANCIENT. Why, no; he put himself down that time:

I happened to be there, and I saw the performance. I guess that you and the Gannet have been repeating your usual tilt; why not say, as Goethe did of the comparisons made between himself and Schiller, "Instead of quarreling about which of us is the greater, people ought simply to be thankful for having us both"? Thirty or forty years ago, when Lowell and Whipple were boys, Longfellow and Holmes young authors, Emerson considered little better than daft, and Whittier almost outlawed on account of his anti-slavery opinions, the literary society here included Irving, Cooper, Bryant, Willis, and Halleck, then the foremost American authors. The chief literary periodicals were here and in Philadelphia; and Boston, although the average of intellectual culture was always higher there than elsewhere, occupied quite a secondary place. But I don't remember that there was ever any jealousy or rivalry; and I confess I can't understand the spirit which fosters such a feeling now.

ZoïLUS. You have passed the age when you care for recognition.

THE ANCIENT. Have I, indeed? Pray, when does that age cease? If I had a more general recognition at present— by which I mean the ascription to me of exactly the literary qualities which I think I possess—I should be stimulated to do more and possibly better work. I began authorship at a time when there was not much discrimination between varieties of literary talent, when such fearful stuff as *Agathé, a Necromant: in Three Chimæras,* by a man named Tasistro, was published in *Graham's Magazine,* and when a dentist in Rhode Island wrote a poem in heroic verse, called *The Dentiad.*

THE GANNET. What was his name?

THE ANCIENT. Solyman Brown. I must quote to you an exquisite passage:

> Whene'er along the ivory disks are seen
> The rapid traces of the dark gangrene,
> When caries come, with stealthy pace, to throw
> Corrosive ink-spots on those banks of snow,
> Brook no delay, ye trembling, suffering Fair,
> But fly for refuge to the dentist's care.

His practised hand, obedient to his will,
Employs the slender file with nicest skill;
Just sweeps the germin of disease away,
And stops the fearful progress of decay.

ZOÏLUS. The latest nursling of Darwin's *Botanic Garden!*
It is not antithetical enough for Pope. Surely, that was not
a popular poem?

THE ANCIENT. I was too young to know. I only mention
it as one of the chaotic elements out of which has grown
what little permanent literature we now have. Probably
three-fourths of the writers then commencing their career
might have developed some sound practical ability, with a
little intelligent guidance; they were not strong enough to
beat their own way out of the wilderness. When I look back
upon the time, I can see the bones of immortal works
bleaching on all sides.

THE GANNET. As ours will bleach for the young fellows
who sit here in 1900! While you were speaking, the thought
occurred to me that no young poet in England can possibly
be as green at his entrance into literature as the most of us
must inevitably be. I begin to see that a conventional
standard is better than none; for if it does not guide, it provokes resistance; either way, therefore, the neophyte acquires a definite form and style.

THE ANCIENT. To that extent, I agree with you. But we
also have a standard, only those who accept it are fewer,
and so scattered over the whole country that their authority
is not immediately felt. They distinguish between what is
temporary and what is permanent, in spite of the general
public. And this ought to be our great comfort, if we are in
earnest, that no power on earth can keep alive a sensational
reputation.

ZOÏLUS. How do you account for the popularity of such
single poems as *The River of Time* (is that the title of it?),
and *Beautiful Snow,* and *Rock Me to Sleep, Mother?* Why,
hardly a week passes but I see a newspaper dispute about
the authorship of one or the other of them! To me they are
languishing sentiment, not poetry.

THE ANCIENT. "Sentiment" sufficiently accounts for their

popularity. Put some tender, thoroughly obvious sentiment into rhyme which sounds like the melody of a popular song, and it will go through hides which are impervious to the keenest arrows of the imagination. But how much more unfortunate for us if it were not so! This gives us just the fulcrum we need if our literature is ever to be an Archimedean lever. I find myself a great deal happier since I have set about discovering the reason of these manifestations of immature taste, instead of lamenting over them, or cursing them, as I once did.

Zoïlus (*ironically*). Then I have not attained your higher standpoint?

The Gannet (*offering him the hat*). Here, pick out one of the caged birds, and make him sing! The prelude of chords and discords has lasted long enough; let the orchestra now fall into a lively melody.

Zoïlus. Ha! How shall I manage Bryant?

Galahad. Or I, Oliver Wendell Holmes?

The Gannet. Or I, N. P. Willis?

Galahad. Let us either exchange or deal again!

The Ancient. No! As chairman, I declare such a proposition out of order. You must not pick out those authors with whose manner you are most familiar, or whom you could most easily imitate. That would be no fair and equal test; and there must be a little emulation, to keep your faculties in nimble playing condition. I am as oddly tasked as either of you,—see, I have drawn Tennyson!—yet, for the sake of good example, I'll work with you this time. Let us surrender ourselves, like spiritual mediums, to the control of the first stray idea that enters our brains; anything whatever will do for a point to start from. I am curious to know what will come of it.

Zoïlus. So am I. Here goes. (*Writes*.)

The Gannet. We must first have our glasses filled; Galahad, ring for the waiter!

(*A silence of fifteen or twenty minutes follows. As the first one who has completed his task lifts his head with a sigh of relief, the others write with a nervous haste; but all wait for the last one.*)

THE GANNET. You were ready first, Zoïlus.

ZOÏLUS. Then it was not because I had the least difficult task. Perhaps our Ancient can tell me why it is so difficult to make an echo for Bryant's verse. To parody any particular poem, such as *The Death of the Flowers,* would be easy enough, I should think; but I was obliged to write something independent in Bryant's manner. Now, when I asked myself, "What is his manner?" I could only answer, "Gravity of subject and treatment, pure rhythm, choice diction, and a mixture more or less strong of the moral element."

THE ANCIENT. You have fairly stated his prominent characteristics, and your difficulty came from the fact that they are all so evenly and exquisitely blended in his verse that no single one seems salient enough to take hold of. Bryant's range of subjects is not wide, but within that range he is a most admirable artist. He is of the same blood with Wordsworth—a brother, not a follower—and oftentimes seems cold, because his intellectual pitch is high. I confess *I* find the powers of control, temperance, self-repression, abnegation of sentiment for a purpose which aims beyond it, in his poems, rather than a negative coldness. His literary position, it is true, is very isolated. He has both kept aloof from the temporary excitements in our poetic atmosphere, and he has rarely given any direct expression of an aspiration for the general literary development of our people, or of sympathy with those who felt and fostered it. Nevertheless, we cannot fairly go beyond an author's works in our judgments; and I suspect we shall all agree, as Americans, in estimating the amount of our debt to Bryant.

GALAHAD. You have so put down my natural reverence that I don't dare to protest. But when I see Bryant in Broadway, with his magnificent Homeric beard, I wonder the people don't take off their hats as he passes. Why, seventy years ago the stolid Berliners almost carried Schiller on their shoulders as he came out of the theater; the raging mob of '48 did homage to Humboldt; and every other people, it seems to me, in every other civilized land, has rendered some sort of honor to its minstrels. But I cannot recollect that we have ever done anything.

THE GANNET. Yes, we have done a little, but not much,—after death. A few men have given Halleck a monument, and two men have put up busts of Irving and Bryant in our parks. There was a public commemoration of Cooper, at which Webster (who knew nothing and cared nothing about our literature) officiated; but that was the end of it. The Bryant Festival was almost a private matter; the public was not represented, and one author belonging to the same club refused to take any part in it, on account of the political views of the poet!

THE ANCIENT. We are forgetting our business.

ZOÏLUS. I told you I had a hard task; therefore I shall not be vexed if you tell me I have failed. (*Reads.*)

THE DESERTED BARN

Against the gray November sky,
　　Beside the weedy lane, it stands;
To newer fields they all pass by,
　　The farmers and their harvest hands.

There is no hay within the mow;
　　The racks and mangers fall to dust;
The roof is crumbling in, but thou,
　　My soul, inspect it and be just.

Once from the green and winding vale
　　The sheaves were borne to deck its floor;
The blue-eyed milkmaid filled her pail,
　　Then gently closed the stable-door.

Once on the frosty winter air
　　The sound of flails afar was borne,
And from his natural pulpit there
　　The preacher cock called up the morn.

But all are gone: the harvest men
　　Work elsewhere now for higher pay;
The blue-eyed milkmaid married Ben,
　　The hand, and went to Ioway.

The flails are banished by machines,
　　Which thrash the grain with equine power;
The senile cock no longer weans
　　The folk from sleep at dawning hour.

They slumber late beyond the hill,
    In that new house which spurns the old;
In gorgeous stalls the kine are still,
    The horse is blanketed from cold.

But I from ostentatious pride
    And hollow pomp of riches turn,
To muse that ancient barn beside:
    Pause, pilgrim, and its lesson learn;

So live, that thou shalt never make
    A mill-pond of the mountain-tarn,
Nor for a gaudy stable take
    The timbers of thy ruined barn!

GALAHAD. I vow I don't know whether that is serious or a burlesque imitation!

THE ANCIENT. Then Zoïlus has fairly succeeded. The grave autumnal tone was indispensable, for it stamps itself on the minds of nine out of ten who read Bryant; just as we always associate Wordsworth with mountain walks and solitary musings. Did you ever see Kuntze's statuette of Bryant? He is sitting, and beside him on the ground there is only a buffalo skull. Of course, you at once imagine a prairie mound, with nothing in sight,—which is carrying the impression altogether too far; for his poems on the apple-tree and the bobolink are entirely human.

GALAHAD (earnestly). There is much more than that in his poetry! There is the evidence of a high imaginative quality, which, for some reason or other, he seems to hold in check! Read The Land of Dreams and his poem on Earth, where there is something about the

Hollows of the great invisible hills
    Where darkness dwells all day—

I can't remember all the passage, but it is exceedingly fine! Generally, he reins himself up so tightly that you cannot feel the fretting of the bit; but rarely, when he lets himself go for a few lines, you get a glimpse of another nature.

THE ANCIENT. Just therein, I think, lies his greatest service to American literature. There have always been, and always will be, enough of wild mustangs, unbridled foals, who dash off at a gallop and can't stop themselves at the proper goal, but pant and stagger a mile beyond it. With Bryant's genius, he might have undertaken much more; but he has hoarded his power, and how freshly it serves him still!

> No waning of fire, no quenching of ray,
> But rising, still rising, then passing away.

Who wrote those lines?

THE GANNET. He who speaks through me tonight,—Willis. But Galahad comes next in order.

GALAHAD. I have really a better right to complain of the severity of my task than Zoïlus. One can't imitate humor without possessing it,—which I'm not sure that I do. Between *Old Ironsides* and the *One-Horse Shay,* Holmes has played in a great many keys, and I was forced to echo that one which seemed easiest to follow. *(Reads.)*

THE PSYCHO-PHYSICAL MUSE

O Muse, descend, or, stay!—evolve thy presence from within,
For all conditions now combine, and so I must begin:
The wind is fresh from west-nor' west, the sky is deepest blue,
Thermometer at seventy, and pulse at seventy-two.

At breakfast fish-balls I consumed; the phosphates are supplied!
The peccant acid in my blood by Selters alkalied;
As far as I can see the works, my old machine of thought
Runs with its cogs and pivots oiled, as if in Waltham bought.

The main-spring is elastic yet, the balance-wheel is trim,
And if "full-jeweled" one should think, let no man scoff at him!
Odi profanum vulgus,—well! the truth is t'other way;
But one eupeptic as myself can always have his say.

Suppose I let the wheels run on, till fancy's index-hand
Points to a verse-inspiring theme and there inclines to stand?
Between the thought and rhythmic speech there often yawns
    a chasm;
To bridge it o'er we only need a vigorous protoplasm.

With an unconscious sinciput, a cerebellum free,
I don't see why the loftiest lays should not be sung by me:
The fitful flushes of the Muse my diagnosis own:
I test her symptoms in the air as surely as ozone.

There's just one thing that fails me yet; the fancies dart around
Like skittish swallows on the wing, but none will touch the
    ground.
With such conditions 'twere a sin to lay the pen aside,
But, with the mind close-girt to run, direction is denied.

I've waited, now, an hour or more: I'd take a glass of wine,
Save that I fear 'twould send the pulse to seventy-eight or nine;
'Tis that capricious jade, the Muse!—I know her tricks of old:
Just when my house is warm for her, she *will* prefer the cold!

THE GANNET. Ah, you've only caught some general characteristics, not the glitter and flash of Holmes's lines! His humor is like a Toledo blade; it may be sheathed in a circular scabbard, but it always springs out straight and keen, and fit for a direct lunge. He is the only poet in the country who can write good "occasionals" without losing faith in the finer inspiration, or ceasing to obey it.

GALAHAD. You very well know we have no time for selection. I have been reading lately his *Mechanism in Thought and Morals,* so that my imitation was really suggested by his prose.

THE ANCIENT. That is permitted. For my part, though I like Holmes's songs in all keys, I have always wished that he had written more such poems as *La Grisette,* wherein we have, first of all, ease and grace, then just enough of sentiment, of humor, and of a light, sportive fancy to make a mixture wholly delightful,—a beverage that cheers, but not inebriates, in which there is neither headache nor morbid tears. Hood had the same quality, though he doesn't often reveal it; so had Praed; so, I feel sure, had Willis, but in his case it was a neglected talent. When I say that we most sorely need this naïve, playful element in our literature, you may not agree with me; but oh, how tired I am of hearing that every poem should "convey a lesson," should "inculcate a truth," should "appeal to the moral sense." Why, half our self-elected critics seem to be blind to the purely aesthetic character of our art! No man—not even the greatest —can breathe a particular atmosphere all his life without taking some of its ingredients into his blood; and just those which seem best may be most fatal to the imaginative faculty. I suspect there has been more of battle in the intellectual life of Holmes than any of us knows.

ZoÏLUS. Now let us hear the Gannet.

THE GANNET. If it had been a leader for the *Home Journal*, I should have found the task light enough; but Willis' poetic style is—as he would have said—rather uncome-at-able. *(Reads.)*

KEREN-HAPPUCH

The comforters of Job had come and gone.
They were anhungered; for the eventide
Sank over Babylon, and smokes arose
From pottage cooked in palace and in tent.
Then Keren-happuch, from her lordly bower
Of gem-like jasper, and the porphyry floors
Swept by the satins of her trailing robe,
Came forth, and sat beside her father Job,
And gave him comfort, mid his painful boils,
And scraped him with a potsherd; and her soul
Rebelled at his unlovely misery,
And from her lips, that parted like a cleft
Of ripe pomegranates o'er their ruby teeth,
Broke forth a wail:

"Alas for thee, my sire!
And for the men and maidens of thy train,
And for thy countless camels on the plain,
      More than thou didst require;
Thou mightst have sold them at the morning dawn
For heavy gold: at even they were gone!

"And they who dressed thy hair
With agate braids and pearls from Samarcand
Have died; there is no handmaid in the land,
      To make my visage fair:
Unpainted and unpowdered, lo! I come,
Gray with the ashes of my gorgeous home!

"Yea, thou and I are lone:
The prince who wooed me fled in haste away
From thine infection: hungered here I stray,
      And find not any bone;
For famished cats have ravaged shelf and plate:
The larder, like my heart, is desolate!

      "And it is very drear,
My sire, whose wealth and beauty were my pride,
To see thee so disfigured at my side,
      Nor leech nor poultice near,
To save thy regal skin from later scars:
Yea, thou art loathsome by the light of stars!

      "Go, hie thee to thy room,
And I will gather marjoram and nard,
And mix their fragrance with the cooling lard,
      And thus avert thy doom.
A daughter's sacrifice no tongue can tell:
The prince will not return till thou art well!"

GALAHAD. Now I must say, although I have enjoyed the travesty with you, that this gives me a pang. I can't forget Willis' sunny, kindly, and sympathetic nature, and the dreary clouding of his mind at the last. There was something very tragic in the way in which he clung to the fragments that remained, as one faculty after another failed him, and strove to be still the cheerful, sparkling author of old. I was hardly more than a boy when I first went to him, a few years ago, and no brother could have been kinder to me.

THE ANCIENT. There never was a poet more free from jealousy or petty rivalry, none more ready to help or encourage. As an author, he was damaged by too early popularity, and he made the mistake of trying to retain it through exaggerating the features of his style which made him popular; but neither homage nor defamation—and he received both in full measure—ever affected the man's heart in his breast. There was often an affectation of aristocratic elegance in his writings; yet, in his life, he was as natural a democrat as Walt Whitman, gentle, considerate, and familiar with the lowest whom he met, and only haughty towards ignorant or vulgar pretension. Poe said that he narrowly missed placing himself at the head of American literature, which was true of his career from 1830 to about 1845. By the by, I wish someone would undertake to write our literary history, beginning, say, about 1800.

Zoïlus. Set about it yourself! But, come, we are not to be cheated out of your contribution tonight; where is your Tennyson?

The Ancient. I have added another to his brief modern idyls. (Reads.)

Eustace Green;

or, the medicine-bottle

Here's the right place for lunch; and if, ah me!
The hollies prick, and burr-weed grows too near,
We'll air our eyesight o'er the swelling downs,
And so not mind them. While the Medoc chills
In ice, and yon champagne-flask in the sun
Takes mellower warmth, I'll tell you what I did
To Eustace Green—last Cambridge-term it was,
Just when the snowball by the farmer's gate
Made jokes of winter at the garden rose.

No marvel of much wisdom Eustace was,—
You know him, Hal,—no high-browed intellect,
Such as with easy grab the wrangler's place
Plucks from the clutching hands of college youth,
But home-bred, as it were; and all the stock,
His stalwart dad, and mother Marigold
(We called her), Kate, Cornelia, Joseph, Jane,
A country posy of great boys and girls.
But she, the mother, when the brown ash took
A livelier green beside the meadow-stile,
And celandines, the milky kine of flowers,
Were yellow in the lanes, hung o'er the fire
A caldron huge—Oh me, it was a sight
To see her stir the many herbs therein!
Of yarrow, tansy, thyme, and camomile—
What know I all?—she boiled and slowly brewed
The strange concoction: 'twas an heirloom old,
The recipe, a sovran cure, and famed

From Hants to Yorkshire: this must Eustace take.
Not that the lubber lad was ill—Oh, no!
You did but need to punch him in the ribs,
To feel how muscle overlaid the bone;
And as for trencher-practice,—trust me, Hal,
A donkey-load of lunch were none too much,
Were he here with us. Where was I?—Ah, yes,
The medicine! She gave it me with words
Many, and thrice repeated; he should take,
Eustace, the dose at morn, and noon, and night,
For these were feverous times: she did not know,
Not she, what airs blew o'er the meads of Cam:
Preventive ounces weighed a pound of cure.
At last, I thrust the bottle in my sack,
And left her.
                    Now, returning Cambridge-wards,
Some devil tickled me to turn the thing
To joke, or was it humors in the blood,
Stirring, perchance, when, oysters out of date
And game prohibited, the stomach pines?
Think as you will; but to myself my mind
Thus reasoned: need to him of medicine
Is none, the green cicala in the grass
Chirps not more wholesome: wherefore swiftly I
Will cast this useless brewage to the winds,
Yea, to the thistled downs; and substitute—
Haply some ancient hostel glimmering near—
Laborious Boreal brandy, equal bulk.
And this, the thing accomplished, then did I
Proffer to Eustace Green, all eager he
For news of home and mother Marigold,
His dad and Kate, Cornelia, Joseph, Jane,
And Bloss, the ox, and Bounce, the plough-horse old,
One-eyed, and spavined. But the medicine
He took with: "Pshaw! that beastly stuff again?
Am I a rat that she should send the dose?"
Then I: "Dear Eustace, times are feverous:
Malarial breezes blow across the Cam:
Preventive ounces weigh a pound of cure."
"Oh, damn your ounces!" he profanely cried;
"But if I must, I must; so summon Giles,
The undertaker, when I take this dose,
And gently coffin me when now I die."

So drank; and then, with great eyes all astare,
Cried: "Taste it, you! Fourth-proof, O. P. and S. T. X.!—
We'll have a punch!" And that teetotal dame,
His mother, did we pledge in steaming punch,
She knowing not; and tears of laughter ran
Down both our cheeks, and trickled in the bowl,
Weakening the punch.
                        But now the Medoc's chill,
And warm the sweet champagne; so, while the copse
Clangs round us like the clang of many shields,
Down the long hollows to the dusky sea,
Let us, with sandwich and the hard-boiled egg,
Enjoy both nature's beauty and our own!

OMNES. Well done!

ZOÏLUS. Why, you have caught the very trick of Tennyson's blank verse! If you had only warmed the Medoc and chilled the champagne, I should hardly know the difference. But how did you ever happen to invent a motive, or plot, all complete, on the spur of the moment?

THE ANCIENT. Ah, you force me to confess: I didn't invent it. It was a trick I played myself, on a friend, in our young days; and, by good luck, it came to my memory just at the right time. Therefore, having the subject, the imitation of Tennyson's manner was easy enough. I'm glad, however, that you think it successful; for it justifies me in holding fast to the principle we accepted, and which I was obliged to enforce tonight. You know that my own scattering poems are quite unlike—however long the interval between—anything of Tennyson's; but I have made it a point, for years past, to study the individual characteristics of the poets, and this proves how easily those which are superficial and obvious may be copied.

ZOÏLUS. May I ask what your private estimate of Tennyson, as a poet, is?

THE ANCIENT. Of course! While I might, possibly, agree with his keenest critics in regard to many details of style or expression, especially in his earlier poems, I yield to no one in the profoundest respect for his noble loyalty to his art. Tennyson is a poet, who, recognizing the exact quality of his gift, has given all the forces of his mind, all the energies of his life, to perfect it. I can see that he has allowed no form of knowledge which this age has developed to arise without assimilating, at least, its substance; but all is employed in the sole service of his poetic art. He began with something of the rank, "lush" luxuriance of style which Keats was just leaving behind him when he died: he now rises, often to a majestic simplicity and dignity which nearly remind me of Milton. Not that the two are similar, in any particular; but Tennyson, like scarcely any other except Schiller, has achieved high success as a poet by comprehending clearly both his powers and their limitations. How easily, by mistaking his true work, he might have scattered his rays, instead of gathering them into a clear focus of light! All honor to him, I say, in this age, when so many writers degrade their gift by making it subservient to worldly ends!

GALAHAD (*with enthusiasm*). You make me happy!

THE GANNET. I should say, nevertheless, that he was well paid in ringing guineas. For instance——

ZOÏLUS. "The continuation in next week's *New York Ledger!*" Do you know that it is one o'clock?

OMNES (*starting up*). We go—but we return!

[*Exeunt.*

Night The Fifth

ALL WERE ON HAND at the usual hour, fresh and eager for a continuation of the performances. The Gannet, addressing Zoïlus, opened the conversation:

"I can guess one thing you have been thinking of since we met,—of Tennyson's place in literature?"

ZOÏLUS. You have just hit it! I didn't fully agree with the Ancient, but there was no time left for discussion. There must be some good reason for Tennyson's influence on the poetry of our day; yet, if his is a genuine flower, it couldn't be made a weed by being sown everywhere. There is no doubt of the individuality of his manner, but I am not yet ready to say that it is pure, as Collins', or Gray's, for instance, or even Wordsworth's. He is sometimes like a perfume which cloys the sense from overrichness. Now, a very slight change in the odor of the tuberose might make it unpleasant; and it seems to me that some of Tennyson's younger followers have made just such a change.

GALAHAD. Almost the same thought occurred to me the other day. I was trying to recall some lines of the Ancient's imitation, and then went over in my mind the numbers of blank-verse idyls more or less in Tennyson's manner which have been written by others. He drew from a very far source, as I think Stedman has clearly shown in his paper on *Theocritus and Tennyson;* but they, drawing from him, cannot conceal theirs. I never before felt so keenly the difference between the poetry which rises out of a man's own nature and that which is impressed upon it, or communicated, like an infection, by another mind. I even went so far as to try my hand alone on an imitation of this idyllic school, which I now see is itself an echo.

THE ANCIENT. Read it to us, then! Who was your immediate model?

GALAHAD (*taking a paper from his pocket*). Why, no one in particular. Now that I look over the lines, I see that I must have been thinking of the echoes of the *Princess,* rather than of those of the short idyls of modern life. It is the craziest burlesque of the mediaeval themes, revived in that form: it is absurd, and nothing else.

ZOÏLUS. That will do very well, for variety.

GALAHAD. Then, as Eustace Green says, if I must, I must. (*Reads.*)

SIR EGGNOGG

Forth from the purple battlements he fared,
Sir Eggnogg of the Rampant Lily, named
From that embrasure of his argent shield
Given by a thousand leagues of heraldry
On snuffy parchments drawn,—so forth he fared,
By bosky boles and autumn leaves he fared,
Where grew the juniper with berries black,
The sphery mansions of the future gin.

But naught of this decoyed his mind, so bent
On fair Miasma, Saxon-blooded girl,
Who laughed his loving lullabies to scorn,
And would have snatched his hero-sword to deck
Her haughty brow, or warm her hands withal,
So scornful she: and thence Sir Eggnogg cursed
Between his teeth, and chewed his iron boots
In spleen of love. But ere the morn was high
In the robustious heaven, the postern-tower
Clang to the harsh, discordant, silvering scream
Of the tire-woman, at the window bent
To dress her crispéd hair. She saw, ah woe!
The fair Miasma, overbalanced, hurled
O'er the flamboyant parapet which ridged
The muffled coping of the castle's peak,
Prone on the ivory pavement of the court,
Which caught and cleft her fairest skull, and sent
Her rosy brains to fleck the Orient floor.
This saw Sir Eggnogg, in his stirrups poised,
Saw he and cursed, with many a deep-mouthed oath,
And, finding nothing more could reunite
The splintered form of fair Miasma, rode
On his careering palfrey to the wars,
And there found death, another death than hers.

Zoïlus. After this, write another such idyl yourself, if you dare!

Galahad. I never shall; but when you have done the thing ignorantly, and a magazine wants it on account of the temporary popularity of the theme and manner, is an author much to blame for publishing?

The Gannet. Let your conscience rest, Galahad! "Hunger and request of friends" were always valid pleas. If a poet invariably asked himself, "Is this original? Is it something that *must* be written? Is it likely to be immortal?" I suspect our stock of verse would soon be very short. At least, only the Chiverses and Tuppers and —— would still be fruitful.

The Ancient. Did you ever guess at the probable permanence of the things which seem best when they appear? It is a wholesome experiment. Macaulay first suggested it to me, in speaking of the 3 per cent of Southey which might survive: since then, I have found that the Middle Ages are an immense graveyard of poems, but nothing to what this century will be. I doubt whether many authors would write, in the mere hope of posthumous fame.

THE GANNET. *I* wouldn't! My idea of literature is the possession of a power which you can wield to some purpose while you live. It may also be wealth, another power; it may be yoked with politics, which is better still; it may——

GALAHAD (*interrupting*). Stop! don't make me feel that your gift, which I have believed in, is so entirely selfish!

ZOÏLUS (*shaking the hat*). Here would soon be a precious row between you two; draw your names and go to work!

THE GANNET. What? Henry T. Tuckerman?

ZOÏLUS. To be sure! I have—Longfellow!

GALAHAD. Mine is William D. Howells.

THE ANCIENT. I have drawn Richard Henry Stoddard. Now, no changing, remember! We are better suited than the last time, unless it be Zoïlus, of whom I have my doubts. All imitations cannot be equally fortunate, and I'm not sure that any of us would succeed better if he should take his own time and pains for the task, instead of trusting to the first random suggestion.

ZOÏLUS. Then why are you doubtful about me? I have my random suggestion already.

THE ANCIENT. Work it out! I think you understand my doubt, nevertheless. The Gannet is chuckling to himself, as if he were on the track of something wicked: I foresee that I must use my authority tonight, if I have any left. (*Writes.*)

THE CHORUS (*whispering together*). They are very evenly matched. Could any inference be drawn from the manner of each as he writes? The Gannet has the most sarcastic air, Zoïlus is evidently satisfied with his performance, Galahad seems earnest and a little perplexed, and the Ancient is cool and businesslike. They have all learned something by practice; they work much more rapidly than at first.

THE GANNET (*after all have finished*). When you try to grasp anything smooth, your hand slips. In Tuckerman there is only proper smoothness which can be travestied, and you know how difficult that is. (*Reads.*)

ODE TO PROPRIETY

Thou calm, complacent goddess of the mind,
    Look on me from thine undisturbed domain;
Thy well-adjusted leaflets let me bind,
    As once on youthful, now on manly brain.

Upon thy head there is no hair awry;
    Thy careful drapery falleth as it should:
Thy face is grave; thy scrutinizing eye
    Sees only that which hath been stamped as good.

Thou art no patron of the strenuous thought
    That speaks at will, regardless of old rule;
To thee no neologic lays are brought,
    But models of the strictly classic school.

Thou teachest me the proper way and sure;
    To no imaginative heights misled,
My verse moves onward with a step secure,
    Nor hastes with rapture, nor delays with dread.

I do not need to woo the fickle Muse,
    But am her master, justified by thee:
All measures must obey me as I choose,
    So long as they are thine, Propriety!

For genius is a fever of the blood,
    And lyric rage a strange, disturbing spell;
Let fools attempt the torrent and the flood,
    Beside the pensive, placid pond I dwell!

ZoïLUS. You have too much alliteration in the last line: that is not at all proper.

THE GANNET. Then it shows the impossibility of reproducing the tone of Pope and Gray in our day. I do not know that Tuckerman attempts this in his verse; but I suspect that his prose model is still Addison.

ZoïLUS. That is really getting to be a sign of originality! Mix Addison and Imagination together, and sublimate in a French retort, and where could you have a finer modern style? Tuckerman has all tradition on his side; he represents a conservative element in literature, which—though I don't admire it much—I think necessary, to keep the wild modern schools in order.

GALAHAD. It is something new, to hear you take this side.

ZOÏLUS. You must not always credit me with being wholly in earnest. I think I am a natural iconoclast; but one might as well assail respectability in society as the "classic" spirit in literature. It is impervious to all our shots; every blow slides off its cold polish. But, candidly, there are times when it seems to refresh me, or, at least, to give me a new relish for something warmer and more pungent.

THE ANCIENT. I believe you fully. We should all fare badly, were it not for the colder works which we hear so often depreciated. They make a fireproof temple in which we may build fires at will. Now, let us hear how you have treated an author who is already a classic, though without the *cold* polish of which you speak. Very few poets have been complimented by so many ordinary parodies.

ZOÏLUS. I am aware of that, and I have tried to get as far away as possible from the risk of resembling them. (*Reads.*)

NAUVOO

This is the place: be still for a while, my high-pressure steam-
    boat!
Let me survey the spot where the Mormons builded their
    temple.
Much have I mused on the wreck and ruin of ancient religions,
Scandinavian, Greek, Assyrian, Zend, and the Sanskrit,
Yea, and explored the mysteries hidden in Talmudic targums,
Caught the gleam of Chrysaor's sword and occulted Orion,
Backward spelled the lines of the Hebrew graveyard at New-
    port,
Studied Ojibwa symbols and those of the Quarry of Pipestone,
Also the myths of the Zulus whose questions converted Colenso,
So, methinks, it were well I should muse a little at Nauvoo.
Fair was he not, the primitive Prophet, nor he who succeeded,
Hardly for poetry fit, though using the Urim and Thummim.
Had he but borrowed Levitical trappings, the girdle and ephod,
Fine-twined linen, and ouches of gold, and bells and pome-
    granates,

That, indeed, might have kindled the weird necromancy of
  fancy.
Had he but set up mystical forms, like Astarte or Peor,
Balder, or Freya, Quetzalcoatl, Perun, Manabozho,
Verily though to the sense theologic it might be offensive,
Great were the gain to the pictured, flashing speech of the poet.
Yet the Muse that delights in Mesopotamian numbers,
Vague and vast as the roar of the wind in a forest of pine-trees,
Now must tune her strings to the names of Joseph and Brigham.
Hebrew, the first; and a Smith before the Deluge was Tubal,
Thor of the East, who first made iron ring to the hammer;
So on the iron heads of the people about him, the latter,
Striking the sparks of belief and forging their faith in the
  Good Time
Coming, the Latter Day, as he called it,—the Kingdom of Zion.
Then, in the words of Philip the Eunuch unto Belshazzar,
Came to him multitudes wan, diseased and decrepit of spirit,
Came and heard and believed, and builded the temple at
  Nauvoo.

All is past; for Joseph was smitten with lead from a pistol,
Brigham went with the others over the prairies to Salt Lake.
Answers now to the long, disconsolate wail of the steamer,
Hoarse, inarticulate, shrill, the rolling and bounding of ten-pins,
Answers the voice of the bartender, mixing the smash and the
  julep,
Answers, precocious, the boy, and bites a chew of tobacco.
Lone as the towers of Afrasiab now is the seat of the Prophet,
Mournful, inspiring to verse, though seeming utterly vulgar:
Also—for each thing now is expected to furnish a moral—
Teaching innumerable lessons for whoso believes and is patient.
Thou, that readest, be resolute, learn to be strong and to suffer!
Let the dead Past bury its dead and act in the Present!
Bear a banner of strange devices, "Forever" and "Never!"
Build in the walls of time the fane of a permanent Nauvoo,
So that thy brethren may see it and say, "Go thou and do
  likewise!"

GALAHAD. Zoïlus, you are incorrigible.

ZOÏLUS (*laughing*). Just what I expected you to say. But
it's no easy thing to be funny in hexameters: the Sapphic
verse is much more practicable. I heaped together everything
I could remember, to increase my chances. In some of Long-

fellow's earlier poems the theme and moral are like two sides of a medal; but I couldn't well copy that peculiarity.

THE GANNET. You will only find it in *The Beleaguered City* and *Seaweed*. Longfellow is too genuine an artist to fall into that or any other "peculiarity." Just his best, his most purely imaginative poems are those which have not been popular, because the reader must be half a poet to appreciate them. What do you consider his best work?

ZOÏLUS. *Evangeline*, of course.

THE GANNET. No, it is the *Golden Legend!* That is the spirit of the Middle Ages, and the feeling of all ages, set to modern melodies. I think I could write an imitation of Longfellow's higher strains—not of those which are so well known and so much quoted—which would be fairer than yours.

ZOÏLUS. Do it, and good luck to you. (THE GANNET *writes.*)

THE ANCIENT. Not one of our poets has deserved better of his countrymen than Longfellow: he has advanced the front rank of our culture. His popularity has naturally brought envy and disparagement upon him; but it has carried far and wide among the people the influence of his purity, his refine-ment, and his constant reference to an ideal of life which so many might otherwise forget. As a nation, we are still full of crudity and confusion, and his influence, so sweet and clear and steady, has been, and is, more than a merely poetic leaven.

GALAHAD. I have felt that, without ever thinking of put-ting it into words. The sweetness of Longfellow's verse is its most *necessary* quality, when we consider his literary career in this light; but I never could see how exquisite finish im-plies any lack of power. What was that line of Goethe which you quoted to me once, Ancient?

THE ANCIENT. *Nur aus vollendeter Kraft blicket die Annuth hervor*—only perfect Strength discloses Grace. There are singular ideas in regard to "power" afloat in literary cir-cles. Why, the sunbeam is more powerful than a thousand earthquakes! I judge the power of an author by the influence of his works.

ZOÏLUS. Well, for my part, I don't appreciate "power,"

unless it strikes me square between the eyes. What I understand by "power" is something regardless of elegance, of the conventional ideas of refinement, of what you call "laws of art,"—something primitive, lawless, forcing you, with a strong hand, to recognize its existence.

THE ANCIENT. Give me a few instances!

ZOÏLUS (*after a pause*). Carlyle,—Poe,—Swinburne,—Emily Brontë's *Wuthering Heights!*

GALAHAD. Why not Artemus Ward and Joaquin Miller?

THE GANNET. There! I never quite succeed when I assume a certain ability. I had in my mind *Prometheus and Epimetheus,* the *Palingenesis,* and other poems in the same key; but it was so difficult to imitate them that I came down one grade and struck into a style more easy to be recognized. It may not be better than yours, but it is not so horribly coarse. (*Reads.*)

THE SEWING-MACHINE

A strange vibration from the cottage window
    My vagrant steps delayed,
And half abstracted, like an ancient Hindoo,
    I paused beneath the shade.

What is, I said, this unremitted humming,
    Louder than bees in spring?
As unto prayer the murmurous answer coming,
    Shed from Sandalphon's wing.

Is this the sound of unimpeded labor,
    That now usurpeth play?
Our harsher substitute for pipe and tabor,
    Ghittern and virelay?

Or, is it yearning for a higher vision,
    By spiritual hearing heard?
Nearer I drew, to listen with precision,
    Deciphering not a word.

Then, peering through the pane, as men of sin do,
    Myself the while unseen,
I marked a maiden seated by the window,
    Sewing with a machine.

Her gentle foot propelled the tireless treadle,
  Her gentle hand the seam:
My fancy said, it were a bliss to peddle
  Those shirts, as in a dream!

Her lovely fingers lent to yoke and collar
  Some imperceptible taste;
The rural swain, who buys it for a dollar,
  By beauty is embraced.

O fairer aspect of the common mission!
  Only the Poet sees
The true significance, the high position
  Of such small things as these.

Not now doth Toil, a brutal Boanerges,
  Deform the maiden's hand;
Her implement its soft sonata merges
  In songs of sea and land.

And thus the hum of the unspooling cotton,
  Blent with her rhythmic tread,
Shall still be heard, when virelays are forgotten,
  And troubadours are dead.

ZOÏLUS. Ah, you couldn't avoid the moral application!

THE ANCIENT. Neither can you, in imitating Bryant and Whittier. In Longfellow—excepting some half-dozen of his earlier poems—the moral element is so skillfully interfused with the imaginative that one hardly suspects its presence. I should say, rather, that it is an inherent quality of his genius, and, therefore, can never offend like an assumed purpose. I abominate as much as you, Zoïlus, possibly can, the deliberate intention to preach moral doctrines in poetry. *That* is turning the glorious guild of authors into a higher kind of Tract Society! But the purer the poetic art, the nearer it approaches the loftiest morality; this is a truth which Longfellow illustrates. I have always defended the New England spirit against your prejudices, but this I must admit, that there is a large class of second-rate writers there who insist that every wayward little brook, whose murmur and sparkle are reason enough for its existence, must be made to turn some utilitarian mill. Over and over again I have seen how their literary estimate of our poets is gauged by the assumed relation of the latter to some variety of "Reform." The Abolition of Slavery, first, then Temperance, and now Woman Suffrage, or Spiritualism, or the Labor Question, are dragged by the head and heels into the temple, and sometimes laid upon the very altar, of Letters. The wonder is that this practice doesn't retrospectively affect their judgment and send Dante and Shakespeare and Milton to their chaotic limbo!

Zoïlus. Thanks for that much support; but let us hear Galahad!

Galahad. Howells, at least, has escaped some of the troubles through which the older authors have been obliged to pass. His four years in Venice made a fortunate separation between his youthful period and his true sphere of activity. He did not change front, as the rest of us must do, in the press of battle. I was very much puzzled what to select, as specially distinctive, and allowed myself, at last, to be guided by two or three short poems. (*Reads.*)

PREVARICATION

. . . .

The Ancient. I think I know what you had in your mind. But I was expecting to hear something in hexameters: you know his . . .[1]

Zoïlus. Yes, but . . .

Galahad. It is true to some extent. Still, on the other hand, he . . .

Zoïlus. Well, after all, we seem to agree tolerably well. All our younger poets are tending towards greater finish and elegance. It is about time to expect the appearance of a third generation, with all the beauties and faults of their new

[1]Mr. Howells, as Editor of the *Atlantic Monthly,* insisted that he could not properly allow his name to appear among the poets. I did not agree with him; but I finally compromised our difference by omitting the travesty and the opinions, and adding footnotes apparently written by himself. The latter were accepted as genuine and commented upon, to our mutual amusement. The imitation has been lost, or I should restore it now.—B. T.

youth about them. Why, we have hardly any known writer much less than thirty-five years old! Our lights scarcely begin to burn until the age when Keats's, Shelley's, Byron's, and Burns's went out. Is there something in our atmosphere that hinders development? I always supposed it possessed a greater stimulus.

THE ANCIENT. If you look back a little, you will find that Bryant, Willis, Longfellow, and Lowell were known and popular authors at twenty-five. But I have noticed the lack of a younger generation of poets. It is equally true of England, France, and Germany; none of those who have made a strong impression, whether good or bad, can be called young, with the single exception of Swinburne. Rossetti, though he has appeared so recently, must be forty-five years old; and in Germany the most popular poets—Geibel, Bodenstedt, Hamerling, and Redwitz—are all in middle age. I think a careful study of the literary history of the last hundred years would show that we have had both the heroes and the *epigonoi;* and now nature requires a little rest. Of course, all theories on the subject must be merely fanciful; half-a-dozen young fellows of the highest promise may turn up in a month; but I rather expect to see a good many fallow years.

GALAHAD. Then I, at least, have fallen on evil times. If I live after our stars have set, and no new ones have arisen, it will be——

ZOÏLUS. Your great luck! *Parmi les aveugles,* you know; but we are forgetting the Ancient's imitation.

THE ANCIENT. Stoddard's last volume shows both variety and inequality, but the most of it has the true ring. I was delighted with his gift of poetic narration, in *The Wine Cup* and *The King's Sentinel;* yet, even in them, there is an undertone of sadness. One can only make a recognizable echo of his verse in the minor key. (*Reads.*)

THE CANTELOPE

Side by side in the crowded street,
    Amid its ebb and flow,
We walked together one autumn morn;
    ('Twas many years ago!)

The markets blushed with fruits and flowers;
(Both Memory and Hope!)
You stopped and bought me at the stall
A spicy cantelope.

We drained together its honeyed wine,
We cast the seeds away;
I slipped and fell on the moony rinds,
And you took me home on a dray!

The honeyed wine of your love is drained;
I limp from the fall I had;
The snow-flakes muffle the empty stall,
And everything is sad.

The sky is an inkstand, upside down,
It splashes the world with gloom:
The earth is full of skeleton bones,
And the sea is a wobbling tomb!

ZoÏLUS. I might have written that; what do you say, Galahad?

GALAHAD. It is fully as rollicking as yours, but not quite so coarse. I always find in Stoddard a most true and delicate ear for the melody of verse, and I thoroughly enjoy his brief snatches, or "catches," of song. When I disagree with him, it is usually on account of the theme rather than the execution. His collection of *Melodies and Madrigals* gave me the key to his own taste and talent; he seems to have wandered down to us from the time of Charles I. What has the Gannet been writing all this while?

THE GANNET. Something not on our program. After trying my hand on Tuckerman and then on Longfellow, I felt fresh for one task more; and we have had so few ladies introduced into our diversions that I turned to Mrs. Stoddard for a new inspiration. You know how I like her poems, as the efforts of a not purely rhythmic mind to express itself rhythmically. They interest me greatly, as every embodiment of struggle does. A commonplace, conventional intellect would never dare to do the things she does, both in prose and verse; she defies the usual ways to popularity with a most indomitable perseverance.

GALAHAD. Is not that the way to reach it in the end?

THE GANNET. No man knoweth; because no one can foresee how the tastes or whims of the mercurial public may turn. Some authors predict their own popularity; some secretly expect it, and never get it; and some, again, leave works which may seem dead and buried, but are dug up as if by accident, after two or three centuries, and become new and delightful to a different race of men. Shall I read you my imitation?

THE ANCIENT. We wait.

THE GANNET. (*Reads.*)

THE NETTLE

If days were nights, I could their weight endure.
This darkness cannot hide from me the plant
I seek: I know it by the rasping touch.
The moon is wrapped in bombazine of cloud;
The capes project like crooked lobster-shears
Into the bobbery of the waves; the marsh,
At ebb, has now a miserable smell.
I will not be delayed nor hustled back,
Though every wind should muss my outspread hair.
I snatch the plant that seems my coming fate:
I pass the crinkled satin of the rose,
The violets, frightened out of all their wits,
And other flowers, to me so commonplace,
And cursed with showy mediocrity,
To cull the foliage which repels and stings.
Weak hands may bleed; but mine are tough with pride,
And I but smile where others sob and screech.
The draggled flounces of the willows lash
My neck; I tread upon the bouncing rake,
Which bangs me sorely, but I hasten on,
With teeth firm-set as biting on a wire,
And feet and fingers clinched in bitter pain.
This, few would comprehend; but if they did,
I should despise myself and merit scorn.
We all are riddles which we cannot guess;
Each has his gimcracks and his thingumbobs,
And mine are night and nettles, mud and mist,
Since others hate them, cowardly avoid.

Things are mysterious when you make them so,
And the slow-pacing days are mighty queer;
But Fate is at the bottom of it all,
And something somehow turns up in the end.

Zoïlus. That is an echo with a vengeance! But the exaggeration of peculiarities is the best part of our fun; there
you had the advantage. And this proves what I have said,
that the "classic" style is nearly impregnable. How *could*
you exaggerate it? You might as well undertake an architectural burlesque of the Parthenon. It is the Gothic, Byzan-
tine, Moresque styles in literature which give the true
material for travesty, just as they allow the greatest intellectual freedom.

The Ancient. We shall have to dub you "the Pugin of
Poetry." You've been taking a hint from Clough's *Bothie*.

The Gannet. Which Zoïlus doesn't like because of the
hexameters, although there never were lighter and less encumbered lines. With all Clough's classicism, his is a thoroughly Saxon-Gothic mind. Where will you find a more
remarkable combination of richness and subtlety, of scholarly
finish and the frankest realism? He is the only man who has
ever made English phrase flow naturally in elegiac cadence.
You, certainly, must remember, Ancient?

Where, upon Apennine slope, with the chestnut the oak trees
    immingle,
  Where amid odorous copse bridle-paths wander and wind
Where under mulberry branches the diligent rivulet sparkles,
  Or amid cotton and maize peasants their water-works ply,
Where, over fig-tree and orange in tier upon tier still repeated,
  Garden on garden upreared, balconies step to the sky,—
Ah, that I were far away from the crowd and the streets of the
    city,
  Under the vine-trellis laid, O my beloved, with thee!

Zoïlus. Oh, if you once begin to quote, I surrender.

The Ancient. Let us all part on good terms; that is, each
holding to his own opinion.

[*Exeunt.*

Night The Sixth

(*Enter* Zoïlus, *last, the others being already assembled: he throws down a newspaper on the table.*)

Zoïlus. There! Read the notice of my last article in ——, and tell me whether such criticism is apt to encourage the development of an American literature!

THE GANNET (*taking the paper*). I see where it is, by the dint of your thumbnail; there are only half-a-dozen lines, in what I should call the sneering-oracular style; but, Zoïlus, you have yourself done a great deal of this thing. Now the poisoned chalice is commended to your own lips. It is singular how little sympathy we have for others in such cases. When I am abused, somebody always sends the paper to me with lines drawn around the article, so that I shall not miss it; and all my friends are sure to ask, "Have you seen what So-and-so says?" When I am praised, nobody sends the paper, and my friends take it for granted that I have read the article. I don't complain of them: they are naturally silent when they agree, and aroused when they disagree, with the criticism.

THE ANCIENT. This notice is not fair, of course; but it is only a part of the prevalent fashion of criticism. One never can be sure, in such cases, whether the writer is really sincere in his judgment, or whether he has seized an opportunity to make a little literary capital for himself at the expense of the author. But I firmly believe in the ultimate triumph of *good work* over all these airs of superior knowledge and patronage and contemptuous depreciation. A friend of mine once devoted a great deal of time to a very careful and thorough article upon a poet who wrote in a dialect with which not ten men in this country are familiar. He afterwards showed me the critical notices it drew forth, and those which treated the subject with the coolest possible air of knowledge were written by men who knew nothing whatever about it.

GALAHAD. Then how is the ordinary reader ever to be enlightened?

THE ANCIENT. Most readers, I imagine, simply like, or

dislike, what they read. Authors greatly exaggerate the effect of inadequate criticism. Why, do you know that critical genius is much rarer than poetical? You are not afraid of the crude poets, who publish in newspaper corners, pushing you from your stools of song: why should you be annoyed by the critics who stand upon the same intellectual plane? Let me repeat to you what the greatest of critics, Lessing, said: "What is tolerable in my labors is owing solely to the critical faculty. I am, therefore, always ashamed or grieved whenever I hear anything said to the disadvantage of that faculty. It is said to crush genius, and I flattered myself that I had received in it something akin to genius." After Lessing, we can only accept Jeffrey with certain reservations, until we come to Sainte-Beuve. In this country, I call Lowell the first critic, though Whipple and Ripley have high and honorable places. A true critic must not only be a universal scholar, but as clear-conscienced as a saint and as tenderly impressible as a woman. After that he may be rigid as Minos.

Zoïlus. But you will certainly agree with me that a critical literature of the kind you describe—intelligent, appreciative, sympathetic, and rigidly just—is much needed?

The Ancient. Never more than just now.

Zoïlus. What then, frankly, do you think of the tone of this paper, and the —— and the ——?

The Ancient (smiling). They remind me so much of a little satirical poem of Uhland, The Spring-Song of the Critic, that I am comforted and amused, when I might otherwise be most annoyed. There never was a more admirable picture of that fine, insidious egotism of the spurious critic, which makes him fear to praise, lest admiration should imply inferiority. I can't remember the original lines, or I would translate it for you; but I might try an American paraphrase.

Omnes. By all means! (The Ancient writes.)

Zoïlus. I feel as if I had had whisky poured into an open wound. You made me smart savagely for a few minutes; but I am already getting comfortable.

The Gannet. There is no real comfort until you grow pachydermatous; I don't envy Galahad the seasoning that awaits him.

GALAHAD. I have part of my experience vicariously, in Zoïlus.

ZOÏLUS. The devil you have! Wait, my boy, until you publish your next poem! I'll return it to you, with interest!

THE ANCIENT. Uhland makes the critic walk out in the springtime and patronize Nature in his usual tone, the very tone of which Zoïlus complains. This is a rough imitation:

H'm! Spring? 'Tis popular, we've heard
   And must be noticed, therefore;
Not that a flower, a brook, or bird
   Is what we greatly care for.

The trees are budding: immature!
   Yet them, no doubt, admire some:
One leaf comes like another, sure,
   And on the whole it's tiresome.

What kind of bird is this we hear?
   The song is vague and mystic;
Some notes, we grant, are smooth and clear,
   But not at all artistic.

We're not quite sure we wholly like
   Those ferns that wave and spread so:
'Tis safe to doubt the things that strike
   The eye at once; we've said so.

An odor? H'm! it might be worse;
   There must be violets nigh us:
Quite passable! (For Shakespeare's verse,
   This time, will justify us.)

A native plant! We don't know what:
   Some, now, would call it pleasant,
But, really, we would rather not
   Commit ourselves at present.

But further time we will not waste,
   Neglecting our position:
To scourge the stupid public taste
   Is our peculiar mission.

And if men saw us, and should deem
(Those ignorant human brothers!)
That we the Spring *enjoyed*, we'd seem
No better than the others!

OMNES. Good! It reads like an original.

THE ANCIENT. It is one, properly: I have not translated any of Uhland's phrases. However, let us change the theme, for this is a dangerous hobby of mine, and we have other work before us. How many names are there still undrawn?

THE GANNET (*looking in the hat*). A dozen yet!

THE ANCIENT (*drawing*). James Russell Lowell—I must gird up my loins.

THE GANNET. Bayard Taylor.

ZOÏLUS. Elizabeth Barrett Browning.

GALAHAD. George H. Boker.

THE GANNET. The supply will be exhausted in two or three nights more, and then all our fun must come to an end. There will be nothing left for us but to travesty each other.

THE CHORUS. An excellent idea! Four times four, each doing each other and himself also, will give us sixteen imitations.

ZOÏLUS. No doubt you would enjoy it hugely. Turn to Lucretius for a picture of the delight of sitting on the safe shore and looking at the waves in a storm!

THE CHORUS. "The swelling and falling of the waves is the life of the sea."

ZOÏLUS. Go to, with your quotations! How easy it is to apply a high moral stimulus to somebody else's mind! Every poet, in his secret soul, admits his exquisite, quivering sensitiveness for the children of his brain. He may hide it from the sight of everyone; but it is there, or he would not be a poet; and he is always most artlessly surprised at the betrayal of the same feeling in another. *I*, of course, should coolly bear any amount of travesty; but how would it be with the Ancient, the Gannet, and Galahad?

THE GANNET. Zoïlus, you're a humbug! Take your pencil and begin your work: see how the Ancient is reeling off his lines!

(*They write steadily for fifteen or twenty minutes; then all have finished except* THE ANCIENT.)

THE ANCIENT. Mine is no easy task, and I'm afraid I have laid it out on too extensive a plan.

OMNES. Go on: we will wait.

THE ANCIENT (*ten minutes later*). You will sympathize with me, Galahad, for you know how much I like Lowell's poetry. I have followed him from the start, when he seemed like a vigorous young oak, and like an oak he has grown slowly, strongly, and with ever-broadening branches. But one can sport, as well as pray, under your large trees. (*Reads.*)

THE SAGA OF AHAB DOOLITTLE

Who hath not thought himself a poet? Who,
Feeling the stubbed pin-feathers pricking through
His greenish gosling-down, but straight misdeems
Himself anointed? They must run their course,
These later measles of the fledgling mind,
Pitting the adolescent rose with brown,
And after, leaving scars; and we must bear,
Who come of other stirp, no end of roil,
Slacken our strings, disorient ourselves,
And turn our ears to huge conchyliar valves
To hear the shell-hum that would fain be sea.

O guarding thorn of Life's dehiscent bud,
Exasperation! Did we clip thee close,
Disarm ourselves with non-resistant shears,
And leave our minds demassachusetted,
What fence 'gainst inroad of the spouting throng?
For Fame's a bird that in her wayward sweep
Gossips to all; then, ravenlike, comes home
Hoarse-voiced as autumn, and, as autumn leaves
Behind her, blown by all the postal winds,
Letters and manuscripts from unknown hands.
Thus came not Ahab's: his he brought himself,
One morn, so clear with impecunious gold,
I said: "Chaucer yet lives, and Calderon!"
And, letting down the gangways of the mind
For shipment from the piers of common life,
O'er Learning's ballast meant some lighter freight

To stow, for export to Macarian Isles.
But it was not to be; a tauroid knock
Shook the ash-panels of my door with pain,
And to my vexed "Come in!" Ahab appeared.
Homespun, at least,—thereat I swiftly felt
Somewhat of comfort,—tall, knock-kneed, and gaunt:
Face windy-red, hands horny, large, and loose,
That groped for mine, and finding, dropped at once
As half ashamed; and thereupon he grinned.

I waited, silent, till the silence grew
Oppressive; but he bore it like a man;
Then, as my face still queried, opened wide
The stiff portcullis of his rustic speech,
Whence issued words: "You'd hardly kalkelate
That I'm a poet, but I kind o' guess
I _be_ one; so the people say, to hum."
Then from his cavernous armpit drew and gave
The singing leaves, not such as erst I knew,
But strange, disjointed, where the unmeasured feet
Staggered allwhither in pursuit of rhyme,
And could not find it; assonance instead,
Cases and verbs misplaced—remediable those—
Broad-shouldered coarseness, fondly meant for wit.
I turned the leaves; his small, gray, hungry eye
Stuck like a burr; agape with hope his mouth.
What could I say? the worn conventional phrase
We use on such occasions,—better wait,
Verse must have time; its seed, like timothy-grass,
Sown in the fall to sprout the following spring,
Is often winter-killed; none can decide;
A single rain-drop prints the eocene,
While crow-bars fail on lias: so with song:
The Doom is born in each thing's primitive stuff.

Perchance he understood not; yet I thrust
Some hypodermic hope within his flesh,
Unconsciously; erelong he came again.
Would I but see his latest? I _did_ see;
Shuddered, and answered him in sterner wise.
I love to put the bars up, shutting out
My pasture from the thistle-cropping beasts
Or squealing hybrids, who have range enough

On our New England commons,—whom the Fiend,
Encouragement-of-Native-Talent, feeds
With windy provender, in *Waverley*,
And *Flag*, and *Ledger*, weakly manger racks.

Months passed; the catbird on the elm-tree sang
What "Free from Ahab!" seemed, and I believed.
But, issuing forth one autumn morn, that shone
As Earth were made October twenty-seventh
(Some ancient Bible gives the date), he shot
Across my path as sped from Ensign's bow,
More gruesome, haggard-seeming than before.
Ere from his sinister armpit his right hand
Could pluck the sheets, I thundered forth, "Aroint!"
Not using the Anglo-Saxon Shibboleth,
But exorcismal terms, unusual, fierce,
Such as would make a saint disintimate.
The witless terror in his face nigh stayed
My speech, but I was firm and passed him by.
Ah, not three weeks were sped, ere he again
Waylaid me in the meadows, with these words:
"I saw thet suthin' riled you, the last time;
Be you in sperrits now?"—and drew again—
But why go on? I met him yesterday,
The nineteenth time,—pale, sad, but patient still.
When Hakon steered the dragons, there was place,
Though but a thrall's, beside the eagle-helms,
For him who rhymed instead of rougher work,
For speech is thwarted deed: the Berserk fire
But smolders now in strange attempts at verse,
While hammering sword-blows mend the halting rhyme,
Give mood and tense unto the well-thewed arm,
And turn these ignorant Ahabs into bards!

ZoïLus. Faith! I think each of us imitates most amusingly
the very authors whom he most admires. I might have made
something fiercer, but it wouldn't have been more characteristic.

THE GANNET. When you seem dissatisfied with Lowell's
work, I can still see that you recognize his genius. I agree
with you that he sometimes mistakes roughness for strength,
and is sometimes consciously careless; but neither his faults
nor his virtues are of the common order. I like him for the

very quality out of which both grow,—his evident faith in the inspiration of the poet. In *The Cathedral* he says "second thoughts are prose," which is always true of the prime conception; but he seems often to apply it to the details of verse. His sympathy with the Norse and Nibelungen elements in literature, and with the old English ballads, is natural and very strong. Perhaps it is not always smoothly fused with the other spirit which is born of his scholarship and taste and artistic feeling. I care less for that: to my mind, he is always grandly tonic and stimulating.

THE ANCIENT. I think the objection which Zoïlus makes comes simply from the fact that many of Lowell's poems are overweighted with ideas. Instead of pouring a thin, smooth stream, he tilts the bottle a little too much, and there is an impetuous, uneven crowding of thought. But I should rather say that he is like his own "Cathedral," large, Gothic, with many a flying buttress, pinnacles melting in the air, and now and then a grotesque gargoyle staring down upon you. There is a great range between *Hosea Biglow* and the *Harvard Ode*.

ZOÏLUS. I confess I don't like unmixed enthusiasm, and I'm frequently provoked to spy out the weak points of any author who gets much of it. How I should feel if it were bestowed on me, I can't tell; probably as complacent as the rest of you.

THE GANNET. O Zoïlus, when you know that *I'm* only considered "brilliant," and get the most superficial praise!

THE ANCIENT. Come, come! This is a sort of personality. Who's next?

GALAHAD. Zoïlus was ready first.

ZOÏLUS. Yes, and none too soon. Mrs. Barrett Browning was a tough subject for me, and I was glad to get her off my hands. Do you know that it is much more difficult to travesty a woman's poem than a man's? (*Reads.*)

GWENDOLINE

'Twas not the brown of chestnut boughs
    That shadowed her so finely;
It was the hair that swept her brows,
    And framed her face divinely;

Her tawny hair, her purple eyes,
    The spirit was ensphered in,
That took you with such swift surprise,
    Provided you had peered in.

Her velvet foot amid the moss
    And on the daisies patted,
As, querulous with sense of loss,
    It tore the herbage matted:
"And come he early, come he late,"
    She saith, "it will undo me;
The sharp fore-speeded shaft of fate
    Already quivers through me.

"When I beheld his red-roan steed,
    I knew what aim impelled it;
And that dim scarf of silver brede,
    I guessed for whom he held it:
I recked not, while he flaunted by,
    Of Love's relentless vi'lence,
Yet o'er me crashed the summer sky,
    In thunders of blue silence.

"His hoof-prints crumbled down the vale,
    But left behind their lava;
What should have been my woman's mail
    Grew jellied as guava:
I looked him proud, but 'neath my pride
    I felt a boneless tremor;
He was the Beër, I descried,
    And I was but the Seemer!

"Ah, how to be what then I seemed,
    And bid him seem that is so!
We always tangle threads we dreamed,
    And contravene our bliss so.
I see the red-roan steed again!
    He looks, as something sought he:
Why, hoity-toity!—*he* is fain,
    So *I'll* be cold and haughty!"

THE ANCIENT. You have done about as well as could be
expected; but I am not sure that I should have recognized it,

without the red-roan steed and the thunders of blue silence. However, Mrs. Browning's force is always so truly feminine that one cannot easily analyze it. There is an underlying weakness—or, at least, a sense of reliance—when she is most vigorous, and you feel the beating of an excited pulse when she is most calmly classic. She often slips into questionable epithets and incongruous images, I grant you; but I can see the first form of her thought through them.

GALAHAD. Has any other woman reached an equal height in English poetry?

THE CHORUS. No!

THE GANNET. George Eliot?

ZOÏLUS. Now you bring the two squarely before my mind, I also say, No! I do not rightly know where to place George Eliot.

THE ANCIENT. Among the phenomena,—unsurpassed as a prose writer, and with every quality of the poet except the single one which is born and never acquired. It is amazing to see how admirable her verse is, and how near to high poetry,—as if only a sheet of plate-glass were between,—and yet it is *not* poetry. Her lines are like the dancing figures on a frieze, symmetry itself, but they do not move. When I read them, I am always on the very verge of recognizing her as a poet, always expecting the warm-blooded measures which sing their way into my own blood, and yet I never cross the invisible boundary.

THE GANNET. Shall we go on? I have Bayard Taylor, who took possession of me readily enough. I know his earlier Oriental better than his later poems. He doesn't seem to have any definite place yet as a poet.

ZOÏLUS. Then it comes of having too many irons in the fire.

GALAHAD. He may have made some mistakes; indeed, I think so, myself; but I find signs of a struggle towards some new form of development in his later poems, and mean to give him a little more opportunity. His rhetoric is at the same time his strength and his weakness, for it has often led him away from the true substance of poetry.

THE ANCIENT. There you are right, Galahad. Nature and

the sensuous delight of life for a while got the upper hand of him, and he wrote many things which aimed to be more, and were not. I think better of his later direction; but how far it will carry him depends on his industry and faith. Let us have the echo!

THE GANNET. (*Reads.*)

HADRAMAUT

The grand conglomerate hills of Araby
    That stand empanoplied in utmost thought,
With dazzling ramparts front the Indian sea,
    Down there in Hadramaut.

The sunshine smashes in the doors of morn
    And leaves them open; there the vibrant calm
Of life magniloquent pervades forlorn
    The giant fronds of palm.

The cockatoo upon the upas screams;
    The armadillo fluctuates o'er the hill;
And like a flag, incarnadined in dreams,
    All crimsonly I thrill!

There have iconoclasts no power to harm,
    So, folded grandly in translucent mist,
I let the light stream down my jasper arm,
    And o'er my opal fist.

An Adamite of old, primeval Earth,
    I see the Sphinx upon the porphyry shore,
Deprived of utterance, ages are her birth,
    As I am,—only more!

Who shall ensnare me with invested gold,
    Or paper symbols, backed like malachite?
Let gaunt reformers objurgate and scold,
    I gorge me with delight.

I do not yearn for what I covet most;
    I give the winds the passionate gifts I sought;
And slumber fiercely on the torrid coast,
    Down there in Hadramaut!

GALAHAD. That is extravagantly and absurdly like some of his poems. You seem to have had in your mind the very feature I mentioned,—his rhetoric. I doubt whether I shall succeed as well with Boker. He and Bayard Taylor are both Pennsylvanians, of nearly the same age, yet they are not at all alike.

THE ANCIENT. I remember Boker's first volume. There was a flavor of the Elizabethan English about it, which was unusual at the time. Then came his tragedy of *Calaynos,* one of the few successful modern plays formed on the old classic models; it ran for nearly a hundred nights in England. But you cannot imitate his best work, which is in this and the later plays; you must choose between his ballads and his sonnets.

GALAHAD. I have tried something half ballad and half song, in his style. (*Reads.*)

PHŒBE THE FAIR

I lie and I languish for Phœbe the Fair,
　　　Ah, welladay!
The blue of her eyes, the brown of her hair,
The elbows that dance and the ankles that gleam,
As she bends at her washing-tub there by the stream,
Disdaining to see me, so what can I say
　　　But, ah, welladay!

I met her last night when the moon was at full,
　　　Alas and alack!
Bewitchingly hooded with mufflers of wool;
Her cloak of gray duffle she wore to a charm,
So boldly I offered the maiden my arm,
But she coolly responded, "You take the back track!"
　　　Alas and alack!

Though I'm but a blacksmith and Hugo a lord,
　　　Sing hey, nonny nonny!
Though I've but a hammer and he has a sword,
When he leans from his destrier Phœbe to greet,
I could smash him to cinders before her white feet,
For lords have no business with maidens so bonny,
　　　Sing hey, nonny nonny!

I've given up Margery, given up Maud,
> Ah, welladay, Phœbe!
But the snow of your bosom by love is unthawed.
The hues of my life are all fading, I guess,
As the calico fades in the suds that you press:
You are scouring the heart of your languishing G. B.
> Ah, welladay, Phœbe!

THE GANNET. I remember those ballads, with a curious antique flavor about them; but I am best acquainted with Boker's sonnets. I don't think they have been appreciated as they deserve; but then, there are hardly twelve sonnets in the English language which can be called popular. Take one of Keats, three of Wordsworth, three of Milton, possibly Blanco White's one, and four or five of Shakespeare, and you have nearly all that are familiarly known. I'll try my hand at an imitation of Boker's grave, sustained measure. (*Writes.*)

THE ANCIENT. No one of our authors is so isolated as he, and it is a double disadvantage. When Philadelphia ceased to be a literary center, which happened very suddenly and unexpectedly, the tone of society there seemed to change. Instead of the open satisfaction of Boston in her brilliant circle of authors, or the passive indifference of our New York, there is almost a positive depreciation of home talent in Philadelphia. Boker is most disparaged in his native city, and most appreciated in New England. There is always less of petty envy where the range of culture is highest.

ZOÏLUS. No, there is not less, granting the culture to be higher; there is only more tact and policy in expressing it.

THE GANNET. Listen to Boker's 999th sonnet, dictated through me! (*Reads.*)

> I charge not with degrees of excellence
> That fair revolt which rested on thy name,
> Nor burden with uncomprehended blame
> The speech, which still eludes my swooning sense,
> Though this poor rhyme at least were some defense
> Against thy chill suspicion: yet, if Fame
> Lift up and burnish what is now my shame,
> 'Twould mitigate a passion so intense.
> This trampled verse awhile my heart relieves

From stringent pain, that cleft me as I turned
Away from beauty, graciously displayed;
And still one dominant emotion cleaves
The clouds, whereon thy passing luster burned,
And leaves behind it gulfs of blacker shade.

GALAHAD. How *could* you echo the tone and atmosphere of a sonnet, without adding one particle of sense?

THE GANNET. Attribute it to my empty head, if you please. I really cannot explain how these imitations arise in my mind. In the "trance condition," you know, one is void of all active consciousness.

ZOÏLUS. If you go on indulging such an idea, you will end by becoming a professional medium.

THE GANNET. Well,—at least I'll dictate to the world better verse than has ever yet come, in that way, from the unfortunate dead poets.

GALAHAD. Could you equal Demosthenes?

THE ANCIENT. For the sake of Human Reason let us drop that subject! There are some aberrations which dishearten us, and it is best simply to turn our backs on them. For my part, I crave music. Zoïlus, give us Herrick's *Julia* before the stirrup-cup!

Night The Seventh

THIS NIGHT the Gannet led the way to the more earnest conversation by returning to a point touched by the Ancient at their fifth meeting. He said: "I should like to know wherein the period of fermentation, which precedes the appearance of an important era in literature, and the period of subsidence, or decadence, which follows it, differ from each other."

ZOÏLUS. H'm! that's rather a tough problem to be solved at a moment's warning. I should guess that the difference is something like that between the first and second childhood of an individual. In the first case, the faults are natural, heedless, graceful, and always suggestive of something to be developed; in the latter, they are helpless repetitions, which point only towards the past.

GALAHAD. Are you not taking the correspondence for granted? Is it exactly justified by the history of any great era in literature?

THE ANCIENT. Not entirely. But there is surely an irregular groping for new modes of thought and new forms of expression in advance; and a struggle, after the masters of the age have gone, to keep up their pitch of achievement.

THE GANNET. Very well; you are near enough in accord to consider my next question. In which period are we living at present? The Ancient says that we have had the heroes and the *epigonoi,* and that there will be many fallow years: I, on the contrary, feel very sure that we are approaching another great era; and the confusion of which he spoke the other night is an additional proof of it.

THE ANCIENT. If you remember, I disclaimed any power of prediction.

THE GANNET. So you did; but I insist that the reasons you gave are just as powerful against your conclusions, unless you can show us that the phenomena of our day are those which *invariably* characterize a period of decadence. I have been reflecting upon the subject with more earnestness than is usual to me. In our modern literature I do *not* find echoes of any other than the masters who are still living and producing, especially Browning, Longfellow, and Tennyson; the faint reflections of Poe seem to have ceased; and the chief characteristic of this day, so far as the younger authors are concerned, is a straining after novel effects, new costumes for old thoughts, if you please, but certainly something very different from a mere repetition of forms of style which already exist. That there is confusion, an absence of pure, clearly outlined ideals of art, I am willing to admit. I accept the premises, but challenge the inferences.

GALAHAD. I am only too ready to agree with you.

THE ANCIENT. What I wish is that we should try to comprehend the literary aspects of our time. If we can turn our modern habit of introversion away from our individual selves, and give it more of an objective character (though this sounds rather paradoxical), it will be a gain in every way. A

period of decadence is not necessarily characterized by repetition; it may manifest itself in exactly such straining for
effect as the Gannet admits. Poe, for instance, or Heine, or
Browning, makes a new manner successful; what more natural, then, than that an inferior poet should say to himself:
"The manner is everything; I will invent one for myself!"
I find something too much of this prevalent, and it does not
inspire me with hope.

ZoÏLUS. But the costume of the thought, as of the man,
is really more important than the body it hides. And I insist
that manner is more than symmetry, or even strength, as the
French have been shrewd enough to discover. We are moving towards an equal brilliancy of style, only most of us are
zigzagging on all sides of the true path. But we shall find it,
and then look out for a shining age of literature!

THE GANNET (*to* THE ANCIENT). You were speaking of
the introversion which is such a characteristic of modern
thought. Can a writer avoid it, without showing, in the very
effort, that he possesses it?

THE ANCIENT. I doubt it. Goethe tried the experiment,
and did not fairly succeed. It seems to me that the character
of an author is relative to the highest culture of his generation. I have never found that there was much development
without self-study; for the true artist must know the exact
measure of his qualities, in order to use them in his one true
way. This is a law as applicable to Shakespeare as to you;
but he may choose to conceal the process, and you may
choose to betray it. For a poet to speculate upon his own
nature, in his poems, is a modern fashion, which originated
with Wordsworth. To us it seems an overconsciousness; yet
it may seem the height of naïve candor, and therefore
a delightful characteristic, to the critics of two centuries
hence.

ZoÏLUS. Well, upon my word, Ancient, you are the most
bewildering of guides! You talk of eternal laws, you refer to
positive systems, but when we come to apply them, there is
nothing permanent, nothing settled, only a labyrinth of per-
hapses and may-seems. What are we to do?

THE GANNET (*offering the hat*). To draw your name and write.

ZOÏLUS (*drawing*). Julia Ward Howe: and I feel no mission within me! I shall miserably fail.

THE GANNET. Jean Ingelow: I need no mission.

GALAHAD. The saints help me! Walt Whitman.

THE ANCIENT. Buchanan Read: *I* must call on the Pope, to judge from the last poem of his which I have read. There are but one or two more slips in the hat: whom have we? Piatt, Bret Harte, Joaquin Miller! Galahad, I suggest that you return our yawping cosmos, and take Piatt in his stead; then let us add John Hay, and we shall have all the latest names together for our next and final night of diversions.

THE GANNET. I second your proposal. It will separate the last and most curious phenomena in poetry from those which preceded them. Perhaps we may be able to guess what they portend.

GALAHAD (*changing the name*). I am so grateful for the permission that I will write two; adding to the imitation of Piatt that of the author of *A Woman's Poems*,[1] in whose poetical fortunes, I imagine, he feels more interest than even in his own. I am attracted by her poems as the Gannet is attracted by Mrs. Stoddard's, though the two are wholly unlike. In *The Woman* I also see indications of a struggle between thought and language, a reluctance to catch the flying Psyche by the wings and hold her until every wavering outline is clear. Women poets generally stand in too much awe of their own conceptions.

ZOÏLUS (*solemnly*). I am possessed! *Procul, O procul,*—or at least be silent. (*Writes.*)

(*All write steadily, and finish their tasks nearly at the same time.*)

THE CHORUS. You came up so nearly neck and neck that only we who timed you can decide. The Gannet first.

THE GANNET. Then hearken to Jean Ingelow. (*Reads.*)

[1]Sarah M. B. Piatt. *A Woman's Poems* (1871) had just appeared. E. W.

THE SHRIMP-GATHERERS

Scarlet spaces of sand and ocean,
  Gulls that circle and winds that blow;
Baskets and boats and men in motion,
  Sailing and scattering to and fro.

Girls are waiting, their wimples adorning
  With crimson sprinkles the broad gray flood;
And down the beach the blush of the morning
  Shines reflected from moisture and mud.

Broad from the yard the sail hangs limpy;
  Lightly the steersman whistles a lay;
Pull with a will, for the nets are shrimpy,
  Pull with a whistle, our hearts are gay!

Tuppence a quart; there are more than fifty!
  Coffee is certain, and beer galore:
Coats are corduroy, minds are thrifty,
  Won't we go it on sea and shore!

See, behind, how the hills are freckled
  With low white huts, where the lasses bide!
See, before, how the sea is speckled
  With sloops and schooners that wait the tide!

Yarmouth fishers may rail and roister,
  Tyne-side boys may shout, "Give way!"
Let them dredge for the lobster and oyster,
  Pink and sweet are our shrimps today!

Shrimps and the delicate periwinkle,
  Such are the sea-fruits lasses love:
Ho! to your nets till the blue stars twinkle,
  And the shutterless cottages gleam above!

THE CHORUS. A very courteous echo. The Ancient was next.

THE ANCIENT. I think if Buchanan Read had confined himself to those short, sweet, graceful lyrics by which he first became known, he would have attained a better success. It is singular, by the by, that his art does not color his poetry, as in Rossetti's case; no one could guess that he is also a painter. But I remember that Washington Allston is a similar instance. Read's best poems are those which have a pastoral character, and I have turned to them for his characteristic manner. (*Reads.*)

A SYLVAN SCENE

The moon, a reaper of the ripened stars,
    Held out her silver sickle in the west;
I leaned against the shadowy pasture-bars,
    A hermit, with a burden in my breast.

The lilies leaned beside me as I stood;
    The lilied heifers gleamed beneath the shed;
And spirits from the high ancestral wood
    Cast their articulate benisons on my head.

The twilight oriole sang her valentine
    From pendulous nests above the stable-sill,
And like a beggar, asking alms and wine,
    Came the importunate murmur of the mill.

Love threw his flying shuttle through my woof,
    And made the web a pattern I abhorred;
Wherefore alone I sang, and far aloof,
    My melting melodies, mightier than the sword.

The white-sleeved mowers, coming slowly home,
    With scythes like rainbows on their shoulders hung,
Sniffed not, in passing me, the scent of Rome,
    Nor heard the music trickling from my tongue.

The milkmaid, following, delayed her step,
    Still singing as she left the stable yard:
'Twas *Sheridan's Ride* she sang: I turned and wep',
    For woman's homage soothes the suffering bard!

GALAHAD. Why didn't you take Read's *Drifting?*

THE ANCIENT. It is a beautiful poem, but would betray itself in any imitation. My object was to catch his especial poetic dialect.

THE CHORUS. Now, Zoïlus.

ZOÏLUS. I have followed exactly the Ancient's plan, but with the disadvantage of not having read Mrs. Howe's *Passion Flowers* lately; so I was forced to take whatever features were accessible, from her prose as well as verse. (*Reads.*)

THE COMING RACE

When with crisped fingers I have tried to part
    The petals which compose
The azure flower of high aesthetic art,
    More firmly did they close.

Yet woman is not undeveloped man,—
    So singeth Tennyson:
Desire, that ever Duty's feet outran,
    Begins, but sees not done.

Our life is full of passionate dismay
    At larger schemes grown small;
That which thou doest, do this very day,
    Then art thou known of all.

The thing that was ungerms the thing to be;
    Before reflects Behind;
So blends our moral trigonometry
    With spheroids of the mind.

Time shall transfigure many a paradox,
    Now crushed with hoofs of scorn,
When in the beauty of the hollyhocks
    The Coming Man is born.

His hand the new Evangels then shall hold,
    That make earth epicene,
And on his shoulder, coiffed with chrismal gold,
    The Coming Woman lean!

THE GANNET. Oh, she should not lean on his shoulder! That is a dependent attitude.

ZOÏLUS. I know; but there is the exigency of an immediate rhyme, and "epicene" is a word which I could not sacrifice.

THE ANCIENT. You have hit upon one of the vices of our literary class,—the superficial refinement which vents itself on words and phrases. I have seen expressions of both love and grief which were too elegant for passion. The strong thought always finds the best speech, but as its total form: it does not pause to prink itself by the way, or to study its face in a glass. I beg pardon, Zoïlus; I am not speaking of, but *from,* you.

ZOÏLUS. As the sinner furnishes more texts than the saint.

THE CHORUS. Let us not keep Galahad waiting.

GALAHAD. I promised two, but have only finished the first. The Gannet must keep me company; for we were nigh forgetting William Winter, and he must be entertained before our board is cleared for the last comers. I dare say we shall remember others; indeed, I can think of several who ought to please the Ancient, for they simply give us their ideas without any manner at all.

THE ANCIENT. Sarcasm from Galahad is sarcasm indeed! I am assailed on all sides tonight. But let us have Piatt; we have all looked through his *Western Windows.*

GALAHAD. (*Reads.*)

THE OLD FENCE-RAIL

It lies and rots by the roadside,
    Among the withering weeds;
The blackberry vines run o'er it,
    And the thistles drop their seeds.

Below, the Miami murmurs
    He flows as he always flowed;
And the people, eastward and westward,
    Travel the National Road.

At times a maiden's glances
    Gild it with tints of dawn,
But the schoolboy snorts with his nostrils,
    Kicks it, and hastens on.

Above it the pioneer's chimney,
    Lonely and rickety, leans;
Beside it the pioneer's garden
    Is a wildering growth of greens.

It was built by the stalwart settler,
   One of the ancient race,
And the hands of his tow-haired children
   Lifted it into its place.

Years after the gawky lover
   Sat on it, dangling his heels,
While his girl forgot her milking,
   And the pen, with its hungry squeals.

Ah, the rail has its own romances,
   The scenes and changes of years:
I pause whenever I see it,
   And drop on it several tears.

ZOÏLUS. Don't you all feel, with me, that our imitations become more and more difficult as we take the younger authors who give us sentiment, fancy, pure meters—in short, very agreeable and meritorious work—but who neither conquer us by their daring nor provoke us by offending our tastes?

THE ANCIENT. We foresaw this the first evening, you will remember. There are many excellent poets who cannot be amusingly travestied,—Collins, or Goldsmith, for example. I was just deliberating whether to suggest the names of two women who have written very good poems, Lucy Larcom and she who calls herself "H. H." The former has rhetoric and rhythm, and uses both quite independently; her *Hannah Binding Shoes* struck an original vein, which I wish she had gone on quarrying. But her finest poem, *The Rose Enthroned*, could only be appreciated by about one per cent of her readers. "H. H." shows delicacy and purity of sentiment, yet her verse is not precisely *song*. Her ear fails to catch the rarer music which lurks behind metrical correctness. I don't well see how either could be imitated; so we will leave the Gannet and Galahad to their second task.

THE GANNET (*looking up*). What you have been saying also applies to my present model. Just the best poems in his *Witness* are so simple, so sweetly and smoothly finished, so marked by pure taste and delicate fancy, that a good travesty would have the air of a serious imitation.

Zoïlus (*to* The Ancient). However we may disagree, I heartily join you in relishing a marked individuality in poetry.

The Ancient. When it is honest, when it frankly expresses the individual nature, not too much restricted by the conventionalisms of the day, nor yielding too indolently to the influences of other minds. It is a notable characteristic of nearly all our younger poets that they wander, as if at random, over such a wide field, before selecting their separate paths. One cause of this, I should guess, is the seduction exercised by that refinement in form, that richness and variety of metrical effect, which marks our modern poetry. Twenty years ago our only criticism almost ignored the idea in a poem; it concerned itself with words, lines, or stanzas, italicizing every agreeable little touch of fancy, as a guide to the reader. Leigh Hunt made this fashion popular; Poe imitated him; and our young authors were taught to believe in detached beauties of expression instead of pure and symmetrical conceptions. Take the earlier poems of Stoddard, Read, Aldrich, Bayard Taylor, and others, and you cannot fail to see how they were led astray.

Zoïlus. Then, I suppose, their genuine poetical quality is tested by the extent to which they have emancipated themselves from those early influences, and discovered their proper individualities?

The Ancient. Most certainly; and if you had grown up with the generation, as I have (being very little older), you would see, as I do now, how each is struggling out of the general wilderness. Boker had not far to go; he grew up under the broad wings of the old English dramatists. Stoddard first struck his highest performance in *The Fisher and Charon,* and Stedman in his *Alectryon,* though both are still best known by their lighter lyrics. Aldrich seems now to be aware of his native grace and delicacy of fancy, and Howells of the sportive, lightsome element, which the *Weltschmerz* of youth for a time suppressed. In his *Pastorals,* Bayard Taylor seems inclined to seek for the substance of poetry, rather than the flash and glitter of its rhetorical drapery. Piatt is turning more and more to that which lies nearest him: in short, without pretending to decide how far each is successful, I think that each, now, is attending seriously to his own special work.

ZoïLus. How much longer do you give them, to reach their highest planes of performance?

THE ANCIENT. All their lives; and I refer you to Bryant, Emerson, Longfellow, and Whittier, as instances of continuous development. If our American atmosphere, as you said the other night, retards the growth of literary men, you cannot deny that it wonderfully prolongs the period of their growth.

THE GANNET. Here have Galahad and myself been waiting with our manuscripts, knowing that you two can never agree, but hoping that each might exhaust the other.

ZoïLus. This from you, for whom there is neither time, space, nor place, when you get fairly started! But who are you now?

THE GANNET. William Winter, at your service. (*Reads.*)

LOVE'S DIET

There be who crave the flavors rich
    Of boneless turkey and of beef;
There be who seek the relish which
    To palsied palates brings relief:
But I, in love's most patient hush,
Partake with thee of simple mush.

The pheasant seems so bright of wing,
    Because 'tis wedded with expense;
The rarer Strasburg pasties bring
    But fleet enjoyment to the sense;
Yet common things, that seem too nigh,
Both purse and heart may satisfy.

'Tis sweet to browse on dishes rare,
    When those who give them can afford:
Sweeter this unpretending fare,
    When thou art seated at the board,
With spoony fingers to unfold
The yielding mush's mass of gold.

Thou pour'st the milk that whiter seems
Than is the orbit of thy brow,
And I indulge with lamblike dreams,
And many a white and harmless vow;
I only wish that there could be
One bowl, not two, for thee and me.

ZOÏLUS. I was not expecting even so much success.

THE GANNET. Galahad was generous to give me the lighter task. It would have quite bewildered me to imitate *A Woman's Poems,* because their chief characteristic is a psychological one. If we had taken that wonderful volume of the songstresses of the *South Land,* now——

ZOÏLUS. That reminds me of a graceful Southern singer, who is like a bard alone in the desert,—Paul H. Hayne. Talk of *our* lack of sympathy and encouragement, here, in New York! What mate has he, for hundreds of miles around him? Why, there is not even the challenge of a rival lance; he must ride around the lonely lists, with neither antagonist to prove his mettle nor queen to crown him for success.

THE ANCIENT. An author *must* have an audience, however thin. We are told that Poetry is its own exceeding great reward; very well; but what if you sing your song into the air and never find it again in the heart of a friend! Genius without sympathetic recognition is like a kindled fire without flue or draught: it smolders miserably away instead of leaping, sparkling, and giving cheer. I have seen some parts of the country where a man of sensitive, poetical nature would surely die if he could not escape. We ought to be very tender towards all honest efforts in literature.

GALAHAD. The "Woman" whom I have imitated needs only the encounter of kind, yet positive minds, to give her dreams what they still lack—a distinct reality. I have purposely tried to exaggerate her principal fault, for it was the only thing I could do. (*Reads.*)

THE PLASTER CAST

The white thought sleeps in it enshrined,
Though mean and cheap the substance seems,

As sleep conceptions in the mind,
　　Hardened, and unreleased by dreams.

A parrot only! yet the child
　　Stares with untutored, dim surprise,
And fain would know what secret mild
　　Is ambushed in those moveless eyes.

His cherry from the painted beak
　　Falls, when his gentle hand would give,
So early some return we seek
　　From that which only seems to live.

Ah, let us even these symbols guard,
　　Nor shatter them with curious touch;
For, should we break ideals hard,
　　The fragments would not move us much.

Zoïlus. You have fairly bewildered me, Galahad. I thought there was an actual idea in the verses, but it slips from my hand like an eel.

The Ancient. It would better answer for the travesty of a school which has a limited popularity at present, but to which *A Woman* does not belong.

Galahad. What school? I know of none such.

The Ancient. The most active members would no doubt be much astonished if I were to tell them of it, but it is a kind of school nevertheless. I think it must have originated as long ago as the days of *The Dial,* and has not yet wholly gone out of fashion with a rather large class of readers. You will find plenty of specimens in newspapers of a mixed religious and literary character, and now and then in the magazines.

The Chorus. Give us its peculiarities.

The Ancient. First, great gravity, if not solemnity of tone; a rhythm, sometimes weak, sometimes hard, but usually halting; obscurity and incoherence of thought, and a perpetual reference to abstract morality.

Zoïlus. Don't describe, but imitate.

The Ancient. I could give you a stanza, by way of illustration. Furnish me with a subject—anything you please.

(ZOÏLUS *writes.*) *The Fifth Wheel!* that will answer; for the poets of this school always begin far away from their themes. The first stanza might run thus:

> From sunshine and from moral truth
>   Let Life be woven athwart thy breast!
> The rapid cycles of thy youth
>   But fetter Duty's solemn quest.

OMNES. Go on!

THE ANCIENT. Now I may get a little nearer to the subject, though I don't clearly see how. (*After a pause.*)

> Vibration gives but faint assent
>   To that which in thee seems complete,
> But time evolves the Incident
>   Behind the dust-driven chariot's feet.

> Be well provided! Overplus
>   Is Life's stern law, none can evade;
> Thou to the goal shall hasten thus,
>   When selfish natures' wheels are stayed.

ZOÏLUS. Great Jove! to think that I never discovered the undying Laura Matilda in this prim disguise! It is the languishing creature grown older, with a high-necked dress, a linen collar, and all her curls brushed smooth! Ancient, you have purged mine eyes from visual film; this boon wipes out all remembrance of our strife.

OMNES. Enough for tonight!   [*Exeunt.*]

Night The Eighth

(*All the members promptly on hand.*)

THE CHORUS. How much does any author distinctly know of himself, or the quality of his works?

ZOÏLUS. Not much.

GALAHAD. Everything!

THE GANNET. Only what makes a hit, and what doesn't.

THE ANCIENT. It depends on who and what the author is: you will find both extremes represented.

THE CHORUS. Yourselves, for instance!

ZOÏLUS. To be frank, I think I have more merit than luck. But when I come to contrast the degrees of popularity with the character of the performance, I am puzzled.

GALAHAD. Popularity has nothing to do with it. I know that some of my qualities are genuine, while other necessary ones are weakly represented. Our talk the last night satisfied me that I have not yet found the one best direction; but, on the other hand, one dare not force one's own development, and I think I see whither I am tending.

THE GANNET. Do you want to see where you stand now, or very nearly the spot?

GALAHAD. Show me if you can?

(THE GANNET *takes a sheet of paper and writes.*)

ZOÏLUS (*to* THE ANCIENT). Do you think that a poet is generally a correct judge of his own works?

THE ANCIENT. Please don't repeat that dismal platitude! A genuine poet is *always* the best judge of his own works, simply because he has an ideal standard by which he measures whatever he does. He may not be able to guess what will be most popular; he may attach an exorbitant value to that which is born of some occult individual mood, in which few others can ever share; but in regard to the quality of the calm, ripened product of his brain he cannot be mistaken! To admit that he can be, substitutes chance for law in the poetic art, and brings us down to the vulgar idea of a wayward and accidental inspiration, instead of conscious growth followed by conscious achievement.

ZOÏLUS. You astonish me.

THE ANCIENT. Then be glad; it is a sign that you are not poetically *blasé*.

GALAHAD. Never! One can never be that.

THE GANNET. Wait till you hear how your theorbo sounds in my ears. What I have attempted is a serious, not a comical, echo of your style.

OMNES. Give it to us!

THE GANNET. Keep Galahad's hands off me till I have finished. (*Reads.*)

THE TWO LIVES

Down in the dell I wandered,
  The loneliest of our dells,
Where grow the lowland lilies,
  Dropping their foam-white bells,
And the brook among the grasses
  Toys with its sands and shells.

Fair were the meads and thickets,
  And sumptuous grew the trees,
And the folding hills of harvest
  Were lulled with the fanning breeze,
But I heard, beyond the valley,
  The roar of the plunging seas.

The birds and the vernal grasses,
  They wooed me sweetly and long,
But the magic of ocean called me,
  Murmuring vast and strong;
Here was the flutelike cadence,
  There was the world-wide song!

"Lie in the wood's embraces,
  Sleep in the dell's repose!"
"Float on the limitless azure,
  Flecked with its foamy snows!"
Such were the changing voices
  Heard at the twilight's close.

Free with the winds and waters,
  Nestled in shade and dew:
Bliss in the soft green shelter,
  Fame on the boundless blue;
Which shall I yield forever?
  Which forever pursue?

OMNES (*clapping their hands*). Galahad! Galahad!

GALAHAD (*with a melancholy air*). It is worse than the most savage criticism. There is just enough of my own sentiment and poetical manner in it to show me how monstrously blind I have been in not perceiving that scores of clever fellows may write the same things, if they should choose. I ought to relapse into the corner of a country newspaper.

THE ANCIENT. Take heart, my dear boy! We all begin with sentiment and melodious rhythm,—or what seems to us to be such. We all discover the same old metaphors over again, and they are as new to us as if they had never been used before. Very few young poets have the slightest presentiment of their coming development. They have the keenest delight, the profoundest satisfaction, with their crudest works. With knowledge comes the sense of imperfection, which increases as they rise in performance. Remember that the Gannet is five or six years older than you, and can now write in cold blood what only comes from the summer heat of your mind.

GALAHAD. I understand you, and don't mean to be discouraged. But Zoïlus is fully avenged now.

ZOÏLUS. I'll prove it by my notice of your next poem in the ——. Let us turn to our remaining models. Whatever may be thought of them at home, they have all made a very positive impression in England; how do you account for it, Ancient?

THE ANCIENT. I can only guess at an explanation apart from the merits which three of them certainly possess. While the average literary culture in England was perhaps never so high as now, the prevalent style of writing was never so conventional. The sensational school, which has been so popular here as well as there, is beginning to fatigue the majority of readers, yet it still spoils their enjoyment of simple, honest work; so, every new appearance in literature, which is racy, which carries the flavor of a fresh soil with it, unconventional yet seemingly natural, neither suggesting the superficial refinement of which they are surfeited nor the nobler refinement which they have forgotten how to relish,—all such appearances, I suspect, furnish just the change they crave.

THE GANNET. But the changes of popular taste in the

two countries are very similar. This is evident in the cases of Bret Harte and Hay; but Walt Whitman seems to have a large circle of enthusiastic admirers in England, and only some half-dozen disciples among us. Do you suppose that the passages of his *Leaves of Grass,* which are prose catalogues to us, or the phrases which are our slang, have a kind of poetical charm there, because they are not understood?

Zoïlus. As Tartar or Mongolian *Leaves of Grass* might have to us? Very likely. There are splendid lines and brief passages in Walt Whitman: there is a modern, half-Bowery-boy, half-Emersonian apprehension of the old Greek idea of physical life, which many take to be wholly new on account of the singular form in which it is presented. I will even admit that the elements of a fine poet exist in him, in a state of chaos. It is curious that while he proclaims his human sympathies to be without bounds, his intellectual sympathies should be so narrow. There never was a man at once so arrogant, and so tender towards his fellowmen.

The Ancient. You have very correctly described him. The same art which he despises would have increased his power and influence. He forgets that the poet must not only have somewhat to say, but must strenuously acquire the power of saying it most purely and completely. A truer sense of art would have prevented that fault which has been called immorality, but it is only a coarse, offensive frankness.

The Gannet. Let us divide our labors. There is only one name apiece: how shall we apportion them?

Zoïlus. Take Joaquin Miller, and give Walt Whitman to the Ancient. Choose of these two, Galahad!

Galahad (*opening the paper*). Bret Harte.

Zoïlus. Then Hay remains to me.

(*They all write steadily for half an hour.*)

The Gannet. Our last is our most difficult task; for we have to give the local flavor of the poetry, as well as its peculiar form and tone.

Zoïlus. I should like to know how much of that local flavor is genuine. I am suspicious of Bret Harte's California dialect: some features of it are evidently English, and very suggestive of Dickens. Hay's is nearer the real thing. Miller's scenery and accessories also inspire me with doubt. Now, much of the value of this *genre* poetry (as I should call it) depends upon its fidelity to nature. Sham slang and sham barbarism are worse than sham refinement and luxury.

THE ANCIENT. Harte's use of "which" as an expletive is certainly an English peculiarity, which he may have heard in some individual miner, but which is not a feature of California slang. So, when Miggles says "Oh, if you please, I'm Miggles," it is an English girl who speaks. Aside from a few little details of this kind, Harte's sketches and poems are truly and admirably colored. He deserves his success, for he has separated himself by a broad gulf from all the literary buffoonery of this day, which is sometimes grotesque and always inane. But he is *picturesque,* and the coarsest humor of his characters rests on a pure human pathos.

GALAHAD. Somehow, the use of a vulgar dialect in poetry is always unpleasant to me; it is like a grinning mask over a beautiful face. And yet, how charming is *'Zekel's Courtship!*

THE ANCIENT. Lowell has done all that is possible with the New England dialect. He has now and then steeped it in an odor of poetry which it never before exhaled and perhaps never may again. Compare it, for instance, with the Scotch of Burns, where every elision makes the word sweeter on the tongue, and where the words which are its special property are nearly always musical. The New England changes are generally on the side of roughness and clumsiness. *With* becomes an ugly *'th,* instead of the soft Scotch *wi';* *have* hardens into *hev,* instead of flowing into *hae;* and *got* coarsens into *gut,* instead of the quaint sharpness of *gat.* It is the very opposite of the mellow broadness of the Scotch; it sacrifices the vowels and aggravates the consonants; its raciest qualities hint of prevarication and non-committal, and its sentiment is grotesque even when it is frank and touching. Yet Lowell's genius sometimes so completely transfigures this harsh material that one's ear forgets it and hears only the finer music of his thought.

ZOÏLUS. Shall we read? I suggest that we take the authors,

tonight, in the order of their appearance. Walt Whitman leads.

THE ANCIENT. (*Reads*).

CAMERADOS

Everywhere, everywhere, following me;
Taking me by the buttonhole, pulling off my boots, hustling me with the elbows;
Sitting down with me to clams and the chowder-kettle;
Plunging naked at my side into the sleek, irascible surges;
Soothing me with the strain that I neither permit nor prohibit;
Flocking this way and that, reverent, eager, orotund, irrepressible;
Denser than sycamore leaves when the north-winds are scouring Paumanok;
What can I do to restrain them? Nothing, verily nothing.
Everywhere, everywhere, crying aloud for me;
Crying, I hear; and I satisfy them out of my nature;
And he that comes at the end of the feast shall find something over.
Whatever they want I give; though it be something else, they shall have it.
Drunkard, leper, Tammanyite, smallpox and cholera patient, shoddy, and codfish millionnaire,
And the beautiful young men, and the beautiful young women, all the same,
Crowding, hundreds of thousands, cosmical multitudes,
Buss me and hang on my hips and lean up to my shoulders,
Everywhere listening to my yawp and glad whenever they hear it;
Everywhere saying, say it, Walt, we believe it:
Everywhere, everywhere.

ZOÏLUS. By Jove, Ancient! you could soon develop into a Kosmos.

THE ANCIENT. It would not be difficult, so far as the form is concerned. The immortal Tupper, in his rivalry with Solomon, substituted semi-rhythmical prose lines for verse; but Walt, being thoroughly in earnest, often makes his lines wholly rhythmical. I confess I enjoy his decameters and hecatameters.

THE CHORUS. Bret Harte was the next appearance, after a very long interval. You will have to do your best, Galahad.

GALAHAD. A superficial imitation is easy enough, but I shall certainly fail to reproduce his subtile wit and pathos. (*Reads*).

TRUTHFUL JAMES'S SONG OF THE SHIRT

Which his name it was Sam;
    He had sluiced for a while
Up at Murderer's Dam,
    Till he got a good pile,
And the heft of each dollar,
    Two thousand or more,
He'd put in the Chollar
    For he seed it was ore
That runs thick up and down, without ceilin' or floor.

And, says he, it's a game
    That's got but one stake;
If I put up that same,
    It'll bust me or make.
At fifty the foot
    I've entered my pile,
And the whole derned cahoot
    I'll let soak for a while,
And jest loaf around here,—say, Jim, will you smile?

Tom Fakes was the chum,
    Down in Frisco, of Sam;
And one mornin' there come
    This here telegram:
"You can sell for five hundred,
    Come down by the train!"
Sam By-Joed and By-Thundered,—
    'Twas whistlin' quite plain,
And down to Dutch Flat rushed with might and with main.

He had no time to sarch,
    But he grabbed up a shirt
That showed bilin' and starch,
    And a coat with less dirt.

He jumped on the step
    As the train shoved away,
And likewise was swep',
    All galliant and gay,
Round the edge of the mounting and down to'rds the Bay.

Seven minutes, to pass
    Through the hole by the Flat!
Says he, I'm an ass
    If I can't shift in that!
But the train behind time,
    Only *three* was enough,—
It came pat as a rhyme—
    He was stripped to the buff
When they jumped from the tunnel to daylight! 'Twas rough.

What else? Here's to you!
    Which he sold of his feet
At five hundred, 'tis true,
    And the same I repeat:
But acquaintances, friends,
    They likes to divert,
And the tale never ends
    Of Sam and his shirt,
And to stop it from goin' he'd give all his dirt!

ZoïLus. You were right to take a merely comical incident.
You couldn't possibly have echoed the strong feeling which
underlies the surface slang of such a poem as *Jim*, which I
consider Harte's masterpiece in his special vein.

GALAHAD. He never could have written that if he had
been only a humorist. His later work shows that he is a
genuine poet.

THE ANCIENT. Yes, that special vein is like many in the
Nevada mines, rich on the surface, narrowing as it goes
down, pinched off by the primitive strata, opening again
unexpectedly into a pocket, but never to be fully depended
upon. Harte's instincts are too true not to see this: I believe
he will do still better, and therefore probably less popular
work.

THE GANNET. Now, Zoïlus, give us Hay, and let *me* close
with a war-whoop!

Zoïlus. I'm not quite sure of my Pike dialect, but I fancy the tone is rough enough to satisfy you. (*Reads.*)

Big Bill

There's them that eats till they're bustin',
  And them that drinks till they're blind,
And them that's snufflin' and spooney,
  But the best of all, to my mind
(And I've been around in my time, boys,
  And cavorted with any you like),
Was Big Bill, that lived in the slashes,
  We called him Big Bill o' Pike.

If he put his hand to his bowie
  Or scratched the scruff of his neck,
You could only tell by waitin'
  To see if you bled a peck:
And the way he fired, 'twas lovely!
  Nobody knowed which was dead,
Till Big Bill grinned, and the stiff 'un
  Tumbled over onto his head!

At school he killed his master;
  Courtin', he killed seven more:
And the hearse was always a-waitin'
  A little ways from his door.
There wasn't much growth in the county
  As the census returns will show,
But we had Big Bill we was proud of,
  And that was enough to grow.

And now Big Bill is an angel,—
  Damn me, it makes me cry!
Jist when he was rampin' the roughest,
  The poor fellow had to die.
A thievin' and sneakin' Yankee
  Got the start on our blessed Bill,
And there's no one to do our killin'
  And nobody left to kill!

Zoïlus. Hay's realism, in those ballads, is of the grimmest kind. It is like the old Dance of Death, in a new form.

I have been greatly amused by the actual fury which his *Little Breeches* and *Jim Bludso* have aroused in some sectarian quarters. To read the attacks, one would suppose that Christianity was threatened by the declaration that angels may interpose to save children, or that a man, ignorant or regardless of ordinary morality, may redeem his soul by the noblest sacrifice. Really, it seems to me that to diminish the range of individual damnation renders many good people unhappy.

THE ANCIENT. Hay has made his name known in the most legitimate way,—by representing phenomena of common Western life which he has observed. He might have faintly echoed Shelley or Tennyson for a decade, and accomplished nothing. Those ballads are not, strictly speaking, poetry; but it is impossible that they should not give him a tendency to base his better poems on the realities of our American life.

THE CHORUS. Let us hear the Gannet's war whoop!

THE GANNET. There is nothing easier than to exaggerate exaggeration. (*Reads.*)

THE FATE OF THE FRONTIERSMAN

That whiskey jug! For, dry or wet,
My tale will need its help, you bet!

We made for the desert, she and I,
Though life was loathsome, and love a lie,
And she gazed on me with her glorious eye,
But all the same, I let her die!
For why?—there was barely water for one
In the small canteen, and of provender, none!
A splendid snake, with an emerald scale,
Slid before us along the trail,
With a famished parrot pecking its head;
And, seizing a huge and dark brown rock
In her dark brown hands, as you crush a crock,
With the dark brown rock she crushed it dead.
But ere her teeth in its flesh could meet,
I laid her as dead as the snake at my feet,
And grabbed the snake for myself to eat.

The plain stretched wide, from side to side,
As bare and blistered and cracked and dried
As a moccasin sole of buffalo hide,
And my throat grew hot, as I walked the trail,
My blood in a sizzle, my muscles dry,
A crimson glare in my glorious eye,
And I felt my sinews wither and fail,
Like one who has lavished, for fifty nights,
His pile in a hell of gambling delights,
And is kicked at dawn from bottle and bed,
And sent to the gulches without a red.
There was no penguin to pick or pluck,
No armadillo's throat to be stuck,
Not even a bilberry's ball of blue
To slush my tongue with its indigo dew,
And the dry brown palm-trees rattled and roared
Like the swish and swizzle of Walker's sword.
I was nigh rubbed out; when, far away,
A shanty baked in the furnace of day,
And I petered on, for an hour or more,
Till I dropped, like a mangy hound, at the door.

No soul to be seen; but a basin stood
On the bench, with a mess of dubious food,
Stringy and doughy and lumpy and thick,
As the clay ere flame has turned it to brick.
I gobbled it up with a furious fire,
A prairie squall of hungry desire,
And strength came back; when, lo! a scream
Closed my stomach and burst my dream.
She stood before me, as lithe and tall
As a musqueet-bush on the Pimos wall,
Fierce as the Zuñi panther's leap,
Fair as the slim Apache sheep.
A lariat draped her broad brown hips,
As she stood and glared with parted lips,
While piercing stitches and maddening shoots
Ran through my body, from brain to boots.
I would have clasped her, but, ere I could,
She flung back her hair's tempestuous hood,
And screamed, in a voice like a tiger-cat's:
"You've gone and ett up my pizen for rats!"
My blood grew limp and my hair grew hard

As the steely tail of the desert pard:
I sank at her feet, convulsed and pale,
And kissed in anguish her brown toe-nail.
You may rip the cloud from the frescoed sky,
Or tear the man from his place in the moon,
Fur from the buzzard and plumes from the coon,
But you can't tear me from the truth I cry,
That life is loathsome and love a lie.
She lifted me up to her bare brown face,
She cracked my ribs in her brown embrace,
And there in the shanty, side by side,
Each on the other's bosom died.

She's now the mistress of Buffalo Bill,
And pure as the heart of a lily still;
While I've killed all who have cared for me,
And I'm just as lonely as I can be,
So, pass the whisky,—we'll have a spree!

OMNES. The real thing!

ZOÏLUS. You've beaten us all, but no wonder! Much of Joaquin Miller's verse is in itself a travesty of poetry. Ancient, you talk about high ideals of literary art, and all that sort of thing: can you tell me what Rossetti and the rest of the English critics mean in hailing this man as the great American poet?

THE ANCIENT. One thing, of course, they cannot see,— the thorough spuriousness of his characters, with their costumes, scenery, and all other accessories. Why, he takes Lara and the Giaour, puts them in a fantastic, impossible country called "Arizona" or "California," and describes them with a rhythm borrowed from Swinburne and a frenzy all his own—and we are called upon to accept this as something original and grand! The amazed admiration of a class in England, and the gushing gratitude of one in America, form, together, a spectacle over which the pure, serene gods must bend in convulsions of inextinguishable laughter.

ZOÏLUS. Give me your hand! As Thackeray said, let us swear eternal friendship! You have often provoked me by persistently mollifying my judgments of authors; but, if you had done so in this case, I could not have forgiven you.

Joaquin Miller, and he alone, would prove the decadence of our literature: he is an Indianized copy of Byron, made up of shrieks and war-paint, and the life he describes is too brutal, selfish, and insane ever to have existed anywhere. A few fine lines or couplets, or an occasional glittering bit of description, are not enough make him a genius, or even an unusual talent.

THE GANNET. But the material—not *his,* the true, Arizonian material—is good, and he has shown shrewdness in selecting it. He is clever, in some ways, or he never could have made so much capital in England. His temporary success here is only an echo of his success there.

ZOÏLUS. If he were a young fellow of twenty, I should say, wait; but his is not the exaggeration of youth, it is the affectation of manhood.

GALAHAD. If anybody ever seriously said, "Alas!" I should say it now. I have picked up many a grain of good counsel in the midst of our fun, and the fun itself has become an agreeable stimulus which I shall miss. We must not give up our habit wholly.

ZOÏLUS. There is no end of intellectual and poetic gymnastics which we may try. I propose that we close with a grand satirical American *Walpurgis Night,* modeled on Goethe's Intermezzo in *Faust.*

THE GANNET. That is a good idea, but how shall we carry it out?

ZOÏLUS. Let each write a stanza or two, satirizing some literary school, author, magazine, or newspaper, throw it into the hat, and then take another, as long as we can keep up the game. When all are exhausted, give the hat to the Ancient and let him read the whole collection of squibs, in the order in which they turn up.

OMNES (*eagerly*). Accepted!

[Here, I am compelled to state, my liberty as a reporter ceases. The plan was carried out, and I think it was not entirely unsuccessful. But our mirth was partly at the expense of others: many of the stanzas were only lively and good-humored, but many others thrust out a sharp sting in the last line. As I was not an accomplice, I was perfectly willing that they should all be given to the public. Zoïlus did not seriously object; but the other three were peremptory in their prohibition. Even the Gannet confessed that he was not courageous enough to run the risk of making half-a-dozen permanent enemies by shafts of four lines apiece: he knew how largely the element of *personal* profit and reputation enters into American literary life, and how touchy a sensitiveness it develops. There was no denying this, for they related many instances to prove it. I yielded, of course, although it was a disappointment to me. After having thus entered authorship by a side door, as it were, I find the field very pleasant; and I withdraw now, since there is no alternative, with reluctance.—The Nameless Reporter.]

A FEW of Poe's stories were translated into French and
published in 1847. Charles Baudelaire read them and "experienced a strange commotion." He looked Poe up in American magazines and found poems and stories of which he
said that he had thought of writing them himself. Poe became an obsession with him. In a note in his journal, he
indicates an intention of praying every morning to God, to
his father, and to Poe. He published, between 1856 and
1865, several volumes of translations of the American; and
Poe became one of the chief influences in the Symbolist
Movement of the end of the century.

Stéphane Mallarmé, who translated *The Raven* and *Ulalume*, wrote a very fine sonnet on Poe, which was read at
Baltimore, November 17, 1875, on the occasion of the unveiling of a tombstone for the poet.

Walt Whitman also attended this ceremony and left a
record of his feelings in connection with it. He was obviously
unsympathetic with those elements in Poe which delighted
the French, and he seems rather dismayed that the poetry
of his time was running to "morbidity" and "abnormal
beauty" rather than taking the "democratic" direction which

he had hoped to induce it to follow. But, though Whitman declined to make a speech, he had "felt a strong impulse" to go to the meeting.

The occasion has been described by H. L. Mencken in the First Series of his *Prejudices*:

The myth that there is a monument to Edgar Allan Poe in Baltimore is widely believed; there are even persons who, stopping off in Baltimore to eat oysters, go to look at it. As a matter of fact, no such monument exists. All that the explorer actually finds is a cheap and hideous tombstone in the corner of a Presbyterian churchyard—a tombstone quite as bad as the worst in Père Lachaise. For twenty-six years after Poe's death there was not even this: the grave remained wholly unmarked. Poe had surviving relatives in Baltimore, and they were well-to-do. One day one of them ordered a local stonecutter to put a plain stone over the grave. The stonecutter hacked it out and was preparing to haul it to the churchyard when a runaway freight-train smashed into his stoneyard and broke the stone to bits. Thereafter the Poes seem to have forgotten Cousin Edgar; at all events, nothing further was done.

The existing tombstone was erected by a committee of Baltimore schoolmarms, and cost about $1,000. It took the dear girls ten long years to raise the money. They started out with a "literary entertainment" which yielded $380. This was in 1865. Six years later the fund had made such slow progress that, with accumulated interest, it came to but $587.02. Three years more went by: it now reached $627.55. Then some anonymous Poe-ista came down with $100, two others gave $50 each, one of the devoted schoolmarms raised $52 in nickels and dimes, and George W. Childs agreed to pay any remaining deficit. During all this time not a single American author of position gave the project any aid. And when, finally, a stone was carved and set up and the time came for the unveiling, the only one who appeared at the ceremony was Walt Whitman. All the other persons present were Baltimore nobodies—chiefly schoolteachers and preachers. There were three set speeches—one by the principal of a local high school, the second by a teacher in the same seminary, and the third by a man who was invited to give his "personal recollections" of Poe, but who announced in his third sentence that "I never saw Poe but once, and our interview did not last an hour."

STÉPHANE MALLARMÉ

LE TOMBEAU D'EDGAR POE

Tel qu'en Lui-même enfin l'éternité le change,
Le Poète suscite avec un glaive nu
Son siècle epouvanté de n'avoir pas connu
Que la mort triomphant dans cette voix étrange!

Eux, comme un vil sursaut d'hydre oyant jadis l'ange
Donner un sens plus pur aux mots de la tribu
Proclamèrent très haute le sortilège bu
Dans le flot sans honneur de quelque noir mélange

Du sol et de la nue hostiles, ô grief!
Si notre idée avec ne sculpte un bas-relief
Dont la tombe de Poe éblouissante s'orne

Calme bloc ici-bas chu d'un désastre obscur
Que ce granit du moins montre à jamais sa borne
Aux noirs vols de Blasphème épars dans le futur.

THE TOMB OF EDGAR POE

Translation and Commentary by ROGER FRY

Such as to himself eternity's changed him,
The Poet arouses with his naked sword
His age fright-stricken for not having known
That Death was triumphing in that strange voice!

They, with a Hydra's vile spasm at hearing the angel
Giving a sense more pure to the words of their tribe
Proclaimed aloud the sortilege drunk
In the dishonored flow of some black brew.

Oh, Grief! From soil and from the hostile cloud,
If thence our idea cannot carve a relief
Wherewith to adorn Poe's shining tomb

Calm block fallen down here from some dark disaster
May this granite at least show forever their bourn
To the black flights of Blasphemy sparse in the future.

This piece needs rather a literary commentary than an explanation. It contains two or three of Mallarmé's best-known lines:

"Such as to himself eternity's changed him" might serve as the theme for a dissertation on Death and the Absolute in the poet's works, while "Giving a sense more pure to the words of their tribe" might serve as epigraph to a Mallarméan esthetic.

"This sonnet," writes Mallarmé, "was recited at the unveiling, at Baltimore, of a block of basalt as a monument to Poe, with which America weighted down the poet's light shadow, *in order to make sure that it never reappeared.*" The ironical remark that is here italicized is a trace of the indignation that animates the sonnet.

The two quatrains appear to sketch the bas-reliefs whose absence from the monument the poet regrets in the first tercet. Eternity presents the poet under his true shape, as the angel of death; the age which misunderstood him is the "Hydra's vile spasm." The strangeness of the poet's voice (really an attempt at poetic purity) the vulgar take to be the effect of drink. The world, from earth to sky, shows itself hostile to genius. This hostility should form the subject of the bas-reliefs. If not, we can at least make this block a boundary stone against future stupidity.

There are few obscurities. "They" is an intentionally contemptuous reference to the members of the amorphous crowd, which divides into individuals for an instant, only to reunite with "a Hydra's vile spasm." "The dishonored flow of some dark brew" may, in view of Mallarmé's more than metaphysical poetic habits, mean stout.

It seems harder to explain clearly "Calm block fallen down here from some dark disaster." It may be an allusion to the volcanic origin of basalt. At any rate, this idea of a cosmic catastrophe makes even stranger the notion of this immense, bare block, an erratic rock or giant meteorite. At first apparently meaningless, it rises black, calm, and strange, like Poe himself, "Such as to himself eternity's changed him." This is why we are not astonished at the irrelevance; the overtones of rock and poet are too strongly related. The "dark disaster" whence the block has fallen is subtly confused with the disasters of genius, the struggle of angel and hydra grows more cosmic, and Poe, if possible, more granitic. Thus the last tercet suddenly acquires a terrifying and desolate grandeur. For this idea of an erratic block suggests an immense, empty plain, from which all life has disappeared. (Notice how, in the first tercet, all idea of human beings has disappeared, and there is no longer question of any but elemental forces—rock and cloud.) The spectacle presented to the imagination is that of an empty earth and an atmosphere of desolation. The last line can now display its sinister extent. At the end of the sonnet, "Blasphemy," like a flock of crows, wheels in an empty sky unable to cross a black boundary, over which the wrath of God seems to hang.

WALT WHITMAN

EDGAR POE'S SIGNIFICANCE

Jan. 1, '80.

IN DIAGNOSING this disease called humanity—to assume for
the nonce what seems a chief mood of the personality and
writings of my subject—I have thought that poets, somewhere or other on the list, present the most mark'd indications. Comprehending artists in a mass, musicians, painters,
actors, and so on, and considering each and all of them as
radiations or flanges of that furious whirling wheel, poetry,
the centre and axis of the whole, where else indeed may
we so well investigate the causes, growths, tally-marks of
the time—the age's matter and malady?

By common consent there is nothing better for man or
woman than a perfect and noble life, morally without flaw,
happily balanced in activity, physically sound and pure,
giving its due proportion, and no more, to the sympathetic,
the human emotional element—a life, in all these, unhasting,
unresting, untiring to the end. And yet there is another
shape of personality dearer far to the artist-sense, (which
likes the play of strongest lights and shades) where the
perfect character, the good, the heroic, although never attain'd, is never lost sight of, but through failures, sorrows,
temporary downfalls, is return'd to again and again, and
while often violated, is passionately adhered to as long as
mind, muscles, voice, obey the power we call volition. This

sort of personality we see more or less in Burns, Byron, Schiller, and George Sand. But we do not see it in Edgar Poe. (All this is the result of reading at intervals the last three days a new volume of his poems—I took it on my rambles down by the pond, and by degrees read it all through there.) While to the character first outlined the service Poe renders is certainly that entire contrast and contradiction which is next best to fully exemplifying it.

Almost without the first sign of moral principle, or of the concrete or its heroisms, or the simpler affections of the heart, Poe's verses illustrate an intense faculty for technical and abstract beauty, with the rhyming art to excess, an incorrigible propensity toward nocturnal themes, a demoniac undertone behind every page—and, by final judgment, probably belong among the electric lights of imaginative literature, brilliant and dazzling, but with no heat. There is an indescribable magnetism about the poet's life and reminiscences, as well as the poems. To one who could work out their subtle retracing and retrospect, the latter would make a close tally no doubt between the author's birth and antecedents, his childhood and youth, his physique, his so-call'd education, his studies and associates, the literary and social Baltimore, Richmond, Philadelphia and New York, of those times—not only the places and circumstances in themselves, but often, very often, in a strange spurning of, and reaction from them all.

The following from a report in the Washington *Star* of November 16, 1875, may afford those who care for it something further of my point of view toward this interesting figure and influence of our era. There occurr'd about that date in Baltimore a public reburial of Poe's remains, and dedication of a monument over the grave:

"Being in Washington on a visit at the time, 'the old gray' went over to Baltimore, and though ill from paralysis, consented to hobble up and silently take a seat on the platform, but refused to make any speech, saying, 'I have felt a strong impulse to come over and be here today myself in memory of Poe, which I have obey'd, but not the slightest impulse to make a speech, which, my dear friends, must also be obeyed.' In an informal circle, however, in conversation after the ceremonies, Whitman said: 'For a long while, and until lately, I had a distaste for Poe's writings. I wanted, and still want for poetry, the clear sun shining, and fresh air blowing—the strength and power of health, not of delirium, even amid the stormiest passions—with always the background of the eternal moralities. Non-complying with these requirements, Poe's genius has yet conquer'd a special recognition for itself, and I too have come to fully admit it, and appreciate it and him.

"'In a dream I once had, I saw a vessel on the sea, at midnight, in a storm. It was no great full-rigg'd ship, nor majestic steamer, steering firmly through the gale, but seem'd one of those superb little schooner yachts I had often seen lying anchor'd, rocking so jauntily, in the waters around New York, or up Long Island sound—now flying uncontroll'd with torn sails and broken spars through the wild sleet and winds and waves of the night. On the deck was a slender, slight, beautiful figure, a dim man, apparently enjoying all the terror, the murk, and the dislocation of which he was the center and the victim. That figure of my lurid dream might stand for Edgar Poe, his spirit, his fortunes, and his poems —themselves all lurid dreams.'"

Much more may be said, but I most desired to exploit the idea put at the beginning. By its popular poets the calibers of an age, the weak spots of its embankments, its subcurrents (often more significant than the biggest surface ones), are unerringly indicated. The lush and the weird that have taken such extraordinary possession of nineteenth century verse-lovers—what mean they? The inevitable tendency of poetic culture to morbidity, abnormal beauty—the sickliness of all technical thought or refinement in itself— the abnegation of the perennial and democratic concretes at first hand, the body, the earth and sea, sex and the like— and the substitution of something for them at second or third hand—what bearings have they on current pathological study?

THIS MONOGRAPH by Henry James on Hawthorne, published in 1879, must be the first extended study ever made of an American writer. It still remains one of the best; and it is one of the most satisfactory of the earlier books of James. It is curious to note the various ways in which the other American writers—Poe, Melville, James, and Eliot—deal with Hawthorne. They seem to get out of him rather different things; but they agree in being particularly interested in him and admiring him more, perhaps, than we usually do today. For the Americans who read Hawthorne in his lifetime he was certainly both original and important. The work of all three of these younger writers has certain fundamental features in common with the work of Hawthorne; and even Eliot glances back to pay a tribute to him.

The novel and short story in America had never before the end of the century particularly concerned itself either with personality or with social observation as fiction had in France, England, and Russia. We had regional and professional differences, which our novelists such as Cooper show, and we had *Uncle Tom's Cabin,* and in the latter half of the century we had social novelists of the second rank like

George Cable and William Dean Howells; but social categories were few and fluid, and, except in the South (see Faulkner), we had no such soil for personalities as Dickens or Tolstoy, say, had: where characters could take root and ripen like the cucumbers and vegetable marrows that Mrs. Nickleby's eccentric neighbor used to throw at her over the wall, or perfect themselves each in its species like the bears and the wolves and the woodcock that the country people in Tolstoy love to hunt. All through the nineteenth century our best stories—Poe's tales, *The Scarlet Letter, Moby Dick, Huckleberry Finn*—tend to be symbolical fables, moral parables, fairy tales. The first important exception to this is precisely Henry James, who regarded himself as a realist and set out to become, in the Balzacian sense, the secretary of American society. But some of the earliest of James's stories are poetical-philosophical legends which probably owe as much to Hawthorne as to the Balzacian *Peau de Chagrin* and *Le Chef-d'oeuvre Inconnu;* and he was to revert in *The Golden Bowl,* his last completed novel, to a symbolism that goes straight back to Hawthorne: the golden bowl itself and the curio dealer who sells it belong certainly to the world of *The Birth-Mark* and *The Minister's Black Veil.* And there is also the moral preoccupation, the refinement of the Puritan conscience, of which Hawthorne had been the great exemplar and which was to continue to motivate James through the whole of his literary career— an indication of Hawthorne's authority which is all the more impressive because James was not himself a New Englander but a New Yorker of Irish stock whose father had been a Swedenborgian liberal and who had been educated partly abroad.

HENRY JAMES

HAWTHORNE

I. Early Years

It will be necessary, for several reasons, to give this short
sketch the form rather of a critical essay than of a biography.
The data for a life of Nathaniel Hawthorne are the reverse
of copious, and even if they were abundant they would
serve but in a limited measure the purpose of the biographer.
Hawthorne's career was probably as tranquil and unevent-
ful a one as ever fell to the lot of a man of letters; it was
almost strikingly deficient in incident, in what may be
called the dramatic quality. Few men of equal genius and of
equal eminence can have led on the whole a simpler life.
His six volumes of *Note-Books* illustrate this simplicity; they
are a sort of monument to an unagitated fortune. Hawthorne's career had few vicissitudes or variations; it was
passed for the most part in a small and homogeneous society,
in a provincial, rural community; it had few perceptible
points of contact with what is called the world, with public
events, with the manners of his time, even with the life of
his neighbors. Its literary incidents are not numerous. He
produced, in quantity, but little. His works consist of four
novels and the fragment of another, five volumes of short
tales, a collection of sketches, and a couple of storybooks

for children. And yet some account of the man and the writer is well worth giving. Whatever may have been Hawthorne's private lot, he has the importance of being the most beautiful and most eminent representative of a literature. The importance of the literature may be questioned, but at any rate, in the field of letters, Hawthorne is the most valuable example of the American genius. That genius has not, as a whole, been literary; but Hawthorne was on his limited scale a master of expression. He is the writer to whom his countrymen most confidently point when they wish to make a claim to have enriched the mother tongue, and, judging from present appearances, he will long occupy this honorable position. If there is something very fortunate for him in the way that he borrows an added relief from the absence of competitors in his own line and from the general flatness of the literary field that surrounds him, there is also, to a spectator, something almost touching in his situation. He was so modest and delicate a genius that we may fancy him appealing from the lonely honor of a representative attitude—perceiving a painful incongruity between his imponderable literary baggage and the large conditions of American life. Hawthorne on the one side is so subtle and slender and unpretending, and the American world on the other is so vast and various and substantial, that it might seem to the author of *The Scarlet Letter* and the *Mosses from an Old Manse* that we render him a poor service in contrasting his proportions with those of a great civilization. But our author must accept the awkward as well as the graceful side of his fame; for he has the advantage of pointing a valuable moral. This moral is that the flower of art blooms only where the soil is deep, that it takes a great deal of history to produce a little literature, that it needs a complex social machinery to set a writer in motion. American civilization has hitherto had other things to do than to produce flowers, and before giving birth to writers it has wisely occupied itself with providing something for them to write about. Three or four beautiful talents of trans-Atlantic growth are the sum of what the world usually recognizes, and in this modest nosegay the genius of Hawthorne is admitted to have the rarest and sweetest fragrance.

His very simplicity has been in his favor; it has helped him to appear complete and homogeneous. To talk of his being national would be to force the note and make a mistake of proportion; but he is, in spite of the absence of the realistic quality, intensely and vividly local. Out of the soil of New England he sprang—in a crevice of that immitigable granite he sprouted and bloomed. Half of the interest that he possesses for an American reader with any turn for analysis must reside in his latent New England savor; and I think it no more than just to say that whatever entertainment he may yield to those who know him at a distance, it is an almost indispensable condition of properly appreciating him to have received a personal impression of the manners, the morals, indeed of the very climate, of the great region of which the remarkable city of Boston is the metropolis. The cold, bright air of New England seems to blow through his pages, and these, in the opinion of many people, are the medium in which it is most agreeable to make the acquaintance of that tonic atmosphere. As to whether it is worth while to seek to know something of New England in order to extract a more intimate quality from *The House of the Seven Gables* and *The Blithedale Romance*, I need not pronounce; but it is certain that a considerable observation of the society to which these productions were more directly addressed is a capital preparation for enjoying them. I have alluded to the absence in Hawthorne of that quality of realism which is now so much in fashion, an absence in regard to which there will of course be more to say; and yet I think I am not fanciful in saying that he testifies to the sentiments of the society in which he flourished almost as pertinently (proportions observed) as Balzac and some of his descendants—MM. Flaubert and Zola—testify to the manners and morals of the French people. He was not a man with a literary theory; he was guiltless of a system, and I am not sure that he had ever heard of Realism, this remarkable compound having (although it was invented sometime earlier) come into general use only since his death. He had certainly not proposed to himself to give an account of the social idiosyncrasies of his fellow citizens, for his touch on such points is always light and vague, he has none of the apparatus of an historian, and his shadowy style of portraiture never suggests a rigid standard of accuracy. Nevertheless, he virtually offers the most vivid reflection of New England life that has found its way into literature. His value in this respect is not diminished by the fact that he has not attempted to portray the usual Yankee of comedy, and that he has been almost culpably indifferent to his opportunities for commemorating the variations of colloquial English that may be observed in the New World. His characters do not express themselves in the dialect of the *Biglow Papers*—their language indeed is apt to be too elegant, too delicate. They are not portraits of actual types, and in their phraseology there is nothing imitative. But nonetheless, Hawthorne's work savors thoroughly of the local soil—it is redolent of the social system in which he had his being.

This could hardly fail to be the case, when the man himself was so deeply rooted in the soil. Hawthorne sprang from the primitive New England stock; he had a very definite and conspicuous pedigree. He was born at Salem, Massachusetts, on the 4th of July, 1804, and his birthday was the great American festival, the anniversary of the Declaration of national Independence.[1] Hawthorne was in his disposition an unqualified and unflinching American; he found occasion to give us the measure of the fact during the seven years that he spent in Europe toward the close of his life; and this was no more than proper on the part of

[1]It is proper that before I go further I should acknowledge my large obligations to the only biography of our author, of any considerable length, that has been written—the little volume entitled *A Study of Hawthorne,* by Mr. George Parsons Lathrop, the son-in-law of the subject of the work. (Boston, 1876.) To this ingenious and sympathetic sketch, in which the author has taken great pains to collect the more interesting facts of Hawthorne's life, I am greatly indebted. Mr. Lathrop's work is not pitched in the key which many another writer would have chosen, and his tone is not to my sense the truly critical one; but without the help afforded by his elaborate essay, the present little volume could not have been prepared.

a man who had enjoyed the honor of coming into the world
on the day on which of all the days in the year the great
Republic enjoys her acutest fit of self-consciousness. Moreover, a person who has been ushered into life by the ringing
of bells and the booming of cannon (unless indeed he be
frightened straight out of it again by the uproar of his
awakening) receives by this very fact an injunction to do
something great, something that will justify such striking
natal accompaniments. Hawthorne was by race of the clearest Puritan strain. His earliest American ancestor (who
wrote the name "Hathorne"—the shape in which it was
transmitted to Nathaniel, who inserted the *w*) was the
younger son of a Wiltshire family, whose residence, according to a note of our author's in 1837, was "Wigcastle,
Wigton." Hawthorne, in the note in question, mentions the
gentleman who was at that time the head of the family;
but it does not appear that he at any period renewed acquaintance with his English kinsfolk. Major William Hathorne came out to Massachusetts in the early years of the
Puritan settlement; in 1635 or 1636, according to the note
to which I have just alluded; in 1630, according to information presumably more accurate. He was one of the band of
companions of the virtuous and exemplary John Winthrop,
the almost lifelong royal Governor of the young colony, and
the brightest and most amiable figure in the early Puritan
annals. How amiable William Hathorne may have been I
know not, but he was evidently of the stuff of which the
citizens of the Commonwealth were best advised to be made.
He was a sturdy fighting man, doing solid execution upon
both the inward and outward enemies of the State. The
latter were the savages, the former the Quakers; the energy
expended by the early Puritans in resistance to the tomahawk not weakening their disposition to deal with spiritual
dangers. They employed the same—or almost the same—
weapons in both directions; the flintlock and the halberd
against the Indians, and the cat-o'-nine-tails against the
heretics. One of the longest, though by no means one of
the most successful, of Hawthorne's shorter tales (*The
Gentle Boy*) deals with this pitiful persecution of the least

aggressive of all schismatic bodies. William Hathorne, who
had been made a magistrate of the town of Salem, where a
grant of land had been offered him as an inducement to
residence, figures in New England history as having given
orders that "Anne Coleman and four of her friends" should
be whipped through Salem, Boston, and Dedham. This
Anne Coleman, I suppose, is the woman alluded to in that
fine passage in the Introduction to *The Scarlet Letter,* in
which Hawthorne pays a qualified tribute to the founder
of the American branch of his race:

> The figure of that first ancestor, invested by family tradition
> with a dim and dusky grandeur, was present to my boyish
> imagination as far back as I can remember. It still haunts me,
> and induces a sort of home-feeling with the past, which I
> scarcely claim in reference to the present, phase of the town.
> I seem to have a stronger claim to a residence here on account
> of this grave, bearded, sable-cloaked, and steeple-crowned pro-
> genitor—who came so early, with his Bible and his sword, and
> trod the unworn street with such a stately port, and made so
> large a figure as a man of war and peace—a stronger claim than
> for myself, whose name is seldom heard and my face hardly
> known. He was a soldier, legislator, judge; he was a ruler in the
> church; he had all the Puritanic traits, both good and evil. He
> was likewise a bitter persecutor, as witness the Quakers, who
> have remembered him in their histories, and relate an incident
> of his hard severity towards a woman of their sect which will
> last longer, it is to be feared, than any of his better deeds,
> though these were many.

William Hathorne died in 1681; but those hard qualities
that his descendant speaks of were reproduced in his son
John, who bore the title of Colonel, and who was connected,
too intimately for his honor, with that deplorable episode
of New England history, the persecution of the so-called
Witches of Salem. John Hathorne is introduced into the
little drama entitled *The Salem Farms* in Longfellow's *New
England Tragedies.* I know not whether he had the com-
pensating merits of his father, but our author speaks of him,
in the continuation of the passage I have just quoted, as
having made himself so conspicuous in the martyrdom of

the witches that their blood may be said to have left a stain upon him. "So deep a stain, indeed," Hawthorne adds, characteristically, "that his old dry bones in the Charter Street burial ground must still retain it, if they have not crumbled utterly to dust." Readers of *The House of the Seven Gables* will remember that the story concerns itself with a family which is supposed to be overshadowed by a curse launched against one of its earlier members by a poor man occupying a lowlier place in the world, whom this ill-advised ancestor had been the means of bringing to justice for the crime of witchcraft. Hawthorne apparently found the idea of the history of the Pyncheons in his own family annals. His witch-judging ancestor was reported to have incurred a malediction from one of his victims, in consequence of which the prosperity of the race faded utterly away. "I know not," the passage I have already quoted goes on, "whether these ancestors of mine bethought themselves to repent and ask pardon of Heaven for their cruelties, or whether they are now groaning under the heavy consequences of them in another state of being. At all events, I, the present writer, hereby take shame upon myself for their sakes, and pray that any curse incurred by them—as I have heard, and as the dreary and unprosperous condition of the race for some time back would argue to exist —may be now and henceforth removed." The two first American Hathornes had been people of importance and responsibility; but with the third generation the family lapsed into an obscurity from which it emerged in the very person of the writer who begs so gracefully for a turn in its affairs. It is very true, Hawthorne proceeds, in the Introduction to *The Scarlet Letter,* that from the original point of view such luster as he might have contrived to confer upon the name would have appeared more than questionable.

Either of these stern and black-browed Puritans would have thought it quite a sufficient retribution for his sins that after so long a lapse of years the old trunk of the family tree, with so much venerable moss upon it, should have borne, as its topmost bough, an idler like myself. No aim that I have ever cherished would they recognize as laudable; no success of mine, if my life, beyond its domestic scope, had ever been brightened by success, would they deem otherwise than worthless, if not positively disgraceful. "What is he?" murmurs one gray shadow of my forefathers to the other. "A writer of story-books! What kind of a business in life, what manner of glorifying God, or being serviceable to mankind in his day and generation, may that be? Why, the degenerate fellow might as well have been a fiddler!" Such are the compliments bandied between my great grandsires and myself across the gulf of time! And yet, let them scorn me as they will, strong traits of their nature have intertwined themselves with mine.

In this last observation we may imagine that there was not a little truth. Poet and novelist as Hawthorne was, skeptic and dreamer and little of a man of action, late-coming fruit of a tree which might seem to have lost the power to bloom, he was morally, in an appreciative degree, a chip of the old block. His forefathers had crossed the Atlantic for conscience' sake, and it was the idea of the urgent conscience that haunted the imagination of their so-called degenerate successor. The Puritan strain in his blood ran clear—there are passages in his Diaries, kept during his residence in Europe, which might almost have been written by the grimmest of the old Salem worthies. To him as to them, the consciousness of *sin* was the most importunate fact of life, and if they had undertaken to write little tales, this baleful substantive, with its attendant adjective, could hardly have been more frequent in their pages than in those of their fanciful descendant. Hawthorne had moreover in his composition, contemplator and dreamer as he was, an element of simplicity and rigidity, a something plain and masculine and sensible, which might have kept his black-browed grandsires on better terms with him than he admits to be possible. However little they might have appreciated the artist, they would have approved of the man. The play of Hawthorne's intellect was light and capricious, but the man himself was firm and rational. The imagination was profane, but the temper was not degenerate.

The "dreary and unprosperous condition" that he speaks of in regard to the fortunes of his family is an allusion to the fact that several generations followed each other on the soil in which they had been planted, that during the eighteenth

century a succession of Hathornes trod the simple streets of
Salem without ever conferring any especial luster upon the
town or receiving, presumably, any great delight from it. A
hundred years of Salem would perhaps be rather a dead
weight for any family to carry, and we venture to imagine
that the Hathornes were dull and depressed. They did what
they could, however, to improve their situation; they trod the
Salem streets as little as possible. They went to sea, and made
long voyages; seamanship became the regular profession of
the family. Hawthorne has said it in charming language.
"From father to son, for above a hundred years, they followed the sea; a gray-headed shipmaster, in each generation,
retiring from the quarter-deck to the homestead, while a boy
of fourteen took the hereditary place before the mast, confronting the salt spray and the gale which had blustered
against his sire and grandsire. The boy also, in due time,
passed from the forecastle to the cabin, spent a tempestuous
manhood, and returned from his world-wanderings to grow
old and die and mingle his dust with the natal earth." Our
author's grandfather, Daniel Hathorne, is mentioned by Mr.
Lathrop, his biographer and son-in-law, as a hardy privateer
during the War of Independence. His father, from whom he
was named, was also a shipmaster, and he died in foreign
lands, in the exercise of his profession. He was carried off
by a fever, at Surinam, in 1808. He left three children, of
whom Nathaniel was the only boy. The boy's mother, who
had been a Miss Manning, came of a New England stock
almost as long established as that of her husband; she is
described by our author's biographer as a woman of remarkable beauty, and by an authority whom he quotes as being
"a minute observer of religious festivals," of "feasts, fasts,
new moons, and Sabbaths." Of feasts the poor lady in her
Puritanic home can have had but a very limited number to
celebrate; but of new moons, she may be supposed to have
enjoyed the usual, and of Sabbaths even more than the
usual, proportion.

In quiet provincial Salem, Nathaniel Hawthorne passed
the greater part of his boyhood, as well as many years of his
later life. Mr. Lathrop has much to say about the ancient

picturesqueness of the place, and about the mystic influences it would project upon such a mind and character as Hawthorne's. These things are always relative, and in appreciating them everything depends upon the point of view. Mr. Lathrop writes for American readers, who in such a matter as this are very easy to please.[1] Americans have as a general thing a hungry passion for the picturesque, and they are so fond of local color that they contrive to perceive it in localities in which the amateurs of other countries would detect only the most neutral tints. History, as yet, has left in the United States but so thin and impalpable a deposit that we very soon touch the hard substratum of nature; and nature herself, in the western world, has the peculiarity of seeming rather crude and immature. The very air looks new and young; the light of the sun seems fresh and innocent, as if it knew as yet but few of the secrets of the world and none of the weariness of shining; the vegetation has the appearance of not having reached its majority. A large juvenility is stamped upon the face of things, and in the vividness of the present, the past, which died so young and had time to produce so little, attracts but scanty attention. I doubt whether English observers would discover any very striking trace of it in the ancient town of Salem. Still, with all respect to a York and a Shrewsbury, to a Toledo and a Verona, Salem has a physiognomy in which the past plays a more important part than the present. It is of course a very recent past; but one must remember that the dead of yesterday are not more alive than those of a century ago. I know not of what picturesqueness Hawthorne was conscious in his respectable birthplace; I suspect his perception of it was less keen than his biographer assumes it to have been; but he must have felt at least that of whatever complexity of earlier life there had been in the country, the elm-shadowed streets of Salem were a recognizable memento. He has made considerable mention of the place, here and there, in his tales; but he has nowhere dilated upon it very lovingly, and it is noteworthy that in *The House of the Seven Gables,* the only one of his novels

[1] Henry James's study was written for the English Men of Letters series.

of which the scene is laid in it, he has by no means availed himself of the opportunity to give a description of it. He had of course a filial fondness for it—a deep-seated sense of connection with it; but he must have spent some very dreary years there, and the two feelings, the mingled tenderness and rancor, are visible in the Introduction to *The Scarlet Letter.*

The old town of Salem [he writes] my native place, though I have dwelt much away from it, both in boyhood and in maturer years—possesses, or did possess, a hold on my affections, the force of which I have never realized during my seasons of actual residence here. Indeed, so far as the physical aspect is concerned, with its flat, unvaried surface, covered chiefly with wooden houses, few or none of which pretend to architectural beauty; its irregularity, which is neither picturesque nor quaint, but only tame; its long and lazy street, lounging wearisomely through the whole extent of the peninsula, with Gallows Hill and New Guinea at one end, and a view of the almshouse at the other—such being the features of my native town it would be quite as reasonable to form a sentimental attachment to a disarranged checkerboard.

But he goes on to say that he has never divested himself of the sense of intensely belonging to it—that the spell of the continuity of his life with that of his predecessors has never been broken. "It is no matter that the place is joyless for him; that he is weary of the old wooden houses, the mud and the dust, the dead level of site and sentiment, the chill east wind, and the chilliest of social atmospheres,—all these and whatever faults besides he may see or imagine, are nothing to the purpose. The spell survives, and just as powerfully as if the natal spot were an earthly paradise." There is a very American quality in this perpetual consciousness of a spell on Hawthorne's part; it is only in a country where newness and change and brevity of tenure are the common substance of life that the fact of one's ancestors having lived for a hundred and seventy years in a single spot would become an element of one's morality. It is only an imaginative American that would feel urged to keep reverting to this circumstance, to keep analyzing and cunningly considering it.

The Salem of today has, as New England towns go, a

physiognomy of its own, and in spite of Hawthorne's analogy of the disarranged draughtboard, it is a decidedly agreeable one. The spreading elms in its streets, the proportion of large, square, honorable-looking houses, suggesting an easy, copious material life, the little gardens, the grassy waysides, the open windows, the air of space and salubrity and decency, and above all the intimation of larger antecedents—these things compose a picture which has little of the element that painters call depth of tone, but which is not without something that they would admit to be style. To English eyes the oldest and most honorable of the smaller American towns must seem in a manner primitive and rustic; the shabby, straggling, village-quality appears marked in them, and their social tone is not unnaturally inferred to bear the village stamp. Village-like they are, and it would be no gross incivility to describe them as large, respectable, prosperous, democratic villages. But even a village, in a great and vigorous democracy, where there are no overshadowing squires, where the "county" has no social existence, where the villagers are conscious of no superincumbent strata of gentility, piled upwards into vague regions of privilege—even a village is not an institution to accept of more or less graceful patronage; it thinks extremely well of itself, and is absolute in its own regard. Salem is a seaport, but it is a seaport deserted and decayed. It belongs to that rather melancholy group of old coast towns, scattered along the great sea-face of New England, and of which the list is completed by the names of Portsmouth, Plymouth, New Bedford, Newburyport, Newport—superannuated centers of the traffic with foreign lands, which have seen their trade carried away from them by the greater cities. As Hawthorne says, their ventures have gone "to swell, needlessly and imperceptibly, the mighty flood of commerce at New York or Boston." Salem, at the beginning of the present century, played a great part in the Eastern trade; it was the residence of enterprising shipowners who despatched their vessels to Indian and Chinese seas. It was a place of large fortunes, many of which have remained, though the activity that produced them has passed away. These successful traders constituted what Hawthorne calls "the aristocratic class." He alludes in one of his slighter sketches (*The Sister Years*) to the sway of this class and the "moral influence of wealth" having been more marked in Salem than in any other New England town. The sway, we may believe, was on the whole gently exercised, and the moral influence of wealth was not exerted in the cause of immorality. Hawthorne was probably but imperfectly conscious of an advantage which familiarity had made stale—the fact that he lived in the most democratic and most virtuous of modern communities. Of the virtue it is but civil to suppose that his own family had a liberal share; but not much of the wealth, apparently, came into their way. Hawthorne was not born to a patrimony, and his income, later in life, never exceeded very modest proportions.

Of his childish years there appears to be nothing very definite to relate, though his biographer devotes a good many graceful pages to them. There is a considerable sameness in the behavior of small boys, and it is probable that if we were acquainted with the details of our author's infantine career we should find it to be made up of the same pleasures and pains as that of many ingenuous lads for whom fame has had nothing in keeping.

The absence of precocious symptoms of genius is on the whole more striking in the lives of men who have distinguished themselves than their juvenile promise; though it must be added that Mr. Lathrop has made out, as he was almost in duty bound to do, a very good case in favor of Hawthorne's having been an interesting child. He was not at any time what would be called a sociable man, and there is therefore nothing unexpected in the fact that he was fond of long walks in which he was not known to have had a companion. "Juvenile literature" was but scantily known at that time, and the enormous and extraordinary contribution made by the United States to this department of human happiness was locked in the bosom of futurity. The young Hawthorne, therefore, like many of his contemporaries, was constrained to amuse himself, for want of anything better, with the *Pilgrim's Progress* and the *Faery Queen*. A boy may have worse company than Bunyan and Spenser, and it is

very probable that in his childish rambles our author may
have had associates of whom there could be no record. When
he was nine years old he met with an accident at school
which threatened for a while to have serious results. He was
struck on the foot by a ball and so severely lamed that he
was kept at home for a long time, and had not completely
recovered before his twelfth year. His school, it is to be supposed, was the common day school of New England—the
primary factor in that extraordinarily pervasive system of
instruction in the plainer branches of learning which forms
one of the principal ornaments of American life. In 1818,
when he was fourteen years old, he was taken by his mother
to live in the house of an uncle, her brother, who was
established in the town of Raymond, near Lake Sebago, in
the State of Maine. The immense State of Maine, in the year
1818, must have had an even more magnificently natural
character than it possesses at the present day, and the uncle's
dwelling, in consequence of being in a little smarter style
than the primitive structures that surrounded it, was known
by the villagers as Manning's Folly. Mr. Lathrop pronounces
this region to be of a "weird and woodsy" character; and
Hawthorne, later in life, spoke of it to a friend as the place
where "I first got my cursed habits of solitude." The outlook,
indeed, for an embryonic novelist, would not seem to have
been cheerful; the social dreariness of a small New England
community lost amid the forests of Maine, at the beginning
of the present century, must have been consummate. But
for a boy with a relish for solitude there were many natural
resources, and we can understand that Hawthorne should in
after years have spoken very tenderly of this episode. "I
lived in Maine like a bird of the air, so perfect was the freedom I enjoyed." During the long summer days he roamed,
gun in hand, through the great woods, and during the moonlight nights of winter, says his biographer, quoting another
informant, "he would skate until midnight, all alone, upon
Sebago Lake, with the deep shadows of the icy hills on either
hand."

In 1819 he was sent back to Salem to school, and in the
following year he wrote to his mother, who had remained at

Raymond (the boy had found a home at Salem with another uncle), "I have left school and have begun to fit for college under Benjm. L. Oliver, Lawyer. So you are in danger of having one learned man in your family. . . . I get my lessons at home and recite them to him (Mr. Oliver) at seven o'clock in the morning. . . . Shall you want me to be a Minister, Doctor, or Lawyer? A Minister I will not be." He adds, at the close of this epistle: "O how I wish I was again with you, with nothing to do but to go a-gunning! But the happiest days of my life are gone." In 1821, in his seventeenth year, he entered Bowdoin College, at Brunswick, Maine. This institution was in the year 1821—a quarter of a century after its foundation—a highly honorable, but not a very elaborately organized, nor a particularly impressive, seat of learning. I say it was not impressive, but I immediately remember that impressions depend upon the minds receiving them; and that to a group of simple New England lads, upwards of sixty years ago, the halls and groves of Bowdoin, neither dense nor lofty though they can have been, may have seemed replete with academic stateliness. It was a homely, simple, frugal "country college," of the old-fashioned American stamp; exerting within its limits a civilizing influence, working, amid the forests and the lakes, the log-houses and clearings, toward the amenities and humanities and other collegiate graces, and offering a very sufficient education to the future lawyers, merchants, clergymen, politicians, and editors, of the very active and knowledge-loving community that supported it. It did more than this—it numbered poets and statesmen among its undergraduates, and on the roll call of its sons it has several distinguished names. Among Hawthorne's fellow-students was Henry Wadsworth Longfellow, who divides with our author the honor of being the most distinguished of American men of letters. I know not whether Mr. Longfellow was especially intimate with Hawthorne at this period (they were very good friends later in life), but with two of his companions he formed a friendship which lasted always. One of these was Franklin Pierce, who was destined to fill what Hawthorne calls "the most august position in the world." Pierce was elected President of the

United States in 1852. The other was Horatio Bridge, who afterwards served with distinction in the Navy, and to whom the charming prefatory letter of the collection of tales published under the name of the *Snow Image* is addressed. "If anybody is responsible at this day for my being an author it is yourself. I know not whence your faith came; but while we were lads together at a country college—gathering blueberries in study-hours under those tall academic pines; or watching the great logs as they tumbled along the current of the Androscoggin; or shooting pigeons and gray squirrels in the woods; or bat-fowling in the summer twilight; or catching trout in that shadowy little stream which, I suppose, is still wandering riverward through the forest—though you and I will never cast a line in it again—two idle lads, in short (as we need not fear to acknowledge now), doing a hundred things the faculty never heard of, or else it had been worse for us—still it was your prognostic of your friend's destiny that he was to be a writer of fiction." That is a very pretty picture, but it is a picture of happy urchins at school, rather than of undergraduates "panting," as Macaulay says, "for one and twenty." Poor Hawthorne was indeed thousands of miles away from Oxford and Cambridge; that touch about the blueberries and the logs on the Androscoggin tells the whole story, and strikes the note, as it were, of his circumstances. But if the pleasures at Bowdoin were not expensive, so neither were the penalties. The amount of Hawthorne's collegiate bill for one term was less than 4*l.*, and of this sum more than 9*s.* was made up of fines. The fines, however, were not heavy. Mr. Lathrop prints a letter addressed by the President to "Mrs. Elizabeth C. Hathorne," requesting her co-operation with the officers of this college, "in the attempt to induce your son faithfully to observe the laws of this institution." He has just been fined fifty cents for playing cards for money during the preceding term. "Perhaps he might not have gamed," the professor adds, "were it not for the influence of a student whom we have dismissed from college." The biographer quotes a letter from Hawthorne to one of his sisters, in which the writer says, in allusion to this remark, that it is a great mistake to think that he has been led away by the wicked ones. "I was fully as willing to play as the person he suspects of having enticed me, and would have been influenced by no one. I have a great mind to commence playing again, merely to show him that I scorn to be seduced by another into anything wrong." There is something in these few words that accords with the impression that the observant reader of Hawthorne gathers of the personal character that underlay his duskily-sportive imagination—an impression of simple manliness and transparent honesty.

He appears to have been a fair scholar, but not a brilliant one; and it is very probable that as the standard of scholarship at Bowdoin was not high, he graduated nonetheless comfortably on this account. Mr. Lathrop is able to testify to the fact, by no means a surprising one, that he wrote verses at college, though the few stanzas that the biographer quotes are not such as to make us especially regret that his rhyming mood was a transient one.

> The ocean hath its silent caves,
> Deep, quiet, and alone.
> Though there be fury on the waves,
> Beneath them there is none.

That quatrain may suffice to decorate our page. And in connection with his college days I may mention his first novel, a short romance entitled *Fanshawe*, which was published in Boston in 1828, three years after he graduated. It was probably also written after that event, but the scene of the tale is laid at Bowdoin (which figures under an altered name), and Hawthorne's attitude with regard to the book, even shortly after it was published, was such as to assign it to this boyish period. It was issued anonymously, but he so repented of his venture that he annihilated the edition, of which, according to Mr. Lathrop, "not half-a-dozen copies are now known to be extant." I have seen none of these rare volumes, and I know nothing of *Fanshawe* but what the writer just quoted relates. It is the story of a young lady who goes in rather an odd fashion to reside at "Harley College" (equivalent of Bowdoin), under the care and guardianship of Dr. Melmoth, the President of the institution, a venerable, amiable, unworldly, and henpecked scholar. Here she becomes very naturally an object of interest to two of the students; in regard to whom I cannot do better than quote Mr. Lathrop. One of these young men "is Edward Wolcott, a wealthy, handsome, generous, healthy young fellow from one of the seaport towns; and the other Fanshawe, the hero, who is a poor but ambitious recluse, already passing into a decline through overmuch devotion to books and meditation. Fanshawe, though the deeper nature of the two, and intensely moved by his new passion, perceiving that a union between himself and Ellen could not be a happy one, resigns the hope of it from the beginning. But circumstances bring him into intimate relation with her. The real action of the book, after the preliminaries, takes up only some three days, and turns upon the attempt of a man named Butler to entice Ellen away under his protection, then marry her, and secure the fortune to which she is heiress. This scheme is partly frustrated by circumstances, and Butler's purpose towards Ellen thus becomes a much more sinister one. From this she is rescued by Fanshawe, and knowing that he loves her, but is concealing his passion, she gives him the opportunity and the right to claim her hand. For a moment the rush of desire and hope is so great that he hesitates; then he refuses to take advantage of her generosity, and parts with her for a last time. Ellen becomes engaged to Wolcott, who had won her heart from the first; and Fanshawe, sinking into rapid consumption, dies before his class graduates." The story must have had a good deal of innocent lightness; and it is a proof of how little the world of observation lay open to Hawthorne, at this time, that he should have had no other choice than to make his little drama go forward between the rather naked walls of Bowdoin, where the presence of his heroine was an essential incongruity. He was twenty-four years old, but the "world," in its social sense, had not disclosed itself to him. He had, however, already, at moments, a very pretty writer's touch, as witness this passage, quoted by Mr. Lathrop, and which is worth transcribing. The heroine has gone off with the nefarious Butler, and the good Dr. Melmoth starts in pursuit of her, attended by young Wolcott.

"Alas, youth, these are strange times," observed the President, "when a doctor of divinity and an undergraduate set forth, like a knight-errant and his squire, in search of a stray damsel. Methinks I am an epitome of the church militant, or a new species of polemical divinity. Pray Heaven, however, there be no such encounter in store for us; for I utterly forgot to provide myself with weapons."

"I took some thought for that matter, reverend knight," replied Edward, whose imagination was highly tickled by Dr. Melmoth's chivalrous comparison.

"Aye, I see that you have girded on a sword," said the divine. "But wherewith shall I defend myself? my hand being empty except of this golden-headed staff, the gift of Mr. Langton."

"One of these, if you will accept it," answered Edward, exhibiting a brace of pistols, "will serve to begin the conflict before you join the battle hand to hand."

"Nay, I shall find little safety in meddling with that deadly instrument, since I know not accurately from which end proceeds the bullet," said Dr. Melmoth. "But were it not better, since we are so well provided with artillery, to betake ourselves, in the event of an encounter, to some stone wall or other place of strength?"

"If I may presume to advise," said the squire, "you, as being most valiant and experienced, should ride forward, lance in hand (your long staff serving for a lance), while I annoy the enemy from afar."

"Like Teucer, behind the shield of Ajax," interrupted Dr. Melmoth, "or David with his stone and sling. No, no, young man; I have left unfinished in my study a learned treatise, important not only to the present age, but to posterity, for whose sake I must take heed to my safety. But, lo! who rides yonder?"

On leaving college Hawthorne had gone back to live at Salem.

II. *Early Manhood*

THE twelve years that followed were not the happiest or most brilliant phase of Hawthorne's life; they strike me indeed as having had an altogether peculiar dreariness. They had their uses; they were the period of incubation of the admirable compositions which eventually brought him reputation and prosperity. But of their actual aridity the young man must have had a painful consciousness; he never lost the impression of it. Mr. Lathrop quotes a phrase to this effect from one of his letters, late in life: "I am disposed to thank God for the gloom and chill of my early life, in the hope that my share of adversity came then, when I bore it alone." And the same writer alludes to a touching passage in the English *Note-Books,* which I shall quote entire:

I think I have been happier this Christmas (1854) than ever before—by my own fireside, and with my wife and children about me—more content to enjoy what I have, less anxious for anything beyond it, in this life. My early life was perhaps a good preparation for the declining half of life; it having been such a blank that any thereafter would compare favorably with it. For a long, long while, I have occasionally been visited with a singular dream; and I have an impression that I have dreamed it ever since I have been in England. It is, that I am still at college, or, sometimes, even, at school—and there is a sense that I have been there unconscionably long, and have quite failed to make such progress as my contemporaries have done; and I seem to meet some of them with a feeling of shame and depression that broods over me as I think of it, even when awake. This dream, recurring all through these twenty or thirty years, must be one of the effects of that heavy seclusion in which I shut myself up for twelve years after leaving college, when everybody moved onward and left me behind. How strange that it should come now, when I may call myself famous and prosperous!—when I am happy too.

The allusion here is to a state of solitude which was the young man's positive choice at the time—or into which he drifted at least under the pressure of his natural shyness and reserve. He was not expansive, he was not addicted to experiments and adventures of intercourse, he was not, personally, in a word, what is called sociable. The general impression of this silence-loving and shade-seeking side of his character is doubtless exaggerated, and, in so far as it points to him as a somber and sinister figure, is almost ludicrously at fault. He was silent, diffident, more inclined to hesitate, to watch and wait and meditate, than to produce himself, and fonder, on almost any occasion, of being absent than of being present. This quality betrays itself in all his writings. There is in all of them something cold and light and thin, something belonging to the imagination alone, which indicates a man but little disposed to multiply his relations, his points of contact, with society. If we read the six volumes of Note-Books with an eye to the evidence of this unsocial side of his life, we find it in sufficient abundance. But we find at the same time that there was nothing unamiable or invidious in his shyness, and above all that there was nothing preponderantly gloomy. The qualities to which the Note-Books most testify are, on the whole, his serenity and amenity of mind. They reveal these characteristics indeed in an almost phenomenal degree. The serenity, the simplicity, seem in certain portions almost child-like; of brilliant gaiety, of high spirits, there is little; but the placidity and evenness of temper, the cheerful and contented view of the things he notes, never belie themselves. I know not what else he may have written in this copious record, and what passages of gloom and melancholy may have been suppressed; but as his diaries stand, they offer in a remarkable degree the reflection of a mind whose development was not in the direction of sadness. A very clever French critic, whose fancy is often more lively than his observation is deep, M. Emile Montégut, writing in the Revue des Deux Mondes, in the year 1860, invents for our author the appellation of "Un Romancier Pessimiste." Superficially speaking, perhaps, the title is a happy one; but only superficially. Pessimism consists in having morbid and bitter views and theories about human nature; not in indulging in shadowy fancies and conceits. There is nothing whatever to show that Hawthorne had any such doctrines or convictions; certainly, the note of depression, of despair, of the disposition to undervalue the human race, is never sounded in his diaries. These volumes contain the record of very few convictions or theories of any kind; they move with curious evenness, with a charming, graceful flow, on a level which lies above that of a man's philosophy. They adhere with such persistence to this upper level that they prompt the reader to believe that Hawthorne had no appreciable philosophy at all—no general views that were in the least uncomfortable. They are the exhibition of an unperplexed intellect. I said just now that the development of Hawthorne's mind was not towards sadness; and I should be inclined to go still further, and say that his mind proper—his mind in so far as it was a repository of opinions and articles of faith—had no development that it is of especial importance to look into. What had a development was his imagination—that delicate and penetrating imagination which was always at play, always entertaining itself, always engaged in a game of hide and seek in the region in which it seemed to him that the game could best be played—among the shadows and substructions, the dark-based pillars and supports, of our moral nature. Beneath this movement and ripple of his imagination—as free and spontaneous as that of the sea surface—lay directly his personal affections. These were solid and strong, but, according to my impression, they had the place very much to themselves.

His innocent reserve, then, and his exaggerated, but by no means cynical, relish for solitude, imposed themselves upon him, in a great measure, with a persistency which helped to make the time a tolerably arid one—so arid a one indeed that we have seen that in the light of later happiness he pronounced it a blank. But in truth, if these were dull years, it was not all Hawthorne's fault. His situation was intrinsically poor—poor with a poverty that one almost hesitates to look into. When we think of what the conditions of intellectual life, of taste, must have been in a small New England town fifty years ago; and when we think of a young man of beautiful genius, with a love of literature and romance, of the picturesque, of style and form and color, trying to make a career for himself in the midst of them, compassion for the young man becomes our dominant sentiment, and we see the large dry village picture in perhaps almost too hard a light. It seems to me then that it was possibly a blessing for Hawthorne that he was not expansive and inquisitive, that he lived much to himself and asked but little of his *milieu*. If he had been exacting and ambitious, if his appetite had been large and his knowledge various, he would probably have found the bounds of Salem intolerably narrow. But his culture had been of a simple sort—there was little of any other sort to be obtained in America in those days, and though he was doubtless haunted by visions of more suggestive opportunities, we may safely assume that he was not to his own perception the object of compassion that he appears to a critic who judges him after half a century's civilization has filtered into the twilight of that earlier time. If New England was socially a very small place in those days, Salem was a still smaller one; and if the American tone at large was intensely provincial, that of New England was not greatly helped by having the best of it. The state of things was extremely natural, and there could be now no greater mistake than to speak of it with a redundancy of irony. American life had begun to constitute itself from the foundations; it had begun to *be*, simply; it was at an immeasurable distance from having begun to enjoy. I imagine there was no appreciable group of people in New England at that time proposing to itself to enjoy life; this was not an undertaking for which any provision had been made, or to which any encouragement was offered. Hawthorne must have vaguely entertained some such design upon destiny; but he must have felt that his success would have to depend wholly upon his own ingenuity. I say he must have proposed to himself to enjoy, simply because he proposed to be an artist, and because this enters inevitably into the artist's scheme. There are a thousand ways of enjoying life, and that of the artist is one of the most innocent. But for all that, it connects itself with the idea of pleasure. He proposes to give pleasure, and to give it he must first get it. Where he gets it will depend upon circumstances, and circumstances were not encouraging to Hawthorne.

He was poor, he was solitary, and he undertook to devote himself to literature in a community in which the interest in literature was as yet of the smallest. It is not too much to say that even to the present day it is a considerable discomfort in the United States not to be "in business." The young man who attempts to launch himself in a career that does not belong to the so-called practical order; the young man who has not, in a word, an office in the business quarter of the town, with his name painted on the door, has but a limited place in the social system, finds no particular bough to perch upon. He is not looked at askance, he is not regarded as an idler; literature and the arts have always been held in extreme honor in the American world, and those who practise them are received on easier terms than in other countries. If the tone of the American world is in some respects provincial, it is in none more so than in this matter of the exaggerated homage rendered to authorship. The gentleman or the lady who has written a book is in many circles the object of an admiration too indiscriminating to operate as an encouragement to good writing. There is no reason to suppose that this was less the case fifty years ago; but fifty years ago, greatly more than now, the literary man must have lacked the comfort and inspiration of belonging to a class. The best things come, as a general thing, from the talents that are members of a group; every man works better when he has companions working in the same line, and yielding the stimulus of suggestion, comparison, emulation. Great things of course have been done by solitary workers; but they have usually been done with double the pains they would have cost if they had been produced in more genial circumstances. The solitary worker loses the profit of example and discussion; he is apt to make awkward experiments; he is in the nature of the case more or less of an empiric. The empiric may, as I say, be treated by the world as an expert; but the drawbacks and discomforts of empiricism remain to him, and are in fact increased by the suspicion that is mingled with his gratitude, of a want in the public taste of a sense of the proportions of things. Poor Hawthorne, beginning to write subtle short tales at Salem, was empirical enough; he was one of, at most, some dozen Americans who had taken up literature as a profession. The profession in the United States is still very young, and of diminutive stature; but in the year 1830 its head could hardly have been seen above ground. It strikes the observer of today that Hawthorne showed great courage in entering a field in which the honors and emoluments were so scanty as the profits of authorship must have been at that time. I have said that in the United States at present authorship is a pedestal, and literature is the fashion; but Hawthorne's history is a proof that it was possible, fifty years ago, to write a great many little masterpieces without becoming known. He begins the preface to the *Twice-Told Tales* by remarking that he was "for many years the obscurest man of letters in America." When once this work obtained recognition, the recognition left little to be desired. Hawthorne never, I believe, made large sums of money by his writings, and the early profits of these charming sketches could not have been considerable; for many of them, indeed, as they appeared in journals and magazines, he had never been paid at all; but the honor, when once it dawned—and it dawned tolerably early in the author's career—was never thereafter wanting. Hawthorne's countrymen are solidly proud of him, and the tone of Mr. Lathrop's *Study* is in itself sufficient evidence of the manner in which an American story-teller may in some cases look to have his eulogy pronounced.

Hawthorne's early attempt to support himself by his pen appears to have been deliberate; we hear nothing of those experiments in countinghouses or lawyers' offices, of which a permanent invocation to the Muse is often the inconsequent sequel. He began to write, and to try and dispose of his writings; and he remained at Salem apparently only because his family, his mother and his two sisters, lived there. His mother had a house, of which during the twelve years that elapsed until 1838 he appears to have been an inmate. Mr. Lathrop learned from his surviving sister that after publishing *Fanshawe* he produced a group of short stories entitled *Seven Tales of My Native Land*, and that this lady retained a very favorable recollection of the work, which her brother had given her to read. But it never saw the light; his attempts to get it published were unsuccessful, and at last, in a fit of irritation and despair, the young author burned the manuscript.

There is probably something autobiographic in the striking

little tale of *The Devil in Manuscript*. "They have been offered to seventeen publishers," says the hero of that sketch in regard to a pile of his own lucubrations.

It would make you stare to read their answers. . . . One man publishes nothing but schoolbooks; another has five novels already under examination; . . . another gentleman is just giving up business, on purpose, I verily believe, to avoid publishing my book. In short, of all the seventeen booksellers, only one has vouchsafed even to read my tales; and he—a literary dabbler himself, I should judge—has the impertinence to criticize them, proposing what he calls vast improvements, and concluding, after a general sentence of condemnation, with the definitive assurance that he will not be concerned on any terms. . . . But there does seem to be one righteous man among these seventeen unrighteous ones, and he tells me, fairly, that no American publisher will meddle with an American work—seldom if by a known writer, and never if by a new one—unless at the writer's risk.

But though the *Seven Tales* was not printed, Hawthorne proceeded to write others that were; the two collections of the *Twice-Told Tales* and the *Snow Image* are gathered from a series of contributions to the local journals and the annuals of that day. To make these three volumes, he picked out the things he thought the best. "Some very small part," he says of what remains, "might yet be rummaged out (but it would not be worth the trouble) among the dingy pages of fifteen or twenty-years-old periodicals, or within the shabby morocco covers of faded *Souvenirs*." These three volumes represent no large amount of literary labor for so long a period, and the author admits that there is little to show "for the thought and industry of that portion of his life." He attributes the paucity of his productions to a "total lack of sympathy at the age when his mind would naturally have been most effervescent." "He had no incitement to literary effort in a reasonable prospect of reputation or profit; nothing but the pleasure itself of composition, an enjoyment not at all amiss in its way, and perhaps essential to the merit of the work in hand, but which in the long run will hardly keep the chill out of a writer's heart, or the numbness out of his fingers." These words occur in the preface attached in 1851 to the second edition of the *Twice-Told Tales; à propos* of which I may say that there is always a charm in Hawthorne's prefaces which makes one grateful for a pretext to quote from them. At this time *The Scarlet Letter* had just made his fame, and the short tales were certain of a large welcome; but the account he gives of the failure of the earlier edition to produce a sensation (it had been published in two volumes, at four years apart) may appear to contradict my assertion that, though he was not recognized immediately, he was recognized betimes. In 1850, when *The Scarlet Letter* appeared, Hawthorne was forty-six years old, and this may certainly seem a long-delayed popularity. On the other hand, it must be remembered that he had not appealed to the world with any great energy. The *Twice-Told Tales,* charming as they are, do not constitute a very massive literary pedestal. As soon as the author, resorting to severer measures, put forth *The Scarlet Letter,* the public ear was touched and charmed, and after that it was held to the end. "Well it might have been!" the reader will exclaim. "But what a grievous pity that the dulness of this same organ should have operated so long as a deterrent, and by making Hawthorne wait till he was nearly fifty to publish his first novel, have abbreviated by so much his productive career!" The truth is, he cannot have been in any very high degree ambitious; he was not an abundant producer, and there was manifestly a strain of generous indolence in his composition. There was a lovable want of eagerness about him. Let the encouragement offered have been what it might, he had waited till he was lapsing from middle life to strike his first noticeable blow; and during the last ten years of his career he put forth but two complete works, and the fragment of a third.

It is very true, however, that during this early period he seems to have been very glad to do whatever came to his hand. Certain of his tales found their way into one of the annuals of the time, a publication endowed with the brilliant title of *The Boston Token and Atlantic Souvenir.* The editor of this graceful repository was S. G. Goodrich, a gentleman who, I suppose, may be called one of the pioneers of Amer-

ican periodical literature. He is better known to the world as
Mr. Peter Parley, a name under which he produced a multitude of popular school-books, story-books, and other attempts
to vulgarize human knowledge and adapt it to the infant
mind. This enterprising purveyor of literary wares appears,
incongruously enough, to have been Hawthorne's earliest
protector, if protection is the proper word for the treatment
that the young author received from him. Mr. Goodrich induced him in 1836 to go to Boston to edit a periodical in
which he was interested, *The American Magazine of Useful
and Entertaining Knowledge*. I have never seen the work in
question, but Hawthorne's biographer gives a sorry account
of it. It was managed by the so-called Bewick Company,
which "took its name from Thomas Bewick, the English
restorer of the art of wood engraving, and the magazine was
to do his memory honor by his admirable illustrations. But in
fact it never did anyone honor, nor brought anyone profit.
It was a penny popular affair, containing condensed information about innumerable subjects, no fiction, and little
poetry. The woodcuts were of the crudest and most frightful
sort. It passed through the hands of several editors and several publishers. Hawthorne was engaged at a salary of five
hundred dollars a year; but it appears that he got next to
nothing, and did not stay in the position long." Hawthorne
wrote from Boston in the winter of 1836: "I came here trusting to Goodrich's positive promise to pay me forty-five dollars
as soon as I arrived; and he has kept promising from one day
to another, till I do not see that he means to pay at all. I
have now broke off all intercourse with him, and never think
of going near him. . . . I don't feel at all obliged to him
about the editorship, for he is a stockholder and director in
the Bewick Company . . . and I defy them to get another
to do for a thousand dollars what I do for five hundred."—"I
make nothing," he says in another letter, "of writing a history
or biography before dinner." Goodrich proposed to him to
write a *Universal History* for the use of schools, offering him
a hundred dollars for his share in the work. Hawthorne accepted the offer and took a hand—I know not how large a
one—in the job. His biographer has been able to identify a

single phrase as our author's. He is speaking of George IV:
"Even when he was quite a young man this king cared as
much about dress as any young coxcomb. He had a great
deal of taste in such matters, and it is a pity that he was a
king, for he might otherwise have made an excellent tailor."
The *Universal History* had a great vogue and passed through
hundreds of editions; but it does not appear that Hawthorne
ever received more than his hundred dollars. The writer of
these pages vividly remembers making its acquaintance at an
early stage of his education—a very fat, stumpy-looking book,
bound in boards covered with green paper, and having in the
text very small woodcuts of the most primitive sort. He associates it to this day with the names of Sesostris and Semiramis
whenever he encounters them, there having been, he supposes, some account of the conquests of these potentates that
would impress itself upon the imagination of a child. At the
end of four months, Hawthorne had received but twenty
dollars—four pounds—for his editorship of the *American
Magazine*.

There is something pitiful in this episode, and something
really touching in the sight of a delicate and superior genius
obliged to concern himself with such paltry undertakings.
The simple fact was that for a man attempting at that time
in America to live by his pen, there were no larger openings;
and to live at all Hawthorne had, as the phrase is, to make
himself small. This cost him less, moreover, than it would
have cost a more copious and strenuous genius, for his modesty was evidently extreme, and I doubt whether he had any
very ardent consciousness of rare talent. He went back to
Salem, and from this tranquil standpoint, in the spring of
1837, he watched the first volume of his *Twice-Told Tales*
come into the world. He had by this time been living some
ten years of his manhood in Salem, and an American com-
mentator may be excused for feeling the desire to construct,
from the very scanty material that offers itself, a slight
picture of his life there. I have quoted his own allusions to
its dulness and blankness, but I confess that these observations serve rather to quicken than to depress my curiosity. A
biographer has of necessity a relish for detail; his business is

to multiply points of characterization. Mr. Lathrop tells us that our author "had little communication with even the members of his family. Frequently his meals were brought and left at his locked door, and it was not often that the four inmates of the old Herbert Street mansion met in family circle. He never read his stories aloud to his mother and sisters. . . . It was the custom in this household for the several members to remain very much by themselves; the three ladies were perhaps nearly as rigorous recluses as himself, and, speaking of the isolation which reigned among them, Hawthorne once said, 'We do not even *live* at our house!'" It is added that he was not in the habit of going to church. This is not a lively picture, nor is that other sketch of his daily habits much more exhilarating, in which Mr. Lathrop affirms that though the statement that for several years "he never saw the sun" is entirely an error, yet it is true that he stirred little abroad all day and "seldom chose to walk in the town except at night." In the dusky hours he took walks of many miles along the coast, or else wandered about the sleeping streets of Salem. These were his pastimes, and these were apparently his most intimate occasions of contact with life. Life, on such occasions, was not very exuberant, as anyone will reflect who has been acquainted with the physiognomy of a small New England town after nine o'clock in the evening. Hawthorne, however, was an inveterate observer of small things, and he found a field for fancy among the most trivial accidents. There could be no better example of this happy faculty than the little paper entitled *Night Sketches,* included among the *Twice-Told Tales.* This small dissertation is about nothing at all, and to call attention to it is almost to overrate its importance. This fact is equally true, indeed, of a great many of its companions, which give even the most appreciative critic a singular feeling of his own indiscretion— almost of his own cruelty. They are so light, so slight, so tenderly trivial, that simply to mention them is to put them in a false position. The author's claim for them is barely audible, even to the most acute listener. They are things to take or to leave—to enjoy, but not to talk about. Not to read them would be to do them an injustice (to read them is essentially to relish them), but to bring the machinery of criticism to bear upon them would be to do them a still greater wrong. I must remember, however, that to carry this principle too far would be to endanger the general validity of the present little work—a consummation which it can only be my desire to avert. Therefore it is that I think it permissible to remark that in Hawthorne, the whole class of little descriptive effusions directed upon common things, to which these just-mentioned *Night Sketches* belong, have a greater charm than there is any warrant for in their substance. The charm is made up of the spontaneity, the personal quality, of the fancy that plays through them, its mingled simplicity and subtlety, its purity and its *bonhomie*. The *Night Sketches* are simply the light, familiar record of a walk under an umbrella, at the end of a long, dull, rainy day, through the sloppy, ill-paved streets of a country town, where the rare gas lamps twinkle in the large puddles, and the blue jars in the druggist's window shine through the vulgar drizzle. One would say that the inspiration of such a theme could have had no great force, and such doubtless was the case; but out of the Salem puddles, nevertheless, springs, flowerlike, a charming and natural piece of prose.

I have said that Hawthorne was an observer of small things, and indeed he appears to have thought nothing too trivial to be suggestive. His *Note-Books* give us the measure of his perception of common and casual things, and of his habit of converting them into *memoranda*. These *Note-Books*, by the way—this seems as good a place as any other to say it —are a very singular series of volumes; I doubt whether there is anything exactly corresponding to them in the whole body of literature. They were published—in six volumes, issued at intervals—some years after Hawthorne's death, and no person attempting to write an account of the romancer could afford to regret that they should have been given to the world. There is a point of view from which this may be regretted; but the attitude of the biographer is to desire as many documents as possible. I am thankful, then, as a biographer, for the *Note-Books*, but I am obliged to confess that, though I have just reread them carefully, I am still at a loss to perceive how they came to be written—what was Hawthorne's purpose in carrying on for so many years this minute and often trivial chronicle. For a person desiring information about him at any cost, it is valuable; it sheds a vivid light upon his character, his habits, the nature of his mind. But we find ourselves wondering what was its value to Hawthorne himself. It is in a very partial degree a register of impressions, and in a still smaller sense a record of emotions. Outward objects play much the larger part in it; opinions, convictions, ideas pure and simple, are almost absent. He rarely takes his note-book into his confidence or commits to its pages any reflections that might be adapted for publicity; the simplest way to describe the tone of these extremely objective journals is to say that they read like a series of very pleasant, though rather dullish and decidedly formal, letters, addressed to himself by a man who, having suspicions that they might be opened in the post, should have determined to insert nothing compromising. They contain much that is too futile for things intended for publicity; whereas, on the other hand, as a receptacle of private impressions and opinions, they are curiously cold and empty. They widen, as I have said, our glimpse of Hawthorne's mind (I do not say that they elevate our estimate of it), but they do so by what they fail to contain, as much as by what we find in them. Our business for the moment, however, is not with the light that they throw upon his intellect, but with the information they offer about his habits and his social circumstances.

I know not at what age he began to keep a diary; the first entries in the American volumes are of the summer of 1835. There is a phrase in the preface to his novel of *Transformation,* which must have lingered in the minds of many Americans who have tried to write novels and to lay the scene of them in the western world. "No author, without a trial, can conceive of the difficulty of writing a romance about a country where there is no shadow, no antiquity, no mystery, no picturesque and gloomy wrong, nor anything but a commonplace prosperity, in broad and simple daylight, as is happily the case with my dear native land." The perusal of

Hawthorne's American *Note-Books* operates as a practical commentary upon this somewhat ominous text. It does so at least to my own mind; it would be too much perhaps to say that the effect would be the same for the usual English reader. An American reads between the lines—he completes the suggestions—he constructs a picture. I think I am not guilty of any gross injustice in saying that the picture he constructs from Hawthorne's American diaries, though by no means without charms of its own, is not, on the whole, an interesting one. It is characterized by an extraordinary blankness—a curious paleness of color and paucity of detail. Hawthorne, as I have said, has a large and healthy appetite for detail, and one is therefore the more struck with the lightness of the diet to which his observation was condemned. For myself, as I turn the pages of his journals, I seem to see the image of the crude and simple society in which he lived. I use these epithets, of course, not invidiously, but descriptively; if one desire to enter as closely as possible into Hawthorne's situation, one must endeavor to reproduce his circumstances. We are struck with the large number of elements that were absent from them, and the coldness, the thinness, the blankness, to repeat my epithet, present themselves so vividly that our foremost feeling is that of compassion for a romancer looking for subjects in such a field. It takes so many things, as Hawthorne must have felt later in life, when he made the acquaintance of the denser, richer, warmer European spectacle—it takes such an accumulation of history and custom, such a complexity of manners and types, to form a fund of suggestion for a novelist. If Hawthorne had been a young Englishman, or a young Frenchman of the same degree of genius, the same cast of mind, the same habits, his consciousness of the world around him would have been a very different affair; however obscure, however reserved, his own personal life, his sense of the life of his fellow-mortals would have been almost infinitely more various. The negative side of the spectacle on which Hawthorne looked out, in his contemplative saunterings and reveries, might, indeed, with a little ingenuity, be made almost ludicrous; one might enumerate the items of high civilization, as it exists in other countries, which are absent from the texture of American life, until it should become a wonder to know what was left. No State, in the European sense of the word, and indeed barely a specific national name. No sovereign, no court, no personal loyalty, no aristocracy, no church, no clergy, no army, no diplomatic service, no country gentlemen, no palaces, no castles, nor manors, nor old country houses, nor parsonages, nor thatched cottages, nor ivied ruins; no cathedrals, nor abbeys, nor little Norman churches; no great universities nor public schools—no Oxford, nor Eton, nor Harrow; no literature, no novels, no museums, no pictures, no political society, no sporting class— no Epsom nor Ascot! Some such list as that might be drawn up of the absent things in American life—especially in the American life of forty years ago, the effect of which, upon an English or a French imagination, would probably as a general thing be appalling. The natural remark, in the almost lurid light of such an indictment, would be that if these things are left out, everything is left out. The American knows that a good deal remains; what it is that remains—that is his secret, his joke, as one may say. It would be cruel, in this terrible denudation, to deny him the consolation of his national gift, that "American humor" of which of late years we have heard so much.

But in helping us to measure what remains, our author's diaries, as I have already intimated, would give comfort rather to persons who might have taken the alarm from the brief sketch I have just attempted of what I have called the negative side of the American social situation, than do those reminding themselves of its fine compensations. Hawthorne's entries are to a great degree accounts of walks in the country, drives in stage-coaches, people he met in taverns. The minuteness of the things that attract his attention and that he deems worthy of being commemorated is frequently extreme, and from this fact we get the impression of a general vacancy in the field of vision. "Sunday evening, going by the jail, the setting sun kindled up the windows most cheerfully; as if there were a bright, comfortable light within its darksome stone wall." "I went yesterday with Monsieur S—— to pick raspberries. He fell through an old log bridge, thrown over a hollow; looking back, only his head and shoulders appeared through the rotten logs and among the bushes.—A shower coming on, the rapid running of a little barefooted boy, coming up unheard, and dashing swiftly past us, and showing us the soles of his naked feet as he ran adown the path and up the opposite side." In another place he devotes a page to a description of a dog whom he saw running round after its tail; in still another he remarks, in a paragraph by itself— "The aromatic odor of peat-smoke in the sunny autumnal air is very pleasant." The reader says to himself that when a man turned thirty gives a place in his mind—and his inkstand—to such trifles as these, it is because nothing else of superior importance demands admission. Everything in the notes indicates a simple, democratic, thinly-composed society; there is no evidence of the writer finding himself in any variety or intimacy of relations with anyone or with anything. We find a good deal of warrant for believing that if we add that statement of Mr. Lathrop's about his meals being left at the door of his room, to rural rambles of which an impression of the temporary phases of the local apple-crop were the usual, and an encounter with an organ-grinder, or an eccentric dog, the rarer, outcome, we construct a rough image of our author's daily life during the several years that preceded his marriage. He appears to have read a good deal, and that he must have been familiar with the sources of good English we see from his charming, expressive, slightly self-conscious, cultivated, but not too cultivated, style. Yet neither in these early volumes of his *Note-Books* nor in the later is there any mention of his reading. There are no literary judgments or impressions—there is almost no allusion to works or to authors. The allusions to individuals of any kind are indeed much less numerous than one might have expected; there is little psychology, little description of manners. We are told by Mr. Lathrop that there existed at Salem during the early part of Hawthorne's life "a strong circle of wealthy families," which "maintained rigorously the distinctions of class," and whose "entertainments were splendid, their manners magnificent." This is a rather pictorial way of saying that there were a number of people in the place—the commercial and professional aristocracy, as it were—who lived in high comfort and respectability, and who, in their small provincial way, doubtless had pretensions to be exclusive. Into this delectable company Mr. Lathrop intimates that his hero was free to penetrate. It is easy to believe it, and it would be difficult to perceive why the privilege should have been denied to a young man of genius and culture, who was very good-looking (Hawthorne must have been in these days, judging by his appearance later in life, a strikingly handsome fellow), and whose American pedigree was virtually as long as the longest they could show. But in fact Hawthorne appears to have ignored the good society of his native place almost completely; no echo of its conversation is to be found in his tales or his journals. Such an echo would possibly not have been especially melodious, and if we regret the shyness and stiffness, the reserve, the timidity, the suspicion, or whatever it was, that kept him from knowing what there was to be known, it is not because we have any very definite assurance that his gains would have been great. Still, since a beautiful writer was growing up in Salem, it is a pity that he should not have given himself a chance to commemorate some of the types that flourished in the richest soil of the place. Like almost all people who possess in a strong degree the story-telling faculty, Hawthorne had a democratic strain in his composition and a relish for the commoner stuff of human nature. Thoroughly American in all ways, he was in none more so than in the vagueness of his sense of social distinctions and his readiness to forget them if a moral or intellectual sensation were to be gained by it. He liked to fraternize with plain people, to take them on their own terms, and put himself if possible into their shoes. His *Note-Books,* and even his tales, are full of evidence of this easy and natural feeling about all his unconventional fellow mortals—this imaginative interest and contemplative curiosity—and it sometimes takes the most charming and graceful forms. Commingled as it is with his own subtlety and delicacy, his complete exemption from vulgarity, it is one of the points in his character which his reader comes most to appreciate—that reader I mean for whom he is not, as for some few, a dusky and malarious genius.

But even if he had had, personally, as many pretensions as he had few, he must in the nature of things have been more or less of a consenting democrat, for democracy was the very keystone of the simple social structure in which he played his part. The air of his journals and his tales alike is full of the genuine democratic feeling. This feeling has by no means passed out of New England life; it still flour-ishes in perfection in the great stock of the people, especially in rural communities; but it is probable that at the present hour a writer of Hawthorne's general fastidiousness would not express it quite so artlessly. "A shrewd gentlewoman, who kept a tavern in the town," he says, in *Chippings with a Chisel*, "was anxious to obtain two or three gravestones for the deceased members of her family, and to pay for these solemn commodities by taking the sculptor to board." This image of a gentlewoman keeping a tavern and looking out for boarders seems, from the point of view to which I allude, not at all incongruous. It will be observed that the lady in question was shrewd; it was probable that she was substan-tially educated, and of reputable life, and it is certain that she was energetic. These qualities would make it natural to Hawthorne to speak of her as a gentlewoman; the natural tendency in societies where the sense of equality prevails being to take for granted the high level rather than the low. Perhaps the most striking example of the democratic senti-ment in all our author's tales, however, is the figure of Uncle Venner, in *The House of the Seven Gables*. Uncle Venner is a poor old man in a brimless hat and patched trousers, who picks up a precarious subsistence by rendering, for a compensation, in the houses and gardens of the good people of Salem, those services that are known in New England as "chores." He carries parcels, splits firewood, digs potatoes, collects refuse for the maintenance of his pigs, and looks forward with philosophic equanimity to the time when he shall end his days in the almshouse. But in spite of the very modest place that he occupies in the social scale, he is received on a footing of familiarity in the household of the far-descended Miss Pyncheon; and when this ancient lady and her companions take the air in the garden of a summer evening, he steps into the estimable circle and mingles the smoke of his pipe with their refined conversation. This obviously is rather imaginative—Uncle Venner is a creation with a purpose. He is an original, a natural moralist, a philosopher; and Hawthorne, who knew perfectly what he was about in introducing him—Hawthorne always knew perfectly what he was about—wished to give in his person an example of humorous resignation and of a life reduced to the simplest and homeliest elements, as opposed to the fantastic pretensions of the antiquated heroine of the story. He wished to strike a certain exclusively human and personal note. He knew that for this purpose he was taking a license; but the point is that he felt he was not indulging in any extravagant violation of reality. Giving in a letter, about 1830, an account of a little journey he was making in Connecticut, he says, of the end of a seventeen miles' stage, that "in the evening, however, I went to a Bible class with a very polite and agreeable gentleman, whom I afterwards discovered to be a strolling tailor of very questionable habits."

Hawthorne appears on various occasions to have absented himself from Salem, and to have wandered somewhat through the New England States. But the only one of these episodes of which there is a considerable account in the *Note-Books* is a visit that he paid in the summer of 1837 to his old college-mate, Horatio Bridge, who was living upon his father's property in Maine, in company with an eccentric young Frenchman, a teacher of his native tongue, who was looking for pupils among the northern forests. I have said that there was less psychology in Hawthorne's journals than might have been looked for; but there is nevertheless a certain amount of it, and nowhere more than in a number of pages relating to this remarkable "Monsieur S." (Hawthorne, intimate as he apparently became with him, always calls him "Monsieur," just as throughout all his diaries he invariably speaks of all his friends, even the most familiar, as "Mr." He confers the prefix upon the unconventional Thoreau, his fellow-woodsman at Concord, and upon the emancipated

brethren at Brook Farm.) These pages are completely occupied with Monsieur S., who was evidently a man of character, with the full complement of his national vivacity.
There is an elaborate effort to analyze the poor young
Frenchman's disposition, something conscientious and painstaking, respectful, explicit, almost solemn. These passages
are very curious as a reminder of the absence of the offhand
element in the manner in which many Americans, and
many New Englanders especially, make up their minds about
people whom they meet. This, in turn, is a reminder of
something that may be called the importance of the individual in the American world; which is a result of the newness and youthfulness of society and of the absence of keen
competition. The individual counts for more, as it were, and,
thanks to the absence of a variety of social types and of settled heads under which he may be easily and conveniently
pigeonholed, he is to a certain extent a wonder and a mystery.
An Englishman, a Frenchman—a Frenchman above all—
judges quickly, easily, from his own social standpoint, and
makes an end of it. He has not that rather chilly and isolated
sense of moral responsibility which is apt to visit a New
Englander in such processes; and he has the advantage that
his standards are fixed by the general consent of the society
in which he lives. A Frenchman, in this respect, is particularly happy and comfortable, happy and comfortable to a
degree which I think is hardly to be overestimated; his standards being the most definite in the world, the most easily
and promptly appealed to, and the most identical with what
happens to be the practice of the French genius itself. The
Englishman is not quite so well off, but he is better off than
his poor interrogative and tentative cousin beyond the seas.
He is blessed with a healthy mistrust of analysis, and hair-
splitting is the occupation he most despises. There is always
a little of the Dr. Johnson in him, and Dr. Johnson would
have had wofully little patience with that tendency to weigh
moonbeams which in Hawthorne was almost as much a quality of race as of genius; albeit that Hawthorne has paid to
Boswell's hero (in the chapter on "Lichfield and Uttoxeter,"
in his volume on England) a tribute of the finest appre-

ciation. American intellectual standards are vague, and Hawthorne's countrymen are apt to hold the scales with a rather uncertain hand and a somewhat agitated conscience.

III. Early Writings

THE second volume of the *Twice-Told Tales* was published in 1845, in Boston; and at this time a good many of the stories which were afterwards collected into the *Mosses from an Old Manse* had already appeared, chiefly in *The Democratic Review,* a sufficiently flourishing periodical of that period. In mentioning these things I anticipate; but I touch upon the year 1845 in order to speak of the two collections of *Twice-Told Tales* at once. During the same year Hawthorne edited an interesting volume, the *Journals of an African Cruiser,* by his friend Bridge, who had gone into the Navy and seen something of distant waters. His biographer mentions that even then Hawthorne's name was thought to bespeak attention for a book, and he insists on this fact in contradiction to the idea that his productions had hitherto been as little noticed as his own declaration that he remained "for a good many years the obscurest man of letters in America," might lead one, and has led many people, to suppose. "In this dismal chamber FAME was won," he writes in Salem in 1836. And we find in the *Note-Books* (1840) this singularly beautiful and touching passage:

Here I sit in my old accustomed chamber, where I used to sit in days gone by. . . . Here I have written many tales—many that have been burned to ashes, many that have doubtless deserved the same fate. This claims to be called a haunted chamber, for thousands upon thousands of visions have appeared to me in it; and some few of them have become visible to the world. If ever I should have a biographer, he ought to make great mention of this chamber in my memoirs, because so much of my lonely youth was wasted here, and here my mind and character were formed; and here I have been glad and hopeful, and here I have been despondent. And here I sat a long, long time, waiting patiently for the world to know me, and sometimes wondering why it did not know me sooner, or whether it would ever know me at all—at least till I were in my grave. And sometimes it seems to me as if I were already in the grave, with only life enough to be chilled and benumbed. But oftener I was happy—at least as happy as I then knew how to be, or was aware of the possibility of being. By and by the world found me out in my lonely chamber and called me forth—not indeed with a loud roar of acclamation, but rather with a still small voice— and forth I went, but found nothing in the world I thought preferable to my solitude till now. . . . And now I begin to understand why I was imprisoned so many years in this lonely chamber, and why I could never break through the viewless bolts and bars; for if I had sooner made my escape into the world, I should have grown hard and rough, and been covered with earthly dust, and my heart might have become callous by rude encounters with the multitude. . . . But living in solitude till the fulness of time was come, I still kept the dew of my youth and the freshness of my heart. . . . I used to think that I could imagine all passions, all feelings, and states of the heart and mind; but how little did I know! . . . Indeed, we are but shadows; we are not endowed with real life, and all that seems most real about us is but the thinnest substance of a dream— till the heart be touched. That touch creates us—then we begin to be—thereby we are beings of reality and inheritors of eternity.

There is something exquisite in the soft philosophy of this little retrospect, and it helps us to appreciate it to know that the writer had at this time just become engaged to be married to a charming and accomplished person, with whom his union, which took place two years later, was complete and full of happiness. But I quote it more particularly for the evidence it affords that, already in 1840, Hawthorne could speak of the world finding him out and calling him forth, as of an event tolerably well in the past. He had sent the first of the *Twice-Told* series to his old college friend, Longfellow, who had already laid, solidly, the foundation of his great poetic reputation, and at the time of his sending it had written him a letter from which it will be to our purpose to quote a few lines:

You tell me you have met with troubles and changes. I know not what these may have been; but I can assure you that trouble is the next best thing to enjoyment, and that there is no fate in the world so horrible as to have no share in either its joys or sorrows. For the last ten years I have not lived, but only dreamed of living. It may be true that there may have been some unsubstantial pleasures here in the shade, which I might have missed in the sunshine, but you cannot conceive how utterly devoid of satisfaction all my retrospects are. I have laid up no treasure of pleasant remembrances against old age; but there is some comfort in thinking that future years may be more varied, and therefore more tolerable, than the past. You give me more credit than I deserve in supposing that I have led a studious life. I have indeed turned over a good many books, but in so desultory a way that it cannot be called study, nor has it left me the fruits of study. . . . I have another great difficulty in the lack of materials; for I have seen so little of the world that I have nothing but thin air to concoct my stories of, and it is not easy to give a lifelike semblance to such shadowy stuff. Sometimes, through a peephole, I have caught a glimpse of the real world, and the two or three articles in which I have portrayed these glimpses please me better than the others.

It is more particularly for the sake of the concluding lines that I have quoted this passage; for evidently no portrait of Hawthorne at this period is at all exact which fails to insist upon the constant struggle which must have gone on between his shyness and his desire to know something of life; between what may be called his evasive and his inquisitive tendencies. I suppose it is no injustice to Hawthorne to say that on the whole his shyness always prevailed; and yet, obviously, the struggle was constantly there. He says of his *Twice-Told Tales,* in the preface, "They are not the talk of a secluded man with his own mind and heart (had it been so they could hardly have failed to be more deeply and permanently valuable) but his attempts, and very imperfectly successful ones, to open an intercourse with the world." We are speaking here of small things, it must be remembered— of little attempts, little sketches, a little world. But everything is relative, and this smallness of scale must not render less apparent the interesting character of Hawthorne's efforts. As for the *Twice-Told Tales* themselves, they are an old story now; everyone knows them a little, and those who admire them particularly have read them a great many times.

The writer of this sketch belongs to the latter class, and he has been trying to forget his familiarity with them, and ask himself what impression they would have made upon him at the time they appeared, in the first bloom of their freshness, and before the particular Hawthorne quality, as it may be called, had become an established, a recognized and valued, fact. Certainly, I am inclined to think, if one had encountered these delicate, dusky flowers in the blossomless garden of American journalism, one would have plucked them with a very tender hand; one would have felt that here was something essentially fresh and new; here, in no extraordinary force or abundance, but in a degree distinctly appreciable, was an original element in literature. When I think of it, I almost envy Hawthorne's earliest readers; the sensation of opening upon *The Great Carbuncle, The Seven Vagabonds,* or *The Threefold Destiny* in an American annual of forty years ago must have been highly agreeable.

Among these shorter things (it is better to speak of the whole collection, including the *Snow Image,* and the *Mosses from an Old Manse* at once) there are three sorts of tales, each one of which has an original stamp. There are, to begin with, the stories of fantasy and allegory—those among which the three I have just mentioned would be numbered, and which, on the whole, are the most original. This is the group to which such little masterpieces as *Malvin's Burial, Rappacini's Daughter,* and *Young Goodman Brown* also belong —these two last perhaps representing the highest point that Hawthorne reached in this direction. Then there are the little tales of New England history, which are scarcely less admirable, and of which *The Grey Champion, The Maypole of Merry Mount,* and the four beautiful *Legends of the Province House,* as they are called, are the most successful specimens. Lastly come the slender sketches of actual scenes and of the objects and manners about him, by means of which, more particularly, he endeavored "to open an intercourse with the world," and which, in spite of their slenderness, have an infinite grace and charm. Among these things *A Rill from the Town Pump, The Village Uncle, The Toll-Gatherer's Day,* the *Chippings with a Chisel,* may most naturally be mentioned. As we turn over these volumes we feel that the pieces that spring most directly from his fancy, constitute, as I have said (putting his four novels aside), his most substantial claim to our attention. It would be a mistake to insist too much upon them; Hawthorne was himself the first to recognize that. "These fitful sketches," he says in the preface to the *Mosses from an Old Manse,* "with so little of external life about them, yet claiming no profundity of purpose—so reserved even while they sometimes seem so frank—often but half in earnest, and never, even when most so, expressing satisfactorily the thoughts which they profess to image—such trifles, I truly feel, afford no solid basis for a literary reputation." This is very becomingly uttered; but it may be said, partly in answer to it, and partly in confirmation, that the valuable element in these things was not what Hawthorne put into them consciously, but what passed into them without his being able to measure it—the element of simple genius, the quality of imagination. This is the real charm of Hawthorne's writing—this purity and spontaneity and naturalness of fancy. For the rest, it is interesting to see how it borrowed a particular color from the other faculties that lay near it—how the imagination, in this capital son of the old Puritans, reflected the hue of the more purely moral part, of the dusky, overshadowed conscience. The conscience, by no fault of its own, in every genuine offshoot of that somber lineage, lay under the shadow of the sense of *sin.* This darkening cloud was no essential part of the nature of the individual; it stood fixed in the general moral heaven under which he grew up and looked at life. It projected from above, from outside, a black patch over his spirit, and it was for him to do what he could with the black patch. There were all sorts of possible ways of dealing with it; they depended upon the personal temperament. Some natures would let it lie as it fell, and contrive to be tolerably comfortable beneath it. Others would groan and sweat and suffer; but the dusky blight would remain, and their lives would be lives of misery. Here and there an individual, irritated beyond endurance, would throw it off in anger, plunging probably into what would be deemed deeper abysses of depravity. Hawthorne's way was the best, for he contrived, by an exquisite process, best known to himself, to transmute this heavy moral burden into the very substance of the imagination, to make it evaporate in the light and charming fumes of artistic production. But Hawthorne, of course, was exceptionally fortunate; he had his genius to help him. Nothing is more curious and interesting than this almost exclusively *imported* character of the sense of sin in Hawthorne's mind; it seems to exist there merely for an artistic or literary purpose. He had ample cognizance of the Puritan conscience; it was his natural heritage; it was reproduced in him; looking into his soul, he found it there. But his relation to it was only, as one may say, intellectual; it was not moral and theological. He played with it and used it as a pigment; he treated it, as the metaphysicians say, objectively. He was not discomposed, disturbed, haunted by it, in the manner of its usual and regular victims, who had not the little postern door of fancy to slip through, to the other side of the wall. It was, indeed, to his imaginative vision, the great fact of man's nature; the light element that had been mingled with his own composition always clung to this rugged prominence of moral responsibility, like the mist that hovers about the mountain. It was a necessary condition for a man of Hawthorne's stock that if his imagination should take license to amuse itself, it should at least select this grim precinct of the Puritan morality for its playground. He speaks of the dark disapproval with which his old ancestors, in the case of their coming to life, would see him trifling himself away as a story-teller. But how far more darkly would they have frowned could they have understood that he had converted the very principle of their own being into one of his toys!

It will be seen that I am far from being struck with the justice of that view of the author of the *Twice-Told Tales,* which is so happily expressed by the French critic to whom I alluded at an earlier stage of this essay. To speak of Hawthorne, as M. Emile Montégut does, as a *romancier pessimiste,* seems to me very much beside the mark. He is no more a pessimist than an optimist, though he is certainly not much of either. He does not pretend to conclude, or to have

a philosophy of human nature; indeed, I should even say
that at bottom he does not take human nature as hard as
he may seem to do. "His bitterness," says M. Montégut,
"is without abatement, and his bad opinion of man is
without compensation. . . . His little tales have the air of
confessions which the soul makes to itself; they are so many
little slaps which the author applies to our face." This, it
seems to me, is to exaggerate almost immeasurably the reach
of Hawthorne's relish of gloomy subjects. What pleased him
in such subjects was their picturesqueness, their rich duski-
ness of color, their chiaroscuro; but they were not the expression of a hopeless, or even of a predominantly melancholy, feeling about the human soul. Such at least is my
own impression. He is to a considerable degree ironical—
this is part of his charm—part even, one may say, of his
brightness; but he is neither bitter nor cynical—he is rarely
even what I should call tragical. There have certainly been
story-tellers of a gayer and lighter spirit; there have been observers more humorous, more hilarious—though on the whole
Hawthorne's observation has a smile in it oftener than may
at first appear; but there has rarely been an observer more
serene, less agitated by what he sees, and less disposed to
call things deeply into question. As I have already intimated,
his *Note-Books* are full of this simple and almost childlike
serenity. That dusky preoccupation with the misery of human life and the wickedness of the human heart which such
a critic as M. Emile Montégut talks about, is totally absent
from them; and if we may suppose a person to have read
these diaries before looking into the tales, we may be sure
that such a reader would be greatly surprised to hear the
author described as a disappointed, disdainful genius. "This
marked love of cases of conscience," says M. Montégut, "this
taciturn, scornful cast of mind, this habit of seeing sin everywhere and hell always gaping open, this dusky gaze bent
always upon a damned world and a nature draped in mourning, these lonely conversations of the imagination with the
conscience, this pitiless analysis resulting from a perpetual
examination of one's self, and from the tortures of a heart
closed before men and open to God—all these elements of

the Puritan character have passed into Mr. Hawthorne, or to speak more justly, have *filtered* into him, through a long succession of generations." This is a very pretty and very vivid account of Hawthorne, superficially considered; and it is just such a view of the case as would commend itself most easily and most naturally to a hasty critic. It is all true indeed, with a difference; Hawthorne was all that M. Montégut says, *minus* the conviction. The old Puritan moral sense, the consciousness of sin and hell, of the fearful nature of our responsibilities and the savage character of our Taskmaster—these things had been lodged in the mind of a man of Fancy, whose fancy had straightway begun to take liberties and play tricks with them—to judge them (Heaven forgive him!) from the poetic and aesthetic point of view, the point of view of entertainment and irony. This absence of conviction makes the difference; but the difference is great. Hawthorne was a man of fancy, and I suppose that in speaking of him it is inevitable that we should feel ourselves confronted with the familiar problem of the difference between the fancy and the imagination. Of the larger and more potent faculty he certainly possessed a liberal share; no one can read *The House of the Seven Gables* without feeling it to be a deeply imaginative work. But I am often struck, especially in the shorter tales, of which I am now chiefly speaking, with a kind of small ingenuity, a taste for conceits and analogies, which bears more particularly what is called the fanciful stamp. The finer of the shorter tales are redolent of a rich imagination.

Had Goodman Brown fallen asleep in the forest and only dreamed a wild dream of witch-meeting? Be it so, if you will; but, alas, it was a dream of evil omen for young Goodman Brown! a stern, a sad, a darkly meditative, a distrustful, if not a desperate, man, did he become from the night of that fearful dream. On the Sabbath day, when the congregation were singing a holy psalm, he could not listen, because an anthem of sin rushed loudly upon his ear and drowned all the blessed strain. When the minister spoke from the pulpit, with power and fervid eloquence, and with his hand on the open Bible of the sacred truth of our religion, and of saintlike lives and triumphant

deaths, and of future bliss or misery unutterable, then did Goodman Brown grow pale, dreading lest the roof should thunder
down upon the gray blasphemer and his hearers. Often, awaking
suddenly at midnight, he shrank from the bosom of Faith; and
at morning or eventide, when the family knelt down at prayer,
he scowled and muttered to himself, and gazed sternly at his
wife, and turned away. And when he had lived long, and was
borne to his grave a hoary corpse, followed by Faith, an aged
woman, and children, and grandchildren, a goodly procession,
besides neighbors not a few, they carved no hopeful verse upon
his tombstone, for his dying hour was gloom.

There is imagination in that, and in many another passage
that I might quote; but as a general thing I should characterize the more metaphysical of our author's short stories as
graceful and felicitous conceits. They seem to me to be
qualified in this manner by the very fact that they belong
to the province of allegory. Hawthorne, in his metaphysical
moods, is nothing if not allegorical, and allegory, to my sense,
is quite one of the lighter exercises of the imagination. Many
excellent judges, I know, have a great stomach for it; they
delight in symbols and correspondences, in seeing a story
told as if it were another and a very different story. I frankly
confess that I have as a general thing but little enjoyment
of it and that it has never seemed to me to be, as it were, a
first-rate literary form. It has produced assuredly some first-
rate works; and Hawthorne in his younger years had been a
great reader and devotee of Bunyan and Spenser, the great
masters of allegory. But it is apt to spoil two good things—
a story and a moral, a meaning and a form; and the taste
for it is responsible for a large part of the forcible-feeble
writing that has been inflicted upon the world. The only
case in which it is endurable is when it is extremely spontaneous, when the analogy presents itself with eager promptitude. When it shows signs of having been groped and
fumbled for, the needful illusion is of course absent and
the failure complete. Then the machinery alone is visible, and the end to which it operates becomes a matter
of indifference. There was but little literary criticism in
the United States at the time Hawthorne's earlier works

were published; but among the reviewers Edgar Poe perhaps held the scales the highest. He at any rate rattled them loudest, and pretended, more than anyone else, to conduct the weighing process on scientific principles. Very remarkable was this process of Edgar Poe's, and very extraordinary were his principles; but he had the advantage of being a man of genius, and his intelligence was frequently great. His collection of critical sketches of the American writers flourishing in what M. Taine would call his *milieu* and *moment* is very curious and interesting reading, and it has one quality which ought to keep it from ever being completely forgotten. It is probably the most complete and exquisite specimen of *provincialism* ever prepared for the edification of men. Poe's judgments are pretentious, spiteful, vulgar; but they contain a great deal of sense and discrimination as well, and here and there, sometimes at frequent intervals, we find a phrase of happy insight imbedded in a patch of the most fatuous pedantry. He wrote a chapter upon Hawthorne, and spoke of him on the whole very kindly; and his estimate is of sufficient value to make it noticeable that he should express lively disapproval of the large part allotted to allegory in his tales—in defense of which, he says, "however, or for whatever object employed, there is scarcely one respectable word to be said. . . . The deepest emotion," he goes on, "aroused within us by the happiest allegory *as* allegory, is a very, *very* imperfectly satisfied sense of the writer's ingenuity in overcoming a difficulty we should have preferred his not having attempted to overcome. . . . One thing is clear, that if allegory ever establishes a fact, it is by dint of overturning a fiction"; and Poe has furthermore the courage to remark that the *Pilgrim's Progress* is a "ludicrously overrated book." Certainly, as a general thing, we are struck with the ingenuity and felicity of Hawthorne's analogies and correspondences; the idea appears to have made itself at home in them easily. Nothing could be better in this respect than the *Snow-Image* (a little masterpiece), or *The Great Carbuncle*, or *Doctor Heidegger's Experiment*, or *Rappacini's Daughter*. But in such things as *The Birth-Mark* and *The Bosom-Serpent* we are struck with something stiff and mechanical, slightly incongruous, as if the kernel had not assimilated its envelope. But these are matters of light impression, and there would be a want of tact in pretending to discriminate too closely among things which all, in one way or another, have a charm. The charm—the great charm—is that they are glimpses of a great field, of the whole deep mystery of man's soul and conscience. They are moral, and their interest is moral; they deal with something more than the mere accidents and conventionalities, the surface occurrences of life. The fine thing in Hawthorne is that he cared for the deeper psychology, and that, in his way, he tried to become familiar with it. This natural, yet fanciful familiarity with it, this air, on the author's part, of being a confirmed *habitué* of a region of mysteries and subtleties, constitutes the originality of his tales. And then they have the further merit of seeming, for what they are, to spring up so freely and lightly. The author has all the ease, indeed, of a regular dweller in the moral, psychological realm; he goes to and fro in it, as a man who knows his way. His tread is a light and modest one, but he keeps the key in his pocket.

His little historical stories all seem to me admirable; they are so good that you may reread them many times. They are not numerous, and they are very short; but they are full of a vivid and delightful sense of the New England past; they have, moreover, the distinction, little tales of a dozen and fifteen pages as they are, of being the only successful attempts at historical fiction that have been made in the United States. Hawthorne was at home in the early New England history; he had thumbed its records and he had breathed its air, in whatever odd receptacles this somewhat pungent compound still lurked. He was fond of it, and he was proud of it, as any New Englander must be, measuring the part of that handful of half-starved fanatics who formed his earliest precursors, in laying the foundations of a mighty empire. Hungry for the picturesque as he always was, and not finding any very copious provision of it around him, he turned back into the two preceding centuries, with the earnest determination that the primitive annals of Massachusetts should at least *appear* picturesque. His fancy, which was always alive, played a little with the somewhat meager and angular facts of the colonial period and forthwith converted a great many of them into impressive legends and pictures. There is a little infusion of color, a little vagueness about certain details, but it is very gracefully and discreetly done, and realities are kept in view sufficiently to make us feel that if we are reading romance, it is romance that rather supplements than contradicts history. The early annals of New England were not fertile in legend, but Hawthorne laid his hands upon everything that would serve his purpose, and in two or three cases his version of the story has a great deal of beauty. *The Grey Champion* is a sketch of less than eight pages, but the little figures stand up in the tale as stoutly, at the least, as if they were propped up on half-a-dozen chapters by a dryer annalist, and the whole thing has the merit of those cabinet pictures in which the artist has been able to make his persons look the size of life. Hawthorne, to say it again, was not in the least a realist—he was not to my mind enough of one; but there is no genuine lover of the good city of Boston but will feel grateful to him for his courage in attempting to recount the "traditions" of Washington Street, the main thoroughfare of the Puritan capital. The four *Legends of the Province House* are certain shadowy stories which he professes to have gathered in an ancient tavern lurking behind the modern shop-fronts of this part of the city. The Province House disappeared some years ago, but while it stood it was pointed to as the residence of the Royal Governors of Massachusetts before the Revolution. I have no recollection of it, but it cannot have been, even from Hawthorne's account of it, which is as pictorial as he ventures to make it, a very imposing piece of antiquity. The writer's charming touch, however, throws a rich brown tone over its rather shallow venerableness; and we are beguiled into believing, for instance, at the close of *Howe's Masquerade* (a story of a strange occurrence at an entertainment given by Sir William Howe, the last of the Royal Governors, during the siege of Boston by Washington), that "superstition, among other legends of this mansion, repeats the wondrous tale that on the anniversary night of Britain's discomfiture the ghosts of the ancient governors of Massachusetts still glide through the Province House. And last of all comes a figure shrouded in a military cloak, tossing his clenched hands into the air and stamping his iron-shod boots upon the freestone steps, with a semblance of feverish despair, but without the sound of a foot-tramp." Hawthorne had, as regards the two earlier centuries of New England life, that faculty which is called nowadays the historic consciousness. He never sought to exhibit it on a large scale; he exhibited it indeed on a scale so minute that we must not linger too much upon it. His vision of the past was filled with definite images—images nonetheless definite, that they were concerned with events as shadowy as this dramatic passing away of the last of King George's representatives in his long loyal but finally alienated colony.

I have said that Hawthorne had become engaged in about his thirty-fifth year; but he was not married until 1842. Before this event took place he passed through two episodes which (putting his falling in love aside) were much the most important things that had yet happened to him. They interrupted the painful monotony of his life, and brought the affairs of men within his personal experience. One of these was moreover in itself a curious and interesting chapter of observation, and it fructified, in Hawthorne's memory, in one of his best productions. How urgently he needed at this time to be drawn within the circle of social accidents, a little anecdote related by Mr. Lathrop in connection with his first acquaintance with the young lady he was to marry may serve as an example. This young lady became known to him through her sister, who had first approached him as an admirer of the *Twice-Told Tales* (as to the authorship of which she had been so much in the dark as to have attributed it first, conjecturally, to one of the two Miss Hathornes); and the two Miss Peabodys, desiring to see more of the charming writer, caused him to be invited to a species of *conversazione* at the house of one of their friends, at which they themselves took care to be punctual. Several other ladies, however, were as punctual as they, and Hawthorne presently arriving, and seeing a bevy of admirers where he had expected but three or four, fell into a state of agitation, which is vividly described by his biographer. He "stood perfectly motionless, but with the look of a sylvan creature on the point of fleeing away . . . He was stricken with dismay; his face lost color and took on a warm paleness . . . his agitation was very great; he stood by a table and, taking up some small object that lay upon it, he found his hand trembling so that he was obliged to lay it down." It was desirable, certainly, that something should occur to break the spell of a diffidence that might justly be called morbid. There is another little sentence dropped by Mr. Lathrop in relation to this period of Hawthorne's life, which appears to me worth quoting, though I am by no means sure that it will seem so to the reader. It has a very simple and innocent air, but to a person not without an impression of the early days of "culture" in New England, it will be pregnant with historic meaning. The elder Miss Peabody, who afterwards was Hawthorne's sister-in-law and who acquired later in life a very honorable American fame as a woman of benevolence, of learning, and of literary accomplishment, had invited the Miss Hathornes to come to her house for the evening, and to bring with them their brother, whom she wished to thank for his beautiful tales. "Entirely to her surprise," says Mr. Lathrop, completing thereby his picture of the attitude of this remarkable family toward society—"entirely to her surprise they came. She herself opened the door, and there, before her, between his sisters, stood a splendidly handsome youth, tall and strong, with no appearance whatever of timidity, but instead, an almost fierce determination making his face stern. This was his resource for carrying off the extreme inward tremor which he really felt. His hostess brought out Flaxman's designs for Dante, just received from Professor Felton, of Harvard, and the party made an evening's entertainment out of them." This last sentence is the one I allude to; and were it not for fear of appearing too fanciful I should say that these few words were, to the initiated mind, an unconscious expression of the lonely frigidity which characterized most attempts at social recreation in the New England world some forty years ago. There was at that time a great desire for culture, a great interest in knowledge, in art, in aesthetics, together with a very scanty supply of the materials for such pursuits. Small things were made to do large service; and there is something even touching in the solemnity of consideration that was bestowed by the emancipated New England conscience upon little wandering books and prints, little echoes and rumors of observation and experience. There flourished at that time in Boston a very remarkable and interesting woman, of whom we shall have more to say, Miss Margaret Fuller by name. This lady was the apostle of culture, of intellectual curiosity, and in the peculiarly interesting account of her life, published in 1852 by Emerson and two other of her friends, there are pages of her letters and diaries which narrate her visits to the Boston Athenaeum and the emotions aroused in her mind by turning over portfolios of engravings. These emotions were ardent and passionate—could hardly have been more so had she been prostrate with contemplation in the Sistine Chapel or in one of the chambers of the Pitti Palace. The only analogy I can recall to this earnestness of interest in great works of art at a distance from them is furnished by the great Goethe's elaborate study of plaster casts and pencil drawings at Weimar. I mention Margaret Fuller here because a glimpse of her state of mind—her vivacity of desire and poverty of knowledge—helps to define the situation. The situation lives for a moment in those few words of Mr. Lathrop's. The initiated mind, as I have ventured to call it, has a vision of a little unadorned parlor, with the snow-drifts of a Massachusetts winter piled up about its windows, and a group of sensitive and serious people, modest votaries of opportunity, fixing their eyes upon a bookful of Flaxman's attenuated outlines.

At the beginning of the year 1839 he received, through political interest, an appointment as weigher and gauger in the Boston Custom-house. Mr. Van Buren then occupied the Presidency, and it appears that the Democratic party, whose successful candidate he had been, rather took credit for the patronage it had bestowed upon literary men. Hawthorne was a Democrat, and apparently a zealous one; even in later years, after the Whigs had vivified their principles by the adoption of the Republican platform, and by taking up an honest attitude on the question of slavery, his political faith never wavered. His Democratic sympathies were eminently natural, and there would have been an incongruity in his belonging to the other party. He was not only by conviction, but personally and by association, a Democrat. When in later years he found himself in contact with European civilization, he appears to have become conscious of a good deal of latent radicalism in his disposition; he was oppressed with the burden of antiquity in Europe, and he found himself sighing for lightness and freshness and facility of change. But these things are relative to the point of view, and in his own country Hawthorne cast his lot with the party of conservatism, the party opposed to change and freshness. The people who found something musty and moldy in his literary productions would have regarded this quite as a matter of course; but we are not obliged to use invidious epithets in describing his political preferences. The sentiment that attached him to the Democracy was a subtle and honorable one, and the author of an attempt to sketch a portrait of him should be the last to complain of this adjustment of his sympathies. It falls much more smoothly into his reader's conception of him than any other would do; and if he had had the perversity to be a Republican, I am afraid our ingenuity would have been considerably taxed in devising a proper explanation of the circumstance. At any rate, the Democrats gave him a small post in the Boston Customhouse, to which an annual salary of $1,200 was attached, and Hawthorne appears at first to have joyously welcomed the gift. The duties of the office were not very congruous to the genius of a man of fancy; but it had the advantage that it broke the spell of his cursed solitude, as he called it, drew him away from Salem, and threw him, comparatively speaking, into the world. The first volume of the American *Note-Books* contains some extracts from letters written during his tenure of this modest office, which indicate sufficiently that his occupations cannot have been intrinsically gratifying.

I have been measuring coal all day, he writes, during the winter of 1840, on board of a black little British schooner, in a dismal dock at the north end of the city. Most of the time I paced the deck to keep myself warm; for the wind (northeast, I believe) blew up through the dock as if it had been the pipe of a pair of bellows. The vessel lying deep between two wharves, there was no more delightful prospect, on the right hand and on the left, than the posts and timbers, half immersed in the water and covered with ice, which the rising and falling of successive tides had left upon them, so that they looked like immense icicles. Across the water, however, not more than half a mile off, appeared the Bunker's Hill Monument, and what interested me considerably more, a church-steeple, with the dial of a clock upon it, whereby I was enabled to measure the march of the weary hours. Sometimes I descended into the dirty little cabin of the schooner, and warmed myself by a red-hot stove, among biscuit-barrels, pots and kettles, sea-chests, and innumerable lumber of all sorts—my olfactories meanwhile being greatly refreshed with the odor of a pipe, which the captain, or some one of his crew, was smoking. But at last came the sunset, with delicate clouds, and a purple light upon the islands; and I blessed it, because it was the signal of my release.

A worse man than Hawthorne would have measured coal quite as well, and of all the dismal tasks to which an unremunerated imagination has ever had to accommodate itself, I remember none more sordid than the business depicted in the foregoing lines. "I pray," he writes some weeks later, "that in one year more I may find some way of escaping from this unblest Custom-house; for it is a very grievous thraldom. I do detest all offices; all, at least, that are held on a political tenure, and I want nothing to do with politicians. Their hearts wither away and die out of their bodies. Their consciences are turned to india-rubber, or to some substance as black as that and which will stretch as much. One thing, if no more, I have gained by my Custom-house experience— to know a politician. It is a knowledge which no previous thought or power of sympathy could have taught me; because the animal, or the machine rather, is not in nature." A few days later he goes on in the same strain:

I do not think it is the doom laid upon me of murdering so many of the brightest hours of the day at the Custom-house that makes such havoc with my wits, for here I am again trying to write worthily . . . yet with a sense as if all the noblest part of man had been left out of my composition, or had decayed out of it since my nature was given to my own keeping. . . . Never comes any bird of Paradise into that dismal region. A salt or even a coal-ship is ten million times preferable; for there the sky is above me, and the fresh breeze around me, and my thoughts, having hardly anything to do with my occupation, are as free as air. Nevertheless . . . it is only once in a while that the image and desire of a better and happier life makes me feel the iron of my chain; for after all a human spirit may find no insufficiency of food for it, even in the Custom-house. And with such materials as these I do think and feel and learn things that are worth knowing, and which I should not know unless I had learned them there; so that the present position of my life shall not be quite left out of the sum of my real existence. . . . It is good for me, on many accounts, that my life has had this passage in it. I know much more than I did a year ago. I have a stronger sense of power to act as a man among men. I have gained worldly wisdom, and wisdom also that is not altogether of this world. And when I quit this earthly career where I am now buried, nothing will cling to me that ought to be left behind. Men will not perceive, I trust, by my look or the tenor of my thoughts and feelings, that I have been a Custom-house officer.

He says, writing shortly afterwards, that "When I shall be free again, I will enjoy all things with the fresh simplicity of a child of five years old. I shall grow young again, made all over anew. I will go forth and stand in a summer shower, and all the worldly dust that has collected on me shall be washed away at once, and my heart will be like a bank of fresh flowers for the weary to rest upon."

This forecast of his destiny was sufficiently exact. A year later, in April 1841, he went to take up his abode in the socialistic community of Brook Farm. Here he found himself among fields and flowers and other natural products— as well as among many products that could not very justly be called natural. He was exposed to summer showers in plenty; and his personal associations were as different as possible from those he had encountered in fiscal circles. He

made acquaintance with Transcendentalism and the Transcendentalists.

IV. Brook Farm and Concord

THE HISTORY of the little industrial and intellectual association which formed itself at this time in one of the suburbs
of Boston has not, to my knowledge, been written; though
it is assuredly a curious and interesting chapter in the domestic annals of New England. It would of course be easy
to overrate the importance of this ingenious attempt of a few
speculative persons to improve the outlook of mankind. The
experiment came and went very rapidly and quietly, leaving
very few traces behind it. It became simply a charming personal reminiscence for the small number of amiable enthusiasts who had had a hand in it. There were degrees of
enthusiasm, and I suppose there were degrees of amiability;
but a certain generous brightness of hope and freshness of
conviction pervaded the whole undertaking and rendered it,
morally speaking, important to an extent of which any heed
that the world in general ever gave to it is an insufficient
measure. Of course it would be a great mistake to represent
the episode of Brook Farm as directly related to the manners
and morals of the New England world in general—and in
especial to those of the prosperous, opulent, comfortable part
of it. The thing was the experiment of a coterie—it was unusual, unfashionable, unsuccessful. It was, as would then
have been said, an amusement of the Transcendentalists—a
harmless effusion of Radicalism. The Transcendentalists
were not, after all, very numerous; and the Radicals were
by no means of the vivid tinge of those of our own day. I
have said that the Brook Farm community left no traces
behind it that the world in general can appreciate; I should
rather say that the only trace is a short novel, of which the
principal merits reside in its qualities of difference from the
affair itself. *The Blithedale Romance* is the main result of
Brook Farm; but *The Blithedale Romance* was very properly
never recognized by the Brook Farmers as an accurate portrait of their little colony.

Nevertheless, in a society as to which the more frequent complaint is that it is monotonous, that it lacks variety of incident and of type, the episode, our own business with which is simply that it was the cause of Hawthorne's writing an admirable tale, might be welcomed as a picturesque variation. At the same time, if we do not exaggerate its proportions, it may seem to contain a fund of illustration as to that phase of human life with which our author's own history mingled itself. The most graceful account of the origin of Brook Farm is probably to be found in these words of one of the biographers of Margaret Fuller: "In Boston and its vicinity, several friends, for whose character Margaret felt the highest honor, were earnestly considering the possibility of making such industrial, social, and educational arrangements as would simplify economies, combine leisure for study with healthful and honest toil, avert unjust collisions of caste, equalize refinements, awaken generous affections, diffuse courtesy, and sweeten and sanctify life as a whole." The reader will perceive that this was a liberal scheme, and that if the experiment failed, the greater was the pity. The writer goes on to say that a gentleman, who afterwards distinguished himself in literature (he had begun by being a clergyman), "convinced by his experience in a faithful ministry that the need was urgent for a thorough application of the professed principles of Fraternity to actual relations, was about staking his all of fortune, reputation, and influence, in an attempt to organize a joint-stock company at Brook Farm." As Margaret Fuller passes for having suggested to Hawthorne the figure of Zenobia in *The Blithedale Romance,* and as she is probably, with one exception, the person connected with the affair who, after Hawthorne, offered most of what is called a personality to the world, I may venture to quote a few more passages from her Memoirs —a curious, in some points of view almost a grotesque, and yet, on the whole, as I have said, an extremely interesting book. It was a strange history and a strange destiny, that of this brilliant, restless, and unhappy woman—this ardent New Englander, this impassioned Yankee, who occupied so large a place in the thoughts, the lives, the affections, of an intelligent and appreciative society, and yet left behind her nothing but the memory of a memory. Her function, her reputation, were singular, and not altogether reassuring: she was a talker, she was *the* talker, she was the genius of talk. She had a magnificent, though by no means an unmitigated, egotism; and in some of her utterances it is difficult to say whether pride or humility prevails—as for instance when she writes that she feels "that there is plenty of room in the Universe for my faults, and as if I could not spend time in thinking of them when so many things interest me more." She has left the same sort of reputation as a great actress. Some of her writing has extreme beauty, almost all of it has a real interest, but her value, her activity, her sway (I am not sure that one can say her charm), were personal and practical. She went to Europe, expanded to new desires and interests, and, very poor herself, married an impoverished Italian nobleman. Then, with her husband and child, she embarked to return to her own country, and was lost at sea in a terrible storm, within sight of its coasts. Her tragical death combined with many of the elements of her life to convert her memory into a sort of legend, so that the people who had known her well grew at last to be envied by later comers. Hawthorne does not appear to have been intimate with her; on the contrary, I find such an entry as this in the American *Note-Books* in 1841: "I was invited to dine at Mr. Bancroft's yesterday, with Miss Margaret Fuller; but Providence had given me some business to do; for which I was very thankful!" It is true that, later, the lady is the subject of one or two allusions of a gentler cast. One of them indeed is so pretty as to be worth quoting:

After leaving the book at Mr. Emerson's, I returned through the woods, and, entering Sleepy Hollow, I perceived a lady reclining near the path which bends along its verge. It was Margaret herself. She had been there the whole afternoon, meditating or reading, for she had a book in her hand with some strange title which I did not understand and have forgotten. She said that nobody had broken her solitude, and was just giving utterance to a theory that no inhabitant of Concord ever visited Sleepy Hollow, when we saw a group of people entering the sacred precincts. Most of them followed a path which led them away from us; but an old man passed near us, and smiled to see Margaret reclining on the ground and me standing by her side. He made some remark upon the beauty of the afternoon, and withdrew himself into the shadow of the wood. Then we talked about autumn, and about the pleasures of being lost in the woods, and about the crows, whose voices Margaret had heard; and about the experiences of early childhood, whose influence remains upon the character after the recollection of them has passed away; and about the sight of mountains from a distance, and the view from their summits; and about other matters of high and low philosophy.

It is safe to assume that Hawthorne could not on the whole have had a high relish for the very positive personality of this accomplished and argumentative woman, in whose intellect high noon seemed ever to reign, as twilight did in his own. He must have been struck with the glare of her understanding, and, mentally speaking, have scowled and blinked a good deal in conversation with her. But it is tolerably manifest, nevertheless, that she was, in his imagination, the starting-point of the figure of Zenobia; and Zenobia is, to my sense, his only very definite attempt at the representation of a character. The portrait is full of alteration and embellishment; but it has a greater reality, a greater abundance of detail, than any of his other figures, and the reality was a memory of the lady whom he had encountered in the Roxbury pastoral or among the wood-walks of Concord, with strange books in her hand and eloquent discourse on her lips. *The Blithedale Romance* was written just after her unhappy death, when the reverberation of her talk would lose much of its harshness. In fact, however, very much the same qualities that made Hawthorne a Democrat in politics—his contemplative turn and absence of a keen perception of abuses, his taste for old ideals, and loitering paces, and muffled tones—would operate to keep him out of active sympathy with a woman of the so-called progressive type. We may be sure that in women his taste was conservative.

It seems odd, as his biographer says, "that the least gregarious of men should have been drawn into a socialistic community"; but although it is apparent that Hawthorne went to Brook Farm without any great Transcendental fervor, yet he had various good reasons for casting his lot in this would-be happy family. He was as yet unable to marry, but he naturally wished to do so as speedily as possible, and there was a prospect that Brook Farm would prove an economical residence. And then it is only fair to believe that Hawthorne was interested in the experiment, and that though he was not a Transcendentalist, an Abolitionist, or a Fourierite, as his companions were in some degree or other likely to be, he was willing, as a generous and unoccupied young man, to lend a hand in any reasonable scheme for helping people to live together on better terms than the common. The Brook Farm scheme was, as such things go, a reasonable one; it was devised and carried out by shrewd and sober-minded New Englanders, who were careful to place economy first and idealism afterwards, and who were not afflicted with a Gallic passion for completeness of theory. There were no formulas, doctrines, dogmas; there was no interference whatever with private life or individual habits, and not the faintest adumbration of a rearrangement of that difficult business known as the relations of the sexes. The relations of the sexes were neither more nor less than what they usually are in American life, excellent; and in such particulars the scheme was thoroughly conservative and irreproachable. Its main characteristic was that each individual concerned in it should do a part of the work necessary for keeping the whole machine going. He could choose his work and he could live as he liked; it was hoped, but it was by no means demanded, that he would make himself agreeable, like a gentleman invited to a dinner-party. Allowing, however, for everything that was a concession to worldly traditions and to the laxity of man's nature, there must have been in the enterprise a good deal of a certain freshness and purity of spirit, of a certain noble credulity and faith in the perfectibility of man, which it would have been easier to find in Boston in the year 1840, than in London five-and-thirty years later. If that was the era of Transcendentalism,

Transcendentalism could only have sprouted in the soil peculiar to the general locality of which I speak—the soil of the old New England morality, gently raked and refreshed by an imported culture. The Transcendentalists read a great deal of French and German, made themselves intimate with George Sand and Goethe, and many other writers; but the strong and deep New England conscience accompanied them on all their intellectual excursions, and there never was a so-called "movement" that embodied itself, on the whole, in fewer eccentricities of conduct, or that borrowed a smaller license in private deportment. Henry Thoreau, a delightful writer, went to live in the woods; but Henry Thoreau was essentially a sylvan personage and would not have been, however the fashion of his time might have turned, a man about town. The brothers and sisters at Brook Farm plowed the fields and milked the cows; but I think that an observer from another clime and society would have been much more struck with their spirit of conformity than with their *dérèglements*. Their ardor was a moral ardor, and the lightest breath of scandal never rested upon them, or upon any phase of Transcendentalism.

A biographer of Hawthorne might well regret that his hero had not been more mixed up with the reforming and free-thinking class, so that he might find a pretext for writing a chapter upon the state of Boston society forty years ago. A needful warrant for such regret should be, properly, that the biographer's own personal reminiscences should stretch back to that period and to the persons who animated it. This would be a guarantee of fulness of knowledge and, presumably, of kindness of tone. It is difficult to see, indeed, how the generation of which Hawthorne has given us, in *Blithedale*, a few portraits, should not at this time of day be spoken of very tenderly and sympathetically. If irony enter into the allusion, it should be of the lightest and gentlest. Certainly, for a brief and imperfect chronicler of these things, a writer just touching them as he passes, and who has not the advantage of having been a contemporary, there is only one possible tone. The compiler of these pages, though his recollections date only from a later period, has a memory of a certain number of persons who had been intimately connected, as Hawthorne was not, with the agitations of that interesting time. Something of its interest adhered to them still—something of its aroma clung to their garments; there was something about them which seemed to say that when they were young and enthusiastic, they had been initiated into moral mysteries, they had played at a wonderful game. Their usual mark (it is true I can think of exceptions) was that they seemed excellently good. They appeared unstained by the world, unfamiliar with worldly desires and standards, and with those various forms of human depravity which flourish in some high phases of civilization; inclined to simple and democratic ways, destitute of pretensions and affectations, of jealousies, of cynicism, of snobbishness. This little epoch of fermentation has three or four drawbacks for the critic—drawbacks, however, that may be overlooked by a person for whom it has an interest of association. It bore, intellectually, the stamp of provincialism; it was a beginning without a fruition, a dawn without a noon; and it produced, with a single exception, no great talents. It produced a great deal of writing, but (always putting Hawthorne aside, as a contemporary but not a sharer) only one writer in whom the world at large has interested itself. The situation was summed up and transfigured in the admirable and exquisite Emerson. He expressed all that it contained, and a good deal more, doubtless, besides; he was the man of genius of the moment; he was the Transcendentalist *par excellence*. Emerson expressed, before all things, as was extremely natural at the hour and in the place, the value and importance of the individual, the duty of making the most of one's self, of living by one's own personal light and carrying out one's own disposition. He reflected with beautiful irony upon the exquisite impudence of those institutions which claim to have appropriated the truth, and to dole it out in proportionate morsels, in exchange for a subscription. He talked about the beauty and dignity of life, and about everyone who is born into the world being born to the whole, having an interest and a stake in the whole. He said "all that is clearly due today is not to lie," and a great many other things which it would be still easier to present in a ridiculous light. He insisted upon sincerity and independence and spontaneity, upon acting in harmony with one's nature, and not conforming and compromising for the sake of being more comfortable. He urged that a man should await his call, his finding the thing to do which he should really believe in doing, and not be urged by the world's opinion to do simply the world's work. "If no call should come for years, for centuries, then I know that the want of the Universe is the attestation of faith by my abstinence. . . . If I cannot work, at least I need not lie." The doctrine of the supremacy of the individual to himself, of his originality and, as regards his own character, *unique* quality, must have had a great charm for people living in a society in which introspection, thanks to the want of other entertainment, played almost the part of a social resource.

In the United States, in those days, there were no great things to look out at (save forests and rivers); life was not in the least spectacular; society was not brilliant; the country was given up to a great material prosperity, a homely *bourgeois* activity, a diffusion of primary education and the common luxuries. There was therefore, among the cultivated classes, much relish for the utterances of a writer who would help one to take a picturesque view of one's internal possibilities, and to find in the landscape of the soul all sorts of fine sunrise and moonlight effects. "Meantime, while the doors of the temple stand open, night and day, before every man, and the oracles of this truth cease never, it is guarded by one stern condition; this, namely—it is an intuition. It cannot be received at second hand. Truly speaking, it is not instruction but provocation that I can receive from another soul." To make one's self so much more interesting would help to make life interesting, and life was probably, to many of this aspiring congregation, a dream of freedom and fortitude. There were faulty parts in the Emersonian philosophy; but the general tone was magnificent; and I can easily believe that, coming when it did and where it did, it should have been drunk in by a great many fine moral appetites with a sense of intoxication. One envies, even, I will not say the illusions, of that keenly sentient period, but the convictions and interests—the moral passion. One certainly envies the privilege of having heard the finest of Emerson's orations poured forth in their early newness. They were the most poetical, the most beautiful productions of the American mind, and they were thoroughly local and national. They had a music and a magic, and when one remembers the remarkable charm of the speaker, the beautiful modulation of his utterance, one regrets in especial that one might not have been present on a certain occasion which made a sensation, an era—the delivery of an address to the Divinity School of Harvard University, on a summer evening in 1838. In the light, fresh American air, unthickened and undarkened by customs and institutions established, these things, as the phrase is, told.

Hawthorne appears, like his own Miles Coverdale, to have arrived at Brook Farm in the midst of one of those April snow-storms which, during the New England spring, occasionally diversify the inaction of the vernal process. Miles Coverdale, in *The Blithedale Romance,* is evidently as much Hawthorne as he is anyone else in particular. He is indeed not very markedly anyone, unless it be the spectator, the observer; his chief identity lies in his success in looking at things objectively and spinning uncommunicated fancies about them. This indeed was the part that Hawthorne played socially in the little community at West Roxbury. His biographer describes him as sitting "silently, hour after hour, in the broad old-fashioned hall of the house, where he could listen almost unseen to the chat and merriment of the young people, himself almost always holding a book before him, but seldom turning the leaves." He put his hand to the plow and supported himself and the community, as they were all supposed to do, by his labor; but he contributed little to the hum of voices. Some of his companions, either then or afterwards, took, I believe, rather a gruesome view of his want of articulate enthusiasm, and accused him of coming to the place as a sort of intellectual vampire, for purely psychological purposes. He sat in a ccrner, they declared, and watched the inmates when they were off their

guard, analyzing their characters, and dissecting the amiable
ardor, the magnanimous illusions, which he was too cold-
blooded to share. In so far as this account of Hawthorne's
attitude was a complaint, it was a singularly childish one.
If he was at Brook Farm without being of it, this is a very
fortunate circumstance from the point of view of posterity,
who would have preserved but a slender memory of the
affair if our author's fine novel had not kept the topic open.
The complaint is indeed almost so ungrateful a one as to
make us regret that the author's fellow-communists came off
so easily. They certainly would not have done so if the
author of *Blithedale* had been more of a satirist. Certainly,
if Hawthorne was an observer, he was a very harmless one;
and when one thinks of the queer specimens of the reforming genus with which he must have been surrounded, one
almost wishes that, for our entertainment, he had given his
old companions something to complain of in earnest. There
is no satire whatever in the *Romance;* the quality is almost
conspicuous by its absence. Of portraits there are only two;
there is no sketching of odd figures—no reproduction of
strange types of radicalism; the human background is left
vague. Hawthorne was not a satirist, and if at Brook Farm
he was, according to his habit, a good deal of a mild skeptic,
his skepticism was exercised much more in the interest of
fancy than in that of reality.

There must have been something pleasantly bucolic and
pastoral in the habits of the place during the fine New England summer; but we have no retrospective envy of the
denizens of Brook Farm in that other season which, as
Hawthorne somewhere says, leaves in those regions "so
large a blank—so melancholy a deathspot—in lives so brief
that they ought to be all summertime." "Of a summer night,
when the moon was full," says Mr. Lathrop, "they lit no
lamps, but sat grouped in the light and shadow, while sundry
of the younger men sang old ballads, or joined Tom Moore's
songs to operatic airs. On other nights there would be an
original essay or poem read aloud, or else a play of Shakespeare, with the parts distributed to different members; and
these amusements failing, some interesting discussion was

likely to take their place. Occasionally, in the dramatic season, large delegations from the farm would drive into Boston,
in carriages and wagons, to the opera or the play. Sometimes,
too, the young women sang as they washed the dishes in
the Hive; and the youthful yeomen of the society came in
and helped them with their work. The men wore blouses
of a checked or plaided stuff, belted at the waist, with a
broad collar folding down about the throat, and rough straw
hats; the women, usually, simple calico gowns and hats."
All this sounds delightfully Arcadian and innocent, and it
is certain that there was something peculiar to the clime
and race in some of the features of such a life; in the free,
frank, and stainless companionship of young men and
maidens, in the mixture of manual labor and intellectual
flights—dish-washing and aesthetics, wood-chopping and
philosophy. Wordsworth's "plain living and high thinking"
were made actual. Some passages in Margaret Fuller's journals throw plenty of light on this. (It must be premised that
she was at Brook Farm as an occasional visitor; not as a
laborer in the Hive.)

All Saturday I was off in the woods. In the evening we had
a general conversation, opened by me, upon Education, in its
largest sense, and on what we can do for ourselves and others.
I took my usual ground: The aim is perfection; patience the
road. Our lives should be considered as a tendency, an approximation only. . . . Mr. R. spoke admirably on the nature of
loyalty. The people showed a good deal of the *sans-culotte*
tendency in their manners, throwing themselves on the floor,
yawning, and going out when they had heard enough. Yet as
the majority differ with me, to begin with—that being the reason
this subject was chosen—they showed on the whole more interest and deference than I had expected. As I am accustomed
to deference, however, and need it for the boldness and anima-
tion which my part requires, I did not speak with as much force
as usual. . . . Sunday.—A glorious day; the woods full of
perfume; I was out all the morning. In the afternoon Mrs. R.
and I had a talk. I said my position would be too uncertain here,
as I could not work. —— said "they would all like to work for
a person of genius." . . . "Yes," I told her; "but where would
be my repose when they were always to be judging whether I

was worth it or not? . . . Each day you must prove yourself
anew." . . . We talked of the principles of the community.
I said I had not a right to come, because all the confidence I
had in it was as an *experiment* worth trying, and that it was part
of the great wave of inspired thought. . . . We had valuable
discussion on these points. All Monday morning in the woods
again. Afternoon, out with the drawing party; I felt the evils
of the want of conventional refinement, in the impudence with
which one of the girls treated me. She has since thought of it
with regret, I notice; and by every day's observation of me will
see that she ought not to have done it. In the evening a husking
in the barn . . . a most picturesque scene . . . I stayed and
helped about half an hour, and then took a long walk beneath
the stars. Wednesday. . . . In the evening a conversation on
Impulse . . . I defended nature, as I always do—the spirit
ascending through, not superseding, nature. But in the scale of
Sense, Intellect, Spirit, I advocated the claims of Intellect, because those present were rather disposed to postpone them. On
the nature of Beauty we had good talk. —— seemed in a much
more reverent humor than the other night, and enjoyed the
large plans of the universe which were unrolled. . . . Saturday.—Well, good-by, Brook Farm. I know more about this place
than I did when I came; but the only way to be qualified for a
judge of such an experiment would be to become an active,
though unimpassioned, associate in trying it. . . . The girl
who was so rude to me stood waiting, with a timid air, to bid
me good-by.

The young girl in question cannot have been Hawthorne's
charming Priscilla; nor yet another young lady, of a most
humble spirit, who communicated to Margaret's biographers
her recollections of this remarkable woman's visits to Brook
Farm; concluding with the assurance that "after a while
she seemed to lose sight of my more prominent and disagreeable peculiarities, and treated me with affectionate regard."
Hawthorne's farewell to the place appears to have been
accompanied with some reflections of a cast similar to those
indicated by Miss Fuller; insofar at least as we may attribute
to Hawthorne himself some of the observations that he
fathers upon Miles Coverdale. His biographer justly quotes
two or three sentences from *The Blithedale Romance*, as
striking the note of the author's feeling about the place.

"No sagacious man," says Coverdale, "will long retain his sagacity if he live exclusively among reformers and progressive people, without periodically returning to the settled system of things, to correct himself by a new observation from that old standpoint." And he remarks elsewhere that "it struck me as rather odd that one of the first questions raised, after our separation from the greedy, struggling, self-seeking world, should relate to the possibility of getting the advantage over the outside barbarians in their own field of labor. But to tell the truth, I very soon became sensible that, as regarded society at large, we stood in a position of new hostility rather than new brotherhood." He was doubtless oppressed by the "sultry heat of society," as he calls it in one of the jottings in the *Note-Books*. "What would a man do if he were compelled to live always in the sultry heat of society, and could never bathe himself in cool solitude?" His biographer relates that one of the other Brook Farmers, wandering afield one summer's day, discovered Hawthorne stretched at his length upon a grassy hillside, with his hat pulled over his face, and every appearance, in his attitude, of the desire to escape detection. On his asking him whether he had any particular reason for this shyness of posture— "Too much of a party up there!" Hawthorne contented himself with replying, with a nod in the direction of the Hive. He had nevertheless for a time looked forward to remaining indefinitely in the community; he meant to marry as soon as possible and bring his wife there to live. Some sixty pages of the second volume of the American *Note-Books* are occupied with extracts from his letters to his future wife and from his journal (which appears however at this time to have been only intermittent), consisting almost exclusively of descriptions of the simple scenery of the neighborhood, and of the state of the woods and fields and weather. Hawthorne's fondness for all the common things of nature was deep and constant, and there is always something charming in his verbal touch, as we may call it, when he talks to himself about them. "Oh," he breaks out, of an October afternoon, "the beauty of grassy slopes, and the hollow ways of paths winding between hills, and the intervals between the road and wood-lots, where Summer lingers and sits down, strewing dandelions of gold and blue asters as her parting gifts and memorials!" He was but a single summer at Brook Farm; the rest of his residence had the winter quality.

But if he returned to solitude, it was henceforth to be as the French say, a *solitude à deux.* He was married in July 1842, and betook himself immediately to the ancient village of Concord, near Boston, where he occupied the so-called Manse which has given the title to one of his collections of tales, and upon which this work, in turn, has conferred a permanent distinction. I use the epithets "ancient" and "near" in the foregoing sentence, according to the American measurement of time and distance. Concord is some twenty miles from Boston, and even today, upwards of forty years after the date of Hawthorne's removal thither, it is a very fresh and well-preserved looking town. It had already a local history when, a hundred years ago, the larger current of human affairs flowed for a moment around it. Concord has the honor of being the first spot in which blood was shed in the war of the Revolution; here occurred the first exchange of musket shots between the King's troops and the American insurgents. Here, as Emerson says in the little hymn which he contributed in 1836 to the dedication of a small monument commemorating this circumstance—

> Here once the embattled farmers stood,
> And fired the shot heard round the world.

The battle was a small one, and the farmers were not destined individually to emerge from obscurity; but the memory of these things has kept the reputation of Concord green, and it has been watered, moreover, so to speak, by the lifelong presence there of one of the most honored of American men of letters—the poet from whom I just quoted two lines. Concord is indeed in itself decidedly verdant, and is an excellent specimen of a New England village of the riper sort. At the time of Hawthorne's first going there it must have been an even better specimen than today—more homogeneous, more indigenous, more absolutely democratic. Forty years ago the tide of foreign immigration had scarcely begun to break upon the rural strongholds of the New England race; it had at most begun to splash them with the salt Hibernian spray. It is very possible, however, that at this period there was not an Irishman in Concord; the place would have been a village community operating in excellent conditions. Such a village community was not the least honorable item in the sum of New England civilization. Its spreading elms and plain white houses, its generous summers and ponderous winters, its immediate background of promiscuous field and forest, would have been part of the composition. For the rest, there were the selectmen and the town-meetings, the town-schools and the self-governing spirit, the rigid morality, the friendly and familiar manners, the perfect competence of the little society to manage its affairs itself. In the delightful introduction to the *Mosses*, Hawthorne has given an account of his dwelling, of his simple occupations and recreations, and of some of the characteristics of the place. The Manse is a large, square wooden house, to the surface of which—even in the dry New England air, so unfriendly to mosses and lichens and weather-stains, and the other elements of a picturesque complexion—a hundred and fifty years of exposure have imparted a kind of tone, standing just above the slow-flowing Concord River, and approached by a short avenue of overarching trees. It had been the dwelling-place of generations of Presbyterian ministers, ancestors of the celebrated Emerson, who had himself spent his early manhood and written some of his most beautiful essays there. "He used," as Hawthorne says, "to watch the Assyrian dawn, and Paphian sunset and moonrise, from the summit of our eastern hill." From its clerical occupants the place had inherited a mild mustiness of theological association—a vague reverberation of old Calvinistic sermons, which served to deepen its extramundane and somnolent quality. The three years that Hawthorne passed here were, I should suppose, among the happiest of his life. The future was indeed not in any special manner assured; but the present was sufficiently genial. In the American *Note-Books* there is a charming passage (too long to quote) descriptive of the entertainment the new couple found in renovating and refurnishing the old parsonage, which, at the time of their going into it, was given up to ghosts and cobwebs. Of the little drawing room, which had been most completely reclaimed, he writes that "the shade of our departed host will never haunt it; for its aspect has been as completely changed as the scenery of a theater. Probably the ghost gave one peep into it, uttered a groan, and vanished forever." This departed host was a certain Doctor Ripley, a venerable scholar, who left behind him a reputation of learning and sanctity which was reproduced in one of the ladies of his family, long the most distinguished woman in the little Concord circle. Doctor Ripley's predecessor had been, I believe, the last of the line of the Emerson ministers—an old gentleman who, in the earlier years of his pastorate, stood at the window of his study (the same in which Hawthorne handled a more irresponsible quill) watching, with his hands under his long coat-tails, the progress of the Concord fight. It is not by any means related, however, I should add, that he waited for the conclusion to make up his mind which was the righteous cause.

Hawthorne had a little society (as much, we may infer, as he desired), and it was excellent in quality. But the pages in the *Note-Books* which relate to his life at the Manse, and the introduction to the *Mosses,* make more of his relations with vegetable nature, and of his customary contemplation of the incidents of wood-path and wayside than of the human elements of the scene; though these also are gracefully touched upon. These pages treat largely of the pleasures of a kitchen-garden, of the beauty of summer-squashes, and of the mysteries of apple-raising. With the wholesome aroma of apples (as is indeed almost necessarily the case in any realistic record of New England rural life) they are especially pervaded; and with many other homely and domestic emanations; all of which derive a sweetness from the medium of our author's colloquial style. Hawthorne was silent with his lips; but he talked with his pen. The tone of his writing is often that of charming talk—ingenious, fanciful, slow-flowing, with all the lightness of gossip and none of its vulgarity. In the preface to the tales written at the Manse he talks of many things, and just touches upon some of the members of his circle—especially upon that odd genius, his fellow-villager, Henry Thoreau. I said a little way back that the New England Transcendental movement had suffered in the estimation of the world at large from not having (putting Emerson aside) produced any superior talents. But any reference to it would be ungenerous which should omit to pay a tribute in passing to the author of *Walden*. Whatever question there may be of his talent, there can be none, I think, of his genius. It was a slim and crooked one; but it was eminently personal. He was imperfect, unfinished, inartistic; he was worse than provincial —he was parochial; it is only at his best that he is readable. But at his best he has an extreme natural charm, and he must always be mentioned after those Americans—Emerson, Hawthorne, Longfellow, Lowell, Motley—who have written originally. He was Emerson's independent moral man made flesh—living for the ages, and not for Saturday and Sunday; for the Universe, and not for Concord. In fact, however, Thoreau lived for Concord very effectually, and by his remarkable genius for the observation of the phenomena of woods and streams, of plants and trees, and beasts and fishes, and for flinging a kind of spiritual interest over these things, he did more than he perhaps intended toward consolidating the fame of his accidental human sojourn. He was as shy and ungregarious as Hawthorne; but he and the latter appear to have been sociably disposed towards each other, and there are some charming touches in the preface to the *Mosses* in regard to the hours they spent in boating together on the large, quiet Concord River. Thoreau was a great voyager, in a canoe which he had constructed himself, and which he eventually made over to Hawthorne, and as expert in the use of the paddle as the redmen who had once haunted the same silent stream. The most frequent of Hawthorne's companions on these excursions appears, however, to have been a local celebrity—as well as Thoreau a high Transcendentalist—Mr. Ellery Channing, whom I may mention, since he is mentioned very explicitly in the preface to the *Mosses*, and also because no account of the little Concord world would be complete which should omit him. He was the son of the distinguished Unitarian moralist, and, I believe, the intimate friend of Thoreau, whom he resembled in having produced literary compositions more esteemed by the few than by the many. He and Hawthorne were both fishermen, and the two used to set themselves afloat in the summer afternoons. "Strange and happy times were those," exclaims the more distinguished of the two writers, "when we cast aside all irksome forms and strait-laced habitudes and delivered ourselves up to the free air, to live like the Indians or any less conventional race, during one bright semicircle of the sun. Rowing our boat against the current, between wide meadows, we turned aside into the Assabeth. A more lovely stream than this, for a mile above its junction with the Concord, has never flowed on earth—nowhere indeed except to lave the interior regions of a poet's imagination. . . . It comes flowing softly through the midmost privacy and deepest heart of a wood which whispers it to be quiet; while the stream whispers back again from its sedgy borders, as if river and wood were hushing one another to sleep. Yes; the river sleeps along its course and dreams of the sky and the clustering foliage. . . ." While Hawthorne was looking at these beautiful things, or, for that matter, was writing them, he was well out of the way of a certain class of visitants whom he alludes to in one of the closing passages of this long Introduction. "Never was a poor little country village infested with such a variety of queer, strangely-dressed, oddly-behaved mortals, most of whom took upon themselves to be important agents of the world's destiny, yet were simply bores of a very intense character." "These hobgoblins of flesh and blood," he says in a preceding paragraph, "were attracted thither by the wide-spreading influence of a great original thinker who had his earthly abode at the opposite extremity of our village. . . . People that had lighted on a new thought or a thought they fancied new, came to Emerson, as the finder of a glittering gem hastens to a lapidary, to ascertain its quality and value." And Hawthorne enumerates some of the categories of pilgrims to the shrine of the mystic counselor, who as a general thing was probably far from abounding in their own sense (when this sense was perverted), but gave them a due measure of plain practical advice. The whole passage is interesting, and it suggests that little Concord had not been ill-treated by the fates—with "a great original thinker" at one end of the village, an exquisite teller of tales at the other, and the rows of New England elms between. It contains, moreover, an admirable sentence about Hawthorne's pilgrim-haunted neighbor, with whom, "being happy," as he says, and feeling therefore "as if there were no question to be put," he was not in metaphysical communion. "It was good nevertheless to meet him in the wood-paths, or sometimes in our avenue, with that pure intellectual gleam diffused about his presence, like the garment of a shining one; and he so quiet, so simple, so without pretension, encountering each man alive as if expecting to receive more than he could impart!" One may without indiscretion risk the surmise that Hawthorne's perception of the "shining" element in his distinguished friend was more intense than his friend's appreciation of whatever luminous property might reside within the somewhat dusky envelope of our hero's identity as a collector of "mosses." Emerson, as a sort of spiritual sun-worshiper, could have attached but a moderate value to Hawthorne's catlike faculty of seeing in the dark.

"As to the daily course of our life," the latter writes in the spring of 1843, "I have written with pretty commendable diligence, averaging from two to four hours a day; and the result is seen in various magazines. I might have written more if it had seemed worth while, but I was content to earn only so much gold as might suffice for our immediate wants, having prospect of official station and emolument which would do away with the necessity of writing for bread. These prospects have not yet had their fulfillment; and we are well content to wait, for an office would inevitably remove us from our present happy home—at least from an outward home; for there is an inner one that will accompany us wherever we go. Meantime, the magazine people do not pay their debts; so that we taste some of the inconveniences of poverty. It is an annoyance, not a trouble." And he goes on to give some account of his usual habits. (The passage is from his journal, and the account is given to himself, as it were, with that odd, unfamiliar explicitness which marks the tone of this record throughout.) "Every day I trudge through snow and slosh to the village, look into the post-office, and spend an hour at the reading-room; and then return home, generally without having spoken a word to any human being. . . . In the way of exercise I saw and split wood, and physically I was never in a better condition than now." He adds a mention of an absence he had lately made. "I went alone to Salem, where I resumed all my bachelor habits for nearly a fortnight, leading the same life in which ten years of my youth flitted away like a dream. But how much changed was I! At last I had got hold of a reality which never could be taken from me. It was good thus to get apart from my happiness for the sake of contemplating it."

These compositions, which were so unpunctually paid for, appeared in the *Democratic Review,* a periodical published at Washington, and having, as our author's biographer says, "considerable pretensions to a national character." It is to be regretted that the practice of keeping its creditors waiting should, on the part of the magazine in question, have been thought compatible with these pretensions. The foregoing lines are a description of a very monotonous but a very contented life, and Mr. Lathrop justly remarks upon the dissonance of tone of the tales Hawthorne produced under these happy circumstances. It is indeed not a little of an anomaly. The episode of the Manse was one of the most agreeable he had known, and yet the best of the *Mosses* (though not the greater number of them) are singularly dismal compositions. They are redolent of M. Montégut's pessimism. "The reality of sin, the pervasiveness of evil," says Mr. Lathrop, "had been but slightly insisted upon in the earlier tales: in this series the idea bursts up like a long-buried fire, with earth-shaking strength, and the pits of hell seem yawning beneath us." This is very true (allowing for Mr. Lathrop's rather too emphatic way of putting it); but the anomaly is, I think, on the whole, only superficial. Our writer's imagination, as has been abundantly conceded, was a gloomy one; the old Puritan sense of sin, of penalties to be paid, of the darkness and wickedness of life, had, as I have already suggested, passed into it. It had not passed into the parts of Hawthorne's nature corresponding to those occupied by the same horrible vision of things in his ancestors; but it had still been determined to claim this later comer as its own, and since his heart and his happiness were to escape, it insisted on setting its mark upon his genius—upon his most beautiful organ, his admirable fancy. It may be said that when his fancy was strongest and keenest, when it was most itself, then the dark Puritan tinge showed in it most richly; and there cannot be a better proof that he was not the man of a somber *parti-pris* whom M. Montégut describes, than the fact that these duskiest flowers of his invention sprang straight from the soil of his happiest days. This surely indicates that there was but little direct connection between the products of his fancy and the state of his affections. When he was lightest at heart, he was most creative, and when he was most creative, the moral picturesqueness of the old secret of mankind in general and of the Puritans in particular most appealed to him—the secret that we are really not by any means so good as a well-regulated society requires us to appear. It is not too much to say, even, that the very condition of production of some of these unamiable tales would be that they should be superficial, and, as it were, insincere. The magnificent little romance of *Young Goodman Brown,* for instance, evidently means nothing as regards Hawthorne's own state of mind, his conviction of human depravity and his consequent melancholy; for the simple reason that if it meant anything, it would mean too much. Mr. Lathrop speaks of it as a "terrible and lurid parable"; but this, it seems to me, is just what it is not. It is not a parable, but a picture, which is a very different thing. What does M. Montégut make, one would ask, from the point of view of Hawthorne's pessimism, of the singularly objective and unpreoccupied tone of the Introduction to the *Old Manse,* in which the author speaks from himself, and in which the cry of metaphysical despair is not even faintly sounded?

We have seen that when he went into the village he often came home without having spoken a word to a human being. There is a touching entry made a little later, bearing upon his mild taciturnity. "A cloudy veil stretches across the abyss of my nature. I have, however, no love of secrecy and darkness. I am glad to think that God sees through my heart, and if any angel has power to penetrate into it, he is welcome to know everything that is there. Yes, and so may any mortal who is capable of full sympathy, and therefore worthy to come into my depths. But he must find his own way there; I can neither guide nor enlighten him." It must be acknowledged, however, that if he was not able to open the gate of conversation, it was sometimes because he was disposed to slide the bolt himself. "I had a purpose," he writes, shortly before the entry last quoted, "if circumstances would permit, of passing the whole term of my wife's absence without speaking a word to any human being." He beguiled these incommunicative periods by studying German, in Tieck and Bürger, without apparently making much progress; also in reading French, in Voltaire and Rabelais. "Just now," he writes, one October noon, "I heard a sharp tapping at the window of my study, and, looking up from my book (a volume of Rabelais), behold, the head of a little bird, who seemed to demand admittance." It was a quiet life, of course, in which these diminutive incidents seemed noteworthy; and what is noteworthy here to the observer of Hawthorne's contemplative simplicity, is the fact that though he finds a good deal to say about the little bird (he devotes several lines more to it) he makes no remark upon Rabelais. He had other visitors than little birds, however, and their demands were also not Rabelaisian. Thoreau comes to see him, and they talk "upon the spiritual advantages of change of place, and upon the *Dial*, and upon Mr. Alcott, and other kindred or concatenated subjects." Mr. Alcott was an arch-transcendentalist, living in Concord, and the *Dial* was a periodical to which the illuminated spirits of Boston and its neighborhood used to contribute.

Another visitor comes and talks "of Margaret Fuller, who, he says, has risen perceptibly into a higher state since their last meeting." There is probably a great deal of Concord five-and-thirty years ago in that little sentence!

V. The Three American Novels

THE prospect of official station and emolument which Hawthorne mentions in one of those paragraphs from his journals which I have just quoted, as having offered itself and then passed away, was at last, in the event, confirmed by his receiving from the administration of President Polk the gift of a place in the Custom-house of his native town. The office was a modest one, and "official station" may perhaps appear a magniloquent formula for the functions sketched in the admirable Introduction to *The Scarlet Letter*. Hawthorne's duties were those of Surveyor of the port of Salem, and they had a salary attached, which was the important part; as his biographer tells us that he had received almost nothing for the contributions to the *Democratic Review*. He bade farewell to his ex-parsonage and went back to Salem in 1846, and the immediate effect of his ameliorated fortune was to make him stop writing. None of his journals of the period from his going to Salem to 1850 have been published; from which I infer that he even ceased to journalize. *The Scarlet Letter* was not written till 1849. In the delightful prologue to that work, entitled *The Custom-house*, he embodies some of the impressions gathered during these years of comparative leisure (I say of leisure because he does not intimate in this sketch of his occupations that his duties were onerous). He intimates, however, that they were not interesting, and that it was a very good thing for him, mentally and morally, when his term of service expired—or rather when he was removed from office by the operation of that wonderful "rotatory" system which his countrymen had invented for the administration of their affairs. This sketch of the Custom-house is, as simple writing, one of the most perfect of Hawthorne's compositions, and one of the most gracefully and humorously autobiographic. It would be

interesting to examine it in detail, but I prefer to use my
space for making some remarks upon the work which was
the ultimate result of this period of Hawthorne's residence
in his native town; and I shall, for convenience' sake, say
directly afterwards what I have to say about the two companions of *The Scarlet Letter*—*The House of the Seven
Gables* and *The Blithedale Romance*. I quoted some passages
from the prologue to the first of these novels in the early
pages of this essay. There is another passage, however,
which bears particularly upon this phase of Hawthorne's
career, and which is so happily expressed as to make it a
pleasure to transcribe it—the passage in which he says that
"for myself, during the whole of my Custom-house experience, moonlight and sunshine, and the glow of the firelight,
were just alike in my regard, and neither of them was of
one whit more avail than the twinkle of a tallow candle. An
entire class of susceptibilities, and a gift connected with
them—of no great richness or value, but the best I had—
was gone from me." He goes on to say that he believes that
he might have done something if he could have made up
his mind to convert the very substance of the commonplace
that surrounded him into matter of literature.

I might, for instance, have contented myself with writing out
the narratives of a veteran shipmaster, one of the inspectors,
whom I should be most ungrateful not to mention; since scarcely
a day passed that he did not stir me to laughter and admiration
by his marvelous gift as a story-teller. . . . Or I might readily
have found a more serious task. It was a folly, with the ma-
teriality of this daily life pressing so intrusively upon me, to
attempt to fling myself back into another age; or to insist on
creating a semblance of a world out of airy matter. . . . The
wiser effort would have been to diffuse thought and imagination
through the opaque substance of today, and thus make it a
bright transparency . . . to seek resolutely the true and indestructible value that lay hidden in the petty and wearisome
incidents and ordinary characters with which I was now conversant. The fault was mine. The page of life that was spread
out before me was dull and commonplace, only because I had
not fathomed its deeper import. A better book than I shall ever
write was there. . . . These perceptions came too late. . . . I

had ceased to be a writer of tolerably poor tales and essays, and had become a tolerably good Surveyor of the Customs. That was all. But, nevertheless, it is anything but agreeable to be haunted by a suspicion that one's intellect is dwindling away, or exhaling, without your consciousness, like ether out of a phial; so that at every glance you find a smaller and less volatile residuum.

As, however, it was with what was left of his intellect after three years' evaporation, that Hawthorne wrote *The Scarlet Letter,* there is little reason to complain of the injury he suffered in his surveyorship.

His publisher, Mr. Fields, in a volume entitled *Yesterdays with Authors,* has related the circumstances in which Hawthorne's masterpiece came into the world. "In the winter of 1849, after he had been ejected from the custom house, I went down to Salem to see him and inquire after his health, for we heard he had been suffering from illness. He was then living in a modest wooden house. . . . I found him alone in a chamber over the sitting-room of the dwelling, and as the day was cold he was hovering near a stove. We fell into talk about his future prospects, and he was, as I feared I should find him, in a very desponding mood." His visitor urged him to bethink himself of publishing something, and Hawthorne replied by calling his attention to the small popularity his published productions had yet acquired, and declaring that he had done nothing and had no spirit for doing anything. The narrator of the incident urged upon him the necessity of a more hopeful view of his situation, and proceeded to take leave. He had not reached the street, however, when Hawthorne hurried to overtake him, and, placing a roll of MS. in his hand, bade him to take it to Boston, read it, and pronounce upon it. "It is either very good or very bad," said the author; "I don't know which." "On my way back to Boston," says Mr. Fields, "I read the germ of *The Scarlet Letter;* before I slept that night I wrote him a note all aglow with admiration of the marvelous story he had put into my hands, and told him that I would come again to Salem the next day and arrange for its publication. I went on in such an amazing

state of excitement, when we met again in the little house,
that he would not believe I was really in earnest. He seemed
to think I was beside myself, and laughed sadly at my
enthusiasm." Hawthorne, however, went on with the book
and finished it, but it appeared only a year later. His
biographer quotes a passage from a letter which he wrote
in February 1850 to his friend Horatio Bridge. "I finished
my book only yesterday; one end being in the press at Boston,
while the other was in my head here at Salem, so that, as
you see, my story is at least fourteen miles long. . . . My
book, the publisher tells me, will not be out before April.
He speaks of it in tremendous terms of approbation, so does
Mrs. Hawthorne, to whom I read the conclusion last night.
It broke her heart, and sent her to bed with a grievous headache—which I look upon as a triumphant success. Judging
from the effect upon her and the publisher, I may calculate
on what bowlers call a ten-strike. But I don't make any
such calculation." And Mr. Lathrop calls attention, in regard
to this passage, to an allusion in the English *Note-Books*
(September 14, 1855). "Speaking of Thackeray, I cannot
but wonder at his coolness in respect to his own pathos, and
compare it to my emotions when I read the last scene of
The Scarlet Letter to my wife, just after writing it—tried
to read it rather, for my voice swelled and heaved as if I
were tossed up and down on an ocean as it subsides after
a storm. But I was in a very nervous state then, having gone
through a great diversity of emotion while writing it, for
many months."

The work has the tone of the circumstances in which it
was produced. If Hawthorne was in a somber mood, and if
his future was painfully vague, *The Scarlet Letter* contains
little enough of gaiety or of hopefulness. It is densely dark,
with a single spot of vivid color in it; and it will probably
long remain the most consistently gloomy of English novels
of the first order. But I just now called it the author's masterpiece, and I imagine it will continue to be, for other generations than ours, his most substantial title to fame. The subject had probably lain a long time in his mind, as his subjects
were apt to do; so that he appears completely to possess it,

to know it and feel it. It is simpler and more complete than his other novels; it achieves more perfectly what it attempts, and it has about it that charm, very hard to express, which we find in an artist's work the first time he has touched his highest mark—a sort of straightness and naturalness of execution, an unconsciousness of his public, and freshness of interest in his theme. It was a great success, and he immediately found himself famous. The writer of these lines, who was a child at the time, remembers dimly the sensation the book produced, and the little shudder with which people alluded to it, as if a peculiar horror were mixed with its attractions. He was too young to read it himself, but its title, upon which he fixed his eyes as the book lay upon the table, had a mysterious charm. He had a vague belief indeed that the "letter" in question was one of the documents that come by the post, and it was a source of perpetual wonderment to him that it should be of such an unaccustomed hue. Of course it was difficult to explain to a child the significance of poor Hester Prynne's blood-colored *A*. But the mystery was at last partly dispelled by his being taken to see a collection of pictures (the annual exhibition of the National Academy), where he encountered a representation of a pale, handsome woman, in a quaint black dress and a white coif, holding between her knees an elfish-looking little girl, fantastically dressed and crowned with flowers. Embroidered on the woman's breast was a great crimson *A*, over which the child's fingers, as she glanced strangely out of the picture, were maliciously playing. I was told that this was Hester Prynne and little Pearl, and that when I grew older I might read their interesting history. But the picture remained vividly imprinted on my mind; I had been vaguely frightened and made uneasy by it; and when, years afterwards, I first read the novel, I seemed to myself to have read it before, and to be familiar with its two strange heroines. I mention this incident simply as an indication of the degree to which the success of *The Scarlet Letter* had made the book what is called an actuality. Hawthorne himself was very modest about it; he wrote to his publisher, when there was a question of his undertaking another novel, that what had given the history of Hester Prynne its "vogue" was simply the introductory chapter. In fact, the publication of *The Scarlet Letter* was in the United States a literary event of the first importance. The book was the finest piece of imaginative writing yet put forth in the country. There was a consciousness of this in the welcome that was given it—a satisfaction in the idea of America having produced a novel that belonged to literature, and to the forefront of it. Something might at last be sent to Europe as exquisite in quality as anything that had been received, and the best of it was that the thing was absolutely American; it belonged to the soil, to the air; it came out of the very heart of New England.

It is beautiful, admirable, extraordinary; it has in the highest degree that merit which I have spoken of as the mark of Hawthorne's best things—an indefinable purity and lightness of conception, a quality which in a work of art affects one in the same way as the absence of grossness does in a human being. His fancy, as I just now said, had evidently brooded over the subject for a long time; the situation to be represented had disclosed itself to him in all its phases. When I say in all its phases, the sentence demands modification; for it is to be remembered that if Hawthorne laid his hand upon the well-worn theme, upon the familiar combination of the wife, the lover, and the husband, it was after all but to one period of the history of these three persons that he attached himself. The situation is the situation after the woman's fault has been committed, and the current of expiation and repentance has set in. In spite of the relation between Hester Prynne and Arthur Dimmesdale, no story of love was surely ever less of a "love story." To Hawthorne's imagination the fact that these two persons had loved each other too well was of an interest comparatively vulgar; what appealed to him was the idea of their moral situation in the long years that were to follow. The story indeed is in a secondary degree that of Hester Prynne; she becomes, really, after the first scene, an accessory figure; it is not upon her the *dénouement* depends. It is upon her guilty lover that the author projects most frequently the cold, thin rays of his

fitfully-moving lantern, which makes here and there a little
luminous circle, on the edge of which hovers the livid and
sinister figure of the injured and retributive husband. The
story goes on for the most part between the lover and the
husband—the tormented young Puritan minister, who carries
the secret of his own lapse from pastoral purity locked up beneath an exterior that commends itself to the reverence of
his flock, while he sees the softer partner of his guilt standing in the full glare of exposure and humbling herself to
the misery of atonement—between this more wretched and
pitiable culprit, to whom dishonor would come as a comfort
and the pillory as a relief, and the older, keener, wiser man,
who, to obtain satisfaction for the wrong he has suffered,
devises the infernally ingenious plan of conjoining himself
with his wronger, living with him, living upon him, and
while he pretends to minister to his hidden ailment and to
sympathize with his pain, revels in his unsuspected knowledge of these things and stimulates them by malignant arts.
The attitude of Roger Chillingworth, and the means he
takes to compensate himself—these are the highly original
elements in the situation that Hawthorne so ingeniously
treats. None of his works are so impregnated with that after-
sense of the old Puritan consciousness of life to which allusion has so often been made. If, as M. Montégut says,
the qualities of his ancestors *filtered* down through generations into his composition, *The Scarlet Letter* was, as it were,
the vessel that gathered up the last of the precious drops.
And I say this not because the story happens to be of so-
called historical cast, to be told of the early days of Massachusetts and of people in steeple-crowned hats and sad-
colored garments. The historical coloring is rather weak than
otherwise; there is little elaboration of detail, of the modern
realism of research; and the author has made no great point
of causing his figures to speak the English of their period.
Nevertheless, the book is full of the moral presence of the
race that invented Hester's penance—diluted and complicated
with other things, but still perfectly recognizable. Puritanism, in a word, is there, not only objectively, as Hawthorne
tried to place it there, but subjectively as well. Not, I mean,

in his judgment of his characters, in any harshness of prejudice, or in the obtrusion of a moral lesson; but in the very quality of his own vision, in the tone of the picture, in a certain coldness and exclusiveness of treatment.

The faults of the book are, to my sense, a want of reality and an abuse of the fanciful element—of a certain superficial symbolism. The people strike me not as characters, but as representatives, very picturesquely arranged, of a single state of mind; and the interest of the story lies, not in them, but in the situation, which is insistently kept before us, with little progression, though with a great deal, as I have said, of a certain stable variation; and to which they, out of their reality, contribute little that helps it to live and move. I was made to feel this want of reality, this over-ingenuity, of *The Scarlet Letter,* by chancing not long since upon a novel which was read fifty years ago much more than today, but which is still worth reading—the story of *Adam Blair,* by John Gibson Lockhart. This interesting and powerful little tale has a great deal of analogy with Hawthorne's novel —quite enough, at least, to suggest a comparison between them; and the comparison is a very interesting one to make, for it speedily leads us to larger considerations than simple resemblances and divergences of plot.

Adam Blair, like Arthur Dimmesdale, is a Calvinistic minister who becomes the lover of a married woman, is overwhelmed with remorse at his misdeed, and makes a public confession of it; then expiates it by resigning his pastoral office and becoming a humble tiller of the soil, as his father had been. The two stories are of about the same length, and each is the masterpiece (putting aside, of course, as far as Lockhart is concerned, the *Life of Scott*) of the author. They deal alike with the manners of a rigidly theological society, and even in certain details they correspond. In each of them, between the guilty pair, there is a charming little girl; though I hasten to say that Sarah Blair (who is not the daughter of the heroine but the legitimate offspring of the hero, a widower) is far from being as brilliant and graceful an apparition as the admirable little Pearl of *The Scarlet Letter.* The main difference between the two tales is the fact that in the American story the husband plays an all-important part, and in the Scottish plays almost none at all. *Adam Blair* is the history of the passion, and *The Scarlet Letter* the history of its sequel; but nevertheless, if one has read the two books at a short interval, it is impossible to avoid confronting them. I confess that a large portion of the interest of *Adam Blair,* to my mind, when once I had perceived that it would repeat in a great measure the situation of *The Scarlet Letter,* lay in noting its difference of tone. It threw into relief the passionless quality of Hawthorne's novel, its element of cold and ingenious fantasy, its elaborate imaginative delicacy. These things do not precisely constitute a weakness in *The Scarlet Letter;* indeed, in a certain way they constitute a great strength; but the absence of a certain something warm and straightforward, a trifle more grossly human and vulgarly natural, which one finds in *Adam Blair,* will always make Hawthorne's tale less touching to a large number of even very intelligent readers, than a love story told with the robust, synthetic pathos which served Lockhart so well. His novel is not of the first rank (I should call it an excellent second-rate one), but it borrows a charm from the fact that his vigorous, but not strongly imaginative, mind was impregnated with the reality of his subject. He did not always succeed in rendering this reality; the expression is sometimes awkward and poor. But the reader feels that his vision was clear, and his feeling about the matter very strong and rich. Hawthorne's imagination, on the other hand, plays with his theme so incessantly, leads it such a dance through the moon-lighted air of his intellect, that the thing cools off, as it were, hardens and stiffens, and, producing effects much more exquisite, leaves the reader with a sense of having handled a splendid piece of silversmith's work. Lockhart, by means much more vulgar, produces at moments a greater illusion, and satisfies our inevitable desire for something, in the people in whom it is sought to interest us, that shall be of the same pitch and the same continuity with ourselves. Above all, it is interesting to see how the same subject appears to two men of a thoroughly different cast of mind and of a different race. Lockhart was struck with the warmth of the subject that offered itself to him, and Hawthorne with its coldness; the one with its glow, its sentimental interest— the other with its shadow, its moral interest. Lockhart's story is as decent, as severely draped, as *The Scarlet Letter;* but the author has a more vivid sense than appears to have imposed itself upon Hawthorne, of some of the incidents of the situation he describes; his tempted man and tempting woman are more actual and personal; his heroine in especial, though not in the least a delicate or a subtle conception, has a sort of credible, visible, palpable property, a vulgar roundness and relief, which are lacking to the dim and chastened image of Hester Prynne. But I am going too far; I am comparing simplicity with subtlety, the usual with the refined. Each man wrote as his turn of mind impelled him, but each expressed something more than himself. Lockhart was a dense, substantial Briton, with a taste for the concrete, and Hawthorne was a thin New Englander, with a miasmatic conscience.

In *The Scarlet Letter* there is a great deal of symbolism; there is, I think, too much. It is overdone at times, and becomes mechanical; it ceases to be impressive, and grazes triviality. The idea of the mystic *A* which the young minister finds imprinted upon his breast and eating into his flesh, in sympathy with the embroidered badge that Hester is condemned to wear, appears to me to be a case in point. This suggestion should, I think, have been just made and dropped; to insist upon it and return to it is to exaggerate the weak side of the subject. Hawthorne returns to it constantly, plays with it, and seems charmed by it; until at last the reader feels tempted to declare that his enjoyment of it is puerile. In the admirable scene, so superbly conceived and beautifully executed, in which Mr. Dimmesdale, in the stillness of the night, in the middle of the sleeping town, feels impelled to go and stand upon the scaffold where his mistress had formerly enacted her dreadful penance, and then, seeing Hester pass along the street, from watching at a sick-bed, with little Pearl at her side, calls them both to come and stand there beside him—in this masterly episode the effect is almost spoiled by the introduction of one of these superficial conteits. What leads up to it is very fine—so fine that I cannot do better than quote it as a specimen of one of the striking pages of the book.

But before Mr. Dimmesdale had done speaking, a light gleamed far and wide over all the muffled sky. It was doubtless caused by one of those meteors which the night watcher may so often observe burning out to waste in the vacant regions of the atmosphere. So powerful was its radiance that it thoroughly illuminated the dense medium of cloud, betwixt the sky and earth. The great vault brightened, like the dome of an immense lamp. It showed the familiar scene of the street with the distinctness of midday, but also with the awfulness that is always imparted to familiar objects by an unaccustomed light. The wooden houses, with their jutting stories and quaint gable-peaks; the doorsteps and thresholds, with the early grass springing up about them; the garden-plots, black with freshly-turned earth; the wheel track, little worn, and, even in the market place, margined with green on either side,—all were visible, but with a singularity of aspect that seemed to give another moral interpretation to the things of this world than they had ever borne before. And there stood the minister, with his hand over his heart; and Hester Prynne, with the embroidered letter glimmering on her bosom; and little Pearl, herself a symbol, and the connecting-link between these two. They stood in the noon of that strange and solemn splendor, as if it were the light that is to reveal all secrets, and the daybreak that shall unite all that belong to one another.

That is imaginative, impressive, poetic; but when, almost immediately afterwards, the author goes on to say that "the minister looking upward to the zenith, beheld there the appearance of an immense letter—the letter A—marked out in lines of dull red light," we feel that he goes too far and is in danger of crossing the line that separates the sublime from its intimate neighbor. We are tempted to say that this is not moral tragedy, but physical comedy. In the same way, too much is made of the intimation that Hester's badge had a scorching property, and that if one touched it one would immediately withdraw one's hand. Hawthorne is perpetually looking for images which shall place themselves in picturesque correspondence with the spiritual facts with which he is concerned, and of course the search is of the very essence of poetry. But in such a process discretion is everything, and when the image becomes importunate it is in danger of seeming to stand for nothing more serious than itself. When Hester meets the minister by appointment in the forest, and sits talking with him while little Pearl wanders away and plays by the edge of the brook, the child is represented as at last making her way over to the other side of the woodland stream, and disporting herself there in a manner which makes her mother feel herself, "in some indistinct and tantalizing manner, estranged from Pearl; as if the child, in her lonely ramble through the forest, had strayed out of the sphere in which she and her mother dwelt together, and was now vainly seeking to return to it." And Hawthorne devotes a chapter to this idea of the child's having, by putting the brook between Hester and herself, established a kind of spiritual gulf, on the verge of which her little fantastic person innocently mocks at her mother's sense of bereavement. This conception belongs, one would say, quite to the lighter order of a story-teller's devices, and the reader hardly goes with Hawthorne in the large development he gives to it. He hardly goes with him either, I think, in his extreme predilection for a small number of vague ideas which are represented by such terms as "sphere" and "sympathies." Hawthorne makes too liberal a use of these two substantives; it is the solitary defect of his style, and it counts as a defect partly because the words in question are a sort of specialty with certain writers immeasurably inferior to himself.

I had not meant, however, to expatiate upon his defects, which are of the slenderest and most venial kind. *The Scarlet Letter* has the beauty and harmony of all original and complete conceptions, and its weaker spots, whatever they are, are not of its essence; they are mere light flaws and inequalities of surface. One can often return to it; it supports familiarity and has the inexhaustible charm and mystery of great works of art. It is admirably written. Hawthorne afterwards polished his style to a still higher degree, but in his later productions—it is almost always the case in a writer's later productions—there is a touch of mannerism. In *The Scarlet Letter* there is a high degree of polish, and at the same time a charming freshness; his phrase is less conscious of itself. His biographer very justly calls attention to the fact that his style was excellent from the beginning; that he appeared to have passed through no phase of learning how to write, but was in possession of his means from the first of his handling a pen. His early tales, perhaps, were not of a character to subject his faculty of expression to a very severe test, but a man who had not Hawthorne's natural sense of language would certainly have contrived to write them less well. This natural sense of language—this turn for saying things lightly and yet touchingly, picturesquely yet simply, and for infusing a gently colloquial tone into matter of the most unfamiliar import, he had evidently cultivated with great assiduity. I have spoken of the anomalous character of his *Note-Books*—of his going to such pains often to make a record of incidents which either were not worth remembering or could be easily remembered without its aid. But it helps us to understand the *Note-Books* if we regard them as a literary exercise. They were compositions, as school boys say, in which the subject was only the pretext, and the main point was to write a certain amount of excellent English. Hawthorne must at least have written a great many of these things for practice, and he must often have said to himself that it was better practice to write about trifles, because it was a greater tax upon one's skill to make them interesting. And his theory was just, for he has almost always made his trifles interesting. In his novels his art of saying things well is very positively tested, for here he treats of those matters among which it is very easy for a blundering writer to go wrong—the subtleties and mysteries of life, the moral and spiritual maze. In such a passage as one I have marked for quotation from *The Scarlet Letter* there is the stamp of the genius of style.

Hester Prynne, gazing steadfastly at the clergyman, felt a dreary influence come over her, but wherefore or whence she knew not, unless that he seemed so remote from her own sphere and utterly beyond her reach. One glance of recognition she had imagined must needs pass between them. She thought of the dim forest with its little dell of solitude, and love, and anguish, and the mossy tree-trunk, where, sitting hand in hand, they had mingled their sad and passionate talk with the melancholy murmur of the brook. How deeply had they known each other then! And was this the man? She hardly knew him now! He, moving proudly past, enveloped as it were in the rich music, with the procession of majestic and venerable fathers; he, so unattainable in his worldly position, and still more so in that far vista in his unsympathizing thoughts, through which she now beheld him! Her spirit sank with the idea that all must have been a delusion, and that vividly as she had dreamed it, there could be no real bond betwixt the clergyman and herself. And thus much of woman there was in Hester, that she could scarcely forgive him —least of all now, when the heavy footstep of their approaching fate might be heard, nearer, nearer, nearer!—for being able to withdraw himself so completely from their mutual world, while she groped darkly, and stretched forth her cold hands, and found him not!

The House of the Seven Gables was written at Lenox, among the mountains of Massachusetts, a village nestling, rather loosely, in one of the loveliest corners of New England, to which Hawthorne had betaken himself after the success of The Scarlet Letter became conspicuous, in the summer of 1850, and where he occupied for two years an uncomfortable little red house which is now pointed out to the inquiring stranger. The inquiring stranger is now a frequent figure at Lenox, for the place has suffered the process of lionization. It has become a prosperous watering-place, or at least (as there are no waters), as they say in America, a summer resort. It is a brilliant and generous landscape, and thirty years ago a man of fancy, desiring to apply himself, might have found both inspiration and tranquillity there. Hawthorne found so much of both that he wrote more during his two years of residence at Lenox than at any period of his career. He began with The House of the Seven Gables, which was finished in the early part of 1851. This is the longest of his three American novels, it is the most elaborate, and in the judgment of some persons it is the finest. It is a rich, delightful, imaginative work, larger and more various than its companions, and full of all sorts of deep intentions, of interwoven threads of suggestion. But it is not so rounded and complete as *The Scarlet Letter;* it has always seemed to me more like a prologue to a great novel than a great novel itself. I think this is partly owing to the fact that the subject, the *donnée,* as the French say, of the story, does not quite fill it out, and that we get at the same time an impression of certain complicated purposes on the author's part, which seem to reach beyond it. I call it larger and more various than its companions, and it has indeed a greater richness of tone and density of detail. The color, so to speak, of *The House of the Seven Gables* is admirable. But the story has a sort of expansive quality which never wholly fructifies, and as I lately laid it down, after reading it for the third time, I had a sense of having interested myself in a magnificent fragment. Yet the book has a great fascination, and of all of those of its author's productions which I have read over while writing this sketch, it is perhaps the one that has gained most by re-perusal. If it be true of the others that the pure, natural quality of the imaginative strain is their great merit, this is at least as true of *The House of the Seven Gables,* the charm of which is in a peculiar degree of the kind that we fail to reduce to its grounds—like that of the sweetness of a piece of music, or the softness of fine September weather. It is vague, indefinable, ineffable; but it is the sort of thing we must always point to in justification of the high claim that we make for Hawthorne. In this case, of course, its vagueness is a drawback, for it is difficult to point to ethereal beauties; and if the reader whom we have wished to inoculate with our admiration inform us after looking a while that he perceives nothing in particular, we can only reply that, in effect, the object is a delicate one.

The House of the Seven Gables comes nearer being a picture of contemporary American life than either of its companions; but on this ground it would be a mistake to make a large claim for it. It cannot be too often repeated that Hawthorne was not a realist. He had a high sense of reality —his *Note-Books* superabundantly testify to it; and fond as he was of jotting down the items that make it up, he never at

tempted to render exactly or closely the actual facts of the
society that surrounded him. I have said—I began by saying—
that his pages were full of its spirit, and of a certain reflected
light that springs from it; but I was careful to add that the
reader must look for his local and national quality between
the lines of his writing and in the *indirect* testimony of his
tone, his accent, his temper, of his very omissions and sup-
pressions. *The House of the Seven Gables* has, however,
more literal actuality than the others, and if it were not too
fanciful an account of it, I should say that it renders, to an
initiated reader, the impression of a summer afternoon in an
elm-shadowed New England town. It leaves upon the mind
a vague correspondence to some such reminiscence, and in
stirring up the association it renders it delightful. The comparison is to the honor of the New England town, which
gains in it more than it bestows. The shadows of the elms, in
The House of the Seven Gables, are exceptionally dense and
cool; the summer afternoon is peculiarly still and beautiful;
the atmosphere has a delicious warmth, and the long daylight seems to pause and rest. But the mild provincial quality
is there, the mixture of shabbiness and freshness, the paucity
of ingredients. The end of an old race—this is the situation
that Hawthorne has depicted, and he has been admirably
inspired in the choice of the figures in whom he seeks to
interest us. They are all figures rather than characters—they
are all pictures rather than persons. But if their reality is
light and vague, it is sufficient, and it is in harmony with the
low relief and dimness of outline of the objects that surround
them. They are all types, to the author's mind, of something
general, of something that is bound up with the history, at
large, of families and individuals, and each of them is the
center of a cluster of those ingenious and meditative musings,
rather melancholy, as a general thing, than joyous, which
melt into the current and texture of the story and give it a
kind of moral richness. A grotesque old spinster, simple,
childish, penniless, very humble at heart, but rigidly conscious of her pedigree; an amiable bachelor, of an epicurean
temperament and an enfeebled intellect, who has passed
twenty years of his life in penal confinement for a crime

of which he was unjustly pronounced guilty; a sweet-natured and bright-faced young girl from the country, a poor relation of these two ancient decrepitudes, with whose moral mustiness her modern freshness and soundness are contrasted; a young man still more modern, holding the latest opinions, who has sought his fortune up and down the world, and, though he has not found it, takes a genial and enthusiastic view of the future: these, with two or three remarkable accessory figures, are the persons concerned in the little drama. The drama is a small one, but as Hawthorne does not put it before us for its own superficial sake, for the dry facts of the case, but for something in it which he holds to be symbolic and of large application, something that points a moral and that it behooves us to remember, the scenes in the rusty wooden house whose gables give its name to the story, have something of the dignity both of history and of tragedy. Miss Hepzibah Pyncheon, dragging out a disappointed life in her paternal dwelling, finds herself obliged in her old age to open a little shop for the sale of penny toys and gingerbread. This is the central incident of the tale, and, as Hawthorne relates it, it is an incident of the most impressive magnitude and most touching interest. Her dishonored and vague-minded brother is released from prison at the same moment, and returns to the ancestral roof to deepen her perplexities. But, on the other hand, to alleviate them, and to introduce a breath of the air of the outer world into this long-unventilated interior, the little country cousin also arrives, and proves the good angel of the feebly distracted household. All this episode is exquisite—admirably conceived, and executed with a kind of humorous tenderness, an equal sense of everything in it that is picturesque, touching, ridiculous, worthy of the highest praise. Hepzibah Pyncheon, with her near-sighted scowl, her rusty joints, her antique turban, her map of a great territory to the eastward which ought to have belonged to her family, her vain terrors and scruples and resentments, the inaptitude and repugnance of an ancient gentlewoman to the vulgar little commerce which a cruel fate has compelled her to engage in—Hepzibah Pyncheon is a masterly picture. I repeat that she is a picture, as her companions are pictures; she is a charming piece of descriptive writing, rather than a dramatic exhibition. But she is described, like her companions, too, so subtly and lovingly that we enter into her virginal old heart and stand with her behind her abominable little counter. Clifford Pyncheon is a still more remarkable conception, though he is perhaps not so vividly depicted. It was a figure needing a much more subtle touch, however, and it was of the essence of his character to be vague and unemphasized. Nothing can be more charming than the manner in which the soft, bright, active presence of Phœbe Pyncheon is indicated, or than the account of her relations with the poor dimly-sentient kinsman for whom her light-handed sisterly offices, in the evening of a melancholy life, are a revelation of lost possibilities of happiness. "In her aspect," Hawthorne says of the young girl, "there was a familiar gladness, and a holiness that you could play with, and yet reverence it as much as ever. She was like a prayer offered up in the homeliest beauty of one's mother tongue. Fresh was Phœbe, moreover, and airy, and sweet in her apparel; as if nothing that she wore—neither her gown, nor her small straw bonnet, nor her little kerchief, any more than her snowy stockings—had ever been put on before; or if worn, were all the fresher for it, and with a fragrance as if they had lain among the rosebuds." Of the influence of her maidenly salubrity upon poor Clifford, Hawthorne gives the prettiest description, and then, breaking off suddenly, renounces the attempt in language which, while pleading its inadequacy, conveys an exquisite satisfaction to the reader. I quote the passage for the sake of its extreme felicity, and of the charming image with which it concludes.

But we strive in vain to put the idea into words. No adequate expression of the beauty and profound pathos with which it impresses us is attainable. This being, made only for happiness, and heretofore so miserably failing to be happy—his tendencies so hideously thwarted that some unknown time ago, the delicate springs of his character, never morally or intellectually strong, had given way, and he was now imbecile—this poor forlorn voyager from the Islands of the Blest, in a frail bark, on a tempestuous sea, had been flung by the last mountain-wave of his shipwreck into a quiet harbor. There, as he lay more than half lifeless on the strand, the fragrance of an earthly rose-bud had come to his nostrils, and, as odors will, had summoned up reminiscences or visions of all the living and breathing beauty amid which he should have had his home. With his native susceptibility of happy influences, he inhales the slight ethereal rapture into his soul, and expires!

I have not mentioned the personage in *The House of the Seven Gables* upon whom Hawthorne evidently bestowed most pains, and whose portrait is the most elaborate in the book; partly because he is, in spite of the space he occupies, an accessory figure, and partly because, even more than the others, he is what I have called a picture rather than a character. Judge Pyncheon is an ironical portrait, very richly and broadly executed, very sagaciously composed and rendered— the portrait of a superb, full-blown hypocrite, a large-based, full-nurtured Pharisee, bland, urbane, impressive, diffusing about him a "sultry" warmth of benevolence, as the author calls it again and again, and basking in the noontide of prosperity and the consideration of society; but in reality hard, gross, and ignoble. Judge Pyncheon is an elaborate piece of description, made up of a hundred admirable touches, in which satire is always winged with fancy, and fancy is linked with a deep sense of reality. It is difficult to say whether Hawthorne followed a model in describing Judge Pyncheon; but it is tolerably obvious that the picture is an impression—a copious impression—of an individual. It has evidently a definite starting-point in fact, and the author is able to draw, freely and confidently, after the image established in his mind. Holgrave, the modern young man, who has been a Jack-of-all-trades and is at the period of the story a daguerreotypist, is an attempt to render a kind of national type—that of the young citizen of the United States whose fortune is simply in his lively intelligence, and who stands naked, as it were, unbiased and unencumbered alike, in the center of the far-stretching level of American life. Holgrave is intended as a contrast; his lack of traditions, his democratic stamp, his condensed experience, are opposed to the desic cated prejudices and exhausted vitality of the race of which poor feebly-scowling, rusty-jointed Hepzibah is the most heroic representative. It is perhaps a pity that Hawthorne should not have proposed to himself to give the old Pyncheon qualities some embodiment which would help them to balance more fairly with the elastic properties of the young daguerreotypist—should not have painted a lusty conservative to match his strenuous radical. As it is, the mustiness and moldiness of the tenants of the House of the Seven Gables crumble away rather too easily. Evidently, however, what Hawthorne designed to represent was not the struggle between an old society and a new, for in this case he would have given the old one a better chance; but simply, as I have said, the shrinkage and extinction of a family. This appealed to his imagination; and the idea of long perpetuation and survival always appears to have filled him with a kind of horror and disapproval. Conservative, in a certain degree, as he was himself, and fond of retrospect and quietude and the mellowing influences of time, it is singular how often one encounters in his writings some expression of mistrust of old houses, old institutions, long lines of descent. He was disposed apparently to allow a very moderate measure in these respects, and he condemns the dwelling of the Pyncheons to disappear from the face of the earth because it has been standing a couple of hundred years. In this he was an American of Americans; or rather he was more American than many of his countrymen, who, though they are accustomed to work for the short run rather than the long, have often a lurking esteem for things that show the marks of having lasted. I will add that Holgrave is one of the few figures, among those which Hawthorne created, with regard to which the absence of the realistic mode of treatment is felt as a loss. Holgrave is not sharply enough characterized; he lacks features; he is not an individual, but a type. But my last word about this admirable novel must not be a restrictive one. It is a large and generous production, pervaded with that vague hum, that indefinable echo, of the whole multitudinous life of man, which is the real sign of a great work of fiction.

After the publication of *The House of the Seven Gables,* which brought him great honor, and, I believe, a tolerable share of a more ponderable substance, he composed a couple of little volumes for children—*The Wonder-Book,* and a small collection of stories entitled *Tanglewood Tales.* They are not among his most serious literary titles, but if I may trust my own early impression of them, they are among the most charming literary services that have been rendered to children in an age (and especially in a country) in which the exactions of the infant mind have exerted much too palpable an influence upon literature. Hawthorne's stories are the old Greek myths, made more vivid to the childish imagination by an infusion of details which both deepen and explain their marvels. I have been careful not to read them over, for I should be very sorry to risk disturbing in any degree a recollecton of them that has been at rest since the appreciative period of life to which they are addressed. They seem at that period enchanting, and the ideal of happiness of many American children is to lie upon the carpet and lose themselves in *The Wonder-Book.* It is in its pages that they first make the acquaintance of the heroes and heroines of the antique mythology, and something of the nursery fairy-tale quality of interest which Hawthorne imparts to them always remains.

I have said that Lenox was a very pretty place, and that he was able to work there Hawthorne proved by composing *The House of the Seven Gables* with a good deal of rapidity. But at the close of the year in which this novel was published he wrote to a friend (Mr. Fields, his publisher) that "to tell you a secret I am sick to death of Berkshire, and hate to think of spending another winter here. . . . The air and climate do not agree with my health at all, and for the first time since I was a boy I have felt languid and dispirited. . . . O that Providence would build me the merest little shanty, and mark me out a rood or two of garden ground, near the sea-coast!" He was at this time for a while out of health; and it is proper to remember that though the Massachusetts Berkshire, with its mountains and lakes, was charming during the ardent American summer, there was a reverse to the medal, consisting of December snows prolonged into April and May. Providence failed to provide him with a cottage by the sea; but he betook himself for the winter of 1852 to the little town of West Newton, near Boston, where he brought into the world *The Blithedale Romance*.

This work, as I have said, would not have been written if Hawthorne had not spent a year at Brook Farm, and though it is in no sense of the word an account of the manners or the inmates of that establishment, it will preserve the memory of the ingenious community at West Roxbury for a generation unconscious of other reminders. I hardly know what to say about it save that it is very charming; this vague, unanalytic epithet is the first that comes to one's pen in treating of Hawthorne's novels, for their extreme amenity of form invariably suggests it; but if on the one hand it claims to be uttered, on the other it frankly confesses its inconclusiveness. Perhaps, however, in this case, it fills out the measure of appreciation more completely than in others, for *The Blithedale Romance* is the lightest, the brightest, the liveliest, of this company of unhumorous fictions.

The story is told from a more joyous point of view—from a point of view comparatively humorous—and a number of objects and incidents touched with the light of the profane world—the vulgar, many-colored world of actuality, as distinguished from the crepuscular realm of the writer's own reveries—are mingled with its course. The book indeed is a mixture of elements, and it leaves in the memory an impression analogous to that of an April day—an alternation of brightness and shadow, of broken sun-patches and sprinkling clouds. Its *dénouement* is tragical—there is indeed nothing so tragical in all Hawthorne, unless it be the murder of Miriam's persecutor by Donatello, in *Transformation*, as the suicide of Zenobia; and yet on the whole the effect of the novel is to make one think more agreeably of life. The standpoint of the narrator has the advantage of being a concrete one; he is no longer, as in the preceding tales, a disembodied spirit, imprisoned in the haunted chamber of his own contemplations, but a particular man, with a certain human grossness.

Of Miles Coverdale I have already spoken, and of its being natural to assume that in so far as we may measure this lightly indicated identity of his, it has a great deal in common with that of his creator. Coverdale is a picture of the contemplative, observant, analytic nature, nursing its fancies, and yet, thanks to an element of strong good sense, not bringing them up to be spoiled children; having little at stake in life, at any given moment, and yet indulging, in imagination, in a good many adventures; a portrait of a man, in a word, whose passions are slender, whose imagination is active, and whose happiness lies, not in doing, but in perceiving—half a poet, half a critic, and all a spectator. He is contrasted, excellently, with the figure of Hollingsworth, the heavily treading Reformer, whose attitude with regard to the world is that of the hammer to the anvil, and who has no patience with his friend's indifferences and neutralities. Coverdale is a gentle skeptic, a mild cynic; he would agree that life is a little worth living—or worth living a little, but would remark that, unfortunately, to live little enough, we have to live a great deal. He confesses to a want of earnestness, but in reality he is evidently an excellent fellow, to whom one might look, not for any personal performance on a great scale, but for a good deal of generosity of detail. "As Hollingsworth once told me, I lack a purpose," he writes, at the close of his story. "How strange! He was ruined, morally, by an overplus of the same ingredient the want of which, I occasionally suspect, has rendered my own life all an emptiness. I by no means wish to die. Yet were there any cause in this whole chaos of human struggle, worth a sane man's dying for, and which my death would benefit, then—provided, however, the effort did not involve an unreasonable amount of trouble—methinks I might be bold to offer up my life. If Kossuth, for example, would pitch the battle-field of Hungarian rights within an easy ride of my abode, and choose a mild sunny morning, after breakfast, for the conflict, Miles Coverdale would gladly be his man, for one brave rush upon the leveled bayonets. Further than that I should be loth to pledge myself."

The finest thing in *The Blithedale Romance* is the char-

acter of Zenobia, which I have said elsewhere strikes me as
the nearest approach that Hawthorne has made to the complete creation of a *person*. She is more concrete than Hester
or Miriam, or Hilda or Phœbe; she is a more definite image,
produced by a greater multiplicity of touches. It is idle to
inquire too closely whether Hawthorne had Margaret Fuller
in his mind in constructing the figure of this brilliant specimen of the strong-minded class and endowing her with the
genius of conversation; or, on the assumption that such was
the case, to compare the image at all strictly with the model.
There is no strictness in the representation by novelists of
persons who have struck them in life, and there can in the
nature of things be none. From the moment the imagination
takes a hand in the game, the inevitable tendency is to divergence, to following what may be called new scents. The
original gives hints, but the writer does what he likes with
them, and imports new elements into the picture. If there is
this amount of reason for referring the wayward heroine of
Blithedale to Hawthorne's impression of the most distinguished woman of her day in Boston, that Margaret Fuller
was the only literary lady of eminence whom there is any
sign of his having known, that she was proud, passionate,
and eloquent, that she was much connected with the little
world of Transcendentalism out of which the experiment of
Brook Farm sprung, and that she had a miserable end and a
watery grave—if these are facts to be noted on one side, I say;
on the other, the beautiful and sumptuous Zenobia, with her
rich and picturesque temperament and physical aspects,
offers many points of divergence from the plain and strenuous invalid who represented feminine culture in the suburbs
of the New England metropolis. This picturesqueness of
Zenobia is very happily indicated and maintained; she is a
woman, in all the force of the term, and there is something
very vivid and powerful in her large expression of womanly
gifts and weaknesses. Hollingsworth is, I think, less successful, though there is much reality in the conception of the
type to which he belongs—the strong-willed, narrow-hearted
apostle of a special form of redemption for society. There is
nothing better in all Hawthorne than the scene between him

and Coverdale, when the two men are at work together in the field (piling stones on a dyke), and he gives it to his companion to choose whether he will be with him or against him. It is a pity, perhaps, to have represented him as having begun life as a blacksmith, for one grudges him the advantage of so logical a reason for his roughness and hardness.

Hollingsworth scarcely said a word, unless when repeatedly and pertinaciously addressed. Then indeed he would glare upon us from the thick shrubbery of his meditations, like a tiger out of a jungle, make the briefest reply possible, and betake himself back into the solitude of his heart and mind . . . His heart, I imagine, was never really interested in our socialist scheme, but was forever busy with his strange, and as most people thought, impracticable plan for the reformation of criminals through an appeal to their higher instincts. Much as I liked Hollingsworth, it cost me many a groan to tolerate him on this point. He ought to have commenced his investigation of the subject by committing some huge sin in his proper person, and examining the condition of his higher instincts afterwards.

The most touching element in the novel is the history of the grasp that this barbarous fanatic has laid upon the fastidious and high-tempered Zenobia, who, disliking him and shrinking from him at a hundred points, is drawn into the gulf of his omnivorous egotism. The portion of the story that strikes me as least felicitous is that which deals with Priscilla and with her mysterious relation to Zenobia—with her mesmeric gifts, her clairvoyance, her identity with the Veiled Lady, her divided subjection to Hollingsworth and Westervelt, and her numerous other graceful but fantastic properties—her Sibylline attributes, as the author calls them. Hawthorne is rather too fond of Sibylline attributes—a taste of the same order as his disposition, to which I have already alluded, to talk about spheres and sympathies. As the action advances, in *The Blithedale Romance*, we get too much out of reality, and cease to feel beneath our feet the firm ground of an appeal to our own vision of the world, our observation. I should have liked to see the story concern itself more with the little community in which its earlier scenes are laid, and avail itself of so excellent an opportunity for describing unhackneyed specimens of human nature. I have already spoken of the absence of satire in the novel, of its not aiming in the least at satire, and of its offering no grounds for complaint as an invidious picture. Indeed the brethren of Brook Farm should have held themselves slighted rather than misrepresented, and have regretted that the admirable genius who for a while was numbered among them should have treated their institution mainly as a perch for starting upon an imaginative flight. But when all is said about a certain want of substance and cohesion in the latter portions of *The Blithedale Romance*, the book is still a delightful and beautiful one. Zenobia and Hollingsworth live in the memory, and even Priscilla and Coverdale, who linger there less importunately, have a great deal that touches us and that we believe in. I said just now that Priscilla was infelicitous; but immediately afterwards I open the volume at a page in which the author describes some of the out-of-door amusements at Blithedale, and speaks of a foot-race across the grass, in which some of the slim young girls of the society joined. "Priscilla's peculiar charm in a foot-race was the weakness and irregularity with which she ran. Growing up without exercise, except to her poor little fingers, she had never yet acquired the perfect use of her legs. Setting buoyantly forth therefore, as if no rival less swift than Atalanta could compete with her, she ran falteringly, and often tumbled on the grass. Such an incident—though it seems too slight to think of—was a thing to laugh at, but which brought the water into one's eyes, and lingered in the memory after far greater joys and sorrows were wept out of it, as antiquated trash. Priscilla's life, as I beheld it, was full of trifles that affected me in just this way." That seems to me exquisite, and the book is full of touches as deep and delicate.

After writing it, Hawthorne went back to live in Concord, where he had bought a small house in which, apparently, he expected to spend a large portion of his future. This was in fact the dwelling in which he passed that part of the rest of his days that he spent in his own country. He established himself there before going to Europe, in 1853, and he returned to the Wayside, as he called his house, on coming back to the United States seven years later. Though he actually occupied the place no long time, he had made it his property, and it was more his own home than any of his numerous provisional abodes. I may therefore quote a little account of the house which he wrote to a distinguished friend, Mr. George Curtis.

As for my old house, you will understand it better after spending a day or two in it. Before Mr. Alcott took it in hand, it was a mean-looking affair, with two peaked gables; no suggestiveness about it, and no venerableness, although from the style of its construction it seems to have survived beyond its first century. He added a porch in front, and a central peak, and a piazza at each end, and painted it a rusty olive hue, and invested the whole with a modest picturesqueness; all which improvements, together with its situation at the foot of a wooded hill, make it a place that one notices and remembers for a few moments after passing. Mr. Alcott expended a good deal of taste and some money (to no great purpose) in forming the hillside behind the house into terraces, and building arbors and summerhouses of rough stems and branches and trees, on a system of his own. They must have been very pretty in their day, and are so still, although much decayed, and shattered more and more by every breeze that blows. The hillside is covered chiefly with locust trees, which come into luxuriant blossom in the month of June, and look and smell very sweetly, intermixed with a few young elms, and white pines and infant oaks—the whole forming rather a thicket than a wood. Nevertheless, there is some very good shade to be found there. I spend delectable hours there in the hottest part of the day, stretched out at my lazy length, with a book in my hand, or some unwritten book in my thoughts. There is almost always a breeze stirring along the sides or brow of the hill. From the hill-top there is a good view along the extensive level surfaces and gentle hilly outlines, covered with wood, that characterize the scenery of Concord. . . . I know nothing of the history of the house except Thoreau's telling me that it was inhabited, a generation or two ago by a man who believed he should never die. I believe, however, he is dead; at least, I hope so; else he may probably reappear and dispute my title to his residence.

As Mr. Lathrop points out, this allusion to a man who believed he should never die is "the first intimation of the story of *Septimius Felton*." The scenery of that romance, he adds, "was evidently taken from the Wayside and its hill." *Septimius Felton* is in fact a young man who, at the time of the war of the Revolution, lives in the village of Concord, on the Boston road, at the base of a woody hill which rises abruptly behind his house, and of which the level summit supplies him with a promenade continually mentioned in the course of the tale. Hawthorne used to exercise himself upon this picturesque eminence, and, as he conceived the brooding Septimius to have done before him, to betake himself thither when he found the limits of his dwelling too narrow. But he had an advantage which his imaginary hero lacked; he erected a tower as an adjunct to the house, and it was a jocular tradition among his neighbors, in allusion to his attributive tendency to evade rather than hasten the coming guest, that he used to ascend this structure and scan the road for provocations to retreat.

Insofar, however, as Hawthorne suffered the penalties of celebrity at the hands of intrusive fellow-citizens, he was soon to escape from this honorable incommodity. On the fourth of March, 1853, his old college-mate and intimate friend, Franklin Pierce, was installed as President of the United States. He had been the candidate of the Democratic party, and all good Democrats, accordingly, in conformity to the beautiful and rational system under which the affairs of the great Republic were carried on, began to open their windows to the golden sunshine of Presidential patronage. When General Pierce was put forward by the Democrats, Hawthorne felt a perfectly loyal and natural desire that his good friend should be exalted to so brilliant a position, and he did what was in him to further the good cause, by writing a little book about its hero. His *Life of Franklin Pierce* belongs to that class of literature which is known as the "campaign biography," and which consists of an attempt, more or less successful, to persuade the many-headed monster of universal suffrage that the gentleman on whose behalf it is addressed is a paragon of wisdom and virtue. Of Hawthorne's little book there is nothing particular to say, save that it is in very good taste, that he is a very fairly ingenious advocate, and that if he claimed for the future President qualities which rather faded in the bright light of a high office, this defect of proportion was essential to his undertaking. He dwelt chiefly upon General Pierce's exploits in the war with Mexico (before that, his record, as they say in America, had been mainly that of a successful country lawyer), and exercised his descriptive powers so far as was possible in describing the advance of the United States troops from Vera Cruz to the city of the Montezumas. The mouthpieces of the Whig party spared him, I believe, no reprobation for "prostituting" his exquisite genius; but I fail to see anything reprehensible in Hawthorne's lending his old friend the assistance of his graceful quill. He wished him to be President—he held afterwards that he filled the office with admirable dignity and wisdom—and as the only thing he could do was to write, he fell to work and wrote for him. Hawthorne was a good lover and a very sufficient partisan, and I suspect that if Franklin Pierce had been made even less of the stuff of a statesman, he would still have found in the force of old associations an injunction to hail him as a ruler. Our hero was an American of the earlier and simpler type— the type of which it is doubtless premature to say that it has wholly passed away, but of which it may at least be said that the circumstances that produced it have been greatly modified. The generation to which he belonged, that generation which grew up with the century, witnessed during a period of fifty years the immense, uninterrupted material development of the young Republic; and when one thinks of the scale on which it took place, of the prosperity that walked in its train and waited on its course, of the hopes it fostered and the blessings it conferred, of the broad morning sunshine, in a word, in which it all went forward, there seems to be little room for surprise that it should have implanted a kind of superstitious faith in the grandeur of the country, its duration, its immunity from the usual troubles of earthly empires. This faith was a simple and uncritical one, en-

livened with an element of genial optimism, in the light of
which it appeared that the great American state was not as
other human institutions are, that a special Providence
watched over it, that it would go on joyously forever, and
that a country whose vast and blooming bosom offered a
refuge to the strugglers and seekers of all the rest of the
world, must come off easily, in the battle of the ages. From
this conception of the American future the sense of its having problems to solve was blissfully absent; there were no
difficulties in the program, no looming complications, no
rocks ahead. The indefinite multiplication of the population,
and its enjoyment of the benefits of a common-school education and of unusual facilities for making an income—this
was the form in which, on.the whole, the future most vividly
presented itself, and in which the greatness of the country
was to be recognized of men. There was indeed a faint
shadow in the picture—the shadow projected by the "peculiar
institution" of the Southern states; but it was far from sufficient to darken the rosy vision of most good Americans, and,
above all, of most good Democrats. Hawthorne alludes to it
in a passage of his life of Pierce, which I will quote not only
as a hint of the trouble that was in store for a cheerful race
of men, but as an example of his own easy-going political
attitude.

It was while in the lower house of Congress that Franklin
Pierce took that stand on the Slavery question from which he
has never since swerved by a hair's-breadth. He fully recognized
by his votes and his voice the rights pledged to the South by
the Constitution. This, at the period when he declared himself,
was an easy thing to do. But when it became more difficult,
when the first imperceptible murmur of agitation had grown almost to a convulsion, his course was still the same. Nor did he
ever shun the obloquy that sometimes threatened to pursue the
Northern man who dared to love that great and sacred reality
—his whole united country—better than the mistiness of a phil-
anthropic theory.

This last invidious allusion is to the disposition, not infrequent at the North, but by no means general, to set a
decisive limit to further legislation in favor of the cherished

idiosyncrasy of the other half of the country. Hawthorne takes the license of a sympathetic biographer in speaking of his hero's having incurred obloquy by his conservative attitude on the question of Slavery. The only class in the American world that suffered in the smallest degree, at this time, from social persecution, was the little band of Northern Abolitionists, who were as unfashionable as they were indiscreet—which is saying much. Like most of his fellow-countrymen, Hawthorne had no idea that the respectable institution which he contemplated in impressive contrast to humanitarian "mistiness" was presently to cost the nation four long years of bloodshed and misery, and a social revolution as complete as any the world has seen. When this event occurred, he was therefore proportionately horrified and depressed by it; it cut from beneath his feet the familiar ground which had long felt so firm, substituting a heaving and quaking medium in which his spirit found no rest. Such was the bewildered sensation of that earlier and simpler generation of which I have spoken; their illusions were rudely dispelled, and they saw the best of all possible republics given over to fratricidal carnage. This affair had no place in their scheme, and nothing was left for them but to hang their heads and close their eyes. The subsidence of that great convulsion has left a different tone from the tone it found, and one may say that the Civil War marks an era in the history of the American mind. It introduced into the national consciousness a certain sense of proportion and relation, of the world being a more complicated place than it had hitherto seemed, the future more treacherous, success more difficult. At the rate at which things are going, it is obvious that good Americans will be more numerous than ever; but the good American, in days to come, will be a more critical person than his complacent and confident grandfather. He has eaten of the tree of knowledge. He will not, I think, be a skeptic, and still less, of course, a cynic; but he will be, without discredit to his well-known capacity for action, an observer. He will remember that the ways of the Lord are inscrutable, and that this is a world in which everything happens; and eventualities, as the late Emperor of the French used to say, will not find him intellectually unprepared. The good American of which Hawthorne was so admirable a specimen was not critical, and it was perhaps for this reason that Franklin Pierce seemed to him a very proper President.

The least that General Pierce could do in exchange for so liberal a confidence was to offer his old friend one of the numerous places in his gift. Hawthorne had a great desire to go abroad and see something of the world, so that a consulate seemed the proper thing. He never stirred in the matter himself, but his friends strongly urged that something should be done; and when he accepted the post of consul at Liverpool there was not a word of reasonable criticism to be offered on the matter. If General Pierce, who was before all things good-natured and obliging, had been guilty of no greater indiscretion than to confer this modest distinction upon the most honorable and discreet of men of letters, he would have made a more brilliant mark in the annals of American statesmanship. Liverpool had not been immediately selected, and Hawthorne had written to his friend and publisher, Mr. Fields, with some humorous vagueness of allusion to his probable expatriation.

Do make some inquiries about Portugal; as, for instance, in what part of the world it lies, and whether it is an empire, a kingdom, or a republic. Also, and more particularly, the expenses of living there, and whether the Minister would be likely to be much pestered with his own countrymen. Also, any other information about foreign countries would be acceptable to an inquiring mind.

It would seem from this that there had been a question of offering him a small diplomatic post; but the emoluments of the place were justly taken into account, and it is to be supposed that those of the consulate at Liverpool were at least as great as the salary of the American representative at Lisbon. Unfortunately, just after Hawthorne had taken possession of the former post, the salary attached to it was reduced by Congress, in an economical hour, to less than half the sum enjoyed by his predecessors. It was fixed at $7,500 (£1,500); but the consular fees, which were often copious, were an added resource. At midsummer then, in 1853, Hawthorne was established in England.

VI.   England and Italy

HAWTHORNE was close upon fifty years of age when he came to Europe—a fact that should be remembered when those impressions which he recorded in five substantial volumes (exclusive of the novel written in Italy) occasionally affect us by the rigidity of their point of view. His *Note-Books*, kept during his residence in England, his two winters in Rome, his summer in Florence, were published after his death; his impressions of England, sifted, revised, and addressed directly to the public, he gave to the world shortly before this event. The tone of his European diaries is often so fresh and unsophisticated that we find ourselves thinking of the writer as a young man, and it is only a certain final sense of something reflective and a trifle melancholy that reminds us that the simplicity which is on the whole the leading characteristic of their pages is, though the simplicity of inexperience, not that of youth. When I say inexperience, I mean that Hawthorne's experience had been narrow. His fifty years had been spent, for much the larger part, in small American towns—Salem, the Boston of forty years ago, Concord, Lenox, West Newton—and he had led exclusively what one may call a village life. This is evident, not at all directly and superficially, but by implication and between the lines, in his desultory history of his foreign years. In other words, and to call things by their names, he was exquisitely and consistently provincial. I suggest this fact not in the least in condemnation, but, on the contrary, in support of an appreciative view of him. I know nothing more remarkable, more touching, than the sight of this odd, youthful-elderly mind, contending so late in the day with new opportunities for learning old things, and on the whole profiting by them so freely and gracefully. The *Note-Books* are provincial, and so, in a greatly modified degree, are the sketches of England, in *Our Old Home*; but the beauty and delicacy of this latter work are so interwoven with the author's air of being remotely outside of everything he describes that they count for more, seem more themselves, and finally give the whole thing the appearance of a triumph, not of initiation, but of the provincial point of view itself.

I shall not attempt to relate in detail the incidents of his residence in England. He appears to have enjoyed it greatly, in spite of the deficiency of charm in the place to which his duties chiefly confined him. His confinement, however, was not unbroken, and his published journals consist largely of minute accounts of little journeys and wanderings, with his wife and his three children, through the rest of the country; together with much mention of numerous visits to London, a city for whose dusky immensity and multitudinous interest he professed the highest relish. His *Note-Books* are of the same cast as the two volumes of his American diaries, of which I have given some account—chiefly occupied with external matters, with the accidents of daily life, with observations made during the long walks (often with his son), which formed his most valued pastime. His office, moreover, though Liverpool was not a delectable home, furnished him with entertainment as well as occupation, and it may almost be said that during these years he saw more of his fellow countrymen, in the shape of odd wanderers, petitioners, and inquirers of every kind, than he had ever done in his native land. The paper entitled *Consular Experiences,* in *Our Old Home,* is an admirable recital of these observations, and a proof that the novelist might have found much material in the opportunities of the consul. On his return to America, in 1860, he drew from his journal a number of pages relating to his observations in England, rewrote them (with, I should suppose, a good deal of care), and converted them into articles which he published in a magazine. These chapters were afterwards collected, and *Our Old Home* (a rather infelicitous title) was issued in 1863. I prefer to speak of the book now, however, rather than in touching upon the closing years of his life, for it is a kind of deliberate *résumé* of his impressions of the land of his ancestors. "It is not a good or a weighty book," he wrote to his publisher, who had sent him some reviews of it, "nor does it deserve any great amount

of praise or censure. I don't care about seeing any more
notices of it." Hawthorne's appreciation of his own productions was always extremely just; he had a sense of the
relations of things, which some of his admirers have not
thought it well to cultivate; and he never exaggerated his
own importance as a writer. *Our Old Home* is not a weighty
book; it is decidedly a light one. But when he says it is not
a good one, I hardly know what he means, and his modesty
at this point is in excess of his discretion. Whether good or
not, *Our Old Home* is charming—it is most delectable reading. The execution is singularly perfect and ripe; of all his
productions it seems to be the best written. The touch, as
musicians say, is admirable; the lightness, the fineness, the
felicity of characterization and description, belong to a man
who has the advantage of feeling delicately. His judgment
is by no means always sound; it often rests on too narrow
an observation. But his perception is of the keenest, and
though it is frequently partial, incomplete, it is excellent as
far as it goes. The book gave but limited satisfaction, I believe, in England, and I am not sure that the failure to enjoy
certain manifestations of its sportive irony has not chilled
the appreciation of its singular grace. That English readers,
on the whole, should have felt that Hawthorne did the
national mind and manners but partial justice is, I think,
conceivable; at the same time that it seems to me remarkable
that the tender side of the book, as I may call it, should not
have carried it off better. It abounds in passages more delicately appreciative than can easily be found elsewhere, and
it contains more charming and affectionate things than, I
should suppose, had ever before been written about a country not the writer's own. To say that it is an immeasurably
more exquisite and sympathetic work than any of the numerous persons who have related their misadventures in the
United States have seen fit to devote to that country, is to
say but little, and I imagine that Hawthorne had in mind
the array of English voyagers—Mrs. Trollope, Dickens, Mar-
ryat, Basil Hall, Miss Martineau, Mr. Grattan—when he
reflected that everything is relative and that, as such books
go, his own little volume observed the amenities of criticism

He certainly had it in mind when he wrote the phrase in his preface relating to the impression the book might make in England. "Not an Englishman of them all ever spared America for courtesy's sake or kindness; nor, in my opinion, would it contribute in the least to any mutual advantage and comfort if we were to besmear each other all over with butter and honey." I am far from intending to intimate that the vulgar instinct of recrimination had anything to do with the restrictive passages of *Our Old Home;* I mean simply that the author had a prevision that his collection of sketches would in some particulars fail to please his English friends. He professed, after the event, to have discovered that the English are sensitive, and as they say of the Americans, for whose advantage I believe the term was invented, thin-skinned. "The English critics," he wrote to his publisher, "seem to think me very bitter against their countrymen, and it is perhaps natural that they should, because their self-conceit can accept nothing short of indiscriminate adulation; but I really think that Americans have much more cause than they to complain of me. Looking over the volume I am rather surprised to find that whenever I draw a comparison between the two people, I almost invariably cast the balance against ourselves." And he writes at another time: "I received several private letters and printed notices of *Our Old Home* from England. It is laughable to see the innocent wonder with which they regard my criticisms, accounting for them by jaundice, insanity, jealousy, hatred, on my part, and never admitting the least suspicion that there may be a particle of truth in them. The monstrosity of their self-conceit is such that anything short of unlimited admiration impresses them as malicious caricature. But they do me great injustice in supposing that I hate them. I would as soon hate my own people." The idea of his hating the English was of course too puerile for discussion; and the book, as I have said, is full of a rich appreciation of the finest characteristics of the country. But it has a serious defect—a defect which impairs its value, though it helps to give consistency to such an image of Hawthorne's personal nature as we may by this time have been able to form. It is the work of an outsider, of

a stranger, of a man who remains to the end a mere spectator
(something less even than an observer), and always lacks
the final initiation into the manners and nature of a people
of whom it may most be said, among all the people of the
earth, that to know them is to make discoveries. Hawthorne
freely confesses to this constant exteriority, and appears to
have been perfectly conscious of it. "I remember," he writes
in the sketch of *A London Suburb*, in *Our Old Home*, "I
remember to this day the dreary feeling with which I sat
by our first English fireside and watched the chill and rainy
twilight of an autumn day darkening down upon the garden,
while the preceding occupant of the house (evidently a most
unamiable personage in his lifetime) scowled inhospitably
from above the mantelpiece, as if indignant that an American should try to make himself at home there. Possibly it
may appease his sulky shade to know that I quitted his abode
as much a stranger as I entered it." The same note is struck
in an entry in his journal, of the date of October 6, 1854.

The people, for several days, have been in the utmost anxiety,
and latterly in the highest exultation, about Sebastopol—and all
England, and Europe to boot, have been fooled by the belief that
it had fallen. This, however, now turns out to be incorrect; and
the public visage is somewhat grim in consequence. I am glad
of it. In spite of his actual sympathies, it is impossible for an
American to be otherwise than glad. Success makes an Englishman intolerable, and already, on the mistaken idea that the way
was open to a prosperous conclusion of the war, the *Times* had
begun to throw out menaces against America. I shall never love
England till she sues to us for help, and, in the meantime, the
fewer triumphs she obtains, the better for all parties. An Englishman in adversity is a very respectable character; he does not
lose his dignity, but merely comes to a proper conception of himself. . . . I seem to myself like a spy or traitor when I meet
their eyes, and am conscious that I neither hope nor fear in sympathy with them, although they look at me in full confidence of
sympathy. Their heart "knoweth its own bitterness," and as for
me, being a stranger and an alien, I "intermeddle not with their
joy."

This seems to me to express very well the weak side of
Hawthorne's work—his constant mistrust and suspicion of

the society that surrounded him, his exaggerated, painful, morbid national consciousness. It is, I think, an indisputable fact that Americans are, as Americans, the most self-conscious people in the world, and the most addicted to the belief that the other nations of the earth are in a conspiracy to under-value them. They are conscious of being the youngest of the great nations, of not being of the European family, of being placed on the circumference of the circle of civilization rather than at the center, of the experimental element not having as yet entirely dropped out of their great political undertaking. The sense of this relativity, in a word, replaces that quiet and comfortable sense of the absolute, as regards its own position in the world, which reigns supreme in the British and in the Gallic genius. Few persons, I think, can have mingled much with Americans in Europe without having made this reflection, and it is in England that their habit of looking askance at foreign institutions—of keeping one eye, as it were, on the American personality, while with the other they contemplate these objects—is most to be observed. Add to this that Hawthorne came to England late in life, when his habits, his tastes, his opinions, were already formed, that he was inclined to look at things in silence and brood over them gently, rather than talk about them, discuss them, grow acquainted with them by action; and it will be possible to form an idea of our writer's detached and critical attitude in the country in which it is easiest, thanks to its aristocratic constitution, to the absence of any considerable public fund of entertainment and diversion, to the degree in which the inexhaustible beauty and interest of the place are private property, demanding constantly a special introduc-tion—in the country in which, I say, it is easiest for a stranger to remain a stranger. For a stranger to cease to be a stranger he must stand ready, as the French say, to pay with his person; and this was an obligation that Hawthorne was indisposed to incur. Our sense, as we read, that his re-flections are those of a shy and susceptible man, with nothing at stake, mentally, in his appreciation of the country, is therefore a drawback to our confidence; but it is not a draw-back sufficient to make it of no importance that he is at the same time singularly intelligent and discriminating, with a faculty of feeling delicately and justly, which constitutes in itself an illumination. There is a passage in the sketch entitled *About Warwick* which is a very good instance of what was probably his usual state of mind. He is speaking of the aspect of the High Street of the town.

The street is an emblem of England itself. What seems new in it is chiefly a skillful and fortunate adaptation of what such a people as ourselves would destroy. The new things are based and supported on sturdy old things, and derive a massive strength from their deep and immemorial foundations, though with such limitations and impediments as only an Englishman could endure. But he likes to feel the weight of all the past upon his back; and moreover the antiquity that overburdens him has taken root in his being, and has grown to be rather a hump than a pack, so that there is no getting rid of it without tearing his whole structure to pieces. In my judgment, as he appears to be sufficiently comfortable under the moldy accretion, he had better stumble on with it as long as he can. He presents a spectacle which is by no means without its charm for a disinterested and unincumbered observer.

There is all Hawthorne, with his enjoyment of the picturesque, his relish of chiaroscuro, of local color, of the deposit of time, and his still greater enjoyment of his own dissociation from these things, his "disinterested and unincumbered" condition. His want of incumbrances may seem at times to give him a somewhat naked and attenuated appearance, but on the whole he carries it off very well. I have said that *Our Old Home* contains much of his best writing, and on turning over the book at hazard, I am struck with his frequent felicity of phrase. At every step there is something one would like to quote—something excellently well said. These things are often of the lighter sort, but Hawthorne's charming diction lingers in the memory—almost in the ear. I have always remembered a certain admirable characterization of Doctor Johnson, in the account of the writer's visit to Lichfield—and I will preface it by a paragraph almost as good, commemorating the charms of the hotel in that interesting town.

At any rate I had the great, dull, dingy, and dreary coffee-room, with its heavy old mahogany chairs and tables, all to myself, and not a soul to exchange a word with except the waiter, who, like most of his class in England, had evidently left his conversational abilities uncultivated. No former practice of solitary living, nor habits of reticence, nor well-tested self-dependence for occupation of mind and amusement, can quite avail, as I now proved, to dissipate the ponderous gloom of an English coffee-room under such circumstances as these, with no book at hand save the county directory, nor any newspaper but a torn local journal of five days ago. So I buried myself, betimes, in a huge heap of ancient feathers (there is no other kind of bed in these old inns), let my head sink into an unsubstantial pillow, and slept a stifled sleep, compounded of the night-troubles of all my predecessors in that same unrestful couch. And when I awoke, the odor of a bygone century was in my nostrils—a faint, elusive smell, of which I never had any conception before crossing the Atlantic.

The whole chapter entitled "Lichfield and Uttoxeter" is a sort of graceful tribute to Samuel Johnson, who certainly has nowhere else been more tenderly spoken of.

Beyond all question I might. have had a wiser friend than he. The atmosphere in which alone he breathed was dense; his awful dread of death showed how much muddy imperfection was to be cleansed out of him before he could be capable of spiritual existence; he meddled only with the surface of life, and never cared to penetrate further than to ploughshare depth; his very sense and sagacity were but a one-eyed clear-sightedness. I laughed at him, sometimes standing beside his knee. And yet, considering that my native propensities were toward Fairy Land, and also how much yeast is generally mixed up with the mental sustenance of a New Englander, it may not have been altogether amiss, in those childish and boyish days, to keep pace with this heavy-footed traveler and feed on the gross diet that he carried in his knapsack. It is wholesome food even now! And then, how English! Many of the latent sympathies that enabled me to enjoy the Old Country so well, and that so readily amalgamated themselves with the American ideas that seemed most adverse to them, may have been derived from, or fostered and kept alive by, the great English moralist. Never was a descriptive epithet more nicely appropriate than that! Doctor Johnson's morality was as English an article as a beef-steak.

And for mere beauty of expression I cannot forbear quoting this passage about the days in a fine English summer:

For each day seemed endless, though never wearisome. As far as your actual experience is concerned, the English summer day has positively no beginning and no end. When you awake, at any reasonable hour, the sun is already shining through the curtains; you live through unnumbered hours of Sabbath quietude, with a calm variety of incident softly etched upon their tranquil lapse; and at length you become conscious that it is bedtime again, while there is still enough daylight in the sky to make the pages of your book distinctly legible. Night, if there be any such season, hangs down a transparent veil through which the bygone day beholds its successor; or if not quite true of the latitude of London, it may be soberly affirmed of the more northern parts of the island that Tomorrow is born before its Yesterday is dead. They exist together in the golden twilight, where the decrepit old day dimly discerns the face of the ominous infant; and you, though a mere mortal, may simultaneously touch them both, with one finger of recollection and another of prophecy.

The *Note-Books*, as I have said, deal chiefly with the superficial aspect of English life, and describe the material objects with which the author was surrounded. They often describe them admirably, and the rural beauty of the country has never been more happily expressed. But there are inevitably a great many reflections and incidental judgments, characterizations of people he met, fragments of psychology and social criticism, and it is here that Hawthorne's mixture of subtlety and simplicity, his interfusion of genius with what I have ventured to call the provincial quality, is most apparent. To an American reader this later quality, which is never grossly manifested, but pervades the journals like a vague natural perfume, an odor of purity and kindness and integrity, must always, for a reason that I will touch upon, have a considerable charm; and such a reader will accordingly take an even greater satisfaction in the diaries kept during the two years Hawthorne spent in Italy; for in these volumes the element I speak of is especially striking. He resigned his consulate at Liverpool towards the close of 1857

—whether because he was weary of his manner of life there and of the place itself, as may well have been, or because he wished to anticipate supersession by the new government (Mr. Buchanan's) which was just establishing itself at Washington, is not apparent from the slender sources of information from which these pages have been compiled. In the month of January of the following year he betook himself with his family to the Continent, and, as promptly as possible, made the best of his way to Rome. He spent the remainder of the winter and the spring there, and then went to Florence for the summer and autumn; after which he returned to Rome and passed a second season. His Italian *Note-Books* are very pleasant reading, but they are of less interest than the others, for his contact with the life of the country, its people and its manners, was simply that of the ordinary tourist—which amounts to saying that it was extremely superficial. He appears to have suffered a great deal of discomfort and depression in Rome, and not to have been on the whole in the best mood for enjoying the place and its resources. That he did, at one time and another, enjoy these things keenly is proved by his beautiful romance, *Transformation,* which could never have been written by a man who had not had many hours of exquisite appreciation of the lovely land of Italy. But he took it hard, as it were, and suffered himself to be painfully discomposed by the usual accidents of Italian life, as foreigners learn to know it. His future was again uncertain, and during his second winter in Rome he was in danger of losing his elder daughter by a malady which he speaks of as a trouble "that pierced to my very vitals." I may mention, with regard to this painful episode, that Franklin Pierce, whose presidential days were over, and who, like other ex-presidents, was traveling in Europe, came to Rome at the time, and that the *Note-Books* contain some singularly beautiful and touching allusions to his old friend's gratitude for his sympathy, and enjoyment of his society. The sentiment of friendship has on the whole been so much less commemorated in literature than might have been expected from the place it is supposed to hold in life, that there is always something striking in any frank and ardent expression of it. It occupied, in so far as Pierce was the object of it, a large place in Hawthorne's mind, and it is impossible not to feel the manly tenderness of such lines as these:

I have found him here in Rome, the whole of my early friend, and even better than I used to know him; a heart as true and affectionate, a mind much widened and deepened by the experience of life. We hold just the same relation to one another as of yore, and we have passed all the turning-off places, and may hope to go on together, still the same dear friends, as long as we live. I do not love him one whit the less for having been President, nor for having done me the greatest good in his power; a fact that speaks eloquently in his favor, and perhaps says a little for myself. If he had been merely a benefactor, perhaps I might not have borne it so well; but each did his best for the other, as friend for friend.

The *Note-Books* are chiefly taken up with descriptions of the regular sights and "objects of interest," which we often feel to be rather perfunctory and a little in the style of the traditional tourist's diary. They abound in charming touches, and every reader of *Transformation* will remember the delightful coloring of the numerous pages in that novel which are devoted to the pictorial aspects of Rome. But we are unable to rid ourselves of the impression that Hawthorne was a good deal bored by the importunity of Italian art, for which his taste, naturally not keen, had never been cultivated. Occasionally, indeed, he breaks out into explicit sighs and groans, and frankly declares that he washes his hands of it. Already, in England, he had made the discovery that he could easily feel overdosed with such things. "Yesterday," he wrote in 1856, "I went out at about twelve and visited the British Museum; an exceedingly tiresome affair. It quite crushes a person to see so much at once, and I wandered from hall to hall with a weary and heavy heart, wishing (Heaven forgive me!) that the Elgin marbles and the frieze of the Parthenon were all burnt into lime, and that the granite Egyptian statues were hewn and squared into building stones."

The plastic sense was not strong in Hawthorne; there

can be no better proof of it than his curious aversion to the
representation of the nude in sculpture. This aversion was
deep-seated; he constantly returns to it, exclaiming upon
the incongruity of modern artists making naked figures. He
apparently quite failed to see that nudity is not an incident,
or accident, of sculpture, but its very essense and principle;
and his jealousy of undressed images strikes the reader as
a strange, vague, long-dormant heritage of his straitlaced
Puritan ancestry. Whenever he talks of statues he makes a
great point of the smoothness and whiteness of the marble
—speaks of the surface of the marble as if it were half the
beauty of the image; and when he discourses of pictures,
one feels that the brightness or dinginess of the frame is an
essential part of his impression of the work—as he indeed
somewhere distinctly affirms. Like a good American, he took
more pleasure in the productions of Mr. Thompson and Mr.
Brown, Mr. Powers and Mr. Hart, American artists who
were plying their trade in Italy, than in the works which
adorned the ancient museums of the country. He suffered
greatly from the cold, and found little charm in the climate,
and during the weeks of winter that followed his arrival
in Rome, he sat shivering by his fire and wondering why
he had come to such a land of misery. Before he left Italy
he wrote to his publisher—"I bitterly detest Rome, and shall
rejoice to bid it farewell forever; and I fully acquiesce in
all the mischief and ruin that has happened to it, from
Nero's conflagration downward. In fact, I wish the very
site had been obliterated before I ever saw it." Hawthorne
presents himself to the reader of these pages as the last of
the old-fashioned Americans—and this is the interest which I
just now said that his compatriots would find in his very
limitations. I do not mean by this that there are not still
many of his fellow-countrymen (as there are many natives
of every land under the sun) who are more susceptible of
being irritated than of being soothed by the influences of
the Eternal City. What I mean is that an American of equal
value with Hawthorne, an American of equal genius, imagination, and, as our forefathers said, sensibility, would at
present inevitably accommodate himself more easily to the

idiosyncrasies of foreign lands. An American as cultivated
as Hawthorne is now almost inevitably more cultivated, and,
as a matter of course, more Europeanized in advance, more
cosmopolitan. It is very possible that in becoming so, he has
lost something of his occidental savor, the quality which
excites the good will of the American reader of our author's
journals for the dislocated, depressed, even slightly bewildered diarist. Absolutely the last of the earlier race of Americans Hawthorne was, fortunately, probably far from being.
But I think of him as the last specimen of the more primitive
type of men of letters; and when it comes to measuring
what he succeeded in being, in his unadulterated form,
against what he failed of being, the positive side of the
image quite extinguishes the negative. I must be on my
guard, however, against incurring the charge of cherishing
a national consciousness as acute as I have ventured to pronounce his own.

Out of his mingled sensations, his pleasure and his weariness, his discomforts and his reveries, there sprang another
beautiful work. During the summer of 1858, he hired a picturesque old villa on the hill of Bellosguardo, near Florence,
a curious structure with a crenelated tower, which, after
having in the course of its career suffered many vicissitudes
and played many parts, now finds its most vivid identity in
being pointed out to strangers as the sometime residence of
the celebrated American romancer. Hawthorne took a fancy
to the place, as well he might, for it is one of the loveliest
spots on earth, and the great view that stretched itself before him contains every element of beauty. Florence lay at
his feet with her memories and treasures; the olive-covered
hills bloomed around him, studded with villas as picturesque
as his own; the Apennines, perfect in form and color, disposed themselves opposite, and in the distance, along its
fertile valley, the Arno wandered to Pisa and the sea. Soon
after coming hither he wrote to a friend in a strain of high
satisfaction:

It is pleasant to feel at last that I am really away from America—a satisfaction that I never really enjoyed as long as I stayed
in Liverpool, where it seemed to me that the quintessence of

nasal and hand-shaking Yankeedom was gradually filtered and sublimated through my consulate, on the way outward and homeward. I first got acquainted with my own countrymen there. At Rome too it was not much better. But here in Florence, and in the summer-time, and in this secluded villa, I have escaped out of all my old tracks, and am really remote. I like my present residence immensely. The house stands on a hill, overlooking Florence, and is big enough to quarter a regiment, insomuch that each member of the family, including servants, has a separate suite of apartments, and there are vast wildernesses of upper rooms into which we have never yet sent exploring expeditions. At one end of the house there is a moss-grown tower, haunted by owls and by the ghost of a monk who was confined there in the thirteenth century, previous to being burnt at the stake in the principal square of Florence. I hire this villa, tower and all, at twenty-eight dollars a month; but I mean to take it away bodily and clap it into a romance, which I have in my head, ready to be written out.

This romance was *Transformation,* which he wrote out during the following winter in Rome, and rewrote during the several months that he spent in England, chiefly at Leamington, before returning to America. The Villa Montauto figures, in fact, in this tale as the castle of Monte-Beni, the patrimonial dwelling of the hero. "I take some credit to myself," he wrote to the same friend, on returning to Rome, "for having sternly shut myself up for an hour or two every day, and come to close grips with a romance which I have been trying to tear out of my mind." And later in the same winter he says—"I shall go home, I fear, with a heavy heart, not expecting to be very well contented there. . . . If I were but a hundred times richer than I am, how very comfortable I could be! I consider it a great piece of good fortune that I have had experience of the discomforts and miseries of Italy, and did not go directly home from England. Anything will seem like a Paradise after a Roman winter." But he got away at last, late in the spring, carrying his novel with him, and the book was published, after, as I say, he had worked it over, mainly during some weeks that he passed at the little watering place of Redcar, on the Yorkshire coast, in February of the following year. It was issued primarily in England; the American edition immediately followed. It is an odd fact that in the two countries the book came out under different titles. The title that the author had bestowed upon it did not satisfy the English publishers, who requested him to provide it with another; so that it is only in America that the work bears the name of *The Marble Faun*. Hawthorne's choice of this appellation is, by the way, rather singular, for it completely fails to characterize the story, the subject of which is the living faun, the faun of flesh and blood, the unfortunate Donatello. His marble counterpart is mentioned only in the opening chapter. On the other hand, Hawthorne complained that *Transformation* "gives one the idea of Harlequin in a pantomime." Under either name, however, the book was a great success, and it has probably become the most popular of Hawthorne's four novels. It is part of the intellectual equipment of the Anglo-Saxon visitor to Rome, and is read by every English-speaking traveler who arrives there, who has been there, or who expects to go.

It has a great deal of beauty, of interest and grace; but it has to my sense a slighter value than its companions, and I am far from regarding it as the masterpiece of the author, a position to which we sometimes hear it assigned. The subject is admirable, and so are many of the details; but the whole thing is less simple and complete than either of the three tales of American life, and Hawthorne forfeited a precious advantage in ceasing to tread his native soil. Half the virtue of *The Scarlet Letter* and *The House of the Seven Gables* is in their local quality; they are impregnated with the New England air. It is very true that Hawthorne had no pretension to portray actualities and to cultivate that literal exactitude which is now the fashion. Had this been the case, he would probably have made a still graver mistake in transporting the scene of his story to a country which he knew only superficially. His tales all go on more or less "in the vague," as the French say, and of course the vague may as well be placed in Tuscany as in Massachusetts. It may also very well be urged in Hawthorne's favor here that in *Transformation* he has attempted to deal with actualities more than he did in either of his earlier novels. He has described the streets and monuments of Rome with a closeness which forms no part of his reference to those of Boston and Salem. But for all this he incurs that penalty of seeming factitious and unauthoritative, which is always the result of an artist's attempt to project himself into an atmosphere in which he has not a transmitted and inherited property. An English or a German writer (I put poets aside) may love Italy well enough, and know her well enough, to write delightful fictions about her; the thing has often been done. But the productions in question will, as novels, always have about them something second-rate and imperfect. There is in *Transformation* enough beautiful perception of the interesting character of Rome, enough rich and eloquent expression of it, to save the book, if the book could be saved; but the style, what the French call the *genre*, is an inferior one, and the thing remains a charming romance with intrinsic weaknesses.

Allowing for this, however, some of the finest pages in all Hawthorne are to be found in it. The subject, as I have said, is a particularly happy one, and there is a great deal of interest in the simple combination and opposition of the four actors. It is noticeable that in spite of the considerable length of the story, there are no accessory figures; Donatello and Miriam, Kenyon and Hilda, exclusively occupy the scene. This is the more noticeable as the scene is very large, and the great Roman background is constantly presented to us. The relations of these four people are full of that moral picturesqueness which Hawthorne was always looking for; he found it in perfection in the history of Donatello. As I have said, the novel is the most popular of his works, and everyone will remember the figure of the simple, joyous, sensuous young Italian, who is not so much a man as a child, and not so much a child as a charming, innocent animal, and how he is brought to self-knowledge and to a miserable conscious manhood by the commission of a crime. Donatello is rather vague and impalpable; he says too little in the book, shows himself too little, and falls short, I think, of being a creation. But he is enough of a creation to make us enter into the situation, and the whole history of his rise, or fall, whichever one chooses to call it—his tasting of the tree of knowledge and finding existence complicated with a regret—is unfolded with a thousand ingenious and exquisite touches. Of course, to make the interest complete, there is a woman in the affair, and Hawthorne has done few things more beautiful than the picture of the unequal complicity of guilt between his immature and dimly-puzzled hero, with his clinging, unquestioning, unexacting devotion, and the dark, powerful, more widely-seeing feminine nature of Miriam. Deeply touching is the representation of the manner in which these two essentially different persons—the woman intelligent, passionate, acquainted with life, and with a tragic element in her own career; the youth ignorant, gentle, unworldly, brightly and harmlessly natural—are equalized and bound together by their common secret, which insulates them, morally, from the rest of mankind. The character of Hilda has always struck me as an admirable invention—one of those things that mark the man of genius. It needed a man of genius and of Hawthorne's imaginative delicacy to feel the propriety of such a figure as Hilda's and to perceive the relief it would both give and borrow. This pure and somewhat rigid New England girl, following the vocation of a copyist of pictures in Rome, unacquainted with evil and untouched by impurity, has been accidentally the witness, unknown and unsuspected, of the dark deed by which her friends, Miriam and Donatello, are knit together. This is *her* revelation of evil, her loss of perfect innocence. She has done no wrong, and yet wrongdoing has become a part of her experience, and she carries the weight of her detested knowledge upon her heart. She carries it a long time, saddened and oppressed by it, till at last she can bear it no longer. If I have called the whole idea of the presence and effect of Hilda in the story a trait of genius, the purest touch of inspiration is the episode in which the poor girl deposits her burden. She has passed the whole lonely summer in Rome, and one day, at the end of it, finding herself in St. Peter's, she enters a confessional, strenuous daughter of the Puritans as she is, and pours out her dark knowledge into the bosom of the Church—then comes away with her conscience lightened, not a whit the less a Puritan than before. If the book contained nothing else noteworthy but this admirable scene, and the pages describing the murder committed by Donatello under Miriam's eyes, and the ecstatic wandering, afterwards, of the guilty couple, through the "blood-stained streets of Rome," it would still deserve to rank high among the imaginative productions of our day.

Like all of Hawthorne's things, it contains a great many light threads of symbolism, which shimmer in the texture of the tale, but which are apt to break and remain in our fingers if we attempt to handle them. These things are part of Hawthorne's very manner—almost, as one might say, of his vocabulary; they belong much more to the surface of his work than to its stronger interest. The fault of *Transformation* is that the element of the unreal is pushed too far, and that the book is neither positively of one category nor of another. His "moonshiny romance," he calls it in a letter; and, in truth, the lunar element is a little too pervasive. The action wavers between the streets of Rome, whose literal features the author perpetually sketches, and a vague realm of fancy, in which quite a different verisimilitude prevails. This is the trouble with Donatello himself. His companions are intended to be real—if they fail to be so, it is not for want of intention; whereas he is intended to be real or not, as you please. He is of a different substance from them; it is as if a painter, in composing a picture, should try to give you an impression of one of his figures by a strain of music. The idea of the modern faun was a charming one; but I think it a pity that the author should not have made him more definitely modern, without reverting so much to his mythological properties and antecedents, which are very gracefully touched upon, but which belong to the region of picturesque conceits, much more than to that of real psychology. Among the young Italians of today there are still plenty of models for such an image as Hawthorne appears to have wished to present in the easy and natural Donatello. And since I am speaking critically, I may go on to say that the art of narration, in *Transformation,* seems to

me more at fault than in the author's other novels. The
story straggles and wanders, is dropped and taken up again,
and towards the close lapses into an almost fatal vagueness.

VII. Last Years

OF THE FOUR LAST YEARS of Hawthorne's life there is not
much to tell that I have not already told. He returned to
America in the summer of 1860, and took up his abode in
the house he had bought at Concord before going to Europe, and of which his occupancy had as yet been brief. He
was to occupy it only four years. I have insisted upon the
fact of his being an intense American, and of his looking at
all things, during his residence in Europe, from the standpoint of that little clod of western earth which he carried
about with him as the good Mohammedan carries the strip
of carpet on which he kneels down to face towards Mecca.
But it does not appear, nevertheless, that he found himself
treading with any great exhilaration the larger section of his
native soil upon which, on his return, he disembarked.
Indeed, the closing part of his life was a period of dejection,
the more acute that it followed directly upon seven years of
the happiest opportunities he was to have known. And his
European residence had been brightest at the last; he had
broken almost completely with those habits of extreme seclusion into which he was to relapse on his return to Concord. "You would be stricken dumb," he wrote from London,
shortly before leaving it for the last time, "to see how quietly
I accept a whole string of invitations, and, what is more,
perform my engagements without a murmur. . . . The stir
of this London life, somehow or other," he adds in the same
letter, "has done me a wonderful deal of good, and I feel
better than for months past. This is strange, for if I had my
choice I should leave undone almost all the things I do."
"When he found himself once more on the old ground,"
writes Mr. Lathrop, "with the old struggle for subsistence
staring him in the face again, it is not difficult to conceive
how a certain degree of depression would follow." There is
indeed not a little sadness in the thought of Hawthorne's

literary gift, light, delicate, exquisite, capricious, never too abundant, being charged with the heavy burden of the maintenance of a family. We feel that it was not intended for such grossness, and that in a world ideally constituted he would have enjoyed a liberal pension, an assured subsistence, and have been able to produce his charming prose only when the fancy took him.

The brightness of the outlook at home was not made greater by the explosion of the Civil War in the spring of 1861. These months, and the three years that followed them, were not a cheerful time for any persons but army contractors; but over Hawthorne the war-cloud appears to have dropped a permanent shadow. The whole affair was a bitter disappointment to him, and a fatal blow to that happy faith in the uninterruptedness of American prosperity which I have spoken of as the religion of the old-fashioned American in general, and the old-fashioned Democrat in particular. It was not a propitious time for cultivating the Muse; when history herself is so hard at work, fiction has little left to say. To fiction, directly, Hawthorne did not address himself; he composed first, chiefly during the year 1862, the chapters of which *Our Old Home* was afterwards made up. I have said that, though this work has less value than his purely imaginative things, the writing is singularly good, and it is well to remember, to its greater honor, that it was produced at a time when it was painfully hard for a man of Hawthorne's cast of mind to fix his attention. The air was full of battle-smoke, and the poet's vision was not easily clear. Hawthorne was irritated, too, by the sense of being to a certain extent, politically considered, in a false position. A large section of the Democratic party was not in good odor at the North; its loyalty was not perceived to be of that clear strain which public opinion required. To this wing of the party Franklin Pierce had, with reason or without, the credit of belonging; and our author was conscious of some sharpness of responsibility in defending the illustrious friend of whom he had already made himself the advocate. He defended him manfully, without a grain of concession, and described the ex-president to the public (and to himself), if not as he was, then as he ought to be. *Our Old Home* is dedicated to him, and about this dedication there was some little difficulty. It was represented to Hawthorne that as General Pierce was rather out of fashion, it might injure the success, and, in plain terms, the sale of his book. His answer (to his publisher) was much to the point.

I find that it would be a piece of poltroonery in me to withdraw either the dedication or the dedicatory letter. My long and intimate personal relations with Pierce render the dedication altogether proper, especially as regards this book, which would have had no existence without his kindness; and if he is so exceedingly unpopular that his name ought to sink the volume, there is so much the more need that an old friend should stand by him. I cannot, merely on account of pecuniary profit or literary reputation, go back from what I have deliberately felt and thought it right to do; and if I were to tear out the dedication I should never look at the volume again without remorse and shame. As for the literary public, it must accept my book precisely as I think fit to give it, or let it alone. Nevertheless, I have no fancy for making myself a martyr when it is honorably and conscientiously possible to avoid it; and I always measure out heroism very accurately according to the exigencies of the occasion, and should be the last man in the world to throw away a bit of it needlessly. So I have looked over the concluding paragraph and have amended it in such a way that, while doing what I know to be justice to my friend, it contains not a word that ought to be objectionable to any set of readers. If the public of the North see fit to ostracize me for this, I can only say that I would gladly sacrifice a thousand or two dollars, rather than retain the good will of such a herd of dolts and mean-spirited scoundrels.

The dedication was published, the book was eminently successful, and Hawthorne was not ostracized. The paragraph under discussion stands as follow: "Only this let me say that, with the record of your life in my memory, and with a sense of your character in my deeper consciousness, as among the few things that time has left as it found them, I need no assurance that you continue faithful forever to that grand idea of an irrevocable Union which, as you once told me, was the earliest that your brave father taught you.

For other men there may be a choice of paths—for you but one; and it rests among my certainties that no man's loyalty is more steadfast, no man's hopes or apprehensions on behalf of our national existence more deeply heartfelt, or more closely intertwined with his possibilities of personal happiness, than those of Franklin Pierce." I know not how well the ex-president liked these lines, but the public thought them admirable, for they served as a kind of formal profession of faith, on the question of the hour, by a loved and honored writer. That some of his friends thought such a profession needed is apparent from the numerous editorial ejaculations and protests appended to an article describing a visit he had just paid to Washington, which Hawthorne contributed to the *Atlantic Monthly* for July 1862, and which, singularly enough, has not been reprinted. The article has all the usual merit of such sketches on Hawthorne's part—the merit of delicate, sportive feeling, expressed with consummate grace—but the editor of the periodical appears to have thought that he must give the antidote with the poison, and the paper is accompanied with several little notes disclaiming all sympathy with the writer's political heresies. The heresies strike the reader of today as extremely mild, and what excites his emotion, rather, is the questionable taste of the editorial commentary, with which it is strange that Hawthorne should have allowed his article to be encumbered. He had not been an Abolitionist before the War, and that he should not pretend to be one at the eleventh hour was, for instance, surely a piece of consistency that might have been allowed to pass. "I shall not pretend to be an admirer of old John Brown," he says, in a page worth quoting, "any further than sympathy with Whittier's excellent ballad about him may go; nor did I expect ever to shrink so unutterably from any apothegm of a sage whose happy lips have uttered a hundred golden sentences"—the allusion here, I suppose, is to Mr. Emerson—"as from that saying (perhaps falsely attributed to so honored a name) that the death of this blood-stained fanatic has 'made the Gallows as venerable as the Cross!' Nobody was ever more justly hanged. He won his martyrdom fairly, and took it fairly. He himself, I am persuaded (such was his natural integrity), would have acknowledged that Virginia had a right to take the life which he had staked and lost; although it would have been better for her, in the hour that is fast coming, if she could generously have forgotten the criminality of his attempt in its enormous folly. On the other hand, any common-sensible man, looking at the matter unsentimentally, must have felt a certain intellectual satisfaction in seeing him hanged, if it were only in requital of his preposterous miscalculation of possibilities." Now that the heat of that great conflict has passed away, this is a capital expression of the saner estimate, in the United States, of the dauntless and deluded old man who proposed to solve a complex political problem by stirring up a servile insurrection. There is much of the same sound sense, interfused with light, just appreciable irony, in such a passage as the following:

I tried to imagine how very disagreeable the presence of a Southern army would be in a sober town of Massachusetts; and the thought considerably lessened my wonder at the cold and shy regards that are cast upon our troops, the gloom, the sullen demeanor, the declared, or scarcely hidden, sympathy with rebellion, which are so frequent here. It is a strange thing in human life that the greatest errors both of men and women often spring from their sweetest and most generous qualities; and so, undoubtedly, thousands of warm-hearted, generous, and impulsive persons have joined the Rebels, not from any real zeal for the cause, but because, between two conflicting loyalties, they chose that which necessarily lay nearest the heart. There never existed any other Government against which treason was so easy, and could defend itself by such plausible arguments, as against that of the United States. The anomaly of two allegiances (of which that of the State comes nearest home to a man's feelings, and includes the altar and the hearth, while the General Government claims his devotion only to an airy mode of law, and has no symbol but a flag) is exceedingly mischievous in this point of view; for it has converted crowds of honest people into traitors, who seem to themselves not merely innocent but patriotic, and who die for a bad cause with a quiet conscience as if it were the best. In the vast extent of our country—too vast by far to be taken into one small human heart

—we inevitably limit to our own State, or at farthest, to our own little section, that sentiment of physical love for the soil which renders an Englishman, for example, so intensely sensitive to the dignity and well-being of his little island, that one hostile foot, treading anywhere upon it, would make a bruise on each individual breast. If a man loves his own State, therefore, and is content to be ruined with her, let us shoot him, if we can, but allow him an honorable burial in the soil he fights for.

To this paragraph a line of deprecation from the editor is attached; and indeed from the point of view of a vigorous prosecution of the war it was doubtless not particularly pertinent. But it is interesting as an example of the way an imaginative man judges current events—trying to see the other side as well as his own, to feel what his adversary feels, and present his view of the case.

But he had other occupations for his imagination than putting himself into the shoes of unappreciative Southerners. He began at this time two novels, neither of which he lived to finish, but both of which were published, as fragments, after his death. The shorter of these fragments, to which he had given the name of *The Dolliver Romance,* is so very brief that little can be said of it. The author strikes, with all his usual sweetness, the opening notes of a story of New England life, and the few pages which have been given to the world contain a charming picture of an old man and a child.

The other rough sketch—it is hardly more—is in a manner complete; it was unfortunately deemed complete enough to be brought out in a magazine as a serial novel. This was to do it a great wrong, and I do not go too far in saying that poor Hawthorne would probably not have enjoyed the very bright light that has been projected upon this essentially crude piece of work. I am at a loss to know how to speak of *Septimius Felton, or the Elixir of Life;* I have purposely reserved but a small space for doing so, for the part of discretion seems to be to pass it by lightly. I differ therefore widely from the author's biographer and son-in-law in thinking it a work of the greatest weight and value, offering striking analogies with Goethe's *Faust;* and still more widely from a critic whom Mr. Lathrop quotes, who regards a certain portion of it as "one of the very greatest triumphs in all literature." It seems to me almost cruel to pitch in this exalted key one's estimate of the rough first draught of a tale in regard to which the author's premature death operates, virtually, as a complete renunciation of pretensions. It is plain to any reader that *Septimius Felton,* as it stands, with its roughness, its gaps, its mere allusiveness and slightness of treatment, gives us but a very partial measure of Hawthorne's full intention; and it is equally easy to believe that this intention was much finer than anything we find in the book. Even if we possessed the novel in its complete form, however, I incline to think that we should regard it as very much the weakest of Hawthorne's productions. The idea itself seems a failure, and the best that might have come of it would have been very much below *The Scarlet Letter* or *The House of the Seven Gables.* The appeal to our interest is not felicitously made, and the fancy of a potion, to assure eternity of existence, being made from the flowers which spring from the grave of a man whom the distiller of the potion has deprived of life, though it might figure with advantage in a short story of the pattern of the *Twice-Told Tales,* appears too slender to carry the weight of a novel. Indeed, this whole matter of elixirs and potions belongs to the fairy-tale period of taste, and the idea of a young man enabling himself to live forever by concocting and imbibing a magic draught has the misfortune of not appealing to our sense of reality or even to our sympathy. The weakness of *Septimius Felton* is that the reader cannot take the hero seriously—a fact of which there can be no better proof than the element of the ridiculous which inevitably mingles itself in the scene in which he entertains his lady-love with a prophetic sketch of his occupations during the successive centuries of his earthly immortality. I suppose the answer to my criticism is that this is allegorical, symbolic, ideal; but we feel that it symbolizes nothing substantial, and that the truth—whatever it may be—that it illustrates, is as moonshiny, to use Hawthorne's own expression, as the allegory itself. Another fault of the story is that a great historical event—the war of the Revolution—is introduced in the first few pages, in order to supply the hero with a pretext for killing the young man from whose grave the flower of immortality is to sprout, and then drops out of the narrative altogether, not even forming a background to the sequel. It seems to me that Hawthorne should either have invented some other occasion for the death of his young officer, or else, having struck the note of the great public agitation which overhung his little group of characters, have been careful to sound it through the rest of his tale. I do wrong, however, to insist upon these things, for I fall thereby into the error of treating the work as if it had been cast into its ultimate form and acknowledged by the author. To avoid this error I shall make no other criticism of details, but content myself with saying that the idea and intention of the book appear, relatively speaking, feeble, and that even had it been finished it would have occupied a very different place in the public esteem from the writer's masterpieces.

The year 1864 brought with it for Hawthorne a sense of weakness and depression from which he had little relief during the four or five months that were left him of life. He had his engagement to produce *The Dolliver Romance,* which had been promised to the subscribers of the *Atlantic Monthly* (it was the first time he had undertaken to publish a work of fiction in monthly parts), but he was unable to write, and his consciousness of an unperformed task weighed upon him, and did little to dissipate his physical inertness. "I have not yet had courage to read the Dolliver proof sheet," he wrote to his publisher in December 1863; "but will set about it soon, though with terrible reluctance, such as I never felt before. I am most grateful to you," he went on, "for protecting me from that visitation of the elephant and his cub. If you happen to see Mr. ——, of L——, a young man who was here last summer, pray tell him anything that your conscience will let you, to induce him to spare me another visit, which I know he intended. I really am not well, and cannot be disturbed by strangers, without more suffering than it is worth-while to endure." A month later he was obliged to ask for a further postponement. "I am not quite up to writing yet, but shall make an effort as soon as I see any hope of success. You ought to be thankful that (like most other brokendown authors) I do not pester you with decrepit pages, and insist upon your accepting them as full of the old spirit and vigor. That trouble perhaps still awaits you, after I shall have reached a further stage of decay. Seriously, my mind has, for the time, lost its temper and its fine edge, and I have an instinct that I had better keep quiet. Perhaps I shall have a new spirit of vigor if I wait quietly for it; perhaps not." The winter passed away, but the "new spirit of vigor" remained absent, and at the end of February he wrote to Mr. Fields that his novel had simply broken down, and that he should never finish it. "I hardly know what to say to the public about this abortive romance, though I know pretty well what the case will be. I shall never finish it. Yet it is not quite pleasant for an author to announce himself, or to be announced, as finally broken down as to his literary faculty. . . . I cannot finish it unless a great change comes over me; and if I make too great an effort to do so, it will be my death; not that I should care much for that, if I could fight the battle through and win it, thus ending a life of much smolder and a scanty fire in a blaze of glory. But I should smother myself in mud of my own making. . . . I am not low-spirited, nor fanciful, nor freakish, but look what seem to me realities in the face, and am ready to take whatever may come. If I could but go to England now, I think that the sea-voyage and the 'old Home' might set me all right."

But he was not to go to England; he started three months later upon a briefer journey, from which he never returned. His health was seriously disordered, and in April, according to a letter from Mrs. Hawthorne, printed by Mr. Fields, he had been "miserably ill." His feebleness was complete; he appears to have had no definite malady, but he was, according to the common phrase, failing. General Pierce proposed to him that they should make a little tour together among the mountains of New Hampshire, and Hawthorne consented, in the hope of getting some profit from the change of air. The northern New England spring is not the most genial season in the world, and this was an indifferent substitute for the resource for which his wife had, on his behalf, expressed a wish—a visit to "some island in the Gulf Stream." He was not to go far; he only reached a little place called Plymouth, one of the stations of approach to the beautiful mountain scenery of New Hampshire, when, on the eighteenth of May, 1864, death overtook him. His companion, General Pierce, going into his room in the early morning, found that he had breathed his last during the night—had passed away, tranquilly, comfortably, without a sign or a sound, in his sleep. This happened at the hotel of the place—a vast white edifice, adjacent to the railway station, and entitled the Pemigiwasset House. He was buried at Concord, and many of the most distinguished men in the country stood by his grave.

He was a beautiful, natural, original genius, and his life had been singularly exempt from worldly preoccupations and vulgar efforts. It had been as pure, as simple, as unsophisticated, as his work. He had lived primarily in his domestic affections, which were of the tenderest kind; and then—without eagerness, without pretension, but with a great deal of quiet devotion—in his charming art. His work will remain; it is too original and exquisite to pass away; among the men of imagination he will always have his niche. No one has had just that vision of life, and no one has had a literary form that more successfully expressed his vision. He was not a moralist, and he was not simply a poet. The moralists are weightier, denser, richer, in a sense; the poets are more purely inconclusive and irresponsible. He combined in a singular degree the spontaneity of the imagination with a haunting care for moral problems. Man's conscience was his theme, but he saw it in the light of a creative fancy which added, out of its own substance, an interest, and, I may almost say, an importance.

This ARTICLE by Henry James on Howells was published in
Harper's Weekly of June 19, 1886, and was never reprinted
by James in any of his volumes of criticism. It is interesting
particularly because it was written precisely at the moment
when James, having gone to live in England, had definitely
abandoned the United States as a subject or background
for his fiction. He had just used up, apparently, the last
remnants of his American material in *Impressions of a
Cousin, A New England Winter,* and *The Bostonians;* and
the third of these—the last long novel (till *The Ivory Tower*
at the end of his life) of which the scene was to be laid
in the United States—had just been coming out serially in
The Century. His next two novels, *The Princess Casamas-
sima* and *The Tragic Muse,* were exclusively concerned with
the English and French; and in the fiction he was later to
write after his unsuccessful experiment with the theater,
he was to depart more and more from that field of simple
realistic observation which he and Howells had worked together. This little appreciation of Howells turns out to have
been a kind of farewell—as if he were handing over to
Howells a department in which he had formerly worked.

The nice young American girl, so "innocent," so "extraordinarily good," with her suitors, her engagements, and her moral dilemmas—Daisy Miller and Isabel Archer—is being committed to the protection of his friend, who is comfortably established at home and whom he perfectly trusts to take care of her.

Howells and James remained friends all their lives. They had both—though Howells was seven years the older—made their debuts in the sixties, and Howells as editor of the *Atlantic Monthly* had published Henry James's first stories. They had been up against the same provincial audience. "Harry James has written another story, which I think admirable," Howells had written Charles Eliot Norton in 1867; "but I do not feel sure of the public any longer, since the *Nation* could not see the merit of *Poor Richard*. . . . I cannot doubt that James has every element of success in fiction. But I suspect that he must in a great degree create his audience. In the meantime I rather despise existing readers." He and James had used to talk about fiction together and read one another their stories when the Howellses had lived in Cambridge, on Sunday evenings "after our simple family supper . . . by the light of our kerosene globe-lamp"; and they had taken long walks through the streets, on one of which Henry James had talked at length about his Albany family as possible subjects for fiction. Howells watched James with solicitude for his interest in American material: "I am glad you like *The American*," he wrote John Hay in 1877. "The fact that Harry James could write likingly of such a fellow-countryman as Newman is the most hopeful thing in his literary history since *Gabrielle de Bergerac*." But he did not resent James's going abroad, and did not blame him for it. "The climate was kinder to him than ours," he wrote after James's death, in connection with the latter's ill-health, "and the life was kinder than his native life and his native land. In fact America was never kind to James. It was rude and harsh, unworthily and stupidly so, as we must more and more own, if we would be true to ourselves. We ought to be ashamed of our part in this; the nearest of his friends in Boston would say they liked him, but they could not bear his fiction; and from the people, conscious of culture, throughout New England, especially the women, he had sometimes outright insult."

James, on his side, is always warm and admiring toward Howells. He will declare to his old friend in a letter of 1890 that *A Hazard of New Fortunes* is "simply prodigious, and I should think it would make you as happy as poor happiness will let us be, to turn off from one year to the other, and from a reservoir in daily domestic use, such a free, full, rich flood. . . . I seem to myself, in comparison, to fill mine with a teaspoon and obtain a trickle." This was written in Henry James's leanest period. He may well in such moments have envied Howells his easy command of his American material. But there was a kind of balance between them. If Howells had now the position of accredited social historian at home, Henry James had something else and must have known it. He probes the shallows of Howells' work when he mentions, in this little eassay, his "small perception of evil." James himself, after 1890, when he had recovered from his theatrical disappointments, went on to create a new kind of fiction in which he tended to disregard that social surface of life where Howells was always safest, and where even the personalities of the characters, always so solidly conceived by James, are seen through the equivocal medium of a rhythmic ruminative prose so much of the substance of emotion and dream that it has some of the qualities of poetry; and, equivocal or not, these later stories have a deeper psychological truth than Howells'.

In America through all this period James's novels were little read. The publication in 1901 of *The Sacred Fount*, which nobody understood, seems to have set off a protest against him: he was ridiculed, parodied, denounced. Howells went on praising his friend; he even defended *The Sacred Fount* and asserted that he understood it. The last literary act of his life, when he was dying in 1920 and had, as his daughter says, "to be kept under drugs to deaden his pain," was to work at an article on James *à propos* of the publication of his letters. This article was called *The American James*, and it went back to the days in Cambridge when he and his friend had walked to Fresh Pond and "from whatever strangeness of his French past we now joined in the American present around the airtight stove which no doubt overheated our little parlor." The paper was "an effort," says Miss Howells, "to say that Howells had always felt that James was deeply and entirely American."

HENRY JAMES

WILLIAM DEAN HOWELLS

As THE EXISTENCE of a man of letters (so far as the public is concerned with it) may be said to begin with his first appearance in literature, that of Mr. Howells, who was born at Martinsville, Ohio, in 1837, and spent his entire youth in his native state, dates properly from the publication of his delightful volume on *Venetian Life*—than which he has produced nothing since of a literary quality more pure—which he put forth in 1865, after his return from the consular post in the city of St. Mark which he had filled for four years. He had, indeed, before going to live in Venice, and during the autumn of 1860, published, in conjunction with his friend Mr. Piatt, a so-called "campaign" biography of Abraham Lincoln; but as this composition, which I have never seen, emanated probably more from a good Republican than from a suitor of the Muse, I mention it simply for the sake of exactitude, adding, however, that I have never heard of the Muse having taken it ill. When a man is a born artist, everything that happens to him confirms his perverse tendency; and it may be considered that the happiest thing that could have been invented on Mr. Howells' behalf was his residence in Venice at the most sensitive and responsive period of life; for

Venice, bewritten and bepainted as she has ever been, does
nothing to you unless to persuade you that you also can
paint, that you also can write. Her only fault is that she sometimes too flatteringly—for she is shameless in the exercise of
such arts—addresses the remark to those who cannot. Mr.
Howells could, fortunately, for his writing was painting as
well in those days. The papers on Venice prove it, equally
with the artistic whimsical chapters of the *Italian Journeys,*
made up in 1867 from his notes and memories (the latter as
tender as most glances shot eastward in working hours across
the Atlantic) of the holidays and excursions which carried
him occasionally away from his consulate.

The mingled freshness and irony of these things gave
them an originality which has not been superseded, to my
knowledge, by any impressions of European life from an
American standpoint. At Venice Mr. Howells married a lady
of artistic accomplishment and association, passed through
the sharp alternations of anxiety and hope to which those
who spent the long years of the civil war in foreign lands
were inevitably condemned, and of which the effect was not
rendered less wearing by the perusal of the London *Times*
and the conversation of the British tourist. The irritation, so
far as it proceeded from the latter source, may even yet be
perceived in Mr. Howells' pages. He wrote poetry at Venice,
as he had done of old in Ohio, and his poems were subsequently collected into two thin volumes, the fruit, evidently,
of a rigorous selection. They have left more traces in the
mind of many persons who read and enjoyed them than they
appear to have done in the author's own. It is not nowadays
as a cultivator of rhythmic periods that Mr. Howells most
willingly presents himself. Everything in the evolution, as
we must all learn to call it today, of a talent of this order
is interesting, but one of the things that are most so is the
separation that has taken place, in Mr. Howells' case, between its early and its later manner. There is nothing in
Silas Lapham, or in *Doctor Breen's Practice,* or in *A Modern
Instance,* or in *The Undiscovered Country,* to suggest that
its author had at one time either wooed the lyric Muse or
surrendered himself to those Italian initiations without which

we of other countries remain always, after all, more or less barbarians. It is often a good, as it is sometimes an evil, that one cannot disestablish one's past, and Mr. Howells cannot help having rhymed and romanced in deluded hours, nor would he, no doubt, if he could. The repudiation of the weakness which leads to such aberrations is more apparent than real, and the spirit which made him care a little for the poor factitious Old World and the superstition of "form" is only latent in pages which express a marked preference for the novelties of civilization and a perceptible mistrust of the purist. I hasten to add that Mr. Howells has had moments of reappreciation of Italy in later years, and has even taken the trouble to write a book (the magnificent volume on *Tuscan Cities*) to show it. Moreover, the exquisite tale *A Foregone Conclusion*, and many touches in the recent novel of *Indian Summer* (both this and the *Cities* the fruit of a second visit to Italy), sound the note of a charming inconsistency.

On his return from Venice he settled in the vicinity of Boston, and began to edit the *Atlantic Monthly*, accommodating himself to this grave complication with infinite tact and industry. He conferred further distinction upon the magazine; he wrote the fine series of *Suburban Sketches,* one of the least known of his productions, but one of the most perfect, and on Sunday afternoons he took a suburban walk —perfect also, no doubt, in its way. I know not exactly how long this phase of his career lasted, but I imagine that if he were asked, he would reply, "Oh, a hundred years." He was meant for better things than this—things better, I mean, than superintending the private life of even the most eminent periodical—but I am not sure that I would speak of this experience as a series of wasted years. They were years rather of economized talent, of observation and accumulation. They laid the foundation of what is most remarkable, or most, at least, the peculiar sign, in his effort as a novelist—his unerring sentiment of the American character. Mr. Howells knows more about it than anyone, and it was during this period of what we may suppose to have been rather perfunctory administration that he must have gathered many

of his impressions of it. An editor is in the nature of the
case much exposed, so exposed as not to be protected even
by the seclusion (the security to a superficial eye so complete) of a Boston suburb. His manner of contact with the
world is almost violent, and whatever bruises he may confer,
those he receives are the most telling, inasmuch as the former
are distributed among many, and the latter all to be endured
by one. Mr. Howells' accessibilities and sufferings were
destined to fructify. Other persons have considered and dis-
coursed upon American life, but no one, surely, has *felt* it
so completely as he. I will not say that Mr. Howells feels it
all equally, for are we not perpetually conscious how vast
and deep it is?—but he is an authority upon many of those
parts of it which are most representative.

He was still under the shadow of his editorship when, in
the intervals of his letter writing and reviewing, he made
his first cautious attempts in the walk of fiction. I say
cautious, for in looking back nothing is more clear than
that he had determined to advance only step by step. In his
first story, *Their Wedding Journey,* there are only two persons, and in his next, *A Chance Acquaintance,* which contains one of his very happiest studies of a girl's character,
the number is not lavishly increased.

In *A Foregone Conclusion,* where the girl again is admirable, as well as the young Italian priest, also a kind of
maidenly figure, the actors are but four. Today Mr. Howells
doesn't count, and confers life with a generous and unerring
hand. If the profusion of forms in which it presents itself to
him is remarkable, this is perhaps partly because he had
the good fortune of not approaching the novel until he had
lived considerably, until his inclination for it had ripened.
His attitude was as little as possible that of the gifted young
person who, at twenty, puts forth a work of imagination of
which the merit is mainly in its establishing the presumption
that the next one will be better. It is my impression that long
after he was twenty he still cultivated the belief that the
faculty of the novelist was not in him, and was even capable
of producing certain unfinished chapters (in the candor
of his good faith he would sometimes communicate them to

a listener) in triumphant support of this contention. He believed, in particular, that he could not make people talk, and such have been the revenges of time that a cynical critic might almost say of him today that he cannot make them keep silent. It was life itself that finally dissipated his doubts, life that reasoned with him and persuaded him. The feeling of life is strong in all his tales, and any one of them has this rare (always rarer) and indispensable sign of a happy origin, that it is an impression at firsthand. Mr. Howells is literary, on certain sides exquisitely so, though with a singular and not unamiable perversity he sometimes endeavors not to be; but his vision of the human scene is never a literary reminiscence, a reflection of books and pictures, of tradition and fashion and hearsay. I know of no English novelist of our hour whose work is so exclusively a matter of painting what he sees, and who is so sure of what he sees. People are always wanting a writer of Mr. Howells' temperament to see certain things that he doesn't (that he doesn't sometimes even want to), but I must content myself with congratulating the author of *A Modern Instance* and *Silas Lapham* on the admirable quality of his vision. The American life which he for the most part depicts is certainly neither very rich nor very fair, but it is tremendously positive, and as his manner of presenting it is as little as possible conventional, the reader can have no doubt about it. This is an immense luxury; the ingenuous character of the witness (I can give it no higher praise) deepens the value of the report.

Mr. Howells has gone from one success to another, has taken possession of the field, and has become copious without detriment to his freshness. I need not enumerate his works in their order, for, both in America and in England (where it is a marked feature of the growing curiosity felt about American life that they are constantly referred to for information and verification), they have long been in everybody's hands. Quietly and steadily they have become better and better; one may like some of them more than others, but it is noticeable that from effort to effort the author has constantly enlarged his scope. His work is of a kind of which it is good that there should be much today—work of observation, of patient and definite notation. Neither in theory nor in practice is Mr. Howells a romancer; but the romancers can spare him; there will always be plenty of people to do their work. He has definite and downright convictions on the subject of the work that calls out to be done in opposition to theirs, and this fact is a source of much of the interest that he excites.

It is a singular circumstance that to know what one wishes to do should be, in the field of art, a rare distinction; but it is incontestable that, as one looks about in our English and American fiction, one does not perceive any very striking examples of a vivifying faith. There is no discussion of the great question of how best to write, no exchange of ideas, no vivacity nor variety of experiment. A vivifying faith Mr. Howells may distinctly be said to possess, and he conceals it so little as to afford every facility to those people who are anxious to prove that it is the wrong one. He is animated by a love of the common, the immediate, the familiar and vulgar elements of life, and holds that in proportion as we move into the rare and strange we become vague and arbitrary; that truth of representation, in a word, can be achieved only so long as it is in our power to test and measure it. He thinks scarcely anything too paltry to be interesting, that the small and the vulgar have been terribly neglected, and would rather see an exact account of a sentiment or a character he stumbles against every day than a brilliant evocation of a passion or a type he has never seen and does not even particularly believe in. He adores the real, the natural, the colloquial, the moderate, the optimistic, the domestic, and the democratic; looking askance at exceptions and perversities and superiorities, at surprising and incongruous phenomena in general. One must have seen a great deal before one concludes; the world is very large, and life is a mixture of many things; she by no means eschews the strange, and often risks combinations and effects that make one rub one's eyes. Nevertheless, Mr. Howells' standpoint is an excellent one for seeing a large part of the truth, and even if it were less advantageous, there would be a great deal to admire in the firmness with which he has planted himself. He hates a "story," and (this private feat is not impossible) has probably made up his mind very definitely as to what the pestilent thing consists of. In this respect he is more logical than M. Émile Zola, who partakes of the same aversion, but has greater lapses as well as greater audacities. Mr. Howells hates an artificial fable and a *dénouement* that is pressed into the service; he likes things to occur as they occur in life, where the manner of a great many of them is not to occur at all. He has observed that heroic emotion and brilliant opportunity are not particularly interwoven with our days, and indeed, in the way of omission, he *has* often practiced in his pages a very considerable boldness. It has not, however, made what we find there any less interesting and less human.

The picture of American life on Mr. Howells' canvas is not of a dazzling brightness, and many readers have probably wondered why it is that (among a sensitive people) he has so successfully escaped the imputation of a want of patriotism. The manners he describes—the desolation of the whole social prospect in *A Modern Instance* is perhaps the strongest expression of those influences—are eminently of a nature to discourage the intending visitor, and yet the westward pilgrim continues to arrive, in spite of the Bartley Hubbards and the Laphams, and the terrible practices at the country hotel in *Doctor Breen,* and at the Boston boardinghouse in *A Woman's Reason.* This tolerance of depressing revelations is explained partly, no doubt, by the fact that Mr. Howells' truthfulness imposes itself—the representation is so vivid that the reader accepts it as he accepts, in his own affairs, the mystery of fate—and partly by a very different consideration, which is simply that if many of his characters are disagreeable, almost all of them are extraordinarily good, and with a goodness which is a ground for national complacency. If American life is on the whole, as I make no doubt whatever, more innocent than that of any other country, nowhere is the fact more patent than in Mr. Howells' novels, which exhibit so constant a study of the actual and so small a perception of evil. His women, in particular, are of the best—except, indeed, in the sense of being the best to live with. Purity of life, fineness of conscience, benevolence of motive, decency of speech, good nature, kindness, charity, tolerance (though, indeed, there is little but each other's manners for the people to tolerate), govern all the scene; the only immoralities are aberrations of thought, like that of Silas Lapham, or excesses of beer, like that of Bartley Hubbard. In the gallery of Mr. Howells' portraits there are none more living than the admirable, humorous images of those two ineffectual sinners. Lapham, in particular, is magnificent, understood down to the ground, inside and out— a creation which does Mr. Howells the highest honor. I do not say that the figure of his wife is as good as his own, only because I wish to say that it is as good as that of the minister's wife in the history of *Lemuel Barker,* which is unfolding itself from month to month at the moment I write. These two ladies are exhaustive renderings of the type of virtue that worries. But everything in *Silas Lapham* is superior—nothing more so than the whole picture of casual female youth and contemporaneous "engaging" one's self, in the daughters of the proprietor of the mineral paint.

This production had struck me as the author's high-water mark, until I opened the monthly sheets of *Lemuel Barker,* in which the art of imparting a palpitating interest to common things and unheroic lives is pursued (or is destined, apparently, to be pursued) to an even higher point. The four (or is it eight?) repeated "good mornings" between the liberated Lemuel and the shop-girl who has crudely been the cause of his being locked up by the police all night are a poem, an idyl, a trait of genius, and a compendium of American good nature. The whole episode is inimitable, and I know fellow-novelists of Mr. Howells' who would have given their eyes to produce that interchange of salutations, which only an American reader, I think, can understand.[1] Indeed, the only limitation, in general, to his extreme truthfulness is, I will not say his constant sense of the

[1]The title of this novel was *The Minister's Charge; or the Apprenticeship of Lemuel Barker.* Lemuel Barker is a country boy, who has just come to Boston and gets arrested by mistake as a purse-

comedy of life, for that is irresistible, but the verbal drollery
of many of his people. It is extreme and perpetual, but I fear
the reader will find it a venial sin. Theodore Colville, in
Indian Summer, is so irrepressibly and happily facetious as
to make one wonder whether the author is not prompting
him a little, and whether he could be quite so amusing without help from outside. This criticism, however, is the only
one I find it urgent to make, and Mr. Howells doubtless
will not suffer from my saying that, being a humorist himself,
he is strong in the representation of humorists. There are
other reflections that I might indulge in if I had more space.
I should like, for instance, to allude in passing, for purposes
of respectful remonstrance, to a phrase that he suffered the
other day to fall from his pen (in a periodical, but not in a
novel), to the effect that the style of a work of fiction is a
thing that matters less and less all the while. Why less and
less? It seems to me as great a mistake to say so as it would
be to say that it matters more and more. It is difficult to see
how it can matter either less or more. The style of a novel
is a part of the execution of a work of art; the execution

snatcher. He spends a night in jail, but the case against him is dismissed the next morning. The girl who has brought the charge is
embarrassed at having got him into trouble. The dialogue that James
speaks of follows. It is interesting to learn that it was the kind of
thing that Henry James felt he could not do. E. W.

"She ha'n't got any call to feel bad about it," said Lemuel
clumsily. "It was just a mistake." Then, not knowing what more
to say, he said, being come to the outer door by this time, "Well, I
wish you good morning."

"Well, good morning," said 'Manda Grier, and she thrust her
elbow sharply into Statira Dudley's side, so that she also said faintly—

"Well, good morning!" She was fluent enough on the witness
stand and in the police station, but now she could not find a word
to say.

The three stood together on the threshold of the courthouse, not
knowing how to get away from one another.

'Manda Grier put out her hand to Lemuel. He took it, and,
"Well, good morning," he said again.

"Well, good morning," repeated 'Manda Grier.

Then Statira put out her hand, and she and Lemuel shook hands,
and said together, "Well, good morning," and on these terms of high
civility they parted. . . .

of a work of art is a part of its very essence, and that, it seems to me, must have mattered in all ages in exactly the same degree, and be destined always to do so. I can conceive of no state of civilization in which it shall not be deemed important, though of course there are states in which executants are clumsy. I should also venture to express a certain regret that Mr. Howells (whose style, in practice, after all, as I have intimated, treats itself to felicities which his theory perhaps would condemn) should appear increasingly to hold composition too cheap—by which I mean, should neglect the effect that comes from alternation, distribution, relief. He has an increasing tendency to tell his story altogether in conversations, so that a critical reader sometimes wishes, not that the dialogue might be suppressed (it is too good for that), but that it might be distributed, interspaced with narrative and pictorial matter. The author forgets sometimes to paint, to evoke the conditions and appearances, to build in the subject. He is doubtless afraid of doing these things in excess, having seen in other hands what disastrous effects that error may have; but all the same I cannot help thinking that the divinest thing in a valid novel is the compendious, descriptive, pictorial touch, *à la Daudet*.

It would be absurd to speak of Mr. Howells today in the encouraging tone that one would apply to a young writer who had given fine pledges, and one feels half guilty of that mistake if one makes a cheerful remark about his future. And yet we cannot pretend not to take a still more lively interest in his future than we have done in his past. It is hard to see how it can help being more and more fruitful, for his face is turned in the right direction, and his work is fed from sources which play us no tricks.

THIS LITTLE ESSAY by Mark Twain on Cooper, one of his rare pieces of writing on literary subjects, first appeared in the *North American Review* of July 1895. It has a certain importance as a landmark. What Mark Twain particularly disliked in Cooper was the wooliness of his style—an example of a kind of bad writing, pretentious, verbose, and slovenly, which has especially flourished in this country. Mark Twain himself had perfected a linear and limpid prose, which made use of the simplest words and a syntax consisting mainly of a series of simple declarative statements. This style had come primarily out of the vocabulary and rhythm of Mark Twain's own Western speech. He was substituting for the bad bookish styles of America a good colloquial one; and, though it was at first thought too homely for serious writing, it had eventually a distinguished development. We will meet it again in Sherwood Anderson, and Hemingway was to make it into an instrument of emotions and implications quite out of the range of Mark Twain. We see it today in its decadence in the hands of Hemingway's imitators.

It may be interesting to quote here an opinion on Cooper

from *The Responsibilities of a Novelist,* by Frank Norris, published in 1903. Frank Norris, a follower of Zola, was one of several Americans who were working at the beginning of the century against the taboos of the Howells era for a presentation in fiction of the hard and crude realities of American life. The passage occurs in an essay called *An American School of Fiction?*

"Cooper, you will say, was certainly American in attitude and choice of subject; none more so. None less so, none less American. As a novelist he is saturated with the romance of the contemporary English story-tellers. It is true that his background is American. But his heroes and heroines talk like the characters out of Bulwer in their most vehement moods, while his Indians stalk through all the melodramatic tableaux of Byron, and declaim in the periods of the border nobleman in the pages of Walter Scott."

Both Mark Twain and Norris, however, rather miss the point about Cooper. *The Leatherstocking Tales* have nothing to do with either Mark Twain's or Norris' kind of realism. D. H. Lawrence, in an essay which will be found further on, understands Cooper better. *The Deerslayer* is not a picture of actual life, but a kind of romantic myth like the stories of Poe, Melville, and Hawthorne. And though Cooper wrote clumsily, though he exasperates us by his faulty sense of movement and proportion—his conversations that go on for pages and seem to end exactly where they began—there is always a poet present who redeems the abominable craftsman. The description, at the beginning of *The Deerslayer,* for example, of Glimmerglass Lake, "as limpid as pure air," and of the solitary "castle" in the middle of it owes its power, like Melville's description of the Pacific or one of Poe's pieces on landscape-gardening, to an emotional content which has charged the object and transformed it into a symbol. And the action does have a reality which we recognize and accept as we read: the reality of a dream full of danger.

MARK TWAIN

FENIMORE COOPER'S LITERARY OFFENSES

> *The Pathfinder* and *The Deerslayer* stand at the head of
> Cooper's novels as artistic creations. There are others of his
> works which contain parts as perfect as are to be found in these,
> and scenes even more thrilling. Not one can be compared with
> either of them as a finished whole.
> The defects in both of these tales are comparatively slight.
> They were pure works of art.—Prof. Lounsbury.

> The five tales reveal an extraordinary fullness of invention.
> . . . One of the very greatest characters in fiction, Natty
> Bumppo. . . .
> The craft of the woodsman, the tricks of the trapper, all the
> delicate art of the forest, were familiar to Cooper from his youth
> up.—Prof. Brander Matthews.

> Cooper is the greatest artist in the domain of romantic fiction
> yet produced by America.—Wilkie Collins.

It seems to me that it was far from right for the Professor
of English Literature in Yale, the Professor of English Literature in Columbia, and Wilkie Collins to deliver opinions
on Cooper's literature without having read some of it. It
would have been much more decorous to keep silent and
let persons talk who have read Cooper.

Cooper's art has some defects. In one place in *Deerslayer,* and in the restricted space of two thirds of a page, Cooper has scored 114 offenses against literary art out of a possible 115. It breaks the record.

There are nineteen rules governing literary art in the domain of romantic fiction—some say twenty-two. In *Deerslayer* Cooper violated eighteen of them. These eighteen require:

1. That a tale shall accomplish something and arrive somewhere. But the *Deerslayer* tale accomplishes nothing and arrives in air.

2. They require that the episodes of a tale shall be necessary parts of the tale, and shall help to develop it. But as the *Deerslayer* tale is not a tale, and accomplishes nothing and arrives nowhere, the episodes have no rightful place in the work, since there was nothing for them to develop.

3. They require that the personages in a tale shall be alive, except in the case of corpses, and that always the reader shall be able to tell the corpses from the others. But this detail has often been overlooked in the *Deerslayer* tale.

4. They require that the personages in a tale, both dead and alive, shall exhibit a sufficient excuse for being there. But this detail has also been overlooked in the *Deerslayer* tale.

5. They require that when the personages of a tale deal in conversation, the talk shall sound like human talk, and be talk such as human beings would be likely to talk in the given circumstances, and have a discoverable meaning, also a discoverable purpose, and a show of relevancy, and remain in the neighborhood of the subject in hand, and be interesting to the reader, and help out the tale, and stop when the people cannot think of anything more to say. But this requirement has been ignored from the beginning of the *Deerslayer* to the end of it.

6. They require that when the author describes the character of a personage in his tale, the conduct and conversation of that personage shall justify said description. But this law gets little or no attention in the *Deerslayer* tale, as Natty Bumppo's case will amply prove.

7. They require that when a personage talks like an illustrated, gilt-edged, tree-calf, hand-tooled, seven-dollar Friendship's Offering in the beginning of a paragraph, he shall not talk like a negro minstrel in the end of it. But this rule is flung down and danced upon in the *Deerslayer* tale.

8. They require that crass stupidities shall not be played upon the reader as "the craft of the woodsman, the delicate art of the forest," by either the author or the people in the tale. But this rule is persistently violated in the *Deerslayer* tale.

9. They require that the personages of a tale shall confine themselves to possibilities and let miracles alone; or, if they venture a miracle, the author must so plausibly set it forth as to make it look possible and reasonable. But these rules are not respected in the *Deerslayer* tale.

10. They require that the author shall make the reader feel a deep interest in the personages of his tale and in their fate; and that he shall make the reader love the good people in the tale and hate the bad ones. But the reader of the *Deerslayer* tale dislikes the good people in it, is indifferent to the others, and wishes they would all get drowned together.

11. They require that the characters in a tale shall be so clearly defined that the reader can tell beforehand what each will do in a given emergency. But in the *Deerslayer* tale this rule is vacated.

In addition to these large rules there are some little ones. These require that the author shall

12. *Say* what he is proposing to say, not merely come near it.
13. Use the right word, not its second cousin.
14. Eschew surplusage.
15. Not omit necessary details.
16. Avoid slovenliness of form.
17. Use good grammar.
18. Employ a simple and straightforward style.

Even these seven are coldly and persistently violated in the *Deerslayer* tale.

Cooper's gift in the way of invention was not a rich endowment; but such as it was he liked to work it, he was pleased with the effects, and indeed he did some quite sweet things with it. In his little box of stage properties he kept six or eight cunning devices, tricks, artifices for his savages and woodsmen to deceive and circumvent each other with, and he was never so happy as when he was working these innocent things and seeing them go. A favorite one was to make a moccasined person tread in the tracks of the moc-

casined enemy, and thus hide his own trail. Cooper wore
out barrels and barrels of moccasins in working that trick.
Another stage property that he pulled out of his box pretty
frequently was his broken twig. He prized his broken twig
above all the rest of his effects, and worked it the hardest.
It is a restful chapter in any book of his when somebody
doesn't step on a dry twig and alarm all the reds and whites
for two hundred yards around. Every time a Cooper person
is in peril, and absolute silence is worth four dollars a
minute, he is sure to step on a dry twig. There may be a
hundred handier things to step on, but that wouldn't satisfy
Cooper. Cooper requires him to turn out and find a dry
twig; and if he can't do it, go and borrow one. In fact, the
Leatherstocking Series ought to have been called the Broken
Twig Series.

I am sorry there is not room to put in a few dozen instances
of the delicate art of the forest, as practiced by Natty
Bumppo and some of the other Cooperian experts. Perhaps
we may venture two or three samples. Cooper was a sailor—
a naval officer; yet he gravely tells us how a vessel, driving
towards a lee shore in a gale, is steered for a particular spot
by her skipper because he knows of an *undertow* there which
will hold her back against the gale and save her. For just
pure woodcraft, or sailorcraft, or whatever it is, isn't that
neat? For several years Cooper was daily in the society of
artillery, and he ought to have noticed that when a cannon-
ball strikes the ground it either buries itself or skips a
hundred feet or so; skips again a hundred feet or so—and
so on, till finally it gets tired and rolls. Now in one place
he loses some "females"—as he always calls women—in the
edge of a wood near a plain at night in a fog, on purpose
to give Bumppo a chance to show off the delicate art of the
forest before the reader. These mislaid people are hunting
for a fort. They hear a cannon-blast, and a cannon-ball
presently comes rolling into the wood and stops at their
feet. To the females this suggests nothing. The case is very
different with the admirable Bumppo. I wish I may never
know peace again if he doesn't strike out promptly and *follow the track* of that cannon-ball across the plain through

the dense fog and find the fort. Isn't it a daisy? If Cooper had any real knowledge of Nature's ways of doing things, he had a most delicate art in concealing the fact. For instance: one of his acute Indian experts, Chingachgook (pronounced Chicago, I think) has lost the trail of a person he is tracking through the forest. Apparently that trail is hopelessly lost. Neither you nor I could ever have guessed out the way to find it. It was very different with Chicago. Chicago was not stumped for long. He turned a running stream out of its course, and there, in the slush in its old bed, were that person's moccasin-tracks. The current did not wash them away, as it would have done in all other like cases—no, even the eternal laws of Nature have to vacate when Cooper wants to put up a delicate job of woodcraft on the reader.

We must be a little wary when Brander Matthews tells us that Cooper's books "reveal an extraordinary fulness of invention." As a rule, I am quite willing to accept Brander Matthews' literary judgments and applaud his lucid and graceful phrasing of them; but that particular statement needs to be taken with a few tons of salt. Bless your heart, Cooper hadn't any more invention than a horse; and I don't mean a high-class horse, either; I mean a clothes-horse. It would be very difficult to find a really clever "situation" in Cooper's books, and still more difficult to find one of any kind which he has failed to render absurd by his handling of it. Look at the episodes of "the caves"; and at the celebrated scuffle between Maqua and those others on the table-land a few days later; and at Hurry Harry's queer water transit from the castle to the ark; and at Deerslayer's half-hour with his first corpse, and at the quarrel between Hurry Harry and Deerslayer later; and at—— But choose for yourself; you can't go amiss.

If Cooper had been an observer his inventive faculty would have worked better; not more interestingly, but more rationally, more plausibly. Cooper's proudest creations in the way of "situations" suffer noticeably from the absence of the observer's protecting gift. Cooper's eye was splendidly inaccurate. Cooper seldom saw anything correctly. He saw nearly all things as through a glass eye, darkly. Of course a man who cannot see the commonest little every-day matters accurately is working at a disadvantage when he is constructing a "situation." In the *Deerslayer* tale Cooper has a stream which is fifty feet wide where it flows out of a lake; it presently narrows to twenty as it meanders along for no given reason, and yet when a stream acts like that it ought to be required to explain itself. Fourteen pages later the width of the brook's outlet from the lake has suddenly shrunk thirty feet, and become "the narrowest part of the stream." This shrinkage is not accounted for. The stream has bends in it, a sure indication that it has alluvial banks and cuts them; yet these bends are only thirty and fifty feet long. If Cooper had been a nice and punctilious observer he would have noticed that the bends were oftener nine hundred feet long than short of it.

Cooper made the exit of that stream fifty feet wide, in the first place, for no particular reason; in the second place, he narrowed it to less than twenty to accommodate some Indians. He bends a "sapling" to the form of an arch over this narrow passage, and conceals six Indians in its foliage. They are "laying" for a settler's scow or ark which is coming up the stream on its way to the lake; it is being hauled against the stiff current by a rope whose stationary end is anchored in the lake; its rate of progress cannot be more than a mile an hour. Cooper describes the ark, but pretty obscurely. In the matter of dimensions "it was little more than a modern canal boat." Let us guess, then, that it was about one hundred and forty feet long. It was of "greater breadth than common." Let us guess, then, that it was about sixteen feet wide. This leviathan had been prowling down bends which were but a third as long as itself, and scraping between banks where it had only two feet of space to spare on each side. We cannot too much admire this miracle. A low-roofed log dwelling occupies "two-thirds of the ark's length"—a dwelling ninety feet long and sixteen feet wide, let us say—a kind of vestibule train. The dwelling has two rooms—each forty-five feet long and sixteen feet wide, let us guess. One of them is the bedroom of the Hutter girls,

Judith and Hetty; the other is the parlor in the daytime, at night it is papa's bedchamber. The ark is arriving at the stream's exit now, whose width has been reduced to less than twenty feet to accommodate the Indians—say to eighteen. There is a foot to spare on each side of the boat. Did the Indians notice that there was going to be a tight squeeze there? Did they notice that they could make money by climbing down out of that arched sapling and just stepping aboard when the ark scraped by? No, other Indians would have noticed these things, but Cooper's Indians never notice anything. Cooper thinks they are marvelous creatures for noticing, but he was almost always in error about his Indians. There was seldom a sane one among them.

The ark is one hundred and forty feet long; the dwelling is ninety feet long. The idea of the Indians is to drop softly and secretly from the arched sapling to the dwelling as the ark creeps along under it at the rate of a mile an hour, and butcher the family. It will take the ark a minute and a half to pass under. It will take the ninety-foot dwelling a minute to pass under. Now, then, what did the six Indians do? It would take you thirty years to guess, and even then you would have to give it up, I believe. Therefore, I will tell you what the Indians did. Their chief, a person of quite extraordinary intellect for a Cooper Indian, warily watched the canal-boat as it squeezed along under him, and when he had got his calculations fined down to exactly the right shade, as he judged, he let go and dropped. And *missed the house!* That is actually what he did. He missed the house, and landed in the stern of the scow. It was not much of a fall, yet it knocked him silly. He lay there unconscious. If the house had been ninety-seven feet long he would have made the trip. The fault was Cooper's, not his. The error lay in the construction of the house. Cooper was no architect.

There still remained in the roost five Indians. The boat has passed under and is now out of their reach. Let me explain what the five did—you would not be able to reason it out for yourself. No. 1 jumped for the boat, but fell in the water astern of it. Then No. 2 jumped for the boat, but fell in the water still farther astern of it. Then No. 3 jumped for the boat, and fell a good way astern of it. Then No. 4 jumped for the boat, and fell in the water *away* astern. Then even No. 5 made a jump for the boat—for he was a Cooper Indian. In the matter of intellect, the difference between a Cooper Indian and the Indian that stands in front of the cigar-shop is not spacious. The scow episode is really a sublime burst of invention; but it does not thrill, because the inaccuracy of the details throws a sort of air of fictitiousness and general improbability over it. This comes of Cooper's inadequacy as an observer.

The reader will find some examples of Cooper's high talent for inaccurate observation in the account of the shooting-match in *The Pathfinder*.

"A common wrought nail was driven lightly into the target, its head having been first touched with paint."

The color of the paint is not stated—an important omission, but Cooper deals freely in important omissions. No, after all, it was not an important omission; for this nail-head is *a hundred yards from* the marksmen, and could not be seen by them at that distance, no matter what its color might be. How far can the best eyes see a common house-fly? A hundred yards? It is quite impossible. Very well; eyes that cannot see a house-fly that is a hundred yards away cannot see an ordinary nail-head at that distance, for the size of the two objects is the same. It takes a keen eye to see a fly or a nailhead at fifty yards—one hundred and fifty feet. Can the reader do it?

The nail was lightly driven, its head painted, and game called. Then the Cooper miracles began. The bullet of the first marksman chipped an edge of the nail-head; the next man's bullet drove the nail a little way into the target—and removed all the paint. Haven't the miracles gone far enough now? Not to suit Cooper; for the purpose of this whole scheme is to show off his prodigy, Deerslayer-Hawk-eye-Long-Rifle-Leather-Stocking-Pathfinder-Bumppo before the ladies.

"'Be all ready to clench it, boys!' cried out Pathfinder, stepping into his friend's tracks the instant they were vacant. 'Never mind a new nail; I can see that, though the paint is gone, and what I can see I can hit at a hundred yards, though it were only a mosquito's eye. Be ready to clench!'

"The rifle cracked, the bullet sped its way, and the head of the nail was buried in the wood, covered by the pieces of flattened lead."

There, you see, is a man who could hunt flies with a rifle, and command a ducal salary in a Wild West show today if we had him back with us.

The recorded feat is certainly surprising just as it stands; but it is not surprising enough for Cooper. Cooper adds a touch. He has made Pathfinder do this miracle with another man's rifle; and not only that, but Pathfinder did not even have the advantage of loading it himself. He had everything against him, and yet he made the impossible shot; and not only made it, but did it with absolute confidence, saying, "Be ready to clench." Now a person like that would have undertaken that same feat with a brickbat, and with Cooper to help he would have achieved it, too.

Pathfinder showed off handsomely that day before the ladies. His very first feat was a thing which no Wild West show can touch. He was standing with the group of marksmen, observing—a hundred yards from the target, mind; one Jasper raised his rifle and drove the center of the bull's-eye. Then the Quartermaster fired. The target exhibited no result this time. There was a laugh. "It's a dead miss," said Major Lundie. Pathfinder waited an impressive moment or two; then said, in that calm, indifferent, know-it-all way of his, "No, Major, he has covered Jasper's bullet, as will be seen if anyone will take the trouble to examine the target."

Wasn't it remarkable! How *could* he see that little pellet fly through the air and enter that distant bullet-hole? Yet that is what he did; for nothing is impossible to a Cooper person. Did any of those people have any deep-seated doubts about this thing? No; for that would imply sanity, and these were all Cooper people.

"The respect for Pathfinder's skill and for his *quickness and accuracy of sight* [the italics are mine] was so profound and general, that the instant he made this declaration the spectators began to distrust their own opinions, and a dozen rushed to the target in order to ascertain the fact. There, sure enough, it was found that the Quartermaster's bullet had gone through the hole made by Jasper's, and that, too, so accurately as to require a minute examination to be certain of the circumstance, which, however, was soon clearly established by discovering one bullet over the other in the stump against which the target was placed."

They made a "minute" examination; but never mind, how could they know that there were two bullets in that hole without digging the latest one out? For neither probe nor eyesight could prove the presence of any more than one bullet. Did they dig? No; as we shall see. It is the Pathfinder's turn now; he steps out before the ladies, takes aim, and fires.

But, alas! here is a disappointment; an incredible, an unimaginable disappointment—for the target's aspect is unchanged; there is nothing there but that same old bullet hole!

"'If one dared to hint at such a thing,' cried Major Duncan, 'I should say that the Pathfinder has also missed the target!'"

As nobody had missed it yet, the "also" was not necessary; but never mind about that, for the Pathfinder is going to speak.

"'No, no, Major,' said he, confidently, 'that *would* be a risky declaration. I didn't load the piece, and can't say what was in it; but if it was lead, you will find the bullet driving down those of the Quartermaster and Jasper, else is not my name Pathfinder.'"

"A shout from the target announced the truth of this assertion."

Is the miracle sufficient as it stands? Not for Cooper. The Pathfinder speaks again, as he "now slowly advances towards the stage occupied by the females":

"'That's not all, boys, that's not all; if you find the target touched at all, I'll own to a miss. The Quartermaster cut the wood, but you'll find no wood cut by that last messenger.'"

The miracle is at last complete. He knew—doubtless *saw* —at the distance of a hundred yards—that his bullet had passed into the hole *without fraying the edges*. There were now three bullets in that one hole—three bullets embedded processionally in the body of the stump back of the target. Everybody knew this—somehow or other—and yet nobody had dug any of them out to make sure. Cooper is not a close observer, but he is interesting. He is certainly always that, no matter what happens. And he is more interesting when he is not noticing what he is about than when he is. This is a considerable merit.

The conversations in the Cooper books have a curious sound in our modern ears. To believe that such talk really ever came out of people's mouths would be to believe that there was a time when time was of no value to a person who thought he had something to say; when it was the custom to spread a two-minute remark out to ten; when a man's mouth was a rolling-mill, and busied itself all day long in turning four-foot pigs of thought into thirty-foot bars of conversational railroad iron by attenuation; when subjects were seldom faithfully stuck to, but the talk wandered all around and arrived nowhere; when conversations consisted mainly of irrelevancies, with here and there a relevancy, a relevancy with an embarrassed look, as not being able to explain how it got there.

Cooper was certainly not a master in the construction of dialogue. Inaccurate observation defeated him here as it defeated him in so many other enterprises of his. He even failed to notice that the man who talks corrupt English six days in the week must and will talk it on the seventh, and can't help himself. In the *Deerslayer* story he lets Deerslayer talk the showiest kind of book-talk sometimes, and at other times the basest of base dialects. For instance, when someone asks him if he has a sweetheart, and if so, where she abides, this is his majestic answer:

"'She's in the forest—hanging from the boughs of the trees, in a soft rain—in the dew on the open grass—the clouds that float about in the blue heavens—the birds that sing in the woods—the sweet springs where I slake my thirst—and in all the other glorious gifts that come from God's Providence!'"

And he preceded that, a little before, with this:

" 'It consarns me as all things that touches a fri'nd consarns a fri'nd.' "

And this is another of his remarks:

" 'If I was Injin born, now, I might tell of this, or carry
in the scalp and boast of the expl'ite afore the whole tribe;
or if my inimy had only been a bear' "—and so on.

We cannot imagine such a thing as a veteran Scotch com-
mander-in-chief comporting himself in the field like a windy,
melodramatic actor, but Cooper could. On one occasion
Alice and Cora were being chased by the French through a
fog in the neighborhood of their father's fort:

" '*Point de quartier aux coquins!*' cried an eager pursuer,
who seemed to direct the operations of the enemy.

" 'Stand firm and be ready, my gallant 60ths!' suddenly
exclaimed a voice above them; 'wait to see the enemy; fire
low, and sweep the glacis.'

" 'Father! father!' exclaimed a piercing cry from out the
mist; 'it is I! Alice! thy own Elsie! Spare, O! save your
daughters!'

" 'Hold!' shouted the former speaker, in the awful tones
of parental agony, the sound reaching even to the woods,
and rolling back in solemn echo. ' 'Tis she! God has restored
me my children! Throw open the sally-port; to the field,
60ths, to the field! Pull not a trigger, lest ye kill my lambs!
Drive off these dogs of France with your steel!' "

Cooper's word-sense was singularly dull. When a person
has a poor ear for music he will flat and sharp right along
without knowing it. He keeps near the tune, but it is *not*
the tune. When a person has a poor ear for words, the result is a literary flatting and sharping; you perceive what he
is intending to say, but you also perceive that he doesn't
say it. This is Cooper. He was not a word-musician. His
ear was satisfied with the *approximate* word. I will furnish
some circumstantial evidence in support of this charge. My
instances are gathered from half-a-dozen pages of the tale
called *Deerslayer*. He uses *verbal,* for *oral; precision,* for
facility; phenomena, for *marvels; necessary,* for *predetermined; unsophisticated,* for *primitive; preparation,* for *ex-
pectancy; rebuked,* for *subdued; dependent on,* for *resulting*

from; fact, for *condition; fact,* for *conjecture; precaution,* for *caution; explain,* for *determine; mortified,* for *disappointed; meretricious,* for *factitious; materially,* for *considerably; decreasing,* for *deepening; increasing,* for *disappearing; embedded,* for *enclosed; treacherous,* for *hostile; stood,* for *stooped; softened,* for *replaced; rejoined,* for *remarked; situation,* for *condition; different,* for *differing; insensible,* for *insentient; brevity,* for *celerity; distrusted,* for *suspicious; mental imbecility,* for *imbecility; eyes,* for *sight; counteracting,* for *opposing; funeral obsequies,* for *obsequies.*

There have been daring people in the world who claimed that Cooper could write English, but they are all dead now— all dead but Lounsbury. I don't remember that Lounsbury makes the claim in so many words, still he makes it, for he says that *Deerslayer* is a "pure work of art." Pure, in that connection, means faultless—faultless in all details— and language is a detail. If Mr. Lounsbury had only compared Cooper's English with the English which he writes himself—but it is plain that he didn't; and so it is likely that he imagines until this day that Cooper's is as clean and compact as his own. Now I feel sure, deep down in my heart, that Cooper wrote about the poorest English that exists in our language, and that the English of *Deerslayer* is the very worst that even Cooper ever wrote.

I may be mistaken, but it does seem to me that *Deerslayer* is not a work of art in any sense; it does seem to me that it is destitute of every detail that goes to the making of a work of art; in truth, it seems to me that *Deerslayer* is just simply a literary *delirium tremens.*

A work of art? It has no invention; it has no order, system, sequence, or result; it has no lifelikeness, no thrill, no stir, no seeming of reality; its characters are confusedly drawn, and by their acts and words they prove that they are not the sort of people the author claims that they are; its humor is pathetic; its pathos is funny; its conversations are—oh! indescribable; its love-scenes odious; its English a crime against the language.

Counting these out, what is left is Art. I think we must all admit that.

*A Cooper Indian who has been washed is a poor thing, and commonplace; it is the Cooper Indian in his paint that thrills. Cooper's extra words are Cooper's paint—his paint, his feathers, his tomahawk, his warwhoop.

In the two-thirds of a page elsewhere referred to, wherein Cooper scored 114 literary transgressions out of a possible 115, he appears before us with all his things on. As follows, the italics are mine—they indicate violations of Rule 14:

In a minute he was once more fastened to the tree, *a helpless object of any insult or wrong that might be offered. So eagerly did every one now act, that nothing was said.* The fire was immediately lighted *in the pile, and the end of all was anxiously expected.*

It was not the intention of the Hurons *absolutely* to destroy *the life of* their victim by *means of* fire. They designed merely to put his *physical fortitude* to the severest proofs it could endure, short of that extremity. In the end, they fully intended to carry his scalp into their village, but it was their wish first to break down his resolution, and to reduce him to *the level of* a complaining sufferer. With this view, the pile of brush *and branches* had been placed at a *proper* distance, *or one* at which it was thought the heat would soon become intolerable, though *it might* not *be* immediately dangerous. *As often happened, however, on these occasions,* this distance had been miscalculated, and the flames *began to wave their forked tongues in a proximity to the face of the victim that* would have proved fatal in another instant had not Hetty rushed through the crowd, armed with a stick, and scattered the blazing pile *in a dozen directions.* More than one hand was raised to strike the *presumptuous* intruder to the earth; but the chiefs prevented the blows by reminding their *irritated* followers of the state of her mind. Hetty, herself,

---

* Since the first edition of this volume, some further unpublished pages of Mark Twain's essay have been found among Mark Twain's papers by Mr. Bernard De Voto, who published them in the *New England Quarterly* of September 1946. This new material follows here (copyright 1946 by the Mark Twain Company). The first section of the essay, Mr. De Voto tells us, appears in the manuscript "as Number I in a series called *Studies in Literary Criticism,* which were supposed to have been 'prepared for last term by Mark Twain, M.A., Professor of Belles Lettres in the Veterinary College of Arizona.'" The second section is evidently unfinished. E.W.

was insensible to the risk she ran; but, *as soon as she had performed this bold act, she* stood looking about her in frowning resentment, as if to rebuke the *crowd of attentive* savages *for their cruelty.*

'God bless you, dea*rest sister,* for that brave and ready act,' murmured Judith, *herself unnerved so much as to be incapable of exertion;* 'Heaven itself has sent you on its holy errand.'

Number of words, 320; necessary ones, 220; words wasted by the generous spendthrift, 100.

In our day those 100 unnecessary words would have to come out. We will take them out presently and make the episode approximate the modern requirement in the matter of compression.

If we may consider each unnecessary word in Cooper's report of that barbecue a separate and individual violation of Rule 14, then that rule is violated 100 times in that report. Other rules are violated in it. Rule 12, two instances; [1] Rule 13, three instances; [2] Rule 15, one instance; [3] Rule 16, two instances; [4] Rule 17, one or two little instances; [5] the Report in its entirety is an offense against Rule 18 [6]—also against Rule 16. Total score, about 114 violations of the laws of literary art out of a possible 115.

Let us now bring forward the Report again, with the most of the unnecessary words knocked out. By departing from Cooper's style and manner, all the facts could be put into 150 words, and the effects heightened at the same time —this is manifest, of course—but that would not be desirable. We must stick to Cooper's language as closely as we can:

In a minute he was once more fastened to the tree. The fire was immediately lighted. It was not the intention of the Hurons to destroy Deerslayer's life by fire; they designed merely to put

[1] Rule 12: "*Say* what he is proposing to say, not merely come near it."
[2] Rule 13: "Use the right word, not its second cousin."
[3] Rule 15: "Not omit necessary details."
[4] Rule 16: "Avoid slovenliness of form."
[5] Rule 17: "Use good grammar."
[6] Rule 18: "Employ a simple and straightforward style."

his fortitude to the severest proofs it could endure short of that extremity. In the end, they fully intended to take his life, but it was their wish first to break down his resolution and reduce him to a complaining sufferer. With this view the pile of brush had been placed at a distance at which it was thought the heat would soon become intolerable, without being immediately dangerous. But this distance had been miscalculated; the fire was so close to the victim that he would have been fatally burned in another instant if Hetty had not rushed through the crowd and scattered the brands with a stick. More than one Indian raised his hand to strike her down but the chiefs saved her by reminding them of the state of her mind. Hetty herself was insensible to the risk she ran; she stood looking about her in frowning resentment, as if to rebuke the savages for their cruelty.

'God bless you, dear!' cried Judith, 'for that brave and ready act. Heaven itself has sent you on its holy errand, and you shall have a chromo.'

Number of words, 220—and the facts are all in.

II

In studying Cooper you will find it profitable to study him in detail—word by word, sentence by sentence. For every sentence of his is interesting. Interesting because of its make-up; its peculiar make-up, its original make-up. Let us examine a sentence or two, and see. Here is a passage from Chapter XI of *The Last of the Mohicans,* one of the most famous and most admired of Cooper's books:

Notwithstanding the swiftness of their flight, one of the Indians had found an opportunity to strike a straggling fawn with an arrow, and had borne the more preferable fragments of the victim, patiently on his shoulders, to the stopping-place. Without any aid from the science of cookery, he was immediately employed, in common with his fellows, in gorging himself with this digestible sustenance. Magua alone sat apart, without participating in the revolting meal, and apparently buried in the deepest thought.

This little paragraph is full of matter for reflection and inquiry. The remark about the swiftness of the flight was unnecessary, as it was merely put in to forestall the possible objection of some over-particular reader that the Indian couldn't have found the needed "opportunity" while fleeing swiftly. The reader would not have made that objection. He would care nothing about having that small matter explained and justified. But that is Cooper's way; frequently he will explain and justify little things that do not need it and then make up for this by as frequently failing to explain important ones that do need it. For instance he allowed that astute and cautious person, Deerslayer-Hawkeye, to throw his rifle heedlessly down and leave it lying on the ground where some hostile Indians would presently be sure to find it—a rifle prized by that person above all things else in the earth—and the reader gets no word of explanation of that strange act. There was a reason, but it wouldn't bear exposure. Cooper meant to get a fine dramatic effect out of the finding of the rifle by the Indians, and he accomplished this at the happy time; but all the same, Hawkeye could have hidden the rifle in a quarter of a minute where the Indians could not have found it. Cooper couldn't think of any way to explain why Hawkeye didn't do that, so he just shirked the difficulty and did not explain at all. In another place Cooper allowed Heyward to shoot at an Indian with a pistol that wasn't loaded—and grants us not a word of explanation as to how the man did it.

No, the remark about the swiftness of their flight was not necessary; neither was the one which said that the Indian found an opportunity; neither was the one which said he *struck* the fawn; neither was the one which explained that it was a "straggling" fawn; neither was the one which said the striking was done with an arrow; neither was the one which said the Indian bore the "fragments"; nor the remark that they were preferable fragments; nor the remark that they were *more* preferable fragments; nor the explanation that they were fragments of the "victim"; nor the over-particular explanation that specifies the Indian's "shoulders" as the part of him that supported the fragments; nor the statement that the Indian bore the fragments patiently. None of those details has any value. We don't care what the Indian struck the fawn with; we don't care whether it was a straggling fawn or an unstraggling one; we don't care which fragments the Indian saved; we don't care why he saved the "more" preferable ones when the merely preferable ones would have amounted to just the same thing and couldn't have been told from the more preferable ones by anybody, dead or alive; we don't care whether the Indian carried them on his shoulders or in his handkerchief; and finally, we don't care whether he carried them patiently or struck for higher pay and shorter hours. We are indifferent to that Indian and all his affairs.

There was only one fact in that long sentence that was worth stating, and it could have been squeezed into these few words—and with advantage to the narrative, too: "During the flight one of the Indians had killed a fawn, and he brought it into camp." You will notice that "During the flight one of the Indians had killed a fawn and he brought it into camp," is more straightforward and business-like, and less mincing and smirky, than it is to say "Notwithstanding the swiftness of their flight, one of the Indians had found an opportunity to strike a straggling fawn with an arrow, and had borne the more preferable fragments of the victim, patiently on his shoulders, to the stopping-place." You will notice that the form "During the flight one of the Indians had killed a fawn and he brought it into camp" holds up its chin and moves to the front with the steady stride of a grenadier, whereas the form "Notwithstanding the swiftness of their flight, one of the Indians had found an opportunity to strike a straggling fawn with an arrow, and had borne the more preferable fragments of the victim, patiently on his shoulders, to the stopping-place," simpers along with an airy, complacent, monkey-with-a-parasol gait which is not suited to the transportation of raw meat.

I beg to remind you that an author's way of setting forth a matter is called his Style, and that an author's style is a main part of his equipment for business. The style of some authors has variety in it, but Cooper's style is remarkable for the absence of this feature. Cooper's style is always grand and stately and noble. Style may be likened to an army, the author to its general, the book to the campaign. Some authors proportion an attacking force to the strength or weakness, the importance or unimportance, of the object to be attacked; but Cooper doesn't. It doesn't make any difference to Cooper whether the object of attack is a hundred thousand men or a cow; he hurls his entire force against it. He comes thundering down with all his battalions at his back, cavalry in the van, artillery on the flanks, infantry massed in the middle, forty bands braying, a thousand banners streaming in the wind; and whether the object be an army or a cow you will see him come marching sublimely in, at the end of the engagement, bearing the more preferable fragments of the victim patiently on his shoulders, to the stopping-place. Cooper's style is grand, awful, beautiful; but it is sacred to Cooper, it is his very own, and no student of the Veterinary College of Arizona will be allowed to filch it from him.

In one of his chapters Cooper throws an ungentle slur at one Gamut because he is not exact enough in his choice of words. But Cooper has that failing himself, as was remarked in our first Lecture. If the Indian had "struck" the fawn with a brick, or with a club, or with his fist, no one could find fault with the word used. And one cannot find much fault when he strikes it with an arrow; still it sounds affected, and it might have been a little better to lean to simplicity and say he shot it with an arrow.

"Fragments" is well enough, perhaps, when one is speaking of the parts of a dismembered deer, yet it hasn't just exactly the right sound—and sound is something; in fact sound is a good deal. It makes the difference between good music and poor music, and it can sometimes make the difference between good literature and indifferent literature. "Fragments" sounds all right when we are talking about the wreckage of a breakable thing that has been smashed; it also sounds all right when applied to cat's-meat; but when we use it to describe large hunks and chunks like the fore- and hind-quarters of a fawn, it grates upon the fastidious ear.

"Without any aid from the science of cookery, he was

immediately employed, in common with his fellows, in gorging himself with this digestible sustenance."

This was a mere statistic; just a mere cold, colorless statistic; yet you see Cooper has made a chromo out of it. To use another figure, he has clothed a humble statistic in flowing, voluminous and costly raiment, whereas both good taste and economy suggest that he ought to have saved these splendors for a king, and dressed the humble statistic in a simple breech-clout. Cooper spent twenty-four words here on a thing not really worth more than eight. We will reduce the statistic to its proper proportions and state it in this way:

"He and the others ate the meat raw."

"Digestible sustenance" is a handsome phrase, but it was out of place there, because we do not know these Indians or care for them; and so it cannot interest us to know whether the meat was going to agree with them or not. Details which do not assist a story are better left out.

"Magua alone sat apart, without participating in the revolting meal," is a statement which we understand, but that is our merit, not Cooper's. Cooper is not clear. He does not say who it is that is revolted by the meal. It is really Cooper himself, but there is nothing in the statement to indicate that it isn't Magua. Magua is an Indian and likes raw meat.

The word "alone" could have been left out and space saved. It has no value where it is.

I must come back with some frequency, in the course of these Lectures, to the matter of Cooper's inaccuracy as an Observer. In this way I shall hope to persuade you that it is well to look at a thing carefully before you try to describe it; but I shall rest you between times with other matters and thus try to avoid over-fatiguing you with that detail of our theme. In *The Last of the Mohicans* Cooper gets up a stirring "situation" on an island flanked by great cataracts— a lofty island with steep sides—a sort of tongue which projects downstream from the midst of the divided waterfall. There are caverns in this mass of rock, and a party of Cooper people hide themselves in one of these to get away from some hostile Indians. There is a small exit at each end of this cavern. These exits are closed with blankets and the light excluded. The exploring hostiles back themselves up against the blankets and rave and rage in a blood-curdling way, but they are Cooper Indians and of course fail to discover the blankets; so they presently go away baffled and disappointed. Alice, in her gratitude for this deliverance, flings herself on her knees to return thanks. The darkness in there must have been pretty solid; yet if we may believe Cooper, it was a darkness which could not have been told from daylight; for here are some nice details which were visible in it:

"Both Heyward and the more tempered Cora witnessed the act of involuntary emotion with powerful sympathy, the former secretly believing that piety had never worn a form so lovely as it had now assumed in the youthful person of Alice. Her eyes were radiant with the glow of grateful feelings; the flush of her beauty was again seated on her cheeks, and her whole soul seemed ready and anxious to pour out its thanksgivings, through the medium of her eloquent features. But when her lips moved, the words they should have uttered appeared frozen by some new and sudden chill. Her bloom gave place to the paleness of death; her soft and melting eyes grew hard, and seemed contracting with horror; while those hands which she had raised, clasped in each other, towards heaven, dropped in horizontal lines before her, the fingers pointed forward in convulsed motion."

It is a case of strikingly inexact observation. Heyward and the more tempered Cora could not have seen the half of it in the dark that way.

I must call your attention to certain details of this work of art which invite particular examination. "Involuntary" is surplusage, and violates Rule 14. All emotion is involuntary when genuine, and then the qualifying term is not needed; a qualifying term is needed only when the emotion is pumped-up and ungenuine. "Secretly" is surplusage, too; because Heyward was not believing out loud, but all to himself; and a person cannot believe a thing all to himself without doing it privately. I do not approve of the word "seated," to describe the process of locating a flush. No one

can seat a flush. A flush is not a deposit on an exterior surface, it is a something which squashes out from within.

I cannot approve of the word "new." If Alice had had an
old chill, formerly, it would be all right to distinguish this
one from that one by calling this one the new chill; but she
had not had any old chill, this one was the only chill she
had had, up till now, and so the tacit reference to an old
anterior chill is unwarranted and misleading. And I do not
altogether like the phrase "while those hands which she had
raised." It seems to imply that she had some other hands—
some other ones which she had put on the shelf a minute
so as to give her a better chance to raise those ones; but it
is not true; she had only the one pair. The phrase is in the
last degree misleading. But I like to see her extend these
ones in front of her and work the fingers. I think that that is
a very good effect. And it would have almost doubled the
effect if the more tempered Cora had done it some, too.

can seat a flush. A flush is not a deposit on an exterior surface, it is a something which squashes out from within.

I cannot approve of the word "new". IF Alice had had an
old chill, formerly, it would be all right to distinguish this
one from that one by calling this one the new chill; but she
had not had any old chill, this one was the only chill she
had had, up till now, and so the tacit reference to an old
anterior chill is unwarranted and misleading. And I do not
altogether like the phrase "while those hands which she had
raised." It seems to imply that she had some other hands—
some other ones which she had put on the shelf a minute
so as to give her a better chance to raise those ones; but it
is not true, she had only the one pair. The phrase is in the
last degree misleading. But I like to see her extend these
ones in front of her and work the fingers I think that is
a very good effect. And it would have almost doubled the
effect if the more tempered Cora had done it some, too.

JOHN JAY CHAPMAN'S FINE ESSAY on Emerson came out under the title *Emerson Sixty Years Later,* in the *Atlantic Monthly* of January and February 1897, and was published the next year in a book called *Emerson and Other Essays.* By the nineties, the heroic individualism of Emerson had been pretty well driven underground by the individualism of Big Business, and the artists and literary men had been feeling themselves freer abroad. John Jay Chapman was an exception to this. He denounced the emigration and stood his ground in the United States. His career was a curious one. He was a moralist, a literary critic, a poet, and a political reformer; and his character was passionate, erratic, intransigent, and self-willed. There is in him something of a more limited Tolstoy and something of the traditional American crank. On one occasion, in 1911, when he read that a Negro had been burned alive in a Pennsylvania steel town, he went there, hired a hall, and held a sort of memorial service, which was attended by only two people, one of them a plain-clothes man.

It was a flare-up of the stifled Emersonian idealism as well as an echo of the Abolitionist protest. We are out of touch today with the dynamic elements of Emerson. Though his credit still remains high, we are rather put off from reading him (as is not the case with Thoreau) by his uninviting literary form. In one very important respect he lacks the technique of the prose writer: he cannot carry you from page to page. He had the tendency either to compose a set speech somewhat in the nature of a sermon, in which his matter was drawn up under heads; or to compile under the most general titles—*Love, Friendship, The Oversoul,* etc.— loose collections of aphorisms from his note-books. In these aphorisms he is dazzling, a poet; and there are passages and even whole essays such as the one included here on Thoreau in which we feel a high voltage. But, neglecting him, it is hard for us to realize how stimulating he seemed to his contemporaries, who used to couple his name with Carlyle's; and that he was even one of the influences behind Nietzsche, of whom Charles Andler says that he had absorbed Emerson's thought so thoroughly that he could not always distinguish it from his own.

It is this Nietzschean side of Emerson that Chapman here presents—or rather Chapman and Nietzsche both feed themselves from Emerson's fire and give expression to points of view which, though both are self-assertive and defiant, assert quite distinct selves. And this essay of Chapman's is today perhaps more easily assimilable than Emerson. Chapman's world is closer to our world; and his prose is among the best of his period.

Chapman's grandmother, Maria Weston Chapman, had been a lieutenant of William Lloyd Garrison's; but Chapman was essentially a New Yorker, who had approached the New England culture from outside. In a preface of 1909 he places his point of view as follows:

As I look back over the past, the figure of Emerson looms up in my mind as the first modern man, and the City of Boston as the first living civilization which I knew.

New York is not a civilization; it is a railway station. There are epochs of revolution and convulsion,—times of the migration or expulsion of races, when too much happens in a moment to permit of anything being either understood or recorded. Such times have no history. They are mysteries and remain mysterious. Such an epoch has been passing over New York City ever since I have known it. The present in New York is so powerful that the past is lost. There is no past. Not a bookshelf, nor a cornice, nor a sign, nor a face, nor a type of mind endures for a generation, and a New York boy who goes away to boarding school returns to a new world at each vacation. He finds perhaps on his return from boarding school, that the street where he and his companions used to play ball is given over to a migration of Teutons. When he returns from college, the Teutons have vanished and given place to Italians. When he reaches the Law school, behold no more Italians—Polish Jews to the horizon's verge.

The young person born in New York during the last quarter century has been like a rat in a bag which the rat-catcher keeps agitating lest the creature's teeth get a purchase on the prison. The New York youth cannot be expected to get hold of any idea while the kaleidoscope is turning so furiously. He is numb and dizzy. He cannot connect his reading with his environment; for the books of the world have been projected out of quietude. They reflect stability, depth, relaxation, and all those conditions of peace and harmony which make thought possible. The youth, therefore, discards books as incomprehensible,—foolish, in fact. Education has for the time being lost its significance.

Now in Massachusetts there has been a consecutive development of thought since colonial times. Her links with the past have never been broken. The influx of new blood and new idea has not overwhelmed the old blood and old idea. There is in New England a traceable connection between the whole historic volume and stream of human culture,—that moving treasury of human thought and experience which flows down out of antiquity and involves us, surrounds and supports us and makes us the thing we are, no matter how much we struggle or how little we may understand. In Massachusetts you may still stop the first man you meet in the street and find in his first remark the influence of Wyclif or Samuel Adams. The spiritual life in New England has never been luxuriant. It is one-sided, sad, and inexpressive in many ways. But it has coherence, and this is what makes it valuable for the young American. Every young person in the United States ought to be sent to Massachusetts for some part of his education. The proximity of Harvard College to Boston gives Harvard a natural advantage over our other colleges. You cannot go to Harvard or indeed to any New England college without getting into some sort of contact with a logical civilization.

I had read Emerson's essays as a boy, but it was not till I reached college that they assumed any special significance to me. Then came a time when it seemed as if Emerson were a younger brother to Shakespeare. No book except Shakespeare's plays ever gave me such keen delight. I was intoxicated with Emerson. He let loose something within me which made me in my own eyes as good as anyone else. To express this I invented a phrase which I have always thought equal to any of Emerson's own exhortations to spiritual independence, and much more modest in form. It was this:

"After all it is just as well that there should be *one* person like *me* in the world."

When I was a student at Harvard, Emerson was still living. And I have seen him wandering about the streets of Cambridge in that stage which is called dotage and which often borders on the sublime even in ordinary people. I never met him; but many of his contemporaries were alive and very willing to talk about the early days. My grandmother, a Massachusetts woman, told me that the first time she had ever heard Emerson's name was when a neighbor said to her: "Oh, have you heard? The new minister of the Second Church has gone mad." Out of gossip and observation I put together a picture of Emerson and his times, without the least intention of writing about him, without, indeed, knowing what I was doing; and when, years afterwards, the *Atlantic Monthly* asked me to write about Emerson I said to myself, "Very well, why not? Be bold, be bold, be not too bold."

Not without trepidation did I launch all those generalizations about Emerson and the New England of Emerson's day. My reading was so superficial that I felt almost criminal in adopting that pose of finality which is customary with historians. I secretly wondered whether all historians were as great humbugs as I, or whether they really knew more about the past.

My reassurance, however, came almost at once in the shape of letters from old original Emersonians in all parts of the country, who wrote that I had found the Emerson whom they had known. I knew, of course, that what these ancient people enjoyed had come from themselves. Out of the mouths not of babes and sucklings but of sybils and old prophets had the truth been established. I was at one with these old antebellum enthusiasts. I had climbed up out of the hurly-burly of nine-teenth-century America and was sitting on a sort of bleak Mas-sachusetts Ararat, panting but safe. Dry ground at least was under foot; a consecutive relation to all the past had been established. This much I owe to Emerson and to Massachusetts; and, no doubt, thousands of others before and since have owed the same.

JOHN JAY CHAPMAN

EMERSON

LEAVE this hypocritical prating about the masses. Masses are rude, lame, unmade, pernicious in their demands and influence, and need not to be flattered, but to be schooled. I wish not to concede anything to them, but to tame, drill, divide, and break them up, and draw individuals out of them. The worst of charity is that the lives you are asked to preserve are not worth preserving. Masses! The calamity is the masses. I do not wish any mass at all, but honest men only, lovely, sweet, accomplished women only, and no shovel-handed, narrow-brained, gin-drinking million stockingers or lazzaroni at all. If government knew how, I should like to see it check, not multiply the population. When it reaches its true law of action, every man that is born will be hailed as essential. Away with this hurrah of masses, and let us have the considerate vote of single men spoken on their honor and their conscience.

This extract from *The Conduct of Life* gives fairly enough the leading thought of Emerson's life. The unending warfare between the individual and society shows us in each generation a poet or two, a dramatist or a musician who exalts and deifies the individual, and leads us back again to the only object which is really worthy of enthusiasm or which can permanently excite it,—the character of a man. It is surprising to find this identity of content in all great deliverances. The only thing we really admire is personal liberty. Those who fought for it and those who enjoyed it are our heroes.

But the hero may enslave his race by bringing in a system of tyranny; the battle-cry of freedom may become a dogma which crushes the soul; one good custom may corrupt the world. And so the inspiration of one age becomes the damnation of the next. This crystallizing of life into death has occurred so often that it may almost be regarded as one of the laws of progress.

Emerson represents a protest against the tyranny of democracy. He is the most recent example of elemental hero-worship. His opinions are absolutely unqualified except by his temperament. He expresses a form of belief in the importance of the individual which is independent of any personal relations he has with the world. It is as if a man had been withdrawn from the earth and dedicated to condensing and embodying this eternal idea—the value of the individual soul—so vividly, so vitally, that his words could not die, yet in such illusive and abstract forms that by no chance and by no power could his creed be used for purposes of tyranny. Dogma cannot be extracted from it. Schools cannot be built on it. It either lives as the spirit lives, or else it evaporates and leaves nothing. Emerson was so afraid of the letter that killeth that he would hardly trust his words to print. He was assured there was no such thing as literal truth, but only literal falsehood. He therefore resorted to metaphors which could by no chance be taken literally. And he has probably suceeded in leaving a body of work which cannot be made to operate to any other end than that for which he designed it. If this be true, he has accomplished the inconceivable feat of eluding misconception. If it be true, he stands alone in the history of teachers; he has circumvented fate, he has left an unmixed blessing behind him.

The signs of those times which brought forth Emerson are not wholly undecipherable. They are the same times which gave rise to every character of significance during the period before the war. Emerson is indeed the easiest to understand of all the men of his time, because his life is freest from the tangles and qualifications of circumstance.

He is a sheer and pure type and creature of destiny, and the unconsciousness that marks his development allies him to the deepest phenomena. It is convenient, in describing him, to use language which implies consciousness on his part, but he himself had no purpose, no theory of himself; he was a product.

The years between 1820 and 1830 were the most pitiable through which this country has ever passed. The conscience of the North was pledged to the Missouri Compromise, and that Compromise neither slumbered nor slept. In New England, where the old theocratical oligarchy of the colonies had survived the Revolution and kept under its own water-locks the new flood of trade, the conservatism of politics reinforced the conservatism of religion; and as if these two inquisitions were not enough to stifle the soul of man, the conservatism of business self-interest was superimposed. The history of the conflicts which followed has been written by the radicals, who negligently charge up to self-interest all the resistance which establishments offer to change. But it was not solely self-interest, it was conscience that backed the Missouri Compromise, nowhere else, naturally, so strongly as in New England. It was conscience that made cowards of us all. The white-lipped generation of Edward Everett were victims, one might even say martyrs, to conscience. They suffered the most terrible martyrdom that can fall to man, a martyrdom which injured their immortal volition and dried up the springs of life. If it were not that our poets have too seldom designed to dip into real life, I do not know what more awful subject for a poem could have been found than that of the New England judge enforcing the Fugitive Slave Law. For lack of such a poem the heroism of these men has been forgotten, the losing heroism of conservatism. It was this spiritual power of a committed conscience which met the new forces as they arose, and it deserves a better name than these new forces afterward gave it. In 1830 the social fruits of these heavy conditions could be seen in the life of the people. Free speech was lost.

"I know no country," says Tocqueville, who was here in 1831, "in which there is so little independence of mind and freedom of discussion as in America." Tocqueville recurs to the point again and again. He cannot disguise his surprise at it, and it tinged his whole philosophy and his book. The timidity of the Americans of this era was a thing which intelligent foreigners could not understand. Miss Martineau wrote in her *Autobiography*:

It was not till months afterwards that I was told that there were two reasons why I was not invited there [Chelsea] as elsewhere. One reason was that I had avowed, in reply to urgent questions, that I was disappointed in an oration of Mr. Everett's; and another was that I had publicly condemned the institution of slavery. I hope the Boston people have outgrown the childishness of sulking at opinions not in either case volunteered, but obtained by pressure. But really, the subservience. to opinion at that time seemed a sort of mania.

The mania was by no means confined to Boston, but qualified this period of our history throughout the Northern States. There. was no literature. "If great writers have not at present existed in America, the reason is very simply given in the fact that there can be no literary genius without freedom of opinion, and freedom of opinion does not exist in America," wrote Tocqueville. There were no amusements, neither music nor sport nor pastime, indoors or out-of-doors. The whole life of the community was a life of the intelligence, and upon the intelligence lay the weight of intellectual tyranny. The pressure kept on increasing, and the suppressed forces kept on increasing, till at last, as if to show what gigantic power was needed to keep conservatism dominant, the Merchant Province put forward Daniel Webster.

The worst period of panic seems to have preceded the anti-slavery agitations. of 1831, because these agitations soon demonstrated that the sky did not fall nor the earth yawn and swallow Massachusetts because of Mr. Garrison's opinions, as most people had sincerely believed would be the case. Some semblance of free speech was therefore gradually regained.

Let us remember the world upon which the young Emerson's eyes opened. The South was a plantation. The North crooked the hinges of the knee where thrift might follow fawning. It was the era of *Martin Chuzzlewit*, a malicious caricature,—founded on fact. This time of humiliation, when there was no free speech, no literature, little manliness, no reality, no simplicity, no accomplishment, was the era of American brag. We flattered the foreigner and we boasted of ourselves. We were oversensitive, insolent, and cringing. As late as 1845, G. P. Putnam, a most sensible and modest man, published a book to show what the country had done in the field of culture. The book is a monument of the age. With all its good sense and good humor, it justifies foreign contempt because it is explanatory. Underneath everything lay a feeling of unrest, an instinct—"this country cannot permanently endure half slave and half free"—which was the truth, but which could not be uttered.

So long as there is any subject which men may not freely discuss, they are timid upon all subjects. They wear an iron crown and talk in whispers. Such social conditions crush and maim the individual, and throughout New England, as throughout the whole North, the individual was crushed and maimed.

The generous youths who came to manhood between 1820 and 1830, while this deadly era was maturing, seem to have undergone a revulsion against the world almost before touching it; at least two of them suffered, revolted, and condemned, while still boys sitting on benches in school, and came forth advancing upon this old society like gladiators. The activity of William Lloyd Garrison, the man of action, preceded by several years that of Emerson, who is his prophet. Both of them were parts of one revolution. One of Emerson's articles of faith was that a man's thoughts spring from his actions rather than his actions from his thoughts, and possibly the same thing holds good for society at large. Perhaps all truths, whether moral or economic, must be worked out in real life before they are discovered by the student, and it was therefore necessary that Garrison should be evolved earlier than Emerson.

The silent years of early manhood, during which Emerson passed through the Divinity School and to his ministry, known by few, understood by none, least of all by himself, were years in which the revolting spirit of an archangel thought out his creed. He came forth perfect, with that serenity of which we have scarce another example in history —that union of the man himself, his beliefs, and his vehicle of expression that makes men great because it makes them comprehensible. The philosophy into which he had already transmuted all his earlier theology at the time we first meet him consisted of a very simple drawing together of a few ideas, all of which had long been familiar to the world. It is the wonderful use he made of these ideas, the closeness with which they fitted his soul, the tact with which he took what he needed, like a bird building its nest, that make the originality, the man.

The conclusion of Berkeley, that the external world is known to us only through our impressions, and that there-fore, for aught we know, the whole universe exists only in our own consciousness, cannot be disproved. It is so simple a conception that a child may understand it; and it has prob-ably been passed before the attention of every thinking man since Plato's time. The notion is in itself a mere philosophical catch or crux to which there is no answer. It may be true. The mystics made this doctrine useful. They were not con-tent to doubt the independent existence of the external world. They imagined that this external world, the earth, the planets, the phenomena of nature, bore some relation to the emotions and destiny of the soul. The soul and the cosmos were somehow related, and related so intimately that the cosmos might be regarded as a sort of projection or dia-gram of the soul.

Plato was the first man who perceived that this idea could be made to provide the philosopher with a vehicle of ex-pression more powerful than any other. If a man will once plant himself firmly on the proposition that *he is* the uni-verse, that every emotion or expression of his mind is cor-related in some way to phenomena in the external world, and that he shall say how correlated, he is in a position where the power of speech is at a maximum. His figures of speech, his tropes, his witticisms, take rank with the law of gravity and the precession of the equinoxes. Philosophical exaltation of the individual cannot go beyond this point. It is the climax.

This is the school of thought to which Emerson belonged. The sun and moon, the planets, are mere symbols. They signify whatever the poet chooses. The planets for the most part stay in conjunction just long enough to flash his thought through their symbolism, and no permanent relation is established between the soul and the zodiac. There is, however, one link of correlation between the external and internal worlds which Emerson considered established, and in which he believed almost literally, namely, the moral law. This idea he drew from Kant through Coleridge and Wordsworth, and it is so familiar to us all that it hardly needs stating. The fancy that the good, the true, the beautiful— all things of which we instinctively approve—are somehow connected together and are really one thing; that our appreciation of them is in its essence the recognition of a law; that this law, in fact all law and the very idea of law, is a mere subjective experience; and that hence any external sequence which we coördinate and name, like the law of gravity, is really intimately connected with our moral nature —this fancy has probably some basis of truth. Emerson adopted it as a corner stone of his thought.

Such are the ideas at the basis of Emerson's philosophy, and it is fair to speak of them in this place because they antedate everything else which we know of him. They had been for years in his mind before he spoke at all. It was in the armor of this invulnerable idealism and with weapons like shafts of light that he came forth to fight.

In 1836, at the age of thirty-three, Emerson published the little pamphlet called *Nature,* which was an attempt to state his creed. Although still young, he was not without experience of life. He had been assistant minister to the Rev. Dr. Ware from 1829 to 1832, when he resigned his ministry on account of his views regarding the Lord's Supper. He had married and lost his first wife in the same interval. He had been abroad and had visited Carlyle in 1833. He had returned and settled in Concord, and had taken up the profession of lecturing, upon which he in part supported himself ever after. It is unnecessary to review these early lectures. "Large portions of them," says Mr. Cabot, his biographer, "appeared afterwards in the *Essays*, especially those of the first series." Suffice it that through them Emerson had become so well known that although *Nature* was published anonymously, he was recognized as the author. Many people had heard of him at the time he resigned his charge, and the story went abroad that the young minister of the Second Church had gone mad. The lectures had not discredited the story, and *Nature* seemed to corroborate it. Such was the impression which the book made upon Boston in 1836. As we read it today, we are struck by its extraordinary beauty of language. It is a supersensuous, lyrical, and sincere rhapsody, written evidently by a man of genius. It reveals a nature compelling respect,—a Shelley, and yet a sort of Yankee Shelley, who is mad only when the wind is nor'-nor'west; a mature nature which must have been nourished for years upon its own thoughts, to speak this new language so eloquently, to stand so calmly on its feet. The deliverance of his thought is so perfect that this work adapts itself to our mood and has the quality of poetry. This fluency Emerson soon lost; it is the quality missing in his poetry. It is the efflorescence of youth.

In good health, the air is a cordial of incredible virtue. Crossing a bare common, in snow puddles, at twilight, under a clouded sky, without having in my thoughts any occurrence of special good fortune, I have enjoyed a perfect exhilaration. I am glad to the brink of fear. In the woods, too, a man casts off his years, as the snake his slough, and at what period soever of life is always a child. In the woods is perpetual youth. Within these plantations of God, a decorum and sanctity reign, a perennial festival is dressed, and the guest sees not how he should tire of them in a thousand years. . . . It is the uniform effect of culture on the human mind, not to shake our faith in the stability of particular phenomena, as heat, water, azote, but to lead us to regard nature as phenomenon, not a substance; to attribute necessary existence to spirit; to esteem nature as an accident and an effect.

Perhaps these quotations from the pamphlet called *Nature* are enough to show the clouds of speculation in which

Emerson had been walking. With what lightning they were charged was soon seen.

In 1837 he was asked to deliver the Phi Beta Kappa oration at Cambridge. This was the opportunity for which he had been waiting. The mystic and eccentric young poet-preacher now speaks his mind, and he turns out to be a man exclusively interested in real life. This recluse, too tender for contact with the rough facts of the world, whose conscience has retired him to rural Concord, pours out a vial of wrath. This cub puts forth the paw of a full-grown lion.

Emerson has left behind him nothing stronger than this address, *The American Scholar*. It was the first application of his views to the events of his day, written and delivered in the heat of early manhood while his extraordinary powers were at their height. It moves with a logical progression of which he soon lost the habit. The subject of it, the scholar's relation to the world, was the passion of his life. The body of his belief is to be found in this address, and in any adequate account of him the whole address ought to be given.

Thus far, our holiday has been simply a friendly sign of the survival of the love of letters amongst a people too busy to give to letters any more. As such it is precious as the sign of an indestructible instinct. Perhaps the time is already come when it ought to be, and will be, something else; when the sluggard intellect of this continent will look from under its iron lids and fill the postponed expectation of the world with something better than the exertions of mechanical skill. . . . The theory of books is noble. The scholar of the first age received into him the world around; brooded thereon; gave it the new arrangement of his own mind, and uttered it again. It came into him life; it went out from him truth. . . . Yet hence arises a grave mischief. The sacredness which attaches to the act of creation, the act of thought, is transferred to the record. The poet chanting was felt to be a divine man: henceforth the chant is divine, also. The writer was a just and wise spirit: henceforward it is settled the book is perfect; as love of the hero corrupts into worship of his statue. Instantly the book becomes noxious: the guide is a tyrant. . . . Books are the best of things, well used; abused, among the worst. What is the right use? What is the one end which all means go to effect? They are for nothing but to inspire. . . . The one thing in the world, of value, is the active soul. This every man is entitled to; this every man contains within him, although in almost all men obstructed, and as yet unborn. The soul active sees absolute truth and utters truth, or creates. In this action it is genius; not the privilege of here and there a favorite, but the sound estate of every man. . . . Genius is always sufficiently the enemy of genius by over-influence. The literature of every nation bears me witness. The English dramatic poets have Shakespearized now for two hundred years. . . . These being his functions, it becomes him to feel all confidence in himself, and to defer never to the popular cry. He, and he only, knows the world. The world of any moment is the merest appearance. Some great decorum, some fetish of a government, some ephemeral trade, or war, or man, is cried up by half mankind and cried down by the other half, as if all depended on this particular up or down. The odds are that the whole question is not worth the poorest thought which the scholar has lost in listening to the controversy. Let him not quit his belief that a popgun is a popgun, though the ancient and honorable of the earth affirm it to be the crack of doom.

Dr. Holmes called this speech of Emerson's our "intellectual Declaration of Independence," and indeed it was. "The Phi Beta Kappa speech," says Mr. Lowell, "was an event without any former parallel in our literary annals,—a scene always to be treasured in the memory for its picturesqueness and its inspiration. What crowded and breathless aisles, what windows clustering with eager heads, what enthusiasm of approval, what grim silence of foregone dissent!"

The authorities of the Divinity School can hardly have been very careful readers of *Nature* and *The American Scholar*, or they would not have invited Emerson, in 1838, to deliver the address to the graduating class. This was Emerson's second opportunity to apply his beliefs directly to society. A few lines out of the famous address are enough to show that he saw in the church of his day signs of the same decadence that he saw in the letters:

The prayers and even the dogmas of our church are like the zodiac of Denderah and the astronomical monuments of the

Hindoos, wholly insulated from anything now extant in the life and business of the people. They mark the height to which the waters once rose. . . . It is the office of a true teacher to show us that God is, not was; that he speaketh, not spake. The true Christianity—a faith like Christ's in the infinitude of man—is lost. None believeth in the soul of man, but only in some man or person old and departed. Ah me! no man goeth alone. All men go in flocks to this saint or that poet, avoiding the God who seeth in secret. They cannot see in secret; they love to be blind in public. They think society wiser than their soul, and know not that one soul, and their soul, is wiser than the whole world.

It is almost misleading to speak of the lofty utterances of these early addresses as attacks upon society, but their reception explains them. The element of absolute courage is the same in all natures. Emerson himself was not unconscious of what function he was performing.

The "storm in our wash-bowl" which followed this Divinity School address, the letters of remonstrance from friends, the advertisements by the Divinity School of "no complicity," must have been cheering to Emerson. His unseen yet dominating ambition is shown throughout the address, and in this note in his diary of the following year:

August 31. Yesterday at the Phi Beta Kappa anniversary. Steady, steady. I am convinced that if a man will be a true scholar he shall have perfect freedom. The young people and the mature hint at odium and the aversion of forces to be presently encountered in society. I say No; I fear it not.

The lectures and addresses which form the latter half of the first volume in the collected edition show the early Emerson in the ripeness of his powers. These writings have a lyrical sweep and a beauty which the later works often lack. Passages in them remind us of Hamlet:

How silent, how spacious, what room for all, yet without space to insert an atom;—in graceful succession, in equal fullness, in balanced beauty, the dance of the hours goes forward still. Like an odor of incense, like a strain of music, like a sleep, it is inexact and boundless. It will not be dissected, nor unraveled, nor shown. . . . The great Pan of old, who was clothed in a leopard skin to signify the beautiful variety of things and the

firmament, his coat of stars,—was but the representative of thee,
O rich and various man! thou palace of sight and sound, carrying in thy senses the morning and the night and the unfathomable galaxy; in thy brain, the geometry of the City of God; in
thy heart, the bower of love and the realms of right and wrong.
. . . Every star in heaven is discontent and insatiable. Gravi-
tation and chemistry cannot content them. Ever they woo and
court the eye of the beholder. Every man who comes into the
world they seek to fascinate and possess, to pass into his mind,
for they desire to republish themselves in a more delicate world
than that they occupy. . . . So it is with all immaterial objects.
These beautiful basilisks set their brute glorious eyes on the
eye of every child, and, if they can, cause their nature to pass
through his wondering eyes into him, and so all things are
mixed.

Emerson is never far from his main thought:
"The universe does not attract us till it is housed in an individual." "A man, a personal ascendancy, is the only great
phenomenon." "I cannot find language of sufficient energy to
convey my sense of the sacredness of private integrity."

On the other hand, he is never far from his great fear:
"But Truth is such a fly-away, such a sly-boots, so untrans-
portable and unbarrelable a commodity, that it is as bad to
catch as light." "Let him beware of proposing to himself any
end. . . . I say to you plainly, there is no end so sacred or so
large that if pursued for itself will not become carrion and an
offense to the nostril."

There can be nothing finer than Emerson's knowledge
of the world, his sympathy with young men and with the
practical difficulties of applying his teachings. We can see
in his early lectures before students and mechanics how
much he had learned about the structure of society from his
own short contact with the organized church.

Each finds a tender and very intelligent conscience a dis-
qualification for success. Each requires of the practitioner a
certain shutting of the eyes, a certain dapperness and com-
pliance, an acceptance of customs, a sequestration from the
sentiments of generosity and love, a compromise of private
opinion and lofty integrity. . . . The fact that a new thought
and hope have dawned in your breast, should apprise you that

in the same hour a new light broke in upon a thousand private hearts. . . . And further I will not dissemble my hope that each person whom I address has felt his own call to cast aside all evil customs, timidity, and limitations, and to be in his place a free and helpful man, a reformer, a benefactor, not content to slip along through the world like a footman or a spy, escaping by his nimbleness and apologies as many knocks as he can, but a brave and upright man who must find or cut a straight road to everything excellent in the earth, and not only go honorably himself, but make it easier for all who follow him to go in honor and with benefit. . . .

Beneath all lay a greater matter—Emerson's grasp of the forms and conditions of progress, his reach of intellect, which could afford fair play to everyone.

His lecture on *The Conservative* is not a puzzling *jeu d'esprit*, like *Bishop Blougram's Apology*, but an honest attempt to set up the opposing chessmen of conservatism and reform so as to represent real life. Hardly can such a brilliant statement of the case be found elsewhere in literature. It is not necessary to quote here the reformer's side of the question, for Emerson's whole life was devoted to it. The conservatives' attitude he gives with such accuracy and such justice that the very bankers of State Street seem to be speaking:

The order of things is as good as the character of the population permits. Consider it as the work of a great and beneficent and progressive necessity, which, from the first pulsation in the first animal life up to the present high culture of the best nations, has advanced thus far. . . .

The conservative party in the universe concedes that the radical would talk sufficiently to the purpose if we were still in the garden of Eden; he legislates for man as he ought to be; his theory is right, but he makes no allowance for friction, and this omission makes his whole doctrine false. The idealist retorts that the conservative falls into a far more noxious error in the other extreme. The conservative assumes sickness as a necessity, and his social frame is a hospital, his total legislation is for the present distress, a universe in slippers and flannels, with bib and pap-spoon, swallowing pills and herb tea. Sickness gets organized as well as health, the vice as well as the virtue

It is unnecessary to go, one by one, through the familiar essays and lectures which Emerson published between 1838 and 1875. They are in everybody's hands and in everybody's thoughts. In 1840 he wrote in his diary:

In all my lectures I have taught one doctrine, namely, the infinitude of the private man. This the people accept readily enough, and even with commendation, as long as I call the lecture Art or Politics, or Literature or the Household; but the moment I call it Religion they are shocked, though it be only the application of the same truth which they receive elsewhere to a new class of facts.

To the platform he returned, and left it only once or twice during the remainder of his life.

His writings vary in coherence. In his early occasional pieces, like the Phi Beta Kappa address, coherence is at a maximum. They were written for a purpose, and were perhaps struck off all at once. But he earned his living by lecturing, and a lecturer is always recasting his work and using it in different forms. A lecturer has no prejudice against repetition. It is noticeable that in some of Emerson's important lectures the logical scheme is more perfect than in his essays. The truth seems to be that in the process of working up and perfecting his writings, in revising and filing his sentences, the logical scheme became more and more obliterated. Another circumstance helped make his style fragmentary. He was by nature a man of inspirations and exalted moods. He was subject to ecstasies, during which his mind worked with phenomenal brilliancy. Throughout his works and in his diary we find constant reference to these moods, and to his own inability to control or recover them. "But what we want is consecutiveness. 'Tis with us a flash of light, then a long darkness, then a flash again. Ah! could we turn these fugitive sparkles into an astronomy of Copernican worlds!"

In order to take advantage of these periods of divination, he used to write down the thoughts that came to him at such times. From boyhood onward he kept journals and commonplace books, and in the course of his reading and meditation he collected innumerable notes and quotations which he indexed for ready use. In these mines he "quarried," as Mr. Cabot says, for his lectures and essays. When he needed a lecture he went to the repository, threw together what seemed to have a bearing on some subject, and gave it a title. If any other man should adopt this method of composition, the result would be incomprehensible chaos; because most men have many interests, many moods, many and conflicting ideas. But with Emerson it was otherwise. There was only one thought which could set him aflame, and that was the thought of the unfathomed might of man. This thought was his religion, his politics, his ethics, his philosophy. One moment of inspiration was in him own brother to the next moment of inspiration, although they might be separated by six weeks. When he came to put together his star-born ideas, they fitted well, no matter in what order he placed them, because they were all part of the same idea.

His works are all one single attack on the vice of the age, moral cowardice. He assails it not by railings and scorn, but by positive and stimulating suggestion. The imagination of the reader is touched by every device which can awake the admiration for heroism, the consciousness of moral courage. Wit, quotation, anecdote, eloquence, exhortation, rhetoric, sarcasm, and very rarely denunciation, are launched at the reader, till he feels little lambent flames beginning to kindle in him. He is perhaps unable to see the exact logical connection between two paragraphs of an essay, yet he feels they are germane. He takes up Emerson tired and apathetic, but presently he feels himself growing heady and truculent, strengthened in his most inward vitality, surprised to find himself again master in his own house.

The difference between Emerson and the other moralists is that all these stimulating pictures and suggestions are not given by him in illustration of a general proposition. They have never been through the mill of generalization in his own mind. He himself could not have told you their logical bearing on one another. They have all the vividness of disconnected fragments of life, and yet they all throw light on one another, like the facets of a jewel. But whatever cause it was that led him to adopt his method of writing, it is certain that he succeeded in delivering himself of his thought with an initial velocity and carrying power such as few men ever attained. He has the force at his command of the thrower of the discus.

His style is American, and beats with the pulse of the climate. He is the only writer we have had who writes as he speaks, who makes no literary parade, has no pretensions of any sort. He is the only writer we have had who has wholly subdued his vehicle to his temperament. It is impossible to name his style without naming his character: they are one thing.

Both in language and in elocution Emerson was a practiced and consummate artist, who knew how both to command his effects and to conceal his means. The casual, practical, disarming directness with which he writes puts any honest man at his mercy. What difference does it make whether a man who can talk like this is following an argument or not? You cannot always see Emerson clearly; he is hidden by a high wall; but you always know exactly on what spot he is standing. You judge it by the flight of the objects he throws over the wall—a bootjack, an apple, a crown, a razor, a volume of verse. With one or other of these missiles, all delivered with a very tolerable aim, he is pretty sure to hit you. These catchwords stick in the mind. People are not in general influenced by long books or discourses, but by odd fragments of observation which they overhear, sentences or headlines which they read while turning over a book at random or while waiting for dinner to be announced. These are the oracles and orphic words that get lodged in the mind and bend a man's most stubborn will. Emerson called them the Police of the Universe. His works are a treasury of such things. They sparkle in the mine, or you may carry them off in your pocket. They get driven into your mind like nails, and on them catch and hang your own experiences, till what was once his thought has become your character.

"God offers to every mind its choice between truth and repose. Take which you please; you can never have both."

"Discontent is want of self-reliance; it is infirmity of will."
"It is impossible for a man to be cheated by anyone but
himself."

The orchestration with which Emerson introduces and
sustains these notes from the spheres is as remarkable as
the winged things themselves. Open his works at a hazard.
You hear a man talking.

A garden is like those pernicious machineries we read of
every month in the newspapers, which catch a man's coat-skirt
or his hand, and draw in his arm, his leg, and his whole body
to irresistible destruction. In an evil hour he pulled down his
wall and added a field to his homestead. No land is bad, but
land is worse. If a man own land, the land owns him. Now
let him leave home if he dare. Every tree and graft, every hill
of melons, row of corn, or quickset hedge, all he has done and
all he means to do, stand in his way like duns, when he would
go out of his gate.

Your attention is arrested by the reality of this gentleman
in his garden, by the firsthand quality of his mind. It matters not on what subject he talks. While you are musing,
still pleased and patronizing, he has picked up the bow of
Ulysses, bent it with the ease of Ulysses, and sent a shaft
clear through the twelve axes, nor missed one of them. But
this, it seems, was mere byplay and marksmanship; for
before you have done wondering, Ulysses rises to his feet
in anger, and pours flight after flight, arrow after arrow,
from the great bow. The shafts sing and strike, the suitors
fall in heaps. The brow of Ulysses shines with unearthly
splendor. The air is filled with lightning. After a little, without shock or transition, without apparent change of tone,
Mr. Emerson is offering you a biscuit before you leave, and
bidding you mind the last step at the garden end. If the
man who can do these things be not an artist, then must we
have a new vocabulary and rename the professions.

There is, in all this effectiveness of Emerson, no pose, no
literary art; nothing that corresponds even remotely to the
pretended modesty and ignorance with which Socrates lays
pitfalls for our admiration in Plato's dialogues.

It was the platform which determined Emerson's style.

He was not a writer, but a speaker. On the platform his manner of speech was a living part of his words. The pauses and hesitation, the abstraction, the searching, the balancing, the turning forward and back of the leaves of his lecture, and then the discovery, the illumination, the gleam of lightning which you saw before your eyes descend into a man of genius,—all this was Emerson. He invented this style of speaking, and made it express the supersensuous, the incommunicable. Lowell wrote, while still under the spell of the magician:

> Emerson's oration was more disjointed than usual, even with him. It began nowhere, and ended everywhere, and yet, as always with that divine man, it left you feeling that something beautiful had passed that way, something more beautiful than anything else, like the rising and setting of stars. Every possible criticism might have been made on it but one—that it was not noble. There was a tone in it that awakened all elevating associations. He boggled, he lost his place, he had to put on his glasses; but it was as if a creature from some fairer world had lost his way in our fogs, and it was *our* fault, not his. It was chaotic, but it was all such stuff as stars are made of, and you couldn't help feeling that, if you waited awhile, all that was nebulous would be whirled into planets, and would assume the mathematical gravity of system. All through it I felt something in me that cried, "Ha! ha!" to the sound of the trumpets.

It is nothing for any man sitting in his chair to be overcome with the sense of the immediacy of life, to feel the spur of courage, the victory of good over evil, the value, now and forever, of all great-hearted endeavor. Such moments come to us all. But for a man to sit in his chair and write what shall call up these forces in the bosoms of others—that is desert, that is greatness. To do this was the gift of Emerson. The whole earth is enriched by every moment of converse with him. The shows and shams of life become transparent, the lost kingdoms are brought back, the shutters of the spirit are opened, and provinces and realms of our own existence lie gleaming before us.

It has been necessary to reduce the living soul of Emerson to mere dead attributes like "moral courage" in order that we might talk about him at all. His effectiveness comes from his character; not from his philosophy, nor from his rhetoric nor his wit, nor from any of the accidents of his education. He might never have heard of Berkeley or Plato. A slightly different education might have led him to throw his teaching into the form of historical essays or of stump speeches. He might, perhaps, have been bred a stone-mason, and have done his work in the world by traveling with a panorama. But he would always have been Emerson. His weight and his power would always have been the same. It is solely as character that he is important. He discovered nothing; he bears no relation whatever to the history of philosophy. We must regard him and deal with him simply as a man.

Strangely enough, the world has always insisted upon accepting him as a thinker: and hence a great coil of misunderstanding. As a thinker, Emerson is difficult to classify. Before you begin to assign him a place, you must clear the ground by a disquisition as to what is meant by "a thinker," and how Emerson differs from other thinkers. As a man, Emerson is as plain as Ben Franklin.

People have accused him of inconsistency; they say that he teaches one thing one day, and another the next day. But from the point of view of Emerson there is no such thing as inconsistency. Every man is each day a new man. Let him be today what he is today. It is immaterial and waste of time to consider what he once was or what he may be.

His picturesque speech delights in fact and anecdote and a public which is used to treatises and deduction cares always to be told the moral. It wants everything reduced to a generalization. All generalizations are partial truths, but we are used to them, and we ourselves mentally make the proper allowance. Emerson's method is, not to give a generalization and trust to our making the allowance, but to give two conflicting statements and leave the balance of truth to be struck in our own minds on the facts. There is no inconsistency in this. It is a vivid and very legitimate method of procedure. But he is much more than a theorist: he is a practitioner. He does not merely state a theory of agitation: he proceeds to agitate. "Do not," he says, "set the least value on what I do, or the least discredit on what I do not, as if I pretended to settle anything as false or true. I unsettle all things. No facts are to me sacred, none are profane. I simply experiment, an endless seeker with no past at my back." He was not engaged in teaching many things, but one thing,—Courage. Sometimes he inspires it by pointing to great characters,— Fox, Milton, Alcibiades; sometimes he inspires it by bidding us beware of imitating such men, and, in the ardor of his rhetoric, even seems to regard them as hindrances and dangers to our development. There is no inconsistency here. Emerson might logically have gone one step further and raised inconsistency into a jewel. For what is so useful, so educational, so inspiring, to a timid and conservative man, as to do something inconsistent and regrettable? It lends character to him at once. He breathes freer and is stronger for the experience.

Emerson is no cosmopolitan. He is a patriot. He is not like Goethe, whose sympathies did not run on national lines. Emerson has America in his mind's eye all the time. There is to be a new religion, and it is to come from America; a new and better type of man, and he is to be an American. He not only cared little or nothing for Europe, but he cared not much for the world at large. His thought was for the future of this country. You cannot get into any chamber in his mind which is below this chamber of patriotism. He loves the valor of Alexander and the grace of the Oxford athlete; but he loves them not for themselves. He has a use for them. They are grist to his mill and powder to his gun. His admiration of them he subordinates to his main purpose, —they are his blackboard and diagrams. His patriotism is the backbone of his significance. He came to his countrymen at a time when they lacked, not thoughts, but manliness. The needs of his own particular public are always before him.

It is odd that our people should have, not water on the brain, but a little gas there. A shrewd foreigner said of the Americans that "whatever they say has a little the air of a speech."

I shall not need to go into an enumeration of our national defects and vices which require this Order of Censors in the

State. . . . The timidity of our public opinion is our disease, or, shall I say, the publicness of opinion, the absence of private opinion.

Our measure of success is the moderation and low level of an individual's judgment. Dr. Channing's piety and wisdom had such weight in Boston that the popular idea of religion was whatever this eminent divine held.

Let us affront and reprimand the smooth mediocrity, the squalid contentment of the times.

The politicians he scores constantly.

"Who that sees the meanness of our politics but congratulates Washington that he is long already wrapped in his shroud and forever safe." The following is his description of the social world of his day: "If any man consider the present aspects of what is called by distinction *society*, he will see the need of these ethics. The sinew and heart of man seem to be drawn out, and we are become timorous, desponding whimperers."

It is the same wherever we open his books. He must spur on, feed up, bring forward the dormant character of his countrymen. When he goes to England, he sees in English life nothing except those elements which are deficient in American life. If you wish a catalogue of what America has not, read *English Traits*. Emerson's patriotism had the effect of expanding his philosophy. Today we know the value of physique, for science has taught it, but it was hardly discovered in his day, and his philosophy affords no basis for it. Emerson in this matter transcends his philosophy. When in England, he was fairly made drunk with the physical life he found there. He is like Casper Hauser gazing for the first time on green fields. *English Traits* is the ruddiest book he ever wrote. It is a hymn to force, honesty, and physical well-being, and ends with the dominant note of his belief: "By this general activity and by this sacredness of individuals, they [the English] have in seven hundred years evolved the principles of freedom. It is the land of patriots, martyrs, sages, and bards, and if the ocean out of which it emerged should wash it away, it will be remembered as an island famous for immortal laws, for the announcements of original right which make the stone tables of liberty."

He had found in England free speech, personal courage, and reverence for the individual.

No convulsion could shake Emerson or make his view unsteady even for an instant. What no one else saw, he saw, and he saw nothing else. Not a boy in the land welcomed the outbreak of the war so fiercely as did this shy village philosopher, then at the age of fifty-eight. He saw that war was the cure for cowardice, moral as well as physical. It was not the cause of the slave that moved him; it was not the cause of the Union for which he cared a farthing. It was something deeper than either of these things for which he had been battling all his life. It was the cause of character against convention. Whatever else the war might bring, it was sure to bring in character, to leave behind it a file of heroes; if not heroes, then villains, but in any case strong men. On the ninth of April 1861, three days before Fort Sumter was bombarded, he had spoken with equanimity of "the downfall of our character-destroying civilization. . . . We find that civilization crowed too soon, that our triumphs were treacheries; we had opened the wrong door and let the enemy into the castle."

"Ah," he said, when the firing began, "sometimes gunpowder smells good." Soon after the attack on Sumter he said in a public address, "We have been very homeless for some years past, say since 1850; but now we have a country again. . . . The war was an eye opener, and showed men of all parties and opinions the value of those primary forces that lie beneath all political action." And it was almost a personal pledge when he said at the Harvard Commemoration in 1865, "We shall not again disparage America, now that we have seen what men it will bear."

The place which Emerson forever occupies as a great critic is defined by the same sharp outlines that mark his work, in whatever light and from whatever side we approach it. A critic in the modern sense he was not, for his point of view is fixed, and he reviews the world like a searchlight placed on the top of a tall tower. He lived too early and at too great a distance from the forum of European thought to absorb the ideas of evolution and give place to them in his philosophy. Evolution does not graft well upon the Platonic Idealism, nor are physiology and the kindred sciences sympathetic. Nothing aroused Emerson's indignation more than the attempts of the medical faculty and of phrenologists to classify, and therefore limit individuals. "The grossest ignorance does not disgust me like this ignorant knowingness."

We miss in Emerson the underlying conception of growth, of development, so characteristic of the thought of our own day, and which, for instance, is found everywhere latent in Browning's poetry. Browning regards character as the result of experience and as an ever-changing growth. To Emerson, character is rather an entity complete and eternal from the beginning. He is probably the last great writer to look at life from a stationary standpoint. There is a certain lack of the historic sense in all he has written. The ethical assumption that all men are exactly alike permeates his work. In his mind, Socrates, Marco Polo, and General Jackson stand surrounded by the same atmosphere, or rather stand as mere naked characters surrounded by no atmosphere at all. He is probably the last great writer who will fling about classic anecdotes as if they were club gossip. In the discussion of morals, this assumption does little harm. The stories and proverbs which illustrate the thought of the moralist generally concern only those simple relations of life which are common to all ages. There is charm in this familiar dealing with antiquity. The classics are thus domesticated and made real to us. What matter if Æsop appear a little too much like an American citizen, so long as his points tell?

It is in Emerson's treatment of the fine arts that we begin to notice his want of historic sense. Art endeavors to express subtle and ever-changing feelings by means of conventions which are as protean as the forms of a cloud; and the man who in speaking on the plastic arts makes the assumption that all men are alike will reveal before he has uttered three sentences that he does not know what art is, that he has never experienced any form of sensation from it. Emerson lived in a time and clime where there was no plastic art, and he was obliged to arrive at his ideas about art by means of a highly complex process of reasoning. He dwelt constantly in a spiritual place which was the very focus of high moral fervor. This was his enthusiasm, this was his revelation, and from it he reasoned out the probable meaning of the fine arts. "This," thought Emerson, his eye rolling in a fine frenzy of moral feeling, "this must be what Apelles experienced, this fervor is the passion of Bramante. I understand the Parthenon." And so he projected his feelings about morality into the field of the plastic arts. He deals very freely and rather indiscriminately with the names of artists —Phidias, Raphael, Salvator Rosa—and he speaks always in such a way that it is impossible to connect what he says with any impression we have ever received from the works of those masters.

In fact, Emerson has never in his life felt the normal appeal of any painting, or any sculpture, or any architecture, or any music. These things, of which he does not know the meaning in real life, he yet uses, and uses constantly, as symbols to convey ethical truths. The result is that his books are full of blind places, like the notes which will not strike on a sick piano.

It is interesting to find that the one art of which Emerson did have a direct understanding, the art of poetry, gave him some insight into the relation of the artist to his vehicle. In his essay on Shakespeare there is a full recognition of the debt of Shakespeare to his times. This essay is filled with the historic sense. We ought not to accuse Emerson because he lacked appreciation of the fine arts, but rather admire the truly Goethean spirit in which he insisted upon the reality of arts of which he had no understanding. This is the same spirit which led him to insist on the value of the Eastern poets. Perhaps there exist a few scholars who can tell us how far Emerson understood or misunderstood Saadi and Firdusi and the Koran. But we need not be disturbed for his learning. It is enough that he makes us recognize that these men were men, too, and that their writings mean something not unknowable to us. The East added nothing to Emerson, but gave him a few trappings of speech. The whole of his mysticism is to be found in *Nature*, written before he knew the sages of the Orient, and it is not improbable that there is some real connection between his own mysticism and the mysticism of the Eastern poets.

Emerson's criticism on men and books is like the test of a great chemist who seeks one or two elements. He burns a bit of the stuff in his incandescent light, shows the lines of it in his spectrum, and there an end.

It was a thought of genius that led him to write *Representative Men*. The scheme of this book gave play to every illumination of his mind, and it pinned him down to the objective, to the field of vision under his microscope. The table of contents of *Representative Men* is the dial of his education. It is as follows: Uses of Great Men; Plato, or The Philosopher; Plato, New Readings; Swedenborg, or The Mystic; Montaigne, or The Skeptic; Shakespeare, or The Poet; Napoleon, or The Man of the World; Goethe, or The Writer. The predominance of the writers over all other types of men is not cited to show Emerson's interest in The Writer, for we know his interest centered in the practical man,—even his ideal scholar is a practical man,—but to show the sources of his illustration. Emerson's library was the old-fashioned gentleman's library. His mines of thought were the world's classics. This is one reason why he so quickly gained an international currency. His very subjects in *Representative Men* are of universal interest, and he is limited only by certain inevitable local conditions. *Representative Men* is thought by many persons to be his best book. It is certainly filled with the strokes of a master. There exists no more profound criticism than Emerson's analysis of Goethe and of Napoleon, by both of whom he was at once fascinated and repelled.

II

The attitude of Emerson's mind toward reformers results so logically from his philosophy that it is easily understood. He saw in them people who sought something as a panacea or as an end in itself. To speak strictly and not irreverently, he had his own panacea—the development of each individual; and he was impatient of any other. He did not believe in association. The very idea of it involved a surrender by the individual of some portion of his identity, and of course all the reformers worked through their associations. With their general aims he sympathized. "These reforms," he wrote, "are our contemporaries; they are ourselves, our own light and sight and conscience; they only name the relation which subsists between us and the vicious institutions which they go to rectify."

But with the methods of the reformers he had no sympathy: "He who aims at progress should aim at an infinite, not at a special benefit. The reforms whose fame now fills the land with temperance, anti-slavery, non-resistance, no-government, equal labor, fair and generous as each appears, are poor bitter things when prosecuted for themselves as an end." Again: "The young men who have been vexing society for these last years with regenerative methods seem to have made this mistake: they all exaggerated some special means, and all failed to see that the reform of reforms must be accomplished without means."

Emerson did not at first discriminate between the movement of the Abolitionists and the hundred and one other reform movements of the period; and in this lack of discrimination lies a point of extraordinary interest. The Abolitionists, as it afterwards turned out, had in fact got hold of the issue which was to control the fortunes of the republic for thirty years. The difference between them and the other reformers was this: that the Abolitionists were men set in motion by the primary and unreasoning passion of pity. Theory played small part in the movement. It grew by the excitement which exhibitions of cruelty will arouse in the minds of sensitive people.

It is not to be denied that the social conditions in Boston in 1831 foreboded an outbreak in some form. If the abolition excitement had not drafted off the rising forces, there might have been a Merry Mount, an epidemic of crime or insanity, or a mob of some sort. The abolition movement afforded the purest form of an indulgence in human feeling that was ever offered to men. It was intoxicating. It made the agitators perfectly happy. They sang at their work and bubbled over with exhilaration. They were the only people in the United States, at this time, who were enjoying an exalted, glorifying, practical activity.

But Emerson at first lacked the touchstone, whether of intellect or of heart, to see the difference between this particular movement and the other movements then in progress. Indeed, in so far as he sees any difference between the Abolitionists and the rest, it is that the Abolitionists were more objectionable and distasteful to him. "Those," he said, "who are urging with most ardor what are called the greatest benefits to mankind are narrow, conceited, self-pleasing men, and affect us as the insane do." And again: "By the side of these men [the idealists] the hot agitators have a certain cheap and ridiculous air; they even look smaller than others. Of the two, I own I like the speculators the best. They have some piety which looks with faith to a fair future unprofaned by rash and unequal attempts to realize it." He was drawn into the abolition cause by having the truth brought home to him that these people were fighting for the Moral Law. He was slow in seeing this, because in their methods they represented everything he most condemned. As soon, however, as he was convinced, he was ready to lecture for them and to give them the weight of his approval. In 1844 he was already practically an Abolitionist, and his feelings upon the matter deepened steadily in intensity ever after.

The most interesting page of Emerson's published journal is the following, written at some time previous to 1844; the exact date is not given. A like page, whether written or unwritten, may be read into the private annals of every man who lived before the war. Emerson has, with unconscious mastery, photographed the half-specter that stalked in the minds of all. He wrote:

I had occasion to say the other day to Elizabeth Hoar that I like best the strong and worthy persons, like her father, who support the social order without hesitation or misgiving. I like these; they never incommode us by exciting grief, pity, or perturbation of any sort. But the professed philanthropists, it is strange and horrible to say, are an altogether odious set of people, whom one would shun as the worst of bores and canters. But my conscience, my unhappy conscience respects that hapless class who see the faults and stains of our social order, and who pray and strive incessantly to right the wrong; this annoying class of men and women, though they commonly find the work altogether beyond their faculty, and their results are, for the present, distressing. They are partial, and apt to magnify their own. Yes, and the prostrate penitent, also—he is not comprehensive, he is not philosophical in those tears and groans. Yet I feel that under him and his partiality and exclusiveness is the earth and the sea and all that in them is, and the axis around which the universe revolves passes through his body where he stands.

It was the defection of Daniel Webster that completed the conversion of Emerson and turned him from an adherent into a propagandist of abolition. Not pity for the slave, but indignation at the violation of the Moral Law by Daniel Webster, was at the bottom of Emerson's anger. His abolitionism was secondary to his main mission, his main enthusiasm. It is for this reason that he stands on a plane of intellect where he might, under other circumstances, have met and defeated Webster. After the seventh of March 1850 he recognized in Webster the embodiment of all that he hated. In his attacks on Webster, Emerson trembles to his inmost fiber with antagonism. He is savage, destructive, personal, bent on death.

This exhibition of Emerson as a fighting animal is magnificent, and explains his life. There is no other instance of his ferocity. No other nature but Webster's ever so moved him; but it was time to be moved, and Webster was a man of his size. Had these two great men of New England been matched in training as they were matched in endowment, and had they then faced each other in debate, they would not have been found to differ so greatly in power. Their natures were electrically repellent, but from which did the greater force radiate? Their education differed so radically that it is impossible to compare them, but if you translate the Phi Beta Kappa address into politics, you have something stronger than Webster,—something that recalls Chatham; and Emerson would have had this advantage,—that he was not afraid. As it was, he left his library and took the stump. Mr. Cabot has given us extracts from his speeches:

The tameness is indeed complete; all are involved in one hot haste of terror,—presidents of colleges and professors, saints and brokers, lawyers and manufacturers; not a liberal recollection, not so much as a snatch of an old song for freedom, dares intrude on their passive obedience. . . . Mr. Webster, perhaps, is only following the laws of his blood and constitution. I suppose his pledges were not quite natural to him. He is a man who lives by his memory; a man of the past, not a man of faith and of hope. All the drops of his blood have eyes that look downward, and his finely developed understanding only works truly and with all its force when it stands for animal good; that is, for property. He looks at the Union as an estate, a large farm, and is excellent in the completeness of his defense of it so far. What he finds already written he will defend. Lucky that so much had got well written when he came, for he has no faith in the power of self-government. Not the smallest municipal provision, if it were new, would receive his sanction. In Massachusetts, in 1776, he would, beyond all question, have been a refugee. He praises Adams and Jefferson, but it is a past Adams and Jefferson. A present Adams or Jefferson he would denounce. . . . But one thing appears certain to me: that the Union is at an end as soon as an immoral law is enacted. He who writes a crime into the statute book digs under the foundations of the Capitol. . . . The words of John Randolph, wiser than he knew, have been ringing ominously in all echoes for thirty years. "We do not govern the people of the North by our black slaves, but by their own white slaves." . . . They come down now like the cry of fate, in the moment when they are fulfilled.

The exasperation of Emerson did not subside, but went on increasing during the next four years, and on March 7, 1854, he read his lecture on the Fugitive Slave Law at the New York Tabernacle:

I have lived all my life without suffering any inconvenience from American Slavery. I never saw it; I never heard the whip; I never felt the check on my free speech and action, until the other day, when Mr. Webster, by his personal influence, brought the Fugitive Slave Law on the country. I say Mr. Webster, for though the bill was not his, it is yet notorious that he was the life and soul of it, that he gave it all he had. It cost him his life, and under the shadow of his great name inferior men sheltered themselves, threw their ballots for it, and made the law. . . . Nobody doubts that Daniel Webster could make a good speech. Nobody doubts that there were good and plausible things to be said on the part of the South. But this is not a question of ingenuity, not a question of syllogisms, but of sides. *How came he there?* . . . But the question which history will ask is broader. In the final hour when he was forced by the peremptory necessity of the closing armies to take a side,—did he take the part of great principles, the side of humanity and justice, or the side of abuse, and oppression and chaos? . . . He did as immoral men usually do,—made very low bows to the Christian Church and went through all the Sunday decorums, but when allusion was made to the question of duty and the sanctions of morality, he very frankly said, at Albany, "Some higher law, something existing somewhere between here and the heaven—I do not know where." And if the reporters say true, this wretched atheism found some laughter in the company.

It was too late for Emerson to shine as a political debater. On May 14, 1857, Longfellow wrote in his diary: "It is rather painful to see Emerson in the arena of politics, hissed and hooted at by young law students." Emerson records a similar experience at a later date: "If I were dumb, yet would I have gone and mowed and muttered or made signs. The mob roared whenever I attempted to speak, and after several beginnings I withdrew." There is nothing "painful" here: it is the sublime exhibition of a great soul in bondage to circumstance.

The thing to be noted is that this is the same man, in the same state of excitement about the same idea, who years before spoke out in *The American Scholar,* in the *Essays,* and in the *Lectures.*

What was it that had aroused in Emerson such Promethean antagonism in 1837 but those same forces which in 1850 came to their culmination and assumed visible shape in the person of Daniel Webster? The formal victory of Webster drew Emerson into the arena, and made a dramatic episode in his life. But his battle with those forces had begun thirteen years earlier, when he threw down the gauntlet to them in his Phi Beta Kappa oration. Emerson by his writings did more than any other man to rescue the youth of the next generation and fit them for the fierce times to follow. It will not be denied that he sent ten thousand sons to the war.

In speaking of Emerson's attitude toward the anti-slavery cause, it has been possible to dispense with any survey of that movement, because the movement was simple and specific and is well remembered. But when we come to analyze the relations he bore to some of the local agitations of his day, it becomes necessary to weave in with the matter a discussion of certain tendencies deeply imbedded in the life of his times, and of which he himself was in a sense an outcome. In speaking of the Transcendentalists, who were essentially the children of the Puritans, we must begin with some study of the chief traits of Puritanism.

What parts the factors of climate, circumstance, and religion have respectively played in the development of the New England character no analysis can determine. We may trace the imaginary influence of a harsh creed in the lines of the face. We may sometimes follow from generation to generation the course of a truth which at first sustained the spirit of man, till we see it petrify into a dogma which now kills the spirits of men. Conscience may destroy the character. The tragedy of the New England judge enforcing the Fugitive Slave Law was no new spectacle in New England. A dogmatic crucifixion of the natural instincts had been in progress there for two hundred years. Emerson, who is more free from dogma than any other teacher that can be named, yet comes very near being dogmatic in his reiteration of the Moral Law.

Whatever volume of Emerson we take up, the Moral Law holds the same place in his thoughts. It is the one statable revelation of truth which he is ready to stake his all upon. "The illusion that strikes me as the masterpiece in that ring of illusions which our life is, is the timidity with which we assert our moral sentiment. We are made of it, the world is built by it, things endure as they share it; all beauty, all health, all intelligence exist by it; yet we shrink to speak of it or range ourselves by its side. Nay, we presume strength of him or them who deny it. Cities go against it, the college goes against it, the courts snatch any precedent at any vicious form of law to rule it out; legislatures listen with appetite to declamations against it and vote it down."

With this very beautiful and striking passage no one will quarrel, nor will anyone misunderstand it.

The following passage has the same sort of poetical truth: "Things are saturated with the moral law. There is no escape from it. Violets and grass preach it; rain and snow, wind and tides, every change, every cause in Nature is nothing but a disguised missionary. . . ."

But Emerson is not satisfied with metaphor. "We affirm that in all men is this majestic perception and command; that it is the presence of the eternal in each perishing man; that it distances and degrades all statements of whatever saints, heroes, poets, as obscure and confused stammerings before its silent revelation. *They* report the truth. *It* is the truth." In this last extract we have Emerson actually affirming that his dogma of the Moral Law is Absolute Truth. He thinks it not merely a form of truth, like the old theologies, but very distinguishable from all other forms in the past.

Curiously enough, his statement of the law grows dogmatic and incisive in proportion as he approaches the borderland between his law and the natural instincts: "The last revelation of intellect and of sentiment is that in a manner it severs the man from all other men; makes known to him *that the spiritual powers are sufficient to him if no other being existed;* that he is to deal absolutely in the world, as if he alone were a system and a state, and though all should perish could make all anew." Here we have the dogma applied, and we see in it only a new form of old Calvinism as cruel as Calvinism, and not much different from its original. The italics are not Emerson's, but are inserted to bring out an idea which is everywhere prevalent in his teaching.

In this final form, the Moral Law, by insisting that sheer conscience can slake the thirst that rises in the soul, is convicted of falsehood; and this heartless falsehood is the same falsehood that has been put into the porridge of every Puritan child for six generations. A grown man can digest doctrine and sleep at night. But a young person of high purpose and strong will, who takes such a lie as this half-truth and feeds on it as on the bread of life, will suffer. It will injure the action of his heart. Truly the fathers have eaten sour grapes, therefore the children's teeth are set on edge.

To understand the civilization of cities, we must look at the rural population from which they draw their life. We have recently had our attention called to the last remnants of that village life so reverently gathered up by Miss Wilkins, and of which Miss Emily Dickinson was the last authentic voice. The spirit of this age has examined with an almost pathological interest this rescued society. We must go to it if we would understand Emerson, who is the blossoming of its culture. We must study it if we would arrive at any intelligent and general view of that miscellaneous crop of individuals who have been called the Transcendentalists.

Between 1830 and 1840 there were already signs in New England that the nutritive and reproductive forces of society were not quite wholesome, not exactly well adjusted. Self-repression was the religion which had been inherited. "Distrust Nature" was the motto written upon the front of the temple. What would have happened to that society if left to itself for another hundred years no man can guess. It was rescued by the two great regenerators of mankind, new land and war. The dispersion came, as Emerson said of the barbarian conquests of Rome, not a day too soon. It happened that the country at large stood in need of New England as much as New England stood in need of the country. This congested virtue, in order to be saved, must be scattered. This ferment, in order to be kept wholesome, must be used as leaven to leaven the whole lump. "As you know," says Emerson in his Eulogy on Boston, "New England supplies annually a large detachment of preachers and schoolmasters and private tutors to the interior of the South and West. . . . We are willing to see our sons emigrate, as to see our hives swarm. That is what they were made to do, and what the land wants and invites."

For purposes of yeast, there was never such leaven as the Puritan stock. How little the natural force of the race had really abated became apparent when it was placed under healthy conditions, given land to till, foes to fight, the chance to renew its youth like the eagle. But during this period the relief had not yet come. The terrible pressure of Puritanism and conservatism in New England was causing a revolt not only of the Abolitionists, but of another class of people of a type not so virile as they. The times have been smartly described by Lowell in his essay on Thoreau:

Every possible form of intellectual and physical dyspepsia brought forth its gospel. Bran had its prophets. . . . Everybody had a Mission (with a capital M) to attend to everybody else's business. No brain but had its private maggot, which must have found pitiably short commons sometimes. Not a few impecunious zealots abjured the use of money (unless earned by other people), professing to live on the internal revenues of the spirit. Some had an assurance of instant millennium so soon as hooks and eyes should be substituted for buttons. Communities were established where everything was to be common but common sense. . . . Conventions were held for every hitherto inconceivable purpose.

Whatever may be said of the Transcendentalists, it must not be forgotten that they represented an elevation of feeling, which through them qualified the next generation, and can be traced in the life of New England today. The strong intrinsic character lodged in these recusants was later made manifest; for many of them became the best citizens of the commonwealth,—statesmen, merchants, soldiers, men and women of affairs. They retained their idealism while becoming practical men. There is hardly an example of what we should have thought would be common in their later lives, namely, a reaction from so much ideal effort, and a plunge into cynicism and malice, scoundrelism, and the flesh-pots. In their early life they resembled the Abolitionists in their devotion to an idea; but with the Transcendentalists self-culture and the aesthetic and sentimental education took the place of more public aims. They seem also to have been persons of greater social refinement than the Abolitionists.

The Transcendentalists were sure of only one thing,—that society as constituted was all wrong. In this their main belief they were right. They were men and women whose fundamental need was activity, contact with real life, and the opportunity for social expansion; and they keenly felt the chill and fictitious character of the reigning conventionalities. The rigidity of behavior which at this time characterized the Bostonians seemed sometimes ludicrous and sometimes disagreeable to the foreign visitor. There was great gravity, together with a certain pomp and dumbness, and these things were supposed to be natural to the inhabitants and to give them joy. People are apt to forget that such masks are never worn with ease. They result from the application of an inflexible will, and always inflict discomfort. The Transcendentalists found themselves all but stifled in a society as artificial in its decorum as the court of France during the last years of Louis XIV.

Emerson was in no way responsible for the movement, although he got the credit of having evoked it by his teaching. He was elder brother to it, and was generated by its parental forces; but even if Emerson had never lived, the Transcendentalists would have appeared. He was their victim rather than their cause. He was always tolerant of them and sometimes amused at them, and disposed to treat them lightly. It is impossible to analyze their case with more astuteness than he did in an editorial letter in *The Dial*. The letter is cold, but is a masterpiece of good sense. He had, he says, received fifteen letters on the Prospects of Culture.

"Excellent reasons have been shown us why the writers, obviously persons of sincerity and elegance, should be dissatisfied with the life they lead, and with their company. . . . They want a friend to whom they can speak and from whom they may hear now and then a reasonable word." After discussing one or two of their proposals,—one of which was that the tiresome "uncles and aunts" of the enthusiasts should be placed by themselves in one delightful village, the dough, as Emerson says, be placed in one pan and the leaven in another,—he continues: "But it would be unjust not to remind our younger friends that whilst this aspiration has always made its mark in the lives of men of thought, in vigorous individuals it does not remain a detached object, but is satisfied along with the satisfaction of other aims." Young Americans "are educated above the work of their times and country, and disdain it. Many of the more acute minds pass into a lofty criticism . . . which only embitters their sensibility to the evil, and widens the feeling of hostility between them and the citizens at large. . . . We should not know where to find in literature any record of so much unbalanced intellectuality, such undeniable apprehension without talent, so much power without equal applicability, as our young men pretend to. . . . The balance of mind and body will redress itself fast enough. Superficialness is the real distemper. . . . It is certain that speculation is no succedaneum for life." He then turns to find the cure for these distempers in the farm lands of Illinois, at that time already being fenced in "almost like New England itself," and closes with a suggestion that so long as there is a woodpile in the yard, and the "wrongs of the Indian, of the Negro, of the emigrant, remain unmitigated," relief might be found even nearer home.

In his lecture on the Transcendentalists he says: ". . . But their solitary and fastidious manners not only withdraw them from the conversation, but from the labors of the world: they are not good citizens, not good members of society; unwillingly they bear their part of the public and private burdens; they do not willingly share in the public charities, in the public religious rites, in the enterprises of education, of missions foreign and domestic, in the abolition of the slave-trade, or in the temperance society. They do not even like to vote."

A less sympathetic observer, Harriet Martineau, wrote of

them: "While Margaret Fuller and her adult pupils sat 'gorgeously dressed,' talking about Mars and Venus, Plato and Goethe, and fancying themselves the elect of the earth in intellect and refinement, the liberties of the republic were running out as fast as they could go at a breach which another sort of elect persons were devoting themselves to repair; and my complaint against the 'gorgeous' pedants was that they regarded their preservers as hewers of wood and drawers of water, and their work as a less vital one than the pedantic orations which were spoiling a set of well-meaning women in a pitiable way." Harriet Martineau, whose whole work was practical, and who wrote her journal in 1855 and in the light of history, was hardly able to do justice to these unpractical but sincere spirits.

Emerson was divided from the Transcendentalists by his common sense. His shrewd business intellect made short work of their schemes. Each one of their social projects contained some covert economic weakness, which always turned out to lie in an attack upon the integrity of the individual, and which Emerson of all men could be counted on to detect. He was divided from them also by the fact that he was a man of genius, who had sought out and fought out his means of expression. He was a great artist, and as such he was a complete being. No one could give to him nor take from him. His yearnings found fruition in expression. He was sure of his place and of his use in this world. But the Transcendentalists were neither geniuses nor artists nor complete beings. Nor had they found their places or uses as yet. They were men and women seeking light. They walked in dry places, seeking rest and finding none. The Transcendentalists are not collectively important because their *Sturm und Drang* was intellectual and bloodless. Though Emerson admonish and Harriet Martineau condemn, yet from the memorials that survive, one is more impressed with the sufferings than with the ludicrousness of these persons. There is something distressing about their letters, their talk, their memoirs, their interminable diaries. They worry and contort and introspect. They rave and dream. They peep and theorize. They cut open the bellows of life to see where the wind comes from. Margaret Fuller analyzes Emerson, and Emerson Margaret Fuller. It is not a wholesome ebullition of vitality. It is a nightmare, in which the emotions, the terror, the agony, the rapture, are all un-real, and have no vital content, no consequence in the world outside. It is positively wonderful that so much excitement and so much suffering should have left behind nothing in the field of art which is valuable. All that intelligence could do toward solving problems for his friends Emerson did. But there are situations in life in which the intelligence is help-less, and in which something else, something perhaps pos-sessed by a plowboy, is more divine than Plato.

If it were not pathetic, there would be something cruel—indeed there is something cruel—in Emerson's incapacity to deal with Margaret Fuller. He wrote to her on October 24, 1840:

My dear Margaret, I have your frank and noble and affecting letter, and yet I think I could wish it unwritten. I ought never to have suffered you to lead me into any conversation or writing on our relation, a topic from which with all persons my Genius warns me away.

The letter proceeds with unimpeachable emptiness and integrity in the same strain. In 1841 he writes in his diary:

Strange, cold-warm, attractive-repelling conversation with Margaret, whom I always admire, most revere when I nearest see, and sometimes love; yet whom I freeze and who freezes me to silence when we promise to come nearest.

Human sentiment was known to Emerson mainly in the form of pain. His nature shunned it; he cast it off as quickly as possible. There is a word or two in the essay on *Love* which seems to show that the inner and diaphanous core of this seraph had once, but not for long, been shot with blood: he recalls only the pain of it. His relations with Mar-garet Fuller seem never normal, though they lasted for years. This brilliant woman was in distress. She was asking for bread, and he was giving her a stone, and neither of them was conscious of what was passing. This is pitiful. It makes us clutch about us to catch hold, if we somehow may, of the hand of a man.

There was manliness in Horace Greeley, under whom Miss Fuller worked on the New York *Tribune* not many years afterward. She wrote:

Mr. Greeley I like—nay, more, love. He is in his habit a plebeian, in his heart a nobleman. His abilities in his own way are great. He believes in mine to a surprising degree. We are true friends.

This anaemic incompleteness of Emerson's character can be traced to the philosophy of his race; at least it can be followed in that philosophy. There is an implication of a fundamental falsehood in every bit of Transcendentalism, including Emerson. That falsehood consists in the theory of the self-sufficiency of each individual, men and women alike. Margaret Fuller is a good example of the effect of this philosophy, because her history afterward showed that she was constituted like other human beings, was dependent upon human relationship, and was not only a very noble, but also a very womanly creature. Her marriage, her Italian life, and her tragic death light up with the splendor of reality the earlier and unhappy period of her life. This woman had been driven into her vagaries by the lack of something which she did not know existed, and which she sought blindly in metaphysics. Harriet Martineau writes of her:

It is the most grievous loss I have almost ever known in private history, the deferring of Margaret Fuller's married life so long. That noble last period of her life is happily on record as well as the earlier.

The hardy Englishwoman has here laid a kind human hand on the weakness of New England, and seems to be unconscious that she is making a revelation as to the whole Transcendental movement. But the point is this: there was no one within reach of Margaret Fuller, in her early days, who knew what was her need. One offered her Kant, one Comte, one Fourier, one Swedenborg, one the Moral Law. You cannot feed the heart on these things.

Yet there is a bright side to this New England spirit, which seems, if we look only to the graver emotions, so dry, dismal, and deficient. A bright and cheery courage appears in certain natures of which the sun has made conquest, that almost reconciles us to all loss, so splendid is the outcome. The practical, dominant, insuppressible active temperaments who have a word for every emergency, and who carry the controlled force of ten men at their disposal, are the fruits of this same spirit. Emerson knew not tears, but he and the hundred other beaming and competent characters which New England has produced make us almost envy their state. They give us again the old Stoics at their best.

Very closely connected with this subject—the crisp and cheery New England temperament—lies another which any discussion of Emerson must bring up—namely, Asceticism. It is probable that in dealing with Emerson's feelings about the plastic arts we have to do with what is really the inside, or metaphysical side, of the same phenomena which present themselves on the outside, or physical side, in the shape of asceticism.

Emerson's natural asceticism is revealed to us in almost every form in which history can record a man. It is in his philosophy, in his style, in his conduct, and in his appearance. It was, however, not in his voice. Mr. Cabot, with that reverence for which everyone must feel personally grateful to him, has preserved a description of Emerson by the New York journalist, N. P. Willis:

It is a voice with shoulders in it, which he has not; with lungs in it far larger than his; with a walk which the public never see; with a fist in it which his own hand never gave him the model for; and with a gentleman in it which his parochial and "bare-necessaries-of-life" sort of exterior gives no other betrayal of. We can imagine nothing in nature (which seems too to have a type for everything) like the want of correspondence between the Emerson that goes in at the eye and the Emerson that goes in at the ear. A heavy and vaselike blossom of a magnolia, with fragrance enough to perfume a whole wilderness, which should be lifted by a whirlwind and dropped into a branch of aspen, would not seem more as if it could never have grown there than Emerson's voice seems inspired and foreign to his visible and natural body.

Emerson's ever-exquisite and wonderful good taste seems closely connected with this asceticism, and it is probable that his taste influenced his views and conduct to some small extent.

The anti-slavery people were not always refined. They were constantly doing things which were tactically very effective, but were not calculated to attract the oversensitive. Garrison's rampant and impersonal egotism was good politics, but bad taste. Wendell Phillips did not hesitate upon occasion to deal in personalities of an exasperating kind. One sees a certain shrinking in Emerson from the taste of the Abolitionists. It was not merely their doctrines or their methods which offended him. He at one time refused to give Wendell Phillips his hand because of Phillips' treatment of his friend, Judge Hoar. One hardly knows whether to be pleased at Emerson for showing a human weakness, or annoyed at him for not being more of a man. The anecdote is valuable in both lights. It is like a tiny speck on the crystal of his character which shows us the exact location of the orb, and it is the best illustration of the feeling of the times which has come down to us.

If by "asceticism" we mean an experiment in starving the senses, there is little harm in it. Nature will soon reassert her dominion, and very likely our perceptions will be sharpened by the trial. But "natural asceticism" is a thing hardly to be distinguished from functional weakness. What is natural asceticism but a lack of vigor? Does it not tend to close the avenues between the soul and the universe? "Is it not so much death?" The accounts of Emerson show him to have been a man in whom there was almost a hiatus between the senses and the most inward spirit of life. The lower register of sensations and emotions which domesticate a man into fellowship with common life was weak. Genial familiarity was to him impossible; laughter was almost a pain. "It is not the sea and poverty and pursuit that separate us. Here is Alcott by my door,—yet is the union more profound? No! the

sea, vocation, poverty, are seeming fences, but man is insular
and cannot be touched. Every man is an infinitely repellent
orb, and holds his individual being on that condition. . . .
Most of the persons whom I see in my own house I see
across a gulf; I cannot go to them nor they come to me."

This aloofness of Emerson must be remembered only as
blended with his benignity. "His friends were all that knew
him," and, as Dr. Holmes said, "his smile was the well-
remembered line of Terence written out in living features."
Emerson's journals show the difficulty of his intercourse even
with himself. He could not reach himself at will, nor could
another reach him. The sensuous and ready contact with
nature which more carnal people enjoy was unknown to
him. He had eyes for the New England landscape, but for
no other scenery. If there is one supreme sensation reserved
for man, it is the vision of Venice seen from the water. This
sight greeted Emerson at the age of thirty. The famous city,
as he approached it by boat, "looked for some time like nothing but New York. It is a great oddity, a city for beavers,
but to my thought a most disagreeable residence. You feel
always in prison and solitary. It is as if you were always at
sea. I soon had enough of it."

Emerson's contempt for travel and for the "rococo toy,"
Italy, is too well known to need citation. It proceeds from
the same deficiency of sensation. His eyes saw nothing; his
ears heard nothing. He believed that men traveled for distraction and to kill time. The most vulgar plutocrat could
not be blinder to beauty nor bring home less from Athens
than this cultivated saint. Everything in the world which
must be felt with a glow in the breast, in order to be understood, was to him dead-letter. Art was a name to him; music
was a name to him; love was a name to him. His essay on
Love is a nice compilation of compliments and elegant
phrases ending up with some icy morality. It seems very well
fitted for a gift-book or an old-fashioned lady's annual.

The lovers delight in endearments, in avowals of love, in
comparisons of their regards. . . . The soul which is in the
soul of each, craving a perfect beatitude, detects incongruities,
defects, and disproportion in the behavior of the other. Hence

arise surprise, expostulation, and pain. Yet that which drew them to each other was signs of loveliness, signs of virtue; and these virtues are there, however eclipsed. They appear and reappear and continue to attract; but the regard changes, quits the sign, and attaches to the substance. This repairs the wounded affection. Meantime, as life wears on, it proves a game of permutation and combination of all possible positions of the parties, to employ all the resources of each, and acquaint each with the weakness of the other. . . . At last they discover that all which at first drew them together—those once sacred features, that magical play of charms—was deciduous, had a prospective end like the scaffolding by which the house was built, and the purification of the intellect and the heart from year to year is the real marriage, foreseen and prepared from the first, and wholly above their consciousness. . . . Thus are we put in training for a love which knows not sex nor person nor partiality, but which seeks wisdom and virtue everywhere, to the end of increasing virtue and wisdom. . . . There are moments when the affections rule and absorb the man, and make his happiness dependent on a person or persons. But in health the mind is presently seen again, *etc.*

All this is not love, but the merest literary coquetry. Love is different from this. Lady Burton, when a very young girl, and six years before her engagement, met Burton at Boulogne. They met in the street, but did not speak. A few days later they were formally introduced at a dance. Of this she writes: "That was a night of nights. He waltzed with me once, and spoke to me several times. I kept the sash where he put his arm around me and my gloves, and never wore them again."

A glance at what Emerson says about marriage shows that he suspected that institution. He can hardly speak of it without some sort of caveat or precaution. "Though the stuff of tragedy and of romances is in a moral union of two superior persons whose confidence in each other for long years, out of sight and in sight, and against all appearances, is at last justified by victorious proof of probity to gods and men, causing joyful emotions, tears, and glory—though there be for heroes this *moral union,* yet they too are as far as ever from an intellectual union, and the moral is for low and external purposes, like the corporation of a ship's company or of a fire club." In speaking of modern novels, he says: "There is no new element, no power, no furtherance. 'Tis only confectionery, not the raising of new corn. Great is the poverty of their inventions. *She was beautiful, and he fell in love.* . . . Happy will that house be in which the relations are formed by character; after the highest and not after the lowest; the house in which character marries and not confusion and a miscellany of unavowable motives. . . . To each occurs soon after puberty, some event, or society or way of living, which becomes the crisis of life and the chief fact in their history. In women it is love and marriage (which is more reasonable), and yet it is pitiful to date and measure all the facts and sequel of an unfolding life from such a youthful and generally inconsiderate period as the age of courtship and marriage. . . . Women more than all are the element and kingdom of illusion. Being fascinated they fascinate. They see through Claude Lorraines. And how dare anyone, if he could, pluck away the coulisses, stage effects, and ceremonies by which they live? Too pathetic, too pitiable, is the region of affection, and its atmosphere always liable to mirage."

We are all so concerned that a man who writes about love shall tell the truth that if he chance to start from premises which are false or mistaken, his conclusions will appear not merely false, but offensive. It makes no matter how exalted the personal character of the writer may be. Neither sanctity nor intellect nor moral enthusiasm, though they be intensified to the point of incandescence, can make up for a want of nature.

This perpetual splitting up of love into two species, one of which is condemned, but admitted to be useful—is it not degrading? There is in Emerson's theory of the relation between the sexes neither good sense, nor manly feeling, nor sound psychology. It is founded on none of these things. It is a pure piece of dogmatism, and reminds us that he was bred to the priesthood. We are not to imagine that there was in this doctrine anything peculiar to Emerson. But we are surprised to find the pessimism inherent in the doctrine over come Emerson, to whom pessimism is foreign. Both doctrine and pessimism are a part of the Puritanism of the times. They show a society in which the intellect had long been used to analyze the affections, in which the head had become dislocated from the body. To this disintegration of the simple passion of love may be traced the lack of maternal tenderness characteristic of the New England nature. The relation between the blood and the brain was not quite normal in this civilization, nor in Emerson, who is its most remarkable representative.

If we take two steps backward from the canvas of this mortal life and glance at it impartially, we shall see that these matters of love and marriage pass like a pivot through the lives of almost every individual, and are, sociologically speaking, the *primum mobile* of the world. The books of any philosopher who slurs them or distorts them will hold up a false mirror to life. If an inhabitant of another planet should visit the earth, he would receive, on the whole, a truer notion of human life by attending an Italian opera than he would by reading Emerson's volumes. He would learn from the Italian opera that there were two sexes; and this, after all, is probably the fact with which the education of such a stranger ought to begin.

In a review of Emerson's personal character and opinions, we are thus led to see that his philosophy, which finds no room for the emotions, is a faithful exponent of his own and of the New England temperament, which distrusts and dreads the emotions. Regarded as a sole guide to life for a young person of strong conscience and undeveloped affections, his works might conceivably be even harmful because of their unexampled power of purely intellectual stimulation.

Emerson's poetry has given rise to much heart-burning and disagreement. Some people do not like it. They fail to find the fire in the ice. On the other hand, his poems appeal not only to a large number of professed lovers of poetry, but also to a class of readers who find in Emerson an element for which they search the rest of poesy in vain.

It is the irony of fate that his admirers should be more

than usually sensitive about his fame. This prophet who desired not to have followers, lest he too should become a cult and a convention, and whose main thesis throughout life was that piety is a crime, has been calmly canonized and embalmed in amber by the very forces he braved. He is become a tradition and a sacred relic. You must speak of him under your breath, and you may not laugh near his shrine.

Emerson's passion for nature was not like the passion of Keats or of Burns, of Coleridge or of Robert Browning; compared with these men he is cold. His temperature is below blood-heat, and his volume of poems stands on the shelf of English poets like the icy fish which in *Caliban upon Setebos* is described as finding himself thrust into the warm ooze of an ocean not his own.

But Emerson is a poet, nevertheless, a very extraordinary and rare man of genius, whose verses carry a world of their own within them. They are overshadowed by the greatness of his prose, but they are authentic. He is the chief poet of that school of which Emily Dickinson is a minor poet. His poetry is a successful spiritual deliverance of great interest. His worship of the New England landscape amounts to a religion. His poems do that most wonderful thing, make us feel that we are alone in the fields and with the trees,—not English fields nor French lanes, but New England meadows and uplands. There is no human creature in sight, not even Emerson is there, but the wind and the flowers, the wild birds, the fences, the transparent atmosphere, the breath of nature. There is a deep and true relation between the intellectual and almost dry brilliancy of Emerson's feelings and the landscape itself. Here is no defective English poet, no Shelley without the charm, but an American poet, a New England poet with two hundred years of New England culture and New England landscape in him.

People are forever speculating upon what will last, what posterity will approve, and some people believe that Emerson's poetry will outlive his prose. The question is idle. The poems are alive now, and they may or may not survive the race whose spirit they embody; but one thing is plain: they have qualities which have preserved poetry in the past. They are utterly indigenous and sincere. They are short. They represent a civilization and a climate.

His verse divides itself into several classes. We have the single lyrics, written somewhat in the style of the later seventeenth century. Of these *The Humble Bee* is the most exquisite, and although its tone and imagery can be traced to various well-known and dainty bits of poetry, it is by no means an imitation, but a masterpiece of fine taste. *The Rhodora* and *Terminus* and perhaps a few others belong to that class of poetry which, like *Abou Ben Adhem*, is poetry because it is the perfection of statement. The *Boston Hymn*, the *Concord Ode*, and the other occasional pieces fall in another class, and do not seem to be important. The first two lines of the *Ode*,

> O tenderly the haughty day
> Fills his blue urn with fire,

are for their extraordinary beauty worthy of some mythical Greek, some Simonides, some Sappho, but the rest of the lines are commonplace. Throughout his poems there are good bits, happy and golden lines, snatches of grace. He himself knew the quality of his poetry, and wrote of it,

> All were sifted through and through,
> Five lines lasted sound and true.

He is never merely conventional, and his poetry, like his prose, is homespun and sound. But his ear was defective: his rhymes are crude, and his verse is often lame and unmusical, a fault which can be countervailed by nothing but force, and force he lacks. To say that his ear was defective is hardly strong enough. Passages are not uncommon which hurt the reader and unfit him to proceed; as, for example:

> Thorough a thousand voices
> Spoke the universal dame:
> "Who telleth one of my meanings
> Is master of all I am."

He himself has very well described the impression his verse is apt to make on a new reader when he says,

> Poetry must not freeze, but flow.

The lovers of Emerson's poems freely acknowledge all these defects, but find in them another element, very subtle and rare, very refined and elusive, if not altogether unique. This is the mystical element or strain which qualifies many of his poems, and to which some of them are wholly devoted.

There has been so much discussion as to Emerson's relation to the mystics that it is well here to turn aside for a moment and consider the matter by itself. The elusiveness of "mysticism" arises out of the fact that it is not a creed, but a state of mind. It is formulated into no dogmas, but, in so far as it is communicable, it is conveyed, or sought to be conveyed, by symbols. These symbols to a skeptical or an unsympathetic person will say nothing, but the presumption among those who are inclined toward the cult is that if these symbols convey anything at all, that thing is mysticism. The mystics are right. The familiar phrases, terms, and symbols of mysticism are not meaningless, and a glance at them shows that they do tend to express and evoke a somewhat definite psychic condition.

There is a certain mood of mind experienced by most of us in which we feel the mystery of existence; in which our consciousness seems to become suddenly separated from our thoughts, and we find ourselves asking, "Who am I? What are these thoughts?" The mood is very apt to overtake us while engaged in the commonest acts. In health it is always momentary, and seems to coincide with the instant of the transition and shift of our attention from one thing to another. It is probably connected with the transfer of energy from one set of faculties to another set, which occurs, for instance, on our waking from sleep, on our hearing a bell at night, on our observing any common object, a chair or a pitcher, at a time when our mind is or has just been thoroughly preoccupied with something else. This displacement of the attention occurs in its most notable form when we walk from the study into the open fields. Nature then attacks us on all sides at once, overwhelms, drowns, and destroys our old thoughts, stimulates vaguely and all at once a thousand new ideas, dissipates all focus of thought, and dissolves our attention. If we happen to be mentally fatigued, and we take a walk in the country, a sense of immense relief, of rest and joy, which nothing else on earth can give, accompanies this distraction of the mind from its problems. The reaction fills us with a sense of mystery and expansion. It brings us to the threshold of those spiritual experiences which are the obscure core and reality of our existence, ever alive within us, but generally veiled and subconscious. It brings us, as it were, into the antechamber of art, poetry, and music. The condition is one of excitation and receptiveness, where art may speak and we shall understand. On the other hand, the condition shows a certain dethronement of the will and attention which may ally it to the hypnotic state.

Certain kinds of poetry imitate this method of nature by calling on us with a thousand voices at once. Poetry deals often with vague or contradictory statements, with a jumble of images, a throng of impressions. But in true poetry the psychology of real life is closely followed. The mysticism is momentary. We are not kept suspended in a limbo, "trembling like a guilty thing surprised," but are ushered into another world of thought and feeling. On the other hand, a mere statement of inconceivable things is the *reductio ad absurdum* of poetry, because such a statement puzzles the mind, scatters the attention, and does to a certain extent superinduce the "blank misgivings" of mysticism. It does this, however, *without* going further and filling the mind with new life. If I bid a man follow my reasoning closely, and then say, "I am the slayer and the slain, I am the doubter and the doubt," I puzzle his mind, and may succeed in reawakening in him the sense he has often had come over him that we are ignorant of our own destinies and cannot grasp the meaning of life. If I do this, nothing can be a more legitimate opening for a poem, for it is an opening of the reader's mind. Emerson, like many other highly organized persons, was acquainted with the mystic mood. It was not momentary with him. It haunted him, and he seems to have believed that the whole of poetry and religion was contained in the mood. And no one can gainsay that this mental condition is intimately connected with our highest feelings and leads directly into them.

The fault with Emerson is that he stops in the ante-chamber of poetry. He is content if he has brought us to the hypnotic point. His prologue and overture are excellent, but where is the argument? Where is the substantial artistic content that shall feed our souls?

The *Sphinx* is a fair example of an Emerson poem. The opening verses are musical, though they are handicapped by a reminiscence of the German way of writing. In the succeeding verses we are lapped into a charming reverie, and then at the end suddenly jolted by the question, "What is it all about?" In this poem we see expanded into four or five pages of verse an experience which in real life endures an eighth of a second, and when we come to the end of the mood we are at the end of the poem.

There is no question that the power to throw your sitter into a receptive mood by a pass or two which shall give you his virgin attention is necessary to any artist. Nobody has the knack of this more strongly than Emerson in his prose writings. By a phrase or a common remark he creates an ideal atmosphere in which his thought has the directness of great poetry. But he cannot do it in verse. He seeks in his verse to do the very thing which he avoids doing in his prose: follow a logical method. He seems to know too much what he is about, and to be content with doing too little. His mystical poems, from the point of view of such criticism as this, are all alike in that they all seek to do the same thing. Nor does he always succeed. How does he sometimes fail in verse to say what he conveys with such everlasting happiness in prose!

> I am owner of the sphere,
> Of the seven stars and the solar year,
> Of Cæsar's hand and Plato's brain,
> Of Lord Christ's heart and Shakespeare's strain.

In these lines we have the same thought which appears a few pages later in prose: "All that Shakespeare says of the king, yonder slip of a boy that reads in the corner feels to be true of himself." He has failed in the verse because he has thrown a mystical gloss over a thought which was stronger in its simplicity; because in the verse he states an abstraction instead of giving an instance. The same failure follows him sometimes in prose when he is too conscious of his machinery.

Emerson knew that the sense of mystery accompanies the shift of an absorbed attention to some object which brings the mind back to the present. "There are times when the cawing of a crow, a weed, a snowflake, a boy's willow whistle, or a farmer planting in his field is more suggestive to the mind than the Yosemite gorge or the Vatican would be in another hour. In like mood, an old verse, or certain words, gleam with rare significance." At the close of his essay on *History* he is trying to make us feel that all history, in so far as we can know it, is within ourselves, and is in a certain sense autobiography. He is speaking of the Romans, and he suddenly pretends to see a lizard on the wall, and proceeds to wonder what the lizard has to do with the Romans. For this he has been quite properly laughed at by Dr. Holmes, because he has resorted to an artifice and has failed to create an illusion. Indeed, Dr. Holmes is somewhere so irreverent as to remark that a gill of alcohol will bring on a psychical state very similar to that suggested by Emerson; and Dr. Holmes is accurately happy in his jest, because alcohol does dislocate the attention in a thoroughly mystical manner.

There is throughout Emerson's poetry, as throughout all of the New England poetry, too much thought, too much argument. Some of his verse gives the reader a very curious and subtle impression that the lines are a translation. This is because he is closely following a thesis. Indeed, the lines are a translation. They were thought first, and poetry afterwards. Read off his poetry, and you see through the scheme of it at once. Read his prose, and you will be put to it to make out the connection of ideas. The reason is that in the poetry the sequence is intellectual, in the prose the sequence is emotional. It is no mere epigram to say that his poetry is governed by the ordinary laws of prose writing, and his prose by the laws of poetry.

The lines entitled *Days* have a dramatic vigor, a mystery, and a music all their own:

> Daughters of Time, the hypocritic Days,
> Muffled and dumb like barefoot dervishes,
> And marching single in an endless file,
> Bring diadems and fagots in their hands.
> To each they offer gifts after his will,
> Bread, kingdoms, stars, and sky that holds them all.
> I, in my pleachèd garden, watched the pomp,
> Forgot my morning wishes, hastily
> Took a few herbs and apples, and the Day
> Turned and departed silent. I, too late,
> Under her solemn fillet saw the scorn.

The prose version of these lines, which in this case is inferior, is to be found in *Works and Days:*

He only is rich who owns the day. . . . They come and go like muffled and veiled figures, sent from a distant friendly party; but they say nothing, and if we do not use the gifts they bring, they carry them as silently away.

That Emerson had within him the soul of a poet no one will question, but his poems are expressed in prose forms. There are passages in his early addresses which can be matched in English only by bits from Sir Thomas Browne or Milton, or from the great poets. Heine might have written the following parable into verse, but it could not have been finer. It comes from the very bottom of Emerson's nature. It is his uttermost. Infancy and manhood and old age, the first and the last of him, speak in it.

Every god is there sitting in his sphere. The young mortal enters the hall of the firmament; there is he alone with them alone, they pouring on him benedictions and gifts, and beckoning him up to their thrones. On the instant, and incessantly, fall snowstorms of illusions. He fancies himself in a vast crowd which sways this way and that, and whose movements and doings he must obey; he fancies himself poor, orphaned, insignificant. The mad crowd drives hither and thither, now furiously commanding this thing to be done, now that. What is he that he should resist their will, and think or act for himself? Every moment new changes and new showers of deceptions to baffle and distract him. And when, by and by, for an instant, the air clears and the cloud lifts a little, there are the gods still sitting around him on their thrones—they alone with him alone.

With the war closes the colonial period of our history, and with the end of the war begins our national life. Before that time it was not possible for any man to speak for the nation, however much he might long to, for there was no nation; there were only discordant provinces held together by the exercise on the part of each of a strong and conscientious will. It is too much to expect that national character shall be expressed before it is developed, or that the arts shall flourish during a period when everybody is preoccupied with the fear of revolution. The provincial note which runs through all our literature down to the war resulted in one sense from our dependence upon Europe. "All American manners, language, and writings," says Emerson, "are derivative. We do not write from facts, but we wish to state the facts after the English manner. It is the tax we pay for the splendid inheritance of English Literature." But in a deeper sense this very dependence upon Europe was due to our disunion among ourselves. The equivocal and unhappy self-assertive patriotism to which we were consigned by fate, and which made us perceive and resent the condescension of foreigners, was the logical outcome of our political situation.

The literature of the Northern states before the war, although full of talent, lacks body, lacks courage. It has not a full national tone. The South is not in it. New England's share in this literature is so large that small injustice will be done if we give her credit for all of it. She was the Academy of the land, and her scholars were our authors. The country at large has sometimes been annoyed at the self-consciousness of New England, at the atmosphere of clique, of mutual admiration, of isolation, in which all her scholars, except Emerson, have lived, and which notably enveloped the last little distinguished group of them. The circumstances which led to the isolation of Lowell, Holmes,

Longfellow, and the Saturday Club fraternity are instructive. The ravages of the war carried off the poets, scholars, and philosophers of the generation which immediately followed these men, and by destroying their natural successors left them standing magnified beyond their natural size, like a grove of trees left by a fire. The war did more than kill off a generation of scholars who would have succeeded these older scholars. It emptied the universities by calling all the survivors into the field of practical life; and after the war ensued a period during which all the learning of the land was lodged in the heads of these older worthies who had made their mark long before. A certain complacency which piqued the country at large was seen in these men. An ante-bellum colonial posing, inevitable in their own day, survived with them. When Jared Sparks put Washington in the proper attitude for greatness by correcting his spelling, Sparks was in cue with the times. It was thought that a great man must have his hat handed to him by his biographer, and be ushered on with decency toward posterity. In the lives and letters of some of our recent public men there has been a reminiscence of this posing, which we condemn as absurd because we forget it is merely archaic. Provincial manners are always a little formal, and the pomposity of the colonial governor was never quite worked out of our literary men.

Let us not disparage the past. We are all grateful for the New England culture, and especially for the little group of men in Cambridge and Boston who did their best according to the light of their day. Their purpose and taste did all that high ideals and good taste can do, and no more eminent literati have lived during this century. They gave the country songs, narrative poems, odes, epigrams, essays, novels. They chose their models well, and drew their materials from decent and likely sources. They lived stainless lives, and died in their professors' chairs honored by all men. For achievements of this sort we need hardly use as strong language as Emerson does in describing contemporary literature: "It exhibits a vast carcass of tradition every year with as much solemnity as a new revelation."

The mass and volume of literature must always be traditional, and the secondary writers of the world do neverthe-less perform a function of infinite consequence in the spread of thought. A very large amount of first-hand thinking is not comprehensible to the average man until it has been distilled and is fifty years old. The men who welcome new learning as it arrives are the picked men, the minor poets of the next age. To their own times these secondary men often seem great because they are recognized and understood at once. We know the disadvantage under which these Humanists of ours worked. The shadow of the time in which they wrote hangs over us still. The conservatism and timidity of our politics and of our literature today are due in part to that fearful pressure which for sixty years was never lifted from the souls of Americans. That conservatism and timidity may be seen in all our past. They are in the rhetoric of Webster and in the style of Hawthorne. They killed Poe. They cre-ated Bryant.

Since the close of our most blessed war, we have been left to face the problems of democracy, unhampered by the ter-rible complications of sectional strife. It has happened, however, that some of the tendencies of our commercial civilization go toward strengthening and riveting upon us the very traits encouraged by provincial disunion. Wendell Phillips, with a cool grasp of understanding for which he is not generally given credit, states the case as follows:

The general judgment is that the freest possible government produces the freest possible men and women, the most indi-vidual, the least servile to the judgment of others. But a mo-ment's reflection will show any man that this is an unreason-able expectation, and that, on the contrary, entire equality and and freedom in political forms almost invariably tend to make the individual subside into the mass and lose his identity in the general whole. Suppose we stood in England tonight. There is the nobility, and here is the church. There is the trading class, and here is the literary. A broad gulf separates the four; and provided a member of either can conciliate his own section, he can afford in a very large measure to despise the opinions of the other three. He has to some extent a refuge and a breakwater against the tyranny of what we call public opinion. But in a country like ours, of absolute democratic equality, public opinion is not only omnipotent, it is omnipresent. There is no refuge from its tyranny, there is no hiding from its reach; and the result is that if you take the old Greek lantern and go about to seek among a hundred, you will find not one single American who has not, or who does not fancy at least that he has, something to gain or lose in his ambition, his social life, or his business, from the good opinion and the votes of those around him. And the consequence is that instead of being a mass of individuals, each one fearlessly blurting out his own convictions, as a nation, compared to other nations, we are a mass of cowards. More than all other people, we are afraid of each other.

If we take a bird's-eye view of our history, we shall find that this constant element of democratic pressure has always been so strong a factor in molding the character of our citizens that there is less difference than we could wish to see between the types of citizenship produced before the war and after the war.

Charles Follen, that excellent and worthy German who came to this country while still a young man and who lived in the midst of the social and intellectual life of Boston, felt the want of intellectual freedom in the people about him. If one were obliged to describe the America of today in a single sentence, one could hardly do it better than by a sentence from a letter of Follen to Harriet Martineau written in 1837, after the appearance of one of her books: "You have pointed out the two most striking national characteristics, 'Deficiency of individual moral independence and extraordinary mutual respect and kindness.'"

Much of what Emerson wrote about the United States in 1850 is true of the United States today. It would be hard to find a civilized people who are more timid, more cowed in spirit, more illiberal, than we. It is easy today for the educated man who has read Bryce and Tocqueville to account for the mediocrity of American literature. The merit of Emerson was that he felt the atmospheric pressure without knowing its reason. He felt he was a cabined, cribbed, confined creature, although every man about him was celebrating Liberty and Democracy, and every day was Fourth of July.

He taxes language to its limits in order to express his revolt. He says that no man should write except what he has discovered in the process of satisfying his own curiosity, and that every man will write well in proportion as he has contempt for the public.

Emerson seems really to have believed that if any man would only resolutely be himself, he would turn out to be as great as Shakespeare. He will not have it that anything of value can be monopolized. His review of the world, whether under the title of Manners, Self-Reliance, Fate, Experience, or what-not, leads him to the same thought. His conclusion is always the finding of eloquence, courage, art, intellect, in the breast of the humblest reader. He knows that we are full of genius and surrounded by genius, and that we have only to throw something off, not to acquire any new thing, in order to be bards, prophets, Napoleons, and Goethes. This belief is the secret of his stimulating power. It is this which gives his writings a radiance like that which shone from his personality.

The deep truth shadowed forth by Emerson when he said that "all the American geniuses lacked nerve and dagger" was illustrated by our best scholar. Lowell had the soul of the Yankee, but in his habits of writing he continued English tradition. His literary essays are full of charm. The *Commemoration Ode* is the high-water mark of the attempt to do the impossible. It is a fine thing, but it is imitative and secondary. It has paid the inheritance tax. Twice, however, at a crisis of pressure, Lowell assumed his real self under the guise of a pseudonym; and with his own hand he rescued a language, a type, a whole era of civilization from oblivion. Here gleams the dagger and here is Lowell revealed. His limitations as a poet, his too much wit, his too much morality, his mixture of shrewdness and religion, are seen to be the very elements of power. The novelty of the *Biglow Papers* is as wonderful as their world-old naturalness. They take rank with greatness, and they were the strongest political tracts of their time. They imitate nothing; they are real.

Emerson himself was the only man of his times who consistently and utterly expressed himself, never measuring himself for a moment with the ideals of others, never troubling himself for a moment with what literature was or how literature should be created. The other men of his epoch, and among whom he lived, believed that literature was a very desirable article, a thing you could create if you were only smart enough. But Emerson had no literary ambition. He cared nothing for belles-lettres. The consequence is that he stands above his age like a colossus. While he lived his figure could be seen from Europe towering like Atlas over the culture of the United States.

Great men are not always like wax which their age imprints. They are often the mere negation and opposite of their age. They give it the lie. They become by revolt the very essence of all the age is not, and that part of the spirit which is suppressed in ten thousand breasts gets lodged, isolated, and breaks into utterance in one. Through Emerson spoke the fractional spirits of a multitude. He had not time, he had not energy left over to understand himself; he was a mouthpiece.

If a soul be taken and crushed by democracy till it utter a cry, that cry will be Emerson. The region of thought he lived in, the figures of speech he uses, are of an intellectual plane so high that the circumstances which produced them may be forgotten; they are indifferent. The Constitution, Slavery, the War itself, are seen as mere circumstances. They did not confuse him while he lived; they are not necessary to support his work now that it is finished. Hence comes it that Emerson is one of the world's voices. He was heard afar off. His foreign influence might deserve a chapter by itself. Conservatism is not confined to this country. It is the very basis of all government. The bolts Emerson forged, his thought, his wit, his perception, are not provincial. They were found to carry inspiration to England and Germany. Many of the important men of the last half century owe him a debt. It is not yet possible to give any account of his influence abroad, because the memoirs which will show it are only beginning to be published. We shall have them in due time; for Emerson was an outcome of the world's progress. His appearance marks the turning-point in the history of that enthusiasm

for pure democracy which has tinged the political thought
of the world for the past one hundred and fifty years. The
youths of England and Germany may have been surprised
at hearing from America a piercing voice of protest against
the very influences which were crushing them at home. They
could not realize that the chief difference between Europe
and America is a difference in the rate of speed with which
revolutions in thought are worked out.

While the radicals of Europe were revolting in 1848
against the abuses of a tyranny whose roots were in feudal-
ism, Emerson, the great radical of America, the arch-radical
of the world, was revolting against the evils whose roots were
in universal suffrage. By showing the identity in essence of
all tyranny, and by bringing back the attention of political
thinkers to its starting-point, the value of human character,
he has advanced the political thought of the world by one
step. He has pointed out for us in this country to what ends
our efforts must be bent.

IT HAS BEEN DIFFICULT to find anything about Stephen Crane for the purposes of this book. Thomas Beer's *Stephen Crane* is valuable, but it is simply a sort of memoir written by one who did not know him; and though the collected edition of Crane includes prefaces by Amy Lowell, Willa Cather, Sherwood Anderson and Howells, these are brief and deal with special aspects. One has to go abroad for something better. There are three fine and moving pieces by Joseph Conrad: *Stephen Crane: A Note without Dates* in the volume called *Life and Letters;* and, in *Last Essays, Stephen Crane* and a review of *The Red Badge of Courage.* But these are well known and easily accessible, and it has seemed more appropriate to include this essay by Mr. Wells, which has never before been reprinted. It appeared in the *North American Review* of August 1900. Crane, who had been living in England for more than a year, had died of tuberculosis on June 4.

The end of the century was a moment when the literary migrants from America were beginning to impinge on the consciousness of literary England. The novelists, Harold Frederic and Henry Harland, had already gone to live in England, and Harland had been editor of *The Yellow Book.*

Henry James and Logan Pearsall Smith had been settled there since the eighties. The set of writers to which Crane belonged and which has been so entertainingly and stimulatingly described by the late Ford Madox Ford in his various books of reminiscences, was curiously cosmopolitan; Crane and Henry James were Americans; Conrad was a Pole; and Ford himself (then Hueffer) was part German. All were working in the English language with trained skill and anxious intensity, but they were all outside the English tradition. It seemed to Mr. Wells that Crane had got free of this English tradition as no American had ever done before.

H. G. WELLS

STEPHEN CRANE FROM AN ENGLISH STANDPOINT

THE UNTIMELY DEATH at thirty of Stephen Crane robs English literature of an interesting and significant figure, and the little world of those who write, of a stout friend and a pleasant comrade. For a year and more he had been ailing. The bitter hardships of his Cuban expedition had set its mark upon mind and body alike, and the slow darkling of the shadow upon him must have been evident to all who were not blinded by their confidence in what he was yet to do. Altogether, I knew Crane for less than a year, and I saw him for the last time hardly more than seven weeks ago. He was then in a hotel at Dover, lying still and comfortably wrapped about, before an open window and the calm and spacious sea. If you would figure him as I saw him, you must think of him as a face of a type very typically American, long and spare, with very straight hair and straight features and long, quiet hands and hollow eyes, moving slowly, smiling and speaking slowly, with that deliberate New Jersey manner he had, and lapsing from speech again into a quiet contemplation of his ancient enemy. For it was the sea that had taken his strength, the same sea that now shone, level waters beyond level waters, with here and there a minute, shining ship, warm and tranquil beneath the tran-

quil evening sky. Yet I felt scarcely a suspicion then that this
was a last meeting. One might have seen it all, perhaps. He
was thin and gaunt and wasted, too weak for more than a
remembered jest and a greeting and good wishes. It did not
seem to me in any way credible that he would reach his
refuge in the Black Forest only to die at the journey's end.
It will be a long time yet before I can fully realize that he
is no longer a contemporary of mine; that the last I saw of
him was, indeed, final and complete.

Though my personal acquaintance with Crane was so
soon truncated, I have followed his work for all the four
years it has been known in England. I have always been
proud, and now I am glad, that, however obscurely, I also
was in the first chorus of welcome that met his coming. It is,
perhaps, no great distinction for me; he was abundantly
praised; but, at least, I was early and willing to praise him
when I was wont to be youthfully jealous of my praises. His
success in England began with the *Red Badge of Courage,*
which did, indeed, more completely than any other book has
done for many years, take the reading public by storm. Its
freshness of method, its vigor of imagination, its force of
color and its essential freedom from many traditions that
dominate this side of the Atlantic, came—in spite of the
previous shock of Mr. Kipling—with a positive effect of
impact. It was a new thing, in a new school. When one
looked for sources, one thought at once of Tolstoy; but,
though it was clear that Tolstoy had exerted a powerful
influence upon the conception, if not the actual writing, of
the book, there still remained something entirely original
and novel. To a certain extent, of course, that was the new
man as an individual; but, to at least an equal extent, it was
the new man as a typical young American, free at last, as no
generation of Americans have been free before, of any regard for English criticism, comment, or tradition, and applying to literary work the conception and theories of the
cosmopolitan studio with a quite American directness and
vigor. For the great influence of the studio on Crane cannot
be ignored; in the persistent selection of the essential elements of an impression, in the ruthless exclusion of mere

information, in the direct vigor with which the selected points are made, there is Whistler even more than there is Tolstoy in the *Red Badge of Courage*. And witness this, taken almost haphazard:

At nightfall the column broke into regimental pieces, and the fragments went into the fields to camp. Tents sprang up like strange plants. Camp fires, like red, peculiar blossoms, dotted the night. . . . From this little distance the many fires, with the black forms of men passing to and fro before the crimson rays, made weird and satanic effects.

And here again; consider the daring departure from all academic requirements in this void countenance:

A warm and strong hand clasped the youth's languid fingers for an instant, and then he heard a cheerful and audacious whistling as the man strode away. As he who had so befriended him was thus passing out of his life, it suddenly occurred to the youth that he had not once seen his face.

I do not propose to add anything here to the mass of criticism upon this remarkable book. Like everything else which has been abundantly praised, it has occasionally been praised "all wrong"; and I suppose that it must have been said hundreds of times that this book is a subjective study of the typical soldier in war. But Mr. George Wyndham, himself a soldier of experience, has pointed out in an admirable preface to a re-issue of this and other of Crane's war studies that the hero of the *Red Badge* is, and is intended to be, altogether a more sensitive and imaginative person than the ordinary man. He is the idealist, the dreamer of boastful things brought suddenly to the test of danger and swift occasions and the presence of death. To this theme Crane returned several times, and particularly in a story called *Death and the Child* that was written after the Greek war. That story is considered by very many of Crane's admirers as absolutely his best. I have carefully reread it in deference to opinions I am bound to respect, but I still find it inferior to the earlier work. The generalized application is, to my taste, a little too evidently underlined; there is just that touch of insistence that prevails so painfully at times in Victor Hugo's work, as of a writer not sure of his reader, not happy in his reader, and seeking to drive his implication (of which also he is not quite sure) home. The child is not a natural child; there is no happy touch to make it personally alive; it is THE CHILD, something unfalteringly big; a large, pink, generalized thing, I cannot help but see it, after the fashion of a Vatican cherub. The fugitive runs panting to where, all innocent of the battle about it, it plays; and he falls down breathless to be asked, "Are you a man?" One sees the intention clearly enough; but in the later story it seems to me there is a new ingredient that is absent from the earlier stories, an ingredient imposed on Crane's natural genius from without— a concession to the demands of a criticism it had been wiser, if less modest, in him to disregard—criticism that missed this quality of generalization and demanded it, even though it had to be artificially and deliberately introduced.

Following hard upon the appearance of the *Red Badge of Courage* in England came reprints of two books, *Maggie* and *George's Mother,* that had already appeared in America six years earlier. Their reception gave Crane his first taste of the peculiarities of the new public he had come upon. These stories seem to me in no way inferior to the *Red Badge;* and at times there are passages, the lament of Maggie's mother at the end of *Maggie,* for example, that it would be hard to beat by any passage from the later book. But on all hands came discouragement or tepid praise. The fact of it is, there had been almost an orgy of praise—for England, that is; and ideas and adjectives and phrases were exhausted. To write further long reviews on works displaying the same qualities as had been already amply discussed in the notices of the *Red Badge* would be difficult and laborious; while to admit an equal excellence and deny an equal prominence would be absurd. But to treat these stories as early work, to find them immature, dismiss them and proceed to fresher topics, was obvious and convenient. So it was, I uncharitably imagine, that these two tales have been overshadowed and are still comparatively unknown. Yet they are absolutely essential to a just understanding of Crane. In these stories, and in these alone, he achieved tenderness and a compulsion of sympathy for other than vehement emotions, qualities that the readers of *The Third Violet* and *On Active Service,* his later love stories, might well imagine beyond his reach.

And upon the appearance of these books in England came what, in my present mood, I cannot but consider as the great blunder and misfortune of Crane's life. It is a trait of the public we writers serve that to please it is to run the gravest risk of never writing again. Through a hundred channels and with a hundred varieties of seduction and compulsion, the public seeks to induce its favorite to do something else— to act, to lecture, to travel, to jump down volcanoes or perform in music halls, to do anything, rather than to possess his soul in peace and to pursue the work he was meant to do. Indeed, this modern public is as violently experimental with its writers as a little child with a kitten. It is animated, above all things, by an insatiable desire to plunge its victim into novel surroundings and watch how he feels. And since Crane had demonstrated, beyond all cavil, that he could sit at home and, with nothing but his wonderful brain and his wonderful induction from recorded things, build up the truest and most convincing picture of war; since he was a fastidious and careful worker, intensely subjective in his mental habit; since he was a man of fragile physique and of that unreasonable courage that will wreck the strongest physique; and since, moreover, he was habitually a bad traveler, losing trains and luggage and missing connections even in the orderly circumstances of peace, it was clearly the most reasonable thing in the world to propose, it was received with the applause of two hemispheres as a most right and proper thing, that he should go as a war correspondent, first to Greece and then to Cuba. Thereby, and for nothing but disappointment and bitterness, he utterly wrecked his health. He came into comparison with men as entirely his masters in this work as he was the master of all men in his own; and I read even in the most punctual of his obituary notices the admission of his journalistic failure. I have read, too, that he brought back nothing from these expeditions. But, indeed, even not counting his death, he brought back much. On his way home from Cuba he was wrecked, and he wrote the story of the nights and days that followed the sinking of the ship with a simplicity and vigor that even he cannot rival elsewhere.

The Open Boat is to my mind, beyond all question, the crown of all his work. It has all the stark power of the earlier stories, with a new element of restraint; the color is as full and strong as ever, fuller and stronger, indeed; but those chromatic splashes that at times deafen and confuse in the *Red Badge,* those images that astonish rather than enlighten, are disciplined and controlled. "That and *Flanagan,*" he told me, with a philosophical laugh, "was all I got out of Cuba." I cannot say whether they were worth the price, but I am convinced that these two things are as immortal as any work of any living man. And the way *The Open Boat* begins, no stress, plain—even a little gray and flattish:

None of them knew the color of the sky. Their eyes glanced level, and were fastened upon the waves that swept toward them. These waves were of the hue of slate, save for the tops, which were of foaming white, and all of the men knew the color of the sea. The horizon narrowed and widened, and dipped and rose, and at all times its edge was jagged with waves that seemed thrust up in points like rocks.

Many a man ought to have a bathtub larger than the boat which here rode upon the sea. These waves were most wrongfully and barbarously abrupt and tall, and each froth top was a problem in small-boat navigation.

The cook squatted in the bottom, and looked with both eyes at the six inches of gunwale which separated him from the ocean. His sleeves were rolled over his fat forearms, and the two flaps of his unbuttoned vest dangled as he bent to bail out the boat. Often he said, "Gawd! That was a narrow clip." As he remarked it, he invariably gazed eastward over the broken sea.

The oiler, steering with one of the two oars in the boat, sometimes raised himself suddenly to keep clear of the water that swirled in over the stern. It was a thin little oar and it seemed often ready to snap.

The correspondent, pulling at the other oar, watched the waves and wondered why he was there.

From that beginning, the story mounts and mounts over the waves, wave frothing after wave, each wave a threat, and the men toil and toil and toil again; by insensible degrees the day lights the waves to green and olive, and the foam grows dazzling. Then as the long day draws out, they come toward the land.

"Look! There's a man on the shore!"

"Where?"

"There! See 'im?"

"Yes, sure! He's walking along."

"Now he's stopped. Look! He's facing us!"

"So he is, by thunder!"

"Ah, now we're all right! Now we're all right! There'll be a boat out here for us in half an hour."

"He's going on. He's running. He's going up to that house there."

The remote beach seemed lower than the sea, and it required a searching glance to discern the little black figure. The captain saw a floating stick and they rowed to it. A bath towel was by some weird chance in the boat, and, tying this on the stick, the captain waved it. The oarsman did not dare turn his head, so he was obliged to ask questions.

"What's he doing now?"

"He's standing still again. He's looking, I think. . . . There he goes again. Towards the house. Now he's stopped again."

"Is he waving at us?"

"No, not now! he was, though."

"Look! There comes another man!"

"He's running."

.   .   .   .

"Well, I wish I could make something out of those signals. What do you suppose he means?"

"He don't mean anything. He's just playing."

"Well, if he'd just signal us to try the surf again, or to go to sea and wait, or go north, or go south, or go to hell—there would be some reason in it. But look at him. He just stands there and keeps his coat revolving like a wheel. The ass!"

"There come more people."

"Now there's quite a mob. Look! Isn't that a boat?"

"Where? Oh, I see where you mean. No, that's no boat."

"That fellow is still waving his coat."

"He must think we like to see him do that. Why don't he quit it? It don't mean anything."

"I don't know. I think he's trying to make us go north. It must be that there's a life saving station there somewhere."

"Say, he ain't tired yet. Look at 'im wave."

. . . .

"Holy smoke!" said one, allowing his voice to express his impious mood. "If we keep on monkeying out here! If we've got to flounder out here all night!"

"Oh, we'll never have to stay here all night! Don't you worry. They've seen us now, and it won't be long before they'll come chasing out after us."

The shore grew dusky. The man waving a coat blended gradually into this gloom, and it swallowed in the same manner the omnibus and the group of people. The spray, when it dashed uproariously over the side, made the voyagers shrink and swear like men who were being branded.

"I'd like to catch the chump who waved the coat. I feel like soaking him one, just for luck."

"Why? What did he do?"

. . . .

In the meantime the oiler rowed, and then the correspondent rowed, and then the oiler rowed. Gray-faced and bowed forward, they mechanically, turn by turn, plied the leaden oars. The form of the lighthouse had vanished from the southern horizon, but finally a pale star appeared, just lifting from the sea. The streaked saffron in the west passed before the all-merging darkness, and the sea to the east was black. The land had vanished, and was expressed only by the low and dread thunder of the surf.

The Open Boat gives its title to a volume containing, in addition to that and *Flanagan,* certain short pieces. One of these others, at least, is also to my mind a perfect thing, *The Wise Men.* It tells of the race between two bartenders in the city of Mexico, and I cannot imagine how it could possibly have been better told. And in this volume, too, is that other masterpiece—the one I deny—*Death and the Child.*

Now I do not know how Crane took the reception of this book, for he was not the man to babble of his wrongs; but I cannot conceive how it could have been anything but a grave disappointment to him. To use the silly phrase of the literary shopman, "the vogue of the short story" was already over; rubbish, pure rubbish, provided only it was lengthy, had resumed its former precedence again in the reviews, in the publishers' advertisements, and on the library and book-sellers' counters. The book was taken as a trivial by-product, its author was exhorted to abandon this production of "brilliant fragments"—anything less than fifty thousand words is a fragment to the writer of literary columns—and to make that "sustained effort," that architectural undertaking, that alone impresses the commercial mind. Of course, the man who can call *The Open Boat* a brilliant fragment would reproach Rodin for not completing the edifice his brilliant fragments of statuary are presumably intended to adorn, and would sigh, with the late Mr. Ruskin, for the day when Mr. Whistler would "finish" his pictures. Moreover, he was strongly advised—just as they have advised Mr. Kipling—to embark upon a novel. And from other quarters, where a finer wisdom might have been displayed, he learned that the things he had written were not "short stories" at all; they were "sketches" perhaps, "anecdotes"—just as they call Mr. Kipling's short stories "anecdotes"; and it was insinuated that for him also the true, the ineffable "short story" was beyond his reach. I think it is indisputable that the quality of this reception, which a more self-satisfied or less sensitive man than Crane might have ignored, did react very unfavorably upon his work. They put him out of conceit with these brief intense efforts in which his peculiar strength was displayed.

It was probably such influence that led him to write *The Third Violet*. I do not know certainly, but I imagine, that the book was to be a demonstration, and it is not a successful demonstration, that Crane could write a charming love story. It is the very simple affair of an art student and a summer boarder, with the more superficial incidents of their petty encounters set forth in a forcible, objective manner that is curiously hard and unsympathetic. The characters act, and on reflection one admits they act, *true,* but the play of their emotions goes on behind the curtain of the style, and all the enrichments of imaginative appeal that make love beautiful are omitted. Yet, though the story as a whole fails to satisfy, there are many isolated portions of altogether happy effectiveness, a certain ride behind an ox cart, for example. Much more surely is *On Active Service* an effort, and in places a painful effort, to fit his peculiar gift to the uncongenial conditions of popular acceptance. It is the least capable and least satisfactory of all Crane's work.

While these later books were appearing, and right up to his last fatal illness, Crane continued to produce fresh war pictures that show little or no falling off in vigor of imagination and handling; and, in addition, he was experimenting with verse. In that little stone-blue volume, *War Is Kind*, and in the earlier *Black Riders*, the reader will find a series of acute and vivid impressions and many of the finer qualities of Crane's descriptive prose, but he will not find any novel delights of melody or cadence or any fresh aspects of Crane's personality. There remain some children's stories to be published and an unfinished romance. With that the tale of his published work ends, and the career of one of the most brilliant, most significant, and most distinctively American of all English writers comes to its unanticipated *finis*.

It would be absurd, here and now, to attempt to apportion any relativity of importance to Crane, to say that he was greater than A or less important than B. That class-list business is, indeed, best left forever to the newspaper plebiscite and the library statistician; among artists, whose sole, just claim to recognition and whose sole title to immortality must necessarily be the possession of unique qualities, that is to say, of unclassifiable factors, these gradations are absurd. Suffice it that, even before his death, Crane's right to be counted in the hierarchy of those who have made a permanent addition to the great and growing fabric of English letters was not only assured, but conceded. To define his position in time, however, and in relation to periods and modes of writing will be a more reasonable undertaking; and it seems to me that, when at last the true proportions can be seen, Crane will be found to occupy a position singularly cardinal. He was a New Englander of Puritan lineage,[1] and

[1] Stephen Crane was not a New Englander. He was born in Newark, New Jersey, and his family, says Thomas Beer, "was old in the State of New Jersey."—E. W.

the son of a long tradition of literature. There had been many Cranes who wrote before him. He has shown me a shelf of books, for the most part the pious and theological works of various antecedent Stephen Cranes. He had been at some pains to gather together these alien products of his kin. For the most part they seemed little, insignificant books, and one opened them to read the beaten *clichés,* the battered, outworn phrases, of a movement that has ebbed. Their very size and binding suggested a dying impulse, that very same impulse that in its prime had carried the magnificence of Milton's imagery and the pomp and splendors of Milton's prose. In Crane that impulse was altogether dead. He began stark—I find all through this brief notice I have been repeating that in a dozen disguises, "freedom from tradition," "absolute directness," and the like—as though he came into the world of letters without ever a predecessor. In style, in method, and in all that is distinctively *not* found in his books, he is sharply defined, the expression in literary art of certain enormous repudiations. Was ever a man before who wrote of battles so abundantly as he has done, and never had a word, never a word from first to last, of the purpose and justification of the war? And of the God of Battles, no more than the battered name; "Hully Gee!"—the lingering trace of the Deity! And of the sensuousness and tenderness of love, so much as one can find in *The Third Violet!* Any richness of allusion, any melody or balance of phrase, the half quotation that refracts and softens and enriches the statement, the momentary digression that opens like a window upon beautiful or distant things, are not merely absent, but obviously and sedulously avoided. It is as if the racial thought and tradition had been razed from his mind and its site plowed and salted. He is more than himself in this; he is the first expression of the opening mind of a new period, or, at least, the early emphatic phase of a new initiative—beginning, as a growing mind must needs begin, with the record of impressions, a record of a vigor and intensity beyond all precedent.

WILLIAM DEAN HOWELLS (1837–1920) presided over American literature through the half-century after the Civil War. He was our always tactful toastmaster, our clearing-house, our universal solvent, our respecter of the distinguished veteran, our encourager of the promising young. He had been the son of a printer in Ohio, an American consul in Venice, the editor of the *Atlantic Monthly* in Boston, an editor of *Harper's* in New York, and something of a publicist for social reform. He knew how to be discreet in Cambridge and was on excellent terms with Lowell and Aldrich; he was delighted to greet gifted Middle Westerners like Booth Tarkington and Hamlin Garland; he was on charming terms with John Hay and usually *persona grata* at the White House; he paid attention to the new plays of Clyde Fitch and George Ade; and he did his best for the realism of the end of the century, advising Henry B. Fuller to stick to Chicago, reviewing and praising Frank Norris' *McTeague*, and trying to persuade the New York bookdealers to handle Stephen Crane's *Maggie*. During Howells' later years one heard a great deal of complaint that his natural prudery and primness rather neutralized his advanced opinions. If one goes back over his criticism today, one does find it rather watery and uninteresting; yet one is brought to the realization that, all through that period of our history when letters were so far from enjoying their earlier exalted prestige, Howells did serve us pretty well. He did want to see good writing get published and read, no matter what it was about or who wrote it; and he cared little about conventional opinion. His instinctive respect for the proprieties and his deference to his feminine audience were a more serious handicap in his fiction than in the exercise of his literary taste.

Howells' most remarkable feat was to appreciate and remain on close terms with both the two great men of our letters who seemed, with their so different publics, antipodal and mutually repellent: Mark Twain and Henry James. Mark Twain till almost the end of his career was much under suspicion of "vulgarity": famous as a popular humorist and in demand as an after-dinner speaker, he was not generally accepted as a serious writer. But Howells had not only taken him seriously—reviewed his books and criticized his manuscripts; he had felt Clemens' strange superiority to even the revered masters of Boston. Mark Twain's disastrous *gaffe* at the Whittier dinner (described in the memoir that follows)—which must, however, have had behind it some real unconscious antagonism on Mark Twain's part—could embarrass Howells but could not scare him. *My Mark Twain*, written when Clemens died in 1910, is probably the best "character" of Mark Twain we have; and it is certainly one of the works of Howells in which he rises to something of intensity both of expression and of feeling.

MY MARK TWAIN[1]

IT WAS in the little office of James T. Fields, over the bookstore of Ticknor & Fields, at 124 Tremont Street, Boston, that I first met my friend of now forty-four years, Samuel L. Clemens. Mr. Fields was then the editor of the *Atlantic Monthly,* and I was his proud and glad assistant, with a pretty free hand as to manuscripts, and an unmanacled command of the book-notices at the end of the magazine. I wrote nearly all of them myself, and in 1869 I had written rather a long notice of a book just winning its way to universal favor. In this review I had intimated my reservations concerning the *Innocents Abroad,* but I had the luck, if not the sense, to recognize that it was such fun as we had not had before. I forget just what I said in praise of it, and it does not matter; it is enough that I praised it enough to satisfy the author. He now signified as much, and he stamped his gratitude into my memory with a story wonderfully allegorizing the situation, which the mock modesty of print forbids my repeating here. Throughout my long acquaintance with him his graphic touch was always allowing itself a freedom which I cannot bring my fainter pencil to illustrate. He had the Southwestern, the Lincolnian, the Elizabethan breadth of parlance, which I suppose one ought not to call coarse without calling one's self prudish; and I was often hiding away in discreet holes and corners the letters in which he had loosed his bold fancy to stoop on rank suggestion; I could not bear to burn them, and I could not, after the first reading, quite bear to look at them. I shall best give my feeling on this point by saying that in it he was Shakespearian, or if his ghost will not suffer me the word, then he was Baconian.

At the time of our first meeting, which must have been well toward the winter, Clemens (as I must call him instead of Mark Twain, which seemed always somehow to mask him from my personal sense) was wearing a sealskin coat, with the fur out, in the satisfaction of a caprice, or the love of strong effect which he was apt to indulge through life. I do not know what droll comment was in Fields's mind with respect to this garment, but probably he felt that here was an original who was not to be brought to any Bostonian book in the judgment of his vivid qualities. With his crest of dense red hair, and the wide sweep of his flaming mustache, Clemens was not discordantly clothed in that sealskin coat, which afterward, in spite of his own warmth in it, sent the cold chills through me when I once accompanied it down Broadway, and shared the immense publicity it won him. He had always a relish for personal effect, which expressed itself in the white suit of complete serge which he wore in his last years, and in the Oxford gown which he put on for every possible occasion, and said he would like to wear all the time. That was not vanity in him, but a keen feeling for costume which the severity of our modern tailoring forbids men, though it flatters women to every excess in it; yet he also enjoyed the shock, the offense, the pang which it gave the sensibilities of others. Then there were times he played these pranks for pure fun, and for the pleasure of the witness. Once I remember seeing him come into his drawing-room at Hartford in a pair of white cowskin slippers, with the hair out, and do a crippled colored uncle to the joy of all beholders. Or, I must not say all, for I remember also the dismay of Mrs. Clemens, and her low, despairing cry of, "Oh, Youth!" That was her name for him among their friends, and it fitted him as no other would, though I fancied with her it was a shrinking from his baptismal Samuel, or the vernacular Sam of his earlier companionships. He was a youth to the end of his days, the heart of a boy with the head of a sage; the heart of a good boy, or a bad boy, but always a wilful boy, and wilfulest to show himself out at every time for just the boy he was.

II

There is a gap in my recollections of Clemens, which I think is of a year or two, for the next thing I remember of him is meeting him at a lunch in Boston given us by that genius of hospitality, the tragically destined Ralph Keeler, author of one of the most unjustly forgotten books, *Vagabond Adventures,* a true bit of picaresque autobiography. Keeler never had any money, to the general knowledge, and he never borrowed, and he could not have had credit at the restaurant where he invited us to feast at his expense. There was T. B. Aldrich, there was J. T. Fields, much the oldest of our company, who had just freed himself from the trammels of the publishing business, and was feeling his freedom in every word; there was Bret Harte, who had lately come East in his princely progress from California; and there was Clemens. Nothing remains to me of the happy time but a sense of idle and aimless and joyful talk-play, beginning and ending nowhere, of eager laughter, of countless good stories from Fields, of a heat-lightning shimmer of wit from Aldrich, of an occasional concentration of our joint mockeries upon our host, who took it gladly; and amid the discourse, so little improving, but so full of good fellowship, Bret Hart's fleering dramatization of Clemens' mental attitude toward a symposium of Boston illuminates. "Why, fellows," he spluttered, "this is the dream of Mark's life," and I remember the glance from under Clemens' feathery eyebrows which betrayed his enjoyment of the fun. We had beefsteak with mushrooms, which in recognition of their shape Aldrich hailed as shoe-pegs, and to crown the feast we had an omelette soufflé, which the waiter brought in as flat as a pancake, amid our shouts of congratulations to poor Keeler, who took them with appreciative submission. It was in every way what a Boston literary lunch ought not to have been in the popular ideal which Harte attributed to Clemens.

Our next meeting was at Hartford, or, rather, at Springfield, where Clemens greeted us on the way to Hartford. Aldrich was going on to be his guest, and I was going to be Charles Dudley Warner's, but Clemens had come part way to welcome us both. In the good fellowship of that cordial neighborhood we had two such days as the aging sun no longer shines on in his round. There was constant running in and out of friendly houses where the lively hosts and guests called one another by their Christian names or nicknames, and no such vain ceremony as knocking or ringing at doors. Clemens was then building the stately mansion in which he satisfied his love of magnificence as if it had been another sealskin coat, and he was at the crest of the prosperity which enabled him to humor every whim or extravagance. The house was the design of that most original artist, Edward Potter, who once, when hard pressed by incompetent curiosity for the name of his style in a certain church, proposed that it should be called the English violet order of architecture; and this house was so absolutely suited to the owner's humor that I suppose there never was another house like it; but its character must be for recognition farther along in these reminiscences. The vividest impression which Clemens gave us two ravenous young Boston authors was of the satisfying, the surfeiting nature of subscription publication. An army of agents was overrunning the country with the prospectuses of his books, and delivering them by the scores of thousands in completed sale. Of the *Innocents Abroad* he said, "It sells right along just like the Bible," and *Roughing It* was swiftly following, without perhaps ever quite overtaking it in popularity. But he lectured Aldrich and me on the folly of that mode of publication in the trade which we had thought it the highest success to achieve a chance in. "Anything but subscription publication is printing for private circulation," he maintained, and he so won upon our greed and hope that on the way back to Boston we planned the joint authorship of a volume adapted to subscription publication. We got a very good name for it, as we believed, in *Memorable Murders*, and we never got farther with it, but by the time we reached Boston we were rolling in wealth so deep that we could hardly walk home in the frugal fashion by which we still thought it best to spare carfare; carriage fare we did not dream of even in that opulence.

III

The visits to Hartford which had begun with this affluence continued without actual increase of riches for me, but now I went alone, and in Warner's European and Egyptian absences I formed the habit of going to Clemens. By this time he was in his new house, where he used to give me a royal chamber on the ground floor, and come in at night after I had gone to bed to take off the burglar alarm so that the family should not be roused if anybody tried to get in at my window. This would be after we had sat up late, he smoking the last of his innumerable cigars, and soothing his tense nerves with a mild hot Scotch, while we both talked and talked and talked, of everything in the heavens and on the earth, and the waters under the earth. After two days of this talk I would come away hollow, realizing myself best in the image of one of those locust-shells which you find sticking to the bark of trees at the end of summer. Once, after some such bout of brains, we went down to New York together, and sat facing each other in the Pullman smoker without passing a syllable till we had occasion to say, "Well, we're there." Then, with our installation in a now vanished hotel (the old Brunswick, to be specific), the talk began again with the inspiration of the novel environment, and went on and on. We wished to be asleep, but we could not stop, and he lounged through the rooms in the long nightgown which he always wore in preference to the pajamas which he despised, and told the story of his life, the inexhaustible, the fairy, the Arabian Nights story, which I could never tire of even when it began to be told over again. Or at times he would reason high—

> Of Providence, foreknowledge, will and fate,
> Fixed fate, free will, foreknowledge absolute,

walking up and down, and halting now and then, with a fine toss and slant of his shaggy head, as some bold thought or splendid joke struck him.

He was in those days a constant attendant at the church of his great friend, the Rev. Joseph H. Twichell, and at least tacitly far from the entire negation he came to at last. I should say he had hardly yet examined the grounds of his passive acceptance of his wife's belief, for it was hers and not his, and he held it unscanned in the beautiful and tender loyalty to her which was the most moving quality of his most faithful soul. I make bold to speak of the love between them, because without it I could not make him known to others as he was known to me. It was a greater part of him than the love of most men for their wives, and she merited all the worship he could give her, all the devotion, all the implicit obedience, by her surpassing force and beauty of character. She was in a way the loveliest person I have ever seen, the gentlest, the kindest, without a touch of weakness; she united wonderful tact with wonderful truth; and Clemens not only accepted her rule implicitly, but he rejoiced, he gloried in it. I am not sure that he noticed all her goodness in the actions that made it a heavenly vision to others, he so had the habit of her goodness; but if there was any forlorn and helpless creature in the room Mrs. Clemens was somehow promptly at his side or hers; she was always seeking occasion of kindness to those in her household or out of it; she loved to let her heart go beyond the reach of her hand, and imagined the whole hard and suffering world with compassion for its structural as well as incidental wrongs. I suppose she had her ladyhood limitations, her female fears of etiquette and convention, but she did not let them hamper the wild and splendid generosity with which Clemens rebelled against the social stupidities and cruelties. She had been a lifelong invalid when he met her, and he liked to tell the beautiful story of their courtship to each new friend whom he found capable of feeling its beauty or worthy of hearing it. Naturally, her father had hesitated to give her into the keeping of the young strange Westerner, who had risen up out of the unknown with his giant reputation of burlesque humorist, and demanded guaranties, demanded proofs. "He asked me," Clemens would say, "if I couldn't give him the names of people who knew me in California, and when it was time to hear from them I heard from him. 'Well, Mr. Clemens,' he said, 'nobody seems to have a very good word for you.' I hadn't referred him to people that I thought were going to whitewash me. I thought it was all up with me, but I was disappointed. 'So I guess I shall have to back you myself.'"

Whether this made him faithfuler to the trust put in him I cannot say, but probably not; it was always in him to be faithful to any trust, and in proportion as a trust of his own was betrayed he was ruthlessly and implacably resentful. But I wish now to speak of the happiness of that household in Hartford which responded so perfectly to the ideals of the mother when the three daughters, so lovely and so gifted, were yet little children. There had been a boy, and "Yes, I killed him," Clemens once said, with the unsparing self-blame in which he would wreak an unavailing regret. He meant that he had taken the child out imprudently, and the child had taken the cold which he died of, but it was by no means certain this was through its father's imprudence. I never heard him speak of his son except that once, but no doubt in his deep heart his loss was irreparably present. He was a very tender father and delighted in the minds of his children, but he was wise enough to leave their training altogether to the wisdom of their mother. He left them to that in everything, keeping for himself the pleasure of teaching them little scenes of drama, learning languages with them, and leading them in singing. They came to the table with their parents, and could have set him an example in behavior when, in moments of intense excitement, he used to leave his place and walk up and down the room, flying his napkin and talking and talking.

It was after his first English sojourn that I used to visit him, and he was then full of praise of everything English: the English personal independence and public spirit, and hospitality, and truth. He liked to tell stories in proof of their virtues, but he was not blind to the defects of their virtues: their submissive acceptance of caste, their callousness with strangers, their bluntness with one another. Mrs. Clemens had been in a way to suffer socially more than he, and she praised the English less. She had sat after dinner with ladies who snubbed and ignored one another, and left her to find her own amusement in the absence of the attention with which Americans perhaps cloy their guests, but which she could not help preferring. In their successive sojourns among them I believe he came to like the English less and she more; the fine delight of his first acceptance among them did not renew itself till his Oxford degree was given him; then it made his cup run over, and he was glad the whole world should see it.

His wife would not chill the ardor of his early Anglomania, and in this, as in everything, she wished to humor him to the utmost. No one could have realized more than she his essential fineness, his innate nobleness. Marriages are what the parties to them alone really know them to be, but from the outside I should say that this marriage was one of the most perfect. It lasted in his absolute devotion to the day of her death, that delayed long in cruel suffering, and that left one side of him in lasting night. From Florence there came to me heartbreaking letters from him about the torture she was undergoing, and at last a letter saying she was dead, with the simple-hearted cry, "I wish I was with Livy." I do not know why I have left saying till now that she was a very beautiful woman, classically regular in features, with black hair smooth over her forehead, and with tenderly peering, myopic eyes, always behind glasses, and a smile of angelic kindness. But this kindness went with a sense of humor which qualified her to appreciate the self-lawed genius of a man who will be remembered with the great humorists of all time, with Cervantes, with Swift, or with any others worthy his company; none of them was his equal in humanity.

IV

Clemens had appointed himself, with the architect's connivance, a luxurious study over the library in his new house, but as his children grew older this study, with its carved and cushioned armchairs, was given over to them for a schoolroom, and he took the room above his stable, which had been intended for his coachman. There we used to talk together, when we were not walking and talking together, until he discovered that he could make a more commodious use of the billiard room at the top of his house, for the purposes of literature and friendship. It was pretty cold up there in the early spring and late fall weather with which I chiefly associate the place, but by lighting up all the gas burners and kindling a reluctant fire on the hearth we could keep it well above freezing. Clemens could also push the balls about, and, without rivalry from me, who could no more play billiards than smoke, could win endless games of pool, while he carried points of argument against imaginable differers in opinion. Here he wrote many of his tales and sketches, and for anything I know some of his books. I particularly remember his reading me here his first rough sketch of *Captain Stormfield's Visit to Heaven,* with the real name of the captain, whom I knew already from his many stories about him.

We had a peculiar pleasure in looking off from the high windows on the pretty Hartford landscape, and down from them into the tops of the trees clothing the hillside by which his house stood. We agreed that there was a novel charm in trees seen from such a vantage, far surpassing that of the farther scenery. He had not been a country boy for nothing; rather he had been a country boy, or, still better, a village boy, for everything that Nature can offer the young of our species, and no aspect of her was lost on him. We were natives of the same vast Mississippi Valley; and Missouri was not so far from Ohio but that we were akin in our first knowledges of woods and fields as we were in our early parlance. I had outgrown the use of mine through my greater bookishness, but I gladly recognized the phrases which he employed for their lasting juiciness and the long-remembered savor they had on his mental palate.

I have elsewhere sufficiently spoken of his unsophisticated use of words, of the diction which forms the backbone of his manly style. If I mention my own greater bookishness, by which I mean his less quantitative reading, it is to give myself better occasion to note that he was always reading some vital book. It might be some out-of-the-way book, but it had the root of the human matter in it: a volume of great trials; one of the supreme autobiographies; a signal passage of history, a narrative of travel, a story of captivity, which gave him life at first-hand. As I remember, he did not care much for fiction, and in that sort he had certain distinct loathings; there were certain authors whose names he seemed not so much to pronounce as to spew out of his mouth. Goldsmith was one of these, but his prime abhorrence was my dear and honored prime favorite, Jane Austen. He once said to me, I suppose after he had been reading some of my unsparing praises of her—I am always praising her, "You seem to think that woman could write," and he forebore withering me with his scorn, apparently because we had been friends so long, and he more pitied than hated me for my bad taste. He seemed not to have any preferences among novelists; or at least I never heard him express any. He used to read the modern novels I praised, in or out of print; but I do not think he much liked reading fiction. As for plays, he detested the theater, and said he would as lief do a sum as follow a plot on the stage. He could not, or did not, give any reasons for his literary abhorrences, and perhaps he really had none. But he could have said very distinctly, if he had needed, why he liked the books he did. I was away at the time of his great Browning passion, and I know of it chiefly from hearsay; but at the time Tolstoy was doing what could be done to make me over Clemens wrote, "That man seems to have been to you what Browning was to me."

I do not know that he had other favorites among the poets, but he had favorite poems which he liked to read to you, and he read, of course, splendidly. I have forgotten what piece of John Hay's it was that he liked so much, but I remember how he fiercely reveled in the vengefulness of William Morris' *Sir Guy of the Dolorous Blast,* and how he especially exulted in the lines which tell of the supposed speaker's joy in slaying the murderer of his brother:

> I am threescore years and ten,
>   And my hair is nigh turned gray,
> But I am glad to think of the moment when
>   I took his life away.

Generally, I fancy his pleasure in poetry was not great, and I do not believe he cared much for the conventionally accepted masterpieces of literature. He liked to find out good things and great things for himself; sometimes he would discover these in a masterpiece new to him alone, and then, if you brought his ignorance home to him, he enjoyed it, and enjoyed it the more the more you rubbed it in.

Of all the literary men I have known he was the most unliterary in his make and manner. I do not know whether he had any acquaintance with Latin, but I believe not the least; German he knew pretty well, and Italian enough late in life to have fun with it; but he used English in all its alien derivations as if it were native to his own air, as if it had come up out of American, out of Missourian ground. His style was what we know, for good and for bad, but his manner, if I may difference the two, was as entirely his own as if no one had ever written before. I have noted before this how he was not enslaved to the consecutiveness in writing which the rest of us try to keep chained to. That is, he wrote as he thought, and as all men think, without sequence, without an eye to what went before or should come after. If something beyond or beside what he was saying occurred to him, he invited it into his page, and made it as much at home there as the nature of it would suffer him. Then, when he was through with the welcoming of this casual and unexpected guest, he would go back to the company he was entertaining, and keep on with what he had been talking about. He observed this manner in the construction of his sentences, and the arrangement of his chapters, and the ordering or disordering of his compilations. I helped him with a Library of Humor, which he once edited, and when I had done my work according to tradition, with authors, times, and topics carefully studied in due sequence, he tore it all apart, and "chucked" the pieces in wherever the fancy for them took him at the moment. He was right: we were not making a textbook, but a book for the pleasure rather than the instruction of the reader, and he did not see why the principle on which he built his travels and reminiscences and tales and novels should not apply to it; and I do not now see, either, though at the time it confounded me. On minor points he was, beyond any author I have known, without favorite phrases or pet words. He utterly despised the avoidance of repetitions out of fear of tautology. If a word served his turn better than a substitute, he would use it as many times in a page as he chose.

v

At that time I had become editor of the *Atlantic Monthly*, and I had allegiances belonging to the conduct of what was and still remains the most scrupulously cultivated of our periodicals. When Clemens began to write for it he came willingly under its rules, for with all his wilfulness there never was a more biddable man in things you could show him a reason for. He never made the least of that trouble which so abounds for the hapless editor from narrower-minded contributors. If you wanted a thing changed, very good, he changed it; if you suggested that a word or a sentence or a paragraph had better be struck out, very good, he struck it out. His proof sheets came back each a veritable "mush of concession," as Emerson says. Now and then he would try a little stronger language than the *Atlantic* had stomach for, and once when I sent him a proof I made him observe that I had left out the profanity. He wrote back: "Mrs. Clemens opened that proof, and lit into the room with danger in her eye. What profanity? You see, when I read the manuscript to her I skipped that." It was part of his joke to pretend a violence in that gentlest creature which the more amusingly realized the situation to their friends.

I was always very glad of him and proud of him as a contributor, but I must not claim the whole merit, or the first merit of having him write for us. It was the publisher, the late H. O. Houghton, who felt the incongruity of his absence from the leading periodical of the country, and was always urging me to get him to write. I will take the credit of being eager for him, but it is to the publisher's credit that he tried, so far as the modest traditions of the *Atlantic* would permit, to meet the expectations in pay which the colossal profits of Clemens' books might naturally have bred in him. Whether he was really able to do this he never knew from Clemens himself, but probably twenty dollars a page did not surfeit the author of books that "sold right along just like the Bible."

We had several short contributions from Clemens first, all of capital quality, and then we had the series of papers which went mainly to the making of his great book, *Life on the Mississippi*. Upon the whole I have the notion that Clemens thought this his greatest book, and he was supported in his opinion by that of the *portier* in his hotel at Vienna, and that of the German Emperor, who, as he told me with equal respect for the preference of each, united in thinking it his best; with such far-sundered social poles approaching in its favor, he apparently found himself without standing for opposition. At any rate, the papers won instant appreciation from his editor and publisher, and from the readers of their periodical, which they expected to prosper beyond precedent in its circulation. But those were days of simpler acceptance of the popular rights of newspapers than these are, when magazines strictly guard their vested interests against them. The New York *Times* and the St. Louis *Democrat* profited by the advance copies of the magazine sent them to reprint the papers month by month. Together they covered nearly the whole reading territory of the Union, and the terms of their daily publication enabled them to anticipate the magazine in its own restricted field. Its subscription list was not enlarged in the slightest measure, and the *Atlantic Monthly* languished on the newsstands as undesired as ever.

VI

It was among my later visits to Hartford that we began to talk up the notion of collaborating a play, but we did not arrive at any clear intention, and it was a telegram out of the clear sky that one day summoned me from Boston to help with a continuation of *Colonel Sellers.* I had been a witness of the high joy of Clemens in the prodigious triumph of the first *Colonel Sellers,* which had been dramatized from the novel of *The Gilded Age.* This was the joint work of Clemens and Charles Dudley Warner, and the story had been put upon the stage by someone in Utah, whom Clemens first brought to book in the courts for violation of his copyright, and then indemnified for such rights as his adaptation of the book had given him. The structure of the play as John T. Raymond gave it was substantially the work of this unknown dramatist. Clemens never pretended, to me at any rate, that he had the least hand in it; he frankly owned that he was incapable of dramatization; yet the vital part was his, for the characters in the play were his as the book embodied them, and the success which it won with the public was justly his. This he shared equally with the actor, following the company with an agent, who counted out the author's share of the gate money, and sent him a note of the amount every day by postal card. The postals used to come about dinner-time, and Clemens would read them aloud to us in wild triumph. One hundred and fifty dollars—two hundred dollars—three hundred dollars were the gay figures which they bore, and which he flaunted in the air before he sat down at table, or rose from it to brandish, and then, flinging his napkin into his chair, walked up and down to exult in.

By and by the popularity of the play waned, and the time came when he sickened of the whole affair, and withdrew his agent, and took whatever gain from it the actor apportioned him. He was apt to have these sudden surceases, following upon the intensities of his earlier interest; though he seemed always to have the notion of making something more of *Colonel Sellers*. But when I arrived in Hartford in answer to his summons, I found him with no definite idea of what he wanted to do with him. I represented that we must have some sort of plan, and he agreed that we should both jot down a scenario overnight and compare our respective schemes the next morning. As the author of a large number of little plays which have been privately presented throughout the United States and in parts of the United Kingdom, without ever getting upon the public stage except for the noble ends of charity, and then promptly getting off it, I felt authorized to make him observe that his scheme was as nearly nothing as chaos could be. He agreed hilariously with me, and was willing to let it stand in proof of his entire dramatic inability. At the same time he liked my plot very much, which ultimated Sellers, according to Clemens' intention, as a man crazed by his own inventions and by his superstition that he was the rightful heir to an English earldom. The exuberant nature of Sellers and the vast range of his imagination served our purpose in other ways. Clemens made him a spiritualist, whose specialty in the occult was materialization; he became on impulse an ardent temperance reformer, and he headed a procession of temperance ladies after disinterestedly testing the deleterious effects of liquor upon himself until he could not walk straight; always he wore a marvelous fire-extinguisher strapped on his back, to give proof in any emergency of the effectiveness of his invention in that way.

We had a jubilant fortnight in working the particulars of these things out. It was not possible for Clemens to write like anybody else, but I could very easily write like Clemens, and we took the play scene and scene about, quite secure of coming out in temperamental agreement. The characters remained for the most part his, and I varied them only to make them more like his than, if possible, he could. Several years after, when I looked over a copy of the play, I could not always tell my work from his; I only knew that I had done certain scenes. We would work all day long at our several tasks, and then at night, before dinner, read them over to each other. No dramatists ever got greater joy out of their creations, and when I reflect that the public never had the chance of sharing our joy I pity the public from a full heart. I still believe that the play was immensely funny; I still believe that if it could once have got behind the foot-lights it would have continued to pack the house before them for an indefinite succession of nights. But this may be my fondness.

At any rate, it was not to be. Raymond had identified himself with Sellers in the playgoing imagination, and whether consciously or unconsciously we constantly worked with Raymond in our minds. But before this time bitter displeasures had risen between Clemens and Raymond, and Clemens was determined that Raymond should never have the play. He first offered it to several other actors, who eagerly caught at it, only to give it back with the despairing renunciation, "That is a Raymond play." We tried managers with it, but their only question was whether they could get Raymond to do it. In the meantime Raymond had provided himself with a play for the winter—a very good play, by Demarest Lloyd; and he was in no hurry for ours. Perhaps he did not really care for it; perhaps he knew when he heard of it that it must come to him in the end. In the end it did, from my hand, for Clemens would not meet him. I found him in a mood of sweet reasonableness, perhaps the more softened by one of those lunches which our publisher, the hospitable James R. Osgood, was always bringing people together over in Boston. He said that he could not do the play that winter, but he was sure that he should like it, and he had no doubt he would do it the next winter. So I gave him the manuscript, in spite of Clemens' charges, for his suspicions and rancors were such that he would not have had me leave it for a moment in the actor's hands. But it seemed a conclusion that involved success and fortune for us. In due time, but I do not remember now long after, Raymond declared himself delighted with the piece; he entered into a satisfactory agreement for it, and at the beginning of the next season he started with it to Buffalo, where he was to give a first production. At Rochester he paused long enough to return it, with the explanation that a friend had noted to him the fact that Colonel Sellers in the play was a lunatic, and insanity was so serious a thing that it could not be represented on the stage without outraging the sensibilities of the audience; or words to that effect. We were too far off to allege Hamlet to the contrary, or King Lear, or to instance the delight which generations of readers throughout the world had taken in the mad freaks of Don Quixote.

Whatever were the real reasons of Raymond for rejecting the play, we had to be content with those he gave, and to set about getting it into other hands. In this effort we failed even more signally than before, if that were possible. At last a clever and charming elocutionist, who had long wished to get himself on the stage, heard of it and asked to see it. We would have shown it to anyone by this time, and we very willingly showed it to him. He came to Hartford and did some scenes from it for us. I must say he did them very well, quite as well as Raymond could have done them, in whose manner he did them. But now, late toward spring, the question was where he could get an engagement with the play, and we ended by hiring a theater in New York for a week of trial performances.

Clemens came on with me to Boston, where we were going to make some changes in the piece, and where we made them to our satisfaction, but not to the effect of that high rapture which we had in the first draft. He went back to Hartford, and then the cold fit came upon me, and "in visions of the night, in slumberings upon the bed," ghastly forms of failure appalled me, and when I rose in the morning I wrote him: "Here is a play which every manager has put out-of-doors and which every actor known to us has refused, and now we go and give it to an elocutioner. We are fools." Whether Clemens agreed with me or not in my conclusion, he agreed with me in my premises, and we promptly bought our play off the stage at a cost of seven hundred dollars, which we shared between us. But Clemens was never a man to give up. I relinquished gratis all right and title I had in the play, and he paid its entire expenses for a week of one-night stands in the country. It never came to New York; and yet I think now that if it had come, it would have succeeded. So hard does the faith of the unsuccessful dramatist in his work die!

VII

There is an incident of this time so characteristic of both men that I will yield to the temptation of giving it here. After I had gone to Hartford in response to Clemens' telegram, Matthew Arnold arrived in Boston, and one of my family called on him, to explain why I was not at home to receive his introduction: I had gone to see Mark Twain. "Oh, but he doesn't like *that* sort of thing, does he?" "He likes Mr. Clemens very much," my representative answered, "and he thinks him one of the greatest men he ever knew." I was still Clemens' guest at Hartford when Arnold came there to lecture, and one night we went to meet him at a reception. While his hand laxly held mine in greeting, I saw his eyes fixed intensely on the other side of the room. "Who—who in the world is that?" I looked and said, "Oh, that is Mark Twain." I do not remember just how their instant encounter was contrived by Arnold's wish, but I have the impression that they were not parted for long during the evening, and the next night Arnold, as if still under the glamour of that potent presence, was at Clemens' house. I cannot say how they got on, or what they made of each other; if Clemens ever spoke of Arnold, I do not recall what he said, but Arnold had shown a sense of him from which the incredulous sniff of the polite world, now so universally exploded, had already perished. It might well have done so with his first dramatic vision of that prodigious head. Clemens was then hard upon fifty, and he had kept, as he did to the end, the slender figure of his youth, but the ashes of the burnt-out years were beginning to gray the fires of that splendid shock of red hair which he held to the height of a stature apparently greater than it was, and tilted from side to side in his undulating walk. He glimmered at you from the narrow slits of fine blue-greenish eyes, under branching brows, which with age grew more and more like a sort of plumage, and he was apt to smile into your face with a subtle but amiable perception, and yet with a sort of remote absence; you were all there for him, but he was not all there for you.

VIII

I shall not try to give chronological order to my recollections of him, but since I am just now with him in Hartford I will speak of him in association with the place. Once when I came on from Cambridge he followed me to my room to see that the water was not frozen in my bath, or something of the kind, for it was very cold weather, and then hospitably lingered. Not to lose time in banalities I began at once from the thread of thought in my mind. "I wonder why we hate the past so," and he responded from the depths of his own consciousness, "It's so damned humiliating," which is what any man would say of his past if he were honest; but honest men are few when it comes to themselves. Clemens was one of the few, and the first of them among all the people I have known. I have known, I suppose, men as truthful, but not so promptly, so absolutely, so positively, so almost aggressively truthful. He could lie, of course, and did to save others from grief or harm; he was not stupidly truthful; but his first impulse was to say out the thing and everything that was in him. To those who can understand it will not be contradictory of his sense of humiliation from the past that he was not ashamed for anything he ever did to the point of wishing to hide it. He could be, and he was, bitterly sorry for his errors, which he had enough of in his life, but he was not ashamed in that mean way. What he had done he owned to, good, bad, or indifferent, and if it was bad he was rather amused than troubled as to the effect in your mind. He would not obtrude the fact upon you, but if it were in the way of personal history he would not dream of withholding it, far less of hiding it.

He was the readiest of men to allow an error if he were found in it. In one of our walks about Hartford, when he was in the first fine flush of his agnosticism, he declared that Christianity had done nothing to improve morals and conditions, and that the world under the highest pagan civilization was as well off as it was under the highest Christian influences. I happened to be fresh from the reading of Charles Loring Brace's *Gesta Christi; or, History of Humane Progress,* and I could offer him abundant proofs that he was wrong. He did not like that evidently, but he instantly gave way, saying he had not known those things. Later he was more tolerant in his denials of Christianity, but just then he was feeling his freedom from it, and rejoicing in having broken what he felt to have been the shackles of belief worn so long. He greatly admired Robert Ingersoll, whom he called an angelic orator, and regarded as an evangel of a new gospel—the gospel of free thought. He took the warmest interest in the newspaper controversy raging at the time as to the existence of a hell; when the noes carried the day, I suppose that no enemy of perdition was more pleased. He still loved his old friend and pastor, Mr. Twichell, but he no longer went to hear him preach his sane and beautiful sermons, and was, I think, thereby the greater loser. Long before that I had asked him if he went regularly to church, and he groaned out: "Oh yes, I go. It 'most kills me, but I go," and I did not need his telling me to understand that he went because his wife wished it. He did tell me, after they both ceased to go, that it had finally come to her saying, "Well, if you are to be lost, I want to be lost with you." He could accept that willingness for supreme sacrifice and exult in it because of the supreme truth as he saw it. After they had both ceased to be formal Christians, she was still grieved by his denial of immortality, so grieved that he resolved upon one of those heroic lies, which for love's sake he held above even the truth, and he went to her, saying that he had been thinking the whole matter over, and now he was convinced that the soul did live after death. It was too late. Her keen vision pierced through his ruse, as it did when he brought the doctor who had diagnosticated her case as organic disease of the heart, and, after making him go over the facts of it again with her, made him declare it merely functional.

To make an end of these records as to Clemens' beliefs, so far as I knew them, I should say that he never went back to anything like faith in the Christian theology, or in the notion of life after death, or in a conscious divinity. It is best to be honest in this matter; he would have hated anything else, and I do not believe that the truth in it can hurt anyone. At one period he argued that there must have been a cause, a conscious source of things; that the universe could not have come by chance. I have heard also that in his last hours or moments he said, or his dearest ones hoped he had said, something about meeting again. But the expression, of which they could not be certain, was of the vaguest, and it was perhaps addressed to their tenderness out of his tenderness. All his expressions to me were of a courageous renunciation of any hope of living again, or elsewhere seeing those he had lost. He suffered terribly in their loss, and he was not fool enough to try ignoring his grief. He knew that for this there were but two medicines; that it would wear itself out with the years, and that meanwhile there was nothing for it but those respites in which the mourner forgets himself in slumber. I remember that in a black hour of my own when I was called down to see him, as he thought from sleep, he said with an infinite, an exquisite compassion, "Oh, did I wake you, did I *wake* you?" Nothing more, but the look, the voice, were everything; and while I live they cannot pass from my sense.

IX

He was the most caressing of men in his pity, but he had the fine instinct, which would have pleased Lowell, of never putting his hands on you—fine, delicate hands, with taper fingers, and pink nails, like a girl's, and sensitively quivering in moments of emotion; he did not paw you with them to show his affection, as so many of us Americans are apt to

do. Among the half-dozen, or half-hundred, personalities
that each of us becomes, I should say that Clemens' central
and final personality was something exquisite. His casual
acquaintance might know him, perhaps, from his fierce intensity, his wild pleasure in shocking people with his ribaldries and profanities, or from the mere need of loosing his
rebellious spirit in that way, as anything but exquisite, and
yet that was what in the last analysis he was. They might
come away loathing or hating him, but one could not know
him well without realizing him the most serious, the most
humane, the most conscientious of men. He was Southwestern, and born amid the oppression of a race that had
no rights as against ours, but I never saw a man more regard-
ful of negroes. He had a yellow butler when I first began
to know him, because he said he could not bear to order
a white man about, but the terms of his ordering George
were those of the softest entreaty which command ever
wore. He loved to rely upon George, who was such a broken
reed in some things, though so stanch in others, and the
fervent Republican in politics that Clemens then liked him
to be. He could interpret Clemens' meaning to the public
without conveying his mood, and could render his roughest
answer smooth to the person denied his presence. His general instructions were that this presence was to be denied
all but personal friends, but the soft heart of George was
sometimes touched by importunity, and once he came up
into the billiard-room saying that Mr. Smith wished to see
Clemens. Upon inquiry, Mr. Smith developed no ties of
friendship, and Clemens said, "You go and tell Mr. Smith
that I wouldn't come down to see the Twelve Apostles."
George turned from the threshold where he had kept
himself, and framed a paraphrase of this message which apparently sent Mr. Smith away content with himself and all
the rest of the world.

The part of him that was Western in his Southwestern
origin Clemens kept to the end, but he was the most de-
southernized Southerner I ever knew. No man more perfectly sensed and more entirely abhorred slavery, and no
one has ever poured such scorn upon the second-hand,

Walter-Scotticized, pseudo-chivalry of the Southern ideal. He held himself responsible for the wrong which the white race had done the black race in slavery, and he explained, in paying the way of a negro student through Yale, that he was doing it as his part of the reparation due from every white to every black man. He said he had never seen this student, nor ever wished to see him or know his name; it was quite enough that he was a negro. About that time a colored cadet was expelled from West Point for some point of conduct "unbecoming an officer and gentleman," and there was the usual shabby philosophy in a portion of the press to the effect that a negro could never feel the claim of honor. The man was fifteen parts white, but, "Oh yes," Clemens said, with bitter irony, "it was that one part black that undid him." It made him a "nigger" and incapable of being a gentleman. It was to blame for the whole thing. The fifteen parts white were guiltless.

Clemens was entirely satisfied with the result of the Civil War, and he was eager to have its facts and meanings brought out at once in history. He ridiculed the notion, held by many, that "it was not yet time" to philosophize the events of the great struggle; that we must "wait till its passions had cooled," and "the clouds of strife had cleared away." He maintained that the time would never come when we should see its motives and men and deeds more clearly, and that now, now, was the hour to ascertain them in lasting verity. Picturesquely and dramatically he portrayed the imbecility of deferring the inquiry at any point to the distance of future years when inevitably the facts would begin to put on fable.

He had powers of sarcasm and a relentless rancor in his contempt which those who knew him best appreciated most. The late Noah Brooks, who had been in California at the beginning of Clemens' career, and had witnessed the effect of his ridicule before he had learned to temper it, once said to me that he would rather have anyone else in the world down on him than Mark Twain. But as Clemens grew older he grew more merciful, not to the wrong, but

to the men who were in it. The wrong was often the source
of his wildest drolling. He considered it in such hopelessness
of ever doing it justice that his despair broke in laughter.

X

I go back to that house in Hartford, where I was so often
a happy guest, with tenderness for each of its endearing
aspects. Over the chimney in the library which had been
cured of smoking by so much art and science, Clemens had
written in perennial brass the words of Emerson, "The ornament of a house is the friends who frequent it," and he
gave his guests a welcome of the simplest and sweetest cor-
diality: but I must not go aside to them from my recollections of him, which will be of sufficient garrulity, if I give
them as fully as I wish. The windows of the library looked
northward from the hillside above which the house stood,
and over the little valley with the stream in it, and they
showed the leaves of the trees that almost brushed them as
in a Claude Lorraine glass. To the eastward the dining-
room opened amply, and to the south there was a wide hall,
where the voices of friends made themselves heard as they
entered without ceremony and answered his joyous hail. At
the west was a little semicircular conservatory of a pattern
invented by Mrs. Harriet Beecher Stowe, and adopted in
most of the houses of her kindly neighborhood. The plants
were set in the ground, and the flowering vines climbed up
the sides and overhung the roof above the silent spray of a
fountain companied by callas and other water-loving lilies.
There, while we breakfasted, Patrick came in from the barn
and sprinkled the pretty bower, which poured out its responsive perfume in the delicate accents of its varied blossoms.
Breakfast was Clemens' best meal, and he sat longer at his
steak and coffee than at the courses of his dinner; luncheon
was nothing to him, unless, as might happen, he made it
his dinner, and reserved the later repast as the occasion of
walking up and down the room, and discoursing at large
on anything that came into his head. Like most good talkers,

he liked other people to have their say; he did not talk them down; he stopped instantly at another's remark and gladly or politely heard him through; he even made believe to find suggestion or inspiration in what was said. His children came to the table, as I have told, and after dinner he was apt to join his fine tenor to their trebles in singing.

Fully half our meetings were at my house in Cambridge, where he made himself as much at home as in Hartford. He would come ostensibly to stay at the Parker House, in Boston, and take a room, where he would light the gas and leave it burning, after dressing, while he drove out to Cambridge and stayed two or three days with us. Once, I suppose it was after a lecture, he came in evening dress and passed twenty-four hours with us in that guise, wearing an overcoat to hide it when we went for a walk. Sometimes he wore the slippers which he preferred to shoes at home, and if it was muddy, as it was wont to be in Cambridge, he would put a pair of rubbers over them for our rambles. He liked the lawlessness and our delight in allowing it, and he rejoiced in the confession of his hostess, after we had once almost worn ourselves out in our pleasure with the intense talk, with the stories and the laughing, that his coming almost killed her, but it was worth it.

In those days he was troubled with sleeplessness, or, rather, with reluctant sleepiness, and he had various specifics for promoting it. At first it had been champagne just before going to bed, and we provided that, but later he appeared from Boston with four bottles of lager beer under his arms; lager beer, he said now, was the only thing to make you go to sleep, and we provided that. Still later, on a visit I paid him at Hartford, I learned that hot Scotch was the only soporific worth considering, and Scotch whisky duly found its place on our sideboard. One day, very long afterward, I asked him if he were still taking hot Scotch to make him sleep. He said he was not taking anything. For a while he had found going to bed on the bathroom floor a soporific; then one night he went to rest in his own bed at ten o'clock, and had gone promptly to sleep without anything. He had done the like with the like effect ever since. Of course, it amused him; there were few experiences of life, grave or gay, which did not amuse him, even when they wronged him.

He came on to Cambridge in April 1875 to go with me to the centennial ceremonies at Concord in celebration of the battle of the Minute Men with the British troops a hundred years before. We both had special invitations, including passage from Boston; but I said, Why bother to go into Boston when we could just as well take the train for Concord at the Cambridge station? He equally decided that it would be absurd; so we breakfasted deliberately, and then walked to the station, reasoning of many things as usual. When the train stopped, we found it packed inside and out. People stood dense on the platforms of the cars; to our startled eyes they seemed to project from the windows, and unless memory betrays me they lay strewn upon the roofs like brakemen slain at the post of duty. Whether this was really so or not, it is certain that the train presented an impenetrable front even to our imagination, and we left it to go its way without the slightest effort to board. We remounted the fame-worn steps of Porter's Station, and began exploring North Cambridge for some means of transportation overland to Concord, for we were that far on the road by which the British went and came on the day of the battle. The liverymen whom we appealed to received us, some with compassion, some with derision, but in either mood convinced us that we could not have hired a cat to attempt our conveyance, much less a horse, or vehicle of any description. It was a raw, windy day, very unlike the exceptionally hot April day when the routed redcoats, pursued by the Colonials, fled panting back to Boston, with "their tongues hanging out like dogs," but we could not take due comfort in the vision of their discomfiture; we could almost envy them, for they had at least got to Concord. A swift procession of coaches, carriages, and buggies, all going to Concord, passed us, inert and helpless, on the sidewalk in the peculiarly cold mud of North Cambridge. We began to wonder if we might not stop one of them and bribe it to take us, but we had not the courage to try, and

Clemens seized the opportunity to begin suffering with an acute indigestion, which gave his humor a very dismal cast. I felt keenly the shame of defeat, and the guilt of responsibility for our failure, and when a gay party of students came toward us on the top of a tallyho, luxuriously empty inside, we felt that our chance had come, and our last chance. He said that if I would stop them and tell them who I was they would gladly, perhaps proudly, give us passage; I contended that if with his far vaster renown he would approach them, our success would be assured. While we stood, lost in this "contest of civilities," the coach passed us, with gay notes blown from the horns of the students, and then Clemens started in pursuit, encouraged with shouts from the merry party who could not imagine who was trying to run them down, to a rivalry in speed. The unequal match could end only in one way, and I am glad I cannot recall what he said when he came back to me. Since then I have often wondered at the grief which would have wrung those blithe young hearts if they could have known that they might have had the company of Mark Twain to Concord that day and did not.

We hung about, unavailingly, in the bitter wind a while longer, and then slowly, very slowly, made our way home. We wished to pass as much time as possible, in order to give probability to the deceit we intended to practice, for we could not bear to own ourselves baffled in our boasted wisdom of taking the train at Porter's Station, and had agreed to say that we had been to Concord and got back. Even after coming home to my house, we felt that our statement would be wanting in verisimilitude without further delay, and we crept quietly into my library, and made up a roaring fire on the hearth, and thawed ourselves out in the heat of it before we regained our courage for the undertaking. With all these precautions we failed, for when our statement was imparted to the proposed victim she instantly pronounced it unreliable, and we were left with it on our hands intact. I think the humor of this situation was finally a greater pleasure to Clemens than an actual visit to Concord would have been; only a few weeks before his death he laughed our defeat over with one of my family in Bermuda, and exulted in our prompt detection.

XI

From our joint experience in failing I argue that Clemens' affection for me must have been great to enable him to condone in me the final defection which was apt to be the end of our enterprises. I have fancied that I presented to him a surface of such entire trustworthiness that he could not imagine the depths of unreliability beneath it; and that never realizing it, he always broke through with fresh surprise but unimpaired faith. He liked, beyond all things, to push an affair to the bitter end, and the end was never too bitter unless it brought grief or harm to another. Once in a telegraph office at a railway station he was treated with such insolent neglect by the young lady in charge, who was preoccupied in a flirtation with a "gentleman friend," that emulous of the public spirit which he admired in the English, he told her he should report her to her superiors, and (probably to her astonishment) he did so. He went back to Hartford, and in due time the poor girl came to me in terror and in tears; for I had abetted Clemens in his action, and had joined my name to his in his appeal to the authorities. She was threatened with dismissal unless she made full apology to him and brought back assurance of its acceptance. I felt able to give this, and, of course, he eagerly approved; I think he telegraphed his approval. Another time, some years afterward, we sat down together in places near the end of a car, and a brakeman came in looking for his official note-book. Clemens found that he had sat down upon it, and handed it to him; the man scolded him very abusively, and came back again and again, still scolding him for having no more sense than to sit down on a note-book. The patience of Clemens in bearing it was so angelic that I saw fit to comment, "I suppose you will report this fellow." "Yes," he answered, slowly and sadly. "That's what I should have done once. But now I remember that he gets twenty dollars a month."

Nothing could have been wiser, nothing tenderer, and his humanity was not for humanity alone. He abhorred the dull and savage joy of the sportsman in a lucky shot, an unerring aim, and once when I met him in the country he had just been sickened by the success of a gunner in bringing down a blackbird, and he described the poor, stricken, glossy thing, how it lay throbbing its life out on the grass, with such pity as he might have given a wounded child. I find this a fit place to say that his mind and soul were with those who do the hard work of the world, in fear of those who give them a chance for their livelihoods and underpay them all they can. He never went so far in socialism as I have gone, if he went that way at all, but he was fascinated with *Looking Backward* and had Bellamy to visit him; and from the first he had a luminous vision of organized labor as the only present help for working-men. He would show that side with such clearness and such force that you could not say anything in hopeful contradiction; he saw with that relentless insight of his that in the unions was the working-man's only present hope of standing up like a man against money and the power of it. There was a time when I was afraid that his eyes were a little holden from the truth; but in the very last talk I heard from him I found that I was wrong, and that this great humorist was as great a humanist as ever. I wish that all the work-folk could know this, and could know him their friend in life as he was in literature; as he was in such a glorious gospel of equality as the *Connecticut Yankee in King Arthur's Court.*

XII

Whether I will or no I must let things come into my story thoughtwise, as he would have let them, for I cannot remember them in their order. One night, while we were giving a party, he suddenly stormed in with a friend of his and mine, Mr. Twichell, and immediately began to eat and drink of our supper, for they had come straight to our house from walking to Boston, or so great a part of the way as to be ahungered and athirst. I can see him now as he stood up in the midst of our friends, with his head thrown back, and in his hand a dish of those escalloped oysters without which no party in Cambridge was really a party, exulting in the tale of his adventure, which had abounded in the most original characters and amusing incidents at every mile of their progress. They had broken their journey with a night's rest, and they had helped themselves lavishly out by rail in the last half; but still it had been a mighty walk to do in two days. Clemens was a great walker in those years, and was always telling of his tramps with Mr. Twichell to Talcott's Tower, ten miles out of Hartford. As he walked of course he talked, and of course he smoked. Whenever he had been a few days with us, the whole house had to be aired, for he smoked all over it from breakfast to bedtime. He always went to bed with a cigar in his mouth, and sometimes, mindful of my fire insurance, I went up and took it away, still burning, after he had fallen asleep. I do not know how much a man may smoke and live, but apparently he smoked as much as a man could, for he smoked incessantly.

He did not care much to meet people, as I fancied, and we were greedy of him for ourselves; he was precious to us; and I would not have exposed him to the critical edge of that Cambridge acquaintance which might not have appreciated him at, say, his transatlantic value. In America his popularity was as instant as it was vast. But it must be acknowledged that for a much longer time here than in England polite learning hesitated his praise. In England rank, fashion, and culture rejoiced in him. Lord mayors, lord chief justices, and magnates of many kinds were his hosts; he was desired in country houses, and his bold genius captivated the favor of periodicals which spurned the rest of our nation. But in his own country it was different. In proportion as people thought themselves refined they questioned that quality which all recognize in him now, but which was then the inspired knowledge of the simple-hearted multitude. I went with him to see Longfellow, but I do not think Longfellow made much of him, and Lowell made less. He stopped as if with the long Semitic curve of

Clemens' nose, which in the indulgence of his passion for finding everyone more or less a Jew he pronounced unmistakably racial. It was two of my most fastidious Cambridge friends who accepted him with the English, the European entirety—namely, Charles Eliot Norton and Professor Francis J. Child. Norton was then newly back from a long sojourn abroad, and his judgments were delocalized. He met Clemens as if they had both been in England, and rejoiced in his bold freedom from environment, and in the rich variety and boundless reach of his talk. Child was of a personal liberty as great in its fastidious way as that of Clemens himself, and though he knew him only at second-hand, he exulted in the most audacious instance of his grotesquery, as I shall have to tell by and by, almost solely. I cannot say just why Clemens seemed not to hit the favor of our community of scribes and scholars, as Bret Harte had done, when he came on from California, and swept them before him, disrupting their dinners and delaying their lunches with impunity; but it is certain he did not, and I had better say so.

I am surprised to find from the bibliographical authorities that it was so late as 1875 when he came with the manuscript of *Tom Sawyer,* and asked me to read it, as a friend and critic, and not as an editor. I have an impression that this was at Mrs. Clemens' instance in his own uncertainty about printing it. She trusted me, I can say with a satisfaction few things now give me, to be her husband's true and cordial adviser, and I was so. I believe I never failed him in this part, though in so many of our enterprises and projects I was false as water through my temperamental love of backing out of any undertaking. I believe this never ceased to astonish him, and it has always astonished me; it appears to me quite out of character; though it is certain that an undertaking, when I have entered upon it, holds me rather than I it. But however this immaterial matter may be, I am glad to remember that I thoroughly liked *Tom Sawyer,* and said so with every possible amplification. Very likely, I also made my suggestions for its improvement; I could not have been a real critic without that; and I have no doubt they were gratefully accepted and, I hope, never acted upon. I went with him to the horse-car station in Harvard Square, as my frequent wont was, and put him aboard a car with his MS. in his hand, stayed and reassured, so far as I counted, concerning it. I do not know what his misgivings were; perhaps they were his wife's misgivings, for she wished him to be known not only for the wild and boundless humor that was in him, but for the beauty and tenderness and "natural piety"; and she would not have had him judged by a too close fidelity to the rude conditions of Tom Sawyer's life. This is the meaning that I read into the fact of his coming to me with those doubts.

XIII

Clemens had then and for many years the habit of writing to me about what he was doing, and still more of what he was experiencing. Nothing struck his imagination, in or out of the daily routine, but he wished to write me of it, and he wrote with the greatest fulness and a lavish dramatization, sometimes to the length of twenty or forty pages, so that I have now perhaps fifteen hundred pages of his letters. They will no doubt someday be published, but I am not even referring to them in these records, which I think had best come to the reader with an old man's falterings and uncertainties. With his frequent absences and my own abroad, and the intrusion of calamitous cares, the rich tide of his letters was more and more interrupted. At times it almost ceased, and then it would come again, a torrent. In the very last weeks of his life he burst forth, and, though too weak himself to write, he dictated his rage with me for recommending to him a certain author whose truthfulness he could not deny, but whom he hated for his truthfulness to sordid and ugly conditions. At heart Clemens was romantic, and he would have had the world of fiction stately and handsome and whatever the real world was not; but he was not romanticistic, and he was too helplessly an artist not to wish his own work to show life as he had seen it. I was preparing to rap him back for these letters when I read that he had got home to die; he would have liked the rapping back.

He liked coming to Boston, especially for those luncheons and dinners in which the fertile hospitality of our publisher, Osgood, abounded. He dwelt equidistant from Boston and New York, and he had special friends in New York, but he said he much preferred coming to Boston; of late years he never went there, and he had lost the habit of it long before he came home from Europe to live in New York. At these feasts, which were often of after-dinner-speaking measure, he could always be trusted for something of amazing delightfulness. Once, when Osgood could think of no other occasion for a dinner, he gave himself a birthday dinner, and asked his friends and authors. The beautiful and splendid trooperlike Waring was there, and I recall how in the long, rambling speech in which Clemens went round the table hitting every head at it, and especially visiting Osgood with thanks for his ingenious pretext for our entertainment, he congratulated Waring upon his engineering genius and his hypnotic control of municipal governments. He said that if there was a plan for draining a city at a cost of a million, by seeking the level of the water in the downhill course of the sewers, Waring would come with a plan to drain that town uphill at twice the cost and carry it through the Common Council without opposition. It is hard to say whether the time was gladder at these dinners, or at the small lunches at which Osgood and Aldrich and I foregathered with him and talked the afternoon away till well toward the winter twilight.

He was a great figure, and the principal figure, at one of the first of the now worn-out Authors' Readings, which was held in the Boston Museum to aid a Longfellow memorial. It was the late George Parsons Lathrop (everybody seems to be late in these sad days) who imagined the reading, but when it came to a price for seats I can always claim the glory of fixing it at five dollars. The price if not the occasion proved irresistible, and the museum was packed from the floor to the topmost gallery. Norton presided, and when it came Clemens' turn to read he introduced him with such

exquisite praises as he best knew how to give, but before
he closed he fell a prey to one of those lapses of tact which
are the peculiar peril of people of the greatest tact. He was
reminded of Darwin's delight in Mark Twain, and how
when he came from his long day's exhausting study, and
sank into bed at midnight, he took up a volume of Mark
Twain, whose books he always kept on a table beside him,
and whatever had been his tormenting problem, or excess
of toil, he felt secure of a good night's rest from it. A sort
of blank ensued which Clemens filled in the only possible
way. He said he should always be glad that he had contributed to the repose of that great man, whom science
owed so much, and then without waiting for the joy in
every breast to burst forth, he began to read. It was curious
to watch his triumph with the house. His carefully studied
effects would reach the first rows in the orchestra first, and
ripple in laughter back to the standees against the wall, and
then with a fine resurgence come again to the rear orchestra
seats, and so rise from gallery to gallery till it fell back, a
cataract of applause from the topmost rows of seats. He was
such a practiced speaker that he knew all the stops of that
simple instrument man, and there is no doubt that these results were accurately intended from his unerring knowledge. He was the most consummate public performer I
ever saw, and it was an incomparable pleasure to hear him
lecture; on the platform he was the great and finished actor
which he probably would not have been on the stage. He
was fond of private theatricals, and liked to play in them
with his children and their friends, in dramatizations of
such stories of his as *The Prince and the Pauper;* but I
never saw him in any of these scenes. When he read his
manuscript to you, it was with a thorough, however involuntary, recognition of its dramatic qualities; he held that
an actor added fully half to the character the author created.
With my own hurried and half-hearted reading of passages
which I wished to try on him from unprinted chapters (say,
out of *The Undiscovered Country* or *A Modern Instance*)
he said frankly that my reading could spoil anything. He
was realistic, but he was essentially histrionic, and he was

rightly so. What we have strongly conceived we ought to make others strongly imagine, and we ought to use every genuine art to that end.

XIV

There came a time when the lecturing which had been the joy of his prime became his loathing, loathing unutterable, and when he renounced it with indescribable violence. Yet he was always hankering for those fleshpots whose savor lingered on his palate and filled his nostrils after his withdrawal from the platform. The Authors' Readings when they had won their brief popularity abounded in suggestion for him. Reading from one's book was not so bad as giving a lecture written for a lecture's purpose, and he was willing at last to compromise. He had a magnificent scheme for touring the country with Aldrich and Mr. G. W. Cable and myself, in a private car, with a cook of our own, and every facility for living on the fat of the land. We should read only four times a week, in an entertainment that should not last more than an hour and a half. He would be the impresario, and would guarantee us others at least seventy-five dollars a day, and pay every expense of the enterprise, which he provisionally called the Circus, himself. But Aldrich and I were now no longer in those earlier thirties when we so cheerfully imagined *Memorable Murders* for subscription publication; we both abhorred public appearances, and, at any rate, I was going to Europe for a year. So the plan fell through except as regarded Mr. Cable, who, in his way, was as fine a performer as Clemens, and could both read and sing the matter of his books. On a far less stupendous scale they two made the rounds of the great lecturing circuit together. But I believe a famous lecture-manager had charge of them and traveled with them.

He was a most sanguine man, a most amiable person, and such a believer in fortune that Clemens used to say of him, as he said of one of his early publishers, that you could rely upon fifty per cent of everything he promised. I myself many years later became a follower of this hopeful prophet, and I can testify that in my case at least he was able to keep ninety-nine, and even a hundred, per cent of his word. It was I who was much nearer failing of mine, for I promptly began to lose sleep from the nervous stress of my lecturing and from the gratifying but killing receptions afterward, and I was truly in that state from insomnia which Clemens recognized in the brief letter I got from him in the Western city, after half-a-dozen wakeful nights. He sardonically congratulated me on having gone into "the lecture field," and then he said: "I know where you are *now*. You are in hell."

It was this perdition which he re-entered when he undertook that round-the-world lecturing tour for the payment of the debts left to him by the bankruptcy of his firm in the publishing business. It was not purely perdition for him, or, rather, it was perdition for only one half of him, the author half; for the actor half it was paradise. The author who takes up lecturing without the ability to give histrionic support to the literary reputation which he brings to the crude test of his reader's eyes and ears invokes a peril and a misery unknown to the lecturer who has made his first public from the platform. Clemens was victorious on the platform from the beginning, and it would be folly to pretend that he did not exult in his triumphs there. But I suppose, with the wearing nerves of middle life, he hated more and more the personal swarming of interest upon him, and all the inevitable clatter of the thing. Yet he faced it, and he labored round our tiresome globe that he might pay the uttermost farthing of debts which he had not knowingly contracted, the debts of his partners who had meant well and done ill, not because they were evil, but because they were unwise, and as unfit for their work as he was. "Pay what thou owest." That is right, even when thou owest it by the error of others, and even when thou owest it to a bank, which had not lent it from love of thee, but in the hard line of business and thy need.

Clemens' behavior in this matter redounded to his glory among the nations of the whole earth, and especially in this nation, so wrapped in commerce and so little used to honor among its many thieves. He had behaved like Walter Scott, as millions rejoiced to know, who had not known how Walter Scott had behaved till they knew it was like Clemens. No doubt it will be put to his credit in the books of the Recording Angel, but what the Judge of all the Earth will say of it at the Last Day there is no telling. I should not be surprised if He accounted it of less merit than some other things that Clemens did and was: less than his abhorrence of the Spanish War, and the destruction of the South-African republics, and our deceit of the Filipinos, and his hate of slavery, and his payment of his portion of our race's debt to the race of the colored student whom he saw through college, and his support of a poor artist for three years in Paris, and his loan of opportunity to the youth who became the most brilliant of our actor-dramatists, and his eager pardon of the thoughtless girl who was near paying the penalty of her impertinence with the loss of her place, and his remembering that the insolent brakeman got so few dollars a month, and his sympathy for working-men standing up to money in their unions, and even his pity for the wounded bird throbbing out its little life on the grass for the pleasure of the cruel fool who shot it. These and the thousand other charities and beneficences in which he abounded, openly or secretly, may avail him more than the discharge of his firm's liabilities with the Judge of all the Earth, who surely will do right, but whose measures and criterions no man knows, and I least of all men.

He made no great show of sympathy with people in their anxieties, but it never failed, and at a time when I lay sick for many weeks his letters were of comfort to those who feared I might not rise again. His hand was out in help for those who needed help, and in kindness for those who needed kindness. There remains in my mind the dreary sense of a long, long drive to the uttermost bounds of the South End at Boston, where he went to call upon some obscure person whose claim stretched in a lengthening chain from his early days in Missouri—a most inadequate person, in whose vacuity the gloom of the dull day deepened till it was almost too deep for tears. He bore the ordeal with grim heroism, and silently smoked away the sense of it, as we drove back to Cambridge, in his slippered feet, somberly musing, somberly swearing. But he knew he had done the right, the kind thing, and he was content. He came the whole way from Hartford to go with me to a friendless play of mine, which Alessandro Salvini was giving in a series of matinees to houses never enlarging themselves beyond the count of the grave two hundred who sat it through, and he stayed my fainting spirit with a cheer beyond flagons, joining me in my joke at the misery of it, and carrying the fun farther.

Before that he had come to witness the aesthetic suicide of Anna Dickinson, who had been a flaming light of the political platform in the war days, and had been left by them consuming in a hapless ambition for the theater. The poor girl had had a play written especially for her, and as Anne Boleyn she ranted and exhorted through the five acts, drawing ever nearer the utter defeat of the anticlimax. We could hardly look at each other for pity, Clemens sitting there in the box he had taken, with his shaggy head out over the corner and his slippered feet curled under him: he either went to a place in his slippers or he carried them with him, and put them on as soon as he could put off his boots. When it was so that we could not longer follow her failure and live, he began to talk of the absolute close of her career which the thing was, and how probably she had no conception that it was the end. He philosophized the mercifulness of the fact, and of the ignorance of most of us, when mortally sick or fatally wounded. We think it is not the end, because we have never ended before, and we do not see how we can end. Some can push by the awful hour and live again, but for Anna Dickinson there could be, and was, no such palingenesis. Of course we got that solemn joy out of reading her fate aright which is the compensation of the wise spectator in witnessing the inexorable doom of others.

XV

When Messrs. Houghton & Mifflin became owners of the *Atlantic Monthly,* Mr. Houghton fancied having some breakfasts and dinners, which should bring the publisher and the editor face to face with the contributors, who were bidden from far and near. Of course, the subtle fiend of advertising, who has now grown so unblushing bold, lurked under the covers at these banquets, and the junior partner and the young editor had their joint and separate fine anguishes of misgiving as to the taste and the principle of them; but they were really very simple-hearted and honestly meant hospitalities, and they prospered as they ought, and gave great pleasure and no pain. I forget some of the "emergent occasions," but I am sure of a birthday dinner most unexpectedly accepted by Whittier, and a birthday luncheon to Mrs. Stowe, and I think a birthday dinner to Longfellow; but the passing years have left me in the dark as to the pretext of that supper at which Clemens made his awful speech, and came so near being the death of us all. At the breakfasts and luncheons we had the pleasure of our lady contributors' company, but that night there were only men, and because of our great strength we survived.

I suppose the year was about 1879, but here the almanac is unimportant, and I can only say that it was after Clemens had become a very valued contributor of the magazine, where he found himself to his own great explicit satisfaction. He had jubilantly accepted our invitation, and had promised a speech, which it appeared afterward he had prepared with unusual care and confidence. It was his custom always to think out his speeches, mentally wording them, and then memorizing them by a peculiar system of mnemonics which he had invented. On the dinner-table a certain succession of knife, spoon, salt-cellar, and butter-plate symbolized a train of ideas, and on the billiard-table a ball, a cue, and a piece of chalk served the same purpose. With a diagram of these printed on the brain he had full command of the phrases which his excogitation had attached to them, and which embodied the ideas in perfect form. He believed he had been particularly fortunate in his notion for the speech of that evening, and he had worked it out in joyous self-reliance. It was the notion of three tramps, three dead-beats, visiting a California mining-camp, and imposing themselves upon the innocent miners as respectively Ralph Waldo Emerson, Henry Wadsworth Longfellow, and Oliver Wendell Holmes. The humor of the conception must prosper or must fail according to the mood of the hearer, but Clemens felt sure of compelling this to sympathy, and he looked forward to an unparalleled triumph.

But there were two things that he had not taken into account. One was the species of religious veneration in which these men were held by those nearest them, a thing that I should not be able to realize to people remote from them in time and place. They were men of extraordinary dignity, of the thing called *presence,* for want of some clearer word, so that no one could well approach them in a personally light or trifling spirit. I do not suppose that anybody more truly valued them or more piously loved them than Clemens himself, but the intoxication of his fancy carried him beyond the bounds of that regard, and emboldened him to the other thing which he had not taken into account —namely, the immense hazard of working his fancy out before their faces, and expecting them to enter into the delight of it. If neither Emerson, nor Longfellow, nor Holmes had been there, the scheme might possibly have carried, but even this is doubtful, for those who so devoutly honored them would have overcome their horror with difficulty, and perhaps would not have overcome it at all.

The publisher, with a modesty very ungrateful to me, had abdicated his office of host, and I was the hapless president, fulfilling the abhorred function of calling people to their feet and making them speak. When I came to Clemens I introduced him with the cordial admiring I had for him as one of my greatest contributors and dearest friends. Here, I said, in sum, was a humorist who never left you hanging your head for having enjoyed his joke; and then the amazing mistake, the bewildering blunder, the cruel catastrophe was upon us. I believe that after the scope of the burlesque made itself clear, there was no one there, including the burlesquer himself, who was not smitten with a desolating dismay. There fell a silence, weighing many tons to the square inch, which deepened from moment to moment, and was broken only by the hysterical and bloodcurdling laughter of a single guest, whose name shall not be handed down to infamy. Nobody knew whether to look at the speaker or down at his plate. I chose my plate as the least affliction, and so I do not know how Clemens looked, except when I stole a glance at him, and saw him standing solitary amid his appalled and appalling listeners, with his joke dead on his hands. From a first glance at the great three whom his jest had made its theme, I was aware of Longfellow sitting upright, and regarding the humorist with an air of pensive puzzle, of Holmes busily writing on his menu, with a well-feigned effect of preoccupation, and of Emerson, holding his elbows, and listening with a sort of Jovian oblivion of this nether world in that lapse of memory which saved him in those later years from so much bother. Clemens must have dragged his joke to the climax and left it there, but I cannot say this from any sense of the fact. Of what happened afterward at the table where the immense, the wholly innocent, the truly unimagined affront was offered, I have no longer the least remembrance. I next remember being in a room of the hotel, where Clemens was not to sleep, but to toss in despair, and Charles Dudley Warner's saying, in the gloom, "Well, Mark, *you're* a funny fellow." It was as well as anything else he could have said, but Clemens seemed unable to accept the tribute.

I stayed the night with him, and the next morning, after a haggard breakfast, we drove about and he made some purchases of bric-à-brac for his house in Hartford, with a soul as far away from bric-à-brac as ever the soul of man was. He went home by an early train, and he lost no time in writing back to the three divine personalities which he had so involuntarily seemed to flout. They all wrote back to him, making it as light for him as they could. I have heard that Emerson was a good deal mystified, and in his sublime forgetfulness asked, Who was this gentleman who appeared to think he had offered him some sort of annoyance? But I am not sure that this is accurate. What I am sure of is that Longfellow, a few days after, in my study, stopped before a photograph of Clemens and said, "Ah, he is a *wag!*" and nothing more. Holmes told me, with deep emotion, such as a brother humorist might well feel, that he had not lost an instant in replying to Clemens' letter, and assuring him that there had not been the least offense, and entreating him never to think of the matter again. "He said that he was a fool, but he was God's fool," Holmes quoted from the letter, with a true sense of the pathos and the humor of the self-abasement.

To me Clemens wrote a week later, "It doesn't get any better; it burns like fire." But now I understand that it was not shame that burnt, but rage for a blunder which he had so incredibly committed. That to have conceived of those men, the most dignified in our literature, our civilization, as impersonable by three hoboes, and then to have imagined that he could ask them personally to enjoy the monstrous travesty, was a break, he saw too late, for which there was no repair. Yet the time came, and not so very long afterward, when some mention was made of the incident as a mistake, and he said, with all his fierceness, "But I don't admit that it *was* a mistake," and it was not so in the minds of all witnesses at second hand. The morning after the dreadful dinner there came a glowing note from Professor Child, who had read the newspaper report of it, praising Clemens' burlesque as the richest piece of humor in the world, and betraying no sense of incongruity in its perpetration in the presence of its victims. I think it must always have ground in Clemens' soul that he was the prey of circumstances, and that if he had some more favoring occasion he could retrieve his loss in it by giving the thing the right setting. Not more than two or three years ago, he came to try me as to trying it again at a meeting of newspaper-men in Washington. I had to own my fears, while I alleged Child's note on the other hand, but in the end he did not try it with the newspaper-men. I do not know whether he has ever printed it or not, but since the thing happened I have often wondered how much offense there really was in it. I am not sure but the horror of the spectators read more indignation into the subjects of the hapless drolling than they felt. But it must have been difficult for them to bear it with equanimity. To be sure, they were not themselves mocked; the joke was, of course, beside them; nevertheless, their personality was trifled with, and I could only end by reflecting that if I had been in their place I should not have liked it myself. Clemens would have liked it himself, for he had the heart for that sort of wild play, and he so loved a joke that even if it took the form of a liberty, and was yet a good joke, he would have loved it. But perhaps this burlesque was not a good joke.

XVI

Clemens was oftenest at my house in Cambridge, but he was also sometimes at my house in Belmont; when, after a year in Europe, we went to live in Boston, he was more rarely with us. We could never be long together without something out of the common happening, and one day something far out of the common happened, which fortunately refused the nature of absolute tragedy, while remaining rather the saddest sort of comedy. We were looking out of my library window on that view of the Charles which I was so proud of sharing with my all-but-next-door neighbor, Doctor Holmes, when another friend who was with us called out with curiously impersonal interest, "Oh, see that woman getting into the water!" This would have excited curiosity and alarmed anxiety far less lively than ours, and Clemens and I rushed downstairs and out through my basement and back gate. At the same time a coachman came out of a stable next door, and grappled by the shoulders a woman who was somewhat deliberately getting down the steps to the water over the face of the embankment. Before we could reach them he had pulled her up to the driveway, and stood holding her there while she crazily grieved at her rescue. As soon as he saw us he went back into his stable, and left us with the poor wild creature on our hands. She

was not very young and not very pretty, and we could not
have flattered ourselves with the notion of anything romantic
in her suicidal mania, but we could take her on the broad
human level, and on this we proposed to escort her up
Beacon Street till we could give her into the keeping of
one of those kindly policemen whom our neighborhood
knew. Naturally there was no policeman known to us or
unknown the whole way to the Public Garden. We had to
circumvent our charge in her present design of drowning
herself, and walk her past the streets crossing Beacon to
the river. At these points it needed considerable reasoning
to overcome her wish and some active maneuvering in both
of us to enforce our arguments. Nobody else appeared to
be interested, and though we did not court publicity in the
performance of the duty so strangely laid upon us, still it
was rather disappointing to be so entirely ignored.

There are some four or five crossings to the river between
302 Beacon Street and the Public Garden, and the suggestions at our command were pretty well exhausted by the
time we reached it. Still the expected policeman was nowhere in sight; but a brilliant thought occurred to Clemens.
He asked me where the nearest police station was, and when
I told him, he started off at his highest speed, leaving me
in sole charge of our hapless ward. All my powers of
suasion were now taxed to the utmost, and I began attracting attention as a short, stout gentleman in early middle
life endeavoring to distrain a respectable female of her
personal liberty, when his accomplice had abandoned him
to his wicked design. After a much longer time than I
thought I should have taken to get a policeman from the
station, Clemens reappeared in easy conversation with an
officer who had probably realized that he was in the company of Mark Twain, and was in no hurry to end the
interview. He took possession of our captive, and we saw
her no more. I now wonder that with our joint instinct for
failure we ever got rid of her; but I am sure we did, and
few things in life have given me greater relief. When we
got back to my house we found the friend we had left
there quite unruffled and not much concerned to know

the facts of our adventure. My impression is that he had been taking a nap on my lounge; he appeared refreshed and even gay; but if I am inexact in these details he is alive to refute me.

XVII

A little after this Clemens went abroad with his family, and lived several years in Germany. His letters still came, but at longer intervals, and the thread of our intimate relations was inevitably broken. He would write me when something I had written pleased him, or when something signal occurred to him, or some political or social outrage stirred him to wrath, and he wished to free his mind in pious profanity. During this sojourn he came near dying of pneumonia in Berlin, and he had slight relapses from it after coming home. In Berlin also he had the honor of dining with the German Emperor at the table of a cousin married to a high officer of the court. Clemens was a man to enjoy such a distinction; he knew how to take it as a delegated recognition from the German people; but as coming from a rather cockahoop sovereign who had as yet only his sovereignty to value himself upon, he was not very proud of it. He expressed a quiet disdain of the event as between the imperiality and himself, on whom it was supposed to confer such glory, crowning his life with the topmost leaf of laurel. He was in the same mood in his account of an English dinner many years before, where there was a "little Scotch lord" present, to whom the English tacitly referred Clemens' talk, and laughed when the lord laughed, and were grave when he failed to smile. Of all the men I have known he was the farthest from a snob, though he valued recognition, and liked the flattery of the fashionable fair when it came in his way. He would not go out of his way for it, but like most able and brilliant men he loved the minds of women, their wit, their agile cleverness, their sensitive perception, their humorous appreciation, the saucy things they would say, and their pretty, temerarious defiances. He had, of course, the keenest sense of what was truly dignified and truly undignified in people; but he was not really interested in what we call society affairs; they scarcely existed for him, though his books witness how he abhorred the dreadful fools who through some chance of birth or wealth hold themselves different from other men.

Commonly he did not keep things to himself, especially dislikes and condemnations. Upon most current events he had strong opinions, and he uttered them strongly. After a while he was silent in them, but if you tried him you found him in them still. He was tremendously worked up by a certain famous trial, as most of us were who lived in the time of it. He believed the accused guilty, but when we met some months after it was over, and I tempted him to speak his mind upon it, he would only say, The man had suffered enough; as if the man had expiated his wrong, and he was not going to do anything to renew his penalty. I found that very curious, very delicate. His continued blame could not come to the sufferer's knowledge, but he felt it his duty to forbear it.

He was apt to wear himself out in the vehemence of his resentments; or, he had so spent himself in uttering them that he had literally nothing more to say. You could offer Clemens offenses that would anger other men and he did not mind; he would account for them from human nature; but if he thought you had in any way played him false you were anathema and maranatha forever. Yet not forever, perhaps, for by and by, after years, he would be silent. There were two men, half a generation apart in their succession, whom he thought equally atrocious in their treason to him, and of whom he used to talk terrifyingly, even after they were out of the world. He went farther than Heine, who said that he forgave his enemies, but not till they were dead. Clemens did not forgive his dead enemies; their death seemed to deepen their crimes, like a base evasion, or a cowardly attempt to escape; he pursued them to the grave; he would like to dig them up and take vengeance upon their clay. So he said, but no doubt he would not have hurt them if he had had them living before him. He was generous without stint; he trusted without measure, but where his generosity was abused, or his trust betrayed, he was a fire of vengeance, a consuming flame of suspicion that no sprinkling of cool patience from others could quench; it had to burn itself out. He was eagerly and lavishly hospitable, but if a man seemed willing to batten on him, or in any way to lie down upon him, Clemens despised him unutterably. In his frenzies of resentment or suspicion he would not, and doubtless could not, listen to reason. But if between the paroxysms he were confronted with the facts he would own them, no matter how much they told against him. At one period he fancied that a certain newspaper was hounding him with biting censure and poisonous paragraphs, and he was filling himself up with wrath to be duly discharged on the editor's head. Later, he wrote me with a humorous joy in his mistake that Warner had advised him to have the paper watched for these injuries. He had done so, and how many mentions of him did I reckon he had found in three months? Just two, and they were rather indifferent than unfriendly. So the paper was acquitted, and the editor's life was spared. The wretch never knew how near he was to losing it, with incredible preliminaries of obloquy, and a subsequent devotion to lasting infamy.

XVIII

His memory for favors was as good as for injuries, and he liked to return your friendliness with as loud a band of music as could be bought or bribed for the occasion. All that you had to do was to signify that you wanted his help. When my father was consul at Toronto during Arthur's administration, he fancied that his place was in danger, and he appealed to me. In turn I appealed to Clemens, bethinking myself of his friendship with Grant and Grant's friendship with Arthur. I asked him to write to Grant in my father's behalf, but No, he answered me, I must come to Hartford, and we would go on to New York together and see Grant personally. This was before, and long before, Clemens became Grant's publisher and splendid benefactor, but the men liked each other as such men could not help doing. Clemens made the appointment, and we went to find Grant in his business office, that place where his business innocence was afterward so betrayed. He was very simple and very cordial, and I was instantly the more at home with him, because his voice was the soft, rounded, Ohio River accent to which my years were earliest used from my steamboating uncles, my earliest heroes. When I stated my business he merely said, Oh no; that must not be; he would write to Mr. Arthur; and he did so that day; and my father lived to lay down his office, when he tired of it, with no urgence from above.

It is not irrelevant to Clemens to say that Grant seemed to like finding himself in company with two literary men, one of whom at least he could make sure of, and unlike that silent man he was reputed, he talked constantly, and so far as he might he talked literature. At least he talked of John Phœnix, that delightfulest of the early Pacific Slope humorists, whom he had known under his real name of George H. Derby, when they were fellow-cadets at West Point. It was mighty pretty, as Pepys would say, to see the delicate deference Clemens paid our plain hero, and the manly respect with which he listened. While Grant talked, his luncheon was brought in from some unassuming restaurant near by, and he asked us to join him in the baked beans and coffee which were served us in a little room out of the office with about the same circumstance as at a railroad refreshment-counter. The baked beans and coffee were of about the railroad-refreshment quality; but eating them with Grant was like sitting down to baked beans and coffee with Julius Cæsar, or Alexander, or some other great Plutarchan captain.

One of the highest satisfactions of Clemens' often supremely satisfactory life was his relation to Grant. It was his proud joy to tell how he found Grant about to sign a contract for his book on certainly very good terms, and said to him that he would himself publish the book and give him a percentage three times as large. He said Grant seemed to doubt whether he could honorably withdraw from the negotiation at that point, but Clemens overbore his scruples, and it was his unparalleled privilege, his princely pleasure, to pay the author a far larger check for his work than had ever been paid to an author before. He valued even more than this splendid opportunity the sacred moments in which their business brought him into the presence of the slowly dying, heroically living man whom he was so befriending; and he told me in words which surely lost none of their simple pathos through his report how Grant described his suffering.

The prosperity of this venture was the beginning of Clemens' adversity, for it led to excesses of enterprise which were forms of dissipation. The young sculptor who had come back to him from Paris modeled a small bust of Grant, which Clemens multiplied in great numbers to his great loss, and the success of Grant's book tempted him to launch on publishing seas where his bark presently foundered. The first and greatest of his disasters was the *Life of Pope Leo XIII*, which he came to tell me of, when he had imagined it, in a sort of delirious exultation. He had no words in which to paint the magnificence of the project, or to forecast its colossal success. It would have a currency bounded only by the number of Catholics in Christendom. It would be translated into every language which was anywhere written or printed; it would be circulated literally in every country of the globe, and Clemens' book agents would carry the prospectuses and then the bound copies of the work to the ends of the whole earth. Not only would every Catholic buy it, but every Catholic must, as he was a good Catholic, as he hoped to be saved. It was a magnificent scheme, and it captivated me, as it had captivated Clemens; it dazzled us both, and neither of us saw the fatal defect in it. We did not consider how often Catholics could not read, how often when they could, they might not wish to read. The event proved that whether they could read or not the immeasurable majority did not wish to read the life of the Pope, though it was written by a dignitary of the Church and issued to the world with every sanction from the Vatican. The failure was incredible to Clemens; his sanguine soul was utterly confounded, and soon a silence fell upon it where it had been so exuberantly jubilant.

XIX

The occasions which brought us to New York together were not nearly so frequent as those which united us in Boston, but there was a dinner given him by a friend which remains memorable from the fatuity of two men present, so different in everything but their fatuity. One was the sweet old comedian Billy Florence, who was urging the unsuccessful dramatist across the table to write him a play about Oliver Cromwell, and giving the reasons why he thought himself peculiarly fitted to portray the character of Cromwell. The other was a modestly millioned rich man who was then only beginning to amass the moneys afterward heaped so high, and was still in the condition to be flattered by the condescension of a yet greater millionaire. His contribution to our gaiety was the verbatim report of a call he had made upon William H. Vanderbilt, whom he had found just about starting out of town, with his trunks actually in the front hall, but who had stayed to receive the narrator. He had, in fact, sat down on one of the trunks, and talked with the easiest friendliness, and quite, we were given to infer, like an ordinary human being. Clemens often kept on with some thread of the talk when we came away from a dinner, but now he was silent, as if "high sorrowful and cloyed"; and it was not till well afterward that I found he had noted the facts from the bitterness with which he mocked the rich man, and the pity he expressed for the actor.

He had begun before that to amass those evidences against mankind which eventuated with him in his theory of what he called "the damned human race." This was not an expression of piety, but of the kind contempt to which he was driven by our follies and iniquities as he had observed them in himself as well as in others. It was as mild a misanthropy, probably, as ever caressed the objects of its malediction. But I believe it was about the year 1900 that his sense of our perdition became insupportable and broke out in a mixed abhorrence and amusement which spared no occasion, so that I could quite understand why Mrs. Clemens should have found some compensation, when kept to her room by sickness, in the reflection that now she should not hear so much about "the damned human race." He told of that with the same wild joy that he told of overhearing her repetition of one of his most inclusive profanities, and her explanation that she meant him to hear it so that he might know how it sounded. The contrast of the lurid blasphemy with her heavenly whiteness should have been enough to cure anyone less grounded than he in what must be owned was as fixed a habit as smoking with him. When I first knew him he rarely vented his fury in that sort, and I fancy he was under a promise to her which he kept sacred till the wear and tear of his nerves with advancing years disabled him. Then it would be like him to struggle with himself till he could struggle no longer and to ask his promise back, and it would be like her to give it back. His profanity was the heritage of his boyhood and young manhood in social conditions and under the duress of exigencies in which everybody swore about as impersonally as he smoked. It is best to recognize the fact of it, and I do so the more readily because I cannot suppose the Recording Angel really minded it much more than that Guardian Angel of his. It probably grieved them about equally, but they could equally forgive it. Nothing came of his pose regarding "the damned human race" except his invention of the Human Race Luncheon Club. This was confined to four persons who were never all got together, and it soon perished of their indifference.

In the earlier days that I have more specially in mind one of the questions that we used to debate a good deal was whether every human motive was not selfish. We inquired as to every impulse, the noblest, the holiest in effect, and he found them in the last analysis of selfish origin. Pretty nearly the whole time of a certain railroad run from New York to Hartford was taken up with the scrutiny of the self-sacrifice of a mother for her child, of the abandon of the lover who dies in saving his mistress from fire or flood, of the hero's courage in the field and the martyr's at the stake. Each he found springing from the unconscious love of self and the dread of the greater pain which the self-sacrificer would suffer in forbearing the sacrifice. If we had any time left from this inquiry that day, he must have devoted it to a high regret that Napoleon did not carry out his purpose of invading England, for then he would have destroyed the feudal aristocracy, or "reformed the lords," as it might be called now. He thought that would have been an incalculable blessing to the English people and the world. Clemens was always beautifully and unfalteringly a republican. None of his occasional misgivings for America implicated a return to monarchy. Yet he felt passionately the splendor of the English monarchy, and there was a time when he gloried in that figurative poetry by which the king was phrased as "the Majesty of England." He rolled the words deep-throatedly out, and exulted in their beauty as if it were beyond any other glory of the world. He read, or read *at*, English history a great deal, and one of the by-products of his restless invention was a game of English Kings (like the game of Authors) for children. I do not know whether he ever perfected this, but I am quite sure it was not put upon the market. Very likely he brought it to a practicable stage, and then tired of it, as he was apt to do in the ultimation of his vehement undertakings.

XX

He satisfied the impassioned demand of his nature for incessant activities of every kind by taking a personal as well as a pecuniary interest in the inventions of others. At one moment "the damned human race" was almost to be redeemed by a process of founding brass without air bubbles in it; if this could once be accomplished, as I understood, or misunderstood, brass could be used in art-printing to a degree hitherto impossible. I dare say I have got it wrong, but I am not mistaken as to Clemens' enthusiasm for the process, and his heavy losses in paying its way to ultimate failure. He was simultaneously absorbed in the perfection of a type-setting machine, which he was paying the inventor a salary to bring to a perfection so expensive that it was practically impracticable. We were both printers by trade, and I could take the same interest in this wonderful piece of mechanism that he could; and it was so truly wonderful that it did everything but walk and talk. Its ingenious creator was so bent upon realizing the highest ideal in it that he produced a machine of quite unimpeachable efficiency. But it was so costly, when finished, that it could not be made for less than twenty thousand dollars, if the parts were made by hand. This sum was prohibitive of its introduction, unless the requisite capital could be found for making the parts by machinery, and Clemens spent many months in vainly trying to get this money together. In the meantime simpler machines had been invented and the market filled, and his investment of three hundred thousand dollars in the beautiful miracle remained permanent but not profitable. I once went with him to witness its performance, and it did seem to me the last word in its way, but it had been spoken too exquisitely, too fastidiously. I never heard him devote the inventor to the infernal gods, as he was apt to do with the geniuses he lost money by, and so I think he did not regard him as a traitor.

In these things, and in his other schemes for the *subiti guadagni* of the speculator and the "sudden making of splendid names" for the benefactors of our species, Clemens satisfied the Colonel Sellers nature in himself (from which he drew the picture of that wild and lovable figure), and perhaps made as good use of his money as he could. He did not care much for money in itself, but he luxuriated in the lavish use of it, and he was as generous with it as ever a man was. He liked giving it, but he commonly wearied of giving it himself, and wherever he lived he established an almoner, whom he fully trusted to keep his left hand ignorant of what his right hand was doing. I believe he felt no finality in charity, but did it because in its provisional way it was the only thing a man could do. I never heard him go really into any sociological inquiry, and I have a feeling that that sort of thing baffled and dispirited him. No one can read *The Connecticut Yankee* and not be aware of the length and breadth of his sympathies with poverty, but apparently he had not thought out any scheme for righting the economic wrongs we abound in. I cannot remember our ever getting quite down to a discussion of the matter; we came very near it once in the day of the vast wave of emotion sent over the world by *Looking Backward,* and again when we were all so troubled by the great coal strike in Pennsylvania; in considering that he seemed to be for the time doubtful of the justice of the working-man's cause. At all other times he seemed to know that whatever wrongs the working-man committed work was always in the right.

When Clemens returned to America with his family, after lecturing round the world, I again saw him in New York, where I so often saw him while he was shaping himself for that heroic enterprise. He would come to me, and talk sorrowfully over his financial ruin, and picture it to himself as the stuff of some unhappy dream, which, after long prosperity, had culminated the wrong way. It was very melancholy, very touching, but the sorrow to which he had come home from his long journey had not that forlorn bewilderment in it. He was looking wonderfully well, and when I wanted the name of his elixir, he said it was plasmon. He was apt, for a man who had put faith so decidedly away from him, to take it back and pin it to some superstition, usually of a hygienic sort. Once, when he was well on in years, he came to New York without glasses, and announced that he and all his family, so astigmatic and myopic and old-sighted, had, so to speak, burned their spectacles behind them upon the instruction of some sage who had found out that they were a delusion. The next time he came he wore spectacles freely, almost ostentatiously, and I heard from others that the whole Clemens family had been near losing their eyesight by the miracle worked in their behalf. Now, I was not surprised to learn that "the damned human race" was to be saved by plasmon, if anything, and that my first duty was to visit the plasmon agency with him, and procure enough plasmon to secure my family against the ills it was heir to forevermore. I did not immediately understand that plasmon was one of the investments which he had made from "the substance of things hoped for," and in the destiny of a disastrous disappointment. But after paying off the creditors of his late publishing firm, he had to do something with his money, and it was not his fault if he did not make a fortune out of plasmon.

XXI

For a time it was a question whether he should not go back with his family to their old home in Hartford. Perhaps the father's and mother's hearts drew them there all the more strongly because of the grief written ineffaceably over it, but for the younger ones it was no longer the measure of the world. It was easier for all to stay on indefinitely in New York, which is a sojourn without circumstance, and equally the home of exile and of indecision. The Clemenses took a pleasant, spacious house at Riverdale, on the Hudson, and there I began to see them again on something like the sweet old terms. They lived far more unpretentiously than they used, and I think with a notion of economy, which they had never very successfully practiced. I recall that at the end of a certain year in Hartford, when they had been saving and paying cash for everything, Clemens wrote, reminding me of their avowed experiment, and asking me to guess how many bills they had at New Year's; he hastened to say that a horse-car would not have held them. At Riverdale they kept no carriage, and there was a snowy night when I drove up to their handsome old mansion in the station carryall, which was crusted with mud as from the going down of the Deluge after transporting Noah and his family from the Ark to whatever point they decided to settle at provisionally. But the good talk, the rich talk, the talk that could never suffer poverty of mind or soul, was there, and we jubilantly found ourselves again in our middle youth. It was the mighty moment when Clemens was building his engines of war for the destruction of Christian

Science, which superstition nobody, and he least of all, expected to destroy. It would not be easy to say whether in his talk of it his disgust for the illiterate twaddle of Mrs. Eddy's book, or his admiration of her genius for organization was the greater. He believed that as a religious machine the Christian Science Church was as perfect as the Roman Church and destined to be more formidable in its control of the minds of men. He looked for its spread over the whole of Christendom, and throughout the winter he spent at Riverdale he was ready to meet all listeners more than half-way with his convictions of its powerful grasp of the average human desire to get something for nothing. The vacuous vulgarity of its texts was a perpetual joy to him, while he bowed with serious respect to the sagacity which built so securely upon the everlasting rock of human credulity and folly.

An interesting phase of his psychology in this business was not only his admiration for the masterly policy of the Christian Science hierarchy, but his willingness to allow the miracles of its healers to be tried on his friends and family, if they wished it. He had a tender heart for the whole generation of empirics, as well as the newer sorts of scienti-tians, but he seemed to base his faith in them largely upon the failure of the regulars rather than upon their own successes, which also he believed in. He was recurrently, but not insistently, desirous that you should try their strange magics when you were going to try the familiar medicines.

XXII

The order of my acquaintance, or call it intimacy, with Clemens was this: our first meeting in Boston, my visits to him in Hartford, his visits to me in Cambridge, in Belmont, and in Boston, our briefer and less frequent meetings in Paris and New York, all with repeated interruptions through my absences in Europe, and his sojourns in London, Berlin, Vienna, and Florence, and his flights to the many ends, and odds and ends, of the earth. I will not try to follow the events, if they were not rather the subjective experiences, of those different periods and points of time which I must not fail to make include his summer at York Harbor, and his divers residences in New York, on Tenth Street and on Fifth Avenue, at Riverdale, and at Stormfield, which his daughter has told me he loved best of all his houses and hoped to make his home for long years.

Not much remains to me of the week or so that we had together in Paris early in the summer of 1904. The first thing I got at my bankers was a cable message announcing that my father was stricken with paralysis, but urging my stay for further intelligence, and I went about, till the final summons came, with my head in a mist of care and dread. Clemens was very kind and brotherly through it all. He was living greatly to his mind in one of those arcaded little hotels in the Rue de Rivoli, and he was free from all household duties to range with me. We drove together to make calls of digestion at many houses where he had got indigestion through his reluctance from their hospitality, for he hated dining out. But, as he explained, his wife wanted him to make these visits, and he did it, as he did everything she wanted. At one place, some suburban villa, he could get no answer to his ring, and he "hove" his cards over the gate just as it opened, and he had the shame of explaining in his unexplanatory French to the man picking them up. He was excruciatingly helpless with his cabmen, but by very cordially smiling and casting himself on the drivers' mercy he always managed to get where he wanted. The family was on the verge of their many moves, and he was doing some small errands; he said that the others did the main things, and left him to do what the cat might.

It was with that return upon the buoyant billow of plasmon, renewed in look and limb, that Clemens' universally pervasive popularity began in his own country. He had hitherto been more intelligently accepted or more largely imagined in Europe, and I suppose it was my sense of this that inspired the stupidity of my saying to him when we came to consider "the state of polite learning" among us, "You mustn't expect people to keep it up here as they do in England." But it appeared that his countrymen were only wanting the chance, and they kept it up in honor of him past all precedent. One does not go into a catalogue of dinners, receptions, meetings, speeches, and the like, when there are more vital things to speak of. He loved these obvious joys, and he eagerly strove with the occasions they gave him for the brilliancy which seemed so exhaustless and was so exhausting. His friends saw that he was wearing himself out, and it was not because of Mrs. Clemens' health alone that they were glad to have him take refuge at Riverdale. The family lived there two happy, hopeless years, and then it was ordered that they should change for his wife's sake to some less exacting climate. Clemens was not eager to go to Florence, but his imagination was taken as it would have been in the old-young days by the notion of packing his furniture into flexible steel cages from his house in Hartford and unpacking it from them untouched at his villa in Fiesole. He got what pleasure any man could out of that triumph of mind over matter, but the shadow was creeping up his life. One sunny afternoon we sat on the grass before the mansion, after his wife had begun to get well enough for removal, and we looked up toward a balcony where by and by that lovely presence made itself visible, as if it had stooped there from a cloud. A hand frailly waved a handkerchief; Clemens ran over the lawn toward it, calling tenderly: "What? What?" as if it might be an asking for him instead of the greeting it really was for me. It was the last time I saw her, if indeed I can be said to have seen her then, and long afterward when I said how beautiful we all thought her, how good, how wise, how wonderfully perfect in every relation of life, he cried out in a breaking voice: "Oh, why didn't you ever tell her? She thought you didn't like her." What a pang it was then not to have told her, but how could we have told her? His unreason endeared him to me more than all his wisdom.

To that Riverdale sojourn belong my impressions of his most violent anti-Christian Science rages, which began with the postponement of his book, and softened into acceptance of the delay till he had well nigh forgotten his wrath when it came out. There was also one of those joint episodes of ours, which, strangely enough, did not eventuate in entire failure, as most of our joint episodes did. He wrote furiously to me of a wrong which had been done to one of the most helpless and one of the most helped of our literary brethren, asking me to join with him in recovering the money paid over by that brother's publisher to a false friend who had withheld it and would not give any account of it. Our hapless brother had appealed to Clemens, as he had to me, with the facts, but not asking our help, probably because he knew he need not ask; and Clemens enclosed to me a very taking-by-the-throat message which he proposed sending to the false friend. For once I had some sense, and answered that this would never do, for we had really no power in the matter, and I contrived a letter to the recreant so softly diplomatic that I shall always think of it with pride when my honesties no longer give me satisfaction, saying that this incident had come to our knowledge, and suggesting that we felt sure he would not finally wish to withhold the money. Nothing more, practically, than that, but that was enough; there came promptly back a letter of justification, covering a very substantial check, which we hilariously forwarded to our beneficiary. But the helpless man who was so used to being helped did not answer with the gladness I, at least, expected of him. He acknowledged the check as he would any ordinary payment, and then he made us observe that there was still a large sum due him out of the moneys withheld. At this point I proposed to Clemens that we should let the nonchalant victim collect the remnant himself. Clouds of sorrow had gathered about the bowed head of the delinquent since we began on him, and my fickle sympathies were turning his way from the victim who was really to blame for leaving his affairs so unguardedly to him in the first place. Clemens made some sort of grim assent, and we dropped the matter. He was more used to ingratitude from those he helped than I was, who found being lain down upon not so amusing as he found my revolt. He reckoned I was right, he said, and after that I think we never recurred to the incident. It was not ingratitude that he ever minded; it was treachery that really maddened him past forgiveness.

XXIII

During the summer he spent at York Harbor I was only forty minutes away at Kittery Point, and we saw each other often; but this was before the last time at Riverdale. He had a wide, low cottage in a pine grove overlooking York River, and we used to sit at a corner of the veranda farthest away from Mrs. Clemens' window, where we could read our manuscripts to each other, and tell our stories, and laugh our hearts out without disturbing her. At first she had been about the house, and there was one gentle afternoon when she made tea for us in the parlor, but that was the last time I spoke with her. After that it was really a question of how soonest and easiest she could be got back to Riverdale; but, of course, there were specious delays in which she seemed no worse and seemed a little better, and Clemens could work at a novel he had begun. He had taken a room in the house of a friend and neighbor, a fisherman and boatman; there was a table where he could write, and a bed where he could lie down and read; and there, unless my memory has played me one of those constructive tricks that people's memories indulge in, he read me the first chapters of an admirable story. The scene was laid in a Missouri town, and the characters such as he had known in boyhood; but often as I tried to make him own it, he denied having written any such story; it is possible that I dreamed it, but I hope the MS. will yet be found.

XXIV

I cannot say whether or not he believed that his wife would recover; he fought the fear of her death to the end; for her life was far more largely his than the lives of most men's wives are theirs. For his own life I believe he would never have much cared, if I may trust a saying of one who was so absolutely without pose as he was. He said that he never saw a dead man whom he did not envy for having had it over and being done with it. Life had always amused him, and in the resurgence of its interests after his sorrow had ebbed away he was again deeply interested in the world and in the human race, which, though damned, abounded in subjects of curious inquiry. When the time came for his wife's removal from York Harbor I went with him to Boston, where he wished to look up the best means of her conveyance to New York. The inquiry absorbed him: the sort of invalid-car he could get; how she could be carried to the village station; how the car could be detached from the Eastern train at Boston and carried round to the Southern train on the other side of the city, and then how it could be attached to the Hudson River train at New York and left at Riverdale. There was no particular of the business which he did not scrutinize and master, not only with his poignant concern for her welfare, but with his strong curiosity as to how these unusual things were done with the usual means. With the inertness that grows upon an aging man he had been used to delegating more and more things, but of that thing I perceived that he would not delegate the least detail.

He had meant never to go abroad again, but when it came time to go he did not look forward to returning; he expected to live in Florence always after that; they were used to the life and they had been happy there some years earlier before he went with his wife for the cure of Nauheim. But when he came home again it was for good and all. It was natural that he should wish to live in New York, where they had already had a pleasant year in Tenth Street. I used to see him there in an upper room, looking south over a quiet open space of back yards where we fought our battles in behalf of the Filipinos and the Boers, and he carried on his campaign against the missionaries in China. He had not yet formed his habit of lying for whole days in bed and reading and writing there, yet he was a good deal in bed, from weakness, I suppose, and for the mere comfort of it.

My perspectives are not very clear, and in the foreshortening of events which always takes place in our review of the past I may not always time things aright. But I believe it was not until he had taken his house at 21 Fifth Avenue that he began to talk to me of writing his autobiography. He meant that it should be a perfectly veracious record of his life and period; for the first time in literature there should be a true history of a man and a true presentation of the men the man had known. As we talked it over the scheme enlarged itself in our riotous fancy. We said it should be not only a book, it should be a library, not only a library, but a literature. It should make good the world's loss through Omar's barbarity at Alexandria; there was no image so grotesque, so extravagant that we did not play with it; and the work so far as he carried it was really done on a colossal scale. But one day he said that as to veracity it was a failure; he had begun to lie, and that if no man ever yet told the truth about himself it was because no man ever could. How far he had carried his autobiography I cannot say; he dictated the matter several hours each day; and the public has already seen long passages from it, and can judge, probably, of the make and matter of the whole from these. It is immensely inclusive, and it observes no order or sequence. Whether now, after his death, it will be published soon or late I have no means of knowing. Once or twice he said in a vague way that it was not to be published for twenty years, so that the discomfort of publicity might be minimized for all the survivors. Suddenly he told me he was not working at it; but I did not understand whether he had finished it or merely dropped it; I never asked.

We lived in the same city, but for old men rather far apart, he at Tenth Street and I at Seventieth, and with our colds and other disabilities we did not see each other often. He expected me to come to him, and I would not without some return of my visits, but we never ceased to be friends, and good friends, so far as I know. I joked him once as to how I was going to come out in his autobiography, and he gave me some sort of joking reassurance. There was one incident, however, that brought us very frequently and actively together. He came one Sunday afternoon to have me call with him on Maxim Gorky, who was staying at a hotel a few streets above mine. We were both interested in Gorky, Clemens rather more as a revolutionist and I as a realist, though I too wished the Russian Tsar ill, and the novelist well in his mission to the Russian sympathizers in this republic. But I had lived through the episode of Kossuth's visit to us and his vain endeavor to raise funds for the Hungarian cause in 1851, when we were a younger and nobler nation than now, with hearts if not hands opener to the "oppressed of Europe"; the oppressed of America, the four or five millions of slaves, we did not count. I did not believe that Gorky could get the money for the cause of freedom in Russia which he had come to get; as I told a valued friend of his and mine, I did not believe he could get twenty-five hundred dollars, and I think now I set the figure too high. I had already refused to sign the sort of general appeal his friends were making to our principles and pockets because I felt it so wholly idle, and when the paper was produced in Gorky's presence and Clemens put his name to it I still refused. The next day Gorky was expelled from his hotel with the woman who was not his wife, but who, I am bound to say, did not look as if she were not, at least to me, who am, however, not versed in those aspects of human nature.

I might have escaped unnoted, but Clemens' familiar head gave us away to the reporters waiting at the elevator's mouth for all who went to see Gorky. As it was, a hunt of interviewers ensued for us severally and jointly. I could remain aloof in my hotel apartment, returning answer to such guardians of the public right to know everything that I had nothing to say of Gorky's domestic affairs; for the public interest had now strayed far from the revolution, and centered entirely upon these. But with Clemens it was different; he lived in a house with a street door kept by a single butler, and he was constantly rung for. I forget how long the siege lasted, but long enough for us to have fun with it. That was the moment of the great Vesuvian eruption, and we figured ourselves in easy reach of a volcano which was every now and then "blowing a cone off," as the telegraphic phrase was. The roof of the great market in Naples had just broken in under its load of ashes and cinders, and crushed hundreds of people; and we asked each other if we were not sorry we had not been there, where the pressure would have been far less terrific than it was with us in Fifth Avenue. The forbidden butler came up with a message that there were some gentlemen below who wanted to see Clemens.

"How many?" he demanded.

"Five," the butler faltered.

"Reporters?"

The butler feigned uncertainty.

"What would you do?" he asked me.

"I wouldn't see them," I said, and then Clemens went directly down to them. How or by what means he appeased their voracity I cannot say, but I fancy it was by the confession of the exact truth, which was harmless enough. They went away joyfully, and he came back in radiant satisfaction with having seen them. Of course he was right and I wrong, and he was right as to the point at issue between Gorky and those who had helplessly treated him with such cruel ignominy. In America it is not the convention for men to live openly in hotels with women who are not their wives. Gorky had violated this convention and he had to pay the penalty; and concerning the destruction of his efficiency as an emissary of the revolution, his blunder was worse than a crime.

XXV

To the period of Clemens' residence in Fifth Avenue belongs his efflorescence in white serge. He was always rather aggressively indifferent about dress, and at a very early date in our acquaintance Aldrich and I attempted his reform by clubbing to buy him a cravat. But he would not put away his stiff little black bow, and until he imagined the suit of white serge, he wore always a suit of black serge, truly deplorable in the cut of the sagging frock. After his measure had once been taken he refused to make his clothes the occasion of personal interviews with his tailor; he sent the stuff by the kind elderly woman who had been in the service of the family from the earliest days of his marriage, and accepted the result without criticism. But the white serge was an inspiration which few men would have had the courage to act upon. The first time I saw him wear it was at the authors' hearing before the Congressional Committee on Copyright in Washington. Nothing could have been more dramatic than the gesture with which he flung off his long loose overcoat, and stood forth in white from his feet to the crown of his silvery head. It was a magnificent *coup*, and he dearly loved a *coup*; but the magnificent speech which he made, tearing to shreds the venerable farrago of nonsense about non-property in ideas which had formed the basis of all copyright legislation, made you forget even his spectacularity.

It is well known how proud he was of his Oxford gown, not merely because it symbolized the honor in which he was held by the highest literary body in the world, but because it was so rich and so beautiful. The red and the lavender of the cloth flattered his eyes as the silken black of the same degree of Doctor of Letters, given him years before at Yale, could not do. His frank, defiant happiness in it, mixed with a due sense of burlesque, was something that those lacking his poet-soul could never imagine; they accounted it vain, weak; but that would not have mattered to him if he had known it. In his London sojourn he had formed the top-hat habit, and for a while he lounged splendidly up and down Fifth Avenue in that society emblem; but he seemed to tire of it, and to return kindly to the soft hat of his Southwestern tradition.

He disliked clubs; I don't know whether he belonged to any in New York, but I never met him in one. As I have told, he himself had formed the Human Race Club, but as he never could get it together it hardly counted. There was to have been a meeting of it the time of my only visit to Stormfield in April of last year; but of three who were to have come I alone came. We got on very well without the absentees, after finding them in the wrong, as usual, and the visit was like those I used to have with him so many years before in Hartford, but there was not the old ferment of subjects. Many things had been discussed and put away for good, but we had our old fondness for nature and for each other, who were so differently parts of it. He showed his absolute content with his house, and that was the greater pleasure for me because it was my son who designed it. The architect had been so fortunate as to be able to plan it where a natural avenue of savins, the close-knit, slender, cypresslike cedars of New England, led away from the rear of the villa to the little level of a pergola, meant someday to be wreathed and roofed with vines. But in the early spring days all the landscape was in the beautiful nakedness of the Northern winter. It opened in the surpassing loveliness of wooded and meadowed uplands, under skies that were the first days blue, and the last gray over a rainy and then a snowy floor. We walked up and down, up and down, between the villa terrace and the pergola, and talked with the melancholy amusement, the sad tolerance of age for the sort of men and things that used to excite us or enrage us; now we were far past turbulence or anger. Once we took a walk together across the yellow pastures to a chasmal creek on his grounds, where the ice still knit the clayey banks together like crystal mosses; and the stream far down clashed through and over the stones and the shards of ice. Clemens pointed out the scenery he had bought to give himself elbow-room, and showed me the lot he was going to have me build on. The next day we came again with the geologist he had asked up to Stormfield to analyze its rocks. Truly he loved the place, though he had been so weary of change and so indifferent to it that he never saw it till he came to live in it. He left it all to the architect whom he had known from a child in the intimacy which bound our families together, though we bodily lived far enough apart. I loved his little ones and he was sweet to mine and was their delighted-in and wondered-at friend. Once and once again, and yet again and again, the black shadow that shall never be lifted where it falls, fell in his house and in mine, during the forty years and more that we were friends, and endeared us the more to each other.

XXVI

My visit at Stormfield came to an end with tender relucting on his part and on mine. Every morning before I dressed I heard him sounding my name through the house for the fun of it and I know for the fondness; and if I looked out of my door, there he was in his long nightgown swaying up and down the corridor, and wagging his great white head like a boy that leaves his bed and comes out in the hope of frolic with someone. The last morning a soft sugar-snow had fallen and was falling, and I drove through it down to the station in the carriage which had been given him by his wife's father when they were first married, and been kept all those intervening years in honorable retirement for this final use. Its springs had not grown yielding with time; it had rather the stiffness and severity of age; but for him it must have swung low like the sweet chariot of the Negro "spiritual" which I heard him sing with such fervor, when those wonderful hymns of the slaves began to make their way northward. *Go Down, Daniel,* was one in which I can hear his quavering tenor now. He was a lover of the things he liked, and full of a passion for them which satisfied itself in reading them matchlessly aloud. No one could read *Uncle Remus* like him; his voice echoed the voices of the Negro nurses who told his childhood the wonderful tales. I remember especially his rapture with Mr. Cable's *Old Creole Days,* and the thrilling force with which he gave the forbidding of the leper's brother when the city's survey ran the course of an avenue through the cottage where the leper lived in hiding: "Strit must not pass!"

Out of a nature rich and fertile beyond any I have known, the material given him by the Mystery that makes a man and then leaves him to make himself over, he wrought a character of high nobility upon a foundation of clear and solid truth. At the last day he will not have to confess anything, for all his life was the free knowledge of anyone who would ask him of it. The Searcher of hearts will not bring him to shame at that day, for he did not try to hide any of the things for which he was often so bitterly sorry. He knew where the Responsibility lay, and he took a man's share of it bravely; but not the less fearlessly he left the rest of the answer to the God who had imagined men.

It is in vain that I try to give a notion of the intensity with which he pierced to the heart of life, and the breadth of vision with which he compassed the whole world, and tried for the reason of things, and then left trying. We had other meetings, insignificantly sad and brief; but the last time I saw him alive was made memorable to me by the kind clear judicial sense with which he explained and justified the labor unions as the sole present help of the weak against the strong.

Next I saw him dead, lying in his coffin amid those flowers with which we garland our despair in that pitiless hour. After the voice of his old friend Twichell had been lifted in the prayer which it wailed through in broken-hearted supplication, I looked a moment at the face I knew so well; and it was patient with the patience I had so often seen in it: something of puzzle, a great silent dignity, an assent to what must be from the depths of a nature whose tragical seriousness broke in the laughter which the unwise took for the whole of him. Emerson, Longfellow, Lowell, Holmes—I knew them all and all the rest of our sages, poets, seers, critics, humorists; they were like one another and like other literary men; but Clemens was sole, incomparable, the Lincoln of our literature.

GEORGE CABOT LODGE (1873–1907) belonged to a generation of poets, born in the late sixties or seventies, that never really accomplished its work. Almost all were born in New England and went to Harvard. Many of them died young. William Vaughn Moody, who died at forty-three, is still to some extent read. Trumbull Stickney, who died at thirty, was a more authentic poet, and some of his best pieces survive in anthologies. Edwin Arlington Robinson alone both was a poet of the first rank and completed a life's work. Outliving so many of his coevals, he became the real spokesman for all these men. Though he had moved from New England to New York, he wrote much of the twilight of New England, and he celebrated the dignity of failure. The typical hero of Robinson is the man who has failed but who has "followed the gleam."

In the work of George Cabot Lodge, though he expended in the writing of his verse a good deal of intellectual energy, the gleam does not glow very brilliantly. One cannot say that he was a bad poet: he was hardly a poet at all—though he did some service to poetry in rescuing the work of Stickney. Edith Wharton, who knew him, says in *A Backward Glance* that "he had a naturally scholarly mind, and might have turned in the end to history and archaeology; unless, indeed, he was simply intended to be the most sensitive of contemplators, as he was the most sensitive and dazzling of talkers." The sole interest of Lodge today is a sad typicality which lends itself to the purposes of historians and critics. Santayana, in a letter to William Lyon Phelps on the subject of his novel, *The Last Puritan*, writes that "an important element in the tragedy of 'his hero' is drawn from the fate of a whole string of Harvard poets in the 1880's and 1890's—Sanborn, Philip Savage, Hugh McCulloch, Trumbull Stickney, and Cabot Lodge. . . . Now, all those friends of mine . . . were visibly killed by the lack of air to breathe. People individually were kind and appreciative to them, as they were to me, but the system was deadly, and they hadn't any alternative tradition (as I had) to fall back upon; and of course . . . they hadn't the strength of a great intellectual hero who can stand alone."

But there would, of course, be no point in including a memoir of Lodge in this volume if Henry Adams had not written about him. Anatole France was once demonstrating in a salon that Jesus could never have existed, and Marcel Proust was listening with serious attention, watching the face of the speaker. France noticed this and stopped and asked his opinion of the matter. "It is not Jesus, monsieur," said Proust, "who interests me in this conversation, but Anatole France."

The late Herbert Croly told a curious story about an interview with Henry Adams. Croly had published in 1912 a biography of Mark Hanna; and the family of John Hay, then in search of a biographer for Hay, thought Croly was a possible man. They had been prompted perhaps by Adams: it was at any rate Adams whom Croly saw. He talked, Croly said, with an air of the great world which exercised a certain spell, but the occasion was deeply chilling. By the time he left Adams' presence, Croly had been made to feel that he would not for anything in the world undertake that biography of Hay. Though Adams' ostensible role had been that of a friend of the family who was trying to provide a memorial for an old and valued friend, he had constantly betrayed this purpose by intimating in backhanded but unmistakable fashion his conviction that Hay was a mediocre person, that it would be impossible to write truthfully about him and to satisfy the family at the same time, and that no self-respecting writer ought to think of taking on the job.

Adams had at that time himself just written, at the request of the family of another old friend, Henry Cabot Lodge, the life of Lodge's son; and he had let down the younger Lodge just as he had let down Hay and just as he was to let down Henry Cabot in *The Education of Henry Adams*. This dreary and cold little book—published in 1911, when Adams was seventy-three—is perhaps the most uncanny example of Adams' equivocal attitude in relation to the social world of Boston and to the official world of Washington out of which he had come and to which he had inevitably reverted, but with which he never ceased to express his extreme dissatisfaction. He assumes that Lodge, as a Lodge and the son of a friend of Adams, is worth taking seriously and writing about; but he turns the poor young man into a shadow, and withers up his verse with a wintry pinch.

It is possible to check Henry Adams' account by the portrait left by Edith Wharton. Mrs. Wharton says, for example, that Lodge was "brilliant and exuberant"—which is the kind of fact one does not get from Adams; and her description of the atmosphere of loving protection with which young Lodge was surrounded is strikingly at variance with Adams' picture of a violator of convention and a contender against the times.

His fate [she writes] was the reverse of mine, for he grew up in a hothouse of intensive culture, and was one of the most complete examples I have ever known of the young genius before whom an adoring family unites in smoothing the way. This kept him out of the struggle of life, and consequently out of its experiences, and to the end his intellectual precocity was combined with a boyishness of spirit at once delightful and pathetic. He had always lived in Washington, where, at the time when he was growing up, his father, Henry Adams, John

Hay, and the eccentric Sturgis Bigelow of Boston, whose erudition so far exceeded his mental capacity, formed a close group of intimates. Until Theodore Roosevelt came to Washington theirs were almost the only houses where one breathed a cosmopolitan air, and where such men as Sir Cecil Spring-Rice, J. J. Jusserand, and Lord Bryce felt themselves immediately at home. But Washington, even then, save for the politician and the government official, was a place to retire to, not to be young in; and Bay [as Lodge was called] often complained of the lack of friends of his own age. Even more than from the narrowness of his opportunities he suffered from the slightly rarefied atmosphere of mutual admiration and disdain of the rest of the world that prevailed in his immediate surroundings. John Hay was by nature the most open-minded of the group, and his diplomatic years in London had enlarged his outlook; but the dominating spirits were Henry Adams and Cabot Lodge, and though they were extremely kind to me, and my pleasantest hours in Washington were spent at their houses, I always felt that the influences prevailing there kept Bay in a state of brilliant immaturity.

Lodge, then, was kept under glass, and he dried up from "lack of air to breathe"; and Adams himself was a part of the stifling. He composes for his young friend an epitaph which buries his aspirations with him. The stealthy and elusive malice which lies in *The Education* here colors what is meant as a tribute with an irony so ready and pervasive that it is hardly aware of itself. J. P. Marquand could not do so well: the dismal comments on Lodge's *Wanderjahre*—"At best, the atmosphere of Paris in December lacks gaiety except for Parisians. . . . One founders through it as one best can." . . . "A winter in Berlin is, under the best of circumstances, a grave strain on the least pessimistic temper" . . . ; the chapter called *War and Love,* with its remark that if poets may be judged by the excellence of the women they are attached to, "young Lodge would take rank among the strongest"; the irony of the final picture—how far is it deliberate on Adams' part?—of poor Lodge arriving back in Boston, weighted down with family, nurses and baggage and in a panic for fear he has lost his manuscripts in the confusion of the North Station; and Henry Adams' own gingerly justification of the element of violence in Greek tragedy: "The better informed and the more accomplished the critic may be, who reads the *Herakles* for the first time, knowing nothing of the author, the more disconcerted he is likely to be in reading it a second time. His first doubts of the poet's knowledge or merits will be followed by doubts of his own."

This double-edged doubt, so characteristic of Adams—the doubt that peeled the gilt off the Gilded Age yet despaired of Adams' strength to stand up to it, the doubt which, in envying the faith that had erected the cathedral at Chartres, yet found in the weakness of the church's foundations a symbol for its own painful fears—this doubt is all through the life of Lodge, the last of Adams' published books. One feels that he dislikes Lodge's poetry. He would like to see something in it; but he shrinks—from what?—from finding in the younger man the reflection of his own sterility or from the disquieting possibility that Lodge may have really been a poet and hence have lived in some richer way than Adams had ever known? He wants to think that Lodge was a nonconformist as he imagines himself to have been; yet he meets in him all the old round of the life-cycle of people from Boston, of people like oneself; and he cannot repress a shiver. We people all come to nothing—not, of course, that we aren't better than the others.

With all this, there is even here that candor in dubiety and impotence which has the accents of a kind of strength; and the rare sensitive-cynical Adams who is himself a kind of poet, as it were, signs the little memoir with the passage at the end of the seventh chapter in which he tells of the solitary writer weaving secret enchantments at night like a drug-merchant or a magician.

THE LIFE OF GEORGE CABOT LODGE

I. Childhood

POETS ARE PROVERBIALLY BORN, not made; and, because they have been born rarely, the conditions of their birth are singularly interesting. One imagines that the conditions surrounding the birth of New England poets can have varied little, yet, in shades, these conditions differ deeply enough to perplex an artist who does not know where to look for them. Especially the society of Boston has always believed itself to have had, from the start, a certain complexity—certain rather refined *nuances*—which gave it an avowed right to stand apart; a right which its members never hesitated to assert, if it pleased them to do so, and which no one thought of questioning. One of the best-known and most strongly marked of these numerous families, was—and still is—that of the Cabots, whose early story has been told by Henry Cabot Lodge in his life of the best-known member of the family, his great-grandfather, George Cabot, Senator of the United States.

George Cabot's son Henry married Anna Blake, and had a daughter, Anna Sophia Cabot, who married John Ellerton Lodge. The Lodges were new arrivals in Boston. Giles Lodge, the grandfather, having narrowly escaped with his life from the San Domingo massacre, arrived, a young Englishman and a stranger, in Boston in 1791. There he established himself in business and married Mary Langdon, daughter of John Langdon, an officer of the Continental Army and cousin of President Langdon of Harvard College, who prayed for the troops on the eve of Bunker Hill. Through his mother John Lodge was descended from the Walleys and Brattles and other Puritan families of Boston, now for the most part extinct and forgotten. But despite the paternal grandmother, Henry Cabot Lodge, the only son of John Ellerton Lodge and Anna Cabot, felt himself Bostonian chiefly on the mother's side, as an offshoot of the prolific stock of the Cabots, who were really all of Essex County origin. He marked the point by making for himself a worldwide reputation under the double name of Cabot Lodge. Of him the public needs no biography, since he became a familiar figure to millions of his fellow-citizens from somewhat early youth to a fairly advanced age; and, from the conspicuous stage of the United States Senate, offered a far more conspicuous presence than his great-grandfather, George Cabot, had ever done.

To Bostonians, in general, the Cabots altogether are a stock too strong, too rich, too varied in their family characteristics, to need explanation. Volumes might be written on them, without exhausting the varieties of the strain.

That such a family should produce a poet was not matter for surprise; but as though to make such a product quite natural and normal, Henry Cabot Lodge, who was born May 12, 1850, married, on June 29, 1871, into another Massachusetts family with history and characteristics as marked as those of the Cabots themselves.

The Plymouth Colony produced Davises as freely as the north shore produced Cabots. Daniel Davis, of the Barnstaple stock, was Solicitor-General of Massachusetts in the days, about 1800, when the Reverend James Freeman was the Unitarian minister of King's Chapel; and Daniel Davis married Lois Freeman, who bore him thirteen children. The oldest, Louisa, married William Minot, of a family more thoroughly Bostonian, if possible, than all the rest. The youngest, Charles Henry Davis, born January 16, 1807, in Somerset Street, Boston, and, in due course, sent to Harvard College, left the college, in 1823, to enter the navy as midshipman, in order to cruise in the old frigate, the *United States*, in the Pacific, under the command of his friend and patron, Commodore Isaac Hull.

The life of Admiral Davis has been admirably told elsewhere, and his victories at Hilton Head, in November 1861, at Fort Pillow, in May 1862, at Memphis and Vicksburg, afterwards, rank among the most decisive of the Civil War, as they rank also among the earliest to give some share of hope or confidence to the national government and to the loyal voters; but his brilliant career in the navy concerns his grandson-poet less than the domestic event of his marriage, in 1842, to Harriette Blake Mills, daughter of still another United States Senator, Elijah Hunt Mills, of Northampton, Massachusetts, who was also a conspicuous figure in his day.

The complications of this alliance were curious, and among them was the chance that another daughter of Senator Mills married Benjamin Peirce, the famous Professor of Mathematics at Harvard College, so that the children of Admiral Davis became first cousins of the great mathematician Charles Peirce and his brothers. Among these children of Admiral Davis was a daughter, Anna Cabot Mills Davis, who grew up to girlhood in Cambridge, under the shadow of Harvard College, where her father, the Admiral, lived while not in active service; and when, after his appointment to the Naval Observatory, he transferred his residence to Washington, she made her home there until her marriage, in June 1871, to Henry Cabot Lodge.

Her second child, George Cabot Lodge, the subject of this story, was born in Boston, October 10, 1873.

A poet, born in Boston, in 1873, saw about him a society which commonly bred refined tastes, and often did refined work, but seldom betrayed strong emotions. The excitements of war had long passed; its ideals were forgotten, and no other great ideal had followed. The twenty-five years between 1873 and 1898—years of astonishing scientific and mechanical activity—were marked by a steady decline of literary and artistic intensity, and especially of the feeling for poetry, which, at best, had never been the favorite form of Boston expression. The only poet who could be called strictly Bostonian by birth—Ralph Waldo Emerson—died in the year 1882, before young Lodge was ten years old. Longfellow, who always belonged to Cambridge rather than to Boston, died in the same year. James Russell Lowell survived till 1891, but was also in no strict social sense a Bostonian. Young men growing up on Beacon Hill or the Back Bay never met such characters unless by a rare chance; and as the city became busier and more crowded, the chances became rarer still.

Not the society, therefore, could have inspired a taste for poetry. Such an instinct must have been innate, like his cousin's mathematics. Society could strike him only as the absence of all that he might have supposed it to be, as he read of it in the history and poetry of the past. Even since the youth of R. W. Emerson, the sense of poetry had weakened like the sense of religion. Boston differed little from other American towns with less reputation for intellect, where, as a rule, not many persons entered their neighbors' houses, and these were members of the family. A stranger was unknown.

The classic and promiscuous turmoil of the forum, the theater, or the bath, which trained the Greeks and the Romans, or the narrower contact of the church and the coffee-house, which bred the polished standards of Dryden and Racine, were unknown in America, and nearly extinct in Paris and London. An American boy scarcely conceived of getting social education from contact with his elders. In previous generations he had been taught to get it from books, but the young American of this period was neither a bookish nor a social animal. Climate and custom combined to narrow his horizon.

Commonly the boy was well pleased to have it so; he asked only to play with his fellows, and to escape contact with the world; but the Boston child of the Cabot type was apt to feel himself alone even as a child. Unless singularly fortunate in finding and retaining sympathetic companions, his strong individuality rebelled against its surroundings. Boys are naturally sensitive and shy. Even as men, a certain proportion of society showed, from the time of the Puritans, a marked reserve, so that one could never be quite sure in State Street, more than in Concord, that the lawyer or banker whom one consulted about drawing a deed or nego-tiating a loan might not be unconsciously immersed in intro-spection, as his ancestors, two centuries before, had been absorbed in their chances of salvation. The latent contrasts of character were full of interest, and so well understood that any old Bostonian, familiar with family histories, could recall by scores the comedies and tragedies which had been due to a conscious or unconscious revolt against the sup-pression of instinct and imagination.

Poetry was a suppressed instinct: and except where, as in Longfellow, it kept the old character of ornament, it became a reaction against society, as in Emerson and the Concord school, or, further away and more roughly, in Walt Whit-man. Less and less it appeared, as in earlier ages, the natural, favorite expression of society itself. In the last half of the nineteenth century, the poet became everywhere a rebel against his surroundings. What had been begun by Words-worth, Byron, and Shelley, was carried on by Algernon Swinburne in London or Paul Verlaine in Paris or Walt Whitman in Washington, by a common instinct of revolt. Even the atmosphere of Beacon Street was at times faintly redolent of Schopenhauer.

The tendency of Bostonians to break away from conven-tional society was fostered by the harshness of the climate, but was vastly helped by the neighborhood of the ocean. Snow and ice and fierce northwest gales shut up society within doors during three months of winter; while equally fierce heat drove society to camp within tide-water during three months of summer. There the ocean was the closest of friends. Everyone knows the little finger of granite that points oceanward, some ten miles north of Boston, as though directing the Bostonian homeward. The spot is almost an island, connected with Lynn by a long, narrow strip of sand-beach; but on the island a small township called Nahant has long existed, and the end of this point of Nahant was bought by the grandfather, John Ellerton Lodge, as a country place for summer residence.

The whole coast, for five hundred miles in either direction, has since been seized for summer residence, but Nahant alone seems to be actually the ocean itself, as though it were a ship quitting port, or, better, just stranded on the rocky coast of Cape Ann. There the winds and waves are alone really at home, and man can never by day or night escape their company. At the best of times, and in their most seductive temper, their restlessness carries a suggestion of change, —a warning of latent passion,—a threat of storm. One looks out forever to an infinite horizon of shoreless and shifting ocean.

The sea is apt to revive some primitive instinct in boys, as though in a far-off past they had been fishes, and had never quite forgotten their home. The least robust can feel the repulsion, even when they cannot feel the physical attraction, of the waves playing with the rocks like children never quite sure of their temper; but the Lodge boy, like most other boys of his class and breed, felt the sea as an echo or double of himself. Commonly this instinct of unity with nature dies early in American life; but young Lodge's nature was itself as elementary and simple as the salt water. Throughout life, the more widely his character spread in circumference, the more simply he thought, and even when trying to grow complex—as was inevitable since it was to grow in Boston—the mind itself was never complex, and the complexities merely gathered on it, as something outside, like the sea-weeds gathering and swaying about the rocks. Robust in figure, healthy in appetite, careless of consequences, he could feel complex and introspective only as his ideal, the Norse faun, might feel astonished and angry at finding nature perverse and unintelligible in a tropical jungle. Since nature could not be immoral or futile, the immorality and futility must be in the mind that conceived it. Man became an outrage; society an artificial device for the distortion of truth; civilization a wrong. Many millions of simple natures have thought, and still think, the same thing, and the more complex have never quite made up their minds whether to agree with them or not; but the thought that was simple and sufficient for the Norseman exploring the tropics, or for an exuberant young savage sailing his boat off the rude shores of Gloucester and Cape Ann, could not long survive in the atmosphere of State Street. Commonly the poet dies young.

The Nahant life was intensely home, with only a father and mother for companions, an elder sister, a younger brother, cousins, or boy friends at hazard, and boundless sea and sky. As the boy passed his tenth year, his father—possibly inspired by the same spirit of restlessness—turned much of his time and attention to politics, and the mother became all the more the companion and resource of the children. From the earliest forms of mammal life, the mothers of fauns have been more in love with their offspring than with all else in existence; and when the mother has had the genius of love and sympathy, the passion of altruism, the instinct of taste and high breeding, besides the commoner resources of intelligence and education, the faun returns the love, and is molded by it into shape.

These were the elements of his youth, and the same elements will be found recurring in all that he thought and said during his thirty-six years of life. He was himself, both in fact and in imagination, *The Wave*, whose song he began his literary career by composing:

This is the song of the wave, that died in the fullness of life.
The prodigal this, that lavished its largess of strength
In the lust of achievement.
Aiming at things for Heaven too high,
Sure in the pride of life, in the richness of strength.
So tried it the impossible height, till the end was found,
Where ends the soul that yearns for the fillet of morning stars,
The soul in the toils of the journeying worlds,
Whose eye is filled with the image of God,
    And the end is Death.

Had the *Song of the Wave* been written after death instead of before the beginning of life, the figure could not have been more exact. The young man felt the image as he felt the act; his thought offered itself to him as a wave. From first to last he identified himself with the energies of nature, as the story will show; he did not invent images for amusement, but described himself in describing the energy. Even the figure of the Norse faun was his own figure, and, like the Wave, with which it belongs, was an effort at the first avowal of himself to himself; for these things were of his youth, felt and not feigned:

> These are the men!
> The North has given them name,
> The children of God who dare. . . .
> These are the men!
> In their youth without memory
> They were glad, for they might not see
> The lies that the world has wrought
> On the parchment of God. The tree
> Yielded them ships, and the sky
> Flamed as the waters fought;
> But they knew that death was a lie,
> That the life of man was as nought,
> And they dwelt in the truth of the sea.
> These are the men.

In conditions of life less intimate than those of Boston, such a way of conceiving one's own existence seems natural; indeed almost normal for Wordsworths and Byrons, Victor Hugos and Walter Savage Landors, Algernon Swinburnes, and Robert Louis Stevensons; but to the Bostonian absorbed in the extremely practical problem of effecting some sort of working arrangement between Beacon Street and the universe, the attitude of revolt seemed unnatural and artificial. He could not even understand it. For centuries the Bostonian had done little but wrestle with nature for a bare existence, and his foothold was not so secure, nor had it been so easily acquired, nor was it so victoriously sufficient for his wants, as to make him care to invite the ice or the ocean once more to cover it or himself; while, even more keenly than the Scotchman or Norseman, he felt that he ought not to be reproached for the lies that the world, including himself, had wrought, under compulsion, on the exceedingly rough and scanty parchment of God.

Therefore the gap between the poet and the citizen was so wide as to be impassable in Boston, but it was not a division of society into hostile camps, as it had been in England with Shelley and Keats, or in Boston itself, half a century before, with the anti-slavery outbursts of Emerson and Whittier, Longfellow and Lowell, which shook the foundations of the State. The Bostonian of 1900 differed from his parents and grandparents of 1850, in owning nothing the value of which, in the market, could be affected by the poet. Indeed, to him, the poet's pose of hostility to actual conditions of society was itself mercantile,—a form of drama,—a thing to sell, rather than a serious revolt. Society could safely adopt it as a form of industry, as it adopted other forms of bookmaking.

Therefore, while, for young Lodge and other protestants of his age and type, the contrast between Nahant and Beacon Street was a real one, even a vital one, life in both places was normal, healthy, and quite free from bitterness or social strain. Society was not disposed to defend itself from criticism or attack. Indeed, the most fatal part of the situation for the poet in revolt, the paralyzing drug that made him helpless, was that society no longer seemed sincerely to believe in itself or anything else; it resented nothing, not even praise. The young poet grew up without being able to find an enemy. With a splendid physique, a warmly affectionate nature, a simple but magnificent appetite for all that life could give, a robust indifference or defiance of consequences, a social position unconscious of dispute or doubt, and a large, insatiable ambition to achieve ideals—with these ample endowments and energies, in full consciousness of what he was about to attempt, the young man entered deliberately upon what he was to call his Great Adventure.

II. Cambridge and Paris

To ALL YOUNG BOSTONIANS of a certain age and social position Harvard College opens its doors so genially as to impose itself almost as a necessary path into the simple problems of Boston life; and it has the rather unusual additional merit of offering as much help as the student is willing to accept towards dealing with the more complex problems of life in a wider sense. Like most of his friends and family, young Lodge, at eighteen years old, went to the University, and profited by it in his own way, which was rarely, with Bostonians of his type, precisely the way which the actual standards of American life required or much approved. The first two years seldom profit young men of this class at all, but with the third year, their tastes, if they have any, begin to show themselves, and their minds grope for objects that offer them attraction, or for supports that the young tendrils can grasp. Every instructor has seen this rather blind process going on in generation after generation of students, and is seldom able to lend much help to it; but if he is so fortunate as to teach some subject that attracts the student's fancy, he can have influence. Owing to some innate sympathies, which were apparently not due to inheritance or conditions, Lodge seemed to care less for English than for French or Italian or classic standards; and it happened that the French department was then directed by Professor Bôcher, who took a fancy to the young man, and not only helped him to an acquaintance with the language, but still more with the literature and the thought of France, a subject in which Professor Bôcher was an admirable judge and critic.

At first, the student made the usual conscientious effort to do what did not amuse him. "I am going to acquire the faculty of not minding applying myself to uninteresting subjects, if I can, and I am sure that it is possible," he wrote to his mother, March 21, 1893; and then, pursuing the usual course which started most Harvard students on literary careers, he fell at once into the arms of Thomas Carlyle. "I am making a study of the religious and philosophical side of Carlyle, with a view to writing a book on the same; and it is a most absorbing subject," he wrote on May 6, 1893. "My head is full of ideas which I want to let out in that book. I propose to devote my summer to it. Even if it isn't a success, it is better than doing nothing, and it is profoundly interesting. I have read attentively almost everything he ever wrote except *Cromwell*, and I am taking notes on all the more philosophical ones, like *Sartor Resartus*; and I am also reading and studying conjointly the French philosophers, Descartes, Malebranche, and Spinoza, and the German Schopenhauer and Fichte, and also Plato, so that I shall get an idea of his relations to the celebrated philosophies. I am going to read Froude's life of him." The door by which a student enters the vast field of philosophy matters little, for, whatever it is, the student cannot stay long in it; but for one of such wide views, Carlyle could serve a very short time as the central interest.

"Today Bourget came out here to a lecture in French 7 by Sumichrast, and Sumichrast got him to talk, which he did most charmingly. I have been taking a course of Bourget, among other things, *Mensonges*; and I feel as if I had been living in the mire. Never have I read books whose atmosphere was so unhealthy and fetid." This was written to his mother, December 12, 1893, when he was barely twenty years old, and marks the steady tide of French influence that was carrying him on to its usual stage of restlessness and depression. On February 28, 1894, he wrote again, announcing that he had fairly reached the moral chaos which belonged to his temperament and years: "I am in very good health and very bad spirits, and I am feeling pretty cynical. It is a constant struggle for me to prevent myself from becoming cynical, and when I feel blue and depressed, the dykes break and it all comes to the surface. I suppose I have seen more of the evil and mean side of men and things than most men of my age, which accounts for my having naturally a pessimistic turn. Really, though, I hate cynicism, —it is a compilation of cheap aphorisms that any fool can learn to repeat,—and yet the world does seem a bad place."

A common place rather than a bad place was the next natural and cheap aphorism which every imaginative young man could look with confidence to reach, but the process of reaching it varies greatly with the temperament of the men. In Lodge it soon took the form of philosophic depression accompanied by intense ambition. The combination, at the age of twenty, is familiar in Europeans, but not so common among Americans, who are apt to feel, or to show, diffidence in their own powers. Lodge's letters will reveal himself fully on that side, but what they show still better is the immense appetite of the young man for his intellectual food, once he had found the food he liked.

"Since I got back [to Cambridge]," he wrote to his mother on March 14, 1894, "I have been reading an immense quantity from variegated authors, Balzac especially; also Flaubert, Alfred de Vigny, Leconte de Lisle, and Musset, Hugo, Renan (whom I am going to write a long French theme about), Schopenhauer, and then the Upanishads, etc. Next time French literature is discussed, ask them what living poet equals Sully Prudhomme." He was already in a region where Boston society—or indeed, any other society except perhaps that of Paris—would have been puzzled to answer his questions; but the sense of reaching new regions excited him. "I am beginning to get beautifully into harness now," he wrote on November 16, 1894, "and find that, outside my College work, I can read from one hundred and fifty to two hundred pages a day. . . . If I were living in Gobi or Sahara, with the British Museum next door and the Louvre round the corner, I think I could do almost anything. When I work I have to fill myself full of my subject, and then write everything down without referring to any books. If I am interrupted in the agonies of composition, it takes me some time to get into the vein." The passion for reading passed naturally into the passion for writing, and every new volume read reflected itself in a volume to be written. The last term of college began and ended in this frame of mind. He wrote on January 17, 1895: "I have a scheme of writing essays on Schopenhauer, Swift, Molière, Poe, Leconte de Lisle, Carlyle, Alfred de Vigny, Balzac, Thackeray (perhaps), and any others I may think of, and entitling the collection *Studies in Pessimism,* or some such title, and treat them all, of course, from that point of view. I could write them all except Swift and Thackeray and Balzac with very little preparation; and even with those three I should not need much. I wish you would ask papa what he thinks of my idea. Last night Max Scull and I took Brun (the French teacher) to dinner and the theater afterwards. He was quite entertaining, and I improved my French considerably, as we spoke nothing else. I told him I was going to France next summer, and he told me to write to him and *qu'il me montrerait Paris à fond.* I have been working on my wretched story, and have gone over it about eight times. It now seems to me to be quite valueless. Also I have burst into song several times—rather lamely, I fear."

Then began, still in college, the invariable, never-ending effort of the artist to master his art,—to attain the sureness of hand and the quality of expression which should be himself. Lodge plunged into the difficulties with the same appetite which he felt for the facilities of expression, and felt at once where his personal difficulties were likely to be greatest, in his own exuberance. "I find I cannot polish my verses to any great extent," he continued on March 20, 1895; "I write when I feel in the mood, and then they are done—badly or well, as the case may be. If badly, they must either be all written over, or else burnt, and a new one written, generally the most appropriate fate for most of them. However, I am indeed very glad that you and papa think I am improving, however slightly. I enclose three efforts in a more lyrical strain. I find it rather a relief to be less trammeled, and unfettered to so concrete and absolute a form as the Petrarchan sonnet,—which is the only kind I write now. I have been looking over the few sonnets Shelley wrote. He had no form at all in them. He seems to have built them up with no preconceived idea of form whatever. Take *Ozymandias,* for instance, which I admire intensely, and one finds no structure at all. Yet of course we know that the whole, as read, is superb. I wonder if most people notice the form of a sonnet. I know I didn't, before I began to scribble myself. Still, I do think, other things being equal, that the Petrarchan form adds a dignity and beauty to a sonnet which no other form possesses. The contour is much more harmonious and symmetrical."

Thus the young man had plunged headlong into the higher problems of literary art before he was fairly ac-

quainted with the commoner standards. Whether he ever
framed to himself a reason for pursuing one form rather
than another, might be a curious question. Why should not
Shakespeare and the Elizabethans have appealed to him
first? Was it because the Petrarchan form was more perfect,
or because it was less English? Whatever the answer to this
question may be, the fact is that, throughout life, he turned
away from the English models, and seemed often indifferent
to their existence. The trait was not wholly peculiar to him,
for even in England itself the later Victorian poets, with
Algernon Swinburne at their head, showed a marked disposition to break rather abruptly with the early Victorian poets,
and to wander away after classical or mediaeval standards;
but their example was hardly the influence that affected
Lodge. With him, the English tradition possibly represented
a restraint,—a convention,—a chain that needed to be broken,
—that jarred on his intense ambition.

"Oh, I am devoured by ambition," he wrote in the last
days of his college life, to his mother: "I do so want to do
something that will last,—some man's work in the world,—
that I am constantly depressed by an awful dread that perhaps I shan't be able to. I am never satisfied with what I
do,—never contented with my expression of what I wish to
express, and yet I hope and sometimes feel that it is possible
I may do something permanent in value. I have got at last
a scheme for the future which I think it probable you will
like, and papa also; but I shall be better able to tell you
when I see you. I have read nothing lately outside my work
except the *Theologia Germanica* which Mrs. Wintie [Chan-
ler] sent me, and which has many beautiful things in it.
I have written even less,—just a few scraps of verse (one
of which, a sonnet, is coming out in the next *Monthly* by
the way), and that article on Shakespeare which went to
papa. I am anxious to know what he thinks of it."

With this, the college life closed, having given, liberally
and sympathetically, all it could give, leaving its graduates
free, and fairly fitted, to turn where they chose for their
further food; which meant, for young Lodge, as his letters
have told, the immediate turning to Paris. The choice showed

the definite determination of his thought. England, Germany, Italy, did not, at that stage, offer the kind of education he wanted. He meant to make himself a literary artist, and in Paris alone he could expect to find the technical practice of the literary arts. In Paris alone, a few men survived who talked their language, wrote prose, and constructed drama, as they modeled a statue or planned a structure.

Thus far, as commonly happens even to ambitious young men, the path was easy, and the outlook clear; but the illusion of ease and horizon seldom lasts long in Paris. A few days completely dispel it. Almost instantly the future becomes desperately difficult. Especially to an American, the processes and machinery of a French education are hard to apply in his home work. The French mind thinks differently and expresses its thought differently, so that the American, though he may actually think in French, will express his thought according to an American formula. Merely the language profits him little; the arts not much more; the history not at all; the poetry is ill suited to the genius of the English tongue; the drama alone is capable of direct application; in sum, it is the whole—the combination of tradition, mental habit, association of ideas, labor of technique, criticism, instinct—that makes a school, and the school, once mastered, is of only indirect use to an American. The secret of French literary art is a secret of its own which does not exist in America. Indeed, the American soon begins to doubt whether America has any secrets, either in literary or any other art.

Within a few weeks all these doubts and difficulties had risen in young Lodge's face, and he found himself reduced to the usual helplessness of the art-student in Paris, working without definite purpose in several unrelated directions. At best, the atmosphere of Paris in December lacks gaiety except for Parisians, or such as have made themselves by time and temperament more or less Parisian. One flounders through it as one best can; but in Lodge's case, the strain was violently aggravated by the political storm suddenly roused by President Cleveland's Venezuela message, and sympathy with his father's political responsibilities in the Senate.

PARIS, *December 26, 1895*

The study here is wholly different from anything I have been accustomed to and I am in some ways much alone. It seems to me here as if I was losing my grip, my aggressiveness, my force of mind, and it is a feeling that has been gradually coming over me, and that Venezuela has brought to a crisis. I don't do anything here, nothing tangible. I work five hours a day or six, and what on—a miserable little poetaster. I want to get home and get some place on a newspaper or anything of that kind, and really do something. I spend more money than is necessary, and altogether don't seem to lead a very profitable life. For me, loafing is not fun except in a recognized vacation. I never realized this until now. I thought I should like to take it easy for a while and *soi-disant* amuse myself. I am wretched. I want something real to do. I don't want to become a mere Teutonic grind, and it's necessary to do that if you are going to take degrees here. Both you and papa told me to feel no hesitation in coming home if I wanted to, and so now that I have been here long enough to see I have made an error, I write as I do. I am always slow of comprehension, and if it has taken me a long time to find this out, it's just that I am getting experience—rather slowly and stupidly. I have not yet absolutely decided. If this appears to you hasty or ill-advised, please let me know in the shortest way possible.

Venezuela excites me horribly and my poor mind is rather torn, as you may see by this somewhat incoherent letter.

PARIS, *January 6, 1896*

Since I last wrote you I have quieted down a good deal more. I feel as if I had been through three hideous weeks of madness and were become on a sudden sane. You see the Venezuela affair came on me on a sudden and filled me with such a longing for home that I lost all pleasure in things over here. So my poor mind whirled round and round from one thing to another till I almost went mad. Now Venezuela seems to be a danger only in the future if at all, and I am realizing how much I am getting here.

If papa is willing I should stay I can come back with a good knowledge of German, Italian, and Spanish, and of Romance Philology and Middle Age Literature—all of which things I very much need.

The thing which tore me worst in all this mental struggle I have been going through was the continual thought of money and my crying inability to adapt myself to my time and to become a money-maker. I felt as if it was almost cowardly of me not to turn in and leave all the things I love and the world doesn't, behind, and to adjust myself to my age, and try to take its ideals and live strongly and wholly in its spirit. It seems so useless being an eternal malcontent. Unless one is a Carlyle, to scream on paper generally ends in a thin squeak, and I fought and fought to try to be more a man of my age so that I might work with the tide and not against it. But it's no use, I cannot stifle my own self or alter it in that way. I said to myself that I ought to go home in order to get into the tide of American life if for nothing else; that I oughtn't to be dreaming and shrieking inside and poetizing and laboring on literature here in Paris, supported by my father, and that I ought to go home and live very hard making money. I said to myself that I knew I could not be very quick at money-making, but that at any rate in the eyes of men I should lead a self-respecting life and my hideous, utter failure would only be for myself and you, who understand. But somehow all the while my soul refused to believe the plain facts and illogically clung to the belief that I might do some good in creative work in the world after all, and so I struggled with the facts and my faiths and loves and there was the Devil of a row inside me and I most wretched. Now it seems to me that my staying here can do no harm, as I can just as well begin to be nineteenth century next year as this, and I shall have a very happy winter and acquire some knowledge and much experience. And so now my mind is comparatively calm and I am becoming happy again and seeing things a little more in their proper perspective.

Now like Marcus Aurelius I have come home to my own soul and found there, I am glad to say, sufficient

strength and resource and calm to reëstablish my equilibrium, and make me see how cowardly it is not to have
enough self-reliance to bear such things as these with a
tolerably good grace. . . .

I might entitle this letter: "Of the entering, passing
through, and coming out of, the madness of George Cabot
Lodge." I really feel as if the past two weeks were a great
black hole in my life, in which all my landmarks were
blurred, and I have just found them again.

PARIS, *January 16, 1896*

I am now working principally on Romance Philology,
Spanish, and Italian. I usually go to the Bibliothèque in
the morning and work on Spanish. I am studying the history
of the literature and trying to read the most important
things as I go along. It is hard work reading the old Spanish
of the twelfth to fifteenth centuries, but I am convinced it
is the only way to know the language or literature really
thoroughly. I also work on my Spanish courses. In Italian I
am reading Tiraboschi, *Storia della litteratura Italiana,* which
of course is the great history of the Italian literature. I also
work a good deal on Petrarch: he is one of my courses, you
know. Mr. Stickney sent to Italy for me for a good edition
of Dante, and when it comes I shall begin the study of it.
In the afternoon I go to courses, and sometimes of course
in the morning, too, and play billiards as a rule about five
with Joe, and in the evening work on my Romance Philology. I have procured by good fortune a very good dictionary of the old French.

Thus, you see, my work now is concentrated on the Romance Languages and Literature, especially before the six-
teenth century. I shall keep on principally on them, because
I am sure by so doing I can come home with a more or less
thorough knowledge of the Latin tongues and a little more
than a smattering of their literature. The Latin languages
attract me and I shall work hard on them. As for German,
I shall learn it if I can find time, but I don't know. . . . I
see now that I must do the best in me if I can; and if there

is a best to do; and at any rate I haven't the force or the weakness to renounce everything without having one glorious fight for what I want to do and believe is best to do. It is this realization of my own self that has done me most good, I think.

I went to the Français last night. It was the birthday of Molière and they gave the *École des Femmes* and the *Malade Imaginaire,* and afterwards the ceremony of crowning the bust by all the *Sociétaires* and *pensionnaires* of the Théâtre. It was most interesting. I think the best night of theater I ever had.

PARIS, *January 27, 1896*

My languages get on very well. Italian and Spanish I am really getting very smart in and read with perfect ease, and I am sure when I come back I shall know a good deal about the Romance Languages. My German I am working on, and of course it comes more slowly, but I think I can do it all right.

PARIS, *February 21, 1896*

I have just lived through the Carnival here, which began on Saturday night with the *bal de l'opéra* (third of the name) and continued until Wednesday morning. I took it in with considerable thoroughness. There was the procession of the Bœuf Gras—the first time this has occurred since the Franco-German war. It was very pretty and the crowds in the street tremendous—all throwing paper confetti and long rolls of paper, which one might throw across the boulevards. Now the trees are all covered with long ribbons of papers of all colors. It was a very pretty sight and most amusing. I never imagined such a good-tempered crowd, and one so bound to have a good time. I send by this mail a sort of program with an amusing picture by Caran D'Ache. I was glad of the Carnival. I think one gets into terrible ruts and little habits close around one, and one gets dull and mechanical. The Carnival just broke all that up for me, and for three days I led a wholly irregular life, that had a certain splendor in the unexpectedness of everything I did. . . .

C. and P. both wrote me very nice things about my poems. I have just read over a lot and become drearily conscious that they are far from deserving any praise, so that it rather worries me to have people so kind about them, as it seems as if I could never live up to what they think I ought to do. However, I have become an excellent critic of my own work and diligently weed out from time to time all that seems flat, so that I may someday have something really poetry.

PARIS, *April 5, 1896*

Here it's Easter Sunday and I haven't had a happier day for a long time. The skies have been bright blue and the sun pure gold, and the trees all timidly "uttering leaves" everywhere, and so I want to write to you. Early this morning Joe and I went and rode horses in the Bois, which we had already done last Sunday, and are going to do more often. It was most marvelous—all the little fresh greening things looking out of the earth, and the early sunlight coming wet and mild through the trees, and the rare fresh air, and the sense of physical glow and exercise.

I found an alley with about a dozen jumps in it and whisked my old hired horse over the entire lot, with the surprising result that he jumped rather well, except the water-jump, into which he flatly jumped, managing, however, to stand up. Then I came home and read Petrarch and Ronsard, and in the afternoon took a boat down a bright blue Seine with white bridges spanning it and a Louvre, etc., on either hand. I got off at the Ile St. Louis, and for the pure dramatic effect went into the "Doric little morgue" and saw two terrible dead old women with the lower jaw dropped on the withered breast and the green of decomposition beginning about the open eyes. Then I came out into the broad sunshine, with that blessed Cathedral Apse in front of me, and its little sun-filled garden with the old Gothic fountain running pure water, and felt it was very good to live. Then I went in and heard a splendid mass, with the great organ rolling up by the front rose window, and saw the Host raised and the church full (really full) of people fall on their knees, and the thick incense come slowly out, and felt alas! how far away I was from the substance of the shadow of splendor I was feeling. But I was very happy for all that, and wandered around some more in the sunlight, and then came home, where I am now writing to you.

This winter I have been realizing a copy-book common-place, which is at the same time a metaphysical profundity, viz.: that the present is all that *is* and it is not. One of the crowning metaphysical paradoxes. Of course the present is not. While you are uttering "now," it is fled—it never existed. It is like a geometrical point, non-existent. And the past—that's the cruel thing, the killing memories. Memories of yesterday, of the moment just fled, which are as hopelessly dead, as impossibly distant as memories of ten years gone. The past is like a great pit, and the present like a frittered edge which is continually crumbling and falling utterly down into the pit. . . . For me—my past is all *amoncelé*, nothing nearer, nothing farther. I have a more vivid memory of Sister with long hair, driving old Rab up the sidewalk by the Gibsons' at Nahant on a gray autumn day, than of most things happened within the year. And my memories are all sad—sad with an infinite hopeless regret; that one of Sister, for example, has almost made me cry. And then the present is the past so facilely, so quickly, and I find myself sometimes when I am not doing anything—talking perhaps or sitting idle or even reading, in fact *un peu toujours*—suddenly turning sick and cold and saying to myself, "See, your life goes, goes, goes. Every day you get more memories to dwell about you like mourning creatures, and still nothing done—with your youth, your strength, and every minute the memories thickening and the pain of them increasing, and still nothing done. Man! Man! Your life is very short, already twenty and two years; as many again, and you will be hardened into your mold, and the mold yet unmade! Up, up and do something!"

And the future—it is the veriest of commonplaces to say the future doesn't exist. It is nothing but a probability—at best a hope. And then did it ever occur to you that the present is like a piece of paper on which experience writes

in invisible ink, and that only when the heat of the pain of
memory and regret blows upon it, do the characters come
out and you know how intensely alive, how happy, or at
any rate how miserable, or at least how unbored, you *had
been*.

It seems to me all the happiness (except, of course, physical) which we get is only the more or less incomplete suggestion or partial realization of some remembered happiness.
For instance, the slant of the western sun through green
leaves sometimes brings back one perfectly unimportant afternoon when I was very small, and Sister sat on the grass
under those willows, behind the little toolhouse in front of
Mr. Locke's, and read a story aloud to me.

She left off in the middle, and I can distinctly remember
the last words she said. Now when I can get a vivid suggestion of something intensely happy in my memory, infinitely richer and more happy than I had any idea of when
it occurred, it makes me more happy than anything. Happiness is a continual thinking backward or forward, memory
or expectation.

This may all sound rather rhetorical, but I assure you it
is unintentional. If you knew how intensely I have been
feeling all this and much more that I cannot express, you
would know that this isn't rhetoric, but pure crying out of
the soul—such as I could only say to you.

Thousands of young people, of both sexes, pass through
the same experience in their efforts to obtain education, in
Paris or elsewhere, and are surprised to find at the end that
their education consists chiefly in whatever many-colored
impressions they have accidentally or unconsciously absorbed. In these their stock or capital of experience is apt
to consist, over and above such general training as is the
common stock of modern society; but most of them would
find themselves puzzled to say in what particular class of
impression their gain was greatest. Lodge would have said
at once that his gain was greatest in the friendship with
young Stickney, to which the letters allude.

Joseph Trumbull Stickney, who was then preparing his

thesis for the unusual distinction of doctorate at the Sorbonne —the University of France—was a European in the variety and extent of his education and the purest of Americans by blood, as his name proclaimed. Nearly of Lodge's age, almost identical in tastes and convictions, and looking forward to much the same career, he and his companionship were among those rare fortunes that sometimes bless unusually favored youth when it needs, more than all else, the constant contact with its kind.

III. The Song of the Wave

EARLY in his college course, the young man had acquired a taste for Schopenhauer. The charm of Schopenhauer is due greatly to his clearness of thought and his excellence of style, —merits rare among German philosophers,—but another of his literary attractions is the strong bent of his thought towards oriental and especially Buddhistic ideals and methods. At about the same time it happened that Sturgis Bigelow returned to Boston from a long residence in Japan, and brought with him an atmosphere of Buddhistic training and esoteric culture quite new to the realities of Boston and Cambridge. The mystical side of religion had vanished from the Boston mind, if it ever existed there, which could have been at best only in a most attenuated form; and Boston was as fresh wax to new impressions. The oriental ideas were full of charm, and the oriental training was full of promise. Young Lodge, tormented by the old problems of philosophy and religion, felt the influence of Sturgis Bigelow deeply, for Bigelow was the closest intimate of the family, and during the summer his island of Tuckanuck, near Nantucket, was the favorite refuge and resource for the Lodges. As time went on, more and more of the young man's letters were addressed to Bigelow.

Returning home after the winter of 1895–96 in Paris, he found himself more than ever harrowed by the conflict of interests and tastes. He went to Newport in August, for a few days, and rebelled against all its standards. "I hate the philistine-plutocrat atmosphere of this place, and it tends not to diminish my views anent modern civilization and the money power. I sincerely thank God I shall never be a rich man, and never will I, if my strength holds. The world cannot be fought with its own weapons; David fought Goliath with a sling, and the only way to kill the world is to fight it with one's own toy sword or sling, and deny strenuously contact with, or participation in, the power it cherishes. Much more of the same nature is yearning to be said, but I will spare you. . . . If I haven't it in me to write a poem, what a sordid farce my life will be!" The expression is strong, but in reality the young man had fairly reached the point where his life was staked on literary success. The bent of his energy was fixed beyond change, and as though he meant deliberately to make change impossible, he returned to Europe, to pass the next winter, 1896–97, in Berlin.

A winter in Berlin is, under the best of circumstances, a grave strain on the least pessimistic temper, but to a young poet of twenty-two, fresh from Paris, and exuberant with the full sense of life and health, Berlin required a conscientious sense of duty amounting to self-sacrifice, in order to make it endurable. Socially it was complete solitude except for the presence of Cecil Spring-Rice, an old Washington intimate then in the British Embassy. As a matter of education in art or literature, the study of German had never been thought essential to poets, or even to prose writers, in the English language; and although, at about the middle of the century, many of the best English and French authors, and some American, had insisted that no trained student could afford to be ignorant of so important a branch of human effort, none had ever imposed it on their pupils as a standard of expression. In that respect, a serious devotion to the language was likely to do more harm than good.

The New England conscience is responsible for much that seems alien to the New England nature. Naturally, young Lodge would have gone to Rome to study his art, and no doubt he would have greatly preferred it. He needed to fill out his education on that side,—not on the side of Germany,—and his future work suffered for want of the experience. If he went to Berlin, he did it because in some vague way he hoped that Germany might lead to practical work. His letters show the strenuous conscientiousness with which he labored through the task.

TO HIS MOTHER

BERLIN, *January 1897*

It's a week now since I wrote you and I've not much more news than I had. I am very well off here. All German bedrooms are bad and mine no worse than the rest, I imagine—large enough for a bed and two tables for my books and papers, a porcelain stove and bureau, washstand, etc. To be sure, it has but one window, through which, by leaning uncomfortably to one side, one can perceive the withered corner of a gray garden, but otherwise facing a dirty wall of brick. But, as I say, it seems this is a chronic malady of German bedrooms, and besides I have the use of a very pleasant front room where I work in the morning, and afternoon, too, sometimes. The people here are very nice, and eager to make me comfortable; otherwise all my news is contained in the word work. Nearer ten hours than eight of this have I done every day—written translations from German, reading of German Grammar, reading Schiller with the man or his Frau, talking, going to the theater,—*Faust, The Winter's Tale,* very good, and a translation of the *Dindon,* etc. All German, you observe, and in fact it seemed best at first to let Greek and everything go, and devote every energy to the acquisition of this tongue—infernally hard it is too. I found, right off, I didn't know anything about it, and since then have really made a good deal of progress.

It's wonderful how the soul clears itself up in this sort of solitude in which I am living—picks up all the raveled threads and weaves them carefully together again, and gradually simplifies and straightens itself out. All my life since last April I have been going over, as I have some of my poems, forcing the events into sequence and building a sort of soul-history, fibrous and coherent. It's a wonderful clearing out of refuse, and I feel strong and self-reliant as I never did before. I have acquired the ability to write over

poetry and work it into shape, which is a great step forward,
I believe, and several of my poems have I been over in this
way with much advantage. And so I am almost childishly
contented at getting back to an existence of sleep and food
at a minimum and work at a maximum, and I really think
I have never worked harder or lived more utterly simply.
And oh! It is good with the entire spiritual solitude and
mental solitude that I abide in.

BERLIN, *January 17, 1897*

I am now, after infinite pains and vast expense, matriculate
at the University here, with several large and most beautiful diplomas certifying in Latin that I am in fact matriculate. The diplomas alone are worth the price of admission.
It was heavy, though—four solid mornings' work and about
75 marks. First I went with the man I am living with, and
found I couldn't hear any lectures at all unless I did matriculate and that to matriculate I had to have my degree from
Cambridge, which I had carefully left at home. Then the
next day I went to the Embassy and found Mr. Jackson,
who had very kindly written me a letter already, saying he
hoped I would come to see him when I wanted to. Well, Mr.
Jackson gave me a letter certifying that I had a degree, and
with this and my passport I went again to the University,
and found I was too late that day and must come the next.
So the next—this time alone—I went and passed—oh, such
a morning! First I sat in a room while the Rector went over
my papers; then I and two Germans were called in to the
Rector and he gave us handsome degrees and swore us to
obedience to all the rules of the University, and then we
shook hands with him. Then someone said, "Go to room 4."
So I and the two Germans went, and there they wrote my
name and birthplace and papa's business, which I tried to
explain and failed, and so he is registered in the Berlin
University as anything from a coal-heaver up.

All this time my nerves were rasping like taxed wires for
fear I shouldn't understand what was said to me.

And then I wrote my own name, birthplace, etc., in my

own sweet hand in another big book, and then was given
a little card where I wrote my name again, and a huge card
filled with questions. When I understood them I answered;
when not, I put *ja* and *nein* alternately. Then they said,
"Go to room 15." So I went and gave a man my filled-out
card and he wrote something which he gave me and said,
"Go to room 4 *zurück*"; so I went. There I got a book and
another card—the last one—and then I filled out all sorts of
things in the book and finally went to room 2, where I paid
out vast sums, got some receipts, and—left, a shattered man
in mind and soul. The strain of trying to understand and
write correctly and being always afraid you won't is really
terrible. Then today I had to go again to see the Dean of
the Philosophical Department in which I matriculated, and
he gave me another beautiful degree. And now it's all over.
I am an *academischer Bürger,* and if the police try to arrest
me all I've got to do is to show my card and they can't
touch me. . . .

This place is gray, gray, gray. I have done a constant
stream of work, which has flowed in a steady and almost
uninterrupted course, with six hours' sleep interval in the
twenty-four. I have been theater-going a lot. I have seen a
good deal of Shakespeare, Schiller, and Sudermann.

BERLIN, *January 26, 1897*

It is for the best my being here, of that rest assured. I am
entirely convinced that it was and is the very best thing
possible for me in the circumstances, and I find sufficient
content and interest, and especially work, to keep me far
from stagnant. As I wrote you, I feel a sense of increased
strength and reliance, which I don't explain and don't try
to. Sufficient that so it is. Much of my life have I overlooked and condemned and profited by in this solitude and
I finally begin to feel a certain strength that I trust will urge
into expression fit and simple and sufficient one day, and
not be trampled under in this awful struggle to acquire a
financial independence which I see is inevitable for me.
Writing prose is the only utterly depressing thing I have

done, and that, D. V., I shall learn by mere gritting of teeth.

I've this moment got back from Dresden, where I've been since Friday with Springy[1]—a little vacation. It's very pretty and the gallery very wonderful. Naturally there I spent my days, and twice I went to the opera.

BERLIN, *February 9, 1897*

I have written some new verse and written over with much time and labor a good deal more old. It's with the greatest difficulty that I can take any other form of literary endeavor seriously; and put my heart in it, I can't. I live and breathe in an atmosphere of imagination and verse here, all alone when I am not a working-machine, and it's all around me like a garment. It's hard to express what I mean—but the other day I went early to the University and saw a radiant sunrise through the snowy Thiergarten and sort of sang inside all the rest of the day—odd rhythms with here and there a word. I was so content I didn't even want to write down anything. I wonder if you have ever had the feeling—I suppose you have—of having a beautiful thing compose the scatteredness of your mind into an order, a rhythm, so that you think and feel everything rhythmically. My expression is weak, but if you've had it you'll know what I mean.

I saw the whole of *Wallenstein* the other day—or rather in two successive evenings—first the *Lager* and the *Piccolomini,* and second evening the *Tod,* which is certainly very fine—both dramatically and poetically,—quite the biggest German play I've seen. I'm reading *Faust* with my teacher here, and admiring very much of it.

BERLIN, *February 1897*

I have been reading over some of Schopenhauer and Kant in the German and enjoying it immensely. I think the study and pursuit of pure metaphysical thought makes a man more contentedly, peacefully happy than any other thing. There

[1]Cecil Spring-Rice.

is a white purity consisting in its utter lack of connection
to the particular, in its entire devotion to the pure, syn-
thetical ideas which never touch the feeling, individual
world, which makes metaphysics the nearest approach to
will-lessness, to pure intellectual contemplation, that I know.
And of course, as all suffering is willful (in its essential
meaning) and emotional, pure intellectual contemplation
must be that privation of suffering in which happiness consists—for I become more than ever convinced that in this
world of evil and separation happiness is only the privation
of pain as good is the privation of evil. 'Tis only the transcendent emotion that you get in poetry or in great passions
such as pity and love, that can be called positive happiness.
Pity or love, I mean, so aggrandized that the sense of individuality is lost in the feeling of union with the whole where
there is no space or time or separation. That is, that only
morally and esthetically can one be positively happy—all
other happiness must be simply the denial of pain. Metaphysics is the completest expression of such a denial, I think,
and also with an almost esthetic poetic value sometimes—in
some metaphysicians an undoubted poetic value, as for instance in Plato and Schopenhauer. But it seems I am writing
you an essay on metaphysics, so I will stop.

BERLIN, *February, late, 1897*

I am gradually digging a way into the language, and you'd
be surprised at my fluent inaccuracy in the German tongue,
and I can write it pretty well, too. Reading is thoroughly acquired, and I am more than satisfied with my progress. I
have heard a good deal of music which always does me
good, though, as Joe tells me, I don't in the least understand
it. I saw the Emperor the other day for the first time, and
rather a fine strong face he has.

I really believe that nothing I ever did benefited me as
much as has this short time here. I have grown more rigid
and surer of myself, and withal have acquired a certain
capacity and love of a great deal of work, which I never
had before, and which is only surpassed by my love of not

doing work after I have done a great deal. My poetry, I think, shows that—I have tried to hope so. Please tell me if you think any of the things I sent you show a clearer, firmer touch than before. As I say, I try to think so and almost feel sometimes as if it really was in me after all to speak a strong, sincere word clearly for men to hear; but then, on the other hand, whiles I think I am going to dry up, and in my perfectly lucid moments, I see with a ghostly distinctness how far short all my work falls of what I seem sometimes to know as an ideal.

The dear Springy came to see me yesterday and I had a good talk with him and subsequently dined with him. I've seen very little of him this month, as society has been on the rampage, and he has rampaged with it perforce. He went to London for a week today, but when he comes back, the world will be quiet and I expect to see a great deal of him.

The German experience added little or nothing to his artistic education, for Schopenhauer can be studied anywhere, and neither Goethe nor Schiller needs to be read in Berlin; but his letters show that his enforced, solitary labor during this winter threw him back upon himself, and led him to publish his work before he fairly knew in what direction his strength lay. During these three years of post-graduate education he had toiled, with sure instinct, to learn the use of his tools, and chiefly of his tongue. All art-students must go through this labor, and probably the reason why so many young poets begin by writing sonnets is that the sonnet is the mode of expression best adapted for practice; it insists on high perfection in form; any defect or weakness betrays itself, and the eye can cover fourteen lines at once without too great an effort. Lodge liked the labor of sonnet-writing, and it taught him the intricacies of language and the refinements of expression which every literary artist must try at least to understand, even when he does not choose to practice them; but, at heart, Lodge was less a poet than a dramatist, though he did not yet know it; and the dramatic art is the highest and most exacting in all literature. The crown of genius belongs only to the very rare poets who have written successful plays. They alone win the blue ribbon of literature. This was the prize to which Lodge, perhaps unconsciously, aspired, and his labor in sonnet-writing, however useful as training in verse, was no great advantage for his real purpose, even though he had Shakespeare for his model.

On the other hand, the lack of society in a manner compels the artist to publish before he is ready. The artist, living in a vacuum without connection with free air, is forced by mere want of breath to cry out against the solitude that stifles him; and the louder he cries, the better is his chance of attracting notice. The public resents the outcry, but remembers the name. A few—very few—readers appreciate the work, if it is good, on its merits; but the poet himself gets little satisfaction from it, and, ten years afterwards, will probably think of it only as a premature effort of his youth.

To this rule a few exceptions exist, like Swinburne's *Poems and Ballads,* where the poet, at the first breath, struck a note so strong and so new as to overpower protest; but, as a rule, recognition is slow, and the torpor of the public serves only to discourage the artist, who would have saved his strength and energy had he waited. When young Lodge returned from Germany in the summer of 1897, he felt himself unpleasantly placed between these two needs,—that of justifying his existence, on the one hand, and that of challenging premature recognition, on the other. He chose boldly to assert his claims to literary rank, and justified his challenge by publishing, in the spring of 1898, the volume of a hundred and thirty-five pages, called *The Song of the Wave.*

Here are some eighty short poems, one half of which are sonnets, and all of which reflect the long, tentative, formative effort of the past five years. Most of them have a personal character, like *The Song of the Wave* itself, which has been already quoted. From a simple, vigorous nature like Lodge's, one would have expected, in a first effort, some vehement or even violent outburst of self-assertion; some extravagance, or some furious protest against the age he lived in; but such an attitude is hardly more than indicated by the dedication to Leopardi. The exordium, "Speak, said my soul!" expresses rather his own need of strength and the solitude of his ambitions:

> Speak! thou art lonely in thy chilly mind,
> With all this desperate solitude of wind,
> The solitude of tears that make thee blind,
>   Of wild and causeless tears.
> Speak! thou hast need of me, heart, hand, and head,
> Speak, if it be an echo of thy dread,
> A dirge of hope, of young illusions dead,—
>   Perchance God hears!

Most of these poems are echoes of early youth, of the ocean, of nature: simple and vigorous expressions of physical force, with an occasional recurrence to Schopenhauer and Leopardi; but the verses that most concern the artist are those which show his effort for mastery of his art, and his progress in power of expression. He scattered such verses here and there, for their own sake, on nearly every page, as most young poets do, or try to do, and such verses are more or less a measure, not only of his correctness of ear, but of his patient labor. Take, for instance, the first half-dozen lines of *The Gates of Life,* which happens to be written in a familiar meter:

> Held in the bosom of night, large to the limits of wonder,
> Close where the refluent seas wrinkle the wandering sands,
> Where, with a tenderness torn from the secrets of sorrow, and
>   under
> The pale pure spaces of night felt like ineffable hands,
> The weak strange pressure of winds moved with the moving of
>   waters,
> Vast with their solitude, sad with their silences, strange with
>   their sound,
> Comes like a sigh from the sleep . . .

This meter seems to call for excessive elaboration of phrase; a few pages further, the poet has tried another meter which repels all such refinements; it is called *Age,* and begins:

> Art thou not cold?
> Brother, alone tonight on God's great earth?

The two last stanzas run:

> Shalt thou not die,
> Brother? the chill is fearful on thy life,
> Shalt thou not die?
> Is this a lie?
> This threadbare hope—of death?
> A lie, like God, and human love, and strife
> For pride, and fame,—this soiled and withered wreath.
>
> Art thou not cold?
> Brother? alone on God's great earth tonight;
> Art thou not cold?
> Art thou not old
> And dying and forlorn?
> Art thou not choking in the last stern fight
> While in divine indifference glows the morn?

The sonnet, again, offers a different temptation. The verses tend of their own accord to group themselves about the favorite verse. The first sonnet in this series begins with what Mrs. Wharton calls the magnificent apostrophe to Silence:

> Lord of the deserts, 'twixt a million spheres,

and need go no further; the rest of the lines infallibly group themselves to sustain the level of the first. So, the sonnet to his own Essex begins with the singularly happy line,—

> Thy hills are kneeling in the tardy spring,

which leads to an echo in the last verse:

> We know how wanton and how little worth
> Are all the passions of our bleeding heart
> That vex the awful patience of the earth.

The sonnet to his friend Stickney, after reading the twelfth-century Roman of *Amis and Amile,* begins:

> And were they friends as thou and I art friends,

in order to work out the personal touch of their common ambition:

> Ah, they who walked the sunshine of the world,
> And heard grave angels speaking through a dream,
> Had never their unlaureled brows defiled,
> Nor strove to stem the world's enormous stream.

The form of the sonnet tends to carry such verbal or personal refinements to excess; they become labored; perhaps particularly so in denunciation, like the sonnet, *Aux Modernes,* which begins:

> Only an empty platitude for God;

and ends with the line,

> The hard, gray, tacit distances of dawn.

Such work marks the steps of study and attainment rather than attainment itself, as the second *Nirvana* marks effort:

TO W. STURGIS BIGELOW

December 10, 1897

I will trouble you with this poem, which here I send to you. I wrote it without correction in half an hour before dinner, and I feel of it, as I have felt of so many of my things, that no one will understand it except you; also I know it's my fault and not theirs that no one will understand it—my implements are still so rude—my ideas seem luminous and limpid while they are wordless, and, I think, owing to practice, most ideas come to me now wordless— but in words they become crude, misty, and imperfect; whiles I feel quite hopeless. But you have been there, have seen vividly all I've half perceived, and you can supply my lapses in coherency. This was, I think, the result of an hour's practice last night. Certainly if it has a merit, it is that I have not been economical in this poem, every word seems to me now over-full with meaning. My soul has gone into the writing of it and, good Lord, it's melancholy to feel how it might have been said—luminously and unavoidably—and how it is said—Well! perhaps, someday! . . . if I could only be with you to try to tell you all I have endeavored to say in these fourteen lines!

NIRVANA

Woof of the scenic sense, large monotone
    Where life's diverse inceptions, Death and Birth,
    Where all the gaudy overflow of Earth
    Die—they the manifold, and thou the one.
Increate, complete, when the stars are gone
    In cinders down the void, when yesterday
    No longer spurs desire starvation-gray,
    When God grows mortal in men's hearts of stone;
As each pulsation of the heart divine
    Peoples the chaos, or with falling breath
    Beggars creation, still the soul is thine!
And still, untortured by the world's increase,
    Thy wide harmonic silences of death,
    And last—thy white, uncovered breast of peace!

I will now, as did Michael Angelo, add a commentary:

Nirvana is the woof on which sense traces its scenic patterns; it is the one, the monotone upon which death and birth, both inceptions, in that death is merely the beginning of changed conditions of life, and "the gaudy overflow of earth"—that is, all finite things and emotions—sing their perishable songs and, as rockets disperse their million sparks which die on the universal night blackness, so they die and leave the constant unchanging monotone. Nirvana is increate because never created, and of course complete. Yesterday spurs desire to a state of starvation-grayness because desire and hope look back on every yesterday as a renewed disappointment. The phrase meant life. "When God grows mortal in men's hearts of stone," has two meanings, first that when men grow unbelieving God perishes—God being the creature of belief; and second that Nirvana endureth when God himself perishes. The next three lines are an embodiment of the idea that with every beat of the heart divine a cosmos swells into existence, and with every subsiding of this heart it sinks, perishes into nothingness. Also from line five to line eleven means that after everything and through everything the soul is still Nirvana's, if I can so express myself; thus reiterating the idea suggested in the first quatrain, that the condition of the finite is separateness and of the spiritual, unity; and that all life, though clothed in diverse forms, holds in it the identical soul which is Nirvana's, attained or potential. The world's increase is of course the cycle of life and death in its largest sense. This is of course a mere shadowing forth of the ideas I had in writing the poem. You will see their possible amplifications.

January 1898

Poetry is an absolute necessity for me, but when I think of dumping a volume of verse that nobody will read on to a gorged world, I say to myself: *"A quoi bon?"* The foolish publisher will have to be found first, however, so I don't worry. Does the enclosed (*The Wind of Twilight—Tuckanuck*) say anything to you? The long things (Oh, be thankful) are too long to send, so I send this. I've done several of these sorts of things lately.

To the cold critic, this stage of an artist's life is the most sympathetic, and the one over which he would most gladly linger. He loves the youthful freshness, the candor, the honest workmanship, the naïf self-abandonment of the artist, in proportion as he is weary of the air of attainment, of cleverness, of certainty and completion. He would, for his own amusement, go on quoting verse after verse to show how the artist approaches each problem of his art, what he gains; what he sacrifices; but this is the alphabet of criticism, and can be practiced on Eginetan marbles or early Rembrandts better than on youthful lyrics. The interested reader has only to read for himself.

IV. War and Love

In JANUARY 1898 young Lodge was in Washington, acting as secretary to his father, varying between office-work all day and composition the greater part of the night. The outbreak of the Spanish War drew him at once into the government service, and he obtained a position as cadet on board his uncle Captain Davis's ship, the *Dixie*. During the three summer months that this war in the tropics lasted, he had other things than poems to think about, and his letters convey an idea that perhaps the life of a naval officer actually suited his inherited instincts best.

TO HIS MOTHER

FORTRESS MONROE, *May 1898*

Here I am and here I rest until Saturday, when the ship will probably sail. I am, and feel like, a perfect fool. Everybody knows everything and I don't know anything; but they are kind and I guess I shall get on when the thing gets fairly started. I went over and saw the ship today and she is fine —at any rate while I am here in this business, I am going to learn all I can.

NEWPORT NEWS, *May 20, 1898*

I am getting on as well as possible and learning a good deal all the time. There is plenty of room for learning. These great golden days go over me, and it seems as if all the real imaginative side of me was under lock and key. The practical things occupy me entirely.

FORTRESS MONROE, *June 2, 1898*

We have been taking on coal all day, and before it's all aboard we shall be chock-full. Uncle Harry has got orders to be ready to sail at a moment's notice, and he is going to telegraph tonight that he is all ready. I hope it may mean that we are to be moved out of here very soon toward the scene of action. A day or two ago we went out for thirty-six hours and fired all the big guns. I fired both mine myself, and was surprised to find the shock not at all serious. The whole process was very interesting, and I shall try to remember it all and be able to tell you all about it when I get back. I get on pretty well. There is one thing I am convinced of and that is that I can make my gun crews fight and my guns effective, and that is after all the principal thing.

The internal condition of Spain makes me believe that the war must end soon. I only hope it will last long enough to insure our possession of Cuba, Puerto Rico, and the Philippines, and give me one fight for my money.

OFF CIENFUEGOS, CUBA, *June 25, 1898*

We reached the squadron the day after I wrote from Mole St. Nicolas, and were immediately sent down here to patrol. In fact, the Admiral gave Uncle Harry discretion to do pretty much what he pleased. We came down and on our way destroyed two blockhouses which were at the southern end of the Trocha. The next day we engaged a battery at a place called Trinidad, and yesterday we engaged the same battery, a gunboat in the harbor, and a gunboat that came out at us, and used them up pretty badly. So you see I am in it. Nothing very serious so far, but still we have been under fire and have killed a good many Spaniards. It is a most beautiful coast all along here, great splendid hills close to the water's edge, and splendid vegetation. The weather has been hot, but very fine and to me excessively pleasant, and I am quite happy to be on the scene of action and in the way of seeing all that's going. My two guns have behaved very well and I have had several very nice compliments from the First Lieutenant. We relieved the *Yankee* here and she goes today to Key West for coal, which gives me a chance to send this letter. I really enjoy the life immensely, far more than I thought I should—the work interests me, and I am learning a good deal every day. Last night Uncle Harry and I dined with Captain Brownson on the *Yankee* and it was very interesting.

August 1898

Many thanks for your letter which I have just got today. I am more than delighted we are going to Spain. We came up from Cape Cruz on the sixth and saw the wrecks of

the Spanish fleet lying up on the beach below Santiago—a
great sight. It's a great business to be here and see the wheels
go round and be a wheel one's self, even if not a very big
one. I am very glad on the whole I came as a cadet and
not as an ensign, for as a cadet I am not supposed to know
anything, which puts me in a true position and not a false
one. None of these militia officers know any more than I
do, and they are in false positions. Anyway, I do a lot of
work and I think accomplish something. It hardly seems as
if the war could last now, and I only hope it will hang on
long enough to give us a whack at Camara and the Spanish
coast.

Yesterday we got the first ice we have had since June
15, and today the first mail since we left Old Point.

U. S. S. "Dixie," *August 5, 1898*

We left Guantanamo after having coaled, and went to
Puerto Rico with the troops. On the way we were detached
from the convoy and sent all round the island to hunt up
transports, and so we did not get to Guanica until after the
army had landed. We got there in the morning, and that
afternoon we were sent with the *Annapolis* and the *Wasp*—
Uncle Harry[1] being the senior officer—down to Ponce,
Puerto Rico. We got there about four and went peacefully
into the harbor. Then Uncle Harry sent Mr. Merriam[2] in
to demand the surrender of the place, and I went along. We
landed under a flag of truce, and found that there was a
Spanish Colonel with about 300 men, who said he would
"die at his post." He was back in the town, which is about
two miles inland. However, during the night delegates came
off and surrendered the town, on condition that the troops
be allowed to withdraw, which we granted, and at six o'clock
the next morning we went in again and I myself raised the
flag over the office of the Captain of the Port, amid immense enthusiasm of the populace. Haines,[3] the marine

[1] Captain Davis, commanding the *Dixie*. H. A.
[2] Lieutenant and executive officer of the *Dixie*. H. A.
[3] Lieutenant of Marines on the *Dixie*. H. A.

officer, was put in charge with a file of Marines, and put guards and sentries on the Customs House and other public places; and then two other officers and I got into a carriage, with a Puerto Rican friend, and drove up to the town.

It was most picturesque. The town had been deserted fearing a bombardment, and from every nook and corner crowds appeared cheering and crying, *"Viva los conquistadores Americanos"; "Viva el Puerto Rico libre."* We drove through the town, the crowd and enthusiasm increasing always, and finally returned and got Haines, who had formally delivered the town to General Miles when he landed. . . . We then went back to Ponce with Haines. We were taken to the club and to the headquarters of the fire-brigade—everywhere amid yelling mobs. While we were there I heard that there were some political prisoners confined in the City Hall. I told Haines, who was senior officer, and he went over to see about liberating them.

Ponce is the largest town in Puerto Rico, about 40,000 people. The City Hall stands at one end of a great square —about as large as Lafayette Square. In it is the Mayor's office and the courtroom, with a dais and throne where the judges sat. There Haines liberated sixteen political prisoners; for the army, though supposed to be in possession of the town, had not taken the City Hall. Finding this to be the case, I got an American flag and told Haines I was going to raise it over the City Hall. I then went onto the roof where the flag-staff was, taking with me the Mayor of Ponce. There with great solemnity, the Mayor and I bareheaded, I raised the flag. The whole square was swaying with people, and as the flag went up they cheered—such a noise as I never heard. Then the Mayor and I went below and the Mayor presented me with his staff of office, the Spanish flag which flew over the City Hall, and the banner of Ponce, and formally delivered over to me his authority. I sent to the barracks where were our soldiers, and got some over to occupy the City Hall. I then, with great ceremony, gave back to the Mayor his badge of office and the town of Ponce. Shortly after we left.

GUANTANAMO BAY, CUBA, *August 10, 1898*

I got your letter just a day or two ago, and mighty glad I was to get it. The flagship has just signaled "Associated Press dispatch states that peace protocol has been arranged." I suppose this is the end. If so, if hostilities cease and peace is eventually certain, I wish you would find out if the *Dixie* is to be put out of commission. I suppose it will take three or four months to patch up the treaty and have it ratified, and if the *Dixie* is to lie here or convoy transports during that time, I should like very much to be detached and ordered home on waiting orders, until my resignation is sent in and accepted. I suppose there would be no trouble about this. I came for the war, and as this isn't and never will be my life when the war is over, I want to get home as soon as possible, and pick up life again where I left off. Of course if the *Dixie* is to be put right out of commission, I should much prefer to go out of active service with the ship, and I should think that the Department would not wish to keep these auxiliary ships, manned with militia, in service any longer than was absolutely necessary. Well, I have learned a good deal and I am mighty glad I came. I haven't seen as much fighting as some, but I have had my share of the fun, I think, and anyway one does one's best and takes the chances of war. I really think I have made myself useful, and at least have not encumbered or hurt the service by coming, and that's as much as an amateur can hope for. Anyway I've worked hard. I shall have a great story to tell you about Ponce, of which *"Magna pars fui,"* and I have got some splendid trophies. I have had a good time and am happy now; but as peace grows more certain I long to get home and see you all again. It seems an enormous stretch of time since I left you.

EXTRACT FROM A LETTER OF CAPTAIN DAVIS TO H. C. L.

July 20, 1898

. . . He [G. C. L.] shows unbounded zeal and unflagging industry, and a great aptitude for the profession. He has

already developed the real sailor's trick of being always the
first on hand. No one has ever been known to say, "Where
is Mr. Lodge?" This is not the encomium of a fond uncle.
I see very little of him on duty except in working ship, when
his station is near mine. He is a daily companion to me in
hours of leisure, but on duty he is the First Lieutenant's
man, and I notice he is always called on for duty where
promptness and intelligence are required. I could give you
a much higher estimate of his usefulness if I quoted Merriam, than in recording my own observation.

Brought back again to the chronic divergence between
paths of life, the young man struggled as he best could to
assert his mastery over his own fate, and developed a
persistence of will that amounted to primitive instinct rather
than to reasoning process. Constantly he threw himself with
all his energy in the direction which led away from the
regular paths of modern activity. He was familiar with them
all, if only as Secretary of a Senate Committee, and he read
science quite as seriously as poetry, but when he came to
action he always widened the gap between himself and his
world. *The Song of the Wave* was his first public act of
divorce. Only the difficulty of finding a publisher prevented
him from taking a tone much more hostile to society in
novels which he wrote and burned one after another, because they failed to satisfy him. His letters to his early
friend, Marjorie Nott, have much to say of this phase of
mind. On September 12, 1899, he wrote from Tuckanuck:

TO MISS MARJORIE NOTT

Why do your letters make me so needlessly happy! I
think it's because you believe in so much and because I do,
too, and need to have someone to tell me that it is so. Not
that I doubt,—what would my life be if I doubted! No, it's
only that pretty much everybody believes I'm a crank or
a fool, or asks when I'm going to begin to do something;
to which question, by the way, I invariably respond—never!
and oh! it's so good not to be on the defensive, not to feel

the good anger rising in you, and step on it because you know they won't understand; not to suffer with the desire to insult the whole world; to lay its ugliness naked; to say: "There, there! don't you see all the dust and ashes that we're all admiring? don't you see? don't you understand?" And then not say it, because you know they can't see, and they won't understand. Ah, yes! it's so good to sit here, and write all this rot to you, and think that you'll know, that you'll understand. Isn't it horrible to get your mind twisted into cheap cynicisms while the tears are falling in your heart? and it's what we have to do—*nous autres!* I shall certainly end in publishing my book if I can find a bold enough publisher. The temptation is too immense. I know they won't understand, and yet I'm young enough to hope they will. Do you remember the book I talked to you of last winter? Well, that's it! I've done it over again, and—well! I don't know! I don't know why I write all this. I am here so calm, with my brother the sun and my sister the sea—by the way, Tuckanuck—and I feel as if I was anywhere except in the hither end of the nineteenth century; and my book, I don't think of it at all here. I write verse now—nothing else.

Naturally, since man or bird began to sing, he has sung to the woman,—or the female. The male is seldom a sympathetic listener; he prefers to do his own singing, or not to sing at all. He is not much to blame, but his indifference commonly ends by stifling the song, and the male singer has to turn to the female, or perish. In America, the male is not only a bad listener, but also, for poetry, a distinctly hostile audience; he thinks poorly of poetry and poets, so that the singer has no choice but to appeal to the woman. That young Lodge should have done so with an intensity proportioned to the repression of his instinct for sympathy and encouragement elsewhere was inevitable. Poets have always done it, but they have not shown by any means the surest instinct of poetry in their affairs of love, so that perhaps a woman who should criticize their work might feel tempted to use this test as the surest proof of force or failure in their instinct for art. By such a test, young Lodge would take rank among the strongest. Little credit is due to any man for yielding to altogether extraordinary beauty and charm in the perfection of feminine ideals,—although few men do it,—but it is far from being a rule that young men who rebel against the world's standards, and with infinite effort set up a standard of private war on the world, and maintain it with long and exhausting endurance, should go directly into the heart of the society they are denouncing, and carry off a woman whom lovers less sensitive to beauty, and less youthful in temperament, than poets or artists, might be excused for adoring.

Elizabeth Davis—another survival of rare American stock: Davis of Plymouth, Frelinghuysen of New Jersey, Griswold of Connecticut, with the usual leash of Senators, Cabinet officers, and other such ornaments, in her ancestry—was in truth altogether the highest flight of young Lodge's poetry, as he constantly told her when her own self-confidence naturally hesitated to believe it; and since his letters to her strike a note which rises high above the level of art or education, they cannot be wholly left out of his life. The man or woman who claims to be a poet at all must prove poetry to the heart, and neither Shakespeare nor Shelley can be exempted from the proof,—neither Dante nor Petrarch,—whatever their society might think about it.

Lodge's letters began in March 1899, when he was starting with his father and mother on a trip to Europe, which led to Sicily. From New York he wrote to bid good-by; the engagement was not yet avowed. And from Rome, a month later:

TO MISS DAVIS

I saw the grave of Keats the other day, and also of Shelley. It was a very keen sensation—more living, I think, than anything I have felt since you. My life is happy here, but my soul is very dolorous and strenuous. In life nothing resolves itself well. If a good issue is to come to anything, so much must be struggled with and sacrificed, so much confusion and distress, before serenity comes! When one is very young, it doesn't seem fitting. One wants so much! Heaven and

Earth is hardly enough for the large desire of youth, and
the gates of possible expansion close one by one, until at
last one runs through the last one just closing, without perhaps its being the right one. The period of choice is very
short; then comes the short, sharp stab of necessity, and then
—one has made one's bed, and one must lie in it. It's all very
eager and restless, and perhaps better for being so.

From Rome in April he wrote:

"One makes oneself so very largely, and to make oneself
greater or better, one must believe. Apply your religion: 'Thy
faith has made thee whole!' That's the most wonderful thing
Christ ever said, and it applies everywhere in life. Believe in
yourself! it should be so easy for you. I do it, and it is of
course far harder for me, for I've less to believe in."

The young people had much need to believe in themselves, for, in a worldly point of view, they had not much
else to believe in. He wrote in July:

TO HIS MOTHER

BOSTON, *July 1899*

I am almost crazed with the desire to be independent, and
yet I won't do anything that I don't approve and I won't
give up my writing, God willing. I must keep at it and accomplish what I can in my own way. I feel sure it's the only
way for me, and I know my intention is not low, whatever
my performance may be. I feel desperate sometimes that it
all comes so slowly and that I do no better; but I grit my
teeth and keep at it. The agony of getting a thought into
adequate expression is enormous. However, I feel so much
resolution that I take heart, and now, too, I see my path
clearer ahead of me. I must write and write, and as I say,
I believe my purposes are good.

TUCKANUCK, *September 1899*

I haven't written for a long time, I am afraid, but since I
have been here—the last ten days—I have been so happy in

the sun and sea that I haven't written to anyone at all and have hardly done any work. I have just lived very happily. I have begun to write a tragedy in verse, and it's terrible work and not very encouraging. However, I get along—I have in my head also a plot for a prose play, very good, I think, and some other things besides. Indeed my mind is quite fertile, and physically I am in splendid condition. I got a letter from Mr. Stedman this morning, who is preparing an anthology of American poets and wants to put me in it. *J'apporte un bagage assez mince,* but still if he can find anything he wants to print he is welcome to it.

A few days afterwards, he wrote from Boston:

TO MISS DAVIS

To get away, very far from all this greasy gossip, this world of little motives and little desires! We must do it very soon. Only men who live in the constant strain of feeling alone against the world are forced to concentrate their passions on an object that seems to them above the world.

V. Marriage

NATURALLY, life cannot be lived in heroics. The man who places himself out of line with the current of society sees most the ridiculous or grotesque features of his surroundings, and finds most in them to laugh at. The conviction that either he or society is insane—or perhaps both—becomes a fixed idea, with many humorous sides; and though the humor tends to irony and somewhat cruel satire, it is often genial and sometimes playful. Young Lodge laughed with the rest, at the world or himself by turns. When Bigelow rebelled at his anarchic handwriting, he replied:

TO W. STURGIS BIGELOW

Ballade d'ung excellent poète au Sieur Bigelow au sujet d'ung certain plaint dudit Sieur Bigelow à luy addressé.

BALLADE

I

I like to see the phrases flow
     So smooth in writing round and plain—
Pooh! Hang the time and trouble! Though
     It gave me fever on the brain
     And caused intolerable pain
In hand and wrist—you set at nought
     The beautiful, and still maintain
That writing must be slave to thought.

II

I wrote for beauty and I know
     That beauty is its own best gain;
"Art for art's sake," I cried, and so
     My unintelligible train
     Of words was writ—you grew insane
Trying to read them, for you sought
     A meaning and you swore again
That writing must be slave to thought.

III

You held the sheet above, below
     Your head, and every nerve did strain
To read, and from your lips did go
     Grim curses manifold as rain.
     You should have known your toil was vain;
For Art's sole sake my writing wrought;
     I scorned the axiom with disdain
That writing must be slave to thought.

IV

Prince, speak! Does anything remain
     Now art is gone? No sense you've caught!
Then tell not me, the pure inane,
     That writing must be slave to thought.

*Fin de la Ballade d'ung excellent poète au Sieur Bigelow.
Composée et mise en escript ce neuvième Décembre.* A. D.
MDCCCXCIX.

From Washington, on April 28, he wrote again to Bigelow:

"Well! the point is here! one should learn that it is not life that should be taken seriously, but living. In that way, one gets pleasure if not happiness. I wish I was going to Tuckanuck with you right off; but I'm not, and I have yards and miles of drudgery that maketh the heart sick. I've got to write another play before June. I have written several this winter, all on a steadily decreasing scale of merit, and I hope this one will be bad enough to be successful. The trees are full of leaves, and the air full of sun, and only I am vile. I wish I could pretend it was all somebody else's fault, but I can't. *Voilà!*"

A successful play needs not only to be fairly bad in a literary sense, but bad in a peculiar way which had no relation with any standard of badness that Lodge could reach. He toiled in vain.

When one is twenty-six years old, splendid in health and strength, and still more splendid in love, one enjoys the exuberant energy of complaint with a Gargantuan appetite:

TO W. STURGIS BIGELOW

WASHINGTON, *May 16, 1900*

Here it has been as high as 106°—Why don't you go to Tuckanuck? I would if I could, Gawd knows. It is of course self-evident to you as it is to me, that in the event of one's absence the world will cease to function,—but then who the Devil cares whether it functions or not? Not you, nor yet I. I would willingly barter the tattered remnants of a devilish tried soul to be under one of the great waves on the outside beach and, please Heaven, I soon shall be doing it. Meanwhile I grovel along in the living heat which I like, and do all the work that's in me—but after these months of it, the supply is running a little short, I'm afraid. I suppose I am here for about three weeks more—and then, with your permission, kind Sir! surf, Sir! and sun, Sir! and nakedness! —Oh, Lord! how I want to get my clothes off—alone in natural solitudes. In this heavy springtime I grow to feel exquisitely pagan, and worship the implacable Aphrodite, and read Sappho (with considerable difficulty) in the Greek.

From the beginnings of life, the poet and artist have gone on, surprising themselves always afresh by the discovery that their highest flights of poetry and art end in some simple and primitive emotion; but the credit of seeing and feeling it is the best proof of the poet. In his next volume of Poems, published in 1902, two years afterwards, he put these emotions into verse—"for E. L."—no longer Elizabeth Davis but Elizabeth Lodge.

She moves in the dusk of my mind, like a bell with the sweet-
        ness of singing
In a twilight of summer fulfilled with the joy of the sadness of
        tears;
And the calm of her face, and the splendid, slow smile are as
        memories clinging
Of songs and of silences filling the distance of passionate years.

She moves in the twilight of life like a prayer in a heart that
        is grieving,
And her youth is essential and old as the spring and the fresh-
        ness of spring;
And her eyes watch the world and the little low ways of the
        sons of the living,
As the seraph might watch from the golden grave height of his
        heaven-spread wing.

The variations on this oldest of themes are endless, and yet are eternally new to someone who discovers them afresh; so that very slight differences of expression have artistic value. So, for example, the sonnet beginning:

Why are you gone? I grope to find your hand.
Why are you gone? The large winds seaward-bound,
Tell of long journeying in the endless void.
Why are you gone? I strain to catch the sound
Of footsteps, watch to see the dark destroyed
Before your lustrous fingers that would creep
Over my eyes, and give me strength to sleep.

One does not venture to suggest a famous line of a great poet for the sake of imitating the art, but one does it readily for the sake of rivaling the feeling. "You and I have gone behind the scenes and beyond, where all is light. I say, grip my hand always, for it is always laid in yours. Get from me some of the joy you give—some of the light and strength. I am overflowing with love, which is force, and you must take from me for my sake. Everywhere there is love, vast treasures of love, that people deny and conceal, but cannot kill, and in the earth and sea also. I am there for you, and love is there!"

All this is the purest sentiment, and yet young Lodge was not sentimental, and especially disliked sentimentality in literature. He would have ruthlessly burned any verse that offered to him the suggestion of sentimentalism. His idyl was intense because it was as old and instinctive as nature itself, and as simple. If he ever approached a sentimental expression, it was in the relation between parent and child, not between lover and mistress. Love was to him a passion, and a very real one, not capable of dilution or disguise. Such passions generally have their own way, and force everything to yield. The marriage took place in Boston, August 18, 1900. True to his instinct of shrinking from close and serious contact with the forms and conventions of a society which was to him neither a close nor a serious relation, he was married without previous notice, and without other than the necessary witnesses, at the Church of the Advent. The officiating clergyman is said to have remarked that he had never seen a more beautiful wedding; but he was the only person present to appreciate its beauty.

They went off to Concord to pass the honeymoon, and thence to Tuckanuck. All the practical difficulties in their way were ignored, and remained ignored through life, without interfering with the young couple's happiness. The world is still kind to those who are young, and handsome, and in love, and who trample on respectability. Naturally, as soon as the winter came, they set off for Paris.

PARIS, *January 1901*

We have found a most charming little apartment, furnished—with only the indispensable, thank Heaven! The superfluous in a furnished apartment of modest price is horrible—and for only two hundred francs a month. We took it. It is 46 Rue du Bac. The house is an old palace of the days when the Rue du Bac was a fashionable street. It is built on three sides of an enormous court as wide as Massachusetts Avenue without the sidewalks. At the back of the court are large greenhouses of a florist—very pretty. Our apartment is on the court, on a southwest corner, filled with sun and very nice for us. It is at the top of the house. The staircase is really splendid—very large, with three great windows on every landing and fine wrought-iron railing, the first flight in stone, the other two in bricks. The apartment itself is the funniest, nicest place you ever saw, a sort of *Vie de Bohême* poetry about it, and sun and air to waste. The walls are very thick, so that the place is full of closets and the windows are all in deep recesses. Some of the floors are stone, others hard wood. We are delighted with it. The Rue du Bac runs up from the Pont Royal, if you remember, and 46 is near the river, and in fact within striking distance of everywhere. Well, we got the apartment, and you may imagine we have been busy, and Mrs. Cameron has been kindness itself, lending us things to cover the walls, etc. We are having a bully time getting installed and altogether I never had such fun in my life.

And there's for the practical side of things. I haven't got round to the absorbing psychological problems surrounding me, nor to the theaters we've seen, nor the work I've done, —a good deal,—nor the thoughts we've thought.

PARIS, *1901*

We live quite alone and see hardly anyone. I am hard at work on one or two things. The law against religious associations has at last passed and all socialists are happy. The next move is to confiscate Rothschild, then the manufacturers, then the other bourgeois, and so on to socialism. There are one or two new things here which would interest you, I think—such as casts of some of the things found at Delphi, the new bridge over the Seine, Pont Alexandre III, which is really very good, and some other things too.

PARIS, *1901*

I have sent the Louis to Bourgouin, and I will at once attend to the books. The socialists here have started a *"librairie socialiste."* How it differs from an ordinary bookshop neither they nor I know; but as I live more or less among socialists, I find myself obliged to get my books there and yours will be sent from there. Curiously enough it is an excellent shop. I was very glad to hear that you expect to get through without an extra session. I had been afraid that Cuba and the Philippines might delay you and produce discord. You know, however, how difficult it is to know what is happening *de par le monde* in this most provincial capital. The New York *Herald* has become merely a vulgar sort of *Town Topics,* published every day, and has, I really think, less news than the best French papers. In which connection I should like extremely to know the truth about the row Sampson has got himself into. I saw that Allen attacked him in his usual polished way in the Senate, which, coupled with the fact that I greatly admire Sampson, warmed my heart for him. But it seems impossible to find out what it was all about.

Here the whole of France is shaken over the pending bill confiscating the property of the religious orders. It is going to pass and the Church is pretty sick. The debate has produced one interesting piece of statistics: that there are three times as many monks in France now as there were in 1789, whereas the population has not quite doubled. My friend, Hubert, says, *"C'est curieux, ça démontre que nous retournions à la barbarie."* B—— saw some American colonist lady the other day, who told her that Porter was a very bad

ambassador. *B——*. Why?—*American colonist lady.* Because
he is pro-Boer.—*B——*. But I thought that was popular in
France.—*American colonist lady.* Oh, no, all the Americans
here are pro-English.—This strikes me as a very characteristic
expression of the American colonist point of view.

We see very few people and no society, and less than no
American colony, and we are very happy indeed. We are
looking forward very much to your advent on the scene.
There are some new plays and things which may amuse
you. Also they have at last arranged the great series of
Rubenses in the Louvre, as decorations, which is what they
are meant to be. I am writing a good deal and studying the
rest of the time. Please give my love to Theodore when
he takes the veil. I hope it will be a fine day for him.

PARIS, 1901

I am so glad you got through the session so well, and I
hope you are not worn out. I was very much interested to
see that England had refused our treaty, and I wonder what
is coming next. Is the sentiment strong to abrogate the
Clayton-Bulwer treaty by resolution? I hope so. This refusal
really makes one believe that those whom the Gods wish to
destroy they first make mad.

PARIS, Spring 1901

Many, many thanks for your kind letter, and for all the
trouble you have taken about my novel and my play. I am
very glad indeed to have R. S.'s criticism, and I think that
dramatically you and he are pretty nearly right. Indeed I
think the action in *Villon* is really too subjective for the
stage. It is far more the presentation of an idea than of an
action, and I doubt very much if it can be fitted for acting.
I should be very glad, however, if you would bring it over
when you come. I have so much on my hands now that I
could not attend to it before then.

The other night I went to hear Jaurès, the Socialist, speak.
He is, I think, a very remarkable orator and a very sincere
man.

The salon is open here and I have been through it once. There are seven kilometers of canvas, I think, and it's altogether a pretty poor showing, so it seems to me. There are, however, one or two good things, especially in the sculpture, and many clever things.

I hope you will succeed in getting the Bayreuth tickets. We are all very much looking forward to going.

TO HIS MOTHER

PARIS, Spring 1901

Day before yesterday Hubert took us to St. Germain, where he is *"attaché au Musée."* It was very interesting and we had a drive in the forest—superb. Hubert is the nicest little man in the world—sympathetic, gentle, bright, and with a preposterous amount of learning. He insists he is going to make me collaborate in some scientific magazine on an Egyptian topic. I hope not. However, I am tolerably strong in Egyptian now. I can read the texts with considerable fluency and the inscriptions on tombs, etc., become very intelligible. It is certainly a useless accomplishment, but excessively interesting. At the same time I have been reading up Chaldea and Syria, Babylonia, etc., so that I have a pretty good idea of the classic Orient. It's a point of departure I have always lacked and needed. Meanwhile, I have written considerably. I enclose a couple of things you may like to see. I am very glad the *Atlantic* and *Century* received me so well. I have just received Papa's letter with the letter from Gilder, and shall answer it at once. Gissing has gone away, I am sorry to say. I should have been glad to see more of him. He is a real man.

VI. Cain

THE EUROPEAN PART of the idyl ended with a week at Bayreuth and the return home in August 1901. Thenceforward, the life at Washington in winter, and at Nahant or Tuckanuck in summer—the life of husband and father—becomes only the background for literary work, and the work alone remains to tell of the life. The poet's education was finished; what the poet could do with it remains to be shown.

The first result appeared in the volume already mentioned, entitled *Poems (1899–1902)*, which appeared in the winter of 1902–3. The next was *Cain*, published in November 1904. The first volume, of one hundred and fifty pages, consisted of the short efforts of the poet's youth. The second volume is a single, sustained effort of drama, and claimed attention less for its poetic than for its dramatic qualities.

Like all the poets of the same school, Lodge conceded nothing to mere decoration or ornament. The vigorous standards of this severe Academy regarded a popular or conventional flower as a blot. Every verse must have its stress, or strain, and every thought its intensity. This preliminary condition is something not to be discussed, but to be accepted or rejected in advance, like the conditions of a color scheme, or an architectural or musical composition; and, since few readers are trained to such technical appreciation, at a moment when the public refuses to make any mental effort that it can avoid, the poet's audience is very small. In reality the mental effort of reading is much less than that of listening to Wagner or Debussy; but the poet numbers his audience by scores, while the musician, if he gets any audience at all, numbers it by thousands. These restraints are a part of the given situation under which the dramatic poet works; conditions which he cannot change; they are in reality far more severe and paralyzing than the conditions imposed by the old unities. They must be kept in mind by the reader, unless his reading is to be waste of time.

So, too, the dramatic idea is a condition given beforehand, to be accepted or refused as a whole. The poet does not want an audience that looks for gems,—that selects a pretty song or verse, and rejects the whole,—the unity. He has some one great tragic motive, which he tries to work out in a way he thinks his own, and he wants to be judged by his dramatic effect, as an actor is judged by his power of holding an audience. Properly he would ask, not whether his drama is liked, but whether it is dramatic; not whether the reader was pleased, but whether he was bored.

Lodge's dramatic motive was always the same, whether in *Cain*, or in *Herakles*, or in the minor poems. It was that of Schopenhauer, of Buddhism, of oriental thought everywhere,—the idea of Will, making the universe, but existing only as subject. The Will is God; it is nature; it is all that is; but it is knowable only as ourself. Thus the sole tragic action of humanity is the Ego,—the Me,—always maddened by the necessity of self-sacrifice, the superhuman effort of lifting himself and the universe by sacrifice, and, of course, by destroying the attachments which are most vital, in order to attain. The idea is a part of the most primitive stock of religious and philosophical motives, worked out in many forms, as Prometheus, as Herakles, as Christ, as Buddha,— to mention only the most familiar,—but, in our modern conception of life, impossible to realize except as a form of insanity. All Saviors were anarchists, but Christian anarchists, tortured by the self-contradictions of their role. All were insane, because their problem was self-contradictory, and because, in order to raise the universe in oneself to its highest power, its negative powers must be paralyzed or destroyed. In reality, nothing was destroyed; only the Will —or what we now call Energy—was freed and perfected.

This idea, which probably seemed simpler than shower or sunshine to a Hindoo baby two thousand years ago, has never taken root in the western mind except as a form of mysticism, and need not be labored further. It was what the French call the *donnée* of Lodge's drama,—the condition to be granted from the start; and it had, for a dramatist, the supreme merit of being the most universal tragic motive in the whole possible range of thought. Again and again, from varied points of view, Lodge treated it in varied moods and tempers; but his two dramas, *Cain* and *Herakles*, were elaborately developed expansions of the theme.

The general reader, who reads a Greek drama in the same spirit in which he reads the morning newspaper, can scarcely get beyond the first half-dozen pages of such a theme; and, in fact, the subject was never intended for him. The more serious student, who reads further, can seldom escape a sense of discomfort from the excessive insistence on the motive,—the violence with which it is—over and over again—thrust before his eyes in its crudest form; and, in fact, Lodge has what the French call the faults of his qualities; he is exuberant, and exuberance passes the bounds of *mesure*. Nature herself is apt to exaggerate in the same way. We must take it—or reject it—as we take a thunderstorm or a flood; it may be unnecessary, but is it dramatic?

Every just critic will leave the reader to answer this question for himself. Taste is a matter about which the Gods themselves are at odds. American taste is shocked by every form of paradox except its own. Greek taste was lavish of paradox, especially about the Gods. Saturn ate his children, and Zeus dethroned his father. Questions of taste! while Lodge's paradox, as developed in *Cain,* was a question rather of logic,—even almost of mathematics. Step by step, like a demonstration in geometry, the primitive man is forced into the attitude of submission to destiny or assertion of self, and Lodge develops each step as a necessary sequence, in the nature of the Greek fate, but a result of conscious Will. The paradox that Cain killed Abel because, from the beginning, man had no choice but to make himself slave of nature or its master, is, after all, nothing like so paradoxical as the philanthropist idea that man has gone on killing himself since the world began, without any reason at all.

This, then, is the paradox of Cain which Lodge undertook to work out, as Byron had worked it out before him, in one of his strongest dramas; and the readers who take it in this sense can hardly fail to find it dramatic. They may not like the drama, but they will probably not toss it aside. They will admit its force. They may even, if particularly sensitive to this oldest of emotional motives, follow the poet himself to the end.

> Captain, my Soul, despair is not for thee!
> Thou shalt behold the seals of darkness lift,
> Weather the wrathful tempest and at last,
> Resolute, onward, headlong, dazed and scarred,
> Reel through the gates of Truth's enormous dawn!

To develop this idea in its dramatic form, Lodge took as
his text the words of *Genesis,* and allowed himself only the
four characters, Adam, Eve, Cain, and Abel. He gave himself no favors; he introduced no light tones; on his somber
background the figures move in no more light than is strictly
necessary to see them move at all; they follow the rules
of the mediaeval Mystery Play, rather than those of the
Greek drama. Yet any sympathetic workman of literary
effect will probably admit that they do move, and even that
at certain moments their movement is highly dramatic; so
much so as to be genuinely emotional.

So also with the characters themselves! If there is a character hard to deal with in the whole range of dramatic
effort, Adam is he! No artist has succeeded in making Adam
sympathetic, and very few indeed have tried to do so. "The
woman tempted me and I did eat" has been his sentence
of condemnation as a figure of drama, since drama was
acted. Such a figure could not be heroic, and only with
difficulty could be saved from being ridiculous on the stage.
Even the twelfth-century *Mystery of Adam's Fall* dwelt only
on his weakness and abject submission to Eve on one side,
and to God on the other. Lodge accepted the traditional
figure, and made the best of it.

> Though my life is bruised with sore affliction
> And dire repentance blast my happiness;
> Though in remembrance Paradise forever
> Blooms with fresh light and flowers ineffable,
> Clear pieties and peaceful innocence,
> Against the gloom of this grieved sentience
> Of violence and starvation, yet I bear,
> Scornful of tears, the grief and scorn of life!
> Faith is the stern, austere acknowledgment
> And dumb obedience to the will of God:
> Such faith my soul has kept inviolable!
> What though he crush me, is not He the Lord!

The drama permitted little development of Adam's character: he scarcely appears after the first act, leaving the
stage to the two brothers to work out their inevitable
antagonism and their contradictory conceptions of duty.

Although Cain's character necessarily had to be developed to the point of insanity, it was a logical insanity; while Abel's character remained also true to its logical conditions of submission to a force or will not its own. The two brothers represented two churches, and the strife ended as such strife in history has commonly ended,—in the destruction of one or the other, the victory of faith or free will.

The character which Lodge developed with evident sympathy was not masculine but feminine. Cain might be himself, but Eve was the mother, a nature far more to his liking. Upon her was thrown the whole burden and stress of the men's weakness or insanity. The drama opens upon her, bearing the alternate reproaches and entreaties of Adam, and trying to infuse into him a share of her own courage and endurance; Adam implores her:

> "Hold me—I need thy tenderness, I need
> Thy calm and pitiful hands to comfort me."

Eve answers:

> "Be still a little; all will be well, I know."

A total inversion of roles! and it is carried through consistently to the end. All the men appeal to Eve, and then refuse to listen to her. In the vehement dispute at the end of the first act, Adam at last turns to Eve, and bids her to lecture her son:

> And thou, Eve, Woman, most perilously wandered
> In weak delusion, now I charge thee speak—
> Lest thou should fall again in deathless sin,—
> Of God and man,—God's all, man's nothingness!

EVE

Dear son, we are God's creatures every one—

CAIN

Mother!

EVE

I'll speak no more!—

Except perhaps the somewhat undeveloped figure of Abel, all these characters are personally felt,—to the dramatist they were real and living figures,—but that of Eve is the most personal of all. As the drama opens on the wife bearing the reproaches and supporting the weakness of the husband, so it ends by the mother assuming the insanities of the son. After the traditional development of the mediaeval drama, Eve is reproduced in the Virgin. Lodge adhered closely to the mediaeval scheme except in transposing the roles of the brothers and intensifying the role of the mother. As, in the mediaeval conception, the role of the Virgin almost effaced the role of Christ, the drama of *Cain* ends by almost effacing Cain in the loftier self-sacrifice of the woman:

> "Go forth, go forth, lonely and godlike man!
> My heart will follow tho' my feet must stay.
> Yet in thy solitude shall there be a woman
> To care for thee through the incessant days,
> To lie beside thee in the desolate nights,
> To love thee as thy soul shall love the truth!
> In her thy generation shall conceive
> Passionate daughters, strong and fierce-eyed sons,
> To lift the light and bear the labor of truth
> Whereof the spark is mine, the fire is thine."

Perhaps some readers would find more meaning and higher taste in the drama had Lodge called it *Eve* instead of calling it *Cain;* but here the dramatist was developing his theme in philosophy rather than in poetry, and the two motives almost invariably stand in each other's light. The maternal theme is the more poetic and dramatic, but without the philosophy the poem and the drama have no reason to exist. The reader must take it as it is given, or must throw it aside altogether, and compose a drama of his own, with a totally different *donnée.* In either case, he will search long, and probably in vain, through American literature, for another dramatic effort as vigorous and sustained as that of *Cain,* and, if he finds what he seeks, it is somewhat more than likely that he will end by finding it in *Herakles.*

VII. *The Great Adventure*

COMPOSITION, and especially dramatic composition, is an absorbing task. Night passes rapidly in shaping a single phrase, and dawn brings a harsh light to witness putting it in the fire. Lodge worked habitually by night, and destroyed as freely as he composed. Meanwhile life went on, with such pleasures and pains as American life offers; but, in narrative, the pains take the larger place, and the pleasures are to be understood as a background. The most serious loss to Lodge's life was the illness and death of his friend, Trumbull Stickney, whose companionship had beer. his best support since the early days of Paris and the Latin Quarter. Stickney owned a nature of singular refinement, and his literary work promised to take rank at the head of the work done by his generation of Americans; but he had hardly come home to begin it at Harvard College when he was struck down by fatal disease. Lodge's letters had much to say of the tragedy, and of the volume of verses which he helped to publish afterwards in order to save what relics remained of Stickney's poetry.

From Boston in August 1904 he wrote his wife: "Just after I wrote to you, John called me up on the telephone and told me that Joe [Stickney] was very seriously ill at the Victoria. I went down there at once and saw Lisel, the doctor, and Lucy, and I write to you now, in the greatest agony of mind. Joe has got a tumor on the brain. For ten days he has had almost constant terrific pains in his head. They brought him to Boston last Thursday. You can imagine how dreadful a shock it was to get this frightful news when I had hoped to take Joe to Tuckanuck with us. I am completely unnerved. . . . The doctor told me I should certainly not be able to see him—no one can. . . . I feel at present utterly prostrated. Somehow I have never conceived of Joe's dying."

From Tuckanuck, September 1: "You can imagine better than I can tell you, with what a tense and anxious hope I cling to the possibility that Joe will be saved, and returned to life a well man. I feel almost heartbroken when I think of him, and my mind goes back through all the immense days and ways of life that we have seen together. . . . Doc [Sturgis Bigelow] is, as you may guess, the best and dearest companion in this twilight of grief and anxiety in which I have my present being, and this place is of course more soothing than anywhere else to me. . . ."

From Nahant, November 1904: "Don't get carried away with the idea that Joe's death has set the term to youth or is really the end of anything. Life—our life, his life, the life of the human soul—is quite continuous, I'm convinced: one thing with another, big and little, sad and gay, real and false, and the whole business just life, which is its own punishment and reward, its own beginning and end. . . ."

From Nahant, November 1904: "I've finished rereading the *Republic,* and it is one of the few books in which my sons shall be thoroughly educated if I can manage it. There are not more than a very few books from which every man can catch a glimpse of the Great Idea, for there are only a very few great torchbearers. But the *Republic* is one, and much more accessible than any other, except the *Leaves of Grass;* for Christ is deeply hidden in the rubbish of the Church, and Buddha and Lao Tze are very far removed from the processes of our minds."

From Boston, January 1905: "I've had the most warm and vivid delight in Dok's [Sturgis Bigelow's] company, which has been constantly with me since I came here. He has surpassed himself in kindness and clear, warm, wise sympathy and comprehensiveness. Tonight I have passed a long and superb evening with him, in which we have together, in a manner of speaking, *fait le tour* on the parapets of thought. It has renewed and inspired me, given me, as it were, a new departure and a new vista. . . . I hate to leave tomorrow, for he seems so glad to have me, and I, the Gods know, get everything from being with him. He does, as you might say, continually see me through,—through confusion, and through mistakes and desperations,—in fact, through life. It's immense, what he has done and does for me. In short, after two days of him I feel all straightened out, and you, you best know how badly I needed this beneficent process. Last night we saw Réjane in *L'Hirondelle,* a play not at all superior, not of any brilliancy of merit or originality of human criticism, but so, after all, interesting by virtue of a certain apparent and immense genuine reality, —so 'written,' with such glitter of word and phrase and epigram, and so acted, above all, that we both passed an evening of immense, contented, uncritical delight."

From Mrs. Wharton's, New York, January 1905: "I left Boston rather sadly, for my days there had been marvelous. A real readjustment and recoherence of all the immense pressure of great experience which has, as you know, kept me struggling and a little breathless since Joe's death. With Dok I really found my footing, brushed the night from my eyes, and took a long glance forward. . . . Mrs. Wharton was really glad to see me, and I to see her, and we have had a good deal of the swift, lucid, elliptical conversation which is so perfect and so stimulating and so neatly defined in its range. . . . It is a great delight to be with her, as I am a good deal, and to be clear and orderly and correct in one's thought and speech, as far as one goes. It's good for one, and vastly agreeable besides,—indeed, it is to me a kind of gymnastic excitement, very stimulating."

As these letters show, the death of Stickney threw Lodge rather violently back on himself and his personal surroundings, and he stretched out his hands painfully for intellectual allies. A stroke of rare good fortune threw a new friend in his way, to fill the void in his life that Stickney had left. Langdon Mitchell, another poet and dramatist, with much the same ideals and difficulties, but with ten years' more experience, brought him help and counsel of infinite value, as his letters show:

TO LANGDON MITCHELL

NAHANT (*July 1903*)

DEAR MITCHELL,—Before receiving your letter and in an ecstasy of good manners, I wrote to your wife to ask her if

I might come to you on the seventeenth. I can't very well come earlier for I am by way of seeing my parents off to Europe, where my dad is going to assist in despoiling the virtuous Briton, for whom the wrathful tears of the State Department abundantly flow, of what neither is nor ought to be his except on the theory that everything of value should belong to that people who, when pressed, will blushingly confess that they are the chosen of God. My father starts, then, on this engaging mission[1] on the seventeenth, and after having given him my blessing and those counsels gained only by inexperience, without which no child with any sense of responsibility should take leave of his father, having in fact done all my duty, I shall at once turn myself to pleasure and embark with a mind wholly vague as to direction, you-ward. It's mighty good of you, dear Mitchell, and of your wife too to want me for a few days, and I can't tell you with how great pleasure I look forward to seeing you. We'll have some great days.

1925 F St., *October 1903*

DEAR MITCHELL,—Good! You understand Baudelaire as I do; indeed you say things about him which make me realize as never before my own comprehension of him. I am doubtful about French poetry being, like Latin, "City poetry." Think of Ronsard and his crowd, or Victor Hugo or Leconte de Lisle—but Baudelaire, like Villon, like Verlaine, is certainly a city poet. And why not? The civilization of an old society is, I am certain, the fair material of poems. The best is that Baudelaire has given you pleasure, and I feel that you have appreciated as I do that he is, in his best moments, really a great poet, one of the torchbearers. "*Allons!* after the great companions and to belong to them!" Ah! let us go and be of them if we can, dear Mitchell. At least we can follow on the "great road of the Universe." Which reminds me that I have been reading your verses again and again and I shall have, for what they're worth, some remarks to make when we next meet.

[1]The Alaskan Boundary Tribunal, which met in London in the summer of 1903 and of which his father was a member. H. A.

1925 F St., *Spring, 1904*

Dear Mitchell,—I largely agree with what you say of Vielé's book, though to my mind you rate it a little too high. His delight in words seems to me far his strongest trick. He says not very much. Of course keep *Cain* till April 1st or as long as you wish. As you may imagine, all that you say about it in your letter is deeply interesting to me. As I've said to you, you are the only person from whom I expect genuine criticism and get it. As regards the stage directions I'll say this: Although the thing has no quality of a real play, nevertheless the action—that is, the main points of the action—are essential to the expression of the idea, and therefore it is necessary that there should be some environment indicated, and that the characters should perform certain motions (as few as possible, of course). The question, then, is merely this: whether the poem is more or less interrupted and the reader subjected to more or less of a jar, by having environment and action indicated as briefly and technically as possible, in brackets, or by having them introduced as verse into the body of the poem. It seemed to me, despite the obvious absurdities, the former was the method most frank and honest, and least likely to mar the poetic and intellectual integrity of the whole. Of course the mere technicalities could be eliminated if they seriously jarred. Thank you—I wish I could—for all that you say, which I find very just and of the utmost assistance to me in clarifying and enlightening my own criticism; and thank you, above all, for your interest, which is valuable to me beyond words.

I'm mighty sorry but not very greatly surprised to hear your news of the condition of the stage. It's depressing beyond measure to know that the American theater is reserved exclusively, either for importations, or the worthless manufactures of almost illiterate Americans who regard plays merely as merchandise, and who would manufacture boots with equal enjoyment and success. Indeed it's most depressing; and what is to be done? Your assertion that the American public will take good plays as well as bad is I believe quite correct, but unfortunately it doesn't help as long as they'll take bad plays as well as good. The stage situation is to me merely another sign of the intellectual, moral, and spiritual childishness of the American. Indeed was there ever such an anomaly as the American man? In practical affairs his cynicism, energy, and capacity are simply stupefying, and in every other respect he is a sentimental idiot possessing neither the interest, the capacity, nor the desire for even the most elementary processes of independent thought. Consider for one moment his position as a domestic animal as it was fifty years ago and as it is today. Then he was the unquestioned head of his family, the master of his house, the father of as many children as he wanted to have. His wife's business was to bear his children and manage his household to suit him, and she never questioned it. Today he is absolutely dethroned. A woman rules in his stead. His wife finds him so sexually inapt that she refuses to bear him children and so driveling in every way except as a money-getter that she compels him to expend his energies solely in that direction while she leads a discontented, sterile, stunted life, not because she genuinely prefers it but because she cannot find a first-rate *man* to make her desire to be the mother of his children and to live seriously and happily. I speak of course only of the well-to-do classes, which as a matter of fact comprise most real Americans, and of which the average number of children per family is under two. We are, dear Mitchell, a dying race, as every race must be of which the men are, as men and not accumulators, third-rate. American women don't fall in love with the American men (I mean, really) and they're quite right; only a woman won't have children by a man she's not really in love with, and when you think of the travail and the peril of death can you blame her? It's an odd situation; we are a dying race and really we've never lived.

Forgive this long dissertation. I got started and could not stop.

1925 F St., *April 1904*

Dear Mitchell,—I'm nearly in a position now to answer the question which we discussed—perhaps you remember—

last summer at Tuckanuck: namely whether or not Jesus Christ appeared as the logical outcome of the Jewish religious tradition. You remember I contended he was wholly sporadic and attached to nothing. I begin now to see I was in a measure quite wrong, and perhaps to a small extent right. I am very anxious to talk it over with you when you return here, and also to discuss with you the whole state of thought and feeling in Judaea at the time of Christ's appearance. All this, you will guess, is the result of work I've been doing in preparation for writing the Christ-play of which I spoke to you and which, to my immense delight, you seem to approve —at least the idea—in your last letter. I've already gone far enough to realize that no subject could be more fascinating or more interesting. Jesus Christ and his teachings, which are neglected and unknown, form a background against which the dark threads of the lives and passions and thoughts of worldly men should stand out like the black bars on the solar spectrum. I have reread Renan's *Vie de Jésus* and it's interesting in many ways and a *"beau livre"*; but, dear Mitchell, can you imagine a man spending ten years on the study of Jesus Christ and at last summing up his appreciation of the man in this phrase: *"C'est un charmeur!"* It's staggering.

1925 F St. (*Spring of 1904*)

Dear Mitchell,—I imagine what you say of solitude is very true. *"Tout se paie"*—in one form or another. Certainly you have kept singularly balanced, singularly vital and sane —in the true sense. What I shall be in ten years there's no guessing. One stakes one's life on the chance of ransoming "one lost moment with a rhyme" and the wheel turns——

Of course keep *Cain* as long as you want. I really feel ashamed to bother you with it when you are so busy, but it's vastly important to me to know precisely what you think; whether, in your deliberate opinion, it's the real thing in any degree whatever, and not merely and utterly—literature! But don't, I beg you, look at it until it's convenient. I shan't write another long thing in verse for some time. Since publishing *Cain* I've had a time of horrible reaction and *"abatte-*

ment"—the sort of thing we all go through occasionally. This has become a drearily egotistical and dull letter. . . .

My days in New York were glorious, the only good days I've had since finishing that poem. I need hardly say how deeply I hope you will dispose of your plays to your satisfaction—for your sake and for the sake of the stage.

1925 F St., Washington
(*Spring, 1904*)

I think, dear Mitchell, that we really about agree as to the Sonnet. The first-rate ones are terribly few and in diverse forms. Witness Baudelaire.

.   .   .   .

My dear man, I've got hold of such a splendid thing to write—immense. I'm shutting down on Society, in which we've been wandering this winter to the detriment of all I value in life, and I'm getting to work—God be praised. I wish I could have a talk with you about this and so many other things. One gets glimpses, such glimpses, of incredible, tremendous things. I wish you were by so we might share them. I feel always tempted to run over for a day to see you, but I'm afraid it's quite impossible now. Still if the desire pushes me too hard I'll turn up some afternoon. Spring-Rice has been here for a week and I had one splendid talk with him and wished more than ever you were here. There's a man who does, really, keep up wonderfully and by a very peculiar faculty he has of remaining, *au fond,* quite detached from his own circumstances and experience. He left tonight, alas! He goes back to Russia, about which he had absorbing things to say. Now that he's gone, once more the "void weighs on us,"—the dreadful, blank, mild nothingness of this nice, agreeable, easy, spacious vacuity (comp. James). And here I am again alone beyond belief, but, fortunately, with a very interesting thing to do, so I'm very well off.

Nahant, Mass., *October 1904*

Dear Mitchell,—I was extremely glad to get your note and I would have answered it before had not events compelled me. On the eleventh my friend Stickney died—quite suddenly at the last. On the fourteenth we buried him. He was thirty years old—by far the most promising man I have known, his best work still and surely to come. Under the terrible test of a mortal disease his mind and character rose to higher levels than they had ever touched before. He died, really, at the height of his powers. The future held nothing for him but suffering, mental and physical. He is very well out of it. Dear Mitchell, what a life it is!—what a life! I am having an undoubtedly hard time. So, it must be said, are other people.

I wish I could get to New York now and see you. I feel more deeply than ever how invaluable your friendship is to me and how incalculably better than anything else in life such friendship as I think you and I share together is in the last analysis. I would come if I had the energy, but I am pretty well done up morally and physically. I shall be in New York, though, from November ninth for some days. Couldn't you be there then too? It would be to me so true a happiness to see you again.

Naturally, too, in the social and literary sequence, young Lodge fell under the charm of Henry James:

TO HIS MOTHER

WASHINGTON, *May 1905*

To this even existence of mine there has been one delightful interruption, namely the lecture and subsequent visions of Henry James. The lecture was profoundly, and to one who writes himself, wonderfully interesting; so many splendid things which had been long at home in my own consciousness and which I first heard then, perfectly and irresistibly expressed. The amiable Miss T—— had asked us to tea for the next day; where I went and found, besides James, old Mrs. ——, a most original and charming and distinguished person, conveying, through all her rather stiff but flattering courtesy, the vivid impression that she might be, on occasion, equally original and the reverse of charming. There were besides some unremarkable people who all left, leaving me the chance to talk with James, which I did with the greatest delight then and also the next morning when, at his invitation, I went with him to the Capitol and the Library for two most interesting hours. This, I believe, can be said of James, though it is not the most obvious remark to make of him, and is, at the same time, the rarest and most important compliment that can be paid to any creative artist—namely, that he is, in matters of art, incorruptibly honest, and in consequence hugely expensive. He is, I mean, as an artist, built through and through of the same material—which you like or not according to your fancy. His very style—again whether you like it or not—bears by its mere tortuous originality, if by no other sign, infallible witness that he has, at immense expenditure, done all the work—artistically and intellectually—and that all the work is his own. In ideas and art he lives in a palace built of his own time and thought, while the usual, you might say the ubiquitous, average person and literary prostitute lives contentedly in one of an interminable row of hovels, built, so to speak, on an endless contract from bare material stolen from Time's intellectual scrap-heap. What it all amounts to is that, whether you like James or not, whether you think he is all on the wrong track or not, you are bound to respect him, for if you do not, whom, in this age of universal machine-made cheapness, whom more than James with his immense talent and industry *and* his small sales, are you going to respect?

This is a long, garrulous, egotistical (to a degree), and perhaps you will say, rather incoherent letter. So I will spare you any further palpitating details of my obscure life.

WASHINGTON, *June 1905*

Indeed, I wish I might have been with you, but on the other hand I have done an immense deal by being quietly [?] and in much long solitude just now at this time. I have lived high most of my working hours, and in consequence my volume of sonnets—*The Great Adventure,* I call it, which is,

I think, a good title—lies before me all but finished—seventy-five sonnets or more, with which I am pretty well pleased. I feel lonely, as I always do when I am hard at work, but I also feel much exhilaration. These are my great years. Well, I am sure I must have said all this before to you. My interest in myself is so poignant that I elude it with difficulty.

Joe's volume represents for me a good deal of work and an experience of grief that neither gives nor receives consolation, which has left its indelible mark upon me—which is good. For I believe there are but two ways with real grief: get rid of it if you can; but if you can't, then take all you can get of it, live in it, work in it, experience it as far as you are capable of experiencing anything. Let it nourish you! as it will, as anything will that is real, and in direct proportion to its reality and significance. I'll tell you that I sent my volume of sonnets to Houghton & Mifflin, who wrote me that they held my work in high consideration; which, I suppose, indicates that some people they have seen think well of *Cain.* Also, perhaps you have seen *Moriturus* (by me) in the July *Scribner.*

The Great Adventure was published in October,—a small volume of ninety pages, of which nearly one third were devoted to the memory of Stickney:

> He said: "We are the Great Adventurers;
> This is the Great Adventure: thus to be
> Alive, and, on the universal sea
> Of being, lone yet dauntless mariners.
>
> .   .   .   .
>
> This is the Great Adventure!" All of us
> Who saw his dead, deep-visioned eyes, could see,
> After the Great Adventure, immanent,
> Splendid and strange, the Great Discovery.

Love and Death were the two themes of these sonnets, almost as personal as the *Song of the Wave.* Underneath the phrases and motives of each lay almost always the sense of

striving against the elements, like Odysseus, or against the
mysteries, like Plato:

> "At least," he said, "we spent with Socrates
> Some memorable days, and in our youth
> Were curious and respectful of the Truth,
> Thrilled with perfections and discoveries,
> And with the everlasting mysteries
> We were irreverent and unsatisfied,—
> And so we are!" he said . . .

The irreverence mattered little, since it was mostly the
mere effervescence of youth and health; but the dissatisfaction went deep, and made a serious strain on his energy,—a
strain which Stickney's death first made vital. The verses began to suggest discouragement:

> In Time's cathedral, Memory, like a ghost,
> Crouched in the narrow twilight of the nave,
> Fumbles with thin pathetic hands to save
> Relics of all things lived and loved and lost.
> Life fares and feasts, and Memory counts the cost
> With unrelenting lips that dare confess
> Life's secret failures, sins and loneliness,
> And life's exalted hopes, defiled and crossed.

The Great Adventure probably marked the instant when
life did, in fact, hover between the two motives,—the beginning and the end,—Love and Death. Both were, for the
moment, in full view, equally near, and equally intense,
with the same background of the unknown:

> In the shadow of the Mystery
> We watched for light with sleepless vigilance,
> Yet still, how far soever we climbed above
> The nether levels, always, like a knife,
> We felt the chill of fear's blind bitter breath;
> For still a secret crazed the heart of Love,
> An endless question blurred the eyes of Life,
> A baffling silence sealed the lips of Death.

Meanwhile life went on with what most people would, at
least in retrospect, regard as altogether exceptional happiness.

The small circle of sympathetic companions was immensely strengthened by the addition of Edith Wharton, whose unerring taste and finished workmanship served as a corrective to his youthful passion for license. Her fine appreciation felt this quality as the most insistent mark of his nature:

"Abundance,—that is the word which comes to me whenever I try to describe him. During the twelve years of our friendship,—and from the day that it began,—I had, whenever we were together, the sense of his being a creature as profusely as he was finely endowed. There was an exceptional delicacy in his abundance, and an extraordinary volume in his delicacy."

Life is not wholly thrown away on ideals, if only a single artist's touch catches like this the life and movement of a portrait. Such a picture needs no proof; it is itself convincing.

"The man must have had a sort of aura about him. Perhaps he was one of those who walk on the outer rim of the world, aware of the jumping-off place; which seems the only way to walk—but few take it. Odd that your article should have appealed so much to me, when I know so little of the subject!"

The more competent the reader,—and this reader, though unnamed, was among the most competent,—the more complete is the conviction; and the same simple quality of the truest art runs through the whole of Mrs. Wharton's painting, to which the critic was alluding. Every touch of her hand takes the place of proof.

"All this," she continues, "on the day when he was first brought to see me,—a spring afternoon of the year 1898, in Washington,—was lit up by a beautiful boyish freshness, which, as the years passed, somehow contrived to ripen without fading. In the first five minutes of our talk, he *gave* himself with the characteristic wholeness that made him so rare a friend; showing me all the sides of his varied nature; the grave sense of beauty, the flashing contempt of meanness, and that large spring of kindly laughter that comes to many only as a result of the long tolerance of life. It was one of his gifts thus to brush aside the preliminaries of ac-

quaintance, and enter at once, with a kind of royal ease, on
the rights and privileges of friendship; as though—one might
think—with a foreboding of the short time given him to enjoy
them.

"Aside from this, however, there was nothing of the
pathetically predestined in the young Cabot Lodge. Then—
and to the end—he lived every moment to the full, and the
first impression he made was of a joyous physical life. His
sweet smile, his easy strength, his deep eyes full of laughter
and visions,—these struck one even before his look of intellectual power. I have seldom seen anyone in whom the
natural man was so wholesomely blent with the reflecting
intelligence; and it was not the least of his charms that he
sent such stout roots into the earth, and had such a hearty
love for all he drew from it. Nothing was common or un-
clean to him but the vulgar, the base, and the insincere, and
his youthful impatience at the littleness of human nature
was tempered by an unusually mature sense of its humors."

While young Lodge, or any other young artist, might find
it the most natural thing in the world to give himself without
thought or hesitation to another artist, like Mrs. Wharton, it
by no means followed that he could give himself to men or
women who had not her gifts, or standards, or sympathies.
He could no more do this than he could write doggerel.
However much he tried, and the more he tried, to lessen the
gap between himself—his group of personal friends—and the
public, the gap grew steadily wider; the circle of sympathies
enlarged itself not at all, or with desperate slowness; and
this consciousness of losing ground,—of failure to find a larger
horizon of friendship beyond his intimacy;—the growing fear
that, beyond this narrow range, no friends existed in the immense void of society,—or could exist, in the form of society
which he lived in,—the suffocating sense of talking and singing in a vacuum that allowed no echo to return, grew more
and more oppressive with each effort to overcome it. The
experience is common among artists, and has often led to
violent outbursts of egotism, of self-assertion, of vanity; but
the New England temper distrusts itself as well as the world
it lives in, and rarely yields to eccentricities of conduct. Emer-

son himself, protesting against every usual tendency of society, respected in practice all its standards.

"One is accustomed," continued Mrs. Wharton, "in enjoying the comradeship of young minds, to allow in them for a measure of passing egotism, often the more marked in proportion to their sensitiveness to impressions; but it was Cabot Lodge's special grace to possess the sensitiveness without the egotism. Always as free from pedantry as from conceit, he understood from the first the give and take of good talk, and was not only quick to see the other side of an argument, but ready to reinforce it by his sympathetic interpretation. And because of this responsiveness of mind, and of the liberating, vivifying nature from which it sprang, he must always, to his friends, remain first of all, and most incomparably, a Friend."

This quality was strongly felt by others. One who knew him intimately when he was Secretary of the British Embassy in Washington and later when they were together in Berlin, Sir Cecil Spring-Rice, now Minister of Great Britain in Stockholm, wrote of him after his death:

"The first time I saw him was at Nahant when the children were all there together; and since then I have always seemed to know him closely and intimately. We bathed together there, and I remember so well the immense joy he had in jumping into the water, and then lying out in the sun till he was all browned—as strong and healthy a human creature as I have ever seen, and exulting in his life. Then we rode together at Washington, and I can see him now galloping along in the woody country near Rock Creek. It didn't strike me then that he was anything but a strong healthy boy, absolutely straight, sincere, and natural.

"It wasn't till I saw a good deal of him in Berlin that I realized what a rare and extraordinary mind he had. He was then studying hard at philosophy. In an extraordinarily quick time he learnt German and seemed to take naturally to the most difficult books—just as he had done to the sea, without any conscious effort. We had many talks then, and his talk was most inspiring. He constantly lived face to face with

immense problems, which he thought out thoroughly and
earnestly,—things men often read and study in order to pass
examinations or achieve distinction; but I am quite sure with
him there was no object except just the attainment and the
presence of truth. He had a most living mind, and a character absolutely independent; resolved on finding out things
by himself, and living by his own lights and thinking out his
own problems. Nothing would have stopped him or interfered with him. In all my experience of people about the
world, I never knew anyone so 'detached,' deaf to the usual
voices of the world; and so determined to live in the light of
Truth, taking nothing for granted till he had proved it by
his own original thought. He had greatly developed when I
last saw him in Washington, during the few days I spent
there. I had two long talks with him in his house. I think he
was the sort of stuff that in the middle ages would have
made a great saint or a great heresiarch—I dare say we have
no use for such people now; I wonder if he found he was
born out of his time, and that ours was not a world for him.
I am not thinking of what he wrote or what he said, but of
the atmosphere in which he lived, and the surroundings of
his own soul—what his thoughts lived and moved in.

"In that detachment and independence and courage I
have never known anyone like him. Yet it was hardly courage: for he didn't give the enemy a thought.

"I wonder if one often meets a man in these times who is
literally capable of standing alone, to whom the noises and
sights of the world, which to most people are everything, are
nothing, absolutely nothing—the state of mind of someone
who is madly in love, but with him it seemed normal and
natural, an everyday habit of being.

"It was only last week I had a long think as I was walking
about through these lonely woods here, and I was wondering whether I should see you all soon again, and I was saying
to myself: At any rate Bay will have grown—he won't disappoint me: he is the sort of man who is bound to get bigger
every day—and he is younger and stronger than I and he will
last. And about how many men of his age could one say *that*
with certainty, that time would surely improve and perfect

him, and that with every new meeting one could gain something new?

"And that is how I thought of him naturally."

Like most of the clever young men of his time—Oscar Wilde, Bernard Shaw, Gilbert Chesterton—he loved a good paradox, and liked to chase it into its burrow. "When you are accustomed to anything, you are estranged from it"; and his supreme gift for liking was never to get accustomed to things or people. By way of a historical paradox he maintained that the Church was devised as a protection against the direct rays of Christ's spirit, which, undimmed, would compel to action and change of character. By way of a poetical paradox he loved Walt Whitman to fanaticism, and quoted, as his favorite description of the world, Walt's "little plentiful manikins skipping about in collars and tailcoats." Yet he sometimes declared that his favorite line in poetry was Swinburne's:

Out of the golden remote wild west where the sea without shore
    is,
Full of the sunset, and sad, if at all, with the fullness of joy.

Perhaps, too, if he had chosen a verse of poetry to suggest his own nature, after the description of Mrs. Wharton he might have found it in another line of Swinburne's:

Some dim derision of mysterious laughter.

However remote he thought himself from his world, he was, in fact, very much of his literary time,—and would not have been recognized at all by any other. Like most of his young contemporaries in literature, he loved his paradoxes chiefly because they served as arrows for him to practice his art on the social conventions which served for a target; and the essence of his natural simplemindedness showed itself in his love for this boy's-play of fresh life which he tired of only too soon, as he will himself tell in his *Noctambulist*. He knew, at bottom, that the world he complained of had as little faith in its conventions as he had; but, apart from the fun and easy practice of paradox, Lodge's most marked trait of mind lay in his instinctive love of logic, which he was

probably not even aware of, although often—as is seen every·
where in the *Cain* and *Herakles*—the reasoning is as close
and continuous as it might be in Plato or Schopenhauer.

This contrast of purposes disconcerted most readers. The
usual reader finds the effort of following a single train of
thought too severe for him; but even professional critics rebel
against a paradox almost in the degree that it is logical, and
find the Greek severity of Prometheus, in its motive, a worse
fault than what they call the "excess of loveliness," which, in
Shelley, "militates against the awful character of the drama."
In modern society, the Greek drama is a paradox; which has
not prevented most of the greatest nineteenth-century poets
from putting their greatest poetry into that form; and Lodge
loved it because of its rigorous logic even more than for its
unequaled situations. Lodge could be exuberant enough
when he pleased, but what he exacted from his readers was
chiefly mind.

With this preamble, such readers as care for intellectual
poetry can now take up his work of the years 1906 and 1907,
published under the titles, *The Soul's Inheritance* and
Herakles. *The Soul's Inheritance* appeared only after his
death, but in the natural order of criticism it comes first.
Although the vigor of his verse was greater, there were already signs that his physical strength was less, and that he
was conscious of it. His health had begun to cause uneasi-
ness; his heart warned him against strains; but he scorned
warnings, and insisted that his health was never better. Submission to an obnoxious fact came hard to him, at all times;
but the insidious weakness of literary workmen lies chiefly
in their inability to realize that quiet work like theirs, which
calls for no physical effort, may be a stimulant more exhausting than alcohol, and as morbid as morphine. The fascination of the silent midnight, the veiled lamp, the smoldering
fire, the white paper asking to be covered with elusive words;
the thoughts grouping themselves into architectural forms,
and slowly rising into dreamy structures, constantly changing, shifting, beautifying their outlines,—this is the subtlest
of solitary temptations, and the loftiest of the intoxications
of genius.

VIII. Herakles

"THE SOUL'S INHERITANCE" was a poem delivered before the Phi Beta Kappa Society at Cambridge in 1906, and in delivering it, Lodge discovered in himself a new power that would probably have led him in time into a new field, where he could put himself into closer relations with the world. His delivery was good, his voice admirable, and his power over his audience was evident. He was probably an orator by right of inheritance, though he had never cared to assert the claim, preferring to rest his distinction on his poetry.

In this poem he reiterated his life-long theme that the Soul, or Will, is the supreme energy of life:

> That here and now, no less for each of us,
> That inward voice, cogent as revelation,
> That trance of truth's sublime discovery,
> Which in the soul of Socrates wrought out
> Gold from the gross ore of humanity,
> Still speak, still hold, still work their alchemy;
> That here and now and in the soul's advance,
> And by the soul's perfection, we may feel
> The thought of Buddha in our mortal brain,
> The human heart of Jesus in our breast,
> And in our will the strength of Hercules!

Again, as always in his poetry, he recurred to the sense of struggle, of—

> The multitudinous menace of the night,

and the soul's need to stand out,—

> Importunate and undissuadable,

over the utmost verge of venture:

> There in our hearts the burning lamp of love,
> There in our sense the rhythm and amplitude,
> And startled splendor of the seas of song.

This last verse—the "startled splendor of the seas of song" —was one of the kind in which he delighted, and which he had a rare power of framing, but the thought was ever the same: the Soul of Man was the Soul of God; and it was repeated in various forms in the three sonnets attached to the blank verse:

> Strangely, inviolably aloof, alone,
> Once shall it hardly come to pass that we,
> As with his Cross, as up his Calvary,
> Burdened and blind, ascend and share his throne.

Again it was repeated in the poem called *Pilgrims*, delivered at the annual dinner of the New England Society, in New York, December 1906. The theme, on such an occasion and before such an audience, in the fumes of dinner and tobacco, was adventurous, but Lodge adhered to it bravely, and insisted all the more on its value,

> Lest we grow tired and tame and temperate.

He boldly asserted: "We *are* the Pilgrims," and proved it by attaching to the blank verse three sonnets, as beautiful as he ever wrote:

> They are gone. . . . They have all left us, one by one:
>   Swiftly, with undissuadable strong tread,
>   Cuirassed in song, with wisdom helmeted,
>   They are gone before us, into the dark, alone. . . .
> Upward their wings rushed radiant to the sun;
>   Seaward the ships of their emprise are sped;
>   Onward their starlight of desire is shed;
>   Their trumpet-call is forward;—they are gone!
> Let us take thought and go!—we know not why
>   Nor whence nor where,—let us take wings and fly!
>   Let us take ship and sail, take heart and dare!
> Let us deserve at last, as they have done,
>   To say of all men living and dead who share
>   The soul's supreme adventure,—*We* are gone!

These verses appeared in print only after his death, as though he had intended them for his epitaph; and perhaps he did, for he continued in the same tone:

> Let us go hence!—however dark the way,
>   Haste!—lest we lose the clear, ambitious sense
>   Of what is ours to gain and to gainsay.
> Let us go hence, lest dreadfully we die!

Two poems cast in the same form followed: *Life in Love* and *Love in Life;* which return to the intensely personal theme. Readers who feel the theme will probably feel the poetry as the highest he ever reached in feeling. Again the three sonnets follow, with their studied beauties of expression:

> Her voice is pure and grave as song;
>   Her lips are flushed as sunset skies;
>   The power, the myth, the mysteries
> Of life and death in silence throng
> The secret of her silences;
>   Her face is sumptuous and strong,
>   And twilights far within prolong
>   The spacious glory of her eyes.

On these themes of Love and Life Lodge had dwelt without interruption from the start; and now, suddenly, without apparent steps of transition, he passed to a new motive,—Doubt! *The Noctambulist* suggests some change, physical or moral; some new influence or ripened growth, or fading youth. Perhaps he would himself have traced the influence and the change, to the death of Stickney. Mrs. Wharton says that "in its harmony of thought and form, it remains perhaps the completest product" of his art; and it is certainly the saddest. The note is struck in the first line:

> That night of tempest and tremendous gloom,

when,—

> Across the table, for—it seemed to us—
> An age of silence, in the dim-lit room,
> Tenantless of all humans save ourselves
> Yet seeming haunted, as old taverns are,
> With the spent mirth of unremembered men,
> He mused at us. . . . And then, "I know! . . . ." he said,
> "I know! O Youth! . . . I too have seen the world
> At sunrise, candid as the candid dew;
>   . . . You look abroad,
> And see the new adventure wait for you,
> Splendid with wars and victories; for you

Trust the masked face of Destiny. But I!
I've turned the Cosmos inside out!" he said;
And on his lips the shadow of a smile
Looked hardly human. . . .

Some two hundred lines of unbroken disillusionment follow, which should not be torn to pieces to make easy quotations; but the passages that here and there suggest autobiography may serve as excuse for cutting up such a poem into
fragments which now and then resemble the letters in their
spontaneous outbursts.

Yes! and I feel anew the splendid zest
Of youth's brave service in truth's ancient cause,
When, with the self-same thunders that you use,
Edged with a wit—at no time Greek!—I too
Most pleasurably assailed and tumbled down,
With a fine sense of conquest and release,
The poor, one, old, enfeebled, cheerless God
Left to us of our much be-Deitied
And more be-Deviled past . . .
And all's well done I doubt not; though the times
Of life may well seem all too brief to waste!
But this comes later, when we learn,—as learn
We must, if we go forward still from strength
To strength incessantly,—to wage no more
With phantoms of the past fortunate wars;
To die no longer on the barricades
For the true faith; to spend no more the rich
And insufficient days and powers of life
Striving to shape the world and force the facts,
Tame the strong heart, and stultify the soul,
To fit some creed, some purpose, some design
Ingeniously contrived to spare the weak,
Protect the timid and delude the fools.—
                                    The time must come
When we can deal in partialities
No more, if truth shall prosper; for we stand
Awfully face to face with just the whole
Secret,—our unrestricted Universe,
Spirit and sense! . . . And then, abruptly then
Swift as a passion, brutal as a blow,
The dark shuts down!

Whether he felt the dark already shutting down, brutal as a blow, or only divined it from the fate of Stickney, one need not know. The verses prove that he felt it personally, for he repeated it again and again:

> In the strict silence, while he spoke no more,
> We heard the tumult of our hearts, and feared
> Almost as men fear death, and know not why,
> We feared, . . . until at last, while at the closed
> Windows the wind cried like a frenzied soul,
> He said: "I too have tried, of mortal life,
> The daily brief excursions; . . .
>   and I have felt the one
> Utterly loosed and loving woman's heart,
> There where the twilight failed and night came on,
> Thrill to life's inmost secret on my breast;
> And I have known the whole of life and been
> The whole of man! The Night is best!"

The letters will show that the *Noctambulist* was meant as "a really new and large and valid departure," which, if followed in its natural direction, should have led to dramatic lyrics and problems more or less in the feeling of *Men and Women*; but, immediately, the *Noctambulist* abuts on *Herakles*, which properly closes the cycle. In the *Herakles*, the poet exhausted, once for all, the whole range of thought and expression with which his life had begun; it was an immense effort; and in approaching the analysis of this drama, which, in bulk, is nearly equal to all the rest of the poet's writings together, and in sustained stress stands beyond comparison with them, the critic or biographer is embarrassed, like the poet himself, by the very magnitude of the scheme.

Although no reader can be now safely supposed to know anything of the Greek drama, he must be assumed to have an acquaintance with Æschylus and Euripides at least. Something must be taken for granted, even though it be only the bare agreement that Shelley's *Prometheus Unbound* does not interfere with *Empedocles on Etna* and that neither of these Greek revivals jostles against *Atalanta in Calydon*.

Here are five or six of the greatest masterpieces of literature with which a reader must be supposed to be acquainted; and perhaps he would do well to keep in mind that, in bulk, Browning's *The Ring and the Book* is large enough to contain them all, and the *Herakles* too; while the methods and merits of all are as distinct and personal as the poets.

The reader, too, who takes up the *Herakles* for the first time, must be supposed to know that the plot of the drama is not of the poet's making: it is given,—imposed; and the dramatist has taken care to quote at the outset the words of the historian, Diodorus, whose story he meant to follow. Herakles and Creon and Megara are familiar characters in history as well as on the stage, and as real as historians can make them. Herakles did marry Megara, the daughter of Creon, King of Thebes; he did refuse to obey the orders of Eurystheus, King of Argos; he was actually—according to the historian—seized with frenzy, and pierced his children with arrows; he submitted to the will of God, performed his miracles, freed Prometheus, and became immortal. All this is fact, which the Greeks accepted, as they afterwards accepted the facts of the Christ's life and death, his miracles and immortality; and for the same reasons: for both were Saviors, Pathfinders, and Sacrifices.

Lodge took up this dramatic motive,—the greatest in human experience,—as it was given him; and so the reader must take it,—or leave it,—since he has nothing to do with the argument of the play once he has accepted it. His interest is in the dramatic development of the action and the philosophic development of the thought. As for the thought, something has already been said; but the reader must be assumed to know that it is the oldest thought that seems to have been known to the human mind, and, in the Christian religion, is the substantial fact which every Catholic sees realized before his eyes whenever he goes to mass. The God who sacrifices himself is one with the victim. The reader who does not already know this general law of religion which confounds all the different elements that enter into ordinary sacrifice, can know neither poetry nor religion. Christ carries the whole of humanity in his person. The identification of subject and object, of thought and matter, of will and universe, is a part of the alphabet of philosophy. The conception of a God sacrificing himself for a world of which he is himself a part, may be a mystery,—a confusion of ideas,—a contradiction of terms,—but it has been the most familiar and the highest expression of the highest—and perhaps also of the lowest—civilizations.

The reader's whole concern lies therefore not in the poem's motive but in its action,—the stages of its movement,—the skill and power with which the theme is developed,—the copiousness of the poet's resources,—the art and scope of his presentation. The critic can do no more than sketch an outline of the difficulties; he cannot attempt to discuss the solutions. Scholars seem inclined to think that Euripides himself failed in his treatment of this theme; that Æschylus scarcely rose quite to its level; and that Shelley used it chiefly as a field on which to embroider beauties wholly his own. Where three of the greatest poets that ever lived have found their highest powers taxed to the utmost, a critic can afford to keep silence.

The play opens at Thebes in the empty agora, at sunset, by a dialogue between the eternal poet and the eternal woman, who serve here in the place of the Greek chorus, each seeking, after the way of poet or woman, for something, —the light,—and so introducing the action, which begins abruptly by a feast in the palace of Creon, the king, who has called his people together to witness his abdication in favor of his son-in-law, Herakles.

Creon is a new creation in Lodge's poetry,—a deliberate effort at character-drawing till now unattempted. Creon is the man of the world, the administrator, the humorist and sage, who has accepted all the phases of life, and has reached the end, which he also accepts, whether as a fact or a phantasm,—whatever the world will,—but which has no more value to him than as being the end, neither comprehended nor comprehensible, but human. Perhaps it is only a coincidence that Æschylus vaguely suggested such a critic in

Okeanos, who appears early in the *Prometheus*. Creon speaks, "in an even, clear, quiet voice":

> I am your King; and I am old,—and wise.
>
> .   .   .   .
>
> And I can now afford your censure! Yes,
> I can afford at last expensive things
> Which cost a man the kingdoms of the world,
> And all their glory! I have lived my life;
> —You cannot bribe me now by any threat
> Of ruin to my life's high edifice,
> Or any dazzled prospect of ambition. . . .
> I think despite these skeptical strange words,
> You will respect me,—for I am your King,
> And I have proved myself among you all
> An architect. Therefore you will not say,
> "This is the voice of failure!"—Yet I know
> That you will find some other things to say
> Not half so true! For, when a man is old,
> He knows at least how utterly himself
> Has failed! But say what things of me you will
> And be assured I sympathize! Indeed,
> A voice like mine is no-wise terrible,
> As might be the tremendous voice of truth
> Should it find speech that you could understand.
> Yet it may vex and dreadfully distress
> Reflective men,—if such indeed there be
> Among you all,—and therefore be assured,
> I sympathize!

With that, Creon names Herakles as his successor, and the crowd departs, leaving the family surrounding Herakles and congratulating him, until Herakles, breaking away, turns fiercely on the king with passionate reproaches for sacrificing him to selfish politics:

> Is this your wisdom, Sire? and is it wise,
> Lightly, and thus with calm complacency,
> Now to believe that I, that Herakles
> Should hold himself so cheaply as your price?

The unshaped, mystical consciousness of a destiny to become the Savior, not the Servant,—the creator, not the economist,—the source itself, not the conduit for "these safe human mediocrities,"—forces Herakles to reject the crown. He will be fettered by none of these ties to common, casual supremacies:

> Sire, I will not serve the Gods or you!
> Sire, I will not rule by grace of God
> Or by your grace! I will be Lord of none,
> And thus unto myself be Lord and Law!

Therewith the inexorable, tragic succession of sacrifices, insanities, begins. The dramatist follows up each step in the rising intensities of the theme, with almost as much care as though he were a professional alienist. He builds his climax from the ground,—that is to say, from the family, which is always the first sacrifice in these mystical ideals of the Savior. The first of the scenes is laid at night before the house of Herakles, who listens to Megara within, singing her children to sleep:

> My children sleep, whose lives fulfil
>   The soul's tranquillity and trust;
>   While clothed in life's immortal dust
> The patient earth lies dark and still.
>
> All night they lie against my breast
>   And sleep, whose dream of life begins;
>   Before the time of strife and sins,
> Of tears and truth, they take their rest.

The next scene is laid before a tavern door, at dawn, where Herakles, in his sleepless wandering, stops to listen to the men and women carousing within. The poet is heard singing:

> I know not what it is appears
>   To us so worth the tragic task—
>   I know beneath his ribald masque
> Man's sightless face is gray with tears!

This tavern scene, to readers who know their drama of sacrifice and redemption, "is gray with tears"; and the more because, true to tradition, it is the woman who first recognizes the Savior, and putting an end to his anguish of doubt and self-distrust, draws him on to his fated duty of self-immolation. The messenger from Eurystheus arrives, while Herakles is parting from his wife and children, bringing the order to submit to the King of Argos and the gods, to perform the imposed labors, and to remain a subject man; but the action of the drama is interrupted here by a discussion between Creon and the poet, of the drama itself,—the dilemma of Herakles,—a discussion which is, in a way, more dramatic than the drama because it broadens the interest to embrace humanity altogether. Like the chorus of Okeanids in Æschylus, Creon sees the hero, and admires him, but doubts what good will come of him to man. He lays down the law, as a King and a Judge must:

> Crowds are but numbers; and at last I see
> There are not merely players of the game;
> There is not, high or low, only the one
> Sensible and substantial prize, to which
> The fiat of the world gives currency,
> And which, in various ways, is always won!
> There is, besides, the one, estranged, rare man,
> Whose light of life is splendid in the soul,
> Burns with a kind of glory in his strength,
> And gives such special grandeur to ambition
> That he will make no terms with fortune. . . .

Creon's reply to this "estranged, rare man," is that "all men living are not ever free," and that, if not pliant, they are broken. In a dozen lines, as terse as those of Æschylus, he sums up the law of life:

> Life, like a candle in a starless night,
> Brightens and burns, or flutters and is spent,
> As man's wise weakness spares the guarded flame,
> Or man's rash strength resolves in all despite
> To lift his torch into the spacious winds,
> To blaze his path across the darknesses,
> And force the elements to his own undoing . . .
> Only the strong go forward—and are slain!

Only the strong, defenseless, dare—and die!
Only the strong, free, fain, and fearless—fail!
Remember this! lest a worse thing than mere
Passion and ecstasy of poems befall you!

"Listen to me," says Mercury to Prometheus, at the close of the same dispute in Æschylus; "When misfortune overwhelms you, do not accuse fate; do not upbraid Zeus for striking you an unfair blow! Accuse no one but yourself! You know what threatens you! No surprise! No artifice! Your own folly alone entangles you in these meshes of misery which never release their prey." Creon, as a wise judge, was bound to repeat this warning, and the Poet—in the poem—makes but an unconvincing answer to it,—in fact, loses his temper altogether, until both parties end, as usual, by becoming abusive, in spite of Creon's self-control.

The action of the play repeats the motive of the dialogue. Herakles is exasperated by the insolence of the messenger to the point of striking him, and threatening to destroy his master. Then, overwhelmed by the mortification of having yielded to a degraded human passion, and of having sunk to the level of the servitude against which he had rebelled, he sets out, in fury and despair, to challenge the oracle of the God at Delphi.

The scene in the temple of Apollo at Delphi follows, where Herakles drags the Pythia from her shrine, and finds himself suddenly saluted as the God.

THE PYTHIA

Yours is the resurrection and the life!

HERAKLES

I am the God!

THE PYTHIA

There is no God but I!
I am whatever is!
I am despair and hope and love and hate,
Freedom and fate,

Life's plangent cry, Death's stagnant silences!
I am the earth and sea and sky,
The race, the runner and the goal;—
There is no thought nor thing but I!

To the ecstasy of the Pythia, the chorus responds in the
deepest tones of despair:

Have we not learned in bitterness to know
It matters nothing what we deem or do,
Whether we find the false or seek the true,
The profit of our lives is vain and small?
Have we not found, whatever price is paid,
Man is forever cheated and betrayed?
So shall the soul at last be cheated after all!

"Coward and weak and abject," is the rejoinder of
Herakles, who rises at last to the full consciousness of his
divine mission and of the price he must pay for it:

I am resolved! And I will stand apart,
Naked and perfect in my solitude
Aloft in the clear light perpetually,
Having afforded to the uttermost
The blood-stained, tear-drenched ransom of the soul!
Having by sacrifice, by sacrifice
Severed his bondage and redeemed the God!
The God I am indeed! For man is slain,
And in his death is God illustrious
And lives!

Then follows the Tenth Scene, the killing of the children.
On this, the poet has naturally thrown his greatest effort,
and his rank and standing as a dramatist must finally rest on
it. The reader had best read it for himself; it is hardly suited
to extracts or criticism; but perhaps, for his own convenience,
he had better read first the same scene as Euripides rendered
it. This is one of the rare moments of the dramatic art where
more depends on the audience than on the poet, for the
violence of the dramatic motive—the Sacrifice—carries the
action to a climax beyond expression in words. The ordinary
reader shrinks from it; the tension of the Greek drama over-

strains him; he is shocked at the sight of an insane man killing his children with arrows, and refuses to forgive the
dramatist for putting such a sight before him. Insanity has
always been the most violent of tragic motives, and the insanity of Herakles surpassed all other insanities, as the
Crucifixion of Christ surpassed all other crucifixions. Naturally, the person who objects to the Crucifixion as a *donnée*
of the drama is quite right in staying away from Oberammergau; but if he goes to Oberammergau, he must at least
try to understand what the drama means to the audience,
which feels—or should feel—itself englobed and incarnated
in it. The better-informed and the more accomplished the
critic may be, who reads the *Herakles* for the first time,
knowing nothing of the author, the more disconcerted he is
likely to be in reading it a second time. His first doubts of
the poet's knowledge or merits will be followed by doubts
of his own.

In one respect at least, as a question of dramatic construction, the doubt is well founded. Critics object to the *Herakles*
of Euripides that it consists of two separate dramas. The
same objection applies to the myth itself. The Savior—
whether Greek, or Christian, or Buddhist—always represents two distinct motives—the dramatic and the philosophic.
The dramatic climax in the Christian version is reached in
the Crucifixion; the philosophic climax, in the Resurrection
and Ascension; but the same personal ties connect the whole
action, and give it unity. This is not the case either with
Herakles or Buddha. The climax of the Greek version is
reached in the killing of the children, so far as the climax
is dramatic; while the philosophic climax—the attainment—
is proved by the freeing of Prometheus; and these two
données are dramatically wide apart,—in fact, totally uncon-
nected. Critics are Creons, and object to being tossed from
one motive to another, with an impatient sense of wrong. As
drama, one idea was capable of treatment; the other was not.

Probably the ordinary reader might find an advantage in
reading the Twelfth Scene of *Herakles*,—the Prometheus,—
as a separate poem. After the violent action of killing the
children, the freeing of Prometheus seems cold and uncon-

vincing; much less dramatic than the raising of Lazarus or even the Ascension. The Greek solution of this difficulty seems to be known only through fragments of the lost *Prometheus Unbound* of Æschylus, which are attached to most good editions of the poet. Lodge's solution is the necessary outcome of his philosophy, and is worth noting, if for no other reason, because it is personal to him,—or, more exactly, to his oriental and Schopenhauer idealism. Possibly—perhaps one might almost say probably—it is—both as logic and as history—the more correct solution; but on that point historians and metaphysicians are the proper sources of authority. Literature has no right to interfere, least of all to decide a question disputed since the origin of thought.

The *Prometheus Unbound*—the Twelfth Scene of *Herakles*—opens, then, upon the Attainment. Herakles has, by self-sacrifice, made himself—and the whole of humanity within him—one with the infinite Will which causes and maintains the universe. He has submitted to God by merging himself in God; he has, by his so-called labors, or miracles, raised humanity to the divine level. Æschylus puts in the mouth of Prometheus the claim to have freed man from the terrors of death and inspired him with blind hopes: "And a precious gift it is that you have given them," responds the chorus! Lodge puts the claim into the mouth of Herakles, and with it his own deification:

> Not in vain, out of the night of Hell,
> I drew the Hound of Hell, the ravening Death,
> Into the light of life, and held him forth
> Where the soul's Sun shed lightnings in his eyes,
> And he was like a thing of little meaning,
> Powerless and vain and nowise terrible.—
> While with my inmost heart I laughed aloud
> Into the blind and vacant face of Death,
> And cast him from me, so he fled away
> Screaming into the darkness whence he came!
> Nothing is vain of all that I have done!
> I have prevailed by labors, and subdued
> All that man is below his utmost truth,
> His inmost virtue, his essential strength,
> His soul's transcendent, one pre-eminence!

> Yea, I have brought into the soul's dominion
> All that I am!—and in the Master's House
> There is no strength of all my mortal being
> That does not serve him now; there is no aim,
> There is no secret which He does not know;
> There is no will save one, which is the Lord's!

The Church had said the same thing from the beginning; and the Greek, or oriental, or German philosophy changed the idea only in order to merge the universe in man instead of merging man in the universe. The Man attained, not by absorption of himself in the infinite, but by absorbing the infinite and finite together, in himself, as his own Thought, —his Will,—

> Giving to phases of the senseless flux,
> One after one, the soul's identity;

so that the philosophic climax of the *Prometheus Unbound* suddenly developed itself as a Prometheus bound in fetters only forged by himself; fetters of his own creation which never existed outside his own thought; and which fell from his limbs at once when he attained the force to will it. Prometheus is as much astonished at his own energy as though he were Creon, and, in a dazed and helpless way, asks what he is to do with it:

> I stand in the beginning, stand and weep.
> Here in the new, bleak light of liberty . . .
> And who am I, and what is liberty?

The answer to this question is that liberty, in itself, is the end,—the sufficient purpose of the will. This simple abstract of the simple thought is the theme of the last speech of Herakles on the last page of the drama:

> When the long life of all men's endless lives,
> Its gradual pregnancies, its pangs and throes,
> Its countless multitudes of perished Gods
> And outworn forms and spent humanities—
> When all the cosmic process of the past
> Stands in the immediate compass of our minds;
> When all is present to us, and all is known,

Even to the least, even to the uttermost,
Even to the first and last,—when, over all,
The widening circles of our thought expand
To infinite horizons everywhere,—
Then, tenoned in our foothold on the still,
Supernal, central pinnacle of being,
Shall we not look abroad and look within,
Over the total Universe, the vast,
Complex, and vital sum of force and form
And say in one, sufficient utterance,
The single, whole, transcendent Truth,—"I am!"

Not only philosophers, but also, and particularly, society itself, for many thousands of years, have waged bloody wars over these two solutions of the problem, as Prometheus and Herakles, Buddha and Christ, struggled with them in turn: but while neither solution has ever been universally accepted as convincing, that of Herakles has at least the advantage of being as old as the oldest, and as new as the newest philosophy,—as familiar as the drama of the Savior in all his innumerable forms,—as dramatic as it is familiar,—as poetic as it is dramatic,—and as simple as sacrifice. Paradox for paradox, the only alternative—Creon's human solution—is on the whole rather more paradoxical, and certainly less logical, than the superhuman solution of Herakles.

IX. The End

THIS is the whole story! What other efforts Lodge might have made, if he had lived into another phase of life, the effort he had made in this first phase was fatal and final. He rebelled against admitting it,—refused to see it,—yet was conscious that something hung over him which would have some tragic end. Possibly the encouragement of great literary success might have helped and stimulated the action of the heart, but he steeled himself against the illusion of success, and bore with apparent and outward indifference the total indifference of the public. As early as September 30, 1907, he wrote to Marjorie Nott: "I am, for one thing,—and to open a subject too vast to be even properly hinted at here—drawing to the close of the immense piece of work which has held and compelled me for a year past. The end looms large in my prospect and I am doing my best,—as you shall one day see. You, in fact, will be one of only a half-dozen, at best, who will see it. Which is, I imagine, all to my credit; and certainly as much as I reasonably want. What I have learned in the last year, through the work and the days, I shall never live to express; which is, I take it, illustrative—as so much else is—of the radical inferiority of writing your truth instead of being and living it,—namely, that by writing you can never, at all, keep abreast of it, but inevitably fall more and more behind as your pace betters. So I shall eventually perish having consciously failed, with (like Esmé) 'all my epigrams in me.' I wonder if Jesus consciously failed; I don't mean, of course, his total, obvious, practical failure, which the world for so long has so loudly recorded in blood and misery and ruin; I mean, did he have that consciousness of personal, solitary failure, which one can hardly, with one's utmost imagination, dissociate from the religious being of the soul of man? I believe he did,—though perhaps his mind was too simple and single,—as, to some extent, apparently, was the mind of Socrates. I sometimes think that the peasant of genius is, perhaps, more outside our comprehension than any other type of man. I perceive that I moon, vaguely moon,—and I shall soon be boring you."

In June 1908 he went abroad with his mother and father, for change and rest, but his letters show a growing sense of fatigue and effort. To his wife he wrote from the steamer, before landing in England:

"Our own voyage has come so warmly, so beautifully, back to me in these tranquil sea-days, our own so clear and fine and high adventure into strange new ways, our great adventure which is still in the making. It seems to me, that gay glad beginning, so alone and so one as we were, as something, now, inexpressibly candid and lovely, and humanly brave. And since then, how much, how really much of our young, our confident, and defiant boast,—flung, at that time, so happily, and so, after all, grandly, at large,—has been proved and greatened and amplified!"

From London, in July: "London has given me a new sense of itself, a flavor of romance and adventure, and the pervading sense of a great, dingy charm. Yes! it's all been quite new to me, and wonderfully pleasant; which just satisfactorily means, I surmise, that I come all new to it,—unimpeded by unimportant prejudices, and prepared vastly more than I was, for life in all its varieties and interests."

Later, from Paris: "I've lunched and dined everywhere; I've been to what theater there is, and chiefly I've drifted about the streets. And I find essentially that I seem to demand much more of life than I ever did, and in consequence take it all here with a less perfect gaiety and a more intense reflection. I feel matured to an incredible degree,—as if I did now quite know the whole of life; and when one's matured, really matured, there is, I imagine, not much ahead except work. So, back to you and to work I'm coming soon."

In August, again from Paris: "This whole Paris experience has been queer and wonderful. Joe and you have been with me in all the familiar streets and places, and my youth has appeared to me in colors richer and more comprehensible than ever before. . . ."

He came home, and brought out *Herakles* in November. In reply to a letter of congratulation from Marjorie Nott, he wrote to her, on December 17: "Thank you! You know that I write for myself, of course, and then, as things are in fact, just for you and so few others. Which is enough! and sees me, so to speak, admirably through. Well! I'm glad you like it, and if you ever have anything more to say of it, you know, my dear, that I want to hear it. You'll find it, of course, long; and you'll strike, I guess, sandy places. Perhaps, though, there are some secrets in it, and some liberties. . . ."

Six months afterwards he took up the theme again, in the last few days of his life, making Marjorie Nott his confidante, as he had done since childhood.

He wrote from Nahant July 31, 1909:

"Before all else I must thank you, my dear, for the grave and deep emotions roused within me by your letter with its fine, clear note of serious trust and loving favor towards me.

Than just that, there isn't for me anything better to be had. I derive from it precisely the intimate encouragement which one so perpetually wants and so exceptionally gets. Moreover, in all your letter I don't find a word with which I can possibly disagree. It occurs to me that there may have been, in my pages to you, some note of complaint, which, in sober truth, I didn't intend and don't feel. Every man of us has the Gods to complain of; every man of us, sooner or later, in some shape, experiences the tragedy of life. But that, too obviously, is nothing to cry about, for the tragedy of life is one thing, and my tragedy or yours, his or hers, is another. All of us must suffer in the general human fate, and some must suffer of private wrongs. I've none such to complain of. At all events, I don't, as I said before, disagree with a word of your letter, but I do, my dear, find it dreadfully vague. You surely can't doubt that I deeply realize the value of human communion of any sort; but that doesn't take me far toward getting it. As I understand your letter it says to me: 'Well! you might get more and better if you tried more and better!' Perhaps! at any rate, goodness knows I do try—and more and more—as best I can. And surely I don't complain of the solitude, which has, of course, its high value; but I do, inevitably, well know it's there. I'll spare you more."

His letters to Langdon Mitchell expressed the same ideas, with such slight difference of form as one naturally uses in writing to a man rather than to a woman:

TO LANGDON MITCHELL

WASHINGTON (*Spring, 1906*)

Thank you, my dear Langdon, for your kind and so welcome letters. I want to thank you for your generous offer of help should I try my hand at a play. . . .

I should have but one personal advantage in writing a play, namely a genuine indifference as to its being played or being successful if played. I call this an advantage because it eliminates the possibility of my mind being disturbed and my powers consequently impaired by any influences external to myself. I become so increasingly convinced that precisely

as perfection of being consists in a perfectly transparent
reality, so artistic perfection depends upon the degree to
which the artist speaks his own words in his own voice and
is unhampered by the vocabulary of convention and the
megaphone of oratory—which exists and could exist only on
the theory of an omnipresent multitude. Let any man speak
his own word and he is as original as Shakespeare and as
permanently interesting as Plato. The whole core of the
struggle, for ourselves and for art, is to emerge from the
envelope of thoughts and words and deeds which are not
our own, but the laws and conventions and traditions formed
of a kind of composite of other men's ideas and emotions and
prejudices. Excuse this dissertation! . . .

Your first letter interested me profoundly, for my winter
has been curiously similar to yours as you describe it. I have
had very poignantly the same sense of growth, of a revelation
and of a consequent observable process of maturity. When
shall we meet and make some exchange of thoughts? It seems
absurd that so great a majority of my life should be spent
without you.

I've been asked (peals of Homeric and scornful laughter
from Mitchell) to deliver the poem at the Phi Beta Kappa in
Cambridge this spring—June. (Mitchell chokes with mirth
and shows symptoms of strangulation. Is patted on the back
and recovers. Lodge then good-naturedly continues:) You
observe how low I've sunk and for a punishment for your
superior sneers I'm going to send you my poem for the occasion to read and criticize. (Mitchell sourly admits that the
joke is not entirely on Lodge.) I shall send it soon, in fact
it may arrive any day. So I hope that your condition of health
is improved.

WASHINGTON, 2346 MASSACHUSETTS AVE.
(*Winter, 1908*)

MY DEAR, DEAR LANGDON,—I shall never have words and
ways enough to thank you for your letter. What it meant,
what it means to me—the encouragement, the life, the hope—
and above all the high felicities of friendship—all these

things and other and more things, which you, my dear friend, of your abundance so liberally afford, have enriched and fortified me beyond expression. . . .

My *Herakles* is done to the last three scenes and hastens somewhat to its end. I won't write you about it, for there is too much to say and finally you'll have to read it—however much it's long and dull.

It's too, too bad you should have been having such a devil's time with this world. But, good heavens, I know what it is to wait; how intolerable it may become sometimes just holding on. But the muscles of patience and that true daily courage which patience implies are fine muscles to have well developed even at some cost—isn't this so, dear man? The living bread and the consecrated wine must be earned and eaten day by day and day by day; we are not made free of perfection by any sudden moment's violence of virtue; the key of the gate of Paradise is not purchased in any single payment, however heavy; the travail of God's nativity within us is gradual and slow and laborious. It is the sustained courage, the long stern patience, the intensest daily labor, the clear, perpetual vigilance of thought, the great resolve, tranquil and faithful in its strength,—it is these things, it is the work, in short, the wonderful slow work of man about the soul's business, which accomplishes constantly—as we both know so well—some real thing which makes us, however gradually, other and nobler and greater than we are, because precisely it makes us more than we are. All of which you know better than I, for better than I you do the work and reap the result. But it's a truth nonetheless which takes time to learn—if it is ever learned at all—for the temptation to think that the reward, the advance is tomorrow, and that Paradise is in the next county, and that both can be got by some adventurous extravagance, some single, tense deed of excellence, is very great, I imagine, to us all. We never realize quite at once that only patience can see us through, and that if the moment is not eternity and the place not Paradise it must be just because we are busy about what is not, in the true strict test, our real concern.

WASHINGTON, 2346 MASSACHUSETTS AVE.
(*Spring, 1908*)

O! MY DEAR LANGDON,—Your letter thrilled and moved
me beyond expression. If I do not thank you for it, it is
because it has roused within me emotions nobler and more
profound than gratitude; and it is in the glamor and power
of these emotions—which will remain permanently interfused
with all that I am—that I now write to you. I tried to read
your letter aloud to B. but it moved me so much and to such
depths that I was unable to continue. This may seem strange
to you, for you will not have thought of all that it means to
me; you will not have been aware of the bare fact that,
apart from the immense inward satisfaction which the effort
of expression must always bring, your letter is just all of
real value I shall get for *Herakles*. And it is more, my dear
friend, far more than enough! That is certain. I speak to you
with an open heart and mind, which your letter has liberated, restored, revived, nourished and sustained. You know
as well as I how passionately we have understanding and
sympathy for what is best and noblest within us. The conception of God the Father, I believe, came from this longing
in the human heart. But the habit of solitude and silence,
which in this queer country, we perforce assume, ends by
making us less attentive to the heart's need, and it is only
when we are fed that we realize how consuming was our
hunger. For all that is not what we at best and most truly
are, we find recognition enough, but the very soul within
us is like a solitary stranger in a strange land—and your letter
was to me like a friendly voice speaking the words of my
own tongue and like the lights of welcome. It is perhaps
your criticisms that I rejoice in most, for I know them to
be valid and just. I feel the faults you find as you feel them,
I believe; and I keep alive the hope that I may learn to feel
them with sufficient force and clearness to correct them. It
would be of infinite advantage to me if you would, someday, go over the whole thing with me in detail. Nothing
could so much improve my chances of better work in the
future. In fact it would be to me the most essential assist-

ance that I could possibly receive; for if I had you there to put your finger on the dreadful Saharas and other undeniable shortcomings, it would illuminate my understanding as nothing else could do. . . .

Just one thing more. It was a noble act of friendship for you to write me that letter amid all the labors of your present days. Thanks for that with all my heart.

With this single condition, the happy life went on, filled with affection and humor to the end, as his last letters tell:

TO HIS MOTHER

NAHANT, *June 13, 1909*

Our train was seven hours late to Boston, which fact, when in the East River, after four hours of open sea, at 6:30 A.M., and by the dull glare of the hot sun through a white fog, it first gradually and at last with agonizing completeness possessed my mind, produced in that sensitive organ emotions too vivid to be here described.

I had retired to rest reconciled, or at least steeled, to the thought of a two hours' delay in our journey; and when, on waking (abysmal moment!) in the squalor of my berth I found that the fog had changed the two hours' delay to seven, I felt in the first shock other emotions besides surprise. . . . Before emerging in unwashed squalor from my section, I had determined, however, in view of everything, to suppress my feelings and to be, for my poor good children and their nurses, just the requisite hope, cheer, and comfort—and this determination (it was the one consoling event of the dreadful day) I did, to the end, successfully carry out. Well, when at last from that dreadful boat we were jerkily drawn once more onto firm land, we fell of course inevitably into the mean hands of the N. Y., N. H., and H. R. R., which characteristically decided that it would, of course, be both cheaper and easier, to give us, instead of the dining car to which—Heaven knows—we seemed entitled, a "fifteen minutes for refreshments" at New Haven; and there, at ten o'clock, in the heartbreaking, dingy dreadfulness of the wait-

ing-room, we—that is the passengers of that luckless train—
thronged four deep round a vastly rectangular barrier like a
shop-counter, girdled, for the public, by high, greasy, "fixed"
stools, covered with inedible pseudo-foods under fly-blown
glass bells, and defended, so to speak, by an insufficient and
driven horde of waiters and waitresses. You can imagine
what chance there was *dans cette galère* for the babes!
Fräulein and the nurse secured, by prodigious exertions, and
wonderfully drank, cups of a dim gray fluid which they
believed to be coffee, while I and the children got back to
the train with some apples, oranges, and sinister sandwiches,
which all, later, and with every accompanying degradation
of drip and slop and grease, all mixed with car dirt, we did
devour,—to avoid starvation. I was still further, however,
to be in a position to appreciate the exquisite benefits of
a railroad monopoly, for when at last our interminable
journey did end at Boston, we found, of course, no porters!
And with a heavy microscope, book, coat, and cane, my
three poor unceasingly good, weary, and toy-laden children,
and my two weary and child-laden nurses, were, perforce,
obliged to leave our four bags on the platform, in charge of
the well-feed train porter, to be immediately "called for" by
Moore's man. Which man, young Moore himself, I duly
found and straitly charged about the four bags, as well as
about my seven pieces in the "van." Then, somewhat
cheered, and having renewed to Moore (who, as you will
presently perceive, I have come to regard as an abysmal
though quite well-intentioned young ass) my charge as to
the four bags, I drove off to the North Station, stopping *en
route* merely to reward my lambs for their exemplary conduct by a rubber toy apiece. Well! at that point I think you
will agree with me that the wariest might have been lulled
into a sense that the worst was over and plain sailing ahead.
Such at least was my condition of confidence, and though
in the North Station waiting-room our bedraggled, dirty,
wornout company waited a full hour for Moore and the
trunks, I just put it down as evidence that the benefits of
the railroad we had just left were still accumulating, and
hoped on. And then Moore arrived—arrived, having just

merely forgotten the four bags—having in short left them—
one of them containing Uncle Henry's manuscript and all
of mine, both irreplaceable—just there on the platform where
I couldn't have not left them. Well! for a moment I didn't
"keep up" a bit and addressed to Moore a few—how inadequate!—"feeling words." I then dispatched him back to
recover the bags, packed my poor babes into the 3:20 for
Lynn,—trusting, as I had to, to Fräulein's ability to get them
out at Lynn,—and remained myself at the North Station,
where I waited for Moore for exactly one hour and fifteen
minutes. My state of mind I won't describe. At the end of
that vigil, however, I mounted—always with microscope,
book, coat, and cane—in a taxicab, went to the South Station, found Moore, and after an interval of almost panic,
when I thought all the manuscripts were lost for good, did,
by dint of energy at last—thank Heaven—find the bags. . . .
Well! I felt then a little "gone" and went therefore to the
Club, had a drink and a sandwich, just in time, and got, at
last, to Nahant, at about seven o'clock, to find that, by some
mistake, they had given me, for the nurse's bag, the bag of
a total stranger. In the nurse's bag was, beside her own effects,
some of Helena's, including a silver mug; and so as I lay, at
last, in my bath, I heard, strangely concordant with my whole
horrible day's experience, Fräulein and Hedwig mourning,
in shrill German, the loss. So Monday I go to town to do
some errands and to find if possible the damned bag. The
children are none the worse for the journey and are already
benefited by the good air. The house is incredibly clean and
charming and we are delighted with it.

TUCKANUCK, *July 1909*

I am having the most beautiful days—endless air and sea
and sun and beauty, and best of all with Langdon's splendid
companionship. It's all just what I've wanted and needed
for so long. I have shown Langdon my latest work,—*The
Noctambulist,* etc.,—what I read to you in Washington,—
and he is most splendidly encouraging. He feels as strongly
as I could wish that I have made, both in thought and form,

a really new and large and valid departure. Which endlessly cheers me, as you will believe. We talk together of everything first and last, off and on, but chiefly on, all day and night with the exception of many hours of sleep. I do no work and just take easily all my present blessings as greedily as I can.

Langdon Mitchell was one of the half-dozen readers, as he said, for whose approbation he wrote, and this last companionship with him at Tuckanuck in July gave Lodge keen pleasure. On returning to Nahant he wrote to Sturgis Bigelow, who was then ill in Paris:

"I've just returned home from Tuckanuck, browned to the most beautiful color by ten glorious days of sun. Langdon and I went together, and except for one day of warm, sweet rain, and one morning of fog,—which cleared splendidly in time for the bath,—we had weather of uninterrupted magnificence. Immeasurable sky and sea and sun, warm water, hot clean sand, clear light, transparent air,—Tuckanuck at its perfect best. I've returned made over in mind and body, feeling better in every way than I've felt since I can remember. For this I have to thank you, for Tuckanuck,—and Langdon for his wonderful, interesting, vital companionship. Together—with every variety of the best talk, the finest communion—we lived all day and night long immersed in the beneficent elements, the prodigious light and air, the sounding, sparkling, flowing sea; and the bathing was different and better every day. The sea showed us all its loveliest moods. On one day it was stretched and smooth to the horizon, drawn away from the shore, on a light north wind, in endless fine blue wrinkles, with just the merest crisp, small ripple on the beach. Another day, fresh southwest wind, with a fine, high, lively, light surf. And even on one day the biggest waves of the season—too big for comfort. Well! it was all glorious;—you will understand; we have had it just like that so often together. Indeed your presence was the one thing we longed for, and didn't have, throughout our whole visit. There was hardly an hour down there when I didn't think of you and long for you. . . . Never had I

more needed the restorative magic of nature and companionship than when I set forth for that blessed island, and never
did it more wonderfully work upon me its beneficent spell.
To judge by the way I feel now, I haven't known what it
was to be really rested and well since I finished *Herakles*. I
feel pages more of enthusiasm at the end of my pen, but I
will spare you. I took down to the island with me my winter's work, which has taken the shape of a volume of poems
ready for publication, and read it to Langdon, who, thank
goodness, felt high praise for them—more enthusiastic approval, indeed, than I had dared to hope for."

Langdon Mitchell's encouragement and sympathy were
pathetically grateful to him, so rare was the voice of an impartial and competent judge. He wrote to his wife in the
warmest appreciation of it.

"I have been having such good days! Langdon is of course
the utmost delight to me, and the presence of companionship day by day is fresh and wonderful to me beyond
measure. Also the weather in general has been glorious, and
the whole spectacle of the world clothed in light and beauty.
I lead a sane and hygienic life. We go to bed before twelve,
and sleep all we can. We breakfast, read, write perhaps an
occasional letter, talk for long, fine, clear stretches of thought,
and, regardless of time, play silly but active games on the
grass, swim, bask in the sun, sail, and talk, and read aloud,
and read to ourselves, and talk, and talk. . . . I'm getting
into splendid condition."

When his father, fagged by the long fatigues of the tariff
session, returned North, they went back to Tuckanuck together in August, and there he had the pleasure of a visit
from a new and enthusiastic admirer, Mr. Alfred Brown,
lecturer and critic, who brought him for the first time a
sense of possible appreciation beyond his personal friends.
He never alluded to his own symptoms. Even his father,
though on the watch, noticed only that he spared himself,
and took more frequent rests. To Sturgis Bigelow he wrote
of his anxiety about both Bigelow and his father, whom, he

said, he was helping to "get his much-needed rest and re-
cuperation, and I think he is getting them, both, good and
plenty, but the knowledge that you will probably not get
here this season makes the dear island seem singularly deserted. . . . It's all doing him good, and what is more, he
thinks it is. . . . I read a good deal, and take my swim, and
an occasional sail. Also, after a month's vacation during
which I haven't written a line, I've now begun again, and
write and meditate for four or five hours every day . . . so
that life flows evenly and quietly and cheerfully. Still, lacking the stimulus of your prospective arrival, I shan't be sorry
to get back to my Pussy and my babes."

This seems to have been one of the last letters he wrote.
It was mailed at Nantucket, August 18, and on the nineteenth he was seized at night by violent indigestion, probably
due to some ptomaine poison. The next day he was better.
The distress returned on the night of the twentieth. Twenty-
four hours of suffering ensued; then the heart suddenly
failed and the end came.

THESE PAPERS on Henry James by T. S. Eliot appeared in *The Little Review* of August 1918, and have never been reprinted by Mr. Eliot. The whole number was devoted to James, who had died in 1916.

At this time it still seemed natural for some of the most gifted of American writers to prefer to live in Europe, and Henry James, who had been there since the eighties, was of special interest to them. Ezra Pound—who also contributed to this number of *The Little Review*—had gone abroad in 1908 and remained; and T. S. Eliot went in 1914 and eventually became a British citizen.

T. S. ELIOT

HENRY JAMES

I. *In Memory*

HENRY JAMES has been dead for some time. The current of English literature was not appreciably altered by his work during his lifetime; and James will probably continue to be regarded as the extraordinarily clever but negligible curiosity. The current hardly matters; it hardly matters that very few people will read James. The "influence" of James hardly matters: to be influenced by a writer is to have a chance inspiration from him; or to take what one wants; or to see things one has overlooked; there will always be a few intelligent people to understand James, and to be understood by a few intelligent people is all the influence a man requires. What matters least of all is his place in such a Lord Mayor's show as Mr. Chesterton's procession of Victorian Literature. The point to be made is that James has an importance which has nothing to do with what came before him or what may happen after him; an importance which has been overlooked on both sides of the Atlantic.

I do not suppose that anyone who is not an American can *properly* appreciate James. James's best American figures in the novels, in spite of their trim, definite outlines, the economy of strokes, have a fullness of existence and an ex-

ternal ramification of relationship which a European reader
might not easily suspect. The Bellegarde family, for instance,
are merely good outline sketches by an intelligent foreigner;
when more is expected of them, in the latter part of the
story, they jerk themselves into only melodramatic violence.
In all appearance Tom Tristram is an even slighter sketch.
Europeans can recognize him; they have seen him, known
him, have even penetrated the Occidental Club; but no European has the Tom Tristram element in his composition,
has anything of Tristram from his first visit to the Louvre
to his final remark that Paris is the only place where a white
man can live. It is the final perfection, the consummation of
an American to become, not an Englishman, but a European—something which no born European, no person of any
European nationality, can become. Tom is one of the failures,
one of nature's misfortunes, in this process. Even General
Packard, C. P. Hatch, and Miss Kitty Upjohn have a reality
which Claire de Cintré misses. Noémie, of course, is perfect,
but Noémie is a result of the intelligent eye; her existence is
a triumph of the intelligence, and it does not extend beyond
the frame of the picture.

For the English reader, much of James's criticism of America must merely be something taken for granted. English
readers can appreciate it for what it has in common with criticism everywhere, with Flaubert in France and Turgenev in
Russia. Still, it should have for the English an importance beyond the work of these writers. There is no English equivalent for James, and at least he writes in this language. As a
critic, no novelist in our language can approach James; there
is not even any large part of the reading public which knows
what the word "critic" means. (The usual definition of a critic
is a writer who cannot "create"—perhaps a reviewer of books.)
James was emphatically not a successful *literary* critic. His
criticism of books and writers is feeble. In writing of a novelist, he occasionally produces a valuable sentence out of
his own experience rather than in judgment of the subject.
The rest is charming talk, or gentle commendation. Even
in handling men whom he could, one supposes, have carved
joint from joint—Emerson, or Norton—his touch is uncertain;

there is a desire to be generous, a political motive, an admission (in dealing with American writers) that under the circumstances this was the best possible, or that it has fine qualities. His father was here keener than he. Henry was not a literary critic.

He was a critic who preyed not upon ideas, but upon living beings. It is criticism which is in a very high sense creative. The characters, the best of them, are each a distinct success of creation: Daisy Miller's small brother is one of these. Done in a clean, flat drawing, each is extracted out of a reality of its own, substantial enough; everything given is true for that individual; but what is given is chosen with great art for its place in a general scheme. The general scheme is not one character, nor a group of characters in a plot or merely in a crowd. The focus is a situation, a relation, an atmosphere, to which the characters pay tribute, but being allowed to give only what the writer wants. The real hero, in any of James's stories, is a social entity of which men and women are constituents. It is, in *The Europeans,* that particular conjunction of people at the Wentworth house, a situation in which several memorable scenes are merely timeless parts, only occurring necessarily in succession. In this aspect, you can say that James is dramatic; as what Pinero and Mr. Jones used to do for a large public, James does for the intelligent. It is in the chemistry of these subtle substances, these curious precipitates and explosive gases which are suddenly formed by the contact of mind with mind, that James is unequaled. Compared with James's, other novelists' characters seem to be only accidentally in the same book. Naturally, there is something terrible, as disconcerting as a quicksand, in this discovery, though it only becomes absolutely dominant in such stories as *The Turn of the Screw.* It is partly foretold in Hawthorne, but James carried it much farther. And it makes the reader, as well as the personae, uneasily the victim of a merciless clairvoyance.

James's critical genius comes out most tellingly in his mastery over, his baffling escape from, Ideas; a mastery and an escape which are perhaps the last test of a superior intelligence. He had a mind so fine that no idea could violate it.

Englishmen, with their uncritical admiration (in the present age) for France, like to refer to France as the Home of Ideas; a phrase which, if we could twist it into truth, or at least a compliment, ought to mean that in France ideas are very severely looked after; not allowed to stray, but preserved for the inspection of civic pride in a Jardin des Plantes, and frugally dispatched on occasions of public necessity. England, on the other hand, if it is not the Home of Ideas, has at least become infested with them in about the space of time within which Australia has been overrun by rabbits. In England ideas run wild and pasture on the emotions; instead of thinking with our feelings (a very different thing) we corrupt our feelings with ideas; we produce the political, the emotional idea, evading sensation and thought. George Meredith (the disciple of Carlyle) was fertile in ideas; his epigrams are a facile substitute for observation and inference. Mr. Chesterton's brain swarms with ideas; I see no evidence that it thinks. James in his novels is like the best French critics in maintaining a point of view, a viewpoint untouched by the parasite idea. He is the most intelligent man of his generation.

The fact of being everywhere a foreigner was probably an assistance to his native wit. Since Byron and Landor, no Englishman appears to have profited much from living abroad. We have had Birmingham seen from Chelsea, but not Chelsea seen (really *seen*) from Baden or Rome. There are advantages, indeed, in coming from a large flat country which no one wants to visit: advantages which both Turgenev and James enjoyed. These advantages have not won them recognition. Europeans have preferred to take their notion of the Russian from Dostoevsky and their notion of the American from, let us say, Frank Norris if not O. Henry. Thus, they fail to note that there are many kinds of their fellow-countrymen, and that most of these kinds, similarly to the kinds of *their* fellow-countrymen, are stupid; likewise with Americans. Americans also have encouraged this fiction of a general type, a formula or idea, usually the predaceous square-jawed or thin-lipped. They like to be told that they are a race of commercial buccaneers. It gives them some-

thing easily escaped from, moreover, when they wish to reject America. Thus the novels of Frank Norris have succeeded in both countries; though it is curious that the most
valuable part of *The Pit* is its satire (quite unconscious, I
believe; Norris was simply representing faithfully the life
he knew) of Chicago society after business hours. All this
show of commercialism which Americans like to present to
the foreign eye James quietly waves aside; and in pouncing
upon his fellow-countryman after the stock exchange has
closed, in tracking down his vices and absurdities across the
Atlantic, and exposing them in their highest flights of dignity
or culture, James may be guilty of what will seem to most
Americans scandalously improper behavior. It is too much
to expect them to be grateful. And the British public, had it
been more aware, would hardly have been more comfortable
confronted with a smile which was so far from breaking into
the British laugh. Henry James's death, if it had been more
taken note of, should have given considerable relief "on both
sides of the Atlantic," and cemented the Anglo-American
Entente.

II. *The Hawthorne Aspect*

MY OBJECT is not to discuss critically even one phase or
period of James, but merely to provide a note, *Beitrage*, toward any attempt to determine his antecedents, affinities,
and "place." Presumed that James's relation to Balzac, to
Turgenev, to anyone else on the continent is known and
measured—I refer to Mr. Hueffer's book and to Mr. Pound's
article—and presumed that his relation to the Victorian novel
is negligible, it is not concluded that James was simply a
clever young man who came to Europe and improved himself, but that the soil of his origin contributed a flavor dis-
criminable after transplantation in his latest fruit. We may
even draw the instructive conclusion that this flavor was
precisely improved and given its chance, not worked off, by
transplantation. If there is this strong native taste, there will
probably be some relation to Hawthorne; and if there is any
relation to Hawthorne, it will probably help us to analyze
the flavor of which I speak.

When we say that James is "American," we must mean
that this "flavor" of his, and also more exactly definable
qualities, are more or less diffused throughout the vast continent rather than anywhere else; but we cannot mean that
this flavor and these qualities have found literary expression
throughout the nation, or that they permeate the work of Mr.
Frank Norris or Mr. Booth Tarkington. The point is that
James is positively a continuator of the New England genius;
that there is a New England genius, which has discovered
itself only in a very small number of people in the middle of
the nineteenth century—and which is *not* significantly present in the writings of Miss Sara Orne Jewett, Miss Eliza
White, or the Bard of Appledore, whose name I forget. I
mean whatever we associate with certain purlieus of Boston,
with Concord, Salem, and Cambridge, Mass.: notably Emerson, Thoreau, Hawthorne, and Lowell. None of these men,
with the exception of Hawthorne, is individually very important; they all can, and perhaps ought to be made to look
very foolish; but there is a "something" there, a dignity, about
Emerson, for example, which persists after we have perceived
the taint of commonness about some English contemporary,
as, for instance, the more intelligent, better-educated, more
alert Matthew Arnold. Omitting such men as Bryant and
Whittier as absolutely plebeian, we can still perceive this
halo of dignity around the men I have named, and also
Longfellow, Margaret Fuller and her crew, Bancroft and
Motley, the faces of (later) Norton and Child pleasantly
shaded by the Harvard elms. One distinguishing mark of
this distinguished world was very certainly leisure; and importantly not in all cases a leisure given by money, but insisted upon. There seems no easy reason why Emerson or
Thoreau or Hawthorne should have been men of leisure; it
seems odd that the New England conscience should have
allowed them leisure; yet they *would* have it, sooner or later.
That is really one of the finest things about them, and sets
a bold frontier between them and a world which will at any
price avoid leisure, a world in which Theodore Roosevelt is
a patron of the arts. An interesting document of this latter
world is the *Letters* of a nimbly dull poet of a younger gen-

eration, of Henry James's generation, Richard Watson Gilder, Civil Service Reform, Tenement House Commission, Municipal Politics.

Of course leisure in a metropolis, with a civilized society (the society of Boston was and is quite uncivilized but refined beyond the point of civilization), with exchange of ideas and critical standards, would have been better; but these men could not provide the metropolis, and were right in taking the leisure under possible conditions.

Precisely this leisure, this dignity, this literary aristocracy, this unique character of a society in which the men of letters were also of the best people, clings to Henry James. It is some consciousness of this kinship which makes him so tender and gentle in his appreciations of Emerson, Norton, and the beloved Ambassador. With Hawthorne, as much the most important of these people in any question of literary art, his relation is more personal; but no more in the case of Hawthorne than with any of the other figures of the background is there any consideration of influence. James owes little, very little, to anyone; there are certain writers whom he consciously studied, of whom Hawthorne was not one; but in any case his relation to Hawthorne is on another plane from his relation to Balzac, for example. The influence of Balzac, not on the whole a good influence, is perfectly evident in some of the earlier novels; the influence of Turgenev is vaguer, but more useful. That James was, at a certain period, more moved by Balzac, that he followed him with more concentrated admiration, is clear from the tone of his criticism of that writer compared with the tone of his criticism of either Turgenev or Hawthorne. In *French Poets and Novelists,* though an early work, James's attitude toward Balzac is exactly that of having been very much attracted from his orbit, perhaps very wholesomely stimulated at an age when almost any foreign stimulus may be good, and having afterwards reacted from Balzac, though not to the point of injustice. He handles Balzac shrewdly and fairly. From the essay on Turgenev there is on the other hand very little to be got but a touching sense of appreciation; from the essay on Flaubert even less. The charming study of Haw-

thorne is quite different from any of these. The first conspicuous quality in it is tenderness, the tenderness of a man
who had escaped too early from an environment to be warped
or thwarted by it, who had escaped so effectually that he
could afford the gift of affection. At the same time he places
his finger, now and then, very gently, on some of Hawthorne's more serious defects as well as his limitations.

"The best things come, as a general thing, from the talents that are members of a group; every man works better
when he has companions working in the same line, and
yielding the stimulus of suggestion, comparison, emulation."
Though when he says that "there was manifestly a strain
of generous indolence in his [Hawthorne's] composition"
he is understating the fault of laziness for which Hawthorne
can chiefly be blamed. But gentleness is needed in criticizing
Hawthorne, a necessary thing to remember about whom is
precisely the difficult fact that the soil which produced him
with his essential flavor is the soil which produced, just as
inevitably, the environment which stunted him.

In one thing alone Hawthorne is more solid than James:
he had a very acute historical sense. His erudition in the
small field of American colonial history was extensive, and
he made most fortunate use of it. Both men had that sense
of the past which is peculiarly American, but in Hawthorne
this sense exercised itself in a grip on the past itself; in James
it is a sense of the sense. This, however, need not be dwelt
upon here. The really vital thing, in finding any personal
kinship between Hawthorne and James, is what James
touches lightly when he says that "the fine thing in Hawthorne is that he cared for the deeper psychology, and
that, in his way, he tried to become familiar with it."
There are other points of resemblance, not directly included
under this, but this one is of the first importance. It is, in
fact, almost enough to ally the two novelists, in comparison
with whom almost all others may be accused of either superficiality or aridity. I am not saying that this "deeper
psychology" is essential, or that it can always be had without loss of other qualities, or that a novel need be any the
less a work of art without it. It is a definition; and it sepa-

rates the two novelists at once from the English contemporaries of either. Neither Dickens nor Thackeray, certainly,
had the smallest notion of the "deeper psychology"; George
Eliot had a kind of heavy intellect for it (Tito) but all her
genuine feeling went into the visual realism of *Amos Barton*.
On the continent it is known; but the method of Stendhal
or of Flaubert is quite other. A situation is for Stendhal
something deliberately constructed, often an illustration.
There is a bleakness about it, vitalized by force rather than
feeling, and its presentation is definitely visual. Hawthorne
and James have a kind of sense, a receptive medium, which
is not of sight. Not that they fail to make you *see*, so far as
necessary, but sight is not the essential sense. They perceive
by antennae; and the "deeper psychology" is here. The
deeper psychology indeed led Hawthorne to some of his ab-
surdest and most characteristic excesses; it was forever tailing
off into the fanciful, even the allegorical, which is a lazy
substitute for profundity. The fancifulness is the "strain of
generous indolence," the attempt to get the artistic effect
by meretricious means. On this side a critic might seize hold
of *The Turn of the Screw*, a tale about which I have many
doubts; but the actual working out of this is different from
Hawthorne's, and we are not interested in approximation
of the two men on the side of their weakness. The point is
that Hawthorne was acutely sensitive to the situation; that
he did grasp character through the relation of two or more
persons to each other; and this is what no one else, except
James, has done. Furthermore, he does establish, as James
establishes, a solid atmosphere, and he does, in his quaint
way, get New England, as James gets a larger part of America, and as none of their respective contemporaries get anything above a village or two, or a jungle. Compare, with
anything that any English contemporary could do, the situation which Hawthorne sets up in the relation of Dimmesdale
and Chillingworth. Judge Pyncheon and Clifford, Hepzibah
and Phoebe, are similarly achieved by their relation to each
other; Clifford, for one, being simply the intersection of a
relation to three other characters. The only dimension in
which Hawthorne could expand was the past, his present

being so narrowly barren. It is a great pity, with his remarkable gift of observation, that the present did not offer him more to observe. But he is the one English-writing predecessor of James whose characters are *aware* of each other, the one whose novels were in any deep sense a criticism of even a slight civilization; and here is something more definite and closer than any derivation we can trace from Richardson or Marivaux.

The fact that the sympathy with Hawthorne is most felt in the last of James's novels, *The Sense of the Past,* makes me the more certain of its genuineness. In the meantime, James has been through a much more elaborate development than poor Hawthorne ever knew. Hawthorne, with his very limited culture, was not exposed to any bewildering variety of influences. James, in his astonishing career of self-improvement, touches Hawthorne most evidently at the beginning and end of his course; at the beginning, simply as a young New Englander of letters[1]; at the end, with almost a gesture of approach. *Roderick Hudson* is the novel of a clever and expanding young New Englander; immature, but just coming out to a self-consciousness where Hawthorne never arrived at all. Compared with *Daisy Miller* or *The Europeans* or *The American* its critical spirit is very crude. But *The Marble Faun* (*Transformation*), the only European novel of Hawthorne, is of Cimmerian opacity; the mind of its author was closed to new impressions though with all its Walter Scott-Mysteries of Udolpho upholstery the old man does establish a kind of solid moral atmosphere which the young James does not get. James in *Roderick Hudson* does very little better with Rome than Hawthorne, and as he confesses in the later preface, rather fails with Northampton.[2]

[1]The James family came from Albany, and Henry James was born in New York City. His residence in New England, which was broken by trips abroad, was mostly confined to the years between 1860 and 1875, when James was, however, in the formative period between seventeen and thirty-two. E. W.

[2]Was Hawthorne at all in his mind here? In criticizing the *House of the Seven Gables* he says "it renders, to an initiated reader, the impression of a summer afternoon in an elm-shaded New England

He does in the later edition tone down the absurdities of Roderick's sculpture a little, the pathetic Thirst and the gigantic Adam; Mr. Striker remains a failure, the judgment of a young man consciously humorizing, too suggestive of *Martin Chuzzlewit*. The generic resemblance to Hawthorne is in the occasional heavy facetiousness of the style, the tedious whimsicality how different from the exactitude of *The American Scene,* the verbalism. He too much identifies himself with Rowland, does not see through the solemnity he has created in that character, commits the cardinal sin of failing to "detect" one of his own characters. The failure to create a situation is evident: with Christina and Mary, each nicely adjusted, but never quite set in relation to each other. The interest of the book for our present purpose is what he does *not* do in the Hawthorne way, in the instinctive attempt to get at something larger, which will bring him to the same success with much besides.

The interest in the "deeper psychology," the observation, and the sense for situation, developed from book to book, culminate in *The Sense of the Past* (by no means saying that this is his best), uniting with other qualities both personal and racial. James's greatness is apparent both in his capacity for development as an artist and his capacity for keeping his mind alive to the changes in the world during twenty-five years. It is remarkable (for the mastery of a span of American history) that the man who did the Wentworth family in the eighties could do the Bradhams in the hundreds. In *The Sense of the Past* the Midmores belong to the same generation as the Bradhams; Ralph belongs to the same race as the Wentworths, indeed as the Pyncheons. Compare the book with *The House of the Seven Gables* (Hawthorne's best novel after all); the situation, the "shrinkage and extinction of a family" is rather more complex, on the surface, than James's with (so far as the book was done) fewer character relations. But James's real situation here, to which Ralph's mounting the step is the key, as Hepzibah's opening

town," and in the preface to *Roderick Hudson* he says "what the early chapters of the book most 'render' to me today is not the umbrageous air of their New England town." T. S. E.

of her shop, is a situation of different states of mind. James's situation is the shrinkage and extinction of an idea. The Pyncheon tragedy is simple; the "curse" upon the family a matter of the simplest fairy mechanics. James has taken Hawthorne's ghost-sense and given it substance. At the same time making the tragedy much more ethereal: the tragedy of that "Sense," the hypertrophy, in Ralph, of a partial civilization; the vulgar vitality of the Midmores in their financial decay contrasted with the decay of Ralph in his financial prosperity, when they precisely should have been the civilization he had come to seek. All this watched over by the absent but conscious Aurora. I do not want to insist upon the Hawthorneness of the confrontation of the portrait, the importance of the opening of a door. We need surely not insist that this book is the most important, most substantial sort of thing that James did; perhaps there is more solid wear even in that other unfinished *Ivory Tower*. But I consider that it was an excursion which we could well permit him, after a lifetime in which he had taken talents similar to Hawthorne's and made them yield far greater returns than poor Hawthorne could harvest from his granite soil; a permissible exercise, in which we may by a legitimately cognate fancy seem to detect Hawthorne coming to a mediumistic existence again, to remind a younger and incredulous generation of what he really was, had he had the opportunity, and to attest his satisfaction that that opportunity had been given to James.

THESE ESSAYS by George Santayana on William James and
Josiah Royce appeared in 1920 in *Character and Opinion in
the United States.*

    This book, with *Egotism in German Philosophy,* which
came out a few years before it, was evidently provoked by
World War I, which had stimulated Mr. Santayana to think
of the issues of the war in terms of national points of view.
Both books are examples of an art of which Santayana is a
master but for which he is not much praised or known. In
these essays he is able to derive his subjects from their social
and geographical backgrounds and to paint them in their
local colors as would only be possible for an interested observer of how men actually live and grow; but this spectacle
does not absorb him: he confidently and quietly passes on
to criticize their philosophical positions in an arena where
all minds meet.

    George Santayana was born in Madrid, the child of
Spanish parents, but was brought to the United States at
nine and remained here for forty years. He graduated from
Harvard and returned to teach there in the philosophy department from 1888 to 1912. In 1912 he resigned and went
permanently to live in Europe.

GEORGE SANTAYANA

I. WILLIAM JAMES

WILLIAM JAMES enjoyed in his youth what are called advantages: he lived among cultivated people, traveled, had teachers of various nationalities. His father was one of those somewhat obscure sages whom early America produced: mystics of independent mind, hermits in the desert of business, and heretics in the churches. They were intense individuals, full of veneration for the free souls of their children, and convinced that everyone should paddle his own canoe, especially on the high seas. Williams James accordingly enjoyed a stimulating if slightly irregular education: he never acquired that reposeful mastery of particular authors and those safe ways of feeling and judging which are fostered in great schools and universities. In consequence he showed an almost physical horror of club sentiment and of the stifling atmosphere of all officialdom. He had a knack for drawing, and rather the temperament of the artist; but the unlovely secrets of nature and the troubles of man preoccupied him, and he chose medicine for his profession. Instead of practicing, however, he turned to teaching physiology, and from that passed gradually to psychology and philosophy. In his earlier years he retained some traces of polyglot student days at Paris, Bonn, Vienna, or Geneva; he slipped sometimes into foreign phrases, uttered in their full vernacular; and there was an occasional afterglow of Bohemia about him, in the bright stripe of a shirt or the exuberance of a tie. On points of art or medicine he retained a professional touch and an unconscious ease which he hardly acquired in metaphysics. I suspect he had heartily admired some of his masters in those other subjects, but had never seen a philosopher whom he would have cared to resemble. Of course there was nothing of the artist in William James, as the artist is sometimes conceived in England, nothing of the aesthete, nothing affected or limp. In person he was short rather than tall, erect, brisk, bearded, intensely masculine. While he shone in expression and would have wished his style to be noble if it could also be strong, he preferred in the end to be spontaneous, and to leave it at that; he tolerated slang in himself rather than primness. The rough, homely, picturesque phrase, whatever was graphic and racy, recommended itself to him; and his conversation outdid his writing in this respect. He believed in improvisation, even in thought; his lectures were not minutely prepared. Know your subject thoroughly, he used to say, and trust to luck for the rest. There was a deep sense of insecurity in him, a mixture of humility with romanticism: we were likely to be more or less wrong anyhow, but we might be wholly sincere. One moment should respect the insight of another, without trying to establish too regimental a uniformity. If you corrected yourself tartly, how could you know that the correction was not the worse mistake? All our opinions were born free and equal, all children of the Lord, and if they were not consistent that was the Lord's business, not theirs. In reality, James was consistent enough, as even Emerson (more extreme in this sort of irresponsibility) was too. Inspiration has its limits, sometimes very narrow ones. But James was not consecutive, not insistent; he turned to a subject afresh, without egotism or pedantry; he dropped his old points, sometimes very good ones; and he modestly looked for light from others, who had less light than himself.

His excursions into philosophy were accordingly in the nature of raids, and it is easy for those who are attracted by one part of his work to ignore other parts, in themselves perhaps more valuable. I think that in fact his popularity does not rest on his best achievements. His popularity rests on three somewhat incidental books, *The Will to Believe, Pragmatism,* and *The Varieties of Religious Experience,* whereas, as it seems to me, his best achievement is his *Principles of Psychology.* In this book he surveys, in a way which for him is very systematic, a subject made to his hand. In its ostensible outlook it is a treatise like any other, but what distinguishes it is the author's gift for evoking vividly the very life of the mind. This is a work of imagination; and the subject as he conceived it, which is the flux of immediate experience in men in general, requires imagination to read it at all. It is a literary subject, like autobiography or psychological fiction, and can be treated only poetically; and in this sense Shakespeare is a better psychologist than Locke or Kant. Yet this gift of imagination is not merely literary; it is not useless in divining the truths of science, and it is invaluable in throwing off prejudice and scientific shams. The fresh imagination and vitality of William James led him to break through many a false convention. He saw that experience, as we endure it, is not a mosaic of distinct sensations, nor the expression of separate hostile faculties, such as reason and the passions, or sense and the categories; it is rather a flow of mental discourse, like a dream, in which all divisions and units are vague and shifting, and the whole is continually merging together and drifting apart. It fades gradually in the rear, like the wake of a ship, and bites into the future, like the bow cutting the water. For the candid psychologist, carried bodily on this voyage of discovery, the past is but a questionable report, and the future wholly indeterminate; everything is simply what it is experienced as being.

At the same time, psychology is supposed to be a science, a claim which would tend to confine it to the natural history of man, or the study of behavior, as is actually proposed by Auguste Comte and by some of James's own disciples, more jejune if more clear-headed than he. As matters now stand, however, psychology as a whole is not a science, but a branch of philosophy; it brings together the literary description of mental discourse and the scientific description of material life, in order to consider the relation between them, which is the nexus of human nature.

What was James's position on this crucial question? It is impossible to reply unequivocally. He approached philosophy as mankind originally approached it, without having a philosophy, and he lent himself to various hypotheses in various directions. He professed to begin his study on the assumptions of common sense, that there is a material world which the animals that live in it are able to perceive and to think about. He gave a congruous extension to this view in his theory that emotion is purely bodily sensation, and also in his habit of conceiving the mind as a total shifting sensibility. To pursue this path, however, would have led him to admit that nature was automatic and mind simply cognitive, conclusions from which every instinct in him recoiled. He preferred to believe that mind and matter had independent energies and could lend one another a hand, matter operating by motion and mind by intention. This dramatic, amphibious way of picturing causation is natural to common sense, and might be defended if it were clearly defined; but James was insensibly carried away from it by a subtle implication of his method. This implication was that experience or mental discourse not only constituted a set of substantive facts, but the *only* substantive facts; all else, even that material world which his psychology had postulated, could be nothing but a verbal or fantastic symbol for sensations in their experienced order. So that while nominally the door was kept open to any hypothesis regarding the conditions of the psychological flux, in truth the question was prejudged. The hypotheses, which were parts of this psychological flux, could have no object save other parts of it. That flux itself, therefore, which he could picture so vividly, was the fundamental existence. The *sense* of bounding over the waves, the *sense* of being on an adventurous voyage, was the living fact; the rest was dead reckoning. Where one's gift is, there will one's faith be also; and to this poet appearance was the only reality.

This sentiment, which always lay at the back of his mind,

reached something like formal expression in his latest writings, where he sketched what he called radical empiricism. The word experience is like a shrapnel shell, and bursts into a thousand meanings. Here we must no longer think of its setting, its discoveries, or its march; to treat it radically we must abstract its immediate objects and reduce it to pure data. It is obvious (and the sequel has already proved) that experience so understood would lose its romantic signification, as a personal adventure or a response to the shocks of fortune. "Experience" would turn into a cosmic dance of absolute entities created and destroyed *in vacuo* according to universal laws, or perhaps by chance. No minds would gather this experience, and no material agencies would impose it; but the immediate objects present to anyone would simply be parts of the universal fireworks, continuous with the rest, and all the parts, even if not present to anybody, would have the same status. Experience would then not at all resemble what Shakespeare reports or what James himself had described in his psychology. If it could be experienced as it flows in its entirety (which is fortunately impracticable), it would be a perpetual mathematical nightmare. Every whirling atom, every changing relation, and every incidental perspective would be a part of it. I am far from wishing to deny for a moment the scientific value of such a cosmic system, if it can be worked out; physics and mathematics seem to me to plunge far deeper than literary psychology into the groundwork of this world; but human experience is the stuff of literary psychology; we cannot reach the stuff of physics and mathematics except by arresting or even hypostatizing some elements of appearance, and expanding them on an abstracted and hypothetical plane of their own. Experience, as memory and literature rehearse it, remains nearer to us than that: it is something dreamful, passionate, dramatic, and significative.

Certainly this personal human experience, expressible in literature and in talk, and no cosmic system however profound, was what James knew best and trusted most. Had he seen the developments of his radical empiricism, I cannot help thinking he would have marveled that such logical mechanisms should have been hatched out of that egg. The principal problems and aspirations that haunted him all his life long would lose their meaning in that cosmic atmosphere. The pragmatic nature of truth, for instance, would never suggest itself in the presence of pure data; but a romantic mind soaked in agnosticism, conscious of its own habits and assuming an environment the exact structure of which can never be observed, may well convince itself that, for experience, truth is nothing but a happy use of signs— which is indeed the truth of literature. But if we once accept *any* system of the universe as literally true, the value of convenient signs to prepare us for such experience as is yet absent cannot be called truth: it is plainly nothing but a necessary inaccuracy. So, too, with the question of the survival of the human individual after death. For radical empiricism a human individual is simply a certain cycle or complex of terms, like any other natural fact; that some echoes of his mind should recur after the regular chimes have ceased, would have nothing paradoxical about it. A mathematical world is a good deal like music, with its repetitions and transpositions, and a little trill, which you might call a person, might well peep up here and there all over a vast composition. Something of that sort may be the truth of spiritualism; but it is not what the spiritualists imagine. Their whole interest lies not in the experiences they have, but in the interpretation they give to them, assigning them to troubled spirits in another world; but both another world and a spirit are notions repugnant to a radical empiricism.

I think it is important to remember, if we are not to misunderstand William James, that his radical empiricism and pragmatism were in his own mind only methods; his doctrine, if he may be said to have had one, was agnosticism. And just because he was an agnostic (feeling instinctively that beliefs and opinions, if they had any objective beyond themselves, could never be sure they had attained it), he seemed in one sense so favorable to credulity. He was not credulous himself, far from it; he was well aware that the trust he put in people or ideas might betray him. For that very reason he was respectful and pitiful to the trustfulness

of others. Doubtless they were wrong, but who were we to
say so? In his own person he was ready enough to face the
mystery of things, and whatever the womb of time might
bring forth; but until the curtain was rung down on the
last act of the drama (and it might have no last act!) he
wished the intellectual cripples and the moral hunchbacks
not to be jeered at; perhaps they might turn out to be the
heroes of the play. Who could tell what heavenly influences
might not pierce to these sensitive, half-flayed creatures,
which are lost on the thick-skinned, the sane, and the duly
goggled? We must not suppose, however, that James meant
these contrite and romantic suggestions dogmatically. The
agnostic, as well as the physician and neurologist in him,
was never quite eclipsed. The hope that some new revelation might come from the lowly and weak could never mean
to him what it meant to the early Christians. For him it
was only a right conceded to them to experiment with their
special faiths; he did not expect such faiths to be discoveries
of absolute fact, which everybody else might be constrained
to recognize. If anyone had made such a claim, and had
seemed to have some chance of imposing it universally,
James would have been the first to turn against him; not,
of course, on the ground that it was *impossible* that such
an orthodoxy should be true, but with a profound conviction
that it was to be feared and distrusted. No: the degree of
authority and honor to be accorded to various human faiths
was a moral question, not a theoretical one. All faiths were
what they were experienced as being, in their capacity of
faiths; these faiths, not their objects, were the hard facts
we must respect. We cannot pass, except under the illusion
of the moment, to anything firmer or on a deeper level.
There was accordingly no sense of security, no joy, in
James's apology for personal religion. He did not really
believe; he merely believed in the right of believing that
you might be right if you believed.

It is this underlying agnosticism that explains an incoherence which we might find in his popular works, where the
story and the moral do not seem to hang together. Profess-
edly they are works of psychological observation; but the

tendency and suasion in them seems to run to disintegrating the idea of truth, recommending belief without reason, and encouraging superstition. A psychologist who was not an agnostic would have indicated, as far as possible, whether the beliefs and experiences he was describing were instances of delusion or of rare and fine perception, or in what measure they were a mixture of both. But James—and this is what gives such romantic warmth to these writings of his—disclaims all antecedent or superior knowledge, listens to the testimony of each witness in turn, and only by accident allows us to feel that he is swayed by the eloquence and vehemence of some of them rather than of others. This method is modest, generous, and impartial; but if James intended, as I think he did, to picture the *drama* of human belief, with its risks and triumphs, the method was inadequate. Dramatists never hesitate to assume, and to let the audience perceive, who is good and who bad, who wise and who foolish, in their pieces; otherwise their work would be as impotent dramatically as scientifically. The tragedy and comedy of life lie precisely in the contrast between the illusions or passions of the characters and their true condition and fate, hidden from them at first, but evident to the author and the public. If in our diffidence and scrupulous fairness we refuse to take this judicial attitude, we shall be led to strange conclusions. The navigator, for instance, trusting his "experience" (which here, as in the case of religious people, means his imagination and his art), insists on believing that the earth is spherical; he has sailed round it. That is to say, he has seemed to himself to steer westward and westward, and has seemed to get home again. But how should he know that home is now where it was before, or that his past and present impressions of it come from the same, or from any, material object? How should he know that space is as trim and tri-dimensional as the discredited Euclidians used to say it was? If, on the contrary, my worthy aunt, trusting to her longer and less ambiguous experience of her garden, insists that the earth is flat, and observes that the theory that it is round, which is only a theory, is much less often tested and found useful than her own perception of its flatness, and that moreover that theory is pedantic, intellectualistic, and a product of academies, and a rash dogma to impose on mankind for ever and ever, it might seem that on James's principle we ought to agree with her. But no; on James's real principles we need not agree with her, nor with the navigator either. Radical empiricism, which is radical agnosticism, delivers us from so benighted a choice. For the quarrel becomes unmeaning when we remember that the earth is *both* flat and round, if it is experienced as being both. The substantive fact is not a single object on which both the perception and the theory are expected to converge; the substantive facts are the theory and the perception themselves. And we may note in passing that empiricism, when it ceases to value experience as a means of discovering external things, can give up its ancient prejudice in favor of sense as against imagination, for imagination and thought are immediate experiences as much as sensation is: they are therefore, for absolute empiricism, no less actual ingredients of reality.

In *The Varieties of Religious Experience* we find the same apologetic intention running through a vivid account of what seems for the most part (as James acknowledged) religious disease. Normal religious experience is hardly described in it. Religious experience, for the great mass of mankind, consists in simple faith in the truth and benefit of their religious traditions. But to James something so conventional and rationalistic seemed hardly experience and hardly religious; he was thinking only of irruptive visions and feelings as interpreted by the mystics who had them. These interpretations he ostensibly presents, with more or less wistful sympathy, for what they were worth; but emotionally he wished to champion them. The religions that had sprung up in America spontaneously—communistic, hysterical, spiritistic, or medicinal—were despised by select and superior people. You might inquire into them, as you might go slumming, but they remained suspect and distasteful. This picking up of genteel skirts on the part of his acquaintance prompted William James to roll up his sleeves —not for a knockout blow, but for a thorough clinical demonstration. He would tenderly vivisect the experiences in question, to show how living they were, though of course he could not guarantee, more than other surgeons do, that the patient would survive the operation. An operation that eventually kills may be technically successful, and the man may die cured; and so a description of religion that showed it to be madness might first show how real and how warm it was, so that if it perished, at least it would perish understood.

I never observed in William James any personal anxiety or enthusiasm for any of these dubious tenets. His conception even of such a thing as free will, which he always ardently defended, remained vague; he avoided defining even what he conceived to be desirable in such matters. But he wished to protect the weak against the strong, and what he hated beyond everything was the *non possumus* of any constituted authority. Philosophy for him had a Polish constitution; so long as a single vote was cast against the majority, nothing could pass. The suspense of judgment, which he had imposed on himself as a duty, became almost a necessity. I think it would have depressed him if he had had to confess that any important question was finally settled. He would still have hoped that something might turn up on the other side, and that just as the scientific hangman was about to dispatch the poor convicted prisoner, an unexpected witness would ride up in hot haste, and prove him innocent. Experience seems to most of us to lead to conclusions, but empiricism has sworn never to draw them.

In the discourse on *The Energies of Men,* certain physiological marvels are recorded, as if to suggest that the resources of our minds and bodies are infinite, or can be infinitely enlarged by divine grace. Yet James would not, I am sure, have accepted that inference. He would, under pressure, have drawn in his mystical horns under his scientific shell; but he was not naturalist enough to feel instinctively that the wonderful and the natural are all of a piece, and that only our degree of habituation distinguishes them. A nucleus, which we may poetically call the soul, certainly lies within us, by which our bodies and minds are generated and controlled, like an army by a government. In this nucleus, since nature in a small compass has room for anything, vast quantities of energy may well be stored up, which may be tapped on occasion, or which may serve like an electric spark to let loose energy previously existing in the grosser parts. But the absolute autocracy of this central power, or its success in imposing extraordinary trials on its subjects, is not an obvious good. Perhaps, like a democratic government, the soul is at its best when it merely collects and co-ordinates the impulses coming from the senses. The inner man is at times a tyrant, parasitical, wasteful, and voluptuous. At other times he is fanatical and mad. When he asks for and obtains violent exertions from the body, the question often is, as with the exploits of conquerors and conjurers, whether the impulse to do such prodigious things was not gratuitous, and the things nugatory. Who would wish to be a mystic? James himself, who by nature was a spirited rather than a spiritual man, had no liking for sanctimonious transcendentalists, visionaries, or ascetics; he hated minds that run thin. But he hastened to correct this manly impulse, lest it should be unjust, and forced himself to overcome his repugnance. This was made easier when the unearthly phenomenon had a healing or saving function in the everyday material world; miracle then reëstablished its ancient identity with medicine, and both of them were humanized. Even when this union was not attained, James was reconciled to the miracle-workers partly by his great charity, and partly by his hunter's instinct to follow a scent, for he believed discoveries to be imminent. Besides, a philosopher who is a teacher of youth is more concerned to give people a right start than a right conclusion. James fell in with the hortatory tradition of college sages; he turned his psychology, whenever he could do so honestly, to purposes of edification; and his little sermons on habit, on will, on faith, and this on the latent capacities of men, were fine and stirring, and just the sermons to preach to the young Christian soldier. He was much less skeptical in morals than in science. He seems to have felt sure that certain thoughts and hopes—those familiar to a liberal

Protestantism—were every man's true friends in life. This assumption would have been hard to defend if he or those he habitually addressed had ever questioned it; yet his whole argument for voluntarily cultivating these beliefs rests on this assumption, that they are beneficent. Since, whether we will or no, we cannot escape the risk of error, and must succumb to some human or pathological bias, at least we might do so gracefully and in the form that would profit us most, by clinging to those prejudices which help us to lead what we all feel is a good life. But what is a good life? Had William James, had the people about him, had modern philosophers anywhere, any notion of that? I cannot think so. They had much experience of personal goodness, and love of it; they had standards of character and right conduct; but as to what might render human existence good, excellent, beautiful, happy, and worth having as a whole, their notions were utterly thin and barbarous. They had forgotten the Greeks, or never known them.

This argument accordingly suffers from the same weakness as the similar argument of Pascal in favor of Catholic orthodoxy. You should force yourself to believe in it, he said, because if you do so and are right you win heaven, while if you are wrong you lose nothing. What would Protestants, Mohammedans, and Hindus say to that? Those alternatives of Pascal's are not the sole nor the true alternatives; such a wager—betting on the improbable because you are offered big odds—is an unworthy parody of the real choice between wisdom and folly. There is no heaven to be won in such a spirit, and if there was, a philosopher would despise it. So William James would have us bet on immortality, or bet on our power to succeed, because if we win the wager we can live to congratulate ourselves on our true instinct, while we lose nothing if we have made a mistake; for unless you have the satisfaction of finding that you have been right, the dignity of having been right is apparently nothing. Or if the argument is rather that these beliefs, whether true or false, make life better in this world, the thing is simply false. To be boosted by an illusion is not to live better than to live in harmony with the truth; it is not nearly so safe, not nearly so sweet, and not nearly so fruitful. These refusals to part with a decayed illusion are really an infection to the mind. Believe, certainly; we cannot help believing; but believe rationally, holding what seems certain for certain, what seems probable for probable, what seems desirable for desirable, and what seems false for false.

In this matter, as usual, James had a true psychological fact and a generous instinct behind his confused moral suggestions. It is a psychological fact that men are influenced in their beliefs by their will and desires; indeed, I think we can go further and say that in its essence belief is an expression of impulse, of readiness to act. It is only peripherally, as our action is gradually adjusted to things, and our impulses to our possible or necessary action, that our ideas begin to hug the facts, and to acquire a true, if still a symbolic, significance. We do not need a will to believe; we only need a will to study the object in which we are inevitably believing. But James was thinking less of belief in what we find than of belief in what we hope for: a belief which is not at all clear and not at all necessary in the life of mortals. Like most Americans, however, only more lyrically, James felt the call of the future and the assurance that it could be made far better, totally other, than the past. The pictures that religion had painted of heaven or the millennium were not what he prized, although his Swedenborgian connection might have made him tender to them, as perhaps it did to familiar spirits. It was the moral succor offered by religion, its open spaces, the possibility of miracles *in extremis,* that must be retained. If we recoiled at the thought of being dupes (which is perhaps what nature intended us to be), were we less likely to be dupes in disbelieving these sustaining truths than in believing them? Faith was needed to bring about the reform of faith itself, as well as all other reforms.

In some cases faith in success could nerve us to bring success about, and so justify itself by its own operation. This is a thought typical of James at his worst—a worst in which there is always a good side. Here again psychological observation is used with the best intentions to hearten oneself

and other people; but the fact observed is not at all understood, and a moral twist is given to it which (besides being
morally questionable) almost amounts to falsifying the fact
itself. Why does belief that you can jump a ditch help you
to jump it? Because it is a symptom of the fact that you
could jump it, that your legs were fit and that the ditch was
two yards wide and not twenty. A rapid and just appreciation of these facts has given you your confidence, or at least
has made it reasonable, manly, and prophetic; otherwise you
would have been a fool and got a ducking for it. Assurance
is contemptible and fatal unless it is self-knowledge. If you
had been rattled you might have failed, because that would
have been a symptom of the fact that you were out of gear;
you would have been afraid because you trembled, as James
at his best proclaimed. You would never have quailed if
your system had been reacting smoothly to its opportunities,
any more than you would totter and see double if you were
not intoxicated. Fear is a sensation of actual nervousness and
disarray, and confidence a sensation of actual readiness; they
are not disembodied feelings, existing for no reason, the devil
Funk and the angel Courage, one or the other of whom may
come down arbitrarily into your body, and revolutionize it.
That is childish mythology, which survives innocently
enough as a figure of speech, until a philosopher is found to
take that figure of speech seriously. Nor is the moral suggestion here less unsound. What is good is not the presumption
of power, but the possession of it: a clear head, aware of its
resources, not a fuddled optimism, calling up spirits from
the vasty deep. Courage is not a virtue, said Socrates, unless
it is also wisdom. Could anything be truer both of courage
in doing and of courage in believing? But it takes tenacity,
it takes *reasonable* courage, to stick to scientific insights such
as this of Socrates or that of James about the emotions; it is
easier to lapse into the traditional manner, to search natural
philosophy for miracles and moral lessons, and in morals
proper, in the reasoned expression of preference, to splash
about without a philosophy.

William James shared the passions of liberalism. He belonged to the left, which, as they say in Spain, is the side

of the heart, as the right is that of the liver; at any rate there
was much blood and no gall in his philosophy. He was one
of those elder Americans still disquieted by the ghost of
tyranny, social and ecclesiastical. Even the beauties of the
past troubled him; he had a puritan feeling that they were
tainted. They had been cruel and frivolous, and must have
suppressed far better things. But what, we may ask, might
these better things be? It may do for a revolutionary politician
to say: "I may not know what I want—except office—but I
know what I don't want"; it will never do for a philosopher.
Aversions and fears imply principles of preference, goods
acknowledged; and it is the philosopher's business to make
these goods explicit. Liberty is not an art, liberty must be
used to bring some natural art to fruition. Shall it be simply
eating and drinking and wondering what will happen next?
If there is some deep and settled need in the heart of man,
to give direction to his efforts, what else should a philosopher
do but discover and announce what that need is?

There is a sense in which James was not a philosopher at
all. He once said to me: "What a curse philosophy would be
if we couldn't forget all about it!" In other words, philosophy
was not to him what it has been to so many, a consolation
and sanctuary in a life which would have been unsatisfying
without it. It would be incongruous, therefore, to expect of
him that he should build a philosophy like an edifice to go
and live in for good. Philosophy to him was rather like a
maze in which he happened to find himself wandering, and
what he was looking for was the way out. In the presence
of theories of any sort he was attentive, puzzled, suspicious,
with a certain inner prompting to disregard them. He lived
all his life among them, as a child lives among grown-up
people; what a relief to turn from those stolid giants, with
their prohibitions and exactions and tiresome talk, to another real child or a nice animal! Of course grown-up people
are useful, and so James considered that theories might be;
but in themselves, to live with, they were rather in the way,
and at bottom our natural enemies. It was well to challenge
one or another of them when you got a chance; perhaps
that challenge might break some spell, transform the strange

landscape, and simplify life. A theory while you were creating or using it was like a story you were telling yourself or a game you were playing; it was a warm, self-justifying thing then; but when the glow of creation or expectation was over, a theory was a phantom, like a ghost, or like the minds of other people. To all other people, even to ghosts, William James was the soul of courtesy; and he was civil to most theories as well, as to more or less interesting strangers that invaded him. Nobody ever recognized more heartily the chance that others had of being right, and the right they had to be different. Yet when it came to understanding what they meant, whether they were theories or persons, his intuition outran his patience; he made some brilliant impressionistic sketch in his fancy and called it by their name. This sketch was as often flattered as distorted, and he was at times the dupe of his desire to be appreciative and give the devil his due; he was too impulsive for exact sympathy; too subjective, too romantic, to be just. Love is very penetrating, but it penetrates to possibilities rather than to facts. The logic of opinions, as well as the exact opinions themselves, were not things James saw easily, or traced with pleasure. He liked to take things one by one, rather than to put two and two together. He was a mystic, a mystic in love with life. He was comparable to Rousseau and to Walt Whitman; he expressed a generous and tender sensibility, rebelling against sophistication, and preferring daily sights and sounds, and a vague but indomitable faith in fortune, to any settled intellectual tradition calling itself science or philosophy.

A prophet is not without honor save in his own country; and until the return wave of James's reputation reached America from Europe, his pupils and friends were hardly aware that he was such a distinguished man. Everybody liked him, and delighted in him for his generous, gullible nature and brilliant sallies. He was a sort of Irishman among the Brahmins, and seemed hardly imposing enough for a great man. They laughed at his erratic views and his undisguised limitations. Of course a conscientious professor ought to know everything he professes to know, but then, they thought, a dignified professor ought to seem to know every thing. The precise theologians and panoplied idealists, who exist even in America, shook their heads. What sound philosophy, said they to themselves, could be expected from an irresponsible doctor, who was not even a college graduate, a crude empiricist, and vivisector of frogs? On the other hand, the solid men of business were not entirely reassured concerning a teacher of youth who seemed to have no system in particular—the ignorant rather demand that the learned should have a system in store, to be applied at a pinch; and they could not quite swallow a private gentleman who dabbled in hypnotism, frequented mediums, didn't talk like a book, and didn't write like a book, except like one of his own. Even his pupils, attached as they invariably were to his person, felt some doubts about the profundity of one who was so very natural, and who after some interruption during a lecture—and he said life was a series of interruptions—would slap his forehead and ask the man in the front row, "What *was* I talking about?" Perhaps in the first years of his teaching he felt a little in the professor's chair as a military man might feel when obliged to read the prayers at a funeral. He probably conceived what he said more deeply than a more scholastic mind might have conceived it; yet he would have been more comfortable if someone else had said it for him. He liked to open the window, and look out for a moment. I think he was glad when the bell rang, and he could be himself again until the next day. But in the midst of this routine of the class-room the spirit would sometimes come upon him, and, leaning his head on his hand, he would let fall golden words, picturesque, fresh from the heart, full of the knowledge of good and evil. Incidentally there would crop up some humorous characterization, some candid confession of doubt or of instinctive preference, some pungent scrap of learning; radicalisms plunging sometimes into the sub-soil of all human philosophies; and, on occasion, thoughts of simple wisdom and wistful piety, the most unfeigned and manly that anybody ever had.

II. JOSIAH ROYCE

MEANTIME the mantle of philosophical authority had fallen at Harvard upon other shoulders. A young Californian, Josiah Royce, had come back from Germany with a reputation for wisdom; and even without knowing that he had already produced a new proof of the existence of God, merely to look at him you would have felt that he was a philosopher; his great head seemed too heavy for his small body, and his portentous brow, crowned with thick red hair, seemed to crush the lower part of his face. "Royce," said William James of him, "has an indecent exposure of forehead." There was a suggestion about him of the benevolent ogre or the old child, in whom a preternatural sharpness of insight lurked beneath a grotesque mask. If you gave him any cue, or even without one, he could discourse broadly on any subject; you never caught him napping. Whatever the textbooks and encyclopaedias could tell him, he knew; and if the impression he left on your mind was vague, that was partly because, in spite of his comprehensiveness, he seemed to view everything in relation to something else that remained untold. His approach to anything was oblique; he began a long way off, perhaps with the American preface of a funny story; and when the point came in sight, it was at once enveloped again in a cloud of qualifications, in the parliamentary jargon of philosophy. The tap once turned on, out flowed the stream of systematic disquisition, one hour, two hours, three hours of it, according to demand or opportunity. The voice, too, was merciless and harsh. You felt the overworked, standardized, academic engine, creaking and thumping on at the call of duty or of habit, with no thought of sparing itself or anyone else. Yet a sprightlier soul behind this performing soul seemed to watch and laugh at the process. Sometimes a merry light would twinkle in the little eyes, and a bashful smile would creep over the uncompromising mouth. A sense of the paradox, the irony, the inconclusiveness of the whole argument would pierce to the surface, like

a white-cap bursting here and there on the heavy swell of
the sea.

His procedure was first to gather and digest whatever the
sciences or the devil might have to say. He had an evident
sly pleasure in the degustation and savor of difficulties; bibli-
cal criticism, the struggle for life, the latest German theory
of sexual insanity, had no terrors for him; it was all grist for
the mill, and woe to any tender thing, any beauty or any
illusion, that should get between that upper and that nether
millstone! He seemed to say: If I were not Alexander how
gladly would I be Diogenes, and if I had not a system to
defend, how easily I might tell you the truth. But after the
skeptic had ambled quizzically over the ground, the prophet
would mount the pulpit to survey it. He would then prove
that in spite of all those horrors and contradictions, or rather
because of them, the universe was absolutely perfect. For
behind that mocking soul in him there was yet another, a
devout and heroic soul. Royce was heir to the Calvinistic
tradition; piety, to his mind, consisted in trusting divine
providence and justice, while emphasizing the most terrifying truths about one's own depravity and the sinister holiness of God. He accordingly addressed himself, in his chief
writings, to showing that all lives were parts of a single divine
life in which all problems were solved and all evils justified.

It is characteristic of Royce that in his proof of something
sublime, like the existence of God, his premiss should be
something sad and troublesome, the existence of error. Error
exists, he tells us, and common sense will readily agree, although the fact is not unquestionable, and pure mystics and
pure sensualists deny it. But if error exists, Royce continues,
there must be a truth from which it differs; and the existence
of truth (according to the principle of idealism, that nothing
can exist except for a mind that knows it) implies that someone knows the truth; but as to know the truth thoroughly,
and supply the corrective to every possible error, involves
omniscience, we have proved the existence of an omniscient
mind or universal thought; and this is almost, if not quite,
equivalent to the existence of God.

What carried Royce over the evident chasms and assumptions in this argument was his earnestness and passionate eloquence. He passed for an eminent logician, because he was dialectical and fearless in argument and delighted in the play of formal relations; he was devoted to chess, music, and mathematics; but all this show of logic was but a screen for his heart, and in his heart there was no clearness. His reasoning was not pure logic or pure observation; it was always secretly enthusiastic or malicious, and the result it arrived at had been presupposed. Here, for instance, no unprejudiced thinker, not to speak of a pure logician, would have dreamt of using the existence of error to found the being of truth upon. Error is a biological accident which may any day cease to exist, say at the extinction of the human race; whereas the being of truth or fact is involved indefeasibly and eternally in the existence of anything whatever, past, present, or future; every event of itself renders true or false any proposition that refers to it. No one would conceive of such a thing as error or suspect its presence, unless he had already found or assumed many a truth; nor could anything be an error actually unless the truth was definite and real. All this Royce of course recognized, and it was in some sense the heart of what he meant to assert and to prove; but it does not need proving and hardly asserting. What needed proof was something else, of less logical importance but far greater romantic interest, namely, that the truth was hovering over us and about to descend into our hearts; and this Royce was not disinclined to confuse with the being of truth, so as to bring it within the range of logical argument. He was tormented by the suspicion that he might be himself in the toils of error, and fervently aspired to escape from it. Error to him was no natural, and in itself harmless, incident of finitude; it was a sort of sin, as finitude was too. It was a part of the problem of evil; a terrible and urgent problem when your first postulate or dogma is that moral distinctions and moral experience are the substance of the world, and not merely an incident in it. The mere being of truth, which is all a logician needs, would not help him in this wrestling for personal salvation; as he keenly felt and often said, the truth is like the stars, always laughing at us. Nothing would help him but *possession* of the truth, something eventual and terribly problematic. He longed to believe that all his troubles and questions, someday and somewhere, must find their solution and quietus; if not in his own mind, in some kindred spirit that he could, to that extent, identify with himself. There must be not only cold truth, not even cold truth personified, but victorious *knowledge* of the truth, breaking like a sunburst through the clouds of error. The nerve of his argument was not logical at all; it was a confession of religious experience, in which the agonized consciousness of error led to a strong imaginative conviction that the truth would be found at last.

The truth, as here conceived, meant the whole truth about everything; and certainly, if any plausible evidence for such a conclusion could be adduced, it would be interesting to learn that we are destined to become omniscient, or are secretly omniscient already. Nevertheless, the aspiration of all religious minds does not run that way. Aristotle tells us that there are many things it is better not to know; and his sublime deity is happily ignorant of our errors and of our very existence; more emphatically so the even sublimer deities of Plotinus and the Indians. The omniscience which our religion attributes to God as the searcher of hearts and the judge of conduct has a moral function rather than a logical one; it prevents us from hiding our sins or being unrecognized in our merits; it is not conceived to be requisite in order that it may be true that those sins or merits have existed. Atheists admit the facts, but they are content or perhaps relieved that they should pass unobserved. But here again Royce slipped into a romantic equivocation which a strict logician would not have tolerated. Knowledge of the truth, a passing psychological possession, was substituted for the truth known, and this at the cost of rather serious ultimate confusions. It is the truth itself, the facts in their actual relations, that honest opinion appeals to, not to another opinion or instance of knowledge; and if, in your dream of warm sympathy and public corroboration, you lay up your treasure in some instance of knowledge, which time and doubt might corrupt, you have not laid up your treasure in heaven. In striving to prove the being of truth, the young Royce absurdly treated it as doubtful, setting a bad example to the pragmatists; while in striving to lend a psychological quality to this truth and turning it into a problematical instance of knowledge, he unwittingly deprived it of all authority and sublimity. To personify the truth is to care less for truth than for the corroboration and sympathy which the truth, become human, might bring to our opinions. It is to set up another thinker, ourself enlarged, to vindicate us; without considering that this second thinker would be shut up, like us, in his own opinions, and would need to look to the truth beyond him as much as we do.

To the old problem of evil Royce could only give an old answer, although he rediscovered and repeated it for himself in many ways, since it was the core of his whole system. Good, he said, is essentially the struggle with evil and the victory over it; so that if evil did not exist, good would be impossible. I do not think this answer set him at rest; he could hardly help feeling that all goods are not of that bellicose description, and that not all evils produce a healthy reaction or are swallowed up in victory; yet the fact that the most specious solution to this problem of evil left it unsolved was in its way appropriate; for if the problem had been really solved, the struggle to find a solution and the faith that there was one would come to an end; yet perhaps this faith and this struggle are themselves the supreme good. Accordingly the true solution of this problem, which we may all accept, is that no solution can ever be found.

Here is an example of the difference between the being of truth and the ultimate solution of all our problems. There is certainly a truth about evil, and in this case not an unknown truth; yet it is no solution to the "problem" which laid the indomitable Royce on the rack. If a younger son asks why he was not born before his elder brother, that question may represent an intelligible state of his feelings; but there is no answer to it, because it is a childish question. So the question why it is right that there should be any evil is itself perverse and raised by false presumptions. To an unsophisticated mortal the existence of evil presents a task, never a

problem. Evil, like error, is an incident of animal life, inevitable in a crowded and unsettled world, where one
spontaneous movement is likely to thwart another, and all to
run up against material impossibilities. While life lasts this
task is recurrent, and every creature, in proportion to the
vitality and integrity of his nature, strives to remove or abate
those evils of which he is sensible. When the case is urgent
and he is helpless, he will cry out for divine aid; and (if he
does not perish first) he will soon see this aid coming to him
through some shift in the circumstances that renders his
situation endurable. Positive religion takes a naturalistic
view of things, and requires it. It parts company with a
scientific naturalism only in accepting the authority of instinct or revelation in deciding certain questions of fact,
such as immortality or miracles. It rouses itself to crush evil,
without asking why evil exists. What could be more intelligible than that a deity like Jehovah, a giant inhabitant of the
natural world, should be confronted with rivals, enemies,
and rebellious children? What could be more intelligible
than that the inertia of matter, or pure chance, or some contrary purpose, should mar the expression of any platonic idea
exercising its magic influence over the world? For the Greek
as for the Jew the task of morals is the same: to subdue
nature as far as possible to the uses of the soul, by whatever
agencies material or spiritual may be at hand; and when a
limit is reached in that direction, to harden and cauterize the
heart in the face of inevitable evils, opening it wide at the
same time to every sweet influence that may descend to it
from heaven. Never for a moment was positive religion entangled in a sophistical optimism. Never did it conceive that
the most complete final deliverance and triumph would
justify the evils which they abolished. As William James
put it, in his picturesque manner, if at the last day all creation was shouting hallelujah and there remained one cock-
roach with an unrequited love, *that* would spoil the universal
harmony; it would spoil it, he meant, in truth and for the
tender philosopher, but probably not for those excited saints.
James was thinking chiefly of the present and future, but
the same scrupulous charity has its application to the past.

To remove an evil is not to remove the fact that it has existed. The tears that have been shed were shed in bitterness, even if a remorseful hand afterwards wipes them away. To be patted on the back and given a sugar plum does not reconcile even a child to a past injustice. And the case is much worse if we are expected to make our heaven out of the foolish and cruel pleasures of contrast, or out of the pathetic offuscation produced by a great relief. Such a heaven would be a lie, like the sardonic heavens of Calvin and Hegel. The existence of any evil anywhere at any time absolutely ruins a total optimism.

Nevertheless philosophers have always had a royal road to complete satisfaction. One of the purest of pleasures, which they cultivate above all others, is the pleasure of understanding. Now, as playwrights and novelists know, the intellect is no less readily or agreeably employed in understanding evil than in understanding good—more so, in fact, if in the intellectual man, besides his intelligence, there is a strain of coarseness, irony, or desire to belittle the good things others possess and he himself has missed. Sometimes the philosopher, even when above all meanness, becomes so devoted a naturalist that he is ashamed to remain a moralist, although this is what he probably was in the beginning; and where all is one vast cataract of events, he feels it would be impertinent of him to divide them censoriously into things that ought to be and things that ought not to be. He may even go one step farther. Awestruck and humbled before the universe, he may insensibly transform his understanding and admiration of it into the assertion that the existence of evil is no evil at all, but that the order of the universe is in every detail necessary and perfect, so that the mere mention of the word evil is blind and blasphemous.

This sentiment, which as much as any other deserves the name of pantheism, is often expressed incoherently and with a false afflatus; but when rationally conceived, as it was by Spinoza, it amounts to this: that good and evil are relations which things bear to the living beings they affect. In itself nothing—much less this whole mixed universe—can be either good or bad; but the universe wears the aspect of a good in so far as it feeds, delights, or otherwise fosters any creature within it. If we define the intellect as the power to see things as they are, it is clear that in so far as the philosopher is a pure intellect the universe will be a pure good to the philosopher; everything in it will give play to his exclusive passion. Wisdom counsels us therefore to become philosophers and to concentrate our lives as much as possible in pure intelligence, that we may be led by it into the ways of peace. Not that the universe will be proved thereby to be intrinsically good (although in the heat of their intellectual egotism philosophers are sometimes betrayed into saying so), but that it will have become in that measure a good to us, and we shall be better able to live happily and freely in it. If intelligibility appears in things, it does so like beauty or use, because the mind of man, in so far as it is adapted to them, finds its just exercise in their society.

This is an ancient, shrewd, and inexpugnable position. If Royce had been able to adhere to it consistently, he would have avoided his gratuitous problem of evil without, I think, doing violence to the sanest element in his natural piety, which was joy in the hard truth, with a touch of humor and scorn in respect to mortal illusions. There was an observant and docile side to him; and as a child likes to see things work, he liked to see processions of facts marching on ironically, whatever we might say about it. This was his sense of the power of God. It attached him at first to Spinoza and later to mathematical logic. No small part of his life-long allegiance to the Absolute responded to this sentiment.

The outlook, however, was complicated and half reversed for him by the transcendental theory of knowledge which he had adopted. This theory regards all objects, including the universe, as merely terms posited by the will of the thinker, according to a definite grammar of thought native to his mind. In order that his thoughts may be addressed to any particular object, he must first choose and create it of his own accord; otherwise his opinions, not being directed upon any object in particular within his ken, cannot be either true or false, whatever picture they may frame. What anything external may happen to be, when we do not mean to speak of

it, is irrelevant to our discourse. If, for instance, the real
Royce were not a denizen and product of my mind—of my
deeper self—I could not so much as have a wrong idea of
him. The need of this initial relevance in our judgments
seems to the transcendentalist to drive all possible objects
into the fold of his secret thoughts, so that he has two minds,
one that seeks the facts and another that already possesses
or rather constitutes them.

Pantheism, when this new philosophy of knowledge is
adopted, seems at first to lose its foundations. There is no
longer an external universe to which to bow; no little corner
left for us in the infinite where, after making the great
sacrifice, we may build a safe nest. The intellect to which
we had proudly reduced ourselves has lost its pre-eminence;
it can no longer be called the faculty of seeing things as they
are. It has become what psychological critics of intellectualism, such as William James, understand by it: a mass of
human propensities to abstraction, construction, belief, or
inference, by which imaginary things and truths are posited
in the service of life. It is therefore on the same plane exactly
as passion, music, or aesthetic taste: a mental complication
which may be an index to other psychological facts connected
with it genetically, but which has no valid intent, no ideal
transcendence, no assertive or cognitive function. Intelligence so conceived understands nothing: it is a buzzing
labor in the fancy which, by some obscure causation, helps
us to live on.

To discredit the intellect, to throw off the incubus of an
external reality or truth, was one of the boons which transcendentalism in its beginnings brought to the romantic soul.
But although at first the sense of relief (to Fichte, for instance) was most exhilarating, the freedom achieved soon
proved illusory: the terrible Absolute had been simply transplanted into the self. You were your own master, and
omnipotent; but you were no less dark, hostile, and inexorable to yourself than the gods of Calvin or of Spinoza had
been before. Since every detail of this mock world was your
secret work, you were not only wiser but also more criminal
than you knew. You were stifled, even more than formerly,

in the arms of nature, in the toils of your own unaccountable character, which made your destiny. Royce never recoiled from paradox or from bitter fact; and he used to say that a mouse, when tormented and torn to pieces by a cat, was realizing his own deepest will, since he had subconsciously chosen to be a mouse in a world that should have cats in it. The mouse really, in his deeper self, wanted to be terrified, clawed, and devoured. Royce was superficially a rationalist, with no tenderness for superstition in detail and not much sympathy with civilized religions; but we see here that in his heart he was loyal to the aboriginal principle of all superstition: reverence for what hurts. He said to himself that in so far as God was the devil—as daily experience and Hegelian logic proved was largely the case—devil-worship was true religion.

A protest, however, arose in his own mind against this doctrine. Strong early bonds attached him to moralism—to the opinion of the Stoics and of Kant that virtue is the only good. Yet if virtue were conceived after their manner, as a heroic and sublimated attitude of the will, of which the world hardly afforded any example, how should the whole whirligig of life be good also? How should moralism, that frowns on this wicked world, be reconciled with pantheism and optimism, that hug it to their bosom? By the ingenious if rather melodramatic notion that we should hug it with a bear's hug, that virtue consisted (as Royce often put it) in holding evil by the throat; so that the world was good because it was a good world to strangle, and if we only managed to do so, the more it deserved strangling the better world it was. But this Herculean feat must not be considered as something to accomplish once for all; the labors of Hercules must be not twelve but infinite, since his virtue consisted in performing them, and if he ever rested or was received into Olympus he would have left virtue—the only good—behind. The wickedness of the world was no reason for quitting it; on the contrary, it invited us to plunge into all its depths and live through every phase of it; virtue was severe but not squeamish. It lived by endless effort, turbid vitality, and *Sturm und Drang*. Moralism and an apology for evil could thus be reconciled and merged in the praises of tragic experience.

This had been the burden of Hegel's philosophy of life, which Royce admired and adopted. Hegel and his followers seem to be fond of imagining that they are moving in a tragedy. But because Aeschylus and Sophocles were great poets, does it follow that life would be cheap if it did not resemble their fables? The life of tragic heroes is not good; it is misguided, unnecessary, and absurd. Yet that is what romantic philosophy would condemn us to; we must all strut and roar. We must lend ourselves to the partisan earnestness of persons and nations calling their rivals villains and themselves heroes; but this earnestness will be of the histrionic German sort, made to order and transferable at short notice from one object to another, since what truly matters is not that we should achieve our ostensible aim (which Hegel contemptuously called ideal) but that we should carry on perpetually, if possible with a *crescendo,* the strenuous experience of living in a gloriously bad world, and always working to reform it, with the comforting speculative assurance that we never can succeed. We never can succeed, I mean, in rendering reform less necessary or life happier; but of course in any specific reform we may succeed half the time, thereby sowing the seeds of new and higher evils, to keep the edge of virtue keen. And in reality we, or the Absolute in us, are succeeding all the time; the play is always going on, and the play's the thing.

It was inevitable that Royce should have been at home only in this circle of Protestant and German intuitions; a more refined existence would have seemed to him to elude moral experience. Although he was born in California he had never got used to the sunshine; he had never tasted peace. His spirit was that of courage and labor. He was tender in a bashful way, as if in tenderness there was something pathological, as indeed to his sense there was, since he conceived love and loyalty to be divine obsessions refusing to be rationalized; he saw their essence in the child who clings to an old battered doll rather than accept a new and better one. Following orthodox tradition in philosophy, he insisted on seeing reason at the bottom of things as well as at the top, so that he never could understand either the root or the flower of anything. He watched the movement of events as if they were mysterious music, and instead of their causes and potentialities he tried to divine their *motif*. On current affairs his judgments were highly seasoned and laboriously wise. If anything escaped him, it was only the simplicity of what is best. His reward was that he became a prophet to a whole class of earnest, troubled people who, having discarded doctrinal religion, wished to think their life worth living when, to look at what it contained, it might not have seemed so; it reassured them to learn that a strained and joyless existence was not their unlucky lot, or a consequence of their solemn folly, but was the necessary fate of all good men and angels. Royce had always experienced and seen about him a groping, burdened, mediocre life; he had observed how fortune is continually lying in ambush for us, in order to bring good out of evil and evil out of good. In his age and country all was change, preparation, hurry, material achievement; nothing was an old and sufficient possession; nowhere, or very much in the background, any leisure, simplicity, security, or harmony. The whole scene was filled with arts and virtues which were merely useful or remedial. The most pressing arts, like war and forced labor, presuppose evil, work immense havoc, and take the place of greater possible goods. The most indispensable virtues, like courage and industry, do likewise. But these seemed in Royce's world the only honorable things, and he took them to be typical of all art and virtue—a tremendous error. It is very true, however, that in the welter of material existence no concrete thing can be good or evil in every respect; and so long as our rough arts and virtues do more good than harm we give them honorable names, such as unselfishness, patriotism, or religion; and it remains a mark of good breeding among us to practice them instinctively. But an absolute love of such forced arts and impure virtues is itself a vice; it is, as the case may be, barbarous, vain, or fanatical. It mistakes something specific—some habit or emotion which may be or may have been good in some respect, or under some circumstances the lesser of two evils—for the very principle of excellence. But good and evil, like light and shade, are ethereal; all things, events, persons, and conventional virtues are in themselves utterly valueless, save as an immaterial harmony (of which mind is an expression) plays about them on occasion, when their natures meet propitiously, and bathes them in some tint of happiness or beauty. This immaterial harmony may be made more and more perfect; the difficulties in the way of perfection, either in man, in society, or in universal nature, are physical not logical. Worship of barbarous virtue is the blackest conservatism; it shuts the gate of heaven, and surrenders existence to perpetual follies and crimes. Moralism itself is a superstition. In its abstract form it is moral, too moral; it adores the conventional conscience, or perhaps a morbid one. In its romantic form, moralism becomes barbarous and actually immoral; it obstinately craves action and stress for their own sake, experience in the gross, and a good-and-bad way of living.

Royce sometimes conceded that there might be some pure goods, music, for instance, or mathematics; but the impure moral goods were better and could not be spared. Such a concession, however, if it had been taken to heart, would have ruined his whole moral philosophy. The romanticist must maintain that *only* what is painful can be noble and *only* what is lurid bright. A taste for turbid and contrasted values would soon seem perverse when once anything perfect had been seen and loved. Would it not have been better to leave out the worst of the crimes and plagues that have heightened the tragic value of the world? But if so, why stop before we had deleted them all? We should presently be horrified at the mere thought of passions that before had been found necessary by the barbarous tragedian to keep his audience awake; and the ear at the same time would become sensitive to a thousand harmonies that had been inaudible in the hurly-burly of romanticism. The romanticist thinks he has life by virtue of his confusion and torment, whereas in truth that torment and confusion are his incipient death, and it is only the modicum of harmony he has achieved in his separate faculties that keeps him alive at all. As Aristotle taught, unmixed harmony would be intensest life. The spheres might make a sweet and perpetual music, and a happy God is at least possible.

It was not in this direction, however, that Royce broke away on occasion from his Hegelian ethics; he did so in the direction of ethical dogmatism and downright sincerity. The deepest thing in him personally was conscience, firm recognition of duty, and the democratic and American spirit of service. He could not adopt a moral bias histrionically, after the manner of Hegel or Nietzsche. To those hardened professionals any role was acceptable, the more commanding the better; but the good Royce was like a sensitive amateur, refusing the role of villain, however brilliant and necessary to the play. In contempt of his own speculative insight, or in an obedience to it which forgot it for the time being, he lost himself in his part, and felt that it was infinitely important to be cast only for the most virtuous of characters. He retained inconsistently the Jewish allegiance to a God essentially the vindicator of only one of the combatants, not in this world often the victor; he could not stomach the providential scoundrels which the bad taste of Germany, and of Carlyle and Browning, was wont to glorify. The last notable act of his life was an illustration of this, when he uttered a ringing public denunciation of the sinking of the *Lusitania*. Orthodox Hegelians might well have urged that here, if anywhere, was a plain case of the providential function of what, from a finite merely moral point of view, was an evil in order to make a higher good possible—the virtue of German self-assertion and of American self-assertion in antithesis to it, synthesized in the concrete good of war and victory, or in the perhaps more blessed good of defeat. What could be more unphilosophical and *gedankenlos* than the intrusion of mere morality into the higher idea of world-development? Was not the Universal Spirit compelled to bifurcate into just such Germans and just such Americans, in order to attain self-consciousness by hating, fighting against, and vanquishing itself? Certainly it was American duty to be angry, as it was German duty to be ruthless. The Idea liked to see its fighting-cocks at it in earnest, since that was what it had bred them for; but both were good cocks. Villains, as Hegel had observed in describing Greek tragedy, were not less self-justified than heroes; they were simply the heroes of a lower stage of culture. America and England remained at the stage of individualism; Germany had advanced to the higher stage of organization. Perhaps this necessary war was destined, through the apparent defeat of Germany, to bring England and America up to the German level. Of course; and yet somehow, on this occasion, Royce passed over these profound considerations, which life-long habit must have brought to his lips. A Socratic demon whispered No, No in his ear; it would have been better for such things never to be. The murder of those thousand passengers was not a providential act, requisite to spread abroad a vitalizing war; it was a crime to execrate altogether. It would have been better for Hegel, or whoever was responsible for it, if a millstone had been hanged about his neck and he, and not those little ones, had been drowned at the bottom of the sea. Of this terrestrial cock-pit Royce was willing to accept the agony, but not the ignominy. The other cock was a wicked bird.

This honest lapse from his logic was habitual with him at the sight of sin, and sin in his eyes was a fearful reality. His conscience spoiled the pantheistic serenity of his system; and what was worse (for he was perfectly aware of the contradiction) it added a deep, almost remorseful unrest to his hard life. What calm could there be in the double assurance that it was really right that things should be wrong, but that it was really wrong not to strive to right them? There was no conflict, he once observed, between science and religion, but the real conflict was between religion and morality. There could indeed be no conflict in his mind between faith and science, because his faith began by accepting all facts and all scientific probabilities in order to face them religiously. But there was an invincible conflict between religion as he conceived it and morality, because morality takes sides and regards one sort of motive and one kind of result as better than another, whereas religion according to him gloried in everything, even in the evil, as fulfilling the will of God.

Of course the practice of virtue was not excluded; it was just as needful as evil was in the scheme of the whole; but while the effort of morality was requisite, the judgments of morality were absurd. Now I think we may say that a man who finds himself in such a position has a divided mind, and that while he has wrestled with the deepest questions like a young giant, he has not won the fight. I mean, he has not seen his way to any one of the various possibilities about the nature of things, but has remained entangled, sincerely, nobly, and pathetically, in contrary traditions stronger than himself. In the goodly company of philosophers he is an intrepid martyr.

In metaphysics as in morals Royce perpetually labored the same points, yet they never became clear; they covered a natural complexity in the facts which his idealism could not disentangle. There was a voluminous confusion in his thought; some clear principles and ultimate possibilities turned up in it, now presenting one face and now another, like chips carried down a swollen stream; but the most powerful currents were below the surface, and the whole movement was hard to trace. He had borrowed from Hegel a way of conceiving systems of philosophy, and also the elements of his own thought, which did not tend to clarify them. He did not think of correcting what incoherence there might remain in any view, and then holding it in reserve, as one of the possibilities, until facts should enable us to decide whether it was true or not. Instead he clung to the incoherence as if it had been the heart of the position, in order to be driven by it to some other position altogether, so that while every view seemed to be considered, criticized, and in a measure retained (since the argument continued on the same lines, however ill-chosen they might have been originally), yet justice was never done to it; it was never clarified, made consistent with itself, and then accepted or rejected in view of the evidence. Hence a vicious and perplexing suggestion that philosophies are bred out of philosophies, not out of men in the presence of things. Hence too a sophistical effort to find everything self-contradictory, and in some disquieting way both true and false, as if there were not an infinite number of perfectly consistent systems which the world might have illustrated.

Consider, for instance, his chief and most puzzling contention, that all minds are parts of one mind. It is easy, according to the meaning we give to the word mind, to render this assertion clear and true, or clear and false, or clear and doubtful (because touching unknown facts), or utterly absurd. It is obvious that all minds are parts of one flux or system of experiences, as all bodies are parts of one system of bodies. Again, if mind is identified with its objects, and people are said to be "of one mind" when they are thinking of the same thing, it is certain that many minds are often identical in part, and they would all be identical with portions of an omniscient mind that should perceive all that they severally experienced. The question becomes doubtful if what we mean by oneness of mind is unity of type; our information or plausible guesses cannot assure us how many sorts of experience may exist, or to what extent their development (when they develop) follows the same lines of evolution. The animals would have to be consulted, and the other planets, and the infinite recesses of time. The straitjacket which German idealism has provided is certainly far too narrow even for the varieties of human imagination. Finally, the assertion becomes absurd when it is understood to suggest that an actual instance of thinking, in which something, say the existence of America, is absent or denied, can be part of another actual instance of thinking in which it is present and asserted. But this whole method of treating the matter—and we might add anything that observation might warrant us in adding about multiple personalities— would leave out the problem that agitated Royce and that bewildered his readers. He wanted all minds to be one in some way which should be logically and morally necessary, and which yet, as he could not help feeling, was morally and logically impossible.

For pure transcendentalism, which was Royce's technical method, the question does not arise at all. Transcendentalism is an attitude or a point of view rather than a system. Its Absolute is thinking "as such," wherever thought may exert itself. The notion that there are separate instances of thought is excluded, because space, time, and number belong to the visionary world posited by thought, not to the function of thinking; individuals are figments of constructive fancy, as are material objects. The stress of moral being is the same wherever it may fall, and there are no finite selves, or relations between thinkers; also no infinite self, because on this principle the Absolute is not an existent being, a psychological monster, but a station or office; its essence is a task. Actual thinking is therefore never a part of the Absolute, but always the Absolute itself. Thinkers, finite or infinite, would be existing persons or masses of feelings; such things are dreamt of only. *Any* system of existences, *any* truth or matter of fact waiting to be recognized, contradicts the transcendental insight and stultifies it. The all-inclusive mind is my mind as I think, mind in its living function, and beyond that philosophy cannot go.

Royce, however, while often reasoning on this principle, was incapable of not going beyond it, or of always remembering it. He could not help believing that constructive fancy not only feigns individuals and instances of thought, but is actually seated in them. The Absolute, for instance, must be not merely the abstract subject or transcendental self in all of us (although it was that too), but an actual synthetic universal mind, the God of Aristotle and of Christian theology. Nor was it easy for Royce, a sincere soul and a friend of William James, not to be a social realist; I mean, not to admit that there are many collateral human minds, in temporal existential relations to one another, any of which may influence another, but never supplant it nor materially include it. Finite experience was not a mere element in infinite experience; it was a tragic totality in itself. I was not God looking at myself, I was myself looking for God. Yet this strain was utterly incompatible with the principles of transcendentalism; it turned philosophy into a simple anticipation of science, if not into an indulgence in literary psychology. Knowledge would then have been only faith leaping across the chasm of coexistence and guessing the presence and nature of what surrounds us by some hint of material influence or brotherly affinity. Both the credulity and the finality which such naturalism implies were offensive to Royce, and contrary to his skeptical and mystical instincts. Was there some middle course?

The audience in a theater stand in a transcendental relation to the persons and events in the play. The performance may take place today and last one hour, while the fable transports us to some heroic epoch or to an age that never existed, and stretches through days and perhaps years of fancied time. Just so transcendental thinking, while actually timeless and not distributed among persons, might survey infinite time and rehearse the passions and thoughts of a thousand characters. Thought, after all, needs objects, however fictitious and ideal they may be; it could not think if it thought nothing. This indispensable world of appearance is far more interesting than the reality that evokes it; the qualities and divisions found in the appearance diversify the monotonous function of pure thinking and render it concrete. Instances of thought and particular minds may thus be introduced consistently into a transcendental system, provided they are distinguished not by their own times and places, but only by their themes. The transcendental mind would be a pure poet, with no earthly life, but living only in his works, and in the times and persons of his fable. This view, firmly and consistently held, would deserve the name of absolute idealism, which Royce liked to give to his own system. But he struggled to fuse it with social realism, with which it is radically incompatible. Particular minds and the whole process of time, for absolute idealism, are *ideas* only; they are thought of and surveyed, they never think or lapse actually. For this reason genuine idealists can speak so glibly of the mind of a nation or an age. It is just as real and unreal to them as the mind of an individual; for within the human individual they can trace unities that run through and beyond him, so that parts of him, identical with parts of other people, form units as living as himself; for it is all a web of themes, not a concourse of existences. This is the very essence and pride of idealism, that knowledge is not knowledge of the world but is the world itself, and that the units of discourse, which are interwoven and crossed units, are the only individuals in being. You may call them persons, because "person" means a mask; but you cannot call them souls. They are knots in the web of history. They are words in their context, and the only spirit in them is the sense they have for me.

Royce, however, in saying all this, also wished not to say it, and his two thick volumes on *The World and the Individual* leave their subject wrapped in utter obscurity. Perceiving the fact when he had finished, he very characteristically added a "Supplementary Essay" of a hundred more pages, in finer print, in which to come to the point. Imagine, he said, an absolutely exhaustive map of England spread out upon English soil. The map would be a part of England, yet would reproduce every feature of England, including itself; so that the map would reappear on a smaller scale within itself an infinite number of times, like a mirror reflected in a mirror. In this way we might be individuals within a larger individual, and no less actual and complete than he. Does this solve the problem? If we take the illustration as it stands, there is still only one individual in existence, the material England, all the maps being parts of its single surface; nor will it at all resemble the maps, since it will be washed by the sea and surrounded by foreign nations, and not, like the maps, by other Englands enveloping it. If, on the contrary, we equalize the status of all the members of the series, by making it infinite in both directions, then there would be no England at all, but only map within map of England. There would be no absolute mind inclusive but not included, and the Absolute would be the series as a whole, utterly different from any of its members. It would be a series while they were maps, a truth while they were minds; and if the Absolute from the beginning had been regarded as a truth only, there never would have been any difficulty in the existence of individuals under it. Moreover, if the individuals are all exactly alike, does not their exact similarity defeat the whole purpose of the speculation, which was to vindicate the equal reality of the whole and of its *limited* parts? And if each of us, living through infinite time, goes through precisely the same experiences as every-one else, why this vain repetition? Is it not enough for this insatiable world to live its life once? Why not admit solipsism and be true to the transcendental method? Because of con-science and good sense? But then the infinite series of maps is useless, England is herself again, and the prospect opens before us of an infinite number of supplementary essays.

Royce sometimes felt that he might have turned his hand to other things than philosophy. He once wrote a novel, and its want of success was a silent disappointment to him. Per-haps he might have been a great musician. Complexity, repe-titions, vagueness, endlessness are hardly virtues in writing or thinking, but in music they might have swelled and swelled into a real sublimity, all the more that he was patient, had a voluminous meandering memory, and loved technical devices. But rather than a musician—for he was no artist—he resembled some great-hearted mediaeval peasant visited by mystical promptings, whom the monks should have adopted and allowed to browse among their theological folios; a Duns Scotus earnest and studious to a fault, not having the light-ness of soul to despise those elaborate sophistries, yet minded to ferret out their secret for himself and walk by his inward light. His was a gothic and scholastic spirit, intent on de-vising and solving puzzles, and honoring God in systematic works, like the coral insect or the spider; eventually creating a fabric that in its homely intricacy and fullness arrested and moved the heart, the web of it was so vast, and so full of mystery and yearning.

THE MIGRATION of Americans to Europe began to give way during the twenties to a movement of Europeans toward America. D. H. Lawrence's *Studies in Classic American Literature* did not appear in book-form till 1922; but he had begun them during World War I. In a letter of February 1, 1919, to Harriet Monroe, the editor of the Chicago magazine *Poetry,* he wrote: "I have worked at them for more than four years—hard work. They may not look it."

In September 1922, Lawrence came to America, and he remained here, with one brief visit to England, till October 1925. The instincts and thoughts that appear in these essays are reflected in his letters of this period. "The sense of doom deepens inside me," he wrote to J. Middleton Murry on August 13, 1923, "at the thought of the old world which I loved—and the new world means nothing to me." But he liked the Southwest and Mexico, because they seemed to bring him close to the primitive "dark gods" from which he tended to think the white race was cutting itself off in abstraction. He spent very little time in the East and lived mostly in the country in New Mexico. "I must say I am glad," he wrote Harriet Monroe from Taos, April 8, 1924, "to be out here in the Southwest of America—there is the pristine something, unbroken, unbreakable, and not to be got under even by us awful whites with our machines—for which I thank whatever gods there be."

He tried to formulate his opinion of America in a letter to Gilbert Seldes of February 25, 1923, from Del Monte Ranch, Questa, New Mexico:

No, I am not disappointed in America. I said I was coming to Europe this spring. But I don't want to. We leave in a fortnight for old Mexico. Perhaps I shall came back here. . . .

But I feel about U.S.A., as I vaguely felt a long time ago: that there is a vast unreal intermediary thing intervening between the real thing which was Europe and the next real thing, which will probably be America, but which isn't yet, at all. Seems to me a vast death-happening must come first. But probably it is here, in America (I don't say just U.S.A.), that the quick will keep alive and come through.

The *Studies in Classic American Literature* have shots that do not hit the mark and moments that are quite hysterical; but they remain one of the few first-rate books that have ever been written on the subject. To an American, American literature is a part of his native landscape, and so veiled with associations that he cannot always see what the author is really saying. D. H. Lawrence has here tried to do what it would be difficult for an American to do: read our books for their meaning in the life of the western world as a whole.

And his *Studies* mark the moment when Europe first begins to look toward America, not merely for freedom, not merely for money, not merely from curiosity, but with a desperate need for new ideals to sustain European civilization.

D. H. LAWRENCE

STUDIES IN CLASSIC AMERICAN LITERATURE

I. The Spirit of Place

WE LIKE TO THINK of the old-fashioned American classics as children's books. Just childishness, on our part. The old American art speech contains an alien quality, which belongs to the American continent and to nowhere else. But, of course, so long as we insist on reading the books as children's tales, we miss all that.

One wonders what the proper high-brow Romans of the third and fourth or later centuries read into the strange utterances of Lucretius or Apuleius or Tertullian, Augustine or Athanasius. The uncanny voice of Iberian Spain, the weirdness of old Carthage, the passion of Libya and North Africa; you may bet the proper old Romans never heard these at all. They read old Latin inference over the top of it, as we read old European inference over the top of Poe or Hawthorne.

It is hard to hear a new voice, as hard as it is to listen to an unknown language. We just don't listen. There is a new voice in the old American classics. The world has declined to hear it, and has babbled about children's stories.

Why?—Out of fear. The world fears a new experience

more than it fears anything. Because a new experience displaces so many old experiences. And it is like trying to use muscles that have perhaps never been used, or that have been going stiff for ages. It hurts horribly.

The world doesn't fear a new idea. It can pigeonhole any idea. But it can't pigeonhole a real new experience. It can only dodge. The world is a great dodger, and the Americans the greatest. Because they dodge their own very selves.

There is a new feeling in the old American books, far more than there is in the modern American books, which are pretty empty of any feeling, and proud of it. There is a "different" feeling in the old American classics. It is the shifting over from the old psyche to something new, a displacement. And displacements hurt. This hurts. So we try to tie it up, like a cut finger. Put a rag round it.

It is a cut too. Cutting away the old emotions and consciousness. Don't ask what is left.

Art speech is the only truth. An artist is usually a damned liar, but his art, if it be art, will tell you the truth of his day. And that is all that matters. Away with eternal truth. Truth lives from day to day, and the marvelous Plato of yesterday is chiefly bosh today.

The old American artists were hopeless liars. But they were artists, in spite of themselves. Which is more than you can say of most living practitioners.

And you can please yourself, when you read *The Scarlet Letter*, whether you accept what that sugary, blue-eyed little darling of a Hawthorne has to say for himself, false as all darlings are, or whether you read the impeccable truth of his art speech.

The curious thing about art speech is that it prevaricates so terribly, I mean it tells such lies. I suppose because we always all the time tell ourselves lies. And out of a pattern of lies art weaves the truth. Like Dostoevsky posing as a sort of Jesus, but most truthfully revealing himself all the while as a little horror.

Truly art is a sort of subterfuge. But thank God for it, we can see through the subterfuge if we choose. Art has two great functions. First, it provides an emotional experience.

And then, if we have the courage of our own feelings, it becomes a mine of practical truth. We have had the feelings
ad nauseam. But we've never dared dig the actual truth
out of them, the truth that concerns us, whether it concerns
our grandchildren or not.

The artist usually sets out—or used to—to point a moral
and adorn a tale. The tale, however, points the other way,
as a rule. Two blankly opposing morals, the artist's and the
tale's. Never trust the artist. Trust the tale. The proper
function of a critic is to save the tale from the artist who
created it.

Now we know our business in these studies; saving the
American tale from the American artist.

Let us look at this American artist first. How did he ever
get to America, to start with? Why isn't he a European still,
like his father before him?

Now listen to me, don't listen to him. He'll tell you the
lie you expect. Which is partly your fault for expecting it.

He didn't come in search of freedom of worship. England
had more freedom of worship in the year 1700 than America
had. Won by Englishmen who wanted freedom, and so
stopped at home and fought for it. And got it. Freedom of
worship? Read the history of New England during the first
century of its existence.

Freedom anyhow? The land of the free! This the land
of the free! Why, if I say anything that displeases them,
the free mob will lynch me, and that's my freedom. Free?
Why, I have never been in any country where the individual
has such an abject fear of his fellow-countrymen. Because,
as I say, they are free to lynch him the moment he shows he
is not one of them.

No, no, if you're so fond of the truth about Queen Victoria, try a little about yourself.

Those Pilgrim Fathers and their successors never came
here for freedom of worship. What did they set up when
they got here? Freedom, would you call it?

They didn't come for freedom. Or if they did, they sadly
went back on themselves.

All right then, what did they come for? For lots of reasons.

Perhaps least of all in search of freedom of any sort: positive freedom, that is.

They came largely to get *away*—that most simple of motives. To get away. Away from what? In the long run, away from themselves. Away from everything. That's why most people have come to America, and still do come. To get away from everything they are and have been.

"Henceforth be masterless."

Which is all very well, but it isn't freedom. Rather the reverse. A hopeless sort of constraint. It is never freedom till you find something you really *positively want to be*. And people in America have always been shouting about the things they are *not*. Unless, of course, they are millionaires, made or in the making.

And after all there is a positive side to the movement. All that vast flood of human life that has flowed over the Atlantic in ships from Europe to America has not flowed over simply on a tide of revulsion from Europe and from the confinements of the European ways of life. This revulsion was, and still is, I believe, the prime motive in emigration. But there was some cause, even for the revulsion.

It seems as if at times man had a frenzy for getting away from any control of any sort. In Europe the old Christianity was the real master. The Church and the true aristocracy bore the responsibility for the working out of the Christian ideals: a little irregularly, maybe, but responsible nevertheless.

Mastery, kingship, fatherhood had their power destroyed at the time of the Renaissance.

And it was precisely at this moment that the great drift over the Atlantic started. What were men drifting away from? The old authority of Europe? Were they breaking the bonds of authority, and escaping to a new more absolute unrestrainedness? Maybe. But there was more to it.

Liberty is all very well, but men cannot live without masters. There is always a master. And men either live in glad obedience to the master they believe in, or they live in a frictional opposition to the master they wish to undermine. In America this frictional opposition has been the vital factor. It has given the Yankee his kick. Only the continual influx of more servile Europeans has provided America with an obedient laboring class. The true obedience never outlasting the first generation.

But there sits the old master, over in Europe. Like a parent. Somewhere deep in every American heart lies a rebellion against the old parenthood of Europe. Yet no American feels he has completely escaped its mastery. Hence the slow, smoldering patience of American opposition. The slow, smoldering, corrosive obedience to the old master Europe, the unwilling subject, the unremitting opposition.

Whatever else you are, be masterless.

> Ca Ca Caliban
> Get a new master, be a new man.

Escaped slaves, we might say, people the republics of Liberia or Haiti. Liberia enough! Are we to look at America in the same way? A vast republic of escaped slaves. When you consider the hordes from eastern Europe, you might well say it: a vast republic of escaped slaves. But one dare not say this of the Pilgrim Fathers, and the great old body of idealist Americans, the modern Americans tortured with thought. A vast republic of escaped slaves. Look out, America! And a minority of earnest, self-tortured people.

The masterless.

> Ca Ca Caliban
> Get a new master, be a new man.

What did the Pilgrim Fathers come for, then, when they came so gruesomely over the black sea? Oh, it was in a black spirit. A black revulsion from Europe, from the old authority of Europe, from kings and bishops and popes. And more. When you look into it, more. They were black, masterful men, they wanted something else. No kings, no bishops maybe. Even no God Almighty. But also, no more of this new "humanity" which followed the Renaissance. None of this new liberty which was to be so pretty in Europe. Something grimmer, by no means free-and-easy.

America has never been easy, and is not easy today. Amer-

icans have always been at a certain tension. Their liberty is
a thing of sheer will, sheer tension: a liberty of THOU SHALT
NOT. And it has been so from the first. The land of THOU
SHALT NOT. Only the first commandment is: THOU SHALT
NOT PRESUME TO BE A MASTER. Hence democracy.

"We are the masterless." That is what the American Eagle
shrieks. It's a Hen-Eagle.

The Spaniards refused the post-Renaissance liberty of
Europe. And the Spaniards filled most of America. The
Yankees, too, refused, refused the post-Renaissance humanism of Europe. First and foremost, they hated masters. But
under that, they hated the flowing ease of humor in Europe.
At the bottom of the American soul was always a dark suspense, at the bottom of the Spanish-American soul the same.
And this dark suspense hated and hates the old European
spontaneity, watches it collapse with satisfaction.

Every continent has its own great spirit of place. Every
people is polarized in some particular locality, which is home,
the homeland. Different places on the face of the earth have
different vital effluence, different vibration, different chemical exhalation, different polarity with different stars: call it
what you like. But the spirit of place is a great reality. The
Nile valley produced not only the corn, but the terrific
religions of Egypt. China produces the Chinese, and will go
on doing so. The Chinese in San Francisco will in time
cease to be Chinese, for America is a great melting pot.

There was a tremendous polarity in Italy, in the city of
Rome. And this seems to have died. For even places die.
The Island of Great Britain had a wonderful terrestrial
magnetism or polarity of its own, which made the British
people. For the moment, this polarity seems to be breaking.
Can England die? And what if England dies?

Men are less free than they imagine; ah, far less free. The
freest are perhaps least free.

Men are free when they are in a living homeland, not
when they are straying and breaking away. Men are free
when they are obeying some deep, inward voice of religious
belief. Obeying from within. Men are free when they belong
to a living, organic, *believing* community, active in fulfilling

some unfulfilled, perhaps unrealized purpose. Not when they are escaping to some wild west. The most unfree souls go west, and shout of freedom. Men are freest when they are most unconscious of freedom. The shout is a rattling of chains, always was.

Men are not free when they are doing just what they like. The moment you can do just what you like, there is nothing you care about doing. Men are only free when they are doing what the deepest self likes.

And there is getting down to the deepest self! It takes some diving.

Because the deepest self is way down, and the conscious self is an obstinate monkey. But of one thing we may be sure. If one wants to be free, one has to give up the illusion of doing what one likes, and seek what IT wishes done.

But before you can do what IT likes, you must first break the spell of the old mastery, the old IT.

Perhaps at the Renaissance, when kinship and fatherhood fell, Europe drifted into a very dangerous half-truth: of liberty and equality. Perhaps the men who went to America felt this, and so repudiated the old world altogether. Went one better than Europe. Liberty in America has meant so far the breaking away from *all* dominion. The true liberty will only begin when Americans discover IT, and proceed possibly to fulfill IT. IT being the deepest *whole* self of man, the self in its wholeness, not idealistic halfness.

That's why the Pilgrim Fathers came to America, then; and that's why we come. Driven by IT. We cannot see that invisible winds carry us, as they carry swarms of locusts, that invisible magnetism brings us as it brings the migrating birds to their unforeknown goal. But it is so. We are not the marvelous choosers and deciders we think we are. IT chooses for us, and decides for us. Unless, of course, we are just escaped slaves, vulgarly cocksure of our ready-made destiny. But if we are living people, in touch with the source, IT drives us and decides us. We are free only so long as we obey. When we run counter, and think we will do as we like, we just flee around like Orestes pursued by the Eumenides.

And still, when the great day begins, when Americans have at last discovered America and their own wholeness, still there will be the vast number of escaped slaves to reckon with, those who have no cocksure, ready-made destinies.

Which will win in America, the escaped slaves, or the new whole men?

The real American day hasn't begun yet. Or at least, not yet sunrise. So far it has been the false dawn. That is, in the progressive American consciousness there has been the one dominant desire, to do away with the old thing. Do away with masters, exalt the will of the people. The will of the people being nothing but a figment, the exalting doesn't count for much. So, in the name of the will of the people, get rid of masters. When you have got rid of masters, you are left with this mere phrase of the will of the people. Then you pause and bethink yourself, and try to recover your own wholeness.

So much for the conscious American motive, and for democracy over here. Democracy in America is just the tool with which the old master of Europe, the European spirit, is undermined. Europe destroyed potentially, American democracy will evaporate. America will begin.

American consciousness has so far been a false dawn. The negative ideal of democracy. But underneath, and contrary to this open ideal, the first hints and revelations of IT. IT, the American whole soul.

You have got to pull the democratic and idealistic clothes off American utterance, and see what you can of the dusky body of IT underneath.

"Henceforth be masterless."

Henceforth be mastered.

II. Benjamin Franklin

THE Perfectibility of Man! Ah heaven, what a dreary theme! The perfectibility of the Ford car! The perfectibility of which man? I am many men. Which of them are you going to perfect? I am not a mechanical contrivance.

Education! Which of the various me's do you propose to educate, and which do you propose to suppress?

Anyhow, I defy you. I defy you, oh society, to educate me or to suppress me, according to your dummy standards.

The ideal man! And which is he, if you please? Benjamin Franklin or Abraham Lincoln? The ideal man! Roosevelt or Porfirio Diaz?

There are other men in me, besides this patient ass who sits here in a tweed jacket. What am I doing, playing the patient ass in a tweed jacket? Who am I talking to? Who are you, at the other end of this patience?

Who are you? How many selves have you? And which of these selves do you want to be?

Is Yale College going to educate the self that is the dark of you, or Harvard College?

The ideal self! Oh, but I have a strange and fugitive self shut out and howling like a wolf or a coyote under the ideal windows. See his red eyes in the dark? This is the self who is coming into his own.

The perfectibility of man, dear God! When every man as long as he remains alive is in himself a multitude of conflicting men. Which of these do you choose to perfect, at the expense of every other?

Old Daddy Franklin will tell you. He'll rig him up for you, the pattern American. Oh, Franklin was the first downright American. He knew what he was about, the sharp little man. He set up the first dummy American.

At the beginning of his career this cunning little Benjamin drew up for himself a creed that should "satisfy the professors of every religion, but shock none."

Now wasn't that a real American thing to do?

"*That there is One God, who made all things.*"

(But Benjamin made Him.)

"*That He governs the world by His Providence.*"

(Benjamin knowing all about Providence.)

"*That He ought to be worshiped with adoration, prayer, and thanksgiving.*"

(Which cost nothing.)

"But——" But me no buts, Benjamin, saith the Lord.

"But that the most acceptable service of God is doing good to men."

(God having no choice in the matter.)

"That the soul is immortal."

(You'll see why, in the next clause.)

"And that God will certainly reward virtue and punish vice, either here or hereafter."

Now if Mr. Andrew Carnegie, or any other millionaire, had wished to invent a God to suit his ends, he could not have done better. Benjamin did it for him in the eighteenth century. God is the supreme servant of men who want to get on, to *produce*. Providence. The provider. The heavenly storekeeper. The everlasting Wanamaker.

And this is all the God the grandsons of the Pilgrim Fathers had left. Aloft on a pillar of dollars.

"That the soul is immortal."

The trite way Benjamin says it!

But man has a soul, though you can't locate it either in his purse or his pocket-book or his heart or his stomach or his head. The *wholeness* of a man is his soul. Not merely that nice little comfortable bit which Benjamin marks out.

It's a queer thing is a man's soul. It is the whole of him. Which means it is the unknown him, as well as the known. It seems to me just funny, professors and Benjamins fixing the functions of the soul. Why the soul of man is a vast forest, and all Benjamin intended was a neat back garden. And we've all got to fit into his kitchen-garden scheme of things. Hail Columbia!

The soul of man is a dark forest. The Hercynian Wood that scared the Romans so, and out of which came the white-skinned hordes of the next civilization.

Who knows what will come out of the soul of man? The soul of man is a dark vast forest, with wild life in it. Think of Benjamin fencing it off!

Oh, but Benjamin fenced a little tract that he called the soul of man, and proceeded to get it into cultivation. Providence, forsooth! And they think that bit of barbed wire is going to keep us in pound forever? More fools they.

This is Benjamin's barbed-wire fence. He made himself a list of virtues, which he trotted inside like a gray nag in a paddock.

I
TEMPERANCE

Eat not to fullness; drink not to elevation.

2
SILENCE

Speak not but what may benefit others or yourself; avoid trifling conversation.

3
ORDER

Let all your things have their places; let each part of your business have its time.

4
RESOLUTION

Resolve to perform what you ought; perform without fail what you resolve.

5
FRUGALITY

Make no expense but to do good to others or yourself—i.e., waste nothing.

6
INDUSTRY

Lose no time, be always employed in something useful; cut off all unnecessary action.

7
SINCERITY

Use no hurtful deceit; think innocently and justly, and, if you speak, speak accordingly.

8
JUSTICE

Wrong none by doing injuries, or omitting the benefits that are your duty.

9
MODERATION

Avoid extremes, forbear resenting injuries as much as you think they deserve.

10
CLEANLINESS

Tolerate no uncleanliness in body, clothes, or habitation.

11
TRANQUILLITY

Be not disturbed at trifles, or at accidents common or unavoidable.

12
CHASTITY

Rarely use venery but for health and offspring, never to dullness, weakness, or the injury of your own or another's peace or reputation.

13
HUMILITY

Imitate Jesus and Socrates.

A Quaker friend told Franklin that he, Benjamin, was generally considered proud, so Benjamin put in the Humility touch as an afterthought. The amusing part is the sort of humility it displays. "Imitate Jesus and Socrates," and mind you don't outshine either of these two. One can just imagine Socrates and Alcibiades roaring in their cups over Philadelphian Benjamin, and Jesus looking at him a little puzzled, and murmuring: "Aren't you wise in your own conceit, Ben?"

"Henceforth be masterless," retorts Ben. "Be ye each one his own master unto himself, and don't let even the Lord put His spoke in." "Each man his own master" is but a puffing up of masterlessness.

Well, the first of Americans practiced this enticing list with assiduity, setting a national example. He had the virtues in columns, and gave himself good and bad marks according as he thought his behavior deserved. Pity these conduct charts are lost to us. He only remarks that Order was his stumbling block. He could not learn to be neat and tidy.

Isn't it nice to have nothing worse to confess?

He was a little model, was Benjamin. Doctor Franklin. Snuff-colored little man! Immortal soul and all!

The immortal soul part was a sort of cheap insurance policy.

Benjamin had no concern, really, with the immortal soul. He was too busy with social man.

1. He swept and lighted the streets of young Philadelphia.

2. He invented electrical appliances.

3. He was the center of a moralizing club in Philadelphia, and he wrote the moral humorisms of Poor Richard.

4. He was a member of all the important councils of Philadelphia, and then of the American colonies.

5. He won the cause of American Independence at the French Court, and was the economic father of the United States.

Now what more can you want of a man? And yet he is *infra dig.*, even in Philadelphia.

I admire him. I admire his sturdy courage first of all, then his sagacity, then his glimpsing into the thunders of electricity, then his common-sense humor. All the qualities of a great man, and never more than a great citizen. Middle-sized, sturdy, snuff-colored Doctor Franklin, one of the soundest citizens that ever trod or "used venery."

I do not like him.

And, by the way, I always thought books of Venery were about hunting deer.

There is a certain earnest naïveté about him. Like a child. And like a little old man. He has again become as a little child, always as wise as his grandfather, or wiser.

Perhaps, as I say, the most complete citizen that ever "used venery."

Printer, philosopher, scientist, author and patriot, impeccable husband and citizen, why isn't he an archetype?

Pioneer, Oh, Pioneers! Benjamin was one of the greatest pioneers of the United States. Yet we just can't do with him.

What's wrong with him then? Or what's wrong with us?
I can remember, when I was a little boy, my father used
to buy a scrubby yearly almanac with the sun and moon
and stars on the cover. And it used to prophesy bloodshed
and famine. But also crammed in corners it had little anecdotes and humorisms, with a moral tag. And I used to have
my little priggish laugh at the woman who counted her
chickens before they were hatched and so forth, and I was
convinced that honesty was the best policy, also a little
priggishly. The author of these bits was Poor Richard, and
Poor Richard was Benjamin Franklin, writing in Philadelphia well over a hundred years before.

And probably I haven't got over those Poor Richard tags
yet. I rankle still with them. They are thorns in young
flesh.

Because, although I still believe that honesty is the best
policy, I dislike policy altogether; though it is just as well
not to count your chickens before they are hatched, it's still
more hateful to count them with gloating when they *are*
hatched. It has taken me many years and countless smarts
to get out of that barbed-wire moral enclosure that Poor
Richard rigged up. Here am I now in tatters and scratched
to ribbons, sitting in the middle of Benjamin's America
looking at the barbed wire, and the fat sheep crawling under
the fence to get fat outside, and the watchdogs yelling at
the gate lest by chance anyone should get out by the proper
exit. Oh, America! Oh, Benjamin! And I just utter a long,
loud curse against Benjamin and the American corral.

Moral America! Most moral Benjamin. Sound, satisfied
Ben!

He had to go to the frontiers of his State to settle some
disturbance among the Indians. On this occasion he writes:

We found that they had made a great bonfire in the middle
of the square; they were all drunk, men and women quarreling
and fighting. Their dark-colored bodies, half naked, seen only
by the gloomy light of the bonfire, running after and beating
one another with firebrands, accompanied by their horrid yell-
ings, formed a scene the most resembling our ideas of hell that
could well be imagined. There was no appeasing the tumult,

and we retired to our lodging. At midnight a number of them
came thundering at our door, demanding more rum, of which
we took no notice.

The next day, sensible they had misbehaved in giving us
that disturbance, they sent three of their counselors to make
their apology. The orator acknowledged the fault, but laid it
upon the rum, and then endeavored to excuse the rum by saying: "The Great Spirit, who made all things, made everything
for some use; and whatever he designed anything for, that use
it should always be put to. Now, when he had made the rum, he
said: 'Let this be for the Indians to get drunk with.' And it
must be so."

And, indeed, if it be the design of Providence to extirpate
these savages in order to make room for the cultivators of the
earth, it seems not improbable that rum may be the appointed
means. It has already annihilated all the tribes who formerly
inhabited all the seacoast. . . .

This, from the good doctor with such suave complacency,
is a little disenchanting. Almost too good to be true.

But there you are! The barbed-wire fence. "Extirpate
these savages in order to make room for the cultivators of
the earth." Oh, Benjamin Franklin! He even "used venery"
as a cultivator of seed.

Cultivate the earth, ye gods! The Indians did that, as
much as they needed. And they left off there. Who built
Chicago? Who cultivated the earth until it spawned Pittsburgh, Pa.?

The moral issue! Just look at it! Cultivation included. If
it's a mere choice of Kultur or cultivation, I give it up.

Which brings us right back to our question, what's wrong
with Benjamin, that we can't stand him? Or else, what's
wrong with us, that we find fault with such a paragon?

Man is a moral animal. All right. I am a moral animal.
And I'm going to remain such. I'm not going to be turned
into a virtuous little automaton as Benjamin would have
me. "This is good, that is bad. Turn the little handle and
let the good tap flow," saith Benjamin, and all America
with him. "But first of all extirpate those savages who are
always turning on the bad tap."

I am a moral animal. But I am not a moral machine. I

don't work with a little set of handles or levers. The Temper-
ance-silence-order-resolution-frugality-industry-sincerity-jus-
tice-moderation-cleanliness-tranquillity-chastity-humility keyboard is not going to get me going. I'm really not just an
automatic piano with a moral Benjamin getting tunes out
of me.

Here's my creed, against Benjamin's. This is what I
believe:

> That I am I.
> That my soul is a dark forest.
> That my known self will never be more than a little clearing
> in the forest.
> That gods, strange gods, come forth from the forest into the
> clearing of my known self, and then go back.
> That I must have the courage to let them come and go.
> That I will never let mankind put anything over me, but that
> I will try always to recognize and submit to the gods in me and
> the gods in other men and women.

There is my creed. He who runs may read. He who
prefers to crawl, or to go by gasoline, can call it rot.

Then for a "list." It is rather fun to play at Benjamin.

1
TEMPERANCE

Eat and carouse with Bacchus, or munch dry bread with
Jesus, but don't sit down without one of the gods.

2
SILENCE

Be still when you have nothing to say; when genuine passion
moves you, say what you've got to say, and say it hot.

3
ORDER

Know that you are responsible to the gods inside you and to
the men in whom the gods are manifest. Recognize your
superiors and your inferiors, according to the gods. This is the
root of all order.

4
RESOLUTION

Resolve to abide by your own deepest promptings, and to sacrifice the smaller thing to the greater. Kill when you must, and be killed the same: the *must* coming from the gods inside you, or from the men in whom you recognize the Holy Ghost.

5
FRUGALITY

Demand nothing; accept what you see fit. Don't waste your pride or squander your emotion.

6
INDUSTRY

Lose no time with ideals; serve the Holy Ghost; never serve mankind.

7
SINCERITY

To be sincere is to remember that I am I, and that the other man is not me.

8
JUSTICE

The only justice is to follow the sincere intuition of the soul, angry or gentle. Anger is just, and pity is just, but judgment is never just.

9
MODERATION

Beware of absolutes. There are many gods.

10
CLEANLINESS

Don't be too clean. It impoverishes the blood.

11
TRANQUILLITY

The soul has many motions, many gods come and go. Try and find your deepest issue, in every confusion, and abide by that. Obey the man in whom you recognize the Holy Ghost; command when your honor comes to command.

12
CHASTITY

Never "use" venery at all. Follow your passional impulse, if it be answered in the other being; but never have any motive in mind, neither offspring nor health nor even pleasure, nor even service. Only know that "venery" is of the great gods. An offering-up of yourself to the very great gods, the dark ones, and nothing else.

13
HUMILITY

See all men and women according to the Holy Ghost that is within them. Never yield before the barren.

There's my list. I have been trying dimly to realize it for a long time, and only America and old Benjamin have at last goaded me into trying to formulate it.

And now I, at least, know why I can't stand Benjamin. He tries to take away my wholeness and my dark forest, my freedom. For how can any man be free, without an illimitable background? And Benjamin tries to shove me into a barbed-wire paddock and make me grow potatoes or Chicagoes.

And how can I be free, without gods that come and go? But Benjamin won't let anything exist except my useful fellow-men, and I'm sick of them; as for his Godhead, his Providence, He is Head of nothing except a vast heavenly store that keeps every imaginable line of goods, from victrolas to cat-o'-nine tails.

And how can any man be free without a soul of his own, that he believes in and won't sell at any price? But Benjamin doesn't let me have a soul of my own. He says I am nothing but a servant of mankind—galley-slave I call it—and if I don't get my wages here below—that is, if Mr. Pierpont Morgan or Mr. Nosey Hebrew or the grand United States Government, the great US, US OR SOMEOFUS, manages to scoop in my bit, along with their lump—why, never mind, I shall get my wages HEREAFTER.

Oh, Benjamin! Oh, Binjum! You do NOT suck me in any longer.

And why, oh, why should the snuff-colored little trap have wanted to take us all in? Why did he do it?

Out of sheer human cussedness, in the first place. We do all like to get things inside a barbed-wire corral. Especially our fellow-men. We love to round them up inside the barbed-wire enclosure of FREEDOM, and make 'em work. "*Work, you free jewel*, WORK!" shouts the liberator, cracking his whip. Benjamin, I will not work. I do not choose to be a free democrat. I am absolutely a servant of my own Holy Ghost.

Sheer cussedness! But there was as well the salt of a subtler purpose. Benjamin was just in his eyeholes—to use an English vulgarism, meaning he was just delighted—when he was at Paris judiciously milking money out of the French monarchy for the overthrow of all monarchy. If you want to ride your horse to somewhere you must put a bit in his mouth. And Benjamin wanted to ride his horse so that it would upset the whole apple-cart of the old masters. He wanted the whole European apple-cart upset. So he had to put a strong bit in the mouth of his ass.

"Henceforth be masterless."

That is, he had to break in the human ass completely, so that much more might be broken, in the long run. For the moment it was the British Government that had to have a hole knocked in it. The first real hole it ever had: the breach of the American rebellion.

Benjamin, in his sagacity, knew that the breaking of the old world was a long process. In the depths of his own under-consciousness he hated England, he hated Europe, he hated the whole corpus of the European being. He wanted to be American. But you can't change your nature and mode of consciousness like changing your shoes. It is a gradual shedding. Years must go by, and centuries must elapse before you have finished. Like a son escaping from the domination of his parents. The escape is not just one rupture. It is a long and half-secret process.

So with the American. He was a European when he first went over the Atlantic. He is in the main a recreant European still. From Benjamin Franklin to Woodrow Wilson may be a long stride, but it is a stride along the same road. There is no new road. The same old road, become dreary and futile. Theoretic and materialistic.

Why then did Benjamin set up this dummy of a perfect citizen as a pattern to America? Of course, he did it in perfect good faith, as far as he knew. He thought it simply was the true ideal. But what we *think* we do is not very important. We never really know what we are doing. Either we are materialistic instruments, like Benjamin, or we move in the gesture of creation, from our deepest self, usually unconscious. We are only the actors, we are never wholly the authors of our own deeds or works. IT is the author, the unknown inside us or outside us. The best we can do is to try to hold ourselves in unison with the deeps which are inside us. And the worst we can do is to try to have things our own way, when we run counter to IT, and in the long run get our knuckles rapped for our presumption.

So Benjamin contriving money out of the Court of France. He was contriving the first steps of the overthrow of all Europe, France included. You can never have a new thing without breaking an old. Europe happens to be the old thing. America, unless the people in America assert themselves too much in opposition to the inner gods, should be the new thing. The new thing is the death of the old. But you can't cut the throat of an epoch. You've got to steal the life from it through several centuries.

And Benjamin worked for this both directly and indirectly. Directly, at the Court of France, making a small but very dangerous hole in the side of England, through which hole Europe has by now almost bled to death. And indirectly in Philadelphia, setting up this unlovely, snuff-colored little ideal, or automaton, of a pattern American. The pattern American, this dry, moral, utilitarian little democrat, has done more to ruin the old Europe than any Russian nihilist. He has done it by slow attrition, like a son who has stayed at home and obeyed his parents, all the while silently hating their authority, and silently, in his soul, destroying not only their authority but their whole existence. For the American spiritually stayed at home in Europe. The spiritual home of

America was, and still is, Europe. This is the galling bond-age, in spite of several billions of heaped-up gold. Your heaps of gold are only so many muck-heaps, America, and will remain so till you become a reality to yourselves.

All this Americanizing and mechanizing has been for the purpose of overthrowing the past. And now look at America, tangled in her own barbed wire, and mastered by her own machines. Absolutely got down by her own barbed wire of shalt-nots, and shut up fast in her own "productive" machines like millions of squirrels running in millions of cages. It is just a farce.

Now is your chance, Europe. Now let. Hell loose and get your own back, and paddle your own canoe on a new sea, while clever America lies on her muck-heaps of gold, stran-gled in her own barbed wire of shalt-not ideals and shalt-not moralisms. While she goes out to work like millions of squirrels in millions of cages. Production!

Let Hell loose, and get your own back, Europe!

III. Hector St. John de Crèvecœur

CRÈVECŒUR was born in France, at Caen, in the year 1735. As a boy he was sent over to England and received part of his education there. He went to Canada as a young man, served for a time with Montcalm in the war against the English, and later passed over into the United States, to become an exuberant American. He married a New England girl, and settled on the frontier. During the period of his "cultivating the earth" he wrote the *Letters from an American Farmer,* which enjoyed great vogue in their day, in England espe-cially, among the new reformers like Godwin and Tom Paine.

But Crèvecœur was not a mere cultivator of the earth. That was his best stunt, shall we say. He himself was more concerned with a perfect society and his own manipulation thereof, than with growing carrots. Behold him, then, trot-ting off importantly and idealistically to France, leaving his farm in the wilds to be burnt by the Indians, and his wife to shift as best she might. This was during the American

War of Independence, when the Noble Red Man took to behaving like his own old self. On his return to America, the American Farmer entered into public affairs and into commerce. Again tripping to France, he enjoyed himself as a *littérateur* Child-of-Nature-sweet-and-pure, was a friend of old Benjamin Franklin in Paris, and quite a favorite with Jean Jacques Rousseau's Madame d'Houdetot, that literary soul.

Hazlitt, Godwin, Shelley, Coleridge, the English romanticists, were, of course, thrilled by the *Letters from an American Farmer.* A new world, a world of the Noble Savage and Pristine Nature and Paradisal Simplicity and all that gorgeousness that flows out of the unsullied fount of the ink-bottle. Lucky Coleridge, who got no farther than Bristol. Some of us have gone all the way.

I think this wild and noble America is the thing that I have pined for most ever since I read Fenimore Cooper, as a boy. Now I've got it.

Franklin is the real *practical* prototype of the American. Crèvecœur is the emotional. To the European, the American is first and foremost a dollar-fiend. We tend to forget the emotional heritage of Hector St. John de Crèvecœur. We tend to disbelieve, for example, in Woodrow Wilson's wrung heart and wet hanky. Yet surely these are real enough. Aren't they?

It wasn't to be expected that the dry little snuff-colored Doctor should have it all his own way. The new Americans might use venery for health or offspring, and their time for cultivating potatoes and Chicagoes, but they had got *some* sap in their veins after all. They had got to get a bit of luscious emotion somewhere.

NATURE.

I wish I could write it larger than that.

NATURE.

Benjamin overlooked NATURE. But the French Crèvecœur spotted it long before Thoreau and Emerson worked it up. Absolutely the safest thing to get your emotional reactions over is NATURE.

Crèvecœur's *Letters* are written in a spirit of touching

simplicity, almost better than Chateaubriand. You'd think neither of them would ever know how many beans make five. This American Farmer tells of the joys of creating a home in the wilderness, and of cultivating the virgin soil. Poor virgin, prostituted from the very start.

The Farmer had an Amiable Spouse and an Infant Son, his progeny. He took the Infant Son—who enjoys no other name than this—

> What is thy name?
> I have no name.
> I am the Infant Son——

to the fields with him, and seated the same I. S. on the shafts of the plow whilst he, the American Farmer, plowed the potato patch. He also, the A. F., helped his Neighbors, whom no doubt he loved as himself, to build a barn, and they labored together in the Innocent Simplicity of one of Nature's Communities. Meanwhile the Amiable Spouse, who likewise in Blakean simplicity has No Name, cooked the doughnuts or the pie, though these are not mentioned. No doubt she was a deep-breasted daughter of America, though she may equally well have been a flat-bosomed Methodist. She would have been an Amiable Spouse in either case, and the American Farmer asked no more. I don't know whether her name was Lizzie or Ahoolibah, and probably Crèvecœur didn't. Spouse was enough for him. "Spouse, hand me the carving knife."

The Infant Son developed into Healthy Offspring as more appeared: no doubt Crèvecœur had used venery as directed. And so these Children of Nature toiled in the Wilds at Simple Toil with a little Honest Sweat now and then. You have the complete picture, dear reader. The American Farmer made his own Family Picture, and it is still on view. Of course the Amiable Spouse put on her best apron to be *Im Bild*, for all the world to see and admire.

I used to admire my head off: before I tiptoed into the Wilds and saw the shacks of the Homesteaders. Particularly the Amiable Spouse, poor thing. No wonder *she* never sang the song of Simple Toil in the Innocent Wilds. Poor haggard drudge, like a ghost wailing in the wilderness, nine times out of ten.

Hector St. John, you have lied to me. You lied even more scurrilously to yourself. Hector St. John, you are an emotional liar.

Jean Jacques, Bernardin de St. Pierre, Chateaubriand, exquisite François Le Vaillant, you lying little lot, with your Nature-Sweet-and-Pure! Marie Antoinette got her head off for playing dairymaid, and nobody even dusted the seats of your pants, till now, for all the lies you put over us.

But Crèvecœur was an artist as well as a liar, otherwise we would not have bothered with him. He wanted to put NATURE in his pocket, as Benjamin put the Human Being. Between them, they wanted the whole scheme of things in their pockets, and the things themselves as well. Once you've got the scheme of things in your pocket, you can do as you like with it, even make money out of it, if you can't find in your heart to destroy it, as was your first intention. So H. St. J. de C. tried to put Nature-Sweet-and-Pure in his pocket. But nature wasn't having any, she poked her head out and baa-ed.

This Nature-sweet-and-pure business is only another effort at intellectualizing. Just an attempt to make all nature succumb to a few laws of the human mind. The sweet-and-pure sort of laws. Nature seemed to be behaving quite nicely, for a while. She has left off.

That's why you get the purest intellectuals in a Garden Suburb or a Brook Farm experiment. You bet, Robinson Crusoe was a highbrow of highbrows.

You can idealize or intellectualize. Or, on the contrary, you can let the dark soul in you see for itself. An artist usually intellectualizes on top, and his dark under-consciousness goes on contradicting him beneath. This is almost laughably the case with most American artists. Crèvecœur is the first example. He is something of an artist, Franklin isn't anything.

Crèvecœur the idealist puts over us a lot of stuff about nature and the noble savage and the innocence of toil, etc.,

etc. Blarney! But Crèvecœur the artist gives us glimpses of actual nature, not writ large.

Curious that his vision sees only the lowest forms of natural life. Insects, snakes, and birds he glimpses in their own mystery, their own pristine being. And straightway gives the lie to Innocent Nature.

"I am astonished to see," he writes quite early in the *Letters,* "that nothing exists but what has its enemy, one species pursue and live upon another: unfortunately our king-birds are the destroyers of those industrious insects (the bees); but on the other hand, these birds preserve our fields from the depredations of the crows, which they pursue on the wing with great vigilance and astonishing dexterity."

This is a sad blow to the sweet-and-pureness of Nature. But it is the voice of the artist in contrast to the voice of the ideal turtle. It is the rudimentary American vision. The glimpsing of the king-birds in winged hostility and pride is no doubt the aboriginal Indian vision carrying over. The Eagle symbol in human consciousness. Dark, swinging wings of hawk-beaked destiny, that one cannot help but feel, beating here above the wild center of America. You look round in vain for the "One being Who made all things, and governs the world by His Providence."

"One species pursue and live upon another."

Reconcile the two statements if you like. But, in America, act on Crèvecœur's observation.

The horse, however, says Hector, is the friend of man, and man is the friend of the horse. But then we leave the horse no choice. And I don't see much *friend,* exactly, in my sly old Indian pony, though he is quite a decent old bird.

Man, too, says Hector, is the friend of man. Whereupon the Indians burnt his farm; so he refrains from mentioning it in the *Letters,* for fear of invalidating his premises.

Some great hornets have fixed their nest on the ceiling of the living-room of the American Farmer, and these tiger-striped animals fly round the heads of the Healthy Offspring and the Amiable Spouse, to the gratification of the American Farmer. He liked their buzz and their tiger waspishness. Also, on the utilitarian plane, they kept the house free of flies.

So Hector says. Therefore Benjamin would have approved. But of the feelings of the Amiable S., on this matter, we are not told, and after all, it was she who had to make the jam.

Another anecdote. Swallows built their nest on the veranda of the American Farm. Wrens took a fancy to the nest of the swallows. They pugnaciously (I like the word pugnaciously, it is so American) attacked the harbingers of spring, and drove them away from their nice adobe nest. The swallows returned upon opportunity. But the wrens, coming home, violently drove them forth again. Which continued until the gentle swallows patiently set about to build another nest, while the wrens sat in triumph in the usurped home. The American Farmer watched this contest with delight, and no doubt loudly applauded those little rascals of wrens. For in the Land of the Free, the greatest delight of every man is in getting the better of the other man.

Crèvecœur says he shot a king-bird that had been devouring his bees. He opened the craw and took out a vast number of bees, which little democrats, after they had lain a minute or two stunned, in the sun roused, revived, preened their wings and walked off debonair, like Jonah up the seashore; or like true Yanks escaped from the craw of the king-bird of Europe.

I don't care whether it's true or not. I like the picture, and see in it a parable of the American resurrection.

The humming-bird.

Its bill is as long and as sharp as a coarse sewing needle; like the Bee, Nature has taught it to find out in the calyx of flowers and blossoms those mellifluous particles that can serve it for sufficient food; and yet it seems to leave them untouched, undeprived of anything that the eye can possibly distinguish. Where it feeds it appears as if immovable, though continually on the wing: and sometimes, from what motives I know not, it will tear and lacerate flowers into a hundred pieces; for, strange to tell, they are the most irascible of the feathered tribe. Where do passions find room in so diminutive a body? They often fight with the fury of lions, until one of the combatants falls a sacrifice and dies. When fatigued, it has often perched within a few feet of me, and on such favorable opportunities I have surveyed it with the most minute attention. Its little eyes appear like diamonds, reflecting light on every side; most elegantly finished in all parts, it is a miniature work of our Great Parent, who seems to have formed it smallest, and at the same time most beautiful, of the winged species.

A regular little Tartar, too. Lions no bigger than ink-spots! I have read about humming-birds elsewhere, in Bates and W. H. Hudson, for example. But it is left to the American Farmer to show me the real little raging lion. Birds are evidently no angels in America, or to the true American. He sees how they start and flash their wings like little devils, and stab each other with egoistic sharp bills. But he sees also the reserved, tender shyness of the wild creature, upon occasion. Quails in winter, for instance.

"Often, in the angles of the fences, where the motion of the wind prevents the snow from settling, I carry them both chaff and grain; the one to feed them, the other to prevent their tender feet from freezing fast to the earth, as I have frequently observed them to do."

This is beautiful, and blood-knowledge. Crèvecœur knows the touch of birds' feet, as if they had stood with their vibrating, sharp, cold-cleaving balance, naked-footed on his naked hand. It is a beautiful, barbaric tenderness of the blood. He doesn't after all turn them into "little sisters of the air," like St. Francis, or start preaching to them. He knows them as strange, shy, hot-blooded concentrations of bird presence.

The *Letter* about snakes and humming-birds is a fine essay, in its primal, dark veracity. The description of the fight between two snakes, a great water-snake and a large black serpent, follows the description of the humming-bird: "Strange was this to behold; two great snakes strongly adhering to the ground, mutually fastened together by means of the writhings which lashed them to each other, and stretched at their full length, they pulled, but pulled in vain; and in the moments of greatest exertions that part of their bodies which was entwined seemed extremely small, while the rest appeared inflated, and now and then convulsed with strong undulations, rapidly following each other. Their eyes seemed on fire, and ready to start out of their heads; at one time the conflict seemed decided; the water-snake bent itself into two great folds, and by that operation rendered the other more than commonly outstretched. The next minute the new struggles of the black one gained an unexpected superiority; it acquired two great folds likewise, which necessarily extended the body of its adversary in proportion as it had contracted its own."

This fight, which Crèvecœur describes to a finish, he calls a sight "uncommon and beautiful." He forgets the sweet-and-pureness of Nature, and is for the time a sheer ophiolater, and his chapter is as handsome a piece of ophiolatry, perhaps, as that coiled Aztec rattlesnake carved in stone.

And yet the real Crèvecœur is, in the issue, neither farmer, nor child of Nature, nor ophiolater. He goes back to France, and figures in the literary salons, and is a friend of Rousseau's Madame d'Houdetot. Also he is a good business man, and arranges a line of shipping between France and America. It all ends in materialism, really. But the *Letters* tell us nothing about this.

We are left to imagine him retiring in grief to dwell with his Red Brothers under the wigwams. For the War of Independence has broken out, and the Indians are armed by the adversaries; they do dreadful work on the frontiers. While Crèvecœur is away in France his farm is destroyed, his family rendered homeless. So that the last letter laments bitterly over the war, and man's folly and inhumanity to man.

But Crèvecœur ends his lament on a note of resolution. With his amiable spouse, and his healthy offspring, now rising in stature, he will leave the civilized coasts, where man is sophisticated, and therefore inclined to be vile, and he will go to live with the Children of Nature, the Red Men, under the wigwam. No doubt, in actual life, Crèvecœur made some distinction between the Indians who drank rum à la Franklin, and who burnt homesteads and massacred families, and those Indians, the noble Children of Nature, who peopled his own predetermined fancy. Whatever he did in actual life, in his innermost self he would not give up this self-made world, where the natural man was an object of undefiled brotherliness. Touchingly and vividly he describes his tented home near the Indian village, how he breaks the aboriginal earth to produce a little maize, while his wife weaves within the wigwam. And his imaginary efforts to save his tender offspring from the brutishness of unchristian darkness are touching and puzzling, for how can Nature, so sweet and pure under the greenwood tree, how can it have any contaminating effect?

But it is all a swindle. Crèvecœur was off to France in high-heeled shoes and embroidered waistcoat, to pose as a literary man, and to prosper in the world. We, however, must perforce follow him into the backwoods, where the simple natural life shall be perfected, near the tented village of the Red Man.

He wanted, of course, to imagine the dark, savage way of life, to get it all off pat in his head. He wanted to know as the Indians and savages know, darkly, and in terms of otherness. He was simply crazy, as the Americans say, for this. Crazy enough! For at the same time he was absolutely determined that Nature is sweet and pure, that all men are brothers, and equal, and that they love one another like so many cooing doves. He was determined to have life according to his own prescription. Therefore, he wisely kept away from any too close contact with Nature, and took refuge in commerce and the material world. But yet, he was determined to know the savage way of life, to his own *mind's* satisfaction. So he just faked us the last *Letters*. A sort of wish-fulfillment.

For the animals and savages are isolate, each one in its own pristine self. The animal lifts its head, sniffs, and knows within the dark, passionate belly. It knows at once, in dark mindlessness. And at once it flees in immediate recoil; or it crouches predatory, in the mysterious storm of exultant anticipation of seizing a victim; or it lowers its head in blank indifference again; or it advances in the insatiable wild curiosity, insatiable passion to approach that which is unspeakably strange and incalculable; or it draws near in the slow trust of wild, sensual love.

Crèvecœur wanted this kind of knowledge. But comfortably, in his head, along with his other ideas and ideals. He didn't go too near the wigwam. Because he must have suspected that the moment he saw as the savages saw, all his fraternity and equality would go up in smoke, and his ideal world of pure sweet goodness along with it. And still worse than this, he would have to give up his own will, which insists that the world is so, because it would be nicest if it were so. Therefore he trotted back to France in high-heeled shoes, and imagined America in Paris.

He wanted his ideal state. At the same time he wanted to know the other state, the dark, savage mind. He wanted both.

Can't be done, Hector. The one is the death of the other.

Best turn to commerce, where you may get things your own way.

He hates the dark, pre-mental life, really. He hates the true sensual mystery. But he wants to "know." To KNOW. Oh, insatiable American curiosity!

He's a liar.

But if he won't risk knowing in flesh and blood, he'll risk all the imagination you like.

It is amusing to see him staying away and calculating the dangers of the step which he takes so luxuriously, in his fancy, alone. He tickles his palate with a taste of true wildness, as men are so fond nowadays of tickling their palates with a taste of imaginary wickedness—just self-provoked.

"I must tell you," he says, "that there is something in the proximity of the woods which is very singular. It is with men as it is with the plants and animals that live in the forests; they are entirely different from those that live in the plains. I will candidly tell you all my thoughts, but you are not to expect that I shall advance any reasons. By living in or near the woods, their actions are regulated by the wildness of the neighborhood. The deer often come to eat their grain, the wolves destroy their sheep, the bears kill their hogs, the foxes catch their poultry. This surrounding hostility immediately puts the gun into their hands; they watch these animals, they kill some; and thus by defending their property they soon become professed hunters; this is the progress; once

hunters, farewell to the plow. The chase renders them ferocious, gloomy, unsociable; a hunter wants no neighbors, he
rather hates them, because he dreads the competition. . . .
Eating of wild meat, whatever you may think, tends to alter
their temper. . . ."

Crèvecœur, of course, had never intended to return as a
hunter to the bosom of Nature, only as a husbandman. The
hunter is a killer. The husbandman, on the other hand,
brings about the birth and increase. But even the husbandman strains in dark mastery over the unwilling earth and
beast; he struggles to win forth substance, he must master
the soil and the strong cattle, he must have the heavy blood-
knowledge, and the slow, but deep, mastery. There is no
equality or selfless humility. The toiling blood swamps the
idea, inevitably. For this reason the most idealist nations invent most machines. America simply teems with mechanical
inventions, because nobody in America ever wants to *do*
anything. They are idealists. Let a machine do the doing.

Again, Crèvecœur dwells on "the apprehension lest my
younger children should be caught by that singular charm,
so dangerous to their tender years"—meaning the charm of
savage life. So he goes on: "By what power does it come to
pass that children who have been adopted when young
among these people (the Indians) can never be prevailed
upon to readopt European manners? Many an anxious
parent have I seen last war who, at the return of peace, went
to the Indian villages where they knew their children to have
been carried in captivity, when to their inexpressible sorrow
they found them so perfectly Indianized that many knew
them no longer, and those whose more advanced ages permitted them to recollect their fathers and mothers, absolutely
refused to follow them, and ran to their adopted parents to
protect them against the effusions of love their unhappy real
parents lavished on them! Incredible as this may appear, I
have heard it asserted in a thousand instances, among persons
of credit.

"There must be something in their (the Indians') social
bond singularly captivating, and far superior to anything to
be boasted of among us; for thousands of Europeans are

Indians, and we have no examples of even one of those
aborigines having from choice become Europeans. . . ."

Our cat and another, Hector.

I like the picture of thousands of obdurate offspring, with
faces averted from their natural white father and mother,
turning resolutely to the Indians of their adoption.

I have seen some Indians whom you really couldn't tell
from white men. And I have never seen a white man who
looked really like an Indian. So Hector is again a liar.

But Crèvecœur wanted to be an *intellectual* savage, like a
great many more we have met. Sweet children of Nature.
Savage and bloodthirsty children of Nature.

White Americans do try hard to intellectualize themselves.
Especially white women Americans. And the latest stunt is
this "savage" stunt again.

White savages, with motor-cars, telephones, incomes, and
ideals! Savages fast inside the machine; yet savage enough,
ye gods!

IV. Fenimore Cooper's White Novels

BENJAMIN FRANKLIN had a specious little equation in providential mathemathics:

$$Rum + Savage = o.$$

Awfully nice! You might add up the universe to nought,
if you kept on.

Rum plus Savage may equal a dead savage. But is a dead
savage nought? Can you make a land virgin by killing off its
aborigines?

The Aztec is gone, and the Incas. The Red Indian, the
Esquimo, the Patagonian are reduced to negligible numbers.

Où sont les neiges d'antan?

My dear, wherever they are, they will come down again
next winter, sure as houses.

Not that the Red Indian will ever possess the broad lands
of America. At least I presume not. But his ghost will.

The Red Man died hating the white man. What remnant
of him lives, lives hating the white man. Go near the Indians, and you just feel it. As far as we are concerned, the

Red Man is subtly and unremittingly diabolic. Even when he doesn't know it. He is dispossessed in life, and unforgiving. He doesn't believe in us and our civilization, and so is our mystic enemy, for we push him off the face of the earth.

Belief is a mysterious thing. It is the only healer of the soul's wounds. There is no belief in the world.

The Red Man is dead, disbelieving in us. He is dead and unappeased. Do not imagine him happy in his Happy Hunting Ground. No. Only those that die in belief die happy. Those that are pushed out of life in chagrin come back unappeased, for revenge.

A curious thing about the Spirit of Place is the fact that no place exerts its full influence upon a newcomer until the old inhabitant is dead or absorbed. So America. While the Red Indian existed in fairly large numbers, the new colonials were in a great measure immune from the daimon, or demon, of America. The moment the last nuclei of Red life break up in America, then the white men will have to reckon with the full force of the demon of the continent. At present the demon of the place and the unappeased ghosts of the dead Indians act within the unconscious or under-conscious soul of the white American, causing the great American grouch, the Orestes-like frenzy of restlessness in the Yankee soul, the inner malaise which amounts almost to madness, sometimes. The Mexican is macabre and disintegrated in his own way. Up till now, the unexpressed spirit of America has worked covertly in the American, the white American soul. But within the present generation the surviving Red Indians are due to merge in the great white swamp. Then the Daimon of America will work overtly, and we shall see real changes.

There has been all the time, in the white American soul, a dual feeling about the Indian. First was Franklin's feeling, that a wise Providence no doubt intended the extirpation of these savages. Then came Crèvecœur's contradictory feeling about the noble Red Man and the innocent life of the wigwam. Now we hate to subscribe to Benjamin's belief in a Providence that wisely extirpates the Indian to make room for "cultivators of the soil." In Crèvecœur we meet a sentimental desire for the glorification of the savages. Absolutely sentimental. Hector pops over to Paris to enthuse about the wigwam.

The desire to extirpate the Indian. And the contradictory desire to glorify him. Both are rampant still, today.

The bulk of the white people who live in contact with the Indian today would like to see this Red brother exterminated; not only for the sake of grabbing his land, but because of the silent, invisible, but deadly hostility between the spirit of the two races. The minority of whites intellectualize the Red Man and laud him to the skies. But this minority of whites is mostly a high-brow minority with a big grouch against its own whiteness. So there you are.

I doubt if there is possible any real reconciliation, in the flesh, between the white and the red. For instance, a Red Indian girl who is servant in the white man's home, if she is treated with natural consideration, will probably serve well, even happily. She is happy with the new power over the white woman's kitchen. The white world makes her feel prouder, so long as she is free to go back to her own people at the given times. But she is happy because she is playing at being a white woman. There are other Indian women who would never serve the white people, and who would rather die than have a white man for a lover.

In either case, there is no reconciliation. There is no mystic conjunction between the spirit of the two races. The Indian girl who happily serves white people leaves out her own race-consideration, for the time being.

Supposing a white man goes out hunting in the mountains with an Indian. The two will probably get on like brothers. But let the same white man go alone with two Indians, and there will start a most subtle persecution of the unsuspecting white. If they, the Indians, discover that he has a natural fear of steep places, then over every precipice in the country will the trail lead. And so on. Malice! That is the basic feeling in the Indian heart towards the white. It may even be purely unconscious.

Supposing an Indian loves a white woman, and lives with her. He will probably be very proud of it, for he will be a big man among his own people, especially if the white mistress has money. He will never get over the feeling of pride at dining in a white dining-room and smoking in a white drawing-room. But at the same time he will subtly jeer at his white mistress, try to destroy her white pride. He will submit to her, if he is forced to, with a kind of false, unwilling childishness, and even love her with the same childlike gentleness, sometimes beautiful. But at the bottom of his heart he is gibing, gibing, gibing at her. Not only is it the sex resistance, but the race resistance as well.

There seems to be no reconciliation in the flesh.

That leaves us only expiation, and then reconciliation in the soul. Some strange atonement: expiation and oneing.

Fenimore Cooper has probably done more than any writer to present the Red Man to the white man. But Cooper's presentment is indeed a wish-fulfillment. That is why Fenimore is such a success still.

Modern critics begrudge Cooper his success. I think I resent it a little myself. This popular wish-fulfillment stuff makes it so hard for the real thing to come through, later.

Cooper was a rich American of good family. His father founded Cooperstown, by Lake Champlain. And Fenimore was a gentleman of culture. No denying it.

It is amazing how cultured these Americans of the first half of the eighteenth century were. Most intensely so. Austin Dobson and Andrew Lang are flea-bites in comparison. Volumes of very *raffiné* light verse and finely drawn familiar literature will prove it to anyone who cares to commit himself to these elderly books. The English and French writers of the same period were clumsy and hoydenish, judged by the same standards.

Truly, European decadence was anticipated in America; and American influence passed over to Europe, was assimilated there, and then returned to this land of innocence as something purplish in its modernity and a little wicked. So absurd things are.

Cooper quotes a Frenchman, who says, *"L'Amérique est pourrie avant d'être mûre."* And there is a great deal in it. America was not taught by France—by Baudelaire, for example. Baudelaire learned his lesson from America.

Cooper's novels fall into two classes: his white novels, such as *Homeward Bound, Eve Effingham, The Spy, The Pilot,* and then the *Leatherstocking Series.* Let us look at the white novels first.

The Effinghams are three extremely refined, genteel Americans who are "Homeward Bound" from England to the States. Their party consists of father, daughter, and uncle, and faithful nurse. The daughter has just finished her education in Europe. She has, indeed, skimmed the cream off Europe. England, France, Italy, and Germany have nothing more to teach her. She is bright and charming, admirable creature; a real modern heroine; intrepid, calm, and self-collected, yet admirably impulsive, always in perfectly good taste; clever and assured in her speech, like a man, but withal charmingly deferential and modest before the stronger sex. It is the perfection of the ideal female. We have learned to shudder at her, but Cooper still admired.

On board is the other type of American, the parvenu, the demagogue, who has "done" Europe and put it in his breeches pocket, in a month. Oh, Septimus Dodge, if a European had drawn you, that European would never have been forgiven by America. But an American drew you, so Americans wisely ignore you.

Septimus is the American self-made man. God had no hand in his make-up. He made himself. He has been to Europe, no doubt seen everything, including the Venus de Milo. "What, is *that* the Venus de Milo?" And he turns his back on the lady. He's seen her. He's got her. She's a fish he has hooked, and he's off to America with her, leaving the scum of a statue standing in the Louvre.

That is one American way of Vandalism. The original Vandals would have given the complacent dame a knock with a battle-ax, and ended her. The insatiable American looks at her. "Is *that* the Venus de Milo?—come on!" And the Venus de Milo stands there like a naked slave in a market-place, whom someone has spat on. Spat on!

I have often thought, hearing American tourists in Europe —in the Bargello in Florence, for example, or in the Piazza di San Marco in Venice—exclaiming, "Isn't that just too cunning!" or else, "Aren't you perfectly crazy about Saint Mark's! Don't you think those cupolas are like the loveliest *turnips* upside down, you know"—as if the beautiful things of Europe were just having their guts pulled out by these American admirers. They admire so wholesale. Sometimes they even seem to grovel. But the golden cupolas of St. Mark's in Venice are turnips upside down in a stale stew, after enough American tourists have looked at them. Turnips upside down in a stale stew. Poor Europe!

And there you are. When a few German bombs fell upon Rheims Cathedral up went a howl of execration. But there are more ways than one of vandalism. I should think the American admiration of five-minutes' tourists has done more to kill the sacredness of old European beauty and aspiration than multitudes of bombs would have done.

But there you are. Europe has got a fall, and peace hath her victories.

Behold then Mr. Septimus Dodge returning to Dodge-town victorious. Not crowned with laurel, it is true, but wreathed in lists of things he has seen and sucked dry. Seen and sucked dry, you know: Venus de Milo, the Rhine, or the Coliseum: swallowed like so many clams, and left the shells.

Now the aristocratic Effinghams, Homeward Bound from Europe to America, are at the mercy of Mr. Dodge: Septimus. He is their compatriot, so they may not disown him. Had they been English, of course, they would never once have let themselves become aware of his existence. But no. They are American democrats, and therefore, if Mr. Dodge marches up and says: "Mr. Effingham? Pleased to meet you, Mr. Effingham"—why, then Mr. Effingham is *forced* to reply: "Pleased to meet you, Mr. Dodge." If he didn't, he would have the terrible hounds of democracy on his heels and at his throat, the moment he landed in the Land of the Free. An Englishman is free to continue unaware of the existence of a fellow-countryman, if the looks of that fellow-countryman are distasteful. But every American citizen is free to force his presence upon you, no matter how unwilling you may be.

Freedom!

The Effinghams detest Mr. Dodge. They abhor him. They loathe and despise him. They have an unmitigated contempt for him. Everything he is, says, and does, seems to them too vulgar, too despicable. Yet they are forced to answer, when he presents himself: "Pleased to meet you, Mr. Dodge."

Freedom!

Mr. Dodge, of Dodge-town, alternately fawns and intrudes, cringes and bullies. And the Effinghams, terribly "superior" in a land of equality, writhe helpless. They would fain snub Septimus out of existence. But Septimus is not to be snubbed. As a true democrat, he is unsnubbable. As a true democrat, he has right on his side. And right is might.

Right is might. It is the old struggle for power.

Septimus, as a true democrat, is the equal of any man. As a true democrat with a full pocket, he is, by the amount that fills his pocket, so much the superior of the democrats with empty pockets. Because, though all men are born equal and die equal, you will not get anybody to admit that ten dollars equal ten thousand dollars. No, no, there's a difference there, however far you may push equality.

Septimus has the Effinghams on the hip. He has them fast, and they will not escape. What tortures await them at home, in the Land of the Free, at the hands of the hideously affable Dodge, we do not care to disclose. What was the persecution of a haughty Lord or a marauding Baron or an inquisitorial Abbot compared to the persecution of a million Dodges? The proud Effinghams are like men buried naked to the chin in ant-heaps, to be bitten into extinction by a myriad of ants. Stoically, as good democrats and idealists, they writhe and endure, without making too much moan.

They writhe and endure. There is no escape. Not from that time to this. No escape. They writhed on the horns of the Dodge dilemma.

Since then Ford has gone one worse.

Through these white novels of Cooper runs this acid of ant bites, the formic acid of democratic poisoning. The

Effinghams feel superior. Cooper felt superior. Mrs. Cooper felt superior too. And bitten.

For they were democrats. They didn't believe in kings, or lords, or masters, or real superiority of any sort. Before God, of course. In the sight of God, of course, all men were equal. This they believed. And therefore, though they *felt* terribly superior to Mr. Dodge, yet, since they were his equals in the sight of God, they could not feel free to say to him: "Mr. Dodge, please go to the devil." They had to say: "Pleased to meet you."

What a lie to tell! Democratic lies.

What a dilemma! To feel so superior. To *know* you are superior. And yet to believe that, in the sight of God, you are equal. Can't help yourself.

Why couldn't they let the Lord Almighty look after the equality, since it seems to happen specifically in His sight, and stick themselves to their own superiority? Why couldn't they?

Somehow they daren't.

They were Americans, idealists. How dare they balance a mere intense feeling against an IDEA and an IDEAL?

Ideally—i.e., in the sight of God, Mr. Dodge was their equal.

What a low opinion they held of the Almighty's faculty for discrimination.

But it was so. The IDEAL of EQUALITY.

Pleased to meet you, Mr. Dodge.

We are equal in the sight of God, of course. But er——

Very glad to meet you, Miss Effingham. Did you say—*er*? Well now, I think my bank balance will bear it.

Poor Eve Effingham.

Eve! Think of it. Eve! And birds of paradise. And apples. And Mr. Dodge.

This is where apples of knowledge get you, Miss Eve. You should leave 'em alone.

"Mr. Dodge, you are a hopeless and insufferable inferior."

Why couldn't she say it? She felt it. And she was a heroine.

Alas, she was an American heroine. She was an EDUCATED

WOMAN. She KNEW all about IDEALS. She swallowed the IDEAL of EQUALITY with her first mouthful of KNOWLEDGE. Alas for her and that apple of Sodom that looked so rosy. Alas for all her knowing.

Mr. Dodge (in check knickerbockers): Well, feeling a little uncomfortable below the belt, are you, Miss Effingham?

Miss Effingham (with difficulty withdrawing her gaze from the INFINITE OCEAN): Good morning, Mr. Dodge. I was admiring the dark blue distance.

Mr. Dodge: Say, couldn't you admire something a bit nearer.

Think how easy it would have been for her to say "Go away!" or "Leave me, varlet!"—or "Hence, base-born knave!" Or just to turn her back on him.

But then he would simply have marched round to the other side of her.

Was she his superior, or wasn't she?

Why surely, intrinsically, she *was*. Intrinsically Fenimore Cooper was the superior of the Dodges of his day. He felt it. But he felt he ought not to feel it. And he never had it out with himself.

That is why one rather gets impatient with him. He feels he is superior, and feels he ought *not* to feel so, and is therefore rather snobbish, and at the same time a little apologetic. Which is surely tiresome.

If a man feels superior, he should have it out with himself. "Do I feel superior because I *am* superior? Or is it just the snobbishness of class, or education, or money?"

Class, education, money won't make a man superior. But if he's just *born* superior, in himself, there it is. Why deny it?

It is a nasty sight to see the Effinghams putting themselves at the mercy of a Dodge, just because of a mere idea or ideal. Fools. They ruin more than they know. Because at the same time they are snobbish.

Septimus at the Court of King Arthur.

Septimus: Hello, Arthur! Pleased to meet you. By the way, what's all that great long sword about?

Arthur: This is Excalibur, the sword of my knighthood and my kingship.

Septimus: That so! We're all equal in the sight of God, you know, Arthur.

Arthur: Yes.

Septimus: Then I guess it's about time I had that yard-and-a-half of Excalibur to play with. Don't you think so? We're equal in the sight of God, and you've had it for quite a while.

Arthur: Yes, I agree. (Hands him Excalibur.)

Septimus (prodding Arthur with Excalibur): Say, Art, which is your fifth rib?

Superiority is a sword. Hand it over to Septimus, and you'll get it back between your ribs.—The whole moral of democracy.

But there you are. Eve Effingham had pinned herself down on the *Contrat Social*, and she was prouder of that pin through her body than of any mortal thing else. Her IDEAL. Her IDEAL of DEMOCRACY.

When America set out to destroy Kings and Lords and Masters, and the whole paraphernalia of European superiority, it pushed a pin right through its own body, and on that pin it still flaps and buzzes and twists in misery. The pin of democratic equality. Freedom.

There'll never be any life in America till you pull the pin out and admit natural inequality. Natural superiority, natural inferiority. Till such time, Americans just buzz round like various sorts of propellers, pinned down by their freedom and equality.

That's why these white novels of Fenimore Cooper are only historically and sardonically interesting. The people are all pinned down by some social pin, and buzzing away in social importance or friction, round and round on the pin. Never real human beings. Always things pinned down, choosing to be pinned down, transfixed by the idea or ideal of equality and democracy, on which they turn loudly and importantly, like propellers propelling. These States. Humanly, it is boring. As a historic phenomenon, it is amazing, ludicrous, and irritating.

If you don't pull the pin out in time, you'll never be able
to pull it out. You must turn on it forever, or bleed to death.

> Naked to the waist was I,
> And deep within my breast did lie,
> Though no man any blood could spy,
> The truncheon of a spear——

Is it already too late?

Oh God, the democratic pin!

Freedom, Equality, Equal Opportunity, Education, Rights
of Man.

The pin! The pin!

Well, there buzzes Eve Effingham, snobbishly, impaled.
She is a perfect American heroine, and I'm sure she wore the
first smartly-tailored "suit" that ever woman wore. I'm sure
she spoke several languages. I'm sure she was hopelessly competent. I'm sure she "adored" her husband, and spent masses
of his money, and divorced him because he didn't understand LOVE.

American women in their perfect "suits." American men
in their imperfect coats and skirts!

I feel I'm the superior of most men I meet. Not in birth,
because I never had a great-grandfather. Not in money,
because I've got none. Not in education, because I'm
merely scrappy. And certainly not in beauty or in manly
strength.

Well, what then?

Just in myself.

When I'm challenged, I do feel myself superior to most of
the men I meet. Just a natural superiority.

But not till there enters an element of challenge.

When I meet another man, and he is just himself—even if
he is an ignorant Mexican pitted with small-pox—then there
is no question between us of superiority or inferiority. He is
a man and I am a man. We are ourselves. There is no question between us.

But let a question arise, let there be a challenge, and then
I feel he should do reverence to the gods in me, because they
are more than the gods in him. And he should give reverence

to the very me, because it is more at one with the gods than is his very self.

If this is conceit, I am sorry. But it's the gods in me that matter. And in other men.

As for me, I am so glad to salute the brave, reckless gods in another man. So glad to meet a man who will abide by his very self.

Ideas! Ideals! All this paper between us. What a weariness.

If only people would meet in their very selves, without wanting to put some idea over one another, or some ideal.

Damn all ideas and all ideals. Damn all the false stress, and the pins.

I am I. Here am I. Where are you?

Ah, there you are! Now, damn the consequences, we have met.

That's my idea of democracy, if you can call it an idea.

V. Fenimore Cooper's Leatherstocking Novels

In his Leatherstocking books Fenimore is off on another track. He is no longer concerned with social white Americans that buzz with pins through them, buzz loudly against every mortal thing except the pin itself. The pin of the Great Ideal.

One gets irritated with Cooper because he never for once snarls at the Great Ideal Pin which transfixes him. No, indeed. Rather he tries to push it through the very heart of the Continent.

But I have loved the Leatherstocking books so dearly. Wish-fulfillment!

Anyhow, one is not supposed to take LOVE seriously in these books. Eve Effingham, impaled on the social pin, conscious all the time of her own ego and of nothing else, suddenly fluttering in throes of love: no, it makes me sick. LOVE is never LOVE until it has a pin pushed through it and becomes an IDEAL. The ego, turning on a pin, is wildly IN LOVE, always. Because that's the thing to be.

Cooper was a GENTLEMAN, in the worst sense of the word.

In the nineteenth-century sense of the word. A correct, clockwork man.

Not altogether, of course.

The great national Grouch was grinding inside him. Probably he called it COSMIC URGE. Americans usually do: in capital letters.

Best stick to National Grouch. The great American grouch.

Cooper had it, gentleman that he was. That is why he flitted round Europe so uneasily. Of course, in Europe he could be, and was, a gentleman to his heart's content.

"In short," he says in one of his letters, "we were at table two counts, one monsignore, an English lord, an ambassador, and my humble self."

Were we really!

How nice it must have been to know that oneself, at least, was humble.

And he felt the democratic American tomahawk wheeling over his uncomfortable scalp all the time.

The great American grouch.

Two monsters loomed on Cooper's horizon.

MRS. COOPER   MY WORK
MY WORK   MY WIFE
MY WIFE   MY WORK
THE DEAR CHILDREN
MY WORK!!!

There you have the essential keyboard of Cooper's soul.

If there is one thing that annoys me more than a businessman and his BUSINESS, it is an artist, a writer, painter, musician, and MY WORK. When an artist says MY WORK, the flesh goes tired on my bones. When he says MY WIFE, I want to hit him.

Cooper grizzled about his work. Oh, heaven, he cared so much whether it was good or bad, and what the French thought, and what Mr. Snippy Knowall said, and how Mrs. Cooper took it. The pin, the pin!

But he was truly an artist: then an American: then a gentleman.

And the grouch grouched inside him, through all.

They seem to have been specially fertile in imagining themselves "under the wigwam," do these Americans, just when their knees were comfortably under the mahogany, in Paris, along with the knees of

4 Counts
2 Cardinals
1 Milord
5 Cocottes
1 Humble self

You bet, though, that when the cocottes were being raffled off, Fenimore went home to his WIFE.

Wish-Fulfillment		Actuality
THE WIGWAM	vs.	MY HOTEL
CHINGACHGOOK	vs.	MY WIFE
NATTY BUMPPO	vs.	MY HUMBLE SELF

Fenimore, lying in his Louis Quatorze hotel in Paris, passionately musing about Natty Bumppo and the pathless forest, and mixing his imagination with the Cupids and Butterflies on the painted ceiling, while Mrs. Cooper was struggling with her latest gown in the next room, and the déjeuner was with the Countess at eleven. . . .

Men live by lies.

In actuality, Fenimore loved the genteel continent of Europe, and waited gasping for the newspapers to praise his WORK.

In another actuality he loved the tomahawking continent of America, and imagined himself Natty Bumppo.

His actual desire was to be: *Monsieur Fenimore Cooper, le grand écrivain américain.*

His innermost wish was to be: Natty Bumppo.

Now Natty and Fenimore, arm in arm, are an old couple.

You can see Fenimore: blue coat, silver buttons, silver-and-diamond buckle shoes, ruffles.

You see Natty Bumppo: a grizzled, uncouth old renegade, with gaps in his old teeth and a drop on the end of his nose.

But Natty was Fenimore's great wish: his wish-fulfillment.

"It was a matter of course," says Mrs. Cooper, "that he should dwell on the better traits of the picture rather than on the coarser and more revolting, though more common points. Like West, he could see Apollo in the young Mohawk."

The coarser and more revolting, though more common points.

You see now why he depended so absolutely on MY WIFE. She had to look things in the face for him. The coarser and more revolting, and certainly more common points, she had to see.

He himself did so love seeing pretty-pretty, with the thrill of a red scalp now and then.

Fenimore, in his imagination, wanted to be Natty Bumppo, who, I am sure, belched after he had eaten his dinner. At the same time Mr. Cooper was nothing if not a gentleman. So he decided to stay in France and have it all his own way.

In France, Natty would not belch after eating, and Chingachgook could be all the Apollo he liked.

As if ever any Indian was like Apollo. The Indians, with their curious female quality, their archaic figures, with high shoulders and deep, archaic waists, like a sort of woman! And their natural devilishness, their natural insidiousness.

But men see what they want to see: especially if they look from a long distance, across the ocean, for example.

Yet the Leatherstocking books are lovely. Lovely half-lies. They form a sort of American Odyssey, with Natty Bumppo for Odysseus.

Only, in the original Odyssey, there is plenty of devil, Circes and swine and all. And Ithacus is devil enough to outwit the devils. But Natty is a saint with a gun, and the Indians are gentlemen through and through, though they may take an occasional scalp.

There are five Leatherstocking novels: a *decrescendo* of reality, and a crescendo of beauty.

1. *Pioneers*: A raw frontier village on Lake Champlain, at the end of the eighteenth century. Must be a picture of Cooper's

home, as he knew it when a boy. A very lovely book. Natty Bumppo an old man, an old hunter half civilized.

2. *The Last of the Mohicans:* A historical fight between the British and the French, with Indians on both sides, at a fort by Lake Champlain. Romantic flight of the British general's two daughters, conducted by the scout, Natty, who is in the prime of life; romantic death of the last of the Delawares.

3. *The Prairie:* A wagon of some huge, sinister Kentuckians trekking west into the unbroken prairie. Prairie Indians, and Natty, an old, old man; he dies seated on a chair on the Rocky Mountains, looking east.

4. *The Pathfinder:* The Great Lakes. Natty, a man of about thirty-five, makes an abortive proposal to a bouncing damsel, daughter of the Sergeant at the Fort.

5. *Deerslayer:* Natty and Hurry Harry, both quite young, are hunting in the virgin wild. They meet two white women. Lake Champlain again.

These are the five Leatherstocking books: Natty Bumppo being Leatherstocking, Pathfinder, Deerslayer, according to his ages.

Now let me put aside my impatience at the unreality of this vision, and accept it as a wish-fulfillment vision, a kind of yearning myth. Because it seems to me that the things in Cooper that make one so savage, when one compares them with actuality, are perhaps, when one considers them as presentations of a deep subjective desire, real in their way, and almost prophetic.

The passionate love for America, for the soil of America, for example. As I say, it is perhaps easier to love America passionately, when you look at it through the wrong end of the telescope, across all the Atlantic water, as Cooper did so often, than when you are right there. When you are actually *in* America, America hurts, because it has a powerful dis-integrative influence upon the white psyche. It is full of grinning, unappeased aboriginal demons, too, ghosts, and it persecutes the white men, like some Eumenides, until the white men give up their absolute whiteness. America is tense with latent violence and resistance. The very common sense of white Americans has a tinge of helplessness in it, and deep fear of what might be if they were not common-sensical.

Yet one day the demons of America must be placated, the ghosts must be appeased, the Spirit of Place atoned for. Then the true passionate love for American Soil will appear. As yet, there is too much menace in the landscape.

But probably one day America will be as beautiful in actuality as it is in Cooper. Not yet, however. When the factories have fallen down again.

And again, this perpetual blood-brother theme of the Leatherstocking novels, Natty and Chingachgook, the Great Serpent. At present it is a sheer myth. The Red Man and the White Man are not blood-brothers: even when they are most friendly. When they are most friendly, it is as a rule the one betraying his race-spirit to the other. In the white man—rather high-brow—who "loves" the Indian, one feels the white man betraying his own race. There is something unproud, underhand in it. Renegade. The same with the Americanized Indian who believes absolutely in the white mode. It is a betrayal. Renegade again.

In the actual flesh, it seems to me the white man and the red man cause a feeling of oppression, the one to the other, no matter what the good will. The red life flows in a different direction from the white life. You can't make two streams that flow in opposite directions meet and mingle soothingly.

Certainly, if Cooper had had to spend his whole life in the backwoods, side by side with a Noble Red Brother, he would have screamed with the oppression of suffocation. He had to have Mrs. Cooper, a straight strong pillar of society, to hang on to. And he had to have the culture of France to turn back to, or he would just have been stifled. The Noble Red Brother would have smothered him and driven him mad.

So that the Natty and Chingachgook myth must remain a myth. It is a wish-fulfillment, an evasion of actuality. As we have said before, the folds of the Great Serpent would have been heavy, very heavy, too heavy, on any white man. Unless the white man were a true renegade, hating himself and his own race spirit, as sometimes happens.

It seems there can be no fusion in the flesh. But the spirit can change. The white man's spirit can never become as the red man's spirit. It doesn't want to. But it can cease to be the opposite and the negative of the red man's spirit. It can open out a new great area of consciousness, in which there is room for the red spirit too.

To open out a new wide area of consciousness means to slough the old consciousness. The old consciousness has become a tight-fitting prison to us, in which we are going rotten.

You can't have a new, easy skin before you have sloughed the old, tight skin.

You can't.

And you just can't, so you may as well leave off pretending.

Now the essential history of the people of the United States seems to me just this: At the Renaissance the old consciousness was becoming a little tight. Europe sloughed her last skin, and started a new, final phase.

But some Europeans recoiled from the last final phase. They wouldn't enter the *cul de sac* of post-Renaissance, "liberal" Europe. They came to America.

They came to America for two reasons:

1. To slough the old European consciousness completely.

2. To grow a new skin underneath, a new form. This second is a hidden process.

The two processes go on, of course, simultaneously. The slow forming of the new skin underneath is the slow sloughing of the old skin. And sometimes this immortal serpent feels very happy, feeling a new golden glow of a strangely-patterned skin envelop him: and sometimes he feels very sick, as if his very entrails were being torn out of him, as he wrenches once more at his old skin, to get out of it.

Out! Out! he cries, in all kinds of euphemisms.

He's got to have his new skin on him before ever he can get out.

And he's got to get out before his new skin can ever be his own skin.

So there he is, a torn, divided monster.

The true American, who writhes and writhes like a snake that is long in sloughing.

Sometimes snakes can't slough. They can't burst their old skin. Then they go sick and die inside the old skin, and nobody ever sees the new pattern.

It needs a real desperate recklessness to burst your old skin at last. You simply don't care what happens to you, if you rip yourself in two, so long as you do get out.

It also needs a real belief in the new skin. Otherwise you are likely never to make the effort. Then you gradually sicken and go rotten and die in the old skin.

Now Fenimore stayed very safe inside the old skin: a gentleman, almost a European, as proper as proper can be. And, safe inside the old skin, he *imagined* the gorgeous American pattern of a new skin.

He hated democracy. So he evaded it, and had a nice dream of something beyond democracy. But he belonged to democracy all the while.

Evasion!—Yet even that doesn't make the dream worthless.

Democracy in America was never the same as Liberty in Europe. In Europe Liberty was a great life throb. But in America Democracy was always something anti-life. The greatest democrats, like Abraham Lincoln, had always a sacrificial, self-murdering note in their voices. American Democracy was a form of self-murder, always. Or of murdering somebody else.

Necessarily. It was a *pis aller*. It was the *pis aller* to European Liberty. It was a cruel form of sloughing. Men murdered themselves into this democracy. Democracy is the utter hardening of the old skin, the old form, the old psyche. It hardens till it is tight and fixed and inorganic. Then it *must* burst, like a chrysalis shell. And out must come the soft grub, or the soft damp butterfly of the American-at-last.

America has gone the *pis aller* of her democracy. Now she must slough even that, chiefly that, indeed.

What did Cooper dream beyond democracy? Why, in his immortal friendship of Chingachgook and Natty Bumppo he dreamed the nucleus of a new society. That is, he dreamed a new human relationship. A stark, stripped human relationship of two men, deeper than the deeps of sex. Deeper than property, deeper than fatherhood, deeper than marriage, deeper than love. So deep that it is loveless. The stark, loveless, wordless unison of two men who have come to the bottom of themselves. This is the new nucleus of a new society, the clue to a new world-epoch. It asks for a great and cruel sloughing first of all. Then it finds a great release into a new world, a new moral, a new landscape.

Natty and the Great Serpent are neither equals nor unequals. Each obeys the other when the moment arrives. And each is stark and dumb in the other's presence, starkly himself, without illusion created. Each is just the crude pillar of a man, the crude living column of his own manhood. And each knows the godhead of this crude column of manhood. A new relationship.

The Leatherstocking novels create the myth of this new relation. And they go backwards, from old age to golden youth. That is the true myth of America. She starts old, old, wrinkled and writhing in an old skin. And there is a gradual sloughing of the old skin, towards a new youth. It is the myth of America.

You start with actuality. *Pioneers* is no doubt Cooperstown, when Cooperstown was in the stage of inception: a village of one wild street of log cabins under the forest hills by Lake Champlain: a village of crude, wild frontiersmen, reacting against civilization.

Towards this frontier village in the wintertime, a Negro slave drives a sledge through the mountains, over deep snow. In the sledge sits a fair damsel, Miss Temple, with her handsome pioneer father, Judge Temple. They hear a shot in the trees. It is the old hunter and backwoodsman, Natty Bumppo, long and lean and uncouth, with a long rifle and gaps in his teeth.

Judge Temple is "squire" of the village, and he has a ridiculous, commodious "hall" for his residence. It is still the old English form. Miss Temple is a pattern young lady, like Eve Effingham: in fact, she gets a young and very genteel but impoverished Effingham for a husband. The old world holding its own on the edge of the wild. A bit tiresomely, too, with rather more prunes and prisms than one can digest. Too romantic.

Against the "hall" and the gentry, the real frontiers-folk, the rebels. The two groups meet at the village inn, and at the frozen church, and at the Christmas sports, and on the ice of the lake, and at the great pigeon shoot. It is a beautiful, resplendent picture of life. Fenimore puts in only the glamour.

Perhaps my taste is childish, but these scenes in *Pioneers* seem to me marvelously beautiful. The raw village street, with woodfires blinking through the unglazed window-chinks, on a winter's night. The inn, with the rough woodsman and the drunken Indian John; the church, with the snowy congregation crowding to the fire. Then the lavish abundance of Christmas cheer, and turkey shooting in the snow. Spring coming, forests all green, maple-sugar taken from the trees: and clouds of pigeons flying from the south, myriads of pigeons, shot in heaps; and night-fishing on the teeming, virgin lake; and deer hunting.

Pictures! Some of the loveliest, most glamorous pictures in all literature.

Alas, without the cruel iron of reality. It is all real enough. Except that one realizes that Fenimore was writing from a safe distance, where he would idealize and have his wish-fulfillment.

Because, when one comes to America, one finds that there is always a certain slightly devilish resistance in the American landscape, and a certain slightly bitter resistance in the white man's heart. Hawthorne gives this. But Cooper glosses it over.

The American landscape has never been at one with the white man. Never. And white men have probably never felt so bitter anywhere, as here in America, where the very landscape, in its very beauty, seems a bit devilish and grinning, opposed to us.

Cooper, however, glosses over this resistance, which in actuality can never quite be glossed over. He *wants* the landscape to be at one with him. So he goes away to Europe and sees it as such. It is a sort of vision.

And, nevertheless, the oneing will surely take place—someday.

The myth is the story of Natty. The old, lean hunter and backwoodsman lives with his friend, the gray-haired Indian John, an old Delaware chief, in a hut within reach of the village. The Delaware is christianized and bears the Christian name of John. He is tribeless and lost. He humiliates his gray hairs in drunkenness, and dies, thankful to be dead, in a forest fire, passing back to the fire whence he derived.

And this is Chingachgook, the splendid Great Serpent of the later novels.

No doubt Cooper, as a boy, knew both Natty and the Indian John. No doubt they fired his imagination even then. When he is a man, crystallized in society and sheltering behind the safe pillar of Mrs. Cooper, these two old fellows become a myth to his soul. He traces himself to a new youth in them.

As for the story: Judge Temple has just been instrumental in passing the wise game laws. But Natty has lived by his gun all his life in the wild woods, and simply childishly cannot understand how he can be poaching on the Judge's land among the pine trees. He shoots a deer in the close season. The Judge is all sympathy, but the law *must* be enforced. Bewildered Natty, an old man of seventy, is put in stocks and in prison. They release him as soon as possible. But the thing was done.

The letter killeth.

Natty's last connection with his own race is broken. John, the Indian, is dead. The old hunter disappears, lonely and severed, into the forest, away, away from his race.

In the new epoch that is coming, there will be no letter of the Law.

Chronologically, *The Last of the Mohicans* follows *Pioneers*. But in the myth, *The Prairie* comes next.

Cooper of course knew his own America. He traveled west and saw the prairies, and camped with the Indians of the prairie.

The Prairie, like *Pioneers*, bears a good deal the stamp of actuality. It is a strange, splendid book, full of the sense of doom. The figures of the great Kentuckian men, with their wolf-women, loom colossal on the vast prairie, as they camp with their wagons. These are different pioneers from Judge Temple. Lurid, brutal, tinged with the sinisterness of crime; these are the gaunt white men who push West, push on and on against the natural opposition of the continent. On towards a doom. Great wings of vengeful doom seem spread over the West, grim against the intruder. You feel them again in Frank Norris' novel, *The Octopus*. While in the West of Bret Harte there is a very devil in the air, and beneath him are sentimental, self-conscious people being wicked and goody by evasion.

In *The Prairie* there is a shadow of violence and dark cruelty flickering in the air. It is the aboriginal demon hovering over the core of the continent. It hovers still, and the dread is still there.

Into such a prairie enters the huge figure of Ishmael, ponderous, pariah-like Ishmael and his huge sons and his werewolf wife. With their wagons they roll on from the frontiers of Kentucky, like Cyclops into the savage wilderness. Day after day they seem to force their way into oblivion. But their force of penetration ebbs. They are brought to a stop. They recoil in the throes of murder and entrench themselves in isolation on a hillock in the midst of the prairie. There they hold out like demigods against the elements and the subtle Indian.

The pioneering brute invasion of the West, crime-tinged!

And into this setting, as a sort of minister of peace, enters the old, old hunter Natty, and his suave, horse-riding Sioux Indians. But he seems like a shadow.

The hills rise softly west, to the Rockies. There seems a new peace: or is it only suspense, abstraction, waiting? Is it only a sort of beyond?

Natty lives in these hills, in a village of the suave, horse-riding Sioux. They revere him as an old wise father.

In these hills he dies, sitting in his chair and looking far east, to the forest and great sweet waters, whence he came. He dies gently, in physical peace with the land and the Indians. He is an old, old man.

Cooper could see no further than the foothills where Natty died, beyond the prairie.

The other novels bring us back East.

The Last of the Mohicans is divided between real histori-cal narrative and true "romance." For myself, I prefer the romance. It has a myth meaning, whereas the narrative is chiefly record.

For the first time we get actual women: the dark, hand-some Cora and her frail sister, the White Lily. The good old division, the dark sensual woman and the clinging, submis-sive little blonde, who is so "pure."

These sisters are fugitives through the forest, under the protection of a Major Heyward, a young American officer and Englishman. He is just a "white" man, very good and brave and generous, etc., but limited, most definitely *borné*. He would probably love Cora, if he dared, but he finds it safer to adore the clinging White Lily of a younger sister.

This trio is escorted by Natty, now Leatherstocking, a hunter and scout in the prime of life, accompanied by his inseparable friend Chingachgook, and the Delaware's beau-tiful son—Adonis rather than Apollo—Uncas, the last of the Mohicans.

There is also a "wicked" Indian, Magua, handsome and injured incarnation of evil.

Cora is the scarlet flower of womanhood, fierce, passionate offspring of some mysterious union between the British officer and a Creole woman in the West Indies. Cora loves Uncas, Uncas loves Cora. But Magua also desires Cora, violently desires her. A lurid little circle of sensual fire. So Fenimore kills them all off, Cora, Uncas, and Magua, and leaves the White Lily to carry on the race. She will breed plenty of white children to Major Heyward. These tiresome "lilies that fester," of our day.

Evidently Cooper—or the artist in him—has decided that there can be no blood-mixing of the two races, white and red. He kills 'em off.

Beyond all this heartbeating stand the figures of Natty and Chingachgook: the two childless, womanless men, of oppo-site races. They are the abiding thing. Each of them is alone, and final in his race. And they stand side by side, stark, abstract, beyond emotion, yet eternally together. All the other loves seem frivolous. This is the new great thing, the clue, the inception of a new humanity.

And Natty, what sort of a white man is he? Why, he is a man with a gun. He is a killer, a slayer. Patient and gentle as he is, he is a slayer. Self-effacing, self-forgetting, still he is a killer.

Twice, in the book, he brings an enemy down hurtling in death through the air, downwards. Once it is the beautiful, wicked Magua—shot from a height, and hurtling down ghastly through space, into death.

This is Natty, the white forerunner. A killer. As in *Deerslayer,* he shoots the bird that flies in the high, high sky, so that the bird falls out of the invisible into the visible, dead, he symbolizes himself. He will bring the bird of the spirit out of the high air. He is the stoic American killer of the old great life. But he kills, as he says, only to live.

Pathfinder takes us to the Great Lakes, and the glamour and beauty of sailing the great sweet waters. Natty is now called Pathfinder. He is about thirty-five years old, and he falls in love. The damsel is Mabel Dunham, daughter of Sergeant Dunham of the Fort garrison. She is blonde and in all things admirable. No doubt Mrs. Cooper was very much like Mabel.

And Pathfinder doesn't marry her. She won't have him. She wisely prefers a more comfortable Jasper. So Natty goes off to grouch, and to end by thanking his stars. When he had got right clear, and sat by the campfire with Chingachgook, in the forest, didn't he just thank his stars! A lucky escape!

Men of an uncertain age are liable to these infatuations. They aren't always lucky enough to be rejected.

Whatever would poor Mabel have done, had she been Mrs. Bumppo?

Natty had no business marrying. His mission was elsewhere.

The most fascinating Leatherstocking book is the last, *Deerslayer.* Natty is now a fresh youth, called Deerslayer.

But the kind of silent prim youth who is never quite young, but reserves himself for different things.

It is a gem of a book. Or a bit of perfect paste. And myself, I like a bit of perfect paste in a perfect setting, so long as I am not fooled by pretense of reality. And the setting of *Deerslayer could* not be more exquisite. Lake Champlain again.

Of course it never rains: it is never cold and muddy and dreary: no one has wet feet or toothache: no one ever feels filthy, when they can't wash for a week. God knows what the women would really have looked like, for they fled through the wilds without soap, comb, or towel. They breakfasted off a chunk of meat, or nothing, lunched the same, and supped the same.

Yet at every moment they are elegant, perfect ladies, in correct toilet.

Which isn't quite fair. You need only go camping for a week, and you'll see.

But it is a myth, not a realistic tale. Read it as a lovely myth. Lake Glimmerglass.

Deerslayer, the youth with the long rifle, is found in the woods with a big, handsome, blond-bearded backwoodsman called Hurry Harry. Deerslayer seems to have been born under a hemlock tree out of a pine-cone: a young man of the woods. He is silent, simple, philosophic, moralistic, and an unerring shot. His simplicity is the simplicity of age rather than of youth. He is race-old. All his reactions and impulses are fixed, static. Almost he is sexless, so race-old. Yet intelligent, hardy, dauntless.

Hurry Harry is a big blusterer, just the opposite of Deerslayer. Deerslayer keeps the center of his own consciousness steady and unperturbed. Hurry Harry is one of those floundering people who bluster from one emotion to another, very self-conscious, without any center to them.

These two young men are making their way to a lovely, smallish lake, Lake Glimmerglass. On this water the Hutter family has established itself. Old Hutter, it is suggested, has a criminal, coarse, buccaneering past, and is a sort of fugitive from justice. But he is a good enough father to his two grown-up girls. The family lives in a log hut "castle," built on piles in the water, and the old man has also constructed an "ark," a sort of houseboat, in which he can take his daughters when he goes on his rounds to trap the beaver.

The two girls are the inevitable dark and light. Judith, dark, fearless, passionate, a little lurid with sin, is the scarlet-and-black blossom. Hetty, the younger, blonde, frail and innocent, is the white lily again. But alas, the lily has begun to fester. She is slightly imbecile.

The two hunters arrive at the lake among the woods just as war has been declared. The Hutters are unaware of the fact. And hostile Indians are on the lake already. So, the story of thrills and perils.

Thomas Hardy's inevitable division of women into dark and fair, sinful and innocent, sensual and pure, is Cooper's division too. It is indicative of the desire in the man. He wants sensuality and sin, and he wants purity and "innocence." If the innocence goes a little rotten, slightly imbecile, bad luck!

Hurry Harry, of course, like a handsome, impetuous meat-fly, at once wants Judith, the lurid poppy blossom. Judith rejects him with scorn.

Judith, the sensual woman, at once wants the quiet, reserved, unmastered Deerslayer. She wants to master him. And Deerslayer is half tempted, but never more than half. He is not going to be mastered. A philosophic old soul, he does not give much for the temptations of sex. Probably he dies virgin.

And he is right of it. Rather than be dragged into a false heat of deliberate sensuality, he will remain alone. His soul is alone, forever alone. So he will preserve his integrity, and remain alone in the flesh. It is a stoicism which is honest and fearless, and from which Deerslayer never lapses, except when, approaching middle age, he proposes to the buxom Mabel.

He lets his consciousness penetrate in loneliness into the new continent. His contacts are not human. He wrestles with the spirits of the forest and the American wild, as a hermit wrestles with God and Satan. His one meeting is with Chingachgook, and this meeting is silent, reserved, across an unpassable distance.

Hetty, the White Lily, being imbecile, although full of vaporous religion and the dear, good God, "who governs all things by his providence," is hopelessly infatuated with Hurry Harry. Being innocence gone imbecile, like Dostoevsky's Idiot, she longs to give herself to the handsome meat-fly. Of course he doesn't want her.

And so nothing happens: in that direction. Deerslayer goes off to meet Chingachgook, and help him woo an Indian maid. Vicarious.

It is the miserable story of the collapse of the white psyche. The white man's mind and soul are divided between these two things: innocence and lust, the Spirit and Sensuality. Sensuality always carries a stigma, and is therefore more deeply desired, or lusted after. But spirituality alone gives the sense of uplift, exaltation, and "winged life," with the inevitable reaction into sin and spite. So the white man is divided against himself. He plays off one side of himself against the other side, till it is really a tale told by an idiot, and nauseating.

Against this, one is forced to admire the stark, enduring figure of Deerslayer. He is neither spiritual nor sensual. He is a moralizer, but he always tries to moralize from actual experience, not from theory. He says: "Hurt nothing unless you're forced to." Yet he gets his deepest thrill of gratification, perhaps, when he puts a bullet through the heart of a beautiful buck, as it stoops to drink at the lake. Or when he brings the invisible bird fluttering down in death, out of the high blue. "Hurt nothing unless you're forced to." And yet he lives by death, by killing the wild things of the air and earth.

It's not good enough.

But you have there the myth of the essential white America. All the other stuff, the love, the democracy, the floundering into lust, is a sort of by-play. The essential American soul is hard, isolate, stoic, and a killer. It has never yet melted.

Of course, the soul often breaks down into disintegration,

and you have lurid sin and Judith, imbecile innocence lusting in Hetty, and bluster, bragging, and self-conscious
strength in Harry. But there are the disintegration products.

What true myth concerns itself with is not the disintegration product. True myth concerns itself centrally with the
onward adventure of the integral soul. And this, for America, is Deerslayer. A man who turns his back on white
society. A man who keeps his moral integrity hard and intact.
An isolate, almost selfless, stoic, enduring man, who lives by
death, by killing, but who is pure white.

This is the very intrinsic-most American. He is at the
core of all the other flux and fluff. And when *this* man breaks
from his static isolation, and makes a new move, then look
out, something will be happening.

VI. *Edgar Allan Poe*

POE has no truck with Indians or Nature. He makes no
bones about Red Brothers and Wigwams.

He is absolutely concerned with the disintegration-proc-
esses of his own psyche. As we have said, the rhythm of
American art-activity is dual.

1. A disintegrating and sloughing of the old consciousness.

2. The forming of a new consciousness underneath.

Fenimore Cooper has the two vibrations going on together.
Poe has only one, only the disintegrative vibration. This
makes him almost more a scientist than an artist.

Moralists have always wondered helplessly why Poe's
"morbid" tales need have been written. They need to be
written because old things need to die and disintegrate,
because the old white psyche has to be gradually broken
down before anything else can come to pass.

Man must be stripped even of himself. And it is a painful,
sometimes a ghastly process.

Poe had a pretty bitter doom. Doomed to seethe down his
soul in a great continuous convulsion of disintegration, and
doomed to register the process. And then doomed to be

abused for it, when he had performed some of the bitterest tasks of human experience, that can be asked of a man. Necessary tasks, too. For the human soul must suffer its own disintegration, *consciously*, if ever it is to survive.

But Poe is rather a scientist than an artist. He is reducing his own self as a scientist reduces a salt in a crucible. It is an almost chemical analysis of the soul and consciousness. Whereas in true art there is always the double rhythm of creating and destroying.

This is why Poe calls his things "tales." They are a concatenation of cause and effect.

His best pieces, however, are not tales. They are more. They are ghastly stories of the human soul in its disruptive throes.

Moreover, they are "love" stories.

Ligeia and *The Fall of the House of Usher* are really love stories.

Love is the mysterious vital attraction which draws things together, closer, closer together. For this reason sex is the actual crisis of love. For in sex the two blood-systems, in the male and female, concentrate and come into contact, the merest film intervening. Yet if the intervening film breaks down, it is death.

So there you are. There is a limit to everything. There is a limit to love.

The central law of all organic life is that each organism is intrinsically isolate and single in itself.

The moment its isolation breaks down, and there comes an actual mixing and confusion, death sets in.

This is true of every individual organism, from man to amoeba.

But the secondary law of all organic life is that each organism only lives through contact with other matter, assimilation, and contact with other life, which means assimilation of new vibrations, non-material. Each individual organism is vivified by intimate contact with fellow organisms: up to a certain point.

So man. He breathes the air into him, he swallows food and water. But more than this. He takes into him the life of his fellow-men, with whom he comes into contact, and he gives back life to them. This contact draws nearer and nearer, as the intimacy increases. When it is a whole contact, we call it love. Men live by food, but die if they eat too much. Men live by love, but die, or cause death, if they love too much.

There are two loves: sacred and profane, spiritual and sensual.

In sensual love, it is the two blood-systems, the man's and the woman's, which sweep up into pure contact, and *almost* fuse. Almost mingle. Never quite. There is always the finest imaginable wall between the two blood-waves, through which pass unknown vibrations, forces, but through which the blood itself must never break, or it means bleeding.

In spiritual love, the contact is purely nervous. The nerves in the lovers are set vibrating in unison like two instruments. The pitch can rise higher and higher. But carry this too far, and the nerves begin to break, to bleed, as it were, and a form of death sets in.

The trouble about man is that he insists on being master of his own fate, and he insists on *oneness*. For instance, having discovered the ecstasy of spiritual love, he insists that he shall have this all the time, and nothing but this, for this is life. It is what he calls "heightening" life. He wants his nerves to be set vibrating in the intense and exhilarating unison with the nerves of another being, and by this means he acquires an ecstasy of vision, he finds himself in glowing unison with all the universe.

But as a matter of fact this glowing unison is only a temporary thing, because the first law of life is that each organism is isolate in itself, it must return to its own isolation.

Yet man has tried the glow of unison, called love, and he *likes* it. It gives him his highest gratification. He wants it. He wants it all the time. He wants it and he will have it. He doesn't want to return to his own isolation. Or if he must, it is only as a prowling beast returns to its lair to rest and set out again.

This brings us to Edgar Allan Poe. The clue to him lies

in the motto he chose for *Ligeia,* a quotation from the mystic Joseph Glanville: "And the will therein lieth, which dieth not. Who knoweth the mysteries of the will, with its vigor? For God is but a great Will pervading all things by nature of its intentness. Man doth not yield himself to the angels, nor unto death utterly, save only through the weakness of his feeble will."

It is a profound saying: and a deadly one.

Because if God is a great will, then the universe is but an instrument.

I don't know what God is. But He is not simply a will. That is too simple. Too anthropomorphic. Because a man wants his own will, and nothing but his will, he needn't say that God is the same will, magnified *ad infinitum.*

For me, there may be one God, but He is nameless and unknowable.

For me, there are also many gods, that come into me and leave me again. And they have very various wills, I must say.

But the point is Poe.

Poe had experienced the ecstasies of extreme spiritual love. And he wanted those ecstasies and nothing but those ecstasies. He wanted that great gratification, the sense of flowing, the sense of unison, the sense of heightening of life. He had experienced this gratification. He was told on every hand that this ecstasy of spiritual, nervous love was the greatest thing in life, was life itself. And he had tried it for himself, he knew that for him it *was* life itself. So he wanted it. And he *would have* it. He set up his will against the whole of the limitations of nature.

This is a brave man, acting on his own belief and his own experience. But it is also an arrogant man, and a fool.

Poe was going to get the ecstasy and the heightening, cost what it might. He went on in a frenzy, as characteristic American women nowadays go on in a frenzy, after the very same thing: the heightening, the flow, the ecstasy. Poe tried alcohol, and any drug he could lay his hand on. He also tried any human being he could lay his hands on.

His grand attempt and achievement was with his wife;

his cousin, a girl with a singing voice. With her he went in for the intensest flow, the heightening, the prismatic shades of ecstasy. It was the intensest nervous vibration of unison, pressed higher and higher in pitch, till the blood-vessels of the girl broke, and the blood began to flow out loose. It was love. If you call it love.

Love can be terribly obscene.

It is love that causes the neuroticism of the day. It is love that is the prime cause of tuberculosis.

The nerves that vibrate most intensely in spiritual unisons are the sympathetic ganglia of the breast, of the throat, and the hind brain. Drive this vibration overintensely, and you weaken the sympathetic tissues of the chest—the lungs—or of the throat, or of the lower brain, and the tubercles are given a ripe field.

But Poe drove the vibrations beyond any human pitch of endurance.

Being his cousin, she was more easily keyed to him.

Ligeia is the chief story. Ligeia! A mental-derived name. To him the woman, his wife, was not Lucy. She was Ligeia. No doubt she even preferred it thus.

Ligeia is Poe's love story, and its very fantasy makes it more truly his own story.

It is a tale of love pushed over a verge. And love pushed to extremes is a battle of wills between the lovers.

Love is become a battle of wills.

Which shall first destroy the other, of the lovers? Which can hold out longest against the other?

Ligeia is still the old-fashioned woman. Her will is still to submit. She wills to submit to the vampire of her husband's consciousness. Even death.

"In stature she was tall, somewhat slender, and, in her later days, even emaciated. I would in vain attempt to portray the majesty, the quiet ease, of her demeanor, or the incomprehensible lightness and elasticity of her footfall. I was never made aware of her entrance into my closed study save by the dear music of her low, sweet voice, as she placed her marble hand on my shoulder."

Poe has been so praised for his style. But it seems to me

a meretricious affair. "Her marble hand" and "the elasticity of her footfall" seem more like chair springs and mantel-pieces than a human creature. She never was quite a human creature to him. She was an instrument from which he got his extremes of sensation. His *machine à plaisir,* as somebody says.

All Poe's style, moreover, has this mechanical quality, as his poetry has a mechanical rhythm. He never sees anything in terms of life, almost always in terms of matter, jewels, marble, etc.—or in terms of force, scientific. And his cadences are all managed mechanically. This is what is called "having a style."

What he wants to do with Ligeia is to analyze her, till he knows all her component parts, till he has got her all in his consciousness. She is some strange chemical salt which he must analyze out in the test tubes of his brain, and then—when he's finished the analysis—*E finita la commedia!*

But she won't be quite analyzed out. There is something, something he can't get. Writing of her eyes, he says: "They were, I must believe, far larger than the ordinary eyes of our race"—as if anybody would want eyes "far larger" than other folks'. "They were even fuller than the fullest of the gazelle eyes of the tribe of Nourjahad"—which is blarney. "The hue of the orbs was the most brilliant of black and, far over them, hung jetty lashes of great length"—suggests a whip-lash. "The brows, slightly irregular in outline, had the same tint. The *strangeness,* which I found in the eyes, was of a nature distinct from the formation, or the color, or the brilliancy of the features, and must, after all, be referred to as the *expression.*"—Sounds like an anatomist anatomizing a cat. "Ah, word of no meaning! behind whose vast latitude of sound we entrench our ignorance of so much of the spiritual. The expression of the eyes of Ligeia! How for long hours have I pondered upon it! How have I, through the whole of a midsummer night, struggled to fathom it! What was it—that something more profound than the well of Democritus—which lay far within the pupils of my be loved? What *was* it? I was possessed with a passion to dis cover. . . ."

It is easy to see why each man kills the thing he loves. To *know* a living thing is to kill it. You have to kill a thing to know it satisfactorily. For this reason, the desirous consciousness, the SPIRIT, is a vampire.

One should be sufficiently intelligent and interested to know a good deal *about* any person one comes into close contact with. *About* her. Or *about* him.

But to try to *know* any living being is to try to suck the life out of that being.

Above all things, with the woman one loves. Every sacred instinct teaches one that one must leave her unknown. You know your woman darkly, in the blood. To try to *know* her mentally is to try to kill her. Beware, oh, woman, of the man who wants to *find out what you are*. And, oh, men, beware a thousand times more of the woman who wants to *know* you, or *get* you, what you are.

It is the temptation of a vampire fiend, is this knowledge.

Man does so horribly want to master the secret of life and of individuality *with his mind*. It is like the analysis of protoplasm. You can only analyze *dead* protoplasm, and know its constituents. It is a death process.

Keep KNOWLEDGE for the world of matter, force, and function. It has got nothing to do with being.

But Poe wanted to know—wanted to know what was the strangeness in the eyes of Ligeia. She might have told him it was horror at his probing, horror at being vamped by his consciousness.

But she wanted to be vamped. She wanted to be probed by his consciousness, to be KNOWN. She paid for wanting it, too.

Nowadays it is usually the man who wants to be vamped, to be KNOWN.

Edgar Allan probed and probed. So often he seemed on the verge. But she went over the verge of death before he came over the verge of knowledge. And it is always so.

He decided, therefore, that the clue to the strangeness lay in the mystery of will. "And the will therein lieth, which dieth not . . ."

Ligeia had a "gigantic volition." . . . "An intensity in

thought, action, or speech was possibly, in her, a result, or
at least an index" (he really meant indication) "of that
gigantic volition which, during our long intercourse, failed
to give other and more immediate evidence of its existence."

I should have thought her long submission to him was
chief and ample "other evidence."

"Of all the women whom I have ever known, she, the outwardly calm, the ever-placid Ligeia, was the most violently
a prey to the tumultuous vultures of stern passion. And of
such passion I could form no estimate, save by the miraculous expansion of those eyes which at once so delighted and
appalled me—by the almost magical melody, modulation,
distinctness, and placidity of her very low voice—and by the
fierce energy (rendered doubly effective by contrast with
her manner of utterance) of the wild words which she
habitually uttered."

Poor Poe, he had caught a bird of the same feather as
himself. One of those terrible cravers, who crave the further
sensation. Crave to madness or death. "Vultures of stern
passion" indeed! Condors.

But having recognized that the clue was in her gigantic
volition, he should have realized that the process of this
loving, this craving, this knowing, was a struggle of wills.
But Ligeia, true to the great tradition and mode of womanly
love, by her will kept herself submissive, recipient. She is
the passive body who is explored and analyzed into death.
And yet, at times, her great female will must have revolted.
"Vultures of stern passion!" With a convulsion of desire
she desired his further probing and exploring. To any
lengths. But then, "tumultuous vultures of stern passion."
She had to fight with herself.

But Ligeia wanted to go on and on with the craving, with
the love, with the sensation, with the probing, with the
knowing, on and on to the end.

There is no end. There is only the rupture of death.
That's where men, and women, are "had." Man is always
sold, in his search for final KNOWLEDGE.

"That she loved me I should not have doubted; and I
might have been easily aware that, in a bosom such as hers,

love would have reigned no ordinary passion. But in death only was I fully impressed with the strength of her affection. For long hours, detaining my hand, would she pour out before me the overflowing of a heart whose more than passionate devotion amounted to idolatry." (Oh, the indecency of all this endless intimate talk!) "How had I deserved to be blessed by such confessions?" (Another man would have felt himself cursed.) "How had I deserved to be cursed with the removal of my beloved in the hour of her making them? But upon this subject I cannot bear to dilate. Let me say only that in Ligeia's more than womanly abandonment to a love, alas! unmerited, all unworthily bestowed, I at length recognized the principle of her longing with so wildly earnest a desire for the life which was fleeing so rapidly away. It is this wild longing—it is this vehement desire for life—*but for life*—that I have no power to portray—no utterance capable of expressing."

Well, that is ghastly enough, in all conscience.

"And from them that have not shall be taken away even that which they have."

"To him that hath life shall be given life, and from him that hath not life shall be taken away even that life which he hath."

Or her either.

These terribly conscious birds, like Poe and his Ligeia, deny the very life that is in them; they want to turn it all into talk, into *knowing*. And so life, which will *not* be known, leaves them.

But poor Ligeia, how could she help it. It was her doom. All the centuries of the SPIRIT, all the years of American rebellion against the Holy Ghost, had done it to her.

She dies, when she would rather do anything than die. And when she dies the clue, which he only lived to grasp, dies with her.

Foiled!

Foiled!

No wonder she shrieks with her last breath.

On the last day Ligeia dictates to her husband a poem. As poems go, it is rather false, meretricious. But put your self in Ligeia's place, and it is real enough, and ghastly beyond bearing.

Out, out are all the lights—out all! 17½
And over each quivering form
The curtain, a funeral pall,
Comes down with the rush of a storm,
And the angels, all pallid and wan,
Uprising, unveiling, affirm
That the play is the tragedy "Man,"
And its hero the Conqueror Worm.

Which is the American equivalent for a William Blake poem. For Blake, too, was one of these ghastly, obscene "Knowers."

"'O God!' half shrieked Ligeia, leaping to her feet and extending her arms aloft with a spasmodic movement, as I made an end of these lines. 'O God! O Divine Father!—shall these things be undeviatingly so? Shall this conqueror be not once conquered? Are we not part and parcel in Thee? Who—who knoweth the mysteries of the angels, *nor unto death utterly,* save only through the weakness of his feeble will.'"

So Ligeia dies. And yields to death at least partly. *Anche troppo.*

As for her cry to God—has not God said that those who sin against the Holy Ghost shall not be forgiven?

And the Holy Ghost is within us. It is the thing that prompts us to be real, not to push our own cravings too far, not to submit to stunts and highfalutin, above all, not to be too egoistic and willful in our conscious self, but to change as the spirit inside us bids us change, and leave off when it bids us leave off, and laugh when we must laugh, particularly at ourselves, for in deadly earnestness there is always something a bit ridiculous. The Holy Ghost bids us never be too deadly in our earnestness, always to laugh in time, at ourselves and everything. Particularly at our sublimities. Everything has its hour of ridicule—everything.

Now Poe and Ligeia, alas, couldn't laugh. They were frenziedly earnest. And frenziedly they pushed on this vibration of consciousness and unison in consciousness. They sinned against the Holy Ghost that bids us all laugh and forget, bids us know our own limits. And they weren't forgiven.

Ligeia needn't blame God. She had only her own will, her "gigantic volition" to thank, lusting after more consciousness, more beastly KNOWING.

Ligeia dies. The husband goes to England, vulgarly buys or rents a gloomy, grand old abbey, puts it into some sort of repair, and furnishes it with exotic, mysterious, theatrical splendor. Never anything open and real. This theatrical "volition" of his. The bad taste of sensationalism.

Then he marries the fair-haired, blue-eyed Lady Rowena Trevanion, of Tremaine. That is, she would be a sort of Saxon-Cornish blue-blood damsel. Poor Poe!

"In halls such as these—in a bridal chamber such as this— I passed, with the Lady of Tremaine, the unhallowed hours of the first month of our marriage—passed them with but little disquietude. That my wife dreaded the fierce moodiness of my temper—that she shunned and loved me but little—I could not help perceiving, but it gave me rather pleasure than otherwise. I loathed her with a hatred belonging rather to a demon than a man. My memory flew back (Oh, with what intensity of regret!) to Ligeia, the beloved, the august, the entombed. I reveled in recollections of her purity . . ." etc.

Now the vampire lust is consciously such.

In the second month of the marriage the Lady Rowena fell ill. It is the shadow of Ligeia hangs over her. It is the ghostly Ligeia who pours poison into Rowena's cup. It is the spirit of Ligeia, leagued with the spirit of the husband, that now lusts in the slow destruction of Rowena. The two vampires, dead wife and living husband.

For Ligeia has not yielded unto death *utterly*. Her fixed, frustrated will comes back in vindictiveness. She could not have her way in life. So she, too, will find victims in life. And the husband, all the time, only uses Rowena as a living body on which to wreak his vengeance for his being thwarted with Ligeia. Thwarted from the final KNOWING her.

And at last from the corpse of Rowena, Ligeia rises. Out

of her death, through the door of a corpse they have destroyed between them, reappears Ligeia, still trying to have her will, to have more love and knowledge, the final gratification which is never final, with her husband.

For it is true, as William James and Conan Doyle and the rest allow, that a spirit can persist in the after-death. Persist by its own volition. But usually the evil persistence of a thwarted will, returning for vengeance on life. Lemures, vampires.

It is a ghastly story of the assertion of the human will, the will-to-love and the will-to-consciousness, asserted against death itself. The pride of human conceit in KNOWLEDGE.

There are terrible spirits, ghosts, in the air of America.

Eleanora, the next story, is a fantasy revealing the sensational delights of the man in his early marriage with the young and tender bride. They dwelt, he, his cousin and her mother, in the sequestered Valley of Many-colored Grass, the valley of prismatic sensation, where everything seems spectrum colored. They looked down at their *own images* in the River of Silence, and drew the god Eros from that wave: out of their own self-consciousness, that is. This is a description of the life of introspection and of the love which is begotten by the self in the self, the self-made love. The trees are like serpents worshiping the sun. That is, they represent the phallic passion in its poisonous or mental activity. Everything runs to consciousness: serpents worshiping the sun. The embrace of love, which should bring darkness and oblivion, would with these lovers be a daytime thing bringing more heightened consciousness, visions, spectrum-visions, prismatic. The evil thing that daytime love-making is, and all sex palaver.

In *Berenice* the man must go down to the sepulcher of his beloved and pull out her thirty-two small white teeth, which he carries in a box with him. It is repulsive and gloating. The teeth are the instruments of biting, of resistance, of antagonism. They often become symbols of opposition, little instruments or entities of crushing and destroying. Hence the dragon's teeth in the myth. Hence the man in *Berenice* must take possession of the irreducible part of his mistress.

"*Toutes ses dents étaient des idées*," he says. Then they are little fixed ideas of mordant hate, of which he possesses himself.

The other great story linking up with this group is *The Fall of the House of Usher*. Here the love is between brother and sister. When the self is broken, and the mystery of the recognition of *otherness* fails, then the longing for identification with the beloved becomes a lust. And it is this longing for identification, utter merging, which is at the base of the incest problem. In psychoanalysis almost every trouble in the psyche is traced to an incest-desire. But it won't do. Incest-desire is only one of the modes by which men strive to get their gratification of the intensest vibration of the spiritual nerves, without any resistance. In the family, the natural vibration is most nearly in unison. With a stranger, there is greater resistance. Incest is the getting of gratification and the avoiding of resistance.

The root of all evil is that we all want this spiritual gratification, this flow, this apparent heightening of life, this knowledge, this valley of many-colored grass, even grass and light prismatically decomposed, giving ecstasy. We want all this *without resistance*. We want it continually. And this is the root of all evil in us.

We ought to pray to be resisted, and resisted to the bitter end. We ought to decide to have done at last with craving.

The motto to *The Fall of the House of Usher* is a couple of lines from Béranger.

> *Son cœur est un luth suspendu;*
> *Sitôt qu'on le touche il résonne.*

We have all the trappings of Poe's rather overdone, vulgar fantasy. "I reined my horse to the precipitous brink of a black and lurid tarn that lay in unruffled luster by the dwelling, and gazed down—but with a shudder even more thrilling than before—upon the remodeled and inverted images of the gray sedge, and the ghastly tree stems, and the vacant and eyelike windows." The House of Usher, both dwelling and family, was very old. Minute fungi overspread the exterior of the house, hanging in festoons from the eaves. Gothic archways, a valet of stealthy step, somber tapestries, ebon black floors, a profusion of tattered and antique furniture, feeble gleams of encrimsoned light through latticed panes, and over all "an air of stern, deep, irredeemable gloom"—this makes up the interior.

The inmates of the house, Roderick and Madeline Usher, are the last remnants of their incomparably ancient and decayed race. Roderick has the same large, luminous eye, the same slightly arched nose of delicate Hebrew model, as characterized Ligeia. He is ill with the nervous malady of his family. It is he whose nerves are so strung that they vibrate to the unknown quiverings of the ether. He, too, has lost his self, his living soul, and become a sensitized instrument of the external influences; his nerves are verily like an æolian harp which must vibrate. He lives in "some struggle with the grim phantasm, Fear," for he is only the physical, post-mortem reality of a living being.

It is a question how much, once the true centrality of the self is broken, the instrumental consciousness of man can register. When man becomes selfless, wafting instrumental like a harp in an open window, how much can his elemental consciousness express? The blood as it runs has its own sympathies and responses to the material world, quite apart from seeing. And the nerves we know vibrate all the while to unseen presences, unseen forces. So Roderick Usher quivers on the edge of material existence.

It is this mechanical consciousness which gives "the fervid facility of his impromptus." It is the same thing that gives Poe his extraordinary facility in versification. The absence of real central or impulsive being in himself leaves him inordinately, mechanically sensitive to sounds and effects, associations of sounds, associations of rhyme, for example— mechanical, facile, having no root in any passion. It is all a secondary, meretricious process. So we get Roderick Usher's poem, The Haunted Palace, with its swift yet mechanical subtleties of rhyme and rhythm, its vulgarity of epithet. It is all a sort of dream-process, where the association between parts is mechanical, accidental as far as passional meaning goes.

Usher thought that all vegetable things had sentience. Surely all material things have a *form* of sentience, even the inorganic: surely they all exist in some subtle and complicated tension of vibration which makes them sensitive to external influence and causes them to have an influence on other external objects, irrespective of contact. It is of this vibration or inorganic consciousness that Poe is master: the sleep consciousness. Thus Roderick Usher was convinced that his whole surroundings, the stones of the house, the fungi, the water in the tarn, the very reflected image of the whole, was woven into a physical oneness with the family, condensed, as it were, into one atmosphere—the special atmosphere in which alone the Ushers could live. And it was this atmosphere which had molded the destinies of his family.

But while ever the soul remains alive, it is the molder and not the molded. It is the souls of living men that subtly impregnate stones, houses, mountains, continents, and give these their subtlest form. People only become subject to stones after having lost their integral souls.

In the human realm, Roderick had one connection: his sister Madeline. She, too, was dying of a mysterious disorder, nervous, cataleptic. The brother and sister loved each other passionately and exclusively. They were twins, almost identical in looks. It was the same absorbing love between them, this process of unison in nerve-vibration, resulting in more and more extreme exaltation and a sort of consciousness, and a gradual breakdown into death. The exquisitely sensitive Roger, vibrating without resistance with his sister Madeline, more and more exquisitely, and gradually devouring her, sucking her life like a vampire in his anguish of extreme love. And she asking to be sucked.

Madeline died and was carried down by her brother into the deep vaults of the house. But she was not dead. Her brother roamed about in incipient madness—a madness of unspeakable terror and guilt. After eight days they were suddenly startled by a clash of metal, then a distinct, hollow metallic, and clangorous, yet apparently muffled, reverberation. Then Roderick Usher, gibbering, began to express

himself: *"We have put her living into the tomb!* Said I not
that my senses were acute? I *now* tell you that I heard
her first feeble movements in the hollow coffin. I heard
them—many, many days ago—yet I dared not—*I dared not
speak."*

It is the same old theme of "each man kills the thing he
loves." He knew his love had killed her. He knew she died
at last, like Ligeia, unwilling and unappeased. So, she rose
again upon him. "But then without those doors there *did*
stand the lofty and enshrouded figure of the Lady Madeline
of Usher. There was blood upon her white robes, and the
evidence of some bitter struggle upon every portion of her
emaciated frame. For a moment she remained trembling and
reeling to and fro upon the threshold, then, with a low
moaning cry, fell heavily inward upon the person of her
brother, and in her violent and now final death-agonies bore
him to the floor a corpse, and a victim to the terrors he had
anticipated."

It is lurid and melodramatic, but it is true. It is a ghastly
psychological truth of what happens in the last stages of this
beloved love, which cannot be separate, cannot be isolate,
cannot listen in isolation to the isolate Holy Ghost. For it
is the Holy Ghost we must live by. The next era is the era
of the Holy Ghost. And the Holy Ghost speaks individually
inside each individual: always, forever a ghost. There is no
manifestation to the general world. Each isolate individual
listening in isolation to the Holy Ghost within him.

The Ushers, brother and sister, betrayed the Holy Ghost
in themselves. They would love, love, love, without resistance. They would love, they would merge, they would be as
one thing. So they dragged each other down into death. For
the Holy Ghost says you must *not* be as one thing with
another being. Each must abide by itself, and correspond
only within certain limits.

The best tales all have the same burden. Hate is as inordinate as love, and as slowly consuming, as secret, as underground, as subtle. All this underground vault business in
Poe only symbolizes that which takes place *beneath* the consciousness. On top, all is fair-spoken. Beneath, there is awful

murderous extremity of burying alive. Fortunato, in *The Cask of Amontillado,* is buried alive out of perfect hatred, as the Lady Madeline of Usher is buried alive out of love. The lust of hate is the inordinate desire to consume and unspeakably possess the soul of the hated one, just as the lust of love is the desire to possess, or to be possessed by, the beloved, utterly. But in either case the result is the dissolution of both souls, each losing itself in transgressing its own bounds.

The lust of Montresor is to devour utterly the soul of Fortunato. It would be no use killing him outright. If a man is killed outright his soul remains integral, free to return into the bosom of some beloved, where it can enact itself. In walling up his enemy in the vault, Montresor seeks to bring about the indescribable capitulation of the man's soul, so that he, the victor, can possess himself of the very being of the vanquished. Perhaps this can actually be done. Perhaps, in the attempt, the victor breaks the bonds of his own identity, and collapses into nothingness, or into the infinite. Becomes a monster.

What holds good for inordinate hate holds good for inordinate love. The motto, *Nemo me impune lacessit,* might just as well be *Nemo me impune amat.*

In *William Wilson* we are given a rather unsubtle account of the attempt of a man to kill his own soul. William Wilson the mechanical, lustful ego succeeds in killing William Wilson the living self. The lustful ego lives on, gradually reducing itself towards the dust of the infinite.

In the *Murders in the Rue Morgue* and *The Gold Bug* we have those mechanical tales where the interest lies in the following out of a subtle chain of cause and effect. The interest is scientific rather than artistic, a study in psychologic reactions.

The fascination of murder itself is curious. Murder is not just killing. Murder is a lust to get at the very quick of life itself, and kill it—hence the stealth and the frequent morbid dismemberment of the corpse, the attempt to get at the very quick of the murdered being, to find the quick and to possess it. It is curious that the two men fascinated by the art of murder, though in different ways, should have been De Quincey and Poe, men so different in ways of life, yet perhaps not so widely different in nature. In each of them is traceable that strange lust for extreme love and extreme hate, possession by mystic violence of the other soul, or violent deathly surrender of the soul in the self: an absence of manly virtue, which stands alone and accepts limits.

Inquisition and torture are akin to murder: the same lust. It is a combat between inquisitor and victim as to whether the inquisitor shall get at the quick of life itself, and pierce it. Pierce the very quick of the soul. The evil will of man tries to do this. The brave soul of man refuses to have the life-quick pierced in him. It is strange: but just as the thwarted will can persist evilly, after death, so can the brave spirit preserve, even through torture and death, the quick of life and truth. Nowadays society is evil. It finds subtle ways of torture, to destroy the life-quick, to get at the life-quick in a man. Every possible form. And still a man can hold out, if he can laugh and listen to the Holy Ghost.—But society is evil, evil, and love is evil. And evil breeds evil, more and more.

So the mystery goes on. La Bruyère says that all our human unhappiness *viennent de ne pouvoir être seuls.* As long as man lives he will be subject to the yearning of love or the burning of hate, which is only inverted love.

But he is subject to something more than this. If we do not live to eat, we do not live to love either.

We live to stand alone, and listen to the Holy Ghost. The Holy Ghost, who is inside us, and who is many gods. Many gods come and go, some say one thing and some say another, and we have to obey the God of the innermost hour. It is the multiplicity of gods within us make up the Holy Ghost.

But Poe knew only love, love, love, intense vibrations and heightened consciousness. Drugs, women, self-destruction, but anyhow the prismatic ecstasy of heightened consciousness and sense of love, of flow. The human soul in him was beside itself. But it was not lost. He told us plainly how it was, so that we should know.

He was an adventurer into vaults and cellars and horrible underground passages of the human soul. He sounded the horror and the warning of his own doom.

Doomed he was. He died wanting more love, and love killed him. A ghastly disease, love. Poe telling us of his disease: trying even to make his desease fair and attractive. Even succeeding.

Which is the inevitable falseness, duplicity of art, American art in particular.

VII. *Nathaniel Hawthorne and* The Scarlet Letter

NATHANIEL HAWTHORNE writes romance.

And what's romance? Usually, a nice little tale where you have everything As You Like It, where rain never wets your jacket and gnats never bite your nose and it's always daisy-time. *As You Like It* and *Forest Lovers,* etc. *Morte D'Arthur.*

Hawthorne obviously isn't this kind of romanticist: though nobody has muddy boots in *The Scarlet Letter,* either.

But there is more to it. *The Scarlet Letter* isn't a pleasant, pretty romance. It is a sort of parable, an earthly story with a hellish meaning.

All the time there is this split in the American art and art-consciousness. On the top it is as nice as pie, goody-goody and lovey-dovey. Like Hawthorne being such a blue-eyed darling, in life, and Longfellow and the rest such sucking-doves. Hawthorne's wife said she "never saw him in time," which doesn't mean she saw him too late. But always in the "frail effulgence of eternity."

Serpents they were. Look at the inner meaning of their art and see what demons they were.

You *must* look through the surface of American art, and see the inner diabolism of the symbolic meaning. Otherwise it is all mere childishness.

That blue-eyed darling Nathaniel knew disagreeable things in his inner soul. He was careful to send them out in disguise.

Always the same. The deliberate consciousness of Americans so fair and smooth-spoken, and the under-consciousness so devilish. *Destroy! destroy! destroy!* hums the under-consciousness. *Love and produce! Love and produce!* cackles the upper consciousness. And the world hears only the love-and-produce cackle. Refuses to hear the hum of destruction underneath. Until such time as it will *have* to hear.

The American has got to destroy. It is his destiny. It is his destiny to destroy the whole corpus of the white psyche, the white consciousness. And he's got to do it secretly. As the growing of a dragonfly inside a chrysalis or cocoon destroys the larva grub, secretly.

Though many a dragonfly never gets out of the chrysalis case: dies inside. As America might.

So the secret chrysalis of *The Scarlet Letter*, diabolically destroying the old psyche inside.

Be good! Be good! warbles Nathaniel. *Be good, and never sin! Be sure your sins will find you out.*

So convincingly that his wife never saw him "as in time."

Then listen to the diabolic undertone of *The Scarlet Letter.*

Man ate of the tree of knowledge, and became ashamed of himself.

Do you imagine Adam had never lived with Eve before that apple episode? Yes, he had. As a wild animal with his mate.

It didn't become "sin" till the knowledge-poison entered. That apple of Sodom.

We are divided in ourselves, against ourselves. And that is the meaning of the cross symbol.

In the first place, Adam knew Eve as a wild animal knows its mate, momentaneously, but vitally, in blood-knowledge. Blood-knowledge, not mind-knowledge. Blood-knowledge, that seems utterly to forget, but doesn't. Blood-knowledge, instinct, intuition, all the vast vital flux of knowing that goes on in the dark, antecedent to the mind.

Then came that beastly apple, and the other sort of knowledge started.

Adam began to look at himself. "My hat!" he said.

"What's this? My Lord! What the deuce!—And Eve! I wonder about Eve."

Thus starts KNOWING. Which shortly runs to UNDERSTANDING, when the devil gets his own.

When Adam went and took Eve, *after* the apple, he didn't do any more than he had done many a time before, in act. But in consciousness he did something very different. So did Eve. Each of them kept an eye on what they were doing, they watched what was happening to them. They wanted to KNOW. And that was the birth of sin. Not *doing* it, but KNOWING about it. Before the apple, they had shut their eyes and their minds had gone dark. Now, they peeped and pried and imagined. They watched themselves. And they felt uncomfortable after. They felt self-conscious. So they said, "The *act* is sin. Let's hide. We've sinned."

No wonder the Lord kicked them out of the Garden. Dirty hypocrites.

The sin was the self-watching, self-consciousness. The sin, and the doom. Dirty understanding.

Nowadays men do hate the idea of dualism. It's no good, dual we are. The cross. If we accept the symbol, then, virtually, we accept the fact. We are divided against ourselves.

For instance, the blood *hates* being KNOWN by the mind. It feels itself destroyed when it is KNOWN. Hence the profound instinct of privacy.

And on the other hand, the mind and the spiritual consciousness of man simply *hates* the dark potency of blood-acts: hates the genuine dark sensual orgasms, which do, for the time being, actually obliterate the mind and the spiritual consciousness, plunge them in a suffocating flood of darkness.

You can't get away from this.

Blood-consciousness overwhelms, obliterates, and annuls mind-consciousness.

Mind-consciousness extinguishes blood-consciousness, and consumes the blood.

We are all of us conscious in both ways. And the two ways are antagonistic in us.

They will always remain so.

That is our cross.

The antagonism is so obvious, and so far-reaching, that it extends to the smallest thing. The cultured, highly-conscious person of today *loathes* any form of physical, "menial" work: such as washing dishes or sweeping a floor or chopping wood. This menial work is an insult to the spirit. "When I see men carrying heavy loads, doing brutal work, it always makes me want to cry," said a beautiful, cultured woman to me.

"When you say that, it makes me want to beat you," said I, in reply. "When I see you with your beautiful head pondering heavy thoughts, I just want to hit you. It outrages me."

My father hated books, hated the sight of anyone reading or writing.

My mother hated the thought that any of her sons should be condemned to manual labor. Her sons must have something higher than that.

She won. But she died first.

He laughs longest who laughs last.

There is a basic hostility in all of us between the physical and the mental, the blood and the spirit. The mind is "ashamed" of the blood. And the blood is destroyed by the mind, actually. Hence pale-faces.

At present the mind-consciousness and the so-called spirit triumphs. In America supremely. In America, nobody does anything from the blood. Always from the nerves, if not from the mind. The blood is chemically reduced by the nerves, in American activity.

When an Italian laborer labors, his mind and nerves sleep, his blood acts ponderously.

Americans, when they are *doing* things, never seem really to be doing them. They are "busy about" it. They are always busy "about" something. But truly *immersed* in *doing* something, with the deep blood-consciousness active, that they never are.

They *admire* the blood-conscious spontaneity. And they want to get it in their heads. "Live from the body," they shriek. It is their last mental shriek. *Co-ordinate.*

It is a further attempt still to rationalize the body and blood. "Think about such and such a muscle," they say, "and relax there."

And every time you "conquer" the body with the mind (you can say "heal" it, if you like) you cause a deeper, more dangerous complex or tension somewhere else.

Ghastly Americans, with their blood no longer blood. A yellow spiritual fluid.

The Fall.

There have been lots of Falls.

We *fell* into *knowledge* when Eve bit the apple. Self-conscious knowledge. For the first time the mind put up a fight against the blood. Wanting to UNDERSTAND. That is to intellectualize the blood.

The blood must be *shed*, says Jesus.

Shed on the cross of our own divided psyche.

Shed the blood, and you become mind-conscious. Eat the body and drink the blood, self-cannibalizing, and you become extremely conscious, like Americans and some Hindus. Devour yourself, and God knows what a lot you'll know, what a lot you'll be conscious of.

Mind you don't choke yourself.

For a long time men *believed* that they could be perfected through the mind, through the spirit. They believed, passionately. They had their ecstasy in pure consciousness. They *believed* in purity, chastity, and the wings of the spirit.

America soon plucked the bird of the spirit. America soon killed the *belief* in the spirit. But not the practice. The practice continued with a sarcastic vehemence. America, with a perfect inner contempt for the spirit and the consciousness of man, practices the same spirituality and universal love and KNOWING all the time, incessantly, like a drug habit. And inwardly gives not a fig for it. Only for the *sensation*. The pretty-pretty *sensation* of love, loving all the world. And the nice fluttering aeroplane *sensation* of knowing, knowing, knowing. Then the prettiest of all sensations, the sensation of UNDERSTANDING. Oh, what a lot they understand, the darlings! So good at the trick, they are. Just a trick of self-conceit.

The Scarlet Letter gives the show away.

You have your pure-pure young parson Dimmesdale.

You have the beautiful Puritan Hester at his feet.

And the first thing she does is to seduce him.

And the first thing he does is to be seduced.

And the second thing they do is to hug their sin in secret, and gloat over it, and try to understand.

Which is the myth of New England.

Deerslayer refused to be seduced by Judith Hutter. At least the Sodom apple of sin didn't fetch him.

But Dimmesdale was seduced gloatingly. Oh, luscious Sin!

He was such a pure young man.

That he had to make a fool of purity.

The American psyche.

Of course, the best part of the game lay in keeping up pure appearances.

The greatest triumph a woman can have, especially an American woman, is the triumph of seducing a man: especially if he is pure.

And he gets the greatest thrill of all, in falling.—"Seduce me, Mrs. Hercules."

And the pair of them share the subtlest delight in keeping up pure appearances, when everybody knows all the while. But the power of pure appearances is something to exult in. All America gives in to it. *Look* pure!

To seduce a man. To have everybody know. To keep up appearances of purity. Pure!

This is the great triumph of woman.

A. The Scarlet Letter. Adulteress! The great Alpha, Alpha! Adulteress! The new Adam and Adama! American!

A. Adulteress! Stitched with gold thread, glittering upon the bosom. The proudest insignia.

Put her upon the scaffold and worship her there. Worship her there. The Woman, the Magna Mater. *A.* Adulteress! Abel!

Abel! Abel! Abel! Admirable!

It becomes a farce.

The fiery heart. *A.* Mary of the Bleeding Heart. Mater

Adolerata! *A*. Capital *A*. Adulteress. Glittering with gold thread. Abel! Adultery. Admirable!

It is, perhaps, the most colossal satire ever penned. *The Scarlet Letter*. And by a blue-eyed darling of a Nathaniel.

Not Bumppo, however.

The human spirit, fixed in a lie, adhering to a lie, giving itself perpetually the lie.

All begins with *A*.

Adulteress. Alpha. Abel, Adam. *A*. America.

The Scarlet Letter.

"Had there been a Papist among the crowd of Puritans, he might have seen in this beautiful woman, so picturesque in her attire and mien, and with the infant at her bosom, an object to remind him of the image of Divine Maternity, which so many illustrious painters have vied with one another to represent; something which should remind him, indeed, but only by contrast, of that sacred image of sinless Motherhood, whose infant was to redeem the world."

Whose infant was to redeem the world indeed! It will be a startling redemption the world will get from the American infant.

"Here was a taint of deepest sin in the most sacred quality of human life, working such effect that the world was only the darker for this woman's beauty, and more lost for the infant she had borne."

Just listen to the darling. Isn't he a master of apology? Of symbols, too.

His pious blame is a chuckle of praise all the while.

Oh, Hester, you are a demon. A man *must* be pure, just that you can seduce him to a fall. Because the greatest thrill in life is to bring down the Sacred Saint with a flop into the mud. Then when you've brought him down, humbly wipe off the mud with your hair, another Magdalen. And then go home and dance a witch's jig of triumph, and stitch yourself a Scarlet Letter with gold thread, as duchesses used to stitch themselves coronets. And then stand meek on the scaffold and fool the world. Who will all be envying you your sin, and beating you because you've stolen an advantage over them.

Hester Prynne is the great nemesis of woman. She is the KNOWING Ligeia risen diabolic from the grave. Having her own back. UNDERSTANDING.

This time it is Mr. Dimmesdale who dies. She lives on and is Abel.

His spiritual love was a lie. And prostituting the woman to his spiritual love, as popular clergymen do, in his preachings and loftiness, was a tall white lie. Which came flop.

We are so pure in spirit. Hi-tiddly-i-ty!

Till she tickled him in the right place, and he fell.

Flop.

Flop goes spiritual love.

But keep up the game. Keep up appearances. Pure are the pure. To the pure all things, etc.

Look out, Mister, for the Female Devotee. Whatever you do, don't let her start tickling you. She knows your weak spot. Mind your Purity.

When Hester Prynne seduced Arthur Dimmesdale it was the beginning of the end. But from the beginning of the end to the end of the end is a hundred years or two.

Mr. Dimmesdale also wasn't at the end of his resources. Previously, he had lived by governing his body, ruling it, in the interests of his spirit. Now he has a good time all by himself torturing his body, whipping it, piercing it with thorns, macerating himself. It's a form of masturbation. He wants to get a mental grip on his body. And since he can't quite manage it with the mind, witness his fall—he will give it what for, with whips. His will shall *lash* his body. And he enjoys his pains. Wallows in them. To the pure all things are pure.

It is the old self-mutilation process, gone rotten. The mind wanting to get its teeth in the blood and flesh. The ego exulting in the tortures of the mutinous flesh. I, the ego, I *will* triumph over my own flesh. Lash! Lash! I am a grand free spirit. *Lash!* I am the master of my soul! *Lash! Lash!* I am the captain of my soul. *Lash!* Hurray! "In the fell clutch of circumstance," etc., etc.

Good-by Arthur. He depended on women for his Spiritual Devotees, spiritual brides. So, the woman just touched him in his weak spot, his Achilles Heel of the flesh. Look out for the spiritual bride. She's after the weak spot.

It is the battle of wills.

"For the will therein lieth, which dieth not——"

The Scarlet Woman becomes a Sister of Mercy. Didn't she just, in the late war. Oh, Prophet Nathaniel!

Hester urges Dimmesdale to go away with her, to a new country, to a new life. He isn't having any.

He knows there is no new country, no new life on the globe today. It is the same old thing, in different degrees, everywhere. *Plus ça change, plus c'est la même chose.*

Hester thinks, with Dimmesdale for her husband, and Pearl for her child, in Australia, maybe, she'd have been perfect.

But she wouldn't. Dimmesdale had already fallen from his integrity as a minister of the Gospel of the Spirit. He had lost his manliness. He didn't see the point of just leaving himself between the hands of a woman and going away to a "new country," to be her thing entirely. She'd only have despised him more, as every woman despises a man who has "fallen" to her; despises him with her tenderest lust.

He stood for nothing any more. So let him stay where he was and dree out his weird.

She had dished him and his spirituality, so he hated her. As Angel Clare was dished, and hated Tess. As Jude in the end hated Sue: or should have done. The women make fools of them, the spiritual men. And when, as men, they've gone flop in their spirituality, they can't pick themselves up whole any more. So they just crawl, and die detesting the female, or the females, who made them fall.

The saintly minister gets a bit of his own back, at the last minute, by making public confession from the very scaffold where she was exposed. Then he dodges into death. But he's had a bit of his own back, on everybody.

"Shall we not meet again?" whispered she, bending her face down close to him. "Shall we not spend our immortal life together? Surely, surely we have ransomed one another with all

this woe! Thou lookest far into eternity with those bright dying
eyes. Tell me what thou seest!"

"Hush, Hester—hush," said he, with tremulous solemnity.
"The law we broke!—the sin here so awfully revealed! Let these
alone be in thy thoughts. I fear! I fear!"

So he dies, throwing the "sin" in her teeth, and escaping
into death.

The law we broke, indeed. You bet!

Whose law?

But it is truly a law, that man must either stick to the
belief he has grounded himself on, and obey the laws of
that belief, or he must admit the belief itself to be inadequate, and prepare himself for a new thing.

There was no change in belief, either in Hester or in
Dimmesdale or in Hawthorne or in America. The same old
treacherous belief, which was really cunning disbelief, in
the Spirit, in Purity, in Selfless Love, and in Pure Consciousness. They would go on following this belief, for the
sake of the sensationalism of it. But they would make a fool
of it all the time. Like Woodrow Wilson, and the rest of
modern Believers. The rest of modern Saviors.

If you meet a Savior today, be sure he is trying to make
an innermost fool of you. Especially if the savior be an
UNDERSTANDING WOMAN, offering her love.

Hester lives on, pious as pie, being a public nurse. She
becomes at last an acknowledged saint, Abel of the Scarlet
Letter.

She would, being a woman. She has had her triumph
over the individual man, so she quite loves subscribing to
the whole spiritual life of society. She will make herself as
false as hell, for society's sake, once she's had her real
triumph over Saint Arthur.

Blossoms out into a Sister-of-Mercy Saint.

But it's a long time before she really takes anybody in.
People kept on thinking her a witch, which she was.

As a matter of fact, unless a woman is held, by man, safe
within the bounds of belief, she becomes inevitably a destructive force. She can't help herself. A woman is almost

always vulnerable to pity. She can't bear to see anything *physically* hurt. But let a woman loose from the bounds and restraints of man's fierce belief, in his gods and in himself, and she becomes a gentle devil. She becomes subtly diabolic. The colossal evil of the united spirit of Woman. WOMAN, German woman or American woman, or every other sort of woman, in the last war, was something frightening. As every *man* knows.

Woman becomes a helpless, would-be-loving demon. She is helpless. Her very love is a subtle poison.

Unless a man believes in himself and his gods, *genuinely*: unless he fiercely obeys his own Holy Ghost: his woman will destroy him. Woman is the nemesis of doubting man. She can't help it.

And with Hester, after Ligeia, woman becomes a nemesis to man. She bolsters him up from the outside, she destroys him from the inside. And he dies hating her, as Dimmesdale did.

Dimmesdale's spirituality had gone on too long, too far. It had become a false thing. He found his nemesis in woman. And he was done for.

Woman is a strange and rather terrible phenomenon, to man. When the subconscious soul of woman recoils from its creative union with man, it becomes a destructive force. It exerts, willy-nilly, an invisible destructive influence. The woman herself may be as nice as milk, to all appearance, like Ligeia. But she is sending out waves of silent destruction of the faltering spirit in men, all the same. She doesn't know it. She can't even help it. But she does it. The devil is in her.

The very women who are most busy saving the bodies of men, and saving the children: these women doctors, these nurses, these educationalists, these public-spirited women, these female saviors: they are all, from the inside, sending out waves of destructive malevolence which eat out the inner life of a man, like a cancer. It is so, it will be so, till men realize it and react to save themselves.

God won't save us. The women are so devilish godly.

Men must save themselves in this strait, and by no sugary means either.

A woman can use her sex in sheer malevolence and poison, while she is *behaving* as meek and good as gold. Dear darling, she is really snow-white in her blamelessness. And all the while she is using her sex as a she-devil, for the endless hurt of her man. She doesn't know it. She will never believe it if you tell her. And if you give her a slap in the face for her fiendishness, she will rush to the first magistrate, in indignation. She is so *absolutely* blameless, the she-devil, the dear, dutiful creature.

Give her the great slap, just the same, just when she is being most angelic. Just when she is bearing her cross most meekly.

Oh, woman out of bounds is a devil. But it is man's fault. Woman never *asked*, in the first place, to be cast out of her bit of an Eden of belief and trust. It is man's business to bear the responsibility of belief. If he becomes a spiritual fornicator and liar, like Ligeia's husband and Arthur Dimmesdale, how *can* a woman believe in him? Belief doesn't go by choice. And if a woman doesn't believe in a *man*, she believes, essentially, in nothing. She becomes, willy-nilly, a devil.

A devil she is, and a devil she will be. And most men will succumb to her devilishness.

Hester Prynne was a devil. Even when she was so meekly going round as a sick-nurse. Poor Hester. Part of her wanted to be saved from her own devilishness. And another part wanted to go on and on in devilishness, for revenge. Revenge! REVENGE! It is this that fills the unconscious spirit of woman today. Revenge against man, and against the spirit of man, which has betrayed her into unbelief. Even when she is most sweet and a salvationist, she is her most devilish, is woman. She gives her man the sugar-plum of her own submissive sweetness. And when he's taken this sugar-plum in his mouth, a scorpion comes out of it. After he's taken this Eve to his bosom, oh, so loving, she destroys him inch by inch. Woman and her revenge! She will have it, and go on having it, for decades and decades, unless she's stopped. And to stop her you've got to believe in yourself and your gods, your own Holy Ghost, Sir Man; and then you've got to fight her, and never give in. She's a devil. But in the long run she is conquerable. And just a tiny bit of her wants to be conquered. You've got to fight three quarters of her, in absolute hell, to get at the final quarter of her that wants a release, at last, from the hell of her own revenge. But it's a long last. And not yet.

"She had in her nature a rich, voluptuous, oriental characteristic—a taste for the gorgeously beautiful." This is Hester. This is American. But she repressed her nature in the above direction. She would not even allow herself the luxury of laboring at fine, delicate stitching. Only she dressed her little sin-child Pearl vividly, and the scarlet letter was gorgeously embroidered. Her Hecate and Astarte insignia.

"A voluptuous, oriental characteristic——" That lies waiting in American women. It is probable that the Mormons are the forerunners of the coming real America. It is probable that men will have more than one wife, in the coming America. That you will have again a half-Oriental womanhood, and a polygamy.

The gray nurse, Hester. The Hecate, the hell-cat. The slowly evolving, voluptuous female of the new era, with a whole new submissiveness to the dark, phallic principle.

But it takes time. Generation after generation of nurses and political women and salvationists. And in the end, the dark erection of the images of sex-worship once more, and the newly submissive women. That kind of depth. Deep women in that respect. When we have at last broken this insanity of mental-spiritual consciousness. And the women *choose* to experience again the great submission.

"The poor, whom she sought out to be the objects of her bounty, often reviled the hand that was stretched to succor them."

Naturally. The poor hate a salvationist. They smell the devil underneath.

"She was patient—a martyr indeed—but she forbore to

pray for her enemies, lest, in spite of her forgiving aspirations, the words of the blessing should stubbornly twist
themselves into a curse."

So much honesty, at least. No wonder the old witch-lady
Mistress Hibbins claimed her for another witch.

"She grew to have a dread of children; for they had imbibed from their parents a vague idea of something horrible
in this dreary woman gliding silently through the town, with
never any companion but only one child."

"A vague idea!" Can't you see her "gliding silently"? It's
not a question of a vague idea imbibed, but a definite feeling directly received.

"But sometimes, once in many days, or perchance in
many months, she felt an eye—a human eye—upon the ignominious brand, that seemed to give a momentary relief,
as if half her agony were shared. The next instant, back
it all rushed again, with a still deeper throb of pain; for in
that brief interval she had sinned again. Had Hester sinned
alone?"

Of course not. As for sinning again, she would go on all
her life silently, changelessly "sinning." She never repented.
Not she. Why should she? She had brought down Arthur
Dimmesdale, that too-too snow-white bird, and that was her
life-work.

As for sinning again when she met two dark eyes in a
crowd, why of course. Somebody who understood as she
understood.

I always remember meeting the eyes of a gipsy woman,
for one moment, in a crowd, in England. She knew; and
I knew. What did we know? I was not able to make out.
But we knew.

Probably the same fathomless hate of this spiritual-con-
scious society in which the outcast woman and I both
roamed like meek-looking wolves. Tame wolves waiting to
shake off their tameness. Never able to.

And again, that "voluptuous, oriental" characteristic that
knows the mystery of the ithyphallic gods. She would not
betray the ithyphallic gods to this white, leprous-white

society of "lovers." Neither will I, if I can help it. These leprous-white, seducing, spiritual women, who "understand" so much. One has been too often seduced, and "understood." "I can read him like a book," said my first lover of me. The book is in several volumes, dear. And more and more comes back to me the gulf of dark hate and *other* understanding, in the eyes of the gipsy woman. So different from the hateful white light of understanding which floats like scum on the eyes of white, oh, so white English and American women, with their understanding voices and their deep, sad words, and their profound, *good* spirits. Pfui!

Hester was scared only of one result of her sin: Pearl. Pearl, the scarlet letter incarnate. The little girl. When women bear children, they produce either devils or sons with gods in them. And it is an evolutionary process. The devil in Hester produced a purer devil in Pearl. And the devil in Pearl will produce—she married an Italian count—a piece of purer devilishness still.

And so from hour to hour we ripe and ripe.

And then from hour to hour we rot and rot.

There was that in the child "which often impelled Hester to ask in bitterness of heart, whether it were for good or ill that the poor little creature had been born at all."

For ill, Hester. But don't worry. Ill is as necessary as good. Malevolence is as necessary as benevolence. If you have brought forth, spawned, a young malevolence, be sure there is a rampant falseness in the world against which this malevolence must be turned. Falseness has to be bitten and bitten, till it is bitten to death. Hence Pearl.

Pearl. Her own mother compares her to the demon of plague, or scarlet fever, in her red dress. But then, plague is necessary to destroy a rotten, false humanity.

Pearl, the devilish girl-child, who can be so tender and loving and *understanding,* and then, when she has understood, will give you a hit across the mouth, and turn on you with a grin of sheer diabolic jeering.

Serves you right, you shouldn't be *understood.* That is your vice. You shouldn't want to be loved, and then you'd not get hit across the mouth. Pearl will love you: marvel-

ously. And she'll hit you across the mouth: oh, so neatly.
And serves you right.

Pearl is perhaps the most modern child in all literature.

Old-fashioned Nathaniel, with his little-boy charm, he'll
tell you what's what. But he'll cover it with smarm.

Hester simply *hates* her child, from one part of herself.
And from another, she cherishes her child as her one precious treasure. For Pearl is the continuing of her female
revenge on life. But female revenge hits both ways. Hits
back at its own mother. The female revenge in Pearl hits
back at Hester, the mother, and Hester is simply livid with
fury and "sadness," which is rather amusing.

"The child could not be made amenable to rules. In giving her existence a great law had been broken; and the result was a being whose elements were perhaps beautiful
and brilliant, but all in disorder, or with an order peculiar
to themselves, amidst which the point of variety and arrangement was difficult or impossible to discover."

Of course, the order is peculiar to themselves. But the
point of variety is this: "Draw out the loving, sweet soul,
draw it out with marvelous understanding; and then spit in
its eye."

Hester, of course, didn't at all like it when her sweet child
drew out her motherly soul, with yearning and deep understanding: and then spit in the motherly eye, with a grin.
But it was a process the mother had started.

Pearl had a peculiar look in her eyes: "a look so intelligent, yet so inexplicable, so perverse, sometimes so malicious,
but generally accompanied by a wild flow of spirits, that
Hester could not help questioning at such moments whether
Pearl was a human child."

A little demon! But her mother, and the saintly Dimmesdale, had borne her. And Pearl, by the very openness of her
perversity, was more straightforward than her parents. She
flatly refuses any Heavenly Father, seeing the earthly one
such a fraud. And she has the pietistic Dimmesdale on toast,
spits right in his eye: in both his eyes.

Poor, brave, tormented little soul, always in a state of
recoil, she'll be a devil to men when she grows up. But the

men deserve it. If they'll let themselves be "drawn" by her loving understanding, they deserve that she shall slap them across the mouth the moment they *are* drawn. The chickens! Drawn and trussed.

Poor little phenomenon of a modern child, she'll grow up into the devil of a modern woman. The nemesis of weak-kneed modern men, craving to be love-drawn.

The third person in the diabolic trinity, or triangle, of the Scarlet Letter, is Hester's first husband, Roger Chillingworth. He is an old Elizabethan physician, with a gray beard and a long-furred coat and a twisted shoulder. Another healer. But something of an alchemist, a magician. He is a magician on the verge of modern science, like Francis Bacon.

Roger Chillingworth is of the old order of intellect, in direct line from the mediaeval Roger Bacon alchemists. He has an old, intellectual belief in the dark sciences, the Hermetic philosophies. He is no Christian, no selfless aspirer. He is not an aspirer. He is the old authoritarian in man. The old male authority. But without passional belief. Only intellectual belief in himself and his male authority.

Shakespeare's whole tragic wail is because of the downfall of the true male authority, the ithyphallic authority and masterhood. It fell with Elizabeth. It was trodden underfoot with Victoria.

But Chillingworth keeps on the *intellectual* tradition. He hates the new spiritual aspirers, like Dimmesdale, with a black, crippled hate. He is the old male authority, in intellectual tradition.

You can't keep a wife by force of an intellectual tradition. So Hester took to seducing Dimmesdale.

Yet her only marriage, and her last oath, is with the old Roger. He and she are accomplices in pulling down the spiritual saint.

"Why dost thou smile so at me?" she says to her old, vengeful husband. "Art thou not like the Black Man that haunts the forest around us? Hast thou not enticed me into a bond which will prove the ruin of my soul?"

"Not thy soul!" he answered with another smile. "No, not thy soul!"

It is the soul of the pure preacher, that false thing, which they are after. And the crippled physician—this other healer—blackly vengeful in his old, distorted male authority, and the "loving" woman, they bring down the saint between them.

A black and complementary hatred, akin to love, is what Chillingworth feels for the young, saintly parson. And Dimmesdale responds, in a hideous kind of love. Slowly the saint's life is poisoned. But the black old physician smiles, and tries to keep him alive. Dimmesdale goes in for self-torture, self-lashing, lashing his own white, thin, spiritual savior's body. The dark old Chillingworth listens outside the door and laughs, and prepares another medicine, so that the game can go on longer. And the saint's very soul goes rotten. Which is the supreme triumph. Yet he keeps up appearances still.

The black, vengeful soul of the crippled, masterful male, still dark in his authority: and the white ghastliness of the fallen saint! The two halves of manhood mutually destroying one another.

Dimmesdale has a *"coup"* in the very end. He gives the whole show away by confessing publicly on the scaffold, and dodging into death, leaving Hester dished, and Roger, as it were, doubly cuckolded. It is a neat last revenge.

Down comes the curtain, as in Ligeia's poem.

But the child Pearl will be on in the next act, with her Italian count and a new brood of vipers. And Hester grayly Abelling, in the shadows, after her rebelling.

It is a marvelous allegory. It is to me one of the greatest allegories in all literature, *The Scarlet Letter*. Its marvelous under-meaning! And its perfect duplicity.

The absolute duplicity of that blue-eyed *Wunderkind* of a Nathaniel. The American wonder-child, with his magical allegorical insight.

But even wonder-children have to grow up in a generation or two.

And even SIN becomes stale.

VIII. *Hawthorne's* Blithedale Romance

No OTHER BOOK of Nathaniel Hawthorne is so deep, so dual, and so complete as *The Scarlet Letter:* this great allegory of the triumph of sin.

Sin is a queer thing. It isn't the breaking of divine commandments. It is the breaking of one's own integrity.

For instance, the sin in Hester and Arthur Dimmesdale's case was a sin because they did what they *thought* it *wrong* to do. If they had really *wanted* to be lovers, and if they had had the honest courage of their own passion, there would have been no sin, even had the desire been only momentary.

But if there had been no sin, they would have lost half the fun, or more, of the game.

It was this very doing of the thing that *they themselves* believed to be wrong, that constituted the chief charm of the act. Man invents sin, in order to enjoy the feeling of being naughty. Also, in order to shift the responsibility for his own acts. A Divine Father tells him what to do. And man is naughty and doesn't obey. And then shiveringly, ignoble man lets down his pants for a flogging.

If the Divine Father doesn't bring on the flogging, in this life, then Sinful Man shiveringly awaits his whipping in the afterlife.

Bah, the Divine Father, like so many other Crowned Heads, has abdicated his authority. Man can sin as much as he likes.

There is only one penalty: the loss of his own integrity. Man should *never* do the thing he believes to be wrong. Because if he does, he loses his own singleness, wholeness, natural honor.

If you want to do a thing, you've either got to believe, sincerely, that it's your true nature to do this thing—or else you've got to let it alone.

Believe in your own Holy Ghost. Or else, if you doubt, abstain.

A thing that you sincerely believe in cannot be wrong, because belief does not come at will. It comes only from the

Holy Ghost within. Therefore a thing you truly believe in cannot be wrong.

But there is such a thing as spurious belief. There is such a thing as *evil* belief: a belief that one *cannot do wrong*. There is also such a thing as a half-spurious belief. And this is rottenest of all. The devil lurking behind the cross.

So there you are. Between genuine belief, and spurious belief, and half-genuine belief, you're as likely as not to be in a pickle. And the half-genuine belief is much the dirtiest and most deceptive thing in life.

Hester and Dimmesdale believed in the Divine Father, and almost gloatingly sinned against Him. The Allegory of Sin.

Pearl no longer believes in the Divine Father. She says so. She has no Divine Father. Disowns Papa both big and little.

So she can't sin against him.

What will she do, then, if she's got no god to sin against? Why, of course, she'll not be able to sin at all. She'll go her own way gaily, and do as she likes, and she'll say, afterwards, when she's made a mess: "Yes, I did it. But I acted for the best, and therefore I am blameless. It's the other person's fault. Or else it's Its fault."

She will be blameless, will Pearl, come what may.

And the world is simply a string of Pearls today. And America is a whole rope of these absolutely immaculate Pearls, who can't sin, let them do what they may, because they've no god to sin against. Mere men, one after another. Men with no ghost to their name.

Pearls!

Oh, the irony, the bitter, bitter irony of the name! Oh, Nathaniel, you great man! Oh, America, you Pearl, you Pearl without a blemish!

How *can* Pearl have a blemish, when there's no one but herself to judge Herself? Of course she'll be immaculate, even if, like Cleopatra, she drowns a lover a night in her dirty Nile. The Nilus Flux of her love.

Candida!

By Hawthorne's day it was already Pearl. Before swine,

of course. There never yet was a Pearl that wasn't cast before swine.

It's part of her game, part of her pearldom.

Because when Circe lies with a man, *he's* a swine after it, if he wasn't one before. Not *she*. Circe is the great white impeccable Pearl.

And yet, oh, Pearl, there's a Nemesis even for you.

There's a Doom, Pearl.

Doom! What a beautiful northern word. Doom.

The doom of the Pearl.

Who will write that Allegory?

Here's what the Doom is, anyhow.

When you don't have a Divine Father to sin against; and when you don't sin against the Son; which the Pearls don't, because they all are very strong on LOVE, stronger on LOVE than on anything: then there's nothing left for you to sin against except the Holy Ghost.

Now, Pearl, come, let's drop you in the vinegar.

And it's a ticklish thing sinning against the Holy Ghost. "*It shall not be forgiven him.*"

Didn't I tell you there was Doom.

It shall not be forgiven her.

The Father forgives; the Son forgives; but the Holy Ghost does *not* forgive. So take that.

The Holy Ghost doesn't forgive because the Holy Ghost is within you. The Holy Ghost *is* you: your very You. So if, in your conceit of your ego, you make a break in your own YOU, in your own integrity, how can you be forgiven? You might as well make a rip in your own bowels. You *know* if you rip your own bowels they will go rotten and *you* will go rotten. And there's an end of you, in the body.

The same if you make a breach with your own Holy Ghost. You go soul-rotten. Like the Pearls.

These dear Pearls, they do anything they like, and remain pure. Oh, purity!

But they can't stop themselves from going rotten inside. Rotten Pearls, fair outside. Their *souls* smell, because their souls are putrefying inside them.

The sin against the Holy Ghost.

And gradually, from within outwards, they rot. Some form of dementia. A thing disintegrating. A decomposing psyche. Dementia.

Quos vult perdere Deus, dementat prius.

Watch these Pearls, these Pearls of modern women. Particularly American women. Battening on love. And fluttering in the first batlike throes of dementia.

You *can* have your cake and eat it. But my God, it will go rotten inside you.

Hawthorne's other books are nothing compared to *The Scarlet Letter*.

But there are good parables, and wonderful dark glimpses of early Puritan America, in *Twice-Told Tales*.

The House of the Seven Gables has "atmosphere." The passing of the old order of the proud, bearded, black-browed Father: an order which is slowly ousted from life, and lingeringly haunts the old dark places. But comes a new generation to sweep out even the ghosts, with these new vacuum cleaners. No ghost could stand up against a vacuum cleaner.

The new generation is having no ghosts or cobwebs. It is setting up in the photography line, and is just going to make a sound financial thing out of it. For this purpose all old hates and old glooms, that belong to the antique order of Haughty Fathers, all these are swept up in the vacuum cleaner, and the vendetta-born young couple effect a perfect understanding under the black cloth of a camera and prosperity. *Vivat Industria!*

Oh, Nathaniel, you savage ironist! Ugh, how you'd have *hated* it if you'd had nothing but the prosperous, "dear" young couple to write about! If you'd lived to the day when America was nothing but a Main Street.

The Dark Old Fathers.

The Beloved Wishy-Washy Sons.

The Photography Business.

? ? ?

Hawthorne came nearest to actuality in the *Blithedale Romance*. This novel is a sort of picture of the notorious

Brook Farm experiment. There the famous idealists and transcendentalists of America met to till the soil and hew the timber in the sweat of their own brows, thinking high thoughts the while, and breathing an atmosphere of communal love, and tingling in tune with the Oversoul, like so many strings of a super-celestial harp. An old twang of the Crèvecœur instrument.

Of course they fell out like cats and dogs. Couldn't stand one another. And all the music they made was the music of their quarreling.

You *can't* idealize hard work. Which is why America invents so many machines and contrivances of all sort: so that they need do no physical work.

And that's why the idealists left off brookfarming and took to bookfarming.

You *can't* idealize the essential brute blood-activity, the brute blood desires, the basic, sardonic blood-knowledge.

That you *can't* idealize.

And you can't eliminate it.

So there's the end of ideal man.

Man is made up of a dual consciousness, of which the two halves are most of the time in opposition to one another—and will be so as long as time lasts.

You've got to learn to change from one consciousness to the other, turn and about. Not to try to make either absolute, or dominant. The Holy Ghost tells you the how and when.

Never did Nathaniel feel himself more spectral—of course he went brookfarming—than when he was winding the horn in the morning to summon the transcendental laborers to their tasks, or than when marching off with a hoe ideally to hoe the turnips, "Never did I feel more spectral," says Nathaniel.

Never did I feel such a fool, would have been more to the point.

Farcical fools, trying to idealize labor. You'll never succeed in idealizing hard work. Before you can dig mother earth you've got to take off your ideal jacket. The harder a man works, at brute labor, the thinner becomes his idealism, the darker his mind. And the harder a man works at mental labor, at idealism, at transcendental occupations, the thinner becomes his blood, and the more brittle his nerves.

Oh, the brittle-nerved brookfarmers!

You've got to be able to do both: the mental work, and the brute work. But be prepared to step from one pair of shoes into another. Don't try and make it all one pair of shoes.

The attempt to idealize the blood!

Nathaniel knew he was a fool, attempting it.

He went home to his amiable spouse and his sanctum sanctorum of a study.

Nathaniel!

But the *Blithedale Romance*. It has a beautiful, wintry-evening farm-kitchen sort of opening.

Dramatis Personæ

1. *I.*—The narrator: whom we will call Nathaniel. A wisp of a sensitive, withal deep, literary young man no longer so very young.

2. *Zenobia*: a dark, proudly voluptuous clever woman with a tropical flower in her hair. Said to be sketched from Margaret Fuller, in whom Hawthorne saw some "evil nature." Nathaniel was more aware of Zenobia's voluptuousness than of her "mind."

3. *Hollingsworth*: a black-bearded blacksmith with a deep-voiced lust for saving criminals. Wants to build a great Home for these unfortunates.

4. *Priscilla*: a sort of White Lily, a clinging little medium-istic sempstress who has been made use of in public seances. A sort of prostitute soul.

5. *Zenobia's Husband*: an unpleasant decayed person with magnetic powers and teeth full of gold—or set in gold. It is he who has given public spiritualist demonstrations, with Priscilla for the medium. He is of the dark, sensual, decayed-handsome sort, and comes in unexpectedly by the back door.

Plot I.—I, Nathaniel, at once catch cold, and have to be put to bed. Am nursed with inordinate tenderness by the black-smith, whose great hands are gentler than a woman's, etc.

The two men love one another with a love surpassing

the love of women, so long as the healing-and-salvation business lasts. When Nathaniel wants to get well and have a soul of his own, he turns with hate to this black-bearded, booming salvationist, Hephæstos of the underworld. Hates him for tyrannous monomaniac.

Plot II.—Zenobia, that clever lustrous woman, is fascinated by the criminal-saving blacksmith, and would have him at any price. Meanwhile she has the subtlest current of understanding with the frail but deep Nathaniel. And she takes the White Lily half pityingly, half contemptuously under a rich and glossy dark wing.

Plot III.—The blacksmith is after Zenobia, to get her money for his criminal asylum: of which, of course, he will be the first inmate.

Plot IV.—Nathaniel also feels his mouth watering for the dark-luscious Zenobia.

Plot V.—The White Lily, Priscilla, vaporously festering, turns out to be the famous Veiled Lady of public spiritualist shows: she whom the undesirable Husband, called the Professor, has used as a medium. Also she is Zenobia's half-sister.

Débâcle

Nobody wants Zenobia in the end. She goes off without her flower. The blacksmith marries Priscilla. Nathaniel dribblingly confesses that he, too, has loved Prissy all the while. Boo-hoo!

Conclusion

A few years after, Nathaniel meets the blacksmith in a country lane near a humble cottage, leaning totteringly on the arm of the frail but fervent Priscilla. Gone are all dreams of asylums, and the savior of criminals can't even save himself from his own Veiled Lady.

There you have a nice little bunch of idealists, transcendentalists, brookfarmers, and disintegrated gentry. All going slightly rotten.

Two Pearls: a white Pearl and a black Pearl: the latter more expensive, lurid with money.

The white Pearl, the little medium, Priscilla, the imitation pearl, has truly some "supernormal" powers. She could drain the blacksmith of his blackness and his smith-strength.

Priscilla, the little psychic prostitute. The degenerate descendant of Ligeia. The absolutely yielding, "loving" woman, who abandons herself utterly to her lover. Or even to a gold-toothed "professor" of spiritualism.

Is it all bunkum, this spiritualism? Is it just rot, this Veiled Lady?

Not quite. Apart even from telepathy, the apparatus of human consciousness is the most wonderful message-receiver in existence. Beats a wireless station to nothing.

Put Prissy under the tablecloth then. Miaow!

What happens? Prissy under the tablecloth, like a canary when you cover his cage, goes into a "sleep," a trance.

A trance, not a sleep. A trance means that all her *in-dividual* personal intelligence goes to sleep, like a hen with her head under her wing. But the *apparatus* of consciousness remains working. Without a soul in it.

And what can this apparatus of consciousness do when it works? Why surely something. A wireless apparatus goes tick-tick-tick, taking down messages. So does your human apparatus. All kinds of messages. Only the soul, or the under-consciousness, deals with these messages in the dark, in the under-conscious. Which is the natural course of events.

But what sorts of messages? All sorts. Vibrations from the stars, vibrations from unknown magnetos, vibrations from unknown people, unknown passions. The human apparatus receives them all and they are all dealt with in the under-conscious.

There are also vibrations of thought, many, many. Necessary to get the two human instruments in key.

There may even be vibrations of ghosts in the air. Ghosts being dead *wills*, mind you, not dead souls. The soul has nothing to do with these dodges.

But some unit of force may persist for a time, after the death of an individual—some associations of vibrations may linger like little clouds in the etheric atmosphere after the death of a human being, or an animal. And these little clots of vibration may transfer themselves to the conscious-apparatus of the medium. So that the dead son of a disconsolate widow may send a message to his mourning mother to tell her that he owes Bill Jackson seven dollars: or that Uncle Sam's will is in the back of the bureau: and cheer up, Mother, I'm all right.

There is never much worth in these "messages," because they are never more than fragmentary items of dead, disintegrated consciousness. And the medium has, and always will have, a hopeless job, trying to disentangle the muddle of messages.

Again, coming events *may* cast their shadow before. The oracle may receive on her conscious-apparatus material vibrations to say that the next great war will break out in 1925. And in so far as the realm of cause-and-effect is master of the living soul, in so far as events are mechanically maturing, the forecast may be true.

But the living souls of men may upset the *mechanical* march of events at any moment.

Rien de certain.

Vibrations of subtlest matter. Concatenations of vibrations and shocks! Spiritualism.

And what then? It is all just materialistic, and a good deal is, and always will be, charlatanry.

Because the real human soul, the Holy Ghost, has its own deep prescience, which will not be put into figures, but flows on dark, a stream of prescience.

And the real human soul is too proud, and too sincere in its belief in the Holy Ghost that is within, to stoop to the practices of these spiritualist and other psychic tricks of material vibrations.

Because the first part of reverence is the acceptance of the fact that the Holy Ghost will never materialize: will never be anything but a ghost.

And the second part of reverence is the watchful observance of the motions, the comings and goings within us, of the Holy Ghost, and of the many gods that make up the Holy Ghost.

The Father had his day, and fell.

The Son has had his day, and fell.

It is the day of the Holy Ghost.

But when souls fall corrupt, into disintegration, they have no more day. They have sinned against the Holy Ghost.

These people in *Blithedale Romance* have sinned against the Holy Ghost, and corruption has set in.

All, perhaps, except the I, Nathaniel. He is still a sad, integral consciousness.

But not excepting Zenobia. The Black Pearl is rotting down. Fast. The cleverer she is, the faster she rots.

And they are all disintegrating, so they take to psychic tricks. It is a certain sign of the disintegration of the psyche in a man, and much more so in a woman, when she takes to spiritualism, and table-rapping, and occult messages, or witchcraft and supernatural powers of that sort. When men want to be supernatural, be sure that something has gone wrong in their natural stuff. More so, even, with a woman.

And yet the soul has its own profound subtleties of knowing. And the blood has its strange omniscience.

But this isn't impudent and materialistic, like spiritualism and magic and all that range of pretentious supernaturalism.

IX. *Dana's* Two Years Before the Mast

You CAN'T IDEALIZE brute labor. That is to say, you can't idealize brute labor, without coming undone, as an idealist.

The soil! The great ideal of the soil. Novels like Thomas Hardy's and pictures like the Frenchman Millet's. The soil.

What happens when you idealize the soil, the mother earth, and really go back to it? Then with overwhelming conviction it is borne in upon you, as it was upon Thomas Hardy, that the whole scheme of things is against you. The whole massive rolling of natural fate is coming down on you like a slow glacier, to crush you to extinction. As an idealist.

Thomas Hardy's pessimism is an absolutely true finding. It is the absolutely true statement of the idealist's last realization, as he wrestles with the bitter soil of beloved mother-earth. He loves her, loves her, loves her. And she just entangles and crushes him like a slow Laocoön snake. The idealist must perish, says mother-earth. Then let him perish.

The great imaginative love of the soil itself! Tolstoy had it, and Thomas Hardy. And both are driven to a kind of fanatic denial of life, as a result.

You can't idealize mother-earth. You can try. You can even succeed. But succeeding, you succumb. She will have no pure idealist sons. None.

If you are a child of mother-earth, you must learn to discard your ideal self, in season, as you discard your clothes at night.

Americans have never loved the soil of America as Europeans have loved the soil of Europe. America has never been a blood-homeland. Only an ideal homeland. The homeland of the idea, of the *spirit*. And of the pocket. Not of the blood.

That has yet to come, when the idea and the spirit have collapsed from their false tyranny.

Europe has been loved with a blood love. That has made it beautiful.

In America, you have Fenimore Cooper's beautiful landscape: but that is wish-fulfillment, done from a distance. And you have Thoreau in Concord. But Thoreau sort of isolated his own bit of locality and put it under a lens, to examine it. He almost anatomized it, with his admiration.

America isn't a blood-homeland. For every American, the blood-homeland is Europe. The spirit-homeland is America.

Transcendentalism. Transcend this homeland business, exalt the idea of These States till you have made it a universal idea, says the true American. The oversoul is a world-soul, not a local thing.

So, in the next great move of imaginative conquest, Americans turned to the sea. Not to the land. Earth is too specific, too particular. Besides, the blood of white men is wine of no American soil. No, no.

But the blood of all men is ocean-born. We have our material universality, our blood-oneness, in the sea. The salt water.

You can't idealize the soil. But you've got to try. And

trying, you reap a great imaginative reward. And the greatest reward is failure. To know you have failed, that you *must* fail. That is the greatest comfort of all, at last.

Tolstoy failed with the soil; Thomas Hardy, too; and Giovanni Verga: the three greatest.

The further extreme, the greatest mother, is the sea. Love the great mother of the sea, the Magna Mater. And see how bitter it is. And see how you must fail to win her to your ideal: forever fail. Absolutely fail.

Swinburne tried in England. But the Americans made the greatest trial. The most vivid failure.

At a certain point, human life becomes uninteresting to men. What then? They turn to some universal.

The greatest material mother of us all is the sea.

Dana's eyes failed him when he was studying at Harvard. And suddenly he turned to the sea, the naked Mother. He went to sea as a common sailor before the mast.

You can't idealize brute labor. Yet you can. You can go through with brute labor, and *know* what it means. You can even meet and match the sea, and KNOW her.

This is what Dana wanted: a naked fighting experience with the sea.

KNOW THYSELF. That means, know the earth that is in your blood. Know the sea that is in your blood. The great elementals.

But we must repeat: KNOWING and BEING are opposite, antagonistic states. The more you know, exactly, the less you *are*. The more you *are,* in being, the less you know.

This is the great cross of man, his dualism. The blood-self, and the nerve-brain self.

Knowing, then, is the slow death of being. Man has his epochs of being, his epochs of knowing. It will always be a great oscillation. The goal is to know how not-to-know.

Dana took another great step in knowing: knowing the mother sea. But it was a step also in his own undoing. It was a new phase of dissolution of his own being. Afterwards, he would be a less human thing. He would be a knower: but more near to mechanism than before. That is our cross, our doom.

And so he writes, in his first days at sea, in winter, on the Atlantic:

Nothing can compare with the *early breaking of day* upon the wide, sad ocean. There is something in the first gray streaks stretching along the eastern horizon, and throwing an indistinct light upon the face of the deep, which creates a feeling of loneliness, of dread, and of melancholy foreboding, which nothing else in nature can give.

So he ventures wakeful and alone into the great naked watery universe of the end of life, the twilight place where integral being lapses, and warm life begins to give out. It is man moving on into the face of death, the great adventure, the great undoing, the strange extension of the consciousness. The same in his vision of the albatross. "But one of the finest sights that I have ever seen was an albatross asleep upon the water, off Cape Horn, when a heavy sea was running. There being no breeze, the surface of the water was unbroken, but a long, heavy swell was rolling, and we saw the fellow, all white, directly ahead of us, asleep upon the waves, with his head under his wing; now rising upon the top of a huge billow, and then falling slowly until he was lost in the hollow between. He was undisturbed for some time, until the noise of our bows, gradually approaching, roused him; when lifting his head, he stared upon us for a moment, and then spread his wide wings, and took his flight."

We must give Dana credit for a profound mystic vision. The best Americans are mystics by instinct. Simple and bare as his narrative is, it is deep with profound emotion and stark comprehension. He sees the last light-loving incarnation of life exposed upon the eternal waters: a speck, solitary upon the verge of the two naked principles, aerial and watery. And his own soul is as the soul of the albatross.

It is a storm-bird. And so is Dana. He has gone down to fight with the sea. It is a metaphysical, actual struggle of an integral soul with the vast, non-living, yet potent element. Dana never forgets, never ceases to watch. If Hawthorne was a specter on the land, how much more is

Dana a specter at sea. But he must watch, he must know, he must conquer the sea in his consciousness. This is the poignant difference between him and the common sailor. The common sailor lapses from consciousness, becomes elemental like a seal, a creature. Tiny and alone Dana watches the great seas mount round his own small body. If he is swept away, some other man will have to take up what he has begun. For the sea must be mastered by the human consciousness, in the great fight of the human soul for mastery over life and death, in KNOWLEDGE. It is the last bitter necessity of the Tree. The Cross. Impartial, Dana beholds himself among the elements, calm and fatal. His style is great and hopeless, the style of a perfect tragic recorder.

Between five and six the cry of "All starbowlines ahoy!" summoned our watch on deck, and immediately all hands were called. A great cloud of a dark slate-color was driving on us from the southwest; and we did our best to take in sail before we were in the midst of it. We had got the light sails furled, the courses hauled up, and the topsail reef tackles hauled out, and were just mounting the forerigging when the storm struck us. In an instant the sea, which had been comparatively quiet, was running higher and higher; and it became almost as dark as night. The hail and sleet were harder than I had yet felt them, seeming almost to pin us down to the rigging.

It is in the dispassionate statement of plain material facts that Dana achieves his greatness. Dana writes from the remoter, non-emotional centers of being—not from the passional emotional self.

So the ship battles on, round Cape Horn, then into quieter seas. The island of Juan Fernandez, Crusoe's island, rises like a dream from the sea, like a green cloud, and like a ghost Dana watches it, feeling only a faint, ghostly pang of regret for the life that was.

But the strain of the long sea-voyage begins to tell. The sea is a great disintegrative force. Its tonic quality is its disintegrative quality. It burns down the tissue, liberates energy. And after a long time, this burning-down is destructive. The psyche becomes destroyed, irritable, frayed, almost dehumanized.

So there is trouble on board the ship, irritating discontent, friction unbearable, and at last a flogging. This flogging rouses Dana for the first and last time to human and ideal passion.

Sam was by this time seized up—that is, placed against the shrouds, with his wrists made fast to the shrouds, his jacket off, and his back exposed. The captain stood on the break of the deck, a few feet from him, and a little raised, so as to have a good swing at him, and held in his hand a light, thick rope. The officers stood round, and the crew grouped together in the waist. All these preparations made me feel sick and faint, angry and excited as I was. A man—a human being made in God's likeness—fastened up and flogged like a beast! The first and almost uncontrollable impulse was resistance. But what could be done?—The time for it had gone by——

So Mr. Dana couldn't act. He could only lean over the side of the ship and spew.

Whatever made him vomit?

Why shall man not be whipped?

As long as man has a bottom, he must surely be whipped. It is as if the Lord intended it so.

Why? For lots of reasons.

Man doth not live by bread alone, to absorb it and to evacuate it.

What is the breath of life? My dear, it is the strange current of interchange that flows between men and men, and men and women, and men and things. A constant current of interflow, a constant vibrating interchange. That is the breath of life.

And this interflow, this electric vibration is polarized. There is a positive and a negative polarity. This is a law of life, of vitalism.

Only ideas are final, finite, static, and single.

All life-interchange is a polarized communication. A circuit.

There are lots of circuits. Male and female, for example, and master and servant. The idea, the IDEA, that fixed gorgon monster, and the IDEAL, that great stationary engine, these two gods-of-the-machine have been busy destroying all *natural* reciprocity and *natural* circuits, for centuries. IDEAS have played the very old Harry with sex relationship, that is, with the great circuit of man and woman. Turned the thing into a wheel on which the human being in both is broken. And the IDEAL has mangled the blood-reciprocity of master and servant into an abstract horror.

Master and servant—or master and man relationship is, essentially, a polarized flow, like love. It is a circuit of vitalism which flows between master and man and forms a very precious nourishment to each, and keeps both in a state of subtle, quivering, vital equilibrium. Deny it as you like, it is so. But once you *abstract* both master and man, and make them both serve an *idea*: production, wage, efficiency, and so on: so that each looks on himself as an instrument performing a certain repeated evolution, then you have changed the vital, quivering circuit of master and man into a mechanical machine unison. Just another way of life: or anti-life.

You could never quite do this on a sailing ship. A master had to be master, or it was hell. That is, there had to be this strange interflow of master-and-man, the strange reciprocity of command and obedience.

The reciprocity of command and obedience is a state of unstable vital equilibrium. Everything vital, or natural, is unstable, thank God.

The ship had been at sea many weeks. A great strain on master and men. An increasing callous indifference in the men, an increasing irritability in the master.

And then what?

A storm.

Don't expect me to say *why* storms must be. They just are. Storms in the air, storms in the water, storms of thunder, storms of anger. Storms just are.

Storms are a sort of violent readjustment in some polarized flow. You have a polarized circuit, a circuit of unstable equilibrium. The instability increases till there is a crash. Everything seems to break down. Thunder roars, lightning flashes. The master roars, the whip whizzes. The sky sends down sweet rain. The ship knows a new strange stillness, a readjustment, a refinding of equilibrium.

Ask the Lord Almighty why it is so. I don't know. I know it is so.

But flogging? Why flogging? Why not use reason or take away jam for tea?

Why not? Why not ask the thunder please to abstain from this physical violence of crashing and thumping, please to swale away like thawing snow.

Sometimes the thunder *does* swale away like thawing snow, and then you hate it. Muggy, sluggish, inert, dreary sky.

Flogging.

You have a Sam, a fat slow fellow, who has got slower and more slovenly as the weeks wear on. You have a master who has grown more irritable in his authority. Till Sam becomes simply wallowing in his slackness, makes your gorge rise. And the master is on red-hot iron.

Now these two men, Captain and Sam, are there in a very unsteady equilibrium of command and obedience. A polarized flow. Definitely polarized.

The poles of will are the great ganglia of the voluntary nerve system, located beside the spinal column, in the back. From the poles of will in the backbone of the Captain, to the ganglia of will in the back of the sloucher Sam, runs a frazzled, jagged current, a staggering circuit of vital electricity. This circuit gets one jolt too many, and there is an explosion.

"Tie up that lousy swine!" roars the enraged Captain.

And whack! Whack! down on the bare back of that sloucher Sam comes the cat.

What does it do? By Jove, it goes like ice-cold water into his spine. Down those lashes runs the current of the Captain's rage, right into the blood and into the toneless ganglia of Sam's voluntary system. Crash! Crash! runs the lightning flame, right into the cores of the living nerves.

And the living nerves respond. They start to vibrate. They brace up. The blood begins to go quicker. The nerves begin to recover their vividness. It is their tonic. The man Sam has a new clear day of intelligence, and a smarty back. The

Captain has a new relief, a new ease in his authority, and a sore heart.

There is a new equilibrium, and a fresh start. The *physical* intelligence of a Sam is restored, the turgidity is relieved from the veins of the Captain.

It is a natural form of human coition, interchange.

It is good for Sam to be flogged. It is good, on this occasion, for the Captain to have Sam flogged. I say so. Because they were both in that physical condition.

Spare the rod and spoil the *physical* child.

Use the rod and spoil the *ideal* child.

There you are.

Dana, as an idealist, refusing the blood-contact of life, leaned over the side of the ship powerless, and vomited: or wanted to. His solar plexus was getting a bit of its own back. To him, Sam was an "ideal" being, who should have been approached through the mind, the reason, and the spirit. That lump of a Sam!

But there was another idealist on board, the seaman John, a Swede. He wasn't named John for nothing, this Jack-tar of the Logos. John felt himself called upon to play Mediator, Interceder, Savior, on this occasion. The popular Paraclete.

"Why are you whipping this man, sir?"

But the Captain had got his dander up. He wasn't going to have his natural passion judged and interfered with by these long-nosed salvationist Johannuses. So he had nosey John hauled up and whipped as well.

For which I am very glad.

Alas, however, the Captain got the worst of it in the end. He smirks longest who smirks last. The Captain wasn't wary enough. Natural anger, natural passion has its unremitting enemy in the idealist. And the ship was already tainted with idealism. A good deal more so, apparently, than Herman Melville's ships were.

Which reminds us that Melville was once going to be flogged. In *White Jacket*. And he, too, would have taken it as the last insult.

In my opinion there are worse insults than floggings. I would rather be flogged than have most people "like" me.

Melville, too, had an Interceder: a quiet, self-respecting man, not a savior. The man spoke in the name of Justice. Melville was to be unjustly whipped. The man spoke honestly and quietly. Not in any salvationist spirit. And the whipping did not take place.

Justice is a great and manly thing. Saviorism is a despicable thing.

Sam was justly whipped. It was a passional justice.

But Melville's whipping would have been a cold, disciplinary injustice. A foul thing. Mechanical *justice* even is a foul thing. For true justice makes the heart's fibers quiver. You can't be cold in a matter of real justice.

Already in those days it was no fun to be a captain. You had to learn already to abstract yourself into a machine-part, exerting machine-control. And it is a good deal bitterer to exert machine-control, selfless, ideal control, than it is to have to obey, mechanically. Because the idealists who mechanically obey almost always hate the *man* who must give the orders. Their idealism rarely allows them to exonerate the man for the office.

Dana's captain was one of the real old-fashioned sort. He gave himself away terribly. He should have been more wary, knowing he confronted a shipful of enemies and at least two cold and deadly idealists, who hated all "masters" on principle.

As he went on, his passion increased, and he danced about on the deck, calling out as he swung the rope, "If you want to know what I flog you for, I'll tell you. It's because I like to do it!—Because I like to do it!—It suits me. That's what I do it for!"

The man writhed under the pain. My blood ran cold, I could look no longer. Disgusted, sick, and horror-stricken, I turned away and leaned over the rail and looked down in the water. A few rapid thoughts of my own situation, and the prospect of future revenge, crossed my mind; but the falling of the blows, and the cries of the man called me back at once. At length they ceased, and, turning round, I found that the Mate, at a signal from the Captain, had cut him down.

After all, it was not so terrible. The Captain evidently did not exceed the ordinary measure. Sam got no more than he asked for. It was a natural event. All would have been well, save for the *moral* verdict. And this came from theoretic idealists like Dana and the seaman John, rather than from the sailors themselves. The sailors understood spontaneous *passional* morality, not the artificial ethical. They respected the violent readjustments of the naked force, in man as in nature.

The flogging was seldom, if ever, alluded to by us in the forecastle. If anyone was inclined to talk about it, the other, with a delicacy which I hardly expected to find among them, always stopped him, or turned the subject.

Two men had been flogged: the second and the elder, John, for interfering and asking the Captain why he flogged Sam. It is while flogging John that the Captain shouts, "If you want to know what I flog you for, I'll tell you——"

But the behavior of the two men who were flogged [Dana continues] toward one another, showed a delicacy and a sense of honor which would have been worthy of admiration in the highest walks of life. Sam knew that the other had suffered solely on his account, and in all his complaints he said that if he alone had been flogged it would have been nothing, but that he could never see that man without thinking that he had been the means of bringing that disgrace upon him; and John never, by word or deed, let anything escape him to remind the other that it was by interfering to save his shipmate that he had suffered.

As a matter of fact, it was John who ought to have been ashamed for bringing confusion and false feeling into a clear issue. Conventional morality apart, John is the reprehensible party, not Sam or the Captain. The case was one of passional readjustment, nothing abnormal. And who was the sententious Johannus, that he should interfere in this? And if Mr. Dana had a weak stomach, as well as weak eyes, let him have it. But let this pair of idealists abstain from making all the other men feel uncomfortable and fuzzy about a thing they would have left to its natural course, if they had been allowed. No, your Johannuses and your Danas have to be creating "public opinion," and mugging up the life-issues with their sententiousness. O idealism!

The vessel arrives at the Pacific coast, and the swell of the rollers falls in our blood—the weary coast stretches wonderful, on the brink of the unknown.

Not a human being but ourselves for miles—the steep hill rising like a wall, and cutting us off from all the world—but the "world of waters." I separated myself from the rest, and sat down on a rock, just where the sea ran in and formed a fine spouting horn. Compared with the dull, plain sand beach of the rest of the coast, this grandeur was as refreshing as a great rock in a weary land. It was almost the first time I had been positively alone. . . . My better nature returned strong upon me. I experienced a glow of pleasure at finding that what of poetry and romance I had ever had in me had not been entirely deadened in the laborious life I had been lately leading. Nearly an hour did I sit, almost lost in the luxury of this entire new scene of the play in which I was acting, when I was aroused by the distant shouts of my companions.

So Dana sits and Hamletizes by the Pacific—chief actor in the play of his own existence. But in him, self-consciousness is almost nearing the mark of scientific indifference to self.

He gives us a pretty picture of the then wild, unknown bay of San Francisco—"The tide leaving us, we came to anchor near the mouth of the bay, under a high and beautifully sloping hill, upon which herds of hundreds of red deer and the stag with his high-branching antlers were bounding about, looking at us for a moment, and then starting off affrighted at the noises we made for the purpose of seeing the variety of their beautiful attitudes and motions——"

Think of it now, and the Presidio! The idiotic guns.

Two moments of strong human emotion Dana experiences: one moment of strong but impotent hate for the captain, one strong impulse of pitying love for the Kanaka boy,

Hope—a beautiful South Sea Islander sick of a white man's disease, phthisis or syphilis. Of him Dana writes:

But the other, who was my friend, and aikane—Hope—was the most dreadful object I had ever seen in my life; his hands looking like claws; a dreadful cough, which seemed to rack his whole shattered system; a hollow, whispering voice, and an entire inability to move himself. There he lay, upon a mat on the ground, which was the only floor of the oven, with no medicine, no comforts, and no one to care for or help him but a few Kanakas, who were willing enough, but could do nothing. The sight of him made me sick and faint. Poor fellow! During the four months that I lived upon the beach we were continually together, both in work and in our excursions in the woods and upon the water. I really felt a strong affection for him, and preferred him to any of my own countrymen there. When I came into the oven he looked at me, held out his hand, and said in a low voice, but with a delightful smile, "*Aloha,* Aikane! *Aloha nui!*" I comforted him as well as I could, and promised to ask the captain to help him from the medicine chest.

We have felt the pulse of hate for the Captain—now the pulse of Savior-like love for the bright-eyed man of the Pacific, a real child of the ocean, full of the mystery-being of that great sea. Hope is for a moment to Dana what Chingachgook is to Cooper—the hearts-brother, the answerer. But only for an ephemeral moment. And even then his love was largely pity, tinged with philanthropy. The inevitable saviorism. The ideal being.

Dana was mad to leave the California coast, to be back in the civilized East. Yet he feels the poignancy of departure when at last the ship draws off. The Pacific is his glamour world: the Eastern states his world of actuality, scientific, materially real. He is a servant of civilization, an idealist, a democrat, a hater of master, a KNOWER. Conscious and self-conscious, without ever forgetting.

When all sail had been set and the decks cleared up the *California* was a speck in the horizon, and the coast lay like a low cloud along the northeast. At sunset they were both out of sight, and we were once more upon the ocean, where sky and water meet.

The description of the voyage home is wonderful. It is as if the sea rose up to prevent the escape of this subtle explorer. Dana seems to pass into another world, another life, not of this earth. There is first the sense of apprehension, then the passing right into the black deeps. Then the waters almost swallow him up, with his triumphant consciousness.

The days became shorter and shorter, the sun running lower in its course each day, and giving less and less heat, and the nights so cold as to prevent our sleeping on deck; the Magellan Clouds in sight of a clear night; the skies looking cold and angry; and at times a long, heavy, ugly sea, setting in from the southward, told us what we were coming to.

They were approaching Cape Horn, in the southern winter, passing into the strange, dread regions of the violent waters.

And there lay, floating in the ocean, several miles off, an immense irregular mass, its top and points covered with snow, its center a deep indigo. This was an iceberg, and of the largest size. As far as the eye could reach the sea in every direction was of a deep blue color, the waves running high and fresh, and sparkling in the light; and in the midst lay this immense mountain island, its cavities and valleys thrown into deep shade, and its points and pinnacles glittering in the sun. But no description can give any idea of the strangeness, splendor, and, really, the sublimity of the sight. Its great size—for it must have been two or three miles in circumference, and several hundred feet in height; its slow motion, as its base rose and sunk in the water and its points nodded against the clouds; the lashing of the waves upon it, which, breaking high with foam, lined its base with a white crust; and the thundering sound of the cracking of the mass, and the breaking and the tumbling down of huge pieces; together with its nearness and approach, which added a slight element of fear—all combined to give it the character of true sublimity——

But as the ship ran further and further into trouble, Dana became ill. First it is a slight toothache. Ice and exposure cause the pains to take hold of all his head and face. And then the face so swelled that he could not open his mouth to eat, and was in danger of lockjaw. In this state he was forced to keep his bunk for three or four days.

At the end of the third day, the ice was very thick; a complete fog-bank covered the ship. It blew a tremendous gale from the eastward, with sleet and snow, and there was every promise of a dangerous and fatiguing night. At dark, the captain called the hands aft, and told them that not a man was to leave the deck that night; that the ship was in the greatest danger; any cake of ice might knock a hole in her, or she might run on an island and go to pieces. The lookouts were then set, and every man was put in his station. When I heard what was the state of things, I began to put on my things, to stand it out with the rest of them, when the mate came below, and looking at my face ordered me back to my berth, saying if we went down we should all go down together, but if I went on deck I might lay myself up for life. In obedience to the mate's orders, I went back to my berth; but a more miserable night I never wish to spend.

It is the story of a man pitted in conflict against the sea, the vast, almost omnipotent element. In contest with this cosmic enemy, man finds his further ratification, his further ideal vindication. He comes out victorious, but not till the sea has tortured his living, integral body, and made him pay something for his triumph in consciousness.

The horrific struggle round Cape Horn, homewards, is the crisis of the Dana history. It is an entry into chaos, a heaven of sleet and black ice-rain, a sea of ice and ironlike water. Man fights the element in all its roused, mystic hostility to conscious life. This fight is the inward crisis and triumph of Dana's soul. He goes through it all consciously, enduring, *knowing*. It is not a mere overcoming of obstacles. It is a pitting of the deliberate consciousness against all the roused, hostile, anti-life waters of the Pole.

After this fight, Dana has achieved his success. He knows. He knows what the sea is. He knows what the Cape Horn is. He knows what work is, work before the mast. He knows, he knows a great deal. He has carried his consciousness open-eyed through it all. He has won through. The ideal being.

And from his book we know, too. He has lived this great experience for us; we owe him homage.

The ship passes through the strait, strikes the polar death mystery, and turns northward, home. She seems to fly with new strong plumage, free.

Every rope yarn seemed stretched to the utmost, and every thread of the canvas; and with this sail added to her the ship sprang through the water like a thing possessed. The sail being nearly all forward, it lifted her out of the water, and she seemed actually to jump from sea to sea.

Beautifully the sailing ship nodalizes the forces of sea and wind, converting them to her purpose. There is no violation, as in a steamship, only a winged centrality. It is this perfect adjusting of ourselves to the elements, the perfect equipoise between them and us, which gives us a great part of our life-joy. The more we intervene machinery between us and the naked forces the more we numb and atrophy our own senses. Every time we turn on a tap to have water, every time we turn a handle to have fire or light, we deny ourselves and annul our being. The great elements, the earth, air, fire, water, are there like some great mistress whom we woo and struggle with, whom we heave and wrestle with. And all our appliances do but deny us these fine embraces, take the miracle of life away from us. The machine is the great neuter. It is the eunuch of eunuchs. In the end it emasculates us all. When we balance the sticks and kindle a fire, we partake of the mysteries. But when we turn on an electric tap there is, as it were, a wad between us and the dynamic universe. We do not know what we lose by all our labor-saving appliances. Of the two evils it would be much the lesser to lose all machinery, every bit, rather than to have, as we have, hopelessly too much.

When we study the pagan gods, we find they have now one meaning, now another. Now they belong to the creative essence, and now to the material-dynamic world. First they have one aspect, then another. The greatest god has both aspects. First he is the source of life. Then he is mystic dynamic lord of the elemental physical forces. So Zeus is Father, and Thunderer.

Nations that worship the material-dynamic world, as all nations do in their decadence, seem to come inevitably to worship the Thunderer. He is Ammon, Zeus, Wotan and Thor, Shango of the West Africans. As the creator of man himself, the Father is greatest in the creative world, the Thunderer is greatest in the material world. He is the god of force and of earthly blessing, the god of the bolt and of sweet rain.

So that electricity seems to be the first, intrinsic principle among the Forces. It has a mystic power of readjustment. It seems to be the overlord of the two naked elements, fire and water, capable of mysteriously enchaining them, and of mysteriously sundering them from their connections. When the two great elements become hopelessly clogged, entangled, the sword of the lightning can separate them. The crash of thunder is really not the clapping together of waves of air. Thunder is the noise of the explosion which takes place when the waters are loosed from the elemental fire, when old vapors are suddenly decomposed in the upper air by the electric force. Then fire flies fluid, and the waters roll off in purity. It is the liberation of the elements from hopeless conjunction. Thunder, the electric force, is the counterpart in the material-dynamic world of the life-force, the creative mystery, itself, in the creative world.

Dana gives a wonderful description of a tropical thunderstorm.

When our watch came on deck at twelve o'clock it was as black as Erebus; not a breath was stirring; the sails hung heavy and motionless from the yards; and the perfect stillness, and the darkness, which was almost palpable, were truly appalling. Not a word was spoken, but everyone stood as though waiting for something to happen. In a few minutes the mate came forward, and in a low tone which was almost a whisper, gave the command to haul down the jib. When we got down we found all hands looking aloft, and then, directly over where we had been standing, upon the main topgallant masthead, was a ball of light, which the sailors name a corposant (*corpus sancti*).

They were all watching it carefully, for sailors have a notion that if the corposant rises in the rigging, it is a sign of fair weather; but if it comes lower down, there will be a storm. Unfortunately, as an omen, it came down and showed itself on the topgallant yard.

In a few minutes it disappeared and showed itself again on the fore topgallant yard, and, after playing about for some time, disappeared again, when the man on the forecastle pointed to it upon the flying-jib-boom-end. But our attention was drawn from watching this by the falling of some drops of rain. In a few minutes low growling thunder was heard, and some random flashes of lightning came from the southwest. Every sail was taken in but the topsail. A few puffs lifted the topsails, but they fell again to the mast, and all was as still as ever. A minute more, and a terrific flash and peal broke simultaneously upon us, and a cloud appeared to open directly over our heads and let down the water in one body like a falling ocean. We stood motionless and almost stupefied, yet nothing had been struck. Peal after peal rattled over our heads with a sound which actually seemed to stop the breath in the body. The violent fall of the rain lasted but a few minutes, and was succeeded by occasional drops and showers; but the lightning continued incessant for several hours, breaking the midnight darkness with irregular and blinding flashes.

During all this time hardly a word was spoken, no bell was struck, and the wheel was silently relieved. The rain fell at intervals in heavy showers, and we stood drenched through, and blinded by the flashes, which broke the Egyptian darkness with a brightness which seemed almost malignant, while the thunder rolled in peals, the concussion of which appeared to shake the very ocean. A ship is not often injured by lightning, for the electricity is separated by the great number of points she presents, and the quality of iron which she has scattered in various parts. The electric fluid ran over our anchors, topsail-sheets and ties; yet no harm was done to us. We went below at four o'clock, leaving things in the same state.

Dana is wonderful at relating these mechanical, or dynamic-physical events. He could not tell about the being of men: only about the forces. He gives another curious instance of the process of recreation, as it takes place within the very corpuscles of the blood. It is *salt* this time which arrests the life-activity, causing a static arrest in Matter, after a certain sundering of water from the fire of the warm-substantial body.

The scurvy had begun to show itself on board. One man had it so badly as to be disabled and off duty; and the English lad, Ben, was in a dreadful state, and was gradually growing worse. His legs swelled and pained him so that he could not walk; his flesh lost its elasticity, so that if it were pressed in, it would not return to its shape; and his gums swelled until he could not open his mouth. His breath, too, became very offensive; he lost all strength and spirit; could eat nothing; grew worse every day; and, in fact, unless something was done for him, would be a dead man in a week at the rate at which he was sinking. The medicines were all gone, or nearly all gone; and if we had had a chestful they would have been of no use; for nothing but fresh provisions and terra firma has any effect upon the scurvy.

However, a boat-load of potatoes and onions was obtained from a passing ship. These the men ate raw.

The freshness and crispness of the raw onion, with the earthy state, give it a great relish to one who has been a long time on salt provisions. We were perfectly ravenous after them. We ate them at every meal, by the dozen; and filled our pockets with them, to eat on the watch on deck. The chief use, however, of the fresh provisions was for the men with the scurvy. One was able to eat, and he soon brought himself to by gnawing upon raw potatoes; but the other, by this time, was hardly able to open his mouth; and the cook took the potatoes raw, pounded them in a mortar, and gave him the juice to suck. The strong earthy taste and smell of this extract of the raw potatoes at first produced a shuddering through his whole frame, and after drinking it, an acute pain, which ran through all parts of his body; but knowing by this that it was taking strong hold, he persevered, drinking a spoonful every hour or so, until, by the effect of this drink, and of his own restored hope, he became so well as to be able to move about, and open his mouth enough to eat the raw potatoes and onions pounded into a soft pulp. This course soon restored his appetite and strength; and ten days after we spoke the *Solon*, so rapid was his recovery that, from lying helpless and almost hopeless in his berth, he was at the masthead, furling a royal.

This is the strange result of the disintegrating effect of the sea, and of salt food. We are all sea-born, science tells us. The moon, and the sea, and salt, and phosphorus, and us: it is a long chain of connection. And then the earth: mother-earth. Dana talks of the relish which the *earthy* taste of the onion gives. The taste of created juice, the living milk of Gea. And limes, which taste of the sun.

How much stranger is the interplay of *life* among the elements than any chemical interplay among the elements themselves. Life—and salt—and phosphorus—and the sea— and the moon. Life—and sulphur—and carbon—and volcanoes—and the sun. The way up, and the way down. The strange ways of life.

But Dana went home, to be a lawyer, and a rather dull and distinguished citizen. He was once almost an ambassador. And pre-eminently respectable.

He had been. He KNEW. He had even told us. It is a great achievement.

And then what?—Why, nothing. The old vulgar humdrum. That's the worst of knowledge. It leaves one only the more lifeless. Dana lived his bit in two years, and knew, and drummed out the rest. Dreary lawyer's years, afterwards.

We know enough. We know too much. We know nothing.

Let us smash something. Ourselves included. But the machine above all.

Dana's small book is a very great book: contains a great extreme of knowledge, knowledge of the great element.

And after all, we have to know all before we can know that knowing is nothing.

Imaginatively, we have to know all: even the elemental waters. And know and know on, until knowledge suddenly shrivels and we know that forever we don't know.

Then there is a sort of peace, and we can start afresh, knowing we don't know.

X. *Herman Melville's* Typee *and* Omoo

THE GREATEST SEER and poet of the sea for me is Melville. His vision is more real than Swinburne's, because he doesn't personify the sea, and far sounder than Joseph Conrad's, because Melville doesn't sentimentalize the ocean and the sea's unfortunates. Snivel in a wet hanky like Lord Jim.

Melville has the strange, uncanny magic of sea-creatures, and some of their repulsiveness. He isn't quite a land animal. There is something slithery about him. Something always half-seas-over. In his life they said he was mad—or crazy. He was neither mad nor crazy. But he was over the border. He was half a water animal, like those terrible yellow-bearded Vikings who broke out of the waves in beaked ships.

He was a modern Viking. There is something curious about real blue-eyed people. They are never quite human, in the good classic sense, human as brown-eyed people are human: the human of the living humus. About a real blue-eyed person there is usually something abstract, elemental. Brown-eyed people are, as it were, like the earth, which is tissue of bygone life, organic, compound. In blue eyes there is sun and rain and abstract, uncreate element, water, ice, air, space, but not humanity. Brown-eyed people are people of the old, old world: *Allzu menschlich.* Blue-eyed people tend to be too keen and abstract.

Melville is like a Viking going home to the sea, encumbered with age and memories, and a sort of accomplished despair, almost madness. For he cannot accept humanity. He can't belong to humanity. Cannot.

The great Northern cycle of which he is the returning unit has almost completed its round, accomplished itself. Balder the beautiful is mystically dead, and by this time he stinketh. Forget-me-nots and sea-poppies fall into water. The man who came from the sea to live among men can stand it no longer. He hears the horror of the cracked church bell, and goes back down the shore, back into the ocean again, home, into the salt water. Human life won't do. He turns back to the elements. And all the vast sun-and-wheat con-sciousness of his day he plunges back into the deeps, burying the flame in the deep, self-conscious and deliberate. As blue flax and sea-poppies fall into the waters and give back their created sun-stuff to the dissolution of the flood.

The sea-born people, who can meet and mingle no longer: who turn away from life, to the abstract, to the elements: the sea receives her own.

Let life come asunder, they say. Let water conceive no more with fire. Let mating finish. Let the elements leave off kissing, and turn their backs on one another. Let the merman turn away from his human wife and children, let the seal-woman forget the world of men, remembering only the waters.

So they go down to the sea, the sea-born people. The Vikings are wandering again. Homes are broken up. Cross the seas, cross the seas, urges the heart. Leave love and home. Leave love and home. Love and home are a deadly illusion. Woman, what have I to do with thee? It is finished. *Consummatum est.* The crucifixion into humanity is over. Let us go back to the fierce, uncanny elements: the corrosive vast sea. Or Fire.

Basta! It is enough. It is enough of life. Let us have the vast elements. Let us get out of this loathsome complication of living humanly with humans. Let the sea wash us clean of the leprosy of our humanity and humanness.

Melville was a northerner, sea-born. So the sea claimed him. We are most of us, who use the English language, water-people, sea-derived.

Melville went back to the oldest of all the oceans, to the Pacific. *Der grosse oder stille Ozean.*

Without doubt the Pacific Ocean is æons older than the Atlantic or the Indian Oceans. When we say older, we mean it has not come to any modern consciousness. Strange con-vulsions have convulsed the Atlantic and Mediterranean peoples into phase after phase of consciousness, while the Pacific and the Pacific peoples have slept. To sleep is to dream: you can't stay unconscious. And, oh, heaven, for how many thousands of years has the true Pacific been dreaming,

turning over in its sleep and dreaming again: idyls: nightmares.

The Maoris, the Tongans, the Marquesans, the Fijians,
the Polynesians: holy God, how long have they been turning
over in the same sleep, with varying dreams? Perhaps, to a
sensitive imagination, those islands in the middle of the
Pacific are the most unbearable places on earth. It simply
stops the heart, to be translated there, unknown ages back,
back into that life, that pulse, that rhythm. The scientists
say the South Sea Islanders belong to the Stone Age. It
seems absurd to class people according to their implements.
And yet there is something in it. The heart of the Pacific is
still the Stone Age; in spite of steamers. The heart of the
Pacific seems like a vast vacuum, in which, mirage-like,
continues the life of myriads of ages back. It is a phantom-
persistence of human beings who should have died, by our
chronology, in the Stone Age. It is a phantom, illusion-like
trick of reality: the glamorous South Seas.

Even Japan and China have been turning over in their
sleep for countless centuries. Their blood is the old blood,
their tissue the old soft tissue. Their busy day was myriads
of years ago, when the world was a softer place, more moisture in the air, more warm mud on the face of the earth, and
the lotus was always in flower. The great bygone world,
before Egypt. And Japan and China have been turning over
in their sleep, while we have "advanced." And now they are
starting up into nightmare.

The world isn't what it seems.

The Pacific Ocean holds the dream of immemorial centuries. It is the great blue twilight of the vastest of all
evenings: perhaps of the most wonderful of all dawns. Who
knows?

It must once have been a vast basin of soft, lotus-warm
civilization, the Pacific. Never was such a huge man-day
swung down into slow disintegration, as here. And now the
waters are blue and ghostly with the end of immemorial
peoples. And phantomlike the islands rise out of it, illusions
of the glamorous Stone Age.

To this phantom Melville returned. Back, back, away from

life. Never man instinctively hated human life, our human life, as we have it, more than Melville did. And never was a man so passionately filled with the sense of vastness and mystery of life which is non-human. He was mad to look over our horizons. Anywhere, anywhere out of *our* world. To get away. To get away, out!

To get away, out of our life. To cross a horizon into another life. No matter what life, so long as it is another life.

Away, away from humanity. To the sea. The naked, salt, elemental sea. To go to sea, to escape humanity.

The human heart gets into a frenzy at last, in its desire to dehumanize itself.

So he finds himself in the middle of the Pacific. Truly over a horizon. In another world. In another epoch. Back, far back, in the days of palm trees and lizards and stone implements. The sunny Stone Age.

Samoa, Tahiti, Raratonga, Nukuheva: the very names are a sleep and a forgetting. The sleep-forgotten past magnificence of human history. "Trailing clouds of glory."

Melville hated the world: was born hating it. But he was looking for heaven. That is, choosingly. Choosingly, he was looking for paradise. Unchoosingly, he was mad with hatred of the world.

Well, the world is hateful. It is as hateful as Melville found it. He was not wrong in hating the world. *Delenda est Chicago.* He hated it to a pitch of madness, and not without reason.

But it's no good *persisting* in looking for paradise "regained."

Melville at his best invariably wrote from a sort of dreamself, so that events which he relates as actual fact have indeed a far deeper reference to his own soul, his own inner life.

So in *Typee* when he tells of his entry into the valley of the dread cannibals of Nukuheva. Down this narrow, steep, horrible dark gorge he slides and struggles as we struggle in a dream, or in the act of birth, to emerge in the green Eden of the Golden Age, the valley of the cannibal savages. This is a bit of birth-myth, or rebirth myth, on Melville's part—

unconscious, no doubt, because his running under-consciousness was always mystical and symbolical. He wasn't aware that he was being mystical.

There he is then, in Typee, among the dreaded cannibal savages. And they are gentle and generous with him, and he is truly in a sort of Eden.

Here at last is Rousseau's Child of Nature and Chateaubriand's Noble Savage called upon and found at home. Yes, Melville loves his savage hosts. He finds them gentle, laughing lambs compared to the ravening wolves of his white brothers, left behind in America and on an American whaleship.

The ugliest beast on earth is the white man, says Melville.

In short, Herman found in Typee the paradise he was looking for. It is true, the Marquesans were "immoral," but he rather liked that. Morality was too white a trick to take him in. Then again, they were cannibals. And it filled him with horror even to think of this. But the savages were very private and even fiercely reserved in their cannibalism, and he might have spared himself his shudder. No doubt he had partaken of the Christian Sacraments many a time. "This is my body, take and eat. This is my blood. Drink it in remembrance of me." And if the savages liked to partake of their sacrament without raising the transubstantiation quibble, and if they liked to say, directly: "This is thy body, which I take from thee and eat. This is thy blood, which I sip in annihilation of thee," why surely their sacred ceremony was as awe-inspiring as the one Jesus substituted. But Herman chose to be horrified. I confess, I am not horrified; though, of course, I am not on the spot. But the savage sacrament seems to me more valid than the Christian: less sidetracking about it. Thirdly, he was shocked by their wild methods of warfare. He died before the great European war, so his shock was comfortable.

Three little quibbles: morality, cannibal sacrament, and stone axes. You must have a fly even in Paradisal ointment. And the first was a ladybird.

But Paradise. He insists on it. Paradise. He could even go stark naked, as before the Apple episode. And his Fayaway, a laughing little Eve, naked with him, and hankering after no apple of knowledge, so long as he would just love her when he felt like it. Plenty to eat, needing no clothes to wear, sunny, happy people, sweet water to swim in: everything a man can want. Then why wasn't he happy along with the savages?

Because he wasn't.

He grizzled in secret, and wanted to escape.

He even pined for Home and Mother, the two things he had run away from as far as ships would carry him. HOME and MOTHER. The two things that were his damnation.

There on the island, where the golden-green great palm-trees chinked in the sun, and the elegant reed houses let the sea breeze through, and people went naked and laughed a great deal, and Fayaway put flowers in his hair for him—great red hibiscus flowers, and frangipani—O God, why wasn't he happy? Why wasn't he?

Because he wasn't.

Well, it's hard to make a man happy.

But I should not have been happy either. One's soul seems under a vacuum, in the South Seas.

The truth of the matter is, one cannot go back. Some men can: renegade. But Melville couldn't go back: and Gauguin couldn't really go back: and I know now that I could never go back. Back towards the past, savage life. One cannot go back. It is one's destiny inside one.

There are these peoples, these "savages." One does not despise them. One does not feel superior. But there is a gulf. There is a gulf in time and being. I cannot commingle my being with theirs.

There they are, these South Sea Islanders, beautiful big men with their golden limbs and their laughing, graceful laziness. And they will call you brother, choose you as a brother. But why cannot one truly be brother?

There is an invisible hand grasps my heart and prevents it opening too much to these strangers. They are beautiful, they are like children, they are generous: but they are more than this. They are far off, and in their eyes is an easy dark-ness of the soft, uncreate past. In a way, they are uncreate.

Far be it from me to assume any "white" superiority. But they are savages. They are gentle and laughing and physically very handsome. But it seems to me that in living so far, through all our bitter centuries of civilization, we have still been living onwards, forwards. God knows it looks like a *cul de sac* now. But turn to the first Negro, and then listen to your own soul. And your own soul will tell you that however false and foul our forms and systems are now, still, through the many centuries since Egypt, we have been living and struggling forwards along some road that is no road, and yet is a great life-development. We have struggled on, and on we must still go. We may have to smash things. Then let us smash. And our road may have to take a great swerve, that seems a retrogression.

But we can't go back. Whatever else the South Sea Islander is, he is centuries and centuries behind us in the life struggle, the consciousness-struggle, the struggle of the soul into fullness. There is his woman, with her knotted hair and her dark, inchoate, slightly sardonic eyes. I like her, she is nice. But I would never want to touch her. I could not go back on myself so far. Back to their uncreate condition.

She has soft warm flesh, like warm mud. Nearer the reptile, the Saurian age. *Noli me tangere.*

We can't go back. We can't go back to the savages: not a stride. We can be in sympathy with them. We can take a great curve in their direction, onwards. But we cannot turn the current of our life backwards, back towards their soft warm twilight and uncreate mud. Not for a moment. If we do it for a moment, it makes us sick.

We can only do it when we are renegade. The renegade hates life itself. He wants the death of life. So these many "reformers" and "idealists" who glorify the savages in America. They are death-birds, life-haters. Renegades.

We can't go back, and Melville couldn't. Much as he hated the civilized humanity he knew. He couldn't go back to the savages; he wanted to, he tried to, and he couldn't.

Because, in the first place, it made him sick; it made him physically ill. He had something wrong with his leg, and this would not heal. It got worse and worse, during his four months on the island. When he escaped, he was in a deplorable condition—sick and miserable, ill, very ill.

Paradise!

But there you are. Try to go back to the savages, and you feel as if your very soul was decomposing inside you. That is what you feel in the South Seas, anyhow: as if your soul was decomposing inside you. And with any savages the same, if you try to go their way, take their current of sympathy.

Yet, as I say, we must make a great swerve in our onward-going life-course now, to gather up again the savage mysteries. But this does not mean going back on ourselves.

Going back to the savages made Melville sicker than anything. It made him feel as if he were decomposing. Worse even than Home and Mother.

And that is what really happens. If you prostitute your psyche by returning to the savages, you gradually go to pieces. Before you can go back, you *have* to decompose. And a white man decomposing is a ghastly sight. Even Melville in Typee.

We have to go on, on, on, even if we must smash a way ahead.

So Melville escaped, and threw a boathook full in the throat of one of his dearest savage friends, and sank him, because that savage was swimming in pursuit. That's how he felt about the savages when they wanted to detain him. He'd have murdered them one and all, vividly, rather than be kept from escaping. Away from them—he must get away from them—at any price.

And once he has escaped, immediately he begins to sigh and pine for the "Paradise"—Home and Mother being at the other end even of a whaling voyage.

When he really was Home with Mother, he found it Purgatory. But Typee must have been even worse than Purgatory, a soft hell, judging from the murderous frenzy which possessed him to escape.

But once aboard the whaler that carried him off from Nukuheva, he looked back and sighed for the Paradise he had just escaped from in such a fever.

Poor Melville! He was determined Paradise existed. So he was always in Purgatory.

He was born for Purgatory. Some souls are purgatorial by destiny.

The very freedom of his Typee was a torture to him. Its ease was slowly horrible to him. This time *he* was the fly in the odorous tropical ointment.

He needed to fight. It was no good to him, the relaxation of the non-moral tropics. He didn't really want Eden. He wanted to fight. Like every American. To fight. But with weapons of the spirit, not the flesh.

That was the top and bottom of it. His soul was in revolt, writhing forever in revolt. When he had something definite to rebel against—like the bad conditions on a whaling ship— then he was much happier in his miseries. The mills of God were grinding inside him, and they needed something to grind on.

When they could grind on the injustice and folly of missionaries, or of brutal sea-captains, or of governments, he was easier. The mills of God were grinding inside him.

They are grinding inside every American. And they grind exceeding small.

Why? Heaven knows. But we've got to grind down our old forms, our old selves, grind them very very small, to nothingness. Whether a new somethingness will ever start, who knows? Meanwhile the mills of God grind on, in American Melville, and it was himself he ground small: himself and his wife, when he was married. For the present, the South Seas.

He escapes on to the craziest, most impossible of whaling ships. Lucky for us Melville makes it fantastic. It must have been pretty sordid.

And anyhow, on the crazy *Julia,* his leg, that would never heal in the paradise of Typee, began quickly to get well. His life was falling into its normal pulse. The drain back into past centuries was over.

Yet, oh, as he sails away from Nukuheva, on the voyage that will ultimately take him to America, oh, the acute and intolerable nostalgia he feels for the island he has left.

The past, the Golden Age of the past—what a nostalgia we all feel for it. Yet we don't want it when we get it. Try the South Seas.

Melville had to fight, fight against the existing world, against his own very self. Only he would never quite put the knife in the heart of his paradisal ideal. Somehow, somewhere, somewhen, love should be a fulfillment, and life should be a thing of bliss. That was his fixed ideal. Fata Morgana.

That was the pin he tortured himself on, like a pinned-down butterfly.

Love is never a fulfillment. Life is never a thing of continuous bliss. There is no paradise. Fight and laugh and feel bitter and feel bliss: and fight again. Fight, fight. That is life.

Why pin ourselves down on a paradisal ideal? It is only ourselves we torture.

Melville did have one great experience, getting way from humanity: the experience of the sea.

The South Sea Islands were not his great experience. They were a glamorous world outside New England. Outside. But it was the sea that was both outside and inside: the universal experience.

The book that follows on from *Typee* is *Omoo*.

Omoo is a fascinating book; picaresque, rascally, roving. Melville, as a bit of a beachcomber. The crazy ship *Julia* sails to Tahiti, and the mutinous crew are put ashore. Put in the Tahitian prison. It is good reading.

Perhaps Melville is at his best, his happiest, in *Omoo*. For once he is really reckless. For once he takes life as it comes. For once he is the gallant rascally epicurean, eating the world like a snipe, dirt and all baked into one *bonne bouche*.

For once he is really careless, roving with that scamp, Doctor Long Ghost. For once he is careless of his actions, careless of his morals, careless of his ideals: ironic, as the epicurean must be. The deep irony of your real scamp: your real epicurean of the moment.

But it was under the influence of the Long Doctor. This long and bony Scotsman was not a mere ne'er-do-well. He

was a man of humorous desperation, throwing his life ironically away. Not a mere loose-kneed loafer, such as the South
Seas seem to attract.

That is good about Melville: he never repents. Whatever
he did, in Typee or in Doctor Long Ghost's wicked society,
he never repented. If he ate his snipe, dirt and all, and enjoyed it at the time, he didn't have bilious bouts afterwards,
which is good.

But it wasn't enough. The Long Doctor was really knocking about in a sort of despair. He let his ship drift rudderless.

Melville couldn't do this. For a time, yes. For a time, in
this Long Doctor's company, he was rudderless and reckless.
Good as an experience. But a man who will not. abandon
himself to despair or indifference cannot keep it up.

Melville would never abandon himself either to despair
or indifference. He always cared. He always cared enough
to hate missionaries, and to be touched by a real act of kindness. He always cared.

When he saw a white man really "gone savage," a white
man with a blue shark tattooed over his brow, gone over to
the savages, then Herman's whole being revolted. He
couldn't bear it. He could not bear a renegade.

He enlisted at last on an American man-of-war. You have
the record in *White Jacket*. He was back in civilization, but
still at sea. He was in America, yet loose in the seas. Good
regular days, after Doctor Long Ghost and the *Julia*.

As a matter of fact, a long thin chain was round Melville's
ankle all the time, binding him to America, to civilization, to
democracy, to the ideal world. It was a long chain, and it
never broke. It pulled him back.

By the time he was twenty-five his wild oats were sown;
his reckless wanderings were over. At the age of twenty-five
he came back to Home and Mother, to fight it out at close
quarters. For you can't fight it out by running away. When
you have run a long way from Home and Mother, then you
realize that the earth is round, and if you keep on running
you'll be back on the same old doorstep—like a fatality.

Melville came home to face out the long rest of his life. He married and had an ecstasy of a courtship and fifty years of disillusion.

He had just furnished his home with disillusions. No more Typees. No more paradises. No more Fayaways. A mother: a gorgon. A home: a torture box. A wife: a thing with clay feet. Life: a sort of disgrace. Fame: another disgrace, being patronized by common snobs who just know how to read.

The whole shameful business just making a man writhe. Melville writhed for eighty years.

In his soul he was proud and savage.

But in his mind and will he wanted the perfect fulfillment of love; he wanted the lovey-doveyness of perfect mutual understanding.

A proud savage-souled man doesn't really want any perfect lovey-dovey fulfillment in love: no such nonsense. A mountain lion doesn't mate with a Persian cat; and when a grizzly bear roars after a mate, it is a she-grizzly he roars after—not after a silky sheep.

But Melville stuck to his ideal. He wrote *Pierre* to show that the more you try to be good the more you make a mess of things: that following righteousness is just disastrous. The better you are, the worse things turn out with you. The better you try to be, the bigger mess you make. Your very striving after righteousness only causes your own slow degeneration.

Well, it is true. No men are so evil today as the idealists, and no women half so evil as your earnest woman, who feels herself a power for good. It is inevitable. After a certain point, the ideal goes dead and rotten. The old pure ideal becomes in itself an impure thing of evil. Charity becomes pernicious, the spirit itself becomes foul. The meek are evil. The pure in heart have base, subtle revulsions: like Dostoevsky's Idiot. The whole Sermon on the Mount becomes a litany of white vice.

What then?

It's our own fault. It was *we* who set up the ideals. And if we are such fools, that we aren't able to kick over our ideals in time, the worse for us.

Look at Melville's eighty long years of writhing. And to the end he writhed on the ideal pin.

From the "perfect woman lover" he passed on to the "perfect friend." He looked and looked for the perfect man friend.

Couldn't find him.

Marriage was a ghastly disillusion to him, because he looked for perfect marriage.

Friendship never even made a real start in him—save perhaps his half-sentimental love for Jack Chase, in *White Jacket*.

Yet to the end he pined for this: a perfect relationship; perfect mating; perfect mutual understanding. A perfect friend.

Right to the end he could never accept the fact that *perfect* relationships cannot be. Each soul is alone, and the aloneness of each soul is a double barrier to perfect relationship between two beings.

Each soul *should* be alone. And in the end the desire for a "perfect relationship" is just a vicious, unmanly craving. *"Tous nos malheurs viennent de ne pouvoir être seuls."*

Melville, however, refused to draw his conclusion. *Life* was wrong, he said. He refused Life. But he stuck to his ideal of perfect relationship, possible perfect love. The world *ought* to be a harmonious loving place. And it *can't* be. So life itself is wrong.

It is silly arguing. Because, after all, only temporary man sets up the "oughts."

The world ought *not* to be a harmonious loving place. It ought to be a place of fierce discord and intermittent harmonies: which it is.

Love ought *not* to be perfect. It ought to have perfect moments, and wildernesses of thorn bushes—which it has.

A "perfect" relationship ought *not* to be possible. Every relationship should have its absolute limits, its absolute reserves, essential to the singleness of the soul in each person. A truly perfect relationship is one in which each party leaves great tracts unknown in the other party.

No two persons can meet at more than a few points, con-

sciously. If two people can just be together fairly often, so
that the presence of each is a sort of balance to the other,
that is the basis of perfect relationship. There must be true
separatenesses as well.

Melville was, at the core, a mystic and an idealist.

Perhaps, so am I.

And he stuck to his ideal guns.

I abandon mine.

He was a mystic who raved because the old ideal guns
shot havoc. The guns of the "noble spirit." Of "ideal love."

I say, let the old guns rot.

Get new ones, and shoot straight.

XI. *Herman Melville's* Moby Dick

Moby Dick, or the White Whale.

A hunt. The last great hunt.

For what?

For Moby Dick, the huge white sperm whale: who is old,
hoary, monstrous, and swims alone; who is unspeakably
terrible in his wrath, having so often been attacked; and
snow-white.

Of course he is a symbol.

Of what?

I doubt if even Melville knew exactly. That's the best of
it.

He is warm-blooded, he is lovable. He is lonely Leviathan,
not a Hobbes sort. Or is he?

But he is warm-blooded and lovable. The South Sea Islanders, and Polynesians, and Malays, who worship shark,
or crocodile, or weave endless frigate-bird distortions, why
did they never worship the whale? So big!

Because the whale is not wicked. He doesn't bite. And
their gods had to bite.

He's not a dragon. He is Leviathan. He never coils like
the Chinese dragon of the sun. He's not a serpent of the
waters. He is warm-blooded, a mammal. And hunted, hunted
down.

It is a great book.

At first you are put off by the style. It reads like journalism. It seems spurious. You feel Melville is trying to put something over you. It won't do.

And Melville really is a bit sententious: aware of himself, self-conscious, putting something over even himself. But then it's not easy to get into the swing of a piece of deep mysticism when you just set out with a story.

Nobody can be more clownish, more clumsy and sententiously in bad taste, than Herman Melville, even in a great book like *Moby Dick*. He preaches and holds forth because he's not sure of himself. And he holds forth, often, so amateurishly.

The artist was so *much* greater than the man. The man is rather a tiresome New Englander of the ethical mystical-transcendentalist sort: Emerson, Longfellow, Hawthorne, etc. So unrelieved, the solemn ass even in humor. So hopelessly *au grand serieux*, you feel like saying: Good God, what does it matter? If life is a tragedy, or a farce, or a disaster, or anything else, what do I care! Let life be what it likes. Give me a drink, that's what I want just now.

For my part, life is so many things I don't care what it is. It's not my affair to sum it up. Just now it's a cup of tea. This morning it was wormwood and gall. Hand me the sugar.

One wearies of the *grand serieux*. There's something false about it. And that's Melville. Oh dear, when the solemn ass brays! brays! brays!

But he was a deep, great artist, even if he was rather a sententious man. He was a real American in that he always felt his audience in front of him. But when he ceases to be American, when he forgets all audience, and gives us his sheer apprehension of the world, then he is wonderful, his book commands a stillness in the soul, an awe.

In his "human" self, Melville is almost dead. That is, he hardly reacts to human contacts any more; or only ideally: or just for a moment. His human-emotional self is almost played out. He is abstract, self-analytical, and abstracted. And he is more spellbound by the strange slidings and collidings of Matter than by the things men do. In this he is like Dana. It is the material elements he really has to do with. His drama is with them. He was a futurist long before futurism found paint. The sheer naked slidings of the elements. And the human soul experiencing it all. So often, it is almost over the border: psychiatry. Almost spurious. Yet so great.

It is the same old thing as in all Americans. They keep their old-fashioned ideal frock-coat on, and an old-fashioned silk hat, while they do the most impossible things. There you are: you see Melville hugged in bed by a huge tattooed South Sea Islander, and solemnly offering burnt offering to this savage's little idol, and his ideal frock-coat just hides his shirt-tails and prevents us from seeing his bare posterior as he salaams, while his ethical silk hat sits correctly over his brow the while. That is so typically American: doing the most impossible things without taking off their spiritual get-up. Their ideals are like armor which has rusted in, and will never more come off. And meanwhile in Melville his bodily knowledge moves naked, a living quick among the stark elements. For with sheer physical vibrational sensitiveness, like a marvelous wireless station, he registers the effects of the outer world. And he records also, almost beyond pain or pleasure, the extreme transitions of the isolated, far-driven soul, the soul which is now alone, without any real human contact.

The first days in New Bedford introduce the only human being who really enters into the book, namely, Ishmael, the "I" of the book. And then the moment's hearts-brother, Queequeg, the tattooed, powerful South Sea harpooner, whom Melville loves as Dana loves "Hope." The advent of Ishmael's bedmate is amusing and unforgettable. But later the two swear "marriage," in the language of the savages. For Queequeg has opened again the flood-gates of love and human connection in Ishmael.

As I sat there in that now lonely room, the fire burning low, in that mild stage when, after its first intensity has warmed the air, it then only glows to be looked at; the evening shades and phantoms gathering round the casements, and peering in upon us silent, solitary twain: I began to be sensible of strange feelings. I felt a melting in me. No more my splintered hand and maddened heart was turned against the wolfish world. This soothing savage had redeemed it. There he sat, his very indifference speaking a nature in which there lurked no civilized hypocrisies and bland deceits. Wild he was; a very sight of sights to see; yet I began to feel myself mysteriously drawn towards him.

So they smoked together, and are clasped in each other's arms. The friendship is finally sealed when Ishmael offers sacrifice to Queequeg's little idol, Gogo.

I was a good Christian, born and bred in the bosom of the infallible Presbyterian Church. How then could I unite with the idolater in worshiping his piece of wood? But what is worship?—to do the will of God—*that* is worship. And what is the will of God?—to do to my fellow-man what I would have my fellow-man do to me—*that* is the will of God. [Which sounds like Benjamin Franklin, and is hopelessly bad theology. But it is real American logic.] Now Queequeg is my fellow-man. And what do I wish that this Queequeg would do to me? Why, unite with me in my particular Presbyterian form of worship. Consequently, I must unite with him; ergo, I must turn idolater. So I kindled the shavings; helped prop up the innocent little idol; offered him burnt biscuit with Queequeg; salaamed before him twice or thrice; kissed his nose; and that done, we undressed and went to bed, at peace with our own consciences and all the world. But we did not go to sleep without some little chat. How it is I know not; but there is no place like bed for confidential disclosures between friends. Man and wife, they say, open the very bottom of their souls to each other; and some old couples often lie and chat over old times till nearly morning. Thus, then, lay I and Queequeg—a cozy, loving pair——

You would think this relation with Queequeg meant something to Ishmael. But no. Queequeg is forgotten like yesterday's newspaper. Human things are only momentary excitements or amusements to the American Ishmael. Ishmael, the hunted. But much more Ishmael, the hunter. What's a Queequeg? What's a wife? The white whale must be hunted down. Queequeg must be just "KNOWN," then dropped into oblivion.

And what in the name of fortune is the white whale?

Elsewhere Ishmael says he loved Queequeg's eyes: "large, deep eyes, fiery black and bold." No doubt, like Poe, he wanted to get the "clue" to them. That was all.

The two men go over from New Bedford to Nantucket, and there sign on to the Quaker whaling ship, the *Pequod*. It is all strangely fantastic, phantasmagoric. The voyage of the soul. Yet curiously a real whaling voyage, too. We pass on into the midst of the sea with this strange ship and its incredible crew. The Argonauts were mild lambs in comparison. And Ulysses went *defeating* the Circes and overcoming the wicked hussies of the isles. But the *Pequod's* crew is a collection of maniacs fanatically hunting down a lonely, harmless white whale.

As a soul history, it makes one angry. As a sea yarn, it is marvelous: there is always something a bit over the mark in sea yarns. Should be. Then again the masking up of actual seaman's experience with sonorous mysticism sometimes gets on one's nerves. And again, as a revelation of destiny the book is too deep even for sorrow. Profound beyond feeling.

You are some time before you are allowed to see the captain, Ahab: the mysterious Quaker. Oh, it is a God-fearing Quaker ship.

Ahab, the captain. The captain of the soul.

> I am the master of my fate,
> I am the captain of my soul!

Ahab!

"Oh, captain, my captain, our fearful trip is done."

The gaunt Ahab, Quaker, mysterious person, only shows himself after some days at sea. There's a secret about him! What?

Oh, he's a portentous person. He stumps about on an ivory stump, made from sea-ivory. Moby Dick, the great white whale, tore off Ahab's leg at the knee, when Ahab was attacking him.

Quite right, too. Should have torn off both his legs, and a bit more besides.

But Ahab doesn't think so. Ahab is now a monomaniac.

Moby Dick is his monomania. Moby Dick must DIE, or Ahab can't live any longer. Ahab is atheist by this.

All right.

This *Pequod,* ship of the American soul, has three mates.

1. Starbuck: Quaker, Nantucketer, a good responsible man of reason, forethought, intrepidity, what is called a dependable man. At the bottom, *afraid*.

2. Stubb: "Fearless as fire, and as mechanical." Insists on being reckless and jolly on every occasion. Must be afraid, too, really.

3. Flask: Stubborn, obstinate, without imagination. To him "the wondrous whale was but a species of magnified mouse or water-rat——"

There you have them: a maniac captain and his three mates, three splendid seamen, admirable whalemen, first-class men at their job.

America!

It is rather like Mr. Wilson and his admirable, "efficient" crew at the Peace Conference. Except that none of the Pequodders took their wives along.

A maniac captain of the soul, and three eminently prac-tical mates.

America!

Then such a crew. Renegades, castaways, cannibals: Ishmael, Quakers.

America!

Three giant harpooners, to spear the great white whale.

1. Queequeg, the South Sea Islander, all tattooed, big and powerful.

2. Tashtego, the Red Indian of the sea-coast, where the Indian meets the sea.

3. Daggoo, the huge black Negro.

There you have them, three savage races, under the Amer-ican flag, the maniac captain, with their great keen harpoons, ready to spear the white whale.

And only after many days at sea does Ahab's own boat-crew appear on deck. Strange, silent, secret, black-garbed Malays, fire-worshiping Parsees. These are to man Ahab's boat, when it leaps in pursuit of that whale.

What do you think of the ship *Pequod*, the ship of the soul of an American?

Many races, many peoples, many nations, under the Stars and Stripes. Beaten with many stripes.

Seeing stars sometimes.

And in a mad ship, under a mad captain, in a mad, fanatic's hunt.

For what?

For Moby Dick, the great white whale.

But splendidly handled. Three splendid mates. The whole thing practical, eminently practical in its working. American industry!

And all this practicality in the service of a mad, mad chase.

Melville manages to keep it a real whaling ship, on a real cruise, in spite of all fantastics. A wonderful, wonderful voyage. And a beauty that is so surpassing only because of the author's awful flounderings in mystical waters. He wanted to get metaphysically deep. And he got deeper than metaphysics. It is a surpassingly beautiful book, with an awful meaning, and bad jolts.

It is interesting to compare Melville with Dana, about the albatross—Melville a bit sententious.

I remember the first albatross I ever saw. It was during a prolonged gale in waters hard upon the Antarctic seas. From my forenoon watch below I ascended to the overcrowded deck, and there, lashed upon the main hatches, I saw a regal feathered thing of unspotted whiteness, and with a hooked Roman bill sublime. At intervals it arched forth its vast, archangel wings—wondrous throbbings and flutterings shook it. Though bodily unharmed, it uttered cries, as some King's ghost in supernatural distress. Through its inexpressible strange eyes methought I peeped to secrets not below the heavens—the white thing was so white, its wings so wide, and in those forever exiled waters I had lost the miserable warping memories of traditions and of towns. I assert, then, that in the wondrous bodily whiteness of the bird chiefly lurks the secret of the spell——

Melville's albatross is a prisoner, caught by a bait on a hook.

Well, I have seen an albatross, too: following us in waters hard upon the Antarctic, too, south of Australia. And in the Southern winter. And the ship, a P. and O. boat, nearly empty. And the lascar crew shivering.

The bird with its long, long wings following, then leaving us. No one knows till they have tried, how lost, how lonely those Southern waters are. And glimpses of the Australian coast.

It makes one feel that our day is only a day. That in the dark of the night ahead other days stir fecund, when we have lapsed from existence.

Who knows how utterly we shall lapse.

But Melville keeps up his disquisition about "whiteness." The great abstract fascinated him. The abstract where we end, and cease to be. White or black. Our white, abstract end!

Then again it is lovely to be at sea on the *Pequod*, with never a grain of earth to us.

It was a cloudy, sultry afternoon; the seamen were lazily lounging about the decks, or vacantly gazing over into the lead-coloured waters. Queequeg and I were mildly employed weaving what is called a sword-mat, for an additional lashing to our boat. So still and subdued, and yet somehow preluding was all the scene, and such an incantation of reverie lurked in the air that each silent sailor seemed resolved into his own invisible self——

In the midst of this preluding silence came the first cry:

There she blows! there! there! there! She blows!

And then comes the first chase, a marvelous piece of true sea-writing, the sea, and sheer sea-beings on the chase, sea-creatures chased. There is scarcely a taint of earth—pure sea-motion.

"Give way, men," whispered Starbuck, drawing still further aft the sheet of his sail; "there is time to kill fish yet before the squall comes. There's white water again!—Close to!—Spring!" Soon after, two cries in quick succession on each side of us denoted that the other boats had got fast; but hardly were they overheard, when with a lightninglike hurtling whisper Starbuck said: "Stand up!" and Queequeg, harpoon in hand, sprang to his feet.—Though not one of the oarsmen was then facing the life and death peril so close to them ahead, yet their eyes on the intense countenance of the mate in the stern of the boat, they knew that the imminent instant had come; they heard, too, an enormous wallowing sound, as of fifty elephants stirring in their litter. Meanwhile the boat was still booming through the mist, the waves curbing and hissing around us like the erected crests of enraged serpents.

"That's his hump. *There! There*, give it to him!" whispered Starbuck.—A short rushing sound leapt out of the boat; it was the darted iron of Queequeg. Then all in one welded motion came a push from astern, while forward the boat seemed striking on a ledge; the sail collapsed and exploded; a gush of scalding vapor shot up near by; something rolled and tumbled like an earthquake beneath us. The whole crew were half suffocated as they were tossed helter-skelter into the white curling cream of the squall. Squall, whale, and harpoon had all blended together; and the whale, merely grazed by the iron, escaped——

Melville is a master of violent, chaotic physical motion; he can keep up a whole wild chase without a flaw. He is as perfect at creating stillness. The ship is cruising on the Carrol Ground, south of St. Helena:

It was while gliding through these latter waters that one serene and moonlight night, when all the waves rolled by like scrolls of silver; and by their soft, suffusing seethings, made what seemed a silvery silence, not a solitude; on such a silent night a silvery jet was seen far in advance of the white bubbles at the bow——

Then there is the description of Brit:

Steering northeastward from the Crozello we fell in with vast meadows of brit, the minute, yellow substance upon which the right whale largely feeds. For leagues and leagues it undulated round us, so that we seemed to be sailing through boundless fields of ripe and golden wheat. On the second day, numbers of right whales were seen, secure from the attack of a sperm whaler like the *Pequod*. With open jaws they sluggishly swam through the brit, which, adhering to the fringed fibers of that wondrous Venetian blind in their mouths, was in that manner separated from the water that escaped at the lip. As moving mowers who, side by side, slowly and seethingly advance their scythes through the long wet grass of the marshy meads; even so these monsters swam, making a strange, grassy, cutting sound; and leaving behind them endless swaths of blue on the yellow sea. But it was only the sound they made as they parted the brit which at all reminded one of mowers. Seen from the mastheads, especially when they paused and were stationary for a while, their vast black forms looked more like masses of rock than anything else——

This beautiful passage brings us to the apparition of the squid:

Slowly wading through the meadows of brit, the *Pequod* still held her way northeastward towards the island of Java; a gentle air impelling her keel, so that in the surrounding serenity her three tall, tapering masts mildly waved to that languid breeze, as three mild palms on a plain. And still, at wide intervals, in the silvery night, that lonely, alluring jet would be seen.

But one transparent-blue morning, when a stillness almost preternatural spread over the sea, however unattended with any stagnant calm; when the long burnished sunglade on the waters seemed a golden finger laid across them, enjoining secrecy; when all the slippered waves whispered together as they softly ran on; in this profound hush of the visible sphere a strange specter was seen by Daggoo from the mainmast head.

In the distance, a great white mass lazily rose, and rising higher and higher, and disentangling itself from the azure, at last gleamed before our prow like a snow-slide, new slid from the hills. Thus glistening for a moment, as slowly it subsided, and sank. Then once more arose, and silently gleamed. It seemed not a whale; and yet, is this Moby Dick? thought Daggoo——

The boats were lowered and pulled to the scene.

In the same spot where it sank, once more it slowly rose. Almost forgetting for the moment all thoughts of Moby Dick, we now gazed at the most wondrous phenomenon which the secret seas have hitherto revealed to mankind. A vast pulpy mass, furlongs in length and breadth, of a glancing cream color, lay floating on the water, innumerable long arms radiating from its center, and curling and twisting like a nest of anacondas, as if blindly to clutch at any hapless object within reach. No perceptible face or front did it have; no conceivable token of either sensation or instinct; but undulated there on the billows, an unearthly, formless, chance-like apparition of life. And with a low sucking it slowly disappeared again.

The following chapters, with their account of whale hunts, the killing, the stripping, the cutting up, are magnificent records of actual happening. Then comes the queer tale of the meeting of the *Jeroboam,* a whaler met at sea, all of whose men were under the domination of a religious maniac, one of the ship's hands. There are detailed descriptions of the actual taking of the sperm oil from a whale's head. Dilating on the smallness of the brain of a sperm whale, Melville significantly remarks—

for I believe that much of a man's character will be found betokened in his backbone. I would rather feel your spine than your skull, whoever you are——

And of the whale, he adds:

For, viewed in this light, the wonderful comparative smallness of his brain proper is more than compensated by the wonderful comparative magnitude of his spinal cord.

In among the rush of terrible, awful hunts, come touches of pure beauty.

As the three boats lay there on that gently rolling sea, gazing down into its eternal blue noon; and as not a single groan or cry of any sort, nay not so much as a ripple or a thought, came up from its depths; what landsman would have thought that beneath all that silence and placidity the utmost monster of the seas was writhing and wrenching in agony!

Perhaps the most stupendous chapter is the one called *The Grand Armada,* at the beginning of Volume III. The *Pequod* was drawing through the Sunda Straits towards Java when she came upon a vast host of sperm whales.

Broad on both bows, at a distance of two or three miles, and forming a great semicircle embracing one half of the level horizon, a continuous chain of whale jets were up-playing and sparkling in the noonday air.

Chasing this great herd, past the Straits of Sunda, themselves chased by Javan pirates, the whalers race on. Then the boats are lowered. At last that curious state of inert irresolution came over the whalers, when they were, as the seamen say, gallied. Instead of forging ahead in huge martial array they swam violently hither and thither, a surging sea of whales, no longer moving on. Starbuck's boat, made fast to a whale, is towed in amongst this howling Leviathan chaos. In mad career it cockles through the boiling surge of monsters, till it is brought into a clear lagoon in the very center of the vast, mad, terrified herd. There a sleek, pure calm reigns. There the females swam in peace, and the young whales came snuffing tamely at the boat, like dogs. And there the astonished seamen watched the love-making of these amazing monsters, mammals, now in rut far down in the sea—

But far beneath this wondrous world upon the surface, another and still stranger world met our eyes, as we gazed over the side. For, suspended in these watery vaults, floated the forms of the nursing mothers of the whales, and those that by their enormous girth seemed shortly to become mothers. The lake, as I have hinted, was to a considerable depth exceedingly transparent; and as human infants while sucking will calmly and fixedly gaze away from the breast, as if leading two different lives at a time; and while yet drawing moral nourishment, be still spiritually feasting upon some unearthly reminiscence, even so did the young of these whales seem looking up towards us, but not at us, as if we were but a bit of gulf weed in their new-born sight. Floating on their sides, the mothers also seemed quietly eying us.—Some of the subtlest secrets of the seas seemed divulged to us in this enchanted pond. We saw young Leviathan amours in the deep. And thus, though surrounded by circle upon circle of consternation and affrights, did these inscrutable creatures at the center freely and fearlessly indulge in all peaceful concernments; yea, serenely reveled in dalliance and delight——

There is something really overwhelming in these whale-hunts, almost superhuman or inhuman, bigger than life, more terrific than human activity. The same with the chapter on ambergris: it is so curious, so real, yet so unearthly. And again in the chapter called *The Cassock*—surely the oldest piece of phallicism in all the world's literature.

After this comes the amazing account of the Try-works, when the ship is turned into the sooty, oily factory in mid-ocean, and the oil is extracted from the blubber. In the light of the red furnace burning on deck, at sea, Melville has his startling experience of reversion. He is at the helm, but has turned to watch the fire: when suddenly he feels the ship rushing backward from him, in mystic reversion—

Uppermost was the impression, that whatever swift, rushing thing I stood on was not so much bound to any haven ahead, as rushing from all havens astern. A stark bewildering feeling, as of death, came over me. Convulsively my hands grasped the tiller, but with the crazy conceit that the tiller was, somehow, in some enchanted way, inverted. My God! What is the matter with me, I thought!

This dream-experience is a real soul-experience. He ends with an injunction to all men, not to gaze on the red fire when its redness makes all things look ghastly. It seems to him that his gazing on fire has evoked this horror of reversion, undoing.

Perhaps it had. He was water-born.

After some unhealthy work on the ship, Queequeg caught a fever and was like to die.

How he wasted and wasted in those few, long-lingering days, till there seemed but little left of him but his frame and tattooing. But as all else in him thinned, and his cheek-bones grew sharper, his eyes, nevertheless, seemed growing fuller and fuller; they took on a strangeness of luster; and mildly but deeply looked out at you there from his sickness, a wondrous testimony to that immortal health in him which could not die, or be weakened. And like circles on the water, which as they grow fainter, expand; so his eyes seemed rounding and rounding, like the circles of Eternity. An awe that cannot be named would steal over you as you sat by the side of this waning savage——

But Queequeg did not die—and the *Pequod* emerges from the Eastern Straits, into the full Pacific.

To my meditative Magian rover, this serene Pacific once beheld, must ever after be the sea of his adoption. It rolls the utmost waters of the world——

In this Pacific the fights go on:

It was far down the afternoon, and when all the spearings of the crimson fight were done, and floating in the lovely sunset sea and sky, sun and whale both died stilly together; then such a sweetness and such a plaintiveness, such inwreathing orisons curled up in that rosy air, that it almost seemed as if far over from the deep green convent valleys of the Manila isles, the Spanish land breeze had gone to sea, freighted with these vesper hymns. Soothed again, but only soothed to deeper gloom, Ahab, who has steered off from the whale, sat intently watching his final wanings from the now tranquil boat. For that strange spectacle, observable in all sperm whales dying—the turning of the head sunwards, and so expiring—that strange spectacle, beheld of such a placid evening, somehow to Ahab conveyed wondrousness unknown before. "He turns and turns him to it; how slowly, but how steadfastly, his home-rendering and invoking brow, with his last dying motions. He, too, worships fire . . ."

So Ahab soliloquizes: and so the warm-blooded whale turns for the last time to the sun, which begot him in the waters.

But as we see in the next chapter, it is the Thunder-fire which Ahab really worships: that living, sundering fire of which he bears the brand, from head to foot; it is storm, the electric storm of the *Pequod,* when the corposants burn in high, tapering flames of supernatural pallor upon the masthead, and when the compass is reversed. After this all is fatality. Life itself seems mystically reversed. In these hunters of Moby Dick there is nothing but madness and possession. The captain, Ahab, moves hand in hand with the poor imbecile Negro boy, Pip, who has been so cruelly demented, left swimming alone in the vast sea. It is the imbecile child of the sun hand in hand with the northern monomaniac, captain and master.

The voyage surges on. They meet one ship, then another. It is all ordinary day-routine, and yet all is a tension of pure madness and horror, the approaching horror of the last fight.

Hither and thither, on high, glided the snow-white wings of small unspecked birds; these were the gentle thoughts of the feminine air; but to and fro in the deeps, far down in the bottomless blue, rushed mighty leviathans, sword-fish and sharks; and these were the strong, troubled, murderous thinkings of the masculine sea——

On this day Ahab confesses his weariness, the weariness of his burden.

"But do I look very old, so very, very old, Starbuck? I feel deadly faint, and bowed, and humped, as though I were Adam staggering beneath the piled centuries since Paradise——"

It is the Gethsemane of Ahab, before the last fight: the Gethsemane of the human soul seeking the last self-conquest, the last attainment of extended consciousness—infinite consciousness.

At last they sight the whale. Ahab sees him from his hoisted perch at the masthead:

From this height the whale was now seen some mile or so ahead, at every roll of the sea revealing his high, sparkling hump, and regularly jetting his silent spout into the air.

The boats are lowered, to draw near the white whale.

At length the breathless hunter came so nigh his seemingly unsuspectful prey that his entire dazzling hump was distinctly visible, sliding along the sea as if an isolated thing, and continually set in a revolving ring of finest, fleecy, greenish foam. He saw the vast involved wrinkles of the slightly projecting head, beyond. Before it, far out on the soft, Turkish rugged waters, went the glistening white shadow from his broad, milky forehead, a musical rippling playfully accompanying the shade; and behind, the blue waters interchangeably flowed over the

MELVILLE'S MOBY DICK 1059

moving valley of his steady wake; and on either side bright
bubbles arose and danced by his side. But these were broken
again by the light toes of hundreds of gay fowl softly feathering
the sea, alternate with their fitful flight; and like to some flag-
staff rising from the pointed hull of an argosy, the tall but
shattered pole of a recent lance projected from the white
whale's back; and at intervals one of the clouds of soft-toed
fowls hovering, and to and fro shimmering like a canopy over
the fish, silently perched and rocked on this pole, the long tail-
feathers streaming like pennons.

A gentle joyousness—a mighty mildness of repose in swiftness, invested the gliding whale——

The fight with the whale is too wonderful, and too awful,
to be quoted apart from the book. It lasted three days. The
fearful sight, on the third day, of the torn body of the
Parsee harpooner, lost on the previous day, now seen lashed
on to the flanks of the white whale by the tangle of harpoon
lines, has a mystic dream-horror. The awful and infuriated
whale turns upon the ship, symbol of this civilized world of
ours. He smites her with a fearful shock. And a few minutes
later, from the last of the fighting whale-boats comes the cry:

"The ship! Great God, where is the ship?" Soon they, through
the dim, bewildering mediums, saw her sidelong fading phantom, as in the gaseous Fata Morgana; only the uppermost masts
out of the water; while fixed by infatuation, or fidelity, or fate,
to their once lofty perches, the pagan harpooners still maintained their sinking lookouts on the sea. And now concentric
circles seized the lone boat itself, and all its crew, and each
floating oar, and every lance-pole, and spinning, animate and
inanimate, all round and round in one vortex, carried the
smallest chip of the *Pequod* out of sight——

The bird of heaven, the eagle, St. John's bird, the Red
Indian bird, the American, goes down with the ship, nailed
by Tashtego's hammer, the hammer of the American Indian.
The eagle of the spirit. Sunk!

Now small fowls flew screaming over the yet yawning gulf;
a sullen white surf beat against its steep sides; then all collapsed; and then the great shroud of the sea rolled on as it
rolled five thousand years ago.

So ends one of the strangest and most wonderful books in the world, closing up its mystery and its tortured symbolism. It is an epic of the sea such as no man has equaled; and it is a book of exoteric symbolism of profound significance, and of considerable tiresomeness.

But it is a great book, a very great book, the greatest book of the sea ever written. It moves awe in the soul.

The terrible fatality.

Fatality.

Doom.

Doom! Doom! Doom! Something seems to whisper it in the very dark trees of America. Doom!

Doom of what?

Doom of our white day. We are doomed, doomed. And the doom is in America. The doom of our white day.

Ah, well, if my day is doomed, and I am doomed with my day, it is something greater than I which dooms me, so I accept my doom as a sign of the greatness which is more than I am.

Melville knew. He knew his race was doomed. His white soul, doomed. His great white epoch, doomed. Himself, doomed. The idealist, doomed. The spirit, doomed.

The reversion. "Not so much bound to any haven ahead, as rushing from all havens astern."

That great horror of ours! It is our civilization rushing from all havens astern.

The last ghastly hunt. The White Whale.

What then is Moby Dick? He is the deepest blood-being of the white race; he is our deepest blood-nature.

And he is hunted, hunted, hunted by the maniacal fanaticism of our white mental consciousness. We want to hunt him down. To subject him to our will. And in this maniacal conscious hunt of ourselves we get dark races and pale to help us, red, yellow, and black, east and west, Quaker and fire-worshiper, we get them all to help us in this ghastly maniacal hunt which is our doom and our suicide.

The last phallic being of the white man. Hunted into the death of upper consciousness and the ideal will. Our blood-self subjected to our will. Our blood-consciousness sapped by a parasitic mental or ideal consciousness.

Hot-blooded, sea-born Moby Dick. Hunted by mono-maniacs of the idea.

Oh God, Oh God, what next, when the *Pequod* has sunk?

She sank in the war, and we are all flotsam.

Now what next?

Who knows? *Quien sabe? Quien sabe, señor?*

Neither Spanish nor Saxon America has any answer.

The *Pequod* went down. And the *Pequod* was the ship of the white American soul. She sank, taking with her Negro and Indian and Polynesian, Asiatic and Quaker and good, businesslike Yankees and Ishmael: she sank all the lot of them.

Boom! as Vachel Lindsay would say.

To use the words of Jesus, IT IS FINISHED.

Consummatum est!

But *Moby Dick* was first published in 1851. If the Great White Whale sank the ship of the Great White Soul in 1851, what's been happening ever since?

Post-mortem effects, presumably.

Because, in the first centuries, Jesus was Cetus, the Whale. And the Christians were the little fishes. Jesus, the Redeemer, was Cetus, Leviathan. And all the Christians all his little fishes.

XII. *Whitman*

POST-MORTEM effects?

But what of Walt Whitman?

The "good gray poet."

Was he a ghost, with all his physicality?

The good gray poet.

Post-mortem effects. Ghosts.

A certain ghoulish insistency. A certain horrible pottage of human parts. A certain stridency and portentousness. A luridness about his beatitudes.

DEMOCRACY! THESE STATES! EIDOLONS! LOVERS, ENDLESS LOVERS!

ONE IDENTITY!

ONE IDENTITY!

I AM HE THAT ACHES WITH AMOROUS LOVE.

Do you believe me, when I say post-mortem effects?

When the *Pequod* went down, she left many a rank and dirty steamboat still fussing in the seas. The *Pequod* sinks with all her souls, but their bodies rise again to man innumerable tramp steamers and ocean-crossing liners. Corpses.

What we mean is that people may go on, keep on, and rush on, without souls. They have their ego and their will; that is enough to keep them going.

So that you see, the sinking of the *Pequod* was only a metaphysical tragedy after all. The world goes on just the same. The ship of the *soul* is sunk. But the machine-manipulating body works just the same: digests, chews gum, admires Botticelli and aches with amorous love.

I AM HE THAT ACHES WITH AMOROUS LOVE.

What do you make of that? I AM HE THAT ACHES. First generalization. First uncomfortable universalization. WITH AMOROUS LOVE! O God! Better a bellyache. A bellyache is at least specific. But the ACHE OF AMOROUS LOVE!

Think of having that under your skin. All that!

I AM HE THAT ACHES WITH AMOROUS LOVE.

Walter, leave off. You are not HE. You are just a limited Walter. And your ache doesn't include all Amorous Love, by any means. If you ache you only ache with a small bit of amorous love, and there's so much more stays outside the cover of your ache, that you might be a bit milder about it.

I AM HE THAT ACHES WITH AMOROUS LOVE.

CHUFF! CHUFF! CHUFF!

CHU-CHU-CHU-CHU-CHUFF!

Reminds one of a steam-engine. A locomotive. They're the only things that seem to me to ache with amorous love. All that steam inside them. Forty million foot-pounds pressure. The ache of AMOROUS LOVE. Steam-pressure. CHUFF!

An ordinary man aches with love for Belinda, or his Native Land, or the Ocean, or the Stars, or the Oversoul: if he feels that an ache is in the fashion.

It takes a steam-engine to ache with AMOROUS LOVE. All of it.

Walt was really too superhuman. The danger of the superman is that he is mechanical.

They talk of his "splendid animality." Well, he'd got it on the brain, if that's the place for animality.

> I am he that aches with amorous love:
> Does the earth gravitate, does not all matter, aching, attract all matter?
> So the body of me to all I meet or know.

What can be more mechanical? The difference between life and matter is that life, living things, living creatures, have the instinct of turning right away from *some* matter, and of blissfully ignoring the bulk of most matter, and of turning towards only some certain bits of specially selected matter. As for living creatures all helplessly hurtling together into one great snowball, why, most very living creatures spend the greater part of their time getting out of the sight, smell, or sound of the rest of living creatures. Even bees only cluster on their own queen. And that is sickening enough. Fancy all white humanity clustering on one another like a lump of bees.

No, Walt, you give yourself away. Matter *does* gravitate, helplessly. But men are tricky-tricksy, and they shy all sorts of ways.

Matter gravitates because it *is* helpless and mechanical.

And if you gravitate the same, if the body of you gravitates to all you meet or know, why, something must have gone seriously wrong with you. You must have broken your mainspring.

You must have fallen also into mechanization.

Your Moby Dick must be really dead. That lonely phallic monster of the individual you. Dead mentalized.

I only know that my body doesn't by any means gravitate to all I meet or know. I find I can shake hands with a few people. But most I wouldn't touch with a long prop.

Your mainspring is broken, Walt Whitman. The mainspring of your own individuality. And so you run down with a great whirr, merging with everything.

You have killed your isolate Moby Dick. You have mentalized your deep sensual body, and that's the death of it.

I am everything and everything is me and so we're all One in One Identity, like the Mundane Egg, which has been addled quite a while.

> Whoever you are, to endless announcements——
> And of these one and all I weave the song of myself.

Do you? Well then, it just shows you haven't *got* any self. It's a mush, not a woven thing. A hotch-potch, not a tissue. Your self.

Oh, Walter, Walter, what have you done with it? What have you done with yourself? With your own individual self? For it sounds as if it had all leaked out of you, leaked into the universe.

Post-mortem effects. The individuality had leaked out of him.

No, no, don't lay this down to poetry. These are post-mortem effects. And Walt's great poems are really huge fat tomb-plants, great rank graveyard growths.

All that false exuberance. All those lists of things boiled in one pudding-cloth! No, no!

I don't want all those things inside me, thank you.

"I reject nothing," says Walt.

If that is so, one must be a pipe open at both ends, so everything runs through.

Post-mortem effects.

"I embrace ALL," says Whitman. "I weave all things into myself."

Do you really! There can't be much left of *you* when you've done. When you've cooked the awful pudding of One Identity.

"And whoever walks a furlong without sympathy walks to his own funeral dressed in his own shroud."

Take off your hat then, my funeral procession of one is passing.

This awful Whitman. This post-mortem poet. This poet with the private soul leaking out of him all the time. All his privacy leaking out in a sort of dribble, oozing into the universe.

Walt becomes in his own person the whole world, the whole universe, the whole eternity of time, as far as his rather sketchy knowledge of history will carry him, that is. Because to *be* a thing he had to know it. In order to assume the identity of a thing he had to know that thing. He was not able to assume one identity with Charlie Chaplin, for example, because Walt didn't know Charlie. What a pity! He'd have done poems, pæans and what not, Chants, Songs of Cinematernity.

Oh, Charlie, my Charlie, another film is done——

As soon as Walt *knew* a thing, he assumed a One Identity with it. If he knew that an Eskimo sat in a kyak, immediately there was Walt being little and yellow and greasy, sitting in a kyak.

Now will you tell me exactly what a kyak is?

Who is he that demands petty definition? Let him behold me *sitting in a kyak*.

I behold no such thing. I behold a rather fat old man full of a rather senile, self-conscious sensuosity.

DEMOCRACY. EN MASSE. ONE IDENTITY.

The universe, in short, adds up to ONE.

ONE.

1.

Which is Walt.

His poems, *Democracy, En Masse, One Identity*, they are long sums in addition and multiplication, of which the answer is invariably MYSELF.

He reaches the state of ALLNESS.

And what then? It's all empty. Just an empty Allness. An addled egg.

Walt wasn't an Eskimo. A little, yellow, sly, cunning, greasy little Eskimo. And when Walt blandly assumed All-ness, including Eskimoness, unto himself, he was just sucking the wind out of a blown egg-shell, no more. Eskimos are not minor little Walts. They are something that I am not, I know that. Outside the egg of my Allness chuckles the greasy little Eskimo. Outside the egg of Whitman's Allness too.

But Walt wouldn't have it. He was everything and everything was in him. He drove an automobile with a very fierce headlight, along the track of a fixed idea, through the darkness of this world. And he saw everything that way. Just as a motorist does in the night.

I, who happen to be asleep under the bushes in the dark, hoping a snake won't crawl into my neck; I, seeing Walt go by in his great fierce poetic machine, think to myself: What a funny world that fellow sees!

ONE DIRECTION! toots Walt in the car, whizzing along it.

Whereas there are myriads of ways in the dark, not to mention trackless wildernesses, as anyone will know who cares to come off the road—even the Open Road.

ONE DIRECTION! whoops America, and sets off also in an automobile.

ALLNESS! shrieks Walt at a cross-road, going whizz over an unwary Red Indian.

ONE IDENTITY! chants democratic En Masse, pelting behind in motor-cars, oblivious of the corpses under the wheels.

God save me, I feel like creeping down a rabbit hole, to get away from all these automobiles rushing down the ONE IDENTITY track to the goal of ALLNESS.

A woman waits for me——

He might as well have said: "The femaleness waits for my maleness." Oh, beautiful generalization and abstraction! Oh, biological function.

"Athletic mothers of these States——" Muscles and wombs. They needn't have had faces at all.

As I see myself reflected in Nature,
As I see through a mist, One with inexpressible completeness,
     sanity, beauty,
See the bent head, and arms folded over the breast, the Female
     I see.

Everything was female to him: even himself. Nature just one great function.

This is the nucleus—after the child is born of woman, man is
    born of woman,
This is the bath of birth, the merge of small and large, and the
    outlet again——

"The Female I see——"
If I'd been one of his women, I'd have given him Female, with a flea in his ear.

Always wanting to merge himself into the womb of something or other.
"The Female I see——"
Anything, so long as he could merge himself.
Just a horror. A sort of white flux.
Post-mortem effects.

He found, as all men find, that you can't really merge in a woman, though you may go a long way. You can't manage the last bit. So you have to give it up, and try elsewhere if you *insist* on merging.

In *Calamus* he changes his tune. He doesn't shout and thump and exult any more. He begins to hesitate, reluctant, wistful.

The strange calamus has its pink-tinged root by the pond, and it sends up its leaves of comradeship, comrades from one root, without the intervention of woman, the female.

So he sings of the mystery of manly love, the love of comrades. Over and over he says the same thing: the new world will be built on the love of comrades, the new great dynamic of life will be manly love. Out of this manly love will come the inspiration for the future.

Will it though? Will it?

Comradeship! Comrades! This is to be the new Democracy of Comrades. This is the new cohering principle in the world: Comradeship.

Is it? Are you sure?

It is the cohering principle of true soldiery, we are told in *Drum Taps*. It is the cohering principle in the new unison for creative activity. And it is extreme and alone, touching the confines of death. Something terrible to bear, terrible to be responsible for. Even Walt Whitman felt it. The soul's last and most poignant responsibility, the responsibility of comradeship, of manly love.

Yet you are beautiful to me, you faint-tinged roots, you make
    me think of death.
Death is beautiful from you (what indeed is finally beautiful
    except death and love?)
I think it is not for life I am chanting here my chant of lovers,
    I think it must be for death,
For how calm, how solemn it grows to ascend to the atmosphere
    of lovers,
Death or life, I am then indifferent, my soul declines to prefer
(I am not sure but the high soul of lovers welcomes death most)
Indeed, O death, I think now these leaves mean precisely the
    same as you mean——

This is strange, from the exultant Walt.
Death!
Death is now his chant! Death!
Merging! And Death! Which is the final merge.
The great merge into the womb. Woman.
And after that, the merge of comrades: man-for-man love.
And almost immediately with this, death, the final merge of death.
There you have the progression of merging. For the great mergers, woman at last becomes inadequate. For those who love to extremes. Woman is inadequate for the last merging. So the next step is the merging of man-for-man love. And this is on the brink of death. It slides over into death.
David and Jonathan. And the death of Jonathan.
It always slides into death.
The love of comrades.
Merging.
So that if the new Democracy is to be based on the love of comrades, it will be based on death too. It will slip so soon into death.
The last merging. The last Democracy. The last love. The love of comrades.

Fatality. And fatality.

Whitman would not have been the great poet he is if he had not taken the last steps and looked over into death. Death, the last merging, that was the goal of his manhood.

To the mergers, there remains the brief love of comrades, and then Death.

Whereto answering, the sea
Delaying not, hurrying not
Whispered me through the night, very plainly before daybreak,
Lisp'd to me the low and delicious word death,
And again death, death, death, death.
Hissing melodions, neither like the bird nor like my arous'd
    child's heart,
But edging near as privately for me rustling at my feet,
Creeping thence steadily up to my ears and laving me softly all
    over,
Death, death, death, death, death——

Whitman is a very great poet, of the end of life. A very great post-mortem poet, of the transitions of the soul as it loses its integrity. The poet of the soul's last shout and shriek, on the confines of death. *Après moi le déluge.*

But we have all got to die, and disintegrate.

We have got to die in life, too, and disintegrate while we live.

But even then the goal is not death.

Something else will come.

      Out of the cradle endlessly rocking.

We've got to die first, anyhow. And disintegrate while we still live.

Only we know this much: Death is not the *goal.* And Love, and merging, are now only part of the death-process. Comradeship—part of the death-process. Democracy—part of the death-process. The new Democracy—the brink of death. One Identity—death itself.

We have died, and we are still disintegrating.

But It is finished.

Consummatum est.

Whitman, the great poet, has meant so much to me. Whitman, the one man breaking a way ahead. Whitman, the one pioneer. And only Whitman. No English pioneers, no French. No European pioneer-poets. In Europe the would-be pioneers are mere innovators. The same in America. Ahead of Whitman, nothing. Ahead of all poets, pioneering into the wilderness of unopened life, Whitman. Beyond him, none. His wide, strange camp at the end of the great high-road. And lots of new little poets camping on Whitman's camping ground now. But none going really beyond. Because Whitman's camp is at the end of the road, and on the edge of a great precipice. Over the precipice, blue distances, and the blue hollow of the future. But there is no way down. It is a dead end.

Pisgah. Pisgah sights. And Death. Whitman like a strange, modern, American Moses. Fearfully mistaken. And yet the great leader.

The essential function of art is moral. Not aesthetic, not decorative, not pastime and recreation. But moral. The essential function of art is moral.

But a passionate, implicit morality, not didactic. A morality which changes the blood, rather than the mind. Changes the blood first. The mind follows later, in the wake.

Now Whitman was a great moralist. He was a great leader. He was a great changer of the blood in the veins of men.

Surely it is especially true of American art, that it is all essentially moral. Hawthorne, Poe, Longfellow, Emerson, Melville: it is the moral issue which engages them. They all feel uneasy about the old morality. Sensuously, passionally, they all attack the old morality. But they know nothing better, mentally. Therefore they give tight mental allegiance to a morality which all their passion goes to destroy. Hence the duplicity which is the fatal flaw in them: most fatal in the most perfect American work of art, *The Scarlet Letter*. Tight mental allegiance given to a morality which the passional self repudiates.

Whitman was the first to break the mental allegiance. He

was the first to smash the old moral conception that the soul of man is something "superior" and "above" the flesh. Even Emerson still maintained this tiresome "superiority" of the soul. Even Melville could not get over it. Whitman was the first heroic seer to seize the soul by the scruff of her neck and plant her down among the potsherds.

"There!" he said to the soul. "Stay there!"

Stay there. Stay in the flesh. Stay in the limbs and lips and in the belly. Stay in the breast and womb. Stay there, O Soul, where you belong.

Stay in the dark limbs of Negroes. Stay in the body of the prostitute. Stay in the sick flesh of the syphilitic. Stay in the marsh where the calamus grows. Stay there, Soul, where you belong.

The Open Road. The great home of the Soul is the open road. Not heaven, not paradise. Not "above." Not even "within." The soul is neither "above" nor "within." It is a wayfarer down the open road.

Not by meditating. Not by fasting. Not by exploring heaven after heaven, inwardly, in the manner of the great mystics. Not by exaltation. Not by ecstasy. Not by any of these ways does the soul come into her own.

Only by taking the open road.

Not through charity. Not through sacrifice. Not even through love. Not through good works. Not through these does the soul accomplish herself.

Only through the journey down the open road.

The journey itself, down the open road. Exposed to full contact. On two slow feet. Meeting whatever comes down the open road. In company with those that drift in the same measure along the same way. Towards no goal. Always the open road.

Having no known direction even. Only the soul remaining true to herself in her going.

Meeting all the other wayfarers along the road. And how? How meet them, and how pass? With sympathy, says Whitman. Sympathy. He does not say love. He says sympathy. Feeling with. Feel with them as they feel with themselves. Catching the vibration of their soul and flesh as we pass.

It is a new great doctrine. A doctrine of life. A new great morality. A morality of actual living, not of salvation. Europe has never got beyond the morality of salvation. America to this day is deathly sick with saviorism. But Whitman, the greatest and the first and the only American teacher, was no Savior. His morality was no morality of salvation. His was a morality of the soul living her life, not saving herself. Accepting the contact with other souls along the open way, as they lived their lives. Never trying to save them. As leave try to arrest them and throw them in jail. The soul living her life along the incarnate mystery of the open road.

This was Whitman. And the true rhythm of the American continent speaking out in him. He is the first white aboriginal.

"In my Father's house are many mansions."

"No," said Whitman. "Keep out of mansions. A mansion may be heaven on earth, but you might as well be dead. Strictly avoid mansions. The soul is herself when she is going on foot down the open road."

It is the American heroic message. The soul is not to pile up defenses round herself. She is not to withdraw and seek her heavens inwardly, in mystical ecstasies. She is not to cry to some God beyond, for salvation. She is to go down the open road, as the road opens, into the unknown, keeping company with those whose soul draws them near to her, accomplishing nothing save the journey, and the works incident to the journey, in the long life-travel into the unknown, the soul in her subtle sympathies accomplishing herself by the way.

This is Whitman's essential message. The heroic message of the American future. It is the inspiration of thousands of Americans today, the best souls of today, men and women. And it is a message that only in America can be fully understood, finally accepted.

Then Whitman's mistake. The mistake of his interpretation of his watchword: Sympathy. The mystery of SYMPATHY. He still confounded it with Jesus' LOVE, and with Paul's CHARITY. Whitman, like all the rest of us, was at the end of the great emotional highway of Love. And be-

cause he couldn't help himself, he carried on his Open
Road as a prolongation of the emotional highway of Love,
beyond Calvary. The highway of Love ends at the foot of
the Cross. There is no beyond. It was a hopeless attempt to
prolong the highway of love.

He didn't follow his Sympathy. Try as he might, he
kept on automatically interpreting it as Love, as Charity.
Merging!

This merging, *en masse,* One Identity, Myself monomania
was a carry-over from the old Love idea. It was carrying the
idea of Love to its logical physical conclusion. Like Flaubert
and the leper. The decree of unqualified Charity, as the
soul's one means of salvation, still in force.

Now Whitman wanted his soul to save itself; *he* didn't
want to save it. Therefore he did not need the great Christian receipt for saving the soul. He needed to supersede the
Christian Charity, the Christian Love, within himself, in
order to give his Soul her last freedom. The high-road of
Love is no Open Road. It is a narrow, tight way, where the
soul walks hemmed in between compulsions.

Whitman wanted to take his Soul down the open road.
And he failed in so far as he failed to get out of the old rut
of Salvation. He forced his Soul to the edge of a cliff, and
he looked down into death. And there he camped, powerless.
He had carried out his Sympathy as an extension of Love
and Charity. And it had brought him almost to madness
and soul-death. It gave him his forced, unhealthy, post-
mortem quality.

His message was really the opposite of Henley's rant:

> I am the master of my fate,
> I am the captain of my soul.

Whitman's essential message was the Open Road. The leaving of the soul free unto herself, the leaving of his fate to
her and to the loom of the open road. Which is the bravest
doctrine man has ever proposed to himself.

Alas, he didn't quite carry it out. He couldn't quite break
the old maddening bond of the love-compulsion; he couldn't

quite get out of the rut of the charity habit—for Love and Charity have degenerated now into habit: a bad habit.

Whitman said Sympathy. If only he had stuck to it! Because Sympathy means feeling with, not feeling for. He kept on having a passionate feeling *for* the Negro slave, or the prostitute, or the syphilitic—which is merging. A sinking of Walt Whitman's soul in the souls of these others.

He wasn't keeping to his open road. He was forcing his soul down an old rut. He wasn't leaving her free. He was forcing her into other people's circumstances.

Supposing he had felt true sympathy with the Negro slave? He would have felt *with* the Negro slave. Sympathy —compassion—which is partaking of the passion which was in the soul of the Negro slave.

What was the feeling in the Negro's soul?

"Ah, I am a slave! Ah, it is bad to be a slave! I must free myself. My soul will die unless she frees herself. My soul says I must free myself."

Whitman came along, and saw the slave, and said to himself: "That Negro slave is a man like myself. We share the same identity. And he is bleeding with wounds. Oh, oh, is it not myself who am also bleeding with wounds?"

This was not *sympathy*. It was merging and self-sacrifice. "Bear ye one another's burdens": "Love thy neighbor as thyself": "Whatsoever ye do unto him, ye do unto me."

If Whitman had truly *sympathized,* he would have said: "That Negro slave suffers from slavery. He wants to free himself. His soul wants to free him. He has wounds, but they are the price of freedom. The soul has a long journey from slavery to freedom. If I can help him I will: I will not take over his wounds and his slavery to myself. But I will help him fight the power that enslaves him when he wants to be free, if he wants my help, since I see in his face that he needs to be free. But even when he is free, his soul has many journeys down the open road, before it is a free soul."

And of the prostitute Whitman would have said:

"Look at that prostitute! Her nature has turned evil under her mental lust for prostitution. She has lost her soul. She knows it herself. She likes to make men lose their souls.

If she tried to make me lose my soul, I would kill her. I wish she may die."

But of another prostitute he would have said:

"Look! She is fascinated by the Priapic mysteries. Look, she will soon be worn to death by the Priapic usage. It is the way of her soul. She wishes it so."

Of the syphilitic he would say:

"Look! She wants to infect all men with syphilis. We ought to kill her."

And of still another syphilitic:

"Look! She has a horror of her syphilis. If she looks my way I will help her to get cured."

This is sympathy. The soul judging for herself, and preserving her own integrity.

But when, in Flaubert, the man takes the leper to his naked body; when Bubi de Montparnasse takes the girl because he knows she's got syphilis; when Whitman embraces an evil prostitute: that is not sympathy. The evil prostitute has no desire to be embraced with love; so if you sympathize with her, you won't try to embrace her with love. The leper loathes his leprosy, so if you sympathize with him, you'll loathe it too. The evil woman who wishes to infect all men with her syphilis hates you if you haven't got syphilis. If you sympathize, you'll feel her hatred, and you'll hate, too, you'll hate her. Her feeling is hate, and you'll share it. Only your soul will choose the direction of its own hatred.

The soul is a very perfect judge of her own motions, if your mind doesn't dictate to her. Because the mind says Charity! Charity! you don't have to force your soul into kissing lepers or embracing syphilitics. Your lips are the lips of your soul, your body is the body of your soul; your own single, individual soul. That is Whitman's message. And your soul hates syphilis and leprosy. Because it *is* a soul, it hates these things, which are against the soul. And therefore to force the body of your soul into contact with uncleanness is a great violation of your soul. The soul wishes to keep clean and whole. The soul's deepest will is to preserve its own integrity, against the mind and the whole mass of disintegrating forces.

Soul sympathizes with soul. And that which tries to kill my soul, my soul hates. My soul and my body are one. Soul and body wish to keep clean and whole. Only the mind is capable of great perversion. Only the mind tries to drive my soul and body into uncleanness and unwholesomeness.

What my soul loves, I love.

What my soul hates, I hate.

When my soul is stirred with compassion, I am compassionate.

What my soul turns away from, I turn away from.

That is the *true* interpretation of Whitman's creed: the true revelation of his Sympathy.

And my soul takes the open road. She meets the souls that are passing, she goes along with the souls that are going her way. And for one and all, she has sympathy. The sympathy of love, the sympathy of hate, the sympathy of simple proximity; all the subtle sympathizings of the incalculable soul, from the bitterest hate to passionate love.

It is not I who guide my soul to heaven. It is I who am guided by my own soul along the open road, where all men tread. Therefore, I must accept her deep motions of love, or hate, or compassion, or dislike, or indifference. And I must go where she takes me, for my feet and my lips and my body are my soul. It is I who must submit to her.

This is Whitman's message of American democracy.

The true democracy, where soul meets soul, in the open road. Democracy. American democracy where all journey down the open road, and where a soul is known at once in its going. Not by its clothes or appearance. Whitman did away with that. Not by its family name. Not even by its reputation. Whitman and Melville both discounted that. Not by a progression of piety, or by works of Charity. Not by works at all. Not by anything, but just itself. The soul passing unenhanced, passing on foot and being no more than itself. And recognized, and passed by or greeted according to the soul's dictate. If it be a great soul, it will be worshiped in the road.

The love of man and woman: a recognition of souls, and a communion of worship. The love of comrades: a recognition of souls, and a communion of worship. Democracy: a recognition of souls, all down the open road, and a great soul seen in its greatness, as it travels on foot among the rest, down the common way of the living. A glad recognition of souls, and a gladder worship of great and greater souls, because they are the only riches.

Love, and Merging, brought Whitman to the Edge of Death! Death! Death!

But the exultance of his message still remains. Purified of MERGING, purified of MYSELF, the exultant message of American Democracy, of souls in the Open Road, full of glad recognition, full of fierce readiness, full of the joy of worship, when one soul sees a greater soul.

The only riches, the great souls.

LOBO, NEW MEXICO.

Amy Lowell (1874–1925) was a descendant of John
Lowell, a Massachusetts lawyer and judge who was active
in the Revolutionary cause in the last half of the eighteenth
century. He had a son by each of three wives and founded
three lines of Lowells. James Russell Lowell was John
Lowell's grandson in one of these branches; and Amy Lowell
his great-great-granddaughter in another. Miss Lowell published her first book of verse in 1912, and she became one
of the principal promoters of the new poetry movement in
America that was getting under way at that time. In 1922,
she published *A Critical Fable*, a counterpart to and imitation of J. R. Lowell's *Fable for Critics*.

Miss Lowell falls somewhat below her model. Her versification is even worse than Lowell's, and when she allows
herself doggerel digressions, she is even more obscure and
far-fetched. But she does show quite vividly the difference
between the literary activity of Lowell's time and the poetry
boom of her own; and she gives us an interesting glimpse
of the way the new poetry looked to a lady in Brookline,
Mass., who was herself one of its enthusiastic exponents.
Miss Lowell amuses herself by imagining her cousin's horror

at learning that Whitman and Poe now outrank the other poets of his era, and that Emily Dickinson is taken seriously; but it is doubtful whether she did much better in distinguishing among her contemporaries the poets that were to emerge from the poets that were to be forgotten. One would say at the present time—at the risk of becoming the butt of some subsequent writer on the subject—that, among the writers mentioned in the *Fable,* Robinson, Eliot, and Miss Millay were the most likely to figure to our grandsons as first-rate poets of the full stature. In a letter of January 1924, Miss Lowell wrote to Sara Teasdale: "The one omission I am sorry for is Elinor Wylie, but at the time I wrote it—three years ago—she was not so prominent as she has since become." E. E. Cummings and Marianne Moore were only just beginning to appear in the *Dial* at the time Miss Lowell wrote.

In any case, she does rather well with her portraits of literary personalities; and there is about the whole performance—it was what Amy Lowell contributed to that literary reawakening—something of Lowell's exhilaration in the exercise of literary talent and perhaps something more than his courage in championing the cause of poetry.

A Critical Fable was published anonymously as *A Fable for Critics* had been, and Miss Lowell played out a long comedy of pretending that it had been written by someone else—first by Louis Untermeyer, then by Leonard Bacon, then by an imaginary poet whom she had invented for the occasion. She followed Lowell in every detail except in rhyming the name and address of the publisher—complaining that for Houghton Mifflin there existed no rhyme except "pifflin'."

When she makes Lowell speak of

> escaping the tonic arrears
> Of a grief not lived through,

she refers to the death of his first wife. The effect on Lowell's work of this event has been mentioned in the introduction to his essay on Thoreau.

AMY LOWELL

Dear Sir (or Dear Madam) who happen to glance at this

TITLE-PAGE

Printed you'll see to enhance its æsthetic attraction,
Pray buy, if you're able, this excellent bargain:

A CRITICAL FABLE

The book may be read in the light of
A *Sequel* to the "Fable for Critics"

A volume unequaled (or hitherto so) for its quips and digressions on

The Poets of the Day

WITHOUT UNDUE PROFESSIONS, I WOULD SAY THAT THIS TREATISE
IS FULLY AS LIGHT AS THE FORMER, ITS JUDGMENTS AS
CERTAINLY RIGHT AS NEED BE.

A HODGE-PODGE

Delivered primarily in the hope of instilling instruction
so airily that readers may see, in the persons on view,
a peripatetic, poetic *Who's Who.*

An Account of the Times

By

A POKER OF FUN, WITT D., O.S., A.I.

GENTLE READER,

THE book you're about to peruse has only one object, which
is to amuse. If, as over its pages you may chance to potter,
you discover it's rather more pungent and hotter than this
simple pretension might lead one to think, recollect, if you
please, there's a devil in ink; and a critic who starts without
any intention to do more than recount will find his apprehension of the poets running on to minutely-limned
pictures of the men as he sees them. Neither praises nor
strictures were in my design for I tried to elude them; but
a man, plus his writings, must always include them inferentially, even if nothing be stated. As the picture emerges,
the sitter stands rated.

But who would be backward when others have done the
very same thing in a search of pure fun? Sixty-odd years
ago a volume appeared called *A Fable for Critics*, wherein
were ensphered eighteen authors of merit. The poet who
selected them dared many sly prods just because he respected them. What a serious analysis may fail to discover
is often revealed to a funloving lover.

In the volume before you, you will find twenty-one

modern poets popped off 'twixt a laugh and a pun. I have
spared them no squib and no palm, what I give is a cursory
view of them run through a sieve. As I rattle my poets about
faster and faster, each man shakes more certainly into a
master; to my thinking, at least, for their rich native flavor
gives them all so abundant a claim on my favor that I'm
willing to leave them for sixty-odd years and let my great-
grandchildren foot the arrears.

With the poets I've not noticed, there's a chance for a
sequel, and some other critic who thinks himself equal to
the writing may build on my scaffolding gratis; and for
readers, I really cannot calculate his—with his hundreds
of victims he'll sell each edition as fast as it's printed—I'm
no mathematician. Take the Poetry Society's roster of members, brush away all the laymen and leave just the embers
which spark into verse now and then; for equations, let
A. equal the poet and B. his relations; then his wife and
her friends with their "circles" and "clubs"; and the cultural
ladies, impervious to snubs, who get out long programs of
up-to-date readings which are called "very helpful" in the
printed proceedings of some Woman's Club's "most remarkable year" (one wonders sometimes what the poor creatures
hear, for of course they don't read now books are so dear),
and someone's geometry's needed, it's clear, to post up the
total. I'll not volunteer for a task which requires an expert
cashier. For the ladies I've mentioned, who take what they're
told as immaculate gospel in letters of gold, and rather than
buy prefer to be sold, they'll be moved, I believe, to purchase
his anthology which, like Poe, he might call *A Hand-Book
of Conchology*. Since I've got the pearls, he must e'en take
the shells, but the public at large has no knowledge of sells
—see them gape at the lies which every quack tells—and,
as I said before, on the question of vails, if I collar the
kudos, why he'll gorge the sales.

For I really don't think there's one person in ten who
can tell the first-class from the second-class men. If I've
twenty-one poets and he sixty-four, how many will stop
to consider that more of the very same thing means a well-
watered article? In my book, you'll perceive, there isn't a

particle of stuffing or layers of lath to increase the absolute
weight of my poets, piece by piece. Each is wrapped in tin-
foil and set round the core of a box that I've softened with
excelsior which, as everyone knows, is the lightest of packing and exceedingly cheap; so, if money be lacking, you
have only to take a few useless trees, such as laurel, or willow, or bay, and with these make a bundle of shavings as
thick as you please. The foil, I admit, is a good deal more
trouble. To wrap poets round with tin is like hoisting a
bubble with grapples and rope. Do you notice my drift?
You can't pull at your bubbles or teach your poets thrift.
Having done what you can to arrange them precisely—
and, considering their angles, this is hard to do nicely—
you should view them a moment to be sure that no jutting
or oversized head will prevent the box shutting; then, just
at the last, right under the cover, to offset any jars, put a
thick wad of clover. A few little holes may be left here and
there for the egress of words and the ingress of air, and
your poets are quite ready for nailing and mailing. If you're
sure of your press, the rest is plain sailing.

Having read me so far, you will ask, I am certain, for
just a stray peep round the edge of the curtain I have carefully hung up between us, but this is, Gentle Reader, the
one of all my prejudices I would not depart from by even
a tittle. Suppose, for a moment, the author's a little just-
out-of-the-egg sort of fellow—why then, would you care
half a jot what fell from his pen? Supposing, for naturally
you must suppose at least something or other, he's (under
the rose) a personage proper, whose judgments are wont to
sway many opinions, would you dare to confront so seasoned
a reasoning with your own reflections?

Where's the fun of a book if you can't take objections to
this and to that, call the author a zany, and in doing so
prove to yourself what a brainy person you are, with a tribe
of convictions which only malicious folk speak of as fictions?

Have I labored my point? You'll enjoy me the more if
you hazard a guess between every score or so lines. Why,
it's endless; you'll see in a twinkling how exciting a book
can be when you've no inkling as to who, or to why, or to

whether, or what, the author may be. If it fall to your lot
to unmask him, how deeply you'll relish the jest. No, Kind
Reader, I cannot fulfill your request.

Think again of my poets, each one will be lying in wait
with some sharp, eager weapon. For dying—why, all in good
time, but not plunked on the head by a furious poet who's
disliked what I said. They're all sure to dislike the particular
parts which deal with their own books, own heads, and
own hearts. All poets are the same in one singular trait:
whatever is said of them, that thing they hate. As I wish
to enjoy a life of some quiet, I refuse to be pestered by
poets on the riot. Having opened my heart, I must seek
to preserve it from every result, even though it deserve it.

Then, like most other writers, I've a scant equanimity and
scarcely can hope to retain my sublimity, in spite of all efforts to show magnanimity, if anyone penetrates my ano-
nymity.

One word more, and I'm silent in *propria persona:* If you,
who are reading, should chance to be owner of the volume
in hand and a poet comes to call, fling it into the fire or
over the wall, put it into your work-basket, under your seat;
but, whatever you do, don't permit him to see it.

With which parting remark, I close my introduction and
leave you the book without farther obstruction, only wishing
you joy of my modest production.

A CRITICAL FABLE

THERE are few things so futile, and few so amusing,
As a peaceful and purposeless sort of perusing
Of old random jottings set down in a blank-book
You've unearthed from a drawer as you looked for your
    bank-book,
Or a knife, or a paper of pins, or some string.
The truth is, of course, you'd forgotten the thing,
And all those most vitally important matters
You'd preserved in its pages, just so many spatters
The wheel of your life kicked up in its going

Now hard as caked clay which nothing can grow in.
You raved over Browning, you discovered Euripides,
You devoured all volumes from which you could snip idees
(No one need be surprised if I use the vernacular
Whenever it fits with my text. It's spectacular.
And what smacks of the soil is always tentacular.)—
Astronomy, botany, paleontology—
At least you acquired their strange phraseology
And sprinkled it over your pages in splendid
Profusion because that was what learned men did.
Having one day observed daffodils in a breeze,
You remarked as a brand-new impression that these
Were beautiful objects; you filled quite two pages
With extracts from all those esteemed personages
Whose sayings are found to their last adumbrations
In any respectable book of quotations.
You heard *Pelléas* and returned in a stutter
Of rainbows, and bomb-shells, and thin bread and butter;
And once every twenty-odd entries or so
You recorded a fact it was worth while to know.
At least that was my blank-book, but one of the "odds"
Gave my memory two or three violent prods.
All it said was, "A gentleman taking a walk
Joined me, and we had a most interesting talk."
We certainly did, that day is as clear
As though the whole circumstance happened this year.
But when it did happen I really can't say,
The note is undated, except it says "May."
Put it, then, when you please, whether last year or next
Doesn't matter a rap, and I shall not be vext
If you think I just dreamt it, it swings in my mind
Without root or grapple, a silvery kind
Of antique recollection, that's all I can say.
The sun shone—I remember the scattering way
It shot over the water. I stood by the river.
The plane-trees were just leaving out, and a shiver
Of sunshine and shadow twitched over the grass.
I was poking at something which glittered like glass
With my stick when he joined me and stopped, and his stick

Helped mine to dig up a long bottle-neck, thick,
Brown, and unctuous with memories of cool yellow wine
From some pre-bellum vineyard on the banks of the Rhine:
Berncastler Doctor, perhaps, or *Rüdesheimer*,
Liebfraumilch—could nomenclature ere be sublimer?
Our dear cousins German are so deftly romantic!
Where else in the world could you meet such an antic
Idea, such a sentiment oily to dripping?
The pot-bellied humbugs deserved a good whipping,
With their hands dropping blood and their noses a-sniffle
At some beautiful thought which burns down to mere piffle.
As I rubbed off the dirt (with my handkerchief mainly)
I may have said this, for he answered profanely,
"But their wine was damned good!" I dispensed from
        replying,
His remark held a truth I was far from denying.
The gentleman seemed not to notice my silence.
"Could you tell me," said he, "if that place a short mile
        hence
Is really Mt. Auburn?" I said that it was,
And went on to observe I had never had cause
To enter its precincts. "Why should you?" he said.
"The living have nothing to say to the dead.
The fact is entirely the other way round,
The dead do the speaking, the living are wound
In the coil of their words." Here I greatly demurred.
His expression provoked me to utter absurd
Refutations. "In America," I began, with bombast—
"Tut! Tut!" the old gentleman smiled, "not so fast.
Fold your wings, young spread-eagle, I merely have stated
That the worth of the living is much overrated.
I was young once myself some few decades ago,
And I lived hereabouts, so I really should know.
This parkway, for instance, is simply man's cheating
Himself to believe he is once more repeating
A loveliness ruthlessly uptorn and lost.
Those motor-horns, now, do you really dare boast
That they please you as marsh-larks' and bobolinks' songs
        would?

That shaven grass shore, is it really so good
As the meadows which used to be here, and these plane-
    trees,
Are they half as delightful as those weather-vane trees,
The poplars? I grant you they're quaint, and can please
Like an old gouache picture of some Genevese
Lake-bordering highway; but it is just these
Trans-Atlantic urbanities which crowd out the flavor,
The old native lushness and running-wild savor,
Of mulleins, and choke-cherries in a confusion
So dire that only small boys dared intrusion;
Beyond, where there certainly wasn't a shore,
Just tufted marsh grass for an acre or more
Treading shiftily into the river and drowned
When the high Spring tides turned inconveniently round,
And on the tall grass-sprays, as likely as not,
Red-winged blackbirds, a score of them, all in one spot.
This place had the taste which a boy feels who grapples
With the season's first puckery, bitter-green apples.
Regardless of consequence, he devours and crams on.
Does maturity get the same joy from a damson?
But we, with our marshes, were more certainly urban
Than you with your brummagem, gilded suburban,
Which you wear like a hired theatrical turban.
You move and you act like folk in a play
All carefully drilled to walk the same way.
Just look at this bottle, we were free in my time,
But I think you are free of nothing but rhyme."
Now here was a thing which was not to be stood,
Poking fun at a soul just escaped from the wood
Like a leaf freshly burst from the bark of its twig.
"At least," I said hotly, "we are not a mere sprig
From an overseas' bush, and we don't care a fig
For a dozen dead worthies of classic humdrum,
And each one no bigger than Hop-o'-my-thumb
To our eyes. Why, the curse of their damned rhetoric
Hangs over our writers like a schoolmaster's stick."
Here I caught a few words like "the dead and the quick."
I admit I was stung by his imperturbability

And the hint in his eyes of suppressed risibility.
"We are breaking away..." Here he tossed up the bottle,
Or the poor jagged neck which was left of the hot Hell
Container, as I think Mr. Volstead might say.
How thankful I am I preceded his day
And remember the lovely, suave lines of these flasks.
To piece them together will be one of the tasks
Of thirty-third century museum curators,
Subsidized and applauded by keen legislators.
It flashed in the sun for an instant or two,
And we watched it in silence as men always do
Things that soar, then it turned and fell in chaotic
Uprisings of spray from a sudden aquatic
Suppression beneath the waves of the Charles.
"Yet that, like so much, is but one of the snarls,"
He dusted his fingers. "And if a man flings
His tangles in air, there are so many strings
To a single cat's-cradle of impulse, who knows
When you pull at one end where the other end goes.
We were worthy, respectable, humdrum, quite so,
An admirable portrait of one Edgar Poe."
"Oh, Poe was a bird of a different feather,
We always rank him and Walt Whitman together."
"You do?" The old gentleman tugged at his whisker.
"I could scarcely myself have imagined a brisker
Sarcasm than that to set down in my *Fable*.
I did what I could, but I scarcely was able
To throw leaves of grass to Poe's raven as sops
For his Cerberus master, who would be mad as hops
At a hint of your excellent juxtaposition,
Since that book was not yet in its first slim edition.
You remember I said that Poe was three parts genius.
As to Whitman, can you think of an action more heinous
Than to write the same book every two or three years?
It's enough to reduce any author to tears
At the thought of this crime to the writing fraternity.
A monstrous, continual, delaying paternity.
But I wax somewhat hot, let's have done with the fellows.
Your strange estimation has made me quite jealous

For those of my time whose secure reputations
Gave us no concern. These are trifling vexations,
But they itch my esteem. Is there really not one
You sincerely admire?" "Yes, Miss Dickinson,"
I hastily answered. At this he stopped dead
In his walk and his eyes seemed to pop from his head.
"What," he thundered, "that prim and perverse little person
Without an idea you could hang up a verse on!
Wentworth Higginson did what he could, his tuition
Was ardent, unwearied, but bore no fruition.
You amaze me, young man, where are Longfellow, Lowell,
With Whittier, Bryant, and Holmes? Do you know well
The works of these men? What of Washington Irving,
And Emerson and Hawthorne, are they not deserving
A tithe of your upstart, unfledged admiration?
In the name of the Furies, what's come to the nation!"
Here I thought it was prudent to say, as to prose
I was perfectly willing to hand him the rose.
But I could not admit that our poets were so backward.
I thought, if he knew them, he'd see they'd a knack would
Command his respect. For the matter of liking,
The men he had mentioned might be each a Viking,
While we, very probably, were merely the skippers
Of some rather lively and smartish tea-clippers;
Or, to put it in terms somewhat more up to date,
Our steamers and aeroplanes might be first-rate
As carriers for a particular freight.
Each time for its heroes, and he must excuse
The terms I employed, I'd not meant to abuse
Our forerunners, but only to speak of a preference—
Anno Domini merely. So classic a reference
Should cool him, I thought. Here I went on to better a
Most happy allusion, and continued—*et cætera*.
I will not repeat all the soothing remarks
With which I endeavored to smother the sparks
Of his anger. Suffice it to say I succeeded
In clouding the issue of what had preceded.
I enjoyed it myself and I almost think he did.
I admit there was something a trifle pragmatical

In my method, but who wants the truth mathematical?
It sours good talk as thunder does cream.
I ignore, for the nonce, a disquieting gleam
In his eye. "But your critics," he answered demurely,
"For your poets, by and by; with your critics you surely
Surpass what we did. I was not fond of critics;
If I rightly remember, I gave them some sly ticks.
I called them, I think, poor broken-kneed hacks."
"We've advanced," I replied, "to the office boot-blacks.
We are quite democratic, and the newspapers think
One man is as good as another in ink.
The fluid that's paid for at so much a sprinkling
Is a guaranteed product, quite free of all inkling
That standardized morals, and standardized criticisms,
And a standardized series of cut-and-dried witticisms,
Are poor stuff to purvey as a full reading ration,
Though they suit to a T the views of a nation
Which fears nothing so much as a personal equation.
Subscribers demand that their thoughts be retailed to them
So often and plenteously that they become nailed to them
And when traveling are lost if their journal's not mailed
        to them.
By this safe and sane rule our newspapers get on
Without any gambling, since there's nothing to bet on.
Of course I refer to things of import
Such as stock-exchange news, murders, fashions, and sport,
With a smattering of politics, garbled to fit
Editorial policy; if they admit
Puerilities like music and art, these are extras
Put in to augment, by means of a dexterous
Metropolitan appearance, their own circulation,
For a paper's first duty is self-preservation.
If they will run book columns, why someone must feed
        them,
And, after all, few take the trouble to read them.
With a pastepot and scissors to cut up his betters
And any young numskull is equal to letters.
He scans what the publisher says on the jacket,
Then the first paragraph and the last, and the packet

Goes off to the second-hand bookshop, the bunch
Polished off in the minutes he's waiting for lunch.
I believe there's no record of anyone feeling
As he pockets his pay that he may have been stealing.
The thing would be murder, but that time has gone by
When an author can be made or marred by such fry.
Some good paper is spoiled, that's the long and the short
    of it."
Here I watched the old gentleman to see what he thought
    of it.
"These reviews which you speak of have one great ad-
    vantage,"
He remarked, "they are brief. In our less petulant age
They had not that merit. But I see we agree
On essentials. Yet we had a very few men
Who wielded a passably powerful pen."
"And one woman," I slyly put in. He grimaced.
"That's the second you've dug up and greatly displaced.
Since you criticize thus, do I err if I doubt
Whether you are the boot-black on his afternoon out?"
Fairly touched and I owned it, and let Margaret Fuller
Slide softly to limbo. 'Twas unmanly to rule her
Out of count in this way, but the fish I must fry
Required considerable diplomacy
To keep in the pan and not drop in the fire.
'Twas an expert affair, and might shortly require
I knew not what effort to induce him to grant
That whatever we are is worth more than we aren't.
So I instantly seized on his "very few men"
And assured him that we also, now and again,
Found a youth who was willing to write good reviews
While learning to tickle the publishers' views
And make them believe he was worth-while to back.
"The thing after all is a question of knack,
Ten to one if you have it you turn out a quack;
If you don't, and win through, you've arrived without doubt,
But the luck's on your side if you're not quite worn out."
"Good old world," he remarked, as he prodded the ground
With the point of his cane, "I observe it goes round

In the same soothing, punctual way. This pastiche
Of the quite unfamiliar is merely a bleach,
A veneer, acid-bitten, on a color we knew.
By the way, when it's finished, who reads your review?"
"The fellow who wrote it, on all those occasions
When his fine self-esteem has received some abrasions.
Then the fellow who's written about cons the thing
Over several times in a day till the sting
Of its strictures becomes just the usual pedantic
Outpouring, and its granules of praise grow gigantic.
Once acquire this excellent trick for benumbing
What you don't want to hear by an extra loud strumming
On the things which you do and you fast are becoming
A real going author. Then there are the gentry
Who must read reviews to fill out an entry
In next week's advertisement; and others peruse
The paper with care to note down its abuse
Of their dear brother writer, and suck up each injurious
Phrase to retail with a finely luxurious
Hypocritical pretense of its being unsuitable,
While all the time showing it quite irrefutable.
Then there are the sisters, and cousins, and aunts
Of the writer and wrote about; some sycophants
Who pry into favor by announcing they've read it,
And praise or deride to heighten their credit
With the interested person. There are others who edit
Gossip columns, and who must go through at a deadheat
The news of the day for the spicy tidbits
And who greatly prefer the more virulent hits.
By the time we are through, a fairly large public
Has skimmed through the paper." He gave a quick flick
To a stone which arose with a circular twist
And plopped into the river. "But if I insist
On your people of parts?" "Oh, they do not exist,"
I assured him, "or only as sparsely as daisies
In city back yards. And if one of them raises
His voice it is drowned in the whirligig hazes
Of mob murmurings. If these men hold the key
To the spacious demesne known as posterity

The gate must have shrunk to a postern, I think.
Everyone worth his salt glues his eye to the chink
'Twixt the frame and the door, but it's long to keep looking
With never a chance to get even a hook in
And pull open a door where it's 'Skeletons Only.'
A notice designed to make anyone lonely.
It stares over the gate in huge letters of red:
'No person admitted until he is dead.'
Small wonder if some of them cannot hold out.
As they dwindle away, the watchers, no doubt,
Feel a sort of cold envy creep through their contempt.
Then perhaps the door opens and one is exempt,
Gone over to dust and to fame. As it slams,
The requiem fraternal, a chorus of 'Damns!'
Cracks the silence a moment. More still break away,
But the shriveled remainder waits each one his day.
It takes marvelous force and persistence to tarry on
When your own special corpse may be counted as carrion
And left where it lies to await decomposing
While that devilish door shows no sign of unclosing.
These custodians of keys are ill to rely on
As the last Day of Judgment to the followers of Zion.
There are folk who dress up in the very same guise
And boast of a power that's nothing but lies.
They shout from their chosen, particular steeple
Of some weekly review: 'We are surely the people!
We know what posterity wants, for we know
What other posterities have wanted, and so
We affirm confidently the true cut and fashion
Which the future will certainly dote on with passion.
There is no need at all of making a fuss
For all generations are exactly like us.
We represent that which is known as the *Vox
Populi,* species *Intelligentsia,* or Cocks
Of the Walk on the Dunghill of High Erudition,
Referred to more elegantly as Fields Elysian.'
The matter of clocks may be readily dropped,
Every Ph.D. knows that they long ago stopped.
What are colleges for with their dignified massiveness

But just to reduce all time-pieces to passiveness."
"The picture you draw does not greatly attract
One who seeks for the absolute even in fact.
That fanciful bit you put in about clocks
Borders rather too smartly upon paradox.
We had a few poets, and we had a few colleges,
And something like half of your bundle of knowledges.
We delivered our lectures and wrote our lampoons,
And I venture to say that the fire-balloons
Of our verse made as lively a sputter as yours.
If things are so changed, what, pray, is the cause?"
I groaned. Poor old gentleman, should I be tempted
To tell him the fault was that he had preëmpted,
He and the others, the country's small stock
Of imagination? The real stumbling-block
Was the way they stood up like Blake's angels, a chorus
Of geniuses over our heads, no more porous
Than so much stretched silk; rain, sun, and the stellar
Effulgences balked by our national umbrella
Of perished celebrities. To mention a trifling
Fact, underneath them the air's somewhat stifling.
Youthful lungs need ozone and, considering the tent,
No man can be blamed if he punches a rent
With his fist in the stiff, silken web if he can.
A feat, I assured him, more horrible than
Cataclysmic tidewaters or Vesuvian
Explosions to all those quaint, straitly-laced folk
Who allow a man only the freedom to choke.
"We may buckle the winds and rip open the sea,
But we mayn't poke a finger at authority."
"A nursery game," the old man spoke benignly,
"To all schoolboys, convention's a matter divinely
Ordained, and the youngster who feels himself bold enough
To step out of the ring will soon find himself cold enough.
To be chips from a hardened old tree may be crippling,
But it's nothing compared to the lot of the stripling.
For the sake of the argument, let us agree
That we were the last surge of life which the tree
Could produce, that our heart-wood was long ago rotted,

Our sap-wood decaying, and all our roots spotted
With fungus; the Spring of our flourishing over,
The first Winter storm would most likely have rove a
Great cleft through the trunk, and the next year's outleaving
Would unbalance the whole without hope of retrieving.
The gentlest of breezes would then send it crashing.
Good luck to the striplings if they escape smashing.
When an oak, having lasted its time, is once thrown,
What is left are the acorns it cast, and these grown
Are the forest of saplings in which it lies prone.
But 'twould be a dull acorn who should dare to declare
It was sprung only from earth's connection with air,
The miraculous birth of a marvelous rut.
Such an acorn indeed would be a poor nut."
He quickened his steps and I followed along,
Listening partly to him, and partly to the song
Of the little light leaves in the plane-trees. Said he,
Stopping short quite abruptly, "I think it should be
Somewhere about here that a house I once knew
Used to stand. It was not much to look at, 'tis true,
But its elms were superb and it had a fine view
Of the river. A friend of mine owned it, indeed
He was born here and loved every tree, every weed.
Circumstance loosed his moorings, but he came back to die,
To envisage the past with a chill, older eye,
And dwelt a few years with the bitter-sweet ghosts
Of his earlier dreams, with the shadowless hosts
Of the things he had never brought farther than planning.
How often he wished there were some way of spanning
The past and the present, to go back again
And drink to the dregs the austere cup of pain.
Instead, he allowed the nepenthe of change
To smother that loneliness by which the range
Of his soul might have reached to some highest achieve-
      ment
Through the vision won out of a grievous bereavement.
He'd a wit and a fancy, a hint of some deepness,
An excellent humor quite unmarred by cheapness,
But somehow his work never got beyond soundings.

I wonder sometimes if it was his surroundings
Or the fact that he fled them. With a grim taciturnity,
He admitted no masterpiece owed its paternity
To him. Now they've pulled down his house, I suppose.
Thistles spring up and die, and the thistledown goes
Anywhere the wind blows it." "Wait," I said, "if you mean
James Lowell's house, 'Elmwood,' you can see it between
That brick porch and that window, and those are its chim-
        neys.
The grounds are cut up and built over, their trimness
Is due to that cluster of very new houses.
In its rather bedraggled condition, it rouses
My ire each time I come anywhere near it.
It deserved better treatment." "I fear it! I fear it!"
He murmured. "Was it lack of success, or those years
I spent in escaping the tonic arrears
Of a grief not lived through. I cannot bear more."
He turned and walked rapidly down to the shore
Of the river and seated himself on the bank.
Many minutes went by, then he asked me point-blank
Who were the young poets of the day. "Since my mood
Will admit no more sorrowful past, be so good
As to marshal your forces, I shall find it quite pleasant
To stroll for a little with you in the present.
So bring them out, lock, stock, and barrel, the whole of
        them,
I'm really most anxious to get a good toll of them.
Recount me their merits, their foibles and absurdities,
Such a tale is too saccharine without some acerbities."
His gesture of challenge was so debonnaire
I could only accept with as devil-may-care
A grace as I could. But our Ostrogothic
Modern manners, I fear, made me seem sans-culottic,
I know that I felt supremely idiotic.
Still "out of the mouths of the babes and the sucklings,"
And I was prepared with some brave ugly ducklings
I was willing to swear would prove to be swans,
Or, to tone up the metaphor, Bellerophons.
At least they'd no fear of a chase round the paddock

After Pegasus, who "might be lamed by a bad hock
And so easily mounted"—I can hear the malicious
Sneers of the critics when one dare be ambitious
And attempt a bold thing, yet it's hard to decry a
Flight its existence when above you the flyer
Is gyrating and plunging on his way to the zenith,
And he grins the best who at the last grinneth.
But my unknown old friend seemed to need no acquainting
With this style of horseflesh, he would notice my painting,
No chance then at all to confuse him by feinting.
I must prove that my horse had his quota of wings,
Was sound wind and limb, that his sidles and swings
Were no circus parade, that the man who would stride him
Knew perfectly well why he wanted to ride him.
That 'twas bareback or die, that the fellow was game
For whichever result was the end of his aim.
As I pondered, I harbored no little aversion
At having embarked on so great an excursion,
Nothing less, be it said, than his total conversion.
"Come, come," he urged quickly, "you're taking some time
To trot out your up-to-date dabblers in rhyme."
I pouted, I think. "Ha! Ha! you're offended!
Because I said 'dabblers' or because I pretended
Not to know that rhyme's lost its erstwhile predominance?"
I assured him at once that we gave no prominence
To rhyme or the lack of it. To which he said "Good!
We've got somewhere at last; now let's have the whole
    brood
In their rareness and rawness. I am surely no prude,
I shall not be satisfied if you exclude
Any atom of character, any least mood.
Give your men as you see them from their toes to their chin.
Only, for God's sake, my dear fellow, begin."
Since he and I wanted the same thing exactly,
I started to put it quite matter-of-factly.
He had spoken of acorns, so poets in a nutshell
Should please him, I thought, and they're none of them but
    shell.
To hesitate longer would smack of the boyish,

And a prophet's ill served by an attitude coyish,
Like a diffident girl asked to play the piano.
I detest all such feminine ruses, and so
I hitched up my mind as sailors and whalers
Are reported to do with their trousers (why tailors
Should so fashion these garments that this act must precede
Every truly stupendous and heroic deed
I am quite at a loss to surmise). To continue,
I exerted each muscle and braced every sinew
For the duty in hand. In a fiery burst
Which I hoped might be eloquence, I took up the first
Poet I happened to think of, explaining quite clearly
That my order of precedence meant nothing really.
Number ten might be easily rated as equal
To one or fifteen, if we lived for the sequel.
Here I saw with concern he had fixed both his eyes on
That soothing Nirvana we call the horizon.
There was danger of slumber I felt, so embarking
On my story with gusto, I began by remarking
(And here I must add for my just self-esteem
That the minute I spoke he awoke from his dream
And never thereafter did so much as blink,
Though I thought, once or twice, I detected a wink.)
But I'm straying again. I remarked then succinctly,
Without farther preamble:

                              "To name them distinctly,
There's Frost with his blueberry pastures and hills
All peopled by folk who have so many ills
'Tis a business to count 'em, their subtle insanities.
One half are sheer mad, and the others inanities.
He'll paint you a phobia quick as a wink
Stuffed into a hay-mow or tied to a sink.
And then he'll deny, with a certain rich rapture,
The very perversion he's set out to capture.
Were it not for his flowers, and orchards, and skies,
One would think the poor fellow was blind of both eyes
Or had never read Freud, but it's only his joke.
If we're looking for cheer, he's a pig in a poke.

But he's such a good chap, he is welcome to say
Tweedledum's Tweedledee if he's feeling that way.
When he calls a thing yellow and you know it is pink,
Why, you've purchased his book and you're welcome to
    think.
He's a foggy benignity wandering in space
With a stray wisp of moonlight just touching his face,
Descending to earth when a certain condition
Reminds him that even a poet needs nutrition,
Departing thereafter to rarefied distances
Quite unapproachable to those persistencies,
The lovers of Lions, who shout at his tail—
At least so he says—when he comes within hail.
Majestic, remote, a quite beautiful pose,
(Or escape, or indulgence, or all three, who knows?)
Set solidly up in a niche like an oracle
Dispensing replies which he thinks categorical.
No wonder he cleaves to his leafy seclusion,
Barricading his door to unlawful intrusion,
The goal of the fledgling, a god in a thicket,
To be viewed only Tuesdays and Fridays by ticket.
Yet note, if you please, this is but one degree
Of Frost, there are more as you'll presently see,
And some of them are so vexatiously teasing
All this stored heat is needed to keep him from freezing.
Life is dreadfully hard on a man who can see
A rainbow-clad prophet atop of each tree;
To whom every grass-blade's a telephone wire
With Heaven as central and electrifier.
He has only to ring up the switch-board and hear
A poem lightly pattering into his ear,
But he must be in tune or the thing takes a kink,
An imminent lunch-bell puts it all on the blink.
Someone to be seen in the late afternoon
Throws all his poetical thoughts in a swoon.
He can't walk with one foot on Parnassus, and stutter
Along with the other foot deep in the gutter,
As many poets do, all those who have tamely
Submitted to life as men live it, and lamely

Continue to limp, half man-in-the-street,
Half poet-in-the-air. How often we meet
Such fellows, they throng the bohemian centers,
The 'Blue Cats' and 'Pink Moons' those artistic frequenters
Who eat at the house's expense for the fame
Their presence ensures have conceived as a name
Full of rich innuendo. Though why a strange hue
Connected with something—moons pink or cats blue—
Should make it so vicious, I can't see, can you?
These double-paced bardlings are marvels at talking,
But their writing seems curiously given to balking,
A result, like as not, of their manner of walking.
Not so Frost, he divides his life into two pieces,
Keeping one for himself while the other he leases
To various colleges. He's eclectic in choice
And at least half-a-dozen have cause to rejoice
That he's sojourned among them; for his unique duty,
What they pay him to do and regard as their booty,
Is the odd one of being on hand, nothing more.
He's an unexplored mine you know contains ore;
Or rather, he acts as a landscape may do
Which says one thing to me and another to you,
But which all agree is a very fine view.
Such a sight is experience, a wonderful thing
To have looked at and felt. This establishing
Of a poet in a college like a bird in a cage
Is a happy endowment for art which our age
Is the first to have thought of and made quite the rage.
That the poet cannot function while kept as a zoo,
Does not matter at all to the wiseacres who
Invented the scheme. They secure for the year
That desideratum, a high atmosphere.
If the poet who provides it be drained to the pith,
That is nothing to leaving their college a myth,
A tradition, to hand down to all future classes.
A thing and its shadow are one to the masses.
The man's written his poems, now he can recite them;
As for new ones, he is a great fool to invite them,
Notoriety offers a constant repose,

Like a time-honored rose-bush which now bears no rose.
Instead of one poet, we've a score of poetasters.
Are we wise in our method or ignorant wasters?
Frost suffers himself to be bled for the small fry
While Pegasus, never a quiescent palfrey,
Stamps at the hitching-post. Still, I'm not saying
There is really much harm in this lengthy delaying.
There's the other half-year and his telegraph grasses
And no college thrives on a diet of asses;
A man must be sacrificed now and again
To provide for the next generation of men.
So if, once in a while, a real poet is captured
And bled for the future, we should all be enraptured.
The violence done to his own special nature
Is a thing of no moment if he add to the stature
Of a handful of students, and business is booming
For the troubadour poets in the town he's illuming.
They come, called in shoals by the interest he rouses,
And talk of themselves to preposterous houses.
But who, in the end, has the best of the luck,
The migrating birds or the poor decoy duck?
Small surprise, when Commencement has ended the year,
If our poet's first free action is to disappear.
Chained up on a campus creating diurnal
Poetic fine weather must be an eternal
Annoyance, a horror, growing always more biting.
How pleasant his mountains must look, how exciting
The long leisured moments to think, with no gaping
Importunate youths whose lives he is shaping
Forever observing his least little movement.
Why, a bleak desert island would be an improvement
On such an existence. Though we should be proud
That there is such a man to let loose on a crowd
Of young bears, any one of whom may become President,
We should be even prouder to know him a resident
Of our woods and our hills, a neighbor of neighbors,
A singer of countrysides and country labors,
Like a hermit thrush deep in a wood whose fresh fire
Of song burns the whole air to music, and higher

Upsoars till it seems not one voice but a choir—
The choir of his people whose hearths are the altars
Of that deep race-religion which in him never falters,
His life is its worship, his songs are its psalters.
Prophet, seer, psalmist, is the world so importunate
As to leave you no peace even here? You are fortunate
At least to abide, remote as the fables,
In a place much neglected by railroad time-tables.
I promise, for one, when I turn from the wicket,
That the name of your town will not be on my ticket.
You have as much right to protect your seclusion
As any old monk of the order Carthusian,
Though solitude really is but an illusion
As most men find out to their utter confusion.
To speak of seclusion is to think of a man
Who is built on a toally otherwise plan.
I mean, and I rather imagine you know it,
Edwin Arlington Robinson, excellent poet,
And excellent person, but vague as a wood
Gazed into at dusk. His preponderant mood
Is withdrawal, and why? For a man of his stamp,
So conscious of people, it seems odd to scamp
Experience and contact, to live in a hollow
Between the four winds and perpetually swallow
The back draughts of air from a swift forward motion.
It takes a huge strength to withstand all emotion,
But Robinson stays with his feet planted square
In the middle of nothing, the vacuum where
The world's swinging starts and whirls out, where is left
The dead root of movement, an emptiness cleft
In the heart of an aim, of all aims, peering out
At the dust and the grass-blades that swirl all about.
He notes who is here, who is coming along,
Who has passed by alone, who is one of a throng.
He peers with intentness bent all into seeing,
A critical eye finely pointed on being.
He is cruel with dispassion, as though he most dreaded
Some shiver of feeling might yet be imbedded
Within him. And if this occurrence should happen,

He would probably see himself with a fool's cap on
And feel himself sinking to shipwreck at once;
Of the two, much preferring disaster to dunce.
For the dunce is contingent on a sort of a curse
He thinks he is doomed with. A curious, perverse
Undercutting of Fate which decrees him observer
And hoods him in ice from all possible fervor.
The slightest conceivable hint of a thaw
Wounds his conscience as though he had broken a law
He had sworn to uphold. Are there demons in hiding
Within his ice-mail? Can he feel them abiding
A time to break loose and disrupt into tatters
The scheme of existence he has taught himself matters,
A barrier raised betwixt him and his satyrs?
For he has them; his quaint, artificial control
Is a bandage drawn tightly to hold down his soul.
Should a nail or a thorn tear the least little mesh, it
Would let all his nature go leaping in freshet
Overflowing his banks and engulfing his dams
In a flurry of life. But the desolate calms
He has cherished so long would be lost in the slams,
The torrential vortices of a swift current
Exploding in motion. Some uncouth, deterrent
Complex in his make-up enforces recoil
Before the fatigue and the wrench of turmoil.
He compounds with inertia by calling it Fate,
Deeply dreading the rush of emotion in spate,
Distrusting his power to outwit disaster
In the realization that with him fast means faster,
And refusing to see that a turbulent strife
Is the valuable paradox given to life
Which only the few may possess. With the prize
In his hand, he turns sadly away, crucifies
His manhood each day with the old dog's-eared lies,
The heritage, left by those Puritan heirs.
His bogies and satyrs are grandsons of theirs.
Could he see them as fruit-trees distorted by mist,
He might unknot himself from the terrible twist
He has suffered through fear of them. Now, with vicarious

Experience in verse, he cheats all the various
Impulses within him which make him a poet;
But, try as he will, his poems all show it.
His tight little verses an inch in diameter,
His quatrains and whole-book-long tales in pentameter,
With never a hint of what he'd call a sham meter,
Though some people style his kind *ad nauseam* meter—
With gimlets for eyes and a sensitive heart,
All battened down tight in the box of his art,
And we have his rare merits and his strange deficiencies
Which mix to a porridge of peculiar efficiencies.
Admired by everyone dowered with wit,
He has scarcely the qualifications to hit
The unlettered public, but the fact that his name
Is already spotted with the lichens of fame
Opens up a most fecund and pertinent query
And is one of the pedestals on which my theory
Is based: whether now we have not reached the stage
Of a perfectly genuine coming-of-age.
I am willing to swear that when he has retired
His books will be listed as 'reading required,'
And poor sweltering youths taking examinations
Will crown him with the bays of their wild lamentations.
Our beautiful system is to make every course able
To render delight quite sterile through forcible
Insistence upon it. But these are the laurels
With which no man who's not insane ever quarrels.
Perhaps it's as well not to look at the guerdon
Too closely or no one would shoulder the burden
Of being a poet.

     "The next I shall take up
Is a fellow as utterly different in make-up
As you're likely to see if you scour the land
With field-glasses and microscopes. This is Carl Sand-
burg, a strange, gifted creature, as slow as a fog
Just lifting to sunshine, a roughly hewn Gog,
Shorn of his twin Magog, set over the portal
Through which brawls the stream of everything mortal.

Day and night he observes it, this river of men,
With a weary-sweet, unflagging interest, and ten
Times in a day he seeks to detach
Himself from the plinth where he's destined to watch,
And mingle as one of them, mistaking his stature
To be but that generally ordained by nature
For the run of humanity. His miscalculations
Of the possible height to which civilizations
May rightly aspire are constantly leading
Him into positions whence there's no proceeding.
Because he can easily reach to the stars,
He cannot believe that a short arm debars
Any others from doing the same, and declares
His qualifications assuredly theirs.
Endowing each man whom he meets with his own
Stretch and feeling, he takes for the foundation stone
Of his creed the ability to walk cheek by jowl
With the sun, at the same time not losing control
Of feet always set on the earth. It is droll
To hear him announce neither giants nor pigmies
Exist, that there's only one knowable size,
Which by implication's as tall as the skies.
What he feels about souls, he has brought into speech,
But since perfect English is a hard thing to teach
To those brought up without it, he changes his tactics
And declares correct use the hypochondriactics
Of language too timid for red-blooded slang.
This theory of his is a swift boomerang
Overturning his balance and flooring him pell-mell, he
Presents the strange sight of a man on his belly
Proclaiming that all men walk that way from preference
And the manner, though new, must be treated with defer-
    ence.
Since his own natural speech is correct to a dot,
His theory, to use the red-blooded, is 'rot,'
And as man does not wiggle along like a jelly
When he walks, to affect that laid flat on the belly
Is the easiest position to attain locomotion
Must surely be called a preposterous notion.

But what's the poor fellow to do? It is plain
He overtops folk if he stands; once again
It's the hill and Mohammed, since he can't raise the others
He must lie if he'd be the same height as his brothers.
It may weary his readers to see a true poet
Who apparently has not the instinct to know it,
And so burdens his beauty with wild propaganda
That much of his work is a hideous slander
Against his remarkable genius, but scratch it
With a prudent pen-knife and there's nothing to match it
Going on in the whole world today. He has sight
Of a loveliness no man has seen, and a might,
A great flowing power of words to express
Its hugeness and littleness. All the excess
Of his passion for living leaps out from his pen
In a gush of fresh imminence; again and again
We read him to fill our soul's withering lungs
With the wind-over-water sweep which is his tongue's
Particular gift—though I should have said 'prairies,'
Not 'water,' he is no result of the seas,
But in every whiff of him, flat and extended,
A man of the plains, whose horizons are ended
By the upreach of earth to that sky which he touches
And carries off great fragments of in his clutches.
Wood-smoke, and water-smoke rising from runnels
At sunrise, long lines of black smoke from the funnels
Of engines and factories, steel of man's forging
And steel he's forged into; the slow, passive gorging
Of earth with mankind, blood of souls, blood of hearts,
Swallowed into the fields where the sprouting grain parts
A right rail from a left rail, and always asunder
Go marching the fields cleft in two by the wonder
Of man gauging distance as magic and burning it
Under boot-heels or car-wheels and all the time earning it
For the silt of his mind from which a new soil
Is gradually risen. This turgescent coil
Is the crawling of glaciers, the upheave of hills,
The process of making and change, the huge spills
Of watersheds seeking their oceans, the miracle

Of creeping continuance. This is the lyrical
Stuff Sandburg works into something as lazy
And deep as geology planting its clays, he
Makes keenly, unhastingly, as evolution,
And yet, poor blind eagle, he dreams revolution.
With the centuries his if he could but decide
To pocket his picayune, popular pride,
Give up his day-dreams and his tin-penny logic,
Be Gog as God made him and not demagogic,
Sit solidly down with his eyes and his heart,
And a file and a chisel, to fashion great art—
If he would, but will he? It really is vexing
To see such a fellow perpetually flexing
His knees to false idols, a mere artisan
When he might be an artist. Some historian
Of the future will round him up in an abstract
By denouncing the times as too matter-of-fact,
Not observing what might well be seen for the looking
That it's simply a case of not quite enough cooking.
An accredited hero or a dream-blinded sloven
Is entirely a matter of stoking the oven.
The material's certainly A number one,
It will be his own fault if he dies underdone.

"The man whom I next shall bring to the fore
Is becoming, I fear, an impossible bore.
Some few years ago, Minerva mislaid
Her glasses, and unable to see in the shade,
Feeling also, quite naturally, rather afraid
To proclaim that she wore them, like any old maid
Teaching school—for a Goddess is loath to parade
Her antiquity, even as others—she said
No word of the matter at home on Olympus.
A pity, because a very bad *impasse*
Might have so been averted. The handmaids and lackeys,
Who are always possessed of both front door and back keys,
Would have hunted the palace from cellar to roof
And most probably found them not very aloof
From the spot where poor Vulcan, in playing Tartuffe,

Had received a convincing and permanent proof
That the lady was chaste. Indeed, however frigid,
No woman of spirit admits to the rigid
Mathematical count of the years after forty,
And even immortals, though reputed quite 'sporty,'
And figuring time by the so many centuries,
Still scarcely desire to add up the entries
And publish the total. Minerva, then, hid
The fact that she could not quite see what she did,
And since it would give things away to inquire, 'Oh,
She could not do that!' And after a *giro*
Which blindly confused every main street and by-row,
In the end she conferred a great book on a tyro.
The author in question, though an excellent notary,
Could scarcely be classed at that time as a votary
Worth Minerva's attention. But, however unsuitable,
The deed, once accomplished, became quite immutable.
No matter how foolish she felt, the poor Goddess
Must carry it through in a pitiless progress.
For be sure, when her family learnt of her blunder,
Which they very soon did, she'd have welcomed Jove's thun-
    der
To be quit of his really abominable quizzing.
His jokes were caught up by Neptune and sent whizzing
For Vulcan to cap them, and as he was still smarting
Beneath the rebuke she'd not spared him at parting,
He gave her good measure now he'd got the upper
Hand. Then the women joined in; what at supper
Was observed was rehashed for breakfast and dinner,
Even Venus said 'Minnie, you *have* picked a winner!
From all that I hear, your man is verbose.
He'll print in ten volumes, a very large dose
For you to inspire.' 'Oh, Minnie is game,'
Cried Mercury, kind-hearted boy. 'All the same,'
Growled Vulcan, 'if Min can hold out, 'twould be speedier
To imbue him at once with an encyclopedia.'
Here Minerva, in tears which begemmed her found glasses,
Declared her relations were all of them asses,
That she cared not a fig for their tuppenny threats

Having settled the book to be done in vignettes.
The Gods broke out laughing. 'Give Minnie the handle
And not one of you is worth even her sandal,'
Shouted Jove, 'she's arranged for a *succès de scandal.*'
Which she had, and her poet, never doubting the giver,
Wrote steadily on without the least quiver,
And at last, in due course, was published *Spoon River.*
Now having explained the volume's true genesis,
Let me say it is not for a party where tennis is
In order, or bridge. If you like porcupining
Your soul with your conscience, here's a chance for refining
On misery, and since Minerva'd a hand in it
No person need doubt that there's plenty of sand in it.
Of course the thing's genius no matter how squint-eyed,
And the reader who never once weeps must be flint-eyed.
But hey, Mr. Masters, how weary and dreary
You make all your folk! How impossibly smeary
And sticky they are with old amorous contacts,
A series of ticketed, sexual facts
Tucked away, all unwashed, in the ground. Who once told
     you
The great, biological truths with a few
Dirty smudges you've never forgotten, like plasters
Thumbed tight to your mind? They're the trade-mark of
     'Masters.'
Whatever he's writing—Minerva-inspired
As this book, *Spoon River;* or, nervous and tired,
Worrying his public as a dog does a bone
As in *Domesday Book,* done, you'll agree, quite alone—
They all have the stamp of back-alley lust
Which you stand as you can, for stand it you must
If you'd read him at all. I've no wish to cloud over
The fame of a book which, from cover to cover,
Shows the trace of Minerva's most helpful collusion.
The hall-marks of genius are here in profusion.
People swarm through its pages like ants in a hill,
No one's like the others, a personal will
Makes each man what he is and his life what it was.
The modern Balzac? Not at all—the new 'Boz!'

Where the Frenchman employed an urbane moderation,
The Englishman gloried in exaggeration.
But, in spite of his gargoyles, his fine gift of humor
Kept even his quaintness from the taint of ill-rumor.
In a grin of delight, he played tricks with his drawing,
And no matter how far from the real he was yawing,
His object was merely a louder guffawing.
He never believed his grotesques were true pictures
Of life, he knew perfectly well men are mixtures
Of rather more this or a little less that;
No man is pure angel and none is sheer brat.
Where he painted them so, it was done to enhance
Some meaning he wished to make clear; circumstance
Induced him to stress both the gall and the honey,
And no one knew better just when to be funny.
Mr. Masters, quite otherwise, thinks his creations
Reveal abstract truth in their vilest relations.
He sees everyone as the suffering prey
Of some low, hidden instinct, his business to flay
The decency off them and show them all naked,
A few of them zanies, the rest downright wicked.
In all his vast gallery there's but one exception,
And that, I hold, is to have wrought with deception.
If some excellent sense of the really amusing
Had led him to practice a little more fusing
Of the good and the bad, his book had succeeded
In being the great masterpiece we have needed
Ever since the beginning. As it is, his caprice
Has given us only a great Masters' piece.
How Minerva deserted him all through the sequel,
We can easily see if we hunt for an equal
Success in the list of his subsequent works.
Each hitches along in a series of jerks.
He tries lyrics, and ballads, and novels in verse,
But lacks always the wit to return to the terse.
In the last, *Domesday Book,* he relied upon Browning
To replace Minerva and keep him from drowning.
Shallow hope! He achieved a self-hitting satire,

Mr. Masters looked so odd in Browning's attire.
The huge bulk of his book brought to mind the old fable
Of the bull-frog who, seeing an ox in the stable,
Puffed up till he burst in a vainglorious trying
To attain the same size. But no magnifying
Can make of unripeness a thing brought to a finish,
For blowing it up only makes it look thinnish.
If asked my opinion, I think that Minerva
Was cruel to abandon the role of preserver.
To lift a man suddenly out of obscurity
And leave him quite solus in his prematurity
Was not, I think, cricket. (I like to imply an
Acquaintance with idioms as remote as the Chian,
They read like a dash of the pepper called Cayenne.)
To conclude, I believe, when the Gods have done chaffing,
Minerva will one morning catch herself laughing,
And, as laughing's a good-natured act to fall into,
I should not be surprised if she found she had been too
High-handed and harsh in her speedy desertion
Of an author who might have become her diversion
Had her relatives not been so prompt with their jeers.
Then, totaling up the count of the years
And the works she'd permitted her erstwhile protégé
To publish without her assistance, 'Heyday!'
I can hear her exclaiming. 'This will scarcely redound
To my credit, and since the world knows that I found
Him and helped him, I really think it would be better
If I helped him again to become the begetter
Of another *Spoon River*, or at least some quite fine thing
Which folk will acknowledge to be a divine thing.'
I should not be astonished if, touched to the marrow,
Minerva set out in her largest Pierce Arrow,
Or else (since I would not pretend to a choice)
Departed in her most expensive Rolls-Royce,
With a dozen or two extremely sharp axes,
Three or four different saws, and various waxes,
A hammer and nails, also scissors and strings,
The whole bundle of tools which a good workman brings

To a job who's no wish to go back for his 'things.'
Arriving *chez* Masters, there'll be a short parley,
And I conjure the world not to miss the finale."

At this point in my tale, there suddenly grew
On my ear a low sound like wind sweeping through
Many acres of pine-trees; but, even as I listened,
It changed into bird-calls which merrily glistened
Like sun-spattered feathers of tone through the glancing
Of leaves over water where shadows are dancing.
Once again was a change, and I heard the low roar
Of surf beating up against a rock shore;
This gave place to the clanging of bells over valleys
And the long monotone of horns blown from Swiss chalets.
I'd scarcely determined that fact when again
It transmuted itself into pattering rain,
Which fused in its turn to harsh drums and to blares
Of tin trumpets, the kind that you meet with at fairs.
But before I'd accustomed myself to the noise,
It rose quiet, single, enduring in poise,
Held high to a balance above growling thunder
As though I were harkening to the world's wonder,
The organ at Harlem, while the *Mourning of Rachel*
Was played—and I knew I was listening to Vachel.
"Who else has, or ever has had, such a voice
As is his, Vachel Lindsay's? Whatever his choice,
Be it singing, exhorting, making fun, prophesying,
It is equally lovely and soul-satisfying.
He's a composite choir, whether shouting or chanting,
Whoever's heard once must admit to a haunting
Nostalgia to hear him again. It's enchanting.
A Sunday-school orator, plus inspiration,
The first ballad-singer, bar none, of the Nation.
When he is performing, I acknowledge to being
More delighted with hearing than I am with seeing.
Perhaps I'm self-conscious, but his postures and poses
Do not strike me as happily chosen for Moses
Bearing down from the mountain his Tables of Stone,
Otherwise the part fits him as though 'twere his own.

When he starts in proclaiming his credo of new laws,
They appear to be vaudeville stunts dashed with blue laws.
He's so desperately earnest there's no modifying him,
And that wonderful voice is forever enskying him.
There's a sober old owl and a bright dragonfly in him,
But clearly there's nothing at all of the dry in him.
An odd, antic fellow, but if you insist
On the unvarnished truth, a sublime egotist
Delighting to cover his titles and fly-leaves
With the personal notes his omnipresent 'I' leaves.
This trait should endear him to every collector
Long after his ego's become a mere specter.
If his writing's so *chic* that you can't read a particle,
Why, all the more grist for a bibliophile's article.
He's a sort of mad xylophone, twinkling his bells
Before all the doors of the thirty-six Hells.
No whirligig dervish gyrating his piety
Can ever be less moved than he with anxiety
Lest his furious rhythms may show impropriety
And injure his creed in the eyes of society.
He knows his own heart and its innate sobriety
And cares nothing for fools who may note with dubiety
A worship which ranges through so much variety.
A mighty jazz dancer before the Lord!—
I can think of no happier term to record
His effect when reciting. He's astoundingly mystic
Even when he purports to be most naturalistic,
A queer ancient trait we may call Judaistic,
Engraft on a style which is pure Methodistic.
He is always attempting to fathom his soul,
But he cannot get hold of a long enough pole.
As he uses an ancient one which he inherited,
Perhaps, after all, his failure is merited.
It's a battered old thing might be John Wesley's staff,
Good enough in its day, but too short by half
To reach to his bottom. Still there's something so stable
In his love for the heirloom, it might pass for a label.
The fellow has scarce an iota of logic
Though he leans rather strongly toward the pedagogic.

These two traits make his teaching less vivid than taking,
He appears as the herald of some proud awaking,
But what it's to be, I dare swear he's no whit
More enlightened than we are, not one little bit.
I like his conceit of the amaranth apples,
(The word is so charming, the look of it dapples
His page with sunshine) and his modern Valkyrie,
A cross between Joan of Arc and a fairy—
I, too, should have relished some good latakia
At a table for two behind clumps of spirea
At the top of his Truth Tower cafeteria
With this twenty-first century wise young Medea.
Who wouldn't, indeed! But the sweepings and shavings
I gather up after her talk seem mere ravings,
The opaline fancies of moonlight and youth.
Among them I scarcely can plot out one truth
Plain enough to be platformed by some voting sleuth
And paraded before the precinct polling-booth.
What's the difference, say I, since the book is as airy
As the dew-dripping song of a young wild canary.
Who dotes on perusing economists' tracts?
There are millions of volumes which deal with mere facts.
I prefer this spiced basket of rose and camellia,
And a populace dancing a gay seguidilla
Under Tajes Mahal, with the star-chimes all ringing.
(That term, by the way, simply does its own singing.)
'Amaranth apple-trees, sandal-wood thickets!'
Bless the man who has shown us the way through the
        wickets
Which lead to this pleasance, and haply the leaven
Works none the less well because he calls it Heaven.
The book is the whole of him, minus his rhythm.
But the others—how often I pass a day with them,
Boomlaying and shouting, 'creeping through the black,'
With a whole troop of nigger-gods yelling at my back,
And the motors whizzing with their 'crack-crack-crack,'
Till at last I strike the wheat-ridge track
And up along a mulberry lane
I listen to the song of the Rachel-Jane.

And as I listen, perhaps it is absurd,
The singer changes to a small gray bird,
And then I see the purple quiver
Of a rainbow junk on a silver river.
I know that 'Spring comes on forever.'
I know it by heart, I have heard the tale
From Lindsay's jade-gray nightingale.
I shall never forget it, because I know it
By heart. This tribute? Do I not owe it!
Forgive me then, most fanciful poet,
If I find in you rarest, gravest delight
When you would have brought me to Heaven's height.
I am very well off where I am, I think,
Still you certainly write with a golden ink,
But I wish you would give us more of the Chink."

At which juncture, I paused to see if my friend,
Who had not said a word, might have ceased to attend.
Far from it, his eyes were fixed on my face
With an eager insistence as if he would trace
My meaning beyond the mere words. "What you say,"
He broke silence at last in his impassive way,
"Proves your poets to be certainly not of my day.
You put the fact gently, but we are *passé*.
At least that I presume's what you wish to convey."
With a horrified gesture I started to say—
But what? Thank the Lord I had no time to get in
The something I should have wrapt up my regret in,
Like a pill in a sugar-plum, since he went on:
"I should not be surprised, as your judgment anon,
If I heard you correctly, was for Miss Dickinson,
With Whitman and Poe. To throw off constraint,
I will say I consider your pronouncement quaint.
But I'm not so at sea to account for the cause
As before your narration I certainly was.
For the men, I'll admit there is room for dispute;
But the choice of Miss Dickinson I must refute."
Then seeing me shrug, he observed, "I am human,
And hardly can bear to allow that a woman

Is ever quite equal to man in the arts;
The two sexes cannot be ranked counterparts."
"My dear Sir," I exclaimed, "if you'd not been afraid
Of Margaret Fuller's success, you'd have stayed
Your hand in her case and more justly have rated her."
Here he murmured morosely, "My God, how I hated her!
But have you no women whom you must hate too?
I shall think all the better of you if you do,
And of them, I may add." I assured him, "A few.
But I scarcely think man feels the same contradictory
Desire to love them and shear them of victory?"
"You think wrong, my young friend," he declared with a
      frown,
"Man will always love woman and always pull down
What she does." "Well, of course, if you will hug the
      cynical,
It is quite your affair, but there is the pinnacle.
She's welcome to climb with man if she wishes."
"And fall with a crash like a trayful of dishes,"
He answered at once, "but if there's no gainsaying her,
There's certainly not the least use in delaying her."
"Very well," I assured him, and quite without mockery,
"But I know several women not yet broken crockery.
Amy Lowell, for instance," I spoke a bit clammily.
"Good Heavens!" he shouted, "not one of the family!
I remember they used to be counted by dozens,
But I never was interested in immature cousins."
"They grow, I believe." The retort was so pat
There was nothing to say, and he pulled down his hat.
I continued: "But since this is not genealogy,
You'll permit me to waive any sort of analogy
Between her and your friend. No one likes to be bound
In a sort of perpetual family pound
Tied by *esprit de corps* to the wheels of the dead.
A poet above all people must have his head.
Indeed it's been whispered the lady sees red
When the subject is broached, she will find her own lati-
      tude."
"My friend, were he here, would extol such an attitude,"

He said very gravely. "But proceed, Sir, I pray."
I hastened as fast as I could to obey:
"Conceive, if you can, an electrical storm
Of a swiftness and fury surpassing the norm;
Conceive that this cyclone has caught up the rainbow
And dashed dizzily on with it streaming in tow.
Imagine a sky all split open and scissored
By lightnings, and then you can picture this blizzard.
That is, if you'll also imagine the clashes
Of tropical thunder, the incessant crashes
Which shiver the hearing and leave it in ashes.
Remember, meanwhile, that the sky is prismatic
And outrageous with color. The effect is erratic
And jarring to some, but to others ecstatic,
Depending, of course, on the idiosyncratic
Response of beholders. When you come to think of it,
A good deal is demanded by those on the brink of it.
To be caught in the skirts of a whirling afflatus
One must not suppose is experienced gratis.
Broncho-busting with rainbows is scarcely a game
For middle-aged persons inclined to the tame.
Likewise, who'd enjoy a sunrise from the Matter-
horn—something all travelers agree is the attar
Of distilled perfection—must be ready to reap
The mid-afternoon pangs of too little sleep.
I might go on forever commingling my metaphors,
And verse by this means does undoubtedly get a force,
But persons who so air their fancy are bores,
A thing every bone in my body abhors,
And you'll guess by this time, without farther allusion,
That the lady's unique and surprising profusion
Creates in some minds an unhappy confusion.
No one's to be blamed who's not something and twenty,
But it's lucky for her that young folk are so plenty.
The future's her goose and I daresay she'll wing it,
Though the triumph will need her own power to sing it.
Although I'm no prophet, I'll hazard a guess
She'll be rated by time as more rather than less.
Once accustom yourself to her strange elocution,

And milder verse seems by contrast mere dilution.
Then again (for I've kept back a very great part),
Despite her traducers, there's always a heart
Hid away in her poems for the seeking; impassioned,
Beneath silver surfaces cunningly fashioned
To baffle coarse pryings, it waits for the touch
Of a man who takes surfaces only as such.
Her work's not, if you will, for the glib amateur,
But I wonder, would it be improved if it were?
Must subtlety always be counted a flaw
And poetry not poetry which puzzles the raw?
Let me turn for an instant to note the reverse
Of my poet, who employs many manners of verse
And when not hurricaning's astoundingly terse;
Yet here the poor creature but makes matters worse.
There are plenty of critics who say they can't hear
When she sings *sotto voce,* the sensation's queer
And inspires a species of horrible fear.
To be told there's a sound and catch nothing at all,
Is a circumstance fairly designed to appall
Most casual people, for here is the hitch:
The admission that one's own ears can't grasp a pitch
Clear and lovely to others. Whereupon a bow-wow
Which swells to a perfectly hideous row.
They've accused her of every description of quackery,
Of only concerning herself with knick-knackery,
It has all been enough to set anyone's back awry.
She's a fool to resent it, a man would have grinned?
Quite so, but then poets are created thin-skinned,
And when one is more than a little volcanic,
With a very strong dash of the ultra-tyrannic,
The retort contentious will be simply Titanic.
Behold, then, our poet, by the lash of atrociousness
Goaded into an attitude much like ferociousness.
Every book that she writes has a preface to guard it
Which spits fire and cannon-balls, making each hard hit
Tell, and mow down its swathe of objectors.
But critics have ever been good resurrectors.
Since she keeps the fight going, they rise to do battle,

When the whole mess is only so much tittle-tattle.
So it goes back and forth with the cries and the cheering,
And there's no sign at all of the atmosphere clearing.
Her books follow each other despite all the riot,
For, oddly enough, there's a queer, crumpled quiet
Perpetually round her, a crazy-quilt tent
Dividing her happily from the event.
Armed to the teeth like an old Samurai,
Juggling with jewels like the ancient genii,
Hung all over with mouse-traps of meters, and cages
Of bright-plumaged rhythms, with pages and pages
Of colors slit up into streaming confetti
Which give the appearance of something sunsetty,
And gorgeous, and flowing—a curious sight
She makes in her progress, a modern White Knight,
Forever explaining her latest inventions
And assuring herself of all wandering attentions
By pausing at times to sing, in a duly
Appreciative manner, an aria from Lully.
The horse which she rides will suit any part
Either Peg (with the 'asus') or 'Peg o' my heart.'
To avoid making blunders, he's usually known
Without any suffix as 'Peg' all alone.
This style of address has become a tradition
Most offendingly silly, since no erudition
Unaided can ever produce a magician.
For the magic she has, I see nothing demonic
In the use of free verse (the 'free' is quite comic!)
Or even that mule of the arts, polyphonic.
No matter what pedants may find that's awry in him,
There's plenty of kick and plenty of fly in him.
Taking this thing and that, and considering on it,
I believe there are more guesses under her bonnet
Than in any two hats you are likely to meet
(Straw or felt, take your choice, so the shape be discreet,
Not too flap-brimmed and weird, nor too jaunty and neat)
In any particular city or street
You may happen to pick. Note, I only say questions,
Which leaves the mind open to many suggestions,

Up or down, there's the rub. (The mere matter of hats
Is too nice, by the way, to be dealt with as 'Rats!'
There's a temperature here which the best thermostats
Could not regulate better. We're all diplomats
Now the 'Arrys have ousted the aris-tocrats.)"

I looked at my friend, his face was averted.
"You make it quite clear why we are deserted,
Old men are tough customers. Now, as a foil,
Give me something as smooth and slow-running as oil,
Something clear, uncontentious, it even may be
A bit chilly in beauty perhaps." "There's 'H. D.,'"
I was tempted to shout, she fitted so rightly
His immediate preference: frost falling lightly
In delicate patterns on thin blades of grass.
(Since oil does not fit, I let that figure pass,
Though it did well enough up above where it was.)
"This author's become a species of fable
For she masks her identity under a label.
If others have ancestors, she would forget hers
And appear the spontaneous child of two letters,
The printing of which is the bane of typesetters.
They have called her a dryad just stepped from a bosk,
But I see an ice maiden within an ice kiosk,
With icicle stalactites hanging around her,
And the violets frozen with which they have crowned her--
The man who would filch them would be an icebounder,
Which I surely am not. If each lovely, veined petal
Becomes by the contact a trifle too brittle
And cold to give out its usual warm scent,
They make it up amply by such dazzlement
Of sun-shot-through-ice that the shine of her shrine
Seems the sky-piercing glitter of some Apennine.
I have told you before that my mind teems with similes.
It's a shocking bad habit persists in some families,
I've an uncle—but there, I spread out like a runnel,
When I should flow as straight as though poured through a
        funnel.
So take this digression in the light of an interlude

Leading up to a change which I wish to obtrude
On the form of my speech, for I find I am freezing
Before the remarkably chilly, though pleasing,
Ice image I've painted, and soon shall be sneezing.
My Muse must immediately seek out a clime
Where her trippings and flittings are not above rime,
Or dew that is duly congealed, or hoar-frost.
I'm indifferent to science, so the meaning be tossed
Into some sort of shape which fits well with my pattern,
For, whatever the faults of said Muse, she's no slattern.
My verse, I'll allow, is the species fantastic,
I've been *épris* for years of the style Hudibrastic,
But my rhyming morale is, I trust, inelastic.
Which preamble means I have searched for a week
To rouse neither my Muse's nor heroine's pique
In the matter of climate. I've found it in Greek.
'H. D.' (for it's time we got back to the girl)
Might be some ancient mirror, with mother-of-pearl
Let into its metal, a thing which a nation
Deems well worth the cost of its own exhumation,
A prize to count up to the whole excavation.
This mirror, which carries the breath of the past
On its scarcely stained surface, is no scholiast,
But a living replica of what once was living
At the touch of a rare adoration reviving.
Here youths in scant armor, on the way to the galleys,
Woo maidens in dark ilex-groves; in the valleys,
Anemone-sprinkled, young shepherds guard flocks
Clad in ram's fleeces only; above the sharp rocks
Jutting into the purple Ionian sea
Are the white, fluted columns of—Fiddle-de-dee!
Such lyrical bursts in a mere *jeu d'esprit*
Are like brandy poured into a cup of bohea,
A transaction called 'lacing' in old days, *on dit*.
I can't say for myself, being no devotee
Of either diluted or straight *eau-de-vie*,
And the eighteenth amendment is nothing to me.
Still, I don't like a law couched in hyperbole,
It gets anyone's goat. To return to 'H. D.,'

Whom I've really kept waiting most outrageously,
She's the thing as it was, not the thing we have made it
And with insolent ornament quite overlaid it.
She descends to no commonplace, flock-guarding shepherds.
No pompous Victorian gush ever jeopards
Her reticent, finely drawn line. No Greek marble
Has less of the pueril and less of the garble.
Her sea is the sea of a child or a Neriad,
And yet no false word lifts it out of its period.
Her flowers of shore and of cliff those we seek
On our cliffs and our shores, but hers somehow are Greek.
Her poems are excitement and rest, and the glory
Of living a life and not reading a story.
Archaeology? Yes, in the very same way
That geology's the mountain we climb every day.
The armor she welds, the dyed cloth she weaves,
Are so perfect in artistry, every word cleaves
To the substance as though that would crackle without it
And split. Read her books (there are two) if you doubt it.
Perhaps, after all, this quintessence of Greece
Is the wool on a century-garlanded fleece;
Underneath is, and was, a tough fiber of leather.
Is the Greece she has given us Greece altogether?
As well might one ask if the youth of Praxiteles
Is an everyday chap or a scheme to belittle ease
By exalting the sharp line of young masculinity.
In her method and his is there not some affinity?
Each sheers to the soul, to the base of a nemesis,
And the hard, glancing residue is the ultimate genesis.
For out of the past is the future; a truism,
You must pardon, since man has invented no new 'ism'
Since the days of the cavemen. I wish merely to prove
That this most modern poet runs along an old groove,
That the erudite novelties filling her pages
Are as old as this morning and as new as the ages."

Here a voice interrupted my long peroration,
Speaking, I detected, in some irritation.
"I think," it announced, "though I may be mistaken,

There's a poet whom you've not mentioned yet, Conrad
  Aiken."
Such an ill-governed mind as I've got, and the porter
Never keeps out intruders who call, as he ought to.
(That rhyme will be cursed as "a regular snorter"
By every stand-pat, Tennysonian supporter.
I am sorry myself to be forced to distort a
Fine line unduly, and if I or my thought err
I am willing to own it without the least *hauteur*.
I rhyme as I can, and am never a courter
For all suffrages.) The doorman, I said,
Who, between you and me, is a crass dunderhead,
Had let this extremely irascible gentleman
Pass through the door, and of course he began
At once to upbraid me. It's the method he uses
To force himself into the sight of the Muses.
"Young man," I replied with some heat, "you mistake
My preoccupation. If you wish to make
Your entrance at once with the ladies, I'll see to it,
But I should have supposed you'd immediately veto it."
This was rather a staggerer, to be grouped with the women
Would tax the endurance of any male human;
Yet to wait any longer, when I might be weary
Before his turn came, did not strike him as cheery.
He puffed and he fumed, with pride pulling both ways;
It was pitiable to see the poor fellow's malaise.
But finally, with a great bluffing of chivalry,
He declared he had no sort of feeling of rivalry
Against the fair sex who adorned his profession.
A very neat way, this, to blur a confession,
For the long and the short of it was he'd go on
The carpet at once, if I pleased. Thereupon
I hastily made my excuses to one
Or two ladies I'd meant to have been next presented.
Being sensible persons, they seemed quite contented.
Perhaps 'twas as well, for I'd rather a hunch
The irascible poet might make good with his "Punch"
And land me that terrible "one on the jaw,"
When I'm sure I should "measure my length" in the straw.

It will clearly be seen that my anxious perusal
Of a recent combat has done much to bamboozle
The erstwhile classic grace of my natural diction.
You see I obeyed a strong predilection
In Carpentier's favor to the tune of a tenner
And, with other good sportsmen, I found my Gehenna.
"Mr. Aiken's a poet so cram full of knowledge
He knows all about poetry that's taught in a college.
His versification's as neat as a pin,
His meter so fine it becomes finikin.
I say nothing of rhythm, for he's something fanatical
Anent the advantage of the beat mathematical.
Within his set limits, the pulse of his verse
Is often most subtle, and even his worse
Attempts are by no means either jejune or lacking
In form, one can hardly imagine him slacking
In pains or desire. He's all that a poet
Can make of himself when he sets out to do it
With his heart, and his soul, and his strength, and his mind.
For years now, he's had a most horrible grind
With his work, with the public, but what stands in his way
Is the awkward necessity of something to say.
A man of sensations, of difficult cheerfulness
Which the fog in his brain has tormented to fearfulness,
Possessed of much music and little idea,
Always steeping his soul in the strange undersphere
Of the brain. Since all thought in him tends to grow hazy
When his sentiment's roused, he is lost in a mazy
Vortex where he swings like some pale asteroid.
Seeking orientation, he's stumbled on Freud.
With the Austrian's assistance, he's become neurological,
A terrible fate to befall the illogical.
Being born with an ultra-sensitive cuticle,
We must realize his verse in a sense therapeutical.
If he doesn't quite state any fact, his oblique
Side-glances at subjects are just hide-and-seek
He's playing with all his frustrated ambitions
And gaining, thereby, some vicarious fruitions.
He's so young as to think that he proves his maturity

By boldly colliding with all sorts of impurity.
His ladies are, most of them, a little bit dusty,
But we're learning to think any other kind musty.
The true modern artist would face destitution
Were it not for that universe-wide institution
Plain people frown down on and call prostitution.
No matter how shopworn the plots he has made,
They will always pass muster if he mentions a spade.
At least this is true with that type of Bohemia
Which is not yet aware that such art spells anaemia.
Not so Aiken—his brothels, street-walkers, dope-eaters
Are merely the web he weaves over with meters.
He uses them chiefly because they are easy
And sure to produce an effect on the queasy.
For more than all else he dreads falling flat;
The fear of it teases his brain like a gnat.
He would rather be called wicked, incomprehensible,
Anything, so long as the world's not insensible.
In his anxious desire to escape being tepid,
He makes too great a show of the over-intrepid,
But his real interest lies in quite other directions:
In noting the faintest of fleeting reflections
In tone or in color; in catching the magic
Of words against words; and it simply is tragic
How few apprehend his remarkable quality.
But was ever a public more lost in frivolity
Than ours? It cannot tell feathers from lead
Till you hit it a crack with the last on the head.
His volumes are filled with a sea-green miasma
Shot and sprinkled throughout with the grotesque phan-
    tasma
Of an egoist's brain, or a man's when he's sleepy.
They revolve unrelated and sink into creepy
Sight and sound mutterings, yet sometimes so vivid
They are that they seem to stand out in a livid
And flaming protrusion. Take, for instance, the scene
Of his satyrs and mænads, which is white striped on green,
With red, sudden explosions. Sometimes, more surprising,
The fog lifts a moment before a sun rising

As clear and as thin as though painted on china
By some eighteenth-century Dresden designer.
His sordid back rooms disappear and the groans
Of dying dope-fiends, and we hear 'three clear tones,'
The tones of his bird in the china-berry tree.
What a mercy that such a tree happened to be!
Otherwise, I believe, he must have invented it.
Never mind, here it is, and he's simply cemented it
On the botany of poetry forever and ever.
I say that superbly, without the least quiver.
If the rest of his work's neither Saint Paul's nor Kremlin,
He's built a basilica surely in *Senlin.*
At least in that *Morning Song,* which, until lately,
Was the sole, single fragment he'd done adequately.
Till *Punch,* ah! with *Punch* now, he should achieve fame.
But there's nothing so dogging as a once-come-by name.
If this were his first, he'd be up like a rocket,
Now I think he'll burn steadily on in his socket
Making beautiful poems though the public won't stand 'em
Because he can't drive style and tale in a tandem.
Since the books as they are stick so hard in the gizzard,
The sensible thing is to have each one scissored.
Cut out from each volume the one or two scraps
You might like on a third or fourth reading perhaps;
Paste them into a scrap-book, and some rainy day
Just glance over the lot and I think you will say:
'By Jove! What a fellow he is in his way!'
And I'll thank you for that as a true leaf of bay.
If he, the arch-skeptic, finds other folk doubting,
He makes a mistake to be seen always pouting.
He has not his deserts, yet to publish the fact
Is a childish and most unintelligent act,
But everyone knows he's deficient in tact.
A man who can work with such utter devotion
Can afford to wait patiently for his promotion,
And that it will come, I've a very strong notion.
One thing we can say, he will certainly wait
And either get in or turn dust at the gate.
Since Fame is a very good hand at the shears,

I shall not be surprised if he gets his arrears,
For quality counts in the long run of years."
I turned to the shade in my mind, but unused
To listening with patience, the thing had vamoosed

Not so my old friend, he was listening intensely,
And as I stopped speaking, he said, "I'm immensely
Intrigued by that man, he's a curious fellow.
Too bad he's permitted himself to see yellow.
A jaundiced perspective's a great handicap.
Well, what other poets have you got in your lap?
I commend you, young man, as an excellent etcher."
"The next I shall notice will be John Gould Fletcher,"
I answered, "but before I begin my narration
Don't *think;* if you can, *see* an irradiation
Spreading out over roofs, over trees, over sky,
The gold screen of a moment, on which you descry
Such oddments as heaps of 'vermilion pavilions'
And Gabriel's angels all riding on pillions
On the backs of cloud horses, blowing trumpets of thunder,
Above forests of elephant trees standing under
The precipitous cone of some steep afternoon.
The whirling wind 'screams,' the stars 'shrill,' the streets
    croon.
A cataract of music swirls out of the throats
Of the long scarlet trumpets, the prismatic notes
Sweep over the city like sun spray and laughter,
Embroidered with all colors . . . Then what comes after?
More colors, a rain of them, hanging, delaying,
To sprinkle cool 'jade balustrades' with their staying.
Golden flakes, silver filaments, what pandemonium!
The rainbow joined in wedlock to a bursting harmonium.
Elephantine surrenders, prodigious relapses,
Speech turned to a fire-ball which soars and collapses
And spills down its words like the whole spectrum falling
In a broken excitement: My eye, it's appalling!
Such a chaotic shooting and drifting of particles,
Mere loveliness solus, not stuck tight to articles,
For what it all means does not matter a jot;

You are filled with delight at it, or you are not.
But suppose that you weary of the polychromatic—
Some natures, I realize, are far too lymphatic
To derive any pleasure from what is not static—
There are corners to rest in with fountains, and grass
Streaming up in long slopes, and if you should pass
Just over the hill, there's a house where each column
Is wreathed and entangled with the half-gay, half-solemn
Recollections of childhood. There you can eat luncheon,
And drink slow well-water from some old gray puncheon,
And listen to tales of hobgoblins and genie
Till I venture to say you'll be a bit spleeny
And welcome the rising of white-faced Selene.
(Rather pretty, that last, such touches do garnish
One's writing, I think, and I'm not above varnish.
I like a bright luster in poems or medallions,
The polish one sees in the later Italians.
Here a friend who's dropped in says I've mixed my my-
      thology.
Such a slip, if I've made it, deserves an apology:
Selene, Cybele, Diana—I care
Not at all for mere names. You may take Lemprière
And choose any Goddess you think opportune
So you quite understand I refer to the moon.)
As you sit in the moonlight, the gist of your summary
Will be: Here at last, is a poet without flummery.
A score or two words are his total of plunder,
But the whole is a boyhood imprisoned in wonder.
A boy, and the things all about him—plain stuff,
And not even new, but the measure's enough.
Not the kind which they want for a penny-a-liner;
It's too sharp, and too sheer, but for that all the finer.
Have you ever gone into a dim, disused attic
And poked about there among the erratic
Remains of worn toys, legless soldiers, chipped blocks,
And suddenly come on an old music-box?
As you twist round the handle, the notes seem to squeeze
Through the dust, some are lost and the rest choke and
      wheeze,

But you make out a tune, and the mere broken hint of it
Is the agonized joy of remembrance, by dint of it
You suffer and love with an ache you'd forgotten.
It were wiser, perhaps, were your ears stuffed with cotton.
So Fletcher's not only the rainbow in spate,
He's the soul of a music-box which can create
All our childhood again. If the tune's a bit scrappy,
What's the odds, just so long as the sound makes us happy?
So far, Mr. Fletcher, for that's only a mood,
We'll not whistle until we are out of the wood.
Were your publishers mad, or why bind together
Your *Old House* and *Symphonies?* One wonders whether
You were bent on emptying out your portfolio.
You created, at any rate, quite an imbroglio.
This break-up of feeling with one or two vile hacks
Of discord is as jarring as gumdrops and smilax
Giving suddenly place to red-peppers and asters.
The symphonies, come on this way, call for plasters.
This arrangement, indeed, was the worst of disasters.
Up bright in the morning, shoes tied and hair brushed,
On a Sunday, maybe, when you're not too much rushed,
You can seek ancient China in Symphony Blue;
Or, if you prefer, you may take a stroll through
Any Spring, in the Green; you may sail over oceans
With the Red glare of stoke-holes to thrill your emotions;
You may fight in the Scarlet, and laugh in the Yellow,
You may do what you please in the Gold. A fine fellow
Whose palette is full if a little bit messy.
But you have a good deal of the world here *in esse.*
At least, you would have, were it not for a doubt
About what any symphony's really about.
He writes, it appears, in a prismatic spasm;
This phase of his work is complete protoplasm.
He is whirling his atoms before quite cohering them,
But there's no doubt at all that he soon will be steering
    them.
Yet, hold on a bit, my dear chap, do you think
You can set all America down in cold ink?
Here you are, aeroplaning from Boston to Texas,

And taking snapshots as you fly to perplex us.
If you see a skyscraper, down it goes, and the next
Shot's a square of Chicago—fit it into the text.
Joggle niggers and Mexicans, some of them dead 'uns,
And for spirit, bring in a few battles where reddens
The smoke of proud guns, for your richest of gravies
Is the sauce of Bull Run and the bier of Jeff Davis.
You've done it, my cock, as well as a man
Who is chiefly the slave of his sensations can;
For somehow your genius has a habit of shying
Whenever your heart is involved. It's most trying.
You can work yourself up to a towering passion
Over landscapes and peoples, but when you would fashion
A love lyric—Puff! and the substance dissolves
And melts out of your fingers. A thousand resolves
To break through with yourself, to have done with ob-
    jectives,
Leave you still where you were, exploring perspectives.
I declare I could weep, did I not know that life
Is only achieved through a vast deal of strife.
You stand in the midst of a cosmic heterogeny,
But I do not despair of your rearing a progeny.
If chaos at last jelled into a man,
What a big chaos did, your small chaos can.
You were built, you perceive, as the first of your clan.
And, whatever you want, you've got what no other
Poet ever has had. So a truce to the pother!
Bless the man, you've done something as new as tomorrow,
And I cannot consider your case with much sorrow.
Just wait" . . . But, most gently, my old friend interrupted,
"Don't go on, Sir, I beg, I am being corrupted.
Your poets are so diverse. One thing I can say,
Good or bad, they're more various than poets were in my day.
If you've more in your bag, produce them, I pray."

Thus adjured, I remembered the one or two ladies
I'd deserted, and mentally crying "Oh, Hades!
Will they be mad as hops or affect a quite staid ease?
Whichever it is, I shall get a good wigging,

To be kept waiting's always a bit *infra digging*.
I must cudgel my brain for a really apt whopper,
Women don't pardon blunders when their *amour propre*
Is in question." But all of the chickens I'd counted,
When I'd tallied them up to a total, amounted
To just nothing at all, for your modern Egeria
Is far too advanced to give way to hysteria.
Approaching the first, I said no woman like her
Had yet been considered. She replied "Oh, you piker!
A poet learns to see, and you need not dissemble.
We will go up at once. Grace, here is your thimble."
Then jumping up quickly from where she was sitting
She quite overturned a little girl's knitting
Who was there by some chance, I'll come back to that later.
Said I to myself, no man living can hate her,
She is what I should call a born fascinator.
Upon reaching my friend—and let me explain
That these scenes in the scene all take place in my brain—
I began with a few neatly turned words on love
As the poet's own bourne, and declared that no glove
Ever fitted a hand with less wrinkling and snugger
Than this theme this poet. Here I noticed her shrug her
Shoulders a little, which was rather upsetting.
However, it may have been only coquetting.
Still I thought it was wise to get on with my tale:
"Our love-poet, *par excellence*, Sara Teasdale,"
I said with a flourish. Now that was a whale
Of a compliment, such things deserve an entail,
'Twas so brilliantly super even if it were true,
And I knew very well 'twas but one of a cue.
"This poet," I went on, "is a great niece of Sappho,
I know not how many 'greats' laid in a row
There should be, but her pedigree's perfectly clear;
You can read it in *Magazine Verse* for the year.
She is also a cousin, a few times removed,
Of dear Mrs. Browning, that last can be proved.
The elder poet hid in a shrouding mantilla
Which she called Portuguese. Was ever trick sillier?
Our Sara is bolder, and feels quite at ease

As herself; in her mind there is nothing to tease.
Dale and valley, the country is hers she traverses,
She has mapped it all out in a bushel of verses.
Sara Teasdale she is—was—for our minnesinger,
Behind her front door, is now Mrs. Filsinger.
A hard question this, for a hand-maid of Muses,
When she's once made a name in cold print which she loses
On taking a husband, the law's masculinity
Would seem to demand a perpetual virginity
For all married poets of the downtrodden sex.
To forfeit the sale of a new volume checks
Even marital ardor, to say nothing of checks.
It's just this sort of thing which so frequently wrecks
The artistic composure, and must surely perplex
Any husband who's not in the class of henpecks.
Still I think the poor man should find some consolation
In two or three volumes of sheer adoration.
It's the price he receives for never imposing
Himself on his wife when the lady's composing.
Under whatever name, the world grows awarer
Every year of the prize we have got here in Sara.
She has no colors, no trumpets, no platforms, no skepticisms,
She has no taste for experiments, and joins in no schisms;
She just sings like a bird, and I think you'll agree
This is clearly the place for the china-berry tree—
With a difference, the bird in that pleasant, arboreal
Importation had three tones, while her repertorial
Range is compassed in one, the reflex amatorial.
She loves in a charming, perpetual way,
As thought it just came when she was distrait,
Or quite occupied in affairs of the day.
Or else, and I think the remark's more acute,
She lives as the flower above a deep root.
Like a dedicate nun, she tells bead after bead
At Matins, Tierce, Vespers. You'd think she'd be treed
Just once in a while to find something to say.
Not at all, she's a vast *catalogue raisonnée*
Of the subject. No one's so completely *au fait*.
Her poetry succeeds, in spite of fragility,

Because of her very remarkable agility.
There is no single stunt in the style amatory
Which is not included in her category,
We may as well take that at once *a priori*.
So easy to her seems the work of creation
She might be just jotting down lines from dictation.
There is nothing green here, each poem's of the ripest.
The income tax lists her as Cupid's own typist.
Of course, it is true that she's not intellectual,
But those poets who are, are so apt to subject you all
To theories and treatises, the whole galvanometry
Of the bardling who thinks verse a sort of geometry.
Now Sara's as easy to read as a slip
On a piece of banana, and there's no need to skip,
For each poem's so peculiarly like every other
You may as well stay where you are and not bother.
She's that very rare compost, the dainty erotic;
Such a mixture can't fail to produce a hypnotic
Effect on the reader, whose keenest sensation
Will consist in a perfect identification
Of himself with the poet, and her sorrows and joys
Become his, while he swings to the delicate poise
Of a primitive passion so nicely refined
It could not bring a blush to the most squeamish mind.
Though the poems, I may add, are all interlined
For the ready perusal of those not too blind.
For Sara, if singer, is also a woman,
I know of no creature more thoroughly human.
If woman, she's also a lady who realizes
That a hidden surprise is the best of surprises.
She seems a white statue awaiting unveiling,
But raised on a platform behind a stout railing
Whence she lures and retires, provoking a nearer
Contact which is promised to be even dearer
If we find we have courage enough not to fear her."
I looked at my subject to find she'd departed,
it's a habit of hers when a party's once started
To vanish unnoticed. My poetess had flown.
Seeing which, I remarked that I'd better postpone

The rest of my discourse. "I think you have shown
The outlines at least, my young cicerone,"
Said my friend. "Have you others? I see the sun's setting.
If you have many more, why we must be getting
On faster." I promised to use all despatch
Which I saw was most needed when I took out my watch.

"There's a child here I've not yet had leisure to mention,
Both she and her mother are worth your attention.
And one or two more I can think of, but most of them
Will not take up much time. After that, there's a host of them
We'll consider, if you are agreeable, *en masse.*"
"You spoke of a child, a child in this class!"
He asked me astonished. "I suppose that betrays me
A fogey indeed, but the thing does amaze me."
"No wonder," I answered, "America's youth
Symbolized with a vengeance as plainest of truth.
The poets I've presented may none of them be
Among the top boughs of that flourishing tree,
The *Genus Poeticus, Anglice-folia,*
Whose flowers have rivaled the greater magnolia,
But no shoot we know of has blossomed so early
As ours, and that makes a distinction clearly.
A ten-year-old child, half elf and half sage,
Where else can you find a poet of her age?
This is no little girl, though the critics preëmpt her
As the essence of childhood, but, *caveat emptor;*
It is easy to say, which is all that they care about,
For where is the critic one can see is aware about
Any essence whatever. This child's no more childhood
Than the wolf was the grandmother for donning her mild
    hood.
Hilda Conkling (I see I've forgotten to name her)
Is a greater phenomenon than they would proclaim her.
She is poetry itself, for her slight little soul
Is not yet of a size to encompass the whole
She gives out. Without knowing who really is speaking,
She speaks, and her words fall without the least seeking.

There's no need for allowances, the poems that she writes
May be certainly reckoned among the high lights
Of their *genre*, and although I'm no hyperbolist
I say flatly this child is the first Imagist.
But you will remember that Jove sometimes naps,
And the baby in Hilda not seldom entraps
The genius. But what of that! Such handicaps
May be reckoned as *nil* in the total, perhaps.
If she sometimes descends from Parnassus crescendo
To play with her dolls, why, the greatest of men do
The same in their fashion, and no innuendo
Need follow so natural a way of proceeding.
It is merely the little girl in her stampeding.
Since she's neither a freak, nor a ghoul, nor a Houyhnhnm,
We may thank the good fate which has left her a minim
Of usual childhood—but, bless my soul, what
Has become of her now, she was here, was she not?"
"Oh," her mother joined in, "she ran off to catch
A white kitten she saw. There's no fear of a scratch,
She understands kittens." "Did she hear what I'm saying?"
I asked. "I am really afraid she was paying
But little attention, her fingers were drumming
In time to some sort of a tune she was humming.
Now she and the kitten are disposed to agree,
We have lost her, I fear, so you'll have to take me."

Now what can a gallant gentleman do
On receiving a challenge so couched? *"Entre nous,*
I think you're delightful," I said in aside,
"Your verses have made many poets emerald-eyed.
What you seem to do without turning a hair
Is just the one trick makes the less gifted swear.
Who would copy you, digs for himself a fine snare."
But when a man whispers inside of his mind
He can scarcely expect an onlooker to find
His abstraction amusing. My friend woke me smartly
From my silent flirtation by announcing, quite tartly,
"The child, as you've proved, is a *lusus naturæ*,
A verdict I'm sure any qualified jury

Would agree to at once were her case up for trial.
Why even our feminophobe on the *Dial*
Never dared to bring forward young ladies of ten
As serious rivals to middle-aged men.
Poor Margaret Fuller, how she would have doted on
Your remarkable age, and how happily floated on
Its dawn-colored currents and all its forensical
Preoccupations! We were so common-sensical.
Perhaps we were tainted with some sentimentalism,
But your *beau ideal* seems to be elementalism.
I can cap you, however, by mentioning one
Poet who never grew up, your friend, Miss Dickinson."
"The comparison's just," I declared. "As to Hilda,
Your juxtaposition need never bewilder
The admirers of either. One you failed quite to scotch;
The other, I think, you should certainly watch."
"Well, well," he said hastily, "but I protest
At sitting all night with you and your quest.
Who's the next, and be quick." As if riding a race
I dashed at my subject: "Let me introduce Grace
Conkling, no one is so handy at brooks,
They chatter and spatter through all of her books.
And her fish—every angler is on tenterhooks
Lest they should escape him. The same with her birds.
My land, what a fluttering they make! Quite two thirds
Of her work is concerned with them, so that her pages
Present the appearance of so many cages.
Then mountains—yes, mountains—she crams them in too.
The little near-by ones all green, and all blue
The more distant peaks. She is great on perspective.
And whatever her theme, she is always selective.
Take her love-poems, for instance, she serves, piping hot,
A lyric of passion, and chooses the spot
For its setting somewhere where you go in a yacht:
South America, Mexico, wherever not,
So there is a garden with grapefruit, kumquat,
A score or two peach-trees and some apricot.
For her flowers, one should be an encyclopedia.
No less an abundance of knowledge the medea

Could possibly be to surmount and recount 'em.
(Here I've got in a mess. There's no rhyme except 'fount.'
    Hem!
Take no notice I beg of the exceedingly thin ice
I'm skating on; if you find my heroine nice,
Which she certainly must be to all masculine eyes,
I care not a whit with what names I am twitted.
On account of my subject, the claim's manumitted.)
Now turn back six lines, so you capture the gist
Of my tale where I left it—I will jot down a list
Of a few of her flowers which must not be missed.
There's magnolia first, of the kind grandiflora,
With its moons of blooms scenting the air where Señora
Jimenez, Alcaro—take your pick, I would banish
Such names if I could, but the Señora's Spanish—
Walks under daturas whose cups of perfume
Hang above her, with jasmine so thick there's scant room
To pass down the path to the beds where the lilies
Are standing together in a stately and still ease.
The dates are in blossom, or is it in fruit?—
One should not make a list unless able to do't,
And this Mexican flora trips anyone's foot—
Never mind, it's enough that the lady's en route
To a clandestine tryst, when a tingling *sol fa*
Shakes the garden to life, for he's brought his guitar.
I acknowledge I've taken a few autocratic
Liberties with my author, who's never dramatic,
But the garden alone seemed to me miasmatic,
With its scents and its sounds, but for the rest solus.
If we must not embroider, why she must parole us.
Since I've given no promise, and the scene, without doubt,
Should have been there although the poet left it out,
It shall stand in my version—and there's a night-piece.
But what of the mornings, as soft as crêpe-lisse
Till the mists burn away with the sun and leave staring
A peacock-hued dome, with gilt cornices, flaring
Above an old market-place crowded with fig trees
And the flame-colored awnings of booths where the big
    trees

Make a thunder-cloud shade, and Giuseppe, Felice,
(These Mexican names make our own sound so screechy!)
Are vociferously selling figs, melons, and grapes?
It's the rainbow gone mad in all colors and shapes.
There are smoky blue plums and raw-striped cucumbers,
Red slits of pomegranates, gold loquats, the umbers
Of nuts and the green of almonds not yet husked;
Huge elephant baskets of flowers all betusked
With long sprays of yucca—the poet has attacked us
With all of her armory at once—spears of cactus
Shoot out between passion vines spreading their discus-
Like blooms just above a bouquet of hibiscus.
The trees, I observe, are all festooned with monkeys,
Long necklaces of them, and the square's choked with
      donkeys.
The bell in the peacock dome clatters and clangs,
Parakeets flash through leaves like so many whiz-bangs
On the fourth of July, there are orchids exploding
New flowers each minute over hand-carts unloading
Bread-fruit and bananas, and the hot, dry sirocco
Tips it all to a sparkle so bright and rococo
The book should be bound in a purple morocco
If the contents and cover were made to agree,
This dismal sage-green is a catastrophe;
But what publisher thinks of aught else but his fee.
I have written my best, but it's so multiplex I can
Never compete with her when she's on Mexican
Horticulture, zoölogy, and I don't know what all,
Unless I've Gray's *Botany* handy, and Nuttall,
With Wilson and Chapman close by on the table;
And as to the speech, it is just so much Babel
To me if each word is not tagged with a label
In good easy English. Well, no matter for that,
I've told you she's got every atmosphere pat.
She's as happy with pine-trees and an orchard of apples
And the clouds which a 'slender sky' scatters and dapples
Over grass-and-stone hillsides, as with lotus-brimmed foun-
      tains,
And I'll swear that no poet has done better with mountains.

Her flickers, and veeries, and finches, and thrushes
Are as good as her nightingale hid in a bush is,
And when she would sing of the Old Mohawk Trail
I toss up my hat with a shout of 'All hail!
Troubadour of New England, who knows that white pine is
Her very soul's self,' and I write in gold, 'Finis!'"

"Dear me," said my friend, "so you think she's the laureate
Of poor old New England." "If there's any one bore I hate
More than another," I answered, "it's the man
Who pretends to see farther than anyone can.
Considering we've Robinson, Miss Lowell, and Frost,
Such a statement were rash. I'm afraid you have lost
Just the shade I intended; there's a difference, be sure,
Between a poet laureate and a troubadour."
"The point is well taken," he admitted at once.
"Was I laureate or troubadour? The distinction confronts
Me now rather unpleasantly. For, was I able
To go her one better in my famous *Fable*?
That I loved my New England you'll find by the space
I devoted to her in that book. Face to face
With her new poets, I'm wondering who'll win in the race.
Am I in the lead since they've quickened the pace?
I'm beginning to doubt it as far as mere praise
Counts at least, I was Frost and she mixed, hence my bays,
If I really deserved any. But with this poetess
I find myself back on old ground, none the less
Delightful, be sure, and there is a slight change
In her manner, I do detect that, but her range
Does not carry me out of the depth of my sympathy."
"The next fellow will," was my succinct reply.
"Alfred Kreymborg, deft master of the oddest machine
Made of strings and of gut which I ever have seen.
A hybrid of sorts yclept mandolute.
Queer instrument? Very. His voice is the flute
Playing over the strings, and his songs epigrams
Tinkled up into rhythm. Oh, yes, they're called shams
By the public at large, but who wants a large public?
Kreymborg's manner to his is a kiss and a kick.

He's the monkey of poetry who climbs on a stick,
But that's only his way to conceal by a trick
The real truth he has. Oh, he's impolitic
To a fault, but the fellow is no lunatic,
Nor mountebank either, though some people think
He has squeezed not two drops of his blood in his ink
And regard him as jester with more than suspicion.
The fact is he's an untaught, but natural musician.
His poems and his tunes come straight out of his pestle
And fall as they will. Unbaked clay's not a vessel,
However, and though I believe he has made
Some excellent poems, that's not really his trade,
Which I grieve to admit consists largely of bluffing.
The gems in his books are half smothered in stuffing.
He's an ironist pure, but I can't call him simple;
More than one of his efforts may be classed as a pimple
On the fair face of poetry, but others delight us
As much for their beauty as the first kind affright us
By their horrible ugliness, wry-formed and waxy.
He's a man flinging queer little toys from a taxi.
If you scrabble round fast enough you may pick a good one,
But the chances are ten to one you'll get a wooden
Contraption of rude, creaky springs, badly gilt,
Just words nailed together haphazard, no lilt,
And no sense you can find. It's a real 'hunt the slipper'
To read what he writes, and you may come a tripper
Or you may win a prize, that's the whole proposition.
How does it affect his poetic position?
I tell you quite frankly I feel at a loss
For an answer to give you, we might try a toss
Or leave it in peace on the lap of the Gods.
To put it quite plainly, dear Sir, what's the odds?
When we come to his singing, it's another concern.
However on earth did the chap come to learn
Of those strange sweeping chords and that odd whispered
　　　singing
Which cleaves to the heart and sets the nerves stinging,
And where did he find his sawed-off mandolin
Or guitar, or banjo? Good Lord, it's a sin

When there is such an instrument no one else knows it,
But the luckier for him, I say, and therefore—*prosit!*
The poems he writes down never end, scarce begin,
If the truth must be told; in the music, a thin
Silver chord holds a something, a glitter of fable,
And the tale and its moral lie strung on a cable,
Half-music, half-thought, but what we have heard
Is more echo than music, more music than word.
He's a poet in the core of him, a bit of a clown,
And two-thirds of a vagabond drifting round town,
Seeing whimsical nothings at every street corner.
A lover possessed, an inveterate scorner,
Engaged in a pulling of plums like Jack Horner—
There's the man, Alfred Kreymborg." "We had no counter-
    part
To your monkey-musician. Do you call the thing art
You've been talking about?" The old gentleman's tone
Betrayed just a trace of annoyance. "I've shown
You a figure, make of him whatever you can,
To tag him as this or that's not in my plan.
You asked me to give you each phase of the time."
"And I could not stand Whitman because he'd no rhyme!"
He gasped. "You may banish all verse that's harmonious,
But it's not so far short of being felonious
When you ask us to substitute for it the simious.
You will find what that means in the pages of Linnæus.
We raised roses, but you seem to cultivate zinnias,
Not to call your verse anything more ignominious."
"You forget," I reminded him, "his mandolute;
To judge him without it is hardly acute."
The old gentleman suddenly turned and snapped "Non-
    sense!"
"On the contrary, Sir, it's the *sine quâ non* sense.
We have Lindsay, a voice; and Kreymborg, an instrument."
"Is your poetry a junk-shop? I am now quite convinced
    you meant
All this as hoaxing." I tried to protest.
He went on in a stream like a person possessed:
"A junk-shop indeed! There is Frost, a dim Buddha

Set high on a shelf; there is Sandburg, a cruder
Carved god of some sort, neither English nor Gothic—
Assyrian, Egyptian, perhaps—a huge Thothic
Sacerdotal presentment placed over the door;
There are two Chinese vases, a spy-glass, three score
Or so dog's-eared books, flowerpots, and a spinet,
This odd jumble's Miss Lowell; there's a little green linnet
Hung up in a cage, Sara Teasdale, I think;
And a battered old desk all bespattered with ink,
That's Masters; and just up above is a palette
Smudged over with paint, that is Fletcher; a mallet
Thrown down on a heap of new books which it crushes
Is Aiken; and there is a bundle of rushes
Just picked and brought in to the shop to set off
A stone-lantern—'H. D.'; just behind is a trough
To water poor readers, it's not overflowing
But full to the brim and seems always just going
To spill, but that never quite happens, you guess
At once this is Robinson; in a recess
Just under the counter are two or three chromos
Of tropical scenes, Mrs. Conkling is those;
And the blocks which you see have just come from the
    gilder
I need hardly tell you are your precious Hilda,
They are specially made to build Castles in Spain.
There's your junk-shop of poets, and I tell you again
I don't like to be quizzed." Poor old soul, he was furious,
But when once convinced his suspicions were spurious
He was eager as ever. "For," said I, "there's no quarrel.
The shop sign's a wreath and it's possibly laurel."
"Perhaps I have half a suspicion of that
Myself," he smiled broadly, "now give tit for tat,
And confound all my quondam ridiculous ires
With something so pleasant and . . ."

                    "The Untermeyers!"
The shout which I gave cut his sentence in two,
And we lost the last part in the hullabaloo
I made as I served up my marital dish.

"Two poets, and between them whatever you wish.
If they haven't the depth, they've more range than the
     Brownings,
It runs all the way from complexes to clownings,
With love songs so frank they pursue more than follow man
Being made on the pattern approved by King Soloman.
(My so spelling that name is nothing to look solemn on,
I've a black-letter precedent one might write a column on.
Orthographical pedantry was not in King Solomon.)
At least hers are, a perfectly natural law
Vide Freud, D. H. Lawrence, and George Bernard Shaw.
For woman possesses, it seems, an atomic
Attraction for man, and his serio-comic
Pretense of pursuit is a masculine blind
To keep up his prestige within his own mind.
If the lady appears to be fleeing, the stroke
Is a masterly one and just her little joke.
But when this same woman, in some bright confection
Of boudoir attire, gives herself to reflection
And writes down her heart in a freak of exposure,
The result will most certainly jar the composure
Of elderly persons brought up more demurely,
While youth will retire, with doors locked securely,
And read what to them is a gorgeous display
Of Paradise opened on visiting day.
The best gifts of our time are these pure revelations
Of facts as they are in all human relations
With no understatements or exaggerations.
And the West is the East, with the puritan night
Swallowed up in a gush of approaching daylight—
At least, so our cherished delusion mistakes it,
And since everything is as man's attitude makes it,
What the Orient knew we are learning again
For the next generation to laud with 'Amen!'
In this wise are the poems of Jean Untermeyer,
Though the whole of her output takes less than a quire
Of paper to hold it. Not at all so with Louis,
He's as rich and eclectic as a bowl of chop suey.
If his wife plays a timbrel, he plays a ram's horn,

His ardor for worship is never outworn,
One of Joshua's soldiers, protecting his candle
With the pitcher he eagerly holds by the handle,
Tramping his turn at a long sentry-go
Round and round the high walls of our new Jericho;
Or, again, on a harp which, if slightly archaic,
Has lost nothing in tone or in timbre since Hebraic
Psalmists once plucked it in stern exhortations
Before kneeling hosts of the wandering nations.
Through the streets of today, with his shoulders set square,
He walks, full of business, and yet one's aware
Of a something he sees which surrounds and encloses
His vision, he might be just gazing on Moses
Descending the mountain, but his tables of stone
Have Marx written on them and Debs, while his own
Name has no place at all, and that's characteristic;
His ego's too eager to be egotistic.
When everything beckons, why sit at home brooding
On the opposite wall; he's no taste for secluding
Himself or his interests, and they're only controlled
By the small slice of time which he happens to hold.
Punctiliously present in this exact moment,
His dates began when he learnt what 'proximo' meant.
No glance of his, scanning the past, finds it prizable,
The only real worth is in the realizable;
Neither history nor legend induce him to vary
His perfect allegiance to the mere temporary.
When he takes on himself the role of appraiser,
His words spout and gush like a Yellowstone geyser,
At least for the poet whose political ways err
From those of society, an apt paraphraser
Of the poems of such men, he becomes a sharp razor
To others, no hint of the sham sentimental
Escapes his smooth blade, and he is not gentle
With the scenes or the poses in which 'temperamental'
Poets indulge, and he's scarcely parental
To persons with leanings toward the transcendental.
His dictums, it's true, are less poignant than plenty,
And do not rank too high among *cognoscenti*,

Who are usually college boys not quite turned twenty.
He has a blind spot: he cannot keep his eye on
A world without man. Why, a fresh dandelion
Is nothing to him without someone to pick it,
Observe it alone and he hands you the ticket
For exit at once, and it's not a return check.
He hopes in this way to act as a stern check
On all those untoward imaginative flights
In which he is sure he descries signal-lights
Of a shower of earth-wrecking meteorites.
Now why should a man who is so pyrotechnical
Find a mere meteoric display apoplectical,
While many consider it a beautiful spectacle?
That's a matter for wonder; but, speaking of rockets,
He carries them round like small change in his pockets.
A touch and they're off, and the whiz and the flare
And the burst of bright balls are quite his affair.
What a crackle of rhymes! They go off like red crackers
Beneath a tin pan. And there are some whackers
Exploding at intervals when you least expect them,
And long trailing assonances set to connect them.
His wit is a pin-wheel which at first jerks and spits
Then whirls suddenly round as though ten thousand fits
Were in it, and all is one sparkling gyration
In every known manner of versification.
But the best of his fire-works comprise his set-pieces
Which are really so many bright-colored *esquisses*.
(Please pardon a liberty in pronunciation.
Le mot juste, I believe, needs no justification,
Even when it involves a slight deviation
From the speech of a friendly but jaw-breaking nation,
Who, I trust, will regard this brief explanation
In the light of a willing, though painful, libation.)
But how I run on! To return to my symbol:
A bare two or three poets have ever been nimble
Enough to depict their confrères and show them
Drawn to scale in each feature as all their friends know
    them.
Just glance at them now, each hung on a hook

Awaiting the match—Ftt! Presto! Now, look—
How they flicker and burn, each one to his trick:
There are Robinson's quatrains, Frost's long, pliant stick
Of blank verse which he carries when taking his walks,
And Sandburg with his suitcase all crammed full of talks
With murderers and hobos and such worth-while gentry;
Here is Lindsay retreating at speed to the entry
To stand on the stair and harangue new arrivals
With the very same stunts they employ at revivals,
While Amy Lowell, close by the library door,
Announces her theories and tries hard to score
More disciples than Lindsay; though, with his and her
        medium,
It's a matter of choice which produces least tedium.
Whoever the poet and whatever his foibles,
Even dull ones like—well, I won't say—are enjoyables
When he touches them up to a glare with his slow-match.
At this sort of thing everyone else is no match
For him, and the best simply rank as '—and Other Poets.'
A terrible fellow with his black line to smother poets,
And that line is become the poetical plank
From which he dives into posterity's tank.
It's a curious conceit, and his one bit of swank,
To flaunt himself under a long line of blank.
But what poet, quick or dead, would dare to decline
An immortal existence conferred by one line.
Take it then, Untermeyer, irrepressible Louis,
And observe, as you touch it, that the leaves are still dewy.
That dew is the proof that it's not bombazine,
One has to be careful with a housewife like Jean.
The lady, you know, is a trifle impulsive,
And I should not like my gift to receive a propulsive
Reception. For fame's rather like millinery,
Today it's a blossom, tomorrow a cherry,
The day after, glass flowers in some cemetery.
But who, even in fame, would remain stationary?
Not you certainly, Louis, your deepest devotion
Is involved in this question, but you have no notion
How nearly you come to perpetual motion."

Here I ended abruptly. When he's carried a man
To the center of movement, the historian
Does well to leave off. I left off therefore.
My old friend somewhat wearily asked, "Is there more?"
"A few odds and ends, but not much you need heed,"
I replied. "Very well, run them over at speed,"
He commanded.

    Now if he had wielded a bludgeon
I could not have more quickly obeyed, no curmudgeon
Could have forced my direction more surely than he did.
His imperious courtesy was all that I needed
To start off again with my tale: "The expatriates
Come next," I began, "but the man who expatiates
Upon them must go all yclad in cold steel
Since these young men are both of them most *difficile,*
And each is possessed of a gift for satire.
Their forked barbs would pierce any usual attire.
In order of merit, if not of publicity,
I will take Eliot first, though it smacks of duplicity
To award Ezra Pound the inferior place
As he simply won't run if not first in a race.
Years ago, 'twould have been the other way round,
With Eliot a rather bad second to Pound.
But Pound has been woefully free with the mustard
And so occupied has quite ruined his custard.
No poems from his pen, just spleen on the loose,
And a man who goes on in that way cooks his goose.
T. S. Eliot's a very unlike proposition,
He has simply won through by process of attrition.
Where Pound played the fool, Eliot acted the wiseacre;
Eliot works in his garden, Pound stultifies his acre.
Eliot's always engaged digging fruit out of dust;
Pound was born in an orchard, but his trees have the rust.
Eliot's mind is perpetually fixed and alert;
Pound goes off anywhere, anyhow, like a squirt.
Pound believes he's a thinker, but he's far too romantic;
Eliot's sure he's a poet when he's only pedantic.
But Eliot has raised pedantry to a pitch,

While Pound has upset romance into a ditch.
Eliot fears to abandon an old masquerade;
Pound's one perfect happiness is to parade.
Eliot's learning was won at a very great price;
What Pound calls his learning he got in a trice.
Eliot knows what he knows, though he cannot digest it;
Pound knows nothing at all, but has frequently guessed it.
Eliot builds up his essays by a process of massing;
Pound's are mostly hot air, what the vulgar call 'gassing.'
Eliot lives like a snail in his shell, pen protruding;
Pound struts like a cock, self-adored, self-deluding.
Pound's darling desire is his ego's projection;
Eliot tortures his soul with a dream of perfection.
Pound's an ardent believer in the value of noise;
Eliot strains every nerve to attain a just poise.
Each despises his fellows, for varying reasons;
Each one is a traitor, but with different treasons.
Each has left his own country, but Pound is quite sick of it,
While for Eliot's sojourn, he is just in the nick of it.
Pound went gunning for trouble, and got it, for cause;
Eliot, far more astute, has deserved his applause.
Each has more brain than heart, but while one man s a
    critic
The other is more than two-thirds tympanitic.
Both of them are book-men, but where Eliot has found
A horizon in letters, Pound has only found Pound.
Each man feels himself so little complete
That he dreads the least commerce with the man in the
    street;
Each imagines the world to be leagued in a dim pact
To destroy his immaculate taste by its impact.
To conceive such a notion, one might point out slyly,
Would scarcely occur to an author more highly
Original; such men seldom bother their wits
With outsiders at all, whether fits or misfits.
Where they are, whom they see, is a matter of sheer
Indifference to a poet with his own atmosphere
To exist in, and such have no need to be preachy
Anent commonplaceness since they can't write a *cliché—*

In toto, at least, and it's *toto* that grounds
All meticulous poets like the Eliots and Pounds.
Taking up Eliot's poetry, it's a blend of intensive
And elegant satire with a would-be offensive
Kind of virulent diatribe, and neither sort's lacking
In the high type of polish we demand of shoe-blacking.
Watteau if you like, arm in arm with Laforgue,
And both of these worthies laid out in a morgue.
The poems are expert even up to a vice,
But they're chilly and dead like corpses on ice.
Now a man who's reluctant to heat his work through,
I submit, is afraid of what that work will do
On its own, with its muscles and sinews unfrozen.
Something, I must think, which he would not have chosen.
Is there barely a clue here that the action of heat
Might reveal him akin to the man in the street?
For his brain—there's no doubt that is up on a steeple,
But his heart might betray him as one of the people.
A fearful dilemma! We can hardly abuse him
For hiding the damaging fact and excuse him
If it really be so, and we've more than a hint of it,
Although I, for one, like him better by dint of it.
Since the poet's not the half of him, we must include
The critical anchorite of his *Sacred Wood.*
'This slim duodecimo you must have your eye on
If you'd be up to date,' say his friends. He's a sly one
To have chosen this format—the book's heavy as iron.
I'm acutely aware that its grave erudition
Is quite in the line of a certain tradition,
That one which is commonly known as tuition.
To read it is much like a lengthy sojourning
In at least two or three institutions of learning.
But, being no schoolboy, I find I'm not burning
For this sort of instruction, and vote for adjourning.
What the fellow's contrived to stuff into his skull
May be certainly classed as a pure miracle,
But the way he imparts it is terribly dull.
This may not be fair, for I've only begun it,
And one should not pronounce on a book till one's done it,

But I've started so often, in so many places,
I think, had there been any livelier spaces
I must have encountered at least one of those
Before falling, I say it with shame, in a doze.
We must take Ezra Pound from a different angle:
He's a belfry of excellent chimes run to jangle
By being too often and hurriedly tugged at,
And even, when more noise was wanted, just slugged at
And hammered with anything there was lying round.
Such delicate bells could not stand so much Pound.
Few men have to their credit more excellent verses
Than he used to write, and even his worse is
Much better than most people's good. He'd a flair
For just the one word indispensably there,
But which few could have hit on. Another distinction
Was the way he preserved fledgeling poets from extinction.
Had he never consented to write when the urge
To produce was not on him, he'd have been on the verge
Of a great reputation by now, but his shoulder
Had always its chip, and Ezra's a scolder.
Off he flew, giving nerves and brain up to the business
In a crowing excitement not unmixed with dizziness,
Whenever he could get any sort of newspaper
To lend him a column and just let him vapor.
But while he was worrying his gift of invention
For adequate means to ensure the prevention
Of anyone's getting what he had not got,
His uncherished talent succumbed to dry rot.
When, after the battle, he would have employed her,
He learnt, to his cost, that he had destroyed her.
Now he does with her ghost, and the ghosts of the hosts
Of troubadours, minstrels, and kings, for he boasts
An acquaintance with persons of whose very names
I am totally ignorant, likewise their fames.
The foremost, of course, is Bertrand de Born,
He's a sort of pervasively huge leprechaun
Popping out from Pound's lines where you never expect
    him.
He is our poet's chief lar, so we must not neglect him.

There is Pierre de Maensac, and Pierre won the singing—
Where or how I can't guess, but Pound sets his fame ringing
Because he was *dreitz hom* (whatever that is)
And had De Tierci's wife; what happened to his
We don't know, in fact we know nothing quite clearly,
For Pound always treats his ghosts cavalierly.
There is John Borgia's bath, and be sure that he needed it;
Aurunculeia's shoe, but no one much heeded it.
There's a chap named Navighero and another Barabello,
Who prods a Pope's elephant; and one Mozarello;
Savairic Mauleon—Good Lord, what a dance
Of impossible names! First I think we're in France,
Then he slides in Odysseus, and Eros, and Atthis—
But I'm not to be fooled in my Greek, that's what that is.
Yet, look, there's Italian sticking out in italics
And French in plain type, the foreign vocalics
Do give one the feeling of infinite background,
When it's all just a trick of that consummate quack, Pound,
To cheat us to thinking there's something behind it.
But, when nothing's to find, it's a hard job to find it.
The tragedy lies in the fact that the man
Had a potentiality such as few can
Look back to or forward to; had he but kept it,
There's no bar in all poetry but he might have leapt it.
Even now, I believe, if he'd let himself grow,
He might start again . . ." "We will have no 'although'
In your gamut of poets. Your man is a victim
Of expatriation, and, as usual, it's licked him.
It has happened more times than I care to reflect,
And the general toll is two countries' neglect."
The old gentleman sighed. "I presume that you've finished,"
He went on at last. "The ranks are diminished,"
I answered, "but still there remain one or two
Whose names, at the least, I must pass in review.

"There's William Rose Benét, his poems have no beaters
In their own special *genre;* he's a wonder with meters,
A sleight-of-hand artist, and one of his mysteries
Is his cabinet trick with all the world's histories.

There's Bodenheim, trowel in hand, bent on laying
A tessellate floor with the words he is saying.
Squares of marble, moss-agate, and jade, and carnelian,
Byzantium *in pleno,* never Delphic nor Delian.
A perfect example of contemporaneity,
But with too little force and too much femineity.
The man's a cascade of verbose spontaneity.
Except when he's giving Advice, there he shines
And La Fontaine plays hide and seek in his lines.
As a maker of Fables, no one ever quarrels
With his style, and old Æsop must look to his laurels.
There's another young man who strums a clavier
And prints a new poem every third or fourth year.
Looking back, I don't know that anything since
Has delighted me more than his *Peter Quince.*
He has published no book and adopts this as pose,
But it's rather more likely, I think, to suppose
The particular gift he's received from the Muses
Is a tufted green field under whose grass there oozes
A seeping of poetry, like wind through a cloister;
On occasion it rises, and then the field's moister
And he has a poem if he'll trouble to bale it,
Address it to *Poetry,* and afterwards mail it.
His name, though the odds overbalance the evens
Of those who don't know it as yet's Wallace Stevens,
But it might be John Doe for all he seems to care—
A little fine work scattered into the air
By the wind, it appears, and he quite unaware
Of the fact, since his motto's a cool 'laisser-faire.'
There's Edna Millay with her *Aria da Cap*-
O'h, she dealt all society a pretty sharp rap
With that bauble of hers, be it drama or fable,
Which I certainly trust won't be laid on the table
In my time. Her *Bean-Stalk* is a nice bit of greenery,
For one of her charms is her most charming scenery,
Few can handle more deftly this sort of machinery.
But I must call a halt, or your brain will be flooded
With big poets, and little poets, and poets not yet budded.
"Have you really so many?" my old friend desired

To know. "If you count all the ones who've aspired,
I could go on all night. You see we have got
A Renaissance on." "Dear me, I forgot,"
He remarked somewhat dryly. "We were not renaissant,
But also I note we were far less complacent
Than you seem to be, and this beggar-my-neighbor
Game you all indulge in was no part of our labor."
"No," I told him, "you played on a pipe and a tabor;
We go girt with a shield and drawing a saber.
And yet you, with Miranda . . ." I talked to the swell
Of the wide-running river, to a clock-striking bell.
There was no one beside me. A wave caught the sedge
Of the bank and went ruffling along its soft edge.
Behind me a motor honked twice, and the bridges
Glared suddenly out of the dusk, twinkling ridges
Notched into the dim river-line. Wind was whirling
The plane-trees about, it sent the waves curling
Across one another in a chuckle of laughter—
And I recollect nothing that happened thereafter.
Who my gentleman was, if you hazard a guess,
I will tell you I know nothing more, nothing less,
Than I here have set forth. For I never have met him
From that day to this, or I should have beset him
With questions, I think. My unique perseverance
Kept me haunting the river for his reappearance,
Armed with two or three books which might serve as a
      primer
To point my remarks, for I am no skimmer,
When I push at a wheel it must go or I'll break it,
Once embarked on a mission I never forsake it.
Did he guess my intention and think he'd enough
Of me and my poets, a sufficient rebuff;
But I've never believed he went off in a huff.
Did I dream him perhaps? Was he only a bluff
Of the past making sport with my brain? But that's stuff!
Take it what way you like, if he were a specter
Then the ghosts of old poets have received a correcter
Account than they had of us, and may elect a
Prize winner and vote over post-prandial nectar.

Suppose that, before awarding the prize,
The poets had determined to sift truth from lies
And had sent an ambassador down to enquire
Whose flames were cut tinsel and whose were real fire.
Selecting a man once employed in the trade,
They had only to wait the report that he made
And discuss it at *al fresco* lunch in the shade
Of some cloudy and laurel-embowered arcade.
Supposing it happened that their emissary
Determined to take me as a tutelary
Genius to guide him, and after he'd pumped me
Of all that I knew, quite naturally dumped me
And returned whence he came. You call this bizarre?
But then, after all, so many things are!
If it were so, at least the conclave knows who's who,
And will see there's no reason at all to pooh-pooh.
I, for one, am most eager to know what they'll do.
Aren't you?

H. L. MENCKEN OF BALTIMORE became literary editor of the *Smart Set* in 1908. This monthly magazine was owned by the dubious Colonel Mann of *Town Topics* and had a frivolous cover and cheap paper; but the monthly articles of Mencken and of the dramatic critic, George Jean Nathan, began to attract attention.

The effect of Mencken's criticism was startling to the young people who had been brought up in the Howells era. Howells had tried very hard to be hospitable to new talent from everywhere, but he had himself kept quite close to the genteel tradition. Mencken had the temerity to put his foot through the genteel tradition, and it suddenly turned out that the spell no longer held. The cobwebs dropped away, and we were able to look out across the country and to see what was actually being produced in the way of interesting work—which seemed scarcely at any point to coincide with the kind of thing admired by our most impressive critics, such as W. C. Brownell. There were crude naturalistic novelists writing about the West, like Dreiser and Frank Norris; a romantic of the primitive like Jack London, who wrote about the Yukon and the Klondike and the Oakland water-front; humorists like George Ade, who were turning American slang into a compressed and pungent speech; radi-

cal pamphleteers headed by Upton Sinclair, himself as
well-informed as a reporter and as passionate as a poet;
solitary, gifted Middle Westerners of the type of Ed Howe,
who had stuck to their little cities in the role of the local
heretic; San Francisco Bohemians like Ambrose Bierce, who
shot up the town in the local newspapers; Southerners
like Miss Reese and Cabell, who, more or less unnoticed
by the North, had quietly been cultivating the literary art
in cities like Baltimore and Richmond.

All these people Mencken read and tried to give their
due. He had something that perhaps none of our literary
men had ever had before him: an appetite for American
print that was limitless and omnivorous. He read many
books, magazines, newspapers, pamphlets, and manuscripts,
as they came in to him from all corners of the country;
and he used to say that he even enjoyed reading the
prospectuses put out by bond houses, because everything
written was an attempt to express the aspirations of some
human being. He also had a good prose style of a kind to
which we were quite unaccustomed, though it was immediately imitated to nausea: a blend of American colloquial
speech with a rakish literary English that sounded as if it
had come out of old plays of the period of Congreve and
Wycherley; and a tone that was humorous and brutal in the
combative Germanic manner. By the beginning of the
twenties the Mencken who had begun by merely making a
few protests and declaring a few emphatic preferences in a
quarter of the journalistic world not much frequented by
the literary found himself—now, with Nathan, editor as
well as critic of the *Smart Set*—a sort of central bureau to
which the young looked for tips to guide them in the
cultural confusion and to whom almost everyone who was
trying to write anxiously brought his efforts. The *Smart
Set* was a raffish magazine; but the old magazines with
their editors of the type of Richard Watson Gilder were
so paralyzed by their publics and their publishers that they
could never have let down the bars and given the new
American writers a hearing.

The essays on James Huneker and Theodore Dreiser in-

cluded in this selection came out in *A Book of Prefaces,*
which was published in 1917 and represented Mencken's
first attempt—though he had already published books on
Shaw and on Nietzsche—to put forward his critical point
of view in a book.

The appearance of *A Book of Prefaces* was thus the first
explicit vindication of the dignity of certain figures, with
the tendencies they represented, who had hitherto been
rather ill-regarded.

James Huneker, though he came from Philadelphia, belonged to that Bohemian New York which had rathe↑
dropped into obscurity since the days of Pfaff's beer-cellar
but had persisted and was now reviving, with Luchow's
on Fourteenth Street taking the place of Pfaff's. It was here
that Huneker liked to hold the floor, and there grew up
about him in New York a whole group of critics who had
drunk with him or been nourished by his books. Mencken,
Nathan, Carl Van Vechten, Paul Rosenfeld, and Lawrence
Gilman—all of them had caught from Huneker something of
his crispness and color, something of his special electrical
version of the Manhattan cosmopolitanism. All loved music
as well as literature, and all knew something of painting,
as Huneker did. All liked to go to Europe when they could
and to bring back the news of its triumphs of the opera,
the gallery, the press, the theater, the music-hall, the table.
All contributed to stimulate their readers as the older critics
had never done to a sense of the marvelous things that the
life of art could give, and they differed from the Howells
generation in making one feel that no other kind of life
was comparable to this. They not only said that art was
great, as Charles Eliot Norton would have done, but they
proved that they believed it by being willing to run foul of
respectable social prejudice, provincial ignorance, academic
usage, and puritanical scruple, in the interests of the claims
of good art. Mencken's tribute to Huneker really marks one
of the stages of a campaign the first battle of which had already been won and to which new recruits were streaming.

But Huneker was mainly a music-lover and he did not

find much in America. It was Mencken who first had the courage to open the Hunekerian pantheon: Nietzsche, Wagner, Ibsen, Huysmans, Richard Strauss, George Moore, etc., to candidates from the United States. The first of these candidates, Dreiser, was now looming to conventional criticism like Grendel in *Beowulf*: a huge, bristling, destructive, and formless monster that every instinct told it to kill. But Mencken knew perfectly how to handle the matter. He had always had a sort of relish for the squalid, semi-literate writing of which so much has been produced in the United States. He amused himself by analyzing and exhibiting specimens of this kind of thing, as in the little piece here included on the prose style of President Harding; and he liked to explore this medium for a record of the sad realities of that common and obscure American life which tried thus to describe its experience. In Dreiser, wrapped up in an integument that sounded superficially like the *Family Herald* (and which must have served as one of the models for the cabmen's-shelter chapter in *Ulysses*), he found a man of first-rate ability; and he managed to spike the worst guns of the enemy by admitting Dreiser's technical faults and exposing them with amiable drollery instead of with indignation. Mencken's study of Dreiser's style reminds us of Mark Twain on Cooper; and, after all, we ask ourselves, does Dreiser really write worse than Cooper? It has been one of the misfortunes of American fiction that American life itself has not always provided an instrument worthy of the interest of its new material. Yet as Cooper has his all-suffusing poetry, so Dreiser has his solemn rhythms. If we can get used to the imprecise language, we can hear in the heavy German cadences a music of the sense of doom at the mercy of material forces which has been stirred in a sensitive and reflective mind at the beginning of the nineteenth century by our sprawling and unkempt and mechanized American industrial life.

The best of Mencken's work as a critic both of literature and of society was certainly done in the days of the *Smart Set*. When he and Nathan, in 1923, started the *American*

Mercury, more elegant and more pretentious, Mencken seemed to become less open-minded. His own prejudices and mannerisms had hardened, and he tended to try to impose them on other writers in the magazine; and he became a little excessively indulgent to writers like Sinclair Lewis whom he himself had helped to create. Like every other good thing in the period of the Boom—like Florida real estate and Lindbergh—the public overdid him. When he made a trip West in the later twenties, he was given the triumphal progress of a candidate for the presidency; and when the movie star Rudolph Valentino became worried about his personal life, he came to Mencken for words of healing as if to an accredited wise man. Mencken's preachings of an equanimous hedonism which involved playing Brahms and drinking beer were followed by the debaucheries of the twenties; and he must have been disgusted by the liberated broker who read *Jurgen* and the *American Mercury* and had etchings of wild geese on his walls.

At any rate, he finally withdrew from this national apotheosis. He resigned from the *American Mercury* in 1933, and has since published a new edition of his work on *The American Language* and a series of autobiographical memoirs which contain some of his best writing.

The essays on Lardner and on the death of Howells came out in *Prejudices, Fifth Series,* of 1926; *A Short View of Gamalielese* was published in the *Nation* of April 27, 1921, and has never been reprinted by Mr. Mencken.

H. L. MENCKEN

THEODORE DREISER

1917

OUT OF THE DESERT of American fictioneering, so populous and yet so dreary, Dreiser stands up—a phenomenon unescapably visible, but disconcertingly hard to explain. What forces combined to produce him in the first place, and how has he managed to hold out so long against the prevailing blasts—of disheartening misunderstanding and misrepresentation, of Puritan suspicion and opposition, of artistic isolation, of commercial seduction? There is something downright heroic in the way the man has held his narrow and perilous ground, disdaining all compromise, unmoved by the cheap success that lies so inviting around the corner. He has faced, in his day, almost every form of attack that a serious artist can conceivably encounter, and yet all of them together have scarcely budged him an inch. He still plods along in the laborious, cheerless way he first marked out for himself; he is quite as undaunted by baited praise as by bludgeoning, malignant abuse; his later novels are, if anything, more unyieldingly dreiserian than his earliest. As one who has long sought to entice him in this direction or that, fatuously presuming to instruct him in what would improve him and profit him, I may well bear a reluctant and resigned sort of testimony to his gigantic steadfastness. It is almost as if any change in his manner, any concession to what is usual and esteemed, any amelioration of his blind, relentless exercises of *force majeure,* were a physical impossibility. One feels him at last to be authentically no more than a helpless instrument (or victim) of that inchoate flow of forces which he himself is so fond of depicting as at once the answer to the riddle of life, and a riddle ten times more vexing and accursed.

And his origins, as I say, are quite as mysterious as his motive power. To fit him into the unrolling chart of American or even of English fiction is extremely difficult. Save one thinks of H. B. Fuller (whose *With the Procession* and *The Cliff-Dwellers* are still remembered by Huneker, but by whom else?[1]), he seems to have had no forerunner among us, and for all the discussion of him that goes on, he has few avowed disciples, and none of them gets within miles of him. One catches echoes of him, perhaps, in Willa Sibert Cather, in Mary S. Watts, in David Graham Phillips, in Sherwood Anderson, and in Joseph Medill Patterson, but, after all, they are no more than echoes. In Robert Herrick the thing descends to a feeble parody; in imitators further removed to sheer burlesque. All the latter-day American novelists of consideration are vastly more facile than Dreiser in their philosophy, as they are in their style. In the fact, perhaps, lies the measure of their difference. What they lack, great and small, is the gesture of pity, the note of awe, the profound sense of wonder—in a phrase, that "soberness of mind" which William Lyon Phelps sees as the hallmark of Conrad and Hardy, and which even the most stupid cannot escape in Dreiser. The normal American novel, even in its most serious forms, takes color from the national cocksureness and superficiality. It runs monotonously to ready explanations, a somewhat infantile smug-

[1]Fuller's disappearance is one of the strangest phenomena of American letters. I was astonished some time ago to discover that he was still alive. Back in 1899 he was already so far forgotten that William Archer mistook his name, calling him Henry Y. Puller. *Vide* Archer's pamphlet, *The American Language,* New York, 1899. H. L. M.

ness and hopefulness, a habit of reducing the unknowable to terms of the not worth knowing. What it cannot explain away with ready formulae, as in the later Winston Churchill, it snickers over as scarcely worth explaining at all, as in the later Howells. Such a brave and tragic book as *Ethan Frome* is so rare as to be almost singular, even with Mrs. Wharton. There is, I daresay, not much market for that sort of thing. In the arts, as in the concerns of everyday, the American seeks escape from the insoluble by pretending that it is solved. A comfortable phrase is what he craves beyond all things—and comfortable phrases are surely not to be sought in Dreiser's stock.

I have heard argument that he is a follower of Frank Norris, and two or three facts lend it a specious probability. *McTeague* was printed in 1899; *Sister Carrie* a year later. Moreover, Norris was the first to see the merit of the latter book, and he fought a gallant fight, as literary advisor to Doubleday, Page & Co., against its suppression after it was in type. But this theory runs aground upon two circumstances, the first being that Dreiser did not actually read *McTeague*, nor, indeed, grow aware of Norris, until after *Sister Carrie* was completed, and the other being that his development, once he began to write other books, was along paths far distant from those pursued by Norris himself. Dreiser, in truth, was a bigger man than Norris from the start; it is to the latter's unending honor that he recognized the fact instanter, and yet did all he could to help his rival. It is imaginable, of course, that Norris, living fifteen years longer, might have overtaken Dreiser, and even surpassed him; one finds an arrow pointing that way in *Vandover and the Brute* (not printed until 1914). But it swings sharply around in *The Epic of the Wheat*. In the second volume of that incomplete trilogy, *The Pit*, there is an obvious concession to the popular taste in romance; the thing is so frankly written down, indeed, that a play has been made of it, and Broadway has applauded it. And in *The Octopus*, despite some excellent writing, there is a descent to a mysticism so fantastic and preposterous that it quickly passes beyond serious consideration. Norris, in his day, swung even lower—for example, in *A Man's Woman* and in some of his short stories. He was a pioneer, perhaps only half sure of the way he wanted to go, and the evil lures of popular success lay all about him. It is no wonder that he sometimes seemed to lose his direction.

Emile Zola is another literary father whose paternity grows dubious on examination. I once printed an article exposing what seemed to me to be a Zolaesque attitude of mind, and even some trace of the actual Zola manner, in *Jennie Gerhardt*; there came from Dreiser the news that he had never read a line of Zola, and knew nothing about his novels. Not a complete answer, of course; the influence might have been exerted at second hand. But through whom? I confess that I am unable to name a likely medium. The effects of Zola upon Anglo-Saxon fiction have been almost *nil*; his only avowed disciple, George Moore, has long since recanted and reformed; he has scarcely rippled the prevailing romanticism. . . . Thomas Hardy? Here, I daresay, we strike a better scent. There are many obvious likenesses between *Tess of the D'Urbervilles* and *Jennie Gerhardt* and again between *Jude the Obscure* and *Sister Carrie*. All four stories deal penetratingly and poignantly with the essential tragedy of women; all disdain the petty, specious explanations of popular fiction; in each one finds a poetical and melancholy beauty. Moreover, Dreiser himself confesses to an enchanted discovery of Hardy in 1896, three years before *Sister Carrie* was begun. But it is easy to push such a fact too hard, and to search for likenesses and parallels that are really not there. The truth is that Dreiser's points of contact with Hardy might be easily matched by many striking points of difference, and that the fundamental ideas in their novels, despite a common sympathy, are anything but identical. Nor does one apprehend any ponderable result of Dreiser's youthful enthusiasm for Balzac, which antedated his discovery of Hardy by two years. He got from both men a sense of the scope and dignity of the novel; they taught him that a story might be a good one, and yet considerably more than a story; they showed him the essential drama of the commonplace. But that they had more influence

in forming his point of view, or even in shaping his technique, than any one of half-a-dozen other gods of those
young days—this I scarcely find. In the structure of his
novels, and in their manner of approach to life no less, they
call up the work of Dostoevsky and Turgenev far more than
the work of either of these men—but of all the Russians
save Tolstoy (as of Flaubert) Dreiser himself tells us that
he was ignorant until ten years after *Sister Carrie*. In his
days of preparation, indeed, his reading was so copious and
so disorderly that antagonistic influences must have well-
nigh neutralized one another, and so left the curious youngster to work out his own method and his own philosophy.
Stevenson went down with Balzac, Poe with Hardy, Dumas
fils with Tolstoy. There were even months of delight in
Sienkiewicz, Lew Wallace, and E. P. Roe! The whole
repertory of the pedagogues had been fought through in
school and college: Dickens, Thackeray, Hawthorne, Washington Irving, Kingsley, Scott. Only Irving and Hawthorne
seem to have made deep impressions. "I used to lie under a
tree," says Dreiser, "and read *Twice-Told Tales* by the hour.
I thought *The Alhambra* was a perfect creation, and I still
have a lingering affection for it." Add Bret Harte, George
Ebers, William Dean Howells, Oliver Wendell Holmes,
and you have a literary stew indeed! . . . But for all its
bubbling I see a far more potent influence in the chance
discovery of Spencer and Huxley at twenty-three—the year
of choosing! Who, indeed, will ever measure the effect of
those two giants upon the young men of that era—Spencer
with his inordinate meticulousness, his relentless pursuit
of facts, his overpowering syllogisms, and Huxley with his
devastating agnosticism, his insatiable questionings of the
old axioms, above all, his brilliant style? Huxley, it would
appear, has been condemned to the scientific hulks, along
with bores innumerable and unspeakable; one looks in
vain for any appreciation of him in treatises on beautiful
letters.[1] And yet the man was a superb artist in works, a

[1]For example, in *The Cambridge History of English Literature*,
which runs to fourteen large volumes and a total of nearly 10,000
pages, Huxley receives but a page and a quarter of notice, and his

master-writer even more than a master-biologist, one of the
few truly great stylists that England has produced since the
time of Anne. One can easily imagine the effect of two
such vigorous and intriguing minds upon a youth groping
about for self-understanding and self-expression. They swept
him clean, he tells us, of the lingering faith of his boyhood
—a mediaeval, Rhenish Catholicism;—more, they filled him
with a new and eager curiosity, an intense interest in the
life that lay about him, a desire to seek out its hidden
workings and underlying causes. A young man set afire by
Huxley might perhaps make a very bad novelist, but it is a
certainty that he could never make a sentimental and superficial one. There is no need to go further than this single
moving adventure to find the genesis of Dreiser's disdain
of the current platitudes, his sense of life as a complex
biological phenomenon, only dimly comprehended, and his
tenacious way of thinking things out, and of holding to
what he finds good. Ah, that he had learned from Huxley,
not only how to inquire, but also how to report! That he
had picked up a talent for that dazzling style, so sweet to
the ear, so damnably persuasive, so crystal-clear!

But the more one examines Dreiser, either as writer or as
theorist of man, the more his essential isolation becomes
apparent. He got a habit of mind from Huxley, but he
completely missed Huxley's habit of writing. He got a view
of woman from Hardy, but he soon changed it out of all
resemblance. He got a certain fine ambition and gusto out
of Balzac, but all that was French and characteristic he left
behind. So with Zola, Howells, Tolstoy, and the rest. The
tracing of likenesses quickly becomes rabbinism, almost
cabalism. The differences are huge and sprout up in all
directions. Nor do I see anything save a flaming up of
colonial passion in the current efforts to fit him into a German frame, and make him an agent of Prussian frightfulness
in letters. Such bosh one looks for in the *Nation* and the
Boston *Transcript,* and there is where one actually finds

remarkable mastery of English is barely mentioned in passing. His
two debates with Gladstone, in which he did some of the best writing
of the century, are not noticed at all. H. L. M.

it. Even the *New Republic* has stood clear of it; it is important only as material for that treatise upon the Anglo-Saxon under the terror which remains to be written. The name of the man, true enough, is obviously Germanic, he has told us himself, in *A Traveler at Forty,* how he sought out and found the tombs of his ancestors in some little town of the Rhine country. There are more of these genealogical revelations in *A Hoosier Holiday,* but they show a Rhenish strain that was already running thin in boyhood. No one, indeed, who reads a Dreiser novel can fail to see the gap separating the author from these half-forgotten forbears. He shows even less of German influence than of English influence.

There is, as a matter of fact, little in modern German fiction that is intelligibly comparable to *Jennie Gerhardt* and *The Titan,* either as a study of man or as a work of art. The naturalistic movement of the eighties was launched by men whose eyes were upon the theater, and it is in that field that nine-tenths of its force has been spent. "German naturalism," says George Madison Priest, quoting Gotthold Klee's *Grun-züge der deutschen Literaturgeschichte,* "created a new type only in the drama."[1] True enough, it has also produced occasional novels, and some of them are respectable. Gustav Frenssen's *Jörn Uhl* is a specimen: it has been done into English. Another is Clara Viebig's *Das tägliche Brot,* which Ludwig Lewisohn compares to George Moore's *Esther Waters.* Yet another is Thomas Mann's *Buddenbrooks.* But it would be absurd to cite these works as evidences of a national quality, and doubly absurd to think of them as inspiring such books as *Jennie Gerhardt* and *The Titan,* which excel them in everything save workmanship. The case of Mann reveals a tendency that is visible in nearly all of his contemporaries. Starting out as an agnostic realist not unlike the Arnold Bennett of *The Old Wives' Tale,* he has gradually taken on a hesitating sort of romanticism, and in one of his later books, *Königliche Hoheit* (in English, *Royal Highness*), he ends upon a note of sentimentalism borrowed

[1] *A Brief History of German Literature;* New York, Chas. Scribner's Sons, 1909. H. L. M.

from Wagner's *Ring*. Fräulein Viebig has also succumbed
to banal and extra-artistic purposes. Her *Die Wacht am
Rheim*, for all its merits in detail, is, at bottom, no more
than an eloquent hymn to patriotism—the most doggish and
dubious of all the virtues. As for Frenssen, he is a parson
by trade, and carries over into the novel a good deal of the
windy moralizing of the pulpit. All of these German nat-
uralists—and they are the only German novelists worth
considering—share the weakness of Zola, their *Stammvater*.
They, too, fall into the morass that engulfed *Fécondité*, and
make sentimental propaganda.

I go into this matter in detail, not because it is intrinsically of any moment, but because the effort to depict
Dreiser as a secret agent of the Wilhelmstrasse, told off to
inject subtle doses of *Kultur* into a naïf and pious people,
has taken on the proportions of an organized movement. The
same critical imbecility which detects naught save a tom-cat
in Frank Cowperwood can find naught save an abhorrent
foreigner in Cowperwood's creator. The truth is that the
trembling patriots of letters, male and female, are simply
at their old game of seeing a man under the bed. Dreiser,
in fact, is densely ignorant of German literature, as he is
of the better part of French literature, and of much of English literature. He did not even read Hauptmann until after
Jennie Gerhardt had been written, and such typical German moderns as Ludwig Thoma, Otto Julius Bierbaum, and
Richard Dehmel remain as strange to him as Heliogabalus.

II

In his manner, as opposed to his matter, he is more the
Teuton, for he shows all of the racial patience and pertinacity and all of the racial lack of humor. Writing a novel
is as solemn a business to him as trimming a beard is to a
German barber. He blasts his way through his interminable
stories by something not unlike main strength; his writing,
one feels, often takes on the character of an actual siege
operation, with tunnelings, drum-fire, assaults in close order,
and hand-to-hand fighting. Once, seeking an analogy, I

called him the Hindenburg of the novel. If it holds, then *The "Genius"* is his Poland. The field of action bears the aspect, at the end, of a hostile province meticulously brought under the yoke, with every road and lane explored to its beginning, and every crossroads village laboriously taken, inventoried, and policed. Here is the very negation of Gallic lightness and intuition, and of all other forms of impressionism as well. Here is no series of illuminating flashes, but a gradual bathing of the whole scene with white light, so that every detail stands out.

And many of those details, of course, are trivial; even irritating. They do not help the picture; they muddle and obscure it; one wonders impatiently what their meaning is, and what the purpose may be of revealing them with such a precise, portentous air. . . . Turn to page 703 of *The "Genius."* By the time one gets there, one has hewn and hacked one's way through 702 large pages of fine print— 97 long chapters, more than 250,000 words. And yet, at this hurried and impatient point, with the *coda* already begun, Dreiser halts the whole narrative to explain the origin, nature, and inner meaning of Christian Science, and to make us privy to a lot of chatty stuff about Mrs. Althea Jones, a professional healer, and to supply us with detailed plans and specifications of the apartment house in which she lives, works her tawdry miracles, and has her being. Here, in sober summary, are the particulars:

1. That the house is "of conventional design."
2. That there is "a spacious areaway" between its two wings.
3. That these wings are "of cream-colored pressed brick."
4. That the entrance between them is "protected by a handsome wrought-iron door."
5. That to either side of this door is "an electric lamp support of handsome design."
6. That in each of these lamp supports there are "lovely cream-colored globes, shedding a soft luster."
7. That inside is "the usual lobby."
8. That in the lobby is "the usual elevator."
9. That in the elevator is the usual "uniformed Negro elevator man."

10. That this Negro elevator man (name not given) is "indifferent and impertinent."

11. That a telephone switchboard is also in the lobby.

12. That the building is seven stories in height.

In *The Financier* there is the same exasperating rolling up of irrelevant facts. The court proceedings in the trial of Cowperwood are given with all the exactness of a parliamentary report in the London *Times*. The speeches of the opposing counsel are set down nearly in full, and with them the remarks of the judge, and after that the opinion of the Appellate Court on appeal, with the dissenting opinions as a sort of appendix. In *Sister Carrie* the thing is less savagely carried out, but that is not Dreiser's fault, for the manuscript was revised by some anonymous hand, and the printed version is but little more than half the length of the original. In *The Titan* and *Jennie Gerhardt* no such brake upon exuberance is visible; both books are crammed with details that serve no purpose, and are as flat as ditchwater. Even in the two volumes of personal record, *A Traveler at Forty* and *A Hoosier Holiday,* there is the same furious accumulation of trivialities. Consider the former. It is without structure, without selection, without reticence. One arises from it as from a great babbling, half drunken. On the one hand the author fills a long and gloomy chapter with the story of the Borgias, apparently under the impression that it is news, and on the other hand he enters into intimate and inconsequential confidences about all the persons he meets en route, sparing neither the innocent nor the obscure. The children of his English host at Bridgely Level strike him as fantastic little creatures, even as a bit uncanny—and he duly sets it down. He meets an Englishman on a French train who pleases him much, and the two become good friends and see Rome together, but the fellow's wife is "obstreperous" and "haughty in her manner" and so "loud-spoken in her opinions" that she is "really offensive"—and down it goes. He makes an impression on a Mlle. Marcelle in Paris, and she accompanies him from Monte Carlo to Ventimiglia, and there gives him a parting kiss and whispers, *"Avril-Fontainebleau"*—and lo, this sweet one is duly spread upon the minutes. He permits himself to be arrested by a fair privateer in Piccadilly, and goes with her to one of the dens of sin that suffragettes see in their nightmares, and cross-examines her at length regarding her ancestry, her professional ethics and ideals, and her earnings at her dismal craft—and into the book goes a full report of the proceedings. He is entertained by an eminent Dutch jurist in Amsterdam—and upon the pages of the chronicle it appears that the gentleman is "waxy" and "a little pedantic," and that he is probably the sort of "thin, delicate, well-barbered" professor that Ibsen had in mind when he cast about for a husband for the daughter of General Gabler.

Such is the art of writing as Dreiser understands it and practices it—an endless piling up of minutiae, an almost ferocious tracking down of ions, electrons, and molecules, an unshakable determination to tell it all. One is amazed by the molelike diligence of the man, and no less by his exasperating disregard for the ease of his readers. A Dreiser novel, at least of the later canon, cannot be read as other novels are read—on a winter evening or summer afternoon, between meal and meal, traveling from New York to Boston. It demands the attention for almost a week, and uses up the faculties for a month. If, reading *The "Genius,"* one were to become engrossed in the fabulous manner described in the publishers' advertisements, and so find oneself unable to put it down and go to bed before the end, one would get no sleep for three days and three nights.

Worse, there are no charms of style to mitigate the rigors of these vast steppes and pampas of narration. Joseph Joubert's saying that "words should stand out well from the paper" is quite incomprehensible to Dreiser; he never imitates Flaubert by writing for *"la respiration et l'oreille."* There is no painful groping for the inevitable word, or for what Walter Pater called "the gipsy phrase"; the common, even the commonplace, coin of speech is good enough. On the first page of *Jennie Gerhardt* one encounters "frank, open countenance," "diffident manner," "helpless poor," "untutored mind," "honest necessity," and half-a-dozen other stand-bys of the second-rate newspaper reporter. In *Sister Carrie* one finds "high noon," "hurrying throng," "unassuming restaurant," "dainty slippers," "high-strung nature," and "cool, calculating world"—all on a few pages. Carrie's sister, Minnie Hanson, "gets" the supper. Hanson himself is "wrapped up" in his child. Carrie decides to enter Storm and King's office, "no matter what." In *The Titan* the word "trig" is worked to death; it takes on, toward the end, the character of a banal and preposterous refrain. In the other books one encounters mates for it—words made to do duty in as many senses as the American verb "to fix" or the journalistic "to secure." . . .

I often wonder if Dreiser gets anything properly describable as pleasure out of this dogged accumulation of threadbare, undistinguished, uninspiring nouns, adjectives, verbs, adverbs, pronouns, participles, and conjunctions. To the man with an ear for verbal delicacies—the man who searches painfully for the perfect word, and puts the way of saying a thing above the thing said—there is in writing the constant joy of sudden discovery, of happy accident. A phrase springs up full blown, sweet and caressing. But what joy can there be in rolling up sentences that have no more life and beauty in them, intrinsically, than so many election bulletins? Where is the thrill in the manufacture of such a paragraph as that in which Mrs. Althea Jones's sordid habitat is described with such inexorable particularity? Or in the laborious confection of such stuff as this, from Book I, Chapter IV, of *The "Genius"*:

The city of Chicago—who shall portray it! This vast ruck of life that had sprung suddenly into existence upon the dank marshes of a lake shore!

Or this from the epilogue to *The Financier*:

There is a certain fish whose scientific name is *Mycteroperca Bonaci*, and whose common name is Black Grouper, which is of considerable value as an afterthought in this connection, and which deserves much to be better known. It is a healthy creature, growing quite regularly to a weight of two hundred and fifty pounds, and living a comfortable, lengthy existence

because of its very remarkable ability to adapt itself to conditions. . . .

Or this from his pamphlet, *Life, Art and America:*[1]

Alas, alas! for art in America. It has a hard stubby row to
hoe.

But I offer no more examples. Every reader of the Dreiser
novels must cherish astounding specimens—of awkward,
platitudinous marginalia, of whole scenes spoiled by bad
writing, of phrases as brackish as so many lumps of sodium
hyposulphite. Here and there, as in parts of *The Titan* and
again in parts of *A Hoosier Holiday,* an evil conscience
seems to haunt him and he gives hard striving to his manner, and more than once there emerges something that is
almost graceful. But a backsliding always follows this phos-
phorescence of reform. *The "Genius,"* coming after *The
Titan,* marks the high tide of his bad writing. There are
passages in it so clumsy, so inept, so irritating that they
seem almost unbelievable; nothing worse is to be found in
the newspapers. Nor is there any compensatory deftness in
structure, or solidity of design, to make up for this carelessness in detail. The well-made novel, of course, can be as
hollow as the well-made play of Scribe—but let us at least
have a beginning, a middle, and an end! Such a story as
The "Genius" is as gross and shapeless as Brünnhilde. It
billows and bulges out like a cloud of smoke, and its internal
organization is almost as vague. There are episodes that, with
a few chapters added, would make very respectable novels.
There are chapters that need but a touch or two to be excellent short stories. The thing rambles, staggers, trips, heaves,
pitches, struggles, totters, wavers, halts, turns aside, trembles
on the edge of collapse. More than once it seems to be
foundering, both in the equine and in the maritime senses.
The tale has been heard of a tree so tall that it took two men
to see to the top of it. Here is a novel so brobdingnagian
that a single reader can scarcely read his way through it. . . .

[1]New York, 1917; reprinted from *The Seven Arts* for February,
1917. H. L. M.

III

Of the general ideas which lie at the bottom of all of Dreiser's work it is impossible to be in ignorance, for he has exposed them at length in *A Hoosier Holiday* and summarized them in *Life, Art and America*. In their main outlines they are not unlike the fundamental assumptions of Joseph Conrad. Both novelists see human existence as a seeking without a finding; both reject the prevailing interpretations of its meaning and mechanism; both take refuge in "I do not know." Put *A Hoosier Holiday* beside Conrad's *A Personal Record*, and you will come upon parallels from end to end. Or better still, put it beside Hugh Walpole's *Joseph Conrad*, in which the Conradean metaphysic is condensed from the novels even better than Conrad has done it himself: at once you will see how the two novelists, each a worker in the elemental emotions, each a rebel against the current assurance and superficiality, each an alien to his place and time, touch each other in a hundred ways.

"Conrad," says Walpole, "is of the firm and resolute conviction that life is too strong, too clever, and too remorseless for the sons of men." And then, in amplification: "It is as though, from some high window, looking down, he were able to watch some shore, from whose security men were forever launching little cockleshell boats upon a limitless and angry sea. . . . From his height he can follow their fortunes, their brave struggles, their fortitude to the very end. He admires their courage, the simplicity of their faith, but his irony springs from his knowledge of the inevitable end." . . .

Substitute the name of Dreiser for that of Conrad, and you will have to change scarcely a word. Perhaps one, to wit, "clever." I suspect that Dreiser, writing so of his own creed, would be tempted to make it "stupid," or, at all events, "unintelligible." The struggle of man, as he sees it, is more than impotent; it is gratuitous and purposeless. There is, to his eye, no grand ingenuity, no skillful adaptation of means to end, no moral (or even dramatic) plan in the order of the universe. He can get out of it only a sense of profound and inexplicable *dis*order. The waves which batter the cockleshells change their direction at every instant. Their navigation is a vast adventure, but intolerably fortuitous and inept—a voyage without chart, compass, sun, or stars. . . .

So at bottom. But to look into the blackness steadily, of course, is almost beyond the endurance of man. In the very moment that its impenetrability is grasped the imagination begins attacking it with pale beams of false light. All religions, I daresay, are thus projected from the questioning soul of man, and not only all religions, but also all great agnosticisms. Nietzsche, shrinking from the horror of that abyss of negation, revived the Pythagorean concept of *der ewigen Wiederkunft*—a vain and blood-curdling sort of comfort. To it, after a while, he added explanations almost Christian—a whole repertoire of whys and wherefores, aims and goals, aspirations and significances. The late Mark Twain, in an unpublished work, toyed with an equally daring idea: that men are to some unimaginably vast and incomprehensible Being what the unicellular organisms of his body are to man, and so on *ad infinitum*. Dreiser occasionally inclines to much the same hypothesis; he likens the endless reactions going on in the world we know, the myriadal creation, collision, and destruction of entities, to the slow accumulation and organization of cells *in utero*. He would make us specks in the insentient embryo of some gigantic Presence whose form is still unimaginable and whose birth must wait for Eons and Eons. Again, he turns to something not easily distinguishable from philosophical idealism, whether out of Berkeley or Fichte it is hard to make out—that is, he would interpret the whole phenomenon of life as no more than an appearance, a nightmare of some unseen sleeper or of men themselves, an "uncanny blur of nothingness"—in Euripides' phrase, "a song sung by an idiot, dancing down the wind." Yet again, he talks vaguely of the intricate polyphony of a cosmic orchestra, cacophonous to our dull ears. Finally, he puts the observed into the ordered, reading a purpose in the displayed event: "life was intended to sting and hurt" . . . But these are only gropings, and not to be read too critically. From speculations and explanations he always returns, Conrad-like, to the bald fact: to "the spectacle and stress of life." All he can make out clearly is "a vast compulsion which has nothing to do with the individual desires or tastes or impulses of individuals." That compulsion springs "from the settling processes of forces which we do not in the least understand, over which we have no control, and in whose grip we are as grains of dust or sand, blown hither and thither, for what purpose we cannot even suspect."[1] Man is not only doomed to defeat, but denied any glimpse or understanding of his antagonist. Here we come upon an agnosticism that has almost got beyond curiosity. What good would it do us, asks Dreiser, to know? In our ignorance and helplessness, we may at least get a slave's consolation out of cursing the unknown gods. Suppose we saw them striving blindly, too, and pitied them? . . .

But, as I say, this skepticism is often tempered by guesses at a possibly hidden truth, and the confession that this truth may exist reveals the practical unworkableness of the unconditioned system, at least for Dreiser. Conrad is far more resolute, and it is easy to see why. He is, by birth and training, an aristocrat. He has the gift of emotional detachment. The lures of facile doctrine do not move him. In his irony there is a disdain which plays about even the ironist himself. Dreiser is a product of far different forces and traditions, and is capable of no such escapement. Struggle as he may, and fume and protest as he may, he can no more shake off the chains of his intellectual and cultural heritage than he can change the shape of his nose. What that heritage is you may find out in detail by reading *A Hoosier Holiday*, or in summary by glancing at the first few pages of *Life, Art and America*. Briefly described, it is the burden of a believing mind, a moral attitude, a lingering superstition. One half of the man's brain, so to speak, wars with the other half. He is intelligent, he is thoughtful, he is a sound artist —but there come moments when a dead hand falls upon him, and he is once more the Indiana peasant, snuffing

[1] *Life, Art and America*, p. 5. H. L. M.

absurdly over imbecile sentimentalities, giving a grave ear to quackeries, snorting and eye-rolling with the best of them. One generation spans too short a time to free the soul of man. Nietzsche, to the end of his days, remained a Prussian pastor's son, and hence two-thirds a Puritan; he erected his war upon holiness, toward the end, into a sort of holy war. Kipling, the grandson of a Methodist preacher, reveals the tin-pot evangelist with increasing clarity as youth and its ribaldries pass away and he falls back upon his fundamentals. And that other English novelist who springs from the serv-ants' hall—let us not be surprised or blame him if he some-times writes like a bounder.

The truth about Dreiser is that he is still in the transition stage between Christian Endeavor and civilization, between Warsaw, Indiana, and the Socratic grove, between being a good American and being a free man, and so he sometimes vacillates perilously between a moral sentimentalism and a somewhat extravagant revolt. The "Genius," on the one hand, is almost a tract for rectitude, a Warning to the Young; its motto might be *Scheut die Dirnen!* And on the other hand, it is full of a laborious truculence that can only be explained by imagining the author as heroically deter-mined to prove that he is a plain-spoken fellow and his own man, let the chips fall where they may. So, in spots, in *The Financier* and *The Titan,* both of them far better books. There is an almost moral frenzy to expose and riddle what passes for morality among the stupid. The isolation of irony is never reached; the man is still evangelical; his ideas are still novelties to him; he is as solemnly absurd in some of his floutings of the Code American as he is in his respect for Bouguereau, or in his flirtings with the New Thought, or in his naïf belief in the importance of novel-writing. Some-where or other I have called all this the Greenwich Village complex. It is not genuine artists, serving beauty reverently and proudly, who herd in those cockroached cellars and bawl for art; it is a mob of half-educated yokels and cockneys to whom the very idea of art is still novel, and intoxicating— and more than a little bawdy.

Not that Dreiser actually belongs to this ragamuffin company. Far from it, indeed. There is in him, hidden deep-down, a great instinctive artist, and hence the makings of an aristocrat. In his muddled way, held back by the manacles of his race and time, and his steps made uncertain by a guiding theory which too often eludes his own comprehension, he yet manages to produce works of art of unquestionable beauty and authority, and to interpret life in a manner that is poignant and illuminating. There is vastly more intuition in him than intellectualism; his talent is essentially feminine, as Conrad's is masculine; his ideas always seem to be deduced from his feelings. The view of life that got into *Sister Carrie*, his first book, was not the product of a conscious thinking out of Carrie's problems. It simply got itself there by the force of the artistic passion behind it; its coherent statement had to wait for other and more reflective days. The thing began as a vision, not as a syllogism. Here the name of Franz Schubert inevitably comes up. Schubert was an ignoramus, even in music; he knew less about polyphony, which is the mother of harmony, which is the mother of music, than the average conservatory professor. But nevertheless he had such a vast instinctive sensitiveness to musical values, such a profound and accurate feeling for beauty in tone, that he not only arrived at the truth in tonal relations, but even went beyond what, in his day, was known to be the truth, and so led an advance. Likewise, Giorgione da Castelfranco and Masaccio come to mind: painters of the first rank, but untutored, unsophisticated, uncouth. Dreiser, within his limits, belongs to this sabot-shod company of the elect. One thinks of Conrad, not as artist first, but as savant. There is something of the icy aloofness of the laboratory in him, even when the images he conjures up pulsate with the very glow of life. He is almost as self-conscious as the Beethoven of the last quartets. In Dreiser the thing is more intimate, more disorderly, more a matter of pure feeling. He gets his effects, one might almost say, not by designing them, but by living them.

But whatever the process, the power of the image evoked is not to be gainsaid. It is not only brilliant on the surface, but mysterious and appealing in its depths. One swiftly

forgets his intolerable writing, his mirthless, sedulous, repellent manner, in the face of the Athenian tragedy he in-
stills into his seduced and soul-sick servant-girls, his barbaric
pirates of finances, his conquered and hamstrung supermen,
his wives who sit and wait. He has, like Conrad, a sure
talent for depicting the spirit in disintegration. Old Gerhardt,
in *Jennie Gerhardt*, is alone worth all the *dramatis personae*
of popular American fiction since the days of *Rob o' the
Bowl*; Howells could no more have created him, in his
Rodinesque impudence of outline, than he could have
created Tartuffe or Gargantua. Such a novel as *Sister Carrie*
stands quite outside the brief traffic of the customary stage.
It leaves behind it an unescapable impression of bigness,
of epic sweep and dignity. It is not a mere story, not a novel
in the customary American meaning of the word; it is at
once a psalm of life and a criticism of life—and that criticism
loses nothing by the fact that its burden is despair. Here,
precisely, is the point of Dreiser's departure from his fellows. He puts into his novels a touch of the eternal *Weltschmerz*. They get below the drama that is of the moment
and reveal the greater drama that is without end. They
arouse those deep and lasting emotions which grow out of
the recognition of elemental and universal tragedy. His aim
is not merely to tell a tale; his aim is to show the vast ebb
and flow of forces which sway and condition human destiny.
One cannot imagine him consenting to Conan Doyle's
statement of the purpose of fiction, quoted with characteristic approval by the New York *Times*: "to amuse mankind,
to help the sick and the dull and the weary." Nor is his
purpose to instruct; if he is a pedagogue it is only incidentally and as a weakness. The thing he seeks to do is to stir,
to awaken, to move. One does not arise from such a book
as *Sister Carrie* with a smirk of satisfaction; one leaves it
infinitely touched.

IV

It is, indeed, a truly amazing first book, and one marvels
to hear that it was begun lightly. Dreiser in those days

(*circa* 1899) had seven or eight years of newspaper work behind him, in Chicago, St. Louis, Toledo, Cleveland, Buffalo, Pittsburgh, and New York, and was beginning to feel that reaction of disgust which attacks all newspaper-men when the enthusiasm of youth wears out. He had been successful, but he saw how hollow that success was, and how little surety it held out for the future. The theater was what chiefly lured him; he had written plays in his nonage, and he now proposed to do them on a large scale, and so get some of the easy dollars of Broadway. It was an old friend from Toledo, Arthur Henry, who turned him toward story writing. The two had met while Henry was city editor of the *Blade* and Dreiser a reporter looking for a job.[1] A firm friendship sprang up, and Henry conceived a high opinion of Dreiser's ability, and urged him to try a short story. Dreiser was distrustful of his own skill, but Henry kept at him, and finally, during a holiday the two spent together at Maumee, Ohio, he made the attempt. Henry had the manuscript typewritten and sent it to *Ainslee's Magazine*. A week or so later there came a check for $75.

This was in 1898. Dreiser wrote four more stories during the year following, and sold them all. Henry now urged him to attempt a novel, but again his distrust of himself held him back. Henry finally tried a rather unusual argument: he had a novel of his own on the stocks,[2] and he represented that he was in difficulties with it and in need of company. One day, in September 1899, Dreiser took a sheet of yellow paper and wrote a title at random. That title was *Sister Carrie*, and with no more definite plan than the mere name offered the book began. It went ahead steadily enough until the middle of October, and had come by then to the place where Carrie meets Hurstwood. At that point Dreiser left it in disgust. It seemed pitifully dull and inconsequential, and for two months he put the manuscript away. Then, under renewed urgings by Henry, he resumed the writing, and kept on to the place where Hurstwood steals the money. Here he went aground upon a comparatively simple prob-

[1] The episode is related in *A Hoosier Holiday*. H. L. M.

[2] *A Princess of Arcady*, published in 1900. H. L. M.

lem; he couldn't devise a way to manage the robbery. Late in January he gave it up. But the faithful Henry kept urging him, and in March he resumed work, and soon had the story finished. The latter part, despite many distractions, went quickly. Once the manuscript was complete, Henry suggested various cuts, and in all about 40,000 words came out. The fair copy went to the Harpers. They refused it without ceremony and soon afterward Dreiser carried the manuscript to Doubleday, Page & Co. He left it with Frank Doubleday, and before long there came notice of its acceptance, and, what is more, a contract. But after the story was in type it fell into the hands of the wife of one of the members of the firm, and she conceived so strong a notion of its immorality that she soon convinced her husband and his associates. There followed a series of acrimonious negotiation, with Dreiser holding resolutely to the letter of his contract. It was at this point that Frank Norris entered the combat—bravely but in vain. The pious Barabbases, confronted by their signature, found it impossible to throw up the book entirely, but there was no nomination in the bond regarding either the style of binding or the number of copies to be issued, and so they evaded further dispute by bringing out the book in a very small edition and with modest unstamped covers. Copies of this edition are now eagerly sought by book-collectors, and one in good condition fetches $25 or more in the auction rooms. Even the second edition (1907), bearing the imprint of B. W. Dodge & Co., carries an increasing premium.

The passing years work strange farces. The Harpers, who had refused *Sister Carrie* with a spirit bordering upon indignation in 1900, took over the rights of publication from B. W. Dodge & Co., in 1912, and reissued the book in a new (and extremely hideous) format, with a publisher's note containing smug quotations from the encomiums of the *Fortnightly Review*, the *Athenaeum*, the *Spectator*, the *Academy* and other London critical journals. More, they contrived humorously to push the date of their copyright back to 1900. But this new enthusiasm for artistic freedom did not last long. They had published *Jennie Gerhardt* in

1911 and they did *The Financier* in 1912, but when *The Titan* followed, in 1914, they were seized with qualms, and suppressed the book after it had got into type. In this emergency the English firm of John Lane came to the rescue, only to seek cover itself when the Comstocks attacked *The "Genius"* two years later. . . . For his high services to American letters, Walter H. Page, of Doubleday, Page & Co., was made ambassador to England, where *Sister Carrie* is regarded (according to the Harpers) as "the best story, on the whole, that has yet come out of America." A curious series of episodes. Another proof, perhaps, of that cosmic imbecility upon which Dreiser is so fond of discoursing. . . .

But of all this I shall say more later on, when I come to discuss the critical reception of the Dreiser novels, and the efforts made by the New York Society for the Suppression of Vice to stop their sale. The thing to notice here is that the author's difficulties with *Sister Carrie* came within an ace of turning him from novel-writing completely. Stray copies of the suppressed first edition, true enough, fell into the hands of critics who saw the story's value, and during the first year or two of the century it enjoyed a sort of esoteric vogue, and encouragement came from unexpected sources. Moreover, a somewhat bowdlerized English edition, published by William Heinemann in 1901, made a fair success, and even provoked a certain mild controversy. But the author's income from the book remained almost *nil,* and so he was forced to seek a livelihood in other directions. His history during the next ten years belongs to the tragi-comedy of letters. For five of them he was a Grub Street hack, turning his hand to any literary job that offered. He wrote short stories for the popular magazines, or special articles, or poems, according as their needs varied. He concocted fabulous tales for the illustrated supplements of the Sunday newspapers. He rewrote the bad stuff of other men. He returned to reporting. He did odd pieces of editing. He tried his hand at one-act plays. He even ventured upon advertisement writing. And all the while, the best that he could get out of his industry was a meager living.

In 1905, tiring of the uncertainties of this life, he accepted a post on the staff of Street & Smith, the millionaire publishers of cheap magazines, servant-girl romances, and dime-novels, and here, in the very slums of letters, he labored with tongue in cheek until the next year. The tale of his duties will fill, I daresay, a volume or two in the autobiography on which he is said to be working; it is a chronicle full of achieved impossibilities. One of his jobs, for example, was to reduce a whole series of dime-novels, each 60,000 words in length, to 30,000 words apiece. He accomplished it by cutting each one into halves, and writing a new ending for the first half and a new beginning for the second, with new titles for both. This doubling of their property aroused the admiration of his employers; they promised him an assured and easy future in the dime-novel business. But he tired of it, despite this revelation of a gift for it, and in 1906 he became managing editor of the *Broadway Magazine,* then struggling into public notice. A year later he transferred his flag to the Butterick Building, and became chief editor of the *Delineator,* the *Designer,* and other such gospels for the fair. Here, of course, he was as much out of water as in the dime-novel foundry of Street & Smith, but at all events the pay was good, and there was a certain leisure at the end of the day's work. In 1907, as part of his duties, he organized the National Child Rescue Campaign, which still rages as the *Delineator's* contribution to the Uplift. At about the same time he began *Jennie Gerhardt.* It is curious to note that, during these same years, Arnold Bennett was slaving in London as the editor of *Woman.*

Dreiser left the *Delineator* in 1910, and for the next half year or so endeavored to pump vitality into the *Bohemian Magazine,* in which he had acquired a proprietary interest. But the *Bohemian* soon departed this life, carrying some of his savings with it, and he gave over his enforced leisure to *Jennie Gerhardt,* completing the book in 1911. Its publication by the Harpers during the same year worked his final emancipation from the editorial desk. It was praised, and, what is more, it sold, and royalties began to come in. A new edition of *Sister Carrie* followed in 1912, with *The Financier* hard upon its heels. Since then Dreiser has devoted himself wholly to serious work. *The Financier* was put forth as the first volume of "a trilogy of desire"; the second volume, *The Titan*, was published in 1914; the third is yet to come. *The "Genius"* appeared in 1915; *The Bulwark* is just announced. In 1912, accompanied by Grant Richards, the London publisher, Dreiser made his first trip abroad, visiting England, France, Italy, and Germany. His impressions were recorded in *A Traveler at Forty*, published in 1913. In the summer of 1915, accompanied by Franklin Booth, the illustrator, he made an automobile journey to his old haunts in Indiana, and the record is in *A Hoosier Holiday*, published in 1916. His other writings include a volume of *Plays of the Natural and the Supernatural* (1916); *Life, Art and America*, a pamphlet against Puritanism in letters (1917); a dozen or more short stories and novelettes, a few poems, and a three-act drama, *The Hand of the Potter*.

Dreiser was born at Terre Haute, Indiana, on August 27, 1871, and, like most of us, is of mongrel blood, with the German, perhaps, predominating. He is a tall man, awkward in movement and nervous in habit; the boon of beauty has been denied him. The history of his youth is set forth in full in *A Hoosier Holiday*. It is curious to note that he is a brother to the late Paul Dresser, author of *The Banks of the Wabash* and other popular songs, and that he himself, helping Paul over a hard place, wrote the affecting chorus:

Oh, the moon is fair tonight along the Wabash,
From the fields there comes the breath of new-mown hay;
Through the sycamores the candle lights are gleaming . . .

But no doubt you know it.

v

The work of Dreiser, considered as craftsmanship pure and simple, is extremely uneven, and the distance separating his best from his worst is almost infinite. It is difficult to believe that the novelist who wrote certain extraordinarily vivid chapters in *Jennie Gerhardt*, and *A Hoosier Holiday*, and, above all, in *The Titan*, is the same who achieved the unescapable dullness of parts of *The Financier* and the general stupidity and stodginess of *The "Genius."* Moreover, the tide of his writing does not rise or fall with any regularity; he neither improves steadily nor grows worse steadily. Only half an eye is needed to see the superiority of *Jennie Gerhardt*, as a sheer piece of writing, to *Sister Carrie*, but on turning to *The Financier*, which followed *Jennie Gerhardt* by an interval of but one year, one observes a falling off which, at its greatest, is almost indistinguishable from a collapse. *Jennie Gerhardt* is suave, persuasive, well-ordered, solid in structure, instinct with life. *The Financier*, for all its merits in detail, is loose, tedious, vapid, exasperating. But had any critic, in the autumn of 1912, argued thereby that Dreiser was finished, that he had shot his bolt, his discomfiture would have come swiftly, for *The Titan*, which followed in 1914, was almost as well done as *The Financier* had been ill done, and there are parts of it which remain, to this day, the very best writing that Dreiser has ever achieved. But *The "Genius"*? Aye, in *The "Genius"* the pendulum swings back again! It is flaccid, elephantine, doltish, coarse, dismal, flatulent, sophomoric, ignorant, unconvincing, wearisome. One pities the jurisconsult who is condemned, by Comstockian clamor, to plow through such a novel. In it there is a sort of humorless *reductio ad absurdum*, not only of the Dreiser manner, but even of certain salient tenets of the Dreiser philosophy. At its best it has a moral flavor. At its worst it is almost maudlin. . . .

The most successful of the Dreiser novels, judged by sales, is *Sister Carrie*, and the causes thereof are not far to seek. On the one hand, its suppression in 1900 gave it a whispered fame that was converted into a public celebrity when it was republished in 1907, and on the other hand, it shares with *Jennie Gerhardt* the capital advantage of having a young and appealing woman for its chief figure. The sentimentalists thus have a heroine to cry over, and to put into a familiar pigeonhole; Carrie becomes a sort of Pollyanna. More, it is, at bottom, a tale of love—the one theme of permanent interest to the average American novel reader, the chief stuffing of all our best-selling romances. True enough, it is vastly more than this—there is in it, for example, the astounding portrait of Hurstwood; but it seems to me plain that its relative popularity is by no means a test of its relative merit, and that the causes of that popularity must be sought in other directions. Its defect, as a work of art, is a defect of structure. Like Norris' *McTeague* it has a broken back. In the midst of the story of Carrie, Dreiser pauses to tell the story of Hurstwood—a memorably vivid and tragic story, to be sure, but still one that, considering artistic form and organization, does damage to the main business of the book. Its outstanding merit is its simplicity, its unaffected seriousness and fervor, the spirit of youth that is in it. One feels that it was written, not by a novelist conscious of his tricks, but by a novice carried away by his own flaming eagerness, his own high sense of the interest of what he was doing. In this aspect, it is perhaps more typically Dreiserian than any of its successors. And maybe we may seek here for a good deal of its popular appeal, for there is a contagion in naïveté as in enthusiasm, and the simple novel-reader may recognize the kinship of a simple mind in the novelist.

But it is in *Jennie Gerhardt* that Dreiser first shows his true mettle. . . . "The power to tell the same story in two forms," said George Moore, "is the sign of the true artist." Here Dreiser sets himself that difficult task, and here he carries it off with almost complete success. Reduce the story to a hundred words, and the same words would also describe *Sister Carrie*. Jennie, like Carrie, is a rose grown from turnipseed. Over each, at the start, hangs poverty, ignorance, the dumb helplessness of the Shudra, and yet in each there is that indescribable something, that element of essential gentleness, that innate inward beauty which levels all barriers of caste, and makes Esther a fit queen for Ahasuerus. Some Frenchman has put it into a phrase: *"une âme grande dans un petit destin"*—a great soul in a small destiny. Jennie has some touch of that greatness; Dreiser is forever calling her "a big woman"; it is a refrain almost as irritating as the "trig" of *The Titan*. Carrie, one feels, is of baser metal; her dignity never rises to anything approaching nobility. But the history of each is the history of the other. Jennie, like Carrie, escapes from the physical miseries of the struggle for existence only to taste the worse miseries of the struggle for happiness. Don't mistake me; we have here no maudlin tales of seduced maidens. Seduction, in truth, is far from tragedy for either Jennie or Carrie. The gain of each, until the actual event has been left behind and obliterated by experiences more salient and poignant, is greater than her loss, and that gain is to the soul as well as to the creature. With the rise from want to security, from fear to ease, comes an awakening of the finer perceptions, a widening of the sympathies, a gradual unfolding of the delicate flower called personality, an in-creased capacity for loving and living. But with all this, and as a part of it, there comes, too, an increased capacity for suffering—and so in the end, when love slips away and the empty years stretch before, it is the awakened and super-sentient woman that pays for the folly of the groping, be-wildered girl. The tragedy of Carrie and Jennie, in brief, is not that they are degraded, but that they are lifted up, not that they go to the gutter, but that they escape the gutter and glimpse the stars.

But if the two stories are thus variations upon the same somber theme, if each starts from the same place and arrives at the same dark goal, if each shows a woman heartened by the same hopes and tortured by the same agonies, there is still a vast difference between them, and that difference is the measure of the author's progress in his craft during the eleven years between 1900 and 1911. *Sister Carrie*, at bot-tom, is no more than a first sketch, a rough piling up of observations and ideas, disordered and often incoherent. In the midst of the story, as I have said, the author forgets it, and starts off upon another. In *Jennie Gerhardt* there is no such flaccidity of structure, no such vacillation in aim, no such proliferation of episode. Considering that it is by Dreiser, it is extraordinarily adept and intelligent in design; only in *The Titan* has he ever done so well. From beginning to end the narrative flows logically, steadily, congruously. Episodes there are, of course, but they keep their proper

place and bulk. It is always Jennie that stands at the center
of the traffic; it is in Jennie's soul that every scene is ultimately played out. Her father and mother; Senator Brander,
the god of her first worship; her daughter Vesta, and Lester
Kane, the man who makes and mars her—all these are drawn
with infinite painstaking, and in every one of them there is
the blood of life. But it is Jennie that dominates the drama
from curtain to curtain. Not an event is unrelated to her;
not a climax fails to make clearer the struggles going on in
her mind and heart.

It is in *Jennie Gerhardt* that Dreiser's view of life begins
to take on coherence and to show a general tendency. In
Sister Carrie the thing is still chiefly representation and no
more; the image is undoubtedly vivid, but its significance, in
the main, is left undisplayed. In *Jennie Gerhardt* this pictorial achievement is reinforced by interpretation; one carries away an impression that something has been said; it is
not so much a visual image of Jennie that remains as a sense
of the implacable tragedy that engulfs her. The book is full
of artistic passion. It lives and glows. It awakens recognition
and feeling. Its lucid ideational structure, even more than
the artless gusto of *Sister Carrie,* produces a penetrating and
powerful effect. Jennie is no mere individual; she is a type
of the national character, almost the archetype of the muddled, aspiring, tragic, fate-flogged mass. And the scene in
which she is set is brilliantly national too. The Chicago of
those great days of feverish money-grabbing and crazy aspiration may well stand as the epitome of America, and it is
made clearer here than in any other American novel—clearer
than in *The Pit* or *The Cliff-Dwellers*—clearer than in any
book by an Easterner—almost as clear as the Paris of Balzac
and Zola. Finally, the style of the story is indissolubly wedded to its matter. The narrative, in places, has an almost
scriptural solemnity; in its very harshness and baldness there
is something subtly meet and fitting. One cannot imagine
such a history done in the strained phrases of Meredith or
the fugal manner of Henry James. One cannot imagine that
stark, stenographic dialogue adorned with the tinsel of pretty
words. The thing, to reach the heights it touches, could have

been done only in the way it has been done. As it stands, I
would not take anything away from it, not even its journalistic banalities, its lack of humor, its incessant returns to C
major. A primitive and touching poetry is in it. It is a novel,
I am convinced, of the first consideration. . . .

In *The Financier* this poetry is almost wholly absent, and
fact is largely to blame for the book's lack of charm. By the
time we see him in *The Titan* Frank Cowperwood has taken
on heroic proportions and the romance of great adventure is
in him, but in *The Financier* he is still little more than an
extra-pertinacious money-grubber, and not unrelated to the
average stockbroker or corner grocer. True enough, Dreiser
says specifically that he is more, that the thing he craves is
not money but power—power to force lesser men to execute
his commands, power to surround himself with beautiful and
splendid things, power to amuse himself with women, power
to defy and nullify the laws made for the timorous and
unimaginative. But the intent of the author never really gets
into his picture. His Cowperwood in this first stage is hard,
commonplace, unimaginative. In *The Titan* he flowers out
as a blend of revolutionist and voluptuary, a highly civilized
Lorenzo the Magnificent, an immoralist who would not
hesitate two minutes about seducing a saint, but would turn
sick at the thought of harming a child. But in *The Financier*
he is still in the larval state, and a repellent sordidness hangs
about him.

Moreover, the story of his rise is burdened by two defects
which still further corrupt its effect. One lies in the fact that
Dreiser is quite unable to get the feel, so to speak, of Philadelphia, just as he is unable to get the feel of New York in
The "Genius." The other is that the style of the writing in
the book reduces the dreiserian manner to absurdity, and
almost to impossibility. The incredibly lazy, involved, and
unintelligent description of the trial of Cowperwood I have
already mentioned. We get, in this lumbering chronicle, not
a cohesive and luminous picture, but a dull, photographic
representation of the whole tedious process, beginning with
an account of the political obligations of the judge and dis-
trict attorney, proceeding to a consideration of the habits of

mind of each of the twelve jurymen, and ending with a summary of the majority and minority opinions of the court of appeals, and a discussion of the motives, ideals, traditions, prejudices, sympathies, and chicaneries behind them, each and severally. When Cowperwood goes into the market, his operations are set forth in their last detail; we are told how many shares he buys, how much he pays for them, what the commission is, what his profit comes to. When he comes into chance contact with a politician, we hear all about that politician, including his family affairs. When he builds and furnishes a house, the chief rooms in it are inventoried with such care that not a chair or a rug or a picture on the wall is overlooked. The endless piling up of such nonessentials cripples and incommodes the story; its drama is too copiously swathed in words to achieve a sting; the Dreiser manner devours and defeats itself.

But nonetheless the book has compensatory merits. Its character sketches, for all the cloud of words, are lucid and vigorous. Out of that enormous complex of crooked politics and crookeder finance, Cowperwood himself stands out in the round, comprehensible and alive. And all the others, in their lesser measures, are done almost as well—Cowperwood's pale wife, whimpering in her empty house; Aileen Butler, his mistress; his doddering and eternally amazed old father; his old-fashioned, stupid, sentimental mother; Stener, the City Treasurer, a dish-rag in the face of danger; old Edward Malia Butler, that barbarian in a boiled shirt, with his Homeric hatred and his broken heart. Particularly old Butler. The years pass and he must be killed and put away, but not many readers of the book, I take it, will soon forget him. Dreiser is at his best, indeed, when he deals with old men. In their tragic helplessness they stand as symbols of that unfathomable cosmic cruelty which he sees as the motive power of life itself. More, even, than his women, he makes them poignant, vivid, memorable. The picture of old Gerhardt is full of a subtle brightness, though he is always in the background, as cautious and penny-wise as an ancient crow, trotting to his Lutheran church, pathetically ill-used by the world he never understands. Butler is another such, different in externals, but at bottom the same dismayed, questioning, pathetic old man. . . .

In *The Titan* there is a tightening of the screws, a clarifying of the action, an infinite improvement in the manner. The book, in truth, has the air of a new and clearer thinking out of *The Financier*, as *Jennie Gerhardt* is a new thinking out of *Sister Carrie*. With almost the same materials, the thing is given a new harmony and unity, a new plausibility, a new passion and purpose. In *The Financier* the artistic voluptuary is almost completely overshadowed by the dollar-chaser; in *The Titan* we begin to see clearly that grand battle between artist and man of money, idealist and materialist, spirit and flesh, which is the informing theme of the whole trilogy. The conflict that makes the drama, once chiefly external, now becomes more and more internal; it is played out within the soul of the man himself. The result is a character sketch of the highest color and brilliance, a superb portrait of a complex and extremely fascinating man. Of all the personages in the Dreiser books, the Cowperwood of *The Titan* is perhaps the most radiantly real. He is accounted for in every detail, and yet, in the end, he is not accounted for at all; there hangs about him, to the last, that baffling mysteriousness which hangs about those we know most intimately. There is in him a complete and indubitable masculinity, as the eternal feminine is in Jennie. His struggle with the inexorable forces that urge him on as with whips, and lure him with false lights, and bring him to disillusion and dismay, is as typical as hers is, and as tragic. In his ultimate disaster, so plainly foreshadowed at the close, there is the clearest of all projections of the ideas that lie at the bottom of all Dreiser's work. Cowperwood, above any of them, is his protagonist.

The story, in its plan, is as transparent as in its burden. It has an austere simplicity in the telling that fits the directness of the thing told. Dreiser, as if to clear decks, throws over all the immemorial baggage of the novelist, making short shrift of "heart interest," conventional "sympathy," and even what ordinarily passes for romance. In *Sister Carrie*, as I have pointed out, there is still a sweet dish for the sen

timentalists; if they don't like the history of Carrie as a work
of art they may still wallow in it as a sad, sad love story.
Carrie is appealing, melting; she moves, like Marguerite
Gautier, in an atmosphere of romantic depression. And Jennie Gerhardt, in this aspect, is merely Carrie done over—a
Carrie more carefully and objectively drawn, perhaps, but
still conceivably to be mistaken for a "sympathetic" heroine
in a best-seller. A lady eating chocolates might jump from
Laddie to *Jennie Gerhardt* without knowing that she was
jumping ten thousand miles. The tear jugs are there to cry
into. Even in *The Financier* there is still a hint of familiar
things. The first Mrs. Cowperwood is sorely put upon; old
Butler has the markings of an irate father; Cowperwood
himself suffers the orthodox injustice and languishes in a
cell. But no one, I venture, will ever fall into any such mistake in identity in approaching *The Titan*. Not a single
appeal to facile sentiment is in it. It proceeds from beginning
to end in a forthright, uncompromising, confident manner.
It is an almost purely objective account, as devoid of cheap
heroics as a death certificate, of a strong man's contest with
incontestable powers without and no less incontestable
powers within. There is nothing of the conventional outlaw
about him; he does not wear a red sash and bellow
for liberty; fate wrings from him no melodramatic defiances.
In the midst of the battle he views it with a sort of ironical
detachment, as if lifted above himself by the sheer aesthetic
spectacle. Even in disaster he asks for no quarter, no generosity, no compassion. Up or down, he keeps his zest for
the game that is being played, and is sufficient unto himself.

Such a man as this Cowperwood of the Chicago days,
described romantically, would be indistinguishable from the
wicked earls and seven-foot guardsmen of Ouida, Robert W.
Chambers, and The Duchess. But described realistically and
cold-bloodedly, with all that wealth of minute and apparently inconsequential detail which Dreiser piles up so amazingly, he becomes a figure astonishingly vivid, lifelike, and
engrossing. He fits into no *a priori* theory of conduct or
scheme of rewards and punishments; he proves nothing and
teaches nothing; the forces which move him are never obvi-

ous and frequently unintelligible. But in the end he seems genuinely a man—a man of the sort we see about us in the real world—not a patent and automatic fellow, reacting docilely and according to a formula, but a bundle of complexities and contradictions, a creature oscillating between the light and the shadow—at bottom, for all his typical representation of a race and a civilization, a unique and inexplicable personality. More, he is a man of the first class, an Achilles of his world; and here the achievement of Dreiser is most striking, for he succeeds where all forerunners failed. It is easy enough to explain how John Smith courted his wife, and even how William Brown fought and died for his country, but it is inordinately difficult to give plausibility to the motives, feelings, and processes of mind of a man whose salient character is that they transcend all ordinary experience. Too often, even when made by the highest creative and interpretative talent, the effort has resolved itself into a begging of the question. Shakespeare made Hamlet comprehensible to the groundlings by diluting that half of him which was Shakespeare with a half which was a college sophomore. In the same way he saved Lear by making him, in large part, a tedious and obscene old donkey—the blood brother of any average ancient of any average English taproom. Tackling Caesar, he was rescued by Brutus' knife. George Bernard Shaw, facing the same difficulty, resolved it by drawing a composite portrait of two or three London actor-managers and a half-a-dozen English politicians. But Dreiser makes no such compromise. He bangs into the difficulties of his problem head on, and if he does not solve it absolutely, he at least makes an extraordinarily close approach to a solution. In *The Financier* a certain incredulity still hangs about Cowperwood; in *The Titan* he suddenly comes unquestionably real. If you want to get the true measure of this feat, put it beside the failure of Frank Norris with Curtis Jadwin in *The Pit.* . . .

The "Genius," which interrupted the "trilogy of desire," marks the nadir of Dreiser's accomplishment, as *The Titan* marks its apogee. The plan of it, of course, is simple enough, and it is one that Dreiser, at his best, might have carried out with undoubted success. What he is trying to show, in brief, is the battle that goes on in the soul of every man of active mind between the desire for self-expression and the desire for safety, for public respect, for emotional equanimity. It is, in a sense, the story of Cowperwood told over again, but with an important difference, for Eugene Witla is a much less self-reliant and powerful fellow than Cowperwood, and so he is unable to muster up the vast resolution of spirits that he needs to attain happiness. *The Titan* is the history of a strong man. *The "Genius"* is the history of a man essentially weak. Eugene Witla can never quite choose his route in life. He goes on sacrificing ease to aspiration and aspiration to ease to the end of the chapter. He vacillates abominably and forever between two irreconcilable desires. Even when, at the close, he sinks into a whining sort of resignation, the proud courage of Cowperwood is not in him; he is always a bit despicable in his pathos.

As I say, a story of simple outlines, and well adapted to the dreiserian pen. But it is spoiled and made a mock of by a donkeyish solemnity of attack which leaves it, on the one hand, diffuse, spineless, and shapeless, and, on the other hand, a compendium of platitudes. It is as if Dreiser, suddenly discovering himself a sage, put off the high passion of the artist and took to pounding a pulpit. It is almost as if he deliberately essayed upon a burlesque of himself. The book is an endless emission of the obvious, with touches of the scandalous to light up its killing monotony. It runs to 736 pages of small type; its reading is an unbearable weariness to the flesh; in the midst of it one has forgotten the beginning and is unconcerned about the end. Mingled with all the folderol, of course, there is stuff of nobler quality. Certain chapters stick in the memory; whole episodes lift themselves to the fervid luminosity of *Jennie Gerhardt*; there are character sketches that deserve all praise; one often pulls up with a reminder that the thing is the work of a proficient craftsman. But in the main it lumbers and jolts, wabbles and bores. A sort of ponderous imbecility gets into it. Both in its elaborate devices to shake up the pious and its imposing demonstrations of what everyone knows, it somehow suggests the advanced thinking of Greenwich Village. I suspect, indeed, that the *vin rouge* was in Dreiser's arteries as he concocted it. He was at the intellectual menopause, and looking back somewhat wistfully and attitudinizingly toward the goatish days that were no more.

But let it go! A novelist capable of *Jennie Gerhardt* has rights, privileges, prerogatives. He may, if he will, go on a spiritual drunk now and then, and empty the stale bilges of his soul. Thackeray, having finished *Vanity Fair* and *Pendennis*, bathed himself in the sheep's milk of *The Newcomes*, and after *The Virginians* he did *The Adventures of Philip*. Zola, with *Germinal*, *La Débâcle* and *La Terre* behind him, re-created himself horribly with *Fécondité*. Tolstoy, after *Anna Karenina*, wrote *What Is Art?* Ibsen, after *Et Dukkehjem* and *Gengangere*, wrote *Vildanden*. The good God himself, after all the magnificence of *Kings* and *Chronicles*, turned Dr. Frank Crane and so botched his Writ with *Proverbs*. . . . A weakness that we must allow for. Whenever Dreiser, abandoning his fundamental skepticism, yields to the irrepressible human (and perhaps also divine) itch to label, to moralize, to teach, he becomes a bit absurd. Observe *The "Genius,"* and parts of *A Hoosier Holiday* and of *A Traveler at Forty*, and of *Plays of the Natural and the Supernatural*. But in this very absurdity, it seems to me, there is a subtle proof that his fundamental skepticism is sound. . . .

I mention the *Plays of the Natural and the Supernatural*. They are ingenious and sometimes extremely effective, but their significance is not great. The two that are "of the natural" are *The Girl in the Coffin* and *Old Ragpicker*, the first a laborious evocation of the gruesome, too long by half, and the other an experiment in photographic realism, with a pair of policemen as its protagonists. All five plays "of the supernatural" follow a single plan. In the foreground, as it were, we see a sordid drama played out on the human plane, and in the background (or in the empyrean above, as you choose) we see the operation of the godlike imbecilities which sway and flay us all. The technical trick is well managed. It would be easy for such four-dimensional pieces to fall into burlesque, but in at least two cases, to wit, in *The Blue Sphere* and *In the Dark*, they go off with an air. Superficially, these plays "of the supernatural" seem to show an abandonment to the wheezy, black bombazine mysticism which crops up toward the end of *The "Genius."* But that mysticism, at bottom, is no more than the dreiserian skepticism made visible. "For myself," says Dreiser somewhere, "I do not know what truth is, what beauty is, what love is, what hope is." And in another place: "I admit a vast compulsion which has nothing to do with the individual desires or tastes or impulses." The jokers behind the arras pull the strings. It is pretty, but what is it all about? . . . The criticism which deals only with externals sees *Sister Carrie* as no more than a deft adventure into realism. Dreiser is praised, when he is praised at all, for making Carrie so clear, for understanding her so well. But the truth is, of course, that his achievement consists precisely in making patent the impenetrable mystery of her, and of the tangled complex of striving and aspiration of which she is so helplessly a part. It is in this sense that *Sister Carrie* is a profound work. It is not a book of glib explanations, of ready formulae; it is, above all else, a book of wonder. . . .

Of *A Traveler at Forty* I have spoken briefly. It is heavy with the obvious; the most interesting thing in it is the fact that Dreiser had never seen St. Peter's or Piccadilly Circus until he was too old for either reverence or romance. *A Hoosier Holiday* is far more illuminating, despite its platitudinizing. Slow in tempo, discursive, reflective, intimate, the book covers a vast territory, and lingers in pleasant fields. One finds in it an almost complete confession of faith, artistic, religious, even political. And not infrequently that confession takes the form of ingenuous confidences—about the fortunes of the house of Dreiser, the dispersed Dreiser clan, the old neighbors in Indiana, new friends made along the way. In *A Traveler at Forty* Dreiser is surely frank enough in his vivisections; he seldom forgets a vanity or a wart. In *A Hoosier Holiday* he goes even further; he speculates heavily about all his *dramatis personae*, prodding into the motives behind their acts, wondering what they would do in this or that situation, forcing them painfully into laboratory jars. They become, in the end, not unlike characters in a novel; one misses only the neatness of a plot. Strangely enough, the one personage of the chronicle who remains dim throughout is the artist, Franklin Booth, Dreiser's host and companion on the long motor ride from New York to Indiana, and the maker of the book's excellent pictures. One gets a brilliant etching of Booth's father, and scarcely less vivid portraits of Speed, the chauffeur; of various persons encountered on the way, and of friends and relatives dredged up out of the abyss of the past. But of Booth one learns little save that he is a Christian Scientist and a fine figure of a man. There must have been much talk during those two weeks of careening along the high-road, and Booth must have borne some part in it, but what he said is very meagerly reported, and so he is still somewhat vague at the end—a personality sensed but scarcely apprehended.

However, it is Dreiser himself who is the chief character of the story, and who stands out from it most brilliantly. One sees in the man all the special marks of the novelist: his capacity for photographic and relentless observation, his insatiable curiosity, his keen zest in life as a spectacle, his comprehension of and sympathy for the poor striving of humble folks, his endless mulling of insoluble problems, his recurrent Philistinism, his impatience of restraints, his fascinated suspicion of messiahs, his passion for physical beauty, his relish for the gaudy drama of big cities; his incurable Americanism. The panorama that he enrolls runs the whole scale of the colors; it is a series of extraordinarily vivid pictures. The somber gloom of the Pennsylvania hills, with Wilkes-Barre lying among them like a gem; the procession of little country towns, sleepy and a bit hoggish; the flash of Buffalo, Cleveland, Indianapolis; the gargantuan coal-pockets and ore-docks along the Erie shore; the tinsel summer resorts; the lush Indiana farmlands, with their stodgy, bovine people—all of these things are sketched in simply, and yet almost magnificently. I know, indeed, of no book which better describes the American hinterland. Here we

have no idle spying by a stranger, but a full-length representation by one who knows the thing he describes intimately, and is himself a part of it. Almost every mile of the
road traveled has been Dreiser's own road in life. He knew
those unkempt Indiana towns in boyhood; he wandered in
the Indiana woods; he came to Toledo, Cleveland, Buffalo
as a young man; all the roots of his existence are out there.
And so he does his chronicle *con amore,* with many a sentimental dredging up of old memories, old hopes, and old
dreams.

Save for passages in *The Titan, A Hoosier Holiday* marks
the high tide of Dreiser's writing—that is, as sheer writing.
His old faults are in it, and plentifully. There are empty,
brackish phrases enough, God knows—"high noon" among
them. But for all that, there is an undeniable glow in it; it
shows, in more than one place, an approach to style; the
mere wholesaler of words has become, in some sense a con-
noisseur, even a voluptuary. The picture of Wilkes-Barre
girt in by her hills is simply done, and yet there is imagination in it, and touches of brilliance. The somber beauty of
the Pennsylvania mountains is vividly transferred to the
page. The towns by the wayside are differentiated, swiftly
drawn, made to live. There are excellent sketches of people—
a courtly hotelkeeper in some godforsaken hamlet, his self-
respect triumphing over his wallow; a group of babbling
Civil War veterans, endlessly mouthing incomprehensible
jests; the half-grown beaux and belles of the summer resorts,
enchanted and yet a bit staggered by the awakening of sex;
Booth *père* and his sinister politics; broken and forgotten
men in the Indiana towns; policemen, waitresses, farmers,
country characters; Dreiser's own people—the boys and girls
of his youth; his brother Paul, the Indiana Schneckenburger
and Francis Scott Key; his sisters and brothers; his beaten,
hopeless, pious father; his brave and noble mother. The book
is dedicated to this mother, now long dead, and in a way it is
a memorial to her, a monument to affection. Life bore upon
her cruelly; she knew poverty at its lowest ebb and despair
at its bitterest; and yet there was in her a touch of fineness

that never yielded, a gallant spirit that faced and fought things through. One thinks, somehow, of the mother of Gounod. . . . Her son has not forgotten her. His book is her epitaph. He enters into her presence with love and with reverence and with something not far from awe. . . .

As for the rest of the Dreiser compositions, I leave them to your curiosity.

VI

Dr. William Lyon Phelps, the Lampson professor of English language and literature at Yale, opens his chapter on Mark Twain in his *Essays on Modern Novelists* with a humorous account of the critical imbecility which pursued Mark in his own country down to his last years. The favorite national critics of that era (and it extended to 1895, at the least) were wholly blind to the fact that he was a great artist. They admitted him, somewhat grudgingly, a certain low dexterity as a clown, but that he was an imaginative writer of the first rank, or even of the fifth rank, was something that, in their insanest moments, never so much as occurred to them. Phelps cites, in particular, an ass named Professor Richardson, whose *American Literature,* it appears, "is still a standard work" and "a deservedly high authority"—apparently in colleges. In the 1892 edition of this *magnum opus,* Mark is dismissed with less than four lines, and ranked below Irving, Holmes, and Lowell—nay, actually below Artemus Ward, Josh Billings, and Petroleum V. Nasby! The thing is fabulous, fantastic, *unglaublich*—but nevertheless true. Lacking the "higher artistic or moral purpose of the greater humorists" (*exempli gratia,* Rabelais, Molière, Aristophanes!!), Mark is dismissed by this Professor Balderdash as a hollow buffoon. . . . But stay! Do not laugh yet! Phelps himself, indignant at the stupidity, now proceeds to credit Mark with a moral purpose! . . . Turn to *The Mysterious Stranger,* or *What Is Man? . . .*

College professors, alas, never learn anything. The identical gentleman who achieved this discovery about old Mark in 1910 now seeks to dispose of Dreiser in the exact manner of Richardson. That is to say, he essays to finish him by putting him into Coventry, by loftily passing over him. "Do not speak of him," said Kingsley of Heine; "he was a wicked man!" Search the latest volume of the Phelps revelation, *The Advance of the English Novel,* and you will find that Dreiser is not once mentioned in it. The late O. Henry is hailed as a genius who will have "abiding fame"; Henry Sydnor Harrison is hymned as "more than a clever novelist," nay, "a valuable ally of the angels" (the right-thinker complex! art as a form of snuffling!), and an obscure Pagliaccio named Charles D. Stewart is brought forward as "the American novelist most worthy to fill the particular vacancy caused by the death of Mark Twain"—but Dreiser is not even listed in the index. And where Phelps leads with his baton of birch most of the other drovers of rah-rah boys follow. I turn, for example, to *An Introduction to American Literature,* by Henry S. Pancoast, A.M., L.H.D., dated 1912. There are kind words for Richard Harding Davis, for Amélie Rives, and even for Will N. Harben, but not a syllable for Dreiser. Again, there is *A History of American Literature,* by Reuben Post Halleck, A.M., LL.D., dated 1911. Lew Wallace, Marietta Holley, Owen Wister, and Augusta Evans Wilson have their hearings, but not Dreiser. Yet again, there is *A History of American Literature Since 1870,* by Prof. Fred Lewis Pattee,[1] instructor in "the English language and literature" somewhere in Pennsylvania. Pattee has praises for Marion Crawford, Margaret Deland, and F. Hopkinson Smith, and polite bows for Richard Harding Davis and Robert W. Chambers, but from end to end of his fat tome I am unable to find the slightest mention of Dreiser.

So much for one group of heroes of the new *Dunciad.* That it includes most of the acknowledged heavyweights of the craft—the Babbitts, Mores, Brownells, and so on—goes without saying; as Van Wyck Brooks has pointed out,[2] these magnificoes are austerely above any consideration of the literature that is in being. The other group, more courageous and more honest, proceeds by direct attack; Dreiser is to be

[1] New York, The Century Co., 1916. H. L. M.
[2] In *The Seven Arts,* May 1917. H. L. M.

disposed of by a moral *attentat*. Its leaders are two more professors, Stuart P. Sherman and H. W. Boynton, and in its
ranks march the lady critics of the newspapers, with much
shrill, falsetto clamor. Sherman is the only one of them who
shows any intelligible reasoning. Boynton, as always, is a
mere parroter of conventional phrases, and the objections of
the ladies fade imperceptibly into a pious indignation which
is indistinguishable from that of the professional suppressors
of vice.

What, then, is Sherman's complaint? In brief, that Dreiser
is a liar when he calls himself a realist; that he is actually
a naturalist, and hence accursed. That "he has evaded the
enterprise of representing human conduct, and confined
himself to a representation of animal behavior." That he
"imposes his own naturalistic philosophy" upon his characters, making them do what they ought not to do, and think
what they ought not to think. That "he has just two things
to tell us about Frank Cowperwood: that he has a rapacious
appetite for money, and a rapacious appetite for women."
That this alleged "theory of animal behavior" is not only
incorrect but downright immoral, and that "when one half
the world attempts to assert it, the other half rises in battle."[1]

Only a glance is needed to show the vacuity of all this
brutum fulmen. Dreiser, in point of fact, is scarcely more the
realist or the naturalist, in any true sense, than H. G. Wells
or the later George Moore, nor has he ever announced himself in either the one character or the other—if there be, in
fact, any difference between them that anyone save a pigeon-
holing pedagogue can discern. He is really something quite
different, and, in his moments, something far more stately.
His aim is not merely to record, but to translate and understand; the thing he exposes is not the empty event and act,
but the endless mystery out of which it springs; his pictures
have a passionate compassion in them that it is hard to separate from poetry. If this sense of the universal and inexplicable tragedy, if this vision of life as a seeking without a
finding, if this adept summoning up of moving images, is
mistaken by college professors for the empty, meticulous

[1] The *Nation*, December 2, 1915. H. L. M.

nastiness of Zola in *Pot-Bouille*—in Nietzsche's phrase, for "the delight to stink"—then surely the folly of college professors, as vast as it seems, has been underestimated. What is the fact? The fact is that Dreiser's attitude of mind, his manner of reaction to the phenomena he represents, the whole of his alleged "naturalistic philosophy," stems directly, not from Zola, Flaubert, Augier, and the younger Dumas, but from the Greeks. In the midst of democratic cocksureness and Christian sentimentalism, of doctrinaire shallowness and professorial smugness, he stands for a point of view which at least has something honest and courageous about it; here, at all events, he is a realist. Let him put a motto to his books, and it might be:

Ἰὼ γενεαὶ βροτῶν,

Ὡς ὑμᾶς ἴσα καὶ τὸ μηδὲν ζώσας ἐναριθμῶ.

If you protest against that as too harsh for Christians and college professors, right thinkers and forward lookers, then you protest against *Oedipus Rex*.[1]

As for the animal behavior prattle of the learned headmaster, it reveals, on the one hand, only the academic fondness for seizing upon high-sounding but empty phrases and using them to alarm the populace, and, on the other hand, only the academic incapacity for observing facts correctly and reporting them honestly. The truth is, of course, that the behavior of such men as Cowperwood and Witla and of such women as Carrie and Jennie, as Dreiser describes it, is no more merely animal than the behavior of such acknowledged and undoubted beings as Dr. Woodrow Wilson and Dr. Jane Addams. The whole point of the story of Witla, to take the example which seems to concern the horrified watchmen most, is this: that his life is a bitter conflict between the animal in him and the aspiring soul, between the flesh and the spirit, between what is weak in him and what is strong, between what is base and what is noble. Moreover,

[1] 1186–1189. So translated by Floyd Dell: "O ye deathward-going tribes of man, what do your lives mean except that they go to nothingness?" H. L. M.

the good, in the end, gets its hooks into the bad: as we part
from Witla he is actually bathed in the tears of remorse,
and resolved to be a correct and godfearing man. And what
have we in *The Financier* and *The Titan?* A conflict, in the
ego of Cowperwood, between aspiration and ambition, between the passion for beauty and the passion for power. Is
either passion animal? To ask the question is to answer it.

I single out Dr. Sherman, not because his pompous syllogisms have any plausibility in fact or logic, but simply
because he may well stand as archetype of the booming, indignant corrupter of criteria, the moralist turned critic. A
glance at his paean to Arnold Bennett[1] at once reveals the
true gravamen of his objection to Dreiser. What offends him
is not actually Dreiser's shortcoming as an artist, but Dreiser's
shortcoming as a Christian and an American. In Bennett's
volumes of pseudo-philosophy—*e.g., The Plain Man and
His Wife* and *The Feast of St. Friend*—he finds the intellectual victuals that are to his taste. Here we have a sweet
commingling of virtuous conformity and complacent optimism, of sonorous platitude and easy certainty—here, in
brief, we have the philosophy of the English middle classes
—and here, by the same token, we have the sort of guff that
the half-educated of our own country can understand. It is
the calm, superior numskullery that was Victorian; it is by
Samuel Smiles out of Hannah More. The offense of Dreiser
is that he has disdained this revelation and gone back to the
Greeks. Lo, he reads poetry into "the appetite for women"—
he rejects the Pauline doctrine that all love is below the
diaphragm! He thinks of Ulysses, not as a mere heretic and
criminal, but as a great artist. He sees the life of man, not
as a simple theorem in Calvinism, but as a vast adventure,
an enchantment, a mystery. It is no wonder that respectable
schoolteachers are against him. . . .

The comstockian attack upon *The "Genius"* seems to have
sprung out of the same muddled sense of Dreiser's essential
hostility to all that is safe and regular—of the danger in him
to that mellowed Methodism which has become the national
ethic. The book, in a way, was a direct challenge, for though

[1]The New York *Evening Post*, December 31, 1915. H. L. M.

it came to an end upon a note which even a Methodist might hear as sweet, there were undoubted provocations in detail. Dreiser, in fact, allowed his scorn to make off with his taste— and *es ist nichts fürchtlicher als Einbildungskraft ohne Geschmack*. The Comstocks arose to the bait a bit slowly, but nonetheless surely. Going through the volume with the terrible industry of a Sunday-school boy dredging up pearls of smut from the Old Testament, they achieved a list of no less than 89 alleged floutings of the code—75 described as lewd and 14 as profane. An inspection of these specifications affords mirth of a rare and lofty variety; nothing could more cruelly expose the inner chambers of the moral mind. When young Witla, fastening his best girl's skate, is so overcome by the carnality of youth that he hugs her, it is set down as lewd. On page 51, having become an art student, he is fired by "a great, warm-tinted nude of Bouguereau"—lewd again. On page 70 he begins to draw from the figure, and his instructor cautions him that the female breast is round, not square—more lewdness. On page 151 he kisses a girl on mouth and neck and she cautions him: "Be careful! Mamma may come in"—still more. On page 161, having got rid of mamma, she yields "herself to him gladly, joyously" and he is greatly shocked when she argues that an artist (she is by way of being a singer) had better not marry—lewdness doubly damned. On page 245 he and his bride, being ignorant, neglect the principles laid down by Dr. Sylvanus Stall in his great works on sex hygiene—lewdness most horrible! But there is no need to proceed further. Every kiss, hug, and tickle of the chin in the chronicle is laboriously snouted out, empaneled, exhibited. Every hint that Witla is no vestal, that he indulges his unchristian fleshliness, that he burns in the manner of *I Corinthians*, VII, 9, is uncovered to the moral inquisition.

On the side of profanity there is a less ardent pursuit of evidences, chiefly, I daresay, because their unearthing is less stimulating. (Beside, there is no law prohibiting profanity in books: the whole inquiry here is but so much *lagniappe*.) On page 408, in describing a character called Daniel C. Summerfield, Dreiser says that the fellow is "very much

given to swearing, more as a matter of habit than of foul
intention," and then goes on to explain somewhat lamely
that "no picture of him would be complete without the in-
terpolation of his various expressions." They turn out to be
God damn and *Jesus Christ*—three of the latter and five or
six of the former. All go down; the pure in heart must be
shielded from the knowledge of them. (But what of the
immoral French? They call the English *Goddams*.) Also,
three plain *damns*, eight *hells*, one *my God*, five *by Gods*,
one *go to the devil*, one *God Almighty*, and one plain *God*.
Altogether, 31 specimens are listed. *The "Genius"* runs to
350,000 words. The profanity thus works out to somewhat
less than one word in 10,000. . . . Alas, the comstockian
proboscis, feeling for such offendings, is not as alert as when
uncovering more savory delicacies. On page 191 I find an
overlooked *by God*. On page 372 there are *Oh God, God
curse her,* and *God strike her dead*. On page 373 there are
Ah God, Oh God, and three other invocations of God. On
page 617 there is *God help me*. On page 720 there is *as God
is my judge*. On page 723 there is *I'm no damned good*. . . .
But I begin to blush.

When the Comstock Society began proceedings against
The "Genius," a group of English novelists, including Arnold Bennett, H. G. Wells, W. L. George, and Hugh Walpole, cabled an indignant caveat. This bestirred the Author's
League of America to activity, and its executive committee
issued a minute denouncing the business. Later on a protest
of American *literati* was circulated, and more than 400
signed, including such highly respectable authors as Winston Churchill, Percy MacKaye, Booth Tarkington, and
James Lane Allen, and such critics as Lawrence Gilman,
Clayton Hamilton, and James Huneker, and the editors of
such journals as the *Century,* the *Atlantic Monthly,* and the
New Republic. Among my literary lumber is all the correspondence relating to this protest, not forgetting the letters
of those who refused to sign, and someday I hope to publish
it, that posterity may not lose the joy of an extremely diverting episode. Meanwhile, the case moves with stately dignity
through the interminable corridors of jurisprudence, and the

bulk of the briefs and exhibits that it throws off begins to rival the staggering bulk of *The "Genius"* itself.[1]

[1]Despite the comstockian attack, Dreiser is still fairly well represented on the shelves of American public libraries. A canvass of the libraries of the 25 principal cities gives the following result, an ✕ indicating that the corresponding book is catalogued, and a — that it is not:

	Sister Carrie	Jennie Gerhardt	The Financier	The Titan	A Traveler at Forty	The "Genius"	Plays of the Natural	A Hoosier Holiday
New York	✕	—	—	✕	✕	✕	✕	✕
Boston	—	—	—	—	✕	—	✕	—
Chicago	✕	✕	✕	✕	✕	✕	✕	✕
Philadelphia	✕	✕	✕	✕	✕	✕	✕	✕
Washington	—	—	—	—	✕	—	✕	—
Baltimore	—	—	—	—	✕	—	—	—
Pittsburgh	—	—	✕	✕	✕	✕	—	✕
New Orleans	—	—	—	—	—	—	—	—
Denver	✕	✕	✕	✕	✕	✕	✕	✕
San Francisco	✕	✕	✕	✕	✕	—	—	✕
St. Louis	✕	✕	✕	✕	✕	—	✕	—
Cleveland	✕	✕	✕	✕	—	✕	✕	—
Providence	—	—	—	—	—	—	—	—
Los Angeles	✕	✕	✕	✕	✕	✕	✕	✕
Indianapolis	✕	✕	✕	—	✕	—	✕	✕
Louisville	✕	✕	—	✕	✕	✕	✕	✕
St. Paul	✕	✕	—	—	✕	—	✕	✕
Minneapolis	✕	✕	✕	—	✕	—	✕	—
Cincinnati	✕	✕	✕	—	✕	—	✕	✕
Kansas City	✕	✕	✕	✕	✕	✕	✕	✕
Milwaukee	—	—	—	—	✕	—	✕	✕
Newark	✕	✕	✕	✕	✕	✕	✕	✕
Detroit	✕	✕	✕	—	✕	✕	✕	✕
Seattle	✕	✕	—	—	✕	—	✕	✕
Hartford	—	—	—	—	—	—	—	✕

This table shows that but two libraries, those of Providence and New Orleans, bar Dreiser altogether. The effect of alarms from newspaper reviewers is indicated by the scant distribution of the *The "Genius,"* which is barred by 14 of the 25. It should be noted that some of these libraries issue certain of the books only under restrictions. This I know to be the case in Louisville, Los Angeles, Newark, and Cleveland. The Newark librarian informs me that *Jennie Gerhardt* is to be removed altogether, presumably in response to some protest from local Comstocks. In Chicago *The "Genius"* has been stolen, and on account of the withdrawal of the book the Public Library has been unable to get another copy. H. L. M.

Dreiser, like Mark Twain and Emerson before him, has been far more hospitably greeted in his first stage, now drawing to a close, in England than in his own country. The cause of this, I daresay, lies partly in the fact that *Sister Carrie* was in general circulation over there during the seven years that it remained suppressed on this side. It was during these years that such men as Arnold Bennett, Theodore Watts-Dunton, Frank Harris, and H. G. Wells, and such critical journals as the *Spectator,* the *Saturday Review,* and the *Athenaeum* became aware of him, and so laid the foundations of a sound appreciation of his subsequent work. Since the beginning of the war, certain English newspapers have echoed the alarmed American discovery that he is a literary agent of the Wilhelmstrasse, but it is to the honor of the English that this imbecility has got no countenance from reputable authority and has not injured his position.

At home, as I have shown, he is less fortunate. When criticism is not merely an absurd effort to chase him out of court because his ideas are not orthodox, as the Victorians tried to chase out Darwin and Swinburne, and their predecessors pursued Shelley and Byron, it is too often designed to identify him with some branch or other of "radical" poppy-cock, and so credit him with purposes he has never imagined. Thus Chautauqua pulls and Greenwich Village pushes. In the middle ground there proceeds the pedantic effort to dispose of him by labeling him. One faction maintains that he is a realist; another calls him a naturalist; a third argues that he is really a disguised romanticist. This debate is all sound and fury, signifying nothing, but out of it has come a valuation by Lawrence Gilman[1] which perhaps strikes very close to the truth. He is, says Mr. Gilman, "a sentimental mystic who employs the mimetic gestures of the realist." This judgment is apt in particular and sound in general. No such thing as a pure method is possible in the novel. Plain realism, as in Gorky's *Nachtasyl* and the war stories of Ambrose Bierce, simply wearies us by its vacuity; plain romance, if we ever

[1] The *North American Review,* February 1916. H. L. M.

get beyond our nonage, makes us laugh. It is their artistic combination, as in life itself, that fetches us—the subtle projection of the concrete muddle that is living against the ideal orderliness that we reach out for—the eternal war of experience and aspiration—the contrast between the world as it is and the world as it might be or ought to be. Dreiser describes the thing that he sees, laboriously and relentlessly, but he never forgets the dream that is behind it. "He gives you," continues Mr. Gilman, "a sense of actuality; but he gives you more than that: out of the vast welter and surge, the plethoric irrelevancies, . . . emerges a sense of the infinite sadness and mystery of human life." . . .[1]

"To see truly," said Renan, "is to see dimly." Dimness or mystery, call it what you will: it is in all these overgrown and formless, but profoundly moving books. Just what do they mean? Just what is Dreiser driving at? That such questions should be asked is only a proof of the straits to which pedagogy has brought criticism. The answer is simple: he is driving at nothing, he is merely trying to represent what he sees and feels. His moving impulse is no flabby yearning to teach, to expound, to make simple; it is that "obscure inner necessity" of which Conrad tells us, the irresistible creative passion of a genuine artist, standing spellbound before the impenetrable enigma that is life, enamored by the strange beauty that plays over its sordidness, challenged to a wondering and half-terrified sort of representation of what passes understanding. And *jenseits von Gut und Böse.* "For myself," says Dreiser, "I do not know what truth is, what beauty is, what love is, what hope is. I do not believe anyone absolutely and I do not doubt anyone absolutely. I think people are both evil and well-intentioned." The hatching of the Dreiser bugaboo is here; it is the flat rejection of the rubberstamp formulae that outrages petty minds; not being "good," he must be "evil"—as William Blake said of Milton, a true poet is always "of the devil's party." But in that very groping toward a light but dimly seen there is a measure, it seems to me, of Dreiser's rank and consideration as an artist. "Now

[1]Another competent valuation, by Randolph Bourne, is in *The Dial*, June 14, 1917. H. L. M.

comes the public," says Hermann Bahr, "and demands that we explain what the poet is trying to say. The answer is this: If we knew exactly he would not be a poet. . . ."

JAMES HUNEKER

1917

EDGAR ALLAN POE, I am fond of believing, earned as a critic a good deal of the excess of praise that he gets as a romancer and a poet, and another overestimated American dithyrambist, Sidney Lanier, wrote the best textbook of prosody in English;[1] but in general the critical writing done in the United States has been of a low order, and most American writers of any genuine distinction, like most American painters and musicians, have had to wait for understanding until it appeared abroad. The case of Emerson is typical. At thirty, he was known in New England as a heretical young clergyman and no more, and his fame threatened to halt at the tea-tables of the Boston Brahmins. It remained for Landor and Carlyle, in a strange land, to discern his higher potentialities, and to encourage him to his real life-work. Mark Twain, as I have hitherto shown, suffered from the same lack of critical perception at home. He was quickly recognized as a funny fellow, true enough, but his actual stature was not even faintly apprehended, and even after *Huckleberry Finn* he was still bracketed with such laborious farceurs as Artemus Ward. It was Sir Walter Besant, an Englishman, who first ventured to put him on his right shelf, along with Swift, Cervantes, and Molière. As for Poe and Whitman, the native recognition of their genius was so greatly conditioned by a characteristic horror of their immorality that it would be absurd to say that their own country understood them. Both were better and more quickly apprehended in France, and it was in France, not in Amer-

[1] *The Science of English Verse;* New York, Scribner, 1880.
H. L. M.

ica, that each founded a school. What they had to teach we have since got back at second-hand—the tale of mystery, which was Poe's contribution, through Gaboriau and Boisgobey; and *vers libre,* which was Whitman's, through the French *imagistes.*

The cause of this profound and almost unbroken lack of critical insight and enterprise, this puerile Philistinism and distrust of ideas among us, is partly to be found, it seems to me, in the fact that the typical American critic is quite without any adequate cultural equipment for the office he presumes to fill. Dr. John Dewey, in some late remarks upon the American universities, has perhaps shown the cause thereof. The trouble with our educational method, he argues, is that it falls between the two stools of English humanism and German relentlessness—that it produces neither a man who intelligently feels nor a man who thoroughly knows. Criticism, in America, is a function of this half-educated and conceited class; it is not a popular art, but an esoteric one; even in its crassest journalistic manifestations it presumes to a certain academic remoteness from the concerns and carnalities of everyday. In every aspect it shows the defects of its practitioners. The American critic of beautiful letters, in his common incarnation, is no more than a talented sophomore, or, at best, a somewhat absurd professor. He suffers from a palpable lack of solid preparation; he has no background of moving and illuminating experience behind him; his soul has not sufficiently adventured among masterpieces, nor among men. Imagine a Taine or a Sainte-Beuve or a Macaulay—man of the world, veteran of philosophies, "lord of life"—and you imagine his complete antithesis. Even on the side of mere professional knowledge, the primary material of his craft, he always appears incompletely outfitted. The grand sweep and direction of the literary currents elude him; he is eternally on the surface, chasing bits of driftwood. The literature he knows is the fossil literature taught in colleges—worse, in high schools. It must be dead before he is aware of it. And in particular he appears ignorant of what is going forward in other lands. An exotic idea, to penetrate his consciousness, must first become stale, and even then he is apt to purge it of all its remaining validity and significance before adopting it.

This has been true since the earliest days. Emerson himself, though a man of unusual discernment and a diligent drinker from German spigots, nevertheless remained a *dilettante* in both aesthetics and metaphysics to the end of his days, and the incompleteness of his equipment never showed more plainly than in his criticism of books. Lowell, if anything, was even worse; his aesthetic theory, first and last, was nebulous and superficial, and all that remains of his pleasant essays today is their somewhat smoky pleasantness. He was a Charles Dudley Warner in nobler trappings, but still, at bottom, a Charles Dudley Warner. As for Poe, though he was by nature a far more original and penetrating critic than either Emerson or Lowell, he was enormously ignorant of good books, and, moreover, he could never quite throw off a congenital vulgarity of taste, so painfully visible in the strutting of his style. The man, for all his grand dreams, had a shoddy soul; he belonged authentically to the era of cuspidors, "females," and Sons of Temperance. His occasional affectation of scholarship has deceived no one. It was no more than Yankee bluster; he constantly referred to books that he had never read. Beside, the typical American critic of those days was not Poe, but his arch-enemy, Rufus Wilmot Griswold, that almost fabulous ass—a Baptist preacher turned taster of the beautiful. Imagine a Baptist valuing Balzac, or Molière, or Shakespeare, or Goethe—or Rabelais!

Coming down to our own time, one finds the same endless amateurishness, so characteristic of everything American, from politics to cookery—the same astounding lack of training and vocation. Consider the solemn ponderosities of the pious old maids, male and female, who write book reviews for the newspapers. Here we have a heavy pretension to culture, a campus cocksureness, a laborious righteousness— but of sound aesthetic understanding, of alertness and hospitality to ideas, not a trace. The normal American book reviewer, indeed, is an elderly virgin, a superstitious bluestocking, an apostle of Vassar *Kultur*; and her customary attitude of mind is one of fascinated horror. (The Hamilton Wright Mabie complex! The "white list" of novels!) William Dean Howells, despite a certain jauntiness and even kittenishness of manner, is spiritually of that company. For all his phosphorescent heresies, he is what the uplifters call a right-thinker at heart, and soaked in the national tradition. He is easiest intrigued, not by force and originality, but by a sickly, *Ladies' Home Journal* sort of piquancy; it was this that made him see a genius in the Philadelphia Zola, W. B. Trites, and that led him to hymn an abusive business letter by Frank A. Munsey, author of *The Boy Broker* and *Afloat in a Great City*, as a significant human document. Moreover, Howells runs true to type in another way, for he long reigned as the leading Anglo-Saxon authority on the Russian novelists without knowing, so far as I can make out, more than ten words of Russian. In the same manner, we have had enthusiasts for D'Annunzio and Mathilde Serao who knew no Italian, and celebrants of Maeterlinck and Verhaeren whose French was of the finishing school, and Ibsen authorities without a single word of Dano-Norwegian—I met one once who failed to recognize *Et Dukkehjem* as the original title of *A Doll's House*,—and performers upon Hauptmann who could no more read *Die Weber* than they could decipher a tablet of Tiglath-Pileser III.

Here and there, of course, a more competent critic of beautiful letters flings out his banner—for example, John Macy, Ludwig Lewisohn, André Tridon (it is a pity Tridon writes so little: his slaughter of Maeterlinck was extraordinarily well performed), Otto Heller, J. E. Spingarn, Willard Huntington Wright, the late Percival Pollard. Well-informed, intelligent, wide-eyed men—but only two of them even Americans, and not one of them with a wide audience, or any appreciable influence upon the main stream of American criticism. Pollard's best work is buried in the perfumed pages of *Town Topics;* his book on the Munich wits and dramatists[1] is almost unknown. Heller and Lewisohn make their way slowly; a patriotic wariness, I daresay, mixes itself

[1] *Masks and Minstrels of New Germany;* Boston, John W. Luce & Co., 1911. H. L. M.

up with their acceptance. Wright turns to journalism and to theoretical aesthetics—a colossal dispersal indeed. As for Macy, I recently found his *The Spirit of American Literature*[1] by long odds the soundest, wisest book on its subject, selling for fifty cents on a Fifth Avenue remainder counter.

How many remain? A few competent reviewers who are primarily something else—Gilman, Bourne, Untermeyer and company. A few youngsters on the newspapers, struggling against the business office. And then a leap to the Victorians, the crêpe-clad pundits, the bombastic word-mongers of the *Nation* school—H. W. Boynton, W. C. Brownell, Paul Elmer More, William Lyon Phelps, Frederick Taber Copper, *et al.* Here, undoubtedly, we have learning of a sort. More, it appears, once taught Sanskrit to the adolescent suffragettes of Bryn Mawr—an enterprise as stimulating (and as intelligible) as that of setting off fireworks in a blind asylum. Phelps sits in a chair at Yale. Boynton is a master of arts in English literature, whatever that may mean. Brownell is both L.H.D. and Litt.D., thus surpassing Samuel Johnson by one point, and Hazlitt, Coleridge, and Malone by two. But the learning of these august *umbilicarii,* for all its pretensions, is precisely the sterile, foppish sort one looks for in second-rate college professors. The appearance is there, but not the substance. One ingests a horse doctor's dose of words, but fails to acquire any illumination. Read More on Nietzsche[2] if you want to find out just how stupid criticism can be and yet show the outward forms of sense. Read Phelps's *The Advance of the English Novel*[3] if you would see a fine art treated as a moral matter, and great works tested by the criteria of a small-town Sunday school, and all sorts of childish sentimentality whooped up. And plow through Brownell's *Standards,*[4] if you have the patience, and then try to reduce its sonorous platitudes to straightforward and defensible propositions.

[1] New York, Doubleday, Page & Co., 1913. H. L. M.

[2] *The Drift of Romanticism;* Boston, Houghton Mifflin Co., 1913. H. L. M.

[3] New York, Dodd, Mead & Co., 1916. H. L. M.

[4] New York, Charles Scribner's Sons, 1917. H. L. M.

II

Now for the exception. He is, of course, James Gibbons Huneker, the solitary Iokanaan in this tragic aesthetic wilderness, the only critic among us whose vision sweeps the whole field of beauty, and whose reports of what he sees there show any genuine gusto. That gusto of his, I fancy, is two-thirds of his story. It is unquenchable, contagious, inflammatory; he is the only performer in the commissioned troupe who knows how to arouse his audience to anything approaching enthusiasm. The rest, even including Howells, are pedants lecturing to the pure in heart, but Huneker makes a joyous story of it; his exposition, transcending the merely expository, takes on the quality of an adventure hospitably shared. One feels, reading him, that he is charmed by the men and women he writes about, and that their ideas, even when he rejects them, give him an agreeable stimulation. And to the charm that he thus finds and exhibits in others, he adds the very positive charm of his own personality. He seems a man who has found the world fascinating, if perhaps not perfect; a friendly and good-humored fellow; no frigid scholiast, but something of an epicure; in brief, the reverse of the customary maker of books about books. Compare his two essays on Ibsen, in *Egoists* and *Iconoclasts*, to the general body of American writing upon the great Norwegian. The difference is that between a portrait and a Bertillon photograph, Richard Strauss and Czerny, a wedding and an autopsy. Huneker displays Ibsen, not as a petty mystifier of the women's clubs, but as a literary artist of large skill and exalted passion, and withal a quite human and understandable man. These essays were written at the height of the symbolism madness; in their own way, they even show some reflection of it; but taking them in their entirety, how clearly they stand above the ignorant obscurantism of the prevailing criticism of the time—how immeasurably superior they are, for example, to that favorite hymn-book of the Ibsenites, *The Ibsen Secret* by Jennette Lee! For the causes of this difference one need not seek far. They are to be found in the difference between the bombastic half-knowledge of a schoolteacher and the discreet and complete knowledge of a man of culture. Huneker is that man of culture. He has reported more of interest and value than any other American critic, living or dead, but the essence of his criticism does not lie so much in what he specifically reports as in the civilized point of view from which he reports it. He is a true cosmopolitan, not only in the actual range of his adventurings, but also and more especially in his attitude of mind. His world is not America, nor Europe, nor Christendom, but the whole universe of beauty. As Jules Simon said of Taine: *Aucun écrivain de nos jours n'a . . . découvert plus d'horizons variés et immenses."*

Need anything else be said in praise of a critic? And does an extravagance or an error here and there lie validly against the saying of it? I think not. I could be a professor if I would and show you slips enough—certain ponderous nothings in the Ibsen essays, already mentioned; a too easy bemusement at the hands of Shaw; a vacillating over Wagner; a habit of yielding to the hocus-pocus of the mystics, particularly Maeterlinck. On the side of painting, I am told, there are even worse aberrations; I know too little about painting to judge for myself. But the list, made complete, would still not be overlong, and few of its items would be important. Huneker, like the rest of us, has sinned his sins, but his judgments, in the overwhelming main, hold water. He has resisted the lure of all the wild movements of the generation; the tornadoes of doctrine have never knocked him over. Nine times out of ten, in estimating a new man in music or letters, he has come curiously close to the truth at the first attempt. And he has always announced it in good time; his solo has always preceded the chorus. He was, I believe, the first American (not forgetting William Morton Payne and Hjalmar Hjorth Boyesen, the pioneers) to write about Ibsen with any understanding of the artist behind the prophet's mask; he was the first to see the rising star of Nietzsche (this was back in 1888); he was beating a drum for Shaw the critic before ever Shaw the dramatist and mob philosopher was born (*circa* 1886–90); he was writing about Hauptmann and Maeterlinck before they had got well set on their legs in their own countries; his estimate of Sudermann, bearing date of 1905, may stand with scarcely the change of a word today; he did a lot of valiant pioneering for Strindberg, Hervieu, Stirner, and Gorki, and later on helped in the pioneering for Conrad; he was in the van of the MacDowell enthusiasts; he fought for the ideas of such painters as Davies, Lawson, Luks, Sloan, and Prendergast (Americans all, by the way: an answer to the hollow charge of exotic obsession) at a time when even Manet, Monet, and Degas were laughed at; he was among the first to give a hand to Frank Norris, Theodore Dreiser, Stephen Crane, and H. B. Fuller. In sum, he gave some semblance of reality in the United States, after other men had tried and failed, to that great but ill-starred revolt against Victorian pedantry, formalism, and sentimentality which began in the early nineties. It would be difficult, indeed, to overestimate the practical value to all the arts in America of his intellectual alertness, his catholic hospitality to ideas, his artistic courage, and, above all, his powers of persuasion. It was not alone that he saw clearly what was sound and significant; it was that he managed, by the sheer charm of his writings, to make a few others see and understand it. If the United States is in any sort of contact today, however remotely, with what is aesthetically going on in the more civilized countries—if the Puritan tradition, for all its firm entrenchment, has eager and resourceful enemies besetting it—if the pall of Harvard quasi-culture, by the Oxford manner out of Calvinism, has been lifted ever so little—there is surely no man who can claim a larger share of credit for preparing the way. . . .

III

Huneker comes out of Philadelphia, that depressing intellectual slum, and his first writing was for the Philadelphia *Evening Bulletin.* He is purely Irish in blood, and is of very respectable ancestry, his maternal grandfather and godfather having been James Gibbons, the Irish poet and patriot, and president of the Fenian Brotherhood in America. Once,

in a review of *The Pathos of Distance,* I ventured the guess
that there was a German strain in him somewhere, and
based it upon the beery melancholy visible in parts of that
book. Who but a German sheds tears over the empty bottles
of day before yesterday, the Adelaide Neilson of 1877?
Who but a German goes into woolen undershirts at forty-
five, and makes his will, and begins to call his wife "Mamma"? The green-sickness of youth is endemic from pole to
pole, as much so as measles; but what race save the wicked
one is floored by a blue distemper in middle age, with sentimental burblings *a cappella,* hallucinations of lost loves, and
an unquenchable lacrymorrhea? . . . I made out a good case,
but I was wrong, and the penalty came swiftly and doubly,
for on the one hand the Boston *Transcript* sounded an alarm
against both Huneker and me as German spies, and on the
other hand Huneker himself proclaimed that, even spiritually, he was less German than Magyar, less "Hun" than
Hun. "I am," he said, "a Celto-Magyar: Pilsener at Donney-
brook Fair. Even the German beer and cuisine are not in it
with the Austro-Hungarian." Here, I suspect, he meant to
say Czech instead of Magyar, for isn't Pilsen in Bohemia?
Moreover, turn to the chapter on Prague in *New Cosmopolis,* and you will find out in what highland his heart
really is. In this book, indeed, is a vast hymn to all things
Czechic—the Pilsen *Urquell,* the muffins stuffed with poppy-
seed jam, the spiced chicken liver *en casserole,* the pretty
Bohemian girls, the rose and golden glory of Hradčany Hill.
. . . One thinks of other strange infatuations: the Polish
Conrad's for England, the Scotch Mackay's for Germany,
the Low German Brahms's for Italy. Huneker, I daresay,
is the first Celto-Czech—or Celto-Magyar, as you choose.
(Maybe the name suggests something. It is not to be debased
to *Hoon*-eker, remember, but kept at *Hun*-eker, rhyming
initially with *nun* and *gun.*) An unearthly marriage of
elements, by all the gods! but there are pretty children of
it. . . .

Philadelphia humanely disgorged Huneker in 1878. His
father designed him for the law, and he studied the institutes
at the Philadelphia Law Academy, but, like Schumann, he

was spoiled for briefs by the stronger pull of music and the *cacoëthes scribendi*. (Grandpa John Huneker had been a composer of church music, and organist at St. Mary's.) In the year mentioned he set out for Paris to see Liszt; his aim was to make himself a piano virtuoso. His name does not appear on his own exhaustive list of Liszt pupils, but he managed to quaff of the Pierian spring at second hand, for he had lessons from Theodore Ritter (*né* Bennet), a genuine pupil of the old walrus, and he was also taught by the venerable Georges Mathias, a pupil of Chopin. These days laid the foundations for two subsequent books, the *Chopin: the Man and His Music* of 1900, and the *Franz Liszt* of 1911. More, they prepared the excavations for all of the others, for Huneker began sending home letters to the Philadelphia *Bulletin* on the pictures that he saw, the books that he read, and the music that he heard in Paris, and out of them gradually grew a body of doctrine that was to be developed into full-length criticism on his return to the United States. He stayed in Paris until the middle eighties, and then settled in New York.

All the while his piano studies continued, and in New York he became a pupil of Rafael Joseffy. He even became a teacher himself and was for ten years on the staff of the National Conservatory, and showed himself at all the annual meetings of the Music Teachers' Association. But bit by bit criticism elbowed out music-making, as music-making had elbowed out criticism with Schumann and Berlioz. In 1886 or thereabout he joined the *Musical Courier;* then he went, in succession, to the old *Recorder*, to the *Morning Advertiser*, to the *Sun*, to the *Times*, and finally back to the *Sun*, in whose columns he still occasionally holds forth. Various weeklies and monthlies have also enlisted him: *Mlle. New York*, the *Atlantic Monthly*, the *Smart Set*, the *North American Review*, and *Scribner's*. He has even stooped to *Puck*, vainly trying to make an American *Simplicissimus* of that dull offspring of synagogue and barbershop. He has been, in brief, an extremely busy and not too fastidious journalist, writing first about one of the arts, and then about another, and then about all seven together. But music has been the steadiest of all his loves; his first three books dealt almost wholly with it; of his complete canon more than half have to do with it.

IV

His first book, *Mezzotints in Modern Music*, published in 1899, revealed his predilections clearly, and, what is more, his critical insight and sagacity. One reads it today without the slightest feeling that it is an old story; some of the chapters, obviously reworkings of articles for the papers, must go back to the middle nineties, and yet the judgments they proclaim scarcely call for the change of a word. The single noticeable weakness is a too easy acquiescence in the empty showiness of Saint-Saëns, a tendency to bow to the celebrated French parlor magician too often. Here, I dare-say, is an echo of old Paris days, for Camille was a hero on the Seine in 1880, and there was even talk of pitting him against Wagner. The estimates of other men are judiciously arrived at and persuasively stated. Tschaikowsky is correctly put down as a highly talented but essentially shallow fellow—a blubberer in the regalia of a philosopher. Brahms, then still under attack by Henry T. Finck, of the *Evening Post* (the press-agent of Massenet: ye gods, what Harvard can do, even to a Württemberger!) is subjected to a long, an intelligent, and an extremely friendly analysis; no better has got into English since, despite too much stress on the piano music. And Richard Strauss, yet a nine days' wonder, is described clearly and accurately, and his true stature indicated. The rest of the book is less noteworthy; Huneker says the proper things about Chopin, Liszt, and Wagner, and adds a chapter on piano methods, the plain fruit of his late pedagogy. But the three chapters I have mentioned are enough; they fell, in their time, into a desert of stupidity; they set a standard in musical criticism in America that only Huneker himself has ever exceeded.

The most popular of his music books, of course, is the *Chopin* (1900). Next to *Iconoclasts*, it is the best seller of them all. More, it has been done into German, French, and

Italian, and is chiefly responsible for Huneker's celebrity
abroad as the only critic of music that America has ever
produced. Superficially, it seems to be a monument of
pedantry, a meticulous piling up of learning, but a study
of it shows that it is very much more than that. Compare
it to Sir George Grove's staggering tome on the Beethoven
symphonies if you want to understand the difference between mere scholastic diligence and authentic criticism. The
one is simply a top-heavy mass of disorderly facts and worshiping enthusiasm; the other is an analysis that searches
out every nook and corner of the subject, and brings it into
coherence and intelligibility. The Chopin rhapsodist is always held in check by the sound musician; there is a snout-
ing into dark places as well as a touching up of high lights.
I myself am surely no disciple of the Polish tuberose—his
sweetness, in fact, gags me, and I turn even to Moszkowski
for relief—but I have read and reread this volume with endless interest, and I find it more bethumbed than any other
Huneker book in my library, saving only *Iconoclasts* and
Old Fogy. Here, indeed, Huneker is on his own ground.
One often feels, in his discussions of orchestral music, that
he only thinks orchestrally, like Schumann, with an effort
—that all music, in his mind, gets itself translated into terms
of piano music. In dealing with Chopin no such transvaluation of values is necessary; the raw materials are ready for
his uses without preparation; he is wholly at home among
the black keys and white.

His *Liszt* is a far less noteworthy book. It is, in truth,
scarcely a book at all, but merely a collection of notes for
a book, some of them considerably elaborated, but others set
down in the altogether. One reads it because it is about
Liszt, the most fantastic figure that ever came out of Hun-
gary, half devil and half clown; not because there is any
conflagration of ideas in it. The chapter that reveals most of
Huneker is the appendix on latter-day piano virtuosi, with
its estimates of such men as de Pachmann, Rosenthal,
Paderewski, and Hofmann. Much better stuff is to be found
in *Overtones, The Pathos of Distance* and *Ivory, Apes and
Peacocks*—brilliant, if not always profound studies of Strauss,

Wagner, Schoenberg, Moussorgsky, and even Verdi. But if I had my choice of the whole shelf, it would rest, barring the *Chopin,* on *Old Fogy*—the *scherzo* of the Hunekerian symphony, the critic taking a holiday, the Devil's Mass in the tonal sanctuary. In it Huneker is at his very choicest, making high-jinks with his Davidsbund of one, rattling the skeletons in all the musical closets of the world. Here, throwing off his critic's black gown, he lays about him right and left, knocking the reigning idols off their perches; resurrecting the old, old dead and trying to pump the breath into them; lambasting on one page and lauding on the next; lampooning his fellow critics and burlesquing their rubber-stamp fustian; extolling Dussek and damning Wagner; swearing mighty oaths by Mozart, and after him, Strauss—not Richard, but Johann! The Old Fogy, of course, is the thinnest of disguises, a mere veil of gossamer for "Editor" Huneker. That Huneker in false whiskers is inimitable, incomparable, almost indescribable. On the one hand, he is a prodigy of learning, a veritable warehouse of musical information, true, half-true, and apocryphal; on the other hand, he is a jester who delights in reducing all learning to absurdity. Reading him somehow suggests hearing a Bach mass rescored for two fifes, a tambourine in B, a wind machine, two tenor harps, a contrabass oboe, two banjos, eight tubas, and the usual clergy and strings. The substance is there; every note is struck exactly in the middle—but what outlandish tone colors, what strange, unearthly sounds! It is not Bach, however, who first comes to mind when Huneker is at his tricks, but Papa Haydn—the Haydn of the Surprise symphony and the Farewell. There is the same gargantuan gaiety, the same magnificent irreverence. Haydn did more for the symphony than any other man, but he also got more fun out of it than any other man.

Old Fogy, of course, is not to be taken seriously: it is frankly a piece of fooling. But all the same a serious idea runs through the book from end to end, and that is the idea that music is getting too subjective to be comfortable. The makers of symphonies tend to forget beauty altogether; their one effort is to put all their own petty trials and tribulations, their empty theories and speculations into cacophony. Even so far back as Beethoven's day that autobiographical habit had begun. "Beethoven," says Old Fogy, is "dramatic, powerful, a maker of storms, a subduer of tempests; but his speech is the speech of a self-centered egotist. He is the father of all the modern melomaniacs, who, looking into their own souls, write what they see therein—misery, corruption, slighting selfishness, and ugliness." Old Ludwig's groans, of course, we can stand. He was not only a great musician, but also a great man. It is just as interesting to hear him sigh and complain as it would be to hear the private prayers of Julius Caesar. But what of Tschaikowsky, with his childish Slavic whining? What of Liszt, with his cheap playacting, his incurable lasciviousness, his plebeian warts? What of Wagner, with his delight in imbecile fables, his popinjay vanity, his soul of a *Schnorrer?* What of Richard Strauss, with his warmed-over Nietzscheism, his flair for the merely horrible? Old Fogy sweeps them all into his rag-bag. If art is to be defined as beauty seen through a temperament, then give us more beauty and cleaner temperaments! Back to the old gods, Mozart and Bach, with a polite bow to Brahms and a sentimental tear for Chopin! Beethoven tried to tell his troubles in his music; Mozart was content to ravish the angels of their harps. And as for Johann Sebastian, "there was more real musical feeling, uplifting, and sincerity in the old Thomaskirche in Leipzig . . . than in all your modern symphony and oratorio machine-made concerts put together."

All this is argued, to be sure, in extravagant terms. Wagner is a mere ghoul and impostor: *The Flying Dutchman* is no more than a parody on Weber, and *Parsifal* is "an outrage against religion, morals, and music." Daddy Liszt is "the inventor of the Liszt pupil, a bad piano player, a venerable man with a purple nose—a Cyrano de Cognac nose." Tschaikowsky is the Slav gone crazy on vodka. He transformed Hamlet into "a yelling man" and Romeo and Juliet into "two monstrous Cossacks, who gibber and squeak at each other while reading some obscene volume." "His Manfred is a libel on Byron, who was a libel on God."

And even Schumann is a vanishing star, a literary man turned composer, a pathological case. But, as I have said, a serious idea runs through all this concerto for slapstick and seltzer siphon, and to me, at least, that idea has a plentiful reasonableness. We are getting too much melodrama, too much vivisection, too much rebellion—and too little music. Turn from Tschaikowsky's *Pathétique* or from any of his wailing tone-poems to Schubert's C major, or to Mozart's *Jupiter*, or to Beethoven's *kleine Sinfonie in F dur:* it is like coming out of a *Kaffeeklatsch* into the open air, almost like escaping from a lunatic asylum. The one unmistakable emotion that much of this modern music from the steppes and morgues and *Biertische* engenders is a longing for form, clarity, coherence, a self-respecting tune. The snorts and moans of the pothouse Werthers are as irritating, in the long run, as the bawling of a child, the squeak of a pig under a gate. One yearns unspeakably for a composer who gives out his pair of honest themes, and then develops them with both ears open, and then recapitulates them unashamed, and then hangs a brisk coda to them, and then shuts up.

v

So much for *Old Fogy* and the musical books. They constitute, not only the best body of work that Huneker himself has done, but the best body of musical criticism that any American has done. Musical criticism, in our great Calvinist republic, confines itself almost entirely to transient reviewing, and even when it gets between covers, it keeps its trivial quality. Consider, for example, the published work of Henry Edward Krehbiel, for long the *doyen* of the New York critics. I pick up his latest book, *A Second Book of Operas,*[1] open it at random, and find this:

On January 31, 1893, the Philadelphia singers, aided by the New York Symphony Society, gave a performance of the opera, under the auspices of the Young Men's Hebrew Association, for the benefit of its charities, at the Carnegie Music Hall, New

[1] New York, The Macmillan Company, 1917. H. L. M.

York. Mr. Walter Damrosch was to have conducted, but was detained in Washington by the funeral of Mr. Blaine, and Mr. Hinrichs took his place.

O Doctor *admirabilis, acutus et illuminatissimus!* Needless to say the universities have not overlooked this geyser of buttermilk: he is an honorary A.M. of Yale. His most respectable volume, that on Negro folksong, impresses one principally by its incompleteness. It may be praised as a sketch, but surely not as a book. The trouble with Krehbiel, of course, is that he mistakes a newspaper morgue for Parnassus. He has all of the third-rate German's capacity for unearthing facts, but he doesn't know how either to think or to write, and so his criticism is mere pretense and pishposh. W. J. Henderson, of the *Sun,* doesn't carry that handicap. He is as full of learning as Krehbiel, as his books on singing and on the early Italian opera show, but he also wields a slippery and intriguing pen, and he could be hugely entertaining if he would. Instead, he devotes himself to manufacturing primers for the newly intellectual. I can find little of the charm of his *Sun* articles in his books. Lawrence Gilman? A sound musician but one who of late years has often neglected music for the other arts. Philip H. Goepp? His three volumes on the symphonic repertoire leave twice as much to be said as they say. Carl Van Vechten? A very promising novice, but not yet at full growth. Philip Hale? His gigantic annotations scarcely belong to criticism at all; they are musical talmudism. Beside, they are buried in the program books of the Boston Symphony Orchestra, and might as well be inscribed on the temple walls of Baalbec. As for Upton and other such fellows, they are merely musical chautauquans, and their tedious commentaries have little more value than the literary criticisms in the religious weeklies. One of them, a Harvard *maestro,* has published a book on the orchestra in which, on separate pages, the reader is solemnly presented with pictures of first and second violins! It seems to me that Huneker stands on a higher level than any of these industrious gentlemen, and that his writ-

ings on music are of much more value, despite his divided
allegiance among the *beaux arts*. Whatever may be said
against him, it must at least be admitted that he knows
Chopin, and that he has written the best volumes upon the
tuberculous Pole in English. Vladimir de Pachmann, that
king of all Chopin players, once bore characteristic testimony
to the fact—I think it was in London. The program was
heavy with the études and ballades, and Huneker sat in
the front row of fanatics. After a storm of applause de
Pachmann rose from the piano stool, levelled a bony claw
at Huneker, and pronounced his dictum: *"He* knows more
than *all* of you." Joseffy seems to have had the same opinion,
for he sought the aid of his old pupil in preparing his new
edition of Chopin, the first volume of which is all he lived
to see in print. . . . And, beyond all the others, Huneker
disdains writing for the kindergarten. There is no stooping
in his discourse; he frankly addresses himself to an audience
that has gone through the forms, and so he avoids the
tediousness of the A B C expositors. He is the only American musical critic, save Van Vechten, who thus assumes
invariably that a musical audience exists, and the only one
who constantly measures up to its probable interests, supposing it to be there. Such a book as *Old Fogy,* for all its
buffoonery, is conceivable only as the work of a sound
musician. Its background is one of the utmost sophistication;
in the midst of its wildest extravagances there is always a
profound knowledge of music on tap, and a profound love
of it to boot. Here, perhaps, more than anywhere else,
Huneker's delight in the things he deals with is obvious. It
is not a seminary that he keeps, but a sort of club of tone
enthusiasts, and membership in it is infinitely charming.

VI

This capacity for making the thing described seem important and delightful, this quality of infectious gusto, this
father-talent of all the talents that a critic needs, sets off
his literary criticism no less than his discourse on music and
musicians. Such a book as *Iconoclasts* or *Egoists* is full of

useful information, but it is even more full of agreeable adventure. The style is the book, as it is the man. It is arch, staccato, ironical, witty, galloping, playful, polyglot, allusive —sometimes, alas, so allusive as to reduce the Drama Leaguer and women's clubber to wonderment and ire. In writing of plays or of books, as in writing of cities, tone-poems or philosophies, Huneker always assumes that the elements are already well-grounded, that he is dealing with the initiated, that a pause to explain would be an affront. Sad work for the Philistines—but a joy to the elect! All this polyphonic allusiveness, this intricate fuguing of ideas, is not to be confused, remember, with the hollow showiness of the academic soothsayer. It is as natural to the man, as much a part of him, as the clanging Latin of Johnson, or, to leap from art to art Huneker-wise, the damnable cross-rhythms of Brahms. He could no more write without his stock company of heretic sages than he could write without his ration of malt. And, on examination, all of them turned out to be real. They are far up dark alleys, but they are there! . . . And one finds them, at last, to be as pleasant company as the multilingual puns of Nietzsche or Debussy's chords of the second.

As for the origin of that style, it seems to have a complex ancestry. Huneker's first love was Poe, and even today he still casts affectionate glances in that direction, but there is surely nothing of Poe's elephantine laboring in his skipping, *pizzicato* sentences. Then came Carlyle—the Carlyle of *Sartor Resartus*—a god long forgotten. Huneker's mother was a woman of taste; on reading his first scribblings, she gave him Cardinal Newman, and bade him consider the Queen's English. Newman achieved a useful purging; the style that remained was ready for Flaubert. From the author of *L'Education Sentimentale*, I daresay, came the deciding influence, with Nietzsche's staggering brilliance offering suggestions later on. Thus Huneker, as stylist, owes nearly all to France, for Nietzsche, too, learned how to write there, and to the end of his days he always wrote more like a Frenchman than a German. His greatest service to his own country, indeed, was not as anarch, but as teacher of writing. He

taught the Germans that their language had a snap in it
as well as sighs and gargles—that it was possible to write
German and yet not wander in a wood. There are whole
pages of Nietzsche that suggest such things, say, as the
essay on Maurice Barrès in *Egoists,* with its bold tropes, its
rapid gait, its sharp *sforzandos.* And you will find old Fried-
rich at his tricks from end to end of *Old Fogy.*

Of the actual contents of such books as *Egoists* and
Iconoclasts it is unnecessary to say anything. One no longer
reads them for their matter, but for their manner. Every
flapper now knows all that is worth knowing about Ibsen,
Strindberg, Maeterlinck, and Shaw, and a great deal that
is not worth knowing. We have disentangled Hauptmann
from Sudermann, and, thanks to Dr. Lewisohn, may read
all his plays in English. Even Henri Becque has got into
the vulgate and is familiar to the Drama League. As for
Anatole France, his *Revolt of the Angels* is on the shelves
of the Carnegie Libraries, and the Comstocks have let it
pass. New gods whoop and rage in Valhalla: Verhaeren,
Artzibashef, Przhevalski. Huneker, alas, seems to drop behind the procession. He writes nothing about these second-
hand third-raters. He has come to Wedekind, Schnitzler,
Schoenberg, Korngold, and Moussorgsky, and he has discharged a few rounds of shrapnel at the Gallo-Asiatic petti-
coat philosopher, Henri Bergson, but here he has stopped,
as he has stopped at Matisse, Picasso, Epstein, and Augustus
John in painting. As he says himself, "one must get off
somewhere." . . .

Particularly if one grows weary of criticism—and in Huneker, of late, I detect more than one sign of weariness.
Youth is behind him, and with it some of its zest for ex-
ploration and combat. "The pathos of distance" is a phrase
that haunts him as poignantly as it haunted Nietzsche, its
maker. Not so long ago I tried to induce him to write some
new *Old Fogy* sketches, nominating Puccini, Stravinsky,
Schoenberg, Korngold, Elgar. He protested that the mood
was gone from him forever, that he could not turn the clock
back twenty years. His late work in *Puck,* the *Times,* and
the *Sun,* shows an unaccustomed acquiescence in current

valuations. He praises such one-day masterpieces as McFee's *Casuals of the Sea;* he is polite to the kept idealists of the *New Republic;* he gags a bit at Wright's *Modern Painting;* he actually makes a gingery curtsy to Frank Jewett Mather, a Princeton professor. . . . The pressure in the gauges can't keep up to 250 pounds forever. Man must tire of fighting after awhile, and seek his ease in his inn. . . .

Perhaps the post-bellum transvaluation of all values will bring Huneker to his feet again, and with something of the old glow and gusto in him. And if the new men do not stir up, then assuredly the wrecks of the ancient cities will: the Paris of his youth; Munich, Dresden, Vienna, Brussels, London; above all, Prague. Go to *New Cosmopolis* and you will find where his heart lies, or, if not his heart, then at all events his oesophagus and pylorus. . . . Here, indeed the thread of his meditations is a thread of nutriment. However diverted by the fragrance of the Dutch woods, the church bells of Belgium, the music of Stuttgart, the bad pictures of Dublin, the plays of Paris, the musty romance of old Wien, he always comes back anon to such ease as a man may find in his inn. "The stomach of Vienna," he says, "first interested me, not its soul." And so, after a dutiful genuflexion to St. Stephen's ("Old Steffel," as the Viennese call it), he proceeds to investigate the paprika-chicken, the *Gulyas,* the *Risi-bisi,* the *Apfelstrudel,* the *Kaiserchmarn,* and the native and authentic *Wienerschnitzel.* And from food to drink—specifically, to the haunts of Pilsener, to "certain semi-sacred houses where the ritual of beer-drinking is observed," to the shrines at which beer maniacs meet, to "a little old house near a Greek church" where "the best-kept Pilsener in Vienna may be found."

The best-kept Pilsener in Vienna! The phrase enchants like an entrance of the horns. The best caviare in Russia, the worst actor on Broadway, the most virtuous angel in Heaven! Such superlatives are transcendental. And yet,—so rare is perfection in this world!—the news swiftly follows, unexpected, disconcerting, that the best Pilsener in Vienna is far short of the ideal. For some undetermined reason— the influence of the American tourist? the decay of the

Austrian national character?—the Vienna *Bierwirte* freeze
and paralyze it with too much ice, so that it chills the nerves
it should caress, and fills the heart below with heaviness
and repining. Avoid Vienna, says Huneker, if you are one
who understands and venerates the great Bohemian brew!
And if, deluded, you find yourself there, take the first *D-zug*
for Prague, that lovely city, for in it you will find the Pilsen
Urquell, and in the Pilsen *Urquell* you will find the best
Pilsener in Christendom—its color a phosphorescent, trans-
lucent, golden yellow, its foam like whipped cream, its
temperature exactly and invariably right. Not even at Pilsen
itself (which the Bohemians call Plzeň) is the emperor of
malt liquors more stupendously grateful to the palate. Write
it down before you forget: the Pilsen *Urquell*, Prague,
Bohemia, 120 miles S. S. E. of Dresden, on the river Moldau
(which the natives call the Vltava). Ask for Fräulein Ottilie.
Mention the name of Herr Huneker, the American *Schrift-
steller*.

Of all the eminent and noble cities between the Alleghe-
nies and the Balkans, Prague seems to be Huneker's favorite.
He calls it poetic, precious, delectable, original, dramatic—
a long string of adjectives, each argued for with eloquence
that is unmistakably sincere. He stands fascinated before
the towers and pinnacles of the Hradčany, "a miracle of
tender rose and marble white with golden spots of sunshine
that would have made Claude Monet envious." He pays
his devotions to the Chapel of St. Wenceslaus, "crammed
with the bones of buried kings," or, at any rate, to the shrine
of St. John Nepomucane, "composed of nearly two tons of
silver." He is charmed by the beauty of the stout, black-
haired, red-cheeked Bohemian girls, and hopes that enough
of them will emigrate to the United States to improve the
fading pulchritude of our own houris. But most of all, he
has praises for the Bohemian cuisine, with its incomparable
apple tarts and its dumplings of cream cheese, and for the
magnificent, the overpowering, the ineffable Pilsener of
Prague. This Pilsener motive runs through the book from
cover to cover. In the midst of Dutch tulip-beds, Dublin
cobblestones, Madrid sunlight, and Atlantic City leg-shows,

one hears it insistently, deep down in the orchestra. The cellos weave it into the polyphony, sometimes clearly, sometimes in scarcely recognizable augmentation. It is heard again in the wood-wind; the bassoons grunt it thirstily; it slides around in the violas; it rises to a stately choral in the brass. And chiefly it is in minor. Chiefly it is sounded by one who longs for the Pilsen *Urquell* in a far land, and among a barbarous and teetotaling people, and in an atmosphere as hostile to the recreations of the palate as it is to the recreations of the intellect.

As I say, this Huneker is a foreigner and hence accursed. There is something about him as exotic as a samovar, as essentially un-American as a bashi-bazouk, a nose-ring, or a fugue. He is filled to the throttle with strange and unpatriotic heresies. He ranks Beethoven miles above the national gods, and not only Beethoven, but also Bach and Brahms, and not only Bach and Brahms, but also Berlioz, Bizet, Bruch, and Bülow and perhaps even Balakirev, Bellini, Balfe, Borodin, and Boïeldieu. He regards Budapest as a more civilized city than his native Philadelphia, Stendhal as a greater literary artist than Washington Irving, *Künstler Leben* as better music than *There Is Sunlight in My Soul*. Irish? I still doubt it, despite the *Stammbaum*. Who ever heard of an Irish epicure, an Irish *flâneur*, or, for that matter, an Irish contrapuntist? The arts of the voluptuous category are unknown west of Cherbourg; one leaves them behind with the French pilot. Even the Czech-Irish hypothesis (or is it Magyar-Irish?) has a smell of the lamp. Perhaps it should be Irish-Czech. . . .

VII

There remain the books of stories, *Visionaries* and *Melomaniacs*. It is not surprising to hear that both are better liked in France and Germany than in England and the United States. (*Visionaries* has even appeared in Bohemian.) Both are made up of what the Germans call *Kultur-Novellen*— that is, stories dealing, not with the emotions common to all men, but with the clash of ideas among the civilized and godless minority. In some of them, *e.g.*, *Rebels of the Moon*, what one finds is really not a story at all, but a static discussion, half aesthetic and half lunatic. In others, *e.g.*, *Isolde's Mother*, the whole action revolves around an assumption incomprehensible to the general. One can scarcely imagine most of these tales in the magazines. They would puzzle and outrage the readers of Gouverneur Morris and Gertrude Atherton, and the readers of Howells and Mrs. Wharton no less. Their point of view is essentially the aesthetic one; the overwhelming importance of beauty is never in any doubt. And the beauty thus vivisected and fashioned into new designs is never the simple Wordsworthian article, of fleecy clouds and primroses all compact; on the contrary, it is the highly artificial beauty of pigments and tone-colors, of Cézanne landscapes and the second act of *Tristan und Isolde*, of Dunsanyan dragons and Paracelsian mysteries. Here, indeed, Huneker riots in the aesthetic occultism that he loves. Music slides over into diabolism; the Pobloff symphony rends the firmament of Heaven; the ghost of Chopin drives Mychowski to drink; a single drum-beat finishes the estimable consort of the composer of the Tympani symphony. In *The Eighth Deadly Sin* we have a paean to perfume—the only one, so far as I know, in English. In *The Hall of the Missing Footsteps* we behold the reaction of hasheesh upon Chopin's ballads in F major. . . . Strangely-flavored, unearthly, perhaps unhealthy stuff. I doubt that it will ever be studied for its style in our new Schools of Literature; a devilish cunning is often there, but it leaves a smack of the pharmacopoeia. However, as George Gissing used to say, "the artist should be free from everything like moral prepossession." This lets in the Antichrist.

. . .

Huneker himself seems to esteem these fantastic tales above all his other work. Story-writing, indeed, was his first love, and his Opus 1, a bad imitation of Poe, by name *The Comet*, was done in Philadelphia so long ago as July 4, 1876. (Temperature, 105 degrees Fahrenheit.) One rather marvels that he has never attempted a novel. It would have been as bad, perhaps, as *Love Among the Artists*, but cer-

tainly no bore. He might have given George Moore useful
help with *Evelyn Innes* and *Sister Teresa*: they are about
music, but not by a musician. As for me, I see no great
talent for fiction *qua* fiction in these two volumes of exotic
tales. They are interesting simply because Huneker the story
teller so often yields place to Huneker the playboy of the
arts. Such things as *Antichrist* and *The Woman Who Loved
Chopin* are no more, at bottom, than second-rate anecdotes;
it is the filling, the sauce, the embroidery that counts. But
what filling! What sauce! What embroidery! . . . One never
sees more of Huneker. . . .

VIII

He must stand or fall, however, as critic. It is what he
has written about other men, not what he has concocted
himself, that makes a figure of him, and gives him his unique
place in the sterile literature of the republic's second century. He stands for a *Weltanschauung* that is not only un-
national, but anti-national; he is the chief of all the curbers
and correctors of the American Philistine; in praising the
arts he has also criticized a civilization. In the large sense,
of course, he has had but small influence. After twenty
years of earnest labor he finds himself almost as alone as a
Methodist in Bavaria. The body of native criticism remains
as I have described it; an endless piling up of platitudes, an
homeric mass of false assumptions and jejune conclusions,
an insane madness to reduce beauty to terms of a petty and
pornographic morality. One might throw a thousand bricks
in any American city without striking a single man who
could give an intelligible account of either Hauptmann or
Cézanne, or of the reasons for holding Schumann to have
been a better composer than Mendelssohn. The boys in our
colleges are still taught that Whittier was a great poet and
Fenimore Cooper a great novelist. Nine-tenths of our people—perhaps ninety-nine hundredths of our native-born—
have yet to see their first good picture, or to hear their first
symphony. Our Chamberses and Richard Harding Davises
are national figures; our Norrises and Dreisers are scarcely

tolerated. Of the two undoubted world figures that we have contributed to letters, one was allowed to die like a stray cat up an alley and the other was mistaken for a cheap buffoon. Criticism, as the average American "intellectual" understands it, is what a Frenchman, a German, or a Russian would call donkeyism. In all the arts we still cling to the ideals of the dissenting pulpit, the public cemetery, the electric sign, the bordello parlor.

But for all that, I hang to a somewhat battered optimism, and one of the chief causes of that optimism is the fact that Huneker, after all these years, yet remains unhanged. A picturesque and rakish fellow, a believer in joy and beauty, a disdainer of petty bombast and moralizing, a sworn friend of all honest purpose and earnest striving, he has given his life to a work that must needs bear fruit hereafter. While the college pedagogues of the Brander Matthews type still worshiped the dead bones of Scribe and Sardou, Robertson and Bulwer-Lytton, he preached the new and revolutionary gospel of Ibsen. In the golden age of Rosa Bonheur's *The Horse Fair* he was expounding the principles of the post-impressionists. In the midst of the Sousa marches he whooped for Richard Strauss. Before the rev. professors had come to Schopenhauer, or even to Spencer, he was hauling ashore the devil-fish, Nietzsche. No stranger poisons have ever passed through the customs than those he has brought in his baggage. No man among us has ever urged more ardently, or with sounder knowledge or greater persuasiveness, that catholicity of taste and sympathy which stands in such direct opposition to the booming certainty and snarling narrowness of Little Bethel.

If he bears a simple label, indeed, it is that of anti-Philistine. And the Philistine he attacks is not so much the vacant and harmless fellow who belongs to the Odd Fellows and recreates himself with *Life* and *Leslie's Weekly* in the barber-shop, as that more belligerent and pretentious donkey who presumes to do battle for "honest" thought and a "sound" ethic—the "forward-looking" man, the university ignoramus, the conservator of orthodoxy, the rattler of ancient phrases—what Nietzsche called "the Philistine of culture." It is against this fat milch cow of wisdom that Huneker has brandished a spear since first there was a Huneker. He is a sworn foe to "the traps that snare the attention from poor or mediocre workmanship—the traps of sentimentalism, of false feeling, of cheap pathos, of the cheap moral." He is on the trail of those pious mountebanks who "clutter the market places with their booths, mischievous half-art and tubs of tripe and soft soap." Superficially, as I say, he seems to have made little progress in this benign *pogrom*. But under the surface, concealed from a first glance, he has undoubtedly left a mark—faint, perhaps, but still a mark. To be a civilized man in America is measurably less difficult, despite the war, than it used to be, say, in 1890. One may at least speak of *Die Walküre* without being laughed at as a half-wit, and read Stirner without being confused with Castro and Rasuili, and argue that Huxley got the better of Gladstone without being challenged at the polls. I know of no man who pushed in that direction harder than James Huneker.

A SHORT VIEW OF GAMALIELESE[1]

1921

IN THE FIRST SENTENCE of the historic address from the east front of the Capitol, glowing there like a gem, was that piquant miscegenation of pronouns, the *one-he* combination, for years a favorite of bad newspaper reporters and the inferior clergy. In the fourth sentence of the first message to Congress is *illy*, the passion of rural grammar-teachers and professors of rhetoric in one-building universities. We are, as they say, getting warm. The next great state paper—who knows?—may caress and enchant us with *"Whom* can

[1]This article deals with the inaugural address on March 4, 1921, by Warren Gamaliel Harding, twenty-ninth President of the United States. E. W.

deny?" And the next with "I would *have had* to *have had*."
And the next with "between you and *I*." And the next,
going the whole hog, with *alright*, to date the gaudiest,
loveliest, darnedest flower of the American language, which
God preserve!

Hog: flower? Perhaps the distemper is contagious. But
certainly not uninteresting to study and snuffle over—certainly no dull thing to the specialist in morbid philology.
In the style of the late Woodrow there was nothing, after
all, very remarkable, despite the orgiastic praises of Adolph
Ochs, the Hon. Josephus Daniels, and other such fanatics.
It was simply the style of a somewhat literary and sentimental curate, with borrowings from Moody and Sankey and
Dr. Berthold Baer. Its phrases lisped and cooed; there was
a velvety and funereal gurgling in them; they were made to
be intoned between the second and third lessons by fashionable rectors; aided by fifes and drums, or even by cost-plus
contracts, they were competent to vamp the intellect. But
intrinsically they were hollow. No heart's blood was in
them; no gobs of raw flesh. There was no passion there,
hot, exigent, and challenging. They could not make one
puff and pant. . . . One had to wait for Dr. Harding for
that. In his style there is pressure, ardency, effortcy, gasping,
a high grunting, Cheyne-Stokes breathing. It is a style that
rolls and groans, struggles and complains. It is the style of
a rhinoceros liberating himself by main strength from a lake
of boiling molasses.

In the doctrine that it is obscure I take no stock whatever.
Not a single sentence in the two great papers is incomprehensible to me, even after I have dined. I exhume a sample
strophe from the canto on the budget system in the message:
"It will be a very great satisfaction to know of its early
enactment, so it may be employed in establishing the economies and business methods so necessary in the minimum
of expenditure." This is awful stuff, I grant you, but is it
actually unintelligible? Surely not. Read it slowly and critically, and it may boggle you, but read it at one flash, and
the meaning will be clear enough. Its method is that of
pointillisme. The blotches of color are violent, and, seen

too closely, they appear insane, but stand off a bit and a quite simple and even austere design is at once discerned. "I hope it is adopted soon, so that we may employ the economies and business methods needed to hold down expenses": this is the kernel. What else is there is the style. It is the style of what the textbooks of rhetoric call "elevated" discourse. Its aim is to lend force to a simple hope or plea or asseveration by giving it the dynamic whoop and hoopla of a revival sermon, an auction sale, or a college yell. The nuclear thought is not smothered in the process, as Democratic aesthetes argue, nor is it true that there is sometimes no nuclear thought at all. It is always present, and nine times out of ten it is simple, obvious, and highly respectable. But it lacks punch; it is devoid of any capacity to startle and scorch. To give it the vigor and dignity that a great occasion demands it is carefully encased in those swathings of sonorous polysyllables, and then, the charge being rammed home, it is discharged point-blank into the ears and cerebrums of Christendom.

Such is the Gamalian manner, the secret of the Gamalian style. That style had its origin under circumstances that are surely not unknown to experts in politico-agrarian oratory. It came to birth on the rustic stump, it developed to full growth among the chautauquas, and it got its final polishing in a small-town newspaper office. In brief, it reflects admirably the tastes and traditions of the sort of audience at which it was first aimed, to wit, the yokelry of the hinterland, naïve, agape, thirsty for the prodigious, and eager to yell. Such an audience has no fancy for a well-knit and succinct argument, packed with ideas. Of all ideas, indeed, it is suspicious, but it will at least tolerate those that it knows by long hearing, those that have come to the estate of platitudes, those that fall readily into gallant and highfalutin phrases. Above all, it distrusts perspicuity, for perspicuity is challenging and forces one to think, and hence lays a burden on the mind. What it likes most of all is the roll of incomprehensible polysyllables—the more incomprehensible the better. It wants to be bombarded, bawled at, overwhelmed by mad gusts of the parts of speech. It wants

to be entertained by orators who are manifestly superior—
fellows whose discourse is so all-fired learned and unintelligible, so brilliant with hard words and trombone phrases,
that it leaves them gasping. Let the thunder sound, and it
takes all else on trust. If a sentence ends with a roar, it
does not stop to inquire how it began. If a phrase has punch,
it does not ask that it also have a meaning. If a word stings,
that is enough.

Trained to the service of such connoisseurs, Dr. Harding
carries over the style that they admire into his traffic with
the Congress, the effete *intelligentsia,* and the powers and
principalities of Europe. That style is based upon the simplest of principles. For every idea there is what may be
called a maximum investiture—a garb of words beyond which
it is a sheer impossibility to go in gaudiness. For every plain
word there is a word four times as big. The problem is to
think the thing out in terms of harmless banality, to arrance
a series of obvious and familiar ideas in a logical sequence,
and then to translate them, one by one, into nouns, verbs,
adjectives, adverbs, and pronouns of the highest conceivable
horse-power—to lift the whole discourse to the plane of
artillery practice—to dignify the sense by all the arts of
sorcery. Turn to the two immortal documents. The word
citizen is plainly banal; even a Congressman can understand
it. Very well, then, let us make it *citizenship*—and *citizenship* it becomes every time. But even that is not enough.
There comes a high point in the argument; a few more
pounds of steam must be found. *Citizen* now undergoes a
second proliferation; it becomes *factor in our citizenship.*
"We must invite . . . every factor in our citizenship to join
in the effort"—to restore normalcy. So with *women.* It is a
word in common use, a vulgar word, a word unfit for the
occasion of statecraft. *Also,* it becomes *womanhood.* Again,
there is *reference;* it swells up a bit and becomes *referendum.* Yet again, *civil* becomes *civic*—more scholarly, more
tasty, more nobby. Yet again, *interference* has a low smack;
it suggests plow-horses that interfere. *En avant!* there is
intermediation! And so with whole phrases. "The views of
the world" gives way to "the expressed views of world

opinion." "Heedless of cost" becomes "in heedlessness of cost." "Public conscience" becomes "the expressed conscience of progress." The "uplift," now ancient and a trifle obscene, is triumphantly reincarnated in "our manifestation of human interest." "The Government's duty to develop good citizens" shrieks upward like a rocket and bursts magnificently into "the Government's obligation affirmatively to encourage the development of the highest and most efficient type of citizenship." And so on and on.

Naturally enough, this style has its perils, no less hellish than war's. A man, so blowing up the parts of speech, may have one burst in his face. I discern something of the sort, alas, in "Congress might speed the price readjustment to normal relationship, with helpfulness of both producer and consumer." Here there has been an accident, just what I do not know. I suspect that "normal relationship" was substituted for *normalcy,* and that *normalcy* somehow got its revenge. Or maybe *helpfulness* came to its rescue and did the dirty work. Furthermore, the little word *of* has a suspicious look. I let the problem go. It is not one that a literary man engages with much gusto. He knows by harsh experience that words have a way of playing tricks—that they run amok at times, and toss him in the air, or stand him on his head—that fooling with them is like training leopards and panthers to leap through hoops and play the violoncello. There is, I have a notion, a foul conspiracy among words to pull Dr. Harding's legs from under him. He has tortured them for years—on the stump, in the chautauquas, beside the felled and smoking ox, at the annual banquets of the Chamber of Commerce, the Knights of Pythias, the Rotary Club, the Moose; above all, on the floors of legislative halls and in the columns of the Marion *Star.* He has forced them into strange and abhorrent marriages. He has stretched them as if they were chewing-gum. He has introduced pipes into them and pumped them until they screamed. He has put them to cruel and unusual uses. He has shown them no mercy. . . . Now, at last, they have him before a crowd that loves mirth, and make ready to get their *revanche.* Now they prepare to put the skids under him.

WANT AD

1926

THE DEATH of William Dean Howells in 1920 brought to an end a decorous and orderly era in American letters, and issued in a sort of anarchy. One may best describe the change, perhaps, by throwing it into dramatic form. Suppose Joseph Conrad and Anatole France were still alive and on their way to the United States on a lecture tour, or to study Prohibition or sex hygiene, or to pay their respects to Henry Ford. Suppose they were to arrive in New York at 2 P.M. today. Who would go down the bay on a revenue-cutter to meet them—that is, who in addition to the newspaper reporters and baggage-searchers—who to represent American Literature? I can't think of a single fit candidate. So long as Howells kept to his legs he was chosen almost automatically for all such jobs, for he was the dean of the national letters, and acknowledged to be such by everyone. Moreover, he had experience at the work and a natural gift for it. He looked well in funeral garments. He had a noble and ancient head. He made a neat and caressing speech. He understood etiquette. And before he came to his growth, stretching back into the past, there was a long line precisely like him —Mark Twain, General Lew Wallace, James Russell Lowell, Edmund Clarence Stedman, Richard Watson Gilder, Bryant, Emerson, Irving, Cooper, and so on back to the dark abysm of time.

Such men performed a useful and highly onerous function. They represented letters in all public and official ways. When there was a grand celebration at one of the older universities they were present in their robes, freely visible to the lowliest sophomore. When there was a great banquet, they sat between generals in the Army and members of the firm of J. P. Morgan & Company. When there was a solemn petition or protest to sign—against fiat money, the massacres in Armenia, municipal corruption, or the lack of international copyright—they signed in fine round hands, not for themselves alone, but for the whole fraternity of American literati. Most important of all, when a literary whale from foreign parts was sighted off Fire Island, they jumped into their frock coats, clapped on their plug-hats, and made the damp, windy trip through the Narrows on the revenue-cutter, to give the visitor welcome in the name of the eminent living and the illustrious dead. It was by such men that Dickens was greeted, and Thackeray, and Herbert Spencer, and Max O'Rell, and Blasco Ibáñez, and Matthew Arnold, and James M. Barrie, and Kipling, and (until they found his bootleg wife under his bed) Maxim Gorky. I name names at random. No worthy visitor was overlooked. Always there was the stately committee on the revenue-cutter, always there was the series of polite speeches, and always there was the general feeling that the right thing had been done in the right way—that American literature had been represented in a tasteful and resounding manner.

Who is to represent it today? I search the country without finding a single suitable candidate, to say nothing of a whole posse. Turn, for example, to the mystic nobles of the American Academy of Arts and Letters. I pick out five at random: William C. Brownell, Augustus Thomas, Hamlin Garland, Owen Wister, and Henry van Dyke. What is wrong with them? The plain but dreadful fact that no literary foreigner has even heard of them—that their appearance on the deck of his incoming barge would puzzle and alarm him, and probably cause him to call for the police. These men do not lack the homely virtues. They spell correctly, write neatly, and print nothing that is not constructive. In the five of them there is not enough sin to raise a congressman's temperature one-hundredth of a degree. But they are completely devoid of what is absolutely essential to the official life: they have, so to speak, no stage presence. There is nothing rotund and gaudy about them. No public and unanimous reverence bathes them. What they write or say never causes any talk. To be welcomed by them, jointly or severally, would appear to Thomas Hardy or Gabriel D'Annunzio as equal to being welcomed by representatives of the St. Joe, Mo., Rotary Club. Nor do I find any better stock among their heirs and apprentices in the National Institute. Put Henry Sydnor Harrison, say, against Howells: it is a wart succeeding Ossa. Match Clayton Hamilton with Edmund Clarence Stedman: Broadway against Wall Street. Shove Robert W. Chambers or Herman Hagedorn into the coat of Lowell: he would rattle in one of its pockets.

Worse, there are no better candidates outside the academic cloister. I daresay that most literate foreigners, asked to name the principal American novelist in practice today, would nominate Theodore Dreiser. He would get probably 75 per cent of the votes, with the rest scattered among Upton Sinclair, Sinclair Lewis, Cabell, Hergesheimer, and Sherwood Anderson. But try to imagine any of these gentlemen togged out in a long-tailed coat, shivering on the deck of a revenue-cutter while Gerhart Hauptmann got a grip on himself aboard the *Majestic!* Try to imagine Cabell presiding at a banquet to Knut Hamsun, with Dr. A. Lawrence Lowell to one side of him and Otto Kahn to the other! Try to picture Sinclair handing James Joyce a wreath to put upon the grave of James Whitcomb Riley! The vision, indeed, is more dismal than ludicrous. Howells, the last of his lordly line, is missed tremendously; there is something grievously lacking in the official hospitality of the country. The lack showed itself the instant he was called away. A few weeks later Columbia University gave a soirée in honor of the centenary of Lowell. The president of Columbia, Dr. Nicholas Murray Butler, is a realist. Moreover, he is a member of the American Academy himself, elected as a wet to succeed Edgar Allan Poe. He was thus privy to the deficiencies of his colleagues. To conceal the flabbiness of the evening he shoved them into back seats—and invited John D. Rockefeller, Jr., Tex Rickard, General Pershing, and the board of governors of the New York Stock Exchange to the platform!

I believe that, of living masters of letters, H. G. Wells was the first to feel the new chill. When he last visited the republic he was made welcome by a committee of ship-news reporters. It was as if one of the justices of the King's

Bench, landing in America, had been received by a committee of police-court lawyers from Gary, Ind. Later on
American literature bestirred itself and gave Wells a banquet
in New York. I was present at this feast, and a singular one
it was. Not a single author read in Iowa or taught at Harvard
was present. The principal literatus at the board was the
late Frank A. Munsey, author of *Derringforth* and *The Boy
Broker,* and the principal address was made by Max East-
man, formerly editor of the *Masses!* . . .

I come to a constructive suggestion. Let the literati of
America meet in their respective places of social relaxation,
each gang determining the credentials of its own members,
and elect delegates to a national convention. Then let the
national convention, by open ballot, choose ten spokesmen
and ten alternates to represent the national letters on all
formal occasions—not only when an eminent foreigner is to
be made welcome, but also when Columbia University holds
memorial services, when a President is inaugurated, when
Harvard meets Yale, when monuments are unveiled—in
brief, at all times of solemn public ceremonial. Let these
representatives practice deportment and elocution. Let them
employ good tailors and trustworthy bootleggers. I have,
alas, no candidates for the committee. As I have said, there
is a dreadful dearth of them. Does Dr. Frank Crane wear
whiskers? If so, I nominate him.

RING LARDNER

1926

A FEW YEARS AGO a young college professor, eager to make
a name for himself, brought out a laborious "critical" edition of *Sam Slick,* by Judge Thomas C. Haliburton, eighty-
seven years after its first publication. It turned out to be
quite unreadable—a dreadful series of archaic jocosities about
varieties of *Homo americanus* long perished and forgotten,

in a dialect now intelligible only to paleophilologists. Sometimes I have a fear that the same fate awaits Ring Lardner.
The professors of his own day, of course, are quite unaware
of him, save perhaps as a low zany to be enjoyed behind
the door. They would no more venture to whoop him up
publicly and officially than their predecessors of 1880 would
have ventured to whoop up Mark Twain, or their remoter
predecessors of 1837 would have dared to say anything for
Haliburton. In such matters the academic mind, being
chiefly animated by a fear of sneers, works very slowly.
So slowly, indeed, does it work that it usually works too
late. By the time Mark Twain got into the textbooks for
sophomores two-thirds of his compositions, as the Young
Intellectuals say, had already begun to date; by the time
Haliburton was served up as a sandwich between introduction and notes he was already dead. As I say, I suspect sadly
that Lardner is doomed to go the same route. His stories, it
seems to me, are superbly adroit and amusing; no other contemporary American, sober or gay, writes better. But I doubt
that they last: our grandchildren will wonder what they are
about. It is not only, or even mainly, that the dialect that
fills them will pass, though that fact is obviously a serious
handicap in itself. It is principally that the people they
depict will pass, that Lardner's Low-Down Americans—his
incomparable baseball players, pugs, song-writers, Elks,
small-town Rotarians, and golf caddies—are flitting figures
of a transient civilization, and doomed to be as puzzling and
soporific, in the year 2000, as Haliburton's Yankee clock
peddler is today.

The fact—if I may assume it to be a fact—is certainly not
to be set against Lardner's account; on the contrary, it is, in
its way, highly complimentary to him. For he has deliberately applied himself, not to the anatomizing of the general human soul, but to the meticulous histological study
of a few salient individuals of his time and nation, and he
has done it with such subtle and penetrating skill that one
must belong to his time and nation to follow him. I doubt
that anyone who is not familiar with professional ball-players,
intimately and at first hand, will ever comprehend the full

merit of the amazing sketches in *You Know Me, Al;* I doubt that anyone who has not given close and deliberate attention to the American vulgate will ever realize how magnificently Lardner handles it. He has had more imitators, I suppose, than any other living American writer, but has he any actual rivals? If so, I have yet to hear of them. They all try to write the speech of the streets as adeptly and as amusingly as he writes it, and they all fall short of him; the next best is miles and miles behind him. And they are all inferior in observation, in sense of character, in shrewdness and insight. His studies, to be sure, are never very profound; he makes no attempt to get at the primary springs of human motive; all his people share the same amiable stupidity, the same transparent vanity, the same shallow swinishness; they are all human Fords in bad repair, and alike at bottom. But if he thus confines himself to the surface, it yet remains a fact that his investigations on that surface are extraordinarily alert, ingenious, and brilliant—that the character he finally sets before us, however roughly articulated as to bones, is so astoundingly realistic as to epidermis that the effect is indistinguishable from that of life itself. The old man in *The Golden Honeymoon* is not merely well done; he is perfect. And so is the girl in *Some Like Them Cold.* And so, even, is the idiotic Frank X. Farrell in *Alibi Ike*—an extravagant grotesque and yet quite real from glabella to calcaneum.

Lardner knows more about the management of the short story than all of its professors. His stories are built very carefully, and yet they seem to be wholly spontaneous, and even formless. He has grasped the primary fact that no conceivable ingenuity can save a story that fails to show a recognizable and interesting character; he knows that a good character sketch is always a good story, no matter what its structure. Perhaps he gets less attention than he ought to get, even among the anti-academic critics, because his people are all lowly boors. For your reviewer of books, like every other sort of American, is always vastly impressed by fashionable pretensions. He belongs to the white-collar class of labor, and shares its prejudices. He praises F. Scott Fitzgerald's stories of country-club flappers eloquently, and over-looks Fitzgerald's other stories, most of which are much better. He can't rid himself of the feeling that Edith Wharton, whose people have butlers, is a better novelist than Willa Cather, whose people, in the main, dine in their kitchens. He lingers under the spell of Henry James, whose most humble character, at any rate of the later years, was at least an Englishman, and hence superior. Lardner, so to speak, hits such critics under the belt. He not only fills his stories with people who read the tabloids, say "Shake hands with my friend," and buy diamond rings on the instalment plan; he also shows them having a good time in the world, and quite devoid of inferiority complexes. They amuse him sardonically, but he does not pity them. A fatal error! The moron, perhaps, has a place in fiction, as in life, but he is not to be treated too easily and casually. It must be shown that he suffers tragically because he cannot abandon the plow to write poetry, or the sample-case to study for opera. Lardner is more realistic. If his typical hero has a secret sorrow it is that he is too old to take up osteopathy and too much in dread of his wife to venture into bootlegging.

Of late a sharply acrid flavor has got into Lardner's buffoonery. His baseball players and fifth-rate pugilists, beginning in his first stories as harmless jackasses, gradually convert themselves into loathsome scoundrels. The same change shows itself in Sinclair Lewis; it is difficult, even for an American, to contemplate the American without yielding to something hard to distinguish from moral indignation. Turn, for example, to the sketches in the volume called *The Love Nest*. The first tells the story of a cinema queen married to a magnate of the films. On the surface she seems to be nothing but a noodle, but underneath there is a sewer; the woman is such a pig that she makes one shudder. Again, he investigates another familiar type: the village practical joker. The fellow, in one form or other, has been laughed at since the days of Aristophanes. But here is a mercilessly realistic examination of his dung-hill humor, and of its effects upon decent people. A third figure is a successful theatrical manager: he turns out to have the professional competence of a chiropractor and the honor of a Prohibition agent. A fourth is a writer of popular songs: stealing other men's ideas has become so fixed a habit with him that he comes to believe that he has an actual right to them. A fifth is a trained nurse—but I spare you this dreadful nurse. The rest are bores of the homicidal type. One gets the effect, communing with the whole gang, of visiting a museum of anatomy. They are as shocking as what one encounters there—but in every detail they are as unmistakably real.

Lardner conceals his new savagery, of course, beneath his old humor. It does not flag. No man writing among us has greater skill at the more extravagant varieties of jocosity. He sees startling and revelatory likeness between immensely disparate things, and he is full of pawky observations and bizarre comments. Two baseball-players are palavering, and one of them, Young Jake, is boasting of his conquests during spring practice below the Potomac. "Down South ain't here!" replies the other. "Those dames in some of those swamps, they lose their head when they see a man with shoes on!" The two proceed to the discussion of a third imbecile, guilty of some obscure tort. "Why," inquires Young Jake, "didn't you break his nose or bust him in the chin?" "His nose was already broke," replied the other, "and he didn't have no chin." Such wisecracks seem easy to devise. Broadway diverts itself by manufacturing them. They constitute the substance of half the town shows. But in those made by Lardner there is something far more than mere facile humor: they are all rigidly in character, and they illuminate that character. Few American novelists, great or small, have character more firmly in hand. Lardner does not see situations; he sees people. And what people! They are all as revolting as so many Methodist evangelists, and they are all as thoroughly American.

One of the most important elements in the literary activity that followed the War was the return from military service of a number of first-rate young writers: John Dos Passos, William Faulkner, Ernest Hemingway, E. E. Cummings. These men had had a deeper experience than Stephen Crane and Sherwood Anderson had had in the Spanish War: they had been involved in a world crisis, and they had seen what it meant at first hand. They had come back with a vivid memory of what human society looks like when the laws and the conventions are suspended, and with a conviction that they knew the reality which the civilians at home could not imagine.

This review by Dos Passos of Cummings' book appeared in *The Dial* of July 1922. Cummings had enlisted, during the War, in the Norton Harjes Ambulance Corps, but his unconstrained letters and talk had aroused the suspicions of the French authorities, who charged him with treasonable activity and sent him to a concentration camp. *The Enormous Room* (1922) is the story of the three months he spent there. Dos Passos had published the year before a novel about the War: *Three Soldiers*. Dos Passos at this time was twenty-six; Cummings twenty-seven.

JOHN DOS PASSOS

OFF THE SHOALS: *THE ENORMOUS ROOM*
BY E. E. CUMMINGS

WHEN the American Chicle Company brings out gum of a new shape and unfamiliar flavor gumchewers are delighted and miss their subway trains in rush hour and step on each other's heels crowding round slot machines in their haste to submit to a new sensation. Frequenters of cabarets and jazz palaces shimmy themselves into St. Vitus's dance with delight over a new noise in the band or a novel squirm in the rhythm. People mortgage their houses to be seen in the newest and most bizarre models of autos. Women hock their jewels and their husbands' insurance policies to acquire an unaccustomed shade in hair or *crêpe de chine.* Why, then, is it that when anyone commits anything novel in the arts he should be always greeted by this same peevish howl of pain and surprise? One is led to suspect that the interest people show in these much-talked-of commodities, painting, music, and writing, cannot be very deep or very genuine when they wince so under any unexpected impact.

The man who invented Eskimo Pie made a million dollars, so one is told, but E. E. Cummings, whose verse has been appearing off and on for three years now, and whose experiments should not be more appalling to those interested in poetry than the experiment of surrounding ice-cream with a layer of chocolate was to those interested in soda fountains has hardly made a dent in the doughy minds of our so-called poetry-lovers. Yet one might have thought that the cadences of

> Or with thy mind against my mind, to hear
> nearing our hearts' irrevocable play—
> through the mysterious high futile day
> an enormous stride
>   (and drawing thy mouth toward
> my mouth, steer our lost bodies carefully downward)

would have melted with as brittle freshness on the senses of the readers of the *Dial* as melted the brown-encrusted oblongs of ice cream in the mouths of tired stenographers and their beaux. Can it be that people like ice-cream and only pretend to like poetry?

Therefore it is very fortunate that this book of E. E. Cummings has come out under the disguise of prose. The average reader is less self-conscious and more open to direct impressions when reading prose than verse; the idea that prose is ART will have closed the minds of only a few overeducated people. Here at last is an opportunity to taste without overmuch prejudice a form, an individual's focus on existence, a gesture unforeseen in American writing. The attempt to obscure the issue, on the paper-cover blurb and in the preface, will fool no one who reads beyond the first page. It's not as an account of a war atrocity or as an attack on France or the holy Allies timely to the Genoa Conference that *The Enormous Room* is important, but as a distinct conscious creation separate from anything else under heaven.

Here's a book that has been conceived unashamedly and directly without a thought either of the columnists or the book trade or Mr. Sumner, or of fitting into any one of the neatly labeled pigeonholes of novel, play, essay, history, travel book, a book that exists because the author was so moved, excited, amused by a certain slice of his existence that things happened freely and cantankerously on paper. And he had the nerve to let things happen. In this pattern-cut generation, most writers are too afraid of losing their private reputations as red-blooded, clear-eyed, hundred-per-centers, well-dressed, well-mannered, and thoroughly disinfected fashion plates, to make any attempt to feel and express directly the life about them and in them. They walk in daily fear that someone will call them morbid, and insulate themselves from their work with the rubber raincoat of fiction. *The Enormous Room* seems to me to be the book that has nearest approached the mood of reckless adventure in which men will reach the white heat of imagination needed to fuse the soggy, disjointed complexity of the industrial life about us into seething fluid of creation. There can be no more playing safe. Like the old steamboat captains on the Mississippi we'll have to forget the hissing of the safety-valve and stoke like beavers if we are to get off the sticky shoals into the deeper reaches beyond. And many an old tub will blow sky high with all hands before someone makes the course. *The Enormous Room* for one seems to me at least to have cleared the shoals.

Along with Sandburg and Sherwood Anderson, E. E. Cummings takes the rhythms of our American speech as the material of his prose as of his verse. It is writing created in the ear and lips and jotted down. For accuracy in noting the halting cadences of talk and making music of it, I don't know anything that comes up to these two passages. This is a poem that came out in *The Dial:*

> Buffalo Bill's
> defunct
>   who used to
>   ride a watersmooth-silver
>   stallion
> and break onetwothreefourfive pigeonsjustlikethat
>   Jesus
> he was a handsome man
>   and what i want to know is
> how do you like your blueeyed boy
> Mister Death

This from *The Enormous Room:*

Sunday: green murmurs in coldness. Surplice fiercely fearful, praying on his bony both knees, crossing himself. . . . The

Fake French Soldier, alias Garibaldi, beside him, a little face
filled with terror . . . the Bell cranks the sharp-nosed priest
on his knees . . . titter from bench of whores—

And that reminds me of a Sunday afternoon on our backs
spent with the wholeness of a hill in Chevancourt, discovering
a great apple pie, B. and Jean Stahl and Maurice le Menusier
and myself; and the sun falling roundly before us.

—And then one *Dimanche* a new high old man with a sharp
violet face and green hair—"You are free, my children, to
achieve immortality—*Songez, songez, donc—L'Eternité est une
existence sans durée—Toujours le Paradis, toujours l'Enfer*" (to
the silently roaring whores) "Heaven is made for you"—and the
Belgian ten-foot farmer spat three times and wiped them with
his foot, his nose dripping; and the nigger shot a white oyster
into a far-off scarlet handkerchief—and the priest's strings came
untied and he sidled crablike down the steps—the two candles
wiggle a strenuous softness . . .

In another chapter I will tell you about the nigger.

And another Sunday I saw three tiny old females stumble
forward, three very formerly and even once bonnets perched
upon three wizened skulls, and flop clumsily before the priest,
and take the wafer hungrily into their leathery faces.

This sort of thing knocks literature into a cocked hat. It
has the raucous directness of a song-and-dance act in cheap
vaudeville, the willingness to go the limit in expression and
emotion of a Negro dancing. And in this mode, nearer the
conventions of speech than those of books, in a style infinitely swift and crisply flexible, an individual not ashamed
of his loves and hates, great or trivial, has expressed a bit
of the underside of History with indelible vividness.

The material itself, of course, is superb. The Concentration Camp at La Ferté-Macé was one of those many fantastic
crossroads of men's lives where one lingered for unforgettable
moments, reaching them one hardly knew how, shoved
away from them as mysteriously by some movement of the
pawns on the chessboard, during the fearfully actual nightmare of war. A desperate recklessness in the air made every
moment, every intonation snatched from the fates of absolute importance. In The Wanderer and Jean le Nègre

and Surplice and Mexique and Apollyon and the Machine Fixer and in those grotesque incidents of the fight with the stovepipes and Celina's defiance we have that intense momentary flare in which lifetimes, generations are made manifest. To have made those moments permanent on a printed page is no common achievement.

For some reason there is a crispness and accuracy about these transcripts of the smell and taste and shiver of that great room full of huddled prisoners that makes me think of Defoe. In *The Journal of the Plague Year* or in the description of a night spent among enormous bones and skeletons in the desert journey in *Captain Singleton* one finds passages of a dry definiteness that somehow give the sort of impression that gives this hotly imaged picture of a roadside crucifix:

I banged forward with bigger and bigger feet. A bird, scared, swooped almost into my face. Occasionally some night noise pricked a futile, minute hole in the enormous curtain of soggy darkness. Uphill now. Every muscle thoroughly aching, head spinning, I half-straightened my no longer obedient body; and jumped: face to face with a little wooden man hanging all by itself in a grove of low trees.

—The wooden body, clumsy with pain, burst into fragile legs with absurdly large feet and funny writhing toes; its little stiff arms made abrupt cruel equal angles with the road. About its stunted loins clung a ponderous and jocular fragment of drapery. On one terribly brittle shoulder the droll lump of its neckless head ridiculously lived. There was in this complete silent doll a gruesome truth of instinct, a success of uncanny poignancy, an unearthly ferocity of rectangular emotion.

For perhaps a minute the almost obliterated face and mine eyed one another in the silence of intolerable autumn.

Perhaps one thinks of Defoe because of the unashamed directness with which every twitch of the individual's fibers, stung or caressed by the world's flowing past outside, is noted down. There is no straining through the standard literary sieve.

Of the English eighteenth century, too, is the fine tang of

high adventure along roads among grotesque companions
that comes to the surface in passages like this:

The high-road won, all of us relaxed considerably. The *sac*
full of suspicious letters which I bore on my shoulder was not
so light as I had thought, but the kick of the Briouse *pinard*
thrust me forward at a good clip. The road was absolutely
deserted; the night hung loosely around it, here and there
tattered by attempting moonbeams. I was somewhat sorry to
find the way hilly, and in places bad underfoot; yet the unknown adventure lying before me, and the delicious silence of
the night (in which our words rattled queerly like tin soldiers
in a plush-lined box) boosted me into a condition of mysterious happiness. We talked, the older and I, of strange subjects.
As I suspected he had not always been a *gendarme*. He had
seen service among the Arabs.

and the first description of The Wanderer:

B. called my attention to a figure squatting in the middle of
the *cour* with his broad back against one of the more miserable
trees. This figure was clothed in a remarkably picturesque
manner; it wore a dark sombrerolike hat with a large drooping
brim, a bright red gipsy shirt of some remarkably fine material
with huge sleeves loosely falling, and baggy corduroy trousers
whence escaped two brown, shapely, naked feet. On moving
a little I discovered a face—perhaps the handsomest face that I
have ever seen, of a gold-brown color, framed in an amazingly
large and beautiful black beard. The features were finely
formed and almost fluent, the eyes soft and extraordinarily
sensitive, the mouth delicate and firm beneath a black mustache
which fused with the silky and wonderful darkness falling upon
the breast. The face contained a beauty and dignity which, as
I first saw it, annihilated the surrounding tumult without an
effort. Around the carefully formed nostrils there was something almost of contempt. The cheeks had known suns of
which I might not think. The feet had traveled nakedly in
countries not easily imagined. Seated gravely in the mud and
noise of the *cour* under the pitiful and scraggly *pommier* . . .
behind the eyes lived a world of complete strangeness and
silence. The composure of the body was graceful and Jovelike.
This being might have been a prophet come out of a country
nearer to the sun. Perhaps a god who had lost his road and

allowed himself to be taken prisoner by *le gouvernement français*. At least a prince of a dark and desirable country, a king over a gold-skinned people who would return when he wished to his fountains and his houris. I learned upon inquiry that he traveled in various countries with a horse and cart and his wife and children, selling bright colors to the women and men of these countries. As it turned out he was one of the Delectable Mountains; to discover which I had come a long and difficult way. Wherefore I shall tell you no more about him for the present, except that his name was Joseph Demestre.

We called him The Wanderer.

There is about this sort of writing a gusto, an intense sensitiveness to men and women and colors and stenches and anger and love that, like the face of Joseph Demestre, "annihilates the surrounding tumult without an effort." When a book like *The Enormous Room* manages to emerge from the morass of print that we flounder in, it is time to take off your new straw hat and jump on it.

SHERWOOD ANDERSON died suddenly, March 8, 1941, on a
trip to South America, where he had intended to stay six
months, visiting small towns of the kind that particularly
interested him, and acquainting himself with the literary
world. The effect of the second world war had been to
make the United States feel the need of establishing a
livelier interchange between the two Americas.

This group of letters to Van Wyck Brooks first appeared
in *Story* magazine of September–October 1941—a special
number devoted to Anderson. They are interesting because
they show that Anderson was conscious of a literary tradition based on Lincoln, Mark Twain, and Whitman, and
thought of himself as belonging to it. Brooks's "essay on *Highbrows and Lowbrows*" of which Anderson speaks, is the first
chapter of Brooks's book, *America's Coming of Age*, published in 1915. In this chapter Brooks pointed out that there
were "two main currents in the American mind running side
by side but rarely mingling." On the one hand, you had
"the current of Transcendentalism, originating in the piety
of the Puritans, becoming a philosophy in Jonathan Ed-
vards, passing through Emerson, producing the fastidious

refinement and aloofness of the chief American writers, and, as the coherent ideals and beliefs of Transcendentalism gradually faded out, resulting in the final unreality of most contemporary American culture; and, on the other hand, the current of catchpenny opportunism, originating in the practical shifts of Puritan life, becoming a philosophy in Franklin, passing through the American humorists, and resulting in the atmosphere of contemporary business life."

Brooks regarded these currents as "both equally unsocial." In his time they were beginning to flow together. The moment of his describing the situation, the moment of our feeling it as uncomfortable, was the moment when it was coming to an end. Brooks himself was one of the writers who was helping to bring this about. And yet one still hears in these letters an echo of the imperfect understanding between Walt Whitman and Emerson.

SHERWOOD ANDERSON

LETTERS TO VAN WYCK BROOKS

Introductory Note by Van Wyck Brooks

I FIRST MET Sherwood Anderson in the late winter of 1917 at the office of *The Seven Arts* in New York. I think it was Waldo Frank who brought him into the magazine, of which Frank and I and James Oppenheim were editors. Paul Rosenfeld and Randolph Bourne were also of the circle, and we all became good friends; and I believe that *The Seven Arts* published the first of the Winesburg stories. Sherwood was still at that time in business, but he had written several novels, along with a great number of short stories; and he was eager to break his connection with business and establish himself as a writer. As he said in one of his letters, "I want to quit working for a living and go wander for five years in our towns." I can remember how struck I was by his fresh healthy mind and his true Whitmanian feeling for comradeship, his beautiful humility, his lovely generosity, and the "proud, conscious innocence" of his nature. This was his own phrase for Mark Twain's mind at the time when he was writing *Huckleberry Finn,* and it goes for Sherwood also. He was the most natural of men, as innocent as any animal or flowering tree.

For six or seven years we saw much of each other, and

these letters are the record of our friendship. They are especially interesting because these were the years during which he was discovering himself and his world. He was, as he says, "setting out on new roads," tasting the "Mid-America" that was his land, "the place between mountain and mountain"—touching it, catching its scent, listening, seeing; and his letters bring back the feeling of that time, when we were all of us groping and lonely. We were all trying to understand the nature of America, turning away from "European culture," and we all felt, as Sherwood says, that we were "struggling in a vacuum"—we had that "queer sense of carving a stone" that would be "cast into a stagnant sea." Well I remember these feelings, which Sherwood expresses; and I remember, too, what a boon it was to have a meeting-place at *The Seven Arts*. While most of us were Easterners, we felt that the heart of America lay in the West; and Sherwood was the essence of his West. He was full of Lincoln and especially of Mark Twain, and he wanted to sell me Twain, as he said in a letter. I was writing *The Ordeal of Mark Twain*, and he was anxious for me to understand him; and after I published the book he showed me clearly where my study had fallen short. I had failed to write the most important chapter, in which I should have praised *Huckleberry Finn*. I was too much concerned with the psychological problem, and the psychologist inhibited the poet in me. I regretted this as much as Sherwood, who loved Mark Twain above all writers. The last time I saw Sherwood, about 1939, we were dining in New York in a semipublic room. On the wall hung a life-sized photograph of Mark Twain, sitting in his rocking chair on the piazza at Redding. Sherwood looked up at it and smiled as he said, "There was a lovely man."

Sherwood bewailed Mark Twain's going East, among men from "barren hills and barren towns"; and he wrote to me, "A man cannot be a pessimist who lives near a brook or a cornfield." He never lost his happiness or his faith, for he knew where he belonged and he loved it. He brooded over his own country and sang it. He sang it least well perhaps in the *Mid-American Chants*, which was rather a matrix of poetry than poetry proper. But his short stories were poems.

They were certainly acrid at moments, but there he was always the poet. He suggests in these letters that I questioned his quality now and then, though he said that I was entitled to my personal taste. Well, the only question I felt regarded his novels, and I may have been quite mistaken. I only regretted that he wrote novels when he had a gift for storytelling that was, in its different way, like Chekhov's; for I never could feel that his novels were as good as his stories, and he was the most enthralling teller of tales. Never can I forget an evening, in 1937, which he spent at my house in Westport. For two hours he told stories about the folks at Marion, while we all listened like a three years' child.

CHICAGO—*1918?—19?*

BROOKS:

I cannot resist the temptation to write you a letter induced by a talk Waldo Frank and I had last evening. The talk drifted to Mark Twain and your attitude toward him. Something Waldo said gave me the notion that your digging into his work had made you a little ill—that you had seen, perhaps too clearly, his dreadful vulgarity and cheapness.

Of course your book cannot be written in a cheerful spirit. In facing Twain's life you face a tragedy. How could the man mean what he does to us if it were not a tragedy. Had the man succeeded in breaking through he would not have been a part of us. Can't you take it that way?

America a land of children—broken off from the culture of the world. Twain there—a part of that. Then the coming of industrialism. The putting of the child into the factory.

Mark Twain was a factory child. I am that. I can however stand off and look at him. When it would be second rate and unmanly to weep concerning myself I can think of him. For his very failure I love him. He was maimed, hurt, broken. In some way he got caught up by the dreadful cheap smartness, the shrillness that was a part of the life of the country, that is still its dominant note.

I don't want you to get off Twain. I want your mind on it. Please do not lose courage, do not be frightened away by the muck and ugliness of it.

For the Americans of the future there can be no escape. They have got to, in some way, face themselves. Your book, about the man they love and in a dumb way understand, will help mightily. I do want you to write that book.

SHERWOOD ANDERSON

VAN WYCK BROOKS

DEAR BROOKS:

I am glad you are going to get at Twain. It is absurd that he should have been translated as an artist by a man like Howells or that fellow Paine. There is something about him no one has got hold of. He belonged out here in the Middle West and was only incidentally a writer.

I've a notion that after Twain passed under the influence of Howells and others of the East he began to think of himself as a writer and lost something of his innocence. Should not one go to Huck Finn for the real man, working out of a real people?

Several years ago I tried to write a story concerning Twain. It never got to anything but I have a copy of the attempt in my desk. There is a character in the story—the old cheese maker from Indiana that I will sometime make the central figure in a real story. He is Twain's type of man.

It is odd what literary connections one makes. In my own mind I have always coupled Mark Twain with George Borrow. I get the same quality of honesty in them, the same wholesome disregard of literary precedent.

Lane's[1] have decided to go ahead with my cornfield songs. I call them Mid-American chants. Then I am going to publish the Winesburg tales—some two dozen of them in a book under the title *Winesburg*. When I came to look at my novel *Mary Cochran*—written several years ago—it didn't suit me. I shall hold it back for more work.

[1] John Lane published several of Anderson's books. V. W. B.

One has to realize that although there is truth in the Winesburg things there is another big story to be done. We are no longer the old America. Those are tales of farming people. We've got a new people now. We are a growing, shifting, changing thing. Our life in our factory towns intensifies. It becomes at the same time more ugly and more intense.

God damn it, Brooks, I wish my books would sell for one reason. I want to quit working for a living and go wander for five years in our towns. I want to be a factory hand again and wander from place to place. I want my frame to unbend from the desk and to go look and listen to this new thing.

My songs are going to be widely abused and perhaps rightly. I'm a poor enough singer. But there is a song here and it has been muffed. Masters might get it but he has too keen a quality of hate.

It makes me ill when I think how little I get done and the years hurrying along but I suppose we all know that sickness. I would like you to know I appreciate your interest in my efforts. The fact that you are interested is one of the bright spots. The quality of your mind I have always thought one of the really bully things of my generation.

I'll get to New York again some time. When I do I hope to see and talk with you.

SHERWOOD ANDERSON

59 W. Schiller St.

I'll send you the Twain thing to read, if I can find it, for the sake of the cheese maker.

1918

DEAR BROOKS:

Waldo Frank gave me Charnwood's *Lincoln* when he was out here. Today there came from my bookseller your *America's Coming of Age*—I had not read it.

You and Charnwood are so oddly in the same spirit that I have been thinking of you. At lunch I read your essay on *Highbrows and Lowbrows.*

The conviction grows in me that you are seeing and think ing with extraordinary clearness but I am constantly puzzled by something.

I get in some odd way a sense of the fact that you want constantly to write of men like Twain and Whitman but draw back from their imperfections, their looseness of thought, their vulgarities.

The thought that was in my mind at lunch and that I want to put over to you may have no essential value as it may be an old thought to you.

Is not the tendency to dislike these men's imperfections— if you have it—an inclination in you to drift toward your own Highbrow classification?

I ask hesitatingly. I do not of course know.

I want you to write of Twain. I want to see that book come from you.

Surely the thing has to be undertaken as a labor of love and love should stomach imperfections.

I dare say that as you work you see little result from your work. You can't of course be popular. I believe however that you by some odd chance see the difficulties of the artistic tendency in the midst of American life more clearly than anyone else.

It is always and more than you realize worth while to men deeply involved and perhaps muddied by the looseness and vulgarity of life that you keep going ahead.

Your book is helpful to me as everything of yours I have ever seen is helpful.

S. Anderson

May 23rd, 1918

Dear Brooks:

I cannot resist an impulse I have to write to you again concerning your book—*America's Coming of Age.* Are there any others of your books in which you also develop the theme you have here taken hold of so firmly?

The amazing thing to me about your mind, Brooks, is that

you see so clearly what I did not suppose any man with a background such as I had thought of you as having could see.

I have myself understood the trenchant sadness of Lincoln, the rather childlike pessimism of Twain, the half sullen and dogmatic insistence on the part of Dreiser on the fight with Puritanism and Whitman's windy insistence on America. I thought I understood these things because I have lived in such a barren place, felt myself so futile, because I have really always felt a lack of strength to continue struggling in a vacuum and looked forward hopelessly to the time when some quirk of the mind would lead me to adopt finally some grotesque sectional attitude and spend myself uselessly on that.

When I talked to Waldo out here I felt in him a sense of background I have never had. I wondered if he knew the utter lack of background. It means so very much that you know and of course he must know also.

One works in an oddly futile way. This year, because I have been very tired after ten years of trying to stay among the men about me, to be part and parcel of them, and at the same time to build something a little permanent at odd moments.

One cannot surrender to the cheaper inclinations in writing, to miss perhaps the secondary approval of an ass like Mencken as his reward.

But then one gets this queer sense of carving a stone that will presently be cast into a stagnant sea, into the Sargasso Sea as you suggest.

I am very sure, after reading this book, that you must be sad also, that you also must feel deeply the futility of things.

What I want to ask you is why you do not sympathize with me in such expressions as my essay, *An Apology for Crudity*, or my *Chants?* Where do I hit wrong?

In the chants I reached into my own personal mutterings, half insane and disordered, and tried to take out of them a little something ordered. You should see how I clutched at the ordered cornfields, insisted on them to myself, took them as about the only thing I could see.

I haven't the right to expect much from such mutterings but I have the right to expect that, having written this book I have just read, you would know what I was at.

Forgive me if I sink to the triviality of explanation. Your mind has won my honest respect. I do not so much seek your approval as I do your brotherhood.

May I say that for me yours is the first, the only note in American criticism that I have ever thought worth a damn. It is really and deeply understanding.

SHERWOOD ANDERSON

Do try to form the habit of writing me some of your thoughts occasionally. It is lonely out here.

MY DEAR BROOKS:

Your letter has stirred up a world of thought in me. It isn't Twain I'm thinking of but the profound truth of some of your own observations.

As far as Twain is concerned, we have to remember the influences about him. Remember how he came into literature —the crude buffoon of the early days in the mining camps— the terrible cheap and second-rate humor of much of *Innocents Abroad*. It seems to me that when he began he addressed an audience that gets a big laugh out of the braying of a jackass and without a doubt Mark often brayed at them. He knew that later. There was tenderness and subtility in Mark when he grew older.

You get the picture of him, Brooks—the river man who could write going East and getting in with that New England crowd—the fellows from barren hills and barren towns. The best he got out of the bunch was Howells and Howells did Twain no good.

There's another point, Brooks. I can't help wishing Twain hadn't married such a good woman. There was such a universal inclination to tame the man—to save his soul as it were. Left alone, I fancy Mark might have been willing to throw his soul overboard and then—ye gods what a fellow he might have been, what poetry might have come from him.

The big point is—it seems to me that this salvation of the soul business gets under everybody's skin. With artists it takes the form of being concerned with their occupation as writers. A struggle constantly goes on. Call the poet a poet and he is no longer the poet. You see what I mean.

There is a fellow like X. for example. He writes me long letters. His days are often made happy or miserable according to whether or not he is writing well.

Is it so important? What star dust we are. What does it matter?

The point is that I catch X. so often striving to say things in an unusual way. It makes me cringe. I want to beat him with my fists.

I pick on X. as an example because I love him and I know he feels deeply. He should write with a swing—weeping, praying and crying to the gods on paper instead of making sentences as he so often does.

Well now you see I'm coming around. The cultural fellows got hold of Mark. They couldn't hold him. He was too big and too strong. He brushed their hands aside.

But their words got into his mind. In the effort to get out beyond that he became a pessimist.

Now, Brooks, you know a man cannot be a pessimist who lives near a brook or a cornfield. When the brook chatters or at night when the moon comes up and the wind plays in the corn, a man hears the whispering of the gods.

Mark got to that once—when he wrote *Huck Finn*. He forgot Howells and the good wife and everyone. Again he was the half savage, tender, god-worshiping, believing boy. He had proud conscious innocence.

I believe he wrote that book in a little hut on a hill on his farm. It poured out of him. I fancy that at night he came down from his hill stepping like a king—a splendid playboy, playing with rivers and men, ending on the Mississippi, on the broad river that is the great artery flowing out of the heart of the land.

Well, Brooks, I'm alone in a boat on that stream sometimes. The rhythm and swing of it is in some of my songs that are to be published next month. It sometimes gets into some of the Winesburg things. I'll ride it some more perhaps. It depends on whether or not I can avoid taking myself seriously. Whom the gods wish to destroy they first make dumb with the notion of being a writer.

Waldo is coming out to spend a month with me.

Wish I could see you sometime this summer. I'll be in the East for a month or more in June or July. Why couldn't you come to the mountains and have a few days walk with me?

SHERWOOD ANDERSON

May 31, 1918

DEAR BROOKS:

I know of course what you mean and it is because you have the clearsightedness to see that you are of such very great value. American writers have a trick of doing something it is difficult at first to understand. They harden, ripen out of time. Your notion of the stony field has significance. In such a field corn would come too soon to tassel. It would turn yellow and produce no grain.

You can see for yourself how our critics produce that peculiarly shallow effect. Dell goes that way, Mencken, Hackett, and our newspaper men out here are peculiarly so. Waldo can tell you of them.

It is probably true that the reason our men who are of importance, Lincoln, Whitman, Twain, Dreiser etc., all begin when they are almost old men is that they have to spend so much of their lives putting down roots. The strength goes into that. We have, you see, Lincoln producing a few notable utterances, Whitman some clear stuff out of much windiness; Twain, *Huck Finn*; Dreiser, *Sister Carrie*, etc.

Oddly enough you are the first man I have seen stoutly at it trying to take the stones out of the field—to give the roots a chance.

If you could get at Twain sympathetically and show how

and why he failed it would be lifting a great stone. He, now, you see, is just about to be accepted by the smart alecks as the great man. We shall be clubbed with his failures and the cheap things he did. His bad work will be glorified as it has been by Howells and others.

As for myself, I think there is soil for the raising of a crop if the stones can be taken away. . . .

Your attitude toward my own efforts is generous and helpful. What I am trying to say to you in all this letter writing is aside from that but connected with it too.

Any work accomplished is a thing already half dead. It may concern others but it cannot deeply concern the workman. He has to look ahead to new difficulties, to wading through new times of disillusionment and weariness.

In my own place here, in the distracted crowds and in the midst of distracting things, I have often lived on little protective sayings muttered to myself. "Do not lose the fine edge of your contempt," I say to myself. Other such smart sayings come to my lips. I find myself living on them.

Of the newer men I have met you and Waldo give me something else. What friendship you give strengthens. It is a thing that cuts across the darkness and the mist.

I would not be hurt by any criticism of my efforts coming from either of you. I would like to have you both feel brotherhood for me and give me as much as you can out of your thoughts.

Is it not probably true that men like Z. lose their grip because they do not stay among workers? They cannot stand the brusqueness and hardness with which men speak who have much to do. They go among idlers where soft meaningless flattery takes the place of truth.

Well if you see things in me give me your friendship as Waldo has done. Let me see your mind at work as often as you can.

I go back to your figure of the stony field. Corn is planted there. You go about trying to cultivate, throwing stones aside. Much of the corn will be destroyed. That may be my fate. It matters so damn little.

What would matter is that one should grow into a yellow rare ripe thing, that one should quit striving to put down roots. You get the sense of what I drive at.

SHERWOOD ANDERSON

I take the liberty of sending your note on to Frank. I will get and read the book you mention.

CHICAGO, ILL., *June seventh, Nineteen eighteen.*

DEAR BROOKS:

If I can fix one thought in your mind I will feel more free in approaching you. When I write to men like you and Frank I do it to cut the fog of my own loneliness. If I can make you feel that no letter of mine demands answering I shall feel more freedom.

I have had an experience lately that will be of interest to you. I got suddenly an impulse to read everything I could get hold of on Lincoln. Waldo stirred up the impulse in me by giving me Charnwood's life. I read others.

I am wondering if you might not profitably go to Lincoln for a greater understanding of Twain and Whitman. There is something—a quality there—common to the three men. In Lincoln it is perhaps more out in front of you.

I got a sense of three very honest boys brought suddenly to face the complex and intricate world. There is a stare in their eyes. They are puzzled and confused. You will be inclined to think Whitman the greater man perhaps. He came closer to understanding. He lacked Lincoln's very great honesty of soul.

Twain's way lies somewhere between the roads taken by the other two men.

I am struck with the thought that I would like to have you believe that Twain's cheapness was not really a part of him. It was a thing out of the civilization in which he lived that crept in and invaded him.

Lincoln let it creep in less, because he was less warm and human. He did not love and hate. In a simple solid way he stuck to abstract principles. He squares up to those principles. That's what makes him seem so big.

There is a kind of unconscious dodging in that—the country girl who died—I mean Ann—left Lincoln a thing to love that wasn't living and about. He could reach out his hand to that shadowy thing when he was lonely. It was all very fine for the making of the big stony thing that stood up sometimes before the world.

Twain got more deeply into the complex matter of living. He was more like you and me, facing more nearly our kind of problems.

Here I am going to confess something to you. Whitman does not mean as much to me as do the other two. There is somewhere a pretense about him, even trickiness. When I was a boy and another boy caught me fairly—doing some second-rate thing—I was supposed to do what we called "acknowledge the corn."

Lincoln wouldn't have done the second-rate thing.

Twain would and would have acknowledged the corn.

Whitman wouldn't have owned up.

Well there you are. I am putting Whitman below where he stands in my mind.

It is unfair. It springs from a growing desire I have to sell you Twain.

SHERWOOD ANDERSON

DEAR BROOKS:

I have been back in the grind for two weeks now and am looking forward with joy to the notion of wiping the dust of business off my feet for at least a time. I'll come down to New York this fall and stay two or three months. I want to wander about, readjust myself, get the weariness out of me and see if I cannot face life anew.

One of the things I look forward to most is the chance of seeing more of you fellows and feeding an insistent hunger in me for companionship.

You will be amused by my memorandum of resignation to my general manager here.

SHERWOOD ANDERSON

Chicago, June 25, 1918

To: Mr. Barton
Dear Barton:
You have a man in your employ that I have thought for a long time should be fired. I refer to Sherwood Anderson. He is a fellow of a good deal of ability but for a long time I have been convinced that his heart is not in his work.

There is no question but that this man Anderson has in some ways been an ornament to our organization. His hair, for one thing, being long and mussy, gives an artistic carelessness to his personal appearance that somewhat impresses such men as Frank Lloyd Wright and Mr. Curtenius of Kalamazoo when they come into the office.

But Anderson is not really productive. As I have said his heart is not in his work. I think he should be fired and if you will not do the job I should like permission to fire him myself.

I therefore suggest that Anderson be asked to sever his connections with the Company on August 1st. He is a nice fellow. We will let him down easy but let's can him.

Respectfully Submitted
Sherwood Anderson

NEW YORK, *August 3, 1918*

DEAR BROOKS:
Just got into town and am going into the country. I will be back here on Monday and will call you up. I want to find a hole in which to work and perhaps you can advise me. It will be good to see and talk with you.

SHERWOOD ANDERSON

DEAR BROOKS:
I have got settled in my own hole—427 W. 22nd St. Phone Chelsea 6140. I expect to write here every day until noon so you can reach me any morning. I have two cots so

any time you will stay in town overnight I have a bed for you

SHERWOOD ANDERSON

NEW YORK, *Sept. 9, 1918*

DEAR BROOKS:

I think I have got into a vein that may interest you and may suggest some things to your mind in connection with your thoughts of Mark Twain. I wrote a story called *The Dancer* which has nothing to do with what I have in mind. Then I began writing a story about a figure called Hugh McVey, a Lincolnian type from Missouri. The story is very definite in my mind, in fact is definitely outlined. Perhaps our talk of these men led me to take one of these men up, live with him in his impulses and among his people and show if possible what influences have led him to be the kind of man we are puzzling about. I have written ten or fifteen thousand words of the tale. For the moment I have laid aside the other thing I call *The Romanticist*. This new tale I call *The Poor White*. I shall be glad to show you the outline of it. Tennessee is here and will be for two or three weeks. I want her to know you and Mrs. Brooks. Let's try to get together.

With love,
SHERWOOD ANDERSON

OWENSBORO, KY.,
June 24

DEAR BROOKS:

I have been rereading *Letters and Leadership* on a hot day in the Ohio River Valley and that has reminded me I have not sent on your copy of *Winesburg*. I will send it as soon as I get home.

My mind is a little hopeful that in *Winesburg* and in future novels that come from my hand you will find a real

refusal to accept life on the terms it is usually presented.
If that is true the result is not a conscious effort on my part
but is in fact the way life has come to look to me.

The growth of that point of view is I take it what you
were seeking when you wrote those remarkable papers. I do
hope you will find some realization in *Winesburg*.

SHERWOOD ANDERSON

On train in Kentucky, Wednesday.

DEAR BROOKS:

Beside my own recurring thoughts of you I keep crossing
your trail from time to time. The other day I went into a
hospital to see the wife of a Chicago judge who is Tennessee's friend and who has been ill for a long time. She was
reading your *Letters and Leadership* and said at once your
mind had helped her understand the difficulties of American
writing as nothing else had.

"I have so often not seen what you were driving at, everything you wrote seemed so incomplete. Now I see that you
stand on nothing," she said. I sent her your *America's Coming of Age*.

In a book store I saw a Jew named Larson[1] who is a friend
of yours. We talked of you. It was his notion you were
almost too prolific, wrote too easily.

I hadn't that angle on you. "I thought he was painfully
careful, almost to the point of being constipated sometimes,"
I said.

We discussed the matter but a few minutes. I liked the
looks of him and didn't want to dispute and then I felt that
he might as well as not be right and I wrong. "Everything
you say shows you don't know Brooks," he declared and I
took his word for it.

I have been reading *The Education of Henry Adams* and
feel tremendously its importance as a piece of American
writing. New England can scarcely go further than that.
It must be in its way very complete. We do I am sure both

[1]Properly Max Lippitt Larkin, a Russian. V. W. B.

live and die rather better in the Middle West. Nothing about us is as yet so completely and racially tired.

When you get at your Mark Twain (I suppose you already have) you must do a chapter on the American going East into that tired, thin New England atmosphere and being conquered by its feminine force.

I came West with my new book *Poor White* about laid by —as we out here say of the corn crop in early October. It is in shocks and stood up in the field. The husking is yet to do. I will not attempt it for a time as the proof on *Winesburg* should be along most any time. . . .

I am back at the old place in the advertising office. The moving picture dependence became impossible. That isn't my road out.

Back here I almost feel able to say that I don't care if I never travel again. The place between mountain and mountain I call Mid-America is my land. Good or bad, it's all I'll ever have.

What I want now is to see a magazine started here in the heart of America. I want you fellows from the coast to come here. We have always been going to you. I want it changed if possible.

It isn't impossible. I will get money for the purpose. I have two or three leads that may lead to money. I shall try it out thoroughly.

Do write me the news of yourself. Give my love to Mrs. Brooks. If I were at home Tennessee would want me to wish you a happy year.

SHERWOOD

10th Floor, Brooks Bldg.,
Chicago

HARRODSBURG, KENTUCKY,
Jan. 8, 1919

DEAR VAN WYCK:

I wonder if I hurt you by my letter. I can't quite presume to think so. It would be too absurd.

However I am writing after reading you in Sept. *Dial.*
O, what a relief after so much of the New York smart
befuddled writing. Those clear crisp sentences, clear crisp
thoughts. It is truly the writing, Brooks, I so utterly admire
writing here.

SHERWOOD ANDERSON

I am still planning to hold you to your promise to read
my book.

March 31, 1919

DEAR BROTHER BROOKS:

I am so glad to hear from you that I gladly forgive you
the long silence. The winter has slipped away for me. I went
through *Poor White* for the first writing and then put it
away to ripen a bit. In the meantime I am doing some
experiments.

First, a new book of *Tales* made up of some already written and others that are on the fire.

Second—a purely insane, experimental thing I call *A New
Testament*. It is an attempt to express, largely by indirection,
the purely fanciful side of a man's life, the odds and ends of
thought, the little pockets of thoughts and emotions that are
so seldom touched.

I've a fancy this last experiment would make your hair
stand on end. It is infinitely more difficult than the chants.

Why do I insist on looking upon you as the apostle of
clearness? For some reason you stand in my mind as the
supersensitive of all that is best in what is orthodox and
certain.

I am myself as uncertain as a weathercock. It seems to me
that anything approaching accomplishment grows wearisome.

I want constantly to push out into experimental fields.
"What can be done in prose that has not been done?" I keep
asking myself.

And so I constantly set out on new roads.

What is gained—perhaps nothing but a little colorful
strength in my everyday writing. I push on knowing that

none will perhaps care in the least for these experiments into which I put so much emotional force.

It is at least the adventure. How I wish I could sit with you for an hour and talk of what I mean.

About Twain. I have still the hunch. Do not look too much to him for an explanation of what is not understandable in him. Think of him as a boy whipped and blown about by the winds of his times.

Look to his times, to the men and the emotions of his times. He wanted very much to be respectable. I wonder if there wasn't a touch of the inferiority complex in him. That would explain much.

He never gave himself to a great or a deep emotion, didn't dare, didn't trust himself. Whitman must have seemed a monster to him.

He stood on the doorstep of New England. It's a ridiculous notion but it's a fact. Twain with hat in hand and an apologetic air on New England's doorstep.

Good luck to you and Mrs. Brooks. I could write many pages and not say what I would like to you.

SHERWOOD

December 15, 1919

DEAR BROTHER:

It is a good morning when I have letters from you and Paul,[1] both of you have been silent so long. Well I have thought of you daily and in a way have altogether understood that your not writing was something that had nothing to do with our established feeling for each other. I am so glad about the Twain book and I do like the title. Waldo's book[2] came to me as an amazing, splashing, living, colorful thing. It will do something for him too, to have done this job. It will be good ground under his feet.

I put the *Poor White* book away when I left New York and for a long time after I came back here I was pretty much a blank dumb thing. I had you see to reestablish myself in

[1] Paul Rosenfeld.

[2] *Our America.*

this grim business of making a living in business. It grows constantly more like eating my own vomit.

However I have gone quite a long way with my New Testament book. I am going to print some of it in the *Little Review*. It is a thing without beginning or end—something that in the end I hope will express something of what you and Waldo are driving at in a semi-poetic vein.

I have up also an old book of mine called *Mary Cochran* which I am trying to get ready for publishing. Can't tell when it will be ready. I have little time for sustained work. How eagerly I look forward to seeing your Twain book. You will never know, Brooks, what your mind has meant to me, how many dark paths it has illuminated.

It is good, too, to feel that the blow that fell when *Seven Arts* went down did not destroy; that you, Waldo and sometimes myself too have been swimming.

Paul has his book[1] in the publisher's hands. I had a fine letter from him today.

Waldo is out in Nebraska. There is something quiet and fine growing up in him that was always there but often out of control.

I am going to try to get to New York between Christmas and New Year's for a short stay. A letter from there tells me the *Dial* is going to attempt being artistic and literary and is to throw politics away. Scofield Thayer and J. S. Watson, Jr. have taken over control. Stewart Mitchell is managing editor. I do not know any of them.

Tennessee was ill for a long time but is now well and strong again. If you do come east in the Spring stop for a few days and look about here.

And give my love to Mrs. Brooks.

Write me when you can.

SHERWOOD

DEAR BROOKS:

I've been thinking about your letter of the other day and my answer that didn't say what I wanted it to say. Your

[1] *Musical Portraits.*

not writing letters doesn't bother me. I have no special feeling about it at all.

I would in some way like to know how I feel in another respect.

I dare say your book when it comes will not have the passionate flaming thing in it that Waldo's book often has. But, Brooks, you must realize what an inciter to flame in others you are.

I have a hunch you are doomed to be a man whose voice will not be heard by many here for a long time but you should realize what it means to those who do hear it.

When in speaking of *Winesburg* you used the word adolescence you struck more nearly than you know on the whole note of me. I am immature, will live and die immature. A quite terrible confession that would be if I did not represent so much.

I am conscious I do represent much and often I feel like a very small boy in the presence of your mind and of Waldo's too.

What is true of me is true of Sandburg, but we are different. He is submerged in adolescence. I am in it and of it but I look out. Give Sandburg a mind and you perhaps destroy him. I don't know whether that would be true of me or not.

Be sure of this, Brooks. No matter how much you may seem to yourself to work in isolation, it is not true. Your voice always comes clear to me and will to some others. You have been the bearer of a lamp that has illuminated many a dark place for me.

Nothing that is going to happen next year will mean as much to me as getting my hand on your new book.

You, Waldo and me—could three men be more unlike. How truly I love you two men.

SHERWOOD

I think of my Testament as a passionate attempt to get poetry into the thing you have expressed time and again and that you and Waldo have together made me a little

conscious of. I want to have it be a distillation. God knows
how far I shall succeed.

Sunday
August 24

DEAR VAN WYCK:

A clear beautiful Sunday morning. What a stir I made
within myself by writing you that letter. It was written at a
time when the engine that is myself was running wildly,
grinding no grain.

Someone had told me that your attitude toward my work
was that it was not sound, wholesome. In myself—in my
right mind—I should have paid no attention. It happened I
was spiritually very tired.

There came and still come odd, hurtful reactions from
some things I write—a woman I have once known—strange
men and women I have never seen, write me queer abusive
letters. "Why do you wallow in ugly lies about life?" they
ask. I have got a dozen such letters in a week.

I put them aside—the thought of them. There were certain minds I did not expect to approve what I do. I did
expect they would feel sure I was going on at my work
honestly, with an intent of spiritual integrity.

You must know, must have felt how much I counted on
your mind there.

The slipshod gossip that you had another attitude, joined
these others in the wallowing theory, would, had I not been
spiritually weary, have made no impression on my mind. I
did harbor it a little and am ashamed. After I had written
you the letter I woke at night sick with shame. I couldn't
work because of it.

I won't say I won't do the same again. When I'm tired
I'm no good, a yellow dog sometimes.

As for your not knowing sometimes what I'm driving at,
I don't always myself. God knows too many of my things
don't fully register.

Perhaps I don't care enough. I feel myself often an instrument to adventure in flights along strange paths. Why should you ever under any circumstances feel any obligation to say anything about my work—to approve of it I mean.

A nasty, tired building up of substantiating proofs that the gossip I had heard was true must have gone on within me.

O brother Brooks, please forget my silly letter.

There are lots of sweeter, finer things I can quarrel with you about at the Pittsburg meeting. I could quarrel with you indefinitely as to the value of the whole lot of political-minded magazines.

I am writing a new book I'm sure you are going to love. It really does I feel get hold of a man and woman in American life intimately, intensely. Am I not a lucky dog to have this time to work undisturbed? If my damned books would only sell a little better. Is the *Ordeal* going to sell? I want that book to sell for other reasons than your own interest. I wish to God I could make all Americans read it.

SHERWOOD

FAIRHOPE, ALA., *May 15th*

DEAR BROTHER:

It was a big moment for me when I got your note and found you liked *Poor White*. When the novel was finished some weeks ago I said to Tennessee, "There is one man's mind I would like to have on that book—it's Brooks." I thought of sending it on and asking you to read it but know yours is a busy life and hadn't the nerve. Then Huebsch did it for me and now I have what I want. The gods are good to me. I am also happy about two other things—that your book is at last on the way to me and that you saw what I wanted someone to see in the *Dial* story—*The Triumph of the Egg*. To my mind it was one of the very best things I had ever done but when I showed it to Paul and Waldo they did not seem much impressed. O, Brooks, if you but knew what your own clear fine mind has meant to me these

last two or three years. Well, there's no use trying to tell you.
It has been a wonderful time for me here these three
months. In the first place I persuaded Tennessee to be
utterly reckless, chuck her job and income and run off here
with me. That has worked out. She is getting well and is
happier than I have ever seen her. What a tremendous thing
life is. For several years she has been a tired woman. Here
she rested and then suddenly began to play. There are great
quantities of red, yellow and blue clay here—very fine and
plastic—Tennessee suddenly began working in it and already
she does really remarkable things. What new joy in life that
approach towards beauty coming in a definite form out of
herself has given her. I go about whispering to myself,
"She is going to be well. She is going to be well." O, for a
world of people not tired. What things could come out of
them.

X. has been for a long time silent. Knowing nothing, I
still feel I do know there is something the matter. I am sure
it is about the novel. It is not getting across with people who
have read it and away down underneath has not got across
with him but he is fighting that thought-insisting. Is my
hunch at all correct? If it is I am unspeakably sorry. I love
X. very deeply and the deep-seated desire in him to be a
great man hurts me at times like an open wound.

We will be leaving here in about a week and after that
address me at—Critchfield & Company, 10th Floor, Brooks
Bldg., Chicago. I hope to be in New York for a short stay
early in June and trust I shall see you then. There are many
things I want to talk to you about. Have begun a rollicking,
Rabelaisian book called *Many Marriages,* a thing I have long
hungered to do. It will take marvelous good health and
spirits to carry the thing off but I may never be in better
shape to begin it.

Also I am painting and doing my own kind of poetry. The
two things are much alike in me—mystic, vague impulses.
There is a painter here who looks at my things, shakes his
head and goes home and takes Epsom salts. It is perhaps the
best way to take the two sides of me.

Tennessee sends love to you. Please bear our love to Mrs.

Brooks. Is there any chance I may sell serial rights for *Poor White* to *Freeman* or *Dial*? It would give me some more freedom if I could achieve some money in this way.

With love,

SHERWOOD

EPHRAIM, WIS.—*Tuesday*

DEAR BROOKS:

This is the sort of thing that I thought might go well in the *Freeman*. I would not want however to sell these things at 2c per word. In a way I should rather keep them for a book I hope some day to print than to send them out at such a low price. I should be asking *Dial* $25 for these things. Would that be impossible for you?

Am back in the woods again and happy here. I hope to be writing pretty steadily this summer.

SHERWOOD

Sunday morning

DEAR BROOKS:

There are two reasons why *Freeman* can't use such things as *The Man in the Brown Coat*. First because it isn't any good. That reason don't go. It is. Second because *Freeman* is a political magazine. *New Republic, Nation, Freeman.* None of them give a damn for literature really. They seem to feel that creative writing has nothing to do with revolution. They want to put a new sort of government in at Washington. Well, the *Freeman* permits you. That's a long step.

There remains *Little Review* and *Dial* as voices for what artistic urge there may be in the country. The gods protect and nourish us. Scattered, immature, undignified, pretentious asinine things. I don't look at *Little Review* at all. I throw such things as *Man in the Brown Coat* into it.

Have just looked at the last *Dial*. It's spoiled eggs. Some old castrated babbler named Hueffer—or Heifer—name don't

matter—a lot of other half-baked stuff—no editing—no purpose—hell.

I don't know why I should swear to you about all this—
most of the time I don't think about it but go on working.
It did hurt though when I found you also rather taking
Winesburg for example as a sex book. It got under my hide
a bit. I'm usually thick-skinned.

To me it seems a little as though one were permitted to
talk abstractly of things, to use scientific terms regarding
them—in the new dispensation—but when one attempts to
dip down into the living stuff the same old formula holds.
A really beautiful story like *Hands* for example is—well,
nasty. God help us. Dozens of men have told me privately
they knew Wing Biddlebaum. I tried to present him sympathetically—taboo.

I get so much force and reality in your *Ordeal*. I read it
over and over like a Bible or Shakespeare's *Sonnets*. Twain
is dead—he paid the price of caving in—but I wonder if I
make you feel what I'm talking about.

In the first place I wish you could know how much I have
loved—do love—your mind. I've frankly banked on it more
than the mind of any other American. Am I right in my
secret belief that you, down at bottom, believe me, in my
reactions to life—well, not nice?[1] Can I—have I the privilege
of caressing your mind so?

I'm settled down to a quite new novel—a tale of country
life in Ohio. It has marched steadily along—a living tale I
believe full of winds and farm yards and people. I paint too
quite a lot. Your *Ordeal* has struck deep. It sets people talking and wondering.

SHERWOOD

Does Twain's formula "Freedom and the other precious
things"—still hold?

What a God damn letter. Well, it's off my chest. It's glorious to have a few more months out of doors—steadily at
work.

[1]No, he was wrong here. I had no such thought. V. W. B.

OXFORD, *July* 26

DEAR BROOKS:

I have written a note to Miss Alice Chown[1] and perhaps will see her in London. We will be here all this week, then back to London until sailing time.

The trip has been really wonderful and I for one am bursting full of new impressions. As for Oxford—well you know how unbelievably lovely it is. Saw Stearns in London and he told me of the book by the American intellectual K of Ps.[2] It should be quite a back-breaker.

Will be in New York a few days on my way home and hope I shall see you.

With love,

SHERWOOD

DEAR VAN WYCK:

I think also that *I'm a Fool* is a piece of work that holds water, but do you not think its wide acceptance is largely due to the fact that it is a story of immaturity and poses no problem? After all isn't it, say, Mark Twain at his best, the *Huckleberry Finn* Mark Twain?

In the same book there is a story *There She Is—She Is Taking Her Bath* I would like you to read. And then the story called *The Man Who Became a Woman* and *The Man's Story*.

One doesn't want to go on always with the childlike feeling for surface—not just that. I suppose this is my quarrel with you—which isn't a quarrel because I love you and you have done so much for me, cleared so many paths for me. I mean, I presume that I do not want you to like best of my things the things easiest to like.

I am happy that you are working again and that Paul is working. For a long time after I came out here I was uncomfortable about him, feeling that he was not at work and

[1] An English friend of Randolph Bourne's. V. W. B.

[2] A reference to Harold Stearn's symposium, *Civilization in the United States.* "K of Ps" stands for Knight of Pythias.

was disturbed for some reason. Then at last the beast wrote me and reported himself at work and all right.

You have a kind of power over my mind, Van Wyck, of making me think of what you are thinking and so I got James on my mind after you got to work at him. You may be interested to know my reactions to some solid weeks of James reading—the feeling of him as a man who never found any-one to love—who did not dare love. I really can't care much for any character after he gets through with it—he, in short, takes my love from me too.

I've a fancy—can it be true that he is the novelist of the haters? Oh, the thing infinitely refined and carried far into the field of intellectuality as skillful haters find out how to do.

It is you see but a notion but I thought it might interest you.

I am enthusiastic about Paul's theme—*The Port of New York*—the title is inspired.

Your garden does sound inviting. When will I be where I may talk now and then with the few men who give me most?

I'm working steadily on the book *Straws* and have a new novel stirring and alive in me. I hope strongly I shall be able to get into it this fall and winter.

My regards to Mrs. Brooks. If you get a chance please insult Paul now and then because he does not write to me oftener.

SHERWOOD

33 East Liberty Street, RENO,
July

DEAR VAN WYCK:

I got hold of *Dial* with your first paper on James and it fascinated me. It was so good to find you writing again—with that clear flowing style that so got me when I first came to it.

A strange lad—that Henry—and you make one feel the strangeness and reality of him. For a time—when you were working so steadily—doing the *Freeman* things—I thought something in you had got pretty tired but this seems crisp and alive.

I'm sure it is going to be a fine book and only wish I could read all of it now.

Am working pretty steadily and enjoying the fact of life immensely. Last winter in New York I was tired and petulant and that has pretty much passed. I am out on the desert —plenty of sun and wind and a nice large sense of leisure.

This is another world—very distinct from the East and quite as distinct I fancy from the Pacific coast. At first the land seems dead, an endless sea of sagebrush but as you walk and ride over it the under delicacy of color, plant and flower life comes forth and sometimes—to your amazement—all flames into color.

Love and good wishes,

Sherwood

Reno, Nevada, *July 30, 1923*

Dear Van Wyck:

After all, Van Wyck, the danger is not imminent. The book is one that spreads out and out. I have to confine it. Get and keep it within a channel if I can.

Do I not know there has always been some of my work you do not like? But how could it be otherwise. I dare say if you and I were to see each other more closely, become really personally acquainted—which we never have quite— there would remain a difficulty.

As for myself, Van Wyck—I have seen so much of ugly meaningless, drifting men that I have come to love the men I feel definitely at work and when you write me of your feeling of being crowded inside I am made happy by your letter. The feeling spreads a sense of richness, of fecundity over my consciousness of you just now and I like that.

I want to settle down really and make myself a home

somewhere soon but Westport has its difficulties. Cost for
one thing. You see I can live more economically any number
of other places. I have to consider that.[1]

There are a lot of things I would like to talk with you
about—the attitude of the artist, for one thing. In your Twain
you come so near getting what I feel about the man but you
did miss an essential thing some way.

Do you know I had, Van Wyck, a feeling that it was just
the artist in Twain you in some way resented. There was
somewhat the sense of a just judge trying a criminal rather
than the sympathetic friend or lover.[2]

Can we understand at all, ever, where we do not love?

Perhaps all that struggling side of James you will feel more
fully. He is more of your own world, isn't he? Twain was
more of my world.

You see in my book—which after all I think I shall not
call *Straws*—but *A Modernist Notebook*—I am frankly daring to proclaim myself the American Man.

I mean by that to take all into myself if I can, the sales-
men, business men, laborers, all among whom I have lived.
I do get the feeling that I, in a peculiar way and because of
the accident of my position in letters, am a kind of composite
essence of it all.

And actually there are days when people by thousands
drift in and out of me. On a recent day here when I walked
in the streets this natural physical feeling of being completely in rapport with every man, woman and child along
a street wherein I walked became so intense that I had to go
hide myself—to rest a little.

I speak of this because, when the feeling has leaked over
into expression in my work you have so often said you didn't
understand what I was talking about.

I want you to understand more than I can say.

And God knows I don't say this as an apology for what is

[1] He thought for a long time of living in Westport, Connecticut,
where his brother Karl had long been settled and Paul Rosenfeld and
I also lived. But these were his roaming years. Karl spoke to me once
of Sherwood's liking "to be alone in strange places." V. W. B.

[2] He was right. It was partly the fault of my method. V. W. B.

not fully fruitioned in my work. No one can be more conscious of the failure of the greater part of it than I am.

But I do want you, Van Wyck, to feel for James and his difficulties, give yourself wholly to James. I can't help asking that you do it more fully than you did when you wrote of Twain.

With love,
SHERWOOD A.

Sunday, RENO

DEAR BROOKS:

When, some time ago, I asked you to take a look at this new book of mine I did not realize what a whale it was going to be. There are almost 150,000 words of it and I could not ask you to wade through any such pile. You have enough on your hands as things stand, and an unfinished book waiting. I should so much rather have you spend your time writing so that I may later read. I'll send it along to Otto Liveright, who is to show it to Harpers. They may want a part of it for the magazine.

The book has you in it with many others. It contains no criticism of you but expresses the regret of a middle western workman that you seemed unwilling or unable to respond to his hunger for more intimate contact, as fellow workmen, with some of the more cultured men of the East.

As for the woman's article in *Dial* I did not in any way connect you with it and did not take her quotation of you as intended to suggest you had said that particular thing of me. I do know of course that you have been out of sympathy with some of my work that has meant most to me and that after some years I still think first-rate work, but I can't very well blame you for that.

I might quarrel with such a statement as applied to Lawrence if I had you here to state at length my point of view—which is that no man can be bogged in immaturity who has done as much good work as Mr. Lawrence.

My dear Brooks, isn't there at least a chance that the fear of emotional response to life may be as much a sign of immaturity as anything else? It does seem so to me.

I really think the article in *Dial* was ill-natured and ill-mannered and largely made up of the fragments of ill-natured things that have been said of me ever since I began working. What puzzles me is the *Dial*. The article is so evidently incompetent. Lord, I could have written so much sharper and clearer criticism of myself. What the *Dial* is up to I can't quite make out. They give me their praise and buy my novel and publish it and then seem to devote themselves to a kind of apology to the public for me.

Of course I want more than anything else freedom for you or any other workman who really wants to work. It has been an odd year for me. I have been more or less separated from all the workmen I know except Stieglitz who has written me often and some very beautiful and helpful letters this year. Poor man, he has had a year of suffering, a part of the time being unable to lift his arms because of pain.

I myself have had an unhappy year. I think often that a good many people, perhaps, you dear Brooks, among them, think of me as a mere reckless adventurer but I have been up to something with my life and work. I am not a mere rudderless ship and now and then I do make a port.

Well, I do know that you have and always have had much to give me and I've got some of it. I'll be glad of more. There are not many sincere workmen in the country and in New York in particular there is so often just a superficial slinging of some smart saying at the head of a man, when understanding or the inclination to try to understand fails. But you know these things as well as I do and I dare say have suffered from them as much. It is a part of the artist's life and I escape a good deal by not seeing the more ill-natured and superficial slings.

For me, anyway, work looms ahead, plenty of it. I really do begin to see a great many of my own failings and shortcomings as a workman and am at least trying all the time to shake them off. And I'll be glad when I can be again where I can see and talk to men whose aims are somewhat like my own.

The book is done for better or worse and will be going off to Liveright I think some time next week.

With love,
SHERWOOD

DEAR VAN WYCK:

I am writing to ask something of you. When I have finished my *Straws,* which is a kind of attempt to picture the artist in our American life, I am wondering if it would be too much trouble for you to read it.

I shall be pretty close to it and perhaps cannot judge it. It will be more or less broken and fragmentary but it is all written on a theme that has occupied your own thoughts all your life.

It is just your mind I would like on it. Will you do it?
SHERWOOD

The disaster would not be immediately impending.

DEAR VAN WYCK:

Well, I shall live more like a monk after this I hope. Have got a little farm in the mountains of Virginia. We go there in the spring. Wish you could come there some time for that real getting acquainted.

Your letter only got to me after I had got back here to New Orleans. There would have been no use seeing each other in New York this trip. I saw no one—not really.

God help me, I've been lecturing to help pay for the farm. Paul said he might try it. Tell him—"No."

It's no go.

I saw young Holt[1] and he talked of a book on me in the McBride books. I had the temerity to suggest you. It was nervy of me. He said something had been said to you and you couldn't do it.

---

[1] Guy Holt.

I was glad. Had I been able to saddle you with it, I would have been ashamed.

Lordy, how many people are vulgar.

You find out when you go lecturing.

I hope you will really give me a chance to know you sometime.

The years fly so. There is so little done.

I am venturing a book of notes, comments, etc., this spring. I hope it may have some life in it.

Love to all in your house. We shall have a quiet house in the country soon.

Come sometime—when you want a quiet place to work—both of you.

SHERWOOD

I am consumed with curiosity. When shall we have a new book by you?

November 14, 1925,
ZORLE, PENNA.

DEAR VAN WYCK:

How belated I am. I have just got to your James. One reason is that the bookstores where I have been handle no books.

And what a keen delightful book this is—the same clear beautiful prose and—will you forgive my saying so—much more real sympathy with and understanding of your man than in the Twain.

The book is one I shall want to read again and again.

As ever,
SHERWOOD ANDERSON

We have bought a little farm down in Virginia and will go there to live in the Spring. New Orleans, for all its charm, is too hot for too many months. My new book seems to be selling. Now I am lecturing to pay for the farm and build a house on it. My regards to Mrs. Brooks.

S. A.

[after a long silence]

MARION, VIRGINIA,
August Sixth,
1938

DEAR VAN WYCK BROOKS:

I am fixing up a room in my house with framed pictures of my friends and men I admire. I spend a great deal of time alone in the country and most of you I often want to see I seldom do see. You may think it a poor substitute but a picture framed and hung up in a room I am in and out of every day does seem to bring my friends closer.

Will you please send me a picture of yourself for framing? I will be grateful.

Sincerely,
(signed) SHERWOOD ANDERSON